Adobe Dreamweaver, Excel 2016, & PowerPoint 2016

BCIS 2610

Pinard | Carey | DesJardins | Parsons | Oja | Ageloff | Bishop | Botello | Waxer

CENGAGE
Learning·

Australia • Brazil • Japan • Korea • Mexico • Singapore • Spain • United Kingdom • United States

Adobe Dreamweaver, Excel 2016, & PowerPoint 2016: BCIS 2610

New Perspectives Microsoft® Office 365 & PowerPoint® 2016, Intermediate
Katherine T. Pinard

© 2017 Cengage Learning. All rights reserved.

New Perspectives Microsoft® Office 365 & Excel 2016, Intermediate,
June Jamrich Parsons, Dan Oja, Patrick Carey, Carol A. DesJardins

© 2017 Cengage Learning. All rights reserved.

New Perspectives on Microsoft Excel 2013, Comprehensive
Patrick Carey, June Jamrich Parsons, Dan Oja, Roy Ageloff, Carol A.
DesJardins

© 2014 Cengage Learning. All rights reserved.

Adobe® Creative Suite® 6 Web Tools: Dreamweaver®, Photoshop®, and
Flash®—Illustrated
Bishop, Botello, Waxer

© 2013 Cengage Learning. All rights reserved.

ALL RIGHTS RESERVED. No part of this work covered by the copyright herein may
be reproduced or distributed in any form or by any means, except as permitted by
U.S. copyright law, without the prior written permission of the copyright owner.

For product information and technology assistance, contact us at
Cengage Learning Customer & Sales Support, 1-800-354-9706

For permission to use material from this text or product,
submit all requests online at **cengage.com/permissions**
Further permissions questions can be emailed to
permissionrequest@cengage.com

This book contains select works from existing Cengage Learning resources and
was produced by Cengage Learning Custom Solutions for collegiate use. As such,
those adopting and/or contributing to this work are responsible for editorial
content accuracy, continuity and completeness.

Compilation © 2017 Cengage Learning

ISBN: 978-1-337-70449-6

Cengage Learning
20 Channel Center Street
Boston, MA 02210
USA

Cengage Learning is a leading provider of customized learning solutions with
office locations around the globe, including Singapore, the United Kingdom,
Australia, Mexico, Brazil, and Japan. Locate your local office at:
www.international.cengage.com/region.

Cengage Learning products are represented in Canada by Nelson Education, Ltd.

For your lifelong learning solutions, visit **www.cengage.com/custom.**

Visit our corporate website at **www.cengage.com.**

Brief Contents

From:
Adobe® Creative Suite® 6 Web Tools: Dreamweaver®, Photoshop®, and Flash®—Illustrated
Bishop, Botello, Waxer

From:
New Perspectives Microsoft® Office 365 & Excel 2016, Intermediate
June Jamrich Parsons, Dan Oja, Patrick Carey, Carol A. DesJardins

From:
New Perspectives on Microsoft Excel 2013, Comprehensive
Patrick Carey, June Jamrich Parsons, Dan Oja, Roy Ageloff, Carol A. DesJardins

From:
New Perspectives Microsoft® Office 365 & PowerPoint® 2016, Intermediate
Katherine T. Pinard

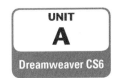

Getting Started with Adobe Dreamweaver CS6

Files You Will Need:

To view a list of files needed for this unit, see the Data Files Grid in the back of the book.

Adobe Dreamweaver CS6 is a web design program used to create media-rich web pages and websites. Its easy-to-use tools let you incorporate sophisticated features, such as animations and interactive forms. In this unit, you learn to start Dreamweaver and examine the workspace. Next, you open a web page and learn how to use the Help feature. Finally, you close the web page and exit the program. You have recently been hired as a manager at The Striped Umbrella, a beach resort in Florida. One of your main responsibilities is to develop the resort's website using Dreamweaver. You begin by familiarizing yourself with the Dreamweaver program.

OBJECTIVES

Define web design software

Start Adobe Dreamweaver CS6

View the Dreamweaver workspace

Work with views and panels

Open a web page

View web page elements

Get help

View a web page in a browser

Close a web page and exit Dreamweaver

Adobe product screenshot(s) reprinted with permission from Adobe Systems Incorporated.

Defining Web Design Software

Adobe Dreamweaver CS6 is a powerful **web design program** that lets you create interactive web pages with text, images, animation, sounds, and video. You can create web page objects in Dreamweaver as well as import objects created using other programs. Although you can create several different types of files with Dreamweaver, you will be saving files with the .html file extension throughout this book. **HTML** is the acronym for **Hypertext Markup Language**, the language web developers use to create web pages. 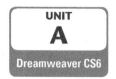 You need to learn some basic Dreamweaver features for your new position.

DETAILS

Using Dreamweaver you can:

* **Create web pages or websites**

  You can use Dreamweaver to create individual web pages or entire websites, depending on your project needs. **Web pages** are pages of text in HTML format combined with images in various image formats. **Websites** are collections of related web pages. Websites are stored on **servers**, which are computers connected to the Internet. Users can view websites using a **web browser**, which is software used to display pages in a website; some of the most popular browsers are Internet Explorer, Mozilla Firefox, Google Chrome, Opera, and Safari. You can also import web pages created in other programs, edit them in Dreamweaver, and then incorporate them into an existing website. Dreamweaver provides predefined page layouts called **templates** that you can apply to existing pages or use as a basis for designing new ones.

QUICK TIP
The Insert panel is collapsed by default. Double-click the panel tab or use the Windows > Insert command to expand it.

* **Add text, images, tables, and media files**

  You can add text, images, tables, and media files to a web page by using the Insert panel. The **Insert panel** (also referred to as the **Insert bar**) contains buttons for creating or inserting objects, such as tables, images, forms, and videos. Using the Insert panel, you can also insert objects made with other Adobe software programs, including Fireworks, Flash, and Photoshop. Table A-1 describes the Insert panel categories.

* **Display web pages as they will appear to users**

  Dreamweaver is a **WYSIWYG** ("What You See Is What You Get") program. As you design a web page in Dreamweaver, you see the page exactly as it will appear in a browser window.

* **Use the Property inspector to view and edit page elements**

  The **Property inspector** (also referred to as the **Properties panel**) is a panel that displays the characteristics of a page's currently selected object. Figure A-1 shows a web page open in Dreamweaver. Note that the properties of the selected text appear in the Property inspector. The Property inspector changes depending upon the type of page object selected. For example, when an image is selected, the Property inspector displays image properties. When text is selected, the Property inspector displays text properties with either the HTML Property inspector or the CSS Property inspector.

* **Manage websites**

  Dreamweaver lets you manage website pages to ensure that all the **links**, or connections among the pages, work properly. The importance of proper site management increases as new pages are added to a website. Part of managing a website involves identifying problems or challenges as content is added and the site becomes more complex. There are several types of reports that you can run to check for problems across the website. Dreamweaver also has special tools that help you manage a site when you are working as part of a team on a project.

FIGURE A-1: Web page open in Dreamweaver

Tab displays filename of open file (Macintosh users will not see tabs unless multiple pages are open.)

Web page

Property inspector showing properties for selected text

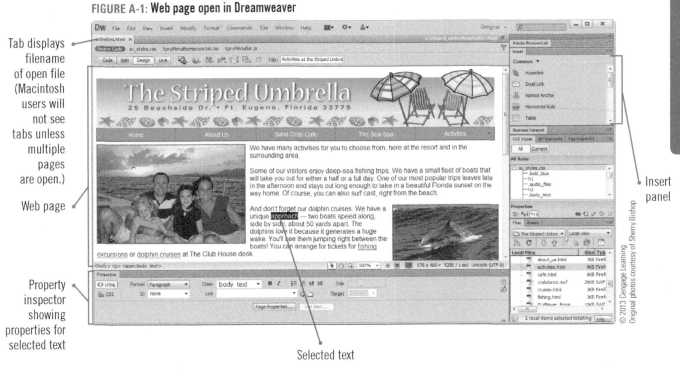

Insert panel

Selected text

TABLE A-1: Insert panel categories and corresponding buttons

category	buttons
Common	Commonly used buttons, such as images, media, and hyperlinks
Layout	Buttons for inserting divs, tables, Spry objects, and frames
Forms	Buttons for inserting form objects, such as check boxes and radio buttons
Data	Buttons for inserting Tabular Data, Dynamic Data, and Recordsets
Spry	Buttons for inserting Spry data sets, Spry validations, and Spry panels
jQuery Mobile	Buttons for inserting widgets in jQuery Mobile Pages
InContext Editing	Buttons for creating editable regions to allow others to add content
Text	Buttons for formatting text; for example, strong, headings, and lists
Favorites	Buttons you can customize; Dreamweaver will add those you use most frequently

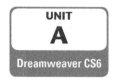

Starting Adobe Dreamweaver CS6

There are several ways to start Dreamweaver, depending on the type of computer you are using and the type of installation you have. Although the steps below start the program using the Start menu (Win) or the hard drive icon (Mac), the fastest way to start Dreamweaver is to place a shortcut (Win) or an alias (Mac) for Adobe Dreamweaver CS6 on your desktop or add it to the taskbar (Win) or Dock (Mac). **Shortcuts** and **aliases** are icons that represent a software program stored on your computer system. When you double-click a shortcut (Win) or an alias (Mac), you do not need to use the Start menu (Win) or open submenus (Mac) to find your program. When you initially open Dreamweaver, the Welcome Screen appears. The Welcome Screen provides shortcuts you can click to open files or to create new files or websites. You are given your first web-related assignment and begin by starting Dreamweaver.

STEPS

WIN

QUICK TIP
Your Start button may look different, depending on your version of Windows and your Windows settings.

1. **Click the** Start button **on the Windows taskbar**
   The Start menu opens, which lists the names of the software programs installed on your computer.

2. **Point to** All Programs, **click** Adobe Web Premium CS6 **or** Adobe Design Premium CS6 **(if you have one of these suites of Adobe products), then click** Adobe Dreamweaver CS6
   Dreamweaver opens and the Welcome Screen appears, as shown in Figure A-2.

3. **Click** HTML **in the Create New column on the Dreamweaver Welcome Screen**
   A new blank HTML document named Untitled-1 opens.

MAC

TROUBLE
Your Adobe Dreamweaver folder may be in a folder other than Applications. See your instructor or technical support contact if you have trouble locating Dreamweaver.

1. **Click** Finder **in the Dock, then click** Applications

2. **Click the** Adobe Dreamweaver CS6 **folder, then double-click the** Adobe Dreamweaver CS6 program
   Dreamweaver opens, and the Welcome Screen appears, as shown in Figure A-2.

3. **Click** HTML **in the Create New column on the Dreamweaver Welcome Screen**
   A blank document named Untitled-1 opens.

Using Dreamweaver layouts

Dreamweaver has several preset workspace layouts that you can choose between. In the **Designer layout**, the panels are docked on the right side of the screen, and Design view is the default view. In the **Coder layout**, the panels are docked on the left side of the screen, and Code view is the default view. The **Dual Screen layout** is used with two monitors: one for the Document window and Property inspector and one for the panels. Other layouts include App Developer, App Developer Plus, Business Catalyst, Classic, Coder Plus, Designer Compact, Fluid Layout, and Mobile Applications. You can change the workspace layout by using a feature called the **Workspace switcher**. The Workspace switcher allows you to quickly change between different preset workspace layouts. You can also create and name your own custom layout with the New Workspace command on the Workspace switcher menu. You can reset your workspace back to the preset Designer layout after you have moved, opened, or closed panels with the 'Reset Designer' command.

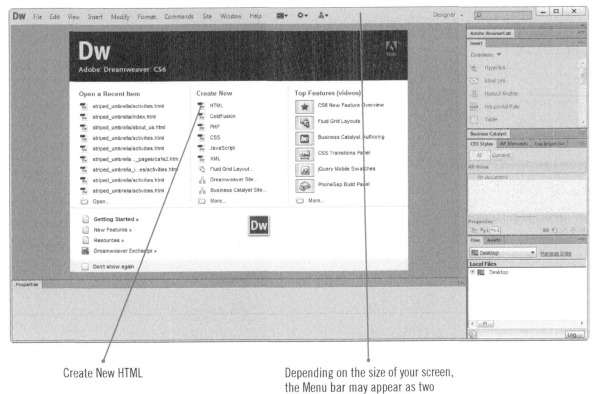

Create New HTML

Depending on the size of your screen,
the Menu bar may appear as two
different bars, one above the other

FIGURE A-2: The Dreamweaver Welcome Screen (Mac)

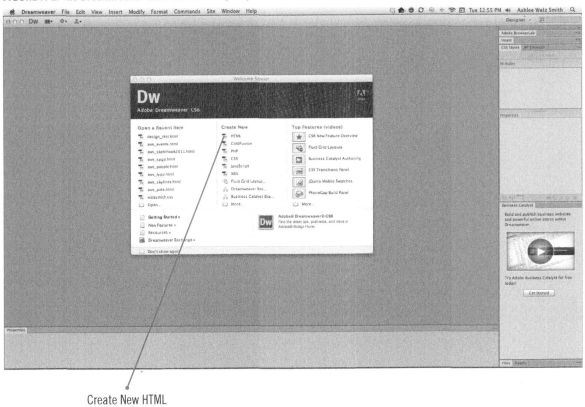

Create New HTML

Viewing the Dreamweaver Workspace

The Dreamweaver **workspace**, shown in Figure A-3, consists of the Document window, the Application bar (Win) or Menu bar (Mac), toolbars, Property inspector, and panels. The default layout in Dreamweaver is called the Designer layout. Other layouts include the Coder and Dual Screen layouts. The Designer and Coder layouts are built with an integrated workspace using the **Multiple Document Interface (MDI)**. This means that all Document windows and panels are positioned within one large application window. **Panel Groups** are sets of related panels that are grouped together. The Property inspector, or Properties panel, is a panel that changes to display the properties of the currently selected web page object. It contains text boxes, shortcut menus, and buttons that allow you to make formatting changes without having to open menus. Its contents vary according to the object currently selected. ▓▓▓ In order to continue with your website project, you want to spend some time familiarizing yourself with the Dreamweaver workspace.

DETAILS

Use Figure A-3 to find many of the elements detailed below.

- When a document is open, the filename, path, and document type appear in the **Browser Navigation toolbar**. This toolbar, located directly above the Document window contains navigation buttons you use when following links on your pages in Live view. **Live view** displays an open document with its interactive elements active and functioning, as if you were viewing the document in an actual browser window.

- The **Application bar** (Win) or **Menu bar** (Mac), located at the top of the Dreamweaver workspace, includes menu names, a Workspace switcher, and other program commands. The Application bar (Win) or Menu bar (Mac) appears as one bar or two bars, depending on your screen size and resolution. You use commands by using shortcut keys or by clicking corresponding buttons on the various panels. We will simply refer to this as the Menu bar from this point forward.

> **TROUBLE**
> If you don't see the Insert panel, click Window on the Menu bar, then click Insert.

- The Insert panel contains buttons that allow you to insert objects, such as images, tables, and horizontal rules. The buttons on the Insert panel change depending on the category you select using a drop-down menu. Each category contains buttons relating to a specific task. When you insert an object using one of the buttons, a dialog box opens, letting you choose the object's characteristics. The last button selected becomes the default button for that category. The Insert panel's drop-down menu also has an option to show the program icons in color.

> **TROUBLE**
> To see hidden toolbars, click View on the Menu bar, point to Toolbars, then click the toolbar name. The Standard and Style Rendering toolbars do not appear by default.

- The **Document toolbar** contains buttons for changing the current web page view, previewing and debugging web pages, and managing files. The Document toolbar buttons are listed in Table A-2.

- The **Standard toolbar** contains buttons for some frequently used commands on the File and Edit menus, such as the Copy and Paste commands.

- The **Style Rendering toolbar** contains buttons that can be used to display different media types.

- The **Coding toolbar** is useful when you are working with HTML code; it can only be accessed in Code view.

- The **Related Files toolbar** displays files related to an open and active file.

- The **Document window** is the large area under the Document toolbar that encompasses most of the Dreamweaver workspace. Web pages that you open in Dreamweaver appear in this area.

> **QUICK TIP**
> To make an open panel active and display its contents, click the panel tab. To expand or collapse a panel, double-click the panel tab.

- The **Status bar** appears under the Document window. The left side displays the **tag selector**, which shows the HTML tags being used at the insertion point location. The right side displays window size data and page download time estimates.

- **Panels** are small windows containing program controls. Related panels appear together in panel groups, such as the CSS Styles panel and the Files panel. You display a panel by choosing its name from the Window menu. You can dock panel groups to the right side of the screen, or undock them by dragging the panel tab. When two or more panels are docked together, you can access the panel you want by clicking its tab name to display its contents.

Getting Started with Adobe Dreamweaver CS6

FIGURE A-3: The Dreamweaver CS6 workspace

Menu bar (Application bar)
File tab with file name
Related Files toolbar
Document toolbar
Style Rendering toolbar

Standard toolbar

Document window

Status bar
Property inspector

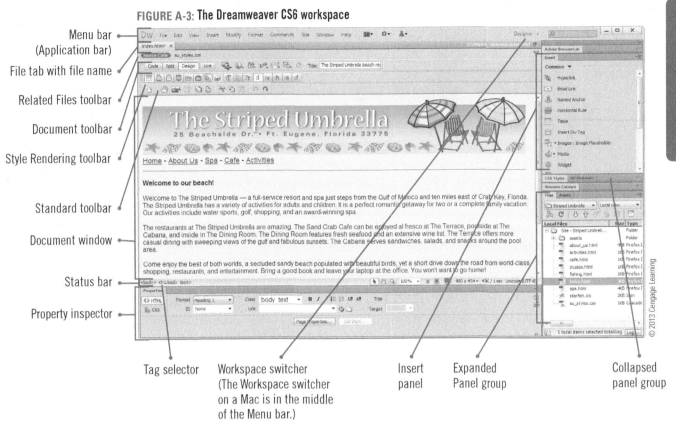

Tag selector
Workspace switcher
(The Workspace switcher on a Mac is in the middle of the Menu bar.)
Insert panel
Expanded Panel group
Collapsed panel group

© 2013 Cengage Learning

TABLE A-2: Document toolbar buttons

button	name	function
Code	Show Code view	Displays only the Code view in the Document window
Split	Show Code and Design views	Displays both the Code and Design views in the Document window
Design	Show Design view	Displays only the Design view in the Document window
Live	Switch Design View to Live View	Displays the page with interactive elements active and functioning
	File management	Displays file management options
	Preview/Debug in browser	Activates the browser for viewing the page
	Multiscreen	Displays the page in three devices in one integrated window; list arrow lets you select options
	W3C Validation	Submits the page to the W3C service for validation
	Check browser compatibility	Checks the page for problems when viewed in browsers
	Visual Aids	Displays options for visual display of information
	Refresh Design View	Reloads the page to reflect any changes made in Code view

Getting Started with Adobe Dreamweaver CS6

Dreamweaver 7

Working with Views and Panels

Dreamweaver has three working views. **Design view** shows a page within the entire Document window and is primarily used when designing and creating a web page. **Code view** fills the Document window with the underlying HTML code for the page and is primarily used when reading or directly editing the code. **Code and Design views** (Split view) is a combination of Code view and Design view; each layout displays in a separate window within the Document window. This view is a good choice for debugging or correcting errors because you can see both the Design and Code views simultaneously. No matter which view you are using, panels and panel groups appear on the right side of the screen by default in the Designer workspace, although you can move them and use them as "floating panels." Panels are individual windows that display information on a particular topic, such as Reference or History. Panel groups, sometimes referred to as Tab groups, are sets of related panels that are grouped together. Panels are listed by groups on the Window menu and are separated by horizontal lines. 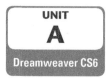 As part of your Dreamweaver exploration, you want to learn how to work with views and organize your screen by opening and closing panels.

STEPS

QUICK TIP

The icons shown in the figures are in color, although the icons by default are not in color. To change to color icons, click the Insert panel drop-down menu, then click Color Icons.

1. **In the Dreamweaver workspace, click the** Show Code view button `Code` **on the Document toolbar**

   The HTML code for the untitled, blank document appears, as shown in Figure A-4. The code for a blank, untitled page is very limited since the page has no content. As content is added, the number of lines of code will increase as well. Notice in the first line of code that this is an XHTML document type, although the file extension is .html.

2. **Click the** Show Code and Design views button `Split` **on the Document toolbar**

   A split screen appears. The left side displays the HTML code, while the right side displays the open page. The open page is blank because the current document, Unitled-1, doesn't have any content.

3. **Click the** Show Design view button `Design` **on the Document toolbar**

   A blank page appears again because there is no page content to view.

TROUBLE

If you don't see the CSS Styles panel, click Window on the Menu bar, then click CSS Styles.

4. **Click the** CSS Styles panel tab, **if necessary, to expand the panel group.**

   The CSS panel group expands so you can see the contents of the active panel. The CSS Styles panel is the active panel in the default Designer workspace when the program is opened initially. An **active panel** is displayed as the front panel in an expanded panel group with the panel options displayed. Panels open in the position they held when the program was last closed. The CSS Styles panel contains two buttons, All and Current, which are used to view specific information in the panel. When two or more panels are docked together, you can access the panel you want by clicking its tab to display its contents.

5. **Click the** AP Elements panel tab **on the CSS Styles panel group**

   AP Elements becomes the active panel with the panel contents displayed. As you click each panel tab, the panel tab changes color and the panel contents are displayed. See Figure A-5.

QUICK TIP

If you want to restore your workspace to the original settings, click Window on the Menu bar, point to Workspace Layout, click Reset 'Designer'; click View on the Menu bar, scroll down, if necessary, then click Color Icons if you want to view your icons in color.

6. **Click the** CSS Styles panel tab **to display it, then double-click the** CSS Styles panel tab

   The panel group collapses. When a panel is collapsed, you click the panel tab to expand it. If a panel group is expanded, you simply click the panel tab to make the panel active.

7. **Click** File **on the Menu bar, click** Close **to close the untitled document, then click** No **if necessary if you are asked about saving the untitled page**

FIGURE A-4: Code view for a blank document

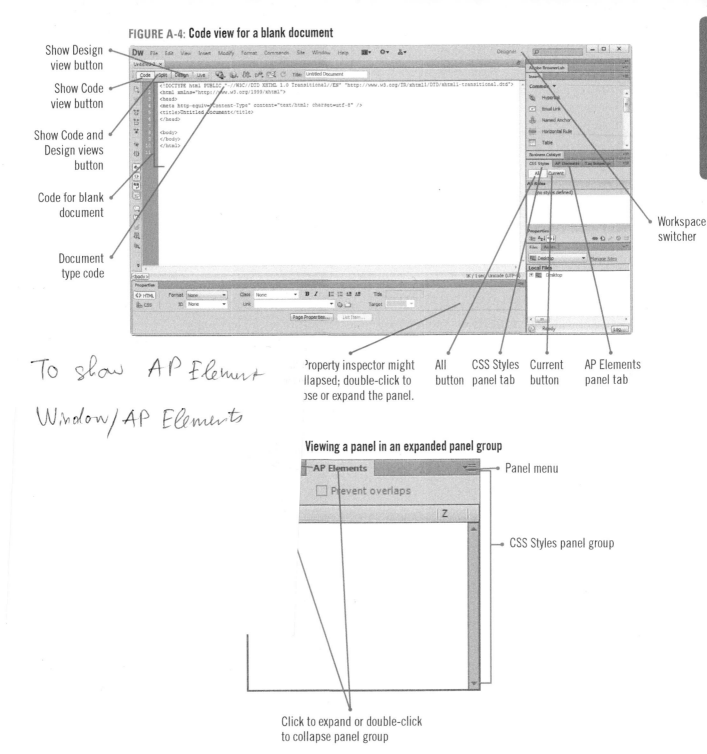

Show Design view button

Show Code view button

Show Code and Design views button

Code for blank document

Document type code

Workspace switcher

Property inspector might [be col]lapsed; double-click to [clo]se or expand the panel.

All button

CSS Styles panel tab

Current button

AP Elements panel tab

To show AP Element
Window/AP Elements

Viewing a panel in an expanded panel group

Panel menu

CSS Styles panel group

Click to expand or double-click to collapse panel group

Using panel groups

By default, the Adobe BrowserLab panel, Insert panel, CSS Styles panel group, Business Catalyst panel, and Files panel group open when you first start Dreamweaver in Windows. The panels will retain their arrangement from one session to the next. For instance, if you open the Files panel and do not close it before exiting Dreamweaver, it will be open the next time you start Dreamweaver. To close a panel group, right-click (Win) or [control]-click (Mac) its title bar, then click Close

Tab Group. The **panel group title bar** is the dark gray bar at the top of each panel group. The Panel menu lets you choose commands related to the currently displayed panel. You can also rearrange the workspace using your own choices for panel placement and save the workspace with a unique name using the "New Workspace" and "Manage Workspaces" commands on the Workspace switcher. The Workspace switcher is shown in Figure A-4.

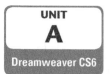
Opening a Web Page

After opening Dreamweaver, you can create a new website or page, or open an existing website or page. The first web page that appears when you access a website is called the **home page**. The home page sets the look and tone of the website and contains a navigation structure that directs the user to the rest of the pages in the website. ████ The resort's marketing firm has designed a new banner for The Striped Umbrella. You begin by opening The Striped Umbrella home page to view the new banner.

STEPS

> **TROUBLE**
> If you do not have your preferences set to show file extensions, you will not see the file extensions for each file. To show file extensions, open Windows Explorer, click Organize, click Folder and search options, click the View tab, then uncheck Hide extensions for known file types.

1. **Click File on the Menu bar, then click Open**
   The Open dialog box opens.

2. **Click the Look in list arrow ⏷ (Win) or click the Current file location list arrow ⏺ (Mac), navigate to the drive and folder where you store your Unit A Data Files, then double-click (Win) or click (Mac) the unit_a folder**
   The list of the data files in the unit_a folder, along with an assets folder where the image files for this unit are stored, appear in the Name column. See Figure A-6.

> **QUICK TIP**
> You can also double-click a file in the Open dialog box to open it. Or click File on the Menu bar, then click one of the recently opened files listed in the Open Recent submenu.

3. **Click the dwa_1.html file, then click Open**
   The document named dwa_1.html opens in the Document window in Design view. Since you are in Design view, all of the page elements appear as if you were viewing the page in a web browser. The interactive elements, however, will not work unless you change to Live View. Since you opened this page as a single page without access to the accompanying pages, the links will not work in Live View or in a browser.

4. **If necessary, click the Maximize button ▭ (Win) or ⊕ (Mac) on the Document window title bar**

5. **Click the Show Code view button ⌑Code⌑ on the Document toolbar**
   The HTML code for the page appears.

6. **Scroll through the code, click the Show Design view button ⌑Design⌑ on the Document toolbar to return to Design view, then, if necessary, scroll to display the top of the page**

Design Matters

Opening or creating different document types with Dreamweaver

You can use either the Welcome Screen or the New command on the File menu to open or create several types of files. For example, you can create HTML documents, XML documents, style sheets, and text files. You can create new documents from scratch, or base them on existing pages. The predesigned CSS page layouts make it easy to design web pages based on Cascading Style Sheets without an advanced level of expertise in writing HTML code. Predesigned templates save you time and promote consistency across a website. As you learn more about Dreamweaver, you will find it worthwhile to explore each category to understand what is available to you as a designer.

FIGURE A-6: Open dialog box (Windows and Mac)

dwa_1.html
data file

Look in list arrow

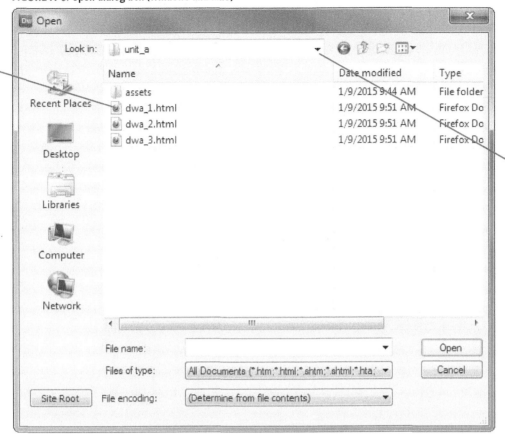

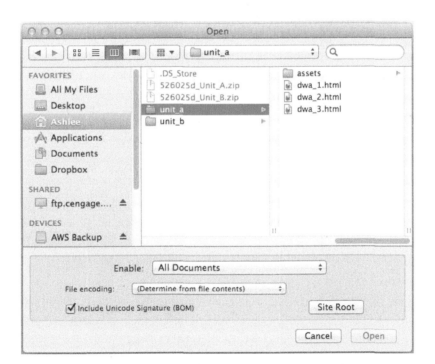

Displaying and docking panel groups

You can move panel groups to a different area on the screen by dragging the panel group title bar. To dock a panel group, drag the panel group to the right side of the screen. A heavy blue bar indicates the position it will take when you release the mouse button. This position is called the **drop zone**. You can also minimize all panels to icons by clicking the Collapse to Icons button in the top-right corner of the top panel. You can hide and show all panels by pressing the F4 key (Win).

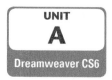
Viewing Web Page Elements

There are many elements that make up web pages. Web pages can be very simple, designed primarily with text, or they can be media-rich with text, images, sound, and videos. You can use the programs shown in Table A-3 to create many of the more common web page elements. Web page elements can be placed directly on the page, or pages can be designed with elements placed in defined areas called **divs** to format and position page elements. Differences in monitor size and settings affect the size of the program and Document windows so your screen may show a larger or smaller area of the document than the figures in this book. ▓▓▓▓▓ To familiarize yourself with web page elements, you examine the various elements on the Striped Umbrella page.

Compare your screen to Figure A-7 as you examine the following:

- **Text**

  Text is the most basic element on a web page. Most information is presented with text. You type or import text onto a web page and then format it with the Property inspector so it is easy to read. Text should be short and to the point so that users can easily skim through it as they browse through websites.

- **Images**

  Images add visual interest to a web page. However, the adage "less is more" is certainly true with images. Too many images cause the page to load too slowly and discourage users from waiting. Many web pages contain **banners**, images that appear across the top of the screen. Banners can incorporate information, such as a company's logo and contact information.

- **Hyperlinks**

  Hyperlinks, also known as **links**, are graphic or text elements on a web page that users click to display another location on the page, another web page within the same website, or a web page in a different website.

- **Divs and AP Divs**

  Divs and AP divs are important page layout options because they allow you to "draw" or insert blocks of content on a page. These content containers can then be used to hold page elements, such as text or images. Because AP divs can "float" over any page element, they are easy to reposition and can be programmed to display according to set criteria. Most designers use divs formatted with Cascading Style Sheets (CSS) for page design. You will learn more about CSS in Unit D.

- **Tables**

  Tables, grids of rows and columns, can be used to hold tabular data on a web page. When used as a design tool, the edges of the table (table borders) can be made invisible to the user. Elements are then placed in table cells to control the placement of each element on the page. Div tags, however, are the best way to display general information that you want to place in columns and rows.

- **Flash movies**

  Flash movies are low-bandwidth animations and interactive elements created using Adobe Flash. These animations use a series of vector-based graphics that load quickly and merge with other graphics and sounds to create short movies. Some websites are built entirely by using Flash, while others may have Flash content in defined areas on individual pages. Most current browsers include Flash player as part of the software. **Flash player** is an Adobe program that is free to download and use. It is required to play Flash animations.

- **Flash video**

  Flash videos are videos that have been converted from a digital video file format to an .flv file using Adobe Flash. The big advantage to Flash videos is that they can be **streamed**, which means that they begin playing before the entire file has been downloaded.

FIGURE A-7: Viewing web page elements

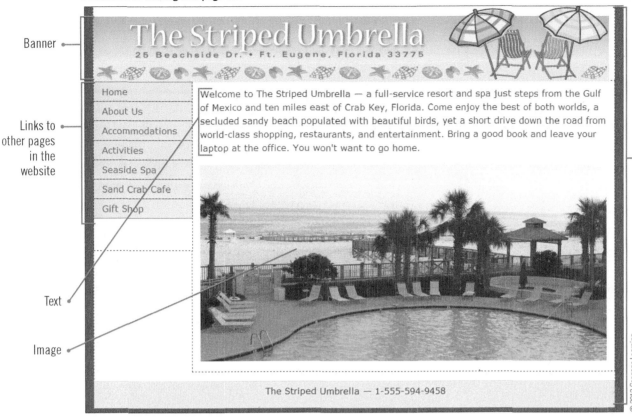

Banner

Links to other pages in the website

Text

Image

Page layout based on divs

Welcome to The Striped Umbrella — a full-service resort and spa just steps from the Gulf of Mexico and ten miles east of Crab Key, Florida. Come enjoy the best of both worlds, a secluded sandy beach populated with beautiful birds, yet a short drive down the road from world-class shopping, restaurants, and entertainment. Bring a good book and leave your laptop at the office. You won't want to go home.

The Striped Umbrella — 1-555-594-9458

© 2013 Cengage Learning
Original photo courtesy of Sherry Bishop

TABLE A-3: Programs used to create web page elements

source program	elements created
Adobe Edge	Used to create animation and interactive content
Adobe Fireworks	Used to create and optimize images for the web
Adobe Flash	Used to create animation and vector graphics
Adobe Illustrator	Used to create and edit vector graphics
Adobe Photoshop	Used to edit and enhance bitmap images

Getting Help

Dreamweaver has an excellent Help feature that is comprehensive and easy to use. When questions or problems arise, you can use the Adobe Community Help window. This window contains two tools that you can use to search for answers in different ways: the link to the PDF and a Search box. Clicking the link to the PDF opens the Dreamweaver Help PDF file that is saved locally on your computer and that contains a list of topics and subtopics by category. The Search box at the top-left corner of the window enables you to enter a keyword to search for a specific topic. You can see context-specific help by clicking the Help button in the Property inspector (Win). The Help feature in Dreamweaver CS6 is based on Adobe Air technology. **Adobe AIR** is an Adobe product used for developing content that can be delivered with a browser or as a desktop application. Context-specific help can be accessed by clicking the Help button on the Property inspector (Win).  You decide to access the Help feature to learn more about Dreamweaver.

STEPS

1. **Click Help on the Menu bar**

   The Help menu appears, displaying the Help categories. See Figure A-8.

2. **Click Dreamweaver Help**

   The Dreamweaver Help/Help and tutorials window opens. Since the help feature is online content, you must have Internet access to use it. This also means that since it is Web content, the pages are live pages subject to change. Your screens will probably not match the figures exactly.

3. **Type "workspace switcher" in the search box on the left side of the window under the words Adobe Community Help, click the drop-down menu next to the search text box, click Dreamweaver if necessary, then press [Enter]**

   A list of topics related to the workspace switcher appears.

4. **Click the option button next to "Only Adobe content" as shown in Figure A-9 then read the information in the Content pane**

   The list repopulates to show only content from the Adobe website. Community content includes content that has been posted from other approved sources outside of Adobe.

5. **Click one of the links listed**

6. **Scroll through and read some of the information, as shown in Figure A-10, then close the Dreamweaver Help window**

Using Adobe Help

When you access the Help feature in Dreamweaver, you have the choice of downloading a PDF for offline help (which is similar to searching in a Dreamweaver manual) or using online help. The online help feature is called Adobe Community Help.

Adobe Community Help is a collection of materials such as tutorials, published articles, or blogs, in addition to the regular help content. All content is monitored and approved by the Adobe Community Expert program.

FIGURE A-8: **Help menu**

Dreamweaver Help	F1
Business Catalyst Help	
Spry Framework Help	
Get started with Business Catalyst InContext Editing	
Reference	Shift+F1
Dreamweaver Support Center	
Dreamweaver Exchange	
Manage Extensions...	
CSS Advisor	
Adobe Online Forums	
Complete/Update Adobe ID Profile...	
Deactivate...	
Updates...	
Adobe Product Improvement Program...	
About Dreamweaver	

Macintosh users will see this on the Dreamweaver menu

FIGURE A-9: **Displaying the Help topics**

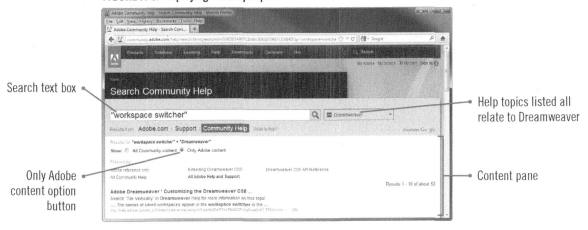

Search text box

Help topics listed all relate to Dreamweaver

Only Adobe content option button

Content pane

FIGURE A-10: **Displaying Help content**

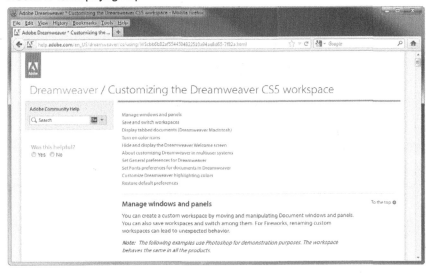

Viewing a Web Page in a Browser

During the process of creating and editing a web page, it is helpful to frequently view the page in a web browser. Dreamweaver also has a view called Live view that displays the page as if it were being viewed using a browser. In Live view, the Browser Navigation toolbar above the Document window becomes active. The **Browser Navigation toolbar** allows you to follow links in Live view as if you were viewing the pages in the browser. Viewing the page in a browser provides visual feedback of what the page will look like when it is published on the Internet. It is best to view a web page using different browsers, screen sizes, and resolutions to ensure the best view based upon your computer's capabilities. It is important to remember that you cannot print a web page in Dreamweaver except in Code view. You use the Print command on your browser toolbar or menu to print the page. 💡 You decide to view The Striped Umbrella home page in your default browser.

STEPS

TROUBLE
If the status bar is out of view, then resize and reposition the Document window as necessary for it to be visible. Drag a corner to resize the window and drag the title bar to reposition it.

1. **In Design view, click the Maximize button ▫ (Win) or ⊕ (Mac) on the Menu bar, then click the Window Size pop-up menu on the right side of the status bar**

   The Window Size pop-up menu appears, as shown in Figure A-11. The Window Size pop-up menu lists several options for simulating commonly used screen sizes. You may need to double-click the right side of the Property inspector to collapse it in order to see the Window Size pop-up menu.

2. **Click 1000 × 620 (1024 × 768, Maximized)**

   The screen size is set to 1000 × 620, which translates to a monitor set at a 1024 × 768 screen resolution. When you choose your screen size, it is important to consider the equipment your users may have when they view your page in their browser. You need to consider how your pages will look, not only with different size desktop monitors, but also on tablets and other mobile devices. The Status bar also has Mobile size ▣, Tablet size ▣, and Desktop size ▣ buttons you can use to view pages with these device sizes. See Table A-4 for window size options.

QUICK TIP
You can change the browser list by using the Edit > Preferences > Preview in Browser command, then using the Add or Remove Browser buttons to add or remove browsers from the list.

3. **Click the Preview/Debug in browser button 🌐 on the Document toolbar, then click Preview in [browser name]**

   The browser opens, and the Striped Umbrella web page previews in the browser, as shown in Figure A-12.

TROUBLE
If you don't see a menu bar, press [Ctrl] [P] to print.

4. **Click File on the browser Menu bar, then click Print**

   The Print dialog box opens.

5. **Click Print**

   A copy of the web page prints. The black background that appears on the web page will not print unless you have selected the Print background colors and images option in your printer settings.

FIGURE A-11: Window size pop-up menu

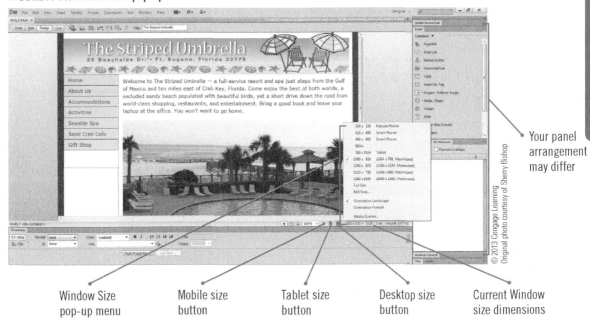

Your panel arrangement may differ

Window Size pop-up menu   Mobile size button   Tablet size button   Desktop size button   Current Window size dimensions

FIGURE A-12: Web page previewed in a browser window

Your path will differ

TABLE A-4: Window size options

window size (inside dimensions of browser window without borders)	corresponding resolution
240 × 320	Feature Phone
320 × 480	Smart Phone
480 × 800	Smart Phone
592w	
768 × 1024	Tablet
1000 × 620	(1024 × 768, Maximized)
1260 × 875	(1280 × 1024, Maximized)
1420 × 750	(1440 × 900, Maximized)
1580 × 1050	(1600 × 1200, Maximized)

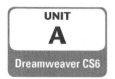

Closing a Web Page and Exiting Dreamweaver

When you are ready to stop working with a file in Dreamweaver, it is a good idea to close the current page or pages you are working on and exit the program. This should prevent data loss if power is interrupted; in some cases, power outages can corrupt an open file and make it unusable. You are finished working for the day so you want to close the web page and exit Dreamweaver.

STEPS

1. **In the browser, click File on the Menu bar, then click Exit (Win), or click [Browser name] on the Menu bar, then click Quit [Browser name] (Mac)**

   The browser closes, and The Striped Umbrella Web page reappears in the Dreamweaver window, as shown in Figure A-13. In this book, screen shots of finished projects feature enlarged windows to display as much content as possible. You may have to scroll to see the same amount of content.

   QUICK TIP
   You may need to click the Dreamweaver CS6 title bar to activate the program.

2. **In the Dreamweaver workspace, click File on the Application bar, then click Exit (Win) or click Dreamweaver on the Menu bar, then click Quit Dreamweaver (Mac)**

   Dreamweaver closes.

Saving and closing Dreamweaver files

It is wise to save a file as soon as you begin creating it and to save frequently as you work. A quick glance at the title bar shows whether you have saved your file. If you haven't saved the file initially, the filename shows "Untitled" rather than a filename. This does not refer to the page title, but the actual filename. After you save the file and make a change to it, an asterisk appears at the end of the filename until you save it again. It is always wise to save and close a page on which you are not actively working. Keeping multiple files open can cause confusion, especially when you are working with multiple websites which have similarly named pages. Each open page has a tab at the top of the page with the filename listed. You use these tabs to switch between each open page to make it the active page. You can also press [Ctrl] [Tab] (Win) or [command][tab] (Mac) to move between open documents.

FIGURE A-13: The finished project in Dreamweaver

The Striped Umbrella

25 Beachside Dr. • Ft. Eugene, Florida 33775

| Home |
| About Us |
| Accommodations |
| Activities |
| Seaside Spa |
| Sand Crab Cafe |
| Gift Shop |

Welcome to The Striped Umbrella — a full-service resort and spa just steps from the Gulf of Mexico and ten miles east of Crab Key, Florida. Come enjoy the best of both worlds, a secluded sandy beach populated with beautiful birds, yet a short drive down the road from world-class shopping, restaurants, and entertainment. Bring a good book and leave your laptop at the office. You won't want to go home.

The Striped Umbrella — 1-555-594-9458

© 2013 Cengage Learning
Original photo courtesy of Sherry Bishop

Design Matters

Designing for multiple window sizes

It is not enough today to simply design for several different screen resolutions and sizes for prospective users using desktop monitors. Although desktop sizes are probably your main focus, you should have a design plan in place for tablet sizes and mobile phone sizes in both portrait and landscape modes. Your first thought may be that your users can just enlarge their screens using gestures. **Gestures** are interactions with a touchscreen, usually with a combination of fingers and a thumb. Gestures can be used to enlarge or reduce a screen. When users pinch their thumb and finger together, the screen zooms out. When users move their thumb and finger apart (a reverse pinch), the screen zooms in. Although most people are familiar with how to use gestures, you should not make them use them in order to read your content. Dreamweaver can help you develop a design plan for multiple window sizes with the new Fluid Grid Layout, a system for designing an adaptive website based on a single fluid grid. Another option is to use Media Queries, a tool that uses CSS3 and HTML5 to identify the device a page is being displayed in and apply the appropriate styles for optimum viewing. We will learn more about Media Queries in Unit J.

Practice

Concepts Review

Label each element in the Dreamweaver window as shown in Figure A-14.

FIGURE A-14

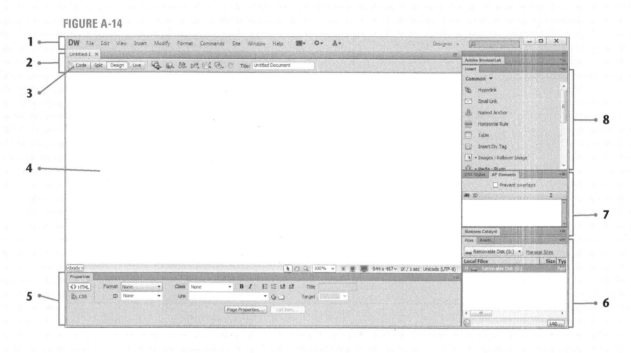

1. _____   5. _____
2. _____   6. _____
3. _____   7. _____
4. _____   8. _____

Match each of the following terms with the statement that best describes its function.

9. **Standard toolbar**
10. **Document toolbar**
11. **Code view**
12. **Tag selector**
13. **Workspace**
14. **Design view**
15. **Insert panel**
16. **Menu bar**

a. The Document window, the menu bar, toolbars, inspectors, and panels
b. Allows you to choose program commands
c. Shows the page layout
d. Contains buttons that allow you to insert objects, such as images
e. Contains buttons for some of the more commonly used options under the File and Edit menus
f. Shows the HTML code
g. Contains buttons for changing the current Dreamweaver view
h. Shows the HTML tags being used at the current insertion point

Select the best answer from the list of choices.

17. You display panels using the _____ menu.
   a. Window
   b. Edit
   c. Panel
   d. View

18. The tool that allows you to show the properties of a selected page element is called the:
   a. Tool inspector.
   b. Element inspector.
   c. Insert panel.
   d. Property inspector or Properties panel.

19. Most information on a web page is presented in the form of:
   a. text.
   b. images.
   c. links.
   d. video.

20. The view that is best for designing and creating a web page is:
   a. Code view.
   b. Design view.
   c. a combination of both Code and Design views.
   d. any of the above.

21. Which of the following is one of the Dreamweaver default panel groups?
   a. History
   b. Design
   c. Application
   d. Files

Skills Review

1. **Define web design software.**
   a. Write a short paragraph describing at least three features of Dreamweaver.
   b. Add another paragraph describing three views that are available in Dreamweaver, then describe when you would use each view.

2. **Start Adobe Dreamweaver CS6.**
   a. Start Dreamweaver and create a new HTML page.
   b. Write a list of the panels that currently appear on the screen.

3. **View the Dreamweaver workspace.**
   a. Locate the document title bar.
   b. Locate the Menu bar.
   c. Locate the Document toolbar.
   d. Locate the Insert panel.
   e. Locate the Property inspector.

4. **Work with views and panels.**
   a. Switch to Code view.
   b. Switch to Code and Design views.
   c. Switch to Design view.
   d. Expand the CSS Styles panel group.
   e. Collapse the CSS Styles panel group.

5. **Open a web page.**
   a. Open dwa_2.html from the drive and folder where you store your Unit A Data Files. Maximize the window, if necessary. (*Hint*: The file will open in the window size last selected. You can change it by using the Window Size menu.)
   b. Display the page in Code view.
   c. Display the page in Design view.
   d. Display the page in Live view, as shown in Figure A-15.
   e. Return to Design view.

6. **View web page elements.**
   a. Locate a banner.
   b. Locate text.
   c. Locate an image.

FIGURE A-15

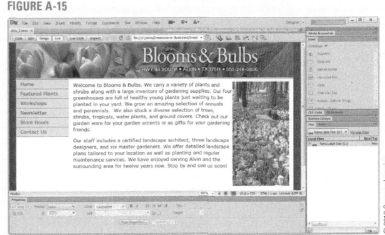

© 2013 Cengage Learning   Original photos courtesy of Sherry Bishop

Skills Review (continued)

7. Get Help.

    a. Use Dreamweaver Help to search for topics relating to the Assets panel.

    b. Display Help information on one of the topics.

    c. Print the topic information.

    d. Close the Help window.

8. View a web page in a browser window.

    a. Note the window size that is currently selected in Dreamweaver.

    b. Change the window size to a different setting.

    c. Preview the page in your web browser.

    d. Print the page.

    e. Close the browser.

9. Close a web page and exit Dreamweaver.

    a. Close the web page.

    b. Exit Dreamweaver.

Independent Challenge 1

You have recently purchased Adobe Dreamweaver CS6 and are eager to learn to use it. You open a web page and view it using Dreamweaver.

    a. Start Dreamweaver.

    b. Open the file dwa_3.html from the drive and folder where you store your Unit A Data Files. Your screen should resemble Figure A-16. (*Hint*: The file will open in the window size last selected. You can change it by using the Window Size menu.)

    c. Change to Code view.

    d. Change back to Design view.

    e. Collapse the Files panel group if necessary.

    f. Expand the Files panel group.

    g. Change the window size, then preview the page in your browser.

    h. Close the browser, close the file, then exit Dreamweaver.

FIGURE A-16

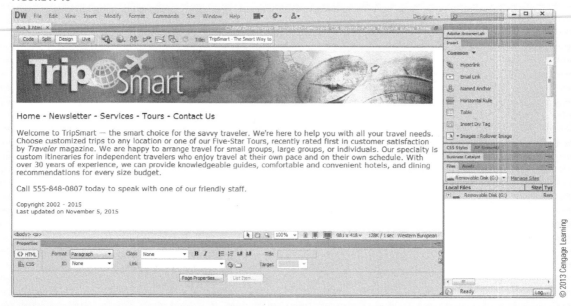

Independent Challenge 2

When you work in Dreamweaver, it is important to organize your panels so that you have the information you need where you can access it quickly.

a. Start Dreamweaver.
b. Use Dreamweaver Help to locate information on how to collapse or expand panel groups.
c. Read and print the information.
d. Close the Help window, then exit Dreamweaver.

 ## Independent Challenge 3

The Adobe website has a feature called Customer Showcase, which includes links to websites that were created using Adobe software such as Dreamweaver, Flash, and Fireworks. The Customer Showcase feature includes the Site of the Day and Customer Showcase Features. The Customer Showcase Features links provide information about spotlighted companies, the challenges that were presented to the design team, the solution, and the resulting benefits to the companies. You visit the Adobe website to look at some of the featured websites to get a feel for what constitutes good page design.

a. Connect to the Internet, then go to the Adobe website at adobe.com.
b. Click the Company link at the top of the screen, then click Customer Showcase. Scroll down and click one of the examples.
c. Read the success story, then print the page from the browser.
d. Close your browser.
e. Using a word processing program or paper, write a short summary (two paragraphs) of the success story, then list three things that you learned about the Adobe software that was used. For example: "I learned that the Adobe Digital Publishing Suite can be used to develop tablet applications."

 ## Real Life Independent Challenge

You are about to begin work on an original website. This site can be about anything you are interested in developing. It can be about you and your family, a hobby, a business, or a fictitious website. There will be no data files supplied. This site will build from unit to unit, so you must do each Real Life Independent Challenge to complete your website.

a. Decide what type of website you would like to build.
b. Find sites on the Internet that are similar to the one you would like to design to gather some ideas.
c. Evaluate what works on these sites and what doesn't work.
d. Write down at least three ideas for your new site.
e. Write down the screen resolutions you will use for designing your pages.

Visual Workshop

Open Dreamweaver, create a new HTML file using the Welcome screen, then use the Window menu to open the panels and document, as shown in Figure A-17. If necessary, collapse or expand the panels into the position on the screen shown in Figure A-17. Exit (Win) or Quit (Mac) Dreamweaver.

FIGURE A-17

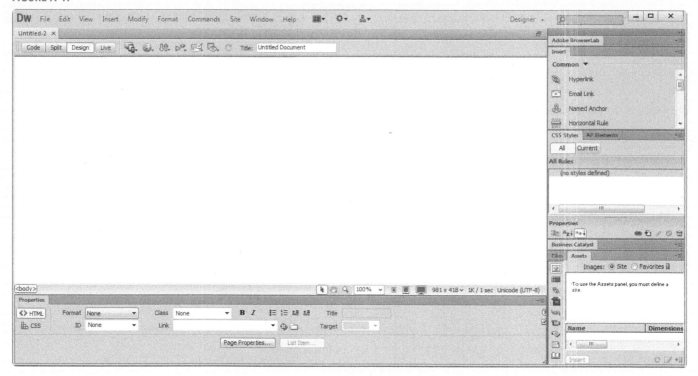

Creating a Website

Files You Will Need:

To view a list of files needed for this unit, see the Data Files Grid in the back of the book.

Creating a website requires lots of thought and careful planning. Dreamweaver CS6 has many tools to help you plan, create, and manage your sites. In this unit, you use these tools to plan and design a new website.  The owners of The Striped Umbrella meet with you to discuss their ideas for a new and improved website. You assure them that you can create a great site for them with Dreamweaver.

OBJECTIVES

Plan a website

Create a folder for website management

Set up a website

Add a folder to a website

Save a web page

Copy a new image to a website

Add new pages to a website

Adobe product screenshot(s) reprinted with permission from Adobe Systems Incorporated.

Planning a Website

Developing a website is a process that begins with careful planning and research. You should plan all development phases before you begin. Figure B-1 illustrates the steps involved in website planning. Your plan should include how you will organize and implement your site. It should also encompass testing your pages on different types of computers and modifying the pages to handle challenges such as page elements appearing inconsistently in different devices or browsers. Careful planning of your website may prevent mistakes that would be costly and time-consuming to correct. After consulting with the lead member of the web development team, you review the steps described below to help you create a plan for The Striped Umbrella site.

DETAILS

QUICK TIP
You can easily create a simple, or low-fidelity, wireframe using a program such as Microsoft PowerPoint, Adobe Illustrator, or Adobe Fireworks. To create a more detailed wireframe that simulates site navigation and user interaction, use a high-fidelity wireframe program such as OverSite, ProtoShare, or Microsoft Visio.

- **Research site goals and needs**

  When you research your website, you determine the site's purpose and requirements. Create a checklist of questions and answer them before you begin work. For example: "What are the company's or client's goals for the website? What tools will I need to construct the site? Will the site require media files? If so, who will create them?" The more questions that you can answer about the site, the more prepared you will be to begin development. Once you have gone through your checklist, create a timeline and a budget for the site.

- **Create a wireframe**

  A **wireframe** can range from a small sketch that represents the relationship between every page of a website to a complex prototype of each page's content on a website, including filenames, navigation, images, text, and link information. Like a flowchart or storyboard, a wireframe shows the relationship of each page to the other pages on the site. Wireframes are used throughout the development process. Consult your wireframe before beginning work on a new page to use as your "blueprint" and compare each completed page to its prototype to make sure you met the specifications. The wireframe example shown in Figure B-2 is helpful during the planning process as it allows you to visualize how each page on the site is linked to the others.

- **Create folders**

  Before you create your website, you can plan for your file storage needs by creating a system of folders for all of the elements you will use in the site. Decide where on your computer you will store your site. Start by creating a folder for the website with a descriptive name, such as the name of the company. Then create a subfolder to store all of the files that are not web pages—for example, images, audio files, and video clips. An organized folder system makes it easier to find files quickly as you develop and edit your website. Figure B-3 shows the folder structure of the Striped Umbrella site.

- **Collect the page content and create the web pages**

  This is the fun part! After studying your wireframe, gather the files you need to create the pages—for example, text, images, buttons, videos, and animations. Some of these elements will be imported from other software programs, and some will be created in Dreamweaver. For instance, you can create text either directly in Dreamweaver or in a word processing program and then import it into Dreamweaver.

- **Test and modify the pages**

  It is important to test your web pages using a variety of web browsers. The four most common browsers are Microsoft Internet Explorer, Apple Safari, Google Chrome, and Mozilla Firefox. You should also test your website using different versions of each browser, a variety of screen resolutions (as discussed in Unit A), and various connection speeds (dial-up modems are considerably slower than cable or DSLs (Digital Subscriber Lines). Your web pages will need to be updated on a regular basis as new information is released and older information becomes outdated. Each time you modify a website element, it is wise to test the site again.

- **Publish the site**

  To publish a website means to make it available for viewing on the Internet or on an **intranet**, an internal website without public access. Many companies have intranets to enable them to share information within their organizations. You publish a website to a **web server**, a computer that is connected to the Internet with an **IP (Internet Protocol) address** and has software that enables it to make files accessible to anyone on the internet or an intranet. Until a website is published, you can only view the site if you have the files stored on a hard drive, USB disk, or other storage device connected to your computer.

FIGURE B-1: **Steps in website planning**

© 2013 Cengage Learning

FIGURE B-2: **The Striped Umbrella website wireframe**

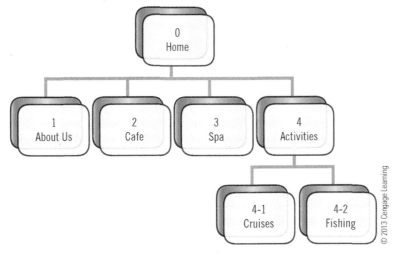

© 2013 Cengage Learning

FIGURE B-3: **Folder and file structure for The Striped Umbrella website**

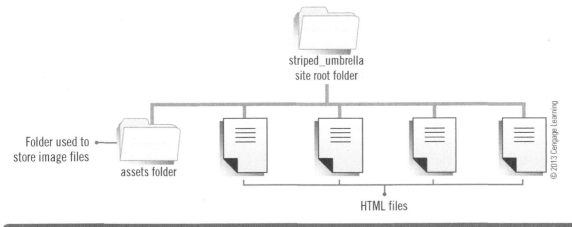

© 2013 Cengage Learning

Design Matters

IP addresses and domain names

To make a website accessible over the Internet, you must publish it to a web server with a permanent IP (Internet Protocol) address. An **IP address** is an assigned series of four numbers, each between 0 and 255 and separated by periods, that indicates the address of a specific computer or other piece of hardware on the Internet or an internal computer network. To access a web page, you enter either an IP address or a domain name in the address box of your browser window. A **domain name** is expressed in letters instead of numbers, and usually reflects the name of the business, individual, or other organization represented by the website. For example the domain name for the Adobe website is adobe.com, but the IP address (at the time of this writing) is 192.150.18.200. Because domain names use descriptive text instead of numbers, they are much easier to remember.

Creating a Folder for Website Management

After composing your checklist, creating wireframes, and gathering the files and resources you need for your website, you then set up the site's folder structure. The first folder you create for the website is called a local site folder, sometimes referred to as the **root folder**. A **local site folder** is a folder on your hard drive, USB disk, or network drive that contains all the files and folders for a website. You can create this folder using Windows Explorer (Win), the Finder (Mac), or the Files panel in Dreamweaver. The **Files panel** is a file management tool similar to Windows Explorer (Win) or Finder (Mac), where Dreamweaver stores and manages your website files and folders. Avoid using spaces, special characters, or uppercase characters when naming files or folders to prevent problems when you publish your website. When you publish the website, you transfer a copy of the local site folder contents to a remote computer, usually hosted by an Internet Service Provider (ISP). ▧▧▧▧ You want to create the local site folder (root folder) for The Striped Umbrella website and name it striped_umbrella.

STEPS

1. **Start Dreamweaver**

   The Dreamweaver Welcome Screen opens. If you don't want the Dreamweaver Welcome Screen to open each time you start Dreamweaver, click the "Don't show again" check box on the Welcome Screen. If you change your mind later, select the Show Welcome Screen check box in the General category of the Preferences dialog box.

QUICK TIP
Determine the location where you will store your new folders and files. Check with your instructor or technical support person if you need assistance.

2. **Click the Files panel tab or expand the Files panel, if necessary, to view its contents**

   The Files panel displays a list of the drives and folders on your computer.

3. **Click the Files panel Site list arrow**

   The drop-down menu displays the list of drives on your computer. See Figure B-4.

TROUBLE
If you see a drive or folder in the list box in the drop-down menu, you do not have a website open.

4. **Click to select the drive, folder, or subfolder in the list where you want your local site root folder to reside**

   The name of the selected drive or folder appears in the Files panel list box. Dreamweaver will store all of the folders and files you create for your websites in this drive or folder.

QUICK TIP
From this point forward, Mac users should know that "right-click" means they should control-click.

5. **Right-click (Win) or control-click (Mac) the drive, folder, or subfolder that you selected in Step 4, then click New Folder**

6. **Type striped_umbrella, then press [Enter] (Win) or [return] (Mac)**

   The local site root folder is named striped_umbrella, as shown in Figure B-5. All of the folders and files for The Striped Umbrella website will be saved in this folder.

FIGURE B-4: Selecting a drive in the Files panel

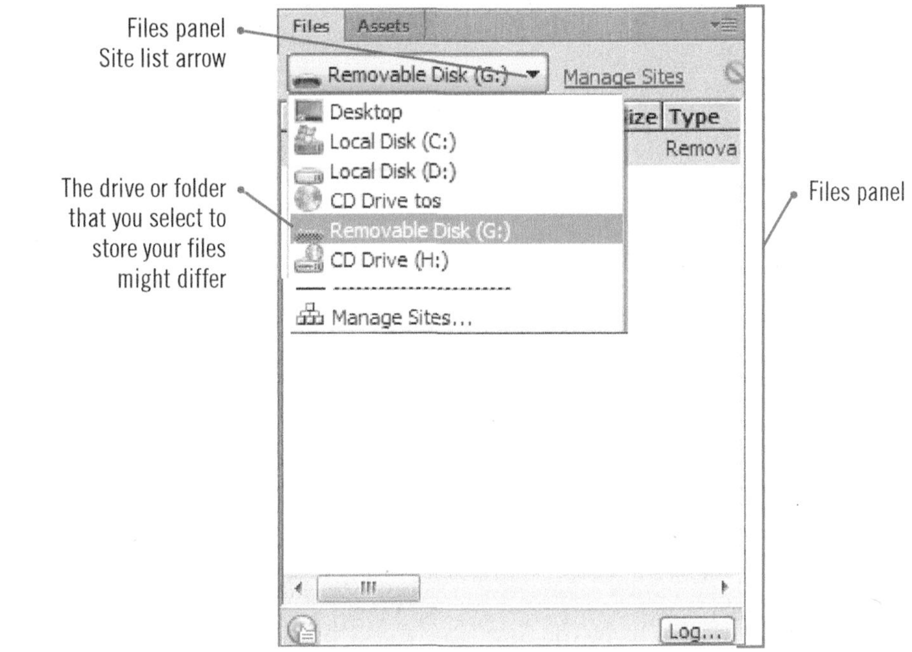

Files panel
Site list arrow

The drive or folder
that you select to
store your files
might differ

Files panel

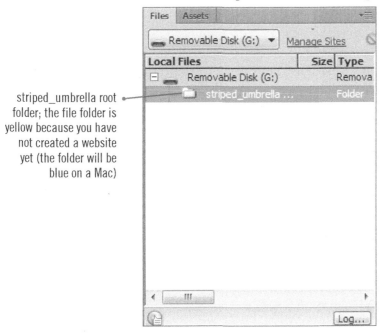

FIGURE B-5: Creating a local site root folder using the Files panel

striped_umbrella root
folder; the file folder is
yellow because you have
not created a website
yet (the folder will be
blue on a Mac)

Design Matters

Managing files

It is imperative that you understand the basics of good file management before you can master Dreamweaver. You should be able to create new folders and new files in a specified location. You should also learn the basic file naming conventions for web content. To ensure that your files are available to all users regardless of their operating system, do not use uppercase letters or spaces in filenames. Although files with uppercase letters or spaces in their names may look fine on your screen, they might not when they are published on a web server and might appear as broken links. If you do not have a basic understanding of file management, a quick review on how to use your operating system will pay big dividends and shorten your Dreamweaver learning curve.

Setting Up a Website

After you create a local site folder, the next step is to define, or set up your website. When you set up a website, you specify the site's local site root folder location to help Dreamweaver keep track of the links among your web pages and related files. After you set up the site, the program displays the local site root folder in the Files panel. The Files panel commands also help you publish your website to a remote computer. See Unit J for more information on publishing your site. 🔴🔴🔴 You are ready to define The Striped Umbrella site.

STEPS

QUICK TIP
If you have created another new site since you have opened Dreamweaver, your Unnamed Site number might be different.

1. **Click Site on the Application bar (Win) or Menu bar (Mac), then click New Site**

   The Site Setup dialog box opens, as shown in Figure B-6. (From this point forward, we will refer to "Application bar (Win) or Menu bar (Mac)" as "Menu bar" to simplify the instructions.)

QUICK TIP
You can also create a new site by clicking Dreamweaver Site under Create New on the Welcome Screen.

2. **Type The Striped Umbrella in the Site Name text box**

   The site is renamed The Striped Umbrella.

QUICK TIP
It is acceptable to use uppercase letters in the site name because it is not the name of a file or folder.

3. **Click the Browse for folder button 📁 to the right of the Local Site Folder text box, click the Select list arrow ▾ (Win) or the Current file location list arrow ⬍ (Mac) in the Choose Root Folder dialog box, navigate to the drive and folder where you created your Local Site Folder, double-click (Win) or click (Mac) the striped_umbrella folder, then click Select (Win) or Choose (Mac)**

   The Choose Root Folder dialog box closes and the Site Setup dialog box reappears with "The Striped Umbrella" as the new name, confirming that you have defined The Striped Umbrella website with the name "The Striped Umbrella". The local site folder, striped_umbrella, is designated as the location for the website files and folders. See Figure B-7.

4. **Click Save in the Site Setup dialog box**

   The Site Setup dialog box closes. Your Files panel should resemble Figure B-8. You can use the Site Setup dialog box at any time to edit your settings. Notice that the striped_umbrella folder is green. In Dreamweaver, this indicates that it is a website folder. Other types of folders are displayed in yellow.

Design Matters

Using the web as your classroom

Throughout this book, you are asked to evaluate real websites. You learn basic design principles parallel to the new skills you learn using Dreamweaver. Learning a new skill, such as inserting an image, will not be very useful if you do not understand how to use images efficiently and effectively on a page.

The best way to learn is to examine how live websites use page elements such as images to convey information. Therefore, you are encouraged to complete the Design Quest Independent Challenges to gain a practical understanding of the skills you learn.

FIGURE B-6: Site Setup dialog box

Your default
Site number
might differ

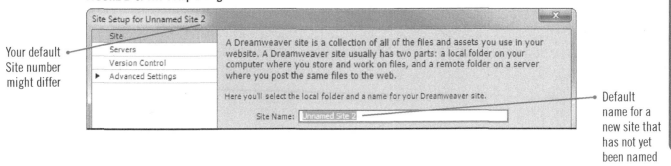

Default
name for a
new site that
has not yet
been named

FIGURE B-7: Site Setup for The Striped Umbrella dialog box

Site Name

The Striped
Umbrella local
site folder
(your path
might differ)

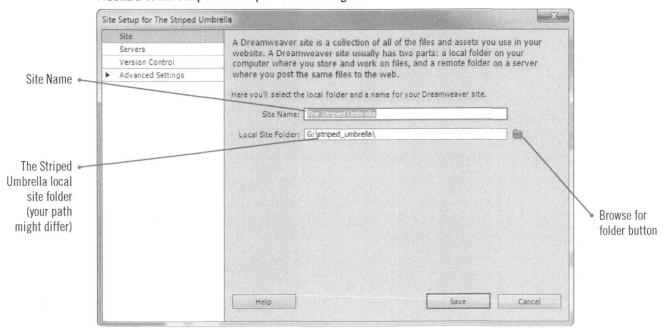

Browse for
folder button

FIGURE B-8: Files panel

The Striped Umbrella local
root folder—your path might
differ—the file folder is now
green, rather than yellow,
indicating that a website has
been created

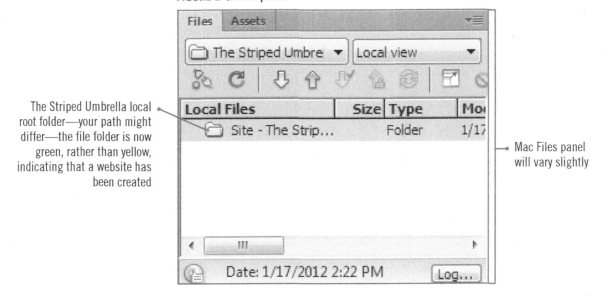

Mac Files panel
will vary slightly

Adding a Folder to a Website

After defining your website, you need to create folders to contain the non-HTML files that will add content to the site. Creating a folder called "assets" or "images" is a good beginning. Complex websites with many types of media or text files may have organizing subfolders within this folder—for example, separate folders for text files, image files, sound files, and video clips. It is better to create these folders in Dreamweaver rather than in Windows Explorer or Macintosh Finder; once you have defined a site, it is much easier to avoid errors if you let Dreamweaver perform all of the file management tasks. ▓▓▓▓ You want to create a folder called assets for The Striped Umbrella website and set this as the default folder for the images you save in the website.

STEPS

1. **If necessary, click the Files panel tab to expand the Files panel, then click the striped_umbrella folder in the Files panel if necessary**

   The striped_umbrella folder is highlighted, indicating that the site is selected.

2. **Click the Panel menu button 🗏 on the Files panel, then point to File**

   See Figure B-9.

3. **Click New Folder, as shown in Figure B-9**

   A new untitled folder appears beneath the striped_umbrella folder in the Files panel.

TROUBLE
If you are using a Mac, you may not see the new folder if the striped_umbrella folder is collapsed. To expand it, click the triangle to the left of the striped_umbrella folder.

4. **Type assets in the folder text box, then press [Enter] (Win) or [return] (Mac)**

   The Files panel displays the assets subfolder indented under the site root folder, as shown in Figure B-10. You will use the assets folder to store images and other elements used in the website. But first the assets folder has to be set as the default folder.

5. **Click Site on the Menu bar, click Manage Sites, then click the Edit the currently selected site button 🖉**

   The Site Setup for The Striped Umbrella dialog box opens with The Striped Umbrella website selected.

6. **Click Advanced Settings from the category list in the left column, click the Browse for folder button 🖿 next to the Default Images folder text box, then click the Select list arrow ▾ (Win) or the Current file location list arrow ◆ (Mac) if necessary to display the striped_umbrella folder in the Select text box**

7. **Click the assets folder**

   The Choose Image Folder dialog box shows the assets folder listed in the Select text box.

8. **Click Select (Win) or Choose (Mac), click Save in the Site Setup for The Striped Umbrella dialog box, then click Done in the Manage Sites dialog box**

   The new folder called "assets" for The Striped Umbrella website is created and established as the default location for saving all images. This will save steps when you copy image files to the website because you will not have to browse to the assets folder each time you save an image. Dreamweaver will save all images automatically in the assets folder. The Files panel shows the assets folder listed under the local site root folder, as shown in Figure B-10.

Design Matters

Why name the folder "assets"?

There is no particular significance to the word *assets* for the name of the folder you will use to store non-HTML files in your websites. Many web designers use the term *images* instead. You can name the folder anything you want, but the term *assets* is a good descriptive word for a folder that can be used to store other types of graphic or media files besides images for your site, such as sound files. The main idea is to organize your files by separating the HTML files from the non-HTML files by using a folder structure with appropriately named folders to reflect the content that they store.

FIGURE B-9: **Creating a new folder in the Files panel**

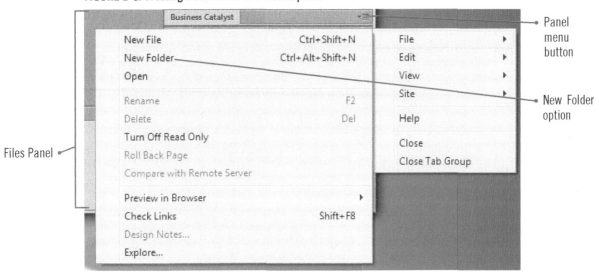

Files Panel

Panel menu button

New Folder option

FIGURE B-10: **Files panel with the assets folder added**

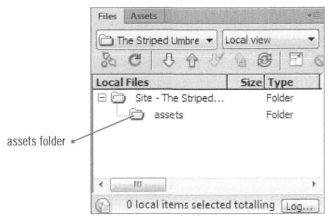

assets folder

Using the Files panel for file management

You can use the Files panel to add, delete, move, or rename files and folders in a website. *It is very important that you perform these file maintenance tasks in the Files panel rather than in Windows Explorer (Win) or the Finder (Mac). If you make changes to the folder structure outside the Files panel, you may experience problems.* If you move or copy the site root folder to a new location, you must define the website again in Dreamweaver, as you did in the lesson on defining a website.

Saving a Web Page

It is wise to save your work frequently. A good practice is to save every five or ten minutes, before you attempt a difficult step, and after you successfully complete a step. This ensures that you do not lose any work in the event of a power outage or computer problem. In this book, you are instructed to use the Save As command after you open each Data File. The Save As command duplicates the open document and allows you to assign the new document a different name. By duplicating the Data Files, you can repeat an exercise or start a lesson over if you make a mistake. ⬛⬛⬛⬛ You are ready to create the first draft of the home page. You want to open a copy of the existing home page from a folder outside the new website, rename it, and then save it in the site root folder for the Striped Umbrella website.

STEPS

1. **Click File on the Menu bar, click Open, navigate to the drive and folder where you store your Unit B Data Files, then double-click dwb_1.html**

   The Striped Umbrella home page opens in the Document window in Design View. This is the home page that users will see when they first visit The Striped Umbrella website.

QUICK TIP
The file extension php stands for PHP: Hypertext Preprocessor. It is a server-side scripting language.

2. **Click File on the Menu bar, click Save As, click the Save in list arrow ⬝ (Win) or the Current file location list arrow ⬍ (Mac) to navigate to the striped_umbrella local site root folder, then double-click (Win) or click (Mac) the striped_umbrella folder**

   The home page will be saved in the Striped Umbrella website root folder, striped_umbrella. Because it will be the home page for your site, you save the file using the name "index.html", the conventional name for a site's home page. Web servers are programmed to search for files named "index.html" or "default.html" to display as the initial page that opens in a website, as well as other file types such as index.php.

QUICK TIP
You can just type the filename "index"; the program automatically adds the .html file extension to the filename after you click Save.

3. **Click in the File name text box (Win) or Save As text box (Mac) if necessary, select the existing file name (dwb_1.html), type index.html, as shown in Figure B-11, click Save, click No in the Update Links dialog box, maximize the Document window if necessary, then click the Show Design view button ⬚ Design ⬚ if necessary**

   The Striped Umbrella home page displays in the Document window, as shown in Figure B-12. If you are not viewing the page in a separate window (Win), the path to the site root folder and the filename is displayed to the right of the document tab. If you are viewing the page in a separate window, this information appears on the document title bar. Mac users point to the file tab to see this information. The drive designator, folder name, subfolder names, and filename is called the **path**, or location of the open file in relation to any folders in the website. The page banner does not appear and is replaced by a gray box, indicating the link is broken. This means the program cannot link to the image, which currently resides in the Data Files folder. In the next lesson you will repair the link so that the image appears.

TROUBLE
If you don't see the index.html file listed in the Files panel, click the Refresh button ⟳.

4. **Click the Close button ⊠ on the dwb_1.html file tab, click the Insert panel drop-down menu, then click Color Icons if necessary to show the icons in color**

   The dwb_1.html page closes. You leave the index.html page open to correct the link to the banner image.

Design Matters

Choosing filenames

When you name a file, you should use a descriptive name that reflects the file's contents. For example, if the page is about a company's products, you could name it "products." You must also follow some general rules for naming web pages. For example, the home page should be named "index.html" or "default.html". You can also use the file extension "htm" instead of "html." Do not use spaces, special characters, regular or back slashes, or punctuation in web page filenames or in the names of any images that will be inserted in your website. Another rule is not to use a number for the first character of a filename. To ensure that everything loads properly on all platforms, including UNIX, assume that filenames are case sensitive and use lowercase characters. A good practice is to limit filenames to eight characters.

FIGURE B-11: The Save As dialog box (Windows and Mac)

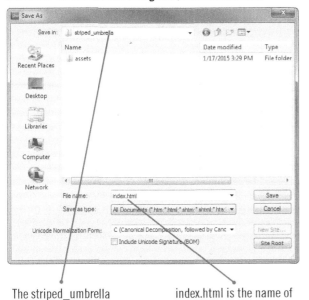

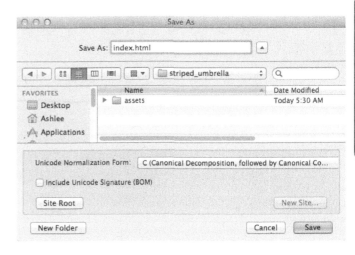

The striped_umbrella
local site root folder

index.html is the name of
the new home page

FIGURE B-12: The Striped Umbrella home page

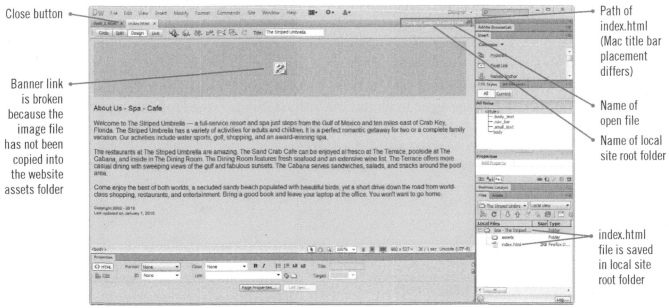

Close button

Banner link
is broken
because the
image file
has not been
copied into
the website
assets folder

Path of
index.html
(Mac title bar
placement
differs)

Name of
open file

Name of local
site root folder

index.html
file is saved
in local site
root folder

Copying a New Image to a Website

When you open a web page in one folder and then save a copy of it in a different folder, you must take care to copy each image on the page from the original folder into the new folder. If you don't do this, the links to each image will be broken when the page is published to a web server and subsequently viewed in a web browser. ██████ You want to identify The Striped Umbrella banner source file and copy it to the website's assets folder.

STEPS

TROUBLE
If your index.html page does not appear in the Files panel, click the Refresh button ⟳ on the Files panel toolbar.

1. **Click the gray box representing the broken image on the index page**

   Selection handles appear on the lower and right edges of the broken image and the Property inspector displays the banner's properties. The Src (Source) text box in the Property inspector displays the location: assets/su-banner.gif, but it is referencing the assets folder in the unit_b Data Files folder, not the assets folder in the website folder. The Striped Umbrella banner, which is the source file, currently resides in the unit_b assets folder. You navigate to the Data Files and select the source file. The concept of broken links will become clearer upon completing Unit F which explores the relationship between absolute and relative links.

TROUBLE
If the path for an image or a link begins with the word *file*, you will have linking problems. Delete all extraneous path information in the Src text box or the browser will not be able to find the image when the website is published. A good practice is to go to Code view and search for the word *file*. If you find *file* in your code, you must evaluate each occurrence to see if you need to remove unnecessary code.

2. **If necessary, double-click the right side of the Property inspector to expand it, click the Browse for File button ⌷ next to the Src text box, click the Look in list arrow ▾ (Win) or the Current file location list arrow ⬍ (Mac) if necessary to navigate to the drive and folder where you store your Data Files, double-click the unit_b folder, double-click the assets folder, then double-click the su_banner.gif file**

   The correct source file is selected from the Data Files folder. Dreamweaver copies the file to the assets folder in the website automatically because you designated the website assets folder as the default location for images when you set up the site. The Src text box in the Property inspector displays the path "assets/su_ banner.gif" without any extra path designation in front of it. If you see a path in front of the word *assets*, Dreamweaver is trying to link the image file to the Data Files folder.

3. **Click anywhere on the page outside of the banner, if necessary, to display the image, select the image again to display the image settings in the Property inspector, click File on the Menu bar, click Save, then compare your screen to Figure B-13**

   The banner now displays correctly on the page which indicates that the source file has been successfully copied to the website assets folder. The Property inspector displays the properties of the selected image.

Design Matters

Making a good first impression

Since the home page is the first page users see as they enter a website, it is important to make a good first impression. When you enter a store, you immediately notice the way the merchandise is displayed, whether the staff is accessible and friendly, and the general overall appearance and comfort of the interior. The same is true of a website. If you see pleasing colors and images, friendly and easy-to-understand text, and a simple navigation system, you are favorably impressed and want to explore the site. If you see poorly organized content, misspelled words, and confusing navigation, you will probably leave the site. It is much faster and easier to leave a website than to leave a store, so you have less time to correct a bad first impression. Have others evaluate your home page before you finalize it so you understand how others see your page.

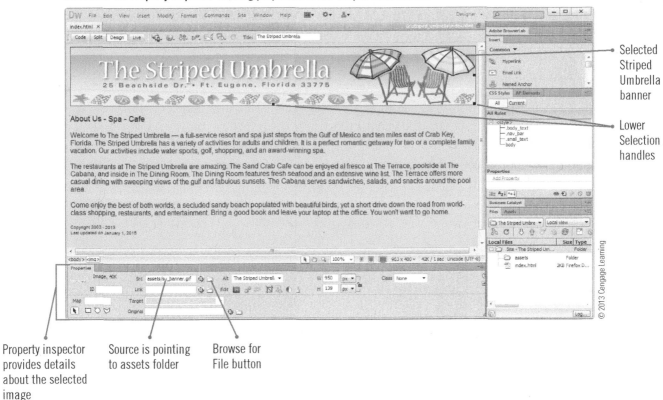

Selected
Striped
Umbrella
banner

Lower
Selection
handles

Property inspector
provides details
about the selected
image

Source is pointing
to assets folder

Browse for
File button

© 2013 Cengage Learning

Design Matters

Planning the page layout

When you begin developing the content for your website, you must decide what to include and how to arrange each element on each page. You must also design the content with the audience in mind. Who is your target audience? What is your audience's age group, sex, race, and residence? What reading and computer literacy level is appropriate? Should pages be simple, containing mostly text, or rich with images and media files? To ensure that users do not get "lost" in your website, make sure all the pages have a consistent look and feel. This can be accomplished easily through the use of templates. **Templates** are web pages that contain the basic layout for each page of a site. You can create original templates with the File menu in Dreamweaver or download them from the Internet. See the Appendix for more information on templates.

Adding New Pages to a Website

Websites may be as small as one page or contain hundreds of pages. In Dreamweaver, you can add new pages to a website, and then add content such as text and images. The blank pages serve as placeholders for pages that you anticipate designing. That way you can set up the navigation structure of the website and test the links between the pages. When you are satisfied with the overall structure, you can then create the content for the pages. You add new pages by using the Files panel. ▓▓▓▓ After consulting your wireframe, you decide to create new web pages to add to The Striped Umbrella website. You create new pages called about_us, spa, cafe, activities, cruises, and fishing, and place them in the site root folder.

STEPS

1. **Click the Refresh button ⟳ on the Files Panel, then click the plus sign (Win) or the triangle (Mac) to the left of the assets folder in the Files panel to expand the folder if necessary**

   The assets folder expands to display its contents, as shown in Figure B-14. The su_banner.gif file is located in the assets folder.

TROUBLE
Be careful not to delete the .html file extension when you name the file.

2. **Click the site folder under the Local Files column to select it, right-click the site folder, click New File, click in the filename text box to select untitled if necessary, type about_us, then press [Enter] (Win) or [return] (Mac)**

   The about us page is added to the website. You can also click the Files panel menu button ▤, point to File, then click New File to create a new file.

3. **Repeat Step 2 to add five more blank pages to The Striped Umbrella website, and name the new files spa.html, cafe.html, activities.html, cruises.html, and fishing.html**

   The new pages appear in the striped_umbrella root folder.

TROUBLE
If you accidentally create your new files in the assets folder rather than the site root folder, select and drag each one to the site root folder.

4. **Click the Refresh button ⟳ on the Files panel toolbar**

   The file listing is refreshed and the files are now sorted in alphabetical order, as shown in Figure B-15.

5. **Click File on the Menu bar, click Close, click File on the Application bar, click Exit (Win) or click Dreamweaver on the Menu bar, then click Quit Dreamweaver (Mac)**

Managing a project with a team

When working with a team, it is essential that you define clear goals for the project and a list of objectives to accomplish those goals. Your plan should be finalized after conferring with both the client and team to make sure that the purpose, scope, and objectives are clear to everyone. Establish the **deliverables**, or products that will be provided to the client upon project completion, such as creation of new pages or graphic elements, and a timeline for their delivery. You should present the web pages to both your team and client for feedback and evaluation at strategic points in the development process. Analyze all feedback objectively, incorporating both the positive and the negative comments to help you make improvements to the site and meet everyone's expectations and goals. A common pitfall in team management is scope creep. **Scope creep** occurs when impromptu changes or additions are made to a project without accounting for corresponding increases in the schedule or budget. Proper project control, resource allocation, and communication between team members and clients can minimize scope creep and achieve the successful and timely completion of a project.

FIGURE B-14: Files panel showing su_banner.gif in the assets folder

assets folder

su_banner.gif file in the assets folder

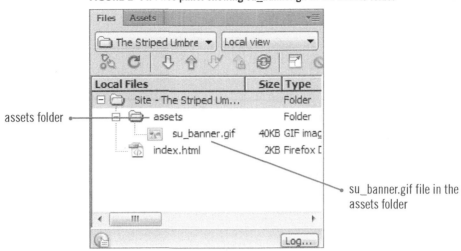

FIGURE B-15: New pages added to The Striped Umbrella website and sorted

Refresh icon

Your image icon for su_banner.gif might differ

New pages added to the striped_umbrella site folder and sorted after the Files panel is refreshed

A Mac Files panel will differ slightly in appearance

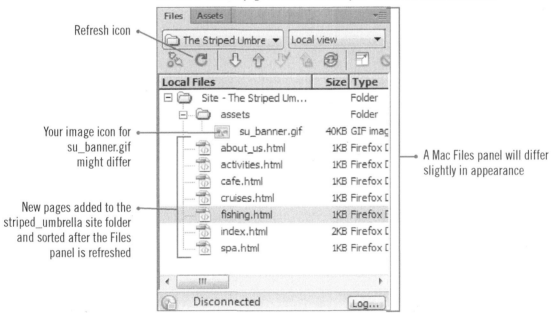

Practice

Concepts Review

Label each element in Figure B-16.

FIGURE B-16

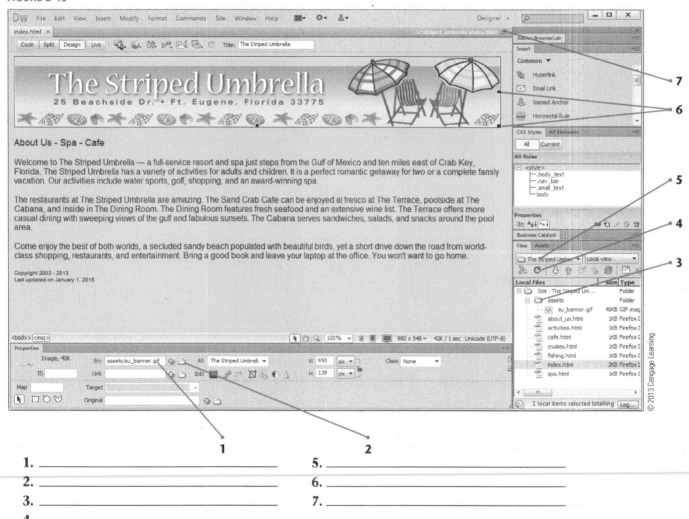

1. _____   5. _____
2. _____   6. _____
3. _____   7. _____
4. _____

Match each of the following terms with the statement that best describes its function.

8. Domain name
9. Wireframe
10. Assets
11. IP address
12. web server
13. Local site folder
14. Intranet
15. Home page
16. Publish a website

a. An address on the web expressed in numbers
b. Computer connected to the Internet with an IP address and software that enables it to make files accessible for viewing on the Internet
c. An internal website without public access
d. To make a website available for viewing on the Internet
e. A folder that holds all the files and folders for a website
f. Usually the first page users see when they visit a website
g. A folder that contains non-HTML files
h. A diagram of a website's folder structure showing links and placement of main page elements
i. An address on the web expressed in letters

Select the best answer from the following list of choices.

17. An internal website without public access is called a(n):

a. Internet

b. Intranet

c. Domain

d. Extension

18. The first step in designing a website should be:

a. Setting up web server access

b. Testing the pages

c. Planning the site

d. Creating the pages and developing the content

19. Which icon or button do you click to refresh the Files panel after you have changed files listed there?

a. 🗂

b. ↻

c. Code

d. 🌐

20. Web pages that contain the basic layout for each page in a website are called:

a. Templates

b. Examples

c. Shells

d. Forms

Skills Review

1. Plan a website.

a. Create a wireframe with five pages for a company called Blooms & Bulbs.

b. Name the pages **index**, **plants**, **workshops**, **newsletter**, and **tips**. (The plants, workshops, newsletter, and tips pages will be linked to the index page.)

2. Create a folder for website management.

a. Start Dreamweaver, then open or expand the Files panel if necessary.

b. Select the drive or folder in the Site list box where you will store your website files.

c. Create a new folder with the name **blooms** to store your website files.

3. Define the website.

a. Create a new site using the Site > New Site command. Name the site **Blooms & Bulbs**.

b. In the Site Setup dialog box, browse to select the root folder you created for the website.

c. Save the site definition and exit the site setup.

4. Add a folder to the website.

a. Use the Files panel to create an assets folder for the website.

b. Use the Site Setup dialog box to set the assets folder as the default images folder for storing your image files.

5. Copy a new image to a website.

a. Open dwb_2.html from the drive and folder where your unit_b Data Files are stored.

b. Save the file as **index.html** in the blooms folder in the Blooms & Bulbs website, and do not update the links.

c. Close the dwb_2.html file.

d. Select the gray box representing the broken link to the banner image on the page.

e. Using the Browse for File button next to the Src text box on the Property inspector, navigate to the assets folder inside the unit_b folder where you store your Data Files, then select blooms_banner.jpg.

f. Refresh the Files panel, click on the page to deselect the banner, then verify that the banner was copied to the assets folder in your Blooms & Bulbs site, then save the index.html file.

Skills Review (continued)

6. **Add new pages to a website.**

   a. Using the Files panel, create a new page called **plants.html**.

   b. Create three more pages, called **workshops.html**, **tips.html**, and **newsletter.html**.

   c. Use the Refresh button to sort the files in alphabetical order, then compare your screen to Figure B-17.

   d. Close the index page, then exit Dreamweaver.

FIGURE B-17

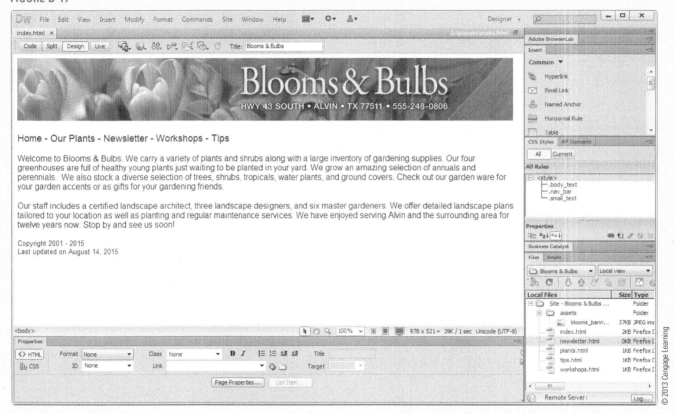

Independent Challenge 1

You have been hired to create a website for a river expedition company named Rapids Transit, located on the Buffalo River in Arkansas. In addition to renting canoes, kayaks, and rafts, they have several types of cabin rentals for overnight stays. River guides are available, if requested, to accompany clients on float trips. The clients range from experienced floaters to beginners. Refer to Figure B-18 as you work through the following steps:

a. Create a website plan and wireframe for this site.

b. Create a folder named **rapids** in the drive and folder where you save your website files.

c. Define the site with the name **Rapids Transit**, setting the rapids folder as the site root folder for the website.

d. Create an **assets** folder, then set it as the default images folder.

e. Open dwb_3.html from the drive and folder where your Unit B Data Files are stored, then save it in the site folder as **index.html**. Do not update the links.

f. Close dwb_3.html.

g. Save the rt_banner.jpg image in the assets folder for your site and save the index.html file. (*Hint*: Use the Browse for File button next to the Src text box to navigate to the unit_b assets folder to locate the image.) Refresh the Files panel and verify that the rt_banner.jpg image was copied to the site assets folder.

h. Create four additional files for the pages in your site plan, and give them the following names: **guides.html**, **rates.html**, **lodging.html**, and **before.html**. Refresh the Files panel to display the files in alphabetical order.

i. Close the index page, then exit Dreamweaver.

FIGURE B-18

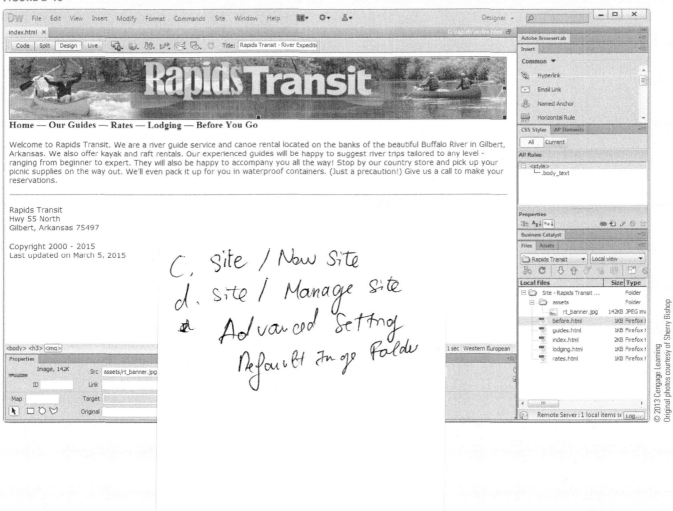

© 2013 Cengage Learning
Original photos courtesy of Sherry Bishop

Independent Challenge 2

Your company is designing a new website for a travel outfitter named TripSmart. TripSmart specializes in travel products and services. In addition to selling travel products such as luggage and accessories, they organize trips and offer travel advice. Their clients range from college students to families to vacationing professionals. The owner, Thomas Howard, has requested a dynamic website that conveys the excitement of traveling. Refer to Figure B-19 as you work through the following steps:

a. Create a website plan and wireframe for this site to present to Thomas.

b. Create a folder named **tripsmart** in the drive and folder where you save your website files.

c. Define the site with the name **TripSmart**, then set the tripsmart folder as the site root folder.

d. Create an assets folder, then set it as the default images folder.

e. Open the file dwb_4.html from the drive and folder where you store your Unit B Data Files, then save it in the site root folder as **index.html**. Do not update the links.

f. Close dwb_4.html.

g. Save the tripsmart_banner.jpg image in the assets folder for the site, save the index.html file, then refresh the Files panel to display the image file in the assets folder.

h. Create four additional files for the pages in your plan, and give them the following names: **catalog.html**, **newsletter.html**, **services.html**, and **tours.html**. Refresh the Files panel to display the files in alphabetical order, then compare your screen to Figure B-19.

i. Close the index page, then exit Dreamweaver.

FIGURE B-19

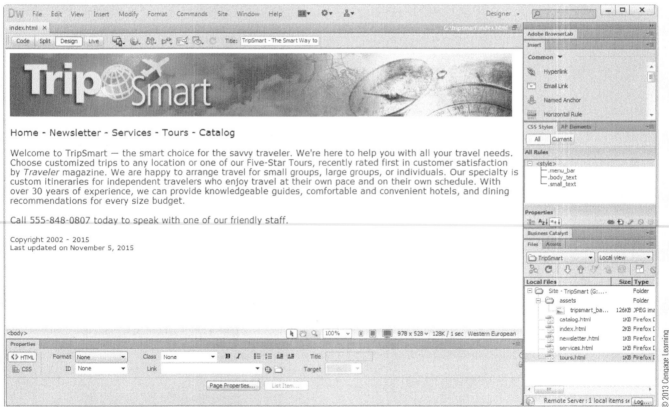

Independent Challenge 3

Patsy Broers is interested in a national program that encourages high school students to memorize and recite poetry. This program is sponsored by the National Endowment for the Arts (NEA), so she goes to the NEA website, shown in Figure B-20, to look for information on the program. (As this is a live site, your figure may differ due to content changes.) Record your answers to the questions below.

FIGURE B-20

National Endowment for the Arts website (nea.gov)

a. Connect to the Internet and go to the NEA website at nea.gov.

b. Click the Site Map link at the bottom of the page. What do you think is the purpose of the site map?

c. How has the NEA organized its information to help you navigate its website?

d. Can you find the information that Patsy needs?

e. Did you feel that the site map helped you navigate the website?

f. Do you feel that the site map link is beneficial for users?

g. Close your browser.

Real Life Independent Challenge

In this assignment, you create a personal website entirely on your own. There will be no Data Files supplied. These Independent Challenges will build from unit to unit, so you must do each unit's Real Life Independent Challenge assignment to complete your website.

a. Decide what type of website you would like to build. It can be a personal website about you and your family, a business website if you have a business you would like to promote, or a fictitious website. Your instructor may direct your choices for this assignment.

b. Create a wireframe for your website and include at least four pages.

c. Create a site root folder where you store your website files and name it appropriately.

d. Define the site with an appropriate name, using the site root folder that you created.

e. Create an assets folder and set it as the default location for images.

f. Begin planning the content you would like to use for the home page and plan how you would like to organize it on the page.

g. Use the Files panel to create the pages you listed in your wireframe.

h. Collect information to use in your website, such as images or text. Store these in a folder (either electronic or paper) that you can bring with you to class as you develop your site.

i. Exit Dreamweaver.

Visual Workshop

Your company has been selected to design a website for a catering business called Carolyne's Creations. In addition to catering, Carolyne's services include cooking classes and daily specials available as take-out meals. She also has a retail shop that stocks gourmet treats and kitchen items. Create the website pictured in Figure B-21, using **Carolyne's Creations** for the site name and **cc** for the site root folder name. Use the files dwb_5.html for the index (home) page and cc_banner.jpg for the banner. These files are located in the drive and folder where you store your Data Files. Next, add the files **catering.html**, **classes.html**, **recipes.html**, and **shop.html** to the local site root folder.

FIGURE B-21

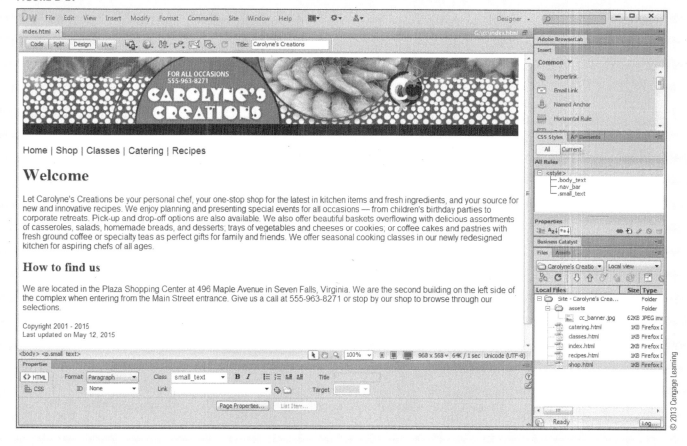

© 2013 Cengage Learning

Developing a Web Page

Files You Will Need:

To view a list of files needed for this unit, see the Data Files Grid in the back of the book.

When you begin developing web pages, you should choose the page content with the purpose of the website and the target audience in mind. A website designed for a large professional corporation should be designed quite differently than an educational website for children. You can use colors, fonts, and images to set a formal or casual tone. In this unit, you learn about planning a website, modifying a web page, and linking it to other pages. Finally, you'll use Code view to modify some of the page code, and test the links to make sure they work.  The Striped Umbrella website should appeal to families, singles, and maturing baby boomers with leisure time and money to spend. You improve the design and content of the home page to attract this broad target audience.

OBJECTIVES

Plan the page layout

Create the head content

Set web page properties

Create and format text

Add links to web pages

Use the History panel

View HTML code

Test and modify web pages

Adobe product screenshot(s) reprinted with permission from Adobe Systems Incorporated.

Planning the Page Layout

When people visit your website, you want them to feel at home, as if they know their way around the pages in your site. You also want to ensure that users will not get lost on the site due to layout inconsistencies. To help maintain a common look for all pages, you can use templates. Templates are web pages that contain basic layouts you can apply to your website pages, standardizing elements, such as the location of a company logo or a menu of buttons. As you will learn in Units D and G, the use of **Cascading Style Sheets (CSS)** provides a way to easily position and format objects or entire pages by providing common formatting characteristics that can be applied to multiple objects. And, as you will learn in Unit G, many designers use tables, simple grids of cells in rows and columns, as a page layout tool to position lists of tabular data on the page easily. Before you begin working on The Striped Umbrella home page, you want to identify key concepts that govern good page layout.

DETAILS

When planning the layout of your web pages, remember the following guidelines:

- **Keep it simple**

  Often the simplest websites are the most appealing. Websites that are simple in layout and design are the easiest to create and maintain. A simple website that works is far superior to a complex one with errors.

- **Use white space effectively**

  Too many text blocks, links, and images can confuse users, and actually make them feel agitated. Consider leaving some white space on each page. **White space** is the area on a web page that is not filled with text or graphics. (Note that white space is not necessarily white in color.) Using white space effectively creates a harmonious balance on the page. Figure C-1 shows how white space can help emphasize strong visual page elements, yet still achieve a simple, clean look for the page.

- **Limit media objects**

  Too many media objects—such as graphics, video clips, or sounds—may result in a page that takes too long to load. Users may tire of waiting for these objects to appear and leave your site before the entire page finishes loading. Placing unnecessary media objects on your page makes your website seem unprofessional.

- **Use an intuitive navigation structure**

  A website's navigational structure should be easy to use. It can be based on text links or a combination of text and graphic links. Users should always know where they are in the website, and be able to find their way back to the home page easily. If users get lost on your website, they may leave the site rather than struggle to find their way around.

- **Apply a consistent theme using templates**

  A theme can be almost anything, from the same background color on each page to common graphics, such as buttons or icons that reflect a collective theme. Common design elements such as borders can also be considered a theme. Templates are a great way to easily incorporate consistent themes in websites.

- **Use CSS for page layout**

  When you use CSS as the basis for page layout, you can control both how the entire page appears in browser windows and how the various page elements are positioned on the page in relation to each other. This allows a page to look the same, regardless of the size of a user's screen.

- **Be conscious of accessibility issues**

  There are several techniques you can use to ensure that your website is accessible to individuals with disabilities. These techniques include using alternate text with images, avoiding certain colors on web pages, and supplying text as an alternate source for information that is presented in audio files. Dreamweaver can display Accessibility dialog boxes to prompt you to insert accessibility information for the page objects, as shown in Figure C-2.

FIGURE C-1: An example of an effective web page layout

First Federal Bank website used with permission from First Federal Bank (ffbh.com)

FIGURE C-2: Accessibility attributes for inserting objects on a page

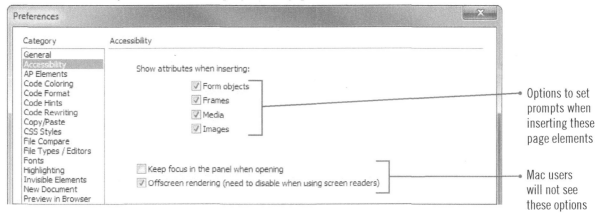

Options to set prompts when inserting these page elements

Mac users will not see these options

Design Matters

Designing for accessibility

It is extremely important to design your website so that individuals with disabilities can successfully navigate and read its web pages. In fact, government websites must be made accessible pursuant to Section 508 of the Workforce Investment Act of 1998, based on the Americans with Disabilities Act (ADA). On May 5, 1999, the first Web Content Accessibility Guidelines (WCAG) were published by the World Wide Web Consortium (W3C). The levels of accessibility are grouped into three priority level checkpoints. Although all websites should comply with the Priority 1 checkpoints, government websites *must* comply with them, such as providing a text equivalent for every non-text element. For more

information about priority level checkpoints, go to w3.org. Adobe's Accessibility Resource Center (adobe.com/accessibility); this site provides specific information about website compliance with Section 508 guidelines, such as suggestions for creating accessible websites, an explanation of Section 508, and information on how people with disabilities use assistive devices to navigate the Internet. These guidelines are based on four principles called the POUR principles: websites should be Perceivable, Operable, Understandable, and Robust. For more information about the POUR principles (Putting People at the Center of the Process) for website accessibility, go to webaim.org.

Creating the Head Content

A web page consists of two sections: the head section and the body. The **body** contains all the page content users see in their browser window, such as text, graphics, and links. The **head section** contains the **head content**, including the page title that is displayed in the browser title bar (not to be confused with the filename which is used to save the page), as well as some very important page elements that are not visible in the browser. These items are called meta tags. **Meta tags** are HTML codes that include information about the page such as keywords and descriptions. **Keywords** are words that are representative to the content of a website. Search engines find web pages by matching the title, description, and keywords in the head content of web pages with keywords users enter in search text boxes. A **description** is a short summary of website content. Before you work on page content for the home page, you modify the page title and add a description and keywords that will draw users to The Striped Umbrella website.

If you don't see the index.html file listed, click the plus sign (Win) or triangle (Mac) next to the striped_umbrella folder to expand the folder contents.

1. **Start Dreamweaver, click the Site list arrow** ⏷ **(Win) or** ⏷ **(Mac) on the Files panel, then click The Striped Umbrella if it isn't already selected**
   The Striped Umbrella website opens in the Files panel.

2. **Double-click index.html in the Files panel, make sure the Document window is maximized and you are in either Design view or Split view, click View on the Menu bar, then if necessary click Head Content to select it**
   The head content section appears at the top of The Striped Umbrella home page, as shown in Figure C-3. The head content section includes the Meta tag icon, the Title tag icon, and the CSS icon.

You can also change the page title using either the Title text box on the Document toolbar or the Page Properties dialog box.

3. **Click the Title icon, place the insertion point after The Striped Umbrella in the Title text box in the Property inspector, press [spacebar], type beach resort and spa, Ft. Eugene, Florida, then press [Enter] (Win) or [return] (Mac)**
   The new page title appears in the Title text box. See Figure C-4. The new title uses the words *beach* and *resort*, which potential guests may use as keywords when using a search engine.

4. **Expand the Insert panel if necessary, click the Insert panel list arrow, then click the Common category (if necessary), scroll down if necessary to locate the Head object, then click the Head button list arrow, as shown in Figure C-3**
   Some buttons on the Insert panel include a list arrow, indicating that there is a menu of choices beneath the current button. The button that was selected last appears on the Insert panel until you select another.

Multiple keywords should always be separated by commas.

5. **Click Keywords, type The Striped Umbrella, beach resort, spa, Ft. Eugene, Florida, Gulf of Mexico, fishing, dolphin cruises (including the commas) in the Keywords text box, as shown in Figure C-5, then click OK**
   The Keywords icon appears selected in the head section, indicating that keywords have been created for the page.

6. **Click the Head button list arrow on the Insert panel, click Description, type The Striped Umbrella is a full-service resort and spa just steps from the Gulf of Mexico in Ft. Eugene, Florida. in the Description dialog box, as shown in Figure C-6, then click OK**
   The Description icon appears selected in the head section, indicating that a description has been entered.

You may see embedded style tags above the title, keywords, and description. Scroll down to see the rest of the head content code.

7. **Click the Show Code view button** Code **on the Document toolbar, click anywhere in the code, then view the head section code, as shown in Figure C-7**
   The title, keywords, and description appear in the head section of the HTML code. The title is surrounded by title tags, and the keywords and description are both surrounded by meta tags.

8. **Click the Show Design view button** Design **on the Document toolbar, click View on the Menu bar, then click Head Content**
   The Striped Umbrella home page redisplays without the head content section visible above the Document window.

Developing a Web Page

FIGURE C-3: Viewing the head content section

Head content section

Meta tag icon   Title icon   CSS icon

Your Head button might differ depending on the option you last selected

© 2013 Cengage Learning

FIGURE C-4: Property inspector displaying new page title

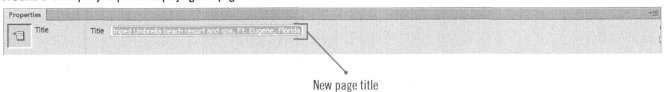

New page title

FIGURE C-5: Keywords dialog box

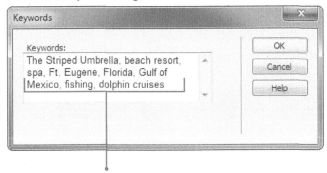

Keywords separated by commas

FIGURE C-6: Description dialog box

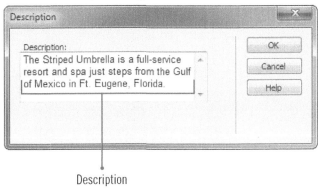

Description

FIGURE C-7: Code view displaying the code for the head content

Your lines of code may appear in a slightly different order

Keywords   Description   Title   Opening head tag

Design Matters

Entering titles, keywords, and descriptions

Search engines use titles, keywords, and descriptions to find pages after the user enters search terms. It is therefore important to anticipate what your potential customers will use for search terms, and to try to include those in the keywords, description, or title. Many search engines print the page titles and descriptions when they list pages in their search results. Some search engines limit the number of keywords that they will index, so again keep your keywords and description to a minimum. It is usually sufficient to enter keywords and a description only for the home page or any other page you want users to find, rather than for every page on the website. To choose effective keywords, many designers use focus groups to learn which words potential customers or clients might use. A **focus group** is a marketing tool that asks a group of people for feedback about a product, such as the impact of a television ad or the effectiveness of a website design.

Setting Web Page Properties

One of the first design decisions that you should make is the background color of your web page. This color should complement the colors used for text, links, and images you place on the page. A strong contrast between the text and background colors makes it easier for users to read the text. You can choose a light background color and a dark text color, or a dark background color and a light text color. A white background, though not terribly exciting, is the easiest to read for most users, and provides good contrast in combination with dark text. The next decision is to choose the default text color. The **default text color** is the color the browser uses to display text when a color is not specified. Settings such as the page background color and the default text color are specified using CSS. You want to set the background color and choose a default text color for The Striped Umbrella home page.

STEPS

QUICK TIP
You can also open the Page Properties dialog box by clicking the Page Properties button on the Property inspector.

1. **Click Modify on the Menu bar, then click Page Properties**

   The Page Properties dialog box opens. You use this dialog box to set page properties, such as the background color and default text color.

2. **Click the Background color box 🔲, as shown in Figure C-8**

   The color picker opens, and the pointer changes to an eyedropper 🖊. When Dreamweaver is first installed, the Background color box appears gray, which represents the default color. This does not mean that the color gray will be applied *unless* gray has previously been selected as the default color for the selected page element. Once you select a color from the color picker, the Background color box changes accordingly.

3. **Click the blue color swatch, #9CF (the fifth color in the last row), as shown in Figure C-8**

   Each color is assigned a **hexadecimal value**, a numerical value that represents the amount of red, green, and blue in the color. For example, white, which is made of equal parts of red, green, and blue, has a hexadecimal value of FFFFFF. Each pair of numbers represents the red, green, and blue values. The hexadecimal number system is based on 16, rather than 10 as in the decimal number system. Since there aren't any digits after reaching the number 9, letters of the alphabet are then used. The letter A represents the number 10, and F represents the number 15 in the hexadecimal number system. The hexadecimal values can be entered in the code using a form of shorthand that shortens the six characters to three characters. For instance: 99CCFF becomes 9CF and FFFFFF becomes FFF. The number value for a color is preceded by a pound sign (#) in HTML code.

4. **Click Apply in the Page Properties dialog box**

   The background color of the web page changes to a different shade of blue while the text color remains the default color, which is black. The Apply button allows you to see changes that you have made to the page without having to close the Page Properties dialog box. The blue background does not provide the best contrast between the page background and the text.

QUICK TIP
The Background color box appears blue (the last color selected) until you click the white color swatch.

5. **Click 🔲 next to Background color, click the white color swatch (the rightmost color in the bottom row), then click Apply**

   The white page background provides a better contrast.

6. **Click the Text color box 🔲, shown in Figure C-9, use the eyedropper 🖊 to select a light shade of blue, then click Apply**

   The light blue text color on the home page is not quite as easy to read as the black text.

7. **Click 🔲 next to Text color, then click the Default Color icon ☑ at the top of the color picker**

   The Page Properties dialog box shows the text color setting restored to the default color. See Figure C-9. The Default Color button restores the default color setting after either the Apply button is clicked or the dialog box is closed.

8. **Click OK**

   The Page Properties dialog box closes and The Striped Umbrella web page redisplays with the default black text color and new white background color.

FIGURE C-8: **Page Properties dialog box**

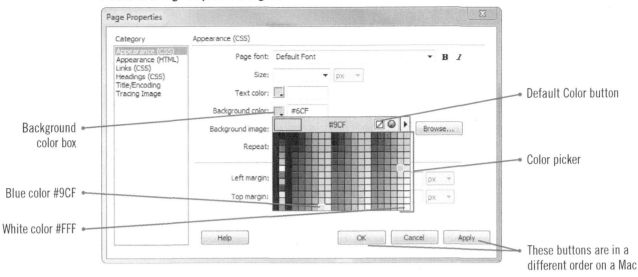

Background color box

Blue color #9CF

White color #FFF

Default Color button

Color picker

These buttons are in a different order on a Mac

FIGURE C-9: **Page Properties dialog box**

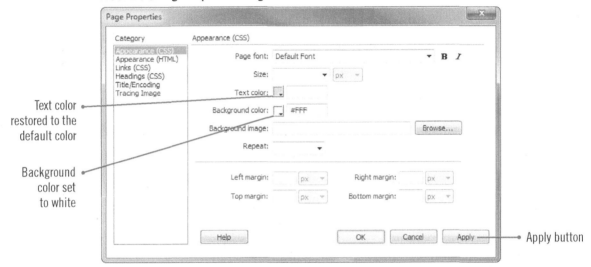

Text color restored to the default color

Background color set to white

Apply button

Design Matters

Choosing Colors to Convey Information

Prior to 1994, colors appeared differently on different types of computers. In 1994, Netscape developed the first **web-safe color palette**, a set of colors that appears consistently in all browsers and on Macintosh, Windows, and UNIX platforms. The evolution of video cards has made this less relevant today, although understanding web-safe colors may still be a factor when you are designing for some devices, such as cell phones and PDAs. The use of appropriate colors is an important factor in creating accessible pages. Be sure to only use colors that provide good contrast on your pages. Dreamweaver has two web-safe color palettes: Color Cubes and Continuous Tone. Each palette contains the 216 web-safe colors. Color Cubes is the default color palette; however, you can choose another one by clicking Modify on the Menu bar, clicking Page Properties, clicking the Appearance (CSS) or (HTML) category, clicking the color box next to the Background or Text color boxes, clicking the color palette list arrow, then clicking the desired color

palette. Figure C-10 shows the list of color palette choices. Another WCAG guideline states that color should never be the only visual means of conveying information. For instance, don't say "Refer to the brown box"; rather, say something like "Refer to the box immediately below this paragraph."

FIGURE C-10: **Color palettes**

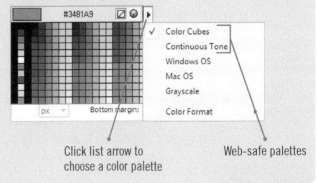

Click list arrow to choose a color palette

Web-safe palettes

Creating and Formatting Text

Text is an important part of any web page. You can enter text directly in Dreamweaver, import it (Win only), or copy and paste text from another document. When you are entering text, each time you press [Enter] (Win) or [return] (Mac), you create a new paragraph in the HTML code. Each paragraph is surrounded by <p> tags. Once you enter or import text, you can format it in Dreamweaver by changing the font, size, and color, just as in other programs. **Headings** are six different HTML text sizes that you can apply to text: Heading 1 (the largest size) through Heading 6 (the smallest size). Using a heading format is a way of showing the importance level of selected text in relation to other text on the page. Examples of tags that show emphasis are the bold tag, <strong>, and the italic tag, <em>. While you can set some formatting characteristics with HTML tags, the preferred practice is to use CSS for most formatting. ▣▣▣ The current menu bar does not include links to all of the main pages so you decide to replace it with a link to each main page and format it using an HTML heading format, then apply the italic setting to the contact information.

Make sure the text is selected properly—the next keystroke will replace the selected items. If you have difficulty selecting text, try [Backspace] or [Delete].

1. **Position the insertion point to the left of A in About Us, then drag to select** About Us - Spa - Cafe, **as shown in Figure C-11**

   The current menu bar is selected. A small icon may appear next to the selected text. If you click this icon, you will bring up the **Code Navigator**, a small window that opens with code for the selected page element. You will learn more about the Code Navigator in Unit D.

2. **Type** Home - About Us - Spa - Cafe - Activities, **using spaces on either side of the hyphens**

   This text becomes the page's new menu bar. A menu bar is a set of text or graphic links that is used to navigate to other pages in your website.

3. **Position the insertion point at the beginning of the first paragraph, type** Welcome to our beach! **then, press [Enter] (Win) or [return] (Mac)**

   Pressing [Enter] (Win) or [return] (Mac) creates a paragraph break represented by a <p> tag. Even a single character is considered a paragraph if it is preceded and followed by a paragraph break. Paragraphs can share common formatting, such as alignment settings.

4. **Click anywhere in the "Welcome!" text you just entered, click the** HTML button `<> HTML` **on the Property inspector to open the HTML Property inspector if necessary, click the** Format list arrow **in the HTML Property inspector, then click** Heading 1

   The Heading 1 format is applied to the text "Welcome to our beach!" as shown in Figure C-12.

Line breaks are useful when you want to apply the same formatting to text but place it on separate lines. The HTML code for a line break is <br />.

5. **Position the insertion point after the period following "...want to go home", as shown in Figure C-12, press [Enter] (Win) or [return] (Mac), then type** The Striped Umbrella

6. **Press and hold [Shift], press [Enter] (Win) or [return] (Mac) to create a line break**

   You can create separate lines within a paragraph by entering a line break after each line. A **line break** places text on separate lines without creating a new paragraph, which enables you to apply common formatting attributes to separate lines of text.

The Italic button is located in both the CSS and HTML Property inspectors, but each one produces different results. The HTML Italic button formats selected text and the CSS Italic button will ask you to create a new CSS rule to use to format the text.

7. **Enter the following information, repeating the instructions in Step 6 to place a line break at the end of each line:** 25 Beachside Drive; Ft. Eugene, Florida 33775; (555) 594-9458

   The semicolons indicate where the line breaks go.

8. **Position the pointer to the left of The Striped Umbrella, click and drag to select it and all of the information you entered in Step 7, click the** Italic button `I` **in the Property inspector, then click anywhere to deselect the text**

   The contact information appears as italicized text. See Figure C-13.

FIGURE C-11: Replacing the current menu bar

© 2013 Cengage Learning

The Striped Umbrella

25 Beachside Dr.™ • Ft. Eugene, Florida 33775

About Us - Spa - Cafe

Welcome to The Striped Umbrella — a full-service resort and spa just steps from the Gulf of Mexico and ten miles east of Crab Key, Florida. The Striped Umbrella has a variety of activities for adults and children. It is a perfect romantic getaway for two or a complete

Selected text

FIGURE C-12: Formatting the new heading

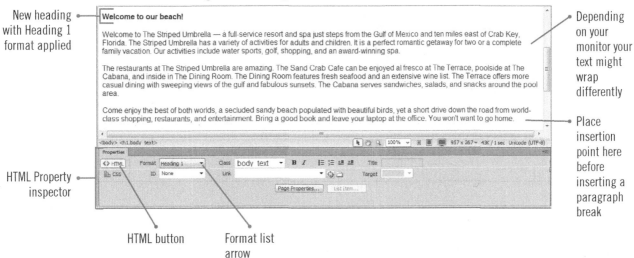

New heading with Heading 1 format applied

HTML Property inspector

HTML button

Format list arrow

Depending on your monitor your text might wrap differently

Place insertion point here before inserting a paragraph break

FIGURE C-13: Adding and formatting the contact information

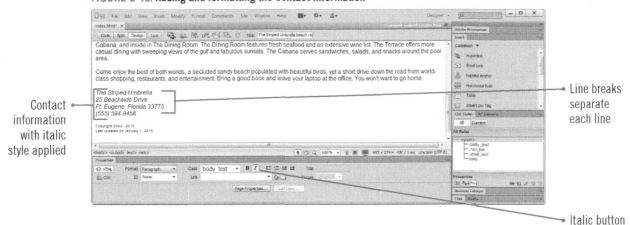

Contact information with italic style applied

Line breaks separate each line

Italic button

Developing a Web Page

UNIT
C
Dreamweaver CS6

Adding Links to Web Pages

Links, or hyperlinks, are specially formatted text or images that users click to navigate through and between websites. Users are more likely to return to sites that have a user-friendly navigation system and interesting links to other web pages or sites. After a link has been clicked in a browser window, it is called a **visited link**, and it changes by default to a purple color in the browser window. The default color for links that have not yet been clicked is blue. When creating web pages, it is important to avoid **broken links**, which are links that are unable to access the intended destination file. In addition to the links that you create to enable users to move from page to page, a helpful link to include is a **point of contact**, a place on a web page that gives users a means of contacting the website if they have questions or problems. A **mailto: link**, an email address for users to contact the website's headquarters, is a common point of contact. You create links for each of the menu items to their respective web pages in The Striped Umbrella website. You also create an email link to the club manager at The Striped Umbrella.

STEPS

1. **Double-click Home in the menu bar**
   You use this selected text to make a link.

> **TROUBLE**
> If your Browse for File button is behind the Panel Groups window, drag the border between the Document window and the panels to resize as necessary.

2. **Click the Browse for File button 📁 next to the Link text box in the HTML Property inspector, as shown in Figure C-14, then navigate to the striped_umbrella site root folder if necessary**
   The Select File dialog box opens. The contents of the striped_umbrella site root folder are listed.

3. **Click index.html, as shown in Figure C-15, verify that Document is selected in the Relative to pop-up menu then click OK (Win) or Open (Mac)**
   The Select File dialog box closes.

> **QUICK TIP**
> When text is selected, you cannot see the text color.

4. **Click anywhere on the home page to deselect Home**
   Home is underlined and blue, the default color for links, indicating that it is a link. When users click the Home link in a browser, the index.html page opens.

5. **Repeat Steps 1–4 to create links for About Us, Spa, Cafe, and Activities, using about_us.html, spa.html, cafe.html, and activities.html as the corresponding files, then click anywhere on the page**
   All five links are now created for The Striped Umbrella home page. See Figure C-16.

> **QUICK TIP**
> If you don't put the insertion point immediately after the last digit in the telephone number, you will not retain the formatting.

6. **Position the insertion point immediately after the last digit in the telephone number, press and hold [Shift], then press [Enter] (Win) or [return] (Mac)**
   A line break is created.

7. **Click the Insert panel list arrow on the Insert panel, click Common if necessary, then click Email Link**
   The Email Link dialog box opens.

> **TROUBLE**
> You can use a descriptive name such as Customer Service in the Text text box for the link text on the page, or you can enter the actual email address.

8. **Type Club Manager in the Text text box, press [Tab], type manager@thestripedumbrella.com in the Email text box, as shown in Figure C-17, then click OK**
   The email link to the Club Manager appears under the telephone number.

9. **If the email link does not appear in italics, position the pointer to the left of Club Manager, click and drag to select the text, click the Italic button *I* in the HTML Property inspector, then click anywhere to deselect the text**
   The Club Manager link appears in italics to match the rest of the contact information.

Developing a Web Page

FIGURE C-14: Creating a link using the Property inspector

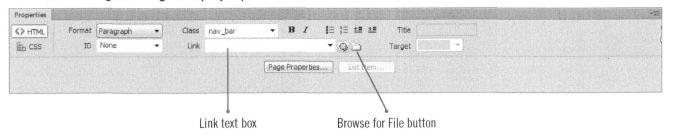

Link text box   Browse for File button

FIGURE C-15: Select File dialog box

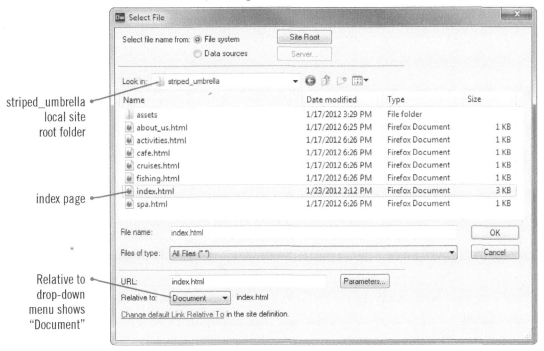

striped_umbrella
local site
root folder

index page

Relative to
drop-down
menu shows
"Document"

FIGURE C-16: Links added to menu bar items

Links to Home, About Us, Spa,
Cafe, and Activities pages

FIGURE C-17: Email Link dialog box

Text for email link
that will appear
on the web page

Email address

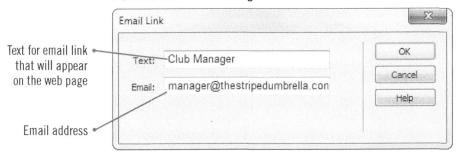

© 2013 Cengage Learning

Using the History Panel

The **History panel** shows the steps that you have performed while editing and formatting a document in Dreamweaver. To **edit** a page means to insert, delete, or change content by, for example, inserting a new image, adding a link, or correcting spelling errors. Remember that formatting, in contrast, means to change just the appearance of page elements. The History panel records all of the tasks that you perform and displays them in the order in which you completed them. If you make a mistake while editing or formatting a page, you can undo your previous steps. Simply drag the slider up next to the step you want to revert to, as shown in Figure C-18. This is a more efficient way to undo steps than using the Edit, Undo command. ⬛⬛⬛⬛ You want to add a horizontal rule to divide the banner and menu bar from the rest of the page as well as use the History panel to undo the changes as you experiment.

1. **Click Window on the Menu bar, then click History**

   The History panel opens, and the steps you have already performed during this session, such as Make Hyperlink and Line Break, display in the panel window.

A horizontal rule can also be inserted by clicking Horizontal rule in the Common category on the Insert panel.

2. **Click the Panel menu ☰ on the History panel title bar, click Clear History, as shown in Figure C-18, then click Yes in the Dreamweaver warning box**

   The steps that were previously listed in the History panel are cleared and the panel is empty.

The preferred way to format horizontal rules is with CSS. After you learn how to use CSS, you will use styles to format your horizontal rules.

3. **Position the insertion point to the left of the words Welcome to our beach! heading, click Insert on the Menu bar, point to HTML, then click Horizontal Rule**

   A horizontal rule, or line, appears on the page above the first paragraph and remains selected.

4. **If "pixels" is not displayed in the width pop-up menu, click the width list arrow in the Property inspector, click pixels, type 950 in the W text box, then press [Enter] (Win) or [return] (Mac)**

   The width of the horizontal rule changes to 950 pixels wide and the step is recorded in the History panel.

5. **Click the Align list arrow in the Property inspector, then click Left**

   The horizontal rule is left-aligned on the page. Compare your Property inspector settings to Figure C-19.

6. **Select 950 in the W text box, type 80, click the Width list arrow, click %, click the Align list arrow, then click Center**

   The horizontal rule is set to 80% of the width of the window and is center-aligned. When you set the width of a horizontal rule as a percentage of the page rather than in pixels, it resizes itself proportionately when viewed on different-sized monitors and resolutions. You prefer the way the rule looked when it was wider, a set width, and left-aligned.

7. **Drag the slider on the History panel up until it is pointing to Set Alignment: left, as shown in Figure C-20, then release it**

   The bottom three steps in the History panel appear gray, indicating that these steps have been undone, and the horizontal rule returns to the left-aligned, 950-pixel width settings.

8. **Click File on the Menu bar, then click Save**

Using the History panel

Dragging the slider up and down in the History panel is a quick way to undo or redo steps. However, the History panel offers much more. It can "memorize" certain steps and consolidate them into one command. This is a useful feature for steps that you need to perform repeatedly. However, some Dreamweaver features, such as steps performed in the Files panel, cannot be recorded in the History panel. The default number of steps that the History panel will record is 50, unless you specify otherwise in the General Preferences dialog box. Setting this number higher requires additional memory, and may affect the speed at which Dreamweaver functions.

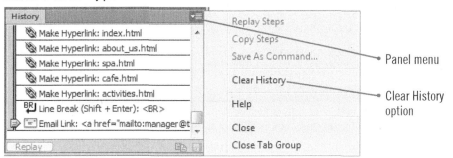

FIGURE C-18: **History panel**

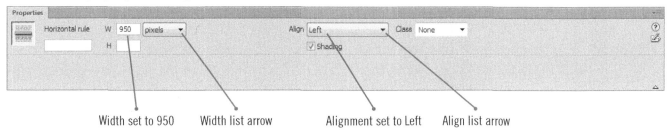

FIGURE C-19: **Property inspector settings for horizontal rule**

Width set to 950   Width list arrow   Alignment set to Left   Align list arrow

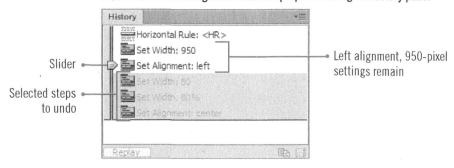

FIGURE C-20: **Resetting horizontal rule properties using the History panel**

Slider

Selected steps to undo

Left alignment, 950-pixel settings remain

Checking your screen against book figures

To show as much of the Document window as possible, most figures appear with the Standard toolbar hidden. Keep in mind that Dreamweaver will "remember" the screen arrangement from the last session when it opens each time. This may mean that you would have to open, close, collapse, or expand the various panels, toolbars, and inspectors to match your screens to the figures in the book. This is not really necessary unless you need a panel that is not open to complete a step. The rulers may also be displayed in figures in Design view. To turn this feature on or off, use the View > Rulers > Show command.

Viewing HTML Code

XHTML is the newest standard for HTML code. Although the default files created in Dreamweaver are XHTML files, the file extension is .html, and the code is referred to as "HTML." It is often helpful to view the code while editing or formatting a web page to understand how the code is working. You can use the **Reference panel** to find answers to coding questions covering topics such as HTML, JavaScript, and accessibility. The built-in electronic reference books supplied with Dreamweaver are available using the Book pop-up menu on the Reference panel. Dreamweaver also has a feature that tells you the last date that changes were made to a web page.  Although you are satisfied with the placement of the horizontal rule on the page, you decide to use the Reference panel to research how to change its color. You also want to add a code so that the date will automatically update each time the page is saved.

1. **Click** Window **on the Menu bar, click** History **to close the History panel, then click the horizontal rule**

   The horizontal rule is selected.

QUICK TIP
[Ctrl] [P] (Win) or [command] [P] (Mac) prints the HTML code for an open page.

2. **Click the** Show Code view button [Code] **on the Document toolbar**

   The highlighted HTML code represents the selected horizontal rule on the page. The Coding toolbar is docked along the left side of the Document window.

3. **If necessary, click to select the** Line Numbers **and** Word Wrap option buttons **on the Coding toolbar, as shown in Figure C-21**

   The option buttons on the Coding toolbar appear with a black border when they are selected. The Line Numbers and Word Wrap options make it easier to navigate code. **Line numbers** provide a point of reference when locating specific sections of code. **Word wrap** keeps all code within the width of the Document window so you don't have to scroll to read long lines of code. It is easier for you to read and select the lines of code as you research the <hr> tag using the Reference panel.

4. **Click** Window **on the Menu bar, point to** Results, **click** Reference, **if necessary click the** Book list arrow **in the Reference Panel to select** O'REILLY HTML Reference, **click the** Tag list arrow **to select** HR **if necessary, as shown in Figure C-22**

   The HR tag appears in the Tag text box in the Reference panel menu bar; HR is the HTML code for horizontal rule tag.

5. **Read the information about horizontal rules**

   The color of rules can be changed by using CSS; this will be covered in Unit D.

QUICK TIP
You can also change the font size with the Results panel menu.

6. **Click the** Panel menu ▥ **on the Results panel title bar, then click** Close Tab Group

   The Results tab group closes.

7. **Scroll down if necessary in the Document window, select** January 1, 2015, **then press** [Delete]

   The date is deleted.

8. **Scroll down the Common category on the Insert panel until the Date object button appears, click** Date **to open the Insert Date dialog box, click** March 7, 1974, **in the Date format options list, click the** Update automatically on save check box **if necessary to select it, as shown in Figure C-23, then click** OK

   The Insert date dialog box closes and the JavaScript code for the date is added to the page. The current date will be placed on the page each time the page is opened and saved.

9. **Click the** Show Design view button [Design] **on the Document toolbar, then save your work**

   The index page appears in Design view in the Document window.

FIGURE C-21: Code view options

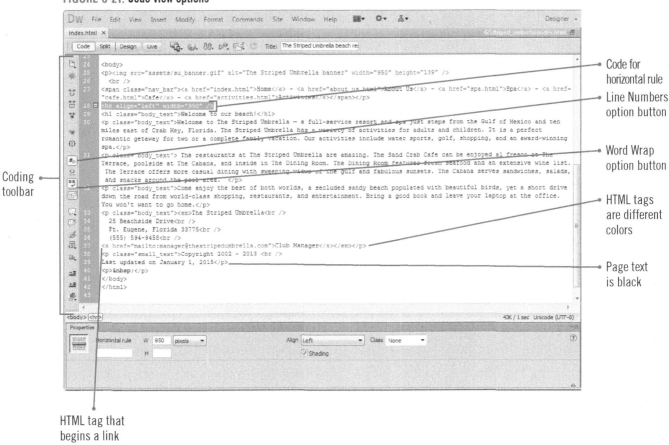

Code for horizontal rule

Line Numbers option button

Word Wrap option button

HTML tags are different colors

Page text is black

Coding toolbar

HTML tag that begins a link

FIGURE C-22: <HR> tag information displayed in the Reference panel

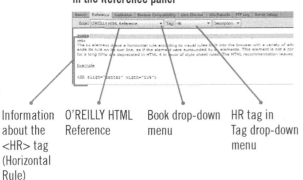

Information about the <HR> tag (Horizontal Rule)

O'REILLY HTML Reference

Book drop-down menu

HR tag in Tag drop-down menu

FIGURE C-23: Insert Date dialog box

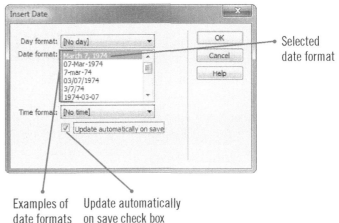

Selected date format

Examples of date formats

Update automatically on save check box

Design Matters

Using Code view to edit pages

Some designers prefer to make changes to their pages by typing directly into the code, rather than working in Design view, because they feel that this gives them more precise control. Some features, such as JavaScript functions, are often added to pages by copying and pasting code into the existing page's HTML code. **JavaScript** is code that adds interaction between the user and the web page,

such as rollovers or interactive forms. **Rollovers** are screen elements that change in appearance as the pointer rests on them. You can view the HTML code in Dreamweaver by using Code view or Code and Design view. This enables you to view the HTML code and the page content in different colors, highlight HTML code that contains errors, and **debug**, or correct, HTML errors.

Testing and Modifying Web Pages

As you develop your web pages, you should test them frequently. The best way to test a web page is to preview it in a browser window to make sure it appears the way you expect it to. You should also check to see that the links work properly, that there are no typographical or grammatical errors, and that you have included all of the necessary information for the page. Dreamweaver has a preview feature that allows you to see what a page would look like if it were viewed on a mobile hand-held device, such as a phone or tablet. This is a feature called the **Multiscreen Preview**. The Multiscreen button is located on the Document toolbar. This button allows you to see the page in three different sizes in the same window, or you can choose one size to preview in the whole Document window. You can also use the Mobile size, the Tablet size, or the Desktop size buttons on the Status bar to simulate page size. You decide to view The Striped Umbrella home page in Dreamweaver to check its appearance in a simulated window size, preview it using your default browser, make adjustments to the page, then preview the changes in the browser.

1. **Click the Tablet size button on the Status bar to see how the page would appear on a tablet using the default tablet settings, as shown in Figure C-24**

   The page is resized to simulate what it would look like in the default Tablet size, (768 × 1024). The Mobile size and Desktop size buttons are on either side of the Tablet size button and are used to view a page in a simulated mobile and desktop screen.

2. **Click the Desktop size button, scroll down if necessary and highlight the period after the "...go home" text, then type !**

   An exclamation point replaces the period after "...go home".

3. **Click File on the Menu bar, click Save, click on the Document toolbar, then click Preview in [your default browser]**

   The Striped Umbrella home page displays in your browser window. See Figure C-25. You can also press the F12 key (Win) to preview a page in the default browser.

4. **Click the About Us link on the menu bar to display one of the blank pages you created in Unit B, then click the Back button on the Address bar (Win) or the Navigation toolbar (Mac)**

   The index page reappears in the browser window.

5. **Repeat Step 4 to test the Spa, Cafe, and Activities links**

   Each link opens a corresponding blank page in the browser window since you haven't placed any text or images on them yet.

6. **Click the Club Manager link**

   The default mail program on your computer opens with a message addressed to manager@thestripedumbrella.com.

7. **Close the email message dialog box, close the browser window, close the index page, then click Exit on the File menu (Win) or Quit on the Dreamweaver menu (Mac) to close the Dreamweaver program**

FIGURE C-24: Using Tablet size to view the page

Multiscreen button

Page viewed in default tablet size

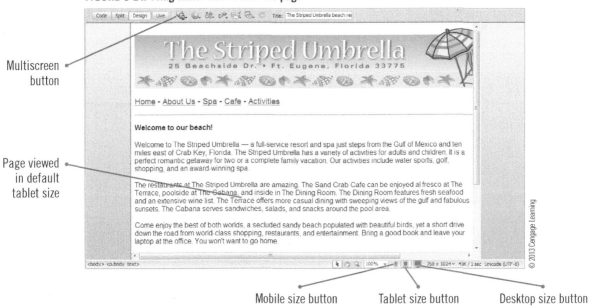

Mobile size button   Tablet size button   Desktop size button

FIGURE C-25: The finished page

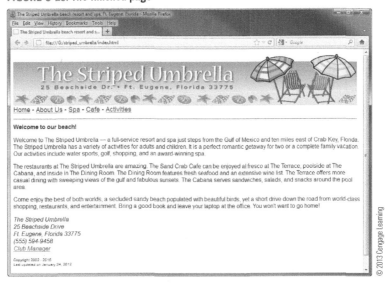

© 2013 Cengage Learning

Design Matters

Using smart design principles

As you view your pages in the browser, take a critical look at the symmetry of the page. Is it balanced? Are there too many images for the amount of text, or too few? Does everything "heavy" seem to be on the top or bottom of the page, or do the page elements seem balanced, with the weight evenly distributed between the top, bottom, and sides? Use design principles to create a site-wide consistency for your pages. **Horizontal symmetry** means that the elements are balanced across the page. **Vertical symmetry** means that they are balanced down the page. **Diagonal symmetry** balances page elements along the invisible diagonal line of the page. **Radial symmetry** runs from the center of the page outward, like the petals of a flower.

These principles all deal with balance; however, too much balance is not good, either. Sometimes it adds interest to place page elements a little off center to have an asymmetrical layout. Color, white space, text, lines, shapes, forms, textures, and images should all complement each other and provide a natural flow across and down the page. The **rule of thirds**—dividing a page into nine squares like a tic-tac-toe grid—states that interest is increased when your focus is on one of the intersections in the grid. The most important information should be at the top of the page where it is visible without scrolling— "above the fold," as they say in the newspaper business. Other design principles include the use of emphasis, movement, unity, proximity, and repetition to place elements attractively on a page.

Practice

Concepts Review

Label each element in the Dreamweaver window shown in Figure C-26.

FIGURE C-26

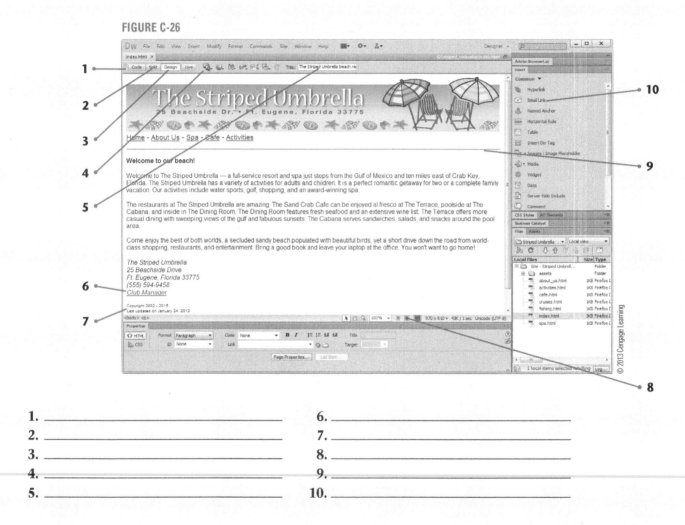

1. _____
2. _____
3. _____
4. _____
5. _____
6. _____
7. _____
8. _____
9. _____
10. _____

Match each of the following terms with the statement that best describes its function.

11. Style
12. Head section
13. Body section
14. Page Properties dialog box
15. Heading 1
16. Heading 6
17. Edit a page
18. Format a page

a. The part of a web page that includes text, graphics, and links

b. A named group of formatting characteristics

c. Includes the default web page settings

d. The smallest heading size

e. Make adjustments in the appearance of page elements

f. Insert, delete, or change page content

g. The largest heading size

h. The part of a web page that includes the page title and meta tags

Select the best answer from the following list of choices.

19. **The head section of a web page can include:**
    a. keywords.
    b. descriptions.
    c. Meta tags.
    d. all of the above.

20. **Links that have been previously clicked are called:**
    a. active links.
    b. links.
    c. visited links.
    d. broken links.

21. **The button that is used to display a web page in Design view in three different sizes is the
    _____ button.**
    a. Multiscreen
    b. Mobile display
    c. Simulated screens
    d. Media

22. **The _____ on the History panel is used to undo or redo several steps.**
    a. scroll bar
    b. pointer
    c. slider
    d. Undo/Redo tool

23. **An example of a point of contact is a:**
    a. heading.
    b. title.
    c. mailto: link.
    d. keywords.

24. **The Dreamweaver default color palette is the:**
    a. Continuous Tone.
    b. Color Cubes.
    c. Windows OS.
    d. Mac OS.

Skills Review

Important: If you did not create the websites used in the preceding exercises in Unit B, you need to create a local site root folder for each website and define the websites using files your instructor provides. See the "Read This Before You Begin" section for more detailed instructions.

1. **Plan the page layout.**
   a. Using a word processor or a piece of paper, list three principles of good page design that you have learned, then list them in order of most important to least important, based on your experiences.
   b. Explain why you chose these three concepts and why you selected the order you did.

2. **Create the head content.**
   a. Start Dreamweaver.
   b. Use the Files panel to open the Blooms & Bulbs website.
   c. Open the index page, then view the head content.
   d. Use the Head button list arrow to insert the following keywords: **Blooms & Bulbs, garden, plants, nursery, flowers, landscape design**, and **greenhouse**.
   e. Insert the following description: **Blooms & Bulbs is a premier supplier of garden plants and trees for both professional and home gardeners.**
   f. Switch to Code view to view the HTML code for the head section.
   g. Switch to Design view.
   h. Save your work, then hide the head content.

3. **Set web page properties.**
   a. View the page properties.
   b. Change the background color to a color of your choice, then apply it to the page, leaving the dialog box open.
   c. Change the background color to white.
   d. Save your work.

4. **Create and format text.**
   a. Replace the hyphens in the current menu bar with a split vertical bar (the top of the backslash key) to separate the items.
   b. Place the insertion point at the end of the last sentence in the second paragraph, then add a paragraph break.
   c. Type the following text, inserting a line break after each line.
      Blooms & Bulbs
      Hwy 43 South
      Alvin, Texas 77511
      555-248-0806
   d. Delete the date in the "Last updated" line, then replace it with a date that will update automatically each time the page is saved, using the March 7, 1974 format.
   e. Using the HTML Property inspector, italicize the copyright statement and last updated statement.
   f. Save your work.

5. **Add links to web pages.**
   a. Link the word *Home* on the menu bar to index.html.
   b. Link *Our Plants* to plants.html.
   c. Link *Newsletter* to newsletter.html.
   d. Link *Workshops* to workshops.html.
   e. Link *Tips* to tips.html.
   f. Using the Insert panel, create an email link under the telephone number with a line break between them; type **Customer Service** in the Text text box and **mailbox@blooms.com** in the Email text box.

Skills Review (continued)

6. **Use the History panel.**
   a. Open and clear the History panel.
   b. Using the Insert menu, insert a horizontal rule right before the first paragraph.
   c. Using the Property inspector, left-align the rule and set the width to 950 pixels.
   d. Edit the horizontal rule to center-align it with a width of 70%.
   e. Use the History panel to change the horizontal rule back to left-aligned with a width of 950 pixels.
   f. Close the History panel.
   g. Save your work.

7. **View HTML code.**
   a. Use Code view to examine the code for the horizontal rule properties, the email link, and the date in the "Last updated" statement.
   b. Return to Design view.

8. **Test and modify web pages.**
   a. Using the Preview buttons on the status bar, view the page at two different preview sizes.
   b. Preview the page in your browser.
   c. Verify that all links work correctly, then close the browser.
   d. Add the text **We are happy to deliver or ship your purchases.** to the end of the first paragraph.
   e. Save your work, preview the page in your browser, compare your screen to Figure C-27, then close your browser.
   f. Close the page, then exit Dreamweaver.

FIGURE C-27

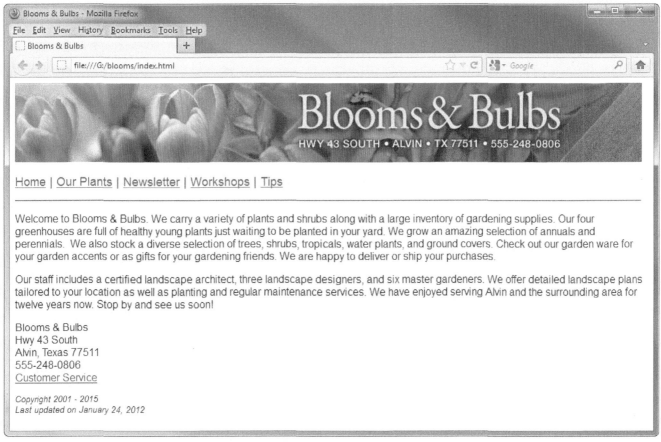

Important: *If you did not create the websites used in the exercises in Unit B, you need to create site root folders for each website and define the websites using files your instructor provides. See the "Read This Before You Begin" section for more detailed instructions.*

Independent Challenge 1

You have been hired to create a website for a river expedition company named Rapids Transit, located on the Buffalo River in Arkansas. In addition to renting canoes, kayaks, and rafts, they have several types of cabin rentals for overnight stays. River guides are available, if requested, to accompany clients on float trips. The owner's name is Mike Andrew.

a. Use the Files panel to open the Rapids Transit website.

b. Open the index page.

c. Create the following keywords: **Rapids Transit, river, rafting, Buffalo River, Arkansas, kayak, canoe,** and **float**.

d. Create the following description: **Rapids Transit is a river expedition company located on the Buffalo River in Arkansas.**

e. Change the page title to **Rapids Transit – Buffalo River Outfitters**.

f. Edit the menu bar below the Rapids Transit banner by changing **Our Guides** to **River Guides**.

g. Enter a line break under the address, then enter the telephone number **(555) 365-5228**.

h. Italicize the company copyright and last updated statements, then, after the phone number, enter a line break and create an email link, using **Mike Andrew** for the text and ***mailbox@rapidstransit.com*** for the email link.

i. Add links to the entries in the menu bar, using the files index.html, guides.html, rates.html, lodging.html, and before.html in the rapids site root folder. (Recall that these files don't have any content yet, but you can still link to them. You will add content to the pages as you work through the remaining units of the book.)

j. Delete the horizontal rule.

k. Delete the date in the last updated statement and change it to a date that will be automatically updated when the page is saved, using the March 7, 1974 data format. Reformat the date to match the rest of the line if necessary.

l. View the HTML code for the page, noting in particular the code for the head section.

m. View the page in Design view in two different screen sizes, save your work, then test the links in your browser, as shown in Figure C-28.

n. Close the browser, close the page, then exit Dreamweaver.

FIGURE C-28

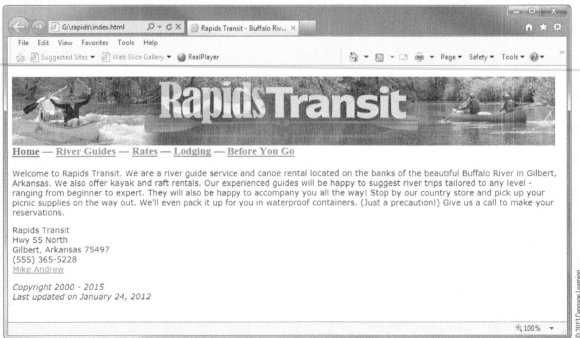

Independent Challenge 2

Your company is designing a new website for a travel outfitter named TripSmart. TripSmart specializes in travel products and services. In addition to selling travel products such as clothing, luggage, and accessories, they promote trips and offer travel advice. Their clients range from college students to families to vacationing professionals. The owner, Thomas Howard, has requested a dynamic website that conveys the excitement of traveling. Refer to Figure C-29 as you work through the following steps.

a. Open the TripSmart website, then open its index page.

b. Create the following keywords: **TripSmart, travel, traveling, tours, trips, vacations**.

c. Create the following description: **TripSmart is a comprehensive travel store. We can help you plan trips, make the arrangements, and supply you with travel gear.**

d. Change the page title to read **TripSmart: Serving all your travel needs**.

e. Change the menu bar below the banner to read **Home - Tours - Newsletter - Services - Catalog**.

f. Add links to the menu bar entries, using the files index.html, tours.html, newsletter.html, services.html, and catalog.html. (Recall that these files don't have any content yet, but you can still link to them. You will add content to the pages as you work through the remaining units of the book.)

g. Replace the date in the "Last updated" statement with a date that will update automatically when the file is saved.

h. Add the following contact information between the last paragraph and copyright statement using line breaks after each line: **TripSmart, 1106 Beechwood, Fayetteville, AR 72604, 555-848–0807**.

i. Immediately beneath the telephone number, place an Email link using **Contact us** as the text and **associate@tripsmart.com** for the link.

j. Insert a horizontal rule that is 950 pixels wide and left-aligned above the contact information.

k. View the HTML code for the page, noting in particular the head section code.

l. View the page in two different screen sizes, save your work, then test the links in your browser window.

m. Close the page and exit Dreamweaver.

FIGURE C-29

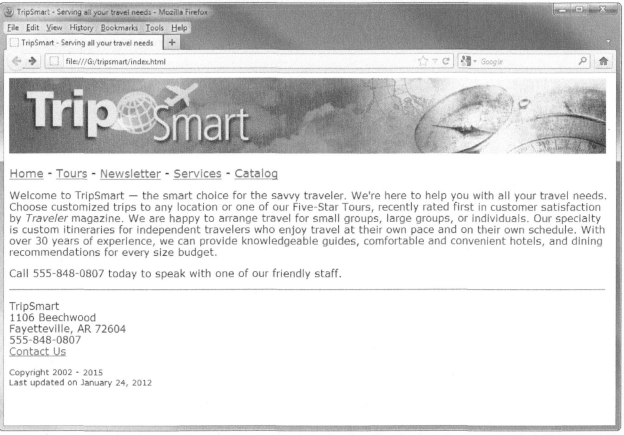

© 2013 Cengage Learning

Independent Challenge 3

Angela Lou is a freelance photographer. She is searching the Internet for a particular type of paper to use in printing her digital images. She knows that websites use keywords and descriptions to increase traffic from search engines such as Google and Bing. She is curious as to how keywords and descriptions work with search engines. Write your answers to these questions on paper or using your word processor.

a. Connect to the Internet, then go to snapfish.com to see the Snapfish website's home page, as shown in Figure C-30.

b. View the page source by clicking View on the menu bar, then clicking Source (Internet Explorer) or Tools > Web Developer > Page Source (Mozilla Firefox). (*Hint*: Press the Alt key if the menu is hidden.)

c. Can you locate a description and keywords?

d. How many keywords do you find?

e. How many words are in the description?

f. In your opinion, is the number of keywords and words in the description about right, too many, or not enough?

g. Use a search engine such as Google (google.com), type the words **photo quality paper** in the Search text box, then press [Enter] (Win) or [Return] (Mac).

h. Choose a link in the list of results and view the source code for that page. Do you see keywords and a description? Do any of them match the words you used in the search? (You may have to scroll down quite a bit to find the keywords. Try using the Find feature to quickly search the code.)

i. If you don't see the search words in keywords or descriptions, do you see them in the body of the pages?

j. Save your work, then exit all programs.

FIGURE C-30

Real Life Independent Challenge

This assignment will continue to build on the personal website that you created in Unit B. In this lesson, you will work with your home page.

a. Insert a brief description and a list of meaningful keywords for your home page in the appropriate locations.

b. Insert an effective title for your home page.

c. Format the home page attractively, creating a strong contrast between your page background and your page content.

d. Add links from the home page to your other pages.

e. Insert an email link.

f. Insert a "Last updated" statement that includes a date that updates automatically when you save the file.

g. Preview the home page in your browser, verifying that each link works correctly.

h. Check the page for errors in content or format and edit as necessary.

i. Save your work, close the page, and exit the program.

Visual Workshop

Your company has been selected to design a website for a catering business named Carolyne's Creations. You are now ready to add content to the home page and apply formatting options to improve the page appearance, using Figure C-31 as a guide. Open your Carolyne's Creations website and modify the index page to duplicate Figure C-31. You can use **carolyne@carolynescreations.com** as the email link. (*Hint*: Remember to add an appropriate description and keywords, and revise the last updated statement so it will automatically update when the page is saved.)

FIGURE C-31

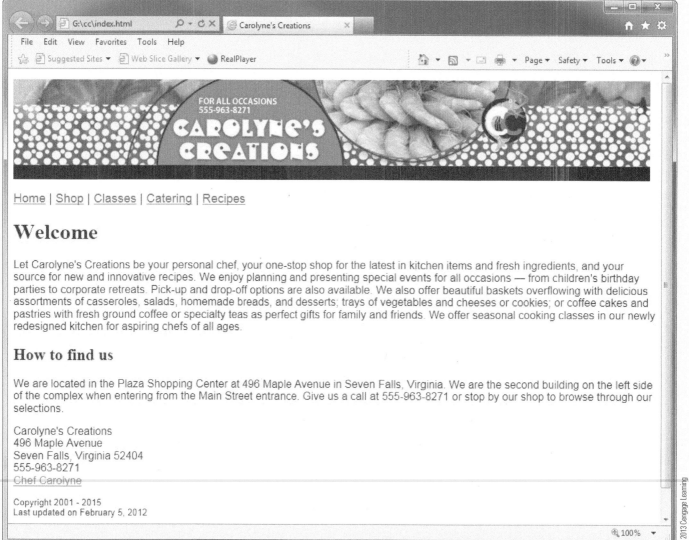

Working with Text and Cascading Style Sheets

Files You Will Need:

To view a list of files needed for this unit, see the Data Files Grid in the back of the book.

The content of most web pages is text-based. Because text on a computer screen can be more tiring to read than text on a printed page, you should strive to make your web page text attractive and easy to read. Dreamweaver has many options for enhancing text, including HTML properties for paragraphs and lists, as well as Cascading Style Sheets (CSS). CSS are used to assign sets of common formatting characteristics to page elements, such as paragraph text, lists, and table data.  You decide to group content on the spa page for The Striped Umbrella website using lists to make the page more readable. Using lists to format text is also considered to be more accessible for users using screen readers. You want to use CSS to make these types of formatting changes consistent throughout the website.

OBJECTIVES

Create a new page

Import text

Set text properties

Create an unordered list

Understand Cascading Style Sheets

Create a rule in a new Cascading Style Sheet

Apply and edit a rule

Add rules to a Cascading Style Sheet

Attach a Cascading Style Sheet to a page

Check for spelling errors

Adobe product screenshot(s) reprinted with permission from Adobe Systems Incorporated.

Creating a New Page

You use the New Document dialog box to create a new page in Dreamweaver. You can create a blank page, a blank template, a fluid grid template, a page from a template, or a page from a sample layout. You have the option of several page types you can create, for example, HTML, CSS, XML, and ASP. Each page type has layout option choices. The HTML page type layouts include one column, two columns, and three columns. The new HTML5 layouts include two or three column layouts. You are ready to create a new page that will replace the placeholder spa page. You decide to use the HTML page type with no preset layout. After you create the page you insert the banner and the spa logo.

STEPS

1. **Start Dreamweaver, click the** Site list arrow (Win) ▼ **or** ▼ **(Mac) on the** Files panel, **then click** The Striped Umbrella, **if it isn't already selected**

   The Striped Umbrella website opens in the Files panel.

2. **Click** File **on the Menu bar, click** New, **click** Blank Page **(if necessary), click** HTML **in the** Page Type **column, click** <none> **in the** Layout **column, click the** DocType **list box, click** HTML 5, **as shown in Figure D-1, click** Create, **then click the** Show Design view button Design **if necessary**

   A new blank page opens in the Document window.

3. **Click** File, **click** Save As, **navigate to your Striped Umbrella local site root folder, then save the file as** spa.html, **overwriting the existing (blank) spa.html file**

4. **Click the** Insert bar menu, **click** Common, **click the** Images list arrow, **then click** Image

   The Select Image Source dialog box opens, as shown in Figure D-2.

   QUICK TIP
   You can also drag the banner image from the Files panel onto the page since it is already saved in the website assets folder.

5. **Browse to and open the website assets folder, double-click** su_banner.gif, **type** The Striped Umbrella banner **in the Alternate text box in the** Image Tag Accessibility Attributes **dialog box, then click** OK

   The banner appears at the top of the new page. You will learn more about the Image Tag Accessibility Attributes dialog box in Unit E.

6. **Click to the right of the banner to deselect it, press** [Enter] **(Win) or** [Return] **(Mac), repeat Step 4 to open the** Select Image Source **dialog box, then navigate to the assets folder in your unit_d Data Files folder**

7. **Double-click** sea_spa_logo.png, **type** The Sea Spa logo **in the Alternate text box in the** Image Tag Accessibility Attributes **dialog box, then click** OK

8. **Click to the right of the logo to place the insertion point on the spa.html page**

   The Sea Spa logo appears under the banner, as shown in Figure D-3.

FIGURE D-1: Creating a new HTML document with the New Document dialog box

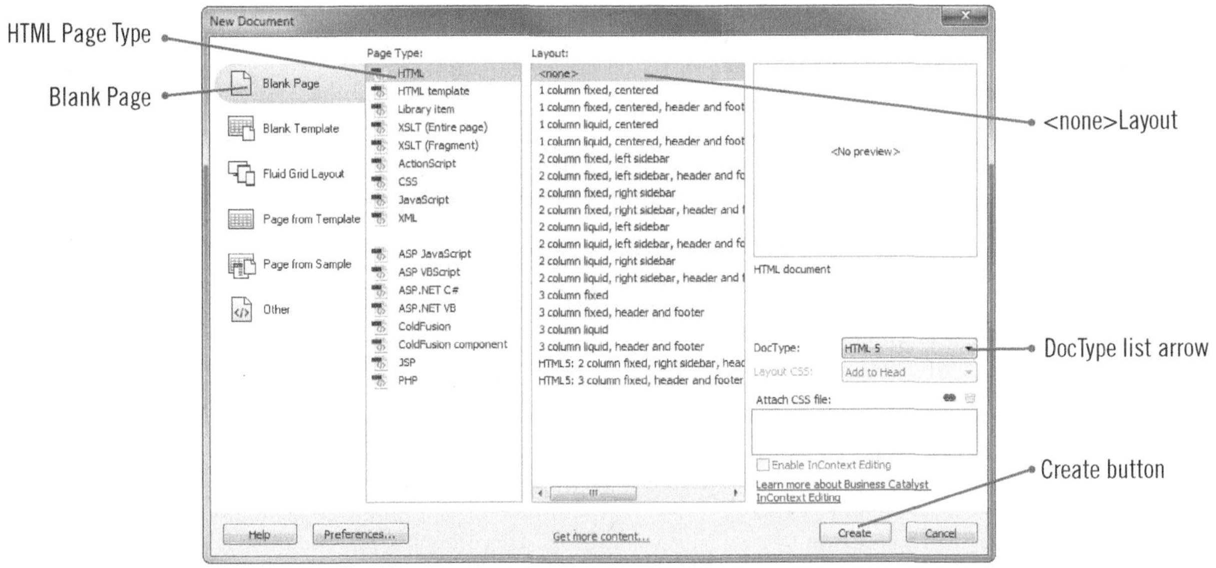

HTML Page Type

Blank Page

<none>Layout

DocType list arrow

Create button

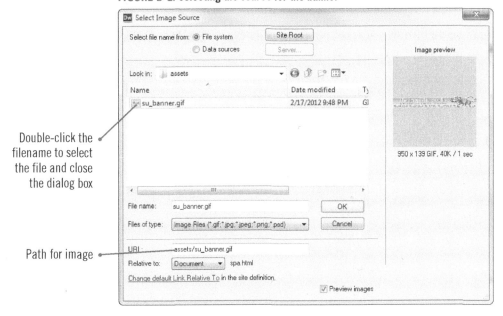

FIGURE D-2: Selecting the source for the banner

Double-click the
filename to select
the file and close
the dialog box

Path for image

FIGURE D-3: Image file added to the Striped Umbrella assets folder

Images
placed on
page

Images listed
in assets
folder

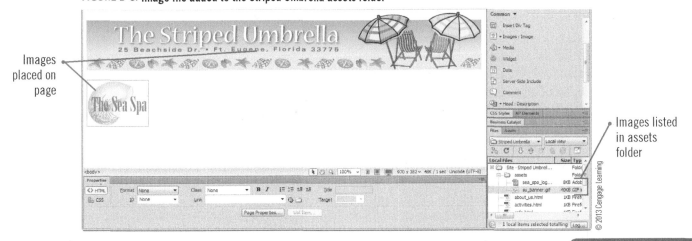

Working with Text and Cascading Style Sheets

© 2013 Cengage Learning

Importing Text

Entering text in Dreamweaver is as easy as entering text in a word processing program. The Dreamweaver text editing features, listed in Table D-1, are similar to those in word processing programs. If you have existing text to place on a page, you can either copy and paste it, or import it from the source program, such as Microsoft Word or Excel. To ensure that text is readable, you can use CSS to set alignment, indentation, headings, and lists to organize the content on the page.  Your manager has given you a list of services to include on The Striped Umbrella spa page. The document, which contains a list of spa services and descriptions, was created in Microsoft Word, then saved as a Word document. You open the spa page, import the text, and use the Clean Up Word HTML command to remove any unnecessary tags.

STEPS

1. **Click File on the Menu bar, point to Import, click Word Document, browse to the folder where you store your Unit D Data Files, then double-click spa.doc (Win); or using Finder, navigate to spa.doc stored in your unit_d data files folder, open spa.doc, select all, copy, close spa.doc, then paste the copied text on the spa page in Dreamweaver (Mac)**

   Mac users cannot use the Import > Word command. The text from the Word file is placed beside and wraps under the logo, as shown in Figure D-4. Although you may not see evidence of unnecessary code on the page, it is always a good idea to remove any unnecessary tags that are added by Microsoft Word.

QUICK TIP
If a dialog box opens stating that Dreamweaver was unable to determine the version of Word used to generate this document, click OK, click the Clean up HTML from list arrow, then select Word 2000 and newer, if necessary.

2. **Click Commands on the Menu bar, then click Clean Up Word HTML**

   The Clean Up Word HTML dialog box opens, as shown in Figure D-5.

3. **Click to select each check box in the Clean Up Word HTML dialog box if necessary, click OK, then click OK again**

   The Clean Up Word HTML dialog box closes.

Importing and linking Microsoft Office documents

Adobe makes it easy to transfer data between Microsoft Office documents and Dreamweaver web pages. To import a Word or Excel document with a PC, click File on the Menu bar, point to Import, then click either Word Document or Excel Document. Select the file you want to import, then click the Formatting list arrow to choose among importing Text only; Text with structure (paragraphs, lists, and tables); Text, structure, basic formatting (bold, italic); or Text, structure, full formatting (bold, italic, styles) before you click Open. The option you choose depends on the importance of the original structure and formatting. Always use the Clean Up Word HTML command after importing a Word file.

On a Mac, open the file you want to import, copy the text, then paste it to an open page in Dreamweaver in Design view.

You can also create a link to a Word or Excel document on your web page. Simply drag the Word or Excel document from its current location to the place on the page you want the link to appear; if the document is located outside the site, you can browse for it using the Site list arrow on the Files panel, Explorer (Win), or Finder (Mac). Next, select the Create a link option button in the Insert Document dialog box, then save the file in your local site root folder so it will be uploaded when you publish your site. If it is not uploaded, the link will be broken.

FIGURE D-4: Spa page with text imported

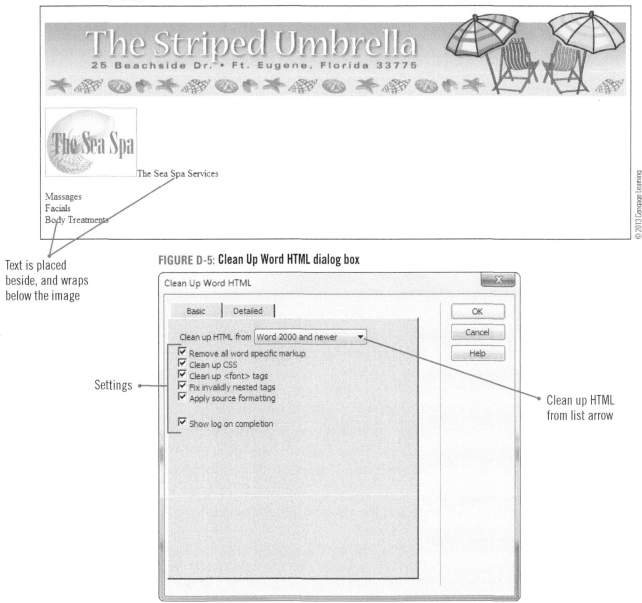

Text is placed beside, and wraps below the image

FIGURE D-5: Clean Up Word HTML dialog box

Settings

Clean up HTML from list arrow

© 2013 Cengage Learning

TABLE D-1: Dreamweaver text editing features

feature	menu	function	feature	menu	function
Find and Replace	Edit	Finds and replaces text on the current web page, the entire website, or in selected files	**Font families**	Modify	Selects font combinations for a browser or allows you to create custom font combinations
Indent and Outdent	Format	Indents selected text to the right or left	**Style**	Format	Sets various styles, such as bold and italic
Paragraph Format	Format	Sets paragraph, H1 through H6, and preformatted text	**CSS Styles**	Format	Provides options for applying a rule, creating a new CSS rule, attaching a style sheet, converting or moving rules, and applying Design-Time Style Sheets
Align	Format	Aligns text with the left or right margin, justifies it, or centers it on the page	**Color**	Format	Sets text color
List	Format	Creates unordered, ordered, or definition lists	**Check Spelling**	Commands	Runs a spell check on the page

Setting Text Properties

After you place text on a page, you format it to enhance its appearance. Text formatting attributes such as paragraph formatting, heading styles, fonts, size, color, alignment, indents, and CSS styles are easy to define by using the CSS Styles panel, the HTML Property inspector, or the CSS Property inspector. Some formatting options are available with both the HTML and CSS Property inspectors, while some are specific to each. Using standard fonts is wise because those set outside the default range may not be available on all computers. Global formatting applied with styles is much preferred over formatting applied directly to text. Styles applied across a website promote a clean and consistent look. As you format your pages, it is important to read the code for each element to see how it is written. The more fluent you are with code, the easier it will be when you have to debug the site (correct coding errors). HTML code is built from a series of **tags** surrounded by < and > symbols. Tags instruct the browser how to display each page element. ▰▰▰ You want to format the new text on the spa page to improve its appearance. You also want to examine the code for the formatting commands to understand the HTML tags that are generated.

STEPS

QUICK TIP

To apply character formats such as bold and italic, you must select the paragraph rather than click within the text.

1. **Click the HTML button ⟨⟩ HTML on the Property inspector if necessary, scroll up if necessary, then click anywhere within the words *The Sea Spa Services***

   The words *The Sea Spa Services* are classified as a paragraph; even a single word is considered a paragraph if there is a hard return or paragraph break after it. Paragraph commands are applied by clicking the insertion point within the paragraph text. The Property inspector shows the settings for the paragraph with the insertion point placed inside of it; Paragraph appears in the Format text box.

2. **Click the Format list arrow on the Property inspector, then click Heading 1**

   The Heading 1 format is applied to the Sea Spa Services paragraph. The HTML code for a Heading 1 tag is <h1>. The tag is then closed with </h1>. The level of the heading tag follows the h, so the code for a Heading 2 tag is <h2>.

3. **Repeat Steps 1 and 2 to add the Heading 2 style to Massages, Facials, and Body Treatments right under the logo**

   The Heading 2 format is applied, as shown in Figure D-6. The H1 and H2 tags make the text a little large for the page, but is more in keeping with semantic markup to begin with level 1 headings and work down. **Semantic markup** means coding to emphasize meaning. You can change the size of the text for each heading using style sheets.

TROUBLE

Mac users may notice that the insertion point does not match when viewing Code and Design view.

4. **Click after the word "Treatments", insert a line break, click the Show Code and Design views button Split on the Document toolbar**

   The HTML code for the headings displays in the left window, as shown in Figure D-7. The first tag in each pair begins the code and the last tag ends the code.

5. **Click the Show Design view button Design on the Document toolbar, then save your work**

   The spa page redisplays in Design view with its changes saved.

FIGURE D-6: Applying paragraph formats

Text with the Heading 1 format applied

Text with the Heading 2 format applied

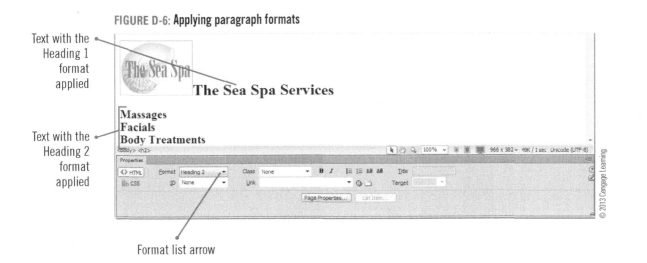

Format list arrow

FIGURE D-7: Show Code and Design views

Show Code and Design views button

The code that is displayed in Code view reflects the position of the insertion point on the page

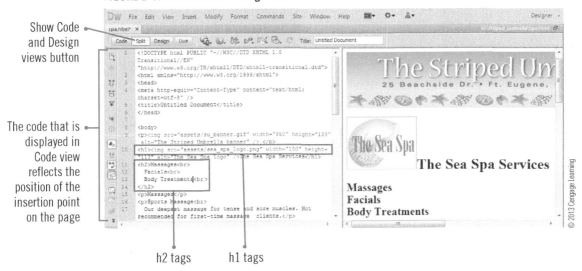

h2 tags   h1 tags

Design Matters

Choosing fonts

There are two classifications of fonts: sans-serif and serif. **Sans-serif** fonts, such as the font you are reading now, are made up of plain characters without any strokes at the top and bottom of letters. They are used frequently for headings and subheadings in printed text. Examples of sans-serif fonts are Arial, Verdana, and Helvetica. **Serif** fonts are more ornate, with small extra strokes at the top and bottom of the characters. They are generally easier to read in printed material because the

extra strokes lead your eye from one character to the next. Examples of serif fonts are Times New Roman, Garamond, and Georgia. Many designers feel that sans-serif fonts are preferable for files read electronically, while serif fonts are preferable for printed materials. When choosing fonts, limit each website to three font variations or less. Avoid using a tiny font size that users will have to enlarge or font colors that are difficult to see against the page background.

Creating an Unordered List

You can break up the monotony of large blocks of text by dividing them into smaller paragraphs or by organizing them as lists. Dreamweaver utilizes three types of lists: unordered lists, ordered lists, and definition lists. **Unordered lists**, also called bulleted lists, are lists of items that do not need to be placed in a specific order. Each item is usually preceded by a small filled circle (known as a **bullet**) or a similar icon. Numbered lists, or **ordered lists,** are lists of items that must be placed in a specific order, and each item is preceded by a number or a letter. **Definition lists** are similar to unordered lists, but do not use numbers or bullets. They are displayed with a hanging indent and are often used with terms and definitions, such as in a dictionary or glossary. ███████ You decide to organize the types of services into logical groups to make them easier to read. You want to create an unordered list for each of the spa service items.

STEPS

QUICK TIP
You can extend an unordered list to add more bullets by pressing [Enter] (Win) or [return] (Mac) once at the end of the list. To end an unordered list, press [Enter] (Win) or [return] (Mac) twice.

1. **Select the three spa service items and their descriptions under the Massages heading**
    Sports Massage, Swedish Massage, and Hot Stone Massage and their descriptions are selected.

2. **Click the** Unordered List button ▤ **on the HTML Property inspector, then deselect the text**
    The spa service items redisplay as an unordered list, as shown in Figure D-8.

TROUBLE
If you accidentally include the contact information/hours paragraph as part of your list, click Edit, Undo, then repeat Step 3.

3. **Repeat Steps 1 and 2 to create unordered lists of the spa service items under the Facials and Body Treatments headings**
    Each group of services redisplays as an unordered list.

4. **Click to place the insertion point before the first item in the first unordered list, then click the** Show Code view button `Code` **on the Document toolbar**
    The page displays in Code view. The HTML tags surrounding the unordered list are `<ul>` and `</ul>`. Each of the list items is surrounded by `<li>` and `</li>` tags, as shown in Figure D-9.

5. **Click the** Show Design view button `Design` **on the Document toolbar to return to Design view, then save your work**

FIGURE D-8: Creating an unordered list

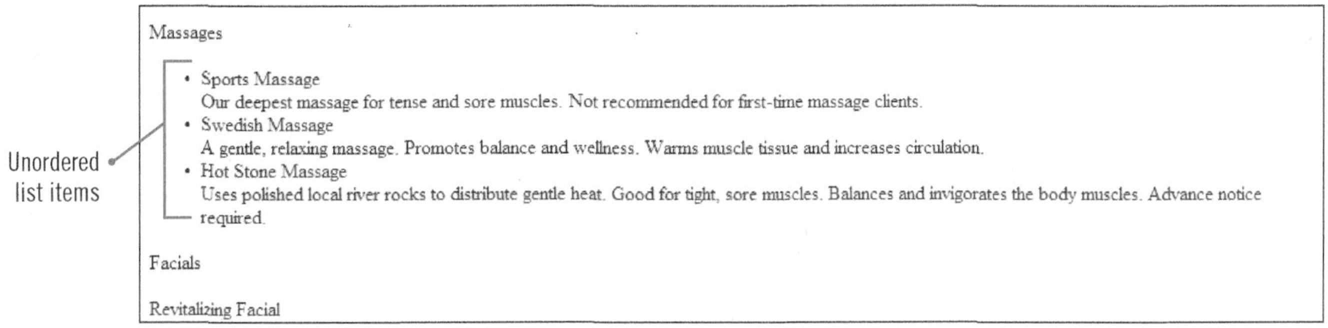

Massages

- Sports Massage
  Our deepest massage for tense and sore muscles. Not recommended for first-time massage clients.
- Swedish Massage
  A gentle, relaxing massage. Promotes balance and wellness. Warms muscle tissue and increases circulation.
- Hot Stone Massage
  Uses polished local river rocks to distribute gentle heat. Good for tight, sore muscles. Balances and invigorates the body muscles. Advance notice required.

Facials

Revitalizing Facial

Unordered list items

FIGURE D-9: Viewing an unordered list in Code view

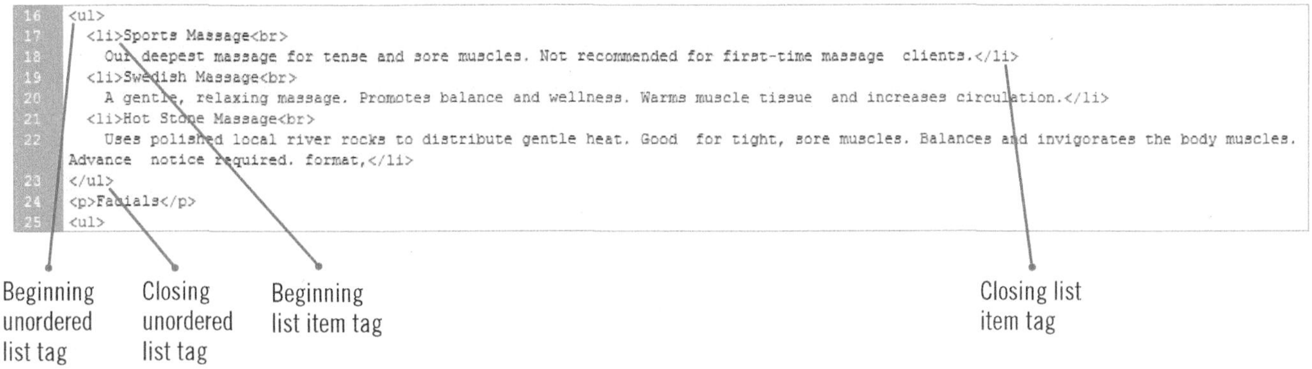

```
16  <ul>
17    <li>Sports Massage<br>
18      Our deepest massage for tense and sore muscles. Not recommended for first-time massage  clients.</li>
19    <li>Swedish Massage<br>
20      A gentle, relaxing massage. Promotes balance and wellness. Warms muscle tissue  and increases circulation.</li>
21    <li>Hot Stone Massage<br>
22      Uses polished local river rocks to distribute gentle heat. Good  for tight, sore muscles. Balances and invigorates the body muscles.
    Advance  notice required. format,</li>
23  </ul>
24  <p>Facials</p>
25  <ul>
```

Beginning unordered list tag

Closing unordered list tag

Beginning list item tag

Closing list item tag

Design Matters

Coding for the semantic web

You read several pages back about semantic markup and have previously heard the term *semantic* web. The word *semantics* refers to the study of word or sentence meanings. So the term **semantic web** refers to the way page content, such as paragraph, text, or list items, can be coded to emphasize their meaning to users. HTML tags such as the <p> tag, used for marking paragraphs, and the <ul> tag, used for marking unordered lists, provide a clear meaning of the function and significance of the paragraphs or lists. **Semantic markup**, or coding to emphasize meaning, is a way to incorporate good accessibility practice. CSS styles affect the appearance of web page content while semantic markup enhances the meaning of the content. Both techniques work together to provide well-designed web pages that are attractive and easy to understand.

Using ordered lists

Ordered lists contain numbered or lettered items that need to appear in a particular order, such as listing the steps to accomplish a task. For example, if you followed directions to drive from point A to point B, each step would have to be executed in order or you would not successfully reach your destination. For this type of sequential information, ordered lists can add more emphasis than bulleted ones. Dreamweaver uses several options for number styles, including Roman and Arabic. The HTML tags that surround ordered lists are <ol> and </ol>.

Understanding Cascading Style Sheets

Cascading Style Sheets (CSS) consist of sets of formatting rules that create styles. You create CSS when you want to apply the same formatting attributes to web page elements, such as text, images, and tables. A style sheet can contain many different rules, such as heading or body text, saved within a descriptive name. You can apply rules to any element in a document or, if you choose, to all of the documents in a website. If you edit an existing rule, all the page elements you have formatted with that rule will automatically update. ███████ You decide to research the ways CSS can save you time and provide your site with a more consistent look.

As you plan to use CSS in a website, keep in mind the following:

Pages formatted with CSS comply with current accessibility standards better than pages that have not used CSS.

- **Advantages of using CSS**

   CSS are made up of individual **rules**, or sets of formatting attributes, such as font-family and font-size. These rules create styles that are applied to individual page elements including text, headings, images, and horizontal rules. CSS are great time-savers and provide continuity across a website by applying the same style to all elements of a given type. After you apply rules, you can edit the rules definition. Once you complete the definition, every item to which you've applied that rule will then be automatically updated to reflect the changes. CSS separate content from layout, which means that you can make editing changes without affecting formatting and vice versa.

While internal styles are useful for creating a quick style that you do not expect to use on other pages, external styles are still preferred because they can be attached to other pages.

- **CSS classified by location**

   One way to categorize styles is by the location where they are stored. An **external style sheet** is a single, separate file with a .css file extension that can be attached to one or all pages in a website. This type of style sheet determines the formatting for various page elements and can contain many individual styles. If you have an external style sheet with 10 styles, you would only need to create one file with 10 styles defined within it, rather than 10 separate style sheet files. You can then attach this style sheet file to all of the pages in the same website (or to pages in other websites) to apply all of the specific styles. **Internal style sheets** are in the code for an individual web page and can either be embedded or inline styles. An **embedded style** consists of code that is stored in a page's head content while an **inline style** is stored in a page's body content. While you are learning, you will create styles of each type. In a work environment, however, you will probably use external styles.

- **CSS classified by function**

   Another way to classify CSS is by their function. A **Class style** can be used to format any page element, such as a paragraph of text or an image. An **HTML style** is used to redefine an HTML tag, such as changing the color of a horizontal rule or the font size for a heading tag. An **Advanced** or **Compound style** is used to format combinations of page elements. For example, you could define an Advanced style that determines how all images are displayed inside a div tag.

- **The CSS Styles panel**

   You use the CSS Styles panel to create, edit, and apply rules. The panel has two views: All (Document) Mode and Current Selection Mode. Figure D-10 shows the CSS Styles panel in All (Document) Mode, which lists all attached and embedded styles. When you select a rule in the All Rules pane, that rule's properties appear in the Properties pane at the bottom of the panel. Figure D-11 shows the CSS Styles panel in Current Selection mode, which shows the properties for the page element at the current position of the insertion point. You can edit the properties for the rule in the Properties pane. The small pane between the Summary for Selection pane and the Properties pane in Current mode is called the Rules pane, which shows the location of the current selected rule in the open document.

FIGURE D-10: **CSS Styles panel in All (Document) Mode**

Switch to All (Document) Mode button

External CSS styles

Properties for selected style are displayed in Properties pane

All Rules pane

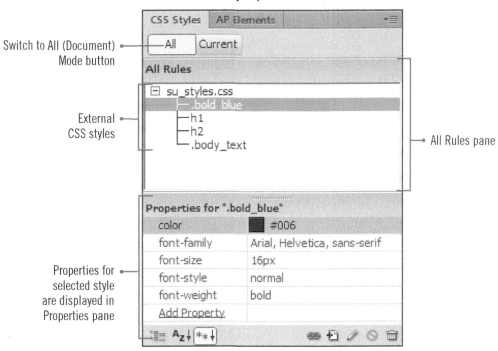

FIGURE D-11: **CSS Styles panel in Current Selection Mode**

Switch to Current Selection Mode button

The insertion point on the page is in a paragraph with the body_text rule applied

Summary for Selection pane

Rules pane

Properties for selected rule are displayed in Properties pane

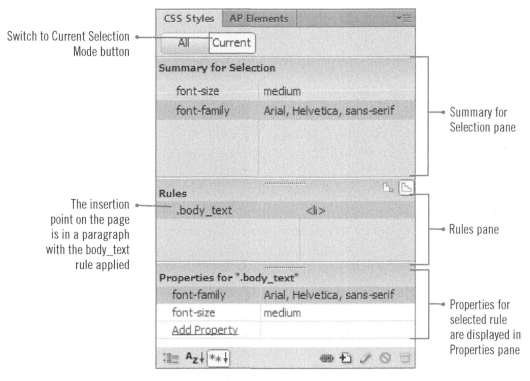

Using the CSS and HTML Property inspector

You apply CSS rules using either the CSS or HTML Property inspectors. You first select the element on the page, then apply a rule from the Property inspector. In the HTML Property inspector, you select a rule from the Class list box. In the CSS Property inspector, you select a rule from the Targeted Rule list box. You change back and forth between the two Property inspectors by clicking the HTML button <> HTML or CSS button ⊞ CSS.

Creating a Rule in a New Cascading Style Sheet

The steps for creating the first rule in a new style sheet are different from the steps for creating additional rules in an existing style sheet. Creating the first rule in a new style sheet is a two-step process. When you create the first rule, you have not yet created the style sheet, so you must first name the style sheet file in which you want to save the first rule. Once you have named and saved the style sheet file, you can then add new rules to it. If you decide to change a rule later, you only have to change the CSS rule and all the items will be updated automatically. 🔲🔲🔲 You decide that the same formatting style should be applied to each of the spa service headings. You want to use CSS to apply the same rule to each item.

STEPS

1. **Click** Window **on the Menu bar, click** CSS Styles **if necessary, then click the** Switch to All (Document) Mode button [All] **under the CSS Styles panel tab**

   The CSS Styles panel opens in the CSS Styles tab group. This panel is where you can add, delete, edit, and apply styles. All (Document) Mode displays all styles in the open document.

QUICK TIP
If you do not create a style before you begin formatting page elements, Dreamweaver will prompt you to create a new rule after you make your first formatting choice.

2. **Click the** New CSS Rule button 🔲 **in the Properties pane on the CSS Styles panel, click the** Selector Type list arrow **in the New CSS Rule dialog box, if necessary, to select** Class (can apply to any HTML element), **then type** bold_blue **in the Selector Name text box**

   The Class option creates a new custom rule that can apply to any HTML tag.

3. **Click the** Rule Definition list arrow, **click** (New Style Sheet File), **compare your screen to Figure D-12, then click** OK

   The Save Style Sheet File As dialog box opens, prompting you to name the Cascading Style Sheet file and store it in the website's root folder. The name of the new rule is bold_blue. The New Style Sheet File option makes the CSS style available for use in the entire website, not just the current document.

QUICK TIP
You can also create a new rule using the New CSS Rule command in the CSS Property inspector.

4. **Type** su_styles **in the File name text box (Win) or the Save As text box (Mac), then click** Save

   The CSS Rule Definition for bold_blue in su_styles.css dialog box opens. This dialog box allows you to choose attributes, such as font color and font size, for the CSS rule.

5. **Click the** Font-family list arrow, **click** Arial, Helvetica, sans-serif; **click the** Font-size list arrow, **click** 14, **leave the size measurement unit as px, click the** Font-style list arrow, **click** normal; **click the** Font-weight list arrow, **then click** bold

   The font-family, size, style, and weight settings are updated. Keeping the measurement at pixels (px) in the size measurement drop-down menu ensures that the text will be an absolute size when viewed in the browser.

TROUBLE
If the CSS rule does not appear, click the plus sign (Win) right-pointing triangle (Mac) next to the CSS file in the CSS Styles panel to expand it and see the styles listed in the file. If the styles do not appear, click [All].

6. **Click the** Color box 🔲 **to open the color picker, type** #006, **as shown in Figure D-13, click** OK, **then click the** Refresh button 🔲 **on the Files panel**

   The CSS rule named bold_blue appears in the CSS Styles panel, preceded by a period in the name. The Related Files toolbar displays under the file tab (Win) or file title bar (Mac) listing the style sheet filename su_styles.css. The Related Files toolbar, which displays the names of files related to the open document file, is used to quickly access files that are linked to the open document. The su_styles.css file appears in the file listing for the website, as shown in Figure D-14, with a different file extension from the HTML files. You may have to scroll down to see the su_styles.css file listed.

7. **Click the** Show Code view button [Code] **on the Document toolbar**

   The HTML code linking to the su_styles.css file appears in the Head section, as shown in Figure D-15. The bold_blue rule appears indented under the file su_styles.css in the CSS Styles panel.

8. **Click** File **on the Menu bar, then click** Save All

Working with Text and Cascading Style Sheets

FIGURE D-12: Adding a new CSS Rule in the New CSS Rule dialog box

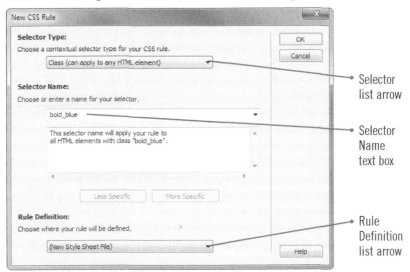

Selector
list arrow

Selector
Name
text box

Rule
Definition
list arrow

FIGURE D-13: CSS Rule Definition for .bold_blue in su_styles.css dialog box

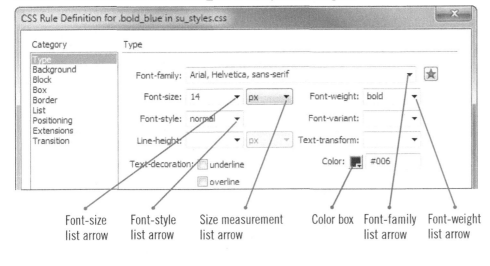

Font-size
list arrow

Font-style
list arrow

Size measurement
list arrow

Color box

Font-family
list arrow

Font-weight
list arrow

FIGURE D-14: The Striped Umbrella site
with the su_styles.css file listed

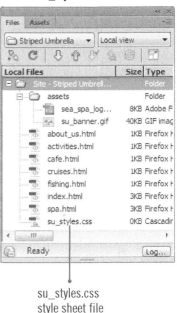

su_styles.css
style sheet file

FIGURE D-15: Code view showing link to style sheet file

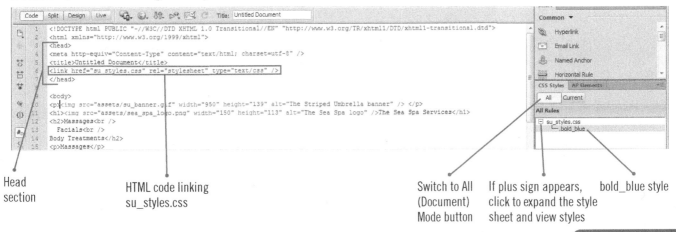

Head
section

HTML code linking
su_styles.css

Switch to All
(Document)
Mode button

If plus sign appears,
click to expand the style
sheet and view styles

bold_blue style

Working with Text and Cascading Style Sheets

Applying and Editing a Rule

After creating a style sheet, it is easy to apply its rules to page elements. If you are not satisfied with the results after applying a rule, you can edit the rule to change the formatting of all elements to which that rule applies. To apply a rule, you select the text or page element to which you want to apply the rule, remove any manual formatting, and then select the rule from the Property inspector. You want to apply a color style to each unordered list heading as well as increase their size to make them stand out.

STEPS

> **QUICK TIP**
> You can also click the Class list arrow in the HTML Property inspector to apply the bold_blue rule.

1. **Click the Show Design view button** `Design` **on the Document toolbar, then click the CSS button** `B. CSS` **to switch to the CSS Property inspector**
   The spa page redisplays in Design view.

2. **Select the unordered list heading Massages, click the Targeted Rule list arrow on the CSS Property inspector, then click bold_blue, as shown in Figure D-17**
   The bold_blue style is applied to the Massages heading. The Font-family, Font-size, Font-weight, Color, and Font-style text boxes on the Property inspector all reflect the bold_blue settings.

> **QUICK TIP**
> You can press [Ctrl][Y] (Win) or [command] [Y] (Mac) to redo (repeat) an action.

3. **Repeat Step 2 to apply the bold_blue style to the Facials and Body Treatment unordered list headings**
   The bold_blue style is applied to each unordered list heading.

> **QUICK TIP**
> If a rule is not selected, the Edit Rule button becomes the Edit Style Sheet button and opens the css file for editing.

4. **Click the bold_blue rule in the CSS Styles panel, then click the Edit Rule button** ✎ **on the CSS Styles panel**
   The CSS Rule Definition for bold_blue in su_styles.css dialog box opens. This same dialog box that you used to create the original rule is used to edit a .css file.

5. **Click the Font-size list arrow, click 16, as shown in Figure D-18, click OK, then deselect the text**
   The unordered list headings appear on the page with a larger text size applied, as shown in Figure D-19.

6. **Click File on the Menu bar, then click Save All**
   The changes to both the spa document file and the style sheet file are saved.

Understanding CSS code

You can also use CSS rules to format page content other than text. For example, you can use CSS to format backgrounds, borders, lists, and images. A CSS rule consists of two parts: the selector and the declaration. The **selector** is the name or the tag to which the style declarations have been assigned. The **declaration** consists of the property and the value. An example of a property would be font-family. An example of a value would be Arial. Figure D-16 shows the coding for three CSS rules in a style sheet.

FIGURE D-16: Code for three rules in the su_styles.css file

Code for heading rules

Code for .body_text rule

```
9   h1 {
10      font-family: Arial, Helvetica, sans-serif;
11      font-size: 24px;
12      font-weight: bold;
13  }
14  h2 {
15      font-family: Arial, Helvetica, sans-serif;
16      font-size: 18px;
17      font-weight: normal;
18  }
19
20
21  .body_text {    font-size: medium;
21      font-family: Arial, Helvetica, sans-serif;
22  }
```

FIGURE D-17: Applying a rule to text

Text is selected

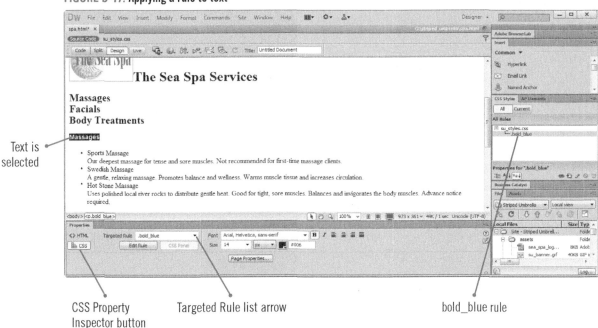

CSS Property Inspector button   Targeted Rule list arrow   bold_blue rule

FIGURE D-18: Editing the bold_blue rule

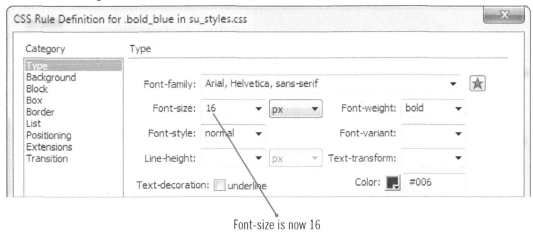

Font-size is now 16

FIGURE D-19: Viewing text after editing the Font-size property

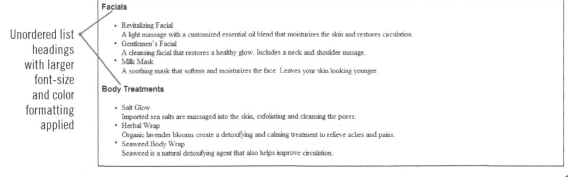

Unordered list headings with larger font-size and color formatting applied

Adding Rules to a Cascading Style Sheet

Once you have created a style sheet, it is easy to add additional rules to it. Generally, the more rules you have defined in a Style Sheet, the more time you can save. Ideally, you should create rules for all page elements. You add rules by using the New CSS Rule button in the CSS Styles panel. You should use the same style sheet for each page to ensure that all your elements have a consistent appearance. You decide to add two new rules in the su_styles.css file, one to modify the <h1> tag and one to modify the <h2> tag. These rules will be Tag selector types, rather than class selector types.

STEPS

1. **Click the New CSS Rule button** 🗗 **on the CSS Styles Panel**
   The New CSS Rule dialog box opens.

2. **Click the Selector Type list arrow, click Tag (redefines an HTML element), type h1 in the Selector Name text box, click the Rule Definition list arrow, click su_styles.css, as shown in Figure D-20, then click OK**
   The CSS Rule Definition for h1 in su_styles.css dialog box opens.

3. **Click the Font-family list arrow, click Arial, Helvetica, sans-serif, click the Font-size list arrow, click 24, click the Font-weight list arrow, then click bold, as shown in Figure D-21, then click OK**
   The font is set to a 24px, bold, Arial, Helvetica, sans-serif font-family. Notice that the heading "The Sea Spa Services" has changed appearance. Since it was originally formatted with the Heading 1 paragraph format, the new <h1> rule properties have been automatically applied to this heading.

QUICK TIP
If you click the insertion point within text or select text that has an applied rule, that rule appears in the Class list box in the HTML Property inspector, or the Targeted Rule list box in the CSS Property inspector.

4. **Repeat Steps 1 through 3 to create a rule to modify the <h2> tag using the following settings: Font-family: Arial, Helvetica, sans-serif; Font-size: 18; Font-weight: normal**
   The headings "Massages", "Facials", and "Body Treatments" have changed appearance. Since they were formatted with a Heading 2 paragraph format, the new <h2> rule properties have been automatically applied, as shown in Figure D-22.

5. **Click File on the Menu bar, then click Save All**
   The changes are saved to both the spa document file and the style sheet file.

Using font combinations in styles

When you are setting rule properties for text, it is wise to apply font combinations. That way, if one font is not available, the browser will apply a similar one. For instance, with the font family "Arial, Helvetica, sans-serif," the browser will first check the user's system for the Arial font, then, if it can't find the Arial font, it will look for the Helvetica font, and so on. If you prefer to use a different set of fonts than the ones Dreamweaver provides, click the Font list arrow on the CSS Property inspector, click Edit Font list, then choose from the available fonts listed. This is also known as a custom font stack. You can also select font combinations in any dialog box with a Font-family option.

Another option for specifying fonts is to use external font libraries. Font libraries are fonts that are downloaded with your page content when viewed in a browser so you are assured that your users will have the correct font applied. Use the @font-face CSS rule to specify fonts from a font library. Go to typekit.com and google.com/webfonts#HomePlace:home for examples of font libraries.

FIGURE D-20: Creating a new CSS rule to define the <h1> rule

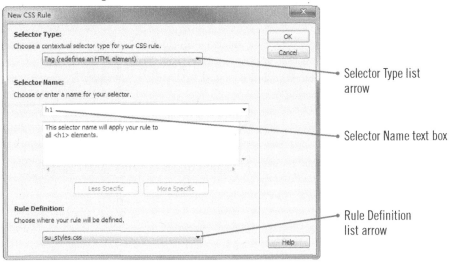

- Selector Type list arrow
- Selector Name text box
- Rule Definition list arrow

FIGURE D-21: Setting the properties for the <h1> rule

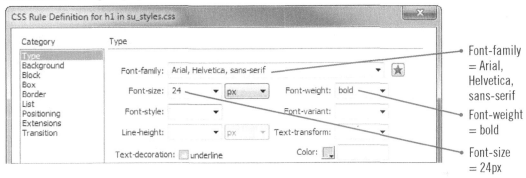

- Font-family = Arial, Helvetica, sans-serif
- Font-weight = bold
- Font-size = 24px

FIGURE D-22: New <h1> and <h2> properties applied to headings

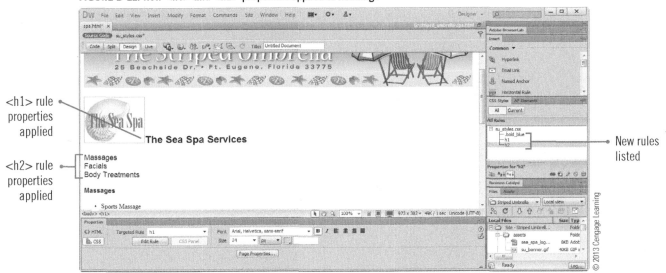

- <h1> rule properties applied
- <h2> rule properties applied
- New rules listed

© 2013 Cengage Learning

Working with Text and Cascading Style Sheets

Attaching a Cascading Style Sheet to a Page

After creating an external style sheet, you should attach it to the rest of the pages in your website to utilize the full benefit. Being able to define a rule and apply it to page elements across all the pages of your site means that you can make hundreds of formatting changes in a few minutes. Style sheets create a more uniform look from page to page and lead to cleaner code. ▰▰▰▰ You decide to attach the su_styles.css file to the home page and use it to format the paragraph text. Since you already have an internal style on the index page, you want to delete it so the external style will be used to format the paragraph text instead.

(Win) To switch between open documents, click the tab for the document you wish to view, or press [Ctrl][Tab].

1. **Open the index.html page**

   Since an external style sheet has yet to be linked to the index page, the external style sheet is not listed in the CSS Styles panel. In order to use an external style sheet with other pages in the website, you must first attach the style sheet file to each page.

2. **Click the Attach Style Sheet button ▣ on the CSS Styles panel**

   The Attach External Style Sheet dialog box opens.

If you don't see your styles listed, click the plus sign (Win) or right-pointing triangle (Mac) next to su_styles.css in the CSS Styles panel.

3. **Click Browse next to the File/URL text box, click su_styles.css in the Select Style Sheet File dialog box if necessary, click OK (Win) or Open (Mac); compare your screen to Figure D-23, then click OK**

   The Attach External Style Sheet dialog box closes and the su_styles.css style sheet file appears in the CSS Styles panel, indicating that the file is attached to the index page. In addition to the su_styles.css external style sheet, some internal styles are also listed in the CSS Styles panel: body_text, nav_bar, small_text, and body.

4. **Right-click the body_text rule under <style> in the CSS Styles Panel in the internal style sheet, click Move CSS Rules, verify that su_styles.css displays in the Move to External Style Sheet dialog box, as shown in Figure D-24, then click OK to close the Move to External Style Sheet dialog box**

   The internal body_text style is moved to the external style sheet, so it can now be used to format the text on all other pages in the website.

5. **Repeat Step 4 to move the nav_bar, small_text, and body rules to the external style sheet, compare your screen to Figure D-25, delete the remaining <style> tag in the CSS Styles panel, save all files, then close the index page**

6. **Select the first unordered list on the spa page, click the Targeted Rule text box on the CSS Property inspector, then click body_text.**

7. **Repeat Step 6 to apply the body_text rule to the rest of the text on the page that does not have a rule applied, click File on the Menu bar, then click Save All**

   The three unordered lists and the last paragraph are now formatted with the body_text rule.

Working with Text and Cascading Style Sheets

FIGURE D-23: Attaching the su_styles.css file to the index page

Name of external style sheet
to attach to the page

Browse button

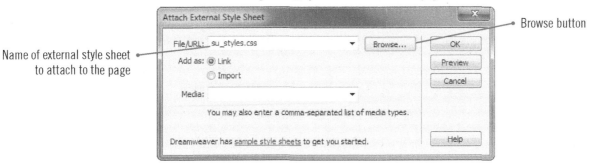

FIGURE D-24: The Move to External Style Sheet dialog box

su_styles.css is
selected for the
destination file

FIGURE D-25: The internal rules moved to the external style sheet

Select and delete
this tag in Step 5

Internal rules
are moved to
the external
style sheet

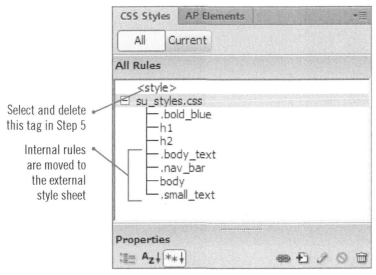

Design Matters

The evolution of CSS3

The use of Cascading Style Sheets has evolved over the years from CSS Level 1 to the present CSS Level 3. Cascading Style Sheets revisions are referenced by "levels" rather than "versions." Each new level builds on the previous level. CSS Level 1 is obsolete today. CSS Level 2 is still used, but CSS Level 3 is the latest W3C (World Wide Web Consortium) standard. With CSS3, several properties are available that promote website accessibility such as the @font-face rule. This rule in CSS2 provided the ability to embed fonts in documents using the WOFF format. WOFF stands for Web Open Font Format and was proposed to the W3C to be a standard format for all web browsers to use. Currently, Firefox Version 3.6 and up, Internet Explorer Version 9 and up, Google Chrome Version 5 and up, and Safari Version 5.1 and up support the WOFF format. The @font-face rule now is used to download a specific font from a font library to render text on a web page if the user does not have that font installed on their system. Examples of font libraries are typekit.com. and google.com/webfonts. For more information about CSS3, go to w3.org/TR/CSS/.

Checking for Spelling Errors

Dreamweaver has a feature for checking spelling errors that is similar to those you have probably used in word processing programs. It is very important to check for spelling and grammatical errors before publishing a page. A page that is published with errors will cause the user to immediately judge the site as unprofessional, and the accuracy of the information presented will be in question. It is a good idea to start a spell check at the top of the document because Dreamweaver searches from the insertion point down. If your insertion point is in the middle of the document, you will receive a message asking if you want to check the rest of the document, which wastes time. If a file you create in a word processor will be imported into Dreamweaver, make sure to run a spell check in the word processing program before you import it. 🔲🔲🔲 You want to check the spelling on the spa page and correct any errors.

STEPS

QUICK TIP
You can also press [Ctrl][Home] to move the insertion point to the top of the document. (Mac users may not have a [home] key depending on their keyboard.)

1. **Place the insertion point in front of The Sea Spa Services heading**

2. **Click Commands on the Menu bar, then click Check Spelling**

   The Check Spelling dialog box opens, as shown in Figure D-26. The word *masage* is highlighted on the spa page, indicating a misspelled word.

3. **Click massage. in the Suggestions list if necessary, click Change, then click Ignore if it stops on any other words that you know are spelled correctly**

   The Check Spelling dialog box closes and a Dreamweaver dialog box opens stating that the Spell check is complete.

4. **Click OK**

   The Dreamweaver dialog box closes and the spa page redisplays with the word *massage* spelled correctly.

5. **Add the page title The Sea Spa to the Title text box on the Document toolbar**

6. **Click File on the Menu bar, click Save, click the Preview/Debug in browser icon 🌐, then preview the spa page in your browser window**

   The spa page opens in your browser window as shown in Figure D-27.

7. **Close your browser, close all open pages, then exit Dreamweaver**

Using Find and Replace

Another useful editing command is Find and Replace, which is located on the Edit menu. You can use this command to make individual or global text edits in either Design or Code view. It is similar to Find and Replace commands in word processing programs, except that there is an added advantage in Dreamweaver. You can use Find and Replace to easily search through code if you are trying to locate and correct coding errors. For example, if you want to find a tag that formats a font with a specific color, you can search for that color number in the code. If you are searching for internal links that are incorrectly set as absolute links, you can enter the search term *src = "file"* to help you to locate them. You will learn more about absolute links in Unit F.

FIGURE D-26: **Using the Check Spelling command**

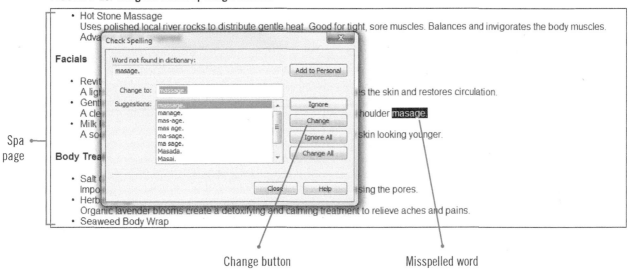

Spa page

Change button   Misspelled word

FIGURE D-27: **The finished product**

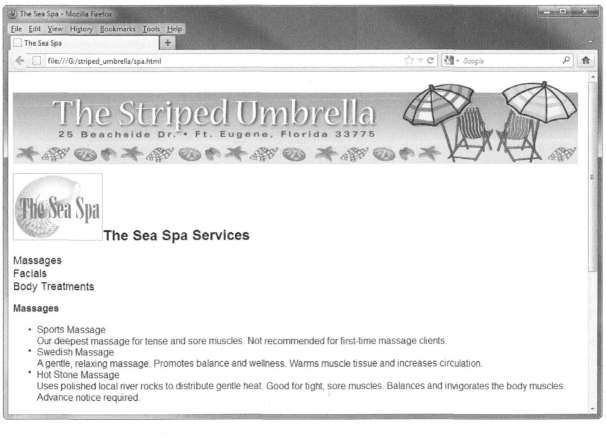

Practice

Concepts Review

Label each element in the Document window, as shown in Figure D-28.

FIGURE D-28

© 2013 Cengage Learning

1. _____	5. _____
2. _____	6. _____
3. _____	7. _____
4. _____	8. _____

Match each of the following terms with the statement that best describes it.

9. **Sans-serif font**

10. **Property inspector**

11. **Ordered lists**

12. **Unordered lists**

13. **CSS styles**

14. **CSS Rule**

15. **External style sheet**

16. **Selector**

17. **Declaration**

18. **Serif font**

a. Numbered lists

b. Font without extra strokes at top and bottom

c. A set of formatting attributes that creates a style

d. A file attached or linked to a web page to format page elements

e. A style property and the value

f. Bulleted lists

g. A panel used for formatting page elements

h. The name or tag to which style declarations have been assigned

i. Font with extra strokes at the top and bottom

j. Sets of formatting attributes to format page elements

Select the best answer from the following list of choices.

19. **The button used to select color is:**
    a. ✎
    b. ▢
    c. ⬒
    d. 🗑

20. **External CSS files are saved with the filename extension:**
    a. .css
    b. .cas
    c. .stl
    d. .csf

21. **A CSS Class Style name in the Styles panel is preceded by a:**
    a. pound sign.
    b. period.
    c. dash.
    d. number.

22. **Styles that are part of the head content of a web page are called:**
    a. external styles.
    b. embedded styles.
    c. inline Styles.
    d. HTML styles.

23. **The type of style used to redefine an HTML tag in the New CSS Rule dialog box is called:**
    a. an Advanced style.
    b. a Class style.
    c. a Tag style.
    d. a Compound style.

Skills Review

Important: *If you did not create this website in Unit B and maintain it in Unit C, you will need to create a local site root folder for this website and define the website using files your instructor will provide. See the "Read This Before You Begin" section of this book for more detailed instructions.*

1. **Create a new page.**
   a. Start Dreamweaver.
   b. Open the Blooms & Bulbs website.
   c. Create a new HTML file and save it as **tips.html** in the Blooms & Bulbs website, overwriting the existing blank file.
   d. Add the page title **Blooms & Bulbs** in the title text box.
   e. Insert the banner from your website assets folder at the top of the page, add appropriate alternate text, then enter a paragraph break after the banner.
   f. Insert the file butterfly.jpg from the assets folder in the drive and folder where you store your Unit D Data Files, then add appropriate alternate text.

2. **Import text.**
   a. With the insertion point to the right of the butterfly image, import (Win) or copy and paste (Mac) the Word document gardening_tips.doc from the drive and folder where you store your Unit D Data Files.
   b. Use the Clean Up Word HTML command on the tips page, then save the tips page.

3. **Set text properties.**
   a. Select the Seasonal Gardening Checklist heading, then format the text with the Heading 1 format.
   b. Select the Basic Gardening Tips heading and format it with a Heading 1 format.
   c. Save your work.

4. **Create an unordered list.**
   a. Select the items under the Seasonal Gardening Checklist.
   b. Format the list of items as an unordered list. (*Hint:* Be sure *not* to select the return at the end of the last line or you will accidentally create a fifth item.)
   c. Select the items under Basic Gardening Tips, then format them as an ordered list. (*Hint:* If you have extra line breaks, you will need to delete them to have only six items in your list.)

5. **Understand Cascading Style Sheets.**
   a. Using a word processor or piece of paper, list the types of CSS categorized by their location in a website.
   b. Using a word processor or piece of paper, list the types of CSS categorized by their function in a website.

6. **Create a Style in a new Cascading Style Sheet.**
   a. Open the CSS Styles panel, if necessary.
   b. Create a new Class style named **bold_gray** in a new style sheet file.
   c. Save the new style sheet file with the name **blooms_styles.css** in the blooms folder.
   d. Set the Font-family for the bold_gray style as Arial, Helvetica, sans-serif.
   e. Set the Font-size as small, the Font-weight as bold, then the Color as #333.
   f. Save all files.

7. **Apply and edit a style.**
   a. Apply the bold_gray style to the words *Fall*, *Winter*, *Spring*, and *Summer*.
   b. Edit the style to increase the text size to medium.
   c. Save all files.

8. Add styles to a Cascading Style Sheet.

a. Create a new Tag selector for the Heading 1 tag in the blooms_styles.css file.

b. Set the Font-family as Arial, Helvetica, sans-serif.

c. Set the Font-size as large, the Font-style as normal, then the Color as #000.

d. Save all files.

9. Attach a Cascading Style Sheet to a page.

a. Open the index page in the Blooms & Bulbs website.

b. Attach the blooms_styles.css file to the index page.

c. Move each of the internal styles to the external style sheet, delete the remaining <style> tag, then save all files and close the index page.

d. On the tips page, apply the body_text rule to all of the text on the page that is not formatted with either a heading format or CSS rule, then save your work.

10. Check for spelling errors.

a. Run a spell check on the tips page, correcting any misspelled words found, then save your work.

b. Preview the page in your browser, then compare your screen to Figure D-29.

c. Close your browser, then Exit (Win) or Quit (Mac) Dreamweaver.

FIGURE D-29

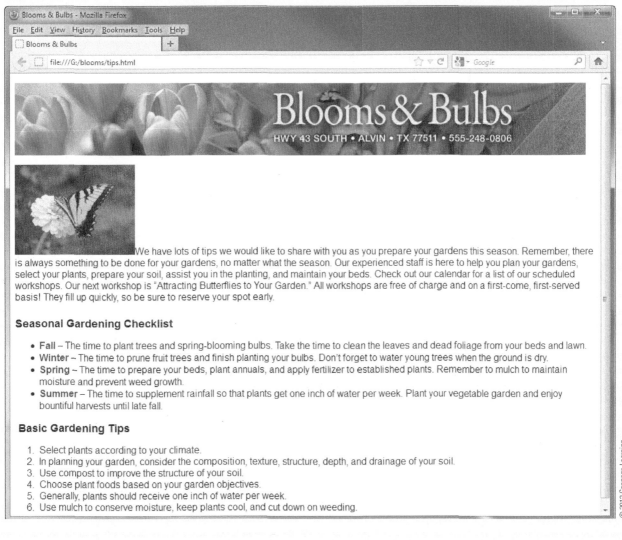

© 2013 Cengage Learning
Original photos courtesy of Sherry Bishop

Important: *If you did not create the following websites in Unit B and maintain them in Unit C, you will need to create a local site root folder for the websites in the following exercises and define the websites using files your instructor will provide. See the "Read This Before You Begin" section in this book for more detailed instructions.*

Independent Challenge 1

You have been hired to create a website for a river expedition company named Rapids Transit, located on the Buffalo River in Arkansas. In addition to renting canoes, kayaks, and rafts, they have several types of cabin rentals for overnight stays. River guides are available, if requested, to accompany clients on float trips. The clients range from beginners to experienced floaters. The owner's name is Mike Andrew. Mike has asked you to add a page to the site that will describe the lodge, cabins, and tents that are available to their customers.

a. Start Dreamweaver.

b. Open the Rapids Transit website.

c. Open the file dwd_1.html from the drive and folder where you store your Unit D Data Files, then save it as **lodging.html** in the Rapids Transit website, replacing the existing file, but not updating links.

d. Close dwd_1.html, then verify that the rapids banner path is set to the assets folder in the website.

e. Create an unordered list from the four types of lodging and their rates.

f. Create a new Tag Selector rule that modifies the Heading 1 tag, then save it in a new style sheet file named **rapids_transit.css** using the following settings: Font-family, Arial, Helvetica, sans-serif; Font-size, 16; Font-weight, bold; Color, #003.

g. Apply the Heading 1 format to the navigation bar text and the first sentence on the page.

h. Create a second Tag selector rule to modify the Heading 2 tag in the rapids_transit.css style sheet.

i. Format the <h2> rule with the following settings: Font-family Arial, Helvetica, sans-serif; Font-size 14; Font-style normal; Font-weight bold; and Color #003.

j. Open the index page, attach the rapids_transit.css file, move the internal body_text rule to the external style sheet, then delete the <style> tag in the CSS Styles panel.

k. Save all files, then on the lodging page, apply the Heading 2 format to the text "Rates are as follows:" and the body_text rule to the rest of the text on the page that is not formatted with a heading format.

l. Create a new class style in the rapids_transit.css style sheet named **contact_info** using Arial, Helvetica sans-serif; italic style; size 14, color #000; then apply it to the contact information on the index page.

m. Apply the Heading 1 format to the navigation bar text on the index page, then save your work using the Save All command on the File menu.

n. Preview the index page in your browser window, click the Lodging link, compare your screen to Figure D-30, close your browser window, close all files, then exit Dreamweaver. (*Hint:* Depending on whether you have clicked other links, your link colors may not match the links in the figure.)

FIGURE D-30

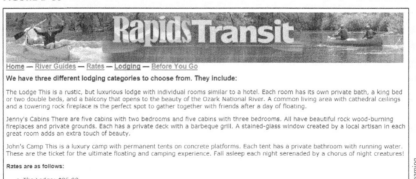

Working with Text and Cascading Style Sheets

Independent Challenge 2

You are a marketing specialist for a travel outfitter named TripSmart. TripSmart specializes in travel products and services. In addition to selling luggage and accessories, they sponsor trips and offer travel advice. Your company is designing a new website and your job is to update the newsletter page on the current website with some timely travel tips.

a. Start Dreamweaver, then open the TripSmart website.

b. Open the file dwd_2.html and save it as **newsletter.html** in the TripSmart website, replacing the existing file, but not updating links, then close dwd_2.html.

c. Verify that the banner path is set to the assets folder of the website.

d. Create an ordered list from the 10 items on the page, starting with Be organized.

e. Create a new Tag Selector rule to modify the Heading 1 format, then save it in a new style sheet named **tripsmart_styles.css**.

f. Choose a font, size, style, color, and weight of your choice for the <h1> rule.

g. Apply the Heading 1 format to the Ten Tips for Stress-Free Travel paragraph heading.

h. Type **TripSmart - Serving all your travel needs** in the document title text box, then save your work.

i. Open the index page, delete the horizontal rule, attach the style sheet, then move the three internal rules to the external style sheet and delete the <style> tag left from the internal styles in the CSS Styles panel.

j. Create another class style in the tripsmart_styles.css style sheet named **contact_info** with settings of your choice, apply it to the contact information on the page, save your work, then close the page.

k. Apply the body_text rule to the two remaining paragraphs without styles applied, preview the newsletter page in your browser window, then compare it to Figure D-31 as an example for a possible solution.

l. Close your browser, close the file, then exit Dreamweaver.

FIGURE D-31

Our staff recently conducted a contest to determine ten top travel tips for stress-free travel. We compiled over forty great tips, but the following were selected as the winners. We hope you will find them useful for your next trip!

Ten Tips for Stress-Free Travel

1. Be organized.
   Make a list of what you want to pack in each bag and check it as you pack. Take this inventory with you in the event your bags are lost or delayed. Then use the list again when you repack, to make sure you haven't left anything behind.
2. Carry important information with you.
   Keep your important travel information in easy reach at all times. Include a list of your flight numbers, confirmation numbers for your travel and hotel reservations, and any car rentals. And don't forget printouts of your itinerary and electronic tickets. Remember to bring your passport, and keep a photocopy of it in another piece of baggage. Be sure to have copies of prescriptions, emergency phone numbers, telephone numbers and addresses of friends and relatives, complete lists of medications, and credit card information. It's not a bad idea to email this information to yourself as a backup if you will have email access.
3. Pack smartly.
   You know the old saying: lay out everything on your bed you plan to take with you, then remove half of it. Pack the remainder and carry your bags around the block once to make sure you can handle them yourself. If in doubt, leave it out! Use packing cubes or zip-top bags to organize your personal items, such as underwear and socks. Make distinctive-looking luggage tags with your name and address for easy identification, and be sure to include the same information inside your luggage.
4. Include basic medical necessities.
   Besides your prescription drugs, take a basic first aid kit with the basics: bandages, anti-nausea medications, anti-diarrhea medications, aspirin, antibiotics, and prescription drugs.
5. Wear comfortable shoes.
   Blisters can ruin a wonderful trip. Wear comfortable shoes and socks. Your priority should be comfortable, dry, warm feet — not fashion. Don't buy new shoes without breaking them in first.

© 2013 Cengage Learning

Independent Challenge 3

Dr. Chappel is a government historian who is conducting research on the separation of church and state. He is using the Library of Congress website to find relevant information. Write your answers to the questions below on paper or using your word processor.

a. Connect to the Internet, then go to The Library of Congress website at www.loc.gov, shown in Figure D-32.

b. Is the content well organized?

c. What font or fonts are used on the pages for the main text? Are the same fonts used consistently on the other pages in the website?

d. Are there any ordered or unordered lists on the website? If so, how are they used?

e. View the source to see if CSS styles are used on the pages in the website.

f. Use a search engine to find another website of interest. Compare and contrast the use of text formatting on this site to that used on the Library of Congress website.

FIGURE D-32

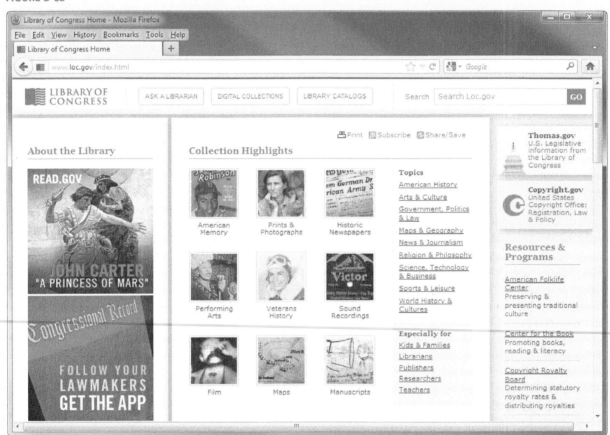

Library of Congress website (loc.gov)

Real Life Independent Challenge

This assignment will continue to build on the personal website that you created in Unit B and modified in Unit C. You have created and developed your index page. In this lesson, you will work with one of the other pages in your website.

a. Consult your wireframe, then decide which page you would like to develop in this lesson.

b. Create content for this page, then format the text attractively on the page using settings for font, size, text color, style, and alignment.

c. Format some of the text on the page as either an ordered or unordered list.

d. Create a style sheet with a minimum of two rules, then apply a rule to all text on the page.

e. Attach the style sheet to any of the pages you have already developed, then apply rules to all text.

f. Save the file, then preview the pages in your browser window.

After you are satisfied with your work, verify the following:

a. Each completed page has a page title.

b. All links work correctly.

c. The completed pages appear correctly using at least two screen resolutions.

d. All images are properly placed with a path to the assets folder of the website.

e. A style sheet is used to format all text.

Visual Workshop

Your company has been selected to design a website for a catering business named Carolyne's Creations. Open the Carolyne's Creations website, open the file dwd_3.html, then save it as **recipes.html** in the Carolyne's Creations website, replacing the original file, and not updating the links. Close dwd_3.html, then format the page using styles so it looks similar to Figure D-33. (The text may wrap slightly different depending on the size of your browser window.) Save the file pie.jpg from the drive and folder where you store your Unit D Data Files to your website assets folder (*Hint*: Use the following styles and settings to match the figure, and save them in a CSS file named cc_styles.css. The small_text rule was not used on the recipes page, but for the copyright and last updated statements on the index page.)

.nav_bar	.body_text	.small_text
Font-family: Arial, Helvetica, sans-serif	Font-family: Arial, Helvetica, sans-serif	Font-family: Arial, Helvetica, sans-serif
Font-size: large	Font-size: medium	Font-size: small

h1	h2	.ingredients_list
Font-family: Verdana, Geneva, sans-serif	Font-family: Verdana, Geneva, sans-serif	Font-family: Arial, Helvetica, sans-serif
Font-size: 18px	Font-size: 16px	Font-size: medium
Font-weight: bold	Font-weight: bold	Text-indent: 30px
Color: #333	Color: #333	List style-type: none

If you have not maintained this website from the previous unit, then contact your instructor for assistance.

FIGURE D-33

Home | Shop | Classes | Catering | Recipes

Caramel Coconut Pie

This is one of our most requested desserts. It is simple, elegant, and refreshing. It is easy to make in advance, because you keep it frozen until just before serving. It makes two pies — one to eat and one to give away!

Ingredients:

¼ cup butter
7 oz. dried coconut
½ cup chopped pecans
1 package (8 oz.) cream cheese, softened
1 can (14 oz.) sweetened condensed milk
1 container (16 oz.) whipped topping, thawed
1 jar (12 oz.) caramel ice cream topping
2 pie shells (9 in.), baked

© 2013 Cengage Learning
Original photos courtesy of Sherry Bishop

Using and Managing Images

Files You Will Need:

To view a list of files needed for this unit, see the Data Files Grid in the back of the book.

Web pages with images are more interesting than pages with just text. You can position images on your web pages, then resize them, add borders, and customize the amount of space around them. You can also use images as a web page, table, or CSS layout block background. In this unit you learn how to incorporate images into a website and how to manage them effectively using the Assets panel. A photographer recently did a photo shoot of The Striped Umbrella property for some new brochures. You decide to incorporate several of the images on the about_us page so that the beauty of the resort comes across.

OBJECTIVES

Insert an image

Align an image

Enhance an image

Use alternate text and set Accessibility preferences

View the Assets panel

Insert a background image

Delete image files from a website

Create and find images for a website

Examine copyright rules

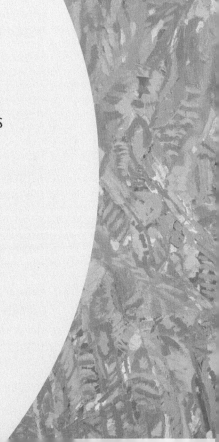

Adobe product screenshot(s) reprinted with permission from Adobe Systems Incorporated.

Inserting an Image

Images you import into a website are automatically added to the Assets panel. The **Assets panel**, located with the other panels on the right side of your workspace, lists the assets of the website, such as images and colors. As you add images to a web page, the page **download time** (the time it takes to transfer the file to a user's computer) increases. Pages that download slowly discourage users from staying on the site. To add an image to a page, you can either use the Insert, Image command on the Menu bar, use the Images button in the Common category on the Insert panel, or drag an image from the Assets panel onto the page. ▰▰▰▰ You want to place several photos of the resort on the about_us web page and check the file size of each in the Assets panel.

TROUBLE

Your download time shown may vary according to the Connection Speed preferences set for your Status bar. To change your settings, click Edit (Win) or Dreamweaver (Mac) on the Menu bar, click Preferences, then click Status Bar.

1. **Start Dreamweaver, switch to Design view if necessary, open The Striped Umbrella website, open dwe_1.html from the drive and folder where you store your Unit E Data Files, save it as about_us.html in the striped_umbrella root folder, overwriting the existing file and not updating the links, then close dwe_1.html**

   The about_us page displays in Design view in your workspace. The Status bar displays the download time for the current web page, as shown Figure E-1.

2. **Click the Attach Style Sheet button ▦ in the CSS Styles panel, attach the su_styles.css style sheet, apply the nav_bar rule to the menu bar, the Heading 1 paragraph format to "Welcome guests!", and the body_text rule to all of the paragraph text on the page**

   The style sheet for the website is attached to the about_us page, and three rules are applied to the menu bar, heading, and two paragraphs.

3. **Click to the left of the word *When* in the first paragraph to place the insertion point, select the Common category on the Insert panel if necessary, scroll down and click the Images list arrow on the Insert panel, then click Image**

   The Select Image Source dialog box opens. This is the same dialog box you have been using to copy images from the Data Files folder to your site assets folder when you save new pages with images.

QUICK TIP

The Image Tag Accessibility Attributes dialog box contains Dreamweaver accessibility features, which you will learn about later in the unit.

4. **Navigate to the drive and folder where you store your Unit E Data Files, double-click club_house.jpg from the assets folder, type Club House as the Alternate text in the Image Tag Accessibility Attributes dialog box if prompted, then click OK**

5. **Expand the assets folder in the Files panel, if necessary, then click the Refresh Button ↻ on the Files panel toolbar if necessary**

   The club house image appears at the beginning of the first paragraph, as shown in Figure E-2. As indicated in the Files panel list, the club house image is located in the website assets folder. This is the location that will be used to load the image in the browser when the page is viewed.

QUICK TIP

You need to select club_house.jpg to see the thumbnail.

6. **Save the file, click the Assets panel tab, click the Images button ▦ on the Assets panel if necessary, then click ↻ at the bottom of the Assets panel, if necessary**

   The three images you added to The Striped Umbrella website—club_house.jpg, sea_spa_logo.jpg, and su_banner.gif—are listed in the Assets panel. When the Images button is selected, the Assets panel displays the images in the current website which, as shown in Figure E-3, is split into two panes. The lower window lists all of the images in the website, while the top window displays a thumbnail of the image currently selected in the list. The Dimensions column lists the height and width of each image.

TROUBLE

If the file names don't appear in the Files or Assets panels, click the Refresh button ↻, or click ↻ while you hold down the [Ctrl] key.

7. **Repeat Steps 3 and 4 to insert the boardwalk.png image at the beginning of the second paragraph, if prompted use Boardwalk to the beach as alternate text, then save your work**

   The boardwalk image appears on the page at the beginning of the second paragraph and boardwalk.png is added to the list of images in the Assets panel. The Assets panel lists the four images shown in Figure E-4.

provides a safe route to the beach for both our guests and the native vegetation. The sea oats and other flora are tender. Please do not step on them or pick them. A lifeguard is on duty from 9:00 a.m. until sunset. Check the flag each time you head for the beach for the status of current swimming conditions and advisories. Jellyfish can be a problem at times, so be careful when you are walking along the beach, especially as the tide is retreating from high tide. We have beach chairs, umbrellas, and towels available to our guests. Check with the attendant on duty. Water, juices, and soft drinks are also available for purchase at the end of the boardwalk. Don't forget your sunglasses, hat, and sunscreen! A sunburn is sure way to ruin a nice vacation. The gift shop in The Club House is a

Your screen size might differ

Page download time (yours might differ, depending on connection speed)

FIGURE E-2: About_us page with image inserted

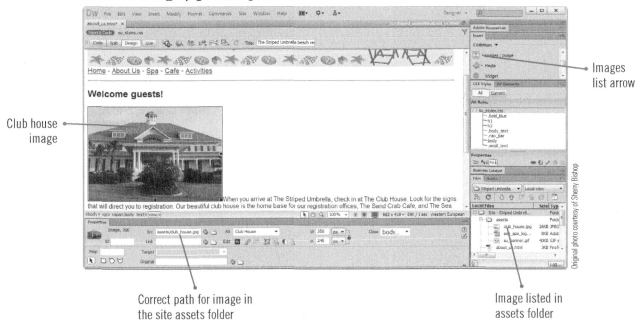

Images list arrow

Club house image

Correct path for image in the site assets folder

Image listed in assets folder

FIGURE E-3: Assets panel listing for The Striped Umbrella website

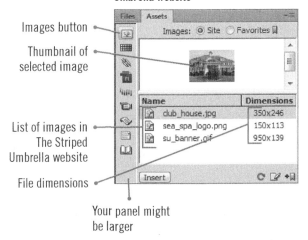

Images button

Thumbnail of selected image

List of images in The Striped Umbrella website

File dimensions

Your panel might be larger

FIGURE E-4: Assets panel with boardwalk.png image included

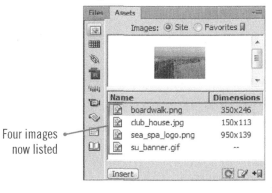

Four images now listed

Using and Managing Images

Dreamweaver 105

Aligning an Image

Like text, images can be positioned on the page in relation to other page elements. Positioning an image is called **aligning** the image. Use CSS to align images. You can use a global rule to modify the <img> tag, or you can create separate rules for individual images. When you first place an image on a page, it has the **Default** alignment which aligns the bottom of the image with the text **baseline**—the bottom of a line of text, not including descending portions of characters such as y or g. You should experiment with CSS rule properties to find the best alignment for your images.  After experimenting with several alignment options, you decide to stagger the alignment of the images on the page to make it appear more balanced.

STEPS

1. **Click the New CSS Rule button 🗗 in the CSS Styles panel**
   The New CSS Rule dialog box opens. You will create a new rule to align images to the left of other page content.

2. **Click Class in the Selector Type list box, type img_left_float for the Selector name, verify that it will be saved in the su_styles.css file, compare your screen to Figure E-5, then click OK**
   The CSS Rule Definition for .img_left_float in su_styles.css dialog box opens. Next, you add the Float property and value.

3. **Click the Box category, click the Float list arrow, click left, as shown in Figure E-6, then click OK**
   The Float property tells the browser to "float" the image to the left of other page content.

> **QUICK TIP**
> You can also right-click an image, point to CSS Styles, then click the rule you want to apply.

4. **Click the club house image if necessary, click the Class list arrow on the right side of the Property inspector, then click img_left_float**
   The text moves to the right side of the image, as shown in Figure E-7.

5. **Repeat Steps 1 through 3 to create another rule named img_right_float with a Float value of right**

6. **Apply the img_right_float rule to the boardwalk image**
   The boardwalk image floats to the right of the text. The images are now aligned on the page in staggered positions.

7. **Click File, Save All to save your work**

Design Matters

Using dynamic images

To make a page even more interesting, you can place images on the page that change frequently, such as a group of several images that are set to automatically cycle on and off the page, called **dynamic images**. You can use dynamic images to display multiple items with a similar layout. For example, a website for a retail store might display images of current sale items in one window on a web page, one item at a time. To insert dynamic images, you must first create a Spry Data Set to store the images using the [+] button in the Bindings panel. You then insert the images on the page using the Data sources option, rather than the File system option, in the Select Image Source dialog box.

FIGURE E-5: New CSS Rule dialog box

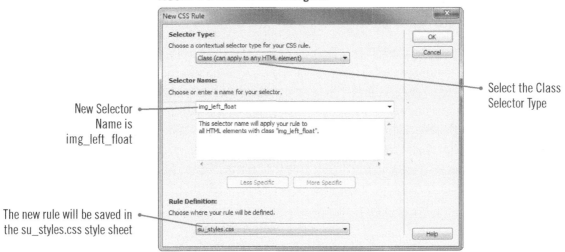

New Selector
Name is
img_left_float

Select the Class
Selector Type

The new rule will be saved in
the su_styles.css style sheet

FIGURE E-6: CSS Rule Definition for img_left_float in su_styles.css dialog box

Select the
Box category

Select the
left Float
value

FIGURE E-7: Club house image with img_left_float rule applied

Image floats
to the left
side of the
text

img_left_float
rule is applied

img_left_float
rule is listed in
the style sheet

Original photos courtesy of Sherry Bishop

Using and Managing Images

Enhancing an Image

After you select, place, and align an image on a web page, you can enhance its appearance. You can improve an image's appearance in Dreamweaver using borders, cropping, resizing, adjusting its brightness and contrast, and adjusting the horizontal and vertical space around an image. **Borders** are like frames that surround an image to make it stand out on the page. **Cropping** an image removes part of the image, both visually (on the page) and physically (the file size). A cropped image is smaller and takes less time to download. **Horizontal** and **vertical space** refers to blank space above, below, or on the sides of an image that separates the image from other elements on the page. You decide to enhance the images on the about_us page by using your image rules to add borders around the images, and adjust the horizontal and vertical space around each image.

STEPS

1. **Click the img_left_float rule in the CSS Styles panel, click the Edit Rule button** 🖉, **click the Border Category, enter the rule properties shown in Figure E-8, then click OK**

2. **Repeat Step 1 to add a border to the img_right_float rule**
   Both images now have a thin border around them.

3. **Edit the img_left_float rule again to add vertical and horizontal space by unchecking the "Same for all" check box under Margin in the Box category, then setting the Box Right Margin to 10 px as shown in Figure E-9, then click OK**
   The text is more evenly wrapped around the image and is easier to read, because it is not so close to the edge of the image.

4. **Using Step 3 as a guide, add a border and a 10 px left margin to the img_right_float rule, then compare your screen to Figure E-10**

5. **Save your work, open the spa page, then apply the img_left_float rule to the spa logo**
   The headings wrap to the right side of the spa logo and look much better on the page.

6. **Click File, Save All, to save all files, then close the spa page**

QUICK TIP
You can use the Brightness and Contrast 🔆, Crop 🔲, and Sharpen 🔺 buttons to slightly adjust images. To perform more complicated adjustments, such as significantly resizing an image, click the Edit button ⏺ to open the image in an editing program such as Adobe Photoshop or Fireworks if they are installed on your computer. Your Edit button will differ in appearance according to your default image editor.

Resizing an image using the Property inspector

To save space on a web page, you can crop an image. If you prefer to keep the entire image, you can resize it on the page instead. Simply select the image, then drag a selection handle toward the center of the image. Since dragging a selection handle can distort an image, press and hold [Shift] then drag a corner selection handle to retain the image's original proportions. (You can also enlarge an image using these methods.) After you drag an image handle to resize it, the image dimensions in the Property inspector appear in bold and a black Refresh icon appears to the right of the dimensions. If you click the Refresh icon, the image reverts to its original size. Do not use this method to significantly resize an image. Instead resize it using an image editor and save a copy of it with the new settings.

FIGURE E-8: CSS Rule Definition for img_left_float dialog box

Same for all check boxes are checked

Border category

Style = solid

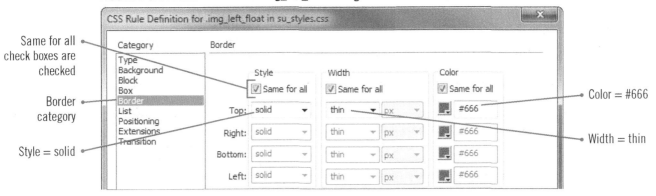

Color = #666

Width = thin

FIGURE E-9: CSS Rule Definition for img_left_float dialog box

Box category

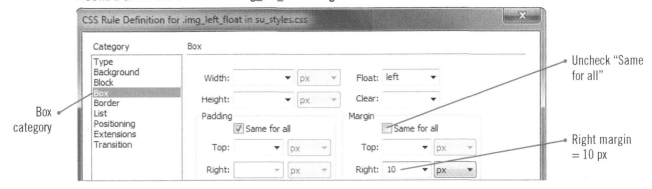

Uncheck "Same for all"

Right margin = 10 px

FIGURE E-10: Viewing the images with borders and margins

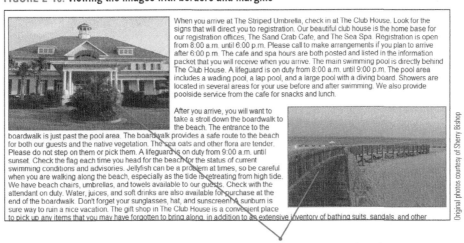

Original photos courtesy of Sherry Bishop

Both images have borders and horizontal space separating them from the text

Design Matters

Resizing images using an external editor

Each image on a web page takes a certain amount of time to download, depending on the size of the file and the speed of the user's Internet connection. Larger files (in terms of kilobytes, not width and height) take longer to download than smaller files. Many designers feel that an ideal page should download in less than five or six seconds; to ensure that your page downloads quickly, your images should have the smallest file size possible while maintaining the necessary level of image quality. If you need to significantly resize an image, use an external image editor

instead of resizing it in Dreamweaver; resizing in Dreamweaver affects how an image appears onscreen, but does not alter the image file itself. Cropping an image in Dreamweaver, however, *will* modify the image file and decrease its overall size. As a general rule, it is better to crop your images using an external editor when you are making a significant change. Always save a copy of the original file before you crop it, then use the copy of the file to make your edits. This will always keep the original file intact in case you need it later.

Using Alternate Text and Setting Accessibility Preferences

One of the easiest ways to make your web page viewer-friendly and more accessible to individuals with disabilities is through the use of alternate text. **Alternate text** is descriptive text that can be set to appear in place of an image while the image is downloading. Some browsers can be set to display only text and to download images manually. In such instances, alternate text is used in place of images. Alternate text can be read by a **screen reader**, a device used by individuals with visual impairments to convert written text on a computer monitor to spoken words. Using a screen reader and alternate text, these users can have an image described to them in detail. You should also use alternate text when inserting form objects, text displayed as images, buttons, frames, and media files to enable screen reader usage. When loading a new installation of Dreamweaver, all the accessibility preferences are turned on by default. To make the alternate text more descriptive for screen readers, you want to edit the alternate text that describes each of the images on the about_us page. You also verify that the Images option in the Accessibility preferences is set so you will not forget to enter alternate text for each image.

1. **Click the** club house image **to select it, select the text in the Alt text box in the Property inspector, type** The Striped Umbrella Club House, **press [Tab], then save the file**
   The alternate text is entered for the image, as shown in Figure E-11.

2. **Repeat Step 1 to edit the alternate text for the boardwalk image to read** Boardwalk to our private beach
   The alternate text is entered for the image, as shown in Figure E-12.

QUICK TIP
Once you set the Accessibility preferences, they will be in effect for all of your websites. You will not have to set each website separately.

3. **Click** Edit **on the Menu bar, (Win) or the Dreamweaver menu (Mac), click** Preferences, **click** Accessibility **in the Category list, click the** Show attributes when inserting check boxes **to select them if necessary, as shown in Figure E-13, then click** OK
   With these options selected, Dreamweaver will prompt you to enter alternate text for new objects you add to the website, including images.

4. **Save your work**

QUICK TIP
If your Save option is not active, you do not need to save your file. However, you can use the Save All command in the File menu to make sure any changes you have made to an open page are saved.

FIGURE E-11: Editing the alternate text for the club house image

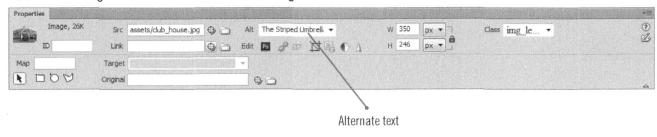

Alternate text

FIGURE E-12: Editing the alternate text for the boardwalk image

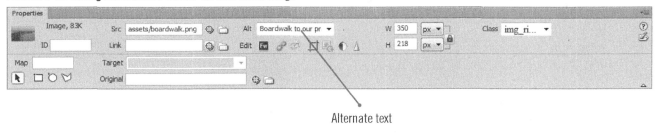

Alternate text

FIGURE E-13: Accessibility Preferences dialog box

Accessibility preferences category

Mac users may not see these options

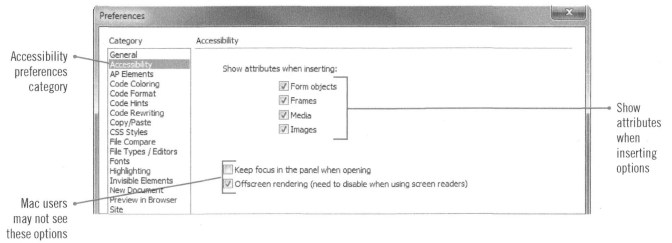

Show attributes when inserting options

Design Matters

Providing for accessibility with alternate text

The use of alternate text is the first checkpoint listed in the web content Accessibility Guidelines (WCAG), Version 2.0, from the World Wide Web Consortium (W3C). It states that a website should "provide text alternatives for any non-text content so that it can be changed into other forms people need, such as large print, Braille, speech, symbols, or simpler language." The twelve WCAG guidelines are grouped together under four principles called the POUR principles: perceivable, operable, understandable, and robust. To view the complete set of accessibility guidelines, go to the Web Accessibility Initiative page (w3.org/WAI). A general rule is that if you need to enter more than 50 characters of alternate text, you should create a separate file with the information you want to convey. Enter the location of the file in the Long Description text box that appears under the Alternate Text text box in the Image Tag Accessibility Attributes dialog box that opens when you insert a new image.

Viewing the Assets Panel

As you have learned, the Assets panel displays all of the assets in a website. It is important to understand how the Assets panel organizes your assets so you can quickly identify and locate the various assets in your site. There are nine categories of assets, each represented by a button on the Assets panel: Images, Colors, URLs, SWF, Shockwave, Movies, Scripts, Templates, and Library. There are two options for viewing the assets in each category. You can click the Site option button to view all the assets in a website, or the Favorites option button to view those assets that you have designated as **favorites**—assets that you expect to use repeatedly while you work on the site. For more information about this topic see the *Using favorites in the Assets panel* Clues to Use box in this lesson. You can also use the Assets panel to insert images on your page by either dragging an asset to the page, or by selecting the image and clicking the Insert button. ▓▓▓ So far, your website includes several images and colors. You explore the Assets panel to understand how Dreamweaver organizes the image files and keeps track of the colors used in the site.

STEPS

QUICK TIP
Make sure that the page you have open is in the current website. If you open a page outside the current website, the Assets panel will not display the assets associated with the open page.

1. Click the Assets tab in the Files Tab group, if necessary

The first time you use the Assets panel, it displays the Images category; after that, it displays the category that was selected during the last Dreamweaver session.

QUICK TIP
You can click the column headings in the Assets panel to sort the files by Name, Dimensions, Size, Type, and Full Path.

2. Click the Images button on the Assets panel, if necessary

Each time you click a category button, the contents in the Assets panel window change. Figure E-14 displays the Images category, and lists the four images in the website. Remember to click the Refresh button ↻ if you don't see all of your assets listed.

TROUBLE
If you see another color listed, click the Refresh button ↻ to remove it. If you still see additional colors, you can either leave them or search for them in Code view and remove them.

3. Click the Colors button ▦ to display the Colors category

Three colors are listed in the website, as shown in Figure E-15. They are gray, blue, and white. The gray and blue colors are used for formatting text and images and are located in the external style sheet. The white color formats the page background color. The Type column shows that each color is listed as Websafe. You learned about websafe colors in Unit C.

Using the terms *graphics* and *images*

In discussing design, people often use the terms **graphics** and **images**. This text uses the term *graphics* to refer to most non-text items on a web page, including photographs, logos, menu bars, Flash animations, graphs, background images, and illustrations. Any of these can be called a **graphic** or a **graphic file**. *Images* is a narrower term, referring to pictures or photographs. **Image files** are referred to by their file type, or file format, such as **JPEG** (Joint

Photographic Experts Group), **GIF** (Graphics Interchange Format), or **PNG** (Portable Network Graphics). See Table E-1 on page 119 for descriptions for each of these formats. This text refers to the pictures that you see on the pages as images. But don't worry too much about which term to use; many people use one term or the other according to habit, region, or type of business, or use them interchangeably.

FIGURE E-14: **Assets panel showing Images category**

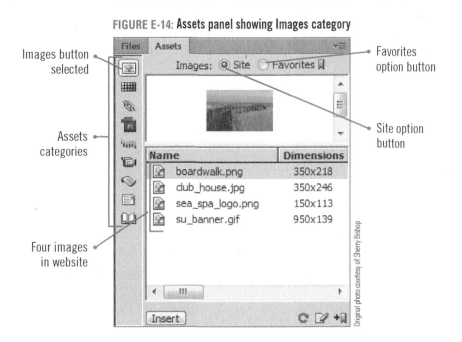

Images button selected

Assets categories

Four images in website

Favorites option button

Site option button

Original photo courtesy of Sherry Bishop

FIGURE E-15: **Assets panel showing Colors category**

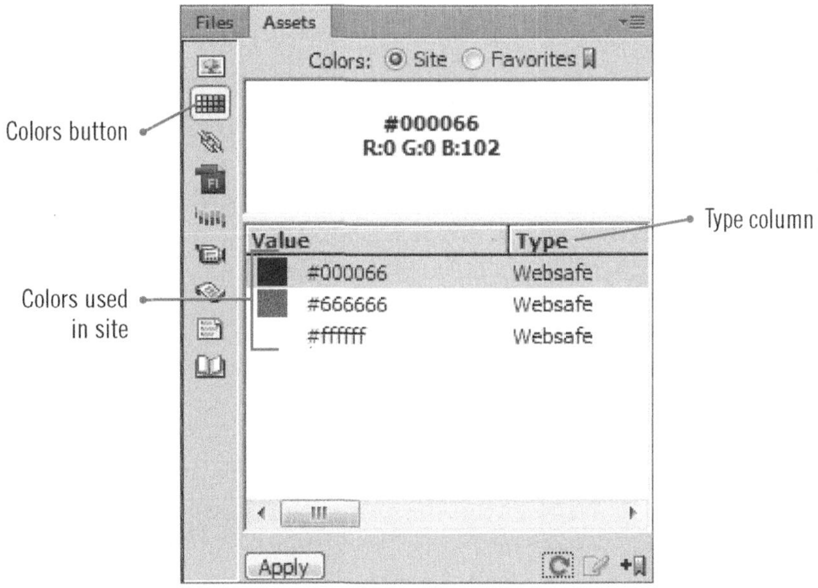

Colors button

Colors used in site

Type column

Using Favorites in the Assets panel

For assets such as images that you plan to use repeatedly, you can place them in the Favorites list in the Assets panel to make them readily available. There are a few ways to add favorites to the Favorites list in the Assets panel. You can right-click an image in Design view, then click Add to Image Favorites. When you subsequently click the Favorites option button in the Assets panel, the image will display in the list. You can also right-click the name of an image in the Site list (when the Site option is selected in the Assets panel), then click Add to

Favorites. In addition, you can create a folder for storing assets by category by clicking the Favorites option in the Assets panel, clicking the Files panel options list arrow on the Files panel group, then clicking New Favorites Folder. You can give the folder a descriptive name, then drag assets from the Favorites list to move them to this folder. You can create nicknames for assets in the Favorites list by right-clicking (Win) or [ctrl]-clicking (Mac) the asset in the Favorites list, then clicking Edit Nickname.

Inserting a Background Image

Although you may consider them too plain, standard white backgrounds are many times the best choice for web pages. Some pages, however, look best when they utilize background colors or images. **Background images** are image files used in place of background colors to provide a depth and visual interest that a one-dimensional background color can't provide. Background images can create a dramatic effect; however, they may also be too distracting on an already full page. You can use background color for some areas of a page and background images on others. If you choose to use a background image, select one that is small in file size so the page will download quickly. Background colors and images are set using CSS. You can create a global rule to modify every page background or layout block or you can create individual rules that format individual sections or page elements. ██████ You are pleased with the current white background color of the about_us page, but want to see what a background image would look like.

1. **Click Modify on the Menu bar, then click Page Properties**

   The Page Properties dialog box opens where you can add a background image to a web page by adding a link to the background image filename.

2. **Click the Appearance (CSS) category, if necessary**

3. **Click Browse next to the Background image text box, navigate to the assets folder in the unit_e folder in the drive and folder where you save your Data Files, double-click water.jpg, then click OK**

   The white background is replaced with a muted water image, as shown in Figure E-16. The color of the water is close to the blue in the banner, so the image fits in well with the other page colors. However, since it flows directly behind the text, it does not provide the good contrast that the white background did.

4. **Expand the CSS Styles panel if necessary, then compare your screen to Figure E-17**

   Since you used the Page Properties dialog box to insert the image background, Dreamweaver created an internal <body> rule to format the page background. Your external style sheet also has a <body> rule that sets a white page background. The internal rule takes precedence over the external rule, so for this page only, the white background is replaced with the water background.

   Even when you remove an image from a web page, it remains in the assets folder in the local site root folder of the website.

5. **Click the <style> tag in the CSS Styles panel, then press the Delete button 🗑 on the CSS Styles panel**

   The about_us page background returns to white, since the external global body tag is again formatting the page background. The internal style is removed from the list in the CSS Styles panel, as shown in Figure E-18.

FIGURE E-16: about_us page with a background image

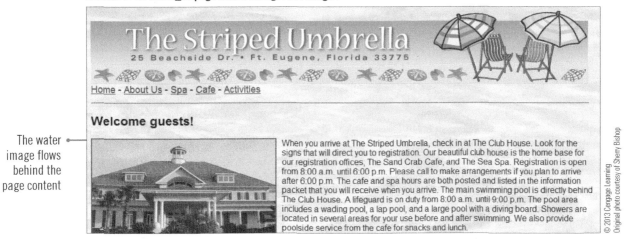

The water image flows behind the page content

© 2013 Cengage Learning
Original photo courtesy of Sherry Bishop

FIGURE E-17: The CSS Styles panel with the new embedded body rule added

Internal rule added to add background image

FIGURE E-18: The CSS Styles panel with the embedded body rule deleted

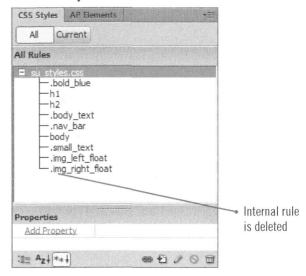

Internal rule is deleted

Integrating Photoshop and Fireworks with Dreamweaver CS6

Dreamweaver has many functions integrated with Photoshop CS6. For example, you can copy and paste images directly from Photoshop into Dreamweaver. Dreamweaver will prompt you to optimize the image by choosing a file format and settings for using the image in a web browser. Then it will paste the image on the page. If you want to edit the image later, select the image, then click the Edit button in the Property inspector to open the image in Photoshop. (The appearance of the Edit button will change according to the default image editor you have specified.) When you edit an image in Photoshop, you can export an updated Smart Object instantly. **Smart Objects** are layers with image source information that allow an image to be modified nondestructively without losing the original data. Photoshop users can set Photoshop as the default image editor in Dreamweaver for specific image file formats. Click Edit on the Menu bar, click Preferences (Win), or click Dreamweaver, click Preferences (Mac), click File Types/Editors, click the Extensions plus sign button, select a file format from the list, click the Editors plus sign button, use the Select External Editor dialog box to browse to Photoshop (if you don't see it listed already), then click Make Primary. Search the Adobe website (adobe.com) for a tutorial on Photoshop and Dreamweaver integration. Fireworks is another commonly used default image editor. Use the same steps to select it rather than Photoshop.

Deleting Image Files from a Website

As you work on a website, it is very common to accumulate files that end up never being used in the site. One way to avoid accumulating unnecessary files is to look at and evaluate an image first, before you copy it to the default images folder. If the file has already been copied to the default images folder, however, you should delete it (or at least move it to another location) to ensure that the Assets panel only lists the assets actually used in the site. This practice is considered good site management. To delete a file from the Assets panel, you can access the Locate in Site command, which is useful if you have a large number of images to search. If you just have a single file to delete, it's faster to just use the Delete command in the Files panel. ████████ Since you decided not to use the background image on the about_us page, you want to delete it from the assets folder.

STEPS

QUICK TIP

⟳ will not appear on the Assets panel when the Favorites option is selected.

1. **Display the Assets panel if necessary, click the Images button ⊞ on the Assets panel, verify that the Site option is selected, then click the Refresh button ⟳ on the Assets panel**
   The background file remains in the Images list on the Assets panel. Even though you have deleted it from the body rule, you have not yet deleted them in the website assets folder.

TROUBLE

If the file is not listed, click ⟳.

2. **Right-click water.jpg in the Assets panel, then click Locate in Site, as shown in Figure E-19**
   The Files panel opens with the water.jpg file selected.

3. **Press [Delete] to delete the file, then click Yes in the confirmation dialog box**
   The water.jpg file is no longer listed in the Assets panel because it has been deleted from the site.

4. **Save your work, then preview your file in your browser**
   Your about_us page is completed and should resemble Figure E-20.

5. **Close the page, then Exit (Win) or Quit (Mac) Dreamweaver**

Inserting files with Adobe Bridge

You can manage project files, including video and Camera Raw files, with a file management tool called Adobe Bridge that is included with Dreamweaver. Bridge provides an easy way to view files outside the website before bringing them into the website. It is an integrated application, working with other Adobe programs, such as Photoshop and Illustrator. You can also use Bridge to add meta tags and search text in your files. To open Bridge, click the Browse in Bridge command on the File menu or click the Browse in Bridge button on the Standard toolbar.

FIGURE E-19: Using the Assets panel to locate a file in a site

water.jpg

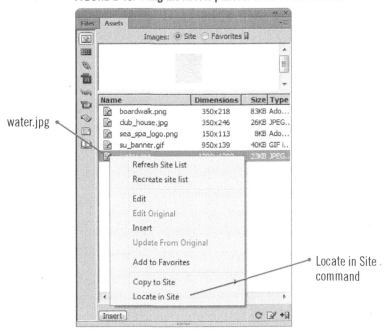

Locate in Site command

FIGURE E-20: The finished page

© 2013 Cengage Learning
Original photos courtesy of Sherry Bishop

Design Matters

Image file management

It is a good idea to have an additional storage location for your image files in addition to the website's assets folder. Keep all original image files outside the website and save them once with their original settings. As you edit them, save them using a different name. This way, you will always be able to find the original file before it is resized or edited. You may also have files you don't want to use now but may need later. Store them outside your website to keep them from cluttering up the assets folder.

Creating and Finding Images for a Website

There are several resources for locating high-quality images for a website. You can create original images using an image editing or drawing program, such as Fireworks, Illustrator, or Photoshop, or use original photographs for colorful, rich images. The Internet, of course, is a great source for finding images. Stock photos are photos on websites that are available to use by either paying a single fee per photo or a subscription fee for downloading multiple images. Table E-1 describes three image types that can be used on web pages.  Now that you understand how to incorporate images into The Striped Umbrella website, you explore the advantages and disadvantages of the different ways to accumulate images.

DETAILS

- **Original images**

  Programs such as Fireworks and Photoshop give you the ability to create and modify original artwork. These image editing programs have numerous features for manipulating images. For example, you can adjust the color, brightness, or size of an image. You can also set a transparent background for an image. **Transparent backgrounds** contain transparent pixels, rather than pixels with color, resulting in images that blend easily on a page background. Only certain file types can be used to create transparent images, such as gifs and pngs. Illustrator is a drawing program that is used to create original vector graphics, which can then be converted to a usable format for the web, such as jpg, gif, or png files.

- **Original photography**

  High-quality photographs can greatly enhance a website. Fortunately, digital cameras and scanners have made this venture much easier than in the past. Once you scan a photograph or shoot it with a digital camera, you can further enhance it using an image editing software program, such as Photoshop or Fireworks. Photographs taken with digital cameras often have large file sizes, so be sure to create resized copies using an image editing program such as Photoshop before placing them on web pages. If you don't have Photoshop or another image editor, many digital cameras come with their own basic software that you can use to resize and enhance images.

- **The Internet**

  There are many websites from which you are able to find images, but look carefully for copyright statements regarding the legal use of images. Stock photos sites, such as iStockphoto, are excellent resources used by many professional designers. To use these sites, you first sign up to become a member, then you either purchase images as you need them, or purchase a subscription, which allows you to pay a set price for the number of files you expect to download each year. There are many collections of images online that are free, but some sites require that you credit them on your website with either a simple statement or a link to their website. Images that are labeled as public domain are free to use without restrictions. Figure E-21 is an example of a source for public domain images. If you are uncertain about whether you may use an image you find on a website, it's best to either contact the site's owner or find another image to use. *If you copy and paste images you find while accessing other websites and use them for your own purposes, you may be violating copyright laws.*

FIGURE E-21: Example of a website with public domain images

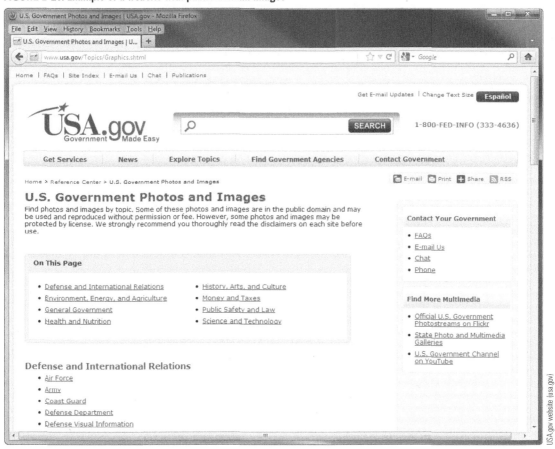

USA.gov website (usa.gov)

TABLE E-1: Common image file formats for images for web publication

format (file extension)	stands for	details
.jpg, .jpeg	Joint Photographic Experts Group	Pixel-based; a web standard. Can set image quality in pixels per inch (ppi), which affects file size. Supports millions of colors. Use for full-color images, such as photographs with large tonal range and those with lifelike artwork. This format is a good choice when targeting mobile devices.
.png	Portable Network Graphics	Can be compressed for storage and quicker download, without loss of picture quality. Supports variable levels of transparency and control of image brightness on different computers. Used for small graphics, such as bullets, as well as for complex photographic images. This format is also a good choice for targeting mobile devices. Not all browsers support the .png file format.
.gif	Graphics Interchange Format	Limited to 256 colors. Low color quality and limited detail are not suitable for printing. Small file size means faster transmission. Suitable for images with only a few colors, such as cartoons, simple illustrations, icons, buttons, and horizontal rules. This format is used for transparent images.

Examine Copyright Rules

The Internet has made it possible to locate compelling and media-rich content to use on websites. But just because you find content does not mean that you can use it however you want or under any circumstance. Learning about copyright law can help you decide whether and how to use content created and published by someone other than yourself. Before you decide whether to use media you find on a website, you must decide whether you can comply with its licensing agreement. A **licensing agreement** is the permission given by a copyright holder that conveys the right to use the copyright holder's work under certain conditions. Websites have rules that govern how a user may use its content, known as **terms of use**. Figures E-22 and E-23 are good examples of clear terms of use for the Library of Congress website. You decide to do some research on copyright law in relation to downloaded content from the Internet. There are several concepts to understand.

DETAILS

- **Intellectual property**

  Intellectual property is a product resulting from human creativity. It can include inventions, movies, songs, designs, clothing, and so on. The purpose of copyright law is to promote progress in society—not expressly to protect the rights of copyright owners. However, you should always assume that the majority of work you might want to download and use in a project is protected by either copyright or trademark law.

- **Copyright**

  A **copyright** protects the particular and tangible expression of an idea, not the idea itself. If you wrote a story about aliens crashing in Roswell, New Mexico, no one could copy or use your specific story without permission. However, anyone could write a story using a similar plot or characters—the actual idea is not copyright-protected. Generally, copyright protection in the United States lasts for the life of the author plus 70 years (most countries have similar regulations). A copyright attaches to a work as soon as it is created; you do not have to register it with the U.S. Copyright Office.

- **Trademark**

  A **trademark** protects an image, word, slogan, symbol, or design used to identify goods or services. For example, the Nike swoosh and the Google logo are images protected by trademark. Trademark protection lasts for 10 years, with 10-year renewal terms; it can last indefinitely provided the trademark is in active use.

- **Fair use**

  The law builds in limitations to copyright protection. One limitation to copyright is fair use. **Fair use** allows limited use of copyright-protected work. For example, you could excerpt short passages of a film or song for a class project. Determining if fair use applies to a work depends on the purpose of its use, the nature of the copyrighted work, how much you want to copy, and the effect on the market or value of the work. There is no clear formula on what constitutes fair use. It is always decided by the courts on a case-by-case basis. Except in cases of fair use, you must obtain permission from the copyright holder to use the work.

- **Derivative work**

  A **derivative work** is a work based on another pre-existing work, such as a movie adaptation of a book or a new musical arrangement of an existing song. Derivative works are included in the six rights of a copyright owner: reproduction (including downloading), creation of derivative works, distribution to the public, public performance, public display, and public performance by digital audio transmission of sound recordings. By default, only a copyright holder can create a derivative work of his or her original work.

QUICK TIP
Even if a site name includes the phrase "public domain," it does not necessarily mean that all content on that site is in the public domain. It is better to err on the side of caution than to risk violating copyright laws.

- **Public domain**

  Work that is not protected by copyright is said to be in the public domain. Anyone can use it however they wish for any purpose, free of charge. In general, photos and other media on federal government websites are in the public domain, but some may have third-party ownership, so it's best to verify before you use them. For instance, there could be a photograph on the page that has a copyright restriction attached to it by the photographer. Websites will often state if their images or other content are in the public domain.

FIGURE E-22: Example of a website with a legal policy statement

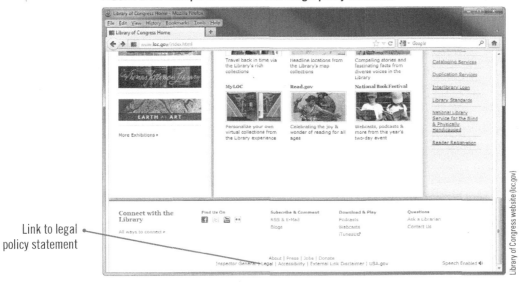

Link to legal
policy statement

Library of Congress website (loc.gov)

FIGURE E-23: Library of Congress legal policies

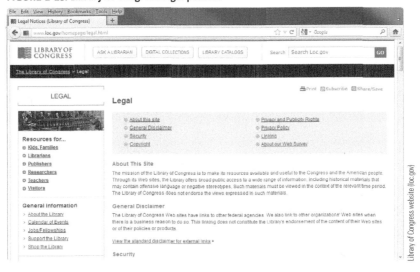

Library of Congress website (loc.gov)

Using proper methods to cite content

The familiar © symbol (or the word *Copyright*) is no longer required to indicate copyrighted materials, nor does it automatically register your work, but it does serve a useful purpose. When you post or publish the copyright term or symbol, you are stating clearly to those who may not know anything about copyright law that this work is claimed by you and is not in the public domain. If someone violates your copyright, your case is made even stronger if your notice is clearly visible. That way, violators can never claim ignorance of the law as an excuse for infringing. Common notification styles include using the word *Copyright* with the year, as in "Copyright 2013, Course Technology," or by using the copyright symbol ©, as in "© 2013 Course Technology."

You must provide proper citation for materials you incorporate into your own work. The following source was used for this lesson content and is referenced as follows:

- Waxer, Barbara M., and Baum, Marsha L. 2006. *Internet Surf and Turf – The Essential Guide to Copyright, Fair Use, and Finding Media*. Boston: Thomson Course Technology.

In addition to words that you quote verbatim, copyrights apply to ideas that you summarize or paraphrase. One prominent set of guidelines for how to cite material found in print or on the web (including text, images, sound, video, blogs, email and text messages, and so forth) is produced by the American Psychological Association (APA). To view these guidelines in detail, go to the APA website at apastyle.org. Other widely used guidelines are available from the Modern Language Association (mla.org) and the Chicago Manual of Style (chicagomanualofstyle.org).

Practice

Concepts Review

Label each element shown in Figure E-24.

FIGURE E-24

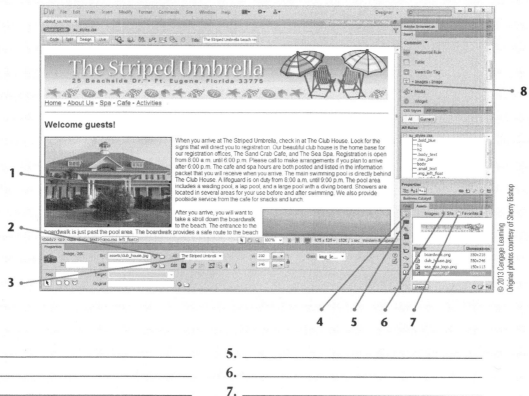

1. _____	5. _____
2. _____	6. _____
3. _____	7. _____
4. _____	8. _____

Match each of the following terms with the statement that best describes it.

9. **Assets panel**

10. **JPG**

11. **Aligning an image**

12. **Derivative work**

13. **Favorites list**

14. **Refresh button**

15. **Trademark**

16. **Copyright**

17. **Alternate text**

18. **Border**

a. Positioning an image on a page

b. Updates the current list of assets in the Assets panel

c. Includes only those assets designated as Favorites

d. Protects an image, word, slogan, symbol, or design used to identify goods or services

e. A work based on another pre-existing work

f. Used by screen readers to describe an image

g. A frame placed around an image

h. An image file format

i. Protects the particular and tangible expression of an idea, not the idea itself

j. Lists all the assets of the website, including favorites

Select the best answer from the list of choices.

19. **The following category is not found on the Assets panel:**
    - **a.** URLs
    - **b.** Colors
    - **c.** Tables
    - **d.** Movies

20. **When you no longer need files in a website, you should:**
    - **a.** leave them in the Assets panel.
    - **b.** drag them off the page to the Recycle bin.
    - **c.** place them in the Site list.
    - **d.** delete them from the site.

21. **Background images:**
    - **a.** are never appropriate.
    - **b.** are always appropriate.
    - **c.** should be used carefully.
    - **d.** cannot be added with a CSS rule.

22. **The following image file format is not appropriate to use for web publication:**
    - **a.** jpg.
    - **b.** gif.
    - **c.** png.
    - **d.** bmp.

Skills Review

Important: If you did not create this website in Unit B and maintain it during the preceding units, you will need to create a local site root folder for this website and define the website using files your instructor will provide. See the "Read This Before You Begin" section in this book for more detailed instructions.

1. **Insert an image.**
   a. Start Dreamweaver.
   b. Open the Blooms & Bulbs website.
   c. Open dwe_2.html from the drive and folder where you store your Unit E Data Files, then save it as **plants.html** in the Blooms & Bulbs website, overwriting the existing plants.html file but not updating the links.
   d. Close dwe_2.html.
   e. Insert the rose_bud.jpg file from the assets folder in the drive and folder where you store your Unit E Data Files, in front of the words *Who can resist....* (Enter alternate text, if prompted.)
   f. Insert the rose_bloom.jpg file in front of the words *For ease of growing....* (Enter alternate text, if prompted.)
   g. Insert the two_roses.jpg file in front of the words *The Candy Cane....* (Enter alternate text, if prompted.)
   h. Attach the blooms_styles.css file to the plants page.
   i. Apply the body_text style to all of the paragraph text on the page.
   j. Apply the HTML Heading 1 format to the text *Featured Spring Plant: Roses!*
   k. Save your work.

2. **Align an image.**
   a. Add a new class rule named img_left_float that adds a float property with a left value.
   b. Add another class rule named img_right_float that adds a float property with a right value.
   c. Apply the img_left_float rule to the rose_bud and two_roses images.
   d. Apply the img_right_float rule to the rose_bloom image, then save your work.

3. **Enhance an image.**
   a. Edit the img_left_float rule to add a border to all sides of an image with the following settings: Style=solid; Width=thin; Color=#333.
   b. Edit the Box Margin property to add a 10px margin to the right side only, then save your changes.
   c. Repeat Step a to add the same border to the img_right_float rule.
   d. Edit the Box Margin property of the img_right_float rule to add a 10px margin to the left side only, then save your changes.
   e. Save your work, preview it in the browser, then compare your screen to Figure E-25.

4. **Use alternate text.**
   a. If you did not add alternate text in Step 1 above, select the rose_bud.jpg image, then use the Property inspector to enter **Rose bud on bird bath** as alternate text.
   b. If necessary, add the alternate text **Rose bloom** for the rose_bloom.jpg image, and **Candy Cane Floribunda** for the two_roses.jpg image.
   c. If necessary, edit the website preferences to set the Accessibility prompt for images.
   d. Save your work.

Skills Review (continued)

5. View the Assets panel.

   a. Display the Assets panel, if necessary.

   b. View the Images list to verify that there are five images in the list. Refresh the Images list, if necessary.

   c. View the Colors list to verify that there are three websafe colors.

6. Insert a background image.

   a. Use Page Properties to insert the lady_in_red file as a background image and refresh the Assets panel. (This file is in the assets folder in the drive and folder where you store your Unit E Data Files.)

   b. Save the page, then view it in your browser.

   c. Close the browser window.

   d. Remove the lady_in_red.jpg image from the background by deleting the internal body rule it created, then save your work.

7. Delete image files from a website.

   a. Delete the lady_in_red.jpg file from the Files panel.

   b. Refresh the Files panel and verify that the lady_in_red.jpg file has been removed from the site. (You may have to re-create the site cache.)

   c. Preview the page in the browser, compare your screen with Figure E-25, and close the browser. (Your text may wrap differently.)

   d. Close the page, Exit (Win) or Quit (Mac) Dreamweaver.

FIGURE E-25

Blooms & Bulbs
HWY 43 SOUTH • ALVIN • TX 77511 • 555-248-0806

Featured Spring Plant: Roses!

Who can resist the romance of roses? Poets have waxed poetically over them throughout the years. Many persons consider the beauty and fragrance of roses to be unmatched in nature. The varieties are endless, ranging from floribunda to hybrid teas to shrub roses to climbing roses. Each variety has its own personality and preference in the garden setting. Pictured on the left is a Summer Breeze Hybrid Tea bud. This variety is fast growing and produces spectacular blooms that are beautiful as cut flowers in arrangements. The enchanting fragrance will fill your home with summer sweetness. They require full sun. Hybrid teas need regular spraying and pruning, but will reward you with classic blooms that will be a focal point in your landscaping and provide you with beautiful arrangements in your home. They are well worth the effort!

For ease of growing, Knock Out® roses are some of our all-time favorites. Even beginners will not fail with these garden delights. They are shrub roses and prefer full sun, but can take partial shade. They are disease resistant and drought tolerant. You do not have to be concerned with either black spot or dead-heading with roses such as the Knock out®, making them an extremely low-maintenance plant. They are also repeat bloomers, blooming into late fall. The shrub can grow quite large, but can be pruned to any size. The one you see on the right is Southern Belle. Check out all our varieties as you will not fail to have great color with these plants.

The Candy Cane Floribunda shown on the left is a beautiful rose with cream, pink, and red stripes and swirls. They have a heavy scent that will remind you of the roses you received on your most special occasions. These blooms are approximately four inches in diameter. They bloom continuously from early summer to early fall. The plants grow up to four feet tall and three feet wide. They are shipped bare root in February.

© 2013 Cengage Learning
Original photos courtesy of Sherry Bishop

Important: *If you did not create the following websites in Unit B and maintain them during the preceding units, you will need to create a local site folder for the websites in the following exercises and define the sites using files your instructor will provide. See the "Read This Before You Begin" section for more detailed instructions.*

Independent Challenge 1

You have been hired to create a website for a river expedition company named Rapids Transit, located on the Buffalo River in Arkansas. In addition to renting canoes, kayaks, and rafts, they have lodging for overnight stays. River guides are available, if requested, to accompany clients on float trips. The clients range from experienced floaters to beginners. The owner's name is Mike Andrew. Mike has asked you to develop the page that introduces the Rapids Transit guides available for float trips. Refer to Figure E-26 as you work on this page.

   a. Start Dreamweaver and open the Rapids Transit website.

   b. Open dwe_3.html from the drive and folder where you store your Unit E Data Files and save it in the Rapids Transit website as **guides.html**, overwriting the existing file but not updating links.

   c. Close dwe_3.html.

   d. Check the path for the Rapids Transit banner and reset the path to the assets folder for the website, if necessary.

   e. Attach the rapids_transit.css style sheet, then save your work.

   f. Insert the image river_guide.jpg at an appropriate place on the page. (This file is in the assets folder in the drive and folder where you store your Unit E Data Files.)

   g. Create alternate text for the river_guide.jpg image, then create a rule to add an image border, float, and margins with settings of your choice, then apply the new rule to the image.

   h. Apply the Heading 1 format to the menu bar and the body_text style to the paragraph text.

   i. Add a heading above the first paragraph and apply the Heading 2 rule to it.

   j. Save your work, preview the page in the browser, then compare your workspace to Figure E-26. (Your image location, border size, and vertical and horizontal space settings may differ.)

   k. Close the browser and Exit (Win) or Quit (Mac) Dreamweaver.

FIGURE E-26

Home — River Guides — Rates — Lodging — Before You Go

Our Guides

We have four of the best river guides you will ever find — Buster, Tucker, Max, and Scarlett. Buster has been with us for fourteen years and was born and raised here on the river. Tucker joined us two years ago "from off" (somewhere up north), but we've managed to make a country boy out of him! Max and Scarlett are actually distant cousins and joined us after they graduated from college last year. They're never happier than when they're out on the water floating and fishing. Each of our guides will show you a great time on the river.

Our guides will pack your supplies, shuttle you to the put-in point, maneuver the raging rapids for you, and then make sure someone is waiting at the take-out point to shuttle you back to the store. They haven't lost a customer yet! Give us a call and we'll set up a date with any of these good people. Here's a photo of Buster showing off his stuff. The river is always faster and higher in the spring. If you want to take it a little slower, come visit us in the summer or fall. Leave your good camera at home, though, no matter what the time of the year. You may get wet! Life jackets are provided and we require that you wear them while on the water. Safety is always our prime concern.

© 2013 Cengage Learning
Original photos courtesy of Sherry Bishop

Independent Challenge 2

Your company is designing a new website for TripSmart, a travel outfitter. TripSmart specializes in travel products and services. In addition to selling travel products, such as luggage and accessories, they sponsor trips and offer travel advice. Their clients range from college students to families and vacationing professionals. You are now ready to work on the destinations page. Refer to Figure E-27 as you work through the following steps.

a. Start Dreamweaver and open the TripSmart website.

b. Open dwe_4.html from the drive and folder where you store your Unit E Data Files and save it in the TripSmart website as **tours.html**, overwriting the existing tours file but not updating links.

c. Close dwe_4.html.

d. Check the path for the TripSmart banner and reset the path to the assets folder for the website, if necessary.

e. Attach the tripsmart_styles.css file to the page, then apply the HTML Heading 1 format to the Destination: The Galapagos heading and the body_text style to the rest of the text on the page. (*Hint*: You probably formatted your styles differently from the example, so your text may look different than Figure E-27.)

f. Change the site preferences to prompt you to add alternate text as you add new images to the website, if necessary.

g. Insert the images iguana_and_lizard.jpg and blue_footed_booby.jpg at the appropriate places on the page, adding alternate text for each image. (These files are in the assets folder in the drive and folder where you store your Unit E Data Files.)

h. Create a new CSS rule to format each image, then apply one to each image.

i. Save your work, preview the page in the browser, then compare your page to Figure E-27 for one possible design solution.

j. Close the browser and Exit (Win) or Quit (Mac) Dreamweaver.

FIGURE E-27

Destination: The Galápagos

We have a really special trip planned for next February. We have reserved ten cabins on the ship *The Wanderer* to explore the Galápagos Islands. The departure date is February 5 and the return date is February 21. This trip of a lifetime begins in Guayaquil, Ecuador. Guayaquil is a seaport on the southern coast of Ecuador. You will find it a vibrant center for business and tourism with lots of sites to explore. Stroll along the riverfront to enjoy colorful shops, lush parks, and street entertainment. After a night's rest, you will board your flight to Baltra Island in the Galápagos archipelago.

After arriving at Baltra's airport, you will board a bus for a short ride to the dock. Here you will find a welcoming committee of iguanas and sea lions. These natives love to sun on the docks and don't seem to mind sharing them with you as long as you don't come too close! *The Wanderer* is an exquisite touring ship licensed to explore the Galápagos by the Ecuadoran government. Tourism to the Galápagos is strictly regulated for the protection of the land, waters, and wildlife. You will use pangas for wet and dry landings to observe the wonderful variety of species of flora and fauna unique to the Galápagos, including the famous blue-footed booby. You will also have opportunities to swim, snorkel, and kayak with penguins. When your time on the ship ends, you will fly to Quito, the second-highest capital city in the world. Quito is a UNESCO World Heritage Site with beautiful colonial architecture. We recommend taking an extra day to explore its rich history and sample Ecuadoran cuisine.

To provide the finest in personal attention, this tour will be limited to no more than twenty people. The price schedule is as follows: Land Tour and Supplemental Group Air, $5,500.00; International Air, $1,350.00; and Single Supplement, $1,000.00. Entrance fees, hotel taxes, and services are included in the Land Tour price. Ship gratuities are also included for the Wanderer crew and guides. A deposit of $500.00 is required at the time the booking is made. Trip insurance and luggage insurance are optional and are also offered for an extra charge. A passport and visa will be required for entry into Ecuador. Call us at 555-555-0807 for further information and the complete itinerary from 8:00 a.m. to 6:00 p.m. (Central Standard Time).

© 2013 Cengage Learning
Original photos courtesy of Sherry Bishop

Independent Challenge 3

Donna Stevens raises and shows horses professionally. She is learning how to use Dreamweaver to be able to create a website to showcase her horses. She would like to look at some other websites about horses to get a feel for the types of images she may want to use in her site. Use a word processor or paper to answer the questions below.

a. Connect to the Internet and go to USHorse.biz (ushorse.biz), as shown in Figure E-28.
b. How are background colors used? Would you have selected different ones? Why, or why not?
c. Evaluate the images used in the site. Do they add interest to the pages? Was alternate text used for any or all of the images?
d. How long did the home page take to download on your computer?
e. Are there too few images, too many, or just enough to add interest?
f. Go to Google (google.com) or Yahoo! (yahoo.com) to find another horse website.
g. Compare the site you found to the USHorse.biz site by answering questions b through e above.

FIGURE E-28

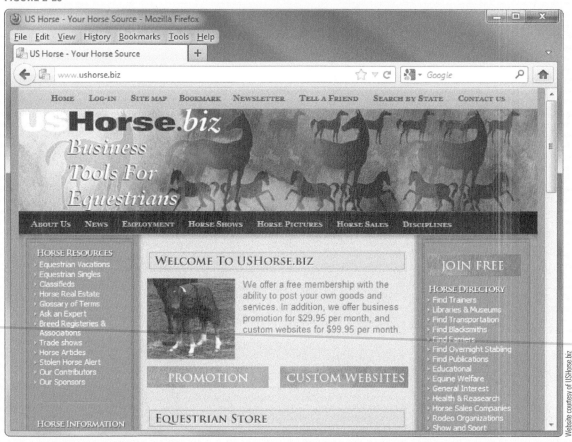

Real Life Independent Challenge

This assignment will continue to build on the personal website that you created in Unit B. You have created and developed your index page. You have also added a page with either an ordered or an unordered list, and a CSS Style Sheet with a minimum of two rules. In this lesson, you work with one of the other pages of your site.

  a. Consult your storyboard and decide which page you would like to develop in this lesson.

  b. Create content for this page and format the text attractively on the page using CSS rules for all formatting.

  c. Set the Accessibility option to prompt you for alternate text for new images added to the website, if necessary.

  d. Add at least two images with appropriate alternate text. Resize the images in an image-editing program if they are too large to place on the page.

  e. Use CSS rules to enhance the images to place them attractively on the page.

  f. Document the source for the images and print some proof that they are in the public domain. Use your own photographs or drawings if you have difficulty obtaining public domain images.

  g. Document the estimated download time for the page and the setting you used to estimate download time.

  h. Save the file and preview the page in a browser.

After you are satisfied with your work, verify the following:

  a. Each completed page has a page title.

  b. All links work correctly.

  c. The completed pages look good using a screen resolution of 1024×768.

  d. All images are properly set showing a path to the assets folder of the website.

  e. All images have alternate text and are legal to use.

Visual Workshop

Your company has been selected to design a website for Carolyne's Creations, a small catering business. Open your Carolyne's Creations website. Chef Carolyne has asked you to create a page that displays featured items in the kitchen shop. Open dwe_5.html from the drive and folder where your Unit E Data Files are stored. Save the file as **shop.html** in the Carolyne's Creations website, then add the peruvian_glass.jpg image from the drive and folder where you store your Unit E Data Files to create the page shown in Figure E-29. (*Hint*: You will need to attach the cc_styles.css style sheet to the page.) Apply the nav_bar rule to the menu bar, the body_text style to the paragraphs, and the Heading 1 HTML format to the heading "June Special: Peruvian Glasses". Use a CSS rule to add horizontal space and a border to the peruvian_glass image.

FIGURE E-29

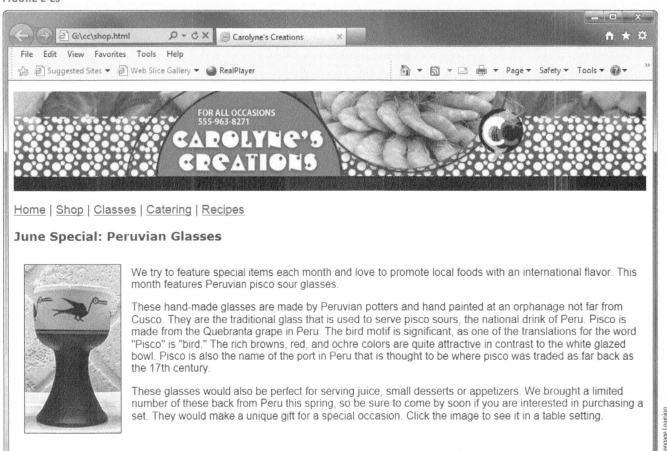

© 2013 Cengage Learning
Original photo courtesy of Sherry Bishop

Creating Links and Menu Bars

Files You Will Need:

To view a list of files needed for this unit, see the Data Files Grid in the back of the book.

As you learned in Unit C, links are the real strength of a website, because they give users the freedom to open various web pages as they choose. You created a menu bar using a group of text links that helps users to navigate between pages of a website. In this unit, you will learn how to create a Spry menu bar and another type of link called an image map. A **Spry menu bar** is one of the preset widgets in Dreamweaver that creates a dynamic, user-friendly menu bar. A **widget** is a piece of code that allows users to interact with the program interface. An **image map** is an image with clickable areas defined on it that, when clicked, serve as links to take the user to another location.  You begin working on the link structure for The Striped Umbrella website. You add links to area attractions on the activities page, create a menu bar that will be used on all pages in the website, create an image map, and run some site management reports.

OBJECTIVES

Understand links and paths

Create an external link

Create an internal link

Insert a named anchor

Create internal links to named anchors

Create a Spry menu bar

Add menu bar items

Format a menu bar

Copy a menu bar to other pages

Create an image map

Manage website links

Adobe product screenshot(s) reprinted with permission from Adobe Systems Incorporated.

Understanding Links and Paths

You can use two types of links (hyperlinks) on web pages. **Internal links** are links to web pages within the same website, and **external links** are links that connect to pages in other websites or to email addresses. Internal and external links both have two important parts that work together. The first part of a link is what the user actually sees and clicks, such as a word, an image, or a button. The second part of a link is the path, which is the name and physical location of the web page file that opens when the link is clicked. A link is classified as internal or external based on the information in its path. External paths reference links with a complete web address, while internal paths reference links with a partial address, based on the relation of the destination page to the page with the link. A link that returns an error message, or a broken link, occurs when files are renamed or deleted from a website, the filename is misspelled, or the website is experiencing technical problems. The majority of the time now you do not have to enter "http://" or "www" before a website URL when you are moving from site to site on the Internet. You spend some time studying the various types of paths used for internal and external links.

DETAILS

TROUBLE

The figures illustrating paths on page 133 are for illustrative purposes only. They are not intended to be working links.

- **Absolute paths**

  Absolute paths are used with external links. They reference links on web pages outside the current website, and include "**http**" (hypertext transfer protocol) and the **URL** (Uniform Resource Locator), or address, of the web page. When necessary, the web page filename and the folder hierarchy are also part of an absolute path. Figure F-1 shows an example of an absolute path.

- **Relative paths**

  Relative paths are used with internal links. They reference web pages and graphic files within one website and include the filename and the folder hierarchy where the file resides. Figure F-2 shows an example of a relative path. Relative paths are further classified as root-relative (relative to the local site root folder) and document-relative (relative to the current document).

- **Root-relative paths**

  Root-relative paths are referenced from a website's local site root folder. As shown in Figure F-3, a root-relative path begins with a forward slash, which represents the website's local site root folder. This method is used when several websites are published to one server, or when a website is so large that it uses more than one server.

- **Document-relative paths**

  Document-relative paths reference the path in relation to the web page that appears, and do not begin with a slash. A document-relative path includes only a filename if the referenced file resides in the same folder as the current web page. For example, index.html and spa.html both reside in the local site root folder for The Striped Umbrella. So you would simply type spa.html to link to the spa page from the index page. However, when an image is referenced in the assets folder, since the assets folder is a subfolder of the local site root folder, you must include the word assets/ (with the slash) in front of the filename, for example, assets/the_spa.jpg. See Figure F-4 for an example of a document-relative path.

  In the exercises in this book, you will use document-relative paths because it is assumed that you will not use more than one server to publish your websites. For this reason, it is very important to make sure that the Relative to text box in the Select File dialog box is set to Document, rather than Site Root, when creating links. This option can also be set in the Site Setup dialog box.

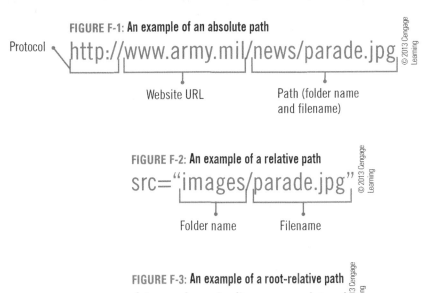

FIGURE F-1: An example of an absolute path

Protocol → http://www.army.mil/news/parade.jpg © 2013 Cengage Learning

Website URL   Path (folder name and filename)

FIGURE F-2: An example of a relative path

src="images/parade.jpg" © 2013 Cengage Learning

Folder name   Filename

FIGURE F-3: An example of a root-relative path

/downloads/lessons.html © 2013 Cengage Learning

Begins with a forward slash

FIGURE F-4: An example of a document-relative path

downloads/lessons.html

© 2013 Cengage Learning

Begins with either a folder name or a filename

Design Matters

Ensuring error-free URLs

It is easy to make mistakes when you type long and complex URLs. One way to minimize errors is to copy and paste the URL of the web page that you would like to include as an external link in your website. To do this, open the web page then copy the link information in the Address text box (Internet Explorer) or the Location bar (Mozilla Firefox). Next, select the link text on your web page, then paste the link information in the Link text box in the HTML Property inspector. When you hear that text is "case sensitive," it means that the text will be treated differently when it is typed using uppercase letters rather than lowercase letters, or vice-versa. With some operating systems, such as Windows, it doesn't matter which case you use when you enter URLs. However, with other systems, such as UNIX, it does matter. To be sure that your links will work with all systems, use lowercase letters for all URLs. This is another good reason to select and copy a URL from the browser address bar, and then paste it in the Link text box or Dreamweaver code when creating an external link. You won't have to worry about missing a case change.

Creating an effective navigation structure

When you create a website, it's important to consider how your users will navigate from page to page within the site. A menu bar is a critical tool for moving around a site, so it's important that all text, buttons, and icons you use on a menu bar have a consistent look across all pages. If you use a complex menu bar, such as one that incorporates JavaScript or Flash, it's a good idea to include plain text links in another location on the page for accessibility. Otherwise, users might become confused or lost within the site.

A navigation structure can include more links than those included on a menu bar, however. For instance, it can contain other sets of links that relate to the content of specific pages. They can be placed at the bottom or sides of a page in a different format. No matter how you decide to design your navigation structure, make sure that every page includes a link back to the home page.

Other good navigation strategies that promote accessibility include adding keyboard equivalents for navigation elements, labeling all links, and incorporating jump menus to enable users to skip to links.

Creating an External Link

As you have learned, external links use absolute paths, which must include the complete name and path of the web address to link to the destination web page successfully. Because the World Wide Web is a constantly changing environment, you should check external links frequently. Websites may be up one day and down the next. If a website changes server locations or shuts down because of technical difficulties, the links to it may become broken. An external link can also become broken when an Internet connection is not working properly. Broken links, like misspelled words on a web page, indicate that the website is not being maintained diligently. 🖲️ Guests staying at The Striped Umbrella often ask for information about family activities in the surrounding area. Links to interesting attractions are helpful not only to currently registered guests, but to attract potential ones as well. You decide to create external links on the activities page that link to two websites for area attractions.

STEPS

1. **Open The Striped Umbrella website, open** dwf_1.html **from the drive and folder where you store your Unit F Data Files, then save it as** activities.html **in the striped_umbrella local site root folder, overwriting the existing file but not updating links**

   The new activities page opens in Design view. The activities page describes two popular area attractions of interest to resort guests. There are two broken image placeholders that represent images that must be copied to the website.

2. **Close** dwf_1.html

TROUBLE
If you don't see the image in the data files folder, remember to browse to the Unit F Data Files assets folder to locate the family_sunset.jpg image.

3. **Select the** first broken image placeholder, **click the** Browse for File button 📁 **next to the** Src text box in the Property inspector, select family_sunset.jpg **from the assets folder in the location where you store your Unit F Data Files, click** OK (Win) or Open (Mac) **to save the image in your assets folder, then click to the right of the placeholder**

   The family_sunset image is copied to the website assets folder and now appears on the page.

4. **Select the** second broken image placeholder, **then repeat Step 3 to place the second image,** two_dolphins.jpg **on the page**

5. **Attach the** su_styles.css **file, then apply the** body_text **style to the paragraphs of text on the page (not to the menu bar)**

6. **Apply the** img_left_float **rule to the first image and the** img_right_float **rule to the second image**

7. **Scroll to the bottom of the page if necessary, then select the** Blue Angels **text in the second to the last paragraph on the page**

   You use the Blue Angels text to create an external link to the Blue Angels website.

8. **Click the** Link text box **in the HTML Property inspector, type** http://www.blueangels.navy.mil, **compare your screen to Figure F-5, then press** [Tab]

   The Blue Angels text is now a link to the Blue Angels website.

9. **Click** File **on the Menu bar, click** Save, **click the** Preview/Debug in browser button 🌐, **click** Preview in [your browser], **click** Blue Angels **on the web page, verify that the link works, then close your browser window**

TROUBLE
If your link does not work correctly, check for typing errors in the link path. If the link is typed correctly, the site may be down and you should remove the link until you can verify that it is working correctly.

10. **Scroll to the bottom of the page if necessary, select the** USS Alabama **text in the last paragraph on the page, then repeat Step 8 to create the link for the USS Alabama text, using the URL** http://www.ussalabama.com

FIGURE F-5: Creating an external link to the Blue Angels website

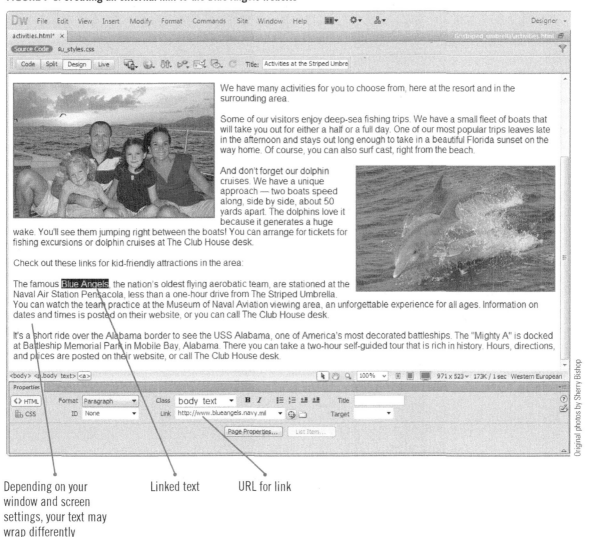

Depending on your window and screen settings, your text may wrap differently

Linked text

URL for link

Original photos by Sherry Bishop

Design Matters

Understanding The Web Accessibility Initiative - Accessible Rich Internet Applications Suite

The Web Accessibility Initiative - Accessible Rich Internet Applications Suite (WAI-ARIA) is a resource for applying best practices when adding advanced user interface controls to a website. Functions such as drag-and-drop or browsing through a menu can be very difficult for users who rely on assistive devices to navigate a site. WAI-ARIA, at w3.org/WAI, provides guidelines and techniques for planning and implementing accessible content. It also provides presentations, handouts, and tutorials for developers who are interested in learning how to provide content that can be easily navigated by all users, such as providing alternative keyboard navigation for web objects primarily designed to function using mouse clicks. The information offered through WAI-ARIA is developed by the Protocols and Formats Working Group (PFWG), a part of the World Wide Web Consortium (W3C).

Creating an Internal Link

As you know, a website usually contains individual pages for each category or major topic covered in the site. Within those pages, internal links are used to provide a way to move quickly from page to page. The home page should provide intuitive navigation to individual pages for each category or major topic covered in a website. A good rule of thumb is to design your site so that users are never more than two or three clicks away from the page they are seeking. Refer to your wireframe frequently as you create pages to help manage your site's navigation structure. ▓▓▓▓▓ You want to create an easy way for users to access the fishing and cruises pages from the activities page, so you create internal links on the activities page that will link to each of them.

STEPS

1. **Using Figure F-6 as a reference, select fishing excursions in the third paragraph**
   You use the fishing excursions text to create an internal link to the fishing page.

QUICK TIP
You can also select the file to which you want to link in the Files panel and drag it to the Link text box or use the Point to File button ⊕ in the Property inspector to create an internal link.

2. **Click the Browse for File button ☐ next to the Link text box in the HTML Property inspector, make sure the Relative to text box is set to Document, then double-click fishing.html in The Striped Umbrella local site root folder in the Select File dialog box**
   Since you designated the fishing.html page as the target for the fishing excursions link, fishing.html is listed in the Link text box in the HTML Property inspector, as shown in Figure F-6.

3. **Select dolphin cruises in the same sentence**
   You use the dolphin cruises text to create an internal link to the cruises page.

4. **Click ☐ in the Property inspector, double-click cruises.html in the Select File dialog box, then save your work**
   The dolphin cruises text is now an internal link to the cruises page in The Striped Umbrella website. There are now nine links on the activities page: seven internal links (five on the menu bar and two in the paragraph text linking to the fishing and cruises pages), and two external links (the Blue Angels and USS Alabama websites), as shown in Figure F-7.

5. **Close the activities page**

Design Matters

Linking to the home page

Every page in your website should include a link to the home page so a user who has become "lost" in your site can quickly go back to the starting point without relying on the Back button. Don't make users rely on the Back button on the browser toolbar to find their way back to the home page. It's possible that the user's current page might have opened as a result of a search and clicking the Back button will take the user out of the your website, which is not a good thing.

FIGURE F-6: Creating an internal link on the activities page

Selected text used for the link

Selected text links to the fishing page

Browse for File button

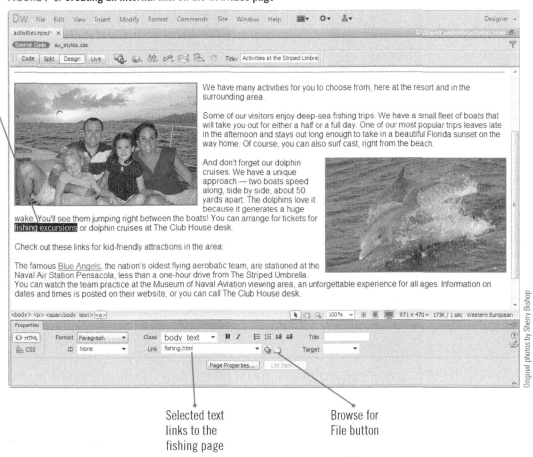

Original photos by Sherry Bishop

FIGURE F-7: Viewing the internal and external links on the activities page

Internal links

External links

© 2013 Cengage Learning
Original photos courtesy of Sherry Bishop

Inserting a Named Anchor

Some web pages have so much content that users must scroll repeatedly to get to information at the top and bottom of the page. To make it easier for users to navigate to specific areas of a page without scrolling, you can use a combination of internal links and named anchors. A **named anchor** is a specific location on a web page that is represented by a tag and an assigned descriptive name. You then create internal links on the page that the user clicks to browse to the named anchor location. For example, you can insert a named anchor called "top" at the top of a web page, then create a link at the bottom of the page that, when clicked, will display the anchor location (the top of the web page) when viewed in the browser. You can also insert named anchors at strategic places on a web page, such as before paragraph headings. The name chosen for a named anchor should be short and reflect its page location. Also, you should use only lowercase characters; do not use spaces or special characters, or begin an anchor name with a number. The logical order for creating and linking to named anchors is to create a named anchor before you create its link to avoid possible errors. 🔷🔷🔷 The Spa Services categories on the spa page contain lists of the names and descriptions of the services offered for each category. To allow users to quickly find the services they are interested in without scrolling up and down the page, you insert four named anchors on the spa page: one for the top of the page and the other three for the Massages, Facials, and Body Treatments lists of services.

STEPS

1. **Open the spa.html page, click View on the Menu bar, point to Visual Aids, then click Invisible Elements to select it, if necessary**
   The Invisible Elements menu item must be selected in order for named anchor locations to be visible on the page in Design view.

2. **Click The Striped Umbrella banner, then press the left arrow key on your keyboard**
   The location for the first named anchor is positioned at the top of the page directly before the banner.

3. **Click the Common category on the Insert panel, if necessary**
   The command for inserting a named anchor object is located in the Common category on the Insert panel.

> **TROUBLE**
> If you don't see the Named Anchor icon on the page, make sure that Invisible Elements is selected in the Visual Aids menu.

4. **Click Named Anchor on the Insert panel, type top in the Anchor name text box in the Named Anchor dialog box, as shown in Figure F-8, then click OK**
   The Named Anchor icon appears before The Striped Umbrella banner. It may be above it or to the left of it depending on the size of your Document window in the workspace.

5. **Click to place the insertion point to the left of the Massages heading above the first unordered list, click Named Anchor on the Insert panel, type massages in the Anchor name text box, then click OK**
   The second named anchor appears before the Massages heading.

6. **Repeat Step 5 to insert named anchors to the left of the Facials and Body Treatments list headings, using the following names: facials and body_treatments, deselect the text, then click the body_treatments named anchor to select it**
   Named anchors appear blue when selected and yellow when not selected, as shown in Figure F-9. The name of the selected anchor appears in the Property inspector.

7. **Save your work**

FIGURE F-8: Named Anchor dialog box

Anchor name text box

Named Anchor command

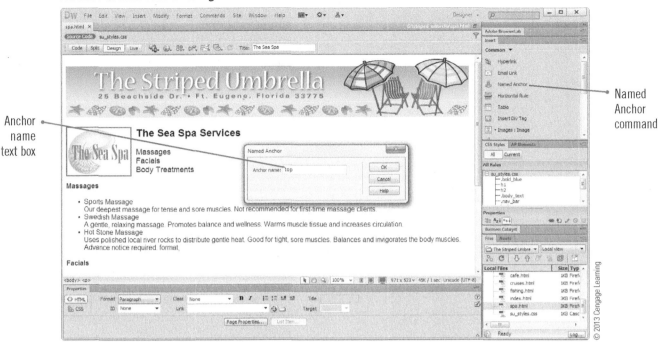

FIGURE F-9: Named anchor icons

Named anchors

Selected named anchor

Name of selected named anchor

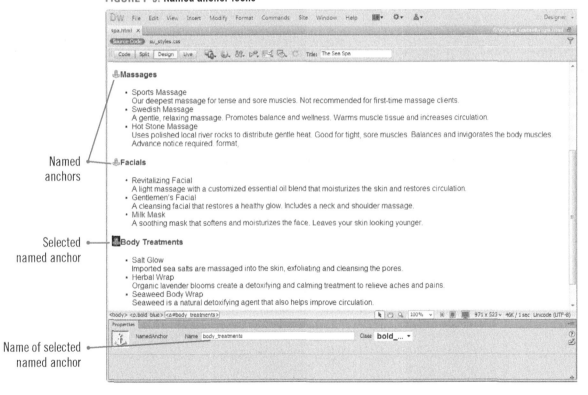

Using Visual Aids

The Visual Aids submenu on the View menu gives you several choices for displaying page elements in Design View, such as named anchor icons. Named anchor icons are considered invisible elements. When you check the Invisible Elements option, you will see the named anchor icons on the page. The icons do not appear when the page is viewed in a browser. Turning on visual aids makes it easier to edit the page. Other options in the Visual Aids menu are Fluid Grid Layout Guides, CSS Layout Backgrounds, CSS Layout Box Model, CSS Layout Outlines, AP Element Outlines, Table Widths, Table Borders, Frame Borders, and Image Maps. The Hide All option hides all of these page elements.

Creating Internal Links to Named Anchors

Named anchors act as targets for internal links. A **target** is the location on a web page that displays in the browser when a link is clicked. You can either drag a filename from the Files panel to selected text or use the Point to File button in the Property inspector to connect an internal link to a named anchor. Now that the named anchors are in place, you are ready to set up links for users to quickly access the information on the spa page. You want to create internal links for the four named anchors and link them to each named anchor on the page. You also decide to create a text link at the bottom of the page to make it easy for users to return to the top of the page.

STEPS

TROUBLE
The line pointing from the Point to File button to the Massages heading may differ slightly in appearance depending on whether you are using a Mac or Windows.

1. **Using Figure F-10 as a guide, select the Massages heading to the right of The Sea Spa logo, then click and drag the Point to File button ⊕ in the HTML Property inspector on top of the massages named anchor in front of the Massages heading, as shown in Figure F-10**

   The named anchor, massages, is the target for the massages link. When viewing the spa page in the browser, the list of massages will display at the top of the window when Massages is clicked. The name of a named anchor is always preceded by a pound (#) sign in the Link text box in the HTML Property inspector, as shown in Figure F-10.

2. **Repeat Step 1 to create internal links for the Facials and Body Treatments headings by first selecting each heading next to the logo, then clicking and dragging ⊕ to the facials and body_treatments named anchors**

   The Facials and Body Treatments headings are now links to the Facials and Body Treatments unordered lists of services.

3. **Click at the end of the last line on the page, press [Enter] (Win) or [return] (Mac), then type Return to top of page**

   The Return to top of page text will be used to link to the named anchor at the top of the page. If the text you want to use for a link to a named anchor and the named anchor itself are far apart on the page, you can scroll up or down the page as much as you need to and still use ⊕ to create the link. As long as the text is still selected, it is not necessary to be able to see it when you point to the named anchor.

4. **Repeat Step 1 again to link the Return to top of page text to the named anchor in front of the banner**

   The top of page text is now a link to the top named anchor to the left of the banner at the top of the page.

QUICK TIP
To enable or disable the Code Navigator, click View on the Menu bar, click Code Navigator, then click the Disable check box. It takes a second or two for the Code Navigator to appear.

5. **Click anywhere in the Return to top of page text, wait for a few seconds until the Click indicator to bring up the Code Navigator icon ✳ appears, then click ✳**

   The Code Navigator, as shown in Figure F-11, indicates that the Return to top of page text has the body and body_text rules applied to it. When you placed the insertion point at the end of the paragraph and entered a paragraph break, the formatting was retained for the Return to top of page text.

6. **Save your work, preview the spa page in your browser, test each link, then close your browser**

   The page can only scroll as far as there is text on the page, so you may not see much change depending on your window size.

FIGURE F-10: Using the Point to File icon

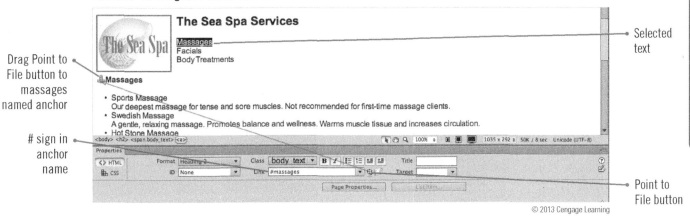

Drag Point to File button to massages named anchor

sign in anchor name

Selected text

Point to File button

© 2013 Cengage Learning

FIGURE F-11: Code Navigator displaying rule name

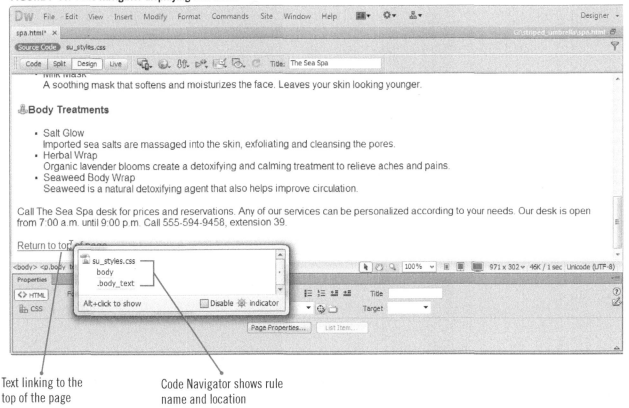

Text linking to the top of the page

Code Navigator shows rule name and location

Using the Code Navigator

When you click on a page element either in Code view or in Design view, wait a second or two; the Click indicator to bring up the Code Navigator icon ![icon] will appear (you can also [Alt]-click (Win) or [Ctrl]-click (Mac) to display it instantly). Clicking ![icon] will open a pop-up window called the Code Navigator. As you recall from Unit C, the Code Navigator lists the CSS rule name linked to the page element, along with the name of the style sheet that contains the rule. Pointing to the rule name will display the properties and values of the rule, as shown in Figure F-12. This is a quick way to view the rule definition. If you click the rule name, the code for the rule will open in Code and Design views, where you can then edit it.

FIGURE F-12: Code Navigator displaying rule properties

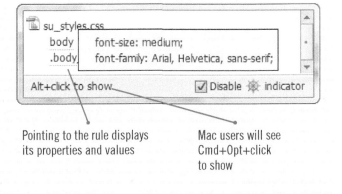

Pointing to the rule displays its properties and values

Mac users will see Cmd+Opt+click to show

Creating a Spry Menu Bar

Recall from Unit C that a menu bar is a set of text or image links that can be used to navigate between pages of a website. To make your site more visually appealing, you can use special effects to create a more professional look for your menu bars. One way to do this is to insert a Spry menu bar. A Spry menu bar is a type of menu bar that uses unordered lists, CSS, and Javascript to create an interactive menu bar with pull-down submenus. **Spry**, or **Spry framework**, is open source code developed by Adobe Systems to help designers quickly incorporate dynamic content on their web pages. Each link in a Spry menu bar is called an **item**. When you add a Spry menu bar, by default it first appears with placeholder text and generic settings for the menu bar properties, such as the width and background color for each item in the menu. The current menu bar for The Striped Umbrella site is a set of five text links. While they work perfectly well, you would like a more professionally designed look. You begin by creating a Spry menu bar that will contain five items: home, about us, cafe, spa, and activities.

STEPS

1. Select the banner on the spa page, press the right arrow key, then press [Shift] [Enter] (Win) or [Shift] [return] (Mac)

   The insertion point is positioned between the banner and the spa logo.

QUICK TIP
The Spry Menu Bar button is also in the Layout category on the Insert panel.

2. Click the Insert panel list arrow on the Insert panel, click the Spry category, scroll down, if necessary, to click Spry Menu Bar, then click to select the Horizontal layout option button in the Spry Menu Bar dialog box, as shown in Figure F-13

   The Horizontal layout option specifies that the menu bar will be placed horizontally on the page.

3. Click OK

   The Spry menu bar, which will be referred to from now on simply as the menu bar, displays selected under the banner. The menu bar contains four items by default and each item contains placeholder text, such as Item 1. Right above the upper left corner of the menu bar is the Spry menu bar label containing the default label name: MenuBar1. The Property inspector shows the menu bar properties. It lists the default items and submenu items, along with text boxes for linking each item and submenu item to the appropriate pages.

4. Select MenuBar1 in the Menu Bar text box in the Property inspector, then type MenuBar

   Item 1 is selected in the Item column (first column on the left) in the Property inspector.

5. Select Item 1 in the Text text box in the right side of the Property inspector, type Home, select Item 1.1 in the first submenu column (second column) in the Property inspector, as shown in Figure F-14, then click the Remove menu Item button ➖ above the first submenu column

   Item 1 is renamed Home and the default submenu item Item 1.1 is deleted.

QUICK TIP
You can add sub-menu items by clicking the Add menu item button ➕.

6. Click ➖ two more times

   The remainder of the default submenu items—Item 1.2 and Item 1.3—for the Home item are deleted as well.

7. Click the Browse for File button 📁 next to the Link text box in the Property inspector, double-click index.html in the local site root folder, then compare your Property inspector to Figure F-15

   The Home item is linked to the home page.

QUICK TIP
If you have a gap between the banner and the menu bar, go to Code view to see if you have a <p> tag around the banner. If you do, delete the beginning and ending tag and the space will be removed.

8. Click to place the insertion point to the right of the menu bar, enter a line break, compare your screen to Figure F-16, save your file, click OK to close the Copy Dependent Files dialog box, then refresh the Files panel if necessary

   The menu bar displays with the first item named Home linked to the home page. The supporting files that are needed to format the Spry menu bar and make it function properly are added to the local site root folder. A new SpryAssets folder is added that contains a JavaScript file, a CSS file, and some images that are used in the Spry menu bar.

FIGURE F-13: Spry Menu Bar dialog box

Horizontal layout option button

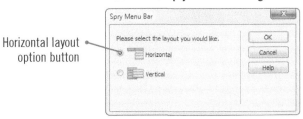

FIGURE F-14: Property inspector with Menu Bar properties

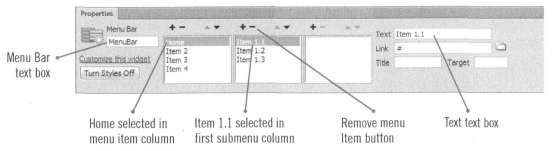

Menu Bar text box

Home selected in menu item column

Item 1.1 selected in first submenu column

Remove menu Item button

Text text box

FIGURE F-15: Home item for the menu bar

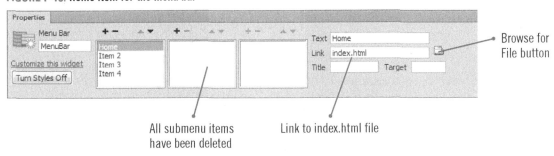

Browse for File button

All submenu items have been deleted

Link to index.html file

FIGURE F-16: The Spry Menu bar on the spa page

The named anchor icon may appear beside the banner, depending on the width of the window

Spry Menu Bar label

Item 1 is renamed "Home"

© 2013 Cengage Learning

Inserting a Fireworks menu bar

Another option for adding a menu bar to your page is to create a menu bar in Adobe Fireworks, open Dreamweaver, then import the menu bar onto the web page. Once you've created the Fireworks menu bar, you export the Fireworks file to a Dreamweaver local site root folder. This file contains the HTML code that defines the menu bar properties. Next, open the appropriate web page in Dreamweaver where you want to insert the menu bar, then use the Insert > Image Objects > Fireworks HTML command to add the HTML code to the page. You can also use Dreamweaver to import rollover images and buttons created in Fireworks.

Adding Menu Bar Items

After you create a menu bar, you can modify it by adding new menu items or submenu items or deleting those that you do not need. Submenus are also called **child menus**. Submenu items can also have submenus under them. The Property inspector is used to add, delete, rename, and link Spry menu items to pages in your website. 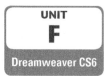 You are ready to add the rest of the menu and submenu items to the menu bar so users will have access to each of the main pages from the menu bar. You want to rename the rest of the default menu items, add one additional menu item, then add two submenu items under the activities item for the cruises and fishing pages.

STEPS

1. **Click the** Spry Menu Bar: MenuBar tab **if necessary, then click** Item 2 **in the Item menu column (first column) in the Property inspector, select** Item 2 **in the Text text box, then type** About Us

   Item 2 is renamed About Us.

2. **Click the** Browse button 🗀 **next to the Link text box, click** about_us.html **in the local site root folder, then click** OK (Win) **or** Open (Mac) **or double-click** about_us.html

   The About Us menu item is linked to the about_us page.

3. **Repeat Steps 1 and 2 to rename Item 3** Sand Crab Cafe **and link it to the cafe.html page in the local site root folder**

4. **Delete each submenu item under the Sand Crab Cafe menu item, then click** OK **to close the warning box confirming the removal of each of the submenus**

   The submenu items under the Sand Crab Cafe menu item are deleted.

5. **Repeat Steps 1 and 2 to rename Item 4** The Sea Spa **and link it to the spa.html page in the local site root folder**

   The Sea Spa menu item is linked to the spa page and remains selected in the Property inspector.

6. **Click the** Add menu item button ➕ **above the Item menu column (first column), select** Untitled Item, **in the Text text box type** Activities, **then link it to the** activities.html **page**

   The new menu item, Activities, is linked to the activities page and remains selected in the Property inspector.

7. **Click** ➕ **above the first submenu column (second column), select** Untitled Item, **type** Cruises **in the Text text box, then link it to the cruises.html page**

   A new submenu item, Cruises, is added under the Activities menu item that will link to the cruises page.

8. **Repeat Step 7 to add another submenu item named** Fishing, **link it to the fishing.html page, save your work, then compare your screen to Figure F-17**

   A second submenu item is added under the Activities menu item that will link to the fishing page.

9. **Create a new Tag rule in the su_styles.css file to modify the <img> tag, then set the Block Vertical-align to** bottom

   This rule will prevent a gap between the banner and menu bar.

TROUBLE
If a message appears that you need to install the Flash plug-in, go to adobe.com to download the plug-in or this feature will not work.

10. **Click the** Switch Design View to Live View button [Live] **on the Document toolbar, view the menu bar, then compare your screen to Figure F-18**

    Live View shows you what the page will look like when opened in a browser. Not only is it a faster way to view your page than previewing it in a browser but it shows the interactive elements functioning. For more information about Live View read the Clues to Use box *Viewing your page in Live View*.

11. **Click** [Live] **again**

    The spa page redisplays in your workspace in Design view without the interactive elements being functional.

FIGURE F-17: Adding menu items and submenu items to the menu bar

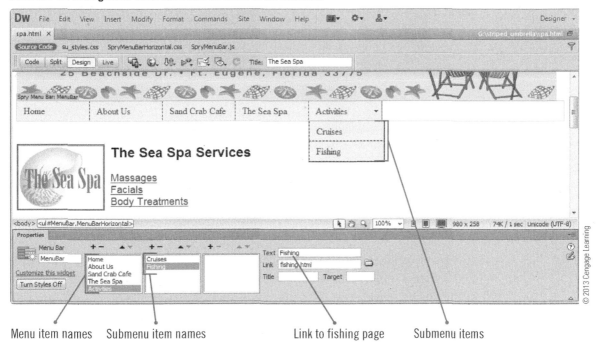

Menu item names   Submenu item names   Link to fishing page   Submenu items

FIGURE F-18: Viewing the spa page in Live View

Switch Design
View to Live
View button

Menu bar as
it will appear
in a browser

Viewing your page in Live View

When you view your web pages in Dreamweaver, the page elements appear similar to the way they will look when viewed in a web browser. Live View gives you a more accurate picture of what the page will actually look like in a browser, with interactive elements active and functioning. You use the Switch Design View to Live View button on the Document toolbar to enable Live View. Next to this button is the Shows the Live View source in code view button, which displays the code. The code remains as read-only until you click the Shows the Live View source in code view

button again. When the Switch Design View to Live View button is active, the Shows the Live View source in code view button can be toggled on or off. If Live View is not active, selecting the Shows the Live View source in code view button will turn it on. When you first click the Live View button, you may see a message that you need to install the Flash plug-in from the Adobe website, adobe.com. Once you download the plug-in, your pages can then be viewed using Live View.

Formatting a Menu Bar

Once you create a Spry menu bar, you'll need to modify the default settings to adjust the appearance of the menu bar and its items. For example, you can adjust their height and width or specify the background color of each menu item. You can add special effects for menu bar items by changing the characteristics for each item's state. A **state** is the condition of the menu item relative to the mouse pointer. You can create a rollover effect by using different background and text colors for each state to represent how the menu item appears when users move their mouse over or away from it. The settings for the menu bar and menu items reside in CSS rules. To change them, you edit the default rules that were automatically created when the Spry menu bar was inserted on the page. *****📖***** You format the Spry menu bar by editing the rules that control the appearance of the Spry menu bar items.

STEPS

TROUBLE
If you don't see the rule listed, click the Switch to All (Document) Mode button [All] in the CSS Styles panel.

1. **Click the plus sign (Win) or right pointing arrow (Mac) next to SpryMenuBarHorizonal.css in the CSS Styles panel if necessary, select the rule ul.MenuBarHorizontal (the first rule listed in the style sheet), then click the Edit Rule button 🖉 on the CSS styles panel**

   The CSS Rule Definition for ul.MenuBarHorizontal in SpryMenuBarHorizontal.css dialog box opens. This is where you define the global settings for all menu and submenu items.

2. **Click Type in the Category list, click the Font-family list arrow, click Arial, Helvetica, sans-serif, click the Font-size list arrow, click 14, click the Font-size unit of measure list arrow, click px, compare your screen to Figure F-19, then click OK**

   The text size of the menu items becomes larger to reflect the new settings, which causes the text on the Sand Crab Cafe button to wrap to two lines. You want the menu bar to revert back to one line.

3. **Select the ul.MenuBarHorizontal li rule (the third rule listed) in the CSS Styles panel, click 🖉, click Box in the Category list, click the Width text box, type 190, click the Width unit of measure list arrow, click px, click in the Height text box, type 25, then compare your screen to Figure F-20**

   The width of each menu item increases to 190 pixels wide and the height is set to 25 pixels.

4. **Click Block in the Category list, click the Text-align text box arrow, select center, then click OK**

   The block settings include properties to change the spacing and alignment of the text in the menu bar. The Text-align setting adjusts the alignment of each text item on its "button." In this case, the menu items are set to appear centered within their button in the menu bar.

TROUBLE
If you don't see the u.MenuBarHorizontal a rule listed in the CSS Styles panel, click the Switch to (All) Document Mode button [All].

5. **Click ul.MenuBarHorizontal a (tenth rule) in the CSS Styles panel, click 🖉, click Type in the Category list, type #FFF in the Color text box replacing the current color, click Background in the Category list, type #09C in the Background-color text box, then click OK**

   The menu items redisplay with white text on a blue background. This is how they appear in the menu bar when the mouse is *not* positioned over them.

QUICK TIP
To locate this rule, which is the longest rule, place your mouse over each rule name to see the extended names. You can also temporarily expand the CSS Styles panel width to see the entire name.

6. **Click ul.MenuBarHorizontal a.MenuBarItemHover, ul.MenuBarHorizontal a.MenuBarItemSubmenuHover, ul.MenuBarHorizontal a.MenuBarSubmenuVisible (twelfth rule) in the CSS Styles panel, then click 🖉**

7. **Click Type in the Category list, type #630 in the Color text box, click Background in the Category list, type #FC9 in the Background-color text box, then click OK**

   The property values for the menu items and submenu items change to a sand background with brown text. This is how they appear when the mouse is positioned over them.

8. **Click File on the Menu bar, click Save All, preview your page in the browser, compare your screen to Figure F-21, test each link to ensure that each works correctly, then close the browser**

   The button background colors are blue with white text when the pointer is not placed over them and sand-colored with brown text when the pointer is positioned over them.

FIGURE F-19: Adding properties for the .ulMenuBarHorizontal rule

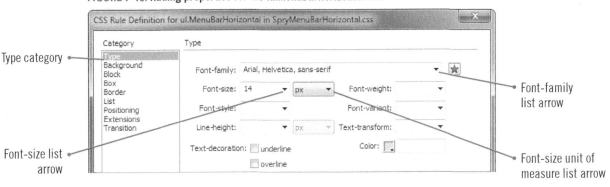

Type category

Font-size list arrow

Font-family list arrow

Font-size unit of measure list arrow

FIGURE F-20: Modifying properties for the ul.MenuBarHorizontal li rule

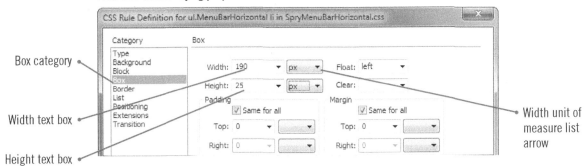

Box category

Width text box

Height text box

Width unit of measure list arrow

FIGURE F-21: Spa page viewed in the browser with the updated menu bar

Menu items and submenu items are blue with white text when the pointer is not placed over them

Menu items and submenu items are sand colored with brown text when the pointer is placed over them

© 2013 Cengage Learning

Copying a Menu Bar to Other Pages

When you create a menu bar for one page in a website, you should copy it to all of the other pages in the site. This practice provides continuity in the navigation structure and makes it easy for users to navigate comfortably through pages in your site. The new Spry menu bar is an improvement over the menu bar with plain text links. You decide to replace all existing menu bars on the pages in the website with this menu bar to improve each page's design and promote consistency. You copy the menu bar to the about_us, index, and activities pages in The Striped Umbrella website.

1. **Click the Spry Menu Bar:MenuBar tab above the top left corner of the menu bar, as shown in Figure F-22, click Edit on the Menu bar, then click Copy**

   The menu bar is ready to be pasted on other pages in the website.

QUICK TIP
When you work on multiple open pages, use the file-name tabs at the top of the Document toolbar or press [Ctrl] [Tab] to move quickly between pages (Win).

2. **Double-click activities.html on the Files panel**

   The activities page opens.

3. **Select the original menu bar on the page, click Edit on the Menu bar, click Paste, click to the right of the menu bar, add a line break, delete the horizontal rule, compare your screen to Figure F-23, then save the page**

   The new menu bar appears on the page in place of the previous one and the new styles are added to the page.

TROUBLE
If you have trouble with the alignment and spacing between the banner and the menu bar, look at the break tag after the banner. If it is on a separate line under the banner, move it to the end of the line of code for the banner.

4. **Open the index page, delete the current menu bar, delete any <p> tags around the banner, click the banner to select it, press the right arrow key, paste the Spry menu bar on the page, delete the horizontal rule, then insert a line break after the menu bar**

   The menu bar is pasted on the index page and the spacing after the menu bar is adjusted to match the other two pages.

5. **Open the about_us page, replace the current menu bar with the new menu bar, add a line break, delete the horizontal rule, then apply the body_text rule to the heading "Welcome guests!"**

   The menu bar is pasted on the about_us page, the horizontal rule is deleted, and the page heading is formatted to match the home, spa, and activities pages.

QUICK TIP
View the pages at a high resolution to ensure that the menu bars do not break into two lines.

6. **Click File on the Menu bar, click Save All, then preview each page in the browser**

   The menu bar appears consistently on the index, about_us, spa, and activities pages of The Striped Umbrella website. Although the cafe, fishing, and activities pages are not designed yet, you see that the links all work correctly. If the spacing between the menu bar and the rest of the page content is not consistent, add or remove <br> tags if necessary to adjust the spacing on each page.

7. **Hold the pointer over the Activities link, as shown in Figure F-24, close the browser, then close all open pages except the about_us page**

   When the pointer is placed over the Activities link, the submenu drops down with the two submenu links visible and active.

FIGURE F-22: Selecting the Spry menu bar on the spa page

Spry Menu
Bar:
MenuBar tab

© 2013 Cengage Learning

FIGURE F-23: Pasting the Spry menu bar on the activities page

Spry Menu
bar copied to
activities
page

© 2013 Cengage Learning
Original photo courtesy of Sherry Bishop

FIGURE F-24: Viewing the activities submenu items in the browser

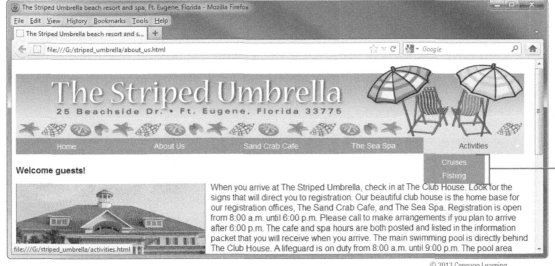

Submenu
items for
Cruises
and Fishing
pages

© 2013 Cengage Learning
Original photo courtesy of Sherry Bishop

Creating an Image Map

Another way to create navigation links for web pages is to create an image map. An image map is an image that has one or more hotspots placed on top of it. A **hotspot** is an active area on an image that, when clicked, links to a different location on the page or to another web page. For example, a map of the world could have a hotspot placed on each individual country so that users could click a country to link to more information. Hotspots are not visible in the browser window, but when users place their pointer over the hotspot, the pointer changes to a pointing finger, indicating the presence of a link. To create a hotspot, select the image on which you want to place the hotspot, draw the hotspot with one of the shape hotspot tools in the Property inspector, then add the link information, alternate text, and target information in the text boxes in the Property inspector. You want to create an image map on the activities page to provide another way for users to link to the index page.

STEPS

1. **Click The Striped Umbrella banner on the about_us page to select it, then double-click a blank area on the right side of the Property inspector to expand it, if necessary**
   The Property inspector displays the drawing tools for creating hotspots on an image in the lower-left corner.

TROUBLE
If you don't see the blue rectangle, click View, point to Visual Aids, then click Image Maps to select it.

2. **Click the Rectangle Hotspot Tool button ▢ on the Property inspector, drag to create a rectangle that encompasses The Striped Umbrella name on the banner, release the mouse button, click OK to close the Dreamweaver dialog box, then compare your screen to Figure F-25**
   A shaded blue rectangle appears within the area that you outlined. This blue rectangle is the hotspot. The dialog box reminds you to add to the alternate text for the hotspot.

3. **Drag the Point to File button ⊕ next to the Link text box in the Property inspector to index.html in the Files panel**
   The hotspot is linked to the index.html file. If the hotspot is clicked, the index file opens.

TROUBLE
If you don't see the Map text box in the Property inspector, click the image map object on the banner to select it.

4. **Select Map in the Map text box in the Property inspector, then type home**
   The image map is named home. Each image map should have a unique name, especially if a page contains more than one image map.

5. **Click the Target list arrow in the Property inspector, then click _self**
   The _self target directs the browser to display the home page in the same browser window as the activities page, rather than opening a separate window. When the hotspot is clicked, the home page opens in the same browser window. See the Clues to Use box *Setting targets for links* to learn more about how the _self property, along with other property options, are used to set targets for links.

QUICK TIP
You should always assign a unique name for each image map to make them more accessible to users utilizing screen readers.

6. **Type Link to home page in the Alt text box in the Property inspector, as shown in Figure F-26**
   The descriptive information placed in the Alt text box provides a brief clue to the user about what further information awaits if the hotspot is clicked. The alternate text is also read by screen readers to tell users what will happen if they click the image map.

7. **Switch to Code view, locate the <br> tag that has been added below the ending </map> tag, then delete it**

QUICK TIP
This additional code will prevent a border appearing around the banner in Internet Explorer.

8. **Place the insertion point right before the closing image tag for the banner, then type style="border:0"**

9. **Return to Design view, save your work, preview the page in your browser window, test the link on the image map, then close the browser**
   The hotspot is not visible in the browser, but if you place the mouse over the hotspot, you will see the pointer change to 🖑 to indicate a link is present.

FIGURE F-25: Drawing a hotspot on The Striped Umbrella banner

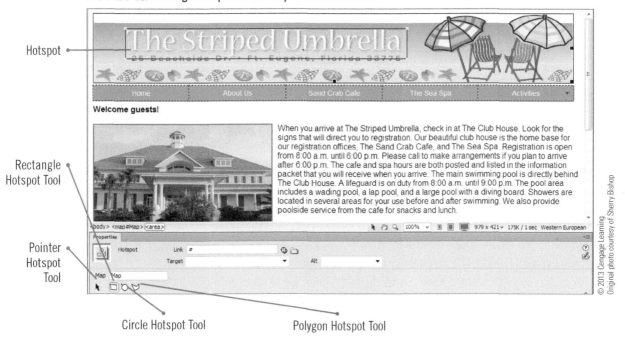

Hotspot

Rectangle Hotspot Tool

Pointer Hotspot Tool

Circle Hotspot Tool

Polygon Hotspot Tool

© 2013 Cengage Learning Original photo courtesy of Sherry Bishop

FIGURE F-26: Adding a link, a target, and alternate text to a hotspot

Link text box

Target text box

Alt text box

Setting targets for links

You can set targets to determine how a new window will display in a browser when links on pages or in frames are clicked. A **frame** is a fixed region in a browser that can display a web page and act independently from other pages displayed in other frames within the browser. When you set a target for a link or frame, you have four options for how the new window will open after the link is clicked. These targets are set by clicking the Target list arrow in the HTML Property inspector and selecting the target you want. The _blank target displays the destination page in a separate browser window and leaves the original window open. The _parent target displays the destination page in the parent window or frameset, replacing the original window or frameset. The _self target displays the destination page in the same window or frame. The _top target displays the destination page in the whole browser window.

Design Matters

Creating and modifying hotspots

In addition to the Rectangle hotspot tool, there are two other helpful shape tools: a Circle hotspot tool and a Polygon hotspot tool. These tools can be used to create any shape hotspot that you need. For instance, the Polygon hotspot tool could be used to draw an outline around each state on a map of the United States. Hotspots can be easily changed and rearranged on an image using the Pointer hotspot tool. First, select the hotspot you would like to edit, then drag one of the hotspot selector handles to change the size or shape of a hotspot. You can also move the hotspot by dragging it to a new position on the image. It is a good idea to limit the number of complex or irregularly shaped hotspots in an image because the code can become too lengthy for the page to download in a reasonable amount of time. You should also make the hotspot boundaries a little larger than they need to be to cover the area you want to set as a link. This allows a little leeway for users when they place their mouse over the hotspot by creating a larger target area for them.

Managing Website Links

As your website grows, so will the number of links on it. Checking links to make sure they work is a crucial and ongoing task that you should perform regularly. The Check Links Sitewide feature is a helpful tool for managing your links. It checks your entire website for the total number of links, categorizing them as OK, external, or broken, and then displays the information in the Link Checker panel. The Link Checker panel also provides a list of all the files used in a website, including those that are **orphaned files**, files that are not linked to any pages in the website. If you find broken internal links (links to files within the website), you should carefully check the code entered in the Link text box for errors. You can either use the Browse for File button in the Link Checker panel to correct the link, or type the correction in the Link text box in the Property inspector. You check broken external links (links to files outside the website) by testing the links in your browser. Due to the volatility of the web, it is important to check external links routinely as websites are often under construction or undergoing address changes. ▰▰▰ You have created three new external links in The Striped Umbrella website: two to external websites and one email link. You want to make sure you entered them correctly, so you run some reports to check the site for any broken links or orphaned files.

STEPS

TROUBLE
If any links are listed under the Broken Links category, click Site on the Menu bar, point to Advanced, click Recreate Site Cache, then run the report again.

1. **Click Site on the Menu bar, then click Check Links Sitewide**

   The Link Checker panel in the Results Tab group opens. By default, the Link Checker panel initially displays any broken internal links found in the website. The Striped Umbrella website has no broken links, as shown in Figure F-27.

QUICK TIP
To view all of the links without scrolling, you can float the Results Tab group.

2. **Click the Show list arrow in the Link Checker panel, click External Links, then compare your screen with Figure F-28**

   Two files are listed: the activities page and the index page. The activities page has two external links listed: one to the Blue Angels website and one to the U.S.S. Alabama website. The index page has an email link listed.

TROUBLE
If any orphaned files are listed under the Files category, click Site on the Menu bar, point to Advanced, click Recreate Site Cache, then run the report again.

3. **Click the Show list arrow, then click Orphaned Files**

   There are no orphaned files displayed in the Link Checker panel for the website, as shown in Figure F-29.

TROUBLE
If you don't see the links, click the Refresh button ↻.

4. **Close the Results Tab Group, click the Assets tab on the Files Tab Group, then click the URLs button ▩ on the Assets panel**

   The list of external links in the Striped Umbrella website displays in the Assets panel. See Figure F-30.

5. **Close the about_us page, then Exit (Win) or Quit (Mac) Dreamweaver**

FIGURE F-27: Link Checker with Broken Links results displayed

Show list
arrow

No broken
links
listed

FIGURE F-28: Link Checker with External Links results displayed

External
links listed

FIGURE F-29: Link Checker with Orphaned Files results displayed

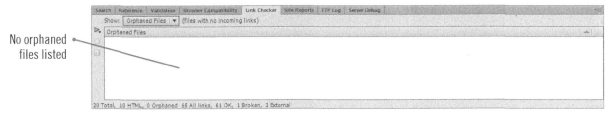

No orphaned
files listed

FIGURE F-30: Assets panel with website external links displayed

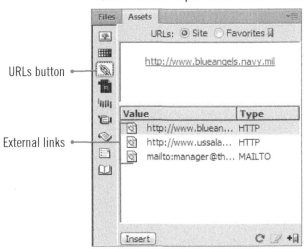

URLs button

External links

Design Matters

Designing for easy navigation

As you work on the navigation structure for a website, you should try to limit the number of internal links on each page. You should also provide visual clues on each page to let users know where they are, much like a "You are here" marker on a store directory at the mall, or a bread crumbs trail. A **bread crumbs trail** is a list of links that provides a path from the initial page you opened in a website to the page that you are currently viewing. Many websites provide a list of all the site's pages, called a **site map**. A site map is similar to a table of contents; it lets users see how the information is divided between the pages and helps them to locate the information they need quickly.

Practice

Concepts Review

Label each element in the Dreamweaver window shown in Figure F-31.

FIGURE F-31

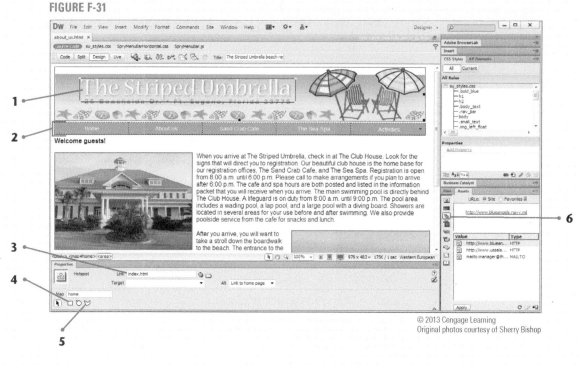

© 2013 Cengage Learning
Original photos courtesy of Sherry Bishop

1. _____	4. _____
2. _____	5. _____
3. _____	6. _____

Match each of the following terms with the statement that best describes its function.

7. **Internal links**

8. **External links**

9. **Broken links**

10. **Named anchor**

11. **Menu bar**

12. **Target**

13. **Image map**

14. **Hotspot**

15. **Orphaned file**

a. Links that do not work correctly

b. A set of text or image links used to navigate between pages of a website

c. An image with hotspots on it

d. Links to pages within the website

e. Active area on an image that serves as a link

f. A location on a web page that browsers will display when a link is clicked

g. A specific location on a web page, represented by a special icon, that will fully display in the browser window when a user clicks the link tagged to it

h. A file that is not linked to any pages on a website

i. Links to pages outside the website

Select the best answer from the following list of choices.

16. **Which type of path begins with a forward slash?**
    a. Document-relative
    b. Root-relative
    c. Absolute
    d. Image-relative

17. **Which button in the Property inspector do you use to connect an internal link to a named anchor?**
    a. Point to File
    b. Point to Anchor
    c. Anchor to File
    d. Point to Named Anchor

18. **The four target options for how a window will display in a browser when a link is clicked are:**
    a. _blank, _parent, _self, _top.
    b. _blank, _child, _self, _top.
    c. _blank, _parent, _child, _top.
    d. _blank, _parent, _self, _new.

19. **To see all links in a website, you click which button on the Assets panel?**
    a. Links
    b. Paths
    c. URLs
    d. Anchors

20. **Which dialog box shows you a list of orphaned files?**
    a. Orphaned Files
    b. Link Checker
    c. Check Links Sitewide
    d. Assets

Skills Review

Important: *If you did not create this website in Unit B and maintain it during the preceding units, you will need to create a local site root folder for this website and define the website using files your instructor will provide. See the "Read This Before You Begin" section for more detailed instructions.*

1. **Understand links and paths.**
   a. Write an example of an absolute path for a link.
   b. Write an example of a relative path for a link.
   c. Write a sentence explaining the difference between a document-relative path and a root-relative path.

2. **Create an external link.**
   a. Start Dreamweaver, then open the Blooms & Bulbs website.
   b. Open dwf_2.html from the drive and folder where you store your Unit F Data Files, save it as **newsletter.html** in the blooms local site root folder, replacing the existing file and not updating links, then close dwf_2.html.
   c. Click the first broken image placeholder for the ruby_grass.jpg file browse to the drive and folder where you store your Unit F Data Files to copy it to your assets folder, then apply the img_left_float rule to it.
   d. Repeat Step c to replace the next two broken image placeholders for the trees.jpg and plants.jpg files, apply the img_right_float rule to the trees image and the img_left_float rule to the plants image.
   e. Scroll to the bottom of the page, then link the National Gardening Association text to **http://www.garden.org**.
   f. Link the Organic Gardening text to **http://www.organicgardening.com**.
   g. Link the Southern Living text to **http://www.southernliving.com/southern**.
   h. Save the file, then preview it in your browser window.
   i. Test the links to make sure they all work correctly, then close the browser.

3. **Create an internal link.**
   a. Select the text "gardening tips" in the last sentence in the Gardening Issues paragraph.
   b. Use the Point to File button to link the text to the tips.html page.
   c. Change the page title to **Gardening Matters**.
   d. Create a new Tag rule in the blooms_styles.css style sheet that modifies the <h2> tag as follows: font-family: Arial, Helvetica, sans-serif font; font-size: medium; font-weight: bold; color: #000.

Skills Review (continued)

  e. Create a new Tag rule in the blooms_styles.css style sheet that modifies the <h3> tag as follows: font-family: Arial, Helvetica, sans-serif; font-size: medium; font-weight: bold; color: #060.

  f. Save all files, test the link in your browser, then close the browser.

  g. Open the plants page, then add a new paragraph to the bottom of the page: **In addition to these marvelous roses, we have many annuals, perennials, and water plants that have just arrived.**

  h. Apply the body_text rule to the paragraph if necessary.

  i. Use the Files panel to create three new blank files in the local site root folder named: annuals.html, perennials.html, and water_plants.html.

  j. Link the "annuals" text in the new paragraph to the annuals.html file, link the "perennials" text to the perennials.html file, then link the "water plants" text to the water_plants.html file.

  k. Save your work, test the links in your browser, then close the browser. (*Hint*: These pages do not have content yet, but are serving as placeholders.)

4. Insert a named anchor.

  a. Switch to the newsletter page, then show the invisible elements if necessary.

  b. Insert a named anchor in front of the Grass subheading, then name it **grass**.

  c. Insert a named anchor in front of the Trees subheading, then name it **trees**.

  d. Insert a named anchor in front of the Plants subheading, then name it **plants**.

  e. Save the file.

5. Create an internal link to a named anchor.

  a. Using the Point to File button in the Property inspector, create a link from the word grass in the Gardening Issues paragraph to the grass named anchor.

  b. Create a link from the word trees in the Gardening Issues paragraph to the trees named anchor.

  c. Create a link from the word plants in the Gardening Issues paragraph to the plants named anchor.

  d. Save the file, then test the links in your browser window.

6. Create a Spry menu bar.

  a. Enter a line break after the banner on the newsletter page.

  b. Use the Spry category on the Insert panel to insert a Spry menu bar with a horizontal layout under the banner.

  c. Replace MenuBar1 in the Menu Bar text box in the Property inspector with the name **MenuBar**.

  d. Replace the name Item 1 in the Text text box with **Home**, then remove all submenu items from the Home item.

  e. Link the Home item to the index.html file.

  f. Switch to Code view, place your insertion point right after the ending tag for the unordered list, switch back to Design view, insert two line breaks, then save the file, copying the dependent files.

7. Add menu bar items.

  a. Rename the Item 2 menu item **Newsletter**, then link it to the newsletter page.

  b. Rename the Item 3 menu item **Plants**, then link it to the plants page.

  c. Rename the Item 4 menu item **Tips**, then link it to the tips page.

  d. With the Tips menu item selected, add a new menu item with the name **Workshops**, then link it to the workshops page.

  e. With the Plants menu item selected, rename submenu Item 3.1 **Annuals**, then link it to the annuals.html page.

  f. With the Plants menu item selected, rename submenu Item 3.2 **Perennials**, then link it to the perennials.html page.

  g. With the Plants menu item selected, rename submenu Item 3.3 **Water Plants**, then link it to the water_plants.html page.

  h. With the Annuals submenu item selected, delete its two submenu items, then save your work.

Skills Review (continued)

8. Format a menu bar.

   a. Expand the SpryMenuBarHorizonal.css style sheet in the CSS Styles panel, then edit the rule ul.MenuBarHorizontal with the following settings: Font-family: Arial, Helvetica, sans-serif; Font-size: 14 px.

   b. Edit the ul.MenuBarHorizontal li rule with the following settings: Box Width: 190 px; Box Height: 25 px; Block Text-align: center.

   c. Edit the following rule: ul.MenuBarHorizontal a with the following settings: Type Color: #030; Background-color: #99F.

   d. Edit the following rule: ul.MenuBarHorizontal a.MenuBarItemHover, ul.MenuBarHorizontal a.MenuBarItemSubmenuHover, ul.MenuBarHorizontal a.MenuBarSubmenuVisible with the following settings: Type Color: #FFC; Background-color: #030.

   e. Create a new Tag rule in the blooms_styles.css file to modify the <img> tag as follows: Block Vertical-align:bottom.

   f. Save your work, then test the menu bar on the page in the browser to make sure everything works correctly.

9. Copy a menu bar to other pages.

   a. Select and copy the menu bar, then open the index page.

   b. Select the banner, press the right arrow key, click the Format list arrow in the HTML Property inspector, then click None if necessary.

   c. Paste the menu bar at the insertion point, then delete the existing menu bar created with text links and the horizontal rule.

   d. Switch to Live View to view the placement of the menu bar on the page.

   e. Return to Design view; when you are satisfied with the page, save your work, then close the index page.

   f. Switch to the plants page, add a line break after the banner, paste the menu bar under the banner, then add another line break.

   g. Switch to Live view to check the placement of the menu bar, then return to Design view and save and close the page.

   h. Repeat Step f to add a menu bar on the tips page, apply the img_left_float to the butterfly image, then save the tips page. (*Hint*: If you see a space between the banner and the menu bar, go to Code view and look for <p> tags around the banner. If you see any, delete them.)

   i. Preview all pages in the browser window, checking the spacing for each page to ensure a uniform look, then close the browser. (*Hint*: The workshops, annuals, perennials, and water_plants pages are serving as placeholder pages and do not have content yet.)

10. Create an image map.

   a. On the newsletter page, create a rectangle hotspot over the words *Blooms & Bulbs* on the Blooms & Bulbs banner.

   b. Name the image map **home**, then link it to the index page.

   c. Set the target as _top.

   d. Enter the alternate text **Link to home page**.

   e. Switch to Code view, locate the <br> tag that has been added below the ending </map> tag, then delete it.

   f. Place the insertion point right before the closing image tag for the banner, then type this code: **style="border:0"**.

   g. Save all pages, then preview the newsletter page in the browser, testing all links. Refer to Figure F-32 to check your work.

FIGURE F-32

Gardening Matters

Welcome, fellow gardeners. My name is Cosie Simmons, the owner of Blooms & Bulbs. My passion has always been my gardens. Ever since I was a small child, I was drawn to my back yard where all varieties of beautiful plants flourished. A lush carpet of thick grass bordered with graceful beds is truly a haven for all living creatures. With proper planning and care, your gardens will draw a variety of birds and butterflies and become a great pleasure to you.

Gardening Issues

There are several areas to concentrate on when formulating your landscaping plans. One is your grass. Another is the number and variety of trees you plant. The third is the combination of plants you select. All of these decisions should be considered in relation to the climate in your area. Be sure and check out our gardening tips before you begin work.

Grass

Lawn experts classify grass into two categories: cool-climate and warm-climate. The northern half of the United States would be considered cool-climate. Examples of cool-climate grass are Kentucky bluegrass and ryegrass. Bermuda grass is a warm-climate grass. Before planting grass, whether by seeding, sodding, sprigging, or plugging, the ground must be properly prepared. The soil should be tested for any nutritional deficiencies and cultivated. Come by or call to make arrangements to have your soil tested. When selecting a lawn, avoid letting personal preferences and the cost of establishment be the overriding factors. Ask yourself these questions. What type of lawn are you expecting? What level of maintenance are you willing to provide? What are the site limitations?

Trees

Before you plant trees, you should evaluate your purpose. Are you interested in shade, privacy, or color? Do you want to attract wildlife? Attract birds? Create a shady play area? Your purpose will determine what variety of tree you should plant. Of course, you also need to consider your climate and available space. Shape is especially important in selecting trees for ornamental and shade purposes. Abundant shade comes from tall trees with long spreading or weeping branches. Ornamental trees will not provide abundant shade. We carry many varieties of trees and are happy to help you make your selections to fit your purpose.

Plants

There are so many types of plants available that it can become overwhelming. Do you want border plants, shrubs, ground covers, annuals, perennials, vegetables, fruits, vines, or bulbs? In reality, a combination of several of these works well. Design aspects such as balance, flow, definition of space and focalization should be considered. Annuals provide brilliant bursts of color in the garden. By selecting flowers carefully to fit the conditions of the site, it is possible to have a beautiful display without an unnecessary amount of work. Annuals are also great as fresh and dry cut flowers. Perennials can greatly improve the quality of your landscape. Perennials have come and gone in popularity, but today are as popular as ever. Water plants are also quite popular now. We will be happy to help you sort out your preferences and select a harmonious combination of plants for you.

Further Research

These are some of my favorite gardening links. Take the time to browse through some of the information they offer, then give me a call at (555) 248-0806 or e-mail me at cosie@blooms4bulbs.com.

National Gardening Association
Organic Gardening
Southern Living

© 2013 Cengage Learning
Original photos courtesy of Sherry Bishop

Skills Review (continued)

11. Manage website links.

 a. Recreate the Site Cache, then use the Check Links Sitewide command to view broken links, external links, and orphaned files.

 b. Refresh the Site list in the Files panel if you see broken links or orphaned files. If any exist, locate them, analyze them, then correct any errors you find.

 c. View the external links in the Assets panel. Exit (Win) or Quit (Mac) Dreamweaver.

Important: *If you did not create the following websites in Unit B and maintain them during the preceding units, you must create a local site root folder for the websites in the following exercises and define the websites using files your instructor will provide. See the "Read This Before You Begin" section for more detailed instructions.*

Independent Challenge 1

You have been hired to create a website for a river expedition company named Rapids Transit, located on the Buffalo River in Gilbert, Arkansas. In addition to renting canoes, kayaks, and rafts, they have lodging available for overnight stays. River guides are available to accompany clients on float trips. The owner's name is Mike Andrew. Mike has asked you to create a new web page that lists helpful links for his customers. Refer to Figure F-33 as you work on this page.

 a. Start Dreamweaver, then open the Rapids Transit website.

 b. Open dwf_3.html in the drive and folder where you store your Unit F Data Files, then save it as **before.html**, replacing the existing file and without updating the links. You need to save the young_paddler.gif file (the photo) in the assets folder of the Rapids Transit website, then correct the path for the banner if necessary.

 c. Close the dwf_3.html file.

 d. Create the following links for the links listed on the page:

  Buffalo National River   http://www.nps.gov/buff/

  Arkansas, the Natural State   http://www.arkansas.com/

  Buffalo River Floater's Guide   http://www.ozarkmtns.com/buffalo/index.asp

 e. Attach the rapids_transit.css style sheet, apply the body_text style to all text on the page, then apply the img_left_float rule to the young_paddler image.

Independent Challenge 1 (continued)

f. Design a Spry menu bar for the page using your choice of settings. The menu bar should include the following items: Home, Our Guides, Rates, Lodging, and Before You Go. Link the menu items to the appropriate files in your Rapids Transit site. Delete all submenus. (Remember to create a new Tag rule in the rapids_transit.css file to modify the `<img>` tag as follows: Block Vertical-align:bottom.)

g. Copy the completed menu bar to the guides, index, and lodging pages. Preview each page in the browser window to make sure the menu bar doesn't "jump," or shift position, when you move from page to page. (*Hint*: If you are having problems with spacing issues, look for stray `<p>`, `<br>`, or heading tags on your pages and remove them if necessary.)

h. Save your work, then test all links in your browser window.

i. Run reports for locate any broken links or orphaned files, then correct any that exist.

j. Exit your browser, then close all files and exit Dreamweaver.

FIGURE F-33

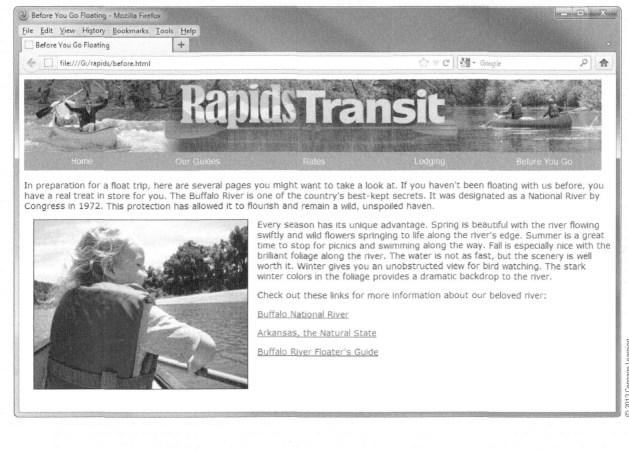

© 2013 Cengage Learning
Original photos courtesy of Sherry Bishop

Independent Challenge 2

Your company is designing a new website for TripSmart, a travel outfitter. TripSmart specializes in travel products and services. In addition to selling travel products, such as luggage and accessories, they sponsor trips and offer travel advice. Their clients range from college students to families to vacationing professionals. You are now ready to work on the services page. This page will include several helpful links for clients to use when planning trips.

a. Start Dreamweaver, then open the TripSmart site.

b. Open the file dwf_4.html from the drive and folder where you store your Unit F Data Files, save it as **services.html** in the tripsmart local site root folder, replacing the existing file but not updating the links, then close dwf_4.html.

c. Apply the Heading 1 format from the attached style sheet to the four paragraph headings, then apply the body_text style to the rest of the text on the page.

d. Create the following links using the text in the unordered list at the bottom of the page:

CNN Travel Channel	http://www.cnn.com/TRAVEL
US Department of State	http://travel.state.gov
Yahoo! Currency Converter	http://finance.yahoo.com/currency-converter
The Weather Channel	http://www.weather.com

e. Create named anchors called **reservations**, **outfitters**, **tours**, and **links** in front of the respective headings on the page, then link each named anchor to "Reservations," "Travel Outfitters," "Escorted Tours," and "Helpful Links in Travel Planning" (respectively) in the first paragraph.

f. Create a Spry menu bar that links to the home, tours, newsletter, services, and catalog pages, replacing any existing menu bars. Delete all submenus.

g. Copy the menu bar to the other completed pages in the website: index, newsletter, and tours pages, replacing any existing menu bars. (*Hint*: If you are having problems with spacing issues, look for stray <p>, <br>, or heading tags on your pages and remove them if necessary.)

h. Add a new Tag rule in the tripsmart_styles.css file to set the Vertical-align for images to bottom.

i. Use the Link Checker to check for broken links and orphaned files.

J. Save any unsaved changes, preview the services page in the browser window, as shown in Figure F-34, then test all links.

k. Exit your browser, then close all files and exit Dreamweaver.

FIGURE F-34

TripSmart has several divisions of customer service to assist you in planning and making reservations for your trip, shopping for your trip wardrobe and providing expert guide services. Give us a call and we will be happy to connect you with one of the following departments: Reservations, Travel Outfitters, or Escorted Tours. If you are not quite ready to talk with one of our departments and would prefer doing some of your own research first, may we suggest beginning with our Helpful Links in Travel Planning.

Reservations

Our Reservations Department is staffed with five Certified Travel Agents, each of whom is eager to assist you in making your travel plans. They have specialty areas in Africa, the Caribbean, South America, Western Europe, Eastern Europe, Asia, Antarctica, and Hawaii and the South Pacific. They also specialize in Senior Travel, Family Travel, Student Travel, and Special Needs Travel. Call us at *(555) 848-0807* extension 75 or e-mail us at *Reservations* to begin making your travel plans now. We will be happy to send you brochures and listings of Internet addresses to help you get started. We are open from 8:00 a.m. until 6:00 p.m. CST.

Travel Outfitters

Our travel outfitters are seasoned travelers that have accumulated a vast amount of knowledge in appropriate travel clothing and accessories for specific destinations. Climate and seasons, of course, are important factors in planning your wardrobe for a trip. Area customs should also be taken in consideration so as not to offend the local residents with inappropriate dress. When traveling abroad, we always hope that our customers will represent our country well as good ambassadors. If they can be comfortable and stylish at the same time, we have succeeded! Our clothing is all affordable and packs well on long trips. Most can be washed easily in a hotel sink and hung to drip-dry overnight. Browse through our on-line catalog, then give us a call at *(555) 433-7844* extension 85. We will also be happy to mail you a catalog of our extensive collection of travel clothing and accessories.

Escorted Tours

Our Escorted Tours department is always hard at work planning the next exciting destination to offer our TripSmart customers. We have seven professional tour guides that accompany our guests from the United States point of departure to their point of return.

Our current feature package tour is to Spain. Our local escort is Don Eugene. Don has traveled Spain extensively and enjoys sharing his love for this exciting country with others. He will be assisted after arrival in Spain with the services of archeologist JoAnne Rife, anthropologist Christina Elizabeth, and naturalist Iris Albert. Call us at *(555) 848-0807* extension 95 for information on the Spain trip or to learn about other destinations being currently scheduled.

Helpful Links in Travel Planning

The following links may be helpful in your travel research. Happy surfing!

- CNN Travel Channel - News affecting travel plans to various destinations
- US Department of State - Travel warnings, passport information, and more
- Yahoo! Currency Converter - Calculate the exchange rate between two currencies
- The Weather Channel - Weather, flight delays, and driving conditions

© 2013 Cengage Learning

Dr. Joan Sullivent's patients often ask her questions about the current treatment protocol for Parkinson's disease, a debilitating neurological disease. She would like to post some helpful links in her clinic website to provide information for her patients. She begins her research at the National Institutes of Health website.

a. Connect to the Internet, then go to the National Institutes of Health website at nih.gov.

b. What do you like or dislike about the menu links?

c. Note the placement and appearance of the menu bar. Does it use text, images, or a combination of the two to form the links?

d. Using your favorite search engine, locate at least five helpful links that Dr. Sullivent should consider for her site, including the National Institutes of Health site pictured in Figure F-35.

FIGURE F-35

National Institutes of Health website (nih.gov)

Real Life Independent Challenge

This assignment will continue to build on the personal website that you created in Unit B. In Unit C you created and developed your index page. In Unit D you added a page with either an ordered or an unordered list, and a CSS style sheet with a minimum of two styles. In Unit E you added a page that included at least two images. In this lesson, you work with one of the other pages in your site.

a. Consult your wireframe and decide which page you would like to develop in this lesson.

b. Create content for this page and format the text attractively on the page using styles.

c. Add at least three external links to this page.

d. Think about a creative use for an image map, then add it to the page.

e. Add at least one named anchor and link to it.

f. Design a menu bar linking to the main pages of your site, then copy it to all of the main pages.

g. Save the file, then preview the page in the browser window.

After you are satisfied with your work, verify the following:

a. Each completed page has a page title.

b. All links work correctly.

c. The completed pages display correctly using a screen resolution of 1024 × 768.

d. All images are properly set showing a path to the website assets folder.

e. All images have alternate text and are legal for you to use.

f. The Link Checker shows no broken links or orphaned files. If there are orphaned files, note your plan to link them.

Visual Workshop

You are continuing your work on the Carolyne's Creations website that you started in Unit B and developed in subsequent units. Chef Carolyne has asked you to create pages describing her cooking classes offered every month. Use the following files for the tasks noted: dwf_5.html to replace the classes.html page; dwf_6.html to create a new children.html page; and dwf_7.html to create a new adults.html page. (Remember not to update the links when prompted.) Copy all new images, including the new banner, cc_banner_with_text.jpg, to the assets folder in the website. Next, create an image map at the bottom of the banner on the classes page with hotspots for each link, add the code **style="border:0"** to the image tag for the banner to prevent a blue outline appearing around the banner in Internet Explorer, and copy it to all pages in the website, replacing all existing menu bars. Create an email link on the classes page using the text "Sign me up!" and carolyne@carolynescreations.com for the link. Create links in the last sentence to the adults' and children's pages, as shown in Figure F-36. Refer to Figures F-36, F-37, and F-38 as you complete this project. Check that each completed page uses styles from the cc_styles.css file, and attach and apply these styles if you find pages without styles. The second image in Figure F-36 was aligned by creating a new rule based on the rule you created in Unit E, but with a different float property. (*Hint*: Remember to remove any formatting around the banners to prevent any pages from appearing to "jump.") Check for broken links and orphaned files. You will see that the former banner, cc_banner.jpg, is now an orphaned file.

FIGURE F-36

FIGURE F-37

© 2013 Cengage Learning
Original photo courtesy of Sherry Bishop

FIGURE F-38

© 2013 Cengage Learning
Original photo courtesy of Sherry Bishop

Using CSS and Tables to Position Content

Files You Will Need:

To view a list of files needed for this unit, see the Data Files Grid in the back of the book.

You have learned how to position elements on a web page using alignment and paragraph settings. These settings let you create simple web pages, but they limit your design choices. The preferred method to position page elements is to use Cascading Style Sheets (CSS). You have already learned to use CSS to format individual page elements. Now you will learn to use CSS to place your content on pages using divs. With CSS layouts, you use blocks of content formatted with CSS rules to place information on web pages. Once you've completed this book, you will have the skills and understanding to efficiently design sites built entirely with CSS. You will also learn to use CSS to position data in tables. In this unit, you use a predesigned CSS layout with divs to create the cafe page for The Striped Umbrella website. You will add a table to the page to list the restaurant hours.

OBJECTIVES

Understand CSS layouts

Create a page using CSS layouts

Add content to CSS layout blocks

Edit content in CSS layout blocks

Edit CSS layout properties

Understand table modes

Insert a table and set table properties

Merge and split table cells

Insert and align images in table cells

Add text

Format and modify cell content

Format cells

Adobe product screenshot(s) reprinted with permission from Adobe Systems Incorporated.

Understanding CSS Layouts

Web pages built with Cascading Style Sheets use div tags to place and format page content. **Div tags** are HTML code segments that set the appearance and position of blocks of web page content. Think of div tags as building blocks. To build a web page with a layout based on CSS, you begin by placing div tags on the page to set up the framework to position the page content. Divs, the page elements created with div tags, can also be referred to as layout blocks, elements, or containers. Next, you add content and format the divs to position them on the page. For beginning designers, the predesigned CSS layouts that are available with Dreamweaver CS6 make creating pages based on CSS easy. You simply choose a predesigned CSS layout, and Dreamweaver places the div tags in the page code for you. [image] You spend some time researching how style sheets are used for page layout.

DETAILS

Before using CSS layouts for page layout, you review the following concepts:

- **Using CSS vs. tables for page layout**

  Table were used previously by designers to position content on web pages. With CSS, designers have moved to positioning most page content with CSS layouts. Tables are still used for some layout purposes, such as placing tabular data on a page. Divs generate pages that are more compliant with current accessibility standards.

QUICK TIP

The Dreamweaver predesigned layouts have been tested using several different browsers.

- **Using Dreamweaver CSS page layouts**

  Dreamweaver offers 18 predesigned layouts in the New Document dialog box, as shown in Figure G-1. These layouts are a great way to learn how to create page layouts based on CSS. As you select each option, a preview of the layout appears on the right side of the New Document dialog box with a description below it. Once you select a layout, you can modify it to fit your needs. The two newest HTML5 page layouts use either a two column or three column layout. These layouts include new HTML tags to support semantic markup such as <section>, < header>, <footer>, <article>, and <aside>. Divs used for page layout are identified by an ID, or name. When the div tag is selected, the ID displays in both the HTML code for the div tag in the Property inspector, and in the CSS Styles panel. In Code view, the code for a div tag named header would be <div id="header">.

- **Using AP divs**

  One type of div is an AP div. AP stands for absolutely positioned, so an **AP div** has a specified position that doesn't change even when viewed in different-sized windows. An AP div creates a container called an **AP element**. You create an AP div by drawing the container with the Draw AP Div button, as shown in Figure G-2. When you create an AP div, a CSS rule is automatically created to apply the property values that determine its size and appearance on the page. You can stack AP divs on top of each other to create interesting effects such as animations. You can also use them to show or hide content on the page by using them with JavaScript behaviors. **JavaScript behaviors** are action scripts that allow you to add dynamic content to your web pages. **Dynamic content** is content that changes either in response to certain conditions or through interaction with the user. For example, the user might enter a zip code to display a local weather forecast. The code in the JavaScript behavior would direct the AP element with the correct forecast to appear after the user enters the corresponding zip code in a text box.

- **Using HTML5 and CSS**

  HTML has been in existence since the 1990s, but it wasn't until 1997 that the then current version, HTML4, became a W3C recommendation. HTML5 introduced new ways to add interactivity and tags that support semantic markup, such as the <nav> tag used for navigation links. Semantic markup refers to coding to convey meaning to other computer programs such as search engines. Semantics, or the meanings of words, when used with syntax, or the actual words and sentence structure, allows the computer to no longer just "read" words, but understand the meaning behind the words. HTML5 also introduces markup for Web applications (apps), an exploding sector of Web development. Other HTML5 tags include <header>, <footer>, <article>, <audio>, <section> and <video>. HTML5 is still a work in progress, but most modern browsers support it.

FIGURE G-1: New Document dialog box

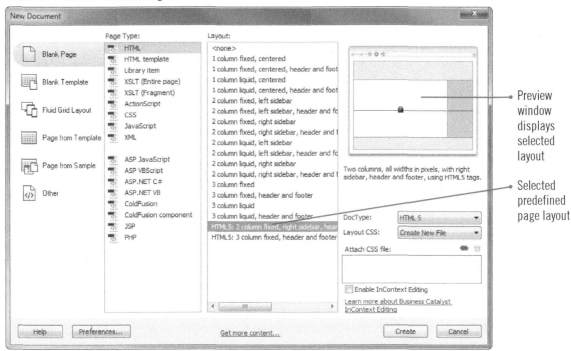

FIGURE G-2: Inserting an AP div Tag using the Draw AP Div button

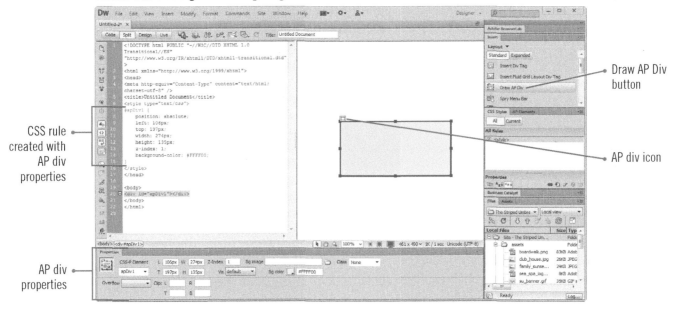

Using Dreamweaver sample pages

You can use either the Welcome Screen or the New Document dialog box, shown in Figure G-1, to create several different types of pages. The predesigned CSS page layouts make it easy for you to design accessible web pages using CSS without being an expert in HTML code. In the Page from Sample category, CSS Style Sheet and Mobile Starters are options that create pages you can use as starting points to develop pages for mobile devices and style sheets. Another choice in the New Document dialog box is the **Fluid Grid Layout**. This layout is used for designing adaptive websites based on a single fluid grid. It is worth the time to explore each category to understand what is available to you as a designer. Once you have selected a sample page, you can customize it to fit your needs and the site design. You can also find a variety of sample pages, or templates, on the Internet. Some sites offer templates free of charge, while others make templates available for purchase.

Creating a Page Using CSS Layouts

With the predesigned CSS layouts available in Dreamweaver, it is easy to create a page using CSS. After you choose a layout for a new page, the page opens with placeholder text displayed in the divs until you replace it with your content. Some divs not only have placeholder text, but also instructional text on how to modify the default settings, such as replacing a placeholder image with your image. Each div has preset styles applied. The properties and values of these styles are displayed in the CSS Styles panel, where you can modify them to fit your needs. Table G-1 lists some of the properties you can use to format divs. Dreamweaver's predesigned CSS layouts include one-, two-, and three-column layouts. Some layouts contain features such as sidebars, headers, and footers, and some are designed with a fixed width, while others are designed to stretch across a browser window. ▰▰▰▰ You decide to create the cafe page for the Striped Umbrella website based on a predesigned CSS HTML5 layout.

STEPS

1. **Start Dreamweaver, open The Striped Umbrella website, then switch to Design view if necessary**

2. **Click File on the Menu bar, click New, verify that Blank Page is highlighted in the left section, click HTML in the Page Type column if necessary, then click HTML5: 2 column fixed, right sidebar, header and footer in the Layout column, as shown in Figure G-3**
   The layout description confirms that this is a fixed layout, measured in pixels. The preview of this page layout is displayed in the preview window. A **fixed layout** has columns expressed in pixels and will not change width when viewed in different window sizes. A **liquid layout** has columns expressed as percents based on the browser window width, so it will change width according to the dimensions of the browser window.

3. **If "Create New File" does not appear in the Layout CSS text box, click the Layout CSS list arrow, click Create New File, then if the su_styles.css file is shown in the Attach CSS file text box in the New Document dialog box, skip to Step 6. If not, click the Attach Style Sheet button 🌐 in the lower-right corner of the dialog box, then click Browse in the Attach External Style Sheet dialog box**
   The Select Style Sheet File dialog box opens.

4. **Click the su_styles.css file in the Select Style Sheet File dialog box, click OK (Win) or Open (Mac), then click OK to close the Dreamweaver confirmation box about the document-relative path**
   The links will not be document-relative until the page is saved in the website.

5. **Verify that the Add as: Link option button is selected in the Attach External Style Sheet dialog box, then click OK**
   The su_styles.css file is attached to the new page, as shown in Figure G-4.

QUICK TIP
The CSS blocks each have a different color background to help you see how the blocks are arranged on the page.

6. **Click Create in the New Document dialog box, verify that the HTML5_twoColFixRtHdr.css file will be saved in the striped_umbrella local site folder in the Save Style Sheet File As dialog box, then click Save to close the Save Style Sheet File As dialog box. Open the CSS Styles panel if necessary, then expand the HTML5_twoColFixRtHdr.css and su_styles.css style sheets**
   A new page opens based on the predesigned CSS layout with blocks of placeholder content as shown in Figure G-5. It contains two columns, as well as a header and footer. Heading formats have been applied to the placeholder headings. There are two style sheets in the CSS Styles panel: the su_styles.css file you imported and the HTML5_twoColFixRtHdr.css style sheet file that was created to format the predesigned page layout.

7. **Save the file as cafe.html, overwriting the existing file**

FIGURE G-3: Predefined layout selected for new page

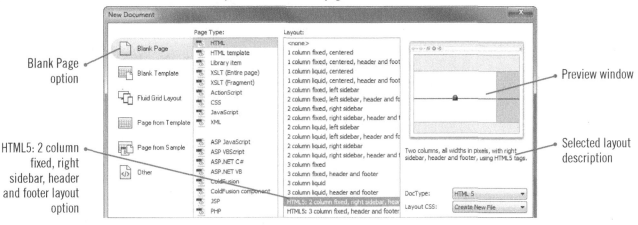

Blank Page option

HTML5: 2 column fixed, right sidebar, header and footer layout option

Preview window

Selected layout description

FIGURE G-4: The su_styles.css file attached to the new page

Choose Create New File

Layout CSS list arrow

Attach Style Sheet button

Attached su_styles.css file

FIGURE G-5: New page based on CSS HTML5 layout with placeholder content

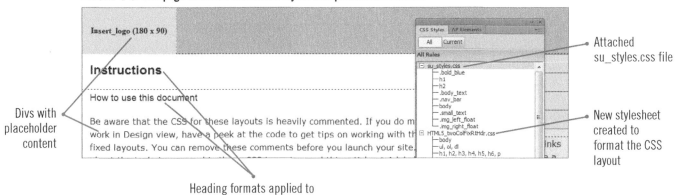

Divs with placeholder content

Attached su_styles.css file

New stylesheet created to format the CSS layout

Heading formats applied to placeholder headings

TABLE G-1: Div tag properties

property	function
ID	Displays the name used to identify the div in the code
Class	Displays the class style currently applied to the div
Float	Sets the float, or position, of the div in relation to adjacent elements as left, right, none, or inherit
Position	Sets the position of the div as absolute, fixed, relative, static, or inherit
Top	Sets the div position in relation to the top of the page or parent element
Right	Sets the right position of the div as either auto or inherit
Bottom	Sets the bottom position of the div as either auto or inherit
Left	Sets the div position in relation to the left side of the page or parent element
Width	Sets the width of the div, in pixels by default
Height	Sets the height of the div, in pixels by default
Overflow	Controls how the div will appear in the browser if the content is larger than the div

Adding Content to CSS Layout Blocks

A page built with all content placed inside divs makes it easy to apply formatting to all page elements. The div style properties and values set background and text colors, container widths, font settings, and alignment settings that are used to format all the images, links, tables, and text. Div styles also determine the content's position on the page. If you have developed your page content already, you can easily copy and paste it into the divs, replacing the placeholder content. **You are ready to place the banner, menu bar, text, and images on the page, replacing the placeholder content.

STEPS

1. **Select all content between the Header and Footer in the main section, as shown in Figure G-6, then press** [Delete]

2. **Change to the HTML Property inspector, click the Format list arrow, then click Paragraph**
   Changing the format to paragraph removed the h1 tag that was left in the content div.

3. **Import the Word document cafe.doc from the drive and folder where you store your Unit G Data Files (Win) or copy and paste it (Mac) at the insertion point**
   The paragraph appears in a div on the new page, replacing the placeholder text. This div is named content.

   QUICK TIP
   Be careful not to delete the beginning and ending div tags.

4. **Switch to Code view, select the code between the beginning and end of the <div class="sidebar1"> tag, as shown in Figure G-7, then press** [Delete]

5. **Return to Design view, then type Reservations are recommended for Beach 25 (our main dining room) during the peak summer season. at the insertion point**

   QUICK TIP
   Press [Ctrl][Tab] to switch between two open pages.

6. **Delete all of the text in the footer block, type Copyright 2002 - 2015 The Striped Umbrella, as shown in Figure G-8, then save your work**

7. **Open the index page and copy both the banner and the menu bar, then close the index page**

   QUICK TIP
   If you struggle with the placement of the banner and menu bar, use Code view to copy the code from the index page then paste it into the code for the cafe page.

8. **Click the placeholder logo image on the cafe page, then paste the banner and menu bar in its place**

9. **Place the insertion point at the end of the paragraph ending with "poolside.", enter a paragraph break, insert cafe_photo.jpg from the assets folder in the drive and folder where you save your Unit G Data Files, then type Sand Crab Cafe photo for the alternate text**
   The content is placed on the page, replacing all placeholder content, as shown in Figure G-9.

Design Matters

Understanding selector types

When you have a mixture of style classifications—embedded styles, external styles, and styles-redefining HTML tags—there is an order of precedence that is followed. Styles are ranked in order of precedence as they are applied to page elements, thus the name "cascading style sheets." The first order of precedence is to find declarations that match the media type being used, such as a computer monitor. The second order of precedence is by importance and origin. The third order of preference is by specificity of

the selector. **Pseudo class styles**, styles that determine the appearance of a page element when certain conditions are met, are considered as normal class styles. Sometimes styles with common formatting properties are grouped together to help reduce the size of style sheets. These styles are called **group selectors**.

Another type of selector is called a **descendant selector**. A descendant selector includes two or more selectors that form a relationship and are separated by white space.

FIGURE G-6: Selected placeholder text in the new cafe page

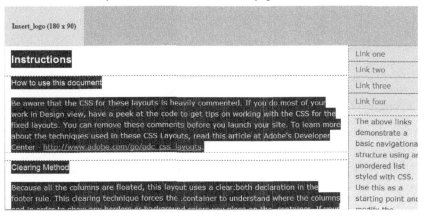

FIGURE G-7: Deleting the sidebar placeholder text

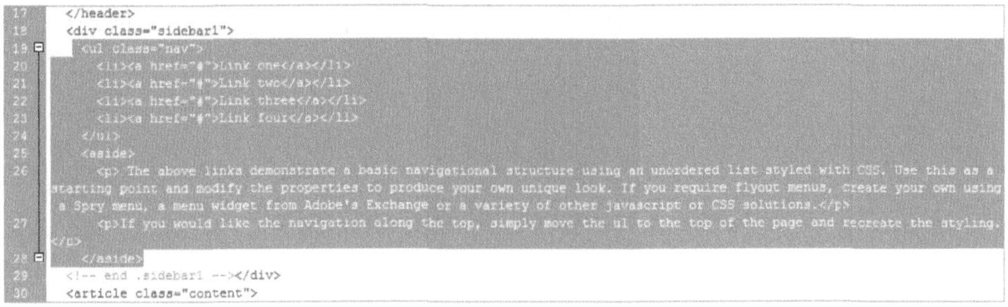

```
17    </header>
18    <div class="sidebar1">
19      <ul class="nav">
20        <li><a href="#">Link one</a></li>
21        <li><a href="#">Link two</a></li>
22        <li><a href="#">Link three</a></li>
23        <li><a href="#">Link four</a></li>
24      </ul>
25      <aside>
26        <p> The above links demonstrate a basic navigational structure using an unordered list styled with CSS. Use this as a
      starting point and modify the properties to produce your own unique look. If you require flyout menus, create your own using
      a Spry menu, a menu widget from Adobe's Exchange or a variety of other javascript or CSS solutions.</p>
27        <p>If you would like the navigation along the top, simply move the ul to the top of the page and recreate the styling.
    </p>
28      </aside>
29      <!-- end .sidebar1 --></div>
30      <article class="content">
```

FIGURE G-8: New text for content, sidebar, and footer divs

New text for content div

New text for sidebar div

New text for footer div

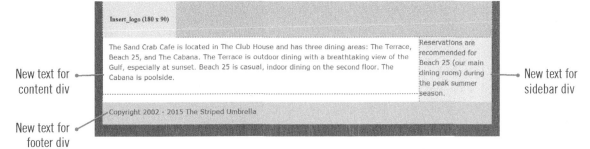

FIGURE G-9: Content added to cafe page

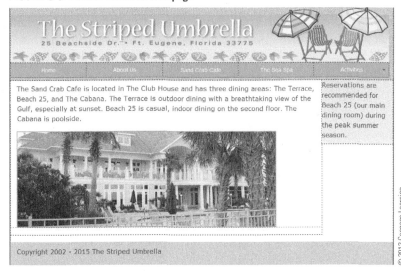

© 2013 Cengage Learning
Original photo courtesy of Sherry Bishop

Editing Content in CSS Layout Blocks

After you replace placeholder content in divs with your website's content, you will probably want to adjust some of the formatting. Styles that you have previously applied might conflict with the div styles, so you may want to remove redundant style properties, such as font and alignment settings. It is generally better to use an external style sheet to format text, to provide consistency across the site. External style sheets use global styles. **Global styles** are styles used to apply common properties for certain page elements, such as text, links, or backgrounds. When you have styles that are defined in both the external style sheet that you created for your site and an external style sheet that was imported into your site after you created a new page based on a predesigned layout, you should evaluate which styles makes the most sense to use, based on the content each is intended to format. The styles for the div tags determine the placement and appearance of the divs, so analyze them carefully before you modify them. ▨▨▨ You continue to work on the new cafe page. You edit the rules for some of the divs to improve the appearance of the content within the divs.

STEPS

1. **Click the .sidebar1 rule in the HTML5_twoColFixRtHdr.css file in the CSS Styles panel, click the Edit Rule button 🖉, click the Block category, click the Text-align list arrow, then click center**
   You can also double-click a rule name to open the rule for editing.

QUICK TIP
You can enter either #FFFFFF or #FFF (the shorthand version).

2. **Click the Box category, change the Float from right to left, click the Background category, change the background color to #FFF, then click OK**
   The sidebar background changes to white, it moves to the left side of the page, and the text is centered inside the div, as shown in Figure G-10.

QUICK TIP
You can edit rule properties in either the CSS Styles Properties pane or by opening the CSS Rule definition dialog box.

3. **Click the header rule in the HTML5_twoColFixRtHdr.css file in the CSS Styles panel to select it, click the Edit Rule button 🖉, click the Background category, change the background color to #FFF, click the Box category, type 5 in the Top Margin text box, verify that the Same for all check box is checked, as shown in Figure G-11, then click OK**
   With the margins added, the banner and menu bar are centered in the header div and the div background is now white.

4. **Click the footer rule in the HTML5_twoColFixRtHdr.css file in the CSS Styles panel to select it, click the Edit Rule button 🖉, click the Background category, change the background color to #FFF, click the Block category, change the Text-align to center, then click OK**
   The footer text is now centered in the footer div with a white background, as shown in Figure G-12.

5. **Save your work**

Using CSS to organize web page layout

You can also use CSS3 to organize content by creating tabs, drop-down menus, and accordions. **Tabs** look similar to file folder tabs and are used for navigation above the top of the page content. You click a tab to display information. **Accordions**, also used for navigation, are buttons that, when clicked, open up like an accordion to display information that drops down below the button. Clicking the button again closes it. These features do not require images or JavaScript to work, but incorporate the animation capabilities of CSS3.

FIGURE G-10: **Editing the properties of the .sidebar1 rule**

© 2013 Cengage Learning

Sidebar moves to left side of the
page, has a white background,
and the content is centered

FIGURE G-11: **Modifying the header rule**

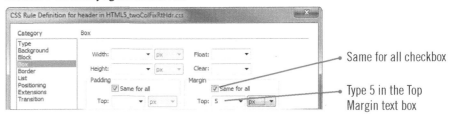

Same for all checkbox

Type 5 in the Top
Margin text box

FIGURE G-12: **Viewing the footer after editing the footer rule**

Banner and menu bar
are centered using
margin settings for the
header rule

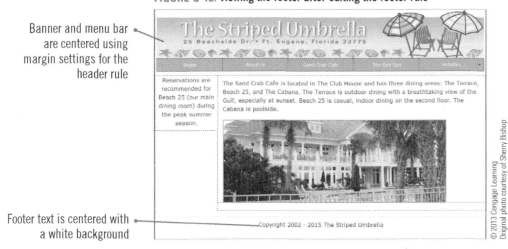

Footer text is centered with
a white background

© 2013 Cengage Learning
Original photo courtesy of Sherry Bishop

Using Visual Aids to work with divs

There are several options for viewing your divs in Design view. You can choose to show or hide outlines, temporarily assign different background colors to each individual div, or view the **CSS Layout Box Model** (padding and margins included) of a selected layout. To change these options, use the View > Visual Aids menu, and then select or deselect the CSS Layout Backgrounds, CSS Layout Box Model, or CSS Layout Outlines menu choice. You can also use the Visual Aids button on the Document toolbar.

Editing CSS Layout Properties

It is unlikely that you will find a predesigned CSS page layout that is exactly what you have in mind for your website. However, once you have created a page with a predesigned CSS layout, it is easy to modify the properties for individual rules to better fit your needs. Ideally, every page element should be formatted using style sheets rather than by applying individual formatting properties with the Property inspector. You can apply the rules in attached external style sheets to format individual page elements with global styles, such as text or horizontal rules. The styles generated by the CSS page layout control the formatting of the divs, including the div width and background color, but, as you have seen, they can also include formatting for the page elements within the divs. **●●▬▬** You continue working on the new cafe page by changing more div properties and the page properties.

1. **Select the body rule in the HTML5_twoColFixRtHdr.css file in the CSS Styles panel, click to select the existing background color in the Properties pane, type #FFF as shown in Figure G-13, then press [Enter] (Win) or [return] (Mac)**
   The body tag is used to format the page body—the area outside the divs. The body tag for the page is set to display a white background.

2. **Click .container in the HTML5_twoColFixRtHdr.css file in the CSS Styles panel, click the Edit rule button 🖉, then click the Border category**
   A border around the page sets it off from the extra space around it when it is viewed in a browser.

3. **Click the Top list arrow in the Style column, click solid, click the Top list arrow in the first text box in the Width column, click thin, click in the First color text box in the Color column, type #033, verify that the Same for all check box is selected in each of the three columns, compare your screen to Figure G-14, then click OK**
   The border properties for the container are set to include a thin solid line with a dark gray color.

4. **Type The Striped Umbrella Beach Resort and Spa, Ft. Eugene, Florida in the Title text box on the Document toolbar**

5. **Click to place the insertion point in front of the word "Reservations" in the sidebar, then enter a line break**

6. **Save your work, preview the page in the browser, compare your screen to Figure G-15, then close the browser**

FIGURE G-13: Editing the properties for the body rule

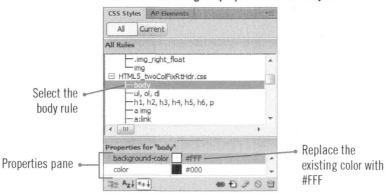

Select the
body rule

Properties pane

Replace the
existing color with
#FFF

FIGURE G-14: Editing the properties for the container rule

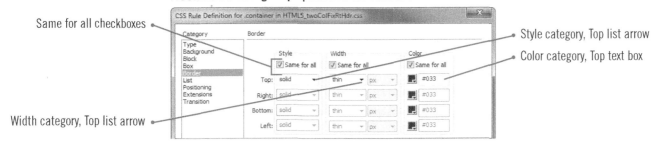

Same for all checkboxes

Width category, Top list arrow

Style category, Top list arrow

Color category, Top text box

FIGURE G-15: Viewing the new cafe page in the browser

Page title

Amount of body
showing differs in
wider or narrower
browser windows

Borders of
container div

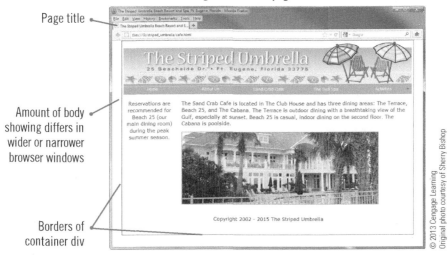

© 2013 Cengage Learning
Original photo courtesy of Sherry Bishop

Design Matters

Using the Adobe CSS Advisor and Adobe BrowserLab for cross-browser rendering issues

You can use the **Browser Compatibility Check (BCC)** feature to check for problematic CSS features that may render differently in multiple browsers. The BCC flags and rates code on three levels: an error that could cause a serious display problem; an error that probably won't cause a serious display problem; or a warning that unsupported code is present, but won't cause a serious display problem. Each bug is linked to the **CSS Advisor**, a part of the Adobe website that offers solutions for that particular bug and other helpful information for resolving any issues with your pages. To use the BCC feature, use the File > Check Page > Browser Compatibility command. Adobe also has an online service called **Adobe BrowserLab** that is a useful tool for cross-browser and cross-platform compatibility testing. Since Adobe BrowserLab is an online service, you can access it from any computer with an Internet connection, but you must have an Adobe ID to use the service. There is no charge to create an Adobe ID. To connect to Adobe BrowserLab, open the Adobe BrowserLab panel, then click Preview. The Adobe BrowserLab panel is located above the Insert panel. The panel contains two buttons: one to connect to the service to preview your pages, and one to choose whether you want to preview the local or server version of your pages.

Understanding Table Modes

Tables are placeholders made up of small boxes called **cells**, which you can use to insert data. Cells are arranged horizontally in rows and vertically in columns. There are two ways to insert a table in Dreamweaver. You can use the Table button in either the Common or Layout category on the Insert panel or use the Menu bar to access the Table commands. When you insert, edit, or format a table, you have a choice of two ways to view the table: Standard mode and Expanded Tables mode. **Standard mode** displays the table with no extra space added between the table cells. **Expanded Tables mode** is similar to Standard mode but has expanded table borders and temporary space between the cells to make it easier to work with individual cells. You choose the mode that you want by clicking the Standard mode button or the Expanded Tables mode button in the Layout category on the Insert panel. It is common to switch between modes as you work with tables in Dreamweaver. Expanded Tables mode is used most often when you are doing precise work with small cells that are difficult to select or move between. You can also use the Import Tabular Data command on the Insert > Table Objects menu to place an existing table with its data on a web page. ▓▓▓ You review the two modes for inserting and viewing tables using the Standard and Expanded Tables modes.

DETAILS

- ### Inserting a table in Standard mode

  To insert a table in Standard mode, you click the Standard mode button in the Layout category on the Insert panel, then click the Table button. You then enter values for the number of rows and columns, the table width, border thickness, cell padding, and cell spacing in the Table dialog box. The **width** refers to the distance across the table, which is expressed either in pixels or as a percentage of page width. This difference is significant. When expressed as a percentage, the table width adjusts to the width of the page in the browser window. When expressed in pixels, the table width does not change, regardless of the size of the browser window. The **border** is the outline or frame around the table and the individual cells. It is expressed in pixels. **Cell padding** is the distance between the cell content and the **cell walls**, the lines inside the cell borders. **Cell spacing** is the distance between cells. Figure G-16 shows an example of a table viewed in Standard mode. You may see the table dimensions at the top, rather than at the bottom, of the table on the open page.

- ### Viewing a table in Expanded Tables mode

  Expanded Tables mode lets you view a table with expanded table borders and temporary cell padding and cell spacing. Since table rows and columns appear magnified when viewed on the page, this mode makes it easier to see how many rows and columns you actually have in your table. It is often difficult, especially after splitting empty cells, to place the insertion point precisely in a table cell, because empty cells can be such small targets. The Expanded Tables mode lets you see each cell clearly. After you select a table item or place the insertion point, it's best to return to Standard mode to maintain the WYSIWYG environment. WYSIWYG is the acronym for "What You See Is What You Get." This means that your web page should look the same in the browser as it does in the web editor. You can toggle between the Expanded Tables mode and Standard mode by pressing [Alt] [F6] (Win) or [option][F6] (Mac). Figure G-17 shows an example of a table in Expanded Tables mode. You can also use the View > Visual Aids > command to hide or show table borders.

Using HTML table tags

When formatting a table, you should understand the basic HTML tags used to define it. The tags that define a table are `<table>` and `</table>`. The tags that define table rows are `<tr>` and `</tr>`. The tags that define table data cells are `<td>` and `</td>`. Dreamweaver places the ` ` code into each empty table cell at the time it is created. The ` ` code inserts a **nonbreaking space**; this is a space that appears in a fixed location to keep a line break from separating text into two lines or, in the case of table cells, to keep an empty cell from collapsing. Some browsers collapse an empty cell, which can ruin the look of a table. The nonbreaking space appears in the cell by default until it is replaced with content.

Using CSS and Tables to Position Content

FIGURE G-16: Table viewed in Standard mode

Layout category

Standard mode button

Table button

Selected table with no additional space between cells

Tag selector

Property inspector expanded to access cell properties

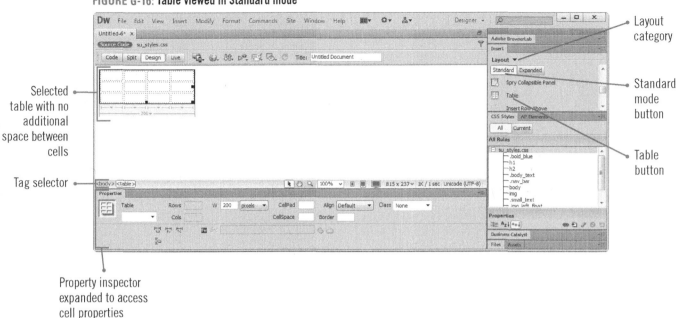

FIGURE G-17: Table viewed in Expanded Tables mode

Expanded Tables mode button

Increased space between table cells

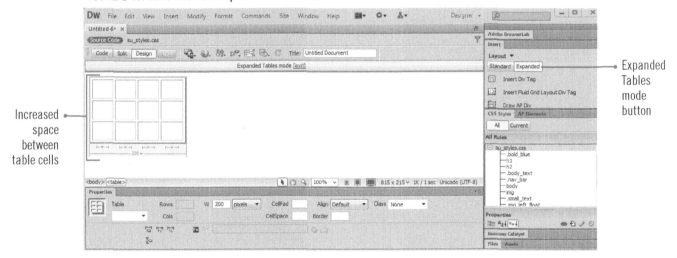

Design Matters

Placing the most important information first

People on the Internet are notoriously hurried and will often read only information that is located on the first screen that they see on a web page, rather than scroll though the entire length of the page. Therefore, it is a good idea to put the most important information at the top of the page. In other words, the most important information should be on the part of the page that is visible before you have to scroll to see the rest. You can use guides to emulate a newspaper fold line, which represents the place where a newspaper is folded. The most important stories are usually printed "above the fold." You create guides by clicking and dragging from the horizontal or vertical ruler, down or across the page.

Inserting a Table and Setting Table Properties

Before you begin creating a table, it is important to decide what information you want to convey and how you want to achieve the desired look. Writing or sketching an overall plan before you begin saves a lot of development time. If you plan to insert images into a table, you should first determine where you want them to appear. You should also consider whether you want the table borders and the cell walls to appear in the browser. If you make a table "invisible" by setting the border value to zero, the user will not be aware that you used a table to arrange the text or images on the page. You format tables with CSS rules, so if you decide to add a table border, be sure to use a style tag rather than the Property inspector or the Table dialog box. ▨▨▨▨ After consulting with the restaurant manager, you have a plan for adding the dining room hours to the page. You begin the process by creating a table with three columns and five rows.

STEPS

QUICK TIP

The Table command is also located in the Layout category of the Insert panel.

1. **With the insertion point to the right of the cafe photo, enter a paragraph break, then click Table in the Common category of the Insert panel**

   The Table dialog box opens.

QUICK TIP

The Table dialog box will retain settings from the last table that was inserted, so be sure to delete any settings that remain in the dialog box that you do not want to use.

2. **Type 5 in the Rows text box, 3 in the Columns text box, click Top in the Header section if necessary, type The Sand Crab Cafe Hours in the Caption text box, compare your screen to Figure G-18, then click OK**

   A table with five rows and three columns displays on the page. The table appears very small because the width for the table has not yet been set. You will define a new Tag Selector rule to use to format the table.

3. **Click the New CSS Rule button 🔲 in the CSS Styles panel, choose Tag (redefines an HTML element) in the Selector Type text box, type table in the Selector Name text box, choose su_styles.css in the Rule Definition list box, then click OK**

   This rule will format the only table in the website. The table appears left-aligned and the table caption appears at the top of the table by default.

4. **Click the Box category, type 600 in the Width text box, verify that px is the unit of measure, change the Float to left, then click OK**

   The <table> rule modified the table by setting the width and alignment on the page, as shown in Figure G-19.

Selecting a table

There are several ways to select a table in Dreamweaver. You can click the insertion point in the table, click Modify on the Menu bar, point to Table, then click Select Table. You can also select a table by moving the pointer slowly to the top or bottom edge of the table, then clicking the table border when the pointer changes to ⬚⊞. Finally, if the insertion point is inside the table, you can click <table> on the tag selector.

FIGURE G-18: Table dialog box

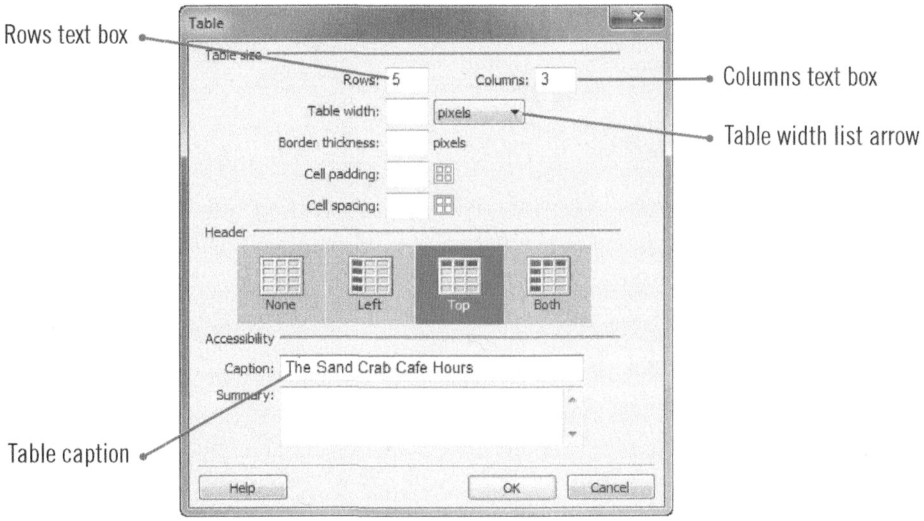

Rows text box

Columns text box

Table width list arrow

Table caption

FIGURE G-19: Table inserted and aligned in the div

Table caption

The Sand Crab Cafe Hours

Original photo courtesy of Sherry Bishop

Design Matters

Formatting Tables with HTML5 and CSS3

Many of the HTML codes used to format tables in HTML4 are now considered to be **deprecated,** or no longer within the current standard and in danger of becoming obsolete. Deprecated tags should be avoided. Deprecated HTML4 table tags include summary, cellpadding, cellspacing, align, width and bgcolor. Rather than format tables using the Table dialog box or the Property inspector, use CSS to format tables by creating a rules to modify table properties and table content. You can either add properties to the <table> tag itself or create new class rules

that can be assigned to specific tables. HTML5 tags you want to use are the <th> and <caption> tags. The table header <th> tag is a type of cell that contains header information. These are like column headings, and identify the content of the data cells below them. The caption <caption> tag is the caption, or title, of a table and describes the table content. These tags provide greater accessibility, as they are used by screen readers. They also add value as semantic markup because they help to label and describe table content.

Merging and Splitting Table Cells

In addition to resizing table columns and rows, you may need to adjust the table cells by splitting or merging them. **Splitting** a cell divides it into multiple rows or columns, while **merging** cells combines multiple adjacent cells into one cell. The ability to split and merge cells gives you more design flexibility for inserting images or text into your table. Merged cells are good placeholders for wide images or headings. For example, you could merge a row of cells to allot space for a heading. You can split merged cells and merge split cells. However, you can only merge cells that, when combined together, form the shape of a rectangle. When cells are merged, the HTML tag used to describe these cells changes from a width size tag to a column span or row span tag. You merge the top row of cells to make room for a heading across the table. You then split one cell to make room for a new image and its descriptive text in the first column. Finally, you merge four cells to create a larger area that will be used to describe room service availability.

STEPS

1. **Click to place the insertion point in the first cell in the top row, then drag the pointer to the right to select all three cells in the top row**

   A black border surrounds the cells, indicating that they are selected.

2. **Click the Merges selected cells using spans button ▣ in the Property inspector**

   The three cells are merged into one cell, as shown in Figure G-20. The heading will display nicely in this area.

3. **Place the insertion point in the first cell in the fifth row, then click the Splits cell into rows or columns button ⬚ in the Property inspector**

   The Split Cell dialog box opens. This is where you select the Rows or Columns option, then specify the number of rows or columns you want as a result of the split.

QUICK TIP

To create a new row identical to the one above it at the end of a table, place the insertion point in the last cell, then press [Tab].

4. **Click the Split cell into: Rows option button to select it if necessary, type 2 in the Number of rows text box if necessary, as shown in Figure G-21, then click OK**

   The dialog box closes, and the bottom-left cell is split into two rows. These rows will eventually contain the photograph of the featured dessert and its description.

5. **Click the Show Code view button ⬚ Code ⬚ on the Document toolbar**

   The code for the split and merged cells displays, as shown in Figure G-22. Table row and table column tags denote the column span and the nonbreaking spaces ( ) inserted in the empty cells. The tag <th colspan="3"> refers to the three top header cells that have been merged into one cell.

6. **Click the Show Design view button ⬚ Design ⬚ on the Document toolbar, select and merge the first cells in rows 2, 3, 4, and 5 in the left column, deselect the cell, compare your screen to Figure G-23, then save your work**

   With the table framework completed, the table is now ready for content.

Using nested tables

Inserting another table inside a cell within another table creates what is called a **nested table**. Nested tables can be used effectively when you want parts of your table data to contain both visible and invisible borders. For example, you can nest a table with red borders inside a table with invisible borders. The process of creating a nested table is similar to the one used to add a new row or column to a table. Simply click to place the insertion point inside the cell where you want the nested table to appear, click Insert on the Menu bar, then click Table, or click the Table button on the Insert panel. A nested table is separate from the original table so you can format it however you wish. The more nested tables you add, however, the more complicated the coding becomes, making it challenging to select and edit each table. You may be able to achieve the same results by adding rows and columns or splitting cells instead of inserting a nested table.

FIGURE G-20: Merging selected cells into one cell

Resulting merged cells

Merges selected cells using spans button

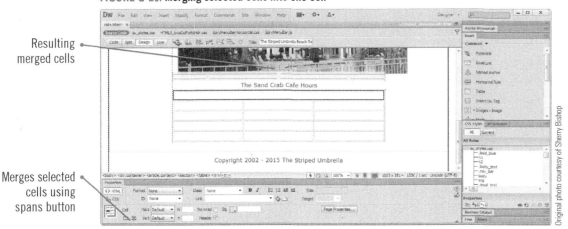

Original photo courtesy of Sherry Bishop

FIGURE G-21: Split Cell dialog box

Rows option button

Number of rows text box

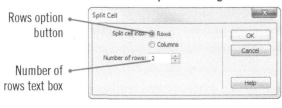

FIGURE G-22: Viewing the code for the merged and split cells

Opening table tag

Code for merged cells

Code for row with split cell

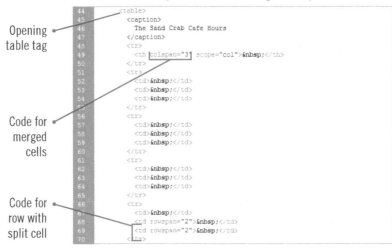

FIGURE G-23: Viewing the table after splitting and merging cells

Merged cells

Split cells

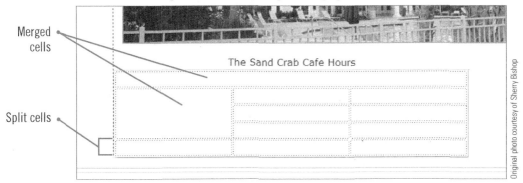

Original photo courtesy of Sherry Bishop

Adding and deleting rows and columns

As you add new content to your table, you may find that you have too many or not enough rows or columns. You can add or delete one row or column at a time or add several at once, using commands on the Modify menu. When you add a new column or row, you must first select an existing column or row to which the new column or row will be adjacent. The Insert Rows or Columns dialog box lets you choose how many rows or columns you want to insert and specify where you want them placed, relative to the selected row or column. To add a new row to the end of a table, simply press [Tab].

Inserting and Aligning Images in Table Cells

You can type, import, or paste text into table cells. You insert images into cells just as you would insert them on a page. Use CSS rules to align the cell content by either creating a rule you apply to the table cell or by creating a rule that you then apply to cell content. Do not use the Property inspector to align cell content or your code will not be HTML5 compliant. As you add content to cells, the cells expand in height to make room for the content. ~~~~~~~ You have a great photograph of a specialty chocolate cake that is featured in two of the dining areas. You insert the new image into the four merged cells in the first column of the table to add visual interest to the cafe page.

STEPS

QUICK TIP

The last button that was selected on the Insert panel becomes the default button that's used until you select another one.

1. **Click to place the insertion point in the first cell in the second row of the table (below the merged cells in the top row), change to the Common category on the Insert panel, if necessary, click the Images button list arrow, click Image, navigate to the drive and folder where you store your Unit G Data Files, then double-click chocolate_cake.jpg from the assets folder**

   The Image Tag Accessibility Attributes dialog box opens. This is where you add the alternate text for screen readers.

TROUBLE

If you do not see an alternate text dialog box, type the text in the Alt text box in the Property inspector.

2. **Type Chocolate Grand Marnier Cake in the alternate text box, click OK, then refresh the Files panel**

   The image of the chocolate cake displays in the merged cells and is saved in the website assets folder.

3. **Click to the right of the chocolate_cake image in the same cell to place the insertion point**

   You will now add code to the table cell with the cake image to center-align the contents of the cell.

TROUBLE

Be sure to click before the ending bracket>.

4. **Switch to Code view, then place the insertion point right after the code "<td rowspan="4"**

   This is the table cell that will be modified by adding a style to center-align the contents.

5. **Press the Spacebar to enter a space, then type style="text-align:center" as shown in Figure G-24**

   Notice how Dreamweaver helps you add code by providing **code hints**. Code hints is an auto-complete feature that displays lists of tags that appear as you type in Code view.

6. **Return to Design view, then save your work**

7. **Preview the page in your browser, view the table with the aligned image, as shown in Figure G-25, then close the browser**

   The image is still not in the exact position you intended. After you add more content to the table, the image will adjust to the correct position. You can also add rules to set the column widths in a table.

Using Live View to check pages

Live View is another option for previewing your pages. It is a quick way to see how your page will look without previewing the page in a browser window. Live View renders the page as though it were being viewed in a browser window with any active objects (such as a Spry menu bar) functioning. To use Live View, open a page in Design view, then click the Switch Design View to Live View button ⌊ Live ⌋. Remember, a page cannot be edited in Live View. You must exit Live View to be able to make changes to the page content.

FIGURE G-24: Aligning the contents of a single cell

```
45        <caption>
46          The Sand Crab Cafe Hours
47        </caption>
48        <tr>
49          <th colspan="3" scope="col"> </th>
50        </tr>
51        <tr>
52          <td rowspan="4" style="text-align:center"> <img src=
    "assets/chocolate_cake.jpg" width="110" height="84" alt="Chocolate Grand Marnier
    Cake"></td>
53          <td> </td>
54          <td> </td>
55        </tr>
```

Code added to
align table cell

FIGURE G-25: Viewing the table in a browser window

The table
borders are not
visible in the
browser

© 2013 Cengage Learning
Original photos courtesy of Sherry Bishop

Design Matters

Recognizing and addressing printing issues

There are many factors that affect how a page will print compared to how it displays in a browser window. While a page background color will display in a browser window, it will not print unless the print option to print background colors is selected by the user. Although the width of the page in the browser window may fit on the screen, it could actually be too wide to print on a standard printer in portrait orientation.

Also, table borders, horizontal rules, and CSS divs may not print exactly how they look in a browser. Printing your pages to see how they actually appear will allow you to address most of these issues. You can also go to a site, such as the World Wide web Consortium (W3C) at w3.org, to find the best solutions to any problems you identify.

Adding Text

You can enter text in table cells by typing it in the cell, copying it from another source and pasting it into the cell, or importing it into the cell from another program. You can then format the text for readability and appearance with CSS. If you import text from another program, you should use the Clean Up HTML or Clean Up Word HTML command to remove unnecessary code. ▰▰▰ You add a heading to the table and a caption for the chocolate cake image. You also add the hours of operation for the three dining areas in the second column. Finally, you include a short description of room service options as well.

TROUBLE

If you can't see the last lines you typed, click the `<div.container>` tag on the Tag selector to refresh the container size on the screen, resize the Dreamweaver application window, or close and reopen the page.

1. **Click in the first cell in the last row (below the chocolate cake image), type** Chocolate, **press [Shift] [Enter] (Win) or [shift] [return] (Mac) to add a line break, type** Grand Marnier, **add another line break, then type** Cake

   The text appears in the first cell in the last row below the chocolate cake image. The cell widths will change as you fill them with content. Don't be concerned about matching the figures exactly until you have completed inserting all content and set the table width.

2. **Click in the top row of the table, then type** Our individual dining areas are listed below:

   The header text appears centered and boldfaced in the table. Note that a header row in a table appears boldfaced and centered by default. Recall that the top row header was selected when the table was created. The caption appears above the table.

QUICK TIP

You can press [Tab] to move your insertion point to the next cell in a row, and press [Shift] [Tab] to move your insertion point to the previous cell.

3. **Enter the names for each dining area and its hours in rows 1 through 3, as shown in Figure G-26**

   The dining room areas and respective hours are listed in the table with the font properties from the body tag applied to them through the rules of inheritance. This means that if formatting is not specified for a child tag inside a parent tag, the parent tag properties and values will format the child tag content.

4. **Merge the second and third cells in the last row, then type the room service information from Figure G-26 with a line break after 12:00 a.m.**

   The room service hours are displayed at the bottom of the table.

TROUBLE

As you add content to the table, the data may not display correctly on the page. Clicking the `<table>` tag or resizing the screen refreshes the display and corrects this.

5. **Click the** `<table>` **tag on the Tag selector**

   The Room service information wraps to a second line, which looks a bit awkward. The width of the table could be extended to the right where there is more room.

6. **Click the** table rule **in the CSS Styles panel, click the** Edit rule button 🖉**, click the** Box category, **change the Box width to** 635 px, **click** OK, **then compare your screen to Figure G-27**

   The table is resized to 635 pixels wide, allowing room for the lengthy sentence to remain on one line.

7. **Save your work**

FIGURE G-26: Table with data entered

Top row header

Original photo courtesy of Sherry Bishop

FIGURE G-27: Increasing the width of the table to accommodate data

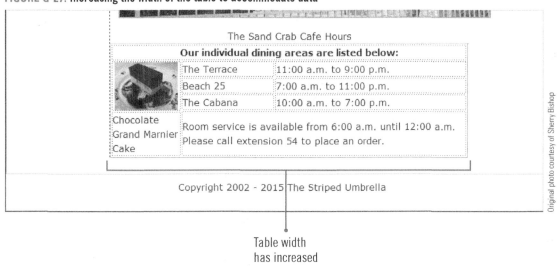

Original photo courtesy of Sherry Bishop

Table width has increased

Importing and exporting tabular data

You can import and export tabular data into and out of Dreamweaver. **Tabular data** is data that is arranged in columns and rows and separated by a **delimiter,** such as a comma, tab, colon, semicolon, or similar character, that tells Dreamweaver where to break the data into table cells. **Importing** means to bring data created in another software program into Dreamweaver, and **exporting** means to save data that was created in Dreamweaver in a different file format so that other programs can read it. Files containing tabular data that are imported into Dreamweaver must first be saved as delimited text files. Programs such as Microsoft Word and Excel offer many file formats for saving files, including saving as delimited text. To import a delimited file, click File on the Menu bar, point to Import, then click Tabular Data. The Import Tabular Data dialog box opens, offering you choices for the resulting table that will appear on the web page. To export a table that you created in Dreamweaver, click File on the Menu bar, point to Export, then click Table. The Export Table dialog box opens, letting you choose the type of delimiter and line breaks you want for the delimited file when you save it.

Formatting and Modifying Cell Content

You format cell content by changing the font, size, or color of the text by applying styles. You can also resize images placed in cells. If you have a simple table that can share the same formatting between all of the table elements, you can add all formatting rules to the table by adding properties and values to the `<table>` tag. ████ Now that you have your text in place, you are ready to format it using CSS. You modify the table tag to set text properties for all table content, then you create a new rule to use for the image caption.

1. **Expand the CSS Styles panel group if necessary**

   Formatting the text in the table cells will make the cafe page look more professional.

2. **Click the table rule in the CSS Styles panel, click the Edit Rule button** 🖉**, click the Type category, click the Font-family list arrow, click Arial, Helvetica, sans-serif, click the Font-size list arrow, click medium, as shown in Figure G-28, then click OK**

   The type in the table changes to assume the properties of the modified table rule. You want the name of the featured dessert, Chocolate Grand Marnier Cake, to stand out on the page but there isn't an existing rule that suits your needs.

3. **Click the New CSS Rule button** 🔲**, then create a new class selector type rule called featured_item in the su_styles.css style sheet file**

   Creating a new style for this specific text will give it a unique look.

4. **In the Type category, set the Font-size to 14, the Font-weight to bold, the Font-style to italic, the Color to #003, as shown in Figure G-29, then click OK**

   Since you did not specify a Font-family in the CSS Rule Definition dialog box, the font will remain the same, as it is inherited from the body rule in the HTML5_twoColFixRtHdr.css file.

5. **Select the Chocolate Grand Marnier Cake text under the chocolate cake image, click the CSS button** 🔳 css **in the Property inspector, then apply the featured_item rule to the text**

   All text on the page now has a rule applied.

6. **Click after the word Cake in the bottom-left cell, then press [Tab]**

   A new row is added. Pressing the Tab key while the insertion point is in the last cell of the table creates a new row. Even though it appears as if the cell with the room service information is the last cell, it is not because of the merged cells.

7. **Merge the cells in the new row, click in the merged cells, click Insert on the Menu bar, point to HTML, then click Horizontal Rule**

   A horizontal rule is displayed in the merged cells in the last row. Horizontal rules are used frequently to set off or divide sections on a page.

8. **Save your work, preview the cafe page in your browser, compare your screen to Figure G-30, then close your browser**

   The page looks much better with the formatted text.

FIGURE G-28: Modifying the table rule

CSS Rule Definition for table in su_styles.css

Category	Type
Type	
Background	Font-family: Arial, Helvetica, sans-serif
Block	
Box	Font-size: medium ▾ px ▾ Font-weight: ▾
Border	

FIGURE G-29: Creating the .featured_item rule

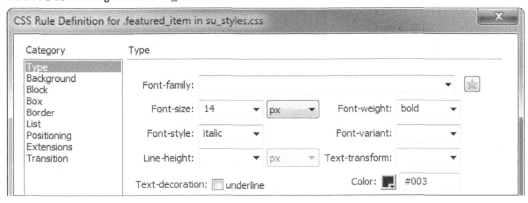

CSS Rule Definition for .featured_item in su_styles.css

Category

Type
Background
Block
Box
Border
List
Positioning
Extensions
Transition

Type

Font-family: ▾

Font-size: 14 ▾ px ▾   Font-weight: bold ▾

Font-style: italic ▾   Font-variant: ▾

Line-height: ▾ px ▾   Text-transform: ▾

Text-decoration: ☐ underline   Color: ■ #003

FIGURE G-30: Rules applied to text and horizontal rule added

body_text
rule applied

featured_items
rule applied

Horizontal rule
added in new row

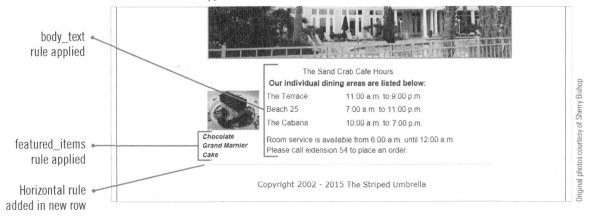

The Sand Crab Cafe Hours
Our individual dining areas are listed below:
The Terrace   11:00 a.m. to 9:00 p.m.
Beach 25   7:00 a.m. to 11:00 p.m.
The Cabana   10:00 a.m. to 7:00 p.m.

Room service is available from 6:00 a.m. until 12:00 a.m.
Please call extension 54 to place an order.

*Chocolate
Grand Marnier
Cake*

Copyright 2002 - 2015 The Striped Umbrella

Original photos courtesy of Sherry Bishop

Design Matters

Setting accessibility preferences for tables

You can make tables more accessible to individuals with disabilities by adding table captions or table headers that can be read by screen readers. A table caption will appear at the top of the table in the browser window and adds to table accessibility. Another way to provide accessibility is by using a **table header**, which is an option used by screen readers to help users identify the content of a table. Table headers are automatically centered, boldfaced, and placed in the top row and/or left column. You create table captions and headers using the settings found in the Table dialog box.

Using CSS and Tables to Position Content

Dreamweaver 187

Dreamweaver CS6

Formatting Cells

Formatting a cell can include setting properties that visually enhance the cell's appearance, such as setting a cell width, assigning a background color, or setting global alignment properties for the cell content. To format a cell, with code that is HTML5 compliant, you can use tags to define a column group style <colgroup>, which will format all cells in a particular column. You can also use the column tag <col> to apply formatting styles to singular cells in a column. Once you have created your rules, you add them to the code for the appropriate columns or cells you wish to format. You can also add code to the tag for an individual cell. Formatting cells is different from formatting cell contents. When you format cell contents, you must select the contents and then apply a rule. See the Clues to Use *Using inherited properties to format cells and cell content* at the bottom of this page for more information. You decide to experiment with the placement and alignment of the current page content. You change the horizontal and vertical alignment settings for some of the table cells to improve the appearance of the cell contents on the page.

STEPS

1. **Click to place the insertion point in the cell with the chocolate cake caption**
   Notice that the .featured_item rule is applied to the text. You will modify the .featured_item rule to add an alignment value.

2. **Click the .featured_item rule in the CSS Styles panel, then click the Edit Rule button** ✎
   The CSS Rule Definition for .featured_item in su_styles.css dialog box opens.

3. **Click the Block Category, click the Text-align list arrow, click center, then click OK**
   The cake text is now centered in the cell, as shown in Figure G-31. Next you will align the contents of the cell describing room service. Since there is not a separate rule applied to this text, you modify the cell tag code to align the cell contents.

4. **Place the insertion point in the cell with the room service information, then switch to Code view**

5. **Place the insertion point at the end of the opening td tag, type** `style="text-align: center"`, **as shown in Figure G-32**
   The page displays as it will appear in your browser. The table looks more organized and professional with the new alignment settings.

6. **Save all files, switch to Design View, click the Switch Design View to Live View button** Live **, then compare your screen to Figure G-33**
   The room service text is centered in the cell.

7. **Return to Design view, close all open pages, then exit Dreamweaver**

Using inherited properties to format cells and cell content

If a table is inside a CSS layout, you can simply let the properties from the existing CSS rules format the content, rather than applying additional rules. This is called inheritance. When a tag is placed, or nested, inside another tag (the parent tag), the properties from the parent tag are inherited by any tags nested within that tag. For example, if you set the Font-family property in the body tag, all content on the page inherits and displays that same font family unless you specify otherwise.

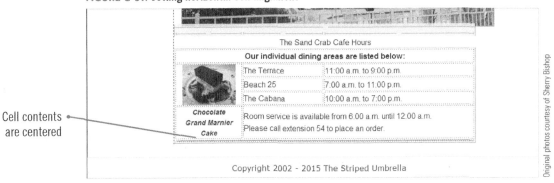

FIGURE G-31: Setting horizontal cell alignment

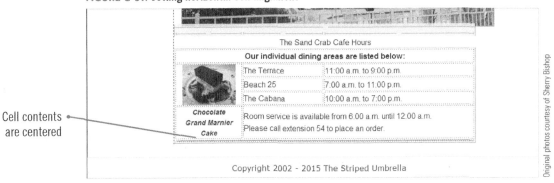

The Sand Crab Cafe Hours

Our individual dining areas are listed below:

The Terrace	11:00 a.m. to 9:00 p.m.
Beach 25	7:00 a.m. to 11:00 p.m.
The Cabana	10:00 a.m. to 7:00 p.m.

Room service is available from 6:00 a.m. until 12:00 a.m.
Please call extension 54 to place an order.

Chocolate Grand Marnier Cake

Copyright 2002 - 2015 The Striped Umbrella

Cell contents are centered

Original photos courtesy of Sherry Bishop

FIGURE G-32: Adding an align property to a cell tag

Add to the code for the cell tag to set the cell alignment to center

```
59    </tr>
60    <tr>
61    <td>The Cabana</td>
62    <td>10:00 a.m. to 7: 00 p.m.</td>
63    </tr>
64    <tr>
65    <td colspan="2" rowspan="2" style="text-align:center">Room service is available from 6:00 a.m. until 12:00 a.m.<br>
66    Please call extension 54 to place an order.</td>
67    </tr>
68    <tr>
69    <td class="featured_item">Chocolate<br>
70    Grand Marnier<br>
71    Cake</td>
72    </tr>
```

FIGURE G-33: The finished product

Original photos courtesy of Sherry Bishop

Using grids and guides for positioning page content

The View menu offers a number of options to help you position your page content more precisely. **Grids** consist of horizontal and vertical lines resembling graph paper that fill the page. You can edit the colors of the lines, the distance between them, whether they are displayed using lines or dots, and whether or not objects "snap" (automatically align) to them. **Guides** are horizontal or vertical lines that you place on the page yourself, by clicking and dragging onto the page from the vertical and horizontal rulers. Unlike grids, which fill the page, you can have as many or as few guides as you need. Both grids and guides are used to position page elements using exact measurements.

You can edit both the color of the guides and the color of the **distance,** a screen tip that shows you the distance between two guides when you hold down the control key (Win) or command key (Mac) and place the mouse pointer between the guides. You can lock the guides so you don't accidentally move them, and you can set them either to snap to page elements or have page elements snap to them. To display grids or guides, click View on the Menu bar, point to either Grid or Guides, then select an option from the displayed menu. Grids and guides only appear in Dreamweaver—they do not display when viewed in the browser.

Dreamweaver CS6

Practice

Concepts Review

Label each element shown in Figure G-34.

FIGURE G-34

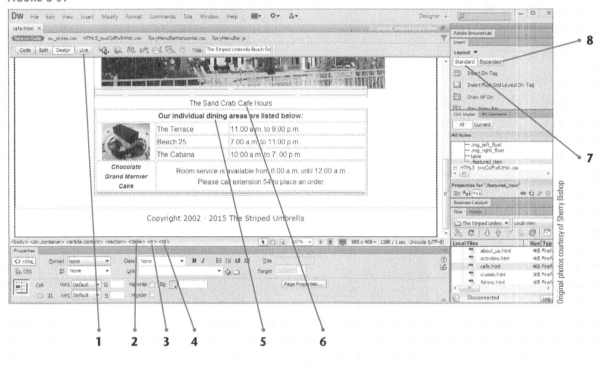

Original photos courtesy of Sherry Bishop

1. _____   5. _____
2. _____   6. _____
3. _____   7. _____
4. _____   8. _____

Match each of the following terms with the statement that best describes its function.

9. Cells
10. Standard mode
11. div tags
12. Import
13. Fixed layout
14. CSS page layouts
15. Deprecated tags
16. CSS Layout box model
17. Export
18. Dynamic content

a. Small boxes arranged in columns and rows
b. Pages built using div tags and CSS
c. Save data that was created in Dreamweaver with a different file format
d. Tags that are no longer considered to be the current standard
e. Page content that changes either in response to certain conditions or through interaction with the user
f. A layout with the width of content blocks based on pixels
g. The mode that does not include temporary cell padding and spacing
h. Bring data into Dreamweaver from another program
i. A view that displays padding and margins for divs
j. HTML tags that determine the appearance and position of containers of content

Skills Review

(If you did not create this website in Unit B and maintain it during the preceding units, you will need to create a local site root folder for this website and define the website using files your instructor will provide. See the "Read This Before You Begin" section for more detailed instructions.)

1. **Create a page using CSS layouts.**
   a. Start Dreamweaver, then open the Blooms & Bulbs website.
   b. Create a new blank HTML5 page with the 2 column fixed, right sidebar, header and footer layout, then attach the blooms_styles.css file to the page and save the new stylesheet file, HTML5_twoColFixRtHdr.css, in the blooms local site folder.
   c. Add the page title **Blooms & Bulbs – Your complete garden center** in the Title text box.
   d. Save the file as **workshops.html**, overwriting the existing workshops page.

2. **Add content to CSS layout blocks.**
   a. Open the index page, then copy the banner and menu bar. (Hint: Select the banner, hold down your Shift key, then click directly under the menu bar to select both.)
   b. Close the index page, then on the workshops page, delete the logo placeholder in the header and paste the banner and menu bar in the header block.
   c. Delete the footer placeholder text, then type **Copyright 2001 – 2015 Blooms & Bulbs** in the footer block.
   d. Delete the placeholder content from the content block.
   e. Type **New Composting Workshop!**, enter a paragraph break, then import the composting.doc file from the drive and folder where you store your Unit G Data Files.
   f. Enter a paragraph break after the last paragraph, then insert the chives.jpg file from the drive and folder where you store your Unit G Data Files. Add the alternate text **Even chives can be beautiful** to the image when prompted.
   g. Save your work.

3. **Edit content in CSS layout blocks.**
   a. Select the footer rule in the CSS Styles panel, then change the Text-align property in the Block category to center.
   b. Select the heading "New Composting Workshop!" and format it using the Heading 1 paragraph format if necessary.

4. **Edit CSS layout properties.**
   a. Select the header rule in the CSS Styles panel and change its background color to #FFF.
   b. Repeat Step a to change the background color of the sidebar1 rule to #FFF and the footer rule to #AFA19E.
   c. Edit the header rule so that the header has a 5-pixel margin on all sides.
   d. Edit the body rule in the HTML5_twoColFixRtHdr.css file to change the Font-size to 14 pixels.
   e. Edit the sidebar1 rule Float to left.
   f. Save your work.

5. **Insert a table and set table properties.**
   a. Delete the placeholder text in the sidebar, including the links, then insert a table with a header at the top of the table, eight rows, and two columns.
   b. Edit the sidebar1 rule to center-align the contents.
   c. Create a new Tag selector in the blooms_styles.css file to modify the table tag by setting the table Box width property to 180 pixels.
   d. Save your work.

Skills Review (continued)

6. **Merge and split cells.**
   a. Merge the two cells in the first row.
   b. Merge the two cells in the last row.
   c. Save your work.

7. **Insert and align images in table cells.**
   a. Use the Insert panel to insert gardening_gloves.gif from the drive and folder where you store your Unit G Data Files in the last row of the table. Add the alternate text **Gardening gloves** to the image when prompted.
   b. Save your work.

8. **Add text.**
   a. Type **Currently Scheduled Workshops** in the merged cells in the first row, using a line break after "Scheduled".
   b. Type the names and dates for the workshops from Figure G-35 in each row of the table.
   c. Save your work.

9. **Format and modify cell content.**
   a. Edit the table rule to center-align the contents.
   b. Save your work.

10. **Format cells.**
    a. Edit the table rule to add a left padding of 5 pixels.
    b. Place the insertion point in the top cell, switch to Code view, and add the following code to the end of the opening table data tag: **style="background-color:#C8DBB5"**. (Hint: When you finish editing the code it will read: <th colspan="2" scope="col" style="background-color:#C8DBB5">)
    c. Save your work, preview the workshops page in the browser, then compare your screen to Figure G-35.
    d. Close the browser and close all open pages.

Skills Review (continued)

FIGURE G-35

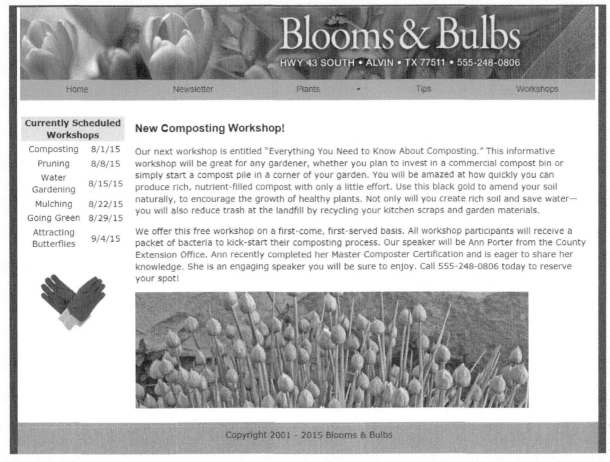

Blooms & Bulbs

HWY 43 SOUTH • ALVIN • TX 77511 • 555-248-0806

Home　　Newsletter　　Plants　▾　Tips　　Workshops

Currently Scheduled Workshops

Composting	8/1/15
Pruning	8/8/15
Water Gardening	8/15/15
Mulching	8/22/15
Going Green	8/29/15
Attracting Butterflies	9/4/15

New Composting Workshop!

Our next workshop is entitled "Everything You Need to Know About Composting." This informative workshop will be great for any gardener, whether you plan to invest in a commercial compost bin or simply start a compost pile in a corner of your garden. You will be amazed at how quickly you can produce rich, nutrient-filled compost with only a little effort. Use this black gold to amend your soil naturally, to encourage the growth of healthy plants. Not only will you create rich soil and save water—you will also reduce trash at the landfill by recycling your kitchen scraps and garden materials.

We offer this free workshop on a first-come, first-served basis. All workshop participants will receive a packet of bacteria to kick-start their composting process. Our speaker will be Ann Porter from the County Extension Office. Ann recently completed her Master Composter Certification and is eager to share her knowledge. She is an engaging speaker you will be sure to enjoy. Call 555-248-0806 today to reserve your spot!

Copyright 2001 - 2015 Blooms & Bulbs

© 2013 Cengage Learning
Original photos courtesy of Sherry Bishop

Important: *If you did not create the websites used in the following exercises in Unit B, you need to create a local site root folder for each website and define the websites using files your instructor provides. See the "Read This Before You Begin" section for more detailed instructions.*

Independent Challenge 1

You continue your work on the Rapids Transit website. After studying Cascading Style Sheets, you decide to experiment with predesigned CSS layouts. You create a new rates page based on a CSS HTML5 layout and add a table to list the equipment rental rates.

a. Open Dreamweaver, then open the Rapids Transit website.

b. Create a new HTML5 page based on the 2 column fixed, right sidebar, header and footer layout, and attach the rapids_transit.css file to the page. Verify that the new HTML5_twoColFixRtHdr.css file will be copied to the local site folder, then save it as rates.html, replacing the blank placeholder page.

c. Add the page title **Rapids Transit – Buffalo River Outfitters**.

d. Copy the banner and menu bar from the index page to the new, untitled page, replacing the logo placeholder, then close the index page.

e. Delete the placeholder text in the main content div, then import the file rentals.doc to take its place.

f. Replace the footer placeholder text with **Copyright 2001 - 2015 Rapids Transit. All rights reserved**.

g. Switch to Code view, delete all the placeholder content in the sidebar1 div, switch back to Design view, then insert girl_floating.jpg from the drive and folder where you store you Unit G Data Files. Add alternate text when prompted.

h. Edit the sidebar1 rule to change the box width to 240 pixels and the background to #FFF.

i. Edit the content rule to change the box width to 720 pixels.

j. Edit the header div to change the background color to #FFF, the text align to center, and add a box margin of 5 pixels on all sides.

k. Save your work.

l. Edit the footer rule to change the text-align to center and the font-style to italic.

m. Place the insertion point at the end of the last paragraph after the word "float" and insert a table with a top header, six rows, and four columns.

n. Create a new Tag Selector rule to modify the table tag with the following settings: Box width: 600 pixels, Box left margin: 60 pixels, Block text-align: left.

o. Merge the cells in the top row and type **Rental Rates per Day**.

p. Enter the rental information listed in Figure G-36 in the next three rows.

q. Merge the third and fourth cells in the fifth row, then insert the image rt_logo.gif. Add alternate text when prompted.

r. Merge the cells in the last row, then insert a horizontal rule.

s. Switch to Code view, then edit the header cell tag by adding following code: `style="text-align:center"`.

t. Edit each of the four cells under the header tag by adding the following code: `style="width:25%"`. (*Hint*: you will not see the column widths change to 25 percent unless you view the page in Live view or in a browser.)

u. Save your work, preview the page in Live view or the browser, compare your screen to Figure G-36, make any spacing adjustments to improve the appearance if necessary, then close all pages and exit Dreamweaver.

Using CSS and Tables to Position Content

Independent Challenge 1 (continued)

FIGURE G-36

Home   Our Guides   Rates   Lodging   Before You Go

You may be wondering why we charge to use our equipment when we are already charging a fee for the float. We do this because we have many repeat customers who have invested in their own gear. We want to be able to charge them a lower price than we charge those who don't own equipment. Therefore, the more you bring along with you, the less your float will cost! Our basic float price is $20.00 without equipment. Add the amounts on the table for the equipment you will need to the basic price, and you will have the total price of the float. We also take an action shot of you on the water that is included in the price of the float.

Rental Rates per Day

Canoe	$15.00	Life Jacket	$3.00
Kayak	$19.00	Helmet	$2.00
Two-man raft	$22.00	Dry Packs	$1.00

Copyright 2001 - 2015 Rapids Transit. All rights reserved.

© 2013 Cengage Learning
Original photo courtesy of Sherry Bishop

Independent Challenge 2

You continue your work on the TripSmart website. You are ready to begin work now on a page featuring a catalog item. You plan to use a CSS HTML5 layout with a table to place the data about the item.

a. Open Dreamweaver, open the TripSmart website, then create a new page based on the HTML5: three column fixed, header and footer CSS layout. Attach the tripsmart_styles.css file, verify that the new style sheet file that formats the page layout will be saved in the tripsmart local site root folder, then save the file as catalog.html, replacing the placeholder catalog page in the website.

b. Open the index page, copy the banner and menu bar, then close the index page.

c. Delete the logo image placeholder in the header, then paste the banner and menu bar in the header block.

d. Replace the placeholder text in the footer rule with **Copyright 2002 – 2015**, then edit the footer rule in the HTML5_thrColFixHdr.css style sheet to center align the content and set the background color to #FFF.

e. Edit the header rule to change the background to #FFF and add margins of 5 pixels to each side.

f. Edit the body rule in the HTML5_thrColFixHdr.css style sheet to change the Font-family to Arial, Helvetica, sans-serif, the Font-size to 14 pixels, and the background color to #FFF.

g. Save your work.

h. Delete the placeholder content in the content block, then type **This Week's Featured Catalog Item**.

i. Delete the placeholder text in the sidebar1 div (first column) and type **These are the lengths available for order:**. (Hint: Remember it is much easier to select all of the placeholder content in Code view.)

j. Delete the placeholder text in the aside div (third column) then type **Special Shipping Offer**, enter a paragraph break, type **Order two or more walking sticks this week and your shipping is free. Enter the code twosticks when you check out to receive free shipping.** then apply the Heading 2 format to the Special Shipping Offer text.

k. Create a new Tag rule in the tripsmart_styles.css style sheet that modifies the Heading 2 tag as follows: Font-family: Arial, Helvetica, sans-serif; Font-size: 16 pixels; Type Color: #54572C, then create a new Tag rule in the tripsmart_styles.css file to modify the Heading 1 tag with settings of your choice.

l. Create a new Class rule called centered_text in the tripsmart_styles.css style sheet and set the Text-align property to center. Select the Special Shipping Offer heading and apply the centered_text rule.

m. Enter a paragraph break after the heading in the second column, then insert the image walking_stick.jpg from the drive and folder where you store your Unit G Data Files, adding appropriate alternate text.

n. Create a new class rule named catalog_images in the tripsmart_styles.css file that will add a border of your choice around the image, set the float to left, and add a margin to all sides with settings of your choice. Apply the catalog_images rule to the walking stick image.

o. Edit the sidebar1 rule and the aside rule to set the background color for each rule to #FFF.

p. Edit the footer rule to add a top border of your choice.

q. Edit the container rule to add a border with your choice of settings around all sides.

r. Edit the content rule to change the width to 580 pixels, 10-pixel padding for all sides, and the file tripsmart_gradient.jpg for a background image.

s. Place the insertion point to the right of the walking stick image, then import the file walking sticks.doc from the drive and folder where you store your Unit G Data Files.

t. Insert a table under the text "These are the lengths available for order." with the following settings: rows: 8, columns: 2, Header: top.

u. Create a rule in the tripsmart_styles.css file to modify the table tag as follows: Box width: 175 px; border: solid; border width: thin; border color: #BABD9F, text-align: center.

v. Insert the data for the table using the information in the table in Figure G-37.

w. Add the page title **TripSmart - Serving all your travel needs.**

x. Save your work, preview the page in the browser, and compare your screen to Figure G-37.

y. Close the browser, close all open pages, then exit Dreamweaver.

FIGURE G-37

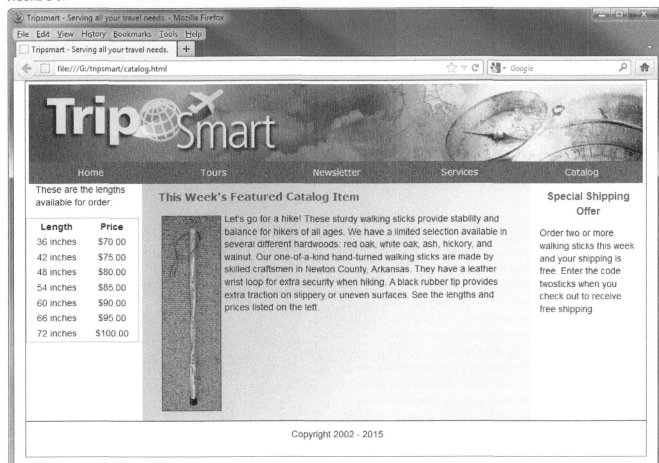

© 2013 Cengage Learning
Original photo courtesy of Sherry Bishop

Independent Challenge 3

Dell Patterson has opened a new shop called CollegeFandz, an online source for college students' clothing and collectibles. She is considering creating a website to promote her products and would like to gather some ideas before she hires a web designer. She decides to visit websites to look for design ideas, and asks you for your help.

a. Connect to the Internet, then go to sfbags.com, as shown in Figure G-38.

b. View the source code for the index page and locate the HTML tags that control the CSS on the page.

c. How is CSS used on this site?

d. List at least five div IDs that you find on the index page.

e. Use the Reference panel in Dreamweaver to look up two sets of code used in this site for page layout that you don't understand.

FIGURE G-38

Real Life Independent Challenge

For this assignment, you will continue to work on the website that you have been developing since Unit A. You are building this website from unit to unit, so you must do each Real Life Independent Challenge to complete your website. There are no Data Files supplied. You will continue building your website by designing and completing a page that uses CSS for page layout.

a. Consult your wireframes to decide which page to create and develop for this unit. Draw a sketch of the page to show how you will use CSS to lay out the content.

b. Create the new page for the site using one of the predesigned CSS layouts. Add or edit the divs on your page, making sure to name each one.

c. Add text, images, or background colors to each div.

d. Copy the menu bar from an existing page to the new page.

e. Update the menu bar, if necessary, to include a link to the new page.

f. Consider using the new page as an example to redesign the existing pages with CSS.

g. Save your work, preview each page in your browser, then make any necessary modifications to achieve a clean, consistent, attractive design for each page.

h. Consult your wireframe to see if you have a need to incorporate a table into one of the pages.

i. If you decide to add a table, create rules to format the table elements.

j. Add the data in your plan to the table cells, modifying the appearance as necessary.

k. View your table in a browser, close your browser, close all open pages, then exit Dreamweaver.

Visual Workshop

Use Figure G-39 as a guide to continue your work on the Carolyne's Creations website. Create a new catering page based on the HTML5: 2 column fixed, right sidebar, header and footer page layout. Remember to attach the website style sheet to the page and save the HTML5_thrColFixHdr.css file in the local site root folder. The image, marshmallows.jpg, is found in the assets folder in the drive and folder where you store your Unit G Data Files. Experiment with your CSS settings to create your unique design for the page.

FIGURE G-39

© 2013 Cengage Learning
Original photo courtesy of Sherry Bishop

Using CSS and Tables to Position Content

Index

tweens, Flash 76
  creating, Flash 80–81
  fixing errors with, Flash 92
  shape, creating, Flash 92–93
  in Timeline, Flash 76–77
tween span, Flash 76
Twitter service, Dreamweaver 218
type. *See* text
typefaces, Flash 42

U

underscores in names, Flash 54–55
ungrouping objects, Flash 64
Uniform Resource Locator (URL),
  Dreamweaver 132, 133
unordered lists, Dreamweaver 80–81
updating files, Dreamweaver 216–217
uploading, Dreamweaver 270
Up state, Flash 130
URL (Uniform Resource Locator),
  Dreamweaver 132, 133
usability testing, integration 3
Use Global Light option, Photoshop 121
user-friendly forms, Dreamweaver 232

V

value element, Flash 32
variables, Flash 161
variable-width text, Flash 40
vector graphics, Photoshop 3, Flash 26,
  Dreamweaver 204
vertical space, Dreamweaver 108
Vibrance adjustment, Photoshop 100–101
vidcasts, Dreamweaver 218
video
  adding to Flash documents, Flash 142
  adding to movies, Flash 144–145
  applications for sharing, Dreamweaver
    218–219
  formats of, Flash 142, Dreamweaver 213
  Import Video Wizard feature, Flash 142–143
  overview, Flash 142, Dreamweaver 212–213
viewing
  using Property inspector, Dreamweaver 2
  web page elements, Dreamweaver 12–13
  web page in browsers, Dreamweaver 16–17
views, Dreamweaver 8–9
view tools, Flash 28
vignette effect, Photoshop 44
visited links, Dreamweaver 56
Visual Aids submenu, Dreamweaver 139
vodcasts, Dreamweaver 218

W

WAI-ARIA (Web Accessibility Initiative -
  Accessible Rich Internet Applications Suite),
  Dreamweaver 135

waveforms, Flash 138
Web 2.0 technology
  blogs, Dreamweaver 218
  collecting feedback for, Dreamweaver
    256–257
  overview, Dreamweaver 218
  podcasts, Dreamweaver 218
  RSS feeds, Dreamweaver 218
  social networking, Dreamweaver 218
  video sharing applications, Dreamweaver
    218–219
  wikis, Dreamweaver 218
Web Accessibility Initiative - Accessible Rich
  Internet Applications Suite (WAI-ARIA),
  Dreamweaver 135
web browsers. *See* browsers
WebDAV (Web-based Distributed Authoring
  and Versioning), Dreamweaver 269
web design
  adding images, Dreamweaver 2
  adding media files, Dreamweaver 2
  adding tables, Dreamweaver 2
  adding text, Dreamweaver 2
  managing websites, Dreamweaver 2–3
  overview, Dreamweaver 2
  using Property inspector to view and edit
    page elements, Dreamweaver 2
  web pages. *See* web pages
web pages
  adding links to, Dreamweaver 56–57
  closing, Dreamweaver 18–19
  creating, Dreamweaver 2
  creating head content, Dreamweaver 50–51
  displaying, Dreamweaver 2
  elements of
    divs and AP divs, Dreamweaver 12
    flash movies, Dreamweaver 12
    flash video, Dreamweaver 12–13
    hyperlinks, Dreamweaver 12
    images, Dreamweaver 12
    overview, Dreamweaver 12
    tables, Dreamweaver 12
    text, Dreamweaver 12
  history panel, Dreamweaver 58–59
  layout of
    accessibility of, Dreamweaver 48–49
    applying themes using templates,
      Dreamweaver 48
    keeping simple, Dreamweaver 48
    media objects, Dreamweaver 48
    navigation structure, Dreamweaver 48
    overview, Dreamweaver 48
    using CSS, Dreamweaver 48
    white space, Dreamweaver 48
  opening, Dreamweaver 10–11
  overview, Dreamweaver 2, Dreamweaver 47
  saving, Dreamweaver 34–35
  setting properties, Dreamweaver 52–53
  testing and modifying, Dreamweaver 62–63

text, creating and formatting,
  Dreamweaver 54–55
  viewing HTML code, Dreamweaver 60–61
  viewing in browsers, Dreamweaver 16–17
web servers, Dreamweaver 26
websites
  adding applications to, Flash 2
  adding folders to, Dreamweaver 32–33
  adding pages to, Dreamweaver 38–39
  color palettes for, Flash 38
  copying images to, Dreamweaver 36–37
  creating and finding images for,
    Dreamweaver 118–119
  creating folder for management of,
    Dreamweaver 28–29
  defined, Dreamweaver 2
  deleting images from, Dreamweaver
    116–117
  links in, Dreamweaver 152–153
  managing, Dreamweaver 2–3
  opening from buttons, Flash 168–169
  overview, Dreamweaver 25
  planning
    creating folders, Dreamweaver 26
    creating wireframes, Dreamweaver 26
    overview, Dreamweaver 26
    page content and web pages,
      Dreamweaver 26
    publishing, Dreamweaver 26–27
    researching goals and needs,
      Dreamweaver 26
    testing and modifying pages,
      Dreamweaver 26
  publishing. *See* publishing
  saving web pages, Dreamweaver 34–35
  setting up, Dreamweaver 30–31
  using CSS in
    advantages of, Dreamweaver 82
    classified by function, Dreamweaver 82
    classified by location, Dreamweaver 82
    styles panel, Dreamweaver 82–83
Welcome Screen, Flash 4
What You See Is What You Get (WYSIWYG)
  programs, Dreamweaver 2
white points, adjusting with levels,
  Photoshop 92–93
white space, Dreamweaver 48
widgets, Dreamweaver 131
width of tables, Dreamweaver 176
Width property (W), Dreamweaver 169,
  Dreamweaver 296
wikis, Dreamweaver 218
windows, designing for different sizes of,
  Dreamweaver 19
Window size options, Dreamweaver 17
wireframes
  creating, Dreamweaver 26
  using for planning, development, and
    presentation, Dreamweaver 266
Word Wrap option, Dreamweaver 60

OBJECTIVES

Session 1.1
- Open and close a workbook
- Navigate through a workbook and worksheet
- Select cells and ranges
- Plan and create a workbook
- Insert, rename, and move worksheets
- Enter text, dates, and numbers
- Undo and redo actions
- Resize columns and rows

Session 1.2
- Enter formulas and the SUM and COUNT functions
- Copy and paste formulas
- Move or copy cells and ranges
- Insert and delete rows, columns, and ranges
- Create patterned text with Flash Fill
- Add cell borders and change font size
- Change worksheet views
- Prepare a workbook for printing
- Save a workbook with a new filename

Getting Started with Excel

Creating a Customer Order Report

Case | *Game Card*

Peter Lewis is part owner of Game Card, a store in Missoula, Montana, that specializes in selling vintage board games. Peter needs to track sales data, generate financial reports, create contact lists for loyal customers, and analyze market trends. He can perform all of these tasks with **Microsoft Excel 2016**, (or just **Excel**), an application used to enter, analyze, and present quantitative data. He wants to create an efficient way of tracking the company inventory and managing customer sales. Peter asks you to use Excel to create a document in which he can enter customer purchases from the store.

STARTING DATA FILES

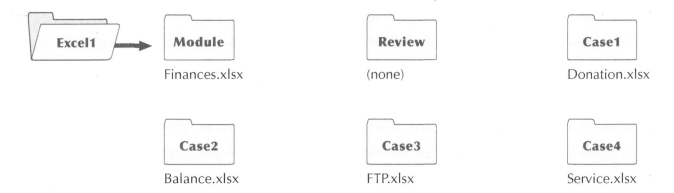

Excel1 → **Module**	**Review**	**Case1**
Finances.xlsx	(none)	Donation.xlsx
Case2	**Case3**	**Case4**
Balance.xlsx	FTP.xlsx	Service.xlsx

Session 1.1 Visual Overview:

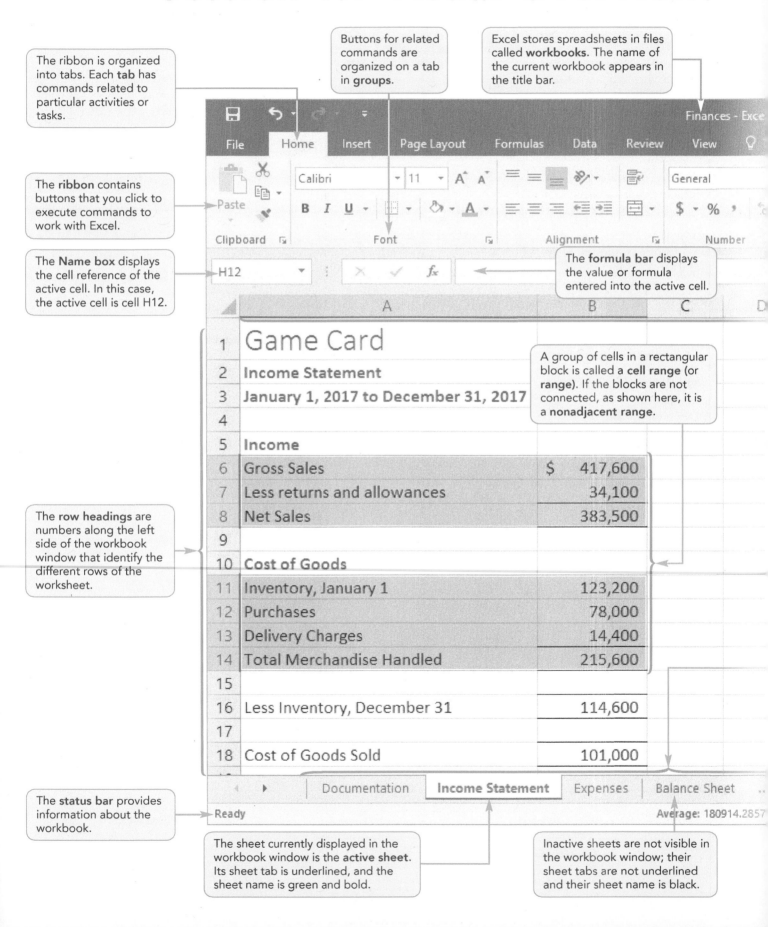

The ribbon is organized into tabs. Each **tab** has commands related to particular activities or tasks.

Buttons for related commands are organized on a tab in **groups**.

Excel stores spreadsheets in files called **workbooks**. The name of the current workbook appears in the title bar.

The **ribbon** contains buttons that you click to execute commands to work with Excel.

The **Name box** displays the cell reference of the active cell. In this case, the active cell is cell H12.

The **formula bar** displays the value or formula entered into the active cell.

A group of cells in a rectangular block is called a **cell range (or range)**. If the blocks are not connected, as shown here, it is a **nonadjacent range**.

The **row headings** are numbers along the left side of the workbook window that identify the different rows of the worksheet.

The **status bar** provides information about the workbook.

The sheet currently displayed in the workbook window is the **active sheet**. Its sheet tab is underlined, and the sheet name is green and bold.

Inactive sheets are not visible in the workbook window; their sheet tabs are not underlined and their sheet name is black.

Finances - Exce

File Home Insert Page Layout Formulas Data Review View

Calibri 11 A A

B I U

General

Paste

Clipboard Font Alignment Number

$ % ,

H12 fx

	A	B	C	D
1	Game Card			
2	Income Statement			
3	January 1, 2017 to December 31, 2017			
4				
5	Income			
6	Gross Sales	$ 417,600		
7	Less returns and allowances	34,100		
8	Net Sales	383,500		
9				
10	Cost of Goods			
11	Inventory, January 1	123,200		
12	Purchases	78,000		
13	Delivery Charges	14,400		
14	Total Merchandise Handled	215,600		
15				
16	Less Inventory, December 31	114,600		
17				
18	Cost of Goods Sold	101,000		

Documentation **Income Statement** Expenses Balance Sheet

Ready Average: 180914.2857

The Excel Workbook

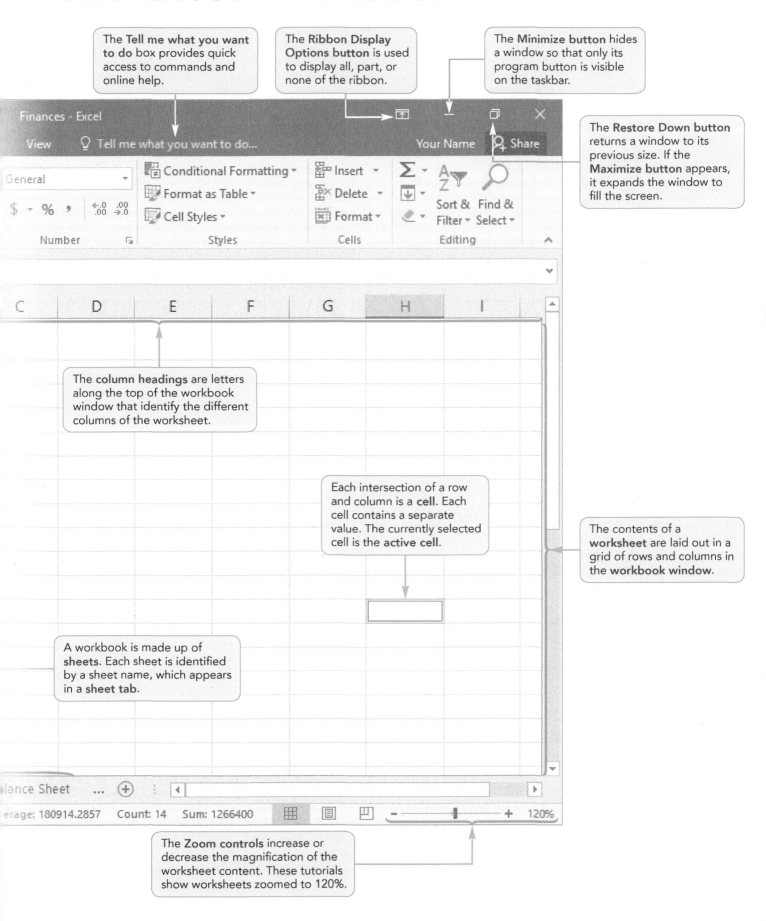

The **Tell me what you want to do** box provides quick access to commands and online help.

The **Ribbon Display Options button** is used to display all, part, or none of the ribbon.

The **Minimize button** hides a window so that only its program button is visible on the taskbar.

The **Restore Down button** returns a window to its previous size. If the **Maximize button** appears, it expands the window to fill the screen.

The **column headings** are letters along the top of the workbook window that identify the different columns of the worksheet.

Each intersection of a row and column is a **cell**. Each cell contains a separate value. The currently selected cell is the **active cell**.

The contents of a **worksheet** are laid out in a grid of rows and columns in the **workbook window**.

A workbook is made up of **sheets**. Each sheet is identified by a sheet name, which appears in a **sheet tab**.

The **Zoom controls** increase or decrease the magnification of the worksheet content. These tutorials show worksheets zoomed to 120%.

Introducing Excel and Spreadsheets

A **spreadsheet** is a grouping of text and numbers in a rectangular grid or table. Spreadsheets are often used in business for budgeting, inventory management, and financial reporting because they unite text, numbers, and charts within one document. They can also be employed for personal use for planning a personal budget, tracking expenses, or creating a list of personal items. The advantage of an electronic spreadsheet is that the content can be easily edited and updated to reflect changing financial conditions.

To start Excel:

▶ **1.** On the Windows taskbar, click the **Start** button ⊞. The Start menu opens.

▶ **2.** Click **All Apps** on the Start menu, scroll the list, and then click **Excel 2016**. Excel starts and displays the Recent screen in Backstage view. **Backstage view** provides access to various screens with commands that allow you to manage files and Excel options. On the left is a list of recently opened workbooks. On the right are options for creating new workbooks. See Figure 1-1.

Figure 1-1	Recent screen in Backstage view

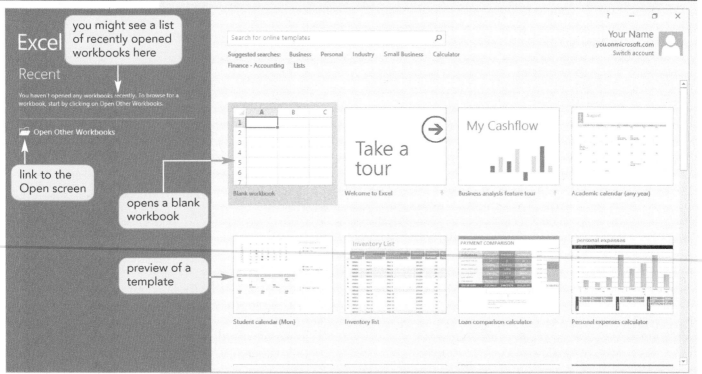

Opening an Existing Workbook

Excel documents are called workbooks. From the Recent screen in Backstage view, you can open a blank workbook, open an existing workbook, or create a new workbook based on a template. A **template** is a preformatted workbook with many design features and some content already filled in. Templates can speed up the process of creating a workbook because much of the effort in designing the workbook and entering its data and formulas is already done for you.

Peter created an Excel workbook that contains several worksheets describing the current financial status of Game Card. You will open that workbook now.

To open the Game Card financial status workbook:

▶ **1.** In the navigation bar on the Recent screen, click the **Open Other Workbooks** link. The Open screen is displayed and provides access to different locations where you might store files. The Recent Workbooks list shows the workbooks that were most recently opened on your computer.

▶ **2.** Click the **Browse** button. The Open dialog box appears.

▶ **3.** Navigate to the **Excel1 > Module** folder included with your Data Files.

Trouble? If you don't have the starting Data Files, you need to get them before you can proceed. Your instructor will either give you the Data Files or ask you to obtain them from a specified location (such as a network drive). If you have any questions about the Data Files, see your instructor or technical support person for assistance.

▶ **4.** Click **Finances** in the file list to select it.

▶ **5.** Click the **Open** button. The workbook opens in Excel.

Trouble? If you don't see the full ribbon as shown in the Session 1.1 Visual Overview, the ribbon may be partially or fully hidden. To pin the ribbon so that the tabs and groups are fully displayed and remain visible, click the Ribbon Display Options button 🔲, and then click Show Tabs and Commands.

▶ **6.** If the Excel window doesn't fill the screen, click the **Maximize** button 🔲 in the upper-right corner of the title bar. See Figure 1-2.

Figure 1-2   **Finances workbook**

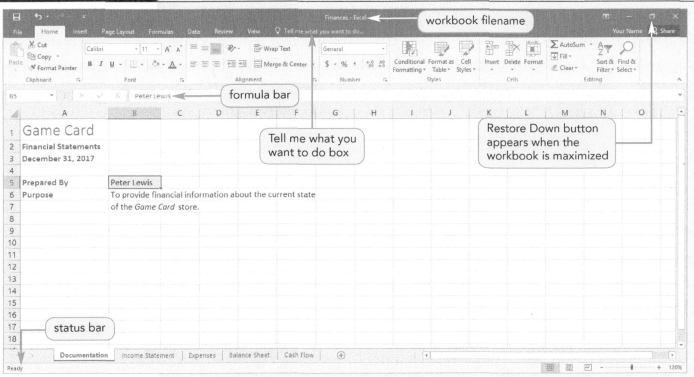

Using Keyboard Shortcuts to Work Faster

Keyboard shortcuts can help you work faster and more efficiently because you can keep your hands on the keyboard. A **keyboard shortcut** is a key or combination of keys that you press to access a feature or perform a command. Excel provides keyboard shortcuts for many commonly used commands. For example, Ctrl+S is the keyboard shortcut for the Save command, which means you hold down the Ctrl key while you press the S key to save the workbook. (Note that the plus sign is not pressed; it is used to indicate that an additional key is pressed.) When available, a keyboard shortcut is listed next to the command's name in a ScreenTip. A **ScreenTip** is a box with descriptive text about a command that appears when you point to a button on the ribbon. Figure 1-3 lists some of the keyboard shortcuts commonly used in Excel. The modules in this text show the corresponding keyboard shortcuts for accomplishing an action when available.

Figure 1-3   Excel keyboard shortcuts

Press	To	Press	To
Alt	Display the Key Tips for the commands and tools on the ribbon	Ctrl+V	Paste content that was cut or copied
Ctrl+A	Select all objects in a range	Ctrl+W	Close the current workbook
Ctrl+C	Copy the selected object(s)	Ctrl+X	Cut the selected object(s)
Ctrl+G	Go to a location in the workbook	Ctrl+Y	Repeat the last command
Ctrl+N	Open a new blank workbook	Ctrl+Z	Undo the last command
Ctrl+O	Open a saved workbook file	F1	Open the Excel Help window
Ctrl+P	Print the current workbook	F5	Go to a location in the workbook
Ctrl+S	Save the current workbook	F12	Save the current workbook with a new name or to a new location

You can also use the keyboard to quickly select commands on the ribbon. First, you press the Alt key to display the **Key Tips**, which are labels that appear over each tab and command on the ribbon. Then, you press the key or keys indicated to access the corresponding tab, command, or button while your hands remain on the keyboard.

Getting Help

If you are unsure about the function of an Excel command or you want information about how to accomplish a particular task, you can use the Help system. To access Excel Help, you either press the F1 key or enter a phrase or keyword into the Tell me what you want to do box next to the tabs on the ribbon. From this search box you can get quick access to detailed information and commands on a wide variety of Excel topics.

Using Excel 2016 in Touch Mode

You can work in Office 2016 with a keyboard and mouse or with touch. If you work with Excel on a touchscreen, you tap objects instead of clicking them. In **Touch Mode**, the ribbon increases in height, the buttons are bigger, and more space appears around each button so you can more easily use your finger or a stylus to tap the button you need.

Although the figures in these modules show the screen with Mouse Mode on, it's helpful to learn how to move between Touch Mode and Mouse Mode. You'll switch to Touch Mode and then back to Mouse Mode. If you are using a touch device, please read these steps, but do not complete them so that you remain working in Touch Mode.

To switch between Touch Mode and Mouse Mode:

▶ **1.** On the Quick Access Toolbar, click the **Customize Quick Access Toolbar** button ⏷. A menu opens, listing buttons you can add to the Quick Access Toolbar as well as other options for customizing the toolbar.

Trouble? If the Touch/Mouse Mode command on the menu has a checkmark next to it, press the Esc key to close the menu, and then skip Step 2.

▶ **2.** Click **Touch/Mouse Mode**. The Quick Access Toolbar now contains the Touch/Mouse Mode button 👆, which you can use to switch between Mouse Mode, the default display, and Touch Mode.

▶ **3.** On the Quick Access Toolbar, click the **Touch/Mouse Mode** button 👆. A menu opens listing Mouse and Touch, and the icon next to Mouse is shaded to indicate it is selected.

Trouble? If the icon next to Touch is shaded, press the Esc key to close the menu and continue with Step 5.

▶ **4.** Click **Touch**. The display switches to Touch Mode with more space between the commands and buttons on the ribbon. See Figure 1-4.

| Figure 1-4 | Ribbon displayed in Touch Mode |

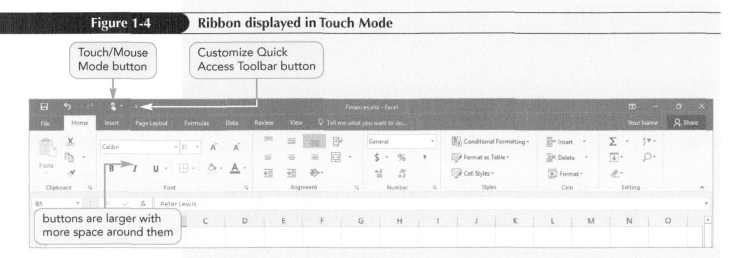

Next, you will switch back to Mouse Mode. If you are working with a touchscreen and want to use Touch Mode, skip Steps 5 and 6.

▶ **5.** On the Quick Access Toolbar, click the **Touch/Mouse Mode** button 👆, and then click **Mouse**. The ribbon returns to Mouse Mode, as shown earlier in Figure 1-2.

▶ **6.** On the Quick Access Toolbar, click the **Customize Quick Access Toolbar** button ⏷, and then click **Touch/Mouse Mode** to deselect it. The Touch/Mouse Mode button is removed from the Quick Access Toolbar.

Exploring a Workbook

Workbooks are organized into separate pages called sheets. Excel supports two types of sheets: worksheets and chart sheets. A worksheet contains a grid of rows and columns into which you can enter text, numbers, dates, and formulas and display charts. A **chart sheet** contains a chart that provides a visual representation of worksheet data. The contents of a workbook are shown in the workbook window.

Changing the Active Sheet

The sheets in a workbook are identified in the sheet tabs at the bottom of the workbook window. The Finances workbook for Game Card includes five sheets labeled Documentation, Income Statement, Expenses, Balance Sheet, and Cash Flow. The sheet currently displayed in the workbook window is the active sheet, which in this case is the Documentation sheet. To make a different sheet active and visible, you click its sheet tab. You can tell which sheet is active because its name appears in bold green.

If a workbook includes so many sheets that not all of the sheet tabs can be displayed at the same time in the workbook window, you can use the sheet tab scrolling buttons to scroll through the list of tabs. Scrolling the sheet tabs does not change the active sheet; it changes only which sheet tabs are visible.

You will view the different sheets in the Finances workbook.

To change the active sheet:

▶ **1.** Click the **Income Statement** sheet tab. The Income Statement worksheet becomes the active sheet, and its name is in bold green type. See Figure 1-5.

| Figure 1-5 | Income Statement worksheet |

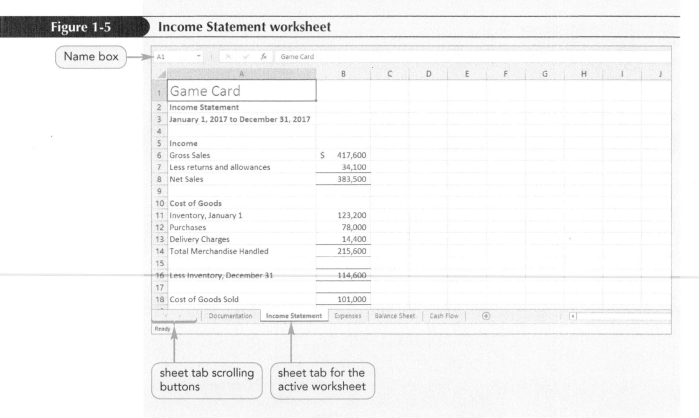

▶ **2.** Click the **Expenses** sheet tab to make it the active sheet. The Expenses sheet is an example of a chart sheet containing only an Excel chart. See Figure 1-6.

Figure 1-6   **Expenses chart sheet**

chart sheet contains a chart but no grid of text and data

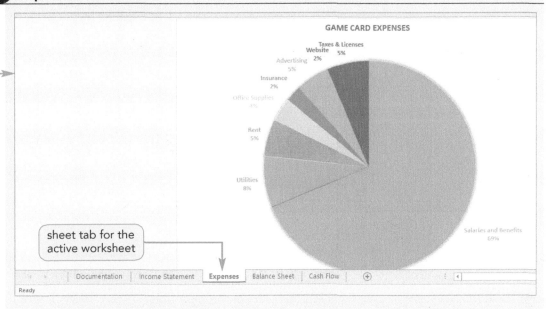

sheet tab for the active worksheet

TIP

You can move to the previous or next sheet in the workbook by pressing the Ctrl+PgUp or Ctrl+PgDn keys.

3. Click the **Balance Sheet** sheet tab to make it the active sheet. Note that this sheet contains charts embedded into the grid of data values. A worksheet can contain data values, embedded charts, pictures, and other design elements.

4. Click the **Cash Flow** sheet tab. The worksheet with information about the company's cash flow is now active.

5. Click the **Income Statement** sheet tab to make the Income Statement worksheet the active sheet.

Navigating Within a Worksheet

A worksheet is organized into a grid of cells. Each cell is identified by a **cell reference**, which indicates the column and row in which the cell is located. For example, in Figure 1-5, the company name, Game Card, is in cell A1, which is the intersection of column A and row 1. The column letter always appears before the row number in any cell reference. The cell that is currently selected in the worksheet is referred to as the active cell. The active cell is highlighted with a thick green border, its cell reference appears in the Name box, and the corresponding column and row headings are highlighted. The active cell in Figure 1-5 is cell A1.

Row numbers range from 1 to 1,048,576, and column labels are letters in alphabetical order. The first 26 column headings range from A to Z. After Z, the next column headings are labeled AA, AB, AC, and so forth. Excel allows a maximum of 16,384 columns in a worksheet (the last column has the heading XFD). This means that you can create large worksheets whose content extends well beyond what is visible in the workbook window.

To move different parts of the worksheet into view, you can use the horizontal and vertical scroll bars located at the bottom and right edges of the workbook window, respectively. A scroll bar has arrow buttons that you can click to shift the worksheet one column or row in the specified direction, and a scroll box that you can drag to shift the worksheet in the direction you drag.

You will scroll the active worksheet so you can review the rest of the Game Card income statement.

To scroll through the Income Statement worksheet:

▶ **1.** On the vertical scroll bar, click the **down arrow** button [▼] to scroll down the Income Statement worksheet until you see cell B36, which displays the company's net income value of $104,200.

▶ **2.** On the horizontal scroll bar, click the **right arrow** button [▶] three times. The worksheet scrolls three columns to the right, moving columns A through C out of view.

▶ **3.** On the horizontal scroll bar, drag the **scroll box** to the left until you see column A.

▶ **4.** On the vertical scroll bar, drag the **scroll box** up until you see the top of the worksheet and cell A1.

Scrolling the worksheet does not change the location of the active cell. Although the active cell might shift out of view, you can always see the location of the active cell in the Name box. To make a different cell active, you can either click a new cell or use the keyboard to move between cells, as described in Figure 1-7.

| Figure 1-7 | Excel navigation keys |

Press	To move the active cell
↑ ↓ ← →	Up, down, left, or right one cell
Home	To column A of the current row
Ctrl+Home	To cell A1
Ctrl+End	To the last cell in the worksheet that contains data
Enter	Down one row or to the start of the next row of data
Shift+Enter	Up one row
Tab	One column to the right
Shift+Tab	One column to the left
PgUp, PgDn	Up or down one screen
Ctrl+PgUp, Ctrl+PgDn	To the previous or next sheet in the workbook

You will use both your mouse and your keyboard to change the location of the active cell in the Income Statement worksheet.

To change the active cell:

▶ **1.** Move your pointer over cell **A5**, and then click the mouse button. The active cell moves from cell A1 to cell A5. A green border appears around cell A5, the column heading for column A and the row heading for row 5 are both highlighted, and the cell reference in the Name box changes from A1 to A5.

▶ **2.** Press the → key. The active cell moves one cell to the right to cell B5.

▶ **3.** Press the **PgDn** key on your keyboard. The active cell moves down one full screen.

▶ **4.** Press the **PgUp** key. The active cell moves up one full screen, returning to cell B5.

▶ **5.** Press the **Ctrl+Home** keys. The active cell returns to the first cell in the worksheet, cell A1.

The mouse and keyboard provide quick ways to navigate the active worksheet. For larger worksheets that span several screens, you can move directly to a specific cell using the Go To command or by typing a cell reference in the Name box. You will try both of these methods.

To use the Go To dialog box and the Name box:

▶ **1.** On the Home tab, in the Editing group, click the **Find & Select** button, and then click **Go To** on the menu that opens (or press the **Ctrl+G** keys). The Go To dialog box opens.

▶ **2.** Type **B34** in the Reference box. See Figure 1-8.

Figure 1-8   Go To dialog box

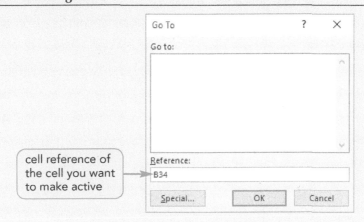

cell reference of the cell you want to make active

▶ **3.** Click the **OK** button. Cell B34 becomes the active cell, displaying 182,000, which is the total expenses for Game Card. Because cell B34 is the active cell, its cell reference appears in the Name box.

▶ **4.** Click in the Name box, type **A1**, and then press the **Enter** key. Cell A1 is again the active cell.

Selecting a Cell Range

Many tasks in Excel require you to work with a group of cells. A group of cells in a rectangular block is called a cell range (or simply a range). Each range is identified with a **range reference** that includes the cell reference of the upper-left cell of the rectangular block and the cell reference of the lower-right cell separated by a colon. For example, the range reference A1:G5 refers to all of the cells in the rectangular block from cell A1 through cell G5.

As with individual cells, you can select cell ranges using your mouse, the keyboard, or commands. You will select a range in the Income Statement worksheet.

To select a cell range:

▶ 1. Click cell **A5** to select it, and without releasing the mouse button, drag down to cell **B8**.

▶ 2. Release the mouse button. The range A5:B8 is selected. The selected cells are highlighted and surrounded by a green border. The first cell you selected in the range, cell A5, is the active cell in the worksheet. The active cell in a selected range is white. The Quick Analysis button appears, providing options for working with the range; you will use this button in another module. See Figure 1-9.

TIP

You can also select a range by clicking its upper-left cell, holding down the Shift key as you click its lower-right cell, and then releasing the Shift key.

Figure 1-9   Range A5:B8 selected

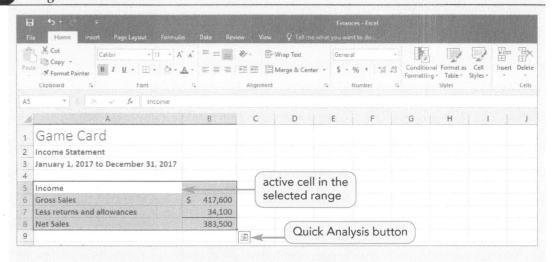

▶ 3. Click cell **A1** to deselect the range.

Another type of range is a nonadjacent range, which is a collection of separate rectangular ranges. The range reference for a nonadjacent range includes the range reference to each range separated by a comma. For example, the range reference A1:G5,A10:G15 includes two ranges—the first range is the rectangular block of cells from cell A1 to cell G5, and the second range is the rectangular block of cells from cell A10 to cell G15.

You will select a nonadjacent range in the Income Statement worksheet.

To select a nonadjacent range in the Income Statement worksheet:

▶ 1. Click cell **A5**, hold down the **Shift** key as you click cell **B8**, and then release the **Shift** key to select the range A5:B8.

▶ 2. Hold down the **Ctrl** key as you drag to select the range **A10:B14**, and then release the **Ctrl** key. The two separate blocks of cells in the nonadjacent range A5:B8,A10:B14 are selected. See Figure 1-10.

Figure 1-10 Nonadjacent range A5:B8,A10:B14 selected

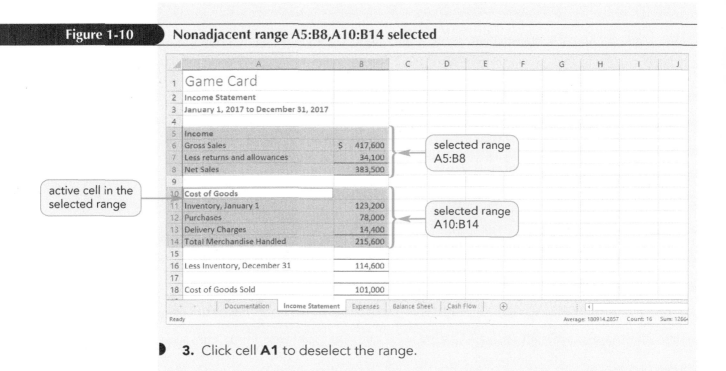

3. Click cell **A1** to deselect the range.

Closing a Workbook

Once you are finished with a workbook you can close it. When you close a workbook, a dialog box might open, asking whether you want to save any changes you may have made to the document. If you have made changes that you want to keep, you should save the workbook. Since you have finished reviewing the financial workbook for Game Card, you will close it without saving any changes you may have inadvertently made to the document contents.

To close the workbook:

1. On the ribbon, click the **File** tab to display Backstage view, and then click **Close** in the navigation bar (or press the **Ctrl+W** keys).

2. If a dialog box opens, asking whether you want to save your changes to the workbook, click the **Don't Save** button. The workbook closes without saving any changes. Excel remains opens, ready for you to create or open another workbook.

Planning a Workbook

It's good practice to plan out your workbooks before you begin creating them. You can do this by using a planning analysis sheet, which includes the following questions that help you think about the workbook's purpose and how to achieve your desired results:

1. **What problems do I want to solve?** The answer identifies the goal or purpose of the workbook. For example, Peter wants you to record customer orders and be able to analyze details from these orders.
2. **What data do I need?** The answer identifies the type of data that you need to collect and enter into the workbook. For example, Peter needs customer contact

information, an order ID number, the date the order shipped, the shipping method, a list of games ordered, the quantity of each item ordered, and the price of each item.

3. **What calculations do I need?** The answer identifies the formulas you need to apply to the data you have collected and entered. For the customer orders, Peter needs to calculate the charge for each item ordered, the total number of items ordered, the shipping cost, the sales tax, and the total cost of the order.

4. **What form should my solution take?** The answer impacts the appearance of the workbook content and how it should be presented to others. For example, Peter wants the order information stored in a single worksheet that is easy to read and prints clearly.

Based on Peter's plan, you will create a workbook containing the details of a recent customer order. Peter will use this workbook as a model for future workbooks detailing other customer orders.

PROSKILLS

Written Communication: Creating Effective Workbooks

Workbooks convey information in written form. As with any type of writing, the final product creates an impression and provides an indicator of your interest, knowledge, and attention to detail. To create the best impression, all workbooks—especially those you intend to share with others such as coworkers and clients—should be well planned, well organized, and well written.

A well-designed workbook should clearly identify its overall goal and present information in an organized format. The data it includes—both the entered values and the calculated values—should be accurate. The process of developing an effective workbook includes the following steps:

- Determine the workbook's purpose, content, and organization before you start.
- Create a list of the sheets used in the workbook, noting each sheet's purpose.
- Insert a documentation sheet that describes the workbook's purpose and organization. Include the name of the workbook author, the date the workbook was created, and any additional information that will help others to track the workbook to its source.
- Enter all of the data in the workbook. Add labels to indicate what the values represent and, if possible, where they originated so others can view the source of your data.
- Enter formulas for calculated items rather than entering the calculated values into the workbook. For more complicated calculations, provide documentation explaining them.
- Test the workbook with a variety of values; edit the data and formulas to correct errors.
- Save the workbook and create a backup copy when the project is completed. Print the workbook's contents if you need to provide a hard-copy version to others or for your files.
- Maintain a history of your workbook as it goes through different versions, so that you and others can quickly see how the workbook has changed during revisions.

By including clearly written documentation, explanatory text, a logical organization, and accurate data and formulas, you will create effective workbooks that others can use easily.

Starting a New Workbook

You create new workbooks from the New screen in Backstage view. Similar to the Recent screen that opened when you started Excel, the New screen includes templates for a variety of workbook types. You can see a preview of what the different workbooks will look like. You will create a new workbook from the Blank workbook template, in which you can add all of the content and design Peter wants for the Game Card customer order worksheet.

To start a new, blank workbook:

1. On the ribbon, click the **File** tab to display Backstage view.

2. Click **New** in the navigation bar to display the New screen, which includes access to templates for a variety of workbooks.

3. Click the **Blank workbook** tile. A blank workbook opens.

   In these modules, the workbook window is zoomed to 120% for better readability. If you want to zoom your workbook window to match the figures, complete Step 4. If you prefer to work in the default zoom of 100% or at another zoom level, read but do not complete Step 4; you might see more or less of the worksheet on your screen, but this will not affect your work in the modules.

4. If you want your workbook window zoomed to 120% to match the figures, on the Zoom slider at the bottom-right of the program window, click the **Zoom In** button ➕ twice to increase the percentage to 120%. The 120% magnification increases the size of each cell but reduces the number of worksheet cells visible in the workbook window. See Figure 1-11.

TIP

You can also create a new, blank workbook by pressing the Ctrl+N keys.

| Figure 1-11 | Blank workbook |

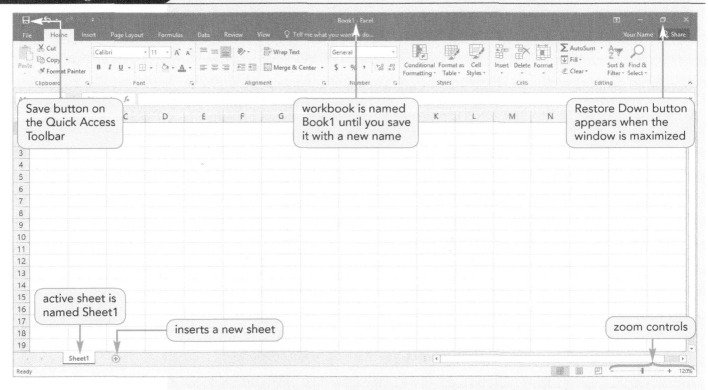

The name of the active workbook, Book1, appears in the title bar. If you open multiple blank workbooks, they are named Book1, Book2, Book3, and so forth until you save them with a more descriptive name.

Renaming and Inserting Worksheets

Blank workbooks open with a single blank worksheet named Sheet1. You can give sheets more descriptive and meaningful names. This is a good practice so that you and others can easily tell what a sheet contains. Sheet names cannot exceed 31 characters, but they can contain blank spaces and include uppercase and lowercase letters.

Because Sheet1 is not a very descriptive name, Peter wants you to rename the worksheet as Customer Order.

To rename the Sheet1 worksheet:

1. Double-click the **Sheet1** tab. The Sheet1 label in the tab is selected.
2. Type **Customer Order** as the new name, and then press the **Enter** key. The width of the sheet tab expands to fit the longer sheet name.

Many workbooks include multiple sheets so that data can be organized in logical groups. A common business practice is to include a worksheet named Documentation that contains a description of the workbook, the name of the person who prepared the workbook, and the date it was created.

Peter wants you to create two new worksheets. You will rename one worksheet as Documentation and the other worksheet as Customer Contact. The Customer Contact worksheet will be used to store the customer's contact information.

To insert and name the Documentation and Customer Contact worksheets:

1. To the right of the Customer Order sheet tab, click the **New sheet** button ⊕. A new sheet named Sheet2 is inserted to the right of the Customer Order sheet.
2. Double-click the **Sheet2** sheet tab, type **Documentation** as the new name, and then press the **Enter** key. The worksheet is renamed.
3. To the right of the Documentation sheet, click the **New sheet** button ⊕, and then rename the inserted Sheet3 worksheet as **Customer Contact**.

Moving Worksheets

A good practice is to place the most important sheets at the beginning of the workbook (the leftmost sheet tabs) and less important sheets at the end (the rightmost sheet tabs). To change the placement of sheets in a workbook, you drag them by their sheet tabs to the new location.

Peter wants you to move the Documentation worksheet to the front of the workbook, so that it appears before the Customer Order sheet.

To move the Documentation worksheet:

1. Point to the **Documentation** sheet tab. The sheet tab name changes to bold.
2. Press and hold the mouse button. The pointer changes to ⬚, and a small arrow appears in the upper-left corner of the tab.
3. Drag to the left until the small arrow appears in the upper-left corner of the Customer Order sheet tab, and then release the mouse button. The Documentation worksheet is now the first sheet in the workbook.

TIP

To copy a sheet, hold down the Ctrl key as you drag and drop its sheet tab.

Deleting Worksheets

In some workbooks, you will want to delete an existing sheet. The easiest way to delete a sheet is by using a **shortcut menu**, which is a list of commands related to a selection that opens when you click the right mouse button. Peter asks you to include the customer's contact information on the Customer Order worksheet so all of the information is on one sheet.

To delete the Customer Contact worksheet from the workbook:

▶ **1.** Right-click the **Customer Contact** sheet tab. A shortcut menu opens.

▶ **2.** Click **Delete**. The Customer Contact worksheet is removed from the workbook.

Saving a Workbook

As you modify a workbook, you should save it regularly—every 10 minutes or so is a good practice. The first time you save a workbook, the Save As dialog box opens so you can name the file and choose where to save it. You can save the workbook on your computer or network or to your account on OneDrive.

To save your workbook for the first time:

▶ **1.** On the Quick Access Toolbar, click the **Save** button 🖫 (or press the **Ctrl+S** keys). The Save As screen in Backstage view opens.

▶ **2.** Click the **Browse** button. The Save As dialog box opens.

▶ **3.** Navigate to the location specified by your instructor.

▶ **4.** In the File name box, select **Book1** (the suggested name) if it is not already selected, and then type **Game Card**.

▶ **5.** Verify that **Excel Workbook** appears in the Save as type box.

▶ **6.** Click the **Save** button. The workbook is saved, the dialog box closes, and the workbook window reappears with the new filename in the title bar.

As you modify the workbook, you will need to resave the file. Because you already saved the workbook with a filename, the next time you save, the Save command saves the changes you made to the workbook without opening the Save As dialog box.

Entering Text, Dates, and Numbers

Workbook content is entered into worksheet cells. Those cells can contain text, numbers, or dates and times. **Text data** is any combination of letters, numbers, and symbols. Text data is often referred to as a **text string** because it contains a series, or string, of text characters. **Numeric data** is any number that can be used in a mathematical calculation. **Date** and **time data** are commonly recognized formats for date and time values. For example, Excel interprets the cell entry April 15, 2017 as a date and not as text. New data is placed into the active cell of the current worksheet. As you enter data, the entry appears in both the active cell and the formula bar. By default, text is left-aligned in cells, and numbers, dates, and times are right-aligned.

Entering Text

Text is often used in worksheets to label other data and to identify areas of a sheet. Peter wants you to enter some of the information from the planning analysis sheet into the Documentation sheet.

To enter text in the Documentation sheet:

▶ **1.** Go to the **Documentation** sheet, and then click the **Ctrl+Home** keys to make sure cell A1 is the active cell.

▶ **2.** Type **Game Card** in cell A1. As you type, the text appears in cell A1 and in the formula bar.

▶ **3.** Press the **Enter** key twice. The text is entered into cell A1, and the active cell moves down two rows to cell A3.

▶ **4.** Type **Author** in cell A3, and then press the **Tab** key. The text is entered and the active cell moves one column to the right to cell B3.

▶ **5.** Type your name in cell B3, and then press the **Enter** key. The text is entered and the active cell moves one cell down and to the left to cell A4.

▶ **6.** Type **Date** in cell A4, and then press the **Tab** key. The text is entered, and the active cell moves one column to the right to cell B4, where you would enter the date you created the worksheet. For now, you will leave the cell for the date blank.

▶ **7.** Press the **Enter** key to make cell A5 the active cell, type **Purpose** in the cell, and then press the **Tab** key. The active cell moves one column to the right to cell B5.

▶ **8.** Type **To record customer game orders** in cell B5, and then press the **Enter** key. Figure 1-12 shows the text entered in the Documentation sheet.

Figure 1-12   **Text entered in the Documentation sheet**

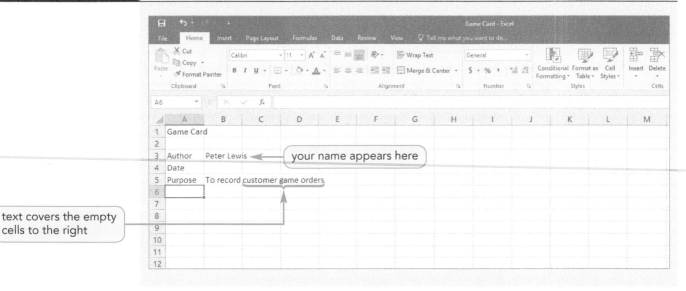

The text strings you entered in cells A1, B3, and B5 are so long that they cover the adjacent cells. Any text you enter in a cell that doesn't fit within that cell will cover the adjacent cells to the right as long as they are empty. If the adjacent cells contain data, only the text that fits into the cell is displayed. The rest of the text entry is hidden from view. The text itself is not affected. The complete text is still entered in the cell; it is just not displayed. (You will learn how to display all text in a cell in the next session.)

Undoing and Redoing an Action

As you enter data in a workbook, you might need to undo a previous action. Excel maintains a list of the actions you performed in the workbook during the current session, so you can undo most of your actions. You can use the Undo button on the Quick Access Toolbar or press the Ctrl+Z keys to reverse your most recent actions one at a time. If you want to undo more than one action, you can click the Undo button arrow and then select the earliest action you want to undo—all of the actions after the earliest action you selected are also undone.

You will undo the most recent change you made to the Documentation sheet— the text you entered into cell B5. Then you will enter more descriptive and accurate description of the worksheet's purpose.

To undo the text entry in cell B5:

▶ 1. On the Quick Access Toolbar, click the **Undo** button 🔙 (or press the **Ctrl+Z** keys). The last action is reversed, removing the text you entered in cell B5.

▶ 2. In cell B5, type **To record purchases of board games from Game Card**, and then press the **Enter** key.

If you want to restore actions you have undone, you can redo them. To redo one action at a time, you can click the Redo button 🔁 on the Quick Access Toolbar or press the Ctrl+Y keys. To redo multiple actions at once, you can click the Redo button arrow 🔁▾ and then click the earliest action you want to redo. After you undo or redo an action, Excel continues the action list starting from any new changes you make to the workbook.

Editing Cell Content

As you continue to create your workbook, you might find mistakes you need to correct or entries that you want to change. To replace all of the content in a cell, you simply select the cell and then type the new entry to overwrite the previous entry. However, if you need to replace only part of a cell's content, you can work in **Edit mode**. To switch to Edit mode, you double-click the cell. A blinking insertion point indicates where the new content you type will be inserted. In the cell or formula bar, the pointer changes to an I-beam, which you can use to select text in the cell. Anything you type replaces the selected content.

Because customers can order more than just games from Game Card, Peter wants you to edit the text in cell B5. You will do that in Edit mode.

To edit the text in cell B5:

▶ 1. Double-click cell **B5** to select the cell and switch to Edit mode. A blinking insertion point appears within the text of cell B5. The status bar displays Edit instead of Ready to indicate that the cell is in Edit mode.

▶ 2. Press the **arrow keys** to move the insertion point directly to the left of the word "from" in the cell text.

▶ 3. Type **and other items** and then press the **spacebar**. The cell now reads "To record purchases of board games and other items from Game Card." See Figure 1-13.

Figure 1-13   **Edited text in the Documentation sheet**

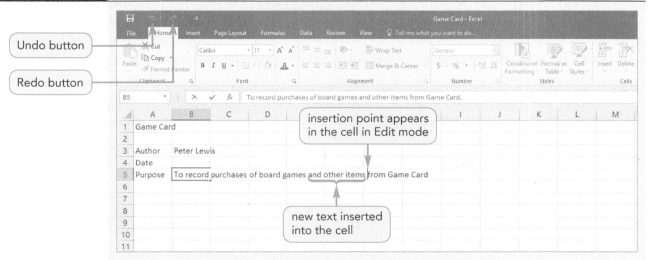

4. Press the **Enter** key to exit the cell and return to Ready mode.

Understanding AutoComplete

As you type text in the active cell, Excel tries to anticipate the remaining characters by displaying text that begins with the same letters as a previous entry in the same column. This feature, known as **AutoComplete**, helps make entering repetitive text easier. To accept the suggested text, press the Tab or Enter key. To override the suggested text, continue to type the text you want to enter in the cell. AutoComplete does not work with dates or numbers or when a blank cell is between the previous entry and the text you are typing.

Next, you will enter the contact information for Leslie Ritter, a customer from Brockton, Massachusetts, who recently placed an order with Game Card. You will enter this information on the Customer Order worksheet.

To enter Leslie Ritter's contact information:

1. Click the **Customer Order** sheet tab to make it the active sheet.

2. In cell A1, type **Customer Order** as the worksheet title, and then press the **Enter** key twice. The worksheet title is entered in cell A1, and the active cell becomes cell A3.

3. Type **Ship To** in cell A3, and then press the **Enter** key. The label is entered in the cell, and the active cell is now cell A4.

4. In the range A4:A10, enter the following labels, pressing the **Enter** key after each entry and ignoring any AutoComplete suggestions: **First Name**, **Last Name**, **Address**, **City**, **State**, **Postal Code**, and **Phone**.

5. Click cell **B4** to make that cell the active cell.

6. In the range B4:B10, enter the following contact information, pressing the **Enter** key after each entry and ignoring any AutoComplete suggestions: **Leslie**, **Ritter**, **805 Mountain St.**, **Brockton**, **MA**, **02302**, and **(508) 555-1072**. See Figure 1-14.

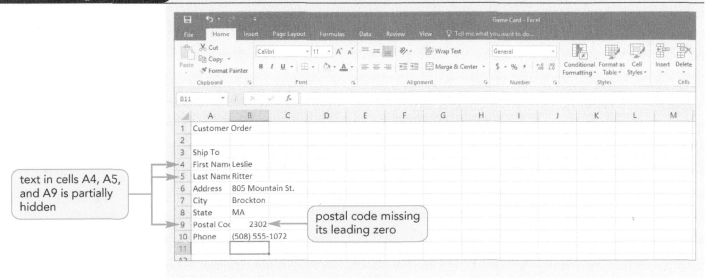

Figure 1-14   **Customer information entered in the Customer Order worksheet**

text in cells A4, A5, and A9 is partially hidden

postal code missing its leading zero

Displaying Numbers as Text

When you enter a number in a cell, Excel treats the entry as a number and ignores any leading zero. For example, in cell B9, the leading zero in the postal code 02302 is missing. Excel displays 2302 because it treats the postal code as a number, and 2302 and 02302 have the same value. To specify that a number entry should be considered text and all digits should be displayed, you include an apostrophe (') before the numbers.

To enter the postal code as text:

1. Click cell **B9** to select it. Notice that the postal code is right-aligned in the cell, unlike the other text entries, which are left-aligned—another indication that the entry is being treated as a number.

2. Type **'02302** in cell B9, and then press the **Enter** key. The text 02302 appears in cell B9 and is left-aligned in the cell, matching all of the other text entries.

3. Click cell **B9** to select it again. See Figure 1-15.

Figure 1-15   **Number entered as text**

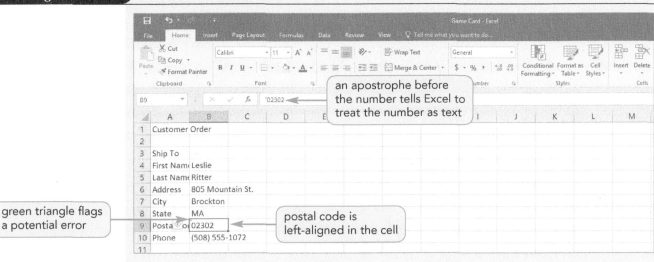

an apostrophe before the number tells Excel to treat the number as text

green triangle flags a potential error

postal code is left-aligned in the cell

TIP

To remove a green triangle, click the cell, click the yellow caution icon that appears to the left of the cell, and then click Ignore Error.

Notice that a green triangle appears in the upper-left corner of cell B9. Excel uses green triangles to flag potential errors in cells. In this case, it is simply a warning that you entered a number as a text string. Because this is intentional, you do not have to edit the cell to fix the "error." Green triangles appear only in the workbook window and not in any printouts of the worksheet.

Entering Dates

You can enter dates in any of the standard date formats. For example, all of the following entries are recognized by Excel as the same date:

- 4/6/2017
- 4/6/17
- 4-6-2017
- April 6, 2017
- 6-Apr-17

Even though you enter a date as text, Excel stores the date as a number equal to the number of days between the specified date and January 0, 1900. Times are also entered as text and stored as fractions of a 24-hour day. For example April 4, 2017 @ 6:00 PM is stored by Excel as 42,842.75 which is 42,842 days after January 0, 1900 plus 3/4 of one day. Dates and times are stored as numbers so that Excel can easily perform date and time calculations, such as determining the elapsed time between one date and another.

Based on the default date format your computer uses, Excel might alter the format of a date after you type it. For example, if you enter the date 4/6/17 into the active cell, Excel might display the date with the four-digit year value, 4/6/2017; if you enter the text April 6, 2017, Excel might change the date format to 6-Apr-17. Changing the date or time format does not affect the underlying date or time value.

INSIGHT

International Date Formats

As business transactions become more international in scope, you may need to adopt international standards for expressing dates, times, and currency values in your workbooks. For example, a worksheet cell might contain 06/05/17. This format could be interpreted as any of the following dates: the 5th of June, 2017; the 6th of May, 2017; and the 17th of May, 2006.

The interpretation depends on which country the workbook has been designed for. You can avoid this problem by entering the full date, as in June 5, 2017. However, this might not work with documents written in foreign languages, such as Japanese, that use different character symbols.

To solve this problem, many international businesses adopt ISO (International Organization for Standardization) dates in the format *yyyy-mm-dd*, where *yyyy* is the four-digit year value, *mm* is the two-digit month value, and *dd* is the two-digit day value. So, a date such as June 5, 2017 is entered as 2017/06/05. If you choose to use this international date format, make sure that people using your workbook understand this format so they do not misinterpret the dates. You can include information about the date format in the Documentation sheet.

For the Game Card workbook, you will enter dates in the format *mm/dd/yyyy*, where *mm* is the two-digit month number, *dd* is the two-digit day number, and *yyyy* is the four-digit year number.

To enter the current date into the Documentation sheet:

1. Click the **Documentation** sheet tab to make the Documentation sheet the active worksheet.

2. Click cell **B4** to make it the active cell, type the current date in the *mm/dd/yyyy* format, and then press the **Enter** key. The date is entered in the cell.

   Trouble? Depending on your system configuration, Excel might change the date to the date format *dd-mmm-yy*. This difference will not affect your work.

3. Click the **Customer Order** sheet tab to return to the Customer Order worksheet.

The next part of the Customer Order worksheet will list the items that customer Leslie Ritter purchased from Game Card. As shown in Figure 1-16, the list includes identifying information about each item, including the item's price, and the quantity of each item ordered.

Figure 1-16   **Customer order from Leslie Ritter**

Stock ID	Category	Manufacturer	Title	Players	Price	Qty
SG71	Strategy Game	Drebeck Brothers	Kings and Jacks: A Medieval Game of Deception	4	$39.95	2
FG14	Family Game	Misty Games	Twirple, Tweedle, and Twaddle	6	$24.55	1
PG05	Party Game	Parlor Vision	Trivia Connection	8	$29.12	1
SU38	Supplies	Parlor Vision	Box of Dice (10)		$9.95	3
SG29	Strategy Game	Drebeck Brothers	Solar Warfare	2	$35.15	1

You will enter the first four columns of the order into the worksheet.

To enter the first part of the customer order:

1. In the Customer Order worksheet, click cell **A12** to make it the active cell, type **Stock ID** as the column label, and then press the **Tab** key to move to cell B12.

2. In the range B12:D12, type the following labels, pressing the **Tab** key to move to the next cell: **Category**, **Manufacturer**, and **Title**.

3. Press the **Enter** key to go to the next row of the worksheet, making cell A13 the active cell.

4. In the range A13:D17, type the Stock ID, Category, Manufacturer, and Title text for the five items purchased by Leslie Ritter listed in Figure 1-16, pressing the **Tab** key to move from one cell to the next, and pressing the **Enter** key to move to a new row. Note that the text in some cells will be partially hidden; you will fix that problem shortly. See Figure 1-17.

Figure 1-17   Partial customer order

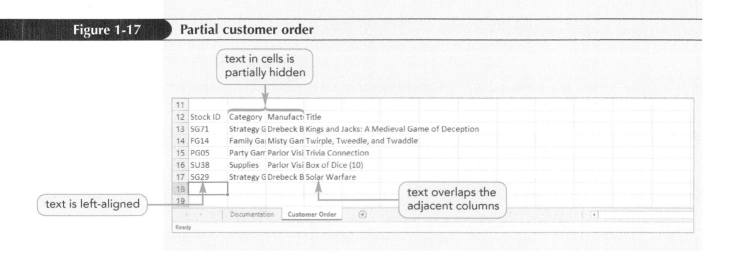

text in cells is partially hidden

text is left-aligned

text overlaps the adjacent columns

Entering Numbers

TIP

If a number exceeds its cell's width, you see ###### instead of the number. You can display the entire number by increasing the column width.

In Excel, numbers can be integers such as 378, decimals such as 1.95, or negatives such as −5.2. In the case of currency and percentages, you can include the currency symbol and percent sign when you enter the value. Excel treats a currency value such as $87.25 as the number 87.25, and a percentage such as 95% as the decimal 0.95. Much like dates, currency and percentages are formatted in a convenient way for you to read, but only the number is stored within the cell. This makes it easier to perform calculations with currency and percentage values.

You will complete Leslie Ritter's order by entering the players, price, and quantity values.

To enter the rest of the customer order:

1. In the range E12:G12, enter **Players**, **Price**, and **Qty** as the labels.

2. In cell E13, enter **4** as the number of players for the game Kings and Jacks.

3. In cell F13, enter **$39.95** as the price of the game. The game price is stored as a number but displayed with the $ symbol.

4. In cell G13, enter **2** as the quantity of the game ordered by Leslie.

5. In the range E14:G17, enter the remaining number of players, prices, and quantities shown earlier in Figure 1-16. See Figure 1-18.

Figure 1-18   Completed customer order

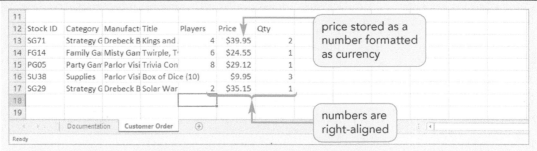

price stored as a number formatted as currency

numbers are right-aligned

6. On the Quick Access Toolbar, click the **Save** button 🖫 (or press the **Ctrl+S** keys) to save the workbook.

Resizing Columns and Rows

Much of the information in the Customer Order worksheet is difficult to read because of the hidden text. You can display all of the cell contents by changing the size of the columns and rows in the worksheet.

Changing Column Widths

Column widths are expressed as the number of characters the column can contain. The default column width is 8.43 standard-sized characters. In general, this means that you can type eight characters in a cell; any additional text is hidden or overlaps the adjacent cell. Column widths are also expressed in terms of pixels. A **pixel** is a single point on a computer monitor or printout. A column width of 8.43 characters is equivalent to 64 pixels.

INSIGHT

Setting Column Widths

On a computer monitor, pixel size is based on screen resolution. As a result, cell contents that look fine on one screen might appear very different when viewed on a screen with a different resolution. If you work on multiple computers or share your workbooks with others, you should set column widths based on the maximum number of characters you want displayed in the cells rather than pixel size. This ensures that everyone sees the cell contents the way you intended.

You will increase the width of column A so that the contact information labels in cells A4, A5, and A9 are completely displayed.

To increase the width of column A:

▶ **1.** Point to the **right border** of the column A heading until the pointer changes to ✛.

▶ **2.** Click and drag to the right until the width of the column heading reaches **15** characters, but do not release the mouse button. The ScreenTip that appears as you resize the column shows the new column width in characters and in pixels. See Figure 1-19.

Figure 1-19   **Width of column A increased to 15 characters**

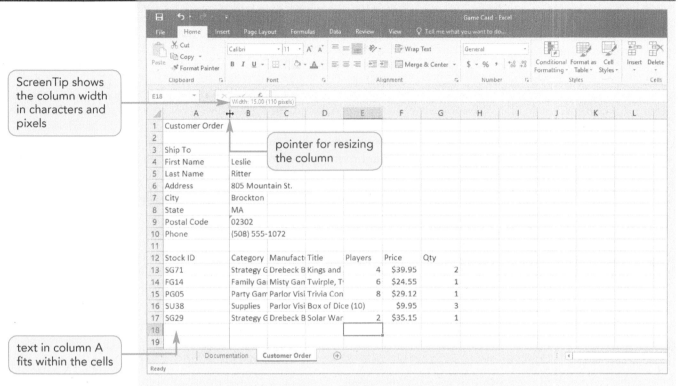

ScreenTip shows the column width in characters and pixels

pointer for resizing the column

text in column A fits within the cells

> **3.** Release the mouse button. The width of column A expands to 15 characters, and all of the text within that column is visible within the cells.

You will increase the widths of columns B and C to 18 characters so that their complete entries are visible. Rather than resizing each column separately, you can select both columns and adjust their widths at the same time.

To increase the widths of columns B and C:

> **1.** Click the **column B** heading. The entire column is selected.

> **2.** Hold down the **Ctrl** key, click the **column C** heading, and then release the **Ctrl** key. Both columns B and C are selected.

> **3.** Point to the **right border** of the column C heading until the pointer changes to ⬌.

> **4.** Drag to the right until the column width changes to **18** characters, and then release the mouse button. Both column widths increase to 18 characters and display all of the entered text.

TIP

To select adjacent columns, you can also click and drag the pointer over multiple column headings.

Using the mouse to resize columns can be imprecise and a challenge to some users with special needs. The Format command on the Home tab gives you precise control over column width and row height settings. You will use the Format command to set the width of column D to exactly 25 characters so that the hidden text is visible.

To set the width of column D using the Format command:

1. Click the **column D** heading. The entire column is selected.

2. On the Home tab, in the Cells group, click the **Format** button, and then click **Column Width.** The Column Width dialog box opens.

3. Type **25** in the Column width box to specify the new column width.

4. Click the **OK** button. The width of column D changes to 25 characters.

5. Click cell **A12** to deselect column D. Figure 1-20 shows the revised column widths for the customer order columns.

| Figure 1-20 | Resized columns |

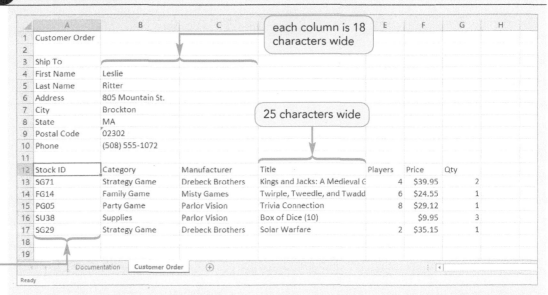

Notice that 25 characters is not wide enough to display all of the characters in each cell of column D. Instead of manually resizing the column width or row height to fit it to the cell contents, you can autofit the column or row. **AutoFit** changes the column width or row height to display the longest or tallest entry within the column or row. You autofit a column or a row by double-clicking the right border of the column heading or the bottom border of the row heading.

TIP

If the row or column is blank, autofitting restores its default height or width.

To autofit the contents of column D:

1. Point to the **right border** of column D until the pointer changes to ↔.

2. Double-click the **right border** of the column D heading. The width of column D increases to about 43 characters so that the longest item title is completely visible.

Wrapping Text Within a Cell

Sometimes, resizing a column width to display all of the text entered in the cells results in a cell that is too wide to read or print nicely. Another way to display long text entries is to wrap text to a new line when it would otherwise extend beyond the cell boundaries. When text wraps within a cell, the row height increases so that all of the text within the cell is displayed.

You will resize column D and then wrap the text entries in the column.

To wrap text in column D:

▶ **1.** Resize the width of column D to **25** characters.

▶ **2.** Select the range **D13:D17**. These cells include the titles that extend beyond the column width.

▶ **3.** On the Home tab, in the Alignment group, click the **Wrap Text** button. The Wrap Text button is toggled on, and text in the selected cells that exceeds the column width wraps to a new line.

▶ **4.** Click cell **A12** to make it the active cell. See Figure 1-21.

Figure 1-21   **Text wrapped within cells**

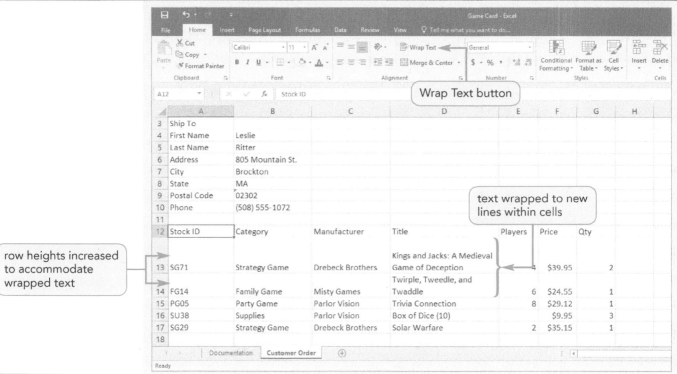

If you want to create a new line within a cell, press the Alt+Enter keys to move the insertion point to the next line within the cell. Whatever you type next will appear on the new line in the cell.

Changing Row Heights

The height of a row is measured in points or pixels. A **point** is approximately 1/72 of an inch. The default row height is 15 points, or 20 pixels. Row heights are set in the same way as column widths. You can drag the bottom border of the row heading to a new row height, specify a row height using the Format command, or autofit the row's height to match its content.

Peter notices that the height of row 13 is a little too tall for its contents. He asks you to change to it 30 points.

To change the height of row 13:

1. Point to the **bottom border** of the row 13 heading until the pointer changes to ✛.

2. Drag the **bottom border** down until the height of the row is equal to **30** points (or **40** pixels), and then release the mouse button. The height of row 13 is set to 30 points.

3. Press the **Ctrl+S** keys to save the workbook.

TIP

You can also set the row height by clicking the Format button in the Cells group on the Home tab and then using the Row Height command.

You have entered most of the data for Leslie Ritter's order at Game Card. In the next session, you will calculate the total charge for the order and print the worksheet.

REVIEW

Session 1.1 Quick Check

1. What are the two types of sheets used in a workbook?
2. What is the cell reference for the cell located in the second column and fifth row of a worksheet?
3. What is the range reference for the block of cells C2 through D10?
4. What is the reference for the nonadjacent block of cells B5 through C10 and cells B15 through D20?
5. What keyboard shortcut makes the active cell to cell A1?
6. What is text data?
7. How do you enter a number so that Excel sees it as text?
8. Cell B2 contains the entry May 3, 2017. Why doesn't Excel consider this a text entry?
9. How do you autofit a column to match the longest cell entry?

Session 1.2 Visual Overview:

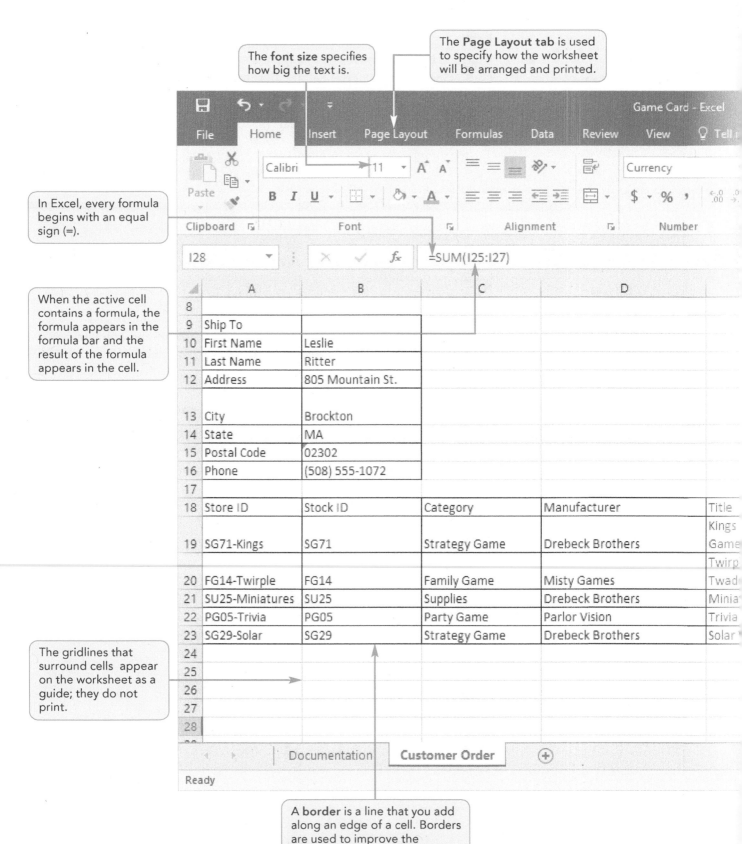

The **font size** specifies how big the text is.

The **Page Layout tab** is used to specify how the worksheet will be arranged and printed.

In Excel, every formula begins with an equal sign (=).

When the active cell contains a formula, the formula appears in the formula bar and the result of the formula appears in the cell.

The gridlines that surround cells appear on the worksheet as a guide; they do not print.

A **border** is a line that you add along an edge of a cell. Borders are used to improve the readability of the worksheet.

Game Card - Excel

I28   =SUM(I25:I27)

	A	B	C	D	
8					
9	Ship To				
10	First Name	Leslie			
11	Last Name	Ritter			
12	Address	805 Mountain St.			
13	City	Brockton			
14	State	MA			
15	Postal Code	02302			
16	Phone	(508) 555-1072			
17					
18	Store ID	Stock ID	Category	Manufacturer	Title
19	SG71-Kings	SG71	Strategy Game	Drebeck Brothers	Kings Game
20	FG14-Twirple	FG14	Family Game	Misty Games	Twirp Twad
21	SU25-Miniatures	SU25	Supplies	Drebeck Brothers	Minia
22	PG05-Trivia	PG05	Party Game	Parlor Vision	Trivia
23	SG29-Solar	SG29	Strategy Game	Drebeck Brothers	Solar
24					
25					
26					
27					
28					

Documentation   **Customer Order**   ⊕

Ready

Excel Formulas and Functions

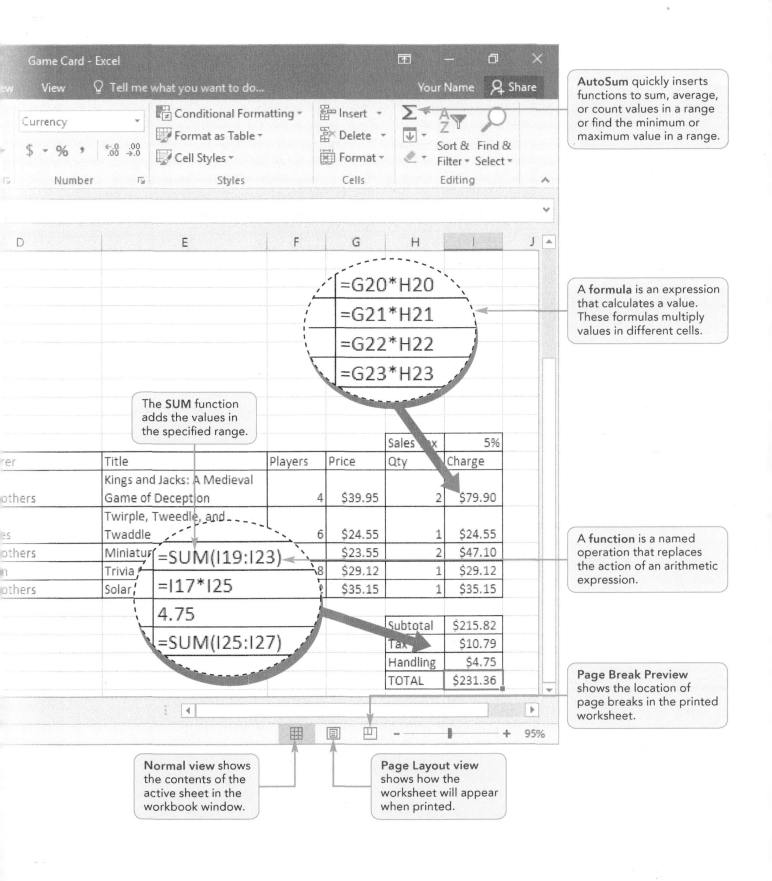

AutoSum quickly inserts functions to sum, average, or count values in a range or find the minimum or maximum value in a range.

A **formula** is an expression that calculates a value. These formulas multiply values in different cells.

The **SUM** function adds the values in the specified range.

A **function** is a named operation that replaces the action of an arithmetic expression.

Page Break Preview shows the location of page breaks in the printed worksheet.

Normal view shows the contents of the active sheet in the workbook window.

Page Layout view shows how the worksheet will appear when printed.

Formulas shown in circle:
=G20*H20
=G21*H21
=G22*H22
=G23*H23

=SUM(I19:I23)
=I17*I25
4.75
=SUM(I25:I27)

Table content:

	Title	Players	Price	Qty	Charge
				Sales Tax	5%
others	Kings and Jacks: A Medieval Game of Deception	4	$39.95	2	$79.90
es	Twirple, Tweedle, and Twaddle	6	$24.55	1	$24.55
others	Miniatu		$23.55	2	$47.10
n	Trivia	8	$29.12	1	$29.12
others	Solar		$35.15	1	$35.15
				Subtotal	$215.82
				Tax	$10.79
				Handling	$4.75
				TOTAL	$231.36

95%

Performing Calculations with Formulas

So far you have entered text, numbers, and dates in the worksheet. However, the main reason for using Excel is to perform calculations and analysis on data. For example, Peter wants the workbook to calculate the number of items that the customer ordered and how much revenue the order will generate. Such calculations are added to a worksheet using formulas and functions.

Entering a Formula

A formula is an expression that returns a value. In most cases, this is a number—though it could also be text or a date. In Excel, every formula begins with an equal sign (=) followed by an expression describing the operation that returns the value. If you don't begin the formula with the equal sign, Excel assumes that you are entering text and will not treat the cell contents as a formula.

A formula is written using **operators** that combine different values, resulting in a single value that is then displayed in the cell. The most common operators are **arithmetic operators** that perform addition, subtraction, multiplication, division, and exponentiation. For example, the following formula adds 3 and 8, returning a value of 11:

=3+8

Most Excel formulas contain references to cells rather than specific values. This allows you to change the values used in the calculation without having to modify the formula itself. For example, the following formula returns the result of adding the values stored in cells C3 and D10:

=C3+D10

If the value 3 is stored in cell C3 and the value 8 is stored in cell D10, this formula would also return a value of 11. If you later changed the value in cell C3 to 10, the formula would return a value of 18. Figure 1-22 describes the different arithmetic operators and provides examples of formulas.

| Figure 1-22 | Arithmetic operators |

Operation	Arithmetic Operator	Example	Description
Addition	+	=B1+B2+B3	Adds the values in cells B1, B2, and B3
Subtraction	–	=C9-B2	Subtracts the value in cell B2 from the value in cell C9
Multiplication	*	=C9*B9	Multiplies the values in cells C9 and B9
Division	/	=C9/B9	Divides the value in cell C9 by the value in cell B9
Exponentiation	^	=B5^3	Raises the value of cell B5 to the third power

If a formula contains more than one arithmetic operator, Excel performs the calculation based on the **order of operations**, which is the sequence in which operators are applied in a calculation:

1. Calculate any operations within parentheses

2. Calculate any exponentiations (^)

3. Calculate any multiplications (*) and divisions (/)

4. Calculate any additions (+) and subtractions (–)

For example, the following formula returns the value 23 because multiplying 4 by 5 takes precedence over adding 3:

=3+4*5

If a formula contains two or more operators with the same level of priority, the operators are applied in order from left to right. In the following formula, Excel first multiplies 4 by 10 and then divides that result by 8 to return the value 5:

=4*10/8

When parentheses are used, the value inside them is calculated first. In the following formula, Excel calculates (3+4) first, and then multiplies that result by 5 to return the value 35:

=(3+4)*5

Figure 1-23 shows how slight changes in a formula affect the order of operations and the result of the formula.

Figure 1-23   **Order of operations applied to Excel formulas**

Formula	Order of Operations	Result
=50+10*5	10*5 calculated first and then 50 is added	100
=(50+10)*5	(50+10) calculated first and then 60 is multiplied by 5	300
=50/10–5	50/10 calculated first and then 5 is subtracted	0
=50/(10–5)	(10–5) calculated first and then 50 is divided by that value	10
=50/10*5	Two operators are at same precedence level, so the calculation is done left to right with 50/10 calculated first and that value is then multiplied by 5	25
=50/(10*5)	(10*5) is calculated first and then 50 is divided by that value	1

Peter wants the Customer Order worksheet to include the total amount charged for each item ordered. The charge is equal to the number of each item ordered multiplied by each item's price. You already entered this information in columns F and G. Now you will enter a formula to calculate the charge for each set of items ordered in column H.

To calculate the charge for the first item ordered:

▶ **1.** If you took a break after the previous session, make sure the Game Card workbook is open and the Customer Order worksheet is active.

▶ **2.** Click cell **H12** to make it the active cell, type **Charge** as the column label, and then press the **Enter** key. The label text is entered in cell H12, and cell H13 is now the active cell.

▶ **3.** Type **=F13*G13** (the price of the Kings and Jacks game multiplied by the number of that game ordered). As you type the formula, a list of Excel function names appears in a ScreenTip, which provides a quick method for entering functions. The list will close when you complete the formula. You will learn more about Excel functions shortly. Also, after you type each cell reference, Excel color codes each cell reference and its cell. See Figure 1-24.

Figure 1-24   **Formula being entered in a cell**

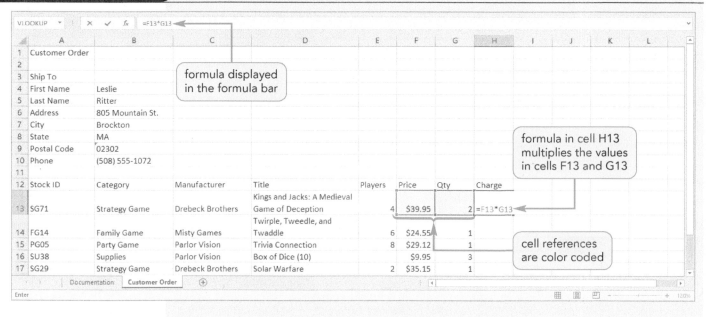

▶ 4. Press the **Enter** key. The formula is entered in cell H13 displaying the value $79.90. The result is displayed as currency because cell F13, which is referenced in the formula, contains a currency value.

▶ 5. Click cell **H13** to make it the active cell. Note that the cell displays the result of the formula, and the formula bar displays the formula you entered.

For the first item, you entered the formula by typing each cell reference in the expression. You can also insert a cell reference by clicking the cell as you type the formula. This technique reduces the possibility of error caused by typing an incorrect cell reference. You will use this method to enter the formula to calculate the charge for the second item on the order.

To enter a formula using the mouse:

▶ 1. Click cell **H14** to make it the active cell.

▶ 2. Type **=**. The equal sign indicates that you are entering a formula. Any cell you click from now on inserts the cell reference of the selected cell into the formula until you complete the formula by pressing the Enter or Tab key.

Be sure to type = first; otherwise, Excel will not recognize the entry as a formula.

▶ 3. Click cell **F14**. The cell reference is inserted into the formula in the formula bar. At this point, any cell you click changes the cell reference used in the formula. The cell reference isn't locked until you type an operator.

▶ 4. Type ***** to enter the multiplication operator. The cell reference for cell F14 is locked in the formula, and the next cell you click will be inserted after the operator.

▶ 5. Click cell **G14** to enter its cell reference in the formula. The formula is complete.

▶ 6. Press the **Enter** key. Cell H14 displays the value $24.55, which is the charge for the second item ordered.

Copying and Pasting Formulas

Sometimes you will need to repeat the same formula throughout a worksheet. Rather than retyping the formula, you can copy a formula from one cell and paste it into another cell. When you copy a formula, Excel places the formula into the **Clipboard**, which is a temporary storage location for text and graphics. When you paste, Excel takes the formula from the Clipboard and inserts it into the selected cell or range. Excel adjusts the cell references in the formula to reflect the formula's new location in the worksheet. This occurs because you usually want to copy the actions of a formula rather than the specific value the formula generates. In this case, the formula's action is to multiply the price of the item ordered by the quantity. By copying and pasting the formula, you can quickly repeat that action for every item listed in the worksheet.

You will copy the formula you entered in cell H14 to the range H15:H17 to calculate the charges on the remaining three items in Leslie Ritter's order. By copying and pasting the formula, you will save time and avoid potential mistakes from retyping the formula.

To copy and paste the formula:

▶ 1. Click cell **H14** to select the cell that contains the formula you want to copy.

▶ 2. On the Home tab, in the Clipboard group, click the **Copy** button (or press the **Ctrl+C** keys). Excel copies the formula to the Clipboard. A blinking green box surrounds the cell being copied.

▶ 3. Select the range **H15:H17**. You want to paste the formula into these cells.

▶ 4. In the Clipboard group, click the **Paste** button (or press the **Ctrl+V** keys). Excel pastes the formula into the selected cells, adjusting each formula so that the charge calculated for each ordered item is based on the corresponding values within that row. A button appears below the selected range, providing options for pasting formulas and values. See Figure 1-25.

| Figure 1-25 | Copied and pasted formula |

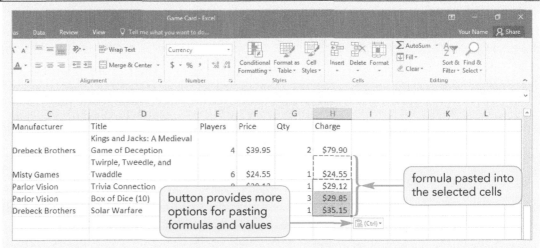

▶ 5. Click cell **H15** and verify that the formula =F15*G15 appears in the formula bar. The formula was updated to reflect the cell references in the corresponding row.

▶ 6. Click the other cells in column H, and verify that the corresponding formulas are entered in those cells.

Simplifying Formulas with Functions

In addition to cell references and operators, formulas can also contain functions. A function is a named operation that replaces the arithmetic expression in a formula. Functions are used to simplify long or complex formulas. For example, to add the values from cells A1 through A10, you could enter the following long formula:

    =A1+A2+A3+A4+A5+A6+A7+A8+A9+A10

Or, you could use the SUM function to calculate the sum of those cell values by entering the following formula:

    =SUM(A1:A10)

In both instances, Excel adds the values in cells A1 through A10, but the SUM function is faster and simpler to enter and less prone to a typing error. You should always use a function, if one is available, in place of a long, complex formula. Excel supports more than 300 different functions from the fields of finance, business, science, and engineering, including functions that work with numbers, text, and dates.

Introducing Function Syntax

Every function follows a set of rules, or **syntax**, which specifies how the function should be written. The general syntax of all Excel functions is

    FUNCTION(arg1,arg2,…)

where *FUNCTION* is the function name, and *arg1*, *arg2*, and so forth are values used by that function. For example, the SUM function shown above uses a single argument, A1:A10, which is the range reference of the cells whose values will be added. Some functions do not require any arguments and are entered as *FUNCTION()*. Functions without arguments still require the opening and closing parentheses but do not include a value within the parentheses.

Entering Functions with AutoSum

A fast and convenient way to enter commonly used functions is with AutoSum. The AutoSum button includes options to insert the following functions into a select cell or cell range:

- SUM—Sum of the values in the specified range
- AVERAGE—Average value in the specified range
- COUNT—Total count of numeric values in the specified range
- MAX—Maximum value in the specified range
- MIN—Minimum value in the specified range

After you select one of the AutoSum options, Excel determines the most appropriate range from the available data and enters it as the function's argument. You should always verify that the range included in the AutoSum function matches the range that you want to use.

You will use AutoSum to enter the SUM function to add the total charges for Leslie Ritter's order.

To use AutoSum to enter the SUM function:

▶ 1. Click cell **G18** to make it the active cell, type **Subtotal** as the label, and then press the **Tab** key to make cell H18 the active cell.

2. On the Home tab, in the Editing group, click the **AutoSum button arrow**. The button's menu opens and displays five common functions: Sum, Average, Count Numbers, Max (for maximum), and Min (for minimum).

3. Click **Sum** to enter the SUM function. The formula =SUM(H13:H17) is entered in cell H18. The cells being summed are selected and highlighted on the worksheet so you can quickly confirm that Excel selected the appropriate range from the available data. A ScreenTip appears below the formula describing the function's syntax. See Figure 1-26.

TIP

You can quickly insert the SUM function by pressing the Alt+= keys.

Figure 1-26   **SUM function being entered with AutoSum button**

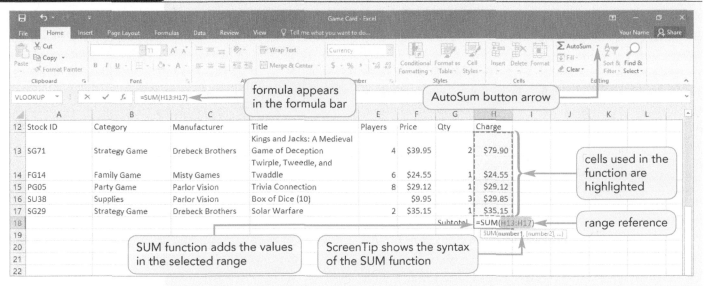

4. Press the **Enter** key to accept the formula. The subtotal of the charges on the order returned by the SUM function is $198.57.

AutoSum makes entering a commonly used formula such as the SUM function fast and easy. However, AutoSum can determine the appropriate range reference to include only when the function is adjacent to the cells containing the values you want to summarize. If you need to use a function elsewhere in the worksheet, you will have to select the range reference to include or type the function yourself.

Each purchase made at Game Card is subject to a 5 percent sales tax and, in the case of online orders, a $4.75 handling fee. You will add these to the Customer Order worksheet so you can calculate the total charge for Leslie Ritter's order.

To add the sales tax and handling fee to the worksheet:

1. Click cell **G11**, type **Sales Tax** as the label, and then press the **Tab** key to make cell H11 the active cell.

2. In cell H11, type **5%** as the sales tax rate, and then press the **Enter** key. The sales tax rate is entered in the cell and can be used in other calculations. The value is displayed with the % symbol but is stored as the equivalent decimal value 0.05.

3. Click cell **G19** to make it the active cell, type **Tax** as the label, and then press the **Tab** key to make cell H19 the active cell.

4. Type **=H11*H18** as the formula to calculate the sales tax on the customer order, and then press the **Enter** key. The formula multiplies the sales tax value in cell H11 by the order subtotal value in cell H18. The value $9.93 is displayed in cell H19, which is 5 percent of the subtotal value of $198.57.

▶ **5.** In cell G20, type **Handling** as the label, and then press the **Tab** key to make cell H20 the active cell. You will enter the handling fee in this cell.

▶ **6.** Type **$4.75** as the handling fee, and then press the **Enter** key.

The last part of the customer order is to calculate the total cost by adding the subtotal, the tax, and the handling fee. Rather than using AutoSum, you will type the SUM function so you can enter the correct range reference for the function. You can type the range reference or select the range in the worksheet. Remember that you must type parentheses around the range reference.

To calculate the total order cost:

▶ **1.** In cell G21, type **TOTAL** as the label, and then press the **Tab** key.

▶ **2.** Type **=SUM(** in cell H21 to enter the function name and the opening parenthesis. As you begin to type the function, a ScreenTip lists the names of all functions that start with S.

Make sure the cell reference in the function matches the range you want to calculate.

▶ **3.** Type **H18:H20** to specify the range reference of the cells you want to add. The cells referenced in the function are selected and highlighted on the worksheet so you can quickly confirm that you entered the correct range reference.

▶ **4.** Type **)** to complete the function, and then press the **Enter** key. The value of the SUM function appears in cell H21, indicating that the total charge for the order is $213.25.

▶ **5.** Click cell **H21** to select the cell and its formula. See Figure 1-27.

| Figure 1-27 | Total charge calculated for the order |

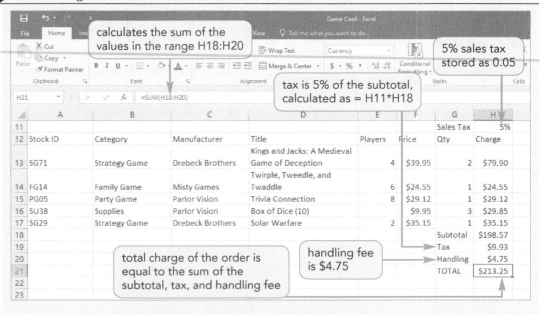

The SUM function makes it simple to quickly add the values in a group of cells.

PROSKILLS

Problem Solving: Writing Effective Formulas

You can use formulas to quickly perform calculations and solve problems. First, identify the problem you need to solve. Then, gather the data needed to solve the problem. Finally, create accurate and effective formulas that use the data to answer or resolve the problem. Follow these guidelines:

- **Keep formulas simple.** Use functions in place of long, complex formulas whenever possible. For example, use the SUM function instead of entering a formula that adds individual cells, which makes it easier to confirm that the formula is making an accurate calculation as it provides answers needed to evaluate the problem.

- **Do not hide data values within formulas.** The worksheet displays formula results, not the actual formula. For example, to calculate a 5 percent interest rate on a currency value in cell A5, you could enter the formula =0.05*A5. However, this doesn't show how the value is calculated. A better approach places the value 0.05 in a cell accompanied by a descriptive label and uses the cell reference in the formula. If you place 0.05 in cell A6, the formula =A6*A5 would calculate the interest value. Other people can then easily see the interest rate as well as the resulting interest, ensuring that the formula is solving the right problem.

- **Break up formulas to show intermediate results.** When a worksheet contains complex computations, other people can more easily comprehend how the formula results are calculated when different parts of the formula are distinguished. For example, the formula =SUM(A1:A10)/SUM(B1:B10) calculates the ratio of two sums but hides the two sum values. Instead, enter each SUM function in a separate cell, such as cells A11 and B11, and use the formula =A11/B11 to calculate the ratio. Other people can see both sums and the value of their ratio in the worksheet and better understand the final result, which makes it more likely that the best problem resolution will be selected.

- **Test formulas with simple values.** Use values you can calculate in your head to confirm that your formula works as intended. For example, using 1s or 10s as the input values lets you easily figure out the answer and verify the formula.

Finding a solution to a problem requires accurate data and analysis. With workbooks, this means using formulas that are easy to understand, clearly showing the data being used in the calculations, and demonstrating how the results are calculated. Only then can you be confident that you are choosing the best problem resolution.

Modifying a Worksheet

As you develop a worksheet, you might need to modify its content and structure to create a more logical organization. Some ways you can modify a worksheet include moving cells and ranges, inserting rows and columns, deleting rows and columns, and inserting and deleting cells.

Moving and Copying a Cell or Range

One way to move a cell or range is to select it, position the pointer over the bottom border of the selection, drag the selection to a new location, and then release the mouse button. This technique is called **drag and drop** because you are dragging the range and dropping it in a new location. If the drop location is not visible, drag the selection to the edge of the workbook window to scroll the worksheet, and then drop the selection.

You can also use the drag-and-drop technique to copy cells by pressing the Ctrl key as you drag the selected range to its new location. A copy of the original range is placed in the new location without removing the original range from the worksheet.

REFERENCE

Moving or Copying a Cell or Range

- Select the cell or range you want to move or copy.
- Move the pointer over the border of the selection until the pointer changes shape.
- To move the range, click the border and drag the selection to a new location (or to copy the range, hold down the Ctrl key and drag the selection to a new location).

or

- Select the cell or range you want to move or copy.
- On the Home tab, in the Clipboard group, click the Cut or Copy button (or right-click the selection, and then click Cut or Copy on the shortcut menu, or press the Ctrl+X or Ctrl+C keys).
- Select the cell or the upper-left cell of the range where you want to paste the content.
- In the Clipboard group, click the Paste button (or right-click the selection and then click Paste on the shortcut menu, or press the Ctrl+V keys).

Peter wants the subtotal, tax, handling, and total values in the range G18:H21 moved down one row to the range G19:H22 to set those calculations off from the list of items in the customer order. You will use the drag-and-drop method to move the range.

To drag and drop the range G18:H21:

1. Select the range **G18:H21**. These are the cells you want to move.

2. Point to the **bottom border** of the selected range so that the pointer changes to ⛏.

3. Press and hold the mouse button to change the pointer to ↖, and then drag the selection down one row. Do not release the mouse button. A ScreenTip appears, indicating that the new range of the selected cells will be G19:H22. A dark green border also appears around the new range. See Figure 1-28.

Figure 1-28	Range being moved

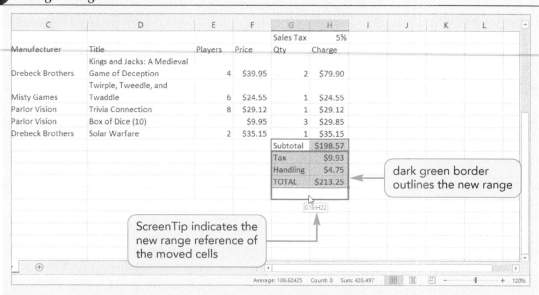

4. Make sure the ScreenTip displays the range G19:H22, and then release the mouse button. The selected cells move to their new location.

Some people find dragging and dropping a select cell range difficult and awkward, particularly if the selected range is large or needs to move a long distance in the worksheet. In those situations, it is often more efficient to cut or copy and paste the cell contents. Cutting moves the selected content, whereas copying duplicates the selected content in the new location.

Peter wants the worksheet to include a summary of the customer order starting in row 3. You will cut the customer contact information and the item listing from range A3:A22 and paste it into range A9:H28, freeing up space for the order information.

To cut and paste the customer contact information:

1. Click cell **A3** to select it.

2. Press the **Ctrl+Shift+End** keys to extend the selection to the last cell in the lower-right corner of the worksheet (cell H22).

3. On the Home tab, in the Clipboard group, click the **Cut** button (or press the **Ctrl+X** keys). The range is surrounded by a moving border, indicating that it has been cut.

4. Click cell **A9** to select it. This is the upper-left corner of the range where you want to paste the range that you cut.

5. In the Clipboard group, click the **Paste** button (or press the **Ctrl+V** keys). The range A3:H22 is pasted into the range A9:H28. Note that the cell references in the formulas were automatically updated to reflect the new location of those cells in the worksheet.

Using the COUNT Function

Sometimes you will want to know how many unique items are included in a range, such as the number of different items in the customer order. To calculate that value, you use the COUNT function

=COUNT(*range*)

TIP

To count cells containing non-numeric values, use the COUNTA function.

where *range* is the range of cells containing numeric values to be counted. Note that any cell in the range containing a non-numeric value is not counted in the final tally.

You will include the count of the number of different items from the order in the summary information. The summary will also display the order ID (a unique number assigned by Game Card to identify the order), the shipping date, and the type of delivery (overnight, two-day, or standard) in the freed-up space at the top of the worksheet. In addition, Peter wants the total charge for the order to be displayed with the order summary so that he does not have to scroll to the bottom of the worksheet to find that value.

To add the order summary:

1. Click cell **A3**, type **Order ID** as the label, press the **Tab** key, type **C10489** in cell B3, and then press the **Enter** key. The order ID is entered, and cell A4 is the active cell.

2. Type **Shipping Date** as the label in cell A4, press the **Tab** key, type **4/3/2017** in cell B4, and then press the **Enter** key. The shipping date is entered, and cell A5 is the active cell.

3. Type **Delivery** as the label in cell A5, press the **Tab** key, type **standard** in cell B5, and then press the **Enter** key. The delivery type is entered, and cell A6 is the active cell.

4. Type **Items Ordered** as the label in cell A6, and then press the **Tab** key. Cell B6 is the active cell. Now you will enter the COUNT function to determine the number of different items ordered.

5. In cell B6, type **=COUNT(** to begin the function.

6. With the insertion point still blinking in cell B6, select the range **G19:G23**. The range reference is entered as the argument for the COUNT function.

7. Type **)** to complete the function, and then press the **Enter** key. Cell B6 displays the value 5, indicating that five items were ordered by Leslie Ritter. Cell A7 is the active cell.

8. Type **Total Charge** as the label in cell A7, and then press the **Tab** key to make cell B7 the active cell.

9. Type **=** to start the formula, and then click cell **H28** to enter its cell reference in the formula in cell B7. The formula you created, =H28, tells Excel to display the contents of cell H28 in the current cell.

10. Press the **Enter** key to complete the formula. The total charge of $213.25 appears in cell B7. See Figure 1-29.

Figure 1-29   **Customer order summary**

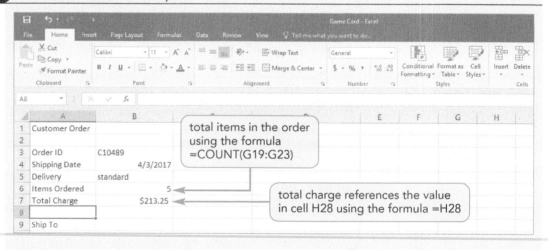

Inserting a Column or Row

You can insert a new column or row anywhere within a worksheet. When you insert a new column, the existing columns are shifted to the right, and the new column has the same width as the column directly to its left. When you insert a new row, the existing rows are shifted down, and the new row has the same height as the row above it. Because inserting a new row or column moves the location of the other cells in the worksheet, any cell references in a formula or function are updated to reflect the new layout.

Inserting or Deleting a Column or Row

REFERENCE

To insert a column or row:
- Select the column(s) or row(s) where you want to insert the new column(s) or row(s). Excel will insert the same number of columns or rows as you select to the left of the selected columns or above the selected rows.
- On the Home tab, in the Cells group, click the Insert button (or right-click a column or row heading or selected column and row headings, and then click Insert on the shortcut menu; or press the Ctrl+Shift+= keys).

To delete a column or row:
- Select the column(s) or row(s) you want to delete.
- On the Home tab, in the Cells group, click the Delete button (or right-click a column or row heading or selected column and row headings, and then click Delete on the shortcut menu; or press the Ctrl+- keys).

Peter informs you that the customer order report for Leslie Ritter is missing an item. You need to insert a new row directly above the entry for the Trivia Connection game in which you'll write the details of the missing item.

To insert a row for the missing order item:

TIP

You can insert multiple columns or rows by selecting that number of column or row headings, and then clicking the Insert button or pressing the Ctrl+Shift+= keys.

1. Click the **row 21** heading to select the entire row.

2. On the Home tab, in the Cells group, click the **Insert** button (or press the **Ctrl+Shift+=** keys). A new row is inserted below row 20 and becomes the new row 21.

3. Enter **SU25** in cell A21, enter **Supplies** in cell B21, enter **Drebeck Brothers** in cell C21, enter **Miniatures Set (12)** in cell D21, leave cell E21 blank, enter **$23.55** in cell F21, and then enter **2** in cell G21.

4. Click cell **H20** to select the cell with the formula for calculating the item charge, and then press the **Ctrl+C** keys to copy the formula in that cell.

5. Click cell **H21** to select the cell where you want to insert the formula, and then press the **Ctrl+V** keys to paste the formula into the cell.

6. Click cell **H26**. See Figure 1-30.

Figure 1-30　　New row inserted into the worksheet

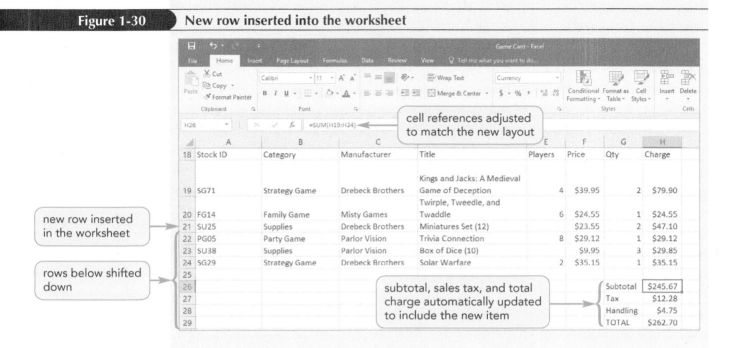

new row inserted
in the worksheet

rows below shifted
down

cell references adjusted
to match the new layout

subtotal, sales tax, and total
charge automatically updated
to include the new item

Notice that the formula in cell H26 is now =SUM(H19:H24). The range reference was updated to reflect the inserted row. Also, the tax amount increased to $12.28 based on the new subtotal value of $245.67, and the total charge increased to $262.70 because of the added item. Also, the result of the COUNT function in cell B6 increased to 6 to reflect the item added to the order.

Deleting a Row or Column

You can also delete rows or columns from a worksheet. **Deleting** removes the data from the row or column as well as the row or column itself. The rows below the deleted row shift up to fill the vacated space. Likewise, the columns to the right of the deleted column shift left to fill the vacated space. Also, all cell references in the worksheet are adjusted to reflect the change. You click the Delete button in the Cells group on the Home tab to delete selected rows or columns.

Deleting a column or row is not the same as clearing a column or row. **Clearing** removes the data from the selected row or column but leaves the blank row or column in the worksheet. You press the Delete key to clear the contents of the selected row or column, which leaves the worksheet structure unchanged.

Leslie Ritter did not order the box of dice created by Parlor Vision. Peter asks you to delete the row containing this item from the report.

To delete the row containing the box of dice from the order:

▶　1. Click the **row 23** heading to select the entire row.

▶　2. On the Home tab, in the Cells group, click the **Delete** button (or press the **Ctrl+-** keys). Row 23 is deleted, and the rows below it shift up to fill the space.

All of the cell references in the worksheet are again updated automatically to reflect the impact of deleting row 23. The subtotal value in cell H25 is now $215.82, which is the sum of the range H19:H23. The sales tax in cell H26 decreases to $10.79. The total cost of the order decreases to $231.36. Also, the result of the COUNT function in cell B6 decreases to 5 to reflect the item deleted from the order. As you can see, one of the great advantages of using Excel is that it modifies the formulas to reflect the additions and deletions you make to the worksheet.

Inserting and Deleting a Range

You can also insert or delete cell ranges within a worksheet. When you use the Insert button to insert a range of cells, the existing cells shift down when the selected range is wider than it is long, and they shift right when the selected range is longer than it is wide, as shown in Figure 1-31. When you use the Insert Cells command, you specify whether the existing cells shift right or down, or whether to insert an entire row or column into the new range.

Figure 1-31   Cells inserted into a worksheet

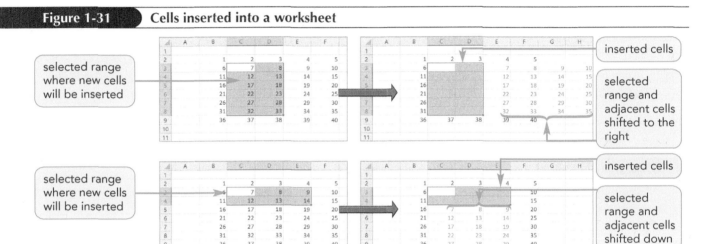

The process works in reverse when you delete a range. As with deleting a row or column, the cells adjacent to the deleted range either move up or left to fill in the space vacated by the deleted cells. The Delete Cells command lets you specify whether you want to shift the adjacent cells left or up or whether you want to delete the entire column or row.

When you insert or delete a range, cells that shift to a new location adopt the width of the columns they move into. As a result, you might need to resize columns and rows in the worksheet.

REFERENCE

Inserting or Deleting a Range

- Select a range that matches the range you want to insert or delete.
- On the Home tab, in the Cells group, click the Insert button or the Delete button.

or

- Select the range that matches the range you want to insert or delete.
- On the Home tab, in the Cells group, click the Insert button arrow and then click Insert Cells, or click the Delete button arrow and then click Delete Cells (or right-click the selected range, and then click Insert or Delete on the shortcut menu).
- Click the option button for the direction to shift the cells, columns, or rows.
- Click the OK button.

Peter wants you to insert a range into the worksheet for the ID that Game Card uses to identify the items it stocks in its store. You will insert these new cells into the range A17:A28, shifting the adjacent cells to the right.

To insert a range for the store IDs:

1. Select the range **A17:A28**.

2. On the Home tab, in the Cells group, click the **Insert button arrow**. A menu of insert options appears.

3. Click **Insert Cells**. The Insert dialog box opens.

4. Verify that the **Shift cells right** option button is selected.

5. Click the **OK** button. New cells are inserted into the selected range, and the adjacent cells move to the right. The cell contents do not fit well in the columns and rows they shifted into, so you will resize the columns and rows.

6. Resize the width of column E to **25** characters. The text is easier to read in the resized columns.

7. Select the row **19** through row **23** headings.

TIP

You can also autofit by double-clicking the bottom border of row 23.

8. In the Cells group, click the **Format** button, and then click **AutoFit Row Height**. The selected rows autofit to their contents.

9. Resize the height of row 19 to **30 (40 pixels)**. Figure 1-32 shows the revised layout of the customer order.

Figure 1-32 | **Range added to worksheet**

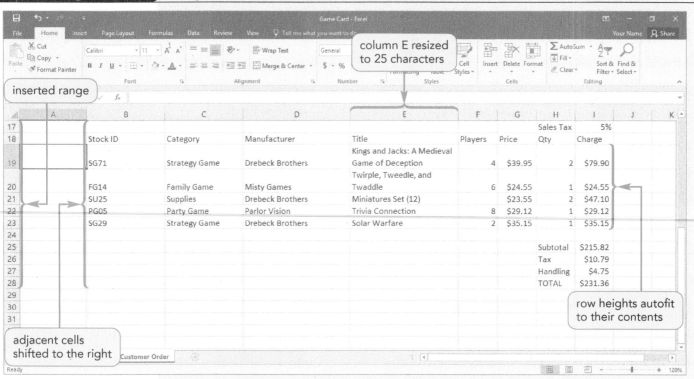

Notice that even though the customer orders will be entered only in the range A18:A23 you selected the range A17:A28 to retain the layout of the page design. Selecting the additional rows ensures that the sales tax and summary values still line up with the Qty and Charge columns. Whenever you insert a new range, be sure to consider its impact on the layout of the entire worksheet.

INSIGHT

Hiding and Unhiding Rows, Columns, and Worksheets

Workbooks can become long and complicated, filled with formulas and data that are important for performing calculations but are of little interest to readers. In those situations, you can simplify these workbooks for readers by hiding rows, columns, and even worksheets. Although the contents of hidden cells cannot be seen, the data in those cells is still available for use in formulas and functions throughout the workbook.

Hiding a row or column essentially decreases that row height or column width to 0 pixels. To a hide a row or column, select the row or column heading, click the Format button in the Cells group on the Home tab, point to Hide & Unhide on the menu that appears, and then click Hide Rows or Hide Columns. The border of the row or column heading is doubled to mark the location of hidden rows or columns.

A worksheet often is hidden when the entire worksheet contains data that is not of interest to the reader and is better summarized elsewhere in the document. To hide a worksheet, make that worksheet active, click the Format button in the Cells group on the Home tab, point to Hide & Unhide, and then click Hide Sheet.

Unhiding redisplays the hidden content in the workbook. To unhide a row or column, click in a cell below the hidden row or to the right of the hidden column, click the Format button, point to Hide & Unhide, and then click Unhide Rows or Unhide Columns. To unhide a worksheet, click the Format button, point to Hide & Unhide, and then click Unhide Sheet. The Unhide dialog box opens. Click the sheet you want to unhide, and then click the OK button. The hidden content is redisplayed in the workbook.

Although hiding data can make a worksheet and workbook easier to read, be sure never to hide information that is important to the reader.

Peter wants you to add the store ID used by Game Card to identify each item it sells. You will use Flash Fill to create these unique IDs.

Using Flash Fill

Flash Fill enters text based on patterns it finds in the data. As shown in Figure 1-33, Flash Fill generates customer names from the first and last names stored in the adjacent columns in the worksheet. To enter the rest of the names, you press the Enter key; to continue typing the names yourself, you press the Esc key.

Figure 1-33   **Text being entered with Flash Fill**

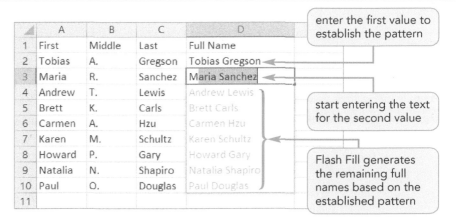

enter the first value to establish the pattern

start entering the text for the second value

Flash Fill generates the remaining full names based on the established pattern

Flash Fill works best when the pattern is clearly recognized from the values in the data. Be sure to enter the data pattern in the column or row right next to the related data. The data used to generate the pattern must be in a rectangular grid and cannot have blank columns or rows.

The store IDs used by Game Card combines the Stock ID and the first name of the item. For example, the Kings and Jacks game has a Stock ID of SG71, so its Store ID is SG71-Kings. Rather than typing this for every item in the customer order, you'll use Flash Fill to complete the data entry.

To enter the Store IDs using Flash Fill:

▶ **1.** Click cell **A18**, type **Store ID** as the label, and then press the **Enter** key. The label is entered in cell A18, and cell A19 is now the active cell.

▶ **2.** Type **SG71-Kings** as the Store ID, and then press **Enter** to make cell A20 active.

▶ **3.** Type **FG** in cell A20. As soon as you complete those two characters Flash Fill generates the remaining entries in the column based on the pattern you entered. See Figure 1-34.

| Figure 1-34 | Store IDs generated by Flash Fill |

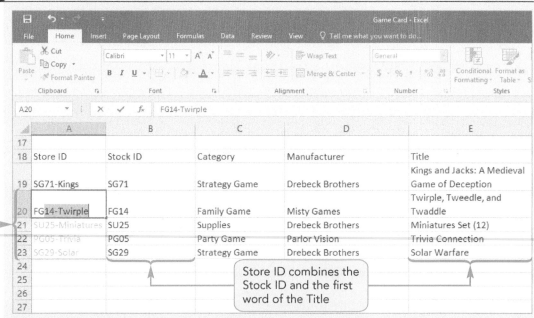

Store ID values suggested by Flash Fill

Store ID combines the Stock ID and the first word of the Title

▶ **4.** Press the **Enter** key to accept the suggested entries.

Note that Flash Fill enters text, not formulas. If you edit or replace an entry originally used by Flash Fill, the content generated by Flash Fill will not be updated.

Formatting a Worksheet

Formatting changes a workbook's appearance to make the content of a worksheet easier to read. Two common formatting changes are adding cell borders and changing the font size of text.

Adding Cell Borders

Sometimes you want to include lines along the edges of cells to enhance the readability of rows and columns of data. You can do this by adding a border to the left, top, right, or bottom edge of a cell or range. You can also specify the thickness of and the number of lines in the border. This is especially helpful when a worksheet is printed because the gridlines that surround the cells are not printed by default; they appear on the worksheet only as a guide.

Peter wants to add borders around the cells that contain content in the Customer Order worksheet to make the content easier to read.

To add borders around the worksheet cells:

1. Select the range **A3:B7**. You will add borders around all of the cells in the selected range.

2. On the Home tab, in the Font group, click the **Borders button arrow** ⊞ ▾, and then click **All Borders**. Borders are added around each cell in the range. The Borders button changes to reflect the last selected border option, which in this case is All Borders. The name of the selected border option appears in the button's ScreenTip.

3. Select the nonadjacent range **A9:B16,H17:I17**. You will add borders around each cell in the selected range.

4. In the Font group, click the **All Borders** button ⊞ to add borders to all of the cells in the selected range.

5. Select the nonadjacent range **A18:I23,H25:I28**, and then click the **All Borders** button ⊞ to add borders to all of the cells in the selected range.

6. Click cell **A28** to deselect the cells. Figure 1-35 shows the borders added to the worksheet cells.

Figure 1-35   **Borders added to cells**

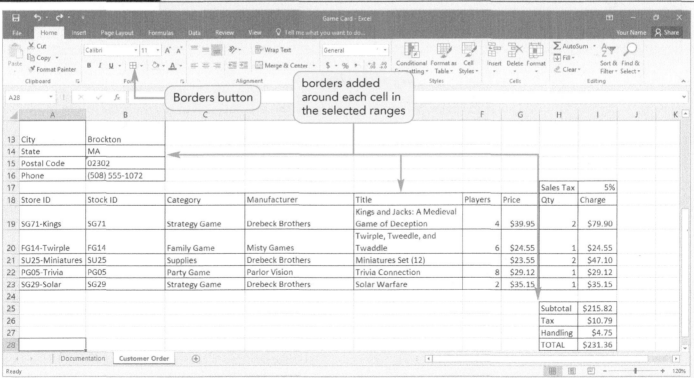

Changing the Font Size

Changing the size of text in a sheet provides a way to identify different parts of a worksheet, such as distinguishing a title or section heading from data. The size of the text is referred to as the font size and is measured in points. The default font size for worksheets is 11 points, but it can be made larger or smaller as needed. You can resize text in selected cells using the Font Size button in the Font group on the Home tab. You can also use the Increase Font Size and Decrease Font Size buttons to resize cell content to the next higher or lower standard font size.

Peter wants you to increase the size of the worksheet title to 26 points to make it more prominent.

To change the font size of the worksheet title:

1. Click cell **A1** to select the cell containing the worksheet title.

2. On the Home tab, in the Font group, click the **Font Size button arrow** [11 ▾] to display a list of font sizes, and then click **28**. The worksheet title changes to 28 points. See Figure 1-36.

| Figure 1-36 | Font size of the cell increased |

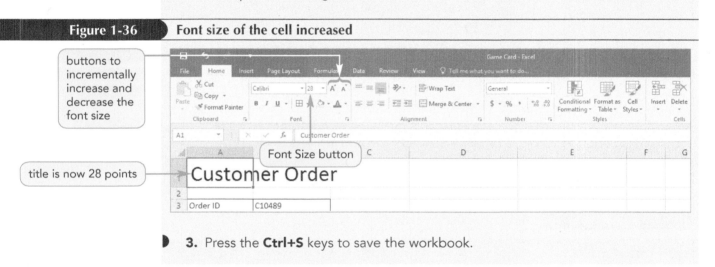

3. Press the **Ctrl+S** keys to save the workbook.

Printing a Workbook

Now that you have finished the workbook, Peter wants you to print a copy of Leslie Ritter's order. Before you print a workbook, you should preview it to ensure that it will print correctly.

Changing Worksheet Views

You can view a worksheet in three ways. Normal view, which you have been using throughout this module, shows the contents of the worksheet. Page Layout view shows how the worksheet will appear when printed. Page Break Preview displays the location of the different page breaks within the worksheet. This is useful when a worksheet will span several printed pages, and you need to control what content appears on each page.

Peter wants you to preview how the Customer Order worksheet will appear when printed. You will do this by switching between views.

To switch the Customer Order worksheet to different views:

1. Click the **Page Layout** button 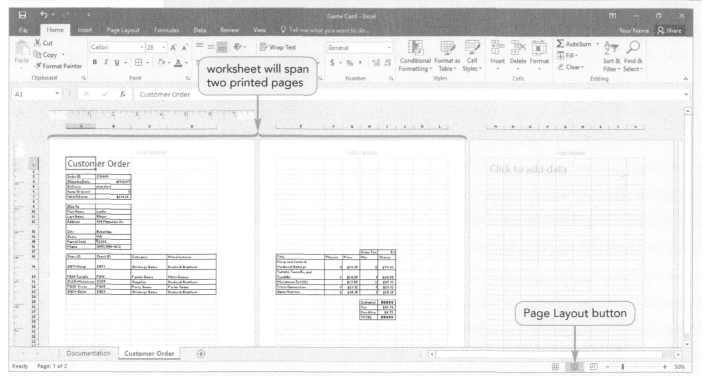 on the status bar. The page layout of the worksheet appears in the workbook window.

2. On the Zoom slider, click the **Zoom Out** button — until the percentage is **50%**. The reduced magnification makes it clear that the worksheet will spread over two pages when printed. See Figure 1-37.

Figure 1-37   Worksheet in Page Layout view

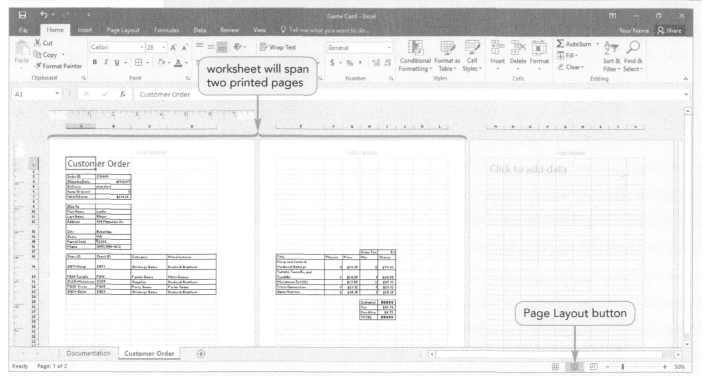

TIP

You can relocate a page break by dragging the dotted blue border in the Page Break Preview window.

3. Click the **Page Break Preview** button on the status bar. The view switches to Page Break Preview, which shows only those parts of the current worksheet that will print. A dotted blue border separates one page from another.

4. Zoom the worksheet to **70%** so that you can more easily read the contents of the worksheet. See Figure 1-38.

Figure 1-38 | **Worksheet in Page Break Preview**

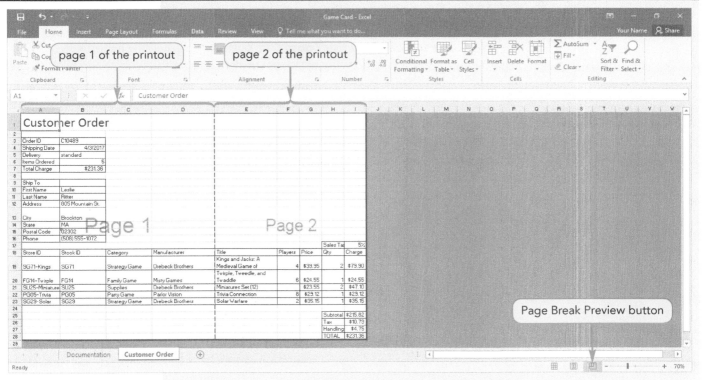

5. Click the **Normal** button ⊞ on the status bar. The worksheet returns to Normal view. Notice that after viewing the worksheet in Page Layout or Page Break Preview, a dotted black line appears in Normal view to show where the page breaks occurs.

Changing the Page Orientation

Page orientation specifies in which direction content is printed on the page. In **portrait orientation**, the page is taller than it is wide. In **landscape orientation**, the page is wider than it is tall. By default, Excel displays pages in portrait orientation. Changing the page orientation affects only the active sheet or sheets.

As you saw in Page Layout view and Page Break Preview, the Customer Order worksheet will print on two pages—columns A through D will print on the first page, and columns E through I will print on the second page, although the columns that print on each page may differ slightly depending on the printer. Peter wants the entire worksheet to print on a single page, so you'll change the page orientation from portrait to landscape.

To change the page orientation of the worksheet:

1. On the ribbon, click the **Page Layout** tab. The tab includes options for changing how the worksheet is arranged.

2. In the Page Setup group, click the **Orientation** button, and then click **Landscape**. The worksheet switches to landscape orientation.

3. Click the **Page Layout** button 🔲 on the status bar to switch to Page Layout view. The worksheet will still print on two pages.

Setting the Scaling Options

You can force the printout to a single page by **scaling** the printed output. There are several options for scaling your printout. You can scale the width or the height of the printout so that all of the columns or all of the rows fit on a single page. You can also scale the printout to fit the entire worksheet (both columns and rows) on a single page. If the worksheet is too large to fit on one page, you can scale the print to fit on the number of pages you select. You can also scale the worksheet to a percentage of its size. For example, scaling a worksheet to 50% reduces the size of the sheet by half when it is sent to the printer. When scaling a printout, make sure that the worksheet is still readable after it is resized. Scaling affects only the active worksheet, so you can scale each worksheet to best fit its contents.

Peter asks you to scale the printout so that all of the Customer Order worksheet fits on one page in landscape orientation.

To scale the printout of the Customer Order worksheet:

1. On the Page Layout tab, in the Scale to Fit group, click the **Width** arrow, and then click **1 page** on the menu that appears. All of the columns in the worksheet now fit on one page.

    If more rows are added to the worksheet, Peter wants to ensure that they still fit within a single sheet.

2. In the Scale to Fit group, click the **Height** arrow, and then click **1 page**. All of the rows in the worksheet now fit on one page. See Figure 1-39.

Figure 1-39   **Printout scaled to fit on one page**

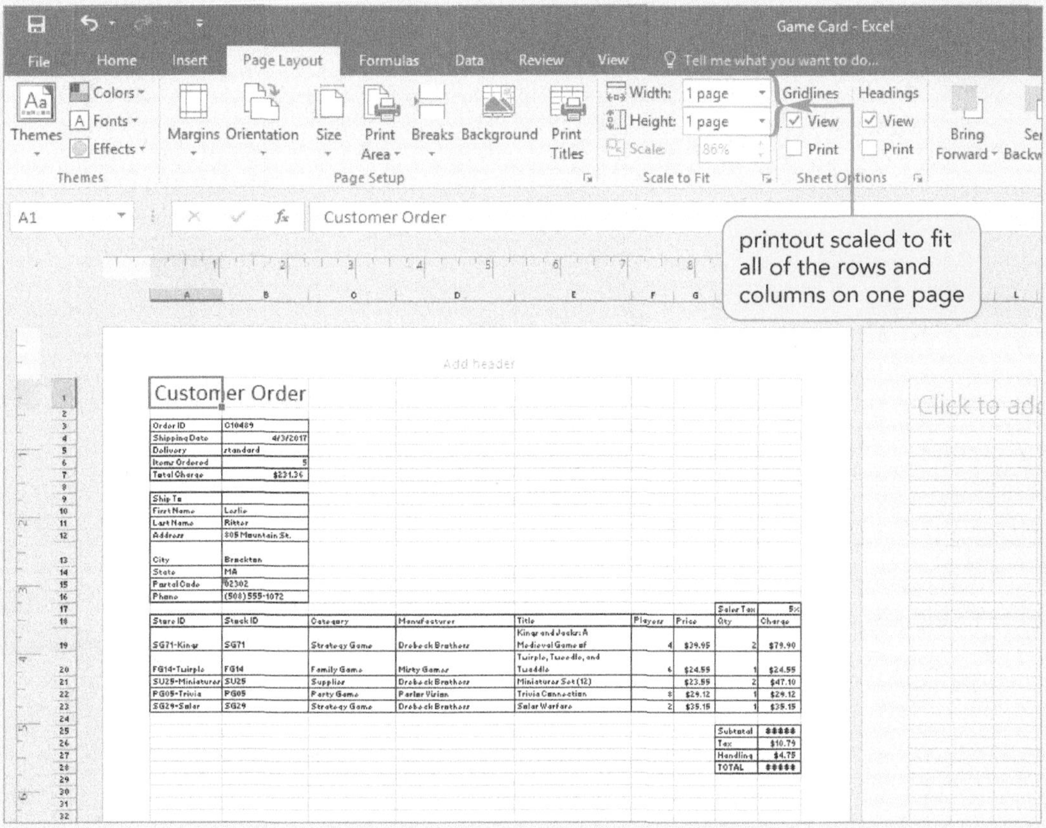

Setting the Print Options

TIP

To print the gridlines or the column and row headings, click the corresponding Print check box in the Sheet Options group on the Page Layout tab.

You can print the contents of a workbook by using the Print screen in Backstage view. The Print screen provides options for choosing where to print, what to print, and how to print. For example, you can specify the number of copies to print, which printer to use, and what to print. You can choose to print only the selected cells, only the active sheets, or all of the worksheets in the workbook that contain data. The printout will include only the data in the worksheet. The other elements in the worksheet, such as the row and column headings and the gridlines around the worksheet cells, will not print by default. The preview shows you exactly how the printed pages will look with the current settings. You should always preview before printing to ensure that the printout looks exactly as you intended and avoid unnecessary reprinting.

Peter asks you to preview and print the customer order workbook now.

Note: Check with your instructor first to make sure you should complete the steps for printing the workbook.

To preview and print the workbook:

▶ **1.** On the ribbon, click the **File** tab to display Backstage view.

▶ **2.** Click **Print** in the navigation bar. The Print screen appears with the print options and a preview of the Customer Order worksheet printout. See Figure 1-40.

Figure 1-40   Print screen in Backstage view

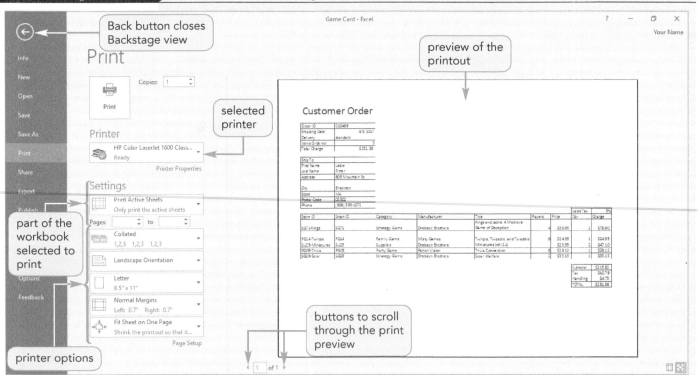

3. Click the **Printer** button, and then click the **printer** to which you want to print, if it is not already selected. By default, Excel will print only the active sheet.

4. In the Settings options, click the top button, and then click **Print Entire Workbook** to print all of the sheets in the workbook—in this case, both the Documentation and the Customer Order worksheets. The preview shows the first sheet in the workbook—the Documentation worksheet. Note that this sheet is still in the default portrait orientation.

5. Below the preview, click the **Next Page** button ▶ to view the Customer Order worksheet. As you can see, the Customer Order worksheet will print on a single page in landscape orientation.

6. If you are instructed to print, click the **Print** button to send the contents of the workbook to the specified printer. If you are not instructed to print, click the **Back** button ⬅ in the navigation bar to exit Backstage view.

Viewing Worksheet Formulas

Most of the time, you will be interested in only the final results of a worksheet, not the formulas used to calculate those results. However, in some cases, you might want to view the formulas used to develop the workbook. This is particularly useful when you encounter unexpected results and you want to examine the underlying formulas, or you want to discuss your formulas with a colleague. You can display the formulas instead of the resulting values in cells.

If you print the worksheet while the formulas are displayed, the printout shows the formulas instead of the values. To make the printout easier to read, you should print the worksheet gridlines as well as the row and column headings so that cell references in the formulas are easy to find in the printed version of the worksheet.

You will look at the Customer Order worksheet with the formulas displayed.

To display the cell formulas:

1. Make sure the Customer Order worksheet is in Page Layout view.

2. Press the **Ctrl+`** keys (the grave accent symbol ` is usually located above the Tab key). The worksheet changes to display all of the formulas instead of the resulting values. Notice that the columns widen to display all of the formula text in the cells.

3. Look at the entry in cell B4. The underlying numeric value of the shipping date (42828) is displayed instead of the formatted date value (4/3/2017). See Figure 1-41.

TIP

You can also display formulas in a worksheet by clicking the Show Formulas button in the Formula Auditing group on the Formulas tab.

Figure 1-41	Worksheet with formulas displayed

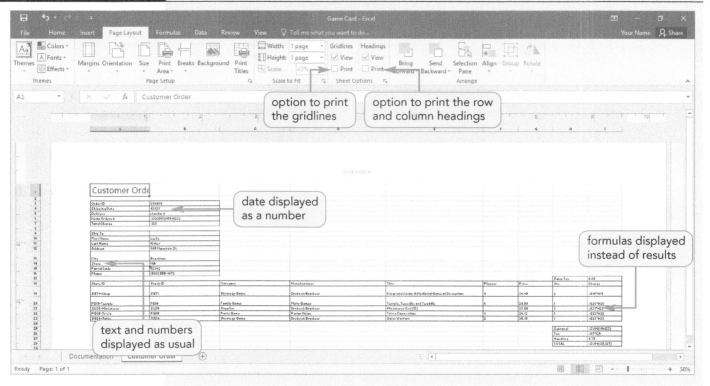

It's good practice to hide the formulas when you are done reviewing them.

4. Press the **Ctrl+`** keys to hide the formulas and display the resulting values.

5. Click the **Normal** button ⊞ on the status bar to return the workbook to Normal view.

Saving a Workbook with a New Filename

Whenever you click the Save button on the Quick Access Toolbar or press the Ctrl+S keys, the workbook file is updated to reflect the latest content. If you want to save a copy of the workbook with a new filename or to a different location, you need to use the Save As command. When you save a workbook with a new filename or to a different location, the previous version of the workbook remains stored as well.

You have completed the customer order workbook for Game Card. Peter wants to use the workbook as a model for other customer order reports. You will save the workbook with a new filename to avoid overwriting the Leslie Ritter order. Then you'll clear the information related to that order, leaving the formulas intact. This new, revised workbook will then be ready for the next customer order.

To save the workbook with a new filename:

1. Press the **Ctrl+S** keys to save the workbook. This ensures that the final copy of the workbook contains the formatted version of Leslie Ritter's order.

2. On the ribbon, click the **File** tab to display Backstage view, and then click **Save As** on the navigation bar. The Save As screen is displayed.

TIP

Save the workbook with the new name before making changes to avoid inadvertently saving your edits to the wrong file.

  3. Click the **Browse** button. The Save As dialog box opens so you can save the workbook with a new filename or to a new location.

  4. Navigate to the location specified by your instructor.

  5. In the File name box, type **Game Card Order** as the new filename.

  6. Click the **Save** button. The workbook is saved with the new filename, and you are returned to the workbook window.

  7. Select the range **B3:B5**, right-click the selected range to open the shortcut menu, and then click **Clear Contents** to clear the contents of the order ID, shipping date, and delivery cells.

  8. Select the nonadjacent range **B10:B16,A19:H23**, and then press the **Delete** key to clear the contact information for Leslie Ritter and the list of items she ordered.

  9. Select cell **I27**, and then clear the handling fee.

  10. Click cell **A3** to make that cell the active cell the next time this workbook is opened.

  11. Press the **Ctrl+S** keys to save the workbook.

  12. Click the **Close** button ⊠ on the title bar (or press the **Ctrl+W** keys). The workbook closes, and the Excel program closes.

Peter is pleased with the workbook you created. With the calculations already in place in the new workbook, he will be able to quickly enter new customer orders and see the calculated charges without having to recreate the worksheet.

Session 1.2 Quick Check

REVIEW

1. What formula would you enter to add the values in cells C1, C2, and C3? What function would you enter to achieve the same result?

2. What formula would you enter to count how many numeric values are in the range D21:D72?

3. If you insert cells into the range C1:D10, shifting the cells to the right, what is the new location of the data that was previously in cell F4?

4. Cell E11 contains the formula =SUM(D1:D20). How does this formula change if a new row is inserted above row 5?

5. Describe four ways of viewing the content of a workbook in Excel.

6. How are page breaks indicated in Page Break Preview?

7. What orientation would you use to make the printed page wider than it is tall?

8. How do you display the formulas used in a worksheet instead of the formula results?

PRACTICE

Review Assignments

There are no Data Files needed for the Review Assignment.

Game Card also buys and resells used games and gaming supplies. Peter wants to use Excel to record recent used purchases made by the store. The workbook should list every item the company has ordered, provide information about the item, and calculate the total order cost. Complete the following:

1. Create a new, blank workbook, and then save the workbook as **Game List** in the location specified by your instructor.
2. Rename the Sheet1 worksheet as **Documentation**, and then enter the data shown in Figure 1-42 in the specified cells.

Figure 1-42   Documentation sheet data

Cell	Text
A1	Game Card
A3	Author
A4	Date
A5	Purpose
B3	*your name*
B4	*current date*
B5	To record game acquisitions for Game Card

3. Set the font size of the title text in cell A1 to **28** points.
4. Add a new worksheet after the Documentation sheet, and then rename the sheet as **Game Purchases**.
5. In cell A1, enter the text **Game Purchases**. Set the font size of this text to **28** points.
6. In cell A3, enter the text **Date** as the label. In cell B3, enter the date **4/3/2017**.
7. In the range A5:F10, enter the data shown in Figure 1-43.

Figure 1-43   Game list

Purchase Number	Category	Manufacturer	Title	Players	Cost
83	Strategy Game	Drebeck Brothers	Secrets of Flight: Building an Airforce	6	$29.54
84	Family Game	Parlor Vision	Brain Busters and Logic Gaming	8	$14.21
85	Strategy Game	Aspect Gaming	Inspection Deduction	3	$18.91
86	Party Game	Miller Games	Bids and Buys	8	$10.81
87	Family Game	Aspect Gaming	Buzz Up	4	$21.43

8. Insert cells into the range A5:A10, shifting the other cells to the right.
9. In cell A5, enter **Stock ID** as the label. In cell A6, enter **SG83** as the first Stock ID, and then type **FG** in cell A7, allowing Flash Fill to enter the remaining Stock IDs.
10. Set the width of column A to **12** characters, columns B through D to **18** characters, and column E to **25** characters.
11. Wrap text in the range E6:E10 so that the longer game titles appear on multiple lines within the cells.

12. Autofit the heights of rows 5 through 10.

13. Move the game list in the range A5:G10 to the range A8:G13.

14. In cell F15, enter **TOTAL** as the label. In cell G15, enter a formula with the SUM function to calculate the sum of the costs in the range G9:G13.

15. In cell A4, enter **Total Items** as the label. In cell B4, enter a formula with the COUNT function to count the number of numeric values in the range G9:G13.

16. In cell A5, enter **Total Cost**. In cell B5, enter a formula to display the value from cell G15.

17. In cell A6, enter **Average Cost** as the label. In cell B6, enter a formula that divides the total cost of the purchased games (listed in cell B5) by the number of games purchased (listed in cell B4).

18. Add borders around each cell in the nonadjacent range A3:B6,A8:G13,F15:G15.

19. For the Game Purchases worksheet, change the page orientation to landscape and scale the worksheet to print on a single page for both the width and the height. If you are instructed to print, print the entire workbook.

20. Display the formulas in the Game Purchases worksheet. If you are instructed to print, print the entire worksheet.

21. Save and close the workbook.

Case Problem 1

APPLY

Data File needed for this Case Problem: Donation.xlsx

Henderson Pediatric Care Center   Kari Essen is a fundraising coordinator for the Pediatric Care Center located in Henderson, West Virginia. Kari is working on a report detailing recent donations to the center and wants you to enter this data into an Excel workbook. Complete the following:

1. Open the **Donation** workbook located in the Excel1 > Case1 folder included with your Data Files. Save the workbook as **Donation List** in the location specified by your instructor.

2. In the Documentation sheet, enter your name in cell B3 and the date in cell B4.

3. Increase the font size of the text in cell A1 to 28 points.

4. Add a new sheet to the end of the workbook, and rename it as **Donor List**.

5. In cell A1 of the Donor List worksheet, enter **Donor List** as the title, and then set the font size to 28 points.

6. In the range A6:H13, enter the donor information shown in Figure 1-44. Enter the ZIP code data as text rather than as numbers.

Figure 1-44   **Donation list**

Last Name	First Name	Street	City	State	ZIP	Phone	Donation
Robert	Richards	389 Felton Avenue	Miami	FL	33127	(305) 555-5685	$150
Barbara	Hopkins	612 Landers Street	Caledonia	IL	61011	(815) 555-5865	$75
Daniel	Vaughn	45 Lyman Street	Statesboro	GA	30461	(912) 555-8564	$50
Parker	Penner	209 South Street	San Francisco	CA	94118	(415) 555-7298	$250
Kenneth	More	148 7th Street	Newberry	IN	47449	(812) 555-8001	$325
Robert	Simmons	780 10th Street	Houston	TX	77035	(713) 555-5266	$75
Donna	Futrell	834 Kimberly Lane	Ropesville	TX	79358	(806) 555-6186	$50

7. Set the width of columns A through D to 25 characters. Set the width of column G to 15 characters.

8. In cell A2, enter the text **Total Donors**. In cell A3, enter the text **Total Donations**. In cell A4, enter the text **Average Donation**.

9. In cell B2, enter a formula that counts how many numeric values are in the range H7:H13.

10. In cell B3, enter a formula that calculates the sum of the donations in the range H7:H13.

11. In cell B4, enter a formula that calculates the average donation by dividing the value in cell B3 by the value in cell B2.

12. Add borders around the nonadjacent range A2:B4,A6:H13.

13. Set the page orientation of the Donor List to landscape.

14. Scale the worksheet to print on a single page for both the width and the height. If you are instructed to print the worksheet, print the Donor List sheet.

15. Display the formulas in the Donor List worksheet. If you are instructed to print, print the worksheet.

16. Save and close the workbook.

Case Problem 2

Data File needed for this Case Problem: Balance.xlsx

Scott Kahne Tool & Die Cheryl Hippe is a financial officer at Scott Kahne Tool & Die, a manufacturing company located in Mankato, Minnesota. Every month the company publishes a balance sheet, a report that details the company's assets and liabilities. Cheryl asked you to create the workbook with the text and formulas for this report. Complete the following:

1. Open the **Balance** workbook located in the Excel1 > Case2 folder included with your Data Files. Save the workbook as **Balance Sheet** in the location specified by your instructor.

2. In the Documentation sheet, enter your name in cell B3 and the date in cell B4.

3. Go to the Balance Sheet worksheet. Set the font size of the title in cell A1 to 28 points.

4. In cell A2, enter the text **Statement for March 2017**.

5. Set the width of columns A and E to 30 characters. Set the width of columns B, C, F, and G to 12 characters. Set the width of column D to 4 characters. (*Hint:* Hold down the Ctrl key as you click the column headings to select both adjacent and nonadjacent columns.)

6. Set the font size of the text in cells A4, C4, E4, and G4 to 18 points.

7. Set the font size of the text in cells A5, E5, A11, E11, A14, E15, A19, E20, and A24 to 14 points.

8. Enter the values shown in Figure 1-45 in the specified cells.

Figure 1-45   Assets and liabilities

Current Assets	Cell	Value
Cash	B6	$123,000
Accounts Receivable	B7	$75,000
Inventories	B8	$58,000
Prepaid Insurance	B9	$15,000
Long-Term Investments	**Cell**	**Value**
Available Securities	B12	$29,000
Tangible Assets	**Cell**	**Value**
Land	B15	$49,000
Building and Equipment	B16	$188,000
Less Accumulated Depreciation	B17	-$48,000
Intangible Assets	**Cell**	**Value**
Goodwill	B20	$148,000
Other Assets	B22	$14,000
Current Liabilities	**Cell**	**Value**
Accounts Payable	F6	$62,000
Salaries	F7	$14,000
Interest	F8	$12,000
Notes Payable	F9	$38,000
Long-Term Liabilities	**Cell**	**Value**
Long-Term Notes Payable	F12	$151,000
Mortgage	F13	$103,000
Stockholders' Equity	**Cell**	**Value**
Capital Stock	F16	$178,000
Retained Earnings	F17	$98,000
Comprehensive Income/Loss	F18	-$5,000

9. In cell C9, enter a formula to calculate the sum of the Current Assets in the range B6:B9.

10. In cell C12, enter a formula to display the value of B12.

11. In cell C17, enter a formula to calculate the sum of the Tangible Assets in the range B15:B17.

12. In cells C20 and C22, enter formulas to display the values of cells B20 and B22, respectively.

13. In cell C24, enter a formula to calculate the total assets in the balance sheet by adding cells C9, C12, C17, C20, and C22. Set the font size of the cell to 14 points.

14. In cell G9, enter a formula to calculate the sum of the Current Liabilities in the range F6:F9.

15. In cell G13, enter a formula to calculate the sum of the Long-Term Liabilities in the range F12:F13.

16. In cell G18, enter a formula to calculate the sum of the Stockholders' Equity in the range F16:F18.

17. In cell G20, calculate the Total Liabilities and Equity for the company by adding the values of cells G9, G13, and G18. Set the font size of the cell to 14 points.

18. Check your calculations. In a balance sheet the total assets (cell C24) should equal the total liabilities and equity (cell G20).

19. Set the page layout orientation to landscape and the Balance Sheet worksheet to print to one page for both the width and height.

20. Preview the worksheet on the Print screen in Backstage view, and then save and close the workbook.

CHALLENGE

Case Problem 3

Data File needed for this Case Problem: FTP.xslx

Succeed Gym Allison Palmer is the owner of Succeed Gym, an athletic club in Austin, Texas, that specializes in coaching men and women aspiring to participate in triathlons, marathons, and other endurance sports. During the winter, Allison runs an indoor cycling class in which she tracks the progress of each student's fitness. One measure of fitness is FTP (Functional Threshold Power). Allison has recorded FTP levels from her students over five races and wants you to use the functions described in Figure 1-46 to analyze this data so that she can track the progress of her class and of individual students.

Figure 1-46   Excel functions

Function	Description
=AVERAGE(*range*)	Calculates the average of the values from the specified *range*
=MEDIAN(*range*)	Calculates the median or midpoint of the values from the specified *range*
=MIN(*range*)	Calculates the minimum of the values from the specified *range*
=MAX(*range*)	Calculates the maximum of the values from the specified *range*

Complete the following:

1. Open the **FTP** workbook located the Excel1 > Case3 folder included with your Data Files. Save the workbook as **FTP Report** in the location specified by your instructor.
2. In the Documentation sheet, enter your name in cell B3 and the date in cell B4.
3. Go to the Race Results worksheet. Change the font size of the title in cell A1 to 28 points.
4. Set the width of column A and B to 15 characters. Set the width of column I to 2 characters.
5. In the range J4:M4, enter the labels **Median**, **Average**, **Min**, and **Max**.
⊕ **Explore** 6. In cell J5, use the MEDIAN function to calculate the median (midpoint) of the FTP values of races 1 through 5 for Diana Bartlett in the range D5:H5. Copy the formula in cell J5 to the range J6:J28 to calculate the median FTP values for the other riders.
⊕ **Explore** 7. In cell K5, use the AVERAGE function to calculate the average the FTP value for races 1 through 5 for Diana Bartlett. Copy the formula to calculate the averages for the other riders.
⊕ **Explore** 8. In cell L5, use the MIN function to return the minimum FTP value for Diana Bartlett. Copy the formula to calculate the minimums for the other riders.
⊕ **Explore** 9. In cell M5, use the MAX function to return the maximum FTP value for Diana Bartlett. Copy the formula to calculate the maximums for the other riders.
10. In the range C30:C33, enter the labels **Median**, **Average**, **Min**, and **Max** to record summary information for each of the five races.
11. In cell D30, use the MEDIAN function to calculate the median FTP value from the range D5:D28. Copy the formula to the range E30:H30 to determine the median values for the other four races.
12. In the range D31:H31, use the AVERAGE function to calculate the average FTP value for each race.
13. In the range D32:H32, use the MIN function to calculate the minimum value for each race.
14. In the range D33:H33, use the MAX function to calculate the maximum FTP value for each race.
15. Move the range A4:M33 to the range A10:M39 to create space for additional summary calculations at the top of the worksheet.

16. In the range A3:A7, enter the labels **Class Size**, **Class Average**, **Class Median**, **Class Minimum**, and **Class Maximum**.

⊕ **Explore** 17. In cell B3, use the COUNTA function to count the number of entries in the range A11:A34.

18. In cell B4, use the AVERAGE function to calculate the average of all FTP values in the range D11:H34.

19. In cell B5, use the MEDIAN function to calculate the median of all FTP values in the range D11:H34.

20. In cell B6, use the MIN function to calculate the minimum FTP value in the range D11:H34.

21. In cell B7, use the MAX function to calculate the maximum FTP value in the range D11:H34.

22. Set the page layout orientation for the Race Results worksheet to portrait and scale the worksheet so that its width and height fit on one page.

23. View the worksheet in Page Layout view, return to Normal view, and then save and close the workbook.

Case Problem 4

Data File needed for this Case Problem: Service.xlsx

Welch Home Appliance Repair   Stefan Welch is the owner of Welch Home Appliance Repair in Trenton, New Jersey. Stefan wants to use Excel to record data from his service calls to calculate the total charge on each service call and the total charges from all service calls within a given period. Unfortunately, the workbook he has created contains several errors. He has asked you to fix the errors and complete the workbook. Complete the following:

1. Open the **Service** workbook located in the Excel1 > Case4 folder included with your Data Files. Save the workbook as **Service Calls** in the location specified by your instructor.

2. In the Documentation sheet, enter your name in cell B3 and the date in cell B4.

3. Go to the Call Sheet worksheet. Insert cells in the range A7:A27, shifting the other cells to the right.

4. In cell A7, enter **Cust ID** as the label. In cell A8, enter **Jensen-5864** (the customer's last name and last four digits on the phone number) as the customer ID for Patricia Jensen. Use Flash Fill to enter in the remaining customer IDs in the column.

5. Resize the columns of the Call Sheet worksheet so that all of the column labels and the cell contents are completely displayed.

⚙ **Troubleshoot** 6. There is a problem with the some of the customer ZIP codes. New Jersey ZIP codes begin with a 0, and these leading zeros are not showing up in the contact information. Revise the text of the ZIP code values to correct this problem.

⚙ **Troubleshoot** 7. The formula in cell L8 that calculates the total number of billable hours for the first customer is not correct. Instead of showing the number of hours, it displays the value as a percentage of a day. Fix this problem by revising the formula so that it multiplies the difference between the value in K8 and J8 by 24. (*Hint:* Use parentheses to enclose the expression that calculates the difference between starting and ending times so that the difference is calculated first.)

8. Copy the formula you entered for cell L8 to calculate the total billable hours for the rest of the entries in column L.

9. The total charge for each service call is equal to the hourly rate multiplied by the number of hours plus the charge for parts. In cell O8, enter a formula to calculate the total service charge for the first customer, and then copy that formula to calculate the rest of the service charges in column O.

10. In cell B4, enter a formula that uses the COUNT function to count the total number of service calls.

⚙ **Troubleshoot** 11. In cell B5, Stefan entered a formula to calculate the total charges from all of the service calls. Examine the formula, and correct the expression so that it adds all of the service call charges.

12. Insert two new rows above row 5.

13. In cell A5, enter the label **Total Hours**. In cell B5, enter function to calculate the total number of hours from all of the service calls.

14. In cell A6, enter the label **Average Charge**. In cell B6, enter a formula that calculates the average charge per call by dividing the total charges by the total number of calls.

15. Add borders around the cells in the nonadjacent range A4:B7,A9:O29.

16. Set the page layout of the Call Sheet worksheet so that it prints on a single page in landscape orientation.

17. View the worksheet in Page Break Preview, return to Normal view, and then save and close the workbook.

OBJECTIVES

Session 2.1
- Change fonts, font style, and font color
- Add fill colors and a background image
- Create formulas to calculate sales data
- Format numbers as currency and percentages
- Format dates and times
- Align, indent, and rotate cell contents
- Merge a group of cells

Session 2.2
- Use the AVERAGE function
- Apply cell styles
- Copy and paste formats with the Format Painter
- Find and replace text and formatting
- Change workbook themes
- Highlight cells with conditional formats
- Format a worksheet for printing
- Set the print area, insert page breaks, add print titles, create headers and footers, and set margins

Formatting Workbook Text and Data

Creating a Sales Report

Case | *Morning Bean*

Carol Evans is a sales manager at Morning Bean, a small but growing chain of shops specializing in coffee, tea, and other hot drinks. Carol needs to develop a workbook for the upcoming sales conference that will provide information on sales and profits for stores located in the Northwest region of the country. Carol already started the workbook by entering sales data for the previous years. She wants you to use this financial data to calculate summary statistics and then format the workbook before it's distributed to stockholders attending the conference.

STARTING DATA FILES

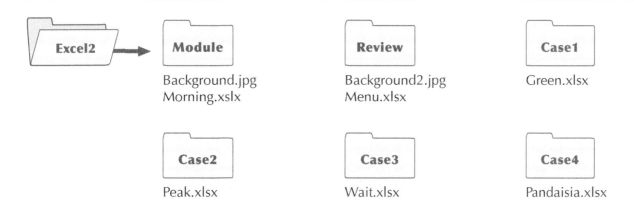

Excel2 →	Module	Review	Case1
	Background.jpg Morning.xslx	Background2.jpg Menu.xlsx	Green.xlsx
	Case2	Case3	Case4
	Peak.xlsx	Wait.xlsx	Pandaisia.xlsx

Session 2.1 Visual Overview:

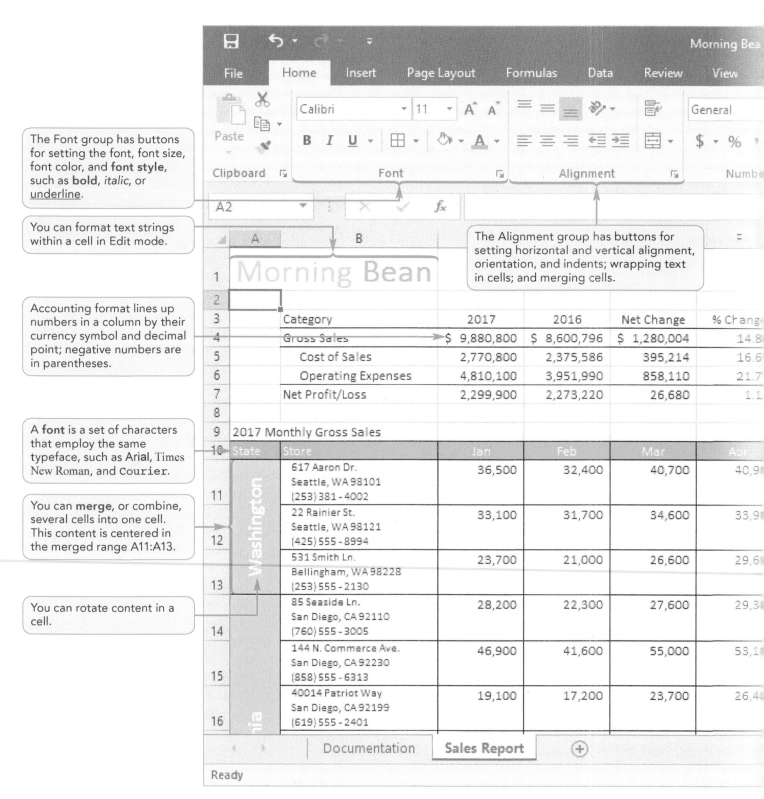

The Font group has buttons for setting the font, font size, font color, and **font style**, such as **bold**, *italic*, or underline.

You can format text strings within a cell in Edit mode.

Accounting format lines up numbers in a column by their currency symbol and decimal point; negative numbers are in parentheses.

A **font** is a set of characters that employ the same typeface, such as Arial, Times New Roman, and Courier.

You can **merge**, or combine, several cells into one cell. This content is centered in the merged range A11:A13.

You can rotate content in a cell.

The Alignment group has buttons for setting horizontal and vertical alignment, orientation, and indents; wrapping text in cells; and merging cells.

Morning Bean

Category	2017	2016	Net Change	% Change
Gross Sales	$ 9,880,800	$ 8,600,796	$ 1,280,004	14.8
Cost of Sales	2,770,800	2,375,586	395,214	16.6
Operating Expenses	4,810,100	3,951,990	858,110	21.7
Net Profit/Loss	2,299,900	2,273,220	26,680	1.1

2017 Monthly Gross Sales

State	Store	Jan	Feb	Mar	Apr
Washington	617 Aaron Dr. Seattle, WA 98101 (253) 381-4002	36,500	32,400	40,700	40,9
	22 Rainier St. Seattle, WA 98121 (425) 555-8994	33,100	31,700	34,600	33,9
	531 Smith Ln. Bellingham, WA 98228 (253) 555-2130	23,700	21,000	26,600	29,6
	85 Seaside Ln. San Diego, CA 92110 (760) 555-3005	28,200	22,300	27,600	29,3
	144 N. Commerce Ave. San Diego, CA 92230 (858) 555-6313	46,900	41,600	55,000	53,1
	40014 Patriot Way San Diego, CA 92199 (619) 555-2401	19,100	17,200	23,700	26,4

Documentation   **Sales Report**

Ready

Formatting a Worksheet

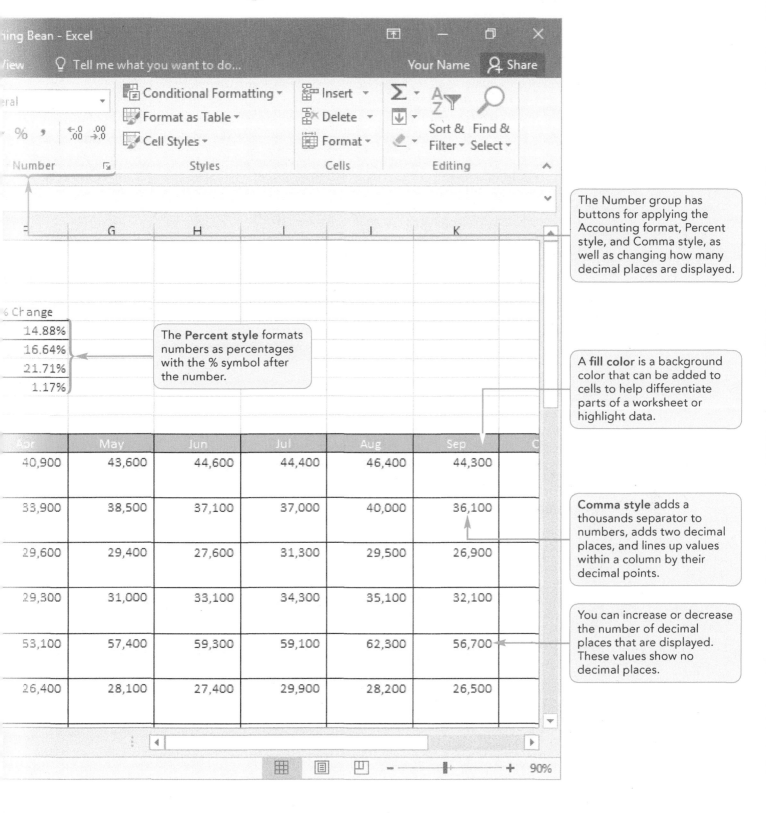

The Number group has buttons for applying the Accounting format, Percent style, and Comma style, as well as changing how many decimal places are displayed.

The **Percent style** formats numbers as percentages with the % symbol after the number.

A **fill color** is a background color that can be added to cells to help differentiate parts of a worksheet or highlight data.

Comma style adds a thousands separator to numbers, adds two decimal places, and lines up values within a column by their decimal points.

You can increase or decrease the number of decimal places that are displayed. These values show no decimal places.

Formatting Cell Text

You can improve the readability of workbooks by choosing the fonts, styles, colors, and decorative features that are used in the workbook and within worksheet cells. Formatting changes only the appearance of the workbook data—it does not affect the data itself.

Excel organizes complementary formatting options into themes. A **theme** is a collection of formatting for text, colors, and effects that give a workbook a unique look and feel. The Office theme is applied to workbooks by default, but you can apply another theme or create your own. You can also add formatting to a workbook using colors, fonts, and effects that are not part of the current theme. Note that a theme is applied to the entire workbook and can be shared between workbooks.

To help you choose the best formatting for your workbooks, **Live Preview** shows the results of each formatting option before you apply it to your workbook.

Carol wants you to format the Morning Bean sales report. You'll use Live Preview to see how the workbook looks with different formatting options.

Applying Fonts and Font Styles

A font is a set of characters that share a common appearance by employing the same typeface. Excel organizes fonts into theme and nontheme fonts. A **theme font** is associated with a particular theme and used for headings and body text in the workbook. Theme fonts change automatically when the theme is changed. Text formatted with a **nontheme font** retains its appearance no matter what theme is used with the workbook.

Fonts are classified based on their character style. **Serif fonts**, such as Times New Roman, have extra strokes at the end of each character that aid in reading passages of text. **Sans serif fonts**, such as Arial, do not include these extra strokes. Other fonts are purely decorative, such as a font used for specialized logos. Every font can be further formatted with a font style such as *italic*, **bold**, or ***bold italic***; with underline; and with special effects such as ~~strikethrough~~ and color. You can also increase or decrease the font size to emphasize the importance of the text within the workbook.

REFERENCE

Formatting Cell Content

- To set the font, select the cell or range. On the Home tab, in the Font group, click the Font arrow, and then select a font.
- To set the font size, select the cell or range. On the Home tab, in the Font group, click the Font Size arrow, and then select a font size.
- To set the font style, select the cell or range. On the Home tab, in the Font group, click the Bold, Italic, or Underline button.
- To set the font color, select the cell or range. On the Home tab, in the Font group, click the Font Color button arrow, and then select a theme or nontheme color.
- To format a text selection, double-click the cell to enter Edit mode, select the text to format, change the font, size, style, or color, and then press the Enter key.

Carol already entered the data and some formulas in her workbook for the upcoming conference. The Documentation sheet describes her workbook's purpose and content. At the top of the sheet is the company name. Carol wants you to format the name in large, bold letters using the default heading font from the Office theme.

To the format the company name:

1. Open the **Morning** workbook located in the **Excel2 > Module** folder included with your Data Files, and then save the workbook as **Morning Bean** in the location specified by your instructor.

2. In the Documentation sheet, enter your name in cell B4 and the date in cell B5.

3. Click cell **A1** to make it the active cell.

4. On the Home tab, in the Font group, click the **Font button arrow** to display a gallery of fonts available on your computer. Each name is displayed in its font. The first two fonts listed are the theme fonts for headings and body text–Calibri Light and Calibri.

5. Scroll down the Fonts gallery until you see Bauhaus 93 in the All Fonts list, and then point to **Bauhaus 93** (or another font). Live Preview shows the effect of the Bauhaus 93 font on the text in cell A1. See Figure 2-1.

Figure 2-1   Font gallery

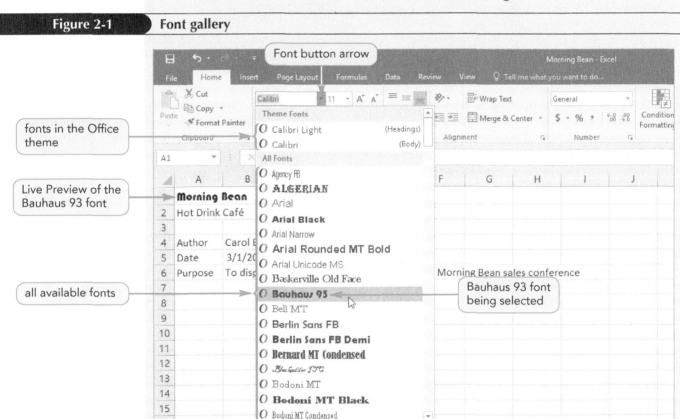

6. Point to three other fonts in the list to see the Live Preview of how the text in cell A1 would look with that font.

7. Click **Calibri Light** in the Theme Fonts list. The company name in cell A1 changes to the Calibri Light Font, the default headings font in the current theme.

8. In the Font group, click the **Font Size button arrow** ⌗ to display a list of font sizes, point to **26** to preview the text in that font size, and then click **26**. The company name changes to 26 points.

9. In the Font group, click the **Bold** button **B** (or press **Ctrl+B** keys). The text changes to bold.

▶ **10.** Click cell **A2** to make it the active cell. The cell with the company description is selected.

▶ **11.** In the Font group, click the **Font Size button arrow** `11 ▾`, and then click **18**. The company description changes to 18 points.

▶ **12.** In the Font group, click the **Italic** button I (or press the **Ctrl+I** keys). The company description in cell A2 is italicized.

▶ **13.** Select the range **A4:A6**, and then press the **Ctrl+B** keys. The text in the selected range changes to bold.

▶ **14.** Click cell **A7** to deselect the range. See Figure 2-2.

| Figure 2-2 | Formatted text in the Documentation sheet |

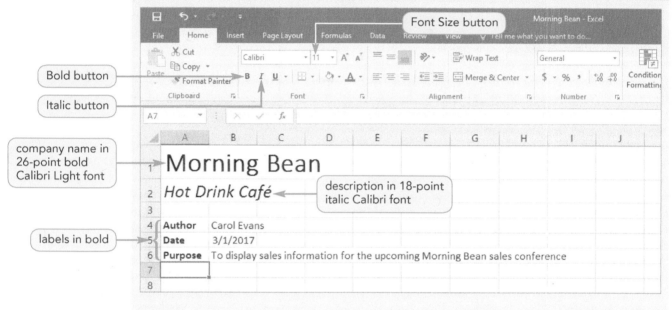

- Font Size button
- Bold button
- Italic button
- company name in 26-point bold Calibri Light font — **Morning Bean**
- description in 18-point italic Calibri font — *Hot Drink Café*
- labels in bold — Author, Date, Purpose

	A	B	C	D	E	F	G
1	Morning Bean						
2	Hot Drink Café						
3							
4	Author	Carol Evans					
5	Date	3/1/2017					
6	Purpose	To display sales information for the upcoming Morning Bean sales conference					
7							
8							

Applying a Font Color

Color can transform a plain workbook filled with numbers and text into a powerful presentation that captures the user's attention and adds visual emphasis to the points you want to make. By default, Excel displays text in a black font color.

Like fonts, colors are organized into theme and nontheme colors. **Theme colors** are the 12 colors that belong to the workbook's theme. Four colors are designated for text and backgrounds, six colors are used for accents and highlights, and two colors are used for hyperlinks (followed and not followed links). These 12 colors are designed to work well together and to remain readable in all combinations. Each theme color has five variations, or accents, in which a different tint or shading is applied to the theme color.

Ten **standard colors**—dark red, red, orange, yellow, light green, green, light blue, blue, dark blue, and purple—are always available regardless of the workbook's theme. You can open an extended palette of 134 standard colors. You can also create a custom color by specifying a mixture of red, blue, and green color values, making available 16.7 million custom colors—more colors than the human eye can distinguish. Some dialog boxes have an automatic color option that uses your Windows default text and background colors, usually black text on a white background.

INSIGHT

Creating Custom Colors

Custom colors let you add subtle and striking colors to a formatted workbook. To create custom colors, you use the **RGB Color model** in which each color is expressed with varying intensities of red, green, and blue. RGB color values are often represented as a set of numbers in the format

`(red, green, blue)`

where `red` is an intensity value assigned to red light, `green` is an intensity value assigned to green light, and `blue` is an intensity value assigned to blue light. The intensities are measured on a scale of 0 to 255—0 indicates no intensity (or the absence of the color) and 255 indicates the highest intensity. So, the RGB color value (255, 255, 0) represents a mixture of high-intensity red (255) and high-intensity green (255) with the absence of blue (0), which creates the color yellow.

To create colors in Excel using the RGB model, click the More Colors option located in a color menu or dialog box to open the Colors dialog box. In the Colors dialog box, click the Custom tab, and then enter the red, green, and blue intensity values. A preview box shows the resulting RGB color.

Carol wants the company name and description in the Documentation sheet to stand out. You will change the text in cell A1 and cell A2 to green.

To change the font color of the company name and description:

▶ **1.** Select the range **A1:A2**.

▶ **2.** On the Home tab, in the Font group, click the **Font Color button arrow** [A·] to display the gallery of theme and standard colors.

▶ **3.** In the Standard Colors section, point to the **Green** color (the sixth color). The color name appears in a ScreenTip, and you see a Live Preview of the text with the green font color. See Figure 2-3.

| Figure 2-3 | Font Color gallery |

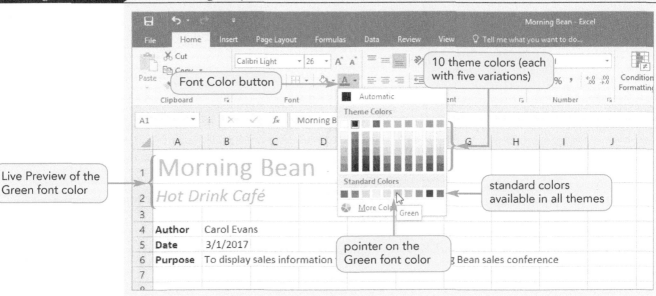

▶ **4.** Click the **Green** color. The company name and description change to green.

Formatting Text Selections Within a Cell

In Edit mode, you can select and format selections of text within a cell. You can make these changes to selected text from the ribbon or from the Mini toolbar. The **Mini toolbar** contains buttons for common formatting options used for that selection. These same buttons appear on the ribbon.

Carol asks you to format the company name in cell A1 so that the text "Morning" appears in gold.

To format part of the company name in cell A1:

▶ **1.** Double-click cell **A1** to select the cell and enter Edit mode (or click cell **A1** and press the **F2** key). The status bar shows Edit to indicate that you are working with the cell in Edit mode. The pointer changes to the I-beam pointer.

▶ **2.** Drag the pointer over the word **Morning** to select it. A Mini toolbar appears above the selected text with buttons to change the font, size, style, and color of the selected text in the cell. In this instance, you want to change the font color.

▶ **3.** On the Mini toolbar, click the **Font Color button arrow** A ·, and then in the Themes Colors section, point to the **Gold, Accent 4** color (the eighth color). Live Preview shows the color of the selected text as gold. See Figure 2-4.

Figure 2-4	Mini toolbar in Edit mode

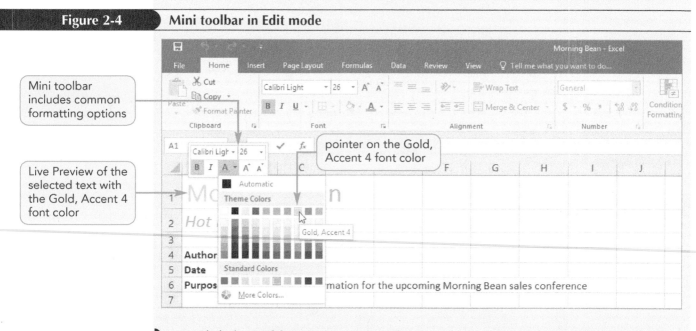

Mini toolbar includes common formatting options

pointer on the Gold, Accent 4 font color

Live Preview of the selected text with the Gold, Accent 4 font color

▶ **4.** Click the **Gold, Accent 4** color. The Mini toolbar closes and the selected text changes to the gold color.

Working with Fill Colors and Backgrounds

Another way to distinguish sections of a worksheet is by formatting the cell background. You can fill the cell background with color or an image.

Changing a Fill Color

TIP

To change a sheet tab's color, right-click its tab, point to Tab Color, and then click a color.

By default, worksheet cells do not include any background color. But background colors, also known as fill colors, can be helpful for distinguishing different parts of a worksheet or adding visual interest. The same selection of colors used to format the color of cell text can be used to format the cell background.

INSIGHT

Using Color to Enhance a Workbook

When used wisely, color can enhance any workbook. However, when used improperly, color can distract the user, making the workbook more difficult to read. As you format a workbook, keep in mind the following tips:

- Use colors from the same theme to maintain a consistent look and feel across the worksheets. If the built-in themes do not fit your needs, you can create a custom theme.
- Use colors to differentiate types of cell content and to direct users where to enter data. For example, format a worksheet so that formula results appear in cells without a fill color and users enter data in cells with a light gray fill color.
- Avoid color combinations that are difficult to read.
- Print the workbook on both color and black-and-white printers to ensure that the printed copy is readable in both versions.
- Understand your printer's limitations and features. Colors that look good on your monitor might not look as good when printed.
- Be sensitive to your audience. About 8 percent of all men and 0.5 percent of all women have some type of color blindness and might not be able to see the text when certain color combinations are used. Red-green color blindness is the most common, so avoid using red text on a green background or green text on a red background.

Carol wants you to change the background color of the range A4:A6 in the Documentation sheet to green and the font color to white.

To change the font and fill colors in the Documentation sheet:

▶ 1. Select the range **A4:A6**.

▶ 2. On the Home tab, in the Font group, click the **Fill Color button arrow** [icon], and then click the **Green** color (the sixth color) in the Standard Colors section.

▶ 3. In the Font group, click the **Font Color button arrow** [icon], and then click the **White, Background 1** color (the first color) in the Theme Colors section. The labels are formatted as white text on a green background.

▶ 4. Select the range **B4:B6**, and then format the cells with the **Green** font color and the **White, Background 1** fill color.

▶ 5. Increase the width of column B to **30** characters, and then wrap the text within the selected range.

▶ 6. Select the range **A4:B6**, and then add all borders around each of the selected cells.

▶ 7. Click cell **A7** to deselect the range. See Figure 2-5.

Figure 2-5 | **Font and fill colors in the Documentation sheet**

width of column B is 30 characters

labels are white text on a green background

green text on a white background

text wrapped in the cell

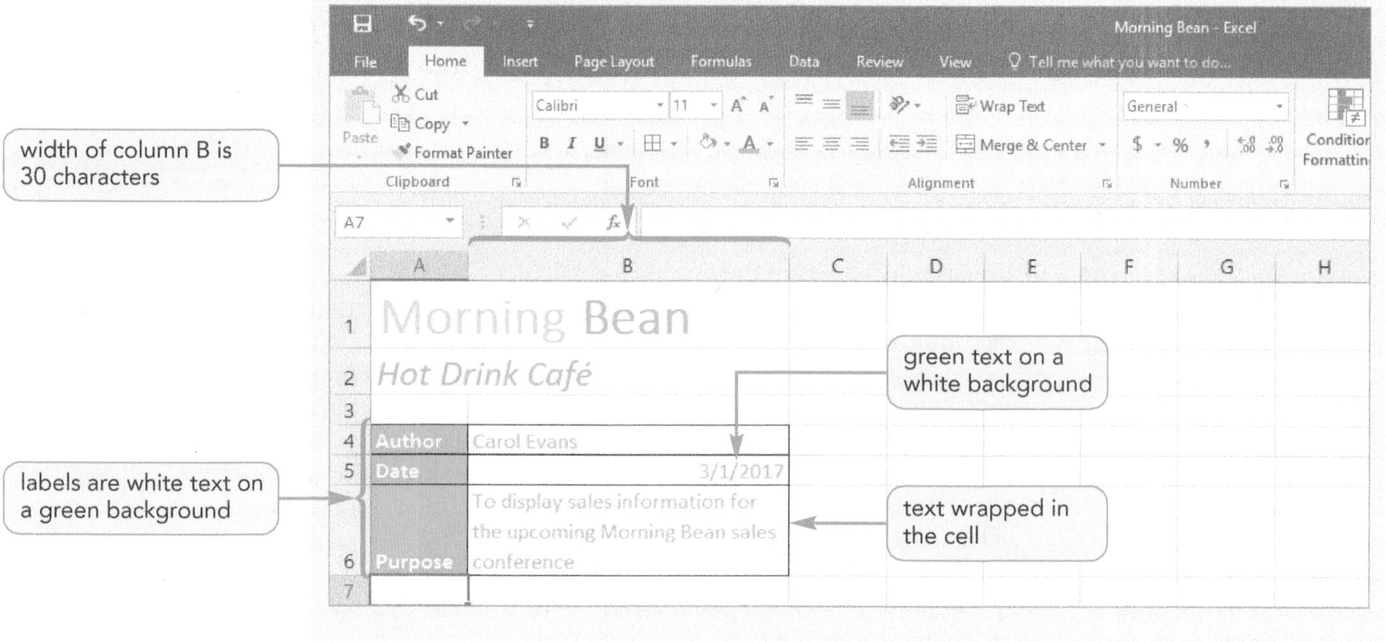

Adding a Background Image

TIP

Background images are usually visible only on the screen; by default they do not print.

Another way to add visual interest to worksheets is with a background image. Many background images are based on textures such as granite, wood, or fibered paper. The image does not need to match the size of the worksheet; a smaller image can be repeated until it fills the entire sheet. Background images do not affect any cell's format or content. Fill colors added to cells appear on top of the image, covering that portion of the image.

Carol has provided an image that she wants you to use as the background of the Documentation sheet.

To add a background image to the Documentation sheet:

1. On the ribbon, click the **Page Layout** tab to display the page layout options.

2. In the Page Setup group, click the **Background** button. The Insert Pictures dialog box opens with options to search for an image file on your computer or local network, or use the Bing Image Search tool.

3. Click the **Browse** button next to the From a file label. The Sheet Background dialog box opens.

4. Navigate to the **Excel2 > Module** folder included with your Data Files, click the **Background** JPEG image file, and then click the **Insert** button. The image is added to the background of the Documentation sheet. The Background button changes to the Delete Background button, which you can click to remove background image. See Figure 2-6.

Figure 2-6   Background image added to the Documentation sheet

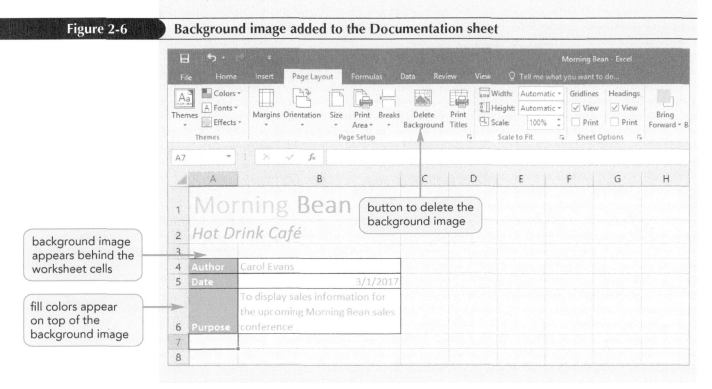

You've completed the formatting the Documentation sheet. Next, you'll work on the Sales Report worksheet.

Using Functions and Formulas to Calculate Sales Data

In the Sales Report worksheet, you will format the data on the gross sales from each of Morning Bean's 20 stores. The worksheet is divided into two areas. The table at the bottom of the worksheet displays gross sales for the past year for each month by store. The section at the top of the worksheet summarizes the sales over the past two years. Carol has compiled the following sales data:

- **Gross Sales**—the total amount of sales at all of the stores
- **Cost of Sales**—the cost of creating Morning Bean products
- **Operating Expenses**—the cost of running the individual stores including the employment and insurance costs
- **Net Profit/Loss**—the difference between the income from the gross sales and the total cost of sales and operating expenses
- **Units Sold**—the total number of menu items sold by Morning Bean during the year
- **Customers Served**—the total number of customers served by Morning Bean during the year

Carol wants you to calculate these sales statistics for the entire company and for each individual store. First, you will calculate Morning Bean's total gross sales from the past year and the company's overall net profit and loss.

To calculate Morning Bean's sales and profit/loss:

▶ **1.** Click the **Sales Report** sheet tab to make the Sales Report worksheet active.

▶ **2.** Click cell **C6**, type the formula **=SUM(C27:N46)** to calculate the total gross sales from all stores in the previous year, and then press the **Enter** key. Cell C6 displays 9880800, indicating that Morning Bean's total gross sales for the year were more than $9.8 million.

▶ **3.** In cell **C9**, enter the formula **=C6-(C7+C8)** to calculate the current year's net profit/loss, which is equal to the difference between the gross sales and the sum of the cost of sales and operating expenses. Cell C9 displays 2299900, indicating that the company's net profit for the year was close to $2.3 million.

▶ **4.** Copy the formula in cell **C9**, and then paste it into cell **D9** to calculate the net profit/loss for the previous year. Cell D9 displays 2273220, indicating that the company's net profit for that year was a little less than $2.3 million.

Morning Bean's net profit increased from the previous year, but it also opened two new stores during that time. Carol wants to investigate the sales statistics on a per-store basis by dividing the statistics you just calculated by the number of stores.

To calculate the per-store statistics:

▶ **1.** In cell **C16**, enter the formula **=C6/C23** to calculate the gross sales per store for the year. The formula returns 494040, indicating each Morning Bean store had, on average, almost $500,000 in gross sales during the year.

▶ **2.** In cell **C17**, enter the formula **=C7/C23** to calculate the cost of sales per store for the year. The formula returns the value 138540, indicating each Morning Bean store had a little more than $138,000 in sales cost.

▶ **3.** In cell **C18**, enter the formula **=C8/C23** to calculate the operating expenses per store for the year. The formula returns the value 240505, indicating that operating expense of a typical store was a little more than $240,000.

▶ **4.** In cell **C19**, enter the formula **=C9/C23** to calculate the net profit/loss per store for the year. The formula returns the value 114995, indicating that the net profit/loss of a typical store was about $115,000.

▶ **5.** In cell **C21**, enter the formula **=C11/C23** to calculate the units sold per store for the year. The formula returns the value 72655, indicating that a typical store sold more than 72,000 units.

▶ **6.** In cell **C22**, enter the formula **=C12/C23** to calculate the customers served per store during the year. The formula returns the value 10255, indicating that a typical store served more than 10,000 customers.

▶ **7.** Copy the formulas in the range **C16:C22** and paste them into the range **D16:D22**. The cell references in the formulas change to calculate the sales data for the previous year.

▶ **8.** Click cell **B24** to deselect the range. See Figure 2-7.

| **Figure 2-7** | **Overall and per-store sales statistics** |

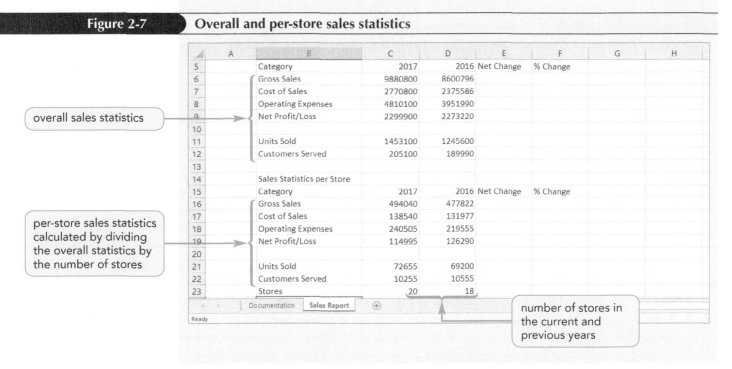

overall sales statistics

per-store sales statistics calculated by dividing the overall statistics by the number of stores

number of stores in the current and previous years

Carol also wants to report how the company's sales and expenses have changed from the previous year to the current year. To do this, you will calculate the net change in the sales statistics as well as the percent change. The percent change is calculated using the following formula:

$$percent\ change = \frac{current\ year\ value - previous\ year\ value}{previous\ year\ value}$$

You will calculate the net change and percentage for all of the statistics in the Sales Report worksheet.

To calculate the net and percent changes:

1. In cell **E6**, enter the formula **=C6–D6** to calculate the difference in gross sales between the previous year and the current year. The formula returns 1280004, indicating that gross sales increased by about $1.28 million.

2. In cell **F6**, enter the formula **=(C6–D6)/D6** to calculate the percent change in gross sales from the previous year to the current year. The formula returns 0.1488239, indicating an increase in gross sales of about 14.88 percent.

   Next, you'll copy and paste the formulas in cells E6 and F6 to the rest of the sales data to calculate the net change and percent change from the previous year to the current year.

3. Select the range **E6:F6**, and then copy the selected range. The two formulas are copied to the Clipboard.

4. Select the nonadjacent range **E7:F9,E11:F12,E16:F19,E21:F23**, and then paste the formulas from the Clipboard into the selected range. The net and percent changes are calculated for the remaining sales data.

5. Click cell **B24** to deselect the range, and then scroll the worksheet up to display row 5. See Figure 2-8.

Be sure to include the parentheses as shown to calculate the percent change correctly.

Figure 2-8   Net change and percent change from 2016 to 2017

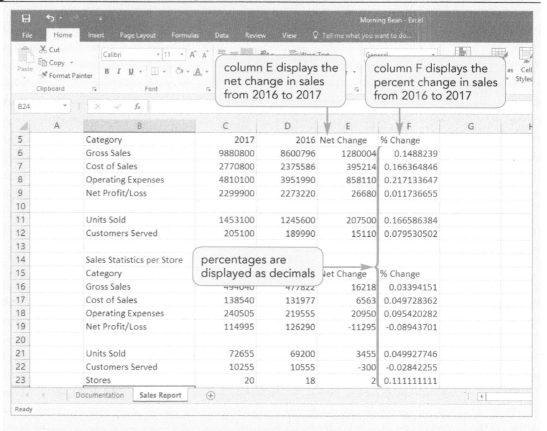

The bottom part of the worksheet contains the sales for each cafe from the current year. You will use the SUM function to calculate the total gross sales for each store during the entire year, the total monthly sales of all 20 stores, and the total gross sales of all stores and months.

To calculate different subtotals of the gross sales:

▶ 1. Click in the **Name** box to select the current cell reference, type **O26**, and then press the **Enter** key. Cell O26 is selected.

▶ 2. Type **TOTAL** as the label, and then press the **Enter** key. Cell O27 is now the active cell.

▶ 3. On the ribbon, click the **Home** tab, if necessary.

▶ 4. In the Editing group, click the **AutoSum** button, and then press the **Enter** key to accept the suggested range reference and enter the formula =SUM(C27:N27) in cell O27. The cell displays 370000, indicating gross sales in 2017 for the 85 Seaside Lane store in San Diego were $370,000.

▶ 5. Copy the formula in cell **O27**, and then paste that formula into the range **O28:O46** to calculate the total sales for each of the remaining 19 stores in the Morning Bean chain.

▶ 6. Click cell **B47**, type **TOTAL** as the label, and then press the **Tab** key. Cell C47 is now the active cell.

▶ 7. Select the range **C47:O47** so that you can calculate the total monthly sales for all of the stores.

8. On the Home tab, in the Editing group, click the **AutoSum** button to calculate the total sales for each month as well as the total sales for all months. For example, cell C47 displays 710900, indicating that monthly sales from all stores in January were $710,900.

9. Click cell **O48** to deselect the range. See Figure 2-9.

Figure 2-9   **Gross sales by store and month**

	E	F	G	H	I	J	K	L			
42	32100	35400	34000	38800	38100	39600	36700	34100	35000	33000	408600
43	46800	49400	48400	52100	54400	51400	49200	52100	47000	48000	578900
44	51700	56400	58400	59100	58200	62100	55900	57400	51000	53000	655400
45	35800	37300	38700	40300	39700	39700	38600	37600	35300	38000	442000
46	56400	55500	58600	57100	61900	61100	58800	60800	53000	57000	675800
47	795500	820000	861600	872900	903000	920000	859800	866200	788900	833100	9880800
48											
49											
50											

gross sales for each store for all months

gross sales for each month for all stores

gross sales for all months and all stores

The Sales Report worksheet contains a lot of information that is difficult to read in its current form. You can improve the readability of the data by adding number formats.

Formatting Numbers

The goal in formatting any workbook is to make the content easier to interpret. For numbers, this can mean adding a comma to separate thousands, setting the number of decimal places, and using percentage and currency symbols to make numbers easier to read and understand. Changing the number format does not affect the value itself, only how that value is displayed in the worksheet.

Applying Number Formats

Cells start out formatted with the **General format**, which, for the most part, displays numbers exactly as they are typed. If a value is calculated from a formula or function, the General format displays as many digits after the decimal point as will fit in the cell and rounds the last digit. Calculated values that are too large to fit into the cell are displayed in scientific notation.

The General format is fine for small numbers, but some values require additional formatting to make the numbers easier to interpret. For example, you might want to:

- Change the number of digits displayed to the right of the decimal point
- Add commas to separate thousands in large numbers
- Include currency symbols to numbers to identify the monetary unit being used
- Identify percentages using the % symbol

TIP

To apply the Currency format, click the Number Format button arrow and click Currency, or press the Ctrl+Shift+$ keys.

Excel supports two monetary formats—currency and accounting. Both formats add a thousands separator to the currency values and display two digits to the right of the decimal point. However, the **Currency format** places a currency symbol directly to the left of the first digit of the currency value and displays negative numbers with a negative sign. The **Accounting format** fixes a currency symbol at the left edge of the column, and displays negative numbers within parentheses and zero values with a dash. It also slightly indents the values from the right edge of the cell to allow room for parentheses around negative values. Figure 2-10 compares the two formats.

Figure 2-10   **Currency and Accounting number formats**

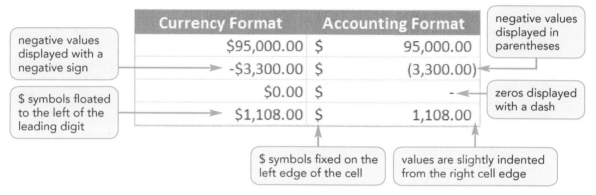

When choosing between the Currency format and the Accounting format for your worksheets, you should consider accounting principles that govern how financial data should be formatted and displayed.

PROSKILLS

Written Communication: Formatting Monetary Values

Spreadsheets commonly include monetary values. To make these values simpler to read and comprehend, keep in mind the following guidelines when formatting the currency data in a worksheet:

- **Format for your audience.** For general financial reports, round values to the nearest hundred, thousand, or million. Investors are generally more interested in the big picture than in exact values. However, for accounting reports, accuracy is important and often legally required. So, for those reports, be sure to display the exact monetary value.

- **Use thousands separators.** Large strings of numbers can be challenging to read. For monetary values, use a thousands separator to make the amounts easier to comprehend.

- **Apply the Accounting format to columns of monetary values.** The Accounting format makes columns of numbers easier to read than the Currency format. Use the Currency format for individual cells that are not part of long columns of numbers.

- **Use only two currency symbols in a column of monetary values.** Standard accounting format displays one currency symbol with the first monetary value in the column and optionally displays a second currency symbol with the last value in that column. Use the Accounting format to fix the currency symbols, lining them up within the column. Following these standard accounting principles will make your financial data easier to read both on the screen and in printouts.

Carol wants you to format the gross sales amounts in the Accounting format so that they are easier to read.

To format the gross sales in the Accounting format:

1. Select the range **C6:E6** containing the gross sales.

2. On the Home tab, in the Number group, click the **Accounting Number Format** button $. The numbers are formatted in the Accounting format. You cannot see the format because the cells display ##########.

TIP

You can click the Accounting Number Format button arrow, and then click a different currency symbol.

The cells display ########## because the formatted numbers don't fit into the columns. One reason for this is that monetary values, by default, show both dollars and cents in the cell. However, you can increase or decrease the number of decimal places displayed in a cell. The displayed value might then be rounded. For example, the stored value 11.7 will appear in the cell as 12 if no decimal places are displayed to the right of the decimal point. Changing the number of decimal places displayed in a cell does not change the value stored in the cell.

Because the conference attendees are interested only in whole dollar amounts, Carol wants you to hide the cents values of the gross sales by decreasing the number of decimal places to zero.

To decrease the number of decimal places displayed in the gross sales:

1. Make sure the range **C6:E6** is still selected.

2. On the Home tab, in the Number group, click the **Decrease Decimal** button twice. The cents are hidden for gross sales.

3. Click cell **C4** to deselect the range. See Figure 2-11.

| Figure 2-11 | Formatted gross sales values |

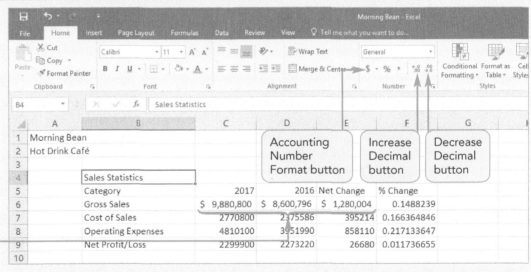

gross sales displayed in the Accounting format with no decimal places

The Comma style is identical to the Accounting format except that it does not fix a currency symbol to the left of the number. The advantage of using the Comma style and the Accounting format together is that the numbers will be aligned in the column.

Carol asks you to apply the Comma style to the remaining sales statistics.

To apply the Comma style to the sales statistics:

▶ **1.** Select the nonadjacent range **C7:E9,C11:E12** containing the sales figures for all stores in 2016 and 2017.

▶ **2.** On the Home tab, in the Number group, click the **Comma Style** button 🔘. In some instances, the number is now too large to be displayed in the cell.

▶ **3.** In the Number group, click the **Decrease Decimal** button 🔘 twice to remove two decimal places. Digits to the right of the decimal point are hidden for all of the selected cells, and all of the numbers are now visible.

▶ **4.** Click cell **C13** to deselect the range. See Figure 2-12.

Figure 2-12	Formatted sales values

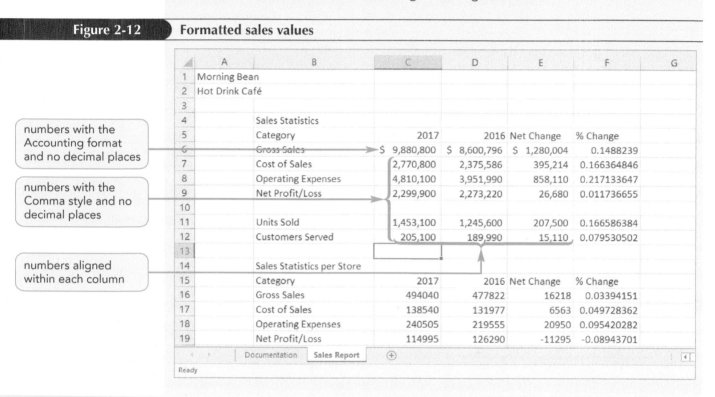

numbers with the Accounting format and no decimal places →

numbers with the Comma style and no decimal places →

numbers aligned within each column →

▲	A	B	C	D	E	F	G
1	Morning Bean						
2	Hot Drink Café						
3							
4		Sales Statistics					
5		Category	2017	2016	Net Change	% Change	
6		Gross Sales	$ 9,880,800	$ 8,600,796	$ 1,280,004	0.1488239	
7		Cost of Sales	2,770,800	2,375,586	395,214	0.166364846	
8		Operating Expenses	4,810,100	3,951,990	858,110	0.217133647	
9		Net Profit/Loss	2,299,900	2,273,220	26,680	0.011736655	
10							
11		Units Sold	1,453,100	1,245,600	207,500	0.166586384	
12		Customers Served	205,100	189,990	15,110	0.079530502	
13							
14		Sales Statistics per Store					
15		Category	2017	2016	Net Change	% Change	
16		Gross Sales	494040	477822	16218	0.03394151	
17		Cost of Sales	138540	131977	6563	0.049728362	
18		Operating Expenses	240505	219555	20950	0.095420282	
19		Net Profit/Loss	114995	126290	-11295	-0.08943701	

Documentation   **Sales Report**   ⊕

Ready

The Percent style formats numbers as percentages with no decimal places so that a number such as 0.124 appears as 12%. You can always change how many decimal places are displayed in the cell if that is important to show with your data.

Carol wants you to format the percent change from the 2016 to 2017 sales statistics with a percent symbol to make the percent values easier to read.

To format the percent change values as percentages:

▶ **1.** Select the nonadjacent range **F6:F9,F11:F12** containing the percent change values.

▶ **2.** On the Home tab, in the Number group, click the **Percent Style** button % (or press the **Ctrl+Shift+%** keys). The values are displayed as percentages with no decimal places.

▶ **3.** In the Number group, click the **Increase Decimal** button 🔘 twice. The displayed number includes two decimal places.

▶ **4.** Click cell **F13** to deselect the range. See Figure 2-13.

Figure 2-13   **Formatted percent change values**

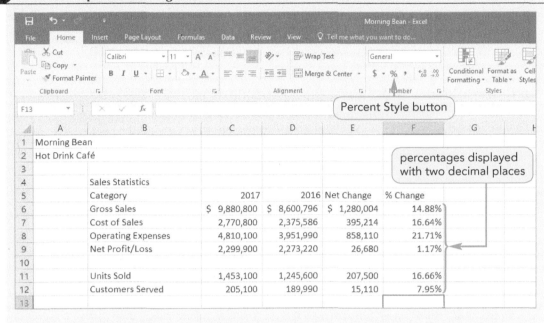

With the data reformatted, the worksheet clearly shows that Morning Bean's gross sales increased from 2016 to 2017 by almost 15 percent, but the company's net profit increased by only 1.17 percent due to increasing expenses in sales costs and operations of 16.64 percent and 21.71 percent, respectively. This type of information is very important to Morning Bean investors and to the company executives as plans are made for the upcoming year.

Formatting Dates and Times

TIP

To view the underlying date and time value, apply the General format to the cell or display the formulas instead of the formula results.

Because Excel stores dates and times as numbers and not as text, you can apply different date formats without affecting the underlying date and time value. The abbreviated format, *mm/dd/yyyy*, entered in the Documentation sheet is referred to as the **Short Date format**. You can also apply a **Long Date format** that displays the day of the week and the full month name in addition to the day of the month and the year. Other built-in formats include formats for displaying time values in 12- or 24-hour time format.

Carol asks you to change the date in the Documentation sheet to the Long Date format.

To format the date in the Long Date format:

▶ **1.** Go to the **Documentation** sheet, and then select cell **B5**.

▶ **2.** On the Home tab, in the Number group, click the **Number Format button arrow** to display a list of number formats, and then click **Long Date**. The date is displayed with the weekday name, month name, day, and year. Notice that the date in the formula bar did not change because you changed only the display format, not the date value.

Formatting Worksheet Cells

You can format the appearance of individual cells by modifying the alignment of text within the cell, indenting cell text, or adding borders of different styles and colors.

Aligning Cell Content

By default, text is aligned with the left edge of the cell, and numbers are aligned with the right edge. You might want to change the alignment to make the text and numbers more readable or visually appealing. In general, you should center column titles, left-align other text, and right-align numbers to keep their decimal places lined up within a column. Figure 2-14 describes the buttons located in the Alignment group on the Home tab that you use to set these alignment options.

Figure 2-14	Alignment buttons

Button	Name	Description
	Top Align	Aligns the cell content with the cell's top edge
	Middle Align	Vertically centers the cell content within the cell
	Bottom Align	Aligns the cell content with the cell's bottom edge
	Align Left	Aligns the cell content with the cell's left edge
	Center	Horizontally centers the cell content within the cell
	Align Right	Aligns the cell content with the cell's right edge
	Decrease Indent	Decreases the size of the indentation used in the cell
	Increase Indent	Increases the size of the indentation used in the cell
	Orientation	Rotates the cell content to any angle within the cell
	Wrap Text	Forces the cell text to wrap within the cell borders
	Merge & Center	Merges the selected cells into a single cell

The date in the Documentation sheet is right-aligned within cell B5 because Excel treats dates and times as numbers. Carol wants you to left-align the date from the Documentation sheet and center the column titles in the Sales Report worksheet.

To left-align the date and center the column titles:

1. In the Documentation sheet, make sure cell **B5** is still selected.

2. On the Home tab, in the Alignment group, click the **Align Left** button. The date shifts to the left edge of the cell.

3. Go to the **Sales Report** worksheet.

4. Select the range **C5:F5** containing the column titles.

5. In the Alignment group, click the **Center** button. The column titles are centered in the cells.

Indenting Cell Content

Sometimes you want a cell's content moved a few spaces from the cell's left edge. This is particularly useful to create subsections in a worksheet or to set off some entries from others. You can increase the indent to shift the contents of a cell away from the left edge of the cell, or you can decrease the indent to shift a cell's contents closer to the left edge of the cell.

Carol wants you to indent the Cost of Sales and Operating Expenses labels in the sales statistics table from the other labels because they represent expenses to the company.

To indent the expense categories:

▶ **1.** Select the range **B7:B8** containing the expense categories.

▶ **2.** On the Home tab, in the Alignment group, click the **Increase Indent** button twice to indent each label two spaces in its cell.

Adding Borders to Cells

Borders are another way to make financial data easier to interpret. Common accounting practices provide guidelines on when to add borders to cells. In general, a single black border should appear above a subtotal, a single bottom border should be added below a calculated number, and a double black bottom border should appear below the total.

Carol wants you to follow common accounting practices in the Sales Report worksheet. You will add borders below the column titles and below the gross sales values. You will add a top border to the net profit/loss values. Finally, you will add a top and bottom border to the Units Sold and Customers Served rows.

To add borders to the sales statistics data:

▶ **1.** Select the range **B5:F5** containing the cell headings.

▶ **2.** On the Home tab, in the Font group, click the **Borders button arrow**, and then click **Bottom Border**. A border is added below the column titles.

▶ **3.** Select the range **B6:F6** containing the gross sales amounts.

▶ **4.** In the Font group, click the **Bottom Border** button to add a border below the selected gross sales amounts.

▶ **5.** Select the range **B9:F9**, click the **Borders button arrow**, and then click **Top Border** to add a border above the net profit/loss amounts.

The Units Sold and Customers Served rows do not contain monetary values as the other rows do. You will distinguish these rows by adding a top and bottom border.

▶ **6.** Select the range **B11:F12**, click the **Borders button arrow**, and then click **Top and Bottom Border** to add a border above the number of units sold and below the number of customers served.

▶ **7.** Click cell **B3** to deselect the range. See Figure 2-15.

Figure 2-15 | **Borders, indents, and alignment added to the sales data**

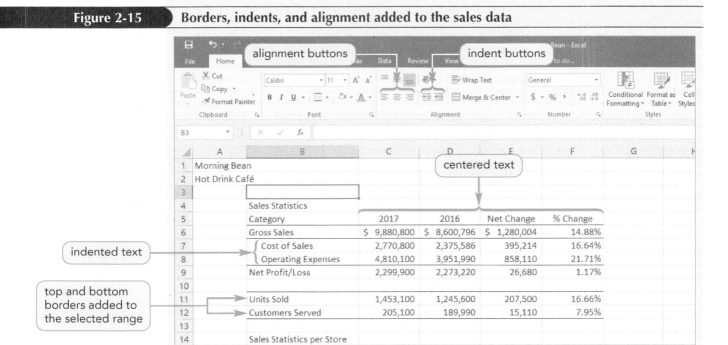

You can apply multiple formats to the same cell to create the look that best fits the data. For example, one cell might be formatted with a number format, alignments, borders, indents, fonts, font sizes, and so on. The monthly sales data needs to be formatted with number styles, alignments, indents, and borders. You'll add these formats now.

To format the monthly sales table:

1. Click in the **Name** box, type **C27:O47**, and then press the **Enter** key. The range C27:O47, containing the monthly gross sales for each store, is selected.

2. On the Home tab, in the Number group, click the **Comma Style** button ![comma] to add a thousands separator to the values.

3. In the Number group, click the **Decrease Decimal** button ![decimal] twice to hide the cents from the sales results.

4. In the Alignment group, click the **Top Align** button ![top align] to align the sales numbers with the top of each cell.

5. Select the range **C26:O26** containing the labels for the month abbreviations and the TOTAL column.

6. In the Alignment group, click the **Center** button ![center] to center the column labels.

7. Select the range **B27:B46** containing the store addresses.

8. Reduce the font size of the store addresses to **9** points.

9. In the Alignment group, click the **Increase Indent** button ![indent] to indent the store addresses.

10. In the Alignment group, click the **Top Align** button ![top align] to align the addresses at the top of each cell.

11. Select the range **B47:O47** containing the monthly totals.

12. In the Font group, click the **Borders button arrow** ![borders], and then click **All Borders** to add borders around each monthly totals cell.

> **13.** Select the range **O26:O46** containing the annual totals for each restaurant, and then click the **All Borders** button ⊞ to add borders around each restaurant total.

> **14.** Click cell **A24** to deselect the range. See Figure 2-16.

| Figure 2-16 | Formatted monthly gross sales |

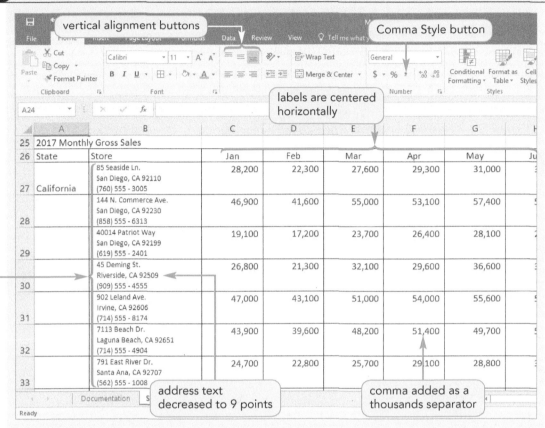

Merging Cells

You can merge, or combine, several cells into one cell. A merged cell contains two or more cells with a single cell reference. When you merge cells, only the content from the upper-left cell in the range is retained. The cell reference for the merged cell is the upper-left cell reference. So, if you merge cells A1 and A2, the merged cell reference is cell A1. After you merge cells, you can align the content within the merged cell. The Merge & Center button in the Alignment group on the Home tab includes the following options:

- **Merge & Center**—merges the range into one cell and horizontally centers the content
- **Merge Across**—merges each row in the selected range across the columns in the range
- **Merge Cells**—merges the range into a single cell but does not horizontally center the cell content
- **Unmerge Cells**—reverses a merge, returning the merged cell to a range of individual cells

The first column of the monthly sales data lists the states in which Morning Bean has stores. You will merge the cells for each state name into a single cell.

To merge the state name cells:

> **1.** Select the range **A27:A33** containing the cells for the California stores. You will merge these seven cells into a single cell.

▶ 2. On the Home tab, in the Alignment group, click the **Merge & Center** button. The range A27:A33 merges into one cell with the cell reference A27, and the text is centered and bottom-aligned within the cell.

▶ 3. Select the range **A34:A36**, and then click the **Merge & Center** button to merge and center the cells for stores in the state of Washington.

▶ 4. Select the range **A37:A40**, and then merge and center the cells for the Oregon stores.

▶ 5. Click cell **A41**, and then click the **Center** button 三 to center the Idaho text horizontally in the cell.

▶ 6. Merge and center the range **A42:A43** containing the Nevada cells.

▶ 7. Merge and center the range **A44:A46** containing the Colorado cells. See Figure 2-17.

Figure 2-17 **Merged cells**

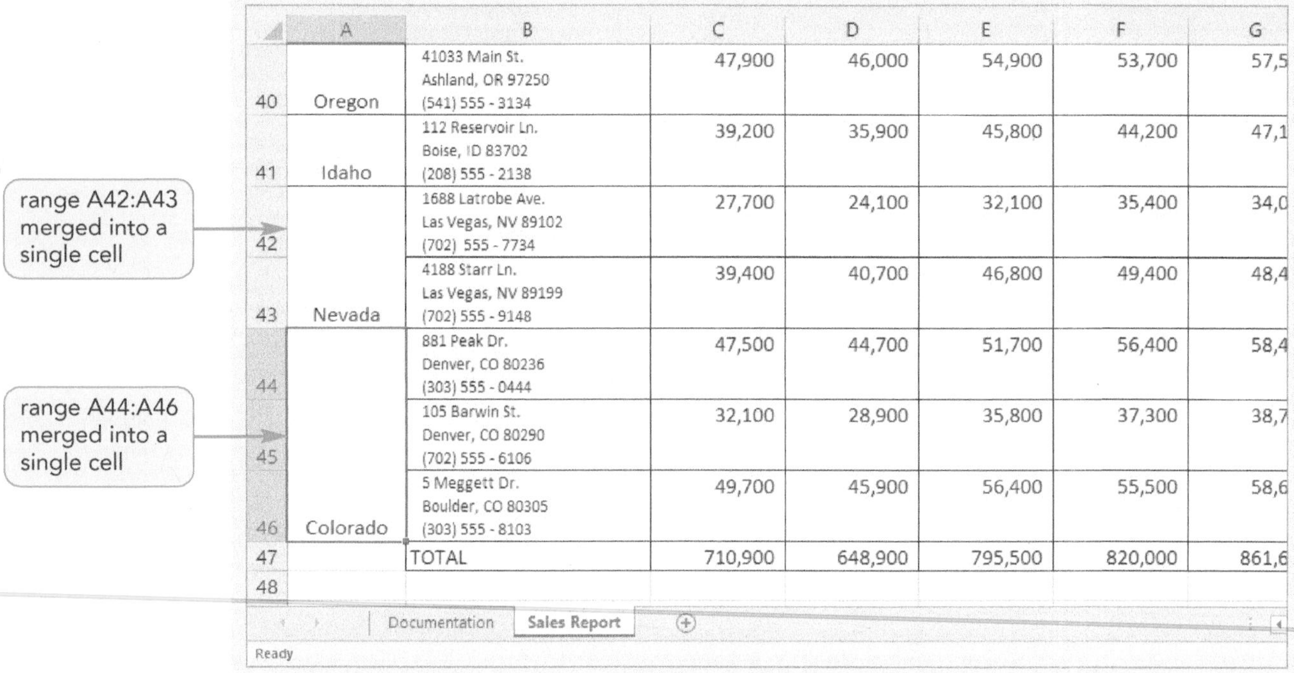

range A42:A43 merged into a single cell

range A44:A46 merged into a single cell

	A	B	C	D	E	F	G
40	Oregon	41033 Main St. Ashland, OR 97250 (541) 555 - 3134	47,900	46,000	54,900	53,700	57,5
41	Idaho	112 Reservoir Ln. Boise, ID 83702 (208) 555 - 2138	39,200	35,900	45,800	44,200	47,1
42		1688 Latrobe Ave. Las Vegas, NV 89102 (702) 555 - 7734	27,700	24,100	32,100	35,400	34,0
43	Nevada	4188 Starr Ln. Las Vegas, NV 89199 (702) 555 - 9148	39,400	40,700	46,800	49,400	48,4
44		881 Peak Dr. Denver, CO 80236 (303) 555 - 0444	47,500	44,700	51,700	56,400	58,4
45		105 Barwin St. Denver, CO 80290 (702) 555 - 6106	32,100	28,900	35,800	37,300	38,7
46	Colorado	5 Meggett Dr. Boulder, CO 80305 (303) 555 - 8103	49,700	45,900	56,400	55,500	58,6
47		TOTAL	710,900	648,900	795,500	820,000	861,6
48							

Documentation | Sales Report | ⊕

Ready

The merged cells make it easier to distinguish restaurants in each state. Next, you will rotate the cells so that the state name rotates up the merged cells.

Rotating Cell Contents

Text and numbers are displayed horizontally within cells. However, you can rotate cell text to any angle to save space or to provide visual interest to a worksheet. The state names at the bottom of the merged cells would look better and take up less room if they were rotated vertically within their cells. Carol asks you to rotate the state names.

To rotate the state names:

▶ 1. Select the merged cell **A27**.

▶ 2. On the Home tab, in the Alignment group, click the **Orientation** button 🔄 to display a list of rotation options, and then click **Rotate Text Up**. The state name rotates 90 degrees counterclockwise.

> **3.** In the Alignment group, click the **Middle Align** button ☰ to vertically center the rotated text in the merged cell.

> **4.** Select the merged cell range **A34:A46**, and then repeat Steps 2 and 3 to rotate and vertically center the rest of the state names in their cells.

> **5.** Reduce the width of column A to **7** characters because the rotated state names take up less space.

> **6.** Select cell **A47**. See Figure 2-18.

Figure 2-18	Rotated cell content

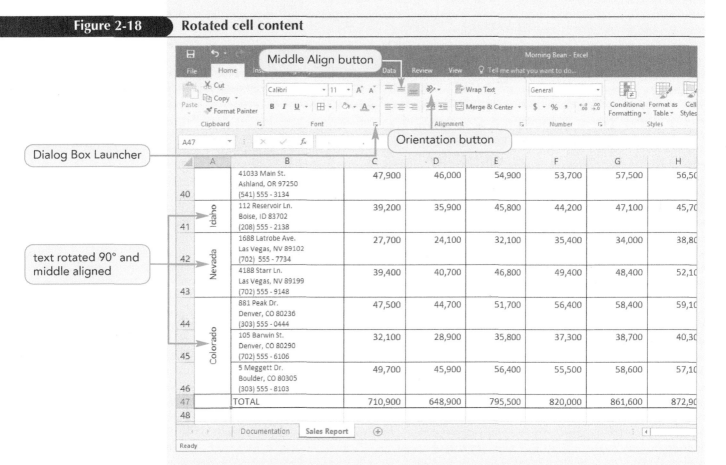

In addition to using the ribbon to apply formatting to a worksheet, you can also use the Format Cells dialog box to apply formatting.

Exploring the Format Cells Dialog Box

The buttons on the Home tab provide quick access to the most commonly used formatting choices. For more options, you can use the Format Cells dialog box. You can apply the formats in this dialog box to the selected worksheet cells. The Format Cells dialog box has six tabs, each focusing on a different set of formatting options, as described below:

- **Number**—provides options for formatting the appearance of numbers, including dates and numbers treated as text such as telephone or Social Security numbers
- **Alignment**—provides options for how data is aligned within a cell
- **Font**—provides options for selecting font types, sizes, styles, and other formatting attributes such as underlining and font colors

- **Border**—provides options for adding and removing cell borders as well as selecting a line style and color
- **Fill**—provides options for creating and applying background colors and patterns to cells
- **Protection**—provides options for locking or hiding cells to prevent other users from modifying their contents

Although you have applied many of these formats from the Home tab, the Format Cells dialog box presents them in a different way and provides more choices. You will use the Font and Fill tabs to format the column titles with a white font on a green background.

To use the Format Cells dialog box to format the column titles:

1. Select the range **A26:O26** containing the column titles for the table.

TIP

Clicking the Dialog Box Launcher in the Font, Alignment, or Number group opens the Format Cells dialog box with that tab displayed.

2. On the Home tab, in the Font group, click the **Dialog Box Launcher** located to the right of the group name (refer to Figure 2-18). The Format Cells dialog box opens with the Font tab displayed.

3. Click the **Color** box to display the available colors, and then click **White, Background 1** in the Theme Color section. The font is set to white. See Figure 2-19.

Figure 2-19   **Font tab in the Format Cells dialog box**

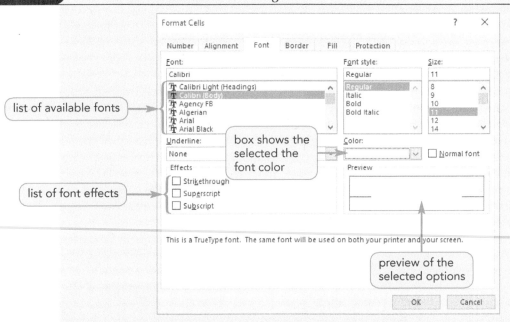

4. Click the **Fill** tab to display background options.

5. In the Background Color section, click the **green** standard color (the sixth color in the last row). The background is set to green, as you can see in the Sample box.

6. Click the **OK** button. The dialog box closes, and the font and fill options you selected are applied to the column titles.

You will also use the Format Cells dialog box to change the appearance of the row titles. You'll format them to be displayed in a larger white font on a gold background.

To format the row titles:

1. Select the range **A27:A46** containing the rotated state names.

2. Right-click the selected range, and then click **Format Cells** on the shortcut menu. The Format Cells dialog box opens with the last tab used displayed—in this case, the Fill tab.

3. In the Background Color section, click the **gold** theme color (the eighth color in the first row). Its preview is shown in the Sample box.

4. Click the **Font** tab to display the font formatting options.

5. Click the **Color** box, and then click the **White, Background 1** theme color to set the font color to white.

6. In the Size box, click **14** to set the font size to 14 points.

7. In the Font style box, click **Bold** to change the font to boldface.

8. Click the **OK** button. The dialog box closes, and the font and fill formats are applied to the state names.

9. Scroll up and click cell **A24** to deselect the A27:A46 range. See Figure 2-20.

| Figure 2-20 | Formatted worksheet cells |

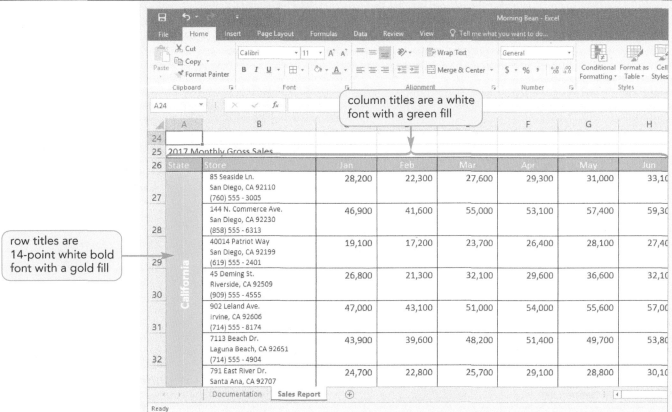

10. Save the workbook.

With the formats you have added to the Sales Report worksheet, readers will be able to more easily read and interpret the large table of store sales.

Written Communication: Formatting Workbooks for Readability and Appeal

Designing a workbook requires the same care as designing any written document or report. A well-formatted workbook is easy to read and establishes a sense of professionalism with readers. Do the following to improve the appearance of your workbooks:

- **Clearly identify each worksheet's purpose.** Include column or row titles and a descriptive sheet name.
- **Include only one or two topics on each worksheet.** Don't crowd individual worksheets with too much information. Place extra topics on separate sheets. Readers should be able to interpret each worksheet with a minimal amount of horizontal and vertical scrolling.
- **Place worksheets with the most important information first in the workbook.** Position worksheets summarizing your findings near the front of the workbook. Position worksheets with detailed and involved analysis near the end as an appendix.
- **Use consistent formatting throughout the workbook.** If negative values appear in red on one worksheet, format them in the same way on all sheets. Also, be consistent in the use of thousands separators, decimal places, and percentages.
- **Pay attention to the format of the printed workbook.** Make sure your printouts are legible with informative headers and footers. Check that the content of the printout is scaled correctly to the page size and that page breaks divide the information into logical sections.

Excel provides many formatting tools. However, too much formatting can be intrusive, overwhelm data, and make the document difficult to read. Remember that the goal of formatting is not simply to make a "pretty workbook" but also to accentuate important trends and relationships in the data. A well-formatted workbook should seamlessly convey your data to the reader. If the reader is thinking about how your workbook looks, it means he or she is not thinking about your data.

You have completed much of the formatting that Carol wants in the Sales Report worksheet for the Morning Bean sales conference. In the next session, you will explore other formatting options.

REVIEW

Session 2.1 Quick Check

1. What is the difference between a serif font and a sans serif font?
2. What is the difference between a theme color and a standard color?
3. A cell containing a number displays #######. Why does this occur, and what can you do to fix it?
4. What is the General format?
5. Describe the differences between Currency format and Accounting format.
6. The range B3:B13 is merged into a single cell. What is its cell reference?
7. How do you format text so that it is set vertically within the cell?
8. Where can you access all the formatting options for worksheet cells?

Session 2.2 Visual Overview:

The Page Layout tab has options for setting how the worksheet will print.

The **Format Painter** copies and pastes formatting from one cell or range to another without duplicating any data.

Print titles are rows and/or columns that are included on every page of the printout. In this case, the text in rows 1 and 2 will print on every page.

A **manual page break** is a page break that you set to indicate where a new page of the printout should start and is identified by a solid blue line.

File   Home   Insert   Page Layout   Formulas   Data   Review   View

Tw Cen MT   26   A⁺ A   General

B I U   A $ %

Clipboard   Font   Alignment   Nu

A1   fx   Morning Bean

	A	B	C	D	E	F
1	Morning Bean					
2	Hot Drink Café					
3						
4		Sales Statistics				
5		Category	2017	2016	Net Change	% Change
6		Gross Sales	$ 9,880,800	$ 8,600,796	$ 1,280,004	14.88%
7		Cost of Sales	2,770,800	2,375,586	395,214	16.64%
8		Operating Expenses	4,810,100	3,951,990	858,110	21.71%
9		Net Profit/Loss	2,299,900	2,273,220	26,680	1.17%
10						
11		Units Sold	1,453,100	1,245,600	207,500	16.66%
12		Customers Served	215,100	189,990	25,110	13.22%
13						
14		Sales Statistics per Store				
15		Category	2017	2016	Net Change	% Change
16		Gross Sales	$ 494,040	$ 477,822	$ 16,218	3.39%
17		Cost of Sales	138,540	131,977	6,563	4.97%
18		Operating Expenses	240,505	219,555	20,950	9.54%
19		Net Profit/Loss	114,995	126,290	(11,295)	-8.94%
20						
21		Units Sold	72,655	69,200	3,455	4.99%
22		Customers Served	10,755	10,555	200	1.89%
23		Stores	20	18	2	11.11%
24						
25	2017 Monthly Gross Sales					
26	State	Store	Jan	Feb	Mar	Apr
27		85 Seaside Lane San Diego, CA 32110 (760) 555 - 3005	28,200	22,300	27,600	29,300
28		144 N. Commerce Avenue San Diego, CA 92230 (858) 555 - 6313	46,900	41,600	55,000	53,100
		40014 Patriot Way	19,100	17,200	23,700	26,400

Page 1

Documentation   Sales Report   ⊕

Ready

Designing a Printout

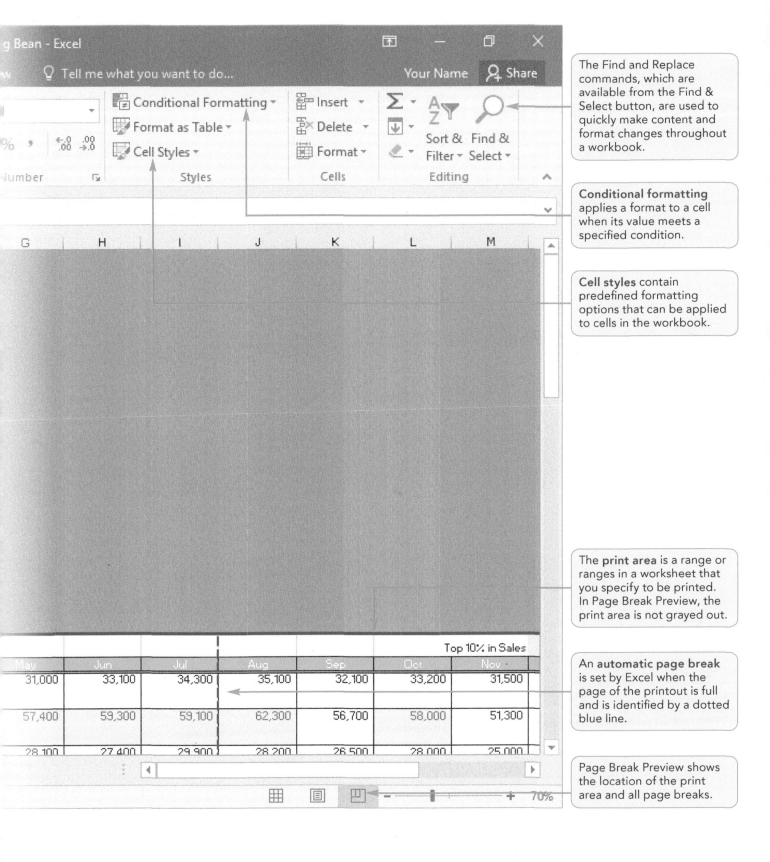

The Find and Replace commands, which are available from the Find & Select button, are used to quickly make content and format changes throughout a workbook.

Conditional formatting applies a format to a cell when its value meets a specified condition.

Cell styles contain predefined formatting options that can be applied to cells in the workbook.

The **print area** is a range or ranges in a worksheet that you specify to be printed. In Page Break Preview, the print area is not grayed out.

An **automatic page break** is set by Excel when the page of the printout is full and is identified by a dotted blue line.

Page Break Preview shows the location of the print area and all page breaks.

Calculating Averages

The **AVERAGE function** calculates the average value from a collection of numbers. It has the syntax

    AVERAGE(number1,number2,number3,…)

where *number1*, *number2*, *number3*, and so forth are either numbers or cell references to the cells or a range where the numbers are stored. For example, the following formula uses the AVERAGE function to calculate the average of 1, 2, 5, and 8, returning the value 4:

    =AVERAGE(1,2,5,8)

However, functions usually reference values entered in a worksheet. So, if the range A1:A4 contains the values 1, 2, 5, and 8, the following formula also returns the value 4:

    =AVERAGE(A1:A4)

The advantage of using cell references is that the values used in the function are visible and can be easily edited.

Carol wants you to calculate the average monthly sales for each of the 20 Morning Bean stores. You will use the AVERAGE function to calculate these values.

To calculate the average monthly sales for each store:

1. If you took a break after the previous session, make sure the Morning Bean workbook is open and the Sales Report worksheet is active.

2. In cell **P26**, enter **AVERAGE** as the column title. The cell is formatted with a green fill and white font color, matching the other column titles.

3. In cell **P27**, enter the formula **=AVERAGE(C27:N27)** to calculate the average of the monthly gross sales values entered in the range C27:N27. The formula returns the value 30,833, which is the average monthly gross sales for the store on 85 Seaside Lane in San Diego, California.

4. Copy the formula in cell **P27**, and then paste the copied formula in the range **P28:P47** to calculate the average monthly gross sales for each of the remaining Morning Bean stores as well as the average monthly sales from all stores. The average monthly gross sales for individual stores range from $25,408 to $56,317. The monthly gross sales from all stores is $823,400.

5. Select the range **P27:P47**. You will format this range of sales statistics.

6. On the Home tab, in the Alignment group, click the **Top Align** button to align each average value with the top edge of its cell.

7. In the Font group, click the **Borders button arrow**, then click **All Borders** to add borders around every cell in the selected range.

8. Click cell **P27** to deselect the range. See Figure 2-21.

Figure 2-21   Average sales results

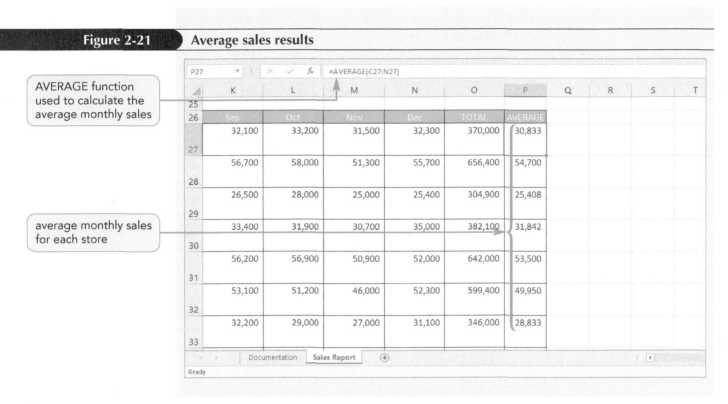

AVERAGE function used to calculate the average monthly sales

average monthly sales for each store

With so many values in the data, Carol wants you to insert double borders around the sales values for each state. The Border tab in the Format Cells dialog box provides options for changing the border style and color and placement.

To add a double border to the state results:

1. Select the range **A27:N33** containing the California monthly sales totals.
2. Open the Format Cells dialog box, and then click the **Border** tab.
3. In the Line section, click the **double line** in the lower-right corner of the Style box.
4. In the Presets section, click the **Outline** option. The double border appears around the selected cells in the Border preview. See Figure 2-22.

Figure 2-22   Border tab in the Format Cells dialog box

Format Cells   ?   ×

Number Alignment Font Border Fill Protection

Line   Presets

Style:

None   None   Outline   Inside

selected border option

Border

Text   Text

Text   Text

preview of the selected border style

selected border style

Color:

Automatic

selected border color

The selected border style can be applied by clicking the presets, preview diagram or the buttons above.

OK   Cancel

5. Click the **OK** button. The selected border is applied to the California monthly sales.

6. Repeat Steps 2 through 5 to apply double borders to the ranges **A34:N36**, **A37:N40**, **A41:N41**, **A42:N43**, and **A44:N46**.

7. Click cell **A48** to deselect the range. See Figure 2-23.

Figure 2-23   Worksheet with font, fill, and border formatting

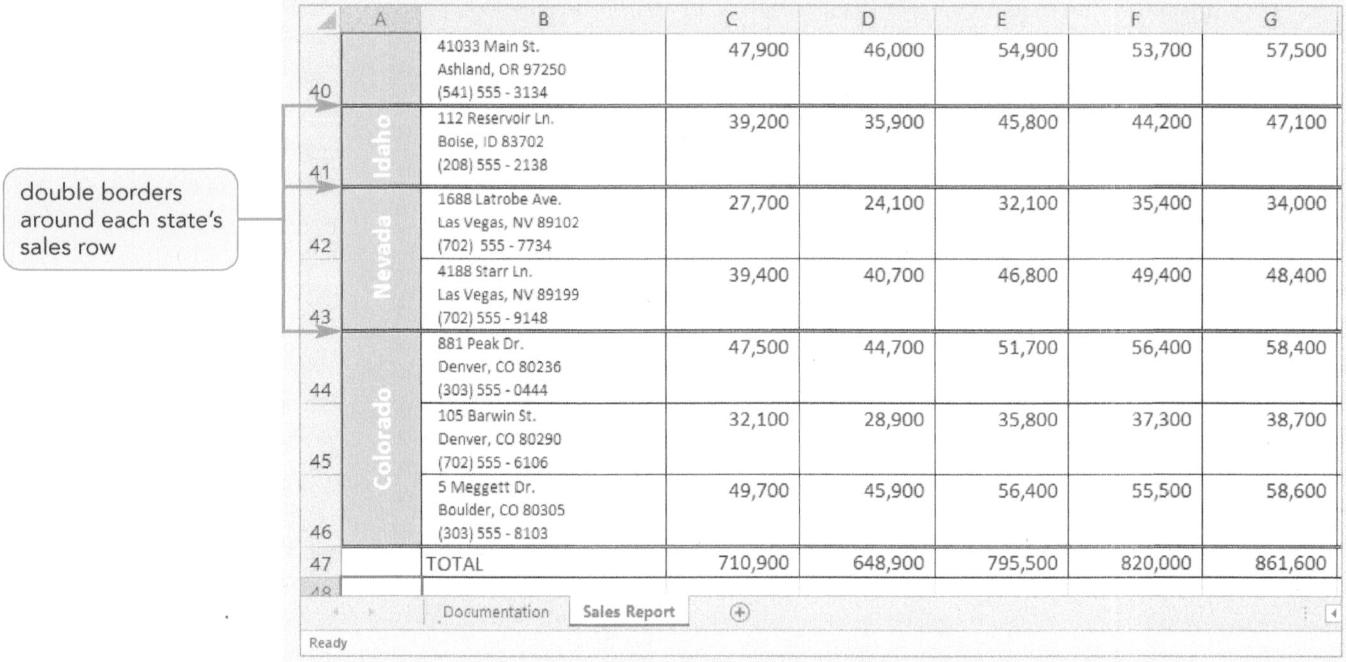

double borders around each state's sales row

	A	B	C	D	E	F	G
40		41033 Main St. Ashland, OR 97250 (541) 555 - 3134	47,900	46,000	54,900	53,700	57,500
41	Idaho	112 Reservoir Ln. Boise, ID 83702 (208) 555 - 2138	39,200	35,900	45,800	44,200	47,100
42	Nevada	1688 Latrobe Ave. Las Vegas, NV 89102 (702) 555 - 7734	27,700	24,100	32,100	35,400	34,000
43		4188 Starr Ln. Las Vegas, NV 89199 (702) 555 - 9148	39,400	40,700	46,800	49,400	48,400
44	Colorado	881 Peak Dr. Denver, CO 80236 (303) 555 - 0444	47,500	44,700	51,700	56,400	58,400
45		105 Barwin St. Denver, CO 80290 (702) 555 - 6106	32,100	28,900	35,800	37,300	38,700
46		5 Meggett Dr. Boulder, CO 80305 (303) 555 - 8103	49,700	45,900	56,400	55,500	58,600
47		TOTAL	710,900	648,900	795,500	820,000	861,600

Documentation   Sales Report   ⊕

Ready

Another way to format worksheet cells is with styles.

Applying Cell Styles

A workbook often contains several cells that store the same type of data. For example, each worksheet might have a cell displaying the sheet title, or a range of financial data might have several cells containing totals and averages. It is good design practice to apply the same format to worksheet cells that contain the same type of data.

One way to ensure that similar data is displayed consistently is with styles. A **style** is a collection of formatting options that include a specified font, font size, font styles, font color, fill color, and borders. The Cell Styles gallery includes a variety of built-in styles that you can use to format titles and headings, different types of data such as totals or calculations, and cells that you want to emphasize. For example, you can use the Heading 1 style to display sheet titles in a bold, blue-gray, 15-point Calibri font with no fill color and a blue bottom border. You can then apply the Heading 1 style to all titles in the workbook. If you later revise the style, the appearance of any cell formatted with that style is updated automatically. This saves you the time and effort of reformatting each cell individually.

You already used built-in styles when you formatted data in the Sales Report worksheet with the Accounting, Comma, and Percent styles. You can also create your own cell styles by clicking New Cell Style at the bottom of the Cell Styles gallery.

Applying a Cell Style

REFERENCE

- Select the cell or range to which you want to apply a style.
- On the Home tab, in the Styles group, click the Cell Styles button.
- Point to each style in the Cell Styles gallery to see a Live Preview of that style on the selected cell or range.
- Click the style you want to apply to the selected cell or range.

Carol wants you to add more color and visual interest to the Sales Report worksheet. You'll use the styles in the Cell Styles gallery to do this.

To apply cell styles to the Sales Report worksheet:

▸ 1. Click cell **B4** containing the text "Sales Statistics."

▸ 2. On the Home tab, in the Styles group, click the **Cell Styles** button. The Cell Styles gallery opens.

▸ 3. Point to the **Heading 1** style in the Titles and Headings section. Live Preview shows cell B4 in a 15-point, bold font with a solid blue bottom border. See Figure 2-24.

Figure 2-24   Cell Styles gallery

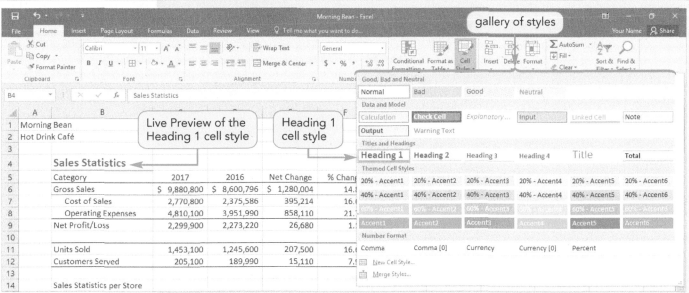

▸ 4. Move the pointer over different styles in the Cell Styles gallery to see cell B4 with a Live Preview of each style.

▸ 5. Click the **Title** style. The Title style—18-point, Blue-Gray, Text 2 Calibri Light font—is applied to cell B4.

▸ 6. Select the range **B5:F5** containing the column titles for the Sales Statistics data.

▸ 7. In the Styles group, click the **Cell Styles** button, and then click the **Accent4** style in the Themed Cell Styles section of the Cell Styles gallery.

▸ 8. Click cell **A25** containing the text "2017 Monthly Gross Sales," and then apply the **Title** cell style to the cell.

▶ **9.** Click cell **A3**. See Figure 2-25.

Figure 2-25   **Cell styles applied to the worksheet**

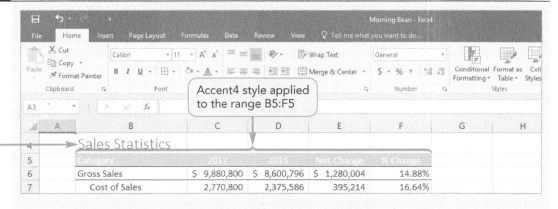

Accent4 style applied to the range B5:F5

Title style applied to cell B4

	A	B	C	D	E	F	G	H
4		Sales Statistics						
5		Category	2017	2016	Net Change	% Change		
6		Gross Sales	$ 9,880,800	$ 8,600,796	$ 1,280,004	14.88%		
7		Cost of Sales	2,770,800	2,375,586	395,214	16.64%		

Copying and Pasting Formats

Large workbooks often use the same formatting on similar data throughout the workbook, sometimes in widely scattered cells. Rather than repeating the same steps to format these cells, you can copy the format of one cell or range and paste it to another.

Copying Formats with the Format Painter

The Format Painter provides a fast and efficient way of copying and pasting formats, ensuring that a workbook has a consistent look and feel. The Format Painter does not copy formatting applied to selected text within a cell, and it does not copy data.

Carol wants the Sales Report worksheet to use the same formats you applied to the Morning Bean company name and description in the Documentation sheet. You will use the Format Painter to copy and paste the formats.

To use the Format Painter to copy and paste a format:

▶ **1.** Go to the **Documentation** worksheet, and then select the range **A1:A2**.

TIP

To paste the same format multiple times, double-click the Format Painter button. Click the button again or press the Esc key to turn it off.

▶ **2.** On the Home tab, in the Clipboard group, click the **Format Painter** button. The formats from the selected cells are copied to the Clipboard, a flashing border appears around the selected range, and the pointer changes to ⊕🖌️.

▶ **3.** Go to the **Sales Report** worksheet, and then click cell **A1**. The formatting from the Documentation worksheet is removed from the Clipboard and applied to the range A1:A2. Notice that gold font color you applied to the text selection "Morning" was not included in the pasted formats.

▶ **4.** Double-click cell **A1** to enter Edit mode, select **Morning**, and then change the font color to the **Gold, Accent 4** theme color. The format for the company title now matches what you applied earlier in the Documentation sheet.

▶ **5.** Press the **Enter** key to exit Edit mode and select cell A2.

You can use the Format Painter to copy all of the formats within a selected range and then apply those formats to another range that has the same size and shape by clicking the upper-left cell of the range. Carol wants you to copy all of the formats that you applied to the Sales Statistics data to the sales statistics per store data.

To copy and paste multiple formats:

1. Select the range **B4:F12** in the Sales Report worksheet.

2. On the Home tab, in the Clipboard group, click the **Format Painter** button.

3. Click cell **B14**. All of the number formats, cell borders, fonts, and fill colors are pasted in the range B14:F22.

4. Select the range **C23:E23**. You'll format this data.

5. On the Home tab, in the Number group, click the **Comma Style** button 〕, and then click the **Decrease Decimal** button twice to remove the decimal places to the right of the decimal point. The numbers are now vertically aligned in their columns.

6. Click cell **F23**.

7. In the Number group, click the **Percent Style** button % to change the number to a percentage, and then click the **Increase Decimal** button twice to display two decimal places in the percentage. The value is now formatted to match the other percentages.

8. Click cell **B24**. See Figure 2-26.

TIP

If the range you paste the formats in is bigger than the range you copied, Format Painter will repeat the copied formats to fill the pasted range.

| Figure 2-26 | Formatting copied and pasted between ranges |

Copying Formats with the Paste Options Button

Another way to copy and paste formats is with the Paste Options button ⬚ (Ctrl)·, which provides options for pasting only values, only formats, or some combination of values and formats. Each time you paste, the Paste Options button appears in the lower-right corner of the pasted cell or range. You click the Paste Options button to open a list of pasting options, shown in Figure 2-27, such as pasting only the values or only the formatting. You can also click the Transpose button to paste the column data into a row, or to paste the row data into a column.

Figure 2-27   Paste Options button

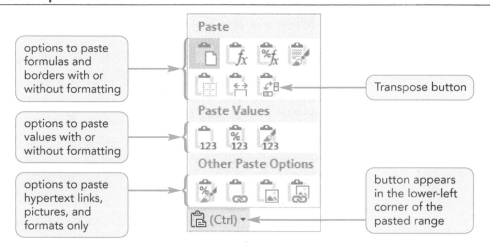

Copying Formats with Paste Special

The Paste Special command provides another way to control what you paste from the Clipboard. To use Paste Special, select and copy a range, select the range where you want to paste the Clipboard contents, click the Paste button arrow in the Clipboard group on the Home tab, and then click Paste Special to open the dialog box shown in Figure 2-28.

Figure 2-28   Paste Special dialog box

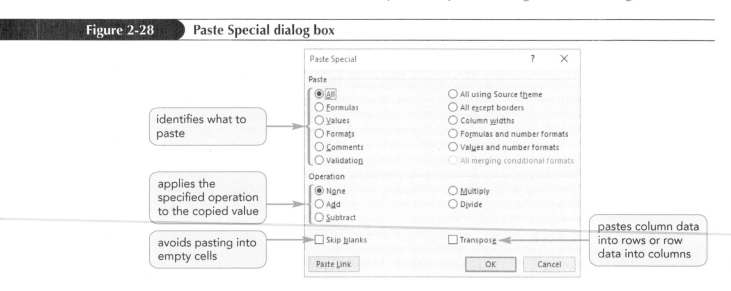

From the Paste Special dialog box, you can control exactly how to paste the copied range.

Finding and Replacing Text and Formats

The Find and Replace commands let you make content and design changes to a worksheet or the entire workbook quickly. The Find command searches through the current worksheet or workbook for the content or formatting you want to locate, and the Replace command then substitutes it with the new content or formatting you specify.

The Find and Replace commands are versatile. You can find each occurrence of the search text one at a time and decide whether to replace it. You can highlight all occurrences of the search text in the worksheet. Or, you can replace all occurrences at once without reviewing them.

Carol wants you to replace all the street title abbreviations (such as Ave.) in the Sales Report with their full names (such as Avenue). You will use Find and Replace to make these changes.

To find and replace the street title abbreviations:

▶ 1. On the Home tab, in the Editing group, click the **Find & Select** button, and then click **Replace** (or press the **Ctrl+H** keys). The Find and Replace dialog box opens.

▶ 2. Type **Ave.** in the Find what box.

▶ 3. Press the **Tab** key to move the insertion point to the Replace with box, and then type **Avenue**. See Figure 2-29.

Figure 2-29	Find and Replace dialog box

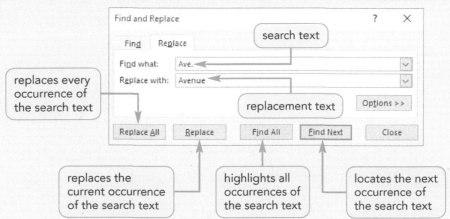

▶ 4. Click the **Replace All** button to replace all occurrences of the search text without reviewing them. A dialog box opens, reporting that three replacements were made in the worksheet.

▶ 5. Click the **OK** button to return to the Find and Replace dialog box.

Next, you will replace the other street title abbreviations.

▶ 6. Repeat Steps 2 through 5 to replace all occurrences of each of the following: **St.** with **Street**, **Ln.** with **Lane,** and **Dr.** with **Drive**.

▶ 7. Click the **Close** button to close the Find and Replace dialog box.

▶ 8. Scroll through the Sales Report worksheet to verify that all street title abbreviations were replaced with their full names.

The Find and Replace dialog box can also be used to replace one format with another or to replace both text and a format simultaneously. Carol wants you to replace all occurrences of the white text on a gold fill in the Sales Report worksheet with blue text on a gold fill. You'll use the Find and Replace dialog box to make this formatting change.

To replace white text with blue text:

▶ 1. On the Home tab, in the Editing group, click the **Find & Select** button, and then click **Replace** (or press the **Ctrl+H** keys). The Find and Replace dialog box opens.

▶ 2. Delete the search text from the Find what and Replace with boxes, leaving those two boxes empty. By not specifying a text string to find and replace, the dialog box will search through all cells regardless of their content.

▶ 3. Click the **Options** button to expand the dialog box.

▶ 4. Click the **Format** button in the Find what row to open the Find Format dialog box, which is similar to the Format Cells dialog box you used earlier to format a range.

▶ 5. Click the **Font** tab to make it active, click the **Color** box, and then click the **White, Background 1** theme color.

▶ 6. Click the **Fill** tab, and then in the Background Color section, click the **gold** color (the eighth color in the first row).

▶ 7. Click the **OK** button to close the Find Format dialog box and return to the Find and Replace dialog box.

▶ 8. Click the **Format** button in the Replace with row to open the Replace Format dialog box.

▶ 9. On the Fill tab, click the **gold** color.

▶ 10. Click the **Font** tab, click the **Color** box, and then click **Blue** in the Standard Colors section.

▶ 11. Click the **OK** button to return to the Find and Replace dialog box. See Figure 2-30.

Figure 2-30   Expanded Find and Replace dialog box

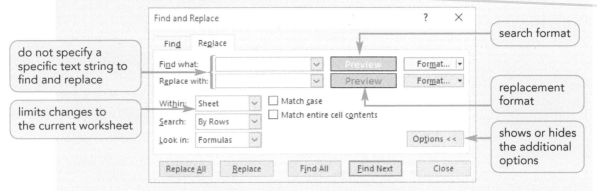

do not specify a specific text string to find and replace

limits changes to the current worksheet

search format

replacement format

shows or hides the additional options

▶ **12.** Click the **Replace All** button to replace all occurrences of white text on a gold fill in the Sales Report worksheet with blue text on a gold fill. A dialog box opens, reporting that 16 replacements were made.

▶ **13.** Click the **OK** button to return to the Find and Replace dialog box.

It is a good idea to clear the find and replace formats after you are done so that they won't affect any future searches and replacements. Carol asks you to remove the formats from the Find and Replace dialog box.

To clear the options from the Find and Replace dialog box:

▶ **1.** In the Find and Replace dialog box, click the **Format button arrow** in the Find what row, and then click **Clear Find Format**. The search format is removed.

▶ **2.** Click the **Format button arrow** in the Replace with row, and then click **Clear Replace Format**. The replacement format is removed.

▶ **3.** Click the **Close** button. The Find and Replace dialog box closes.

Another way to make multiple changes to the formats used in your workbook is through themes.

Working with Themes

Recall that a theme is a coordinated selection of fonts, colors, and graphical effects that are applied throughout a workbook to create a specific look and feel. When you switch to a different theme, the theme-related fonts, colors, and effects change throughout the workbook to reflect the new theme. The appearance of nontheme fonts, colors, and effects remains unchanged no matter which theme is applied to the workbook.

Most of the formatting you have applied to the Sales Report workbook is based on the Office theme. Carol wants you to change the theme to see how it affects the workbook's appearance.

To change the workbook's theme:

▶ **1.** On the ribbon, click the **Page Layout** tab.

▶ **2.** In the Themes group, click the **Themes** button. The Themes gallery opens. Office—the current theme—is the default.

▶ **3.** Point to different themes in the Themes gallery using Live Preview to preview the impact of each theme on the fonts and colors used in the worksheet.

▶ **4.** Click the **Droplet** theme to apply that theme to the workbook. See Figure 2-31.

Figure 2-31	Live Preview of the Droplet theme

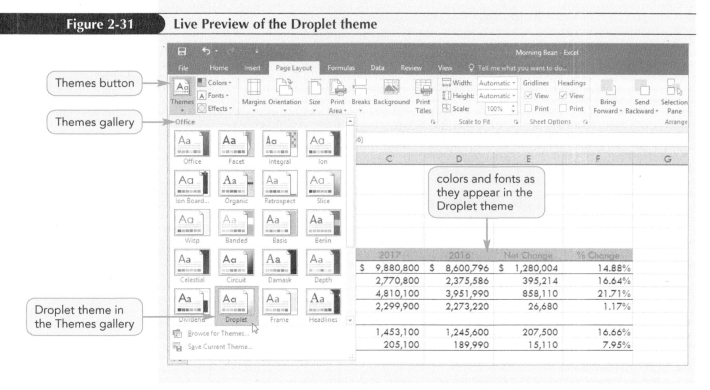

Changing the theme made a significant difference in the worksheet's appearance. The most obvious changes to the worksheet are the fill colors and the fonts. Only formatting options directly tied to a theme change when you select a different theme. Any formatting options you selected that were not theme-based remain unaffected by the change. For example, using a standard color or a nontheme font will not be affected by the choice of theme. In the Sales Report worksheet, the standard green color used for the font of the company description and the fill of the column title cells in the 2017 Monthly Gross Sales data didn't change because that green is not a theme color.

Sharing Styles and Themes

INSIGHT

Using a consistent look and feel for all the files you create in Microsoft Office is a simple way to project a professional image. This consistency is especially important when a team is collaborating on a set of documents. When all team members work from a common set of style and design themes, readers will not be distracted by inconsistent or clashing formatting.

To quickly copy the styles from one workbook to another, open the workbook with the styles you want to copy, and then open the workbook in which you want to copy those styles. On the Home tab, in the Styles group, click the Cell Styles button, and then click Merge Styles. The Merge Styles dialog box opens, listing the currently open workbooks. Select the workbook with the styles you want to copy, and then click the OK button to copy those styles into the current workbook. If you modify any styles, you must copy the styles to the other workbook; Excel does not update styles between workbooks.

Because other Office files, including those created with Word or PowerPoint, use the same file format for themes, you can create one theme to use with all your Office files. To save a theme, click the Themes button in the Themes group on the Page Layout tab, and then click Save Current Theme. The Save Current Theme dialog box opens. Select a save location, type a name in the File name box, and then click the Save button. If you saved the theme file in a default Theme folder, the theme appears in the Themes gallery and affects any Office file that uses that theme.

Highlighting Data with Conditional Formats

Conditional formatting is often used to help analyze data. Conditional formatting applies formatting to a cell when its value meets a specified condition. For example, conditional formatting can be used to format negative numbers in red and positive numbers in black. Conditional formatting is dynamic, which means that the formatting can change when the cell's value changes. Each conditional format has a set of rules that define how the formatting should be applied and under what conditions the format will be changed.

REFERENCE

Highlighting Cells with Conditional Formatting

- Select the range in which you want to highlight cells.
- On the Home tab, in the Styles group, click the Conditional Formatting button, point to Highlight Cells Rules or Top/Bottom Rules, and then click the appropriate rule.
- Select the appropriate options in the dialog box.
- Click the OK button.

Excel has four types of conditional formatting—data bars, highlighting, color scales, and icon sets. In this module, you will use conditional formatting to highlight cells.

Highlighting Cells Based on Their Values

Cell highlighting changes the cell's font color or fill color based on the cell's value, as described in Figure 2-32. You can enter a value or a cell reference if you want to compare other cells with the value in a certain cell.

Figure 2-32   Highlight Cells rules

Rule	Highlights Cell Values
Greater Than	Greater than a specified number
Less Than	Less than a specified number
Between	Between two specified numbers
Equal To	Equal to a specified number
Text that Contains	That contain specified text
A Date Occurring	That contain a specified date
Duplicate Values	That contain duplicate or unique values

Carol wants to highlight important trends and sales values in the Sales Report worksheet. She asks you to highlight sales statistics that show a negative net change or negative percent change from the previous year to the current year. You will use conditional formatting to highlight the negative values in red.

To highlight negative values in red:

1. In the Sales Report worksheet, select the range **E6:F12,E16:F22** containing the net and percent changes overall and per store from the previous year to the current year.

> **2.** On the ribbon, click the **Home** tab.

> **3.** In the Styles group, click the **Conditional Formatting** button, and then point to **Highlight Cells Rules** to display a menu of the available rules.

TIP

To create a format, click the right box arrow, then click Custom Format to open the Format Cells dialog box.

> **4.** Click **Less Than**. The Less Than dialog box opens so you can select the value and formatting to highlight negative values.

> **5.** Make sure the value in the first box is selected, and then type **0** so that cells in the selected range that contain values that are less than 0 are formatted with a light red fill and dark red text. Live Preview shows the conditional formatting applied to the cells with negative numbers. See Figure 2-33.

Figure 2-33 **Live Preview of the Less Than conditional format**

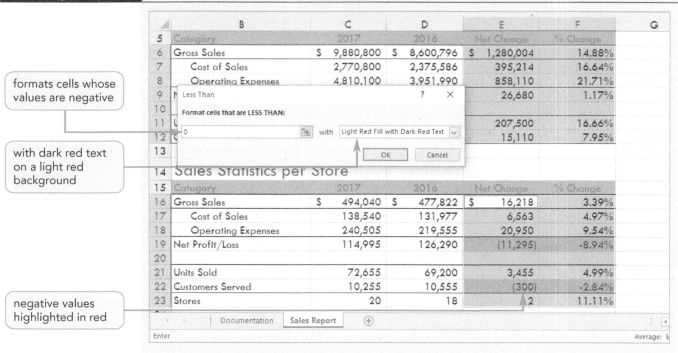

> **6.** Click the **OK** button to apply the highlighting rule.

The conditional formatting highlights that Morning Bean showed a decline from the previous year to the current year for two statistics: The net profit per store declined $11,295 or 8.94 percent, and the number of customers served per store declined by 300 persons or 2.84 percent. These declines occurred because the two new stores that Morning Bean opened in 2017 are still finding a market, resulting in lower profit and customer served per store for the entire franchise.

Conditional formatting is dynamic, which means that changes in the values affect the format of those cells. The total number of customers served in 2017 was incorrectly entered in cell C12 as 205,100. The correct value is 215,100. You will make this change and view its impact on the cells highlighted with conditional formatting.

To view the impact of changing values on conditional formatting:

> **1.** Click cell **C12** to select it.

> **2.** Type **215,100** as the new value, and then press the Enter key. The conditional formatting changes based on the new value. See Figure 2-34.

Figure 2-34   **Cells with conditional formatting**

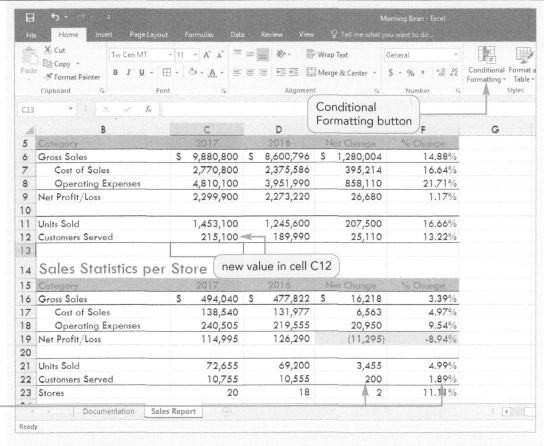

cells E22 and F22 are no longer formatted with red

By changing the value in cell C12 to 215,100, the net change in customers served per store in cell E22 is now 200 and the percentage change in cell F22 is now 1.89%. Because both of these values are now positive, the cells are no longer highlighted in red.

Highlighting Cells with a Top/Bottom Rule

Another way of applying conditional formatting is with the Quick Analysis tool. The **Quick Analysis tool**, which appears whenever you select a range of cells, provides access to the most common tools for data analysis and formatting. The Formatting category includes buttons for the Greater Than and Top 10% conditional formatting rules. You can highlight cells based on their values in comparison to other cells. For example, you can highlight cells with the 10 highest or lowest values in a selected range, or you can highlight the cells with above-average values in a range.

Carol wants to know which stores and which months rank in the top 10 percent of sales. She wants to use this information to identify the most successful stores and learn which months those stores show the highest sales volume. You'll highlight those values using the Quick Analysis tool.

To use a Top/Bottom Rule to highlight stores with the highest average sales:

1. Select the range **C27:N46** containing the monthly sales values for each of the 20 Morning Bean stores.

2. Click the **Quick Analysis** button , and then point to **Top 10%**. Live Preview formats the cells in the top 10 percent with red font and a red fill. See Figure 2-35.

Figure 2-35   Quick Analysis tool applying conditional formatting

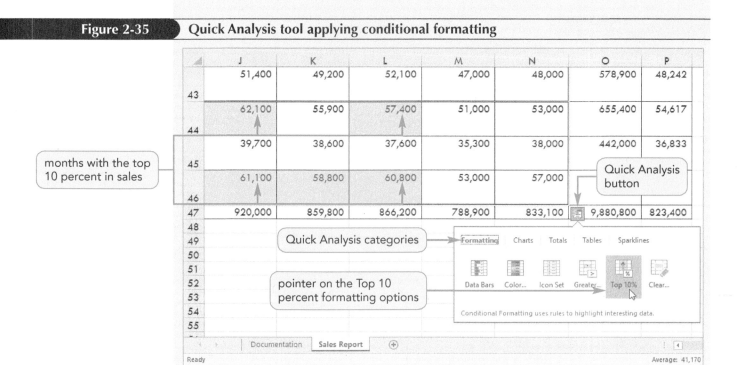

months with the top 10 percent in sales

Quick Analysis button

Quick Analysis categories

pointer on the Top 10 percent formatting options

Carol doesn't like the default format used by the Quick Analysis tool because red is usually applied to negative values and results. Instead, she wants to format the top 10 percent values in green.

3. Press the **Esc** key to close the Quick Analysis tool without applying the conditional format. The range C27:N46 remains selected.

   Trouble? If the conditional formatting was applied to the worksheet, press the Ctrl+Z keys to undo the format, and then continue with Step 4.

4. On the Home tab, in the Styles group, click the **Conditional Formatting** button, and then point to **Top/Bottom Rules** to display a list of available rules.

5. Click **Top 10%** to open the Top 10% dialog box.

6. Click the **with** arrow box and click **Green Fill with Dark Green Text** to apply green to cells with sales value in the top 10 percent. See Figure 2-36.

Figure 2-36   Top 10% dialog box

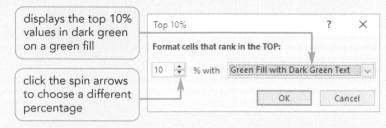

displays the top 10% values in dark green on a green fill

click the spin arrows to choose a different percentage

7. Click the **OK** button, and then click cell **A24** to deselect the cells. Monthly sales that rank in the top 10 percent are formatted with green.

8. Zoom the worksheet to **40%** so you can view all of the monthly gross sales and more easily see the sales pattern. See Figure 2-37.

Figure 2-37   **Top 10 percent highlighted with green conditional formatting**

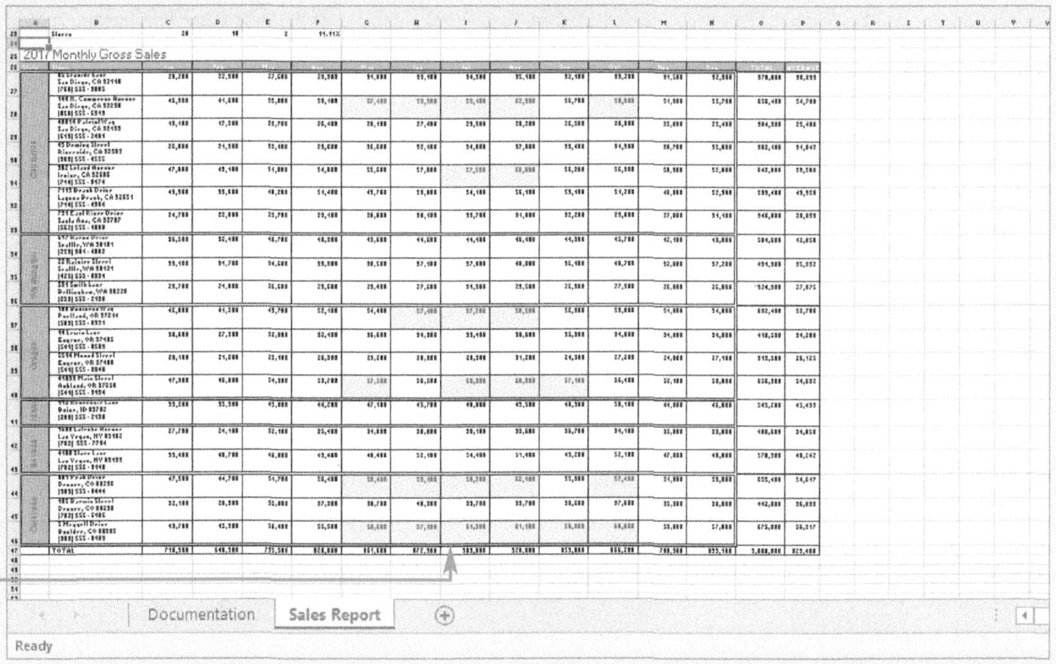

top 10 percent sales occur between May and October and are found in six stores

▶ **9.** Return the zoom to **120%** or whatever zoom is appropriate for your monitor.

The top 10 percent in monthly sales comes from six stores located in San Diego, Irvine, Portland, Ashland, Denver, and Boulder. The highest sales appear to be centered around the months from May to October. This information will be valuable to Carol as she compares the sales performance of different stores and projects monthly cash flows for the company.

Other Conditional Formatting Options

To create dynamic conditional formats that are based on cell values rather than a constant value, you can enter a cell reference in the conditional format dialog box. For example, you can highlight all cells whose value is greater than the value in cell B10. For this type of conditional format, enter the formula =$B$10 in the conditional formatting dialog box. Note that the $ character keeps the cell reference from changing if that formula moves to another cell.

You can remove a conditional format at any time without affecting the underlying data by selecting the range containing the conditional format, clicking the Conditional Formatting button, and then clicking the Clear Rules command. A menu opens, providing options to clear the conditional formatting rules from the selected cells or the entire worksheet. You can also click the Quick Analysis button that appears in the lower-right corner of the selected range and then click the Clear Format button in the Formatting category. Note that you might see only "Clear..." as the button name.

Creating a Conditional Formatting Legend

When you use conditional formatting to highlight cells in a worksheet, the purpose of the formatting is not always immediately apparent. To ensure that everyone knows why certain cells are highlighted, you should include a legend, which is a key that identifies each format and its meaning.

Carol wants you to add a legend to the Sales Report worksheet to document the two conditional formatting rules you created in the worksheet.

To create a conditional formatting legend:

▶ **1.** In cell **M25**, enter the text **Top 10% in Sales**, and then select cell **M25** again.

▶ **2.** On the Home tab, click the **Align Right** button ☰ to right-align the cell contents of the selected cell.

▶ **3.** In cell **N25**, type **green** to identify the conditional formatting color you used to highlight the values in the top 10 percent, and then select cell **N25** again.

▶ **4.** In the Alignment group, click the **Center** button ☰ to center the contents of the cell.

   You will use a highlighting rule to format cell N25 using dark green text on a green fill.

▶ **5.** On the Home tab, in the Styles group, click the **Conditional Formatting** button, point to **Highlight Cells Rules**, and then click **Text that Contains**. The Text That Contains dialog box opens. The text string "green" is automatically entered into the left input box.

▶ **6.** In the right box, click **Green Fill with Dark Green Text**.

▶ **7.** Click the **OK** button to apply the conditional formatting to cell N25. See Figure 2-38.

Figure 2-38   **Conditional formatting legend**

legend explains the purpose of the conditional formatting

	J	K	L	M	N	O	P	Q
22								
23								
24								
25				Top 10% in Sales	green			
26	Aug	Sep	Oct	Nov	Dec	TOTAL	AVERAGE	
27	35,100	32,100	33,200	31,500	32,300	370,000	30,833	
28	62,300	56,700	58,000	51,300	55,700	656,400	54,700	
29	28,200	26,500	28,000	25,000	25,400	304,900	25,408	
30	37,800	33,400	31,900	30,700	35,000	382,100	31,842	
31	60,800	56,200	56,900	50,900	52,000	642,000	53,500	
	56,100	53,100	51,200	46,000	52,300	599,400	49,950	

Documentation   Sales Report   ⊕

Ready

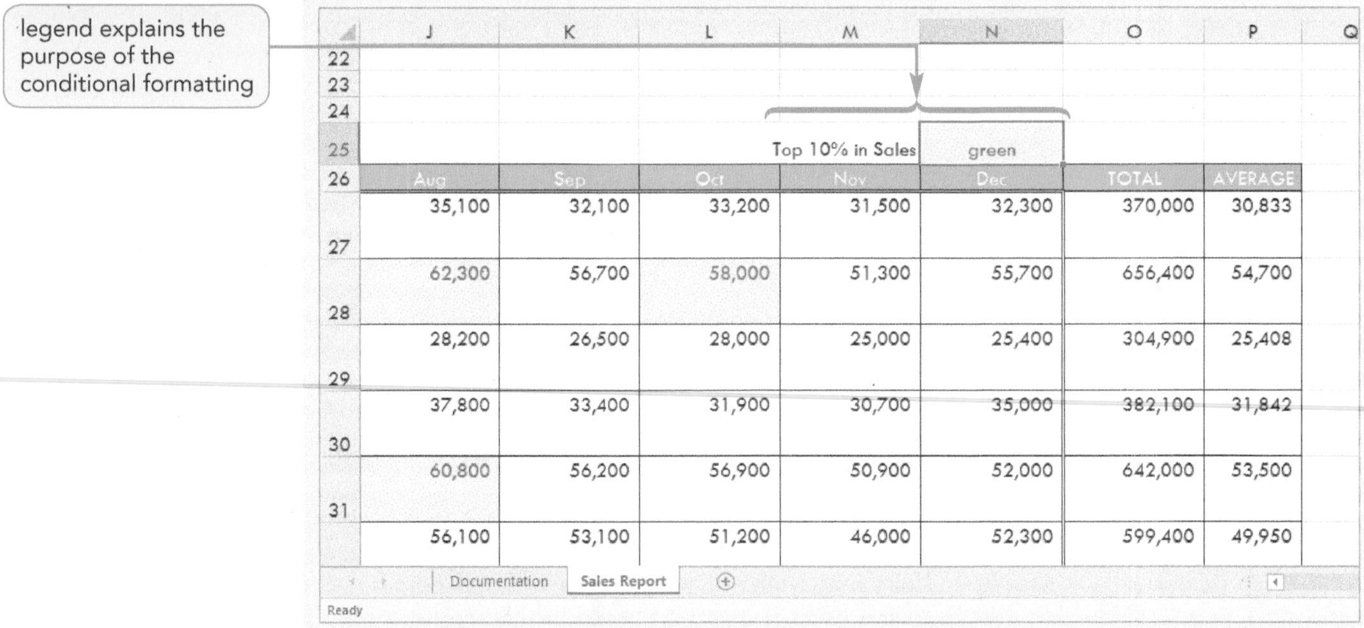

You've completed formatting the appearance of the workbook for the computer screen. Next you'll explore how to format the workbook for the printer.

Written Communication: Using Conditional Formatting Effectively

Conditional formatting is an excellent way to highlight important trends and data values to clients and colleagues. However, be sure to use it judiciously. Overusing conditional formatting might obscure the very data you want to emphasize. Keep in mind the following tips as you make decisions about what to highlight and how it should be highlighted:

- **Document the conditional formats you use.** If a bold, green font means that a sales number is in the top 10 percent of all sales, include that information in a legend in the worksheet.
- **Don't clutter data with too much highlighting.** Limit highlighting rules to one or two per data set. Highlights are designed to draw attention to points of interest. If you use too many, you will end up highlighting everything—and, therefore, nothing.
- **Use color sparingly in worksheets with highlights.** It is difficult to tell a highlight color from a regular fill color, especially when fill colors are used in every cell.
- **Consider alternatives to conditional formats.** If you want to highlight the top 10 sales regions, it might be more effective to simply sort the data with the best-selling regions at the top of the list.

Remember that the goal of highlighting is to provide a strong visual clue to important data or results. Careful use of conditional formatting helps readers to focus on the important points you want to make rather than distracting them with secondary issues and facts.

Formatting a Worksheet for Printing

You should format any worksheets you plan to print so that they are easy to read and understand. You can do this using the print settings, which enable you to set the page orientation, the print area, page breaks, print titles, and headers and footers. Print settings can be applied to an entire workbook or to individual sheets. Because other people will likely see your printed worksheets, you should format the printed output as carefully as you format the electronic version.

Carol wants you to format the Sales Report worksheet so she can distribute the printed version at the upcoming sales conference.

Using Page Break Preview

Page Break Preview shows only those parts of the active sheet that will print and how the content will be split across pages. A dotted blue border indicates a page break, which separates one page from another. As you format the worksheet for printing, you can use this view to control what content appears on each page.

Carol wants to know how the Sales Report worksheet would print in portrait orientation and how many pages would be required. You will look at the worksheet in Page Break Preview to find these answers.

To view the Sales Report worksheet in Page Break Preview:

▶ 1. Click the **Page Break Preview** button 🖥 on the status bar. The worksheet switches to Page Break Preview.

▶ 2. Change the zoom level of the worksheet to **30%** so you can view the entire contents of this large worksheet. See Figure 2-39.

Figure 2-39 Sales Report worksheet in Page Break preview

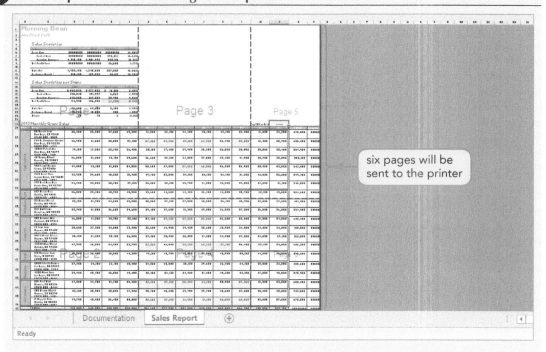

Trouble? If you see a different page layout or the worksheet is split onto a different number of pages, don't worry. Each printer is different, so the layout and pages might differ from what is shown in Figure 2-39.

Page Break Preview shows that a printout of the Sales Report worksheet requires six pages in portrait orientation, and that pages 3 and 5 would be mostly blank. Note that each printer is different, so your Page Break Preview might show a different number of pages. With this layout, each page would be difficult to interpret because the data is separated from the descriptive labels. Carol wants you to fix the layout so that the contents are easier to read and understand.

Defining the Print Area

By default, all cells in a worksheet containing text, formulas, or values are printed. If you want to print only part of a worksheet, you can set a print area, which is the region of the worksheet that is sent to the printer. Each worksheet has its own print area. Although you can set the print area in any view, Page Break Preview shades the areas of the worksheet that are not included in the print area, making it simple to confirm what will print.

Carol doesn't want the empty cells in the range G1:P24 to print, so you will set the print area to exclude those cells.

To set the print area of the Sales Report worksheet:

▶ 1. Change the zoom level of the worksheet to **80%** to make it easier to select cells and ranges.

▶ 2. Select the nonadjacent range **A1:F24,A25:P47** containing the cells with content.

▶ 3. On the ribbon, click the **Page Layout** tab.

4. In the Page Setup group, click the **Print Area** button, and then click **Set Print Area**. The print area changes to cover only the nonadjacent range A1:F24,A25:P47. The rest of the worksheet content is shaded to indicate that it will not be part of the printout.

5. Click cell **A1** to deselect the range.

6. Change the zoom level to **50%** so you can view more of the worksheet. See Figure 2-40.

Figure 2-40   **Print area set for the Sales Report worksheet**

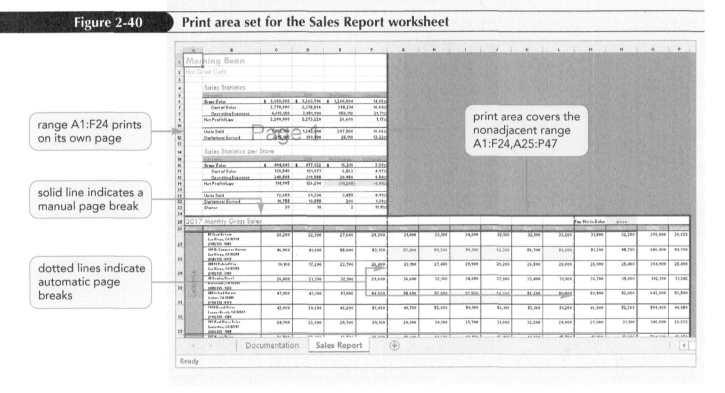

range A1:F24 prints on its own page

solid line indicates a manual page break

dotted lines indicate automatic page breaks

print area covers the nonadjacent range A1:F24,A25:P47

Inserting Page Breaks

Often, the contents of a worksheet will not fit onto a single printed page. When this happens, Excel prints as much of the content that fits on a single page without resizing, and then inserts automatic page breaks to continue printing the remaining worksheet content on successive pages. The resulting printouts might split worksheet content in awkward places, such as within a table of data.

TIP

When you remove a page break, Excel will automatically rescale the printout to fit into the allotted pages.

To split the printout into logical segments, you can insert manual page breaks. Page Break Preview identifies manual page breaks with a solid blue line and automatic page breaks with a dotted blue line. When you specify a print area for a nonadjacent range, as you did for the Sales Report worksheet, you also insert manual page breaks around the adjacent ranges. So a manual page break already appears in the print area you defined (see Figure 2-40). You can remove a page break in Page Break Preview by dragging it out of the print area.

REFERENCE

Inserting and Removing Page Breaks

To insert a page break:
- Click the first cell below the row where you want to insert a page break, click a column heading, or click a row heading.
- On the Page Layout tab, in the Page Setup group, click the Breaks button, and then click Insert Page Break.

To remove a page break:
- Select any cell below or to the right of the page break you want to remove.
- On the Page Layout tab, in the Page Setup group, click the Breaks button, and then click Remove Page Break.

or

- In Page Break Preview, drag the page break line out of the print area.

The Sales Report worksheet has automatic page breaks along columns F and L. Carol wants you to remove these automatic page breaks from the Sales Report worksheet.

To remove the automatic page breaks and insert manual page breaks:

1. Point to the dotted blue page break directly to the right of column L in the 2017 Monthly Gross Sales table until the pointer changes to ↔.

2. Drag the page break to the right and out of the print area. The page break is removed from the worksheet.

3. Point to the page break that is located in column F so that the pointer changes to ↔, and then drag the page break to the right and out of the print area.

4. Click the **I** column heading to select the entire column. You will add a manual page break between columns H and I to split the monthly gross sales data onto two pages so the printout will be larger and easier to read.

5. On the Page Layout tab, in the Page Setup group, click the **Breaks** button, and then click **Insert Page Break**. A manual page break is added between columns H and I, forcing the monthly gross sales onto a new page after the June data.

6. Click cell **A1** to deselect the column. The printout of the Sales Report worksheet is now limited to three pages. However, the gross sales data in the range A25:P47 is split across pages. See Figure 2-41.

Figure 2-41   **Manual page break in the print area**

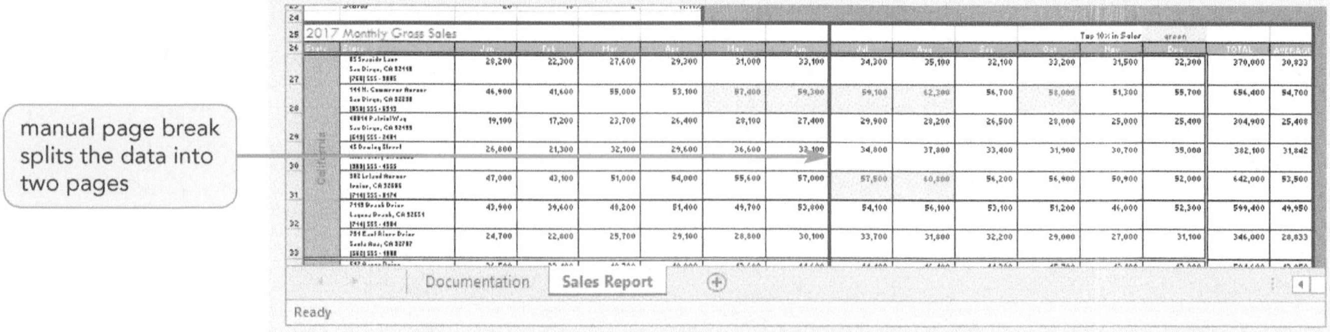

manual page break splits the data into two pages

Adding Print Titles

It is a good practice to include descriptive information such as the company name, logo, and worksheet title on each page of a printout in case a page becomes separated from the other pages. You can repeat information, such as the company name, by specifying which rows or columns in the worksheet act as print titles. If a worksheet contains a large table, you can print the table's column headings and row headings on every page of the printout by designating those columns and rows as print titles.

In the Sales Report worksheet, the company name appears on the first page of the printout but does not appear on subsequent pages. Also, the descriptive row titles for the monthly sales table in column A do not appear on the third page of the printout. You will add print titles to fix these issues.

To set the print titles:

TIP

You can also open the Page Setup dialog box by clicking the Dialog Box Launcher in the Page Setup group on the Page Layout tab.

1. On the Page Layout tab, in the Page Setup group, click the **Print Titles** button. The Page Setup dialog box opens with the Sheet tab displayed.

2. In the Print titles section, click the **Rows to repeat at top** box, move the pointer over the worksheet, and then select the range **A1:A2**. A flashing border appears around the first two rows of the worksheet to indicate that the contents of the first two rows will be repeated on each page of the printout. The row reference $1:$2 appears in the Rows to repeat at top box.

3. Click the **Columns to repeat at left** box, and then select columns A and B from the worksheet. The column reference $A:$B appears in the Columns to repeat at left box. See Figure 2-42.

Figure 2-42   Sheet tab in the Page Setup dialog box

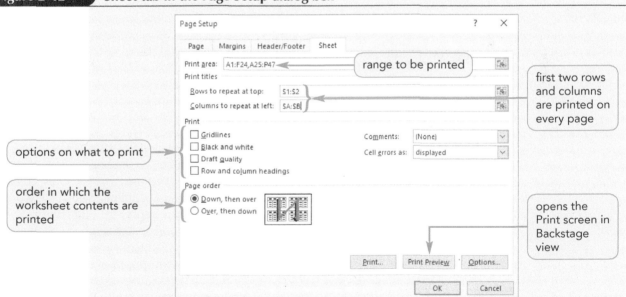

You will next rescale the worksheet so that it doesn't appear too small in the printout.

4. In the Page Setup dialog box, click the **Page** tab.

5. In the Scaling section, change the Adjust to amount to **60%** of normal size.

6. Click the **Print Preview** button to preview the three pages of printed material on the Print screen in Backstage view.

7. Verify that each of the three pages has the Morning Bean title at the top of the page and that the state and store names appear in the leftmost columns of pages 2 and 3. See Figure 2-43.

Figure 2-43 | **Print titles on page 3 of the printout**

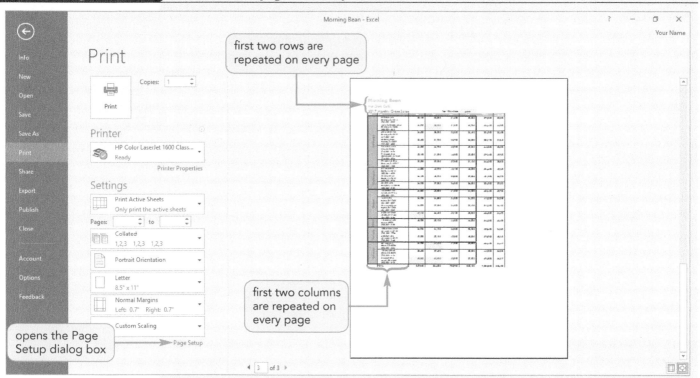

Trouble? If your printout doesn't fit on three pages, reduce the scaling factor from 60 percent to a slightly lower percentage until it does fit on three pages.

Designing Headers and Footers

You can also use headers and footers to repeat information on each printed page. A **header** appears at the top of each printed page; a **footer** appears at the bottom of each printed page. Headers and footers contain helpful and descriptive text that is usually not found within the worksheet, such as the workbook's author, the current date, or the workbook's filename. If the printout spans multiple pages, you can display the page number and the total number of pages in the printout to help ensure you and others have all the pages.

Each header and footer has three sections—a left section, a center section, and a right section. Within each section, you type the text you want to appear, or you insert elements such as the worksheet name or the current date and time. These header and footer elements are dynamic; if you rename the worksheet, for example, the name is automatically updated in the header or footer. Also, you can create one set of headers and footers for even and odd pages, and you can create another set for the first page in the printout.

Carol wants the printout to display the workbook's filename in the header's left section, and the current date in the header's right section. She wants the center footer to display the page number and the total number of pages in the printout, and the right footer to display your name as the workbook's author.

To set up the page header:

1. Near the bottom of the Print screen, click the **Page Setup** link. The Page Setup dialog box opens.

2. Click the **Header/Footer** tab to display the header and footer options.

3. Click the **Different first page** check box to select it. This lets you create one set of headers and footers for the first page, and one set for the rest of the pages.

4. Click the **Custom Header** button to open the Header dialog box. The dialog box contains two tabs—Header and First Page Header—because you selected the Different first page option.

TIP

You can create or edit headers and footers in Page Layout view by clicking in the header/footer section and using the tools on the Design tab.

5. On the Header tab, in the Left section box, type **Filename:**, press the **spacebar**, and then click the **Insert File Name** button. The code &[File], which displays the filename of the current workbook, is added to the left section of the header.

6. Press the **Tab** key twice to move to the right section of the header, and then click the **Insert Date** button. The code &[Date] is added to the right section of the header. See Figure 2-44.

Figure 2-44   Header dialog box

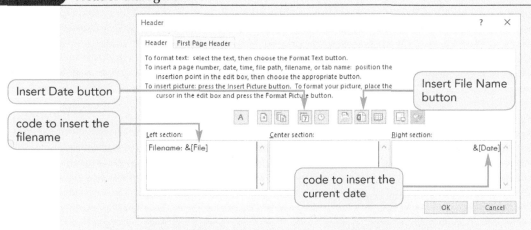

7. Click the **OK** button to return to the Header/Footer tab in the Page Setup dialog box.

You did not define a header for the first page of the printout, so no header information will be added to that page. Next, you will format the footer for all pages of the printout.

To create the page footer:

1. On the Header/Footer tab of the Page Setup dialog box, click the **Custom Footer** button. The Footer dialog box opens.

2. On the Footer tab, click the **Center section** box, type **Page**, press the **spacebar**, and then click the **Insert Page Number** button. The code &[Page], which inserts the current page number, appears after the label "Page."

3. Press the **spacebar**, type **of**, press the **spacebar**, and then click the **Insert Number of Pages** button. The code &[Pages], which inserts the total number of pages in the printout, is added to the Center section box. See Figure 2-45.

Figure 2-45   **Footer dialog box**

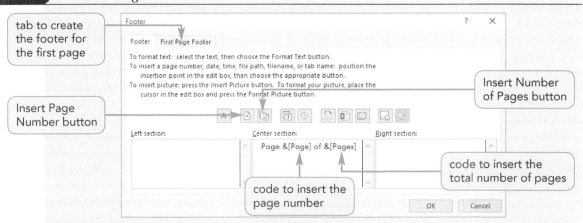

▸ **4.** Click the **First Page Footer** tab so you can create the footer for the first page of the printout.

▸ **5.** Click the **Right section** box, type **Prepared by:**, press the **spacebar**, and then type your name.

▸ **6.** Click the **OK** button to return to the Page Setup dialog box.

You will leave the Page Setup dialog box so you can finish formatting the printout by setting the page margins.

Setting the Page Margins

A **margin** is the space between the page content and the edges of the page. By default, Excel sets the page margins to 0.7 inch on the left and right sides, and 0.75 inch on the top and bottom; and it allows for 0.3-inch margins around the header and footer. You can reduce or increase these margins as needed by selecting predefined margin sizes or setting your own.

Carol's reports need a wider margin along the left side of the page to accommodate the binding. She asks you to increase the left margin for the printout from 0.7 inch to 1 inch.

To set the left margin:

TIP

To select preset margins, click the Margins button in the Page Setup group on the Page Layout tab.

▸ **1.** Click the **Margins** tab in the Page Setup dialog box to display options for changing the page margins.

▸ **2.** Double-click the **Left** box to select the setting, and then type **1** to increase the size of the left margin to 1 inch. See Figure 2-46.

| Figure 2-46 | Margins tab in the Page Setup dialog box |

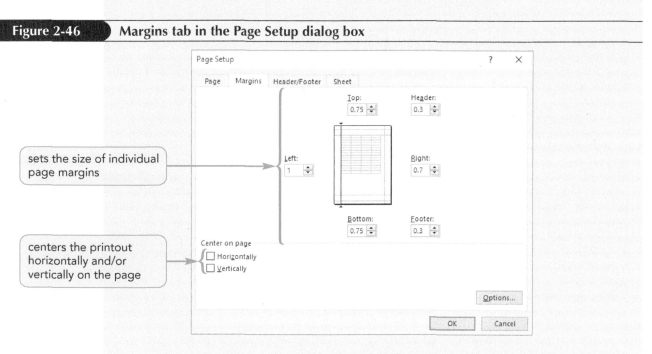

sets the size of individual page margins

centers the printout horizontally and/or vertically on the page

▶ **3.** Click the **OK** button to close the dialog box. You can see the margin change in the preview on the Print screen in Backstage view.

Now that you have formatted the printout, you can print the final version of the worksheet.

To save and print the workbook:

▶ **1.** With the workbook still in the Print screen in Backstage view, click the first box in the Settings section, and then click **Print Entire Workbook**.

Both the Sales Report worksheet and the Documentation sheet appear in the preview. As you can see, the printout will include a header with the filename and date on every page except the first page and a footer with your name on the first page and the page number along with the total number of pages on subsequent pages.

▶ **2.** If you are instructed to print, print the entire workbook.

▶ **3.** Click the **Back** button ⬅ from the Backstage View navigation bar to return to the workbook window.

▶ **4.** Click the **Normal** button ▦ on the status bar to return the view of the workbook to normal.

▶ **5.** Save the workbook, and then close it.

Carol is pleased with the worksheet's appearance and the layout of the printout. The formatting has made the contents easier to read and understand.

REVIEW

Session 2.2 Quick Check

1. Describe two methods of applying the same format to different ranges.

2. Red is a standard color. What happens to red text when you change the workbook's theme?

3. What is a conditional format?

4. How would you highlight the top 10 percent values of the range A1:C20?

5. How do you insert a manual page break in a worksheet?

6. What is a print area?

7. What are print titles?

8. Describe how to add the workbook filename to the center section of the footer on every page of the printout.

Review Assignments

Data Files needed for the Review Assignments: Menu.xlsx, Background2.jpg

Carol created a workbook that tracks the sales of individual items from the Morning Bean menu to share at an upcoming conference. She has already entered most of the financial formulas but wants you to calculate some additional values. She also asks you to format the workbook so that it will look professional and be easy to read and understand. Complete the following:

1. Open the **Menu** workbook located in the Excel2 > Review folder included with your Data Files, and then save the workbook as **Menu Sales** in the location specified by your instructor.
2. In the Documentation sheet, enter your name in cell B4 and the date in cell B5.
3. Change the theme of the workbook to Retrospect.
4. Make the following formatting changes to the Documentation sheet:
   a. Set the background image to the **Background2** JPEG file located in the Excel2 > Review folder.
   b. Format the text in cell A1 in a 26-point bold Calibri Light.
   c. In cell A1, change the font color of the word "Morning" to the Orange, Accent 1 theme color and change the font color of the word "Bean" to the Brown, Accent 3 theme color.
   d. Format the text in cell A2 in 18-point, italic, and change the font color to the Brown, Accent 3 theme color.
   e. Format the range A4:A6 with the Accent 3 cell style.
   f. Change the font color of the range B4:B6 to the Brown, Accent 3 theme color, and change the fill color to the White, Background 1 theme color.
   g. In cell B5, format the date in the Long Date format and left-align the cell contents.
5. Use the Format Painter to copy the formatting in the range A1:A2 in the Documentation sheet and paste it to the same range in the Menu Items worksheet. Change the font colors in cell A1 of the Menu Items worksheet to match the colors used in cell A1 of the Documentation sheet.
6. Apply the Title cell style to cells B4, B12, and A20.
7. Make the following changes to the Units Sold table in the range B5:F10:
   a. Apply the Accent3 cell style to the headings in the range B5:F5. Center the headings in the range C5:F5.
   b. In cell C6, use the SUM function to calculate the total number of specialty drinks sold by the company (found in the range C22:N31 in the Units Sold per Month table). In cell C7, use the SUM function to calculate the total number of smoothies sold (in the range C32:N36). In cell C8, use the SUM function calculate the total number of sandwiches sold (in the range C37:N41). In cell C9, calculate the total number of soups sold (in the range C42:N45).
   c. In cell C10, use the SUM function to calculate the total units sold from all menu types in 2017 (based on the range C6:C9). Copy the formula to cell D10 to calculate the total units sold in 2016.
   d. In each cell of the range E6:E10, calculate the change in units sold between the 2017 and 2016 values. In each cell of the range F6:F10, calculate the percent change from 2016 to 2017. (*Hint:* The percent change is the net change divided by the 2016 value.)
   e. Format the range C6:E10 with the Comma style and no decimal places.
   f. Format the range F6:F10 with the Percent style and two decimal places.
   g. Add a top border to the range B10:F10.
8. Make the following changes to the Gross Sales table in the range B13:F18:
   a. In cells C18 and D18, use the SUM function to calculate the totals of the 2017 and 2016 sales.
   b. In the range E14:F18, enter formulas to calculate the net change and the percent change in sales.
   c. Use the Format Painter to copy the formatting from the range B5:F10 to the range B13:F18.
   d. Format the ranges C14:E14 and C18:E18 with Accounting format and no decimal places.

9. Make the following changes to the Units Sold per Month table in the range A21:O46:

a. In the range O22:O45, use the SUM function to calculate the total units sold for each menu item. In the range C46:O46, use the SUM function to calculate the total items sold per month and overall.

b. Format the headings in the range A21:O21 with the Accent3 cell style. Center the headings in the range C21:O21.

c. Format the units sold values in the range C22:O46 with the Comma style and no decimal places.

d. Change the fill color of the subtotals in the range O22:O45,C46:N46 to the White, Background 1, Darker 15% theme color (the first color in the third row).

e. Merge each of the menu categories in the ranges A22:A31, A32:A36, A37:A41, and A42:A45 into single cells. Rotate the text of the cells up, and middle-align the cell contents.

f. Format cell A22 with the Accent1 cell style. Format cell A32 with the Accent2 cell style. Format cell A37 with the Accent3 cell style. Format cell A42 with the Accent4 cell style. Change the font size of these four merged cells to 14 points.

g. Add thick outside borders around each category of menu item in the ranges A22:O31, A32:O36, A37:O41, and A42:O45.

10. Use conditional formatting to highlight negative values in the range E6:F10,E14:F18 with a light red fill with dark red text to highlight which menu categories showed a decrease in units sold or gross sales from 2016 to 2017.

11. Use conditional formatting to format cells that rank in the top 10 percent of the range C22:N45 with a green fill with dark green text to highlight the menu items and months that are in the top 10 percent of units sold.

12. Create a legend for the conditional formatting you added to the worksheet. In cell O20, enter the text **Top Sellers**. Add thick outside borders around the cell, and then use conditional formatting to display this text with a green fill with dark green text.

13. Set the following print formats for the Menu Items worksheet:

a. Set the print area to the nonadjacent range A1:F19,A20:O46.

b. Switch to Page Break Preview, and then remove any automatic page breaks in the Units Sold per Month table. Insert a manual page break to separate the June and July sales figures. The printout of the Menu Sales worksheet should fit on three pages.

c. Scale the printout to 70 percent.

d. Create print titles that repeat the first three rows at the top of the sheet and the first two columns at the left of the sheet.

e. Increase the left margin of the printout from 0.7 inch to 1 inch.

f. Create headers and footers for the printout with a different first page.

g. For the first page header, print **Prepared by** followed by your name in the right section. For every other page, print **Filename:** followed by the filename in the left section and the date in the right section. (*Hint*: Use the buttons in the Header dialog box to insert the filename and date.)

h. For every footer, including the first page, print **Page** followed by the page number and then **of** followed by the total number of pages in the printout in the center section.

i. Preview the printout to verify that the company name and description appear on every page of the Menu Items worksheet printout and that the menu category and menu item name appear on both pages with the Units Sold table. If you are instructed to print, print the entire workbook in portrait orientation.

14. Save the workbook, and then close it.

Case Problem 1

Data File needed for this Case Problem: Green.xlsx

Green Clean Homes   Sean Patel is developing a business plan for Green Clean Homes, a new professional home cleaning service in Toledo, Ohio. As part of his business plan, Sean needs to predict the company's annual income and expenses. You will help him finalize and format the Excel workbook containing the projected income statement. Complete the following:

1. Open the **Green** workbook located in the Excel2 > Case1 folder, and then save the workbook as **Green Clean** in the location specified by your instructor.
2. In the Documentation sheet, enter your name in cell B3 and the date in cell B4.
3. Display the date in cell B4 in the Long Date format and left-aligned.
4. Change the theme of the workbook to Facet.
5. Make the following formatting changes to the Documentation sheet:
   a. Merge and center cells A1 and B1.
   b. Apply the Accent2 cell style to the merged cell A1 and to the range A3:A5.
   c. In cell A1, set the font size to 22 points and bold the text. Italicize the word "Clean" in the company name.
   d. Add borders around each cell in the range A3:B5. Top-align the text in the range A3:B5.
   e. Change the font color of the text in the range B3:B5 to Dark Green, Accent 2.
6. In the Income Statement worksheet, merge and center the range A1:C1, and then apply the Accent2 cell style to the merged cell. Change the font size to 24 points and the text style to bold. Italicize the word "Clean" within the company name.
7. Make the following changes to the Income Statement worksheet:
   a. Format the range A3:C3 with the Heading 1 cell style.
   b. Format the range A4:C4,A9:C9 with the 40% - Accent1 cell style.
   c. Format cell B5 in the Accounting style with no decimal places.
   d. Format cell B6 and the range B10:B17 in the Comma style with no decimal places.
8. Add the following calculations to the workbook:
   a. In cell C7, calculate the gross profit, which is equal to the gross sales minus the cost of sales.
   b. In cell C18, calculate the company's total operating expenses, which is equal to the sum of the values in the range B10:B17. Format the value in the Accounting format with no decimal places.
   c. In cell C20, calculate the company's operating profit, which is equal to its gross profit minus its total operating expenses.
   d. In cell C21, calculate the company's incomes taxes by multiplying its total operating profit by the corporate tax rate (cell G25). Format the value in the Accounting format with no decimal places.
   e. In cell C22, calculate the company's net profit, which is equal to the total operating profit minus the income taxes.
9. Finalize the formatting of the Projected Income statement by adding the following:
   a. Add a bottom border to the ranges A6:C6, A17:C17, and A20:C20. Add a single top border and a double bottom border to the range A22:C22.
   b. Indent the expenses categories in the range A10:A17 twice.
10. Format the Financial Assumptions section as follows:
    a. Add borders around all of the cells in the range E4:G25.
    b. Format the range E3:G3 with the Heading 1 cell style.
    c. Merge the cells in the ranges E4:E7, E9:E13, E14:E15, E16:E18, and E20:E22.
    d. Top-align and left-align the range E4:E25.
    e. Change the fill color of the range E4:F25 to Green, Accent 1, Lighter 60%.

11. Use conditional formatting to highlight the net profit (cell C22) if its value is less than $50,000 with a light red fill with dark red text.

12. Change the value in cell G9 from 4 to **5**. Observe the impact that hiring another cleaner has on the projected net profit for the company in cell C22.

13. Format the printed version of the Income Statement worksheet as follows:

    a. Add a manual page break between columns D and E.

    b. For the first page, add a header that prints **Prepared by** followed by your name in the left section of the header and the current date in the right section of the header. Do not display header text on any other page.

    c. For every page, add a footer that prints the workbook filename in the left section, **Page** followed by the page number in the center section, and the worksheet name in the right section.

    d. Set the margins to 1 inch on all four sides of the printout, and center the contents of the worksheet horizontally within the printed page.

14. If you are instructed to print, print the entire contents of the workbook in portrait orientation.

15. Save and close the workbook.

Case Problem 2

APPLY

Data File needed for this Case Problem: Peak.xlsx

Peak Bytes   Peter Taylor is an engineer at Peak Bytes, an Internet service provider located in Great Falls, Montana. Part of Peter's job is to track the over-the-air connection speeds from the company's transmitters. Data from an automated program recording Internet access times has been entered into a workbook, but the data is difficult to interpret. He wants you to edit the workbook so that the data is easier to read and the fast and slow connection times are quickly visible. He also wants the workbook to provide summary statistics on the connection speeds. Complete the following:

1. Open the **Peak** workbook located in the Excel2 > Case2 folder, and then save the workbook as **Peak Bytes** in the location specified by your instructor.

2. In the Documentation sheet, enter your name in cell B3 and the date in cell B4.

3. Apply the Banded theme to the workbook.

4. Format the Documentation sheet as follows:

    a. Apply the Title cell style to cell A1. Change the font style to bold and the font size to 24 points.

    b. Add borders around the range A3:B5.

    c. Apply the Accent4 cell style to the range A3:A5.

    d. Top-align the contents in the range A3:B5.

5. In the Speed Test worksheet, move the data from the range A1:D97 to the range A12:D108.

6. Copy cell A1 from the Documentation sheet, and paste it into cell A1 of the Speed Test worksheet.

7. In cell A2, enter **Internet Speed Test Results**. Apply the Heading 1 cell style to the range A2:D2.

8. In cell A4, enter **Date** and format it using the Accent4 cell style. In cell B4, enter **4/8/2017** and format it using the Long Date format. Add a border around the cells in the range A4:B4.

9. Format the data in the Speed Test worksheet as follows:

    a. In the range A13:A108, format the numeric date and time values with the Time format. (*Hint*: The Time format is in the Number Format box in the Number group on the Home tab.)

    b. In the range C13:D108, show the numbers with three decimal places.

    c. In the range A12:D12, apply the Accent4 cell style and center the text.

    d. In the range A12:D108, add borders around all of the cells.

10. Create a table of summary statistics for the Internet Speed Test as follows:

    a. Copy the headings in the range B12:D12, and paste them into the range B6:D6.

    b. In cell A7, enter **Average**. In cell A8, enter **Minimum**. In cell A9, enter **Maximum**. Format the range A7:A9 with the Accent4 cell style.

c. In cell B7, use the AVERAGE function to calculate the average ping value of the values in the range B13:B108. In cell B8, use the MIN function to calculate the minimum ping value of the values in the range B13:B108. In cell B9, use the MAX function to calculate the maximum ping value of the values in the range B13:B108.

d. Copy the formulas from the range B7:B9 to the range C7:D9 to calculate summary statistics for the download and upload speeds from the Internet test.

e. Format the values in the range B7,C7:D9 to show two decimal places.

f. Add borders around all of the cells in the range A6:D9.

11. Use conditional formatting to highlight ping values greater than 70 in the range B13:B108 with a light red fill with dark red text to highlight times when the Internet usually appears to be slow.

12. Use conditional formatting to highlight upload values less than 3.5 in the range C13:C108 with a light red fill with dark red text.

13. Use conditional formatting to highlight download values less than 2 in the range D13:D108 with a light red fill with dark red text.

14. In cell D11, enter the text **Slow Connection**. Use conditional formatting to display this text string with a light red fill with dark red text. Center the text, and add a border around cell D11.

15. Set the print titles to repeat the first 12 rows at the top of every page of the printout.

16. For the first page of the printout, add a header that prints **Prepared by** followed by your name in the left section of the header and the current date in the right section of the header. Do not display header text on any other page.

17. For every page, add a footer that prints the workbook filename in the left section, **Page** followed by the page number followed by **of** followed by the number of pages in the center section, and then the worksheet name in the right section.

18. If you are instructed to print, print the entire contents of the workbook in portrait orientation.

19. Save and close the workbook.

Case Problem 3

Data File needed for this Case Problem: Wait.xlsx

YuriTech   Kayla Schwartz is the customer service manager at YuriTech, an electronics and computer firm located in Scottsdale, Arizona. Kayla is analyzing the calling records for technical support calls to YuriTech to determine which times are understaffed, resulting in unacceptable wait times. She has compiled several months of data and calculated the average wait times in one-hour intervals for each day of the week. You will format Kayla's workbook to make it easier to determine when YuriTech should hire more staff to assist with customer support requests. Complete the following:

1. Open the **Wait** workbook located in the Excel2 > Case3 folder, and then save the workbook as **Wait Times** in the location specified by your instructor.

2. In the Documentation sheet, enter your name in cell B3 and the date in cell B4.

3. Apply the Ion theme to the workbook.

4. Format the Documentation sheet as follows:

a. Format the title in cell A1 using a 36-point Impact font with the Purple, Accent 6 font color.

b. Format the range A3:A5 with the Accent6 cell style.

c. Add a border around the cells in the range A3:B5. Wrap the text within each cell, and top-align the cell text.

5. Copy the format you used in cell A1 of the Documentation sheet, and paste it to cell A1 of the Wait Times worksheet.

6. Format the text in cell A2 with 14-point bold font and the Purple, Accent6 font color.

7. In the range A14:H39, format the average customer wait times for each hour and day of the week data as follows:

   a. Merge and center the range A14:H14, and apply the Title cell style to the merged contents.

   b. Change the number format of the data in the range B16:H39 to show one decimal place.

   c. Format the column and row labels in the range A15:H15, A16:A39 with the Accent6 cell style. Center the column headings in the range B15:H15.

8. In cell B5, enter the value **22** as an excellent wait time. In cell B6, enter **34** as a good wait time. In cell B7, enter **45** as an acceptable wait time. In cell B8, enter **60** as a poor wait time. In cell B9, enter **78** as a very poor wait time. In cell B10, enter **90** as an unacceptable wait time.

9. In the range A4:C10, apply the following formats to the wait time goals:

   a. Merge and center the range A4:C4, and apply the Accent6 cell style to the merged cells.

   b. Add borders around the cells in the range A4:C10.

10. In cell E4, enter the label **Average Wait Time (All Days)**. In cell E7, enter the label **Average Wait Time (Weekdays)**. In cell E10, enter the label **Average Wait Time (Weekends)**.

11. Merge and center the range E4:F6, wrap the text in the merged cell, center the cell content both horizontally and vertically, and then apply the Accent6 cell style to the merged cell.

12. Copy the format from the merged cell E4:F6 to cells E7 and E10.

13. In cell G4, enter a formula to calculate the average of the wait times in the range B16:H39. In cell G7, enter a formula to calculate the average weekday wait times in the range C16:G39. In cell G10, calculate the average weekend rate times in the range B16:B39,H16:H39.

14. Merge and center the ranges G4:G6, G7:G9, and G10:G12, and then center the calculated averages vertically within each merged cell.

15. Add borders around the cells in the range E4:G12.

16. Change the fill color of the range A5:C5 to a medium green, the fill color of the range A6:C6 to a light green, the fill color of the range A7:C7 to a light gold, the fill color of the range A8:C8 to a light red, and the fill color of the range A9:C9 to a medium red. Format the range A10:C10 with white text on a black background.

⊕ **Explore** 17. Use conditional formatting to highlight cells with custom formats as follows:

   a. Select the range G4:G12,B16:H39. Use conditional formatting to highlight cells with values less than 22 with a custom format that matches the fill color used in the range A5:C5.

   b. Use conditional formatting to highlight cells with values greater than 90 in the range G4:G12,B16:H39 with a custom format of a white font on a black fill.

   c. Use conditional formatting to highlight cells with values between 22 and 34 in the range G4:G12,B16:H39 with a custom format that matches the fill color used in the range A6:C6.

   d. Use conditional formatting to highlight cells with values between 34 and 60 in the range G4:G12,B16:H39 with a light gold fill color that matches the cells in the range A7:C7.

   e. Use conditional formatting to highlight cells with values between 60 and 78 in the range G4:G12,B16:H39 with light red, matching the fill color of the cells in the range A8:C8.

   f. Use conditional formatting to highlight cells with values between 78 and 90 in the range G4:G12,B16:H39 with medium red, matching the fill color of the cells in the range A9:C9.

18. In cell A41, enter the label **Notes** and then format it with the Title cell style.

19. Merge the range A42:H50. Top- and left-align the contents of the cell. Turn on text wrapping within the merged cell. Add a thick outside border to the merged cell.

20. Within the merged cell in the range A42:H50, summarize your conclusions about the wait times. Answer whether the wait times are within acceptable limits on average for the entire week, on weekdays, and on weekends. Also indicate whether there are times during the week that customers are experience very poor to unacceptable delays.

21. Format the printed version of the Wait Times worksheet as follows:

   a. Scale the sheet so that it fits on a single page in portrait orientation.

   b. Center the sheet on the page horizontally and vertically.

c. Add the header **Prepared by** followed by your name in the right section.

d. Add a footer that prints the filename in the left section, the worksheet name in the center section, and the date in the right section.

22. If you are instructed to print, print the entire contents of the workbook.

23. Save and close the workbook.

Case Problem 4

Data File needed for this Case Problem: Pandaisia.xlsx

Pandaisia Chocolates   Anne Ambrose is the owner and head chocolatier of Pandaisia Chocolates, a chocolate shop located in Essex, Vermont. Anne has asked you to create an Excel workbook in which she can enter customer orders. She wants the workbook to be easy to use and read. The final design of the order form is up to you. One possible solution is shown in Figure 2-47.

Figure 2-47   **Pandaisia Chocolates order form**

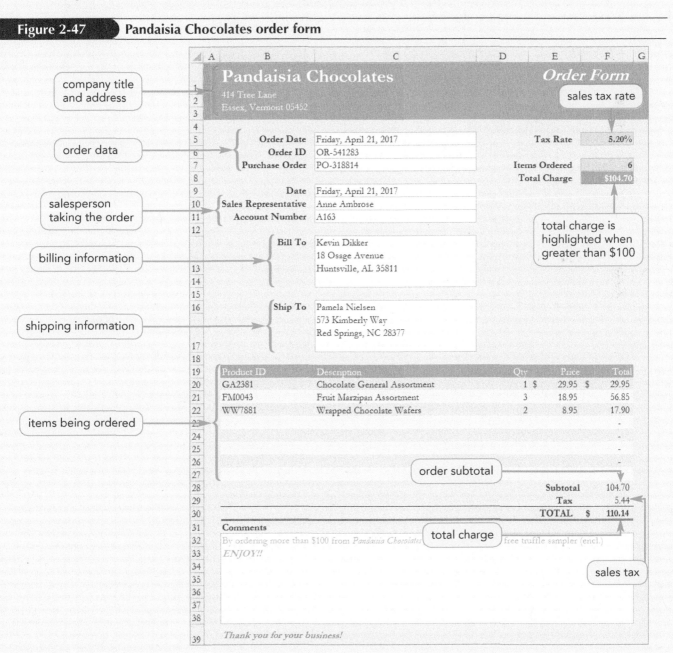

Complete the following:

1. Open the **Pandaisia** workbook located in the Excel2 > Case3 folder, and then save the workbook as **Pandaisia Order** in the location specified by your instructor.
2. In the Documentation sheet, enter your name in cell B3 and the date in cell B4.
3. Insert a worksheet named **Order Form** after the Documentation worksheet.
4. Enter the following information in the order form:
    - The title and address of Pandaisia Chocolates
    - The order date, order ID, and purchase order ID
    - The date, sales representative, and account number for the order
    - The billing address of the order
    - The shipping address of the order
    - A table listing every item ordered including the item's product ID, description, quantity ordered, price, and total charge for the item(s)
    - A comment box where Anne can insert additional information about the order
5. Include formulas in the order form to do the following:
    a. For each item ordered, calculate the cost of the item(s), which is equal to the quantity multiplied by the price.
    b. Calculate the subtotal of the costs for every item ordered by the customer.
    c. Calculate the sales tax for the order, which is equal to 5.2 percent times the subtotal value.
    d. Calculate the total cost of the order, which is equal to the subtotal plus the sale tax.
6. Format the order form by doing the following:
    a. Apply a different built-in Excel theme.
    b. Change the font colors and fill colors.
    c. Format a text string within a cell.
    d. Align content within cells.
    e. Format dates with the Long Date format.
    f. Apply the Percent, Accounting, and Currency formats as appropriate.
    g. Add borders around cells and ranges.
    h. Merge a range into a single cell.
7. Pandaisia Chocolates includes a free complimentary truffle sample for every order over $100. Use conditional formatting to highlight the total charge in bold colored font when it is greater than $100.
8. Test your order form by entering the data shown in Figure 2-47. Confirm that the charge on your order matches that shown in the figure.
9. Set up the print version of the order form so that it prints in portrait orientation on a single sheet. Add a header and/or footer that includes your name, the date, and the name of the workbook.
10. If you are instructed to print, print the entire contents of the workbook.
11. Save and close the workbook.

MODULE **3**

EXCEL

OBJECTIVES

Session 3.1
- Document formulas and data values
- Explore function syntax
- Insert functions from the Formula Library
- Perform a what-if analysis

Session 3.2
- AutoFill series and formulas
- Use relative and absolute cell references
- Use the Quick Analysis tool
- Work with dates and Date functions
- Find values with Lookup functions
- Work with Logical functions

Performing Calculations with Formulas and Functions

Calculating Farm Yield and Revenue

Case | *Wingait Farm*

Jane Wingait is the owner and operator of Wingait Farm, a small farm located outside of Cascade, Iowa. Jane's cash crop is corn, and she has planted almost 140 acres of the sweet corn variety for the past 11 years. Near harvest time every year Jane samples and analyzes a portion of her crop to estimate her farm's total yield for the year. She wants you to help her design an Excel workbook that will calculate her corn yield. As Jane prepares for next year's crop, she also wants to use Excel to track her corn's growth from planting to harvesting. As you create the workbook, you will explore how Jane can use Excel formulas to help her in running her farm.

STARTING DATA FILES

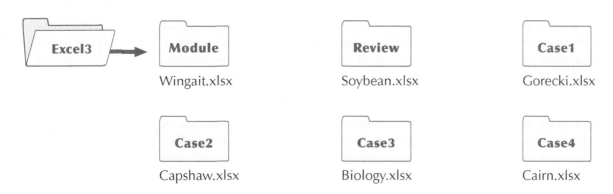

Excel3 →	Module	Review	Case1
	Wingait.xlsx	Soybean.xlsx	Gorecki.xlsx
	Case2	Case3	Case4
	Capshaw.xlsx	Biology.xlsx	Cairn.xlsx

Session 3.1 Visual Overview:

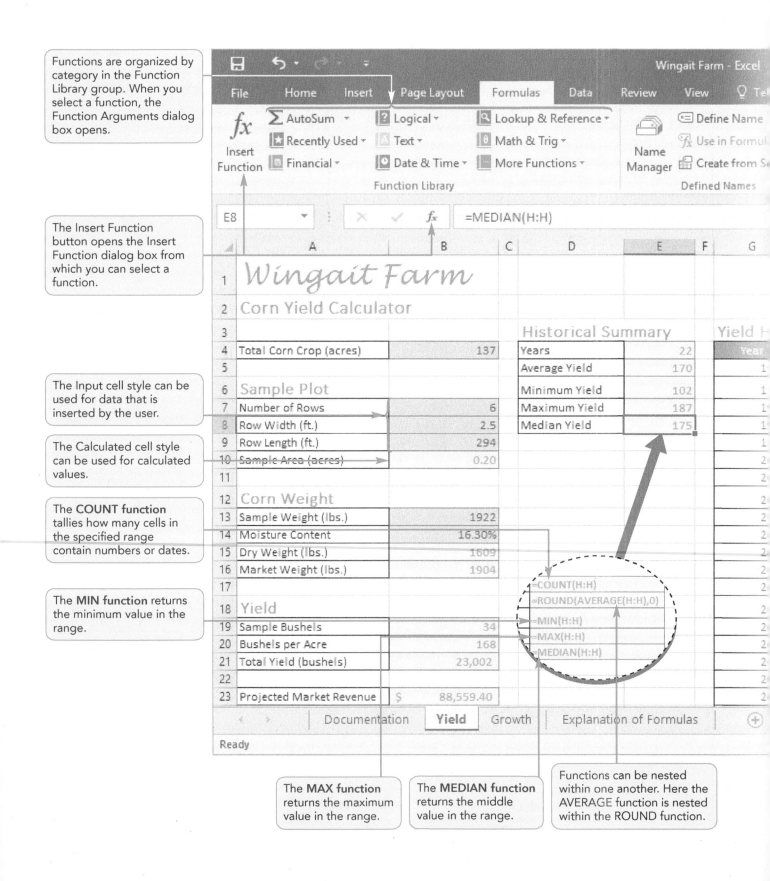

Functions are organized by category in the Function Library group. When you select a function, the Function Arguments dialog box opens.

The Insert Function button opens the Insert Function dialog box from which you can select a function.

The Input cell style can be used for data that is inserted by the user.

The Calculated cell style can be used for calculated values.

The **COUNT function** tallies how many cells in the specified range contain numbers or dates.

The **MIN function** returns the minimum value in the range.

The **MAX function** returns the maximum value in the range.

The **MEDIAN function** returns the middle value in the range.

Functions can be nested within one another. Here the AVERAGE function is nested within the ROUND function.

Formulas and Functions

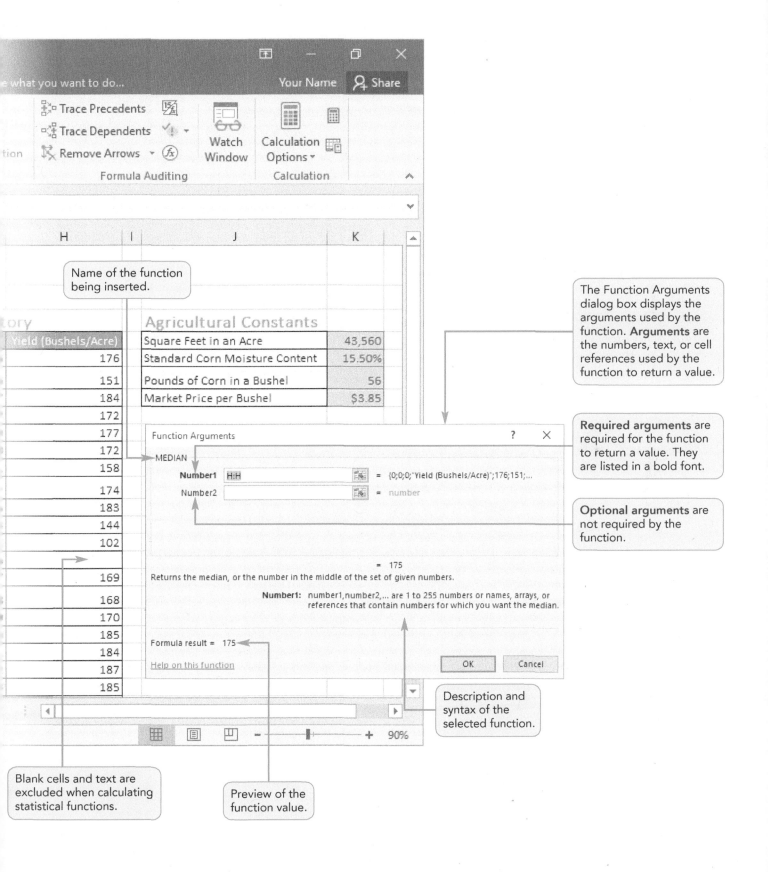

Name of the function being inserted.

The Function Arguments dialog box displays the arguments used by the function. **Arguments** are the numbers, text, or cell references used by the function to return a value.

Required arguments are required for the function to return a value. They are listed in a bold font.

Optional arguments are not required by the function.

Description and syntax of the selected function.

Blank cells and text are excluded when calculating statistical functions.

Preview of the function value.

Agricultural Constants

Square Feet in an Acre	43,560
Standard Corn Moisture Content	15.50%
Pounds of Corn in a Bushel	56
Market Price per Bushel	$3.85

Function Arguments ? ✕

MEDIAN

Number1 H:H = {0;0;0;"Yield (Bushels/Acre)";176;151;...
Number2 = number

= 175

Returns the median, or the number in the middle of the set of given numbers.

Number1: number1,number2,... are 1 to 255 numbers or names, arrays, or references that contain numbers for which you want the median.

Formula result = 175

Help on this function   OK   Cancel

Yield (Bushels/Acre)

176
151
184
172
177
172
158
174
183
144
102
169
168
170
185
184
187
185

90%

Making Workbooks User-Friendly

Excel is a powerful application for interpreting a wide variety of data used in publications from financial reports to scientific articles. To be an effective tool for data analysis, a workbook needs to be easy to use and interpret. This includes defining any technical terms in the workbook and explaining the formulas used in the analysis. In this module, you'll create a workbook to analyze the corn harvest for a farm in Iowa, employing techniques to make the workbook easily accessible to other users.

To open and review the Wingait Farms workbook:

▶ **1.** Open the **Wingait** workbook located in the **Excel3 > Module** folder included with your Data Files, and then save the workbook as **Wingait Farm** in the location specified by your instructor.

▶ **2.** In the Documentation sheet, enter your name in cell B3 and the date in cell B4.

▶ **3.** Go to the **Yield** worksheet.

Jane uses the Yield worksheet to project her farm's entire corn yield based on a small sample of harvested corn. Information about the sample and the calculations that estimate the total yield will be entered in columns A and B. Columns D and E contain important agricultural constants that Jane will use in the workbook's formulas and functions.

Jane uses a sample plot to estimate the farm's total yield. This plot, a small portion of Jane's 137-acre farm, is laid out in six rows of corn with each row 294 feet long and 2.5 feet wide. You will enter information about the size of the sample plot.

To enter data on the sample plot:

▶ **1.** In cell **B4**, enter **137** as the total acreage of the farm that Jane devotes to sweet corn.

▶ **2.** In cell **B7**, enter **6** as the number of corn rows in the sample plot.

▶ **3.** In cell **B8**, enter **2.5** as the width of each row in feet.

▶ **4.** In cell **B9**, enter **294** as the length in feet of each row. See Figure 3-1.

Figure 3-1   Sample plot data entered

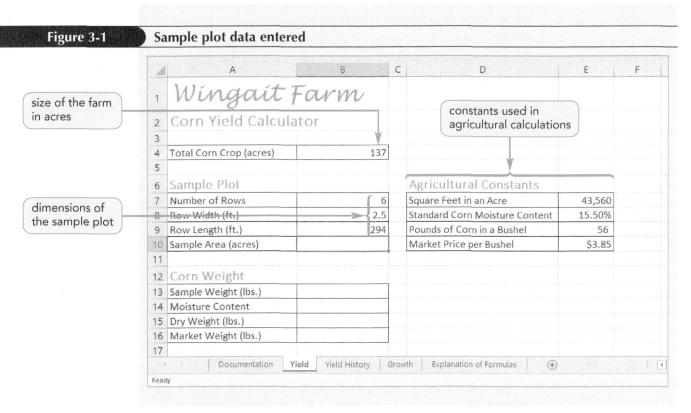

size of the farm in acres

dimensions of the sample plot

constants used in agricultural calculations

Wingait Farm

Corn Yield Calculator

	A	B	C	D	E	F
4	Total Corn Crop (acres)	137				
6	Sample Plot			Agricultural Constants		
7	Number of Rows	6		Square Feet in an Acre	43,560	
8	Row Width (ft.)	2.5		Standard Corn Moisture Content	15.50%	
9	Row Length (ft.)	294		Pounds of Corn in a Bushel	56	
10	Sample Area (acres)			Market Price per Bushel	$3.85	
12	Corn Weight					
13	Sample Weight (lbs.)					
14	Moisture Content					
15	Dry Weight (lbs.)					
16	Market Weight (lbs.)					

Documentation   Yield   Yield History   Growth   Explanation of Formulas   ⊕

Ready

The width and length of the sample rows are measured in feet, but Jane needs the total area expressed in acres. To calculate the area of the sample being tested, you need to refer to the agricultural equations that Jane documented for you.

Documenting Formulas

Documenting the contents of a workbook helps to avoid errors and confusion. It also makes it easier for others to interpret the analysis in the workbook. For workbooks that include many calculations, such as the Wingait Farm workbook, it is helpful to explain the formulas and terms used in the calculations. Such documentation also can serve as a check that the equations are accurate.

Jane has included explanations of equations you'll use in developing her workbook. Before proceeding, you'll review this documentation.

To review the documentation in Wingait Farm workbook:

▶ **1.** Go to the **Explanation of Formulas** worksheet.

▶ **2.** Read the worksheet contents, reviewing the descriptions of common agricultural constants and formulas. As you continue developing the Wingait Farm workbook, you'll learn about these terms and formulas in more detail.

▶ **3.** Go to the **Yield** worksheet.

Using Constants in Formulas

One common skill you need when creating a workbook is being able to translate an equation into an Excel formula. Some equations use **constants**, which are terms in a formula that don't change their value.

The first equation Jane wants you to enter calculates the size of the sample plot in acres, given the number of corn rows and the width and length of each row. The formula is

$$area = \frac{2 \times rows \times width \times length}{43560}$$

where *rows* is the number of corn rows, *width* is the width of the sample rows measured in feet, and *length* is the length of the sample rows measured in feet. In this equation, 43560 is a constant because that value never changes when calculating the sample area.

INSIGHT

Deciding Where to Place a Constant

Should a constant be entered directly into the formula or placed in a separate worksheet cell and referenced in the formula? The answer depends on the constant being used, the purpose of the workbook, and the intended audience. Placing constants in separate cells that you reference in the formulas can help users better understand the worksheet because no values are hidden within the formulas. Also, when a constant is entered in a cell, you can add explanatory text next to each constant to document how it is being used in the formula. On the other hand, you don't want a user to inadvertently change the value of a constant and throw off all the formula results. You will need to evaluate how important it is for other people to immediately see the constant and whether the constant requires any explanation for other people to understand the formula.

To convert the area equation to an Excel formula, you'll replace the *row*, *width*, and *length* values with references to the cells B7, B8, and B9, and you'll replace 43560 with a reference to cell E7. These cells provide the number of rows in the sample plot, the row width in feet, the row length in feet, and the number of square feet in one acre of land.

To calculate the area of the sample plot:

▶ **1.** In cell **B10**, enter the formula **=2*B7*B8*B9/E7** to calculate the area of the sample plot. The formula returns 0.202479339.

Trouble? If your result differs from 0.202479339, you probably entered the formula incorrectly. Edit the formula you entered in cell B10 as needed so that the numbers and cell references match those shown in the formula in Step 1.

Jane does not need to see the acreage of the sample plot with eight decimal places.

TIP

Decreasing the number decimals places rounds the displayed value; the stored value remains unchanged.

▶ **2.** Click cell **B10**, and then decrease the number of decimal places to **2**. The area of the sample plot is displayed as 0.20 acres. See Figure 3-2.

Figure 3-2   Calculated size of the sample plot in acres

formula to calculate
the size of the
sample plot

size of the sample
plot in acres

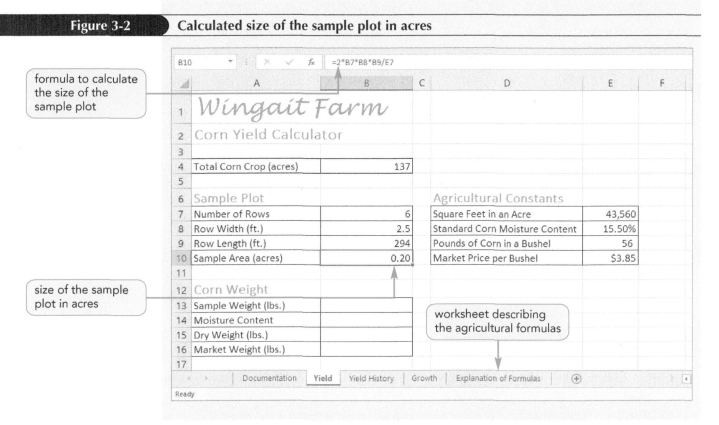

When Jane harvests the corn from the sample plot, she measures the total weight of the corn, which includes its moisture content. She then analyzes the corn to determine what percentage of its weight is due to moisture. The total weight of the corn is 1,922 pounds of which 16.3 percent is moisture. To sell the corn, Jane needs to calculate the dry weight of the corn without the moisture. She can do this with the formula

$$dry\ weight = total\ weight \times (1 - moisture)$$

where *total weight* is the weight of the corn and *moisture* is the percentage of the weight due to moisture. Market prices for corn are standardized at a moisture percentage of 15.5 percent, so to get the correct market weight of her corn, Jane uses the following formula:

$$market\ weight = \frac{dry\ weight}{1 - 0.155}$$

You will enter these two formulas in Jane's workbook to calculate the market weight of the corn she harvested from the sample plot.

To calculate the market weight of the corn:

1. In cell **B13**, enter **1922** as the total weight of the corn sample.

2. In cell **B14**, enter **16.3%** as the moisture content.

3. In cell **B15**, enter the formula **=B13*(1-B14)** to calculate the dry weight of the corn kernels. Based on the formula, the dry weight of the corn harvested from the sample plot is 1608.714 pounds.

Because the expression requires dividing by two terms, you must enclose those terms within parentheses.

▶ **4.** In cell **B16**, enter the formula **=B15/(1-E8)** to calculate the market weight of the corn kernels using the dry weight value in cell B15 and the standard moisture content value in cell E8. Based on the formula, the market weight of the corn is 1903.80355 pounds.

Jane does not need to see such precise weight values, so you will reduce the number of decimal places displayed in the worksheet.

▶ **5.** Select the range **B15:B16**, and then format the numbers with no decimals places to display the dry and market weights of 1609 and 1904 pounds, respectively. See Figure 3-3.

Figure 3-3   Calculated dry and market weights of the corn

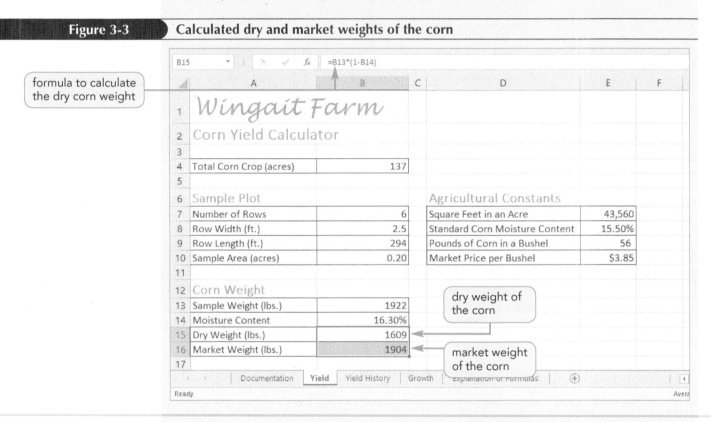

Corn is not sold by the pound but rather by the bushel where 1 bushel contains 56 pounds of corn. You will calculate the number of bushels of corn in the sample plot and then use this number to estimate the farm's total yield and revenue.

To project the farm's total yield and revenue:

▶ **1.** In cell **B19**, enter the formula **=B16/E9** to convert the market weight to bushels. In this case, the market weight is equal to 33.99649197 bushels.

▶ **2.** In cell **B19**, format the number with no decimals places. The number is rounded to 34 bushels.

▶ **3.** In cell **B20**, enter the formula **=B19/B10** to divide the number of bushels in the sample plot by the size of the plot in acres. Based on this calculation, this year's crop has yielded 167.901042 bushels per acre.

▶ **4.** In cell **B20**, format the number with no decimals places. This year's crop yielded about 168 bushels per acre.

Assuming that the rest of the farm is as productive as the sample plot, you can calculate the total bushels that the farm can produce by multiplying the bushels per acre by the total acreage of the farm.

▶ **5.** In cell **B21**, enter the formula **=B20*B4** to multiply the bushels per acre by the total acreage of the farm. Assuming that the rest of the farm is as productive as the sample plot, the total bushels that the farm can produce is 23002.44275 bushels.

▶ **6.** Format cell B21 using the Comma style with no decimal places. Cell B21 displays 23,002.

▶ **7.** In cell **B23**, enter the formula **=B21*E10** to calculate the revenue Jane can expect by selling all of the farm's corn at the market price of $3.85 per bushel.

▶ **8.** Format cell B23 with the Accounting style. The formula result is displayed as $88,559.40. See Figure 3-4.

| Figure 3-4 | **Projected yield and revenue from the corn harvest** |

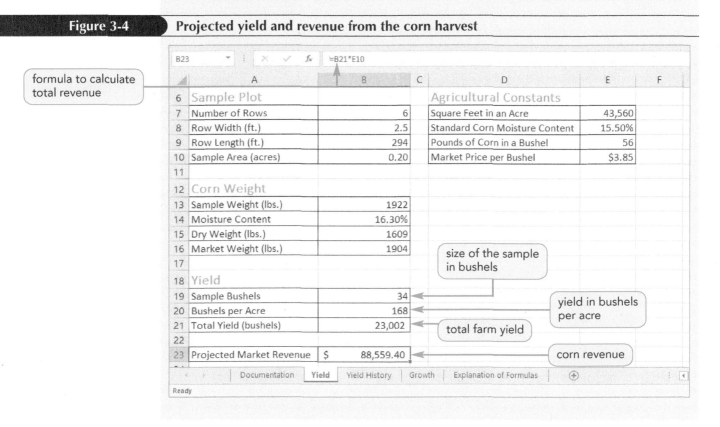

Based on your calculations, Jane projects an income of almost $90,000 from this year's corn crop.

PROSKILLS

Written Communication: Displaying Significant Digits

Excel stores numbers with up to 15 digits and displays as many digits as will fit into the cell. So even the result of a simple formula such as =10/3 will display 3.33333333333333 if the cell is wide enough.

A number with 15 digits is difficult to read, and calculations rarely need that level of accuracy. Many scientific disciplines, such as chemistry or physics, have rules for specifying exactly how many digits should be displayed with any calculation. These digits are called **significant digits** because they indicate the accuracy of the measured and calculated values. For example, an input value of 19.32 has four significant digits.

The rules are based on several factors and vary from one discipline to another. Generally, a calculated value should display no more digits than are found in any of the input values. For example, because the input value 19.32 has four significant digits, any calculated value based on that input should have no more than four significant digits. Showing more digits would be misleading because it implies a level of accuracy beyond that which was actually measured.

Because Excel displays calculated values with as many digits as can fit into a cell, you need to know the standards for your profession and change the display of your calculated values accordingly.

Identifying Notes, Input Values, and Calculated Values

When worksheets involve notes and many calculations, it is useful to distinguish input values that are used in formulas from calculated values that are returned by formulas. Formatting that clearly differentiates input values from calculated values helps others more easily understand the worksheet. Such formatting also helps prevent anyone from entering a value in a cell that contains a formula.

Jane wants to be sure that whenever she and her staff update the workbook, they can easily see where to enter data values. You will apply cell styles to distinguish between input and calculated values.

To apply cell styles to input values and calculated values:

1. Select the nonadjacent range **B4,B7:B9,B13:B14,E7:E10**. These cells contain the data that you entered for Jane.

2. On the Home tab, in the Styles group, click the **Cell Styles** button to open the Cell Styles gallery.

3. In the Data and Model section, click the **Input** cell style. The selected cells are formatted with a light blue font on an orange background, identifying those cells as containing input values.

4. Select the nonadjacent range **B10,B15:B16,B19:B21,B23**. These cells contain the formulas for calculating the weight, yield, and revenue values.

5. Format the selected cells with the **Calculation** cell style located in the Data and Model section of the Cell Styles gallery. The cells with the calculated values are formatted with a bold orange font on a light gray background.

6. Click cell **D12** to deselect the range. See Figure 3-5.

Figure 3-5 **Input and calculated values formatted with cell styles**

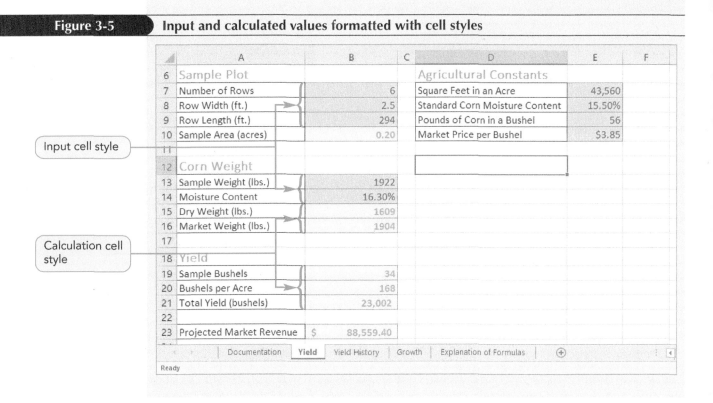

	A	B	C	D	E	F
6	Sample Plot			Agricultural Constants		
7	Number of Rows	6		Square Feet in an Acre	43,560	
8	Row Width (ft.)	2.5		Standard Corn Moisture Content	15.50%	
9	Row Length (ft.)	294		Pounds of Corn in a Bushel	56	
10	Sample Area (acres)	0.20		Market Price per Bushel	$3.85	
11						
12	Corn Weight					
13	Sample Weight (lbs.)	1922				
14	Moisture Content	16.30%				
15	Dry Weight (lbs.)	1609				
16	Market Weight (lbs.)	1904				
17						
18	Yield					
19	Sample Bushels	34				
20	Bushels per Acre	168				
21	Total Yield (bushels)	23,002				
22						
23	Projected Market Revenue	$ 88,559.40				

Input cell style

Calculation cell style

Documentation   Yield   Yield History   Growth   Explanation of Formulas   (+)

Ready

Using Excel Functions

Excel functions can be used in place of long and complicated formulas to simplify your worksheet. Jane wants to compare the estimated yield for this year's crop to historic trends. To make that comparison, you'll work with some Excel functions.

Understanding Function Syntax

Before you use functions, you should understand the function syntax. Recall that the syntax of an Excel function follows the general pattern

> FUNCTION(argument1,argument2,...)

where FUNCTION is the name of the function, and argument1, argument2, and so forth are arguments used by the function. An argument can be any type of value including text, numbers, cell references, or even other formulas or functions. Not all functions require arguments.

Some arguments are optional and can be included with the function or omitted altogether. Most optional arguments will have default values, so that if you omit an argument value, Excel will automatically apply the default. The convention is to show optional arguments within square brackets along with the argument's default value (if any), as

> FUNCTION(argument1[,argument2=value2,...])

where argument1 is a required argument, argument2 is optional, and value2 is the default value for argument2. As you work with specific functions, you will learn which arguments are required and which are optional as well as any default values associated with those optional arguments.

Figure 3-6 describes some of the more commonly used Math, Trig, and Statistical functions and provides the syntax of those functions, including any optional arguments.

TIP

Optional arguments are always placed last in the argument list.

Figure 3-6	Common Math, Trig, and Statistical functions

Function	Description
AVERAGE(number1[,number2,...])	Calculates the average of a collection of numbers, where number1, number2, and so forth are numbers or cell references
COUNT(value1[,value2,...])	Counts how many cells in a range contain numbers, where value1, value2, and so forth are either numbers or cell references
COUNTA(value1[,value2,...])	Counts how many cells are not empty in ranges value1, value2, and so forth including both numbers and text entries
INT(number)	Displays the integer portion of number
MAX(number1[,number2,...])	Calculates the maximum value of a collection of numbers, where number1, number2, and so forth are either numbers or cell references
MEDIAN(number1[,number2,...])	Calculates the median, or middle, value of a collection of numbers, where number1, number2, and so forth are either numbers or cell references
MIN(number1[,number2,...])	Calculates the minimum value of a collection of numbers, where number1, number2, and so forth are either numbers or cell references
RAND()	Returns a random number between 0 and 1
ROUND(number,num_digits)	Rounds number to the number of digits specified by num_digits
SUM(number1[,number2,...])	Adds a collection of numbers, where number1, number2, and so forth are either numbers or cell references

Entering the COUNT function

The following COUNT function is used by Excel to count how many cells in a range contain numbers. The COUNT function syntax is

```
COUNT(value1[,value2,…])
```

where value1 is either a cell reference, range reference, or a number, and value2 and so on are optional arguments that provide additional cell references, range references, or numbers. There are no default values for the optional arguments.

The COUNT function does not include blank cells or cells that contain text in its tally. For example, the following function counts how many cells in the range A1:A10, the range C1:C5, and cell E5 contain numbers or dates:

```
COUNT(A1:A10,C1:C5,E5)
```

The COUNT function is especially helpful when data in the ranges are regularly updated.

INSIGHT

Counting Text

Excel has another important function for counting cells—the **COUNTA function**. This function counts the number of cells that contain any entries, including numbers, dates, or text. The syntax of the COUNTA function is

```
COUNTA(value1[,value2,...])
```

where *value1* is the first item or cell reference containing the entries you want to count. The remaining optional value arguments are used primarily when you want to count entries in nonadjacent ranges. The COUNTA function should be used for text data or for data in which you need to include blanks as part of the total.

You'll use the COUNT function to tally how many years of data are included in the corn yield history.

To count the number of years in the corn yield history:

▶ **1.** Go to the **Yield History** worksheet, and then click cell **B5**. You'll enter the COUNT function in this cell.

▶ **2.** Type **=COUNT(** to begin entering the COUNT function. The first argument, which is the only required argument, is the cell or range reference for the cells to be counted.

   The yield values are stored in the range E5:E27. Instead of referencing this range, you will use column E as the argument for the COUNT function because Jane plans to add data to this column each year as she continues to track the farm's annual corn yield.

▶ **3.** Click the **E** column heading to select the entire column. The column reference E:E is inserted into the function as the first argument.

▶ **4.** Type **)** to end the function, and then press the **Enter** key. The formula =COUNT(E:E) is entered in cell B5 and returns 22, which is the number of years for which Jane has corn yield data.

Nesting the ROUND and AVERAGE Functions

One function can be placed inside, or **nested**, within another function. When a formula contains more than one function, Excel first evaluates the innermost function and then moves outward to evaluate the next function. The inner function acts as an argument value for the outer function. For example, the following expression nests the AVERAGE function within the ROUND function.

```
ROUND(AVERAGE(A1:A100),0)
```

TIP

The ROUND function changes the value stored in the cell, not the number of decimal places displayed in the cell.

Excel first uses the AVERAGE function to calculate the average of the values in the range A1:A100 and then uses the ROUND function to round that average to the nearest integer (where the number of digits to the right of the decimal point is 0.)

   One challenge of nested functions is being sure to include all of the parentheses. You can check this by counting the number of opening parentheses and making sure that number matches the number of closing parentheses. Excel also displays each level of nested parentheses in different colors to make it easier for you to match the opening and closing parentheses. If the number of parentheses doesn't match, Excel will not accept the formula and will provide a suggestion for how to rewrite the formula so the number of opening and closing parentheses does match.

Jane wants you to analyze the corn yield history at Wingait Farm. You'll use the COUNT function to tally the number of years in the historical sample and then use the AVERAGE function to calculate the average yield during those years. Because Jane doesn't need the exact corn yield values, you'll use the ROUND function to round that calculated average to the nearest integer.

To analyze the corn yield history:

▶ **1.** Click cell **B6**. You want to enter the nested function in this cell.

▶ **2.** Type **=ROUND(** to begin the formula with the ROUND function.

▶ **3.** Type **AVERAGE(E:E)** to enter the AVERAGE function as the first argument of the ROUND function.

▶ **4.** Type **,** (a comma) to separate the first and second arguments.

▶ **5.** Type **0)** to specify the number of decimal places to include in the results. In this case, Jane doesn't want to include any decimal places.

▶ **6.** Press the **Enter** key. The nested functions first calculate the average value of the numbers in column E and then round that number to the nearest integer. The formula returns 170, which is the average annual yield of Wingait Farm in bushels per acre rounded to the nearest integer. See Figure 3-7.

Figure 3-7	Nested functions calculate the average annual yield

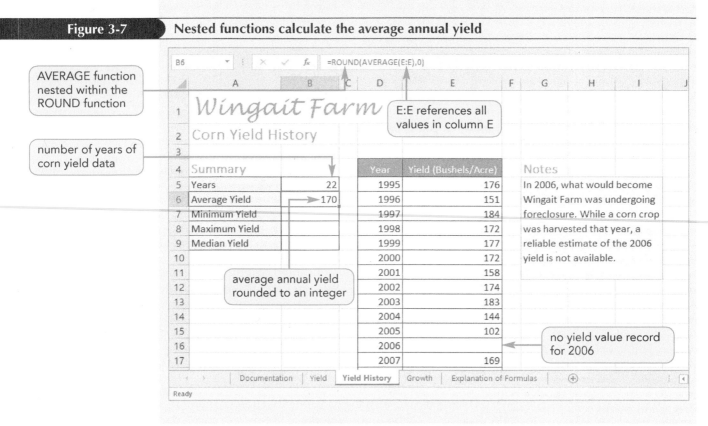

Based on values from 22 seasons of data, Jane expects her farm to yield 170 bushels of corn per acre each year.

Note that in 2006, no data on corn yield was available. Excel ignores nonnumeric data and blank cells when calculating statistical functions such as COUNT and AVERAGE. So, the count and average values in cells B5 and B6 represent only those years containing recorded corn yields. Keep in mind that a blank cell is not the same as a zero value in worksheet calculations. Figure 3-8 shows how function results differ when a zero replaces a blank in the selected range.

| Figure 3-8 | Calculations with blank cells and zero values |

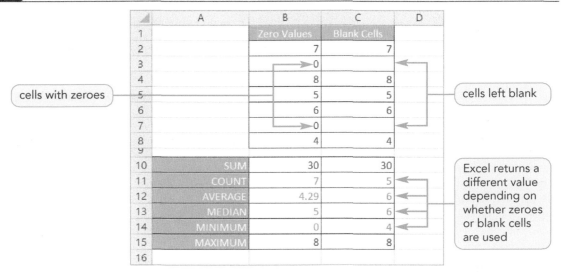

Whether you use a blank or zero depends on what you're trying to measure. For example, if Jane were to calculate average hours worked per day at the Wingait farm store, she could enter 0 for the holidays on which the store is closed, or she could enter a blank and thus calculate the average only for days in which the store is open.

Using the Function Library and the Insert Function Dialog Box

With so many Excel functions, it can difficult to locate the function you want to use for a particular application. Excel organizes its function into the 13 categories described in Figure 3-9. These function categories are available in the Function Library group on the Formulas tab and in the Insert Function dialog box.

| Figure 3-9 | Excel function categories |

Category	Description
Compatibility	Functions from Excel 2010 or earlier, still supported to provide backward compatibility
Cube	Retrieve data from multidimensional databases involving online analytical processing (OLAP)
Database	Retrieve and analyze data stored in databases
Date & Time	Analyze or create date and time values and time intervals
Engineering	Analyze engineering problems
Financial	Analyze information for business and finance
Information	Return information about the format, location, or contents of worksheet cells
Logical	Return logical (true-false) values
Lookup & Reference	Look up and return data matching a set of specified conditions from a range
Math & Trig	Perform math and trigonometry calculations
Statistical	Provide statistical analyses of data sets
Text	Return text values or evaluate text
Web	Provide information on web-based connections

Once you select a function either from the Function Library or the Insert Function dialog box, the Function Arguments dialog box opens, listing all of the arguments associated with that function. Required arguments are in bold type; optional arguments are in normal type.

Jane wants to know the range of annual corn yields, so she asks you to calculate the minimum and maximum yield values from the past 23 years. Because minimums and maximums are statistical measures, you will find them in the Statistics category in the Function Library.

To calculate the minimum and maximum yield:

1. Click cell **B7** if necessary to make it the active cell.

2. On the ribbon, click the **Formulas** tab. The Function Library group has buttons for some of the more commonly used categories of functions.

3. In the Function Library group, click the **More Functions** button, and then point to **Statistical** to open a list of all of the functions in the Statistical category.

4. Scroll down the list, and click **MIN**. The Function Arguments dialog box opens, showing the arguments for the MIN function and a brief description of the function syntax.

5. With the entry for the Number1 argument highlighted, click the **E** column heading to select the entire column and insert the cell reference **E:E** into the Number1 input box. See Figure 3-10.

Figure 3-10 MIN function in the Function Arguments dialog box

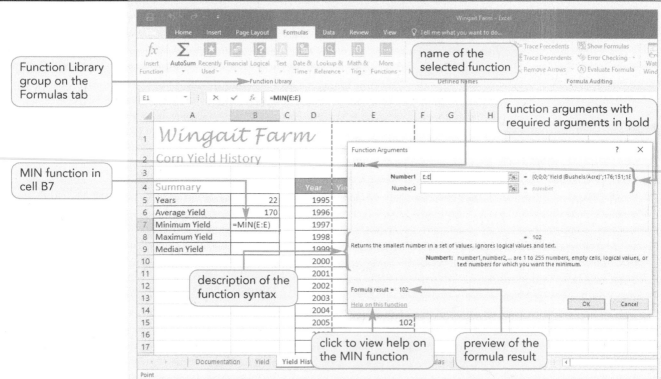

Trouble? You can click and drag the title bar in the Function Arguments dialog box to move it out of the way of the column E heading.

6. Click the **OK** button to insert the formula =MIN(E:E) into cell B7. The formula returns 102, which is the minimum value in column E.

7. Click cell **B8**, and then repeat Steps 3 through 6, selecting the **MAX** function from the Statistical category. The formula =MAX(E:E) entered in cell B8, and returns 187, which is the maximum value in column E. See Figure 3-11.

Figure 3-11   **Results of the MIN and MAX functions**

formula to calculate the maximum value in column E

	A	B	C	D	E	F	G	H	I	J
1	*Wingait Farm*									
2	Corn Yield History									
3										
4	Summary			Year	Yield (Bushels/Acre)		Notes			
5	Years	22		1995	176		In 2006, what would become			
6	Average Yield	170		1996	151		Wingait Farm was undergoing			
7	Minimum Yield	102		1997	184		foreclosure. While a corn crop			
8	Maximum Yield	187		1998	172		was harvested that year, a			
9	Median Yield			1999	177		reliable estimate of the 2006			

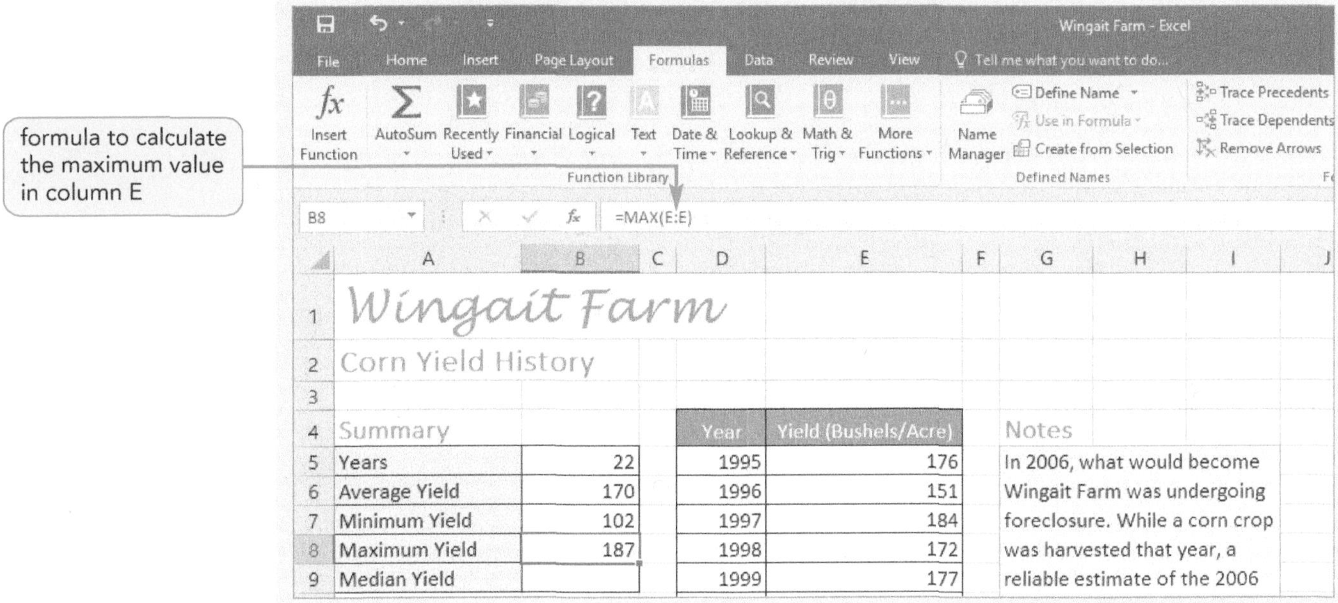

Note that like the COUNT and AVERAGE functions, the MIN and MAX functions ignore cells with text or blank cells in the selected range.

The average is one way of summarizing data from a sample. However, averages are susceptible to the effects of extremely large or extremely small values. For example, imagine calculating the average net worth of 10 people when one of them is a billionaire. An average would probably not be a good representation of the typical net worth of that group. To avoid the effect of extreme values, statisticians often use the middle, or median, value in the sample.

Jane wants you to include the median corn yield value from the farm's history. Rather than inserting the function from the Function Library, you'll search for this function in the Insert Function dialog box.

To find the median corn yield:

1. Click cell **B9** to make it the active cell.

2. Click the **Insert Function** button f_x located to the left of the formula bar. The Insert Function dialog box opens.

3. In the Search for a function box, type **middle value** as the search description, and then click the **Go** button. A list of functions matching that description appears in the Select a function box. See Figure 3-12.

Figure 3-12 Search results in the Insert Function dialog box

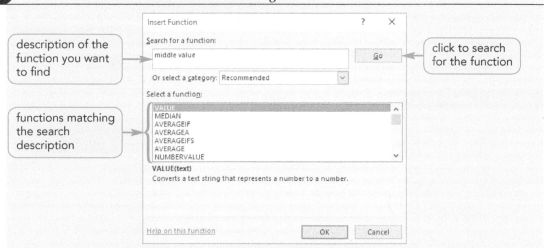

4. In the Select a function box, click **MEDIAN** to select that function, and then click the **OK** button. The Function Arguments dialog box opens with the insertion point in the Number1 box.

5. Click the **E** column heading to insert the reference E:E in the Number1 box.

6. Click the **OK** button. The formula =MEDIAN(E:E) is entered in cell B9. The formula returns 175, which is the middle value from the list of annual corn yields in the farm's history. See Figure 3-13.

Figure 3-13 Median function finds the middle corn yield value

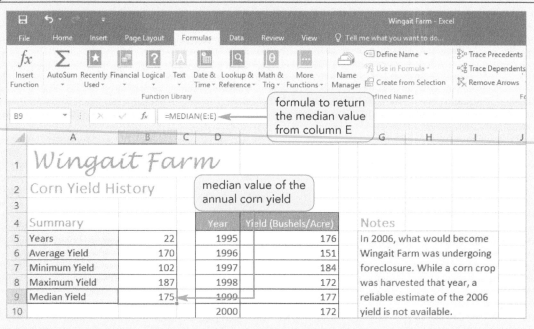

The median estimate of 175 bushels per acre is higher than the average value of 170 bushels per acre. This is due in part to the extremely low yield of 102 bushels per acre in 2005, which brought the overall average value down. Because of this, 175 bushels per acre might be a more reliable estimate of the farm's productivity.

INSIGHT

Methods of Rounding

For cleaner and neater workbooks, you will often want to round your values. There is little need for a large corporation to show revenue to the nearest cents at the annual stockholders' convention. Excel provides several methods for rounding data values. One method is to decrease the number of decimal places displayed in the cell, leaving the underlying value unchanged but rounding the displayed value to a specified number of digits.

Another approach is to use the ROUND function, which rounds the value itself to a specified number of digits. The ROUND function also accepts negative values for the number of digits in order to round the value to the nearest multiple of 10, 100, 1000, and so forth. The formula

```
=ROUND(5241,-2)
```

returns a value of 5200, rounding the value to the nearest hundred. For rounding to the nearest of multiple of a given number, use the function

```
MROUND(number,multiple)
```

where *number* is the number to be rounded and *multiple* is the multiple that the number should be rounded to. For example, the formula

```
=MROUND(5241,25)
```

rounds 5241 to the nearest multiple of 25, returning 5250. Remember though that when you use these rounding methods, you should always have access to the original, unrounded data, in case you need to audit your calculations in the future.

Next Jane wants to explore how to increase the farm's corn revenue in future seasons. You can explore the possibilities with a what-if analysis.

Performing What-If Analyses

A **what-if analysis** explores the impact that changing input values has on calculated values. For example, Jane wants to increase the farm's total revenue from corn, which you calculated as $88,559.40 for the current year, to at least $100,000. The most obvious way to increase the farm's corn revenue is to plant and then harvest more corn. Jane asks you to perform a what-if analysis to determine how many acres of corn would be needed to generate $100,000 of income, assuming conditions remain the same as the current year in which the farm yielded 168 bushels per acre at a selling price of $3.85 per bushel.

Using Trial and Error

One way to perform a what-if analysis is with **trial and error** where you change one or more of the input values to see how they affect the calculated results. Trial and error requires some guesswork as you estimate which values to change and by how much. You will use the trial and error to study the impact of changing the cornfield acreage on the total revenue generated for the farm.

To use trial and error to find how many acres of corn will generate $100,000 revenue:

1. Go to the **Yield** worksheet containing calculations for determining the farm's current corn revenue.

▶ **2.** In cell **B4**, change the farm acreage from 137 to **150**. Cell B23 shows that with 150 acres of corn sold at $3.85 per bushel, the farm's revenue from corn sales would increase from $88,559.40 to $96,962.85.

▶ **3.** In cell **B4**, change the farm acreage from 150 to **175**. Cell B23 shows that if the farm plants 175 acres of corn, the revenue would increase to $113,123.33.

▶ **4.** In cell **B4**, change the farm acreage back to **137**, which is the current acreage of corn on Wingait Farm.

To find the exact acreage that would result in $100,000 of revenue, you would have to continue trying different values in cell B4, gradually closing in on the correct value. This is why the method is called "trial and error." For some calculations, trial and error can be a very time-consuming way to locate the exact input value. A more direct approach to this problem is to use Goal Seek.

Using Goal Seek

TIP

Goal Seek can be used only with calculated numbers, not with text.

Goal Seek automates the trial-and-error process by allowing you to specify a value for a calculated item, which Excel uses to determine the input value needed to reach that goal. In this case, because Jane wants $100,000 of revenue, the question that Goal Seek answers is: "How many acres of corn are needed to generate $100,000?" Goal Seek starts by setting the calculated value and automatically works backward to determine the correct input value.

REFERENCE

Performing What-If Analysis and Goal Seek

To perform a what-if analysis by trial and error:
- Change the value of a worksheet cell (the input cell).
- Observe its impact on one or more calculated cells (the result cells).
- Repeat until the desired results are achieved.

To perform a what-if analysis using Goal Seek:
- On the Data tab, in the Forecast group, click the What-If Analysis button, and then click Goal Seek.
- Select the result cell in the Set cell box, and then specify its value (goal) in the To value box.
- In the By changing cell box, specify the input cell.
- Click the OK button. The value of the input cell changes to set the value of the result cell.

You will use Goal Seek to find how much acreage Wingait Farms must plant with corn to achieve $100,000 of revenue.

To use Goal Seek to find how many acres of corn will generate $100,000 revenue:

▶ **1.** On the ribbon, click the **Data** tab.

▶ **2.** In the Forecast group, click the **What-If Analysis** button, and then click **Goal Seek**. The Goal Seek dialog box opens.

▶ **3.** With Set cell box selected, click cell **B23** in the Yield worksheet. The cell reference $B$23 appears in the Set cell box. The set cell is the calculated value you want Goal Seek to change to meet your goal. (You'll learn about $ symbols in cell references in the next session.)

▶ **4.** Press the **Tab** key to move the insertion point to the To value box, and then type **100000** indicating that you want Goal Seek to set the value in cell B23 value to 100,000.

▶ **5.** Press the **Tab** key to move the insertion point to the By changing cell box.

There are often many possible input values you can change to meet a goal. In this case, you want to change the size of the farm acreage in cell B4.

▶ **6.** Click cell **B4**. The cell reference $B$4 appears in the By changing cell box. See Figure 3-14.

| Figure 3-14 | Goal Seek dialog box |

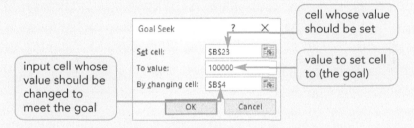

▶ **7.** Click the **OK** button. The Goal Seek dialog box closes, and the Goal Seek Status dialog box opens, indicating that Goal Seek found a solution.

▶ **8.** Click the **OK** button. The value in cell B4 changes to 154.6984204, and the value of cell B23 changes to $100,000.

If Jane increases the acreage devoted to corn production to almost 155 acres, the farm would produce a total revenue from corn of $100,000, assuming a yield of 168 bushels per acre sold at $3.85 per bushel. If the yield or market price increases, the revenue would also increase.

Interpreting Error Values

As you add formulas and values to a workbook, you might make a mistake such as mistyping a formula or entering data as the wrong type. When such errors occur, Excel displays an error value in the cell. An **error value** indicates that some part of a formula is preventing Excel from returning a value. Figure 3-15 lists the common error values you might see in place of calculated values from Excel formulas and functions. For example, the error value #VALUE! indicates that the wrong type of value is used in a function or formula.

Figure 3-15   **Excel error values**

Error Value	Description
#DIV/0!	The formula or function contains a number divided by 0.
#NAME?	Excel doesn't recognize text in the formula or function, such as when the function name is misspelled.
#N/A	A value is not available to a function or formula, which can occur when a workbook is initially set up prior to entering actual data values.
#NULL!	A formula or function requires two cell ranges to intersect, but they don't.
#NUM!	Invalid numbers are used in a formula or function, such as text entered in a function that requires a number.
#REF!	A cell reference used in a formula or function is no longer valid, which can occur when the cell used by the function was deleted from the worksheet.
#VALUE!	The wrong type of argument is used in a function or formula. This can occur when you reference a text value for an argument that should be strictly numeric.

Error values themselves are not particularly descriptive or helpful. To help you locate the error, an error indicator appears in the upper-left corner of the cell with the error value. When you point to the error indicator, a ScreenTip appears with more information about the source of the error. Although the ScreenTips provide hints as to the source of the error, you will usually need to examine the formulas in the cells with error values to determine exactly what went wrong.

Jane wants you to test the workbook. You'll change the value of cell B4 from a number to a text string, creating an error in the Yield worksheet.

To create an error value:

1. In cell **B4**, enter the text string **137 acres**. After you press the Enter key, the #VALUE! error value appears in cells whose formulas use the value in cell B4 either directly or indirectly, indicating that the wrong type of argument is used in a function or formula. In the Yield worksheet, the value in cell B4 affects the values of cells B21 and B23. See Figure 3-16.

Figure 3-16   **Error value in the worksheet**

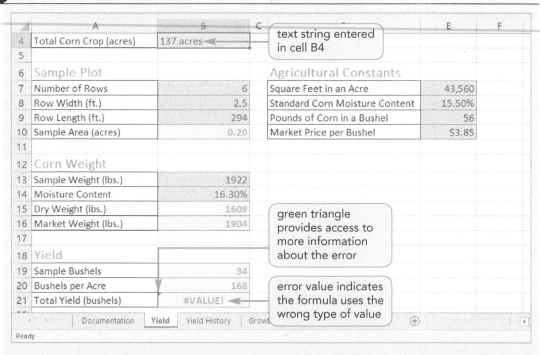

▶   **2.** Click cell **B21**, and then point to the button that appears to the left of the cell. A ScreenTip appears, providing useful information about the cause of the error value. In this case, the ScreenTip is, "A value used in the formula is of the wrong data type."

▶   **3.** Click cell **B4**, enter **137** to change the value back to the current acreage that Wingait Farm devotes to corn. After you press the Enter key, the error values disappear, the total yield in cell B21 returns to 23,002, and the projected revenue in cell B23 returns to $88,559.40.

▶   **4.** Save the workbook.

So far, you have used formulas and functions to analyze the current and past season's crop yield at Wingait Farm. In the next session, you'll use additional formulas and functions to analyze the growth of Wingait Farm's corn crop from planting to harvesting.

REVIEW

Session 3.1 Quick Check

1. Convert the following equation into an Excel formula where the *radius* value is stored in cell E31 and the value of π is stored in cell D12:

$$area = \pi \times radius^2$$

2. In Excel, the PI() function returns the decimal value of π. Rewrite your answer for the previous formula using this function.

3. Write a formula to round the value in cell A5 to the fourth decimal place.

4. Write a formula to return the middle value from the values in the range Y1:Y100.

5. The range of a set of values is defined as the maximum value minus the minimum value. Write a formula to calculate the range of values in the range Y1:Y100 and then to round that value to the nearest integer.

6. Explain the difference between the COUNT function and the COUNTA function.

7. Stephen is entering hundreds of temperature values into an Excel worksheet for a climate research project, and he wants to speed up data entry by leaving freezing point values as blanks rather than typing zeroes. Explain why this will cause complications if he later tries to calculate the average temperature from those data values.

8. What is the difference between a what-if analysis by trial and error and by Goal Seek?

9. Cell B2 contains the formula =SUME(A1:A100) with the name of the SUM function misspelled as SUME. What error value will appear in the cell?

Session 3.2 Visual Overview:

The **VLOOKUP function** returns values from a vertical lookup table by specifying the value to be matched, the location of the lookup table, and the column containing the return values.

The **TODAY function** returns the current date.

A **relative cell reference** is used for references that change when the formula is moved to a new location. For example, E15 is a relative cell reference.

Wingait Farm - Excel

File   Home   Insert   Page Layout   Formulas   Data   Review   View   Tell

Calibri   11   A A   General

Paste   B I U $ - % ,

Clipboard   Font   Alignment   Number

B13   fx   =VLOOKUP($B$12,$N$17:$O$19,2,FALSE)

=TODAY()

	A	B	C	D			G	H	I
1	*Wingait Farm*								
2	Corn Growth Calculator			Day			Tmin	Tmax	GDD
3									
4	Current Date	11/15/2017		Day 1	45	52	50	52	1.0
5				Day 2	42	64	50	64	7.0
6	Estimated Stage Dates			Day 3	38	70	50	70	10.0
7	Planting Date	4/25/2017		Day 4	43	76	50	76	13.0
8	Emergence	4/30/2017		Day 5	47	74	50	74	12.0
9	First Leaf	5/3/2017		Day 6	45	74	50	74	12.0
10				Day 7	47	71	50	71	10.5
11	Hybrid Summary			Day 8	56	68	56	68	12.0
12	Corn Hybrid	CS6489		Day 9	60	85	60	85	22.5
13	Maturity (GDD)	2920		Day 10	61	71	61	71	16.0
14				=MAX(E14,$O7)					
15	Harvesting			=MAX(E15,$O$7)	62	60	62	80	21.0
16	Harvest Date	9/		=MAX(E16,$O$7)		79	65	79	22.0
17				=MAX(E17,$O$7)	67	80	67	80	23.5
18				=MAX(E18,$O$7	56	70	56	70	13.0
19					53	75	53	75	14.0
20				Day 16	59	73	59	73	16.0

Documentation | Yield | Yield History | **Growth** | Explanation o ...

Ready

An **absolute cell reference** is used for references that do not change when the formula is moved to a new location. Absolute references have "$" before the row and column components. For example, $O$7 is an absolute cell reference.

Cell References and Formulas

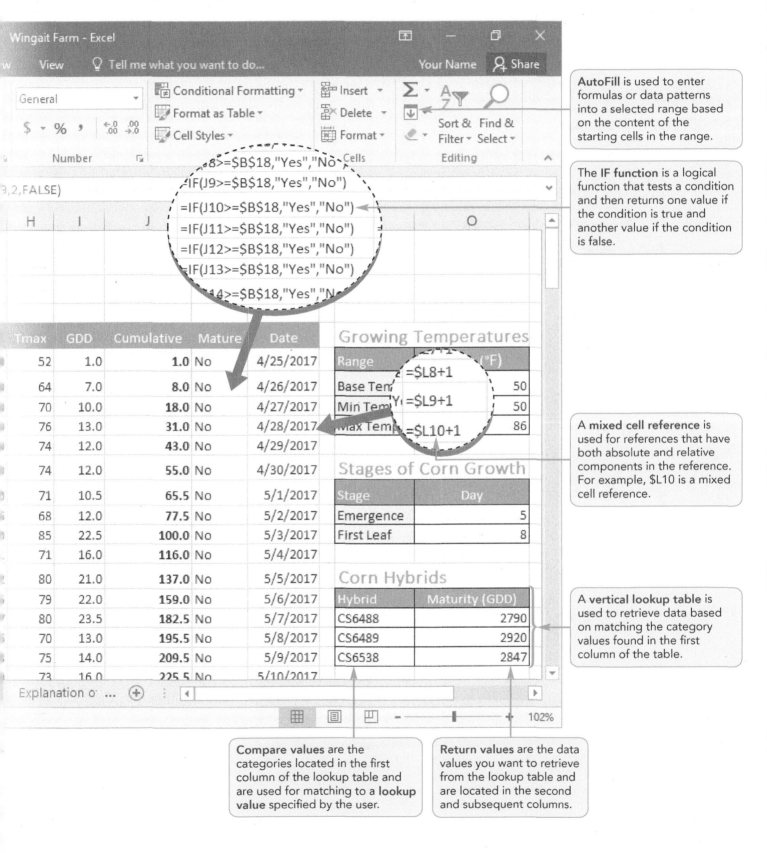

AutoFill is used to enter formulas or data patterns into a selected range based on the content of the starting cells in the range.

The IF function is a logical function that tests a condition and then returns one value if the condition is true and another value if the condition is false.

A mixed cell reference is used for references that have both absolute and relative components in the reference. For example, $L10 is a mixed cell reference.

A vertical lookup table is used to retrieve data based on matching the category values found in the first column of the table.

Compare values are the categories located in the first column of the lookup table and are used for matching to a lookup value specified by the user.

Return values are the data values you want to retrieve from the lookup table and are located in the second and subsequent columns.

AutoFilling Formulas and Data

One way to efficiently enter long columns or rows of data values and formulas is with AutoFill. AutoFill extends formulas or data patterns that were entered in a selected cell or range into adjacent cells. AutoFill is faster than copying and pasting.

Filling a Series

To extend a series of data values with a particular pattern, you enter enough values to establish the pattern, next you select those cells, and then you drag the fill handle across additional cells. The **fill handle** is the box that appears in the lower-right corner of a selected cell or range.

Figure 3-17 shows how AutoFill can be used to extend an initial series of odd numbers into a larger range. The pattern of odd numbers is established in cells A2 and A3. When the user drags the fill handle over the range A4:A9, Excel extends the series into those cells using the same pattern of odd numbers.

Figure 3-17   AutoFill used to extend a series

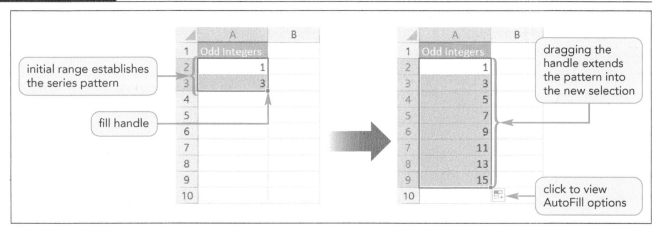

AutoFill can extend a wide variety of series, including dates and times and patterned text. Figure 3-18 shows some examples of series that AutoFill can generate. In each case, you must provide enough information for AutoFill to identify the pattern. AutoFill can recognize some patterns from only a single entry—such as Jan or January to create a series of month abbreviations or names, or Mon or Monday to create a series of the days of the week. A text pattern that includes text and a number such as Region 1, Region 2, and so on can also be automatically extended using AutoFill. You can start the series at any point, such as Weds, June, or Region 10, and AutoFill will complete the next days, months, or text.

Figure 3-18	Series patterns extended with AutoFill

Type	Initial Values	Extended Values
Numbers	1, 2, 3	4, 5, 6, ..
	2, 4, 6	8, 10, 12, ...
Dates and Times	Jan	Feb, Mar, Apr, ...
	January	February, March, April, ...
	15-Jan, 15-Feb	15-Mar, 15-Apr, 15-May, ...
	12/30/2017	12/31/2017, 1/1/2018, 1/2/2018, ...
	12/31/2017, 1/31/2018	2/29/2018, 3/31/2018, 4/30/2018, ...
	Mon	Tue, Wed, Thu, ...
	Monday	Tuesday, Wednesday, Thursday, ...
	11:00AM	12:00PM, 1:00PM, 2:00PM, ...
Patterned Text	1st period	2nd period, 3rd period, 4th period, ...
	Region 1	Region 2, Region 3, Region 4, ...
	Quarter 3	Quarter 4, Quarter 1, Quarter 2, ...
	Qtr3	Qtr4, Qtr1, Qtr2, ...

With AutoFill, you can quickly fill a range with a series of numbers, dates and times, and patterned text.

REFERENCE

Creating a Series with AutoFill

- Enter the first few values of the series into a range.
- Select the range, and then drag the fill handle of the selected range over the cells you want to fill.
- To copy only the formats or only the formulas, click the Auto Fill Options button and select the appropriate option.

or

- Enter the first few values of the series into a range.
- Select the entire range into which you want to extend the series.
- On the Home tab, in the Editing group, click the Fill button, and then click Down, Right, Up, Left, Series, or Justify to set the direction in which you want to extend the series.

Jane wants you to complete the worksheet she started to explore the growth of the Wingait Farm corn crop from planting through harvesting. You need to create a column that labels each day of corn growth starting with Day 1, Day2, and so forth through the end of the season. You will create these labels using AutoFill.

To use AutoFill to extend a series of labels:

1. If you took a break after the previous session, make sure the Wingait Farm workbook is open.

2. Go to the **Growth** worksheet.

3. In cell **D5**, enter the text string **Day 1**. This is the initial label in the series.

4. Click cell **D5** to select the cell, and then drag the **fill handle** (located in the bottom-right corner of the cell) down over the range **D5:D163**.

TIP

You can also fill a series down by selecting the entire range including the initial cell(s) that establish the pattern, and then pressing the Ctrl+D keys.

▶ **5.** Release the mouse button. AutoFill enters the labels Day1 through Day 159 in the selected range. See Figure 3-19.

Figure 3-19   **Farm Day pattern extended with AutoFill**

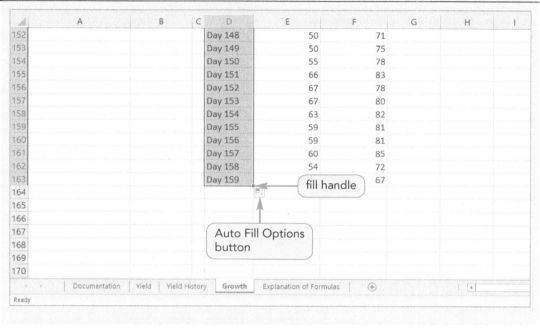

Exploring Auto Fill Options

By default, AutoFill copies both the content and the formatting of the original range to the selected range. However, sometimes you might want to copy only the content or only the formatting. The Auto Fill Options button that appears after you release the mouse button lets you specify what is copied. Figure 3-20 shows the Auto Fill Options menu for an extended series of patterned text.

Figure 3-20   **Auto Fill Options menu**

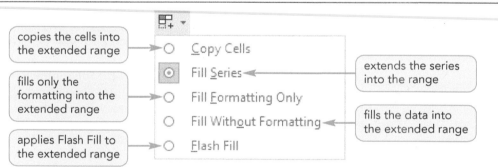

The Copy Cells option copies both the cell content and formatting but does not extend a series based on the initial values. The Fill Series option (the default) extends the initial series values into the new range. Other options allow you to fill in the values with or without the formatting used in the initial cells. Additional options (not shown in Figure 3-20) are provided when extending date values, allowing AutoFill to extend the initial dates by days, weekdays, months, or years.

The Series dialog box provides other options for how AutoFill is applied. To open the Series dialog box, click the Fill button in the Editing group on the Home tab, and then click Series. You can specify a linear or growth series for numbers; a date series for dates that increase by day, weekday, month, or year; or an AutoFill series for patterned text. With numbers, you can also specify the step value (how much each number increases over the previous entry) and a stop value (the endpoint for the entire series). See Figure 3-21.

Figure 3-21   Series dialog box

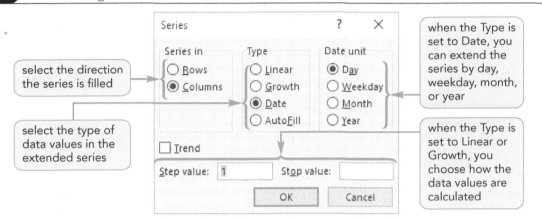

Filling Formulas

You can also use AutoFill to extend formulas into a range. AutoFill copies the formula in the initial cell or range into the extended range. Excel modifies the cell references in the formulas based on the location of the cells in the extended range.

Jane wants the Growth worksheet to include the date of each growing day starting from the planting date and extending to the last day of recorded data. Because dates are stored as numbers, you can fill in the calendar days by adding 1 to the date displayed in the previous row. Jane wants to use the date 4/15/2017 as the starting date of when the farm began planting corn.

To copy the formula with the dates for the growing season with AutoFill:

1. In cell **B7**, enter the date **4/15/2017** as the starting date of when the farm began planting corn.

2. In cell **L5**, enter the formula **=B7**. After you press the Enter key, cell L5 displays 4/15/2017, which is the first date of the growing season for corn.

3. In cell **L6**, enter the formula **=L5+1** to add one day to the date in cell L5. After you press the Enter key, the date 4/16/2017 appears in cell L6.

4. Click cell **L6** to select it, and then drag the fill handle over the range **L6:L163**. AutoFill copies the formula in cell L6 to the range L7:L163, increasing the date value by one day in each row.

AutoFill extends the formulas to display the date 4/16/2017 in cell L6 through the date 9/20/2017 in cell L163. Each date is calculated by increasing the value in the cell one row above it by one day. The formulas for these calculations are= L5+1 in cell L6, =L6+1 in cell L7, and so forth up to =L162+1 in cell L163.

Jane wants you to change the planting date to 4/25/2017, which is closer to the final date for planting corn at Wingait Farm.

To change the planting date:

▶ **1.** Scroll to the top of the workbook.

▶ **2.** In cell **B7**, change the value from 4/15/2017 to **4/25/2017**. The dates in column L automatically change to reflect the new planting date with the last date in the column changing to 9/30/2017. See Figure 3-22.

Figure 3-22 Date series pattern extended with AutoFill

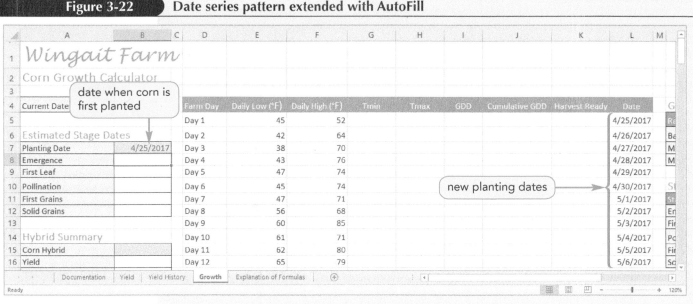

Jane wants to know when the corn crop will reach different stages of growth. In the range N11:O16 of the Growth worksheet, Jane created a table listing the number of days after planting that different growth milestones are reached. For example, the sprouts of the corn plant are often visible five days after planting (cell O12), the first small leaf appears eight days after planting (cell O13), and so forth. You will use the values in the range O12:O16 to estimate the calendar dates for when the first sprouts emerge, the first leaf appears, the corn begins to pollinate, the corn shows its first grains, and finally when the corn shows its solid grains or kernels.

To display the dates for corn growth milestones:

▶ **1.** In cell **B8**, enter the formula **=B7+O12** to add the number of days until emergence to the planting date. The date 4/30/2017, which is the estimated date when the first corn sprouts will appear, is displayed in cell B8.

▶ **2.** Click cell **B8** to select it, and then drag the fill handle over the range **B8:B12** to fill in the dates for the other growth milestones. See Figure 3-23.

| Figure 3-23 | Formula extended with AutoFill |

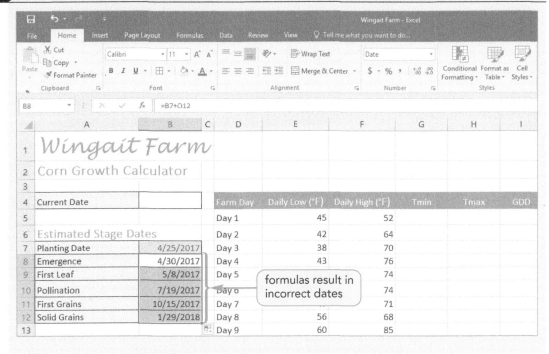

Something is wrong with the formulas that calculate the milestone dates. For example, the date for when the first corn kernels appear is January of the next year. To understand why the formulas resulted in incorrect dates, you need to look at the cell references.

Exploring Cell References

Excel has three types of cell references: relative, absolute, and mixed. Each type of cell reference in a formula is affected differently when the formula is copied and pasted to a new location.

Understanding Relative References

So far, all of the cell references you have worked with are relative cell references. When a formula includes a relative cell reference, Excel interprets the reference to each cell relative to the position of the cell containing the formula. For example, if cell A1 contains the formula =B1+B2, Excel interprets that formula as "Add the value of the cell one column to the right (B1) to the value of the cell one column to the right and one row down (B2)".

This relative interpretation of the cell reference is retained when the formula is copied to a new location. If the formula in cell A1 is copied to cell A3 (two rows down in the worksheet), the relative references also shift two rows down, resulting in the formula =B3+B4.

Figure 3-24 shows another example of how relative references change when a formula is pasted to new locations in the worksheet. In this figure, the formula =A3 entered in cell D6 displays 10, which is the number entered in cell A3. When pasted to a new location, each of the pasted formulas contains a reference to a cell that is three rows up and three rows to the left of the current cell's location.

Figure 3-24 Formulas using relative references

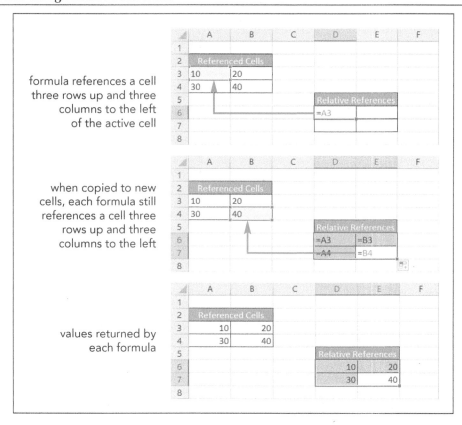

This explains what happened when you used AutoFill to copy the formula =B7+O12 in cell B8 into the range B9:B12. The formula in cell B9 became =B8+O13, the formula in cell B10 became =B9+O14, the formula in cell B11 became =B10+O15, and the formula in cell B12 became =B11+O16. In each case, the stage days were added to the date in the previous row, not the original planting date entered in cell B7. As a result, date calculation for the appearance of the first solid grains was pushed out to January of the following year.

To correct this, you need a cell reference that remains fixed on cell B7 no matter where the formula is pasted. This can be accomplished with an absolute reference.

Understanding Absolute References

An absolute reference is used for a cell reference that remains fixed even when that formula is copied to a new cell. Absolute references include $ (a dollar sign) before each column and row designation. For example, B8 is a relative reference to cell B8, while $B$8 is an absolute reference to that cell.

Figure 3-25 shows an example of how copying a formula with an absolute reference results in the same cell reference being pasted in different cells regardless of their position compared to the location of the original copied cell. In this example, the formula =$A$3 will always reference cell A3 no matter where the formula is copied to.

Figure 3-25 **Formulas using absolute references**

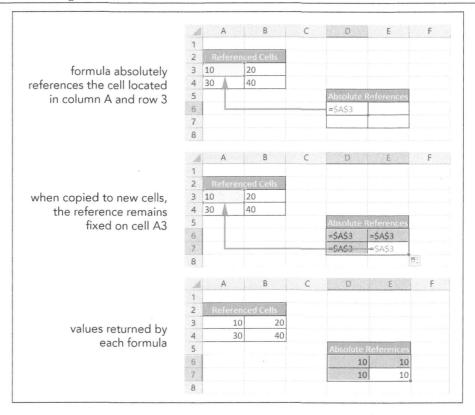

formula absolutely references the cell located in column A and row 3

when copied to new cells, the reference remains fixed on cell A3

values returned by each formula

Sometimes, you'll want only one part of the cell reference to remain fixed. This requires a mixed cell reference.

Understanding Mixed References

A mixed cell reference contains both relative and absolute components. For example, a mixed reference for cell A2 can be either $A2 where the column component is absolute and the row component is relative, or it can be entered as A$2 with a relative column component and a fixed row component. A mixed reference "locks" only one part of the cell reference. When you copy and paste a cell with a mixed reference to a new location, the absolute portion of the cell reference remains fixed, and the relative portion shifts along with the new location of the pasted cell.

Figure 3-26 shows an example of using mixed references to complete a multiplication table. The first cell in the table, cell B3, contains the formula =$A3*B$2, which multiplies the first column entry (cell A3) by the first row entry (cell B2), returning 1. When this formula is copied to another cell, the absolute portions of the cell references remain unchanged, and the relative portions of the references change. For example, if the formula is copied to cell E6, the first mixed cell reference changes to $A6 because the column reference is absolute and the row reference is relative, and the second cell reference changes to E$2 because the row reference is absolute and the column reference is relative. The result is that cell E6 contains the formula =$A6*E$2 and returns a value of 16. Other cells in the multiplication table are similarly modified so that each entry returns the multiplication of the intersection of the row and column headings.

Figure 3-26   **Formulas using mixed references**

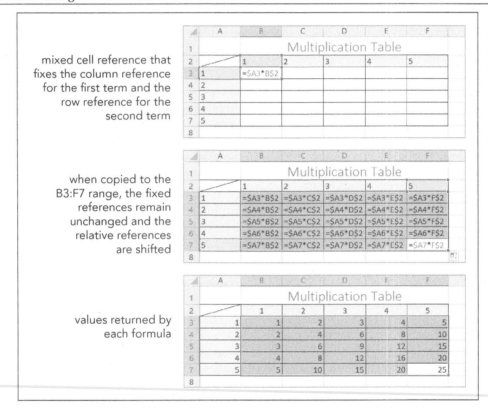

mixed cell reference that fixes the column reference for the first term and the row reference for the second term

when copied to the B3:F7 range, the fixed references remain unchanged and the relative references are shifted

values returned by each formula

Changing Cell References in a Formula

You can quickly switch a cell reference from relative to absolute or mixed. Rather than retyping the formula, you can select the cell reference in Edit mode and then press the F4 key. As you press the F4 key, Excel cycles through the different reference types—starting with the relative reference, followed by the absolute reference, then to a mixed reference with an absolute row component followed by a mixed reference with an absolute column component.

To calculate the correct stage dates in the Growth worksheet, you will change the formula in cell B8 to use an absolute reference to cell B7 and then use AutoFill to copy that formula into range B9:B12.

To correct the stage dates formulas with absolute cell references:

▶ **1.** Double-click cell **B8** to select it and enter Edit mode.

▶ **2.** In cell B8, double-click the **B7** reference to select it, and then press the **F4** key. Excel changes the formula in cell B8 to =$B$7+O12.

▶ **3.** Press the **Enter** key to enter the formula and exit Edit mode.

▶ **4.** Click cell **B8** to select it, and then drag the fill handle over the range **B8:B12**. Figure 3-27 shows the revised dates for the different stages of corn growth.

| Figure 3-27 | Stage dates calculated with absolute cell references |

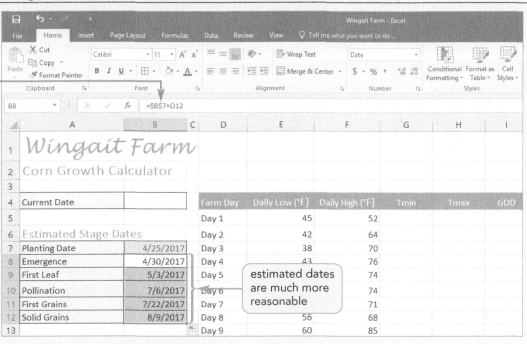

absolute cell reference to the planting date in cell B7

The revised dates for the different stages of the corn maturation are much more reasonable. For example, the date on which solid grains first appear is 8/9/2017, which is more in line with Jane's experience.

PROSKILLS

Problem Solving: When to Use Relative, Absolute, and Mixed References

Part of effective workbook design is knowing when to use relative, absolute, and mixed references. Use relative references when you want to apply the same formula with input cells that share a common layout or pattern. Relative references are commonly used when copying a formula that calculates summary statistics across columns or rows of data values. Use absolute references when you want your copied formulas to always refer to the same cell. This usually occurs when a cell contains a constant value, such as a tax rate, that will be referenced in formulas throughout the worksheet. Mixed references are seldom used other than when creating tables of calculated values such as a multiplication table in which the values of the formula or function can be found at the intersection of the rows and columns of the table.

Calendar days are one way of predicting crop growth, but Jane knows that five days of hot weather will result in more rapid growth than five mild days. A more accurate method to estimate growth is to calculate the crop's Growing Degree Days (GDD), which take into account the range of daily temperatures to which the crop is exposed. GDD is calculated using the formula

$$\text{GDD} = \frac{T_{max} + T_{min}}{2} - T_{base}$$

where T_{max} is the daily high temperature, T_{min} is the daily low temperature, and T_{base} is a baseline temperature for the region. For corn growing in Iowa, T_{min} and T_{max} are limited to the temperature range 50°F to 86°F with a baseline line temperature of 50°F. The limits are necessary because corn does not appreciably grow when the temperature falls below 50°F, nor does a temperature above 86°F increase the rate of growth.

Jane already retrieved meteorological data containing sample low and high temperatures for each day of the growing season in the Cascade, Iowa, region. She stored the limits of the corn's T_{min}, T_{max}, and T_{base} values in the Growth worksheet in the range N5:O8. You will use these values to calculate each day's GDD value for corn growth.

To calculate the GDD value:

▶ 1. Click cell **G5**, and then type the formula **=MAX(E5, $O$7)** to set the T_{min}. value to either that day's minimum temperature or to 50°F, whichever is larger.

▶ 2. Press the **Tab** key. The formula returns a value of 50.

▶ 3. In cell H5, type the formula **=MIN(F5, $O$8)** to set the T_{max} value to that day's maximum temperature or to 86°F, whichever is smaller, and then press the **Tab** key. The formula returns a value of 52.

▶ 4. In cell I5, enter the formula **=(G5+H5)/2-$O$6** to calculate that day's GDD value using the T_{base} value of 50°F stored in cell O6. The formula returns 1.0, indicating that the GDD value for that day is 1.

   Next you'll use AutoFill to copy these formulas into the range G5:I163. Because you used absolute references in the formulas, the copied formulas will continue to reference cells O7, O8, and O6 in the extended range.

▶ 5. Select the range **G5:I5**, and then drag the fill handle down to row **163**. Figure 3-28 shows the first several rows of GDD values for the corn crop's history.

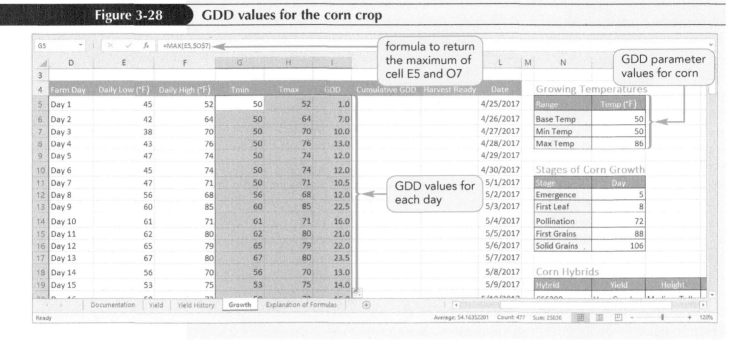

Figure 3-28 GDD values for the corn crop

The first GDD values range between 1 and 22.5, but in July and August, GDD routinely reach the upper 20s and lower 30s, indicating that those hot days result in rapid corn growth.

Summarizing Data with the Quick Analysis Tool

The Quick Analysis tool can generate columns and rows of summary statistics and formulas that can be used for analyzing data. GDD is cumulative, which means that as the crop gains more Growing Degree Days, it continues to grow and mature. Jane needs you to calculate a running total of the GDD value for each day in the season. You will enter this calculation using the Quick Analysis tool.

To calculate a running total of GDD:

1. Select the range **I5:I163** containing the GDD values for day of the growing season.

2. Click the **Quick Analysis** button in the lower-right corner of the select range (or press the **Ctrl+Q** keys) to display the menu of Quick Analysis tools.

3. Click **Totals** from the list of tools. The Quick Analysis tools that calculate summary statistics for the selected data appear. See Figure 3-29.

Figure 3-29   Totals tools on the Quick Analysis tool

adds a row displaying column sums

adds a row of column counts

adds a row of column averages

adds a column displaying row sums

click the scroll arrow to view more Quick Analysis tools for row totals

adds a row displaying percent of the totals

adds a row containing column running totals

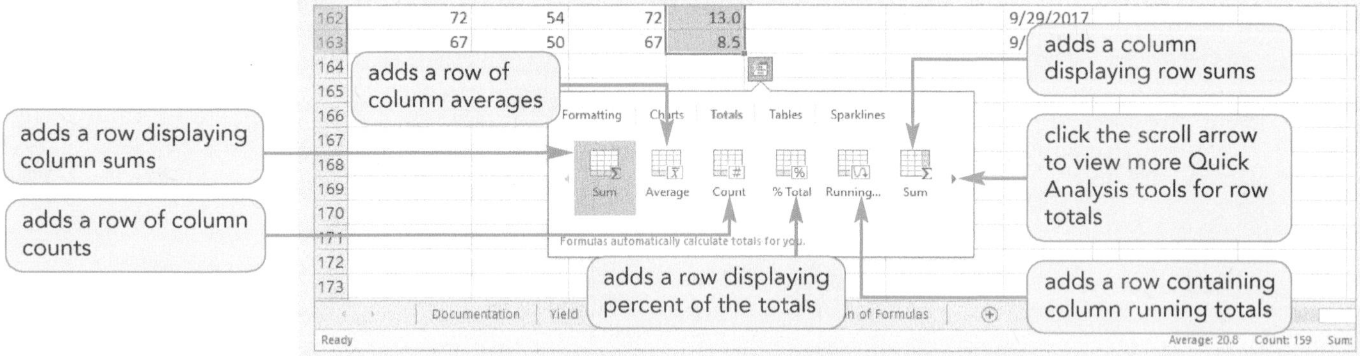

4. Click the **right scroll arrow** ▶ to view additional Quick Analysis tools, and then click **Running** (the last icon in the list). The running total of GDD values through each day of the season appears in a bold font in a new column J to the right of the selected range. See Figure 3-30.

Figure 3-30   Cumulative totals for the GDD values

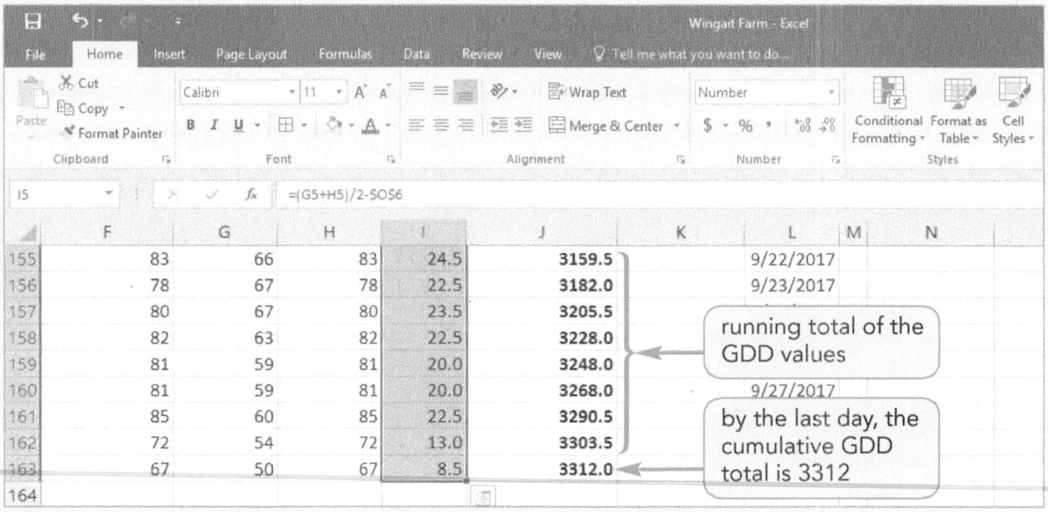

running total of the GDD values

by the last day, the cumulative GDD total is 3312

Based on the running total in column J, Jane projects that by 9/30/2017, the corn crop will have a total of 3312 Growing Degree Days. To create the running total, the Quick Analysis tool added the following formula to cell J5 and then copied that formula over the range J5:J163:

```
=SUM($I$5:I5)
```

Note that this formula uses a combination of absolute and relative cell references. When copied to cell J6 the formula becomes

```
=SUM($I$5:I6)
```

and when copied to J7 the formula is

```
=SUM($I$5:I7)
```

In this formula, the starting cell of the range used with the SUM function is fixed at cell I5, but the ending cell is relative, causing the number of rows in the range to expand to match the cell selection. For the last date in row 163, the formula becomes:

```
=SUM($I$5:I163)
```

This approach shows how a combination of absolute and relative cell references expands the capability of Excel to create formulas for a variety of ranges.

Working with Dates and Date Functions

Excel has several functions that work with dates and times. These functions are particularly useful in workbooks that involve production schedules and calendars. Figure 3-31 describes some of the commonly used date and time functions.

Figure 3-31	Date functions

Function	Description
DATE(*year,month,day*)	Creates a date value for the date represented by the *year*, *month*, and *day* arguments
DAY(*date*)	Extracts the day of the month from *date*
MONTH(*date*)	Extracts the month number from *date* where 1=January, 2=February, and so forth
YEAR(*date*)	Extracts the year number from *date*
NETWORKDAYS(*start,end[,holidays]*)	Calculates the number of whole working days between *start* and *end*; to exclude holidays, add the optional *holidays* argument containing a list of holiday dates to skip
WEEKDAY(*date[,return_type]*)	Calculates the weekday from *date*, where 1=Sunday, 2=Monday, and so forth; to choose a different numbering scheme, set *return_type* to 1 (1=Sunday, 2=Monday, ...), 2 (1=Monday, 2=Tuesday, ...), or 3 (0=Monday, 1=Tuesday, ...)
WORKDAY(*start,days[,holidays]*)	Returns the workday after *days* workdays have passed since the *start* date; to exclude holidays, add the optional *holidays* argument containing a list of holiday dates to skip
NOW( )	Returns the current date and time
TODAY( )	Returns the current date

Many workbooks include the current date so that any reports generated by the workbook are identified by date. To display the current date, you can use the TODAY function:

```
TODAY( )
```

TIP

To display the current date and time, which is updated each time the workbook is reopened, use the NOW function.

Note that although the TODAY function doesn't have any arguments, you still must include the parentheses for the function to work. The date displayed by the TODAY function is updated automatically whenever you reopen the workbook or enter a new calculation.

Jane wants the Growth worksheet to show the current date each time it is used or printed. You will use the TODAY function to display the current date in cell B4.

To display the current date:

1. Scroll to the top of the worksheet, and then click cell **B4**.

2. On the ribbon, click the **Formulas** tab.

3. In the Function Library group, click the **Date & Time** button to display the date and time functions.

4. Click **TODAY**. The Function Arguments dialog box opens and indicates that the TODAY function requires no arguments.

▶ **5.** Click the **OK** button. The formula =TODAY() is entered in cell B4, and the current date is displayed in the cell.

Note that Excel automatically formats cells containing the TODAY function to display the value in Short Date format.

INSIGHT

Date Calculations with Working Days

Businesspeople are often more interested in workdays rather than in all of the days of the week. For example, to estimate a delivery date in which packages are not shipped or delivered on weekends, it is more useful to know the date of the next weekday rather than the date of the next day.

To display the date of a weekday that is a specified number of weekdays past a start date, Excel provides the **WORKDAY function**

    WORKDAY(start,days[,holidays])

where *start* is a start date, *days* is the number of workdays after that starting date, and *holidays* is an optional list of holiday dates to skip. For example, if cell A1 contains the date 12/20/2018, a Thursday, the following formula displays the date 1/2/2019, a Wednesday that is nine working days later:

    =WORKDAY(A1,9)

The optional *holidays* argument references a series of dates that the WORKDAY function will skip in performing its calculations. So, if both 12/25/2018 and 1/1/2019 are entered in the range B1:B2 as holidays, the following function will return the date 1/4/2019, a Friday that is nine working days, excluding the holidays, after 12/20/2018:

    =WORKDAY(A1,9,B1:B2)

To reverse the process and calculate the number of working days between two dates, use the NETWORKDAYS function

    NETWORKDAYS(start,end[,holidays])

where *start* is the starting date and *end* is the ending date. So, if cell A1 contains the date 12/20/2018 and cell A2 contains the date 1/3/2019, the following function returns 9, indicating that there are nine working days between the start and ending, excluding the holidays specified in the range B1:B2:

    =NETWORKDAYS(A1,A2,B1:B2)

For international applications in which the definition of working day differs between one country and another, Excel supports the WORKDAY.INTL function. See Excel Help for more information.

Corn seed is sold in a wide variety of hybrids used to create corn of different quality, size, resistance to parasites, and growth rates. Jane wants the Growth worksheet to display data about the corn hybrid she chose for Wingait Farm. You can retrieve that data using a lookup function.

Using Lookup Functions

A **lookup function** retrieves values from a table of data that match a specified condition. For example, a lookup function can be used to retrieve a tax rate from a tax table for a given annual income or to retrieve shipping rates for different delivery options.

The table that stores the data you want to retrieve is called a **lookup table**. The first row or column of the table contains compare values, which are the values that are being looked up. If the compare values are in the first row, the table is a **horizontal lookup table**; if the compare values are in the first column, the table is a vertical lookup table. The remaining rows or columns contain the return values, which are the data values being retrieved by the lookup function.

Figure 3-32 shows the range N19:Q27 in the Growth worksheet containing information about different corn hybrids. This information is a vertical lookup table because the first column of the table containing the names of the hybrids stores the compare values. The remaining columns containing type of yield, height of the corn stalk, and GDD units until the hybrid reaches maturity are the return values. To look up the Growing Degree Days required until the corn hybrid CS6478 reaches maturity, Excel scans the first column of the lookup table until it finds the entry for CS6478. Excel then moves to the right to the column containing information that needs to be returned.

Figure 3-32   **Finding an exact match from a lookup table**

Lookup tables can be constructed for exact match or approximate match lookups. In an **exact match lookup**, the lookup value must exactly match one of the compare values in the first row or column of the lookup table. Figure 3-32 is an exact match lookup because the name of the corn hybrid must match one of the compare values in the table. An **approximate match lookup** is used when the lookup value falls within a range of compare values. You will work with exact match lookups in this module.

Finding an Exact Match with the VLOOKUP Function

To retrieve the return value from a vertical lookup table, you use the VLOOKUP function

```
VLOOKUP(comp_value,table_array,col_index_num[,range_lookup=TRUE])
```

where *comp_value* is the compare value to find in the first column of the lookup table, *table_array* is the range reference to the lookup table, and *col_index_num* is the number of the column in the lookup table that contains the return value. Keep in mind that *col_index_num* refers to the number of the column within the lookup table, not the worksheet column. So, a *col_index_num* of 2 refers to the lookup table's second column. Finally, *range_lookup* is an optional argument that specifies whether the lookup should be done as an exact match or an approximate match. For an exact match, you set the *range_lookup* value to FALSE. For approximate match lookups, you set the *range_lookup* value to TRUE. The default is to assume an approximate match.

For example, the following formula performs an exact match lookup using the text "CS6478" as the compare value and the data in the range N20:Q27 (shown in Figure 3-32) as the lookup table:

```
=VLOOKUP("CS6478",N20:Q27,4,FALSE)
```

TIP

If the VLOOKUP function cannot find the lookup value in the lookup table, it returns the #N/A error value.

The function looks through the compare values in the first column of the table to locate the "CS6478" entry. When the exact entry is found, the function returns the corresponding value in the fourth column of the table, which in this case is 2795.

Jane wants you to retrieve information about the CS6478 hybrid she uses at Wingait Farm and then display that information in the range B16:B18 on the Growth worksheet. You'll use a VLOOKUP function to retrieve yield information about the hybrid.

To use the VLOOKUP function to find yield information for hybrid CS6478:

1. In cell **B15**, enter the hybrid **CS6478**.

2. Click cell **B16**, and then click the **Insert Function** button f_x to the left of the formula bar. The Insert Function dialog box opens.

3. Click the **Or select a category** box, and then click **Lookup & Reference** in the list of function categories.

4. Scroll down the Select a function box, and then double-click **VLOOKUP**. The Function Arguments dialog box for the VLOOKUP function opens.

5. In the Lookup_value box, type **$B$15** as the absolute reference to the hybrid name, and then press the **Tab** key. The insertion point moves to the Table_array box.

6. In the Growth worksheet, select the range **N20:Q27** as the Table_array value, press the **F4** key to change the range reference to the absolute reference **$N$20:$Q$27**.

7. Press the **Tab** key. The insertion point moves to the Col_index_num box. Yield information is stored in the second column of the lookup table.

8. Type **2** in the Col_index_num box to return information from the second column of the lookup table, and then press the **Tab** key. The insertion point moves to the Range_lookup box.

9. Type **FALSE** in the Range_lookup box to perform an exact match lookup. See Figure 3-33.

TIP

Exact matches are not case sensitive, so the lookup values False, false, and FALSE are considered the same.

Figure 3-33   **Function Arguments dialog box for the VLOOKUP function**

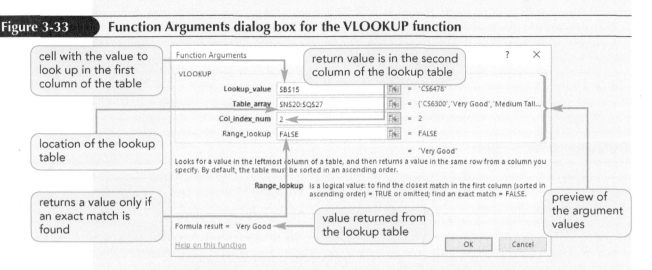

- cell with the value to look up in the first column of the table
- return value is in the second column of the lookup table
- location of the lookup table
- returns a value only if an exact match is found
- value returned from the lookup table
- preview of the argument values

> **10.** Click the **OK** button. The dialog box closes and the formula =VLOOKUP($B$15, $N$20:$Q$27,2,FALSE) is entered in cell B16. "Very Good," which is the yield associated with the CS6478 hybrid, is displayed in the cell. See Figure 3-34.

Figure 3-34   **VLOOKUP function results**

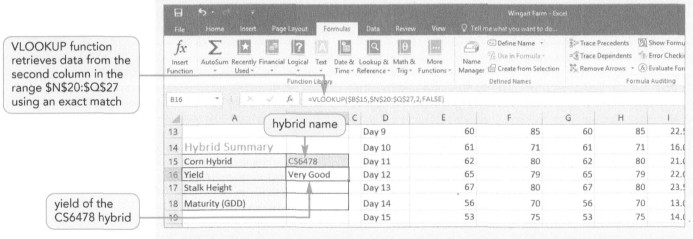

- VLOOKUP function retrieves data from the second column in the range $N$20:$Q$27 using an exact match
- hybrid name
- yield of the CS6478 hybrid

Jane wants to see the stalk height and the GDD information about the hybrid CS6478. You will use AutoFill to copy the VLOOKUP function into the other cells in the Hybrid Summary table.

To display other information about the hybrid CS6478:

> **1.** Click cell **B16** to select it, and then drag the fill handle over the range **B16:B18** to copy the VLOOKUP formula into cells B17 and B18. The text "Very Good" appears in cells B17 and B18, because the formula is set up to retrieve text from the second column of the lookup table.
>
> You need to edit the formulas in cells B17 and B18 to retrieve information from the third and fourth columns of the lookup table, respectively.

> **2.** Double-click cell **B17** to enter into Edit mode, change the third argument from 2 to **3**, and then press the **Enter** key. The value Medium for the hybrid's stalk height appears in cell B17.

> **3.** Double-click cell **B18** to enter Edit mode, change the third argument from 2 to **4**, and then press the **Enter** key. The value 2795 for the hybrid's GDD appears in cell B18. See Figure 3-35.

Figure 3-35   VLOOKUP function results for other columns

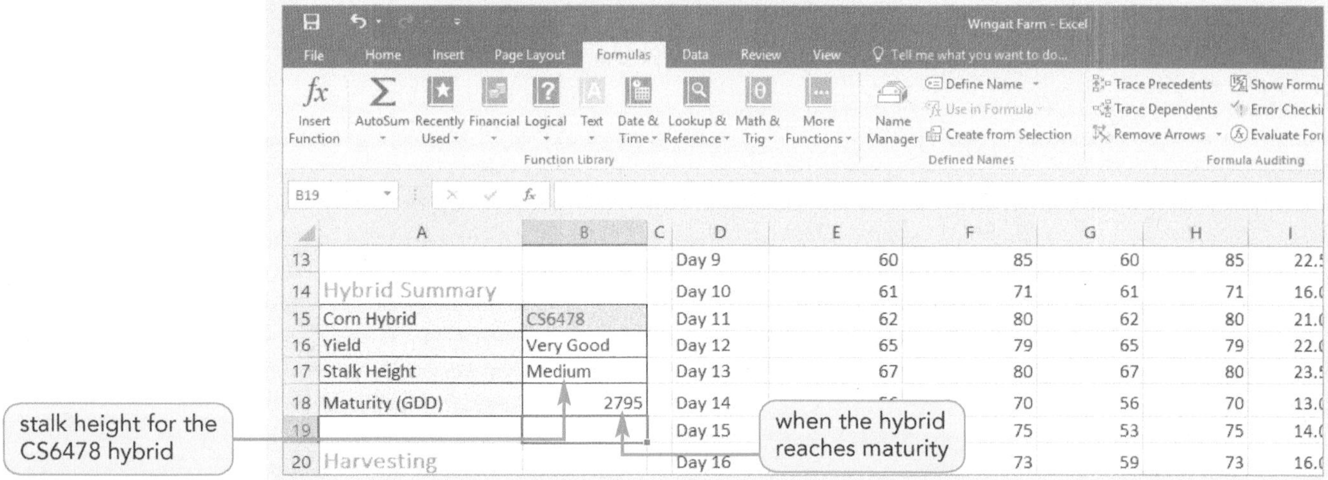

stalk height for the CS6478 hybrid

when the hybrid reaches maturity

Based on the values in the lookup table, the CS6478 hybrid will reach maturity and be ready for harvesting after 2795 Growing Degree Days. Jane wants you to add a column of values to the growth table that indicates for each date, whether the corn crop has reached maturity and is ready for harvesting. To create this column, you will need to use a logical function.

Working with Logical Functions

A **logical function** is a function that returns a different value depending on whether the given condition is true or false. That condition is entered as an expression, such as A5=3. If cell A5 is equal to 3, this expression and condition are true; if cell A5 is not equal to 3, this expression and condition are false. The most commonly used logical function is the IF function. The syntax of the IF function is

```
IF(condition,value_if_true,value_if_false)
```

where `condition` is an expression that is either true or false, `value_if_true` is the value returned by the function if the expression is true, and `value_if_false` is the value returned if the expression is false.

The value returned by the IF function can be a number, text, a date, a cell reference, or a formula. For example, the following formula tests whether the value in cell A1 is equal to the value in cell B1, returning 100 if those two cells are equal and 50 if they're not.

```
=IF(A1=B1,100,50)
```

TIP

To apply multiple logical conditions, you can nest one IF function within another.

In many cases, you will use cell references instead of values in the IF function. The following formula, for example, uses cell references, returning the value of cell C1 if A1 equals B1; otherwise, it returns the value of cell C2:

```
=IF(A1=B1,C1,C2)
```

The = symbol in these formulas is a **comparison operator** that indicates the relationship between two parts of the logical function's condition. Figure 3-36 describes other comparison operators that can be used within logical functions.

Figure 3-36	Logical comparison operators

Operator	Expression	Tests
=	A1 = B1	If the value in cell A1 is equal to the value in cell B1
>	A1 > B1	If the value in cell A1 is greater than the value in cell B1
<	A1 < B1	If the value in cell A1 is less than the value in cell B1
>=	A1 >= B1	If the value in cell A1 is greater than or equal to the value in cell B1
<=	A1 <= B1	If the value in cell A1 is less than or equal to the value in cell B1
<>	A1 <> B1	If the value in cell A1 is not equal to the value in cell B1

The IF function also works with text. For example, the following formula tests whether the value of cell A1 is equal to "yes":

```
=IF(A1="yes","done","restart")
```

If the condition is true (the value of cell A1 is equal to "yes"), then the formula returns the text "done"; otherwise, it returns the text "restart".

For each date in the growth record of the corn crop, Jane wants to know whether the cumulative GDD value is greater than or equal to the GDD value on which the hybrid reaches maturity and is ready for harvesting. If the crop is ready for harvesting, she wants the cell to display the text "Yes"; otherwise, it should display the text "No". You'll use the IF function to do this.

To enter the IF function to specify whether the corn is ready for harvesting:

1. Click cell **K5** to select it. You'll enter the IF function in this cell.

2. On the Formulas tab, in the Function Library group, click the **Logical** button to display the list of logical functions, and then click **IF**. The Function Arguments dialog box for the IF function opens.

3. In the Logical_test box, enter the expression **J5>=$B$18** to test whether the cumulative GDD value is greater than the maturity value in cell B18.

4. Press **Tab** key to move the insertion point to the Value_if_true box, and then type **"Yes"** as the value if the logical test is true.

5. Press **Tab** key to move the insertion point to the Value_if_false box, and then type **"No"** as the value if the logical test is false. See Figure 3-37.

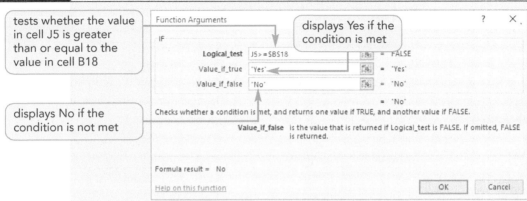

Figure 3-37   Function Arguments dialog box for the IF function

6. Click the **OK** button. The formula =IF(J5>=$B$18,"Yes","No") is entered in cell K5. The cell displays the text "No," indicating that the crop is not harvest ready on this day (a logical result because this is the day when the farm starts planting the corn).

7. Click cell **K5**, and then drag fill handle to select the range **K5:K163**. The formula with the IF function is applied to the remaining days of the growing season. As shown in Figure 3-38, by the end of the growing season, the crop is ready for harvesting because the cumulative GDD value for the hybrid CS6478 has exceeded 2795.

Figure 3-38   IF function evaluates whether the crop is harvest ready

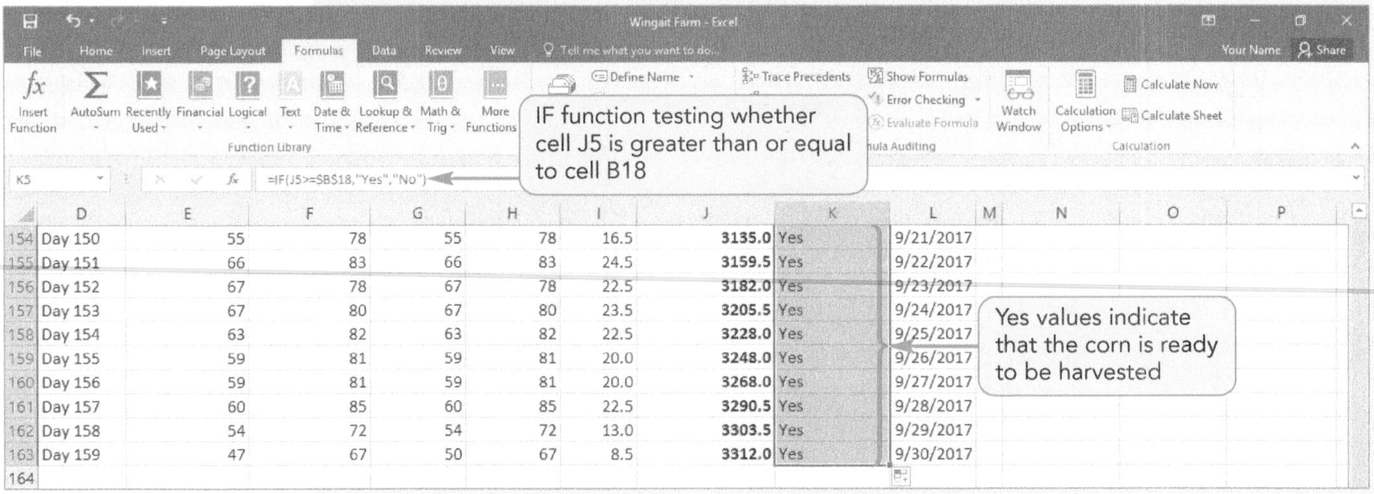

IF function testing whether cell J5 is greater than or equal to cell B18

K5   fx   =IF(J5>=$B$18,"Yes","No")

	D	E	F	G	H	I	J	K	L	M	N	O	P
154	Day 150	55	78	55	78	16.5	3135.0	Yes	9/21/2017				
155	Day 151	66	83	66	83	24.5	3159.5	Yes	9/22/2017				
156	Day 152	67	78	67	78	22.5	3182.0	Yes	9/23/2017				
157	Day 153	67	80	67	80	23.5	3205.5	Yes	9/24/2017				
158	Day 154	63	82	63	82	22.5	3228.0	Yes	9/25/2017				
159	Day 155	59	81	59	81	20.0	3248.0	Yes	9/26/2017				
160	Day 156	59	81	59	81	20.0	3268.0	Yes	9/27/2017				
161	Day 157	60	85	60	85	22.5	3290.5	Yes	9/28/2017				
162	Day 158	54	72	54	72	13.0	3303.5	Yes	9/29/2017				
163	Day 159	47	67	50	67	8.5	3312.0	Yes	9/30/2017				
164													

Yes values indicate that the corn is ready to be harvested

By scrolling up and down the Growth worksheet you can locate the row in which the value in the Harvest Ready column switches from No to Yes. For this data, the switch occurs in row 138 where the cumulative GDD value is equal to 2814, exceeding the minimum GDD value required for this particular hybrid to reach maturity.

Rather than scrolling through the worksheet, Jane wants the worksheet to display the calendar date on which the crop reaches maturity and is ready for harvesting. You can obtain this information by using columns K and L as a lookup table. Recall that Excel scans a lookup table from the top to the bottom and stops when it reaches the first value in the compare column that matches the lookup value. You can use this fact to find the first location in column K where the Harvest Ready value is equal to "Yes" and then apply the VLOOKUP function to return the corresponding calendar date in column L.

To display the harvest date for the corn crop:

1. Near the top of the worksheet, click cell **B21** to select it.

2. Click the **Insert Function** button f_x to the left of the formula bar. The Insert Function dialog box opens.

3. Click the **Or select a category box arrow**, and then click **Most Recently Used** to display a list of the functions you have used most recently.

4. Double-click **VLOOKUP** in the list. The Function Arguments dialog box for the VLOOKUP function opens.

5. In the Lookup_value box, type **"Yes"** and then press the **Tab** key. The insertion point moves to the Table_array box.

6. Select the **K** and **L** column headings to insert the reference K:L in the Table_array box, and then press the **Tab** key. The insertion point moves to the Col_index_num box.

7. Type **2** in the Col_index_num box to retrieve the value from the second column in the lookup table, and then press the **Tab** key. The insertion point moves to the Range_lookup box.

Use FALSE to perform an exact match lookup.

8. Type **FALSE** in the Range_lookup box to apply an exact match lookup. See Figure 3-39.

Figure 3-39 **Function Arguments for the VLOOKUP function**

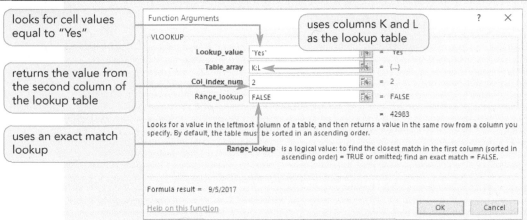

9. Click the **OK** button. The formula =VLOOKUP("Yes",K:L,2,FALSE) is entered in cell B21. The cell displays 9/5/2017, which is the date when the corn crop has reached maturity and is ready for harvesting to begin.

Jane can view the impact of different hybrids on the harvest date by changing the value of cell B15.

10. Click cell **B15**, and then change the corn hybrid from CS6478 to **CS6489**. The results from the lookup and IF functions in the worksheet change to reflect the corn hybrid CS6489. This hybrid has excellent yield and tall stalks and is ready for harvesting on 9/10/2017, five days later than the corn hybrid CS6478. See Figure 3-40.

Figure 3-40   **Summary and harvesting data for the hybrid CS6489**

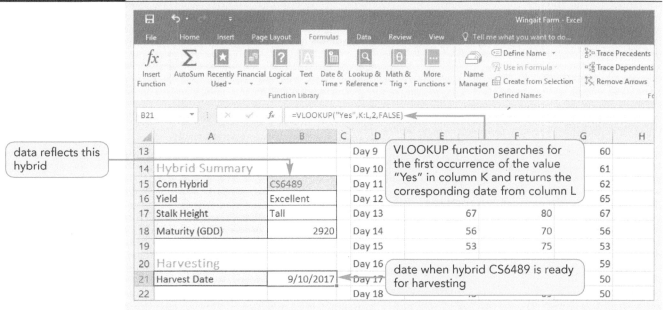

data reflects this hybrid

VLOOKUP function searches for the first occurrence of the value "Yes" in column K and returns the corresponding date from column L

date when hybrid CS6489 is ready for harvesting

11. Save the workbook.

You've completed your work on the Wingait Farm workbook. Jane will use this workbook to analyze next year's crop, entering new values for the daily temperatures and for the hybrid types. By tracking the growth of the corn crop, Jane hopes to more effectively increase her farm's yield and predict when the corn crop is ready for harvesting.

INSIGHT

Managing Error Values with the IF Function

An error value does not mean that you must correct the cell's formula or function. Some error values appear simply because you have not yet entered any data into the workbook. For example, if you use the VLOOKUP function without a lookup value, the #N/A error value appears because Excel cannot look up an empty value. However, as soon as you enter a lookup, the #N/A error value disappears, replaced with the result of the VLOOKUP function.

Error values of this type can make your workbook difficult to read and can confuse other users. One way to avoid error values resulting from missing input values is to nest formulas within an IF function. For example, the following formula first tests whether a value has been entered into cell B2 before attempting to use that cell as a lookup value in the VLOOKUP function:

```
=IF(B2="","",VLOOKUP(B2,$E1:$G$10,3,FALSE)
```

Note that "" is used to represent an empty text string or value. If the IF condition is true because no value has been entered into cell B2, the formula will return an empty text string instead of an error value, but if B2 has a value, the VLOOKUP function is applied using cell B2 as the lookup value. The result is a cleaner workbook that is easier for other people to read and use.

Jane appreciates all of the work you have done in developing the Wingait Farm workbook. She will continue to study the document and get back to you with future projects at the farm.

Session 3.2 Quick Check

1. If 4/30/2017 and 5/31/2017 are the initial values, what are the next two values AutoFill will insert?

2. You need to reference cell Q57 in a formula. What is its relative reference? What is its absolute reference? What are the two mixed references?

3. If cell R10 contains the formula =R1+R2, which is then copied to cell S20, what formula is entered in cell S20?

4. If cell R10 contains the formula =$R1+R$2, which is then copied to cell S20, what formula is entered in cell S20?

5. Explain how to use the Quick Analysis tool to calculate a running total of the values in the range D1:D10.

6. Write the formula to display the current date in the worksheet.

7. Write the formula to display a date that is four workdays after the date in cell A5. Do not assume any holidays in your calculation.

8. Write the formula to perform an exact match lookup with the lookup value from cell G5 using a vertical lookup table located in the range A1:F50. Return the value from the third column of the table.

9. If cell Q3 is greater than cell Q4, you want to display the text "OK"; otherwise, display the text "RETRY". Write the formula that accomplishes this.

Review Assignments

Data File needed for the Review Assignments: Soybean.xlsx

Another cash crop grown at Wingait Farm is soybeans. Jane wants you to create a workbook for the soybean crop similar to the workbook you created for the corn crop. The workbook should estimate the total yield and revenue from a small plot sample and compare that yield to the farm's historic norms. The workbook should also track the soybean growth from planting to harvest. Complete the following:

1. Open the **Soybean** workbook located in the Excel3 > Review folder, and then save the workbook as **Soybean Crop** in the location specified by your instructor.
2. In the Documentation worksheet, enter your name in cell B3 and the date in cell B4.
3. The size of the soybean crop is **72** acres. Enter this value in cell B4 of the Yield worksheet.
4. The soybean sample comes from a plot of **4** rows each **7.5** inches wide and **21** inches long. Enter these values in the range B7:B9.
5. Within the plot, the farm has harvested **400** soybean pods with an average of **2.5** soybeans per pod. Enter these values in the B14:B15 range.
6. Apply the Input cell style to cells B4, B7:B9, and B14:B15.
7. Using the equations described in the Formulas worksheet, enter the following calculations:
   a. In cell B10, calculate the area of the plot sample in inches.
   b. In cell B11, convert the sample area to acres by dividing the value in cell B10 by the number of square inches in an acre (cell H4). Display the result to four decimal places.
   c. In cell B16, calculate the total number of seeds harvested in the sample.
   d. In cell B17, calculate the weight of the sample in pounds by dividing the number of seeds by the number of seeds in one pound (cell H5). Display the value to two decimal places.
   e. In cell B18, convert the weight to bushels by dividing the weight in pounds by the number of pounds of soybeans in one bushel (cell H6). Display the value to four decimal places.
   f. In cell B19, estimate the farm's soybean yield in bushels per acre by dividing the number of bushels in the plot sample by the area of the sample in acres. Display the value as an integer.
8. Calculate the following values for soybean yield and revenue:
   a. In cell B20, calculate the farm's average soybean yield using the values in column E. Use the ROUND function to round that average value to the nearest integer.
   b. In cell B21, calculate the farm's median soybean yield from the values in column E.
   c. In cell B24, calculate the farm's total production of soybeans in bushels by multiplying the bushels per acre value by the total number of acres that the farm devotes to soybeans. Display the value as an integer.
   d. In cell B25, calculate the total revenue from the soybean crop by multiplying the total bushels harvested by the current price per bushel (cell H7). Display the value using the Accounting format style.
9. Apply the Calculation style to the range B10:B11,B16:B21,B24:B25.
10. Use Goal Seek to determine what value in cell B4 (the number of acres devoted to soybeans) will result in a total soybean revenue of $40,000.
11. In the Growth worksheet, in cell B5, enter a formula with a function to display the current date.
12. Use AutoFill to insert the text strings Day 1 through Day 112 in the range D5:D116.
13. In cell G5, calculate the Growing Degree Days (GDD) for the first day of the season using the formula described in the Formulas worksheet and the temperature range values in the range L6:M9. (*Hint*: Use the same formula used in the tutorial for corn, but enter the T_{min}, T_{max}, and *base* values directly in the formula. Be sure to use absolute references for the temperature range values.)
14. Copy the formula in cell G5 to the range G5:G112.

15. Use the Quick Analysis tool to calculate the cumulative total of the GDD values from the range G5:G112, placing those values in the range H5:H112.

16. In cell B9, enter **5/12/2017**, which is the date the farm will start planting the soybean crop.

17. In cell J5, enter a formula to display the date from cell B9. In cell J6, enter a formula to increase the date in cell J5 by one day. Copy the formula in cell J6 to the range J6:J112 to enter the dates for the growing season.

18. In cell B8, enter **M070** as the maturity group for the current soybean hybrid.

19. In cell B10, use the VLOOKUP function to retrieve the cumulative GDD value for the M070 hybrid. (*Hint:* The range L12:M21 displays the cumulative GDD for each maturity group.)

20. In cell I5, enter an IF function that tests whether the cumulative GDD value in cell H5 is greater than the maturity value in cell B10. Use an absolute reference to cell B10. If the condition is true, return the text string "Ready"; otherwise, return the text "Not Ready". Copy the formula to the range I5:I112.

21. In cell B11, insert a VLOOKUP function using the values in the columns I and J that returns the date on which the Harvest Ready value is first equal to the text string "Ready".

22. In cell B12, calculate the number of days between planting and harvesting by subtracting the planting date (cell B9) from the harvest date (cell B11).

23. Save and close the workbook.

Case Problem 1

APPLY

Data File needed for this Case Problem: Gorecki.xlsx

Gorecki Construction   Stefan Gorecki is the owner of Gorecki Construction, a small construction firm in Chester, Pennsylvania. He wants to use Excel to track his company's monthly income and expenses and then use that information to create a monthly budget. Stefan has already entered the raw data values but has asked to you to complete the workbook by adding the formulas and functions to perform the calculations. Complete the following:

1. Open the **Gorecki** workbook located in the Excel3 > Case1 folder, and then save the workbook as **Gorecki Budget** in the location specified by your instructor.

2. In the Documentation worksheet, enter your name in cell B3 and the date in cell B4.

3. The budget values are entered based on the end-of-month values. In the Monthly Budget worksheet, enter the date **31-Jan-18** in cell E4 and **28-Feb-18** in cell F4. Use AutoFill to fill in the remaining end-of-month date in the range G4:P4.

4. Calculate the company's total monthly income by selecting the range E6:P7 and using the Quick Analysis tool to insert the SUM function automatically into the range E8:P8.

5. Calculate the company's total cost of goods sold by selecting values in range E10:P11 and using the Quick Analysis tool to insert the SUM function automatically into the range E12:P12.

6. In the range E14:P14, calculate the company's monthly gross profit, which is equal to the difference between the monthly income and the monthly cost of goods sold.

7. Select the expenses entered in the range E17:P26, and use the Quick Analysis tool to insert the sum of the monthly expenses into the range E27:P27.

8. In the range E29:P29, calculate the company's net income equal to the difference between its gross profit and its total expenses.

9. Select the values in the range E29:P29, and then use the Quick Analysis tool to insert a running total of the company's net income into the range E30:P30.

10. Calculate the year-end totals for all financial categories by selecting the range E6:P29 and using the Quick Analysis tool to insert the sum of each row into the range Q6:Q29. Delete the content of any cells that do not contain financial figures.

11. Stefan wants the monthly averages of each financial category to be displayed in range B6:B29. Select cell B6, and then enter a formula that contains a nested function that first calculates the average of the values in the range E6:P6 and then uses the ROUND function to round that average to the nearest 10 dollars. (*Hint*: Use –1 for the value of the num_digits argument.) Use AutoFill to extend formula over the range B6:B29, deleting any cells corresponding to empty values.

12. Save and close the workbook.

Case Problem 2

Data File needed for this Case Problem: Capshaw.xlsx

Capshaw Family Dentistry   Carol Lemke is a new receptionist at Capshaw Dentistry in East Point, Georgia. She wants to get a rough estimate of what her take-home pay would be after deductions for federal and local taxes. She asks you to set up an Excel worksheet to perform the wage calculations for a sample two-week period. Carol already entered the work schedule and several tables containing the federal and state tax rates but needs you to insert the formulas. (*Note:* The tax rate tables and formulas used in this example are a simplified version of the tax code and should not be used to calculate actual taxes.) Complete the following:

1. Open the **Capshaw** workbook located in the Excel3 > Case2 folder, and then save the workbook as **Capshaw Wages** in the location specified by your instructor.

2. In the Documentation worksheet, enter your name in cell B3 and the date in cell B4.

3. In the Work Schedule worksheet, enter the following information in the range B5:B9: Name **Carol Lemke**; Hourly Rate **$16.25**; Federal Marital Status **Single**; State Marital Status **Single**; and Withholding Allowances **1**.

4. In cell D6, enter the date **4/10/2017**. Use AutoFill to fill in the next day weekdays in the range D6:D15. (*Hint*: Click the AutoFill options button after dragging the fill handle, and then select the Fill Weekdays option button.)

5. In cell G6, calculate the total hours worked on the first day, which is equal to the difference between cell F6 and cell E6 multiplied by 24.

6. Carol will get overtime wages when she works more than eight hours in a day. Calculate the non-overtime hours in cell H6 by using the MIN function to return the minimum of the value in cell G6 and the value 8.

7. In cell I6, calculate the amount of overtime hours by using the IF function to test whether cell G6 is greater than 8. If it is, return the value cell G6 minus 8; otherwise, return the value 0.

8. In cell J6, calculate the salary due on the first day. The salary due is equal to the Straight Time worked multiplied by the hourly rate in cell B6 plus the Overtime multiplied by the hourly rate times 1.5 (Carol will receive time-and-a-half for each overtime hour.) Use an absolute reference to cell B6.

9. Select the range G6:J6, and then use AutoFill to copy the formulas into the range G7:J15 to calculate the salary for each of the ten days in the table.

10. In cell B11, calculate the total straight time hours worked by summing the values in column H. In cell B12, calculate the total overtime hours by summing the values in column I. In cell B13, calculate the total hours worked by summing the value in column G. In cell B14, calculate the total payments by summing the values in column J.

11. In cell B17, calculate the amount of federal tax by multiplying the Total Pay value in cell B14 by the appropriate federal tax rate for an employee with the marital status in cell B7 and withholding allowances in cell B9. (*Hint*: Use the VLOOKUP function with an exact match lookup for the lookup table in the range L6:W8. For the Col_index_num argument, use the value of cell B9 plus 2.)

12. In cell B18, calculate the Social Security tax equal to the value of cell B14 multiplied by the tax rate in cell M16.

13. In cell B19, calculate the Medicare tax equal to the value of cell B14 multiplied by the tax rate in cell M17.

14. In cell B20, calculate the amount of Georgia state tax by multiplying the value of cell B14 by the appropriate state tax rate in the range L12:W14 lookup table using the state marital status in cell B8 and the withholding allowance in cell B9. (*Hint*: Use the same type of VLOOKUP function as you did in Step 10 to retrieve the correct state tax rate.)

15. In cell B22, calculate the total deduction from pay by summing the values in the range B17:B20. In cell B23, calculate the withholding rate by dividing cell B22 by the total pay in cell B14.

16. In cell B24, calculate the take-home pay from subtracting the total withholding in cell B22 from cell B14.

17. Carol wants her take-home pay for the two weeks that she works in the sample schedule to be $1000. Use Goal Seek to find the hourly rate in cell B6 that will result in a take-home pay value of $1000.

18. Save and close the workbook.

Case Problem 3

Data File needed for this Case Problem: Biology.xlsx

CHALLENGE

Biology 221 Daivi Emani teaches biology and life sciences at Milford College in White Plains, New York. She wants to use Excel to track the test scores and calculate final averages for the students in her Biology 221 class. She has already entered the homework, quiz, and final exam scores for 66 students. The overall score is based on weighted average of the individual scores with homework accounting for 10 percent of the final grade, each of three quizzes accounting for 20 percent, and the final exam accounting for 30 percent. To calculate a weighted average you can use the SUMPRODUCT function

    SUMPRODUCT(array1,array2)

where *array1* is the range containing the weights assigned to each score and *array2* is the range containing the scores themselves.

Daivi also wants you to calculate each student's rank in the class based on the student's weighted average. Ranks are calculated using the RANK function

    RANK(number,ref[,order=0])

where *number* is the value to be ranked, *ref* is a reference to the range containing the values against which the ranking is done, and *order* is an optional argument that specifies whether to rank in descending order or ascending order. The default order value is 0 to rank the values in descending order.

Finally, you will create formulas that will look up information on a particular student based on that student's ID so that Daivi doesn't have to scroll through the complete class roster to find a particular student. Complete the following:

1. Open the **Biology** workbook located in the Excel3 > Case3 folder, and then save the workbook as **Biology Grades** in the location specified by your instructor.

2. In the Documentation worksheet, enter your name in cell B3 and the date in cell B4.

3. In the Biology Grades worksheet, in cell B5, calculate the number of students in the class by using the COUNTA function to count up the student IDs in the H column and subtracting 1 from that value (so as to not include cell H2 in the count).

4. In the range B8:F8, enter the weight values **10%**, **20%**, **20%**, **20%**, and **30%**.

5. In the range B9:F9, calculate the average of the numbers in columns K, L, M, N, and O.

6. In the range B10:F10, calculate the minimum values in the corresponding student score columns.

7. In the range B11:F11, use the MEDIAN function to calculate the midpoint of each of the student scores.

8. In the range B12:F12, calculate the maximum values for each of the student scores.

⊕ **Explore** 9. In cell P3, use the SUMPRODUCT function to calculate the weighted average of the scores for the first student in the list. Use an absolute reference to the range B8:F8 for the *array1* argument, and use the relative reference to the student scores in the range K3:O3 for the *array2* argument.

⊕ **Explore** 10. In cell Q3, use the RANK function to calculate the first student's rank in class. Use cell P3 for the *number* argument and column P for the *ref* argument. You do not to specify a value for the *order* argument.

11. Calculate the weighted average and ranks for all of the students by using AutoFill to copy the formulas in the range P3:Q3 to the range P3:Q68.

12. In cell B15, enter the student ID **602-1-99** for Lawrence Fujita.

13. In cell B16, use the VLOOKUP function with the student ID from cell B15 to look up the first name of the student matching that ID. Use the range H:Q as the reference to the lookup table, and retrieve the third column from the table.

14. In the range B17:B24, use lookup functions to retrieve the other data for the student ID entered in cell B15.

15. Test the VLOOKUP function by adding other student IDs in cell B15 to confirm that you can retrieve the record for any student in class based on his or her student ID.

16. Manuel Harmon was not able to take the final exam because of a family crisis. Daivi is scheduling a makeup exam for him. A weighted average of 92.0 will give Manuel an A for the course. Use Goal Seek to determine what grade he would need on the final to get an A for the course.

17. Save and close the workbook.

CHALLENGE

Case Problem 4

Data File needed for this Case Problem: Cairn.xlsx

Cairn Camping Supplies   Diane Cho is the owner of Cairn Camping Supplies, a small camping store she runs out of her home in Fort Smith, Arkansas. To help her manage her inventory and orders, she wants to develop an Excel worksheet for recording orders. The worksheet needs to calculate the cost of each order, including the cost of shipping and sales tax. Shipping costs vary based on whether the customer wants to use standard, three-day, two-day, or overnight shipping. Diane will also offer free shipping for orders that are more than $250. The shipping form worksheet will use lookup functions so that Diane can enter each product's ID code and have the name and price of the product automatically entered into the form. To keep the worksheet clean without distracting error values when no input values have been entered, you'll use IF functions to test whether the user has entered a required value first before applying a formula using that value. Complete the following:

1. Open the **Cairn** workbook located in the Excel3 > Case4 folder, and then save the workbook as **Cairn Camping** in the location specified by your instructor.

2. In the Documentation worksheet, enter your name in cell B3 and the date in cell B4.

3. In the Order Form worksheet, enter the following sample order data: Customer **Dixie Kaufmann**; Order Number **381**; Order Date **4/5/2018**; Street **414 Topeak Lane**; City **Fort Smith**; State **AK**; ZIP **72914**; Phone **(479) 555-2081**; and Delivery Type **3 Day**.

⊕ **Explore** 4. In cell B17, calculate the number of delivery days for the order. Insert an IF function that first tests whether the value in cell B16 is equal to an empty text string (""). If it is, return an empty text string; otherwise, apply a lookup function to retrieve the lookup value from the table in the range F5:H8 using the value of cell B16 as the lookup value.

⊕ **Explore** 5. In cell B18, estimate the date of weekday delivery by inserting an IF function that tests whether cell B16 is equal to an empty text string. If it is, return an empty text string, otherwise apply the WORKDAY function using the values in cell B6 as the starting date and cell B17 as the number of days.

6. In cell D13, enter **p4981** as the initial item ordered by the customer. In cell G13, enter **2** as the number of items ordered.

7. In cell E13, enter an IF function that tests whether the value in cell D13 is equal to an empty text string. If true, return an empty text string. If false, apply the VLOOKUP function to return the name of the product ID entered into cell D13.

8. In cell F13, enter another IF function that tests whether the value in cell D13 is equal to an empty text string. If true, return an empty text string. If false, return the price of the product ID entered in cell D13.

9. In cell H13, enter another IF function to test whether the value in cell D13 is equal to an empty text string. If true, return an empty text string; otherwise, calculate the value of the price of the item multiplied by the number of items ordered.

10. Copy the formula in the range E13:F13 to the range E13:F20. Use AutoFill to copy the formula from cell H13 into the range H13:H20.

11. In cell H22, calculate the sum of the values in the range H13:H20.

12. In cell H23, calculate the sales tax equal to the total cost of the items ordered multiplied by the sales tax rate in cell G10.

13. In cell H24, calculate the shipping cost of the order by inserting an IF function that tests whether the value of cell B16 is an empty text string. If it is, return the value 0; otherwise, use a lookup function to return the shipping cost for the indicated shipping method.

14. In cell H25, insert an IF function that tests whether the value of cell H22 is greater than 250 (the minimum order needed to qualify for free shipping). If it is, return a value of cell H24; otherwise, return a value of 0.

15. In cell H27, calculate the total cost of the order by summing the values in the range H22:H24 and subtracting the value of cell H25.

16. Complete the customer order by adding the following items: Item **t7829** and Qty **1**; Item **led7331** and Qty **3**; and Item **sb8502** and Qty **5**.

17. Confirm that your worksheet correctly calculates the total cost, and then save your workbook.

18. Save the workbook as **Cairn Order Form** in the location specified by your instructor.

19. Create a blank order form sheet by deleting the input values in the ranges B4:B6, B9:B13, B16, D13:D16, G13:G16. Do *not* delete any formulas in the worksheet. Confirm that the worksheet does not show any error values when the input data is removed.

20. Save and close the workbook.

OBJECTIVES

Session 4.1
- Use the PMT function to calculate a loan payment
- Create an embedded pie chart
- Apply styles to a chart
- Add data labels to a pie chart
- Format a chart legend
- Create a clustered column chart
- Create a stacked column chart

Session 4.2
- Create a line chart
- Create a combination chart
- Format chart elements
- Modify the chart's data source
- Create a histogram and Pareto chart
- Add sparklines to a worksheet
- Format cells with data bars

Analyzing and Charting Financial Data

EXCEL

Preparing a Business Plan

Case | *Backspace Gear*

Haywood Mills is the owner of Backspace Gear, a new business in Kennewick, Washington, that manufactures backpacks for work, school, travel, and camping. Haywood has been working from a small shop making specialized packs for friends and acquaintances and wants to expand his business and his customer base. To do that, he needs to secure a business loan. Part of the process of securing a loan is to present a business plan that shows the current state of the market and offers projections about the company's future growth and earnings potential.

In addition to financial tables and calculations, Haywood's presentation needs to include charts and graphics that show a visual picture of the company's current financial status and where he hopes to take it. Haywood has asked for your help in creating the Excel charts and financial calculations he needs to include in his business plan.

STARTING DATA FILES

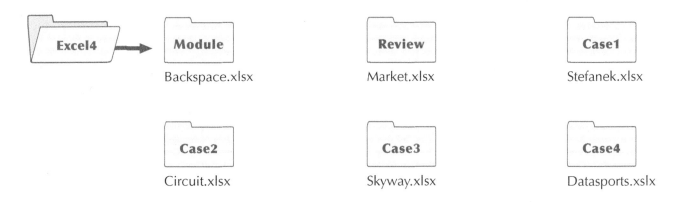

Excel4 → Module	Review	Case1
Backspace.xlsx	Market.xlsx	Stefanek.xlsx

Case2	Case3	Case4
Circuit.xlsx	Skyway.xlsx	Datasports.xslx

Session 4.1 Visual Overview:

A **data series** contains the actual values that are plotted or displayed on the chart. This data series shows the total number of each type of backpack.

The **category values** are the groups or categories to which the data series values belong. These category values show the different backpack types.

Each chart has a **data source**, which is the range that contains the data to display in the chart. The data source in the range A4:B10 is used in the pie chart.

A **chart**, or **graph**, is a visual representation of a set of data values. Charts show trends or relationships that may not be readily apparent from numbers alone.

The **chart area** contains the chart and all of the other chart elements.

A **data label** is text associated with an individual data marker, such as the percentage value next to a pie slice.

Chart **elements** are individual parts of the chart, such as the title or the legend.

The **vertical axis**, or **value axis**, displays the values from the data series.

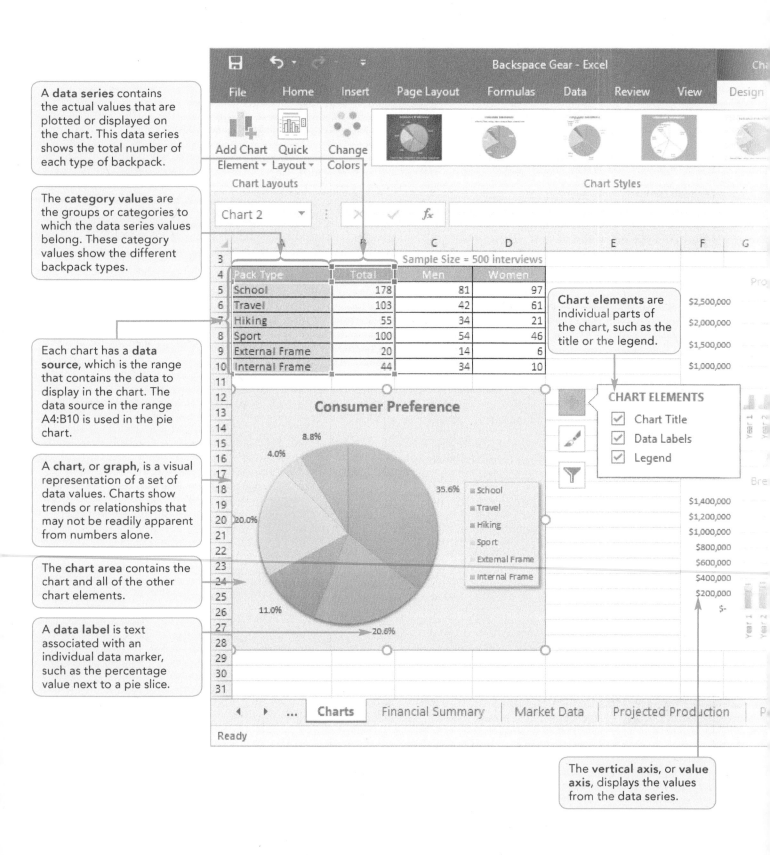

Chart Elements

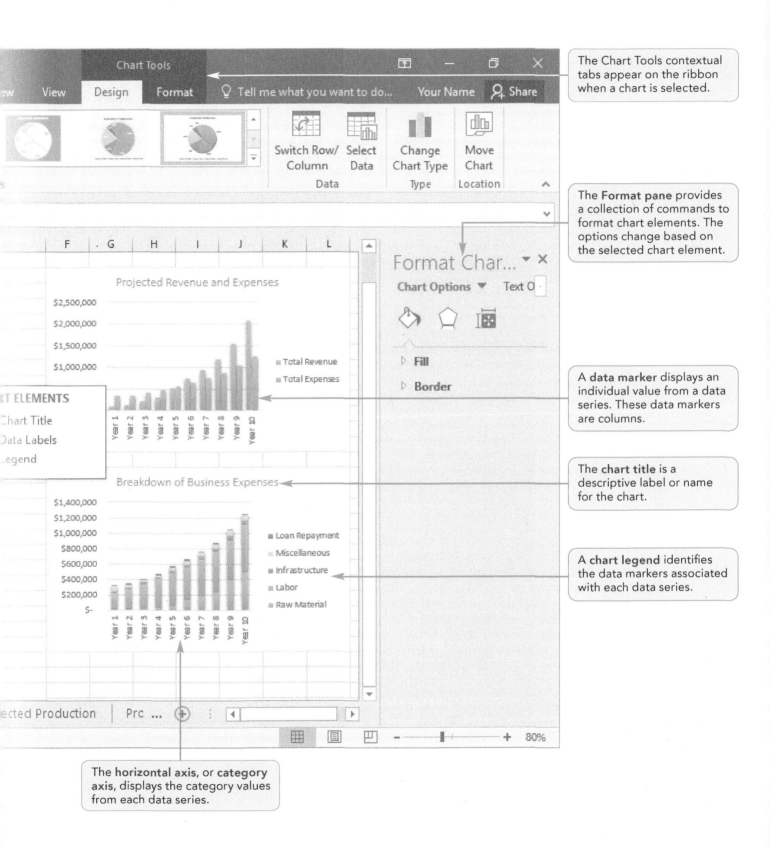

The Chart Tools contextual tabs appear on the ribbon when a chart is selected.

The **Format pane** provides a collection of commands to format chart elements. The options change based on the selected chart element.

A **data marker** displays an individual value from a data series. These data markers are columns.

The **chart title** is a descriptive label or name for the chart.

A **chart legend** identifies the data markers associated with each data series.

The **horizontal axis**, or **category axis**, displays the category values from each data series.

Introduction to Financial Functions

Financial functions are used to analyze loans, investments, and business statistics. Figure 4-1 lists some of the many Excel financial functions that are often used in business applications.

Figure 4-1   Financial functions for loans and investments

Function	Description
FV(rate,nper,pmt [,pv=0][,type=0])	Calculates the future value of an investment, where rate is the interest rate per period, nper is the total number of periods, pmt is the payment in each period, pv is the present value of the investment, and type indicates whether payments should be made at the end of the period (0) or the beginning of the period (1)
PMT(rate,nper,pv [,fv=0][,type=0])	Calculates the payments required each period on a loan or an investment, where fv is the future value of the investment
IPMT(rate,per,nper, pv[,fv=0][,type=0])	Calculates the amount of a loan payment devoted to paying the loan interest, where per is the number of the payment period
PPMT(rate,per,nper, pv[,fv=0][,type=0])	Calculates the amount of a loan payment devoted to paying off the principal of a loan
PV(rate,nper,pmt [,fv=0][,type=0])	Calculates the present value of a loan or an investment based on periodic, constant payments
NPER(rate,pmt,pv [,fv=0][,type=0])	Calculates the number of periods required to pay off a loan or an investment
RATE(nper,pmt,pv [,fv=0][,type=0])	Calculates the interest rate of a loan or an investment based on periodic, constant payments

The **PMT function** is used to calculate the payments required to completely repay a mortgage or other type of loan. Before you can use the PMT function, you need to understand some of the concepts and definitions associated with loans. The cost of a loan to the borrower is largely based on three factors—the principal, the interest, and the time required to repay the loan. **Principal** is the amount of the loan. **Interest** is the amount added to the principal by the lender. You can think of interest as a kind of "user fee" because the borrower is paying for the right to use the lender's money. Generally, interest is expressed at an annual percentage rate, or APR. For example, an 8 percent APR means that the annual interest rate on the loan is 8 percent of the amount owed to the lender.

An annual interest rate is divided by the number of payments per year (often monthly or quarterly). So, if the 8 percent annual interest rate is paid monthly, the resulting monthly interest rate is 1/12 of 8 percent, or about 0.67 percent per month. If payments are made quarterly, then the interest rate per quarter would be 1/4 of 8 percent, or 2 percent per quarter.

The third factor in calculating the cost of a loan is the time required to repay the loan, which is specified as the number of payment periods. The number of payment periods is based on the length of the loan multiplied by the number of payments per year. For example, a 10-year loan that is paid monthly has 120 payment periods (that is, 10 years × 12 months per year). If that same 10-year loan is paid quarterly, it has 40 payment periods (10 years × 4 quarters per year).

Using the PMT Function

To calculate the costs associated with a loan, such as the one that Haywood needs to fund the startup costs for Backspace Gear, you need the following information:

- The annual interest rate
- The number of payment periods per year
- The length of the loan in terms of the total number of payment periods
- The amount being borrowed
- When loan payments are due

The PMT function uses this information to calculate the payment required in each period to pay back the loan. The PMT function syntax is

```
PMT(rate,nper,pv[,fv=0][,type=0])
```

where *rate* is the interest rate for each payment period, *nper* is the total number of payment periods required to repay the loan, and *pv* is the present value of the loan or the amount that needs to be borrowed. The PMT function has two optional values—*fv* and *type*. The *fv* value is the future value of the loan. Because the intent with most loans is to repay them completely, the future value is equal to 0 by default. The *type* value specifies when the interest is charged on the loan, either at the end of the payment period (*type=0*), which is the default, or at the beginning of the payment period (*type=1*).

For example, you can use the PMT function to calculate the monthly payments required to repay a car loan of $15,000 over a five-year period at an annual interest rate of 9 percent. The *rate*, or interest rate per period value, is equal to 9 percent divided by 12 monthly payments, or 0.75 percent per month. The *nper*, or total number of payments value, is equal to 12×5 (12 monthly payments over five years) or 60 payments. The *pv*, or present value of the loan, is 15,000. In this case, because the loan will be repaid completely and payments will be made at the end of the month, you can accept the defaults for the *fv* and *type* values. The resulting PMT function can be written as

```
PMT(0.09/12, 5*12, 15000)
```

returning the value –311.38, or a monthly loan payment of $311.38. The PMT function returns a negative value because the monthly loan payments are treated as an expense to the borrower.

Rather than entering the argument values directly in the PMT function, you should include the loan terms in worksheet cells that are referenced in the function. This makes it clear what values are being used in the loan calculation. It also makes it easier to perform a what-if analysis exploring other loan options.

Haywood wants to borrow $150,000 to help start up his new business at a 6 percent annual interest rate. He plans to repay the loan in 10 years with monthly payments. You will calculate the amount of his monthly loan payment.

To enter the terms of the loan:

1. Open the **Backspace** workbook located in the **Excel4 > Module** folder included with your Data Files, and then save the workbook as **Backspace Gear** in the location specified by your instructor.

2. In the Documentation sheet, enter your name in cell B3 and the date in cell B4.

3. Go to the **Business Loan** worksheet. You'll use this worksheet to calculate the monthly payments that will be due on Haywood's loan.

4. In cell **B4**, enter **$150,000** as the loan amount.

5. In cell **B5**, enter **6.00%** as the annual interest rate.

▶ 6. In cell **B6**, enter **12** as the number of payments per year, indicating that the loan will be repaid monthly.

▶ 7. In cell **B7**, enter the formula **=B5/B6** to calculate the interest rate per period. In this case, the 6 percent interest rate is divided by 12 payments per year, returning a monthly interest rate of 0.50 percent.

▶ 8. In cell **B8**, enter **10** as the number of years in the loan.

▶ 9. In cell **B9**, enter **=B6*B8** to multiply the number of payments per year by the number of years in the loan, returning a value of 120 payments needed to repay the loan.

Next, you will use the PMT function to calculate the monthly payment needed to repay the loan in 10 years.

To calculate the monthly payment:

▶ 1. Select cell **B11** to make it the active cell. You will enter the PMT function in this cell.

▶ 2. On the ribbon, click the **Formulas** tab.

▶ 3. In the Function Library group, click the **Financial** button, and then scroll down and click **PMT** in the list of financial functions. The Function Arguments dialog box opens.

TIP

For the Rate argument, you must enter the interest rate per payment, not the annual interest rate.

▶ 4. With the insertion point in the Rate box, click cell **B7** in the worksheet to enter the reference to the cell with the interest rate per month.

▶ 5. Click in the **Nper** box, and then click cell **B9** in the worksheet to enter the reference to the cell with the total number of monthly payments required to repay the loan.

▶ 6. Click in the **Pv** box, and then click cell **B4** in the worksheet to enter the reference to the cell with the present value of the loan. See Figure 4-2.

Figure 4-2   **Function Arguments dialog box for the PMT function**

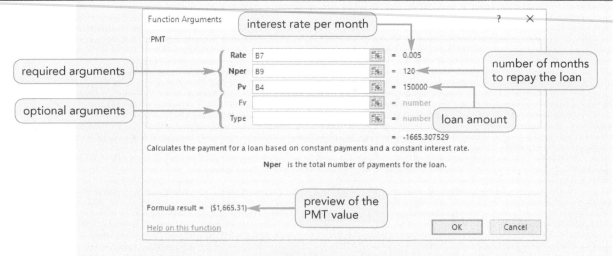

7. Click the **OK** button. The monthly payment amount ($1,665.31) appears in cell B11. The number is displayed in parentheses and in a red font to indicate a negative value because that is the payment that Backspace Gear must make rather than income it receives.

8. In cell B12, enter the formula **=B6*B11** to multiply the number of payments per year by the monthly payment amount, calculating the total payments for the entire year. The annual payments would be ($19,983.69), shown as a negative number to indicate money being paid out.

9. Select cell **B11**. The calculations for the business loan are complete. See Figure 4-3.

| Figure 4-3 | Monthly and annual costs of the business loan |

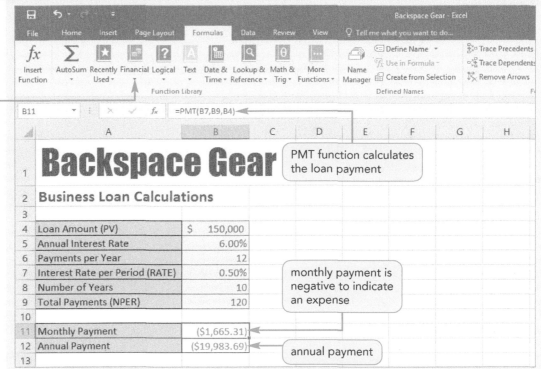

click to view a list of financial functions

B11   =PMT(B7,B9,B4)

PMT function calculates the loan payment

Backspace Gear

Business Loan Calculations

	A	B
4	Loan Amount (PV)	$ 150,000
5	Annual Interest Rate	6.00%
6	Payments per Year	12
7	Interest Rate per Period (RATE)	0.50%
8	Number of Years	10
9	Total Payments (NPER)	120
10		
11	Monthly Payment	($1,665.31)
12	Annual Payment	($19,983.69)
13		

monthly payment is negative to indicate an expense

annual payment

Haywood wants to see the financial impact of taking out a larger loan.

10. In cell **B4**, change the loan amount to **250,000**. With a loan of that size, the monthly payment increases to $2,775.51, and the annual total increases to $33,306.15.

Although a larger loan might help the business get off the ground, Haywood does not want the company to take such a large debt.

11. In cell **B4**, return the loan amount to **150,000**.

Based on your analysis, Backspace Gear would spend about $20,000 a year repaying the $150,000 business loan over the next 10 years. Haywood wants this information included in the Projected Cash Flow worksheet, which estimates Backspace Gear's annual revenue, expenses, and cash flow for the first 10 years of its operation. You will enter that amount as an expense for each year, completing the projected cash flow calculations.

To enter the loan repayment amount in the cash flow projection:

▶ **1.** Go to the **Projected Cash Flow** worksheet, and review the estimated annual revenue, expenses, and cash flow for the next decade.

▶ **2.** In cell **B20**, enter **20,000** as the projected yearly amount of the loan repayment. Because the projected cash flow is a rough estimate of the projected income and expenses, it is not necessary to include the exact dollar-and-cents cost of the loan.

▶ **3.** Copy the annual loan payment in cell **B20** into the range **C20:K20** to enter the projected annual loan payment in each year of the cash flow projections. See Figure 4-4.

Figure 4-4   Completed Projected Cash Flow worksheet

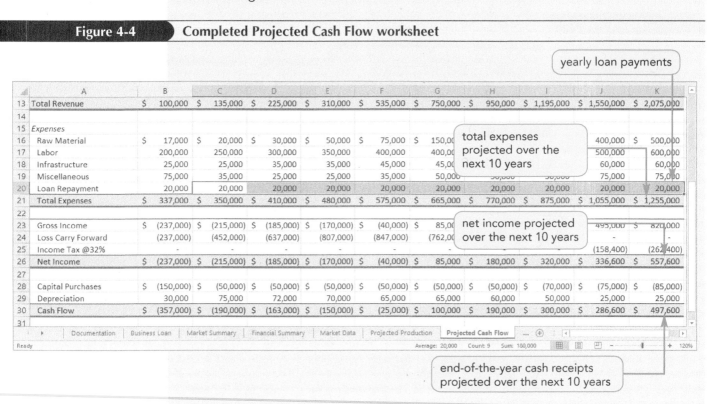

After including the projected annual loan payments, the Projected Cash Flow worksheet shows that Backspace Gear's projected net income at the end of the tenth year would be about $560,000, assuming all of the other projections are accurate. Based on these figures, the company should have almost $500,000 in cash at that time.

INSIGHT

Using Functions to Manage Personal Finances

Excel has many financial functions to manage personal finances. The following list can help you determine which function to use for the most common personal finance calculations:

- To determine how much an investment will be worth after a series of monthly payments at some future time, use the FV (future value) function.
- To determine how much you have to spend each month to repay a loan or mortgage within a set period of time, use the PMT (payment) function.
- To determine how much of your monthly loan payment is used to pay the interest, use the IPMT (interest payment) function.
- To determine how much of your monthly loan payment is used for repaying the principal, use the PPMT (principal payment) function.
- To determine the largest loan or mortgage you can afford given a set monthly payment, use the PV (present value) function.
- To determine how long it will take to pay off a loan with constant monthly payments, use the NPER (number of periods) function.

For most loan and investment calculations, you need to enter the annual interest rate divided by the number of times the interest is compounded during the year. If interest is compounded monthly, divide the annual interest rate by 12; if interest is compounded quarterly, divide the annual rate by four. You must also convert the length of the loan or investment into the number of payments per year. If you will make payments monthly, multiply the number of years of the loan or investment by 12.

Now that you have calculated the cost of the business loan and determined its impact on future cash flows, your next task is to summarize Haywood's business proposal for Backspace Gear. An effective tool for summarizing complex scientific and financial data is a chart.

Getting Started with Excel Charts

Charts show trends or relationships in data that are easier to see than by looking at the actual numbers. Creating a chart is a several-step process that involves choosing the chart type, selecting the data to display in the chart, and formatting the chart's appearance.

REFERENCE

Creating a Chart

- Select the range containing the data you want to chart.
- On the Insert tab, in the Charts group, click the Recommended Charts button or a button representing the general chart type, and then click the chart you want to create (or click the Quick Analysis button, click the Charts category, and then click the chart you want to create).
- On the Chart Tools Design tab, in the Location group, click the Move Chart button, select whether to embed the chart in a worksheet or place it in a chart sheet, and then click the OK button.

Excel provides 59 types of charts organized into the 10 categories described in Figure 4-5. Within each chart category are chart variations called **chart subtypes**. You can also design your own custom chart types to meet the specific needs of your reports and projects.

Figure 4-5 **Excel chart types and subtypes**

Chart Category	Description	Chart Subtypes
Column or Bar	Compares values from different categories. Values are indicated by the height of the columns or the length of a bar.	2-D Column, 3-D Column, 2-D Bar, 3-D Bar
Hierarchy	Displays data that is organized into a hierarchy of categories where the size of the groups is based on a number.	Treemap, Sunburst
Waterfall or Stock	Displays financial cash flow values or stock market data.	Waterfall, Stock
Line	Compares values from different categories. Values are indicated by the height of the lines. Often used to show trends and changes over time.	2-D Line, 3-D Line, 2-D Area, 3-D Area
Statistic	Displays a chart summarizing the distribution of values from a sample population.	Histogram, Pareto, Box and Whisker
Pie	Compares relative values of different categories to the whole. Values are indicated by the areas of the pie slices.	2-D Pie, 3-D Pie, Doughnut
X Y (Scatter)	Shows the patterns or relationship between two or more sets of values. Often used in scientific studies and statistical analyses.	Scatter, Bubble
Surface or Radar	Compares three sets of values in a three-dimensional chart.	Surface, Radar
Combo	Combines two or more chart types to make the data easy to visualize, especially when the data is widely varied.	Clustered Column-Line, Clustered Column-Line on Secondary Axis, Stacked Area-Clustered Column
PivotChart	Creates a chart summarizing data from a PivotTable.	*none*

Sometimes more than one chart can be used for the same data. Figure 4-6 presents the same labor cost data displayed as a line chart, a bar chart, and column charts. The column charts are shown with both a 2-D subtype that has two-dimensional, or flat, columns and a 3-D subtype that gives the illusion of three-dimensional columns. The various charts and chart subtypes are better suited for different data. You should choose the one that makes the data easiest to interpret.

Figure 4-6   Same data displayed as different chart types

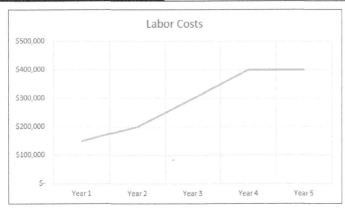

Line chart

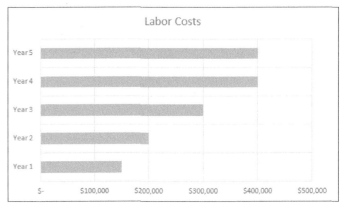

Bar chart

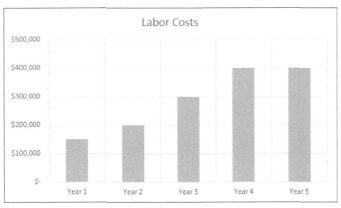

2-D Column chart

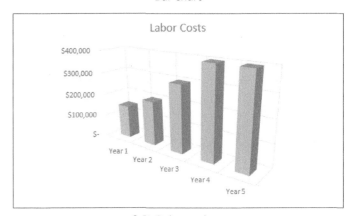

3-D Column chart

Creating a Pie Chart

TIP

Don't include row or column totals in the pie chart data because Excel will treat those totals as another category.

The first chart you will create is a **pie chart**, which is a chart in the shape of a circle divided into slices like a pie. Each slice represents a single value from a data series. Larger data values are represented with bigger pie slices. The relative sizes of the slices let you visually compare the data values and see how much each contributes to the whole. Pie charts are most effective with six or fewer slices and when each slice is large enough to view easily.

Selecting the Data Source

The data displayed in a chart comes from the chart's data source, which includes one or more data series and a series of category values. A data series contains the actual values that are plotted on the chart, whereas the category values provide descriptive labels for each data series and are used to group those series. Category values are usually located in the first column or first row of the data source. The data series are usually placed in subsequent columns or rows. However, you can select category and data values from anywhere within a workbook.

Over the next 10 years Backspace Gear plans to produce school, travel, hiking, sport, external frame (for camping), and internal frame (for camping) packs. Haywood conducted a consumer survey of 500 adults to determine which of these will likely have the greatest demand in the Washington area. You will use the survey results, which Hayward entered in the Market Summary worksheet, as the data source for a pie chart.

To select the survey results as the pie chart's data source:

1. Go to the **Market Summary** worksheet. A summary of the survey results is stored in the range A4:D10.

2. Select the range **A4:B10** containing the overall results of the survey for both men and women. See Figure 4-7.

Figure 4-7   Selected chart data source

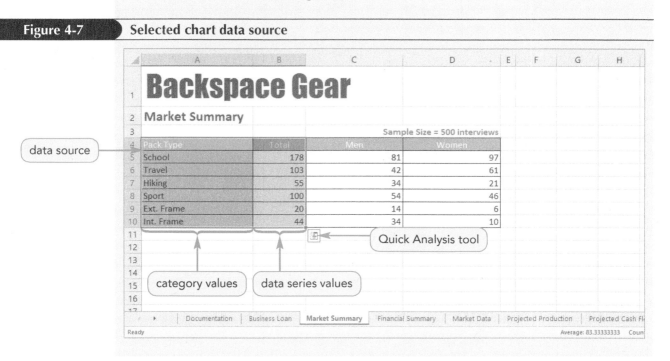

The selected data source covers two columns. The category values are located in the first column, and the data series that you will chart is located in the second column. When the selected range is taller than it is wide, Excel assumes that the category values and data series are laid out in columns. Conversely, a data source that is wider than it is tall is assumed to have the category values and data series laid out in rows. Note that the first row in this selected data source contains labels that identify the category values (Pack Type) and the data series name (Total).

Charting with the Quick Analysis Tool

After you select a data source, the Quick Analysis tool appears. The Charts category contains a list of chart types that are often appropriate for the selected data source. For the market survey results, a pie chart provides the best way to compare the preferences for the six types of packs that Backspace Gear plans to produce. You will use the Quick Analysis tool to generate the pie chart for Haywood.

To create a pie chart with the Quick Analysis tool:

TIP

You can also insert a chart by selecting a chart type in the Charts group on the Insert tab.

1. With the range A4:B10 still selected, click the **Quick Analysis** button 📳 in the lower-right corner of the selected range (or press the **Ctrl+Q** keys) to open the Quick Analysis tool.

2. Click the **Charts** category. The chart types you will most likely want to use with the selected data source are listed. See Figure 4-8.

Figure 4-8

Figure 4-8   **Charts category of the Quick Analysis tool**

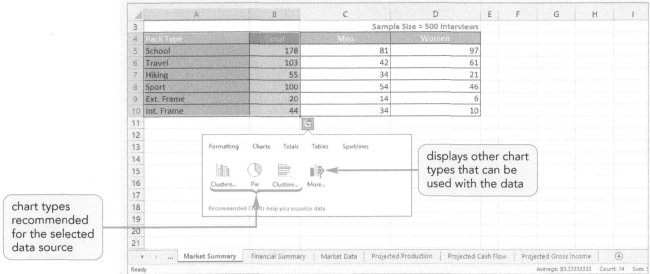

chart types recommended for the selected data source

displays other chart types that can be used with the data

3. Click **Pie**. A pie chart appears in the Market Summary worksheet. Each slice is a different size based on its value in the data series. The biggest slice represents the 178 people in the survey who selected a school pack as their most likely purchase from Backspace Gear. The smallest slice of the pie represents the 20 individuals who selected the external frame pack. See Figure 4-9.

Figure 4-9   **Pie chart in the Market Summary worksheet**

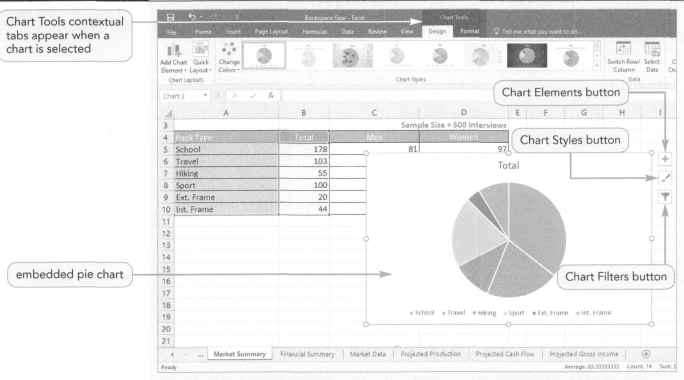

Chart Tools contextual tabs appear when a chart is selected

Chart Elements button

Chart Styles button

Chart Filters button

embedded pie chart

When you create or select a chart, two Chart Tools contextual tabs appear on the ribbon. The Design tab provides commands to specify the chart's overall design. The Format tab supplies the tools needed to format the graphic shapes found in the chart, such as the chart's border or the slices from a pie chart. When you select a worksheet cell or another object that is not a chart, the Chart Tools contextual tabs disappear until you reselect the chart.

Moving and Resizing a Chart

TIP

You can print an embedded chart with its worksheet, or you can print only the selected embedded chart without its worksheet.

Charts are either placed in their own chart sheets or embedded in a worksheet. When you create a chart, it is embedded in the worksheet that contains the data source. For example, the chart shown in Figure 4-9 is embedded in the Market Summary worksheet. The advantage of an **embedded chart** is that you can display the chart alongside its data source and any text that describes the chart's meaning and purpose. Because an embedded chart covers worksheet cells, you might have to move or resize the chart so that important information is not hidden.

Before you can move or resize a chart, it must be selected. A selected chart has a **selection box** around the chart for moving or resizing the chart. **Sizing handles**, which appear along the edges of the selection box, change the chart's width and height.

Haywood wants the pie chart to appear directly below its data source in the Market Summary worksheet. You will move and resize the chart to fit this location.

To move and resize the survey results pie chart:

1. Point to an empty area of the selected chart. The pointer changes to and "Chart Area" appears in a ScreenTip.

Be sure to drag the chart from an empty part of the chart area so the entire chart moves, not just chart elements within the chart.

2. Hold down the **Alt** key, drag the chart until its upper-left corner snaps to the upper-left corner of cell **A12**, and then release the mouse button and the **Alt** key. The upper-left corner of the chart is aligned with the upper-left corner of cell A12.

   Trouble? If the pie chart resizes or does not move to the new location, you probably didn't drag the chart from an empty part of the chart area. Press the Ctrl+Z keys to undo your last action, and then repeat Steps 1 and 2, being sure to drag the pie chart from the chart area.

   The chart moves to a new location, but it still needs to be resized.

3. Point to the sizing handle in the lower-right corner of the selection box until the pointer changes to .

4. Hold down the **Alt** key, drag the sizing handle up to the lower-right corner of cell **D26**, and then release the mouse button and the **Alt** key. The chart resizes to cover the range A12:D26 and remains selected. See Figure 4-10.

Figure 4-10	Moved and resized pie chart

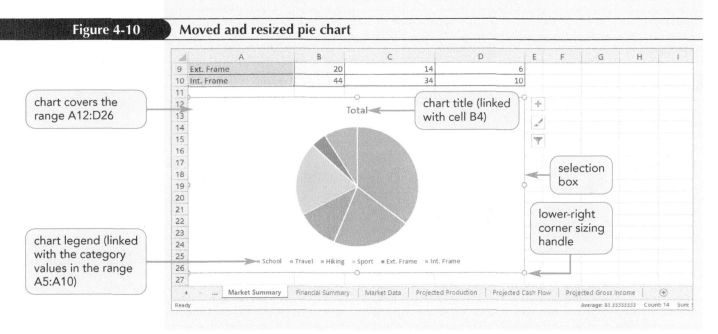

chart covers the range A12:D26

chart title (linked with cell B4)

selection box

lower-right corner sizing handle

chart legend (linked with the category values in the range A5:A10)

Note that three buttons appear to the right of the selected chart: the Chart Elements button, the Chart Styles button, and the Chart Filters button. You will use these to modify the chart's appearance.

Working with Chart Elements

Every chart contains elements that can be formatted individually. For example, a pie chart has three elements—the chart title, the chart legend identifying each pie slice, and data labels that provide a data value associated with each slice. The Chart Elements button that appears to the right of the selected chart lists the elements that can be added or removed from the chart. When you add or remove a chart element, the other elements resize to fit in the unoccupied space in the chart. Live Preview shows how changing an element will affect the chart's appearance so that you can experiment with different formats before applying them.

Haywood doesn't want the pie chart to include a title because the text in cell B4 and the data in the range A5:B10 sufficiently explain the chart's purpose. However, he does want to display the data values next to the pie slices. You will remove the chart title element and add the data labels element.

To remove the chart title and add data labels:

TIP

You can also add and remove chart elements with the Add Chart Element button in the Chart Layouts group on the Chart Tools Design tab.

1. With the pie chart still selected, click the **Chart Elements** button. A menu of chart elements that are available for the pie chart opens. As the checkmarks indicate, only the chart title and the chart legend are displayed in the pie chart.

2. Click the **Chart Title** check box to deselect it. The chart title is removed from the pie chart, and the chart elements resize to fill the space.

3. Point to the **Data Labels** check box. Live Preview shows how the chart will look when the data labels show a count of responses within each category.

4. Click the **Data Labels** check box to select it. The data labels are added to the chart. See Figure 4-11.

| Figure 4-11 | Displayed chart elements |

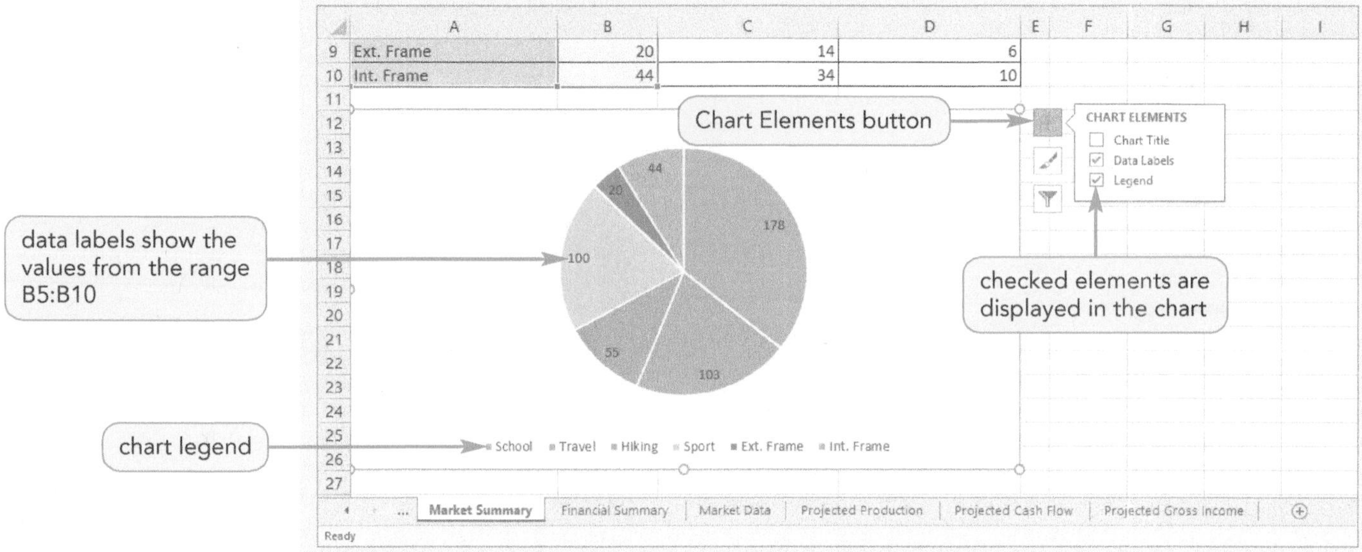

data labels show the values from the range B5:B10

chart legend

Chart Elements button

checked elements are displayed in the chart

Choosing a Chart Style

Chart elements can be formatted individually or as a group using one of the many built-in Excel chart styles. In the pie chart you just created, the format of the chart title, the location of the legend, and the colors of the pie slices are all part of the default pie chart style. You can quickly change the appearance of a chart by selecting a different style from the Chart Styles gallery. Live Preview shows how a chart style will affect the chart.

Haywood wants the pie slices to have a raised, three-dimensional look. You will explore different chart styles to find a style that best fulfills his request.

To choose a different chart style for the backpack production pie chart:

TIP

You can also select a chart style from the Chart Styles gallery in the Chart Styles group on the Chart Tools Design tab.

1. Click the **Chart Styles** button next to the selected pie chart. The Chart Styles gallery opens.

2. Point to different styles in the gallery. Live Preview shows the impact of each chart style on the pie chart's appearance.

3. Scroll to the bottom of the gallery, and then click the **Style 12** chart style. The chart style is applied to the pie chart. See Figure 4-12.

Figure 4-12   **Chart Styles gallery**

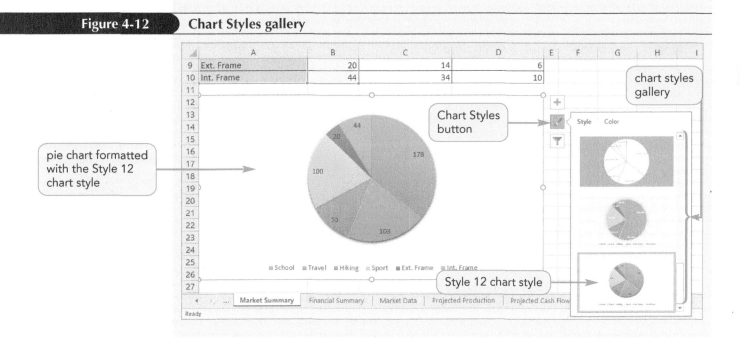

pie chart formatted with the Style 12 chart style

Chart Styles button

chart styles gallery

Style 12 chart style

Formatting a Chart Legend

You can fine-tune a chart style by formatting individual chart elements. Using the Chart Elements button, you can open a submenu for each element that includes formatting options, such as the element's location within the chart. You can also open a Format pane, which has more options for formatting the selected chart element.

The default location for the pie chart legend is alongside the chart's bottom edge. Haywood thinks the chart would look better if the legend were aligned with the right edge of the chart. You'll make that change.

To format the pie chart legend:

▶ **1.** With the pie chart still selected, click the **Chart Elements** button [+].

▶ **2.** Point to **Legend** in the Chart Elements menu, and then click the **right arrow** icon next to the Legend entry, displaying a submenu of formatting options for that chart element.

▶ **3.** Point to **Left** to see a Live Preview of the pie chart with the legend aligned along the left side of the chart area.

▶ **4.** Click **Right** to place the legend along the right side of the chart area. The pie shifts to the left to make room for the legend.

The Chart Elements button also provides access to the Format pane, which has more design options for the selected chart element. Haywood wants you to add a drop shadow to the legend similar to the pie chart's drop shadow, change the fill color to a light gold, and add a light gray border. You'll use the Format pane to make these changes.

To use the Format pane to format the chart legend:

TIP

You can also double-click any chart element to open its Format pane.

1. On the Legend submenu for the entry, click **More Options**. The Format pane opens on the right side of the workbook window. The Format Legend title indicates that the pane contains options relating to chart legend styles.

2. Click the **Fill & Line** button ⬟ near the top of the Format pane to display options for setting the fill color and border style of the legend.

3. Click **Fill** to expand the fill options, and then click the **Solid fill** option button to apply a solid fill color to the legend. Color and Transparency options appear below the fill color options.

4. Click the **Fill Color** button, and then click the **Gold, Accent 4, Lighter 40%** theme color (the fourth color in the eighth column) to apply a light gold fill color to the legend.

5. Click **Border** to display the border options, and then click the **Solid line** option button. Additional border options appear below the border options.

6. Click the **Outline color** button, and then click the **Gray - 50%, Accent 3, Lighter 40%** theme color (the fourth color in the seventh column) to add a gray border around the legend.

7. At the top of the Format Legend pane, click the **Effects** button ⬠ to display options for special visual effects.

8. Click **Shadow** to display the shadow options, and then next to the **Presets** button, click □▾ to display the Shadow gallery. See Figure 4-13.

Figure 4-13   Formatted chart legend

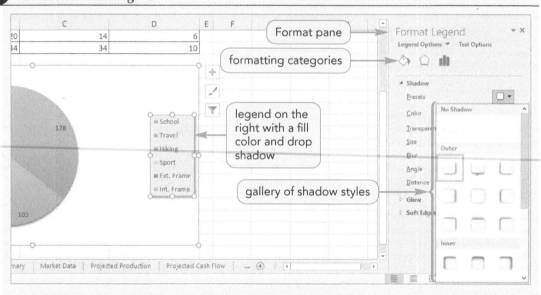

9. Click the **Offset Diagonal Bottom Right** button in the first row and first column to apply the drop shadow effect to the legend.

Formatting Pie Chart Labels

You can modify the content and appearance of data labels, selecting what the labels contain as well as where the labels are positioned. Data labels are placed where they best fit to keep the chart nicely proportioned, but you can change their location. From the Format pane, you can center the labels on the pie slices, place them outside of the slices, or set them as data callouts with each label placed in a text bubble and connected to its slice with a callout line. You can also change the text and number styles used in the data labels. You can also drag and drop individual data labels, placing them anywhere within the chart. When a data label is placed far from its pie slice, a **leader line** is added to connect the data label to its pie slice.

The pie chart data labels display the number of potential customers interested in each pack type, but this information also appears on the worksheet directly above the chart. Haywood wants to include data labels that add new information to the chart—in this case, the percentage that each pack type received in the survey. You'll change the label options.

To display percentage labels in the pie chart:

TIP

You can also format chart elements using the formatting buttons on the Home tab or on the Chart Tools Format tab.

1. At the top of the Format pane, click the **Legend Options** arrow to display a menu of chart elements, and then click **Series "Total" Data Labels** to display the formatting options for data labels. The title of the Format pane changes to Format Data Labels and includes formatting options for data labels. Selection boxes appear around every data label in the pie chart.

2. Near the top of the Format Data Labels pane, click the **Label Options** button [chart icon], and then click **Label Options**, if necessary, to display the options for the label contents and position. Data labels can contain series names, category names, values, and percentages.

3. Click the **Percentage** check box to add the percentage associated with each pie slice to the pie chart.

4. Click the **Value** check box to deselect it, removing the data series values from the data labels and showing only the percentages. For example, the pie chart shows that 35 percent of the survey responders indicated a willingness to buy Backspace Gear packs designed for school use.

5. Click the **Outside End** option button to move the labels outside of the pie slices. The labels are easier to read in this location.

6. Scroll down the Format pane, and then click **Number** to show the number formatting options for the data labels.

7. Click the **Category** box to display the number formats, and then click **Percentage**.

8. In the Decimal places box, select **2**, type **1**, and then press the **Enter** key. The percentages are displayed with one decimal place. See Figure 4-14.

Figure 4-14   **Formatted data labels**

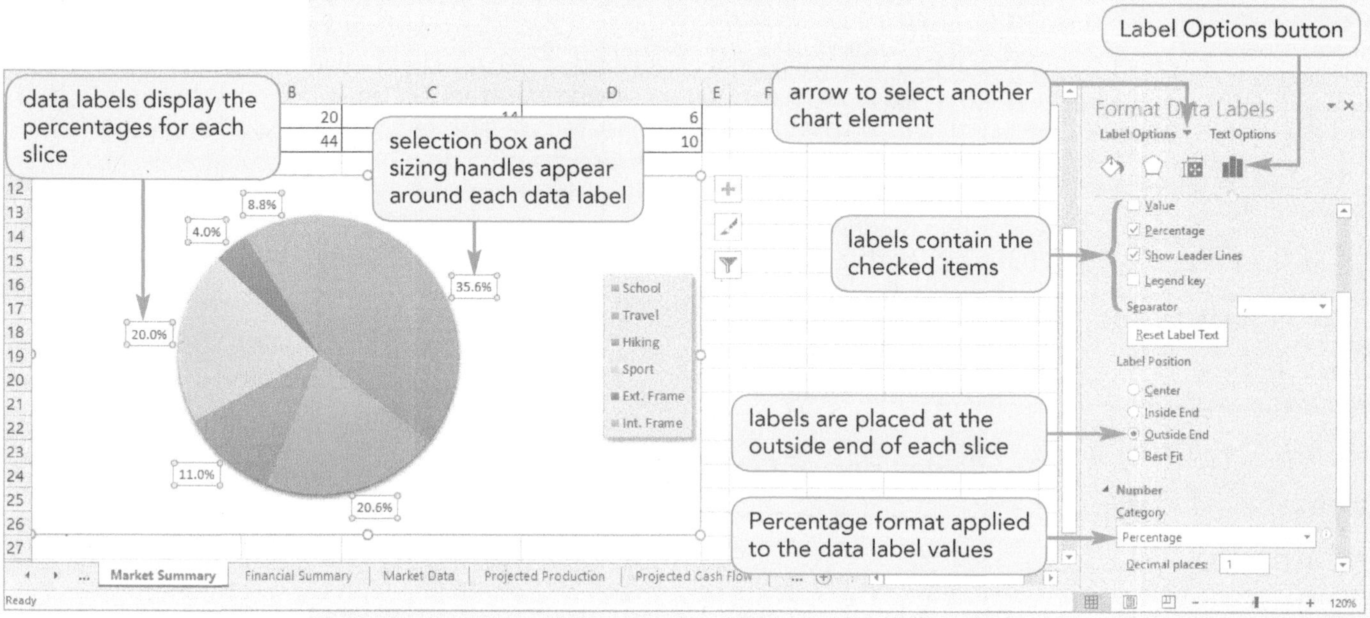

data labels display the percentages for each slice

selection box and sizing handles appear around each data label

arrow to select another chart element

Label Options button

labels contain the checked items

labels are placed at the outside end of each slice

Percentage format applied to the data label values

Changing the Pie Slice Colors

A pie slice is an example of a data marker representing a single data value from a data series. You can format the appearance of individual data markers to make them stand out from the others. Pie slice colors should be as distinct as possible to avoid confusion. Depending on the printer quality or the monitor resolution, it might be difficult to distinguish between similarly colored slices. If data labels are displayed within the slice, you also need enough contrast between the slice color and the data label color to make the text readable.

Haywood is concerned that the dark blue color of the Ext. Frame slice will be too dark when printed. He wants you to change it to a light shade of green.

To change the color of a pie slice:

▶ 1. Click any pie slice to select all of the slices in the pie chart.

▶ 2. Click the **Ext. Frame** slice, which is the darker blue slice that represents 4.0% percent of the pie. Only that slice is selected, as you can see from the sizing handles that appear at each corner of the slice.

▶ 3. On the ribbon, click the **Home** tab.

▶ 4. In the Font group, click the **Fill Color button arrow** ⬛▾, and then click the **Green, Accent 6, Lighter 40%** theme color (the fourth color in the last column) of the gallery. The pie slice changes to a light green, and the chart legend automatically updates to reflect that change.

You can also change the colors of all the pie slices by clicking the Chart Styles button ![icon] next to the selected chart, clicking the Color heading, and then selecting a color scheme.

INSIGHT

Exploding a Pie Chart

Pie slices do not need to be fixed within the pie. An **exploded pie chart** moves one slice away from the others as if someone were taking the piece away from the pie. Exploded pie charts are useful for emphasizing one category above all of the others. For example, to emphasize the fact that Backspace Gear will be producing more school packs than any other type of pack, you could explode that single slice, moving it away from the other slices.

To explode a pie slice, first click the pie to select all of the slices, and then click the single slice you want to move. Make sure that a selection box appears around only that slice. Drag the slice away from the pie to offset it from the others. You can explode multiple slices by selecting each slice in turn and dragging them away. To explode all of the slices, select the entire pie and drag the pointer away from the pie's center. Each slice will be exploded and separated from the others. Although you can explode more than one slice, the resulting pie chart is rarely effective as a visual aid to the reader.

Formatting the Chart Area

The chart's background, which is called the chart area, can also be formatted using fill colors, border styles, and special effects such as drop shadows and blurred edges. The chart area fill color used in the pie chart is white, which blends in with the worksheet background. Haywood wants you to change the fill color to a medium green to match the worksheet's color scheme and to make the chart stand out better.

To change the chart area color:

TIP
You can select any chart element using the Chart Elements box in the Current Selection group on the Chart Tools Format tab.

1. Click a blank area within the chart, not containing either a pie slice or the chart legend. The chart area is selected, which you can verify because the Format pane title changes to "Format Chart Area."

2. On the Home tab, in the Font group, click the **Fill Color button arrow** ![icon], and then click the **Green, Accent 6, Lighter 60%** theme color (the last color in the third row). The chart area fill color is now medium green. See Figure 4-15.

Figure 4-15   **Chart area fill color**

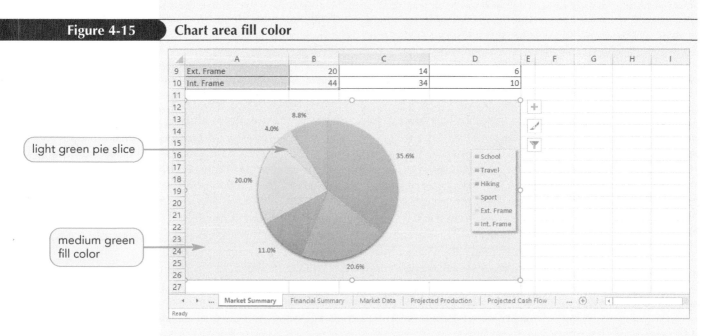

You are done formatting the pie chart, so you will close the Format pane to keep the window uncluttered.

▸ **3.** Click the **Close** button ☒ on the title bar of the Format pane. The pane closes, leaving more space for viewing the worksheet contents.

Performing What-If Analyses with Charts

Because a chart is linked to its data source, any changes in the data source values will be automatically reflected in the chart. For the Market Survey pie chart, the chart title is linked to the text in cell B4, the size of the pie slices is based on the production goals in the range B5:B10, and the category names are linked to the category values in the range A5:A10. Any changes to these cells affect the chart's content and appearance. This makes charts a powerful tool for data exploration and what-if analysis.

Haywood wants to see how the pie chart would change if the survey results were updated.

To apply a what-if analysis to the pie chart:

▸ **1.** In cell **B7**, enter **100** to change the number of individuals who expressed an interest in Backspace hiking packs to 100. The Hiking slice automatically increases in size, changing from 11 percent to 18.3 percent. The size of the remaining slices and their percentages are reduced to compensate.

▸ **2.** In cell **B7**, restore the value to **55**. The pie slices return to their initial sizes, and the percentages return to their initial values.

Haywood wants you to change the category names "Ext. Frame" and "Int. Frame" to "External Frame" and "Internal Frame."

▸ **3.** Click cell **A9**, and then change the text to **External Frame**.

> **4.** Click cell **A10**, and then change the text to **Internal Frame**. The legend text in the pie chart automatically changes to reflect the new text.

Another type of what-if analysis is to **filter** the data source, which limits the data to fewer values. For example, the pie chart shows the survey results for all six types of packs that Backspace Gear will manufacture, but you can filter the pie chart so that it shows only the packs you select.

Haywood wants you to filter the pie chart so that it compares only the packs used for school, travel, and sport.

To filter the pie chart to show only three packs:

> **1.** Click the pie chart to select it.

> **2.** Click the **Chart Filters** button next to the chart to open a menu listing the chart categories.

> **3.** Click the **Hiking**, **External Frame**, and **Internal Frame** check boxes to deselect them, leaving only the School, Travel, and Sport check boxes selected.

> **4.** At the bottom of the Chart Filters menu, click the **Apply** button. Excel filters the chart, showing only the three marked pack types. After filtering the data, the chart shows that 46.7 percent of the survey respondents would buy the School pack out of the choice of school, travel, and sport packs. See Figure 4-16.

| Figure 4-16 | Filtered pie chart |

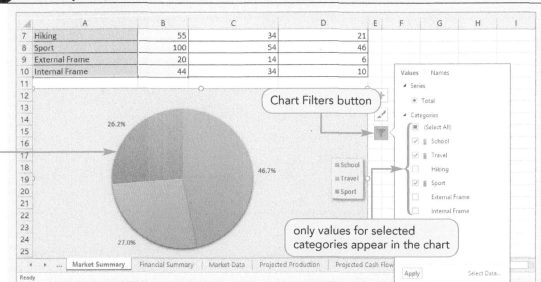

> **5.** In the Categories section of the Chart Filters menu, double-click the **Select All** check box to reselect all six pack types.

> **6.** Click the **Apply** button to update the chart's appearance.

> **7.** Press the **Esc** key to close the menu, leaving the chart selected.

The pie chart is complete. Next you'll create column charts to examine Haywood's proposed production schedule for the next years.

Creating a Column Chart

A **column chart** displays data values as columns with the height of each column based on the data value. A column chart turned on its side is called a **bar chart**, with the length of the bar determined by the data value. It is better to use column and bar charts than pie charts when the number of categories is large or the data values are close in value. Figure 4-17 displays the same data as a pie chart and a column chart. As you can see, it's difficult to determine which pie slice is biggest and by how much. It is much simpler to make those comparisons in a column or bar chart.

Figure 4-17	Data displayed as a pie chart and a column chart

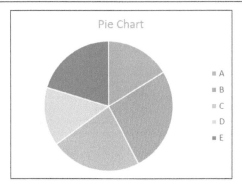
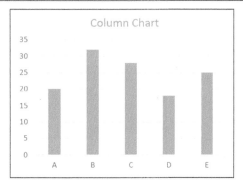

Comparing Column Chart Subtypes

Unlike pie charts, which can show only one data series, column and bar charts can display multiple data series. Figure 4-18 shows three examples of column charts in which four data series named School, Travel, Hiking, and Sport are plotted against one category series (Years).

Figure 4-18	Column chart subtypes

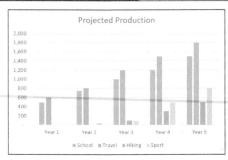
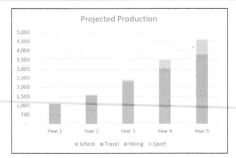
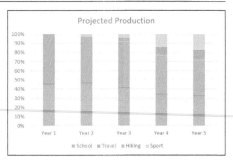

Clustered Column   Stacked Column   100% Stacked Column

The **clustered column chart** displays the data series in separate columns side by side so that you can compare the relative heights of the columns in the three series. The clustered column chart in Figure 4-18 compares the number of packs produced in year 1 through year 5. Note that Backspace Gear mostly produces school and travel packs in years 1 through 3 with hiking and sport packs production increasing in years 4 and 5.

The **stacked column chart** places the data series values within combined columns showing how much is contributed by each series. The stacked column chart in Figure 4-18 gives information on the total number of packs produced each year and how each year's production is split among the four types of packs.

Finally, the **100% stacked column chart** makes the same comparison as the stacked column chart except that the stacked sections are expressed as percentages. As you can see from the 100% stacked column chart in Figure 4-18, school and travel packs account for about 100% of the production in year 1 and steadily decline to 70% of the production in year 5 as Backspace Gear introduces hiking and sport packs.

Creating a Clustered Column Chart

The process for creating a column chart is the same as for creating a pie chart: selecting the data source and choosing a chart type and subtype. After the chart is embedded in the worksheet, you can move and resize the chart as well as change the chart's design, layout, and format.

Haywood wants his business plan to show the projected revenue and expenses for Backspace Gear's first 10 years. Because this requires comparing the data series values, you will create a clustered column chart.

To create a clustered column chart showing projected revenue and expenses:

▶ **1.** Go to the **Projected Cash Flow** worksheet.

▶ **2.** Select the nonadjacent range **A4:K4,A13:K13,A21:K21** containing the Year categories in row 4, the Total Revenue data series in row 13, and the Total Expenses data series in row 21. Because you selected a nonadjacent range, the Quick Analysis tool is not available.

TIP

You can also open the Insert Chart dialog box to see the chart types recommended for the selected data source.

▶ **3.** On the ribbon, click the **Insert** tab. The Charts group contains buttons for inserting different types of charts.

▶ **4.** In the Charts group, click the **Recommended Charts** button. The Insert Chart dialog box opens with a gallery of suggested charts for the selected data. See Figure 4-19.

| Figure 4-19 | Recommended Charts tab in the Insert Chart dialog box |

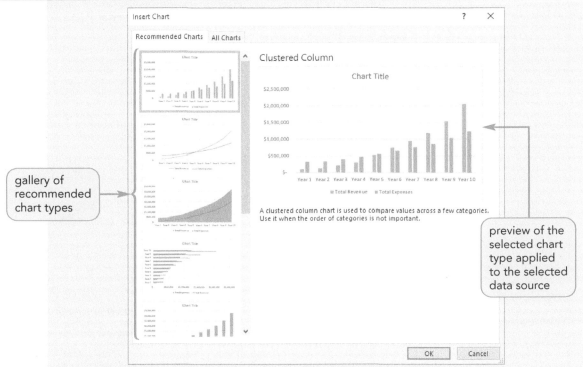

gallery of recommended chart types

preview of the selected chart type applied to the selected data source

▶ **5.** Make sure the **Clustered Column** chart is selected, and then click the **OK** button. The clustered column chart is embedded in the Projected Cash Flow worksheet.

▶ **6.** Click the **Chart Styles** button 🖌 next to the selected column chart.

▶ **7.** In the Style gallery, scroll down, and click the **Style 14** chart style to format the columns with drop shadows.

▶ **8.** Click the **Chart Styles** button ✐ again to close the Style gallery.

Next, you will move the chart to a new location in the workbook.

INSIGHT

Changing a Chart Type

After creating a chart, you can easily switch the chart to a different chart type without having to recreate the chart from scratch. For example, if the data in a column chart would be more effective presented as a line chart, you can change its chart type rather than creating a new chart. Clicking the Change Chart Type button in the Type group on the Chart Tools Design tab opens a dialog box similar to the Insert Chart dialog box, from which you can select a new chart type.

Moving a Chart to a Different Worksheet

The Move Chart dialog box provides options for moving charts between worksheets and chart sheets. You can also cut and paste a chart from one location to another. Haywood wants you to move the column chart of the projected revenue and expenses to the Financial Summary worksheet.

To move the clustered column chart to the Financial Summary worksheet:

▶ **1.** Make sure the clustered column chart is still selected.

▶ **2.** On the Chart Tools Design tab, in the Location group, click the **Move Chart** button. The Move Chart dialog box opens.

▶ **3.** Click the **Object in** arrow to display a list of the worksheets in the active workbook, and then click **Financial Summary**.

▶ **4.** Click the **OK** button. The chart moves from the Projected Cash Flow worksheet to the Financial Summary worksheet and remains selected.

▶ **5.** Hold down the **Alt** key as you drag the chart so that its upper-left corner is aligned with the upper-left corner of cell **E4**, and then release the mouse button and the **Alt** key. The upper-left corner of the chart snaps to the worksheet.

TIP

To set an exact chart size, enter the height and width values in the Size group on the Chart Tools Format tab.

▶ **6.** Hold down the **Alt** key as you drag the lower-right sizing handle of the clustered column chart to the lower-right corner of cell **L20**, and then release the mouse button and the **Alt** key. The chart now covers the range E4:L20.

The revenue and expenses chart shows that Backspace Gear will produce little revenue during its first few years as it establishes itself and its customer base. It is only during year 6 that the revenue will outpace the expenses. After that, Haywood anticipates that the company's revenue will increase rapidly while expenses grow at a more moderate pace.

Editing a Chart Title

When a chart has a single data series, the name of the data series is used for the chart title. When a chart has more than one data series, *Chart Title* appears as the temporary title of the chart. You can replace the placeholder text with a more descriptive title and add a custom format.

Haywood wants you to change the chart title of the clustered column chart to "Projected Revenue and Expenses."

To change the title of the column chart:

1. At the top of the column chart, click **Chart Title** to select the placeholder text.

2. Type **Projected Revenue and Expenses** as the new title, and then press the **Enter** key. The new title is entered into the chart, and the chart title element remains selected.

3. On the ribbon, click the **Home** tab, and then use the buttons in the Font group to remove the bold from the chart title, change the font to **Calibri Light**, change the font size to **16** points, and then change the font color to the **Green, Accent 6, Darker 25%** theme color. See Figure 4-20.

Figure 4-20   Clustered column chart

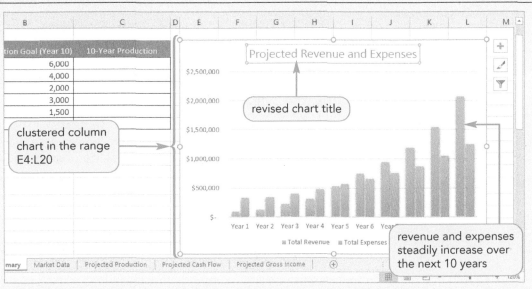

Creating a Stacked Column Chart

The next chart that Haywood wants added to the Financial Summary worksheet is a chart that projects the expenses incurred by the company over the next 10 years broken down by category. Because this chart looks at how different parts of the whole vary across time, that information would be better displayed in a stacked column chart. You will create this chart based on the data located in the Projected Cash Flow worksheet.

To create a stacked column chart:

1. Return to the **Projected Cash Flow** worksheet, and then select the nonadjacent range **A4:K4,A16:K20** containing the year categories and five data series for different types of expenses.

2. On the ribbon, click the **Insert** tab.

3. In the Charts group, click the **Insert Column or Bar Chart** button. A list of column and bar chart subtypes appears.

4. Click the **Stacked Column** icon (the second chart in the 2-D Column section). The stacked column chart is embedded in the Projected Cash Flow worksheet.

5. With the chart still selected, click the **Chart Styles** button, and then apply the **Style 11** chart style (the last style in the gallery).

   You'll move this chart to the Financial Summary worksheet.

6. On the Chart Tools Design tab, in the Location group, click the **Move Chart** button. The Move Chart dialog box opens.

7. Click the **Object in** arrow, and then click **Financial Summary**.

8. Click the **OK** button. The stacked column chart is moved to the Financial Summary worksheet.

As with the clustered column chart, you'll move and resize the stacked column chart in the Financial worksheet and then add a descriptive chart title.

To edit the stacked column chart:

TIP
To retain the chart's proportions as you resize it, hold down the Shift key as you drag the sizing handle.

1. Move and resize the stacked column chart so that it covers the range **E22:L38** in the Financial Summary worksheet. Use the Alt key to help you align the chart's location and size with the underlying worksheet grid.

2. Select the chart title, type **Breakdown of Business Expenses** as the new title, and then press the **Enter** key.

3. With the chart title still selected, change the font style to a nonbold **Green, Accent 6, Darker 25%; Calibri Light** font to match the clustered column chart. See Figure 4-21.

| Figure 4-21 | Stacked column chart |

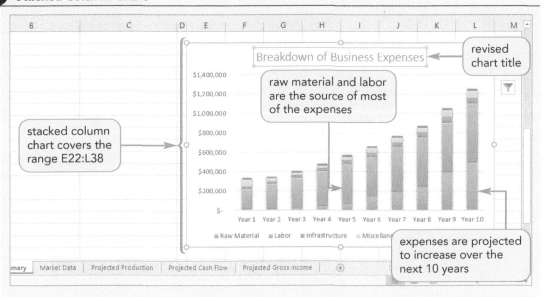

The chart clearly shows that the company's main expenses over the next 10 years will come from the raw material and labor costs. General maintenance, miscellaneous, and the business loan repayment constitute a smaller portion of the company's projected expenses. The overall yearly expense of running the company is expected to increase from about $337,000 in year 1 to $1,255,000 by year 10.

Written Communication: Communicating Effectively with Charts

Studies show that people more easily interpret information when it is presented as a graphic rather than in a table. As a result, charts can help communicate the real story underlying the facts and figures you present to colleagues and clients. A well-designed chart can illuminate the bigger picture that might be hidden by viewing only the numbers. However, poorly designed charts can mislead readers and make it more difficult to interpret data.

To create effective and useful charts, keep in mind the following tips as you design charts:

- **Keep it simple.** Do not clutter a chart with too many graphical elements. Focus attention on the data rather than on decorative elements that do not inform.

- **Focus on the message.** Design the chart to highlight the points you want to convey to readers.

- **Limit the number of data series.** Most charts should display no more than four or five data series. Pie charts should have no more than six slices.

- **Choose colors carefully.** Display different data series in contrasting colors to make it easier to distinguish one series from another. Modify the default colors as needed to make them distinct on the screen and in the printed copy.

- **Limit your chart to a few text styles.** Use a maximum of two or three different text styles in the same chart. Having too many text styles in one chart can distract attention from the data.

The goal of written communication is always to inform the reader in the simplest, most accurate, and most direct way possible. When creating worksheets and charts, everything in the workbook should be directed toward that end.

So far, you have determined monthly payments by using the PMT function and created and formatted a pie chart and two column charts. In the next session, you'll continue your work on the business plan by creating line charts, combination charts, histograms, sparklines, and data bars.

REVIEW

Session 4.1 Quick Check

1. You want to apply for a $225,000 mortgage. The annual interest on the loan is 4.8 percent with monthly payments. You plan to repay the loan in 20 years. Write the formula to calculate the monthly payment required to completely repay the loan under those conditions.

2. What function do you use to determine how many payment periods are required to repay a loan?

3. Why does the PMT function return a negative value when calculating the monthly payment due on a loan or mortgage?

4. What three chart elements are included in a pie chart?

5. A data series contains values grouped into 10 categories. Would this data be better displayed as a pie chart or a column chart? Explain why.

6. A research firm wants to create a chart that displays the total population growth of a county over a 10-year period broken down by five ethnicities. Which chart type best displays this information? Explain why.

7. If the research firm wants to display the changing ethnic profile of the county over time as a percentage of the county population, which chart type should it use? Explain why.

8. If the research firm is interested in comparing the numeric sizes of different ethnic groups over time, which chart should it use? Explain why.

9. If the research firm wants to display the ethnic profile of the county only for the current year, which chart should it use? Explain why.

Session 4.2 Visual Overview:

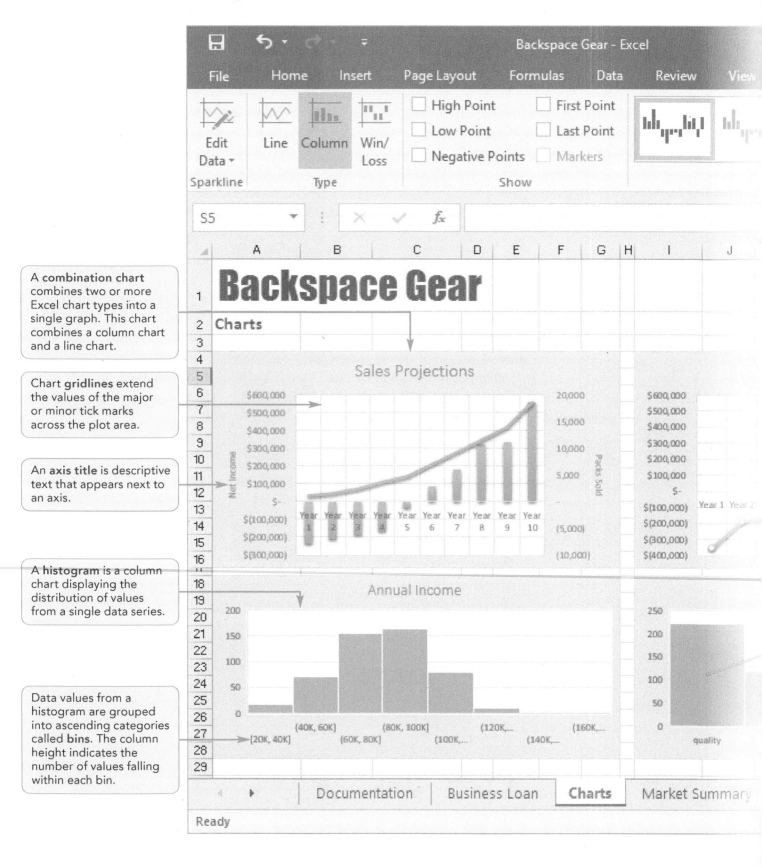

A **combination chart** combines two or more Excel chart types into a single graph. This chart combines a column chart and a line chart.

Chart **gridlines** extend the values of the major or minor tick marks across the plot area.

An **axis title** is descriptive text that appears next to an axis.

A **histogram** is a column chart displaying the distribution of values from a single data series.

Data values from a histogram are grouped into ascending categories called **bins**. The column height indicates the number of values falling within each bin.

Charts, Sparklines, and Data Bars

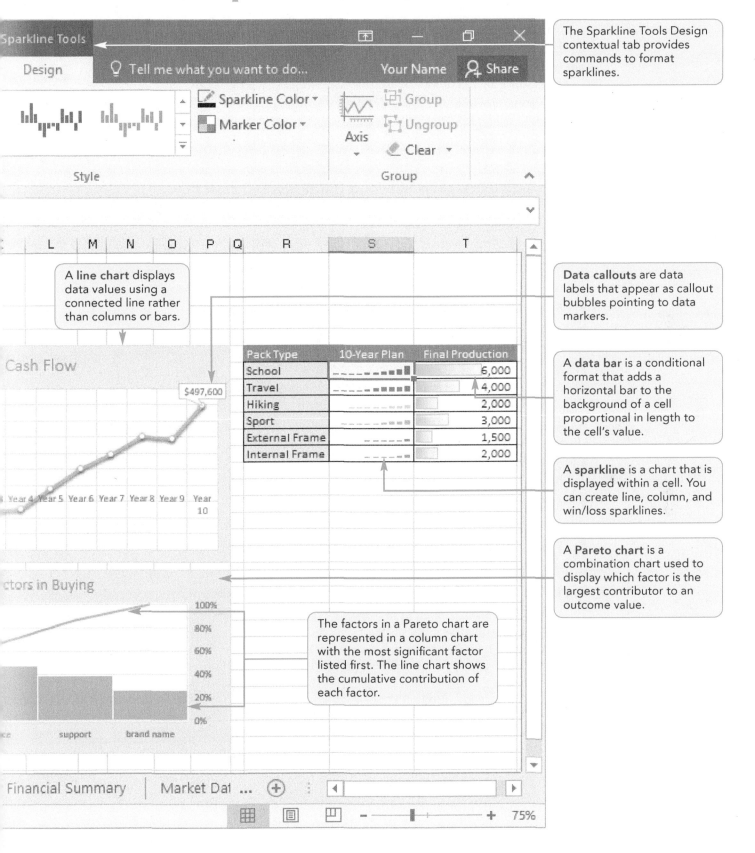

The Sparkline Tools Design contextual tab provides commands to format sparklines.

A **line chart** displays data values using a connected line rather than columns or bars.

Data callouts are data labels that appear as callout bubbles pointing to data markers.

A **data bar** is a conditional format that adds a horizontal bar to the background of a cell proportional in length to the cell's value.

A **sparkline** is a chart that is displayed within a cell. You can create line, column, and win/loss sparklines.

A **Pareto chart** is a combination chart used to display which factor is the largest contributor to an outcome value.

The factors in a Pareto chart are represented in a column chart with the most significant factor listed first. The line chart shows the cumulative contribution of each factor.

Pack Type	10-Year Plan	Final Production
School		6,000
Travel		4,000
Hiking		2,000
Sport		3,000
External Frame		1,500
Internal Frame		2,000

Creating a Line Chart

Line charts are typically used when the data consists of values drawn from categories that follow a sequential order at evenly spaced intervals, such as historical data that is recorded monthly, quarterly, or yearly. Like column charts, a line chart can be used with one or more data series. When multiple data series are included, the data values are plotted on different lines with varying line colors.

Haywood wants to use a line chart to show Backspace Gear's potential cash flow over the next decade. Cash flow examines the amount of cash flowing into and out of a business annually; it is one measure of a business's financial health and ability to make its payments.

To create a line chart showing the projected cash flow:

1. If you took a break at the end of the previous session, make sure the Backspace Gear workbook is open.

2. Go to the **Projected Cash Flow** worksheet, and select the nonadjacent range **A4:K4,A30:K30** containing the Year categories from row 4 and the Cash Flow data series from row 30.

> **TIP**
>
> When charting table values, do not include the summary totals because they will be treated as another category.

3. On the ribbon, click the **Insert** tab.

4. In the Charts group, click the **Recommended Charts** button. The Insert Chart dialog box opens, showing different ways to chart the selected data.

5. Click the second chart (the Line chart), and then click the **OK** button. The line chart of the year-end cash flow values is embedded in the Projected Cash Flow worksheet.

6. On the Home tab, in the Clipboard group, click the **Cut** button ✂ (or press the **Ctrl+X** keys). The selected line chart moves to the Clipboard.

7. Go to the **Financial Summary** worksheet, and then click cell **A12**. You want the upper-left corner of the line chart in cell A12.

8. In the Clipboard group, click the **Paste** button 📋 (or press the **Ctrl+V** keys). The line chart is pasted into the Financial Summary worksheet.

9. Resize the line chart to cover the range **A12:C24**.

10. On the ribbon, click the **Chart Tools Design** tab.

11. In the Chart Styles group, click the **Style 15** chart style (the last style in the style gallery) to format the line chart with a raised 3-D appearance.

12. Format the chart title with the same nonbold **Green, Accent 6, Darker 25%; Calibri Light** font style you applied to the two column charts. See Figure 4-22.

| Figure 4-22 | Line chart showing the projected cash flow |

chart title formatted to match other chart titles

chart moved and resized

chart line has a 3-D appearance

initial cash flow values are negative

later cash flow values are positive

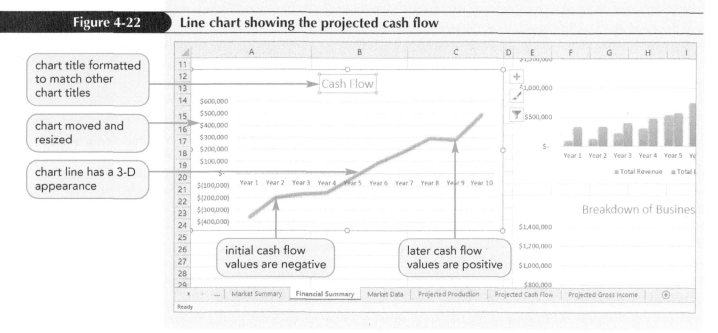

The line chart shows that Backspace Gear will have a negative cash flow in its early years and that the annual cash flow will increase throughout the decade, showing a positive cash flow starting in its sixth year.

INSIGHT

Line Charts and Scatter Charts

Line charts can sometimes be confused with XY (scatter) charts, but they are very different chart types. A line chart is more like a column chart that uses lines instead of columns. In a line chart, the data series are plotted against category values. These categories are assumed to have some sequential order. If the categories represent dates or times, they must be evenly spaced in time. For example, the Cash Flow line chart plotted the cash flow values against categories that ranged sequentially from year 1 to year 10.

A scatter chart has no category values. Instead, one series of data values is plotted against another. For example, if you were analyzing the relationship between height and weight among high school students, you would use a scatter chart because both weight and height are data values. On the other hand, if you charted weight measures against height categories (Short, Average, Tall), a line chart would be more appropriate.

Scatter charts are more often used in statistical analysis and scientific studies in which the researcher attempts to find a relationship between one variable and another. For that purpose, Excel includes several statistical tools to augment scatter charts, such as trendlines that provide the best fitting line or curve to the data. You can add a trendline by right-clicking the data series in the chart, and then clicking Add Trendline on the shortcut menu. From the Format Trendline pane that opens you can select different types of trendlines, including exponential and logarithmic lines as well as linear (straight) lines.

You have created three charts that provide a visual picture of the Backspace Gear business plan. Haywood anticipates lean years as the company becomes established, but he expects that by the end of 10 years, the company will be profitable and stable. Next, you'll look at other tools to fine-tune the formatting of these charts. You'll start by looking at the scale applied to the chart values.

Working with Axes and Gridlines

A chart's vertical and horizontal axes are based on the values in the data series and the category values. In many cases, the axes display the data in the most visually effective and informative way. Sometimes, however, you will want to modify the axes' scale, add gridlines, and make other changes to better highlight the chart data.

Editing the Scale of the Vertical Axis

The range of values, or **scale**, of an axis is based on the values in the data source. The default scale usually ranges from 0 (if the data source has no negative values) to the maximum value. If the scale includes negative values, it ranges from the minimum value to the maximum value. The vertical, or value, axis shows the range of values in the data series; the horizontal, or category, axis shows the category values.

Excel divides the scale into regular intervals, which are marked on the axis with **tick marks** and labels. For example, the scale of the vertical axis for the Projected Revenue and Expenses chart (shown in Figure 4-20) ranges from $0 up to $2,500,000 in increments of $500,000. Having more tick marks at smaller intervals could make the chart difficult to read because the tick mark labels might start to overlap. Likewise, having fewer tick marks at larger intervals could make the chart less informative. **Major tick marks** identify the main units on the chart axis while **minor tick marks** identify the smaller intervals between the major tick marks.

Some charts involve multiple data series that have vastly different values. In those instances, you can create dual axis charts. You can plot one data series against a **primary axis**, which usually appears along the left side of the chart, and the other against a **secondary axis**, which is usually placed on the right side of the chart. The two axes can be based on entirely different scales.

By default, no titles appear next to the value and category axes. This is fine when the axis labels are self-explanatory. Otherwise, you can add descriptive axis titles. In general, you should avoid cluttering a chart with extra elements such as axis titles when that information is easily understood from other parts of the chart.

Haywood thinks the value axis scale for the Projected Revenue and Expenses chart needs more tick marks and asks you to modify the axis so that it ranges from $0 to $2,500,000 in intervals of $250,000.

To change the scale of the vertical axis:

▶ 1. Click the **Projected Revenue and Expenses** chart to select it.

▶ 2. Double-click the vertical axis. The Format Axis pane opens with the Axis Options list expanded.

   Trouble? If you don't see the Axis Options section on the Format Axis pane, click the Axis Options button ▥ near the top of the pane.

   The Bounds section provides the minimum and maximum boundaries of the axis, which in this case are set from 0.0 to 2.5E6 (which stands for 2,500,000). Note that minimum and maximum values are set to Auto, which means that Excel automatically set these boundaries based on the data values.

TIP

To return a scale value to Auto, click the Reset button next to the value in the Format pane.

The Units section provides the intervals between the major tick marks and between minor tick marks. The major tick mark intervals, which are currently 500,000, are also set automatically by Excel.

3. In the Units section, click in the **Major** box, delete the current value, type **250000** as the new interval between major tick marks, and then press the **Enter** key. The scale of the value axis changes. See Figure 4-23.

Figure 4-23   Formatted value axis

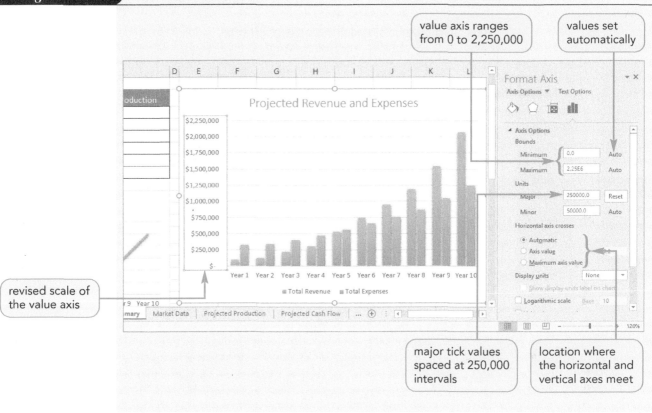

The revised axis scale makes it easier to determine the values displayed in the column chart.

Displaying Unit Labels

When a chart involves large numbers, the axis labels can take up a lot of the available chart area and be difficult to read. You can simplify the chart's appearance by displaying units of measure more appropriate to the data values. For example, you can display the value 20 to represent 20,000 or 20,000,000. This is particularly useful when space is at a premium, such as in an embedded chart confined to a small area of the worksheet.

To display a units label, you double-click the axis to open the Format pane displaying options to format the axis. Select the units type from the Display units box. You can choose unit labels to represent values measured in the hundreds up to the trillions. Excel will modify the numbers on the selected axis and add a label so that readers will know what the axis values represent.

Adding Gridlines to a Chart

Gridlines are horizontal and vertical lines that help you compare data and category values in a chart. Depending on the chart style, gridlines may or may not appear in a chart, though you can add or remove them separately. Gridlines are placed at the major tick marks on the axes, or you can set them to appear at the minor tick marks.

The chart style used for the two column charts and the line chart includes horizontal gridlines. Haywood wants you to add vertical gridlines to the Projected Revenue and Expenses chart to help further separate one set of year values from another.

To add vertical gridlines to a chart:

1. With the Projected Revenue and Expenses chart still selected, click the **Chart Elements** button ⊞ to display the menu of chart elements.

2. Point to **Gridlines**, and then click the **right arrow** that appears to open a submenu of gridline options.

3. Click the **Primary Major Vertical** check box to add vertical gridlines at the major tick marks on the chart. See Figure 4-24.

| Figure 4-24 | Vertical gridlines added to the column chart |

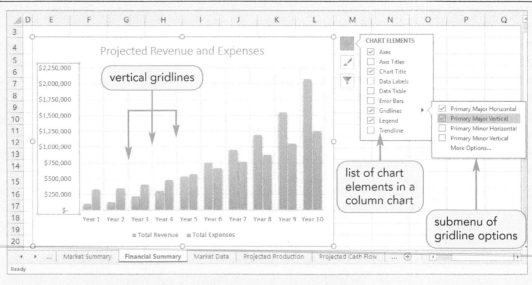

4. Click the **Chart Elements** button ⊞ to close the Chart Elements menu.

Working with Column Widths

Category values do not have the scale options used with data values. However, you can set the spacing between one column and another in your column charts. You can also define the width of the columns. As with the vertical axis, the default spacing and width are set automatically by Excel. A column chart with several categories will naturally make those columns thinner and more tightly packed.

Haywood thinks that the columns in the Projected Revenue and Expenses chart are spaced too closely, making it difficult to distinguish one year's values from another. He wants you to increase the gap between the columns.

To format the chart columns:

▶ **1.** Make sure the Projected Revenue and Expenses chart is still selected and the Format pane is still open.

▶ **2.** Click the **Axis Options arrow** at the top of the Format pane, and then click **Series "Total Revenue"** from the list of chart elements. The Format pane title changes to "Format Data Series," and all of the columns in the chart that show total revenue values are selected.

▶ **3.** In the Format pane, click the **Series Options** button 📊 to display the list of series options.

Series Overlap sets the amount of overlap between columns of different data series. Gap Width sets the amount of space between one group of columns and the next.

TIP

You can use the up and down spin arrows in the Gap Width box to fine-tune the gap width in 1 percent increments.

▶ **4.** Drag the **Gap Width** slider until **200%** appears in the Gap Width box. The gap between groups of columns increases, and the individual column widths decrease to make room for the larger gap. See Figure 4-25.

Figure 4-25   **Gap width between columns**

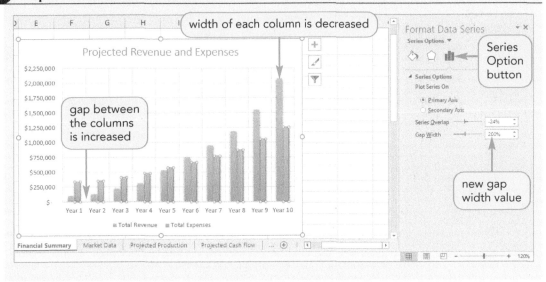

Formatting Data Markers

Each value from a data series is represented by a data marker. In pie charts, the data markers are the individual pie slices. In column charts, the columns are the data markers. In a line chart, the data markers are the points connected by the line. Depending on the line chart style, these data marker points can be displayed or hidden.

In the Cash Flow line chart, the data marker points are hidden, and only the line connecting them is visible. Haywood wants you to display these data markers and change their fill color to white so that they stand out, making the chart easier to understand.

To display and format the line chart data markers:

1. Scroll to view the Cash Flow line chart, and then double-click the line within the chart. The Format pane changes to the Format Data Series pane.

2. Click the **Fill & Line** button ⬧ at the top of the Format pane.

   You can choose to display the format options for lines or data markers.

3. Click **Marker**, and then click **Marker Options** to expand the list of options for the line chart data markers. Currently, the None option button is selected to hide the data markers.

4. Click the **Automatic** option button to automatically display the markers.

   The data markers are now visible in the line chart, but they have a blue fill color. You will change this fill color to white.

5. Click **Fill** to expand the list of fill options, if necessary.

6. Click the **Solid fill** option button, click the **Color** button, and then click the **White, Background 1** theme color. The fill color for the data markers in the line chart changes to white.

In many charts, you will want to highlight an important data point. Data labels provide a way to identify the different values in a chart. Whether you include data labels depends on the chart, the complexity of the data and presentation, and the chart's purpose. You can include data labels for every data marker or just for individual data points.

Haywood wants to highlight that at the end of the tenth year, the company should have an annual cash flow of almost $500,000. He wants you to add a data label that displays the value of the last data marker in the chart at that data point.

To add a data label to the line chart:

1. With the line in the Cash Flow line chart still selected, click the last point on the line to select only that point. Note that selection handles appear around this data marker but not around any of the others.

2. Click the **Chart Elements** button ⊞ next to the line chart, and then click the **Data Labels** check box to select it. The data label appears above only the selected data marker.

3. Click the **Data Labels** arrow to display a menu of data label positions and options, and then click **Data Callout**. The data label is changed to a data callout box that includes both the category value and the data value, displaying "Year 10, $497,600." You will modify this callout to display only the data value.

4. On the Data Labels menu, click **More Options**. The Format pane title changes to "Format Data Label."

5. Click the **Label Options** button 📊, and then click **Label Options**, if necessary, to expand the list of those options.

6. Click the **Category Name** check box to deselect it. The data callout now displays only $497,600. See Figure 4-26.

Figure 4-26   Formatted data markers and data label

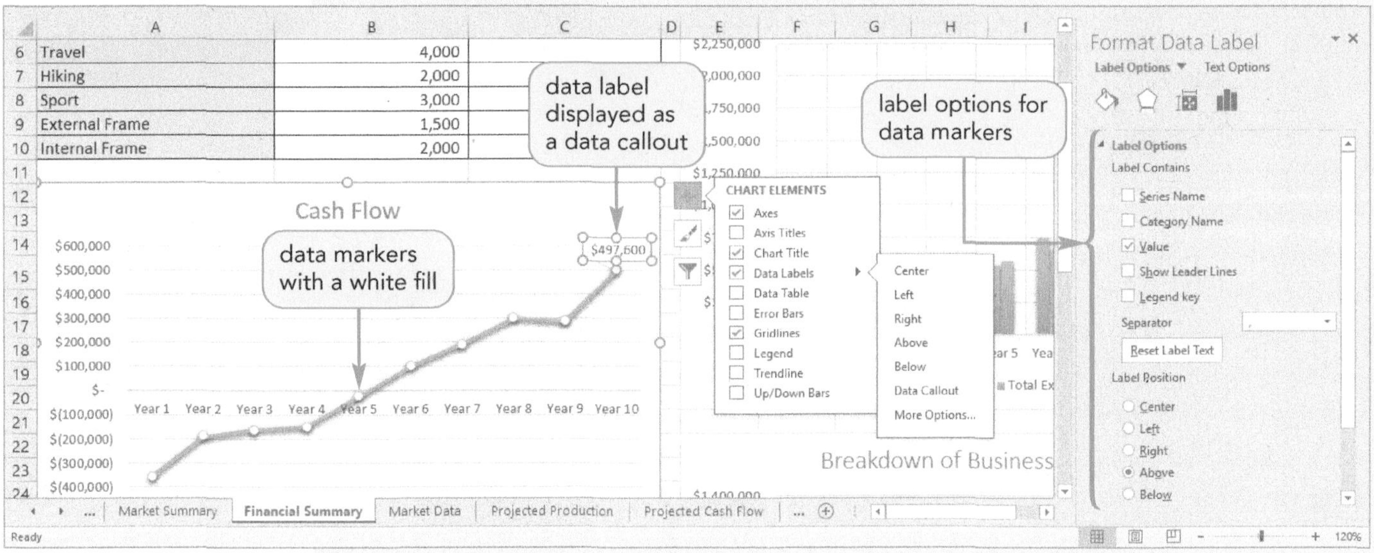

Formatting the Plot Area

The chart area covers the entire background of the chart, whereas the **plot area** includes only that portion of the chart in which the data markers, such as the columns in a column chart, have been placed or plotted. You can format the plot area by changing its fill and borders and by adding visual effects. Changes to the plot area are often made in conjunction with the chart area.

Haywood wants you to format the chart area and plot area of the Projected Revenue and Expenses chart. You will set the chart area fill color to a light green to match the pie chart background color you applied in the last session, and you will change the plot area fill color to white.

To change the fill colors of the chart and plot areas:

1. Click the **Projected Revenue and Expenses** chart to select it.

2. On the ribbon, click the **Chart Tools Format** tab.

3. In the Current Selection group, click the **Chart Elements arrow** to display a list of chart elements in the current chart, and then click **Chart Area**. The chart area is selected in the chart.

4. In the Shape Styles group, click the **Shape Fill button arrow**, and then click the **Green, Accent 6, Lighter 60%** theme color in the third row and last column. The entire background of the chart changes to light green.

5. In the Current Selection group, click the **Chart Elements arrow**, and then click **Plot Area** to select that chart element.

6. Change the fill color of the plot area to the **White, Background 1** theme color. See Figure 4-27.

Figure 4-27   **Final Projected Revenue and Expenses chart**

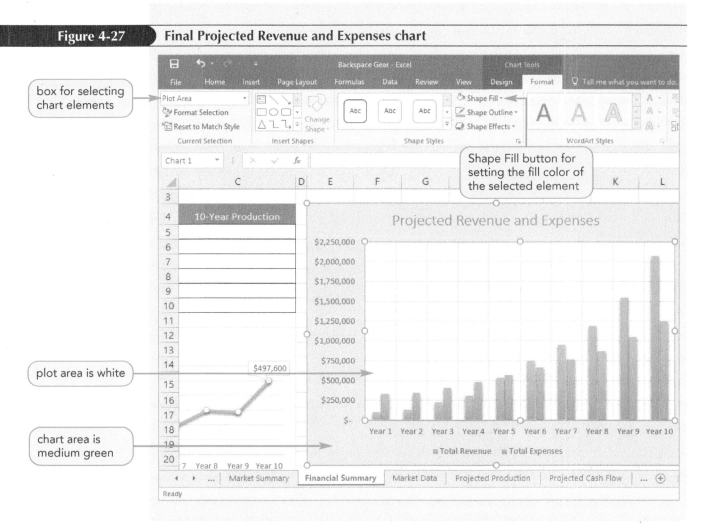

box for selecting chart elements

Shape Fill button for setting the fill color of the selected element

plot area is white

chart area is medium green

Haywood wants to apply the same general design applied to the Breakdown of Business Expenses column chart and the Cash Flow line chart. You will add vertical gridlines to each chart and then change the chart area fill color to light green and the plot area fill color to white.

To format the other charts:

1. Click the **Breakdown of Business Expenses** column chart to select it.

2. Select the **chart area**, and then set the fill color of the chart area to **Green, Accent 6, Lighter 60%** theme color.

3. Select the **plot area**, and then change the fill color to the **White, Background 1** theme color.

   Next, you'll add vertical gridlines to the chart. You can also use the Chart Tools Design tab to add chart elements such as gridlines.

4. On the ribbon, click the **Chart Tools Design** tab.

5. In the Chart Layouts group, click the **Add Chart Element** button, scroll down the chart elements, point to **Gridlines**, and then click **Primary Major Vertical** on the submenu. Vertical gridlines are added to the chart. See Figure 4-28.

| Figure 4-28 | Final Business Expenses chart |

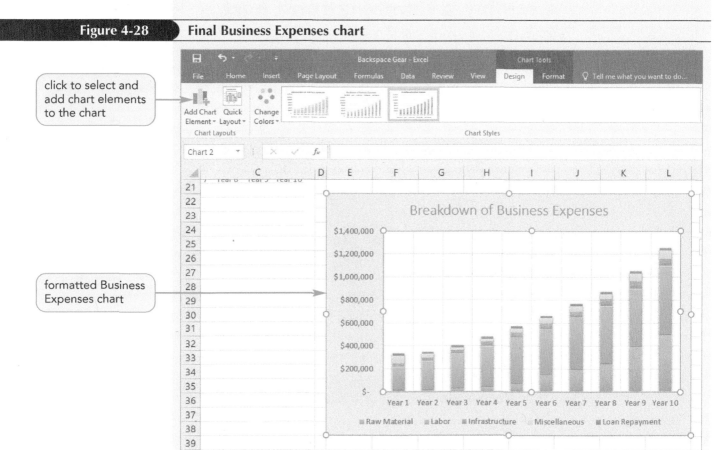

click to select and add chart elements to the chart

formatted Business Expenses chart

▶ **6.** Select the **Cash Flow** line chart, and then repeat Steps 2 through 5 to set the chart area fill color to light green, set the plot area fill color to white, and add major gridlines to the chart's primary axis.

The Breakdown of Business Expenses column chart and the Cash Flow line chart are now formatted with the same design.

Overlaying Chart Elements

INSIGHT

An embedded chart takes up less space than a chart sheet. However, it can be challenging to fit all of the chart elements into that smaller space. One solution is to overlay one element on top of another. The most commonly overlaid elements are the chart title and the chart legend. To overlay the chart title, click the Chart Title arrow from the list of Chart Elements and select Centered Overlay from the list of position options. Excel will place the chart title on top of the plot area, freeing up more space for other chart elements. Chart legends can also be overlaid by opening the Format pane for the legend and deselecting the Show the legend without overlapping the chart check box in the Legend Options section. Other chart elements can be overlaid by dragging them to new locations in the chart area and then resizing the plot area to recover the empty space.

Don't overuse the technique of overlaying chart elements. Too much overlaying of chart elements can make your chart difficult to read.

Creating a Combination Chart

A combination chart combines two chart types, such as a column chart and a line chart, enabling you to display two sets of data using the chart type that is best for each. Because the two data series might have vastly different values, combination charts support two vertical axes labeled the primary axis and the secondary axis, with each axes associated with a different data series.

Haywood wants to include a chart that projects the net income and packs of all types to be sold over the next 10 years by Backspace Gear. Because these two data series are measuring different things (dollars and sales items), the chart might be better understood if the Net Income data series is displayed as a column chart and the Packs Produced and Sold data series is displayed as a line chart.

To create a combination chart:

1. Go to the **Projected Cash Flow** worksheet, and then select the nonadjacent range **A4:K5,A26:K26** containing the Year category values, the data series for Packs Produced and Sold, and the data series for Net Income.

2. On the ribbon, click the **Insert** tab, and then click the **Recommended Charts** button in the Charts group. The Insert Chart dialog box opens.

3. Click the **All Charts** tab to view a list of all chart types and subtypes.

4. Click **Combo** in the list of chart types, and then click the **Custom Combination** subtype (the fourth subtype).

   At the bottom of the dialog box, you choose the chart type for each data series and whether that data series is plotted on the primary or secondary axis.

5. For the Packs Produced and Sold data series, click the **Chart Type arrow**, and then click **Line**.

6. Click the **Secondary Axis** check box to display the values for that series on a secondary axis.

7. For the Net Income data series, click the **Chart Type arrow**, and then click **Clustered Column**. See Figure 4-29.

| Figure 4-29 | Custom Combination chart in the Insert Chart dialog box |

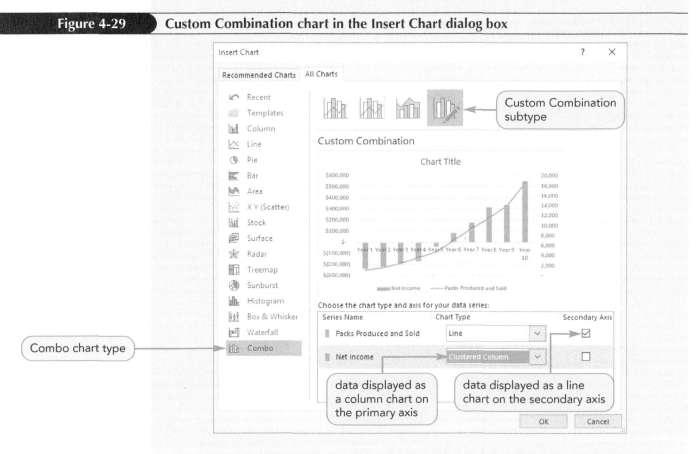

8. Click the **OK** button. The combination chart is embedded in the Projected Cash Flow worksheet.

9. Format the combination chart with the **Style 8** chart style to give both the line and the columns a raised 3-D effect.

Haywood wants the combo chart moved to the Financial Summary worksheet and formatted to match the style used for the other charts.

To move and format the combo chart:

1. Move the combination chart to the **Financial Summary** worksheet, and then resize it cover the range **A26:C38**.

2. Change the title of the combination chart to **Sales Projections**, and then format the title in the same nonbold **Green, Accent 6, Darker 25%**; **Calibri Light** font you used with the other chart titles.

3. Remove the **Legend** chart element from the combination chart.

4. Add **Primary Major Vertical** gridlines to the combination chart.

5. Change the fill color of the plot area to the **White, Background 1** theme color, and then change the fill color of the chart area to the same **Green, Accent 6, Lighter 60%** theme color as the other charts. See Figure 4-30.

Figure 4-30   **Initial Sales Projections combination chart**

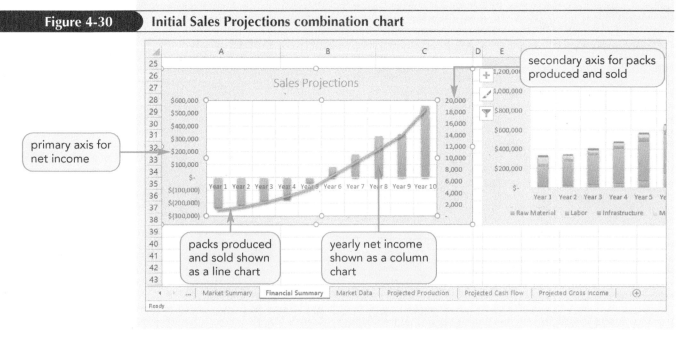

The primary axis scale for the net income values is shown on the left side of the chart; the secondary axis scale for the number of items produced and sold appears on the right side. The chart shows that the Backspace Gear will have a negative income for the first five years, while the number of packs produced and sold will increase steadily to more than 18,000 items by year 10.

Working with Primary and Secondary Axes

With a primary and secondary axis, combo charts can be confusing to the reader trying to determine which axis is associated with each data series. It is helpful to add an axis title to the chart with descriptive text that appears next to the axis values. As with other chart elements, you can add, remove, and format axis titles.

Haywood wants you to edit the Sales Projections chart to include labels describing what is being measured by the primary and secondary axes.

To add titles to the primary and second axes:

1. Click the **Chart Elements** button ⊞ next to the combination chart, and then click the **Axis Titles** check box to select it. Titles with the placeholders "Axis Title" are added to the primary and secondary axes.

2. Click the left axis title to select it, type **Net Income** as the descriptive title, and then press the **Enter** key.

3. With the left axis title selected, change the font color to the **Orange, Accent 2, Darker 25%** theme color to match the color of the columns in the chart.

4. Select the numbers on the left axis scale, and then change the font color to the **Orange, Accent 2, Darker 25%** theme color. The left axis title and scale are now the same color as the columns that reference that axis.

5. Select the **right axis** title, type **Packs Sold** as the descriptive title, and then press the **Enter** key.

6. With the right axis title still selected, change the font color to the **Blue, Accent 1, Darker 25%** theme color to match the color of the line in the chart.

7. On the Home tab, in the Alignment group, click the **Orientation** button , and then click **Rotate Text Down** to change the orientation of the right axis title.

8. Select the numbers on the right axis scale, and then change the font color to the **Blue, Accent 1, Darker 25%** theme color. The right axis title and scale are now the same color as the line that references that axis.

9. Click the horizontal axis title to select it, and then press the **Delete** key. The placeholder is removed from the chart, freeing up more space for other chart elements. See Figure 4-31.

Figure 4-31	Combination chart with axis titles

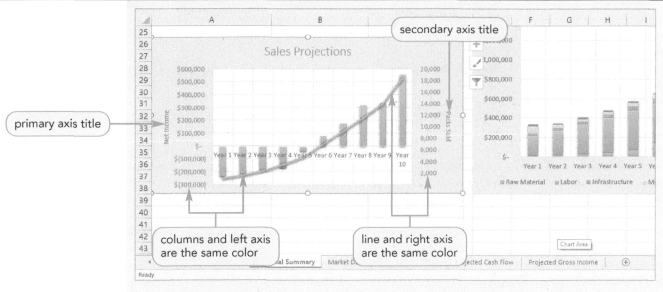

Haywood is concerned that the line chart portion of the graph makes it look as if the number of packs produced and sold was negative for the first five years. This is because the secondary axis scale, which is automatically generated by Excel, goes from a minimum of 0 to a maximum of 20,000. You will change the scale so that the 0 tick mark for Packs Sold better aligns with the $0 for Net Income.

To modify the secondary axis scale:

1. Double-click the secondary axis scale to select it and open the Format pane.

2. Click the **Axis Options** button, if necessary, to display the list of axis options.

▶ **3.** In Axis Options section, click the **Minimum** box, change the value from 0.0 to **–10000**, and then press the **Enter** key. The secondary axis scale is modified. The Packs Sold scale is now better aligned with the Net Income scale, providing a clearer picture of the data.

▶ **4.** Close the Format pane, and then press the **Esc** key to deselect the secondary axis. See Figure 4-32.

Figure 4-32 **Final combination chart**

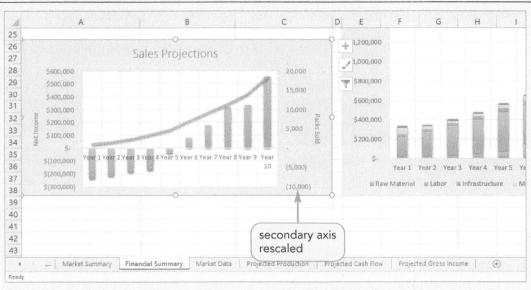

You have completed the charts portion of the Financial Summary worksheet. These charts provide a good overview of the financial picture of the first 10 years of Haywood's proposed business plan for Backspace Gear.

Copying and Pasting a Chart Format

INSIGHT

You will often want to use the same design over and over again for the charts in your worksheet. Rather than repeating the same commands, you can copy the formatting from one chart to another. To copy a chart format, first select the chart with the existing design that you want to replicate, and then click the Copy button in the Clipboard group on the Home tab (or press the Ctrl+C keys). Next, select the chart that you want to format, click the Paste button arrow in the Clipboard group, and then click Paste Special to open the Paste Special dialog box. In the Paste Special dialog box, select the Formats option button, and then click the OK button. All of the copied formats from the original chart—including fill colors, font styles, axis scales, and chart types—are then pasted into the new chart. Be aware that the pasted formats will overwrite any formats previously used in the new chart.

Editing a Chart Data Source

Excel automates most of the process of creating and formatting a chart. However, sometimes the rendered chart does not appear the way you expected. One situation where this happens is when the selected cells contain numbers you want to treat as categories but Excel treats them as a data series. When this happens, you can modify the data source to specify exactly which ranges should be treated as category values and which ranges should be treated as data values.

REFERENCE

Modifying a Chart's Data Source

- Click the chart to select it.
- On the Chart Tools Design tab, in the Data group, click the Select Data button.
- In the Legend Entries (Series) section of the Select Data Source dialog box, click the Add button to add another data series to the chart, or click the Remove button to remove a data series from the chart.
- Click the Edit button in the Horizontal (Category) Axis Labels section to select the category values for the chart.

The Projected Gross Income worksheet contains a table that projects the company's gross income for the next 10 years. Haywood wants you to create a simple line chart of this data.

To create the line chart:

▶ **1.** Go to the **Projected Gross Income** worksheet, and then select the range **A4:B14**.

▶ **2.** On the ribbon, click the **Insert** tab.

▶ **3.** In the Charts group, click the **Insert Line or Area Chart** button.

▶ **4.** In the 2-D Line charts section, click the **Line** subtype (the first subtype in the first row) to create a 2-D line chart.

▶ **5.** Move the chart over the range **D2:J14**. See Figure 4-33.

Figure 4-33   Line chart with Year treated as a data series

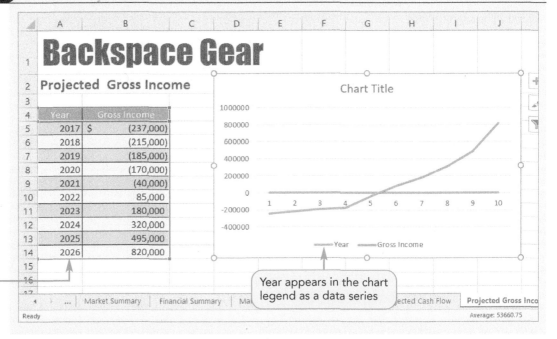

Year values should be treated as categories

Year appears in the chart legend as a data series

The line chart is incorrect because the Year values from the range A5:A14 are treated as another data series rather than category values. The line chart actually doesn't even have category values; the values are charted sequentially from the first value to the tenth. You can correct this problem from the Select Data dialog box by identifying the data series and category values to use in the chart.

To edit the chart's data source:

▶ **1.** On the Chart Tools Design tab, in the Data group, click the **Select Data** button. The Select Data Source dialog box opens. Note that Year is selected as a legend entry and the category values are simply the numbers 1 through 10. See Figure 4-34.

Figure 4-34   **Select Data Source dialog box**

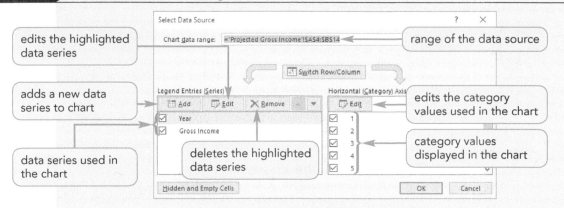

2. With Year selected (highlighted in gray) in the list of legend entries, click the **Remove** button. Year is removed from the line chart.

3. Click the **Edit** button for the Horizontal (Category) Axis Labels. The Axis Labels dialog box opens. You'll specify that Year should be used as the category values.

4. Select the range **A5:A14** containing the years as the axis label range, and then click the **OK** button. The Year values now appear in the list of Horizontal (Category) Axis Labels.

5. Click the **OK** button to close the Select Data Source dialog box. The line chart now displays Year as the category values and Gross Income as the only data series. See Figure 4-35.

TIP

To organize a data series in rows, click the Switch Row/Column button.

Make sure you insert a completely new range for the category values rather than simply adding to the category values already in use.

Figure 4-35   **Revised Gross Income line chart**

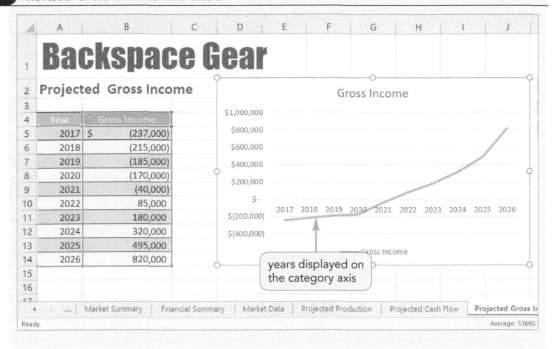

The Select Data Source dialog box is also useful when you want to add more data series to a chart. For example, if Haywood wanted to include other financial estimates in an existing chart, he could add the data series to the existing chart rather than creating a new chart. To add a data series to a chart, select the chart, click the Select Data button in the Data group on the Chart Tools Design tab to open the Select Data Source dialog box, click the Add button, and then select the range for the data series.

Exploring Other Chart Types

Excel provides many chart types tailored to specific needs in finance, statistics, science, and project management. One chart that is often used in finance and statistics is the histogram.

Creating a Histogram

A histogram is a column chart displaying the distribution of values from a single data series. For example, a professor might create a histogram to display the distribution of scores from a midterm exam. There is no category series for a histogram; instead, the data values are automatically grouped into ascending categories, or bins, with the histogram displaying the number of data points falling within the bin. So a histogram of midterm exam scores might consist of four bins corresponding to exam scores of 60 to 70, 70 to 80, 80 to 90, and 90 to 100. The number and placement of the bins is arbitrary and is chosen to best indicate the shape of the distribution.

You will use a histogram chart to summarize data from the market survey. Part of the survey included demographic information such as the respondent's gender and annual income. Haywood wants a histogram displaying the income distribution for Backspace Gear's most likely customers, which will help him better market Backspace Gear to its core customer base.

To create a histogram of income distribution:

▶ **1.** Go to the **Market Data** worksheet.

▶ **2.** In the Market Data worksheet, click the **Name** box, type the range **E6:E506**, and then press the **Enter** key to select the data values containing the annual income of the 500 survey respondents.

▶ **3.** On the ribbon, click the **Insert** tab.

▶ **4.** In the Charts group, click the **Insert Statistic Chart** button to display a list of statistic charts supported by Excel.

▶ **5.** Click the **Histogram** subtype (the first subtype in the Histogram section). The histogram of the income data appears in the Market Data worksheet.

▶ **6.** With the chart selected, click the **Cut** button in the Clipboard group on the Home tab (or press the **Ctrl+X** keys).

▶ **7.** Go to the **Market Summary** worksheet, click cell **F4**, and then click the **Paste** button (or press the **Ctrl+V** keys) to paste the histogram chart at the top of the worksheet.

▶ **8.** Resize the chart so that it covers the range **F4:M14**.

▶ **9.** Change the chart title to **Annual Income**, and then change the color of the chart title to nonbold **Green, Accent 6, Darker 25%; Calibri Light** font.

▶ **10.** Change the fill color of the chart area to the same **Green, Accent 6, Lighter 60%** theme color used with other charts, and then change the plot area fill color to the **White, Background 1** theme color. See Figure 4-36.

Figure 4-36   Histogram of annual income

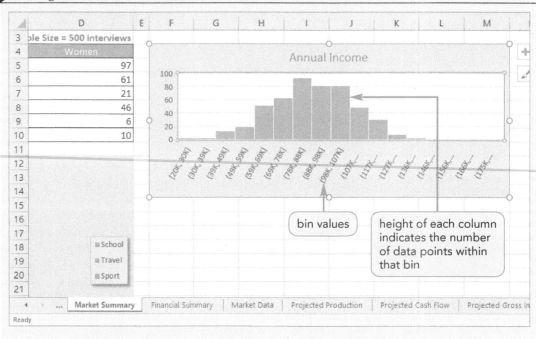

The histogram shows that most of the respondents are clustered around incomes of $59,000 to $100,000 per year. The lowest incomes are in the $20,000 to $30,000 range with some very few respondents having incomes around $175,000. Excel created the histogram with 17 bins. The number of bins is used to cover the range of values from the smallest income value up to the largest. This can result in odd-sized ranges. Haywood suggests that you change the width of each bin to 20,000. You can modify the bins by editing the values in the horizontal axis of the histogram chart.

To modify the bins used in the histogram:

▶ **1.** Double-click the horizontal axis values to select them and open the Format Axis pane.

TIP

To combine bin values, set the Overflow bin and Underflow bin values in Axis Options section.

▶ **2.** Click the **Axis Options** button ![icon] near the top of the Format pane, and then click **Axis Options** to expand the list. Excel displays a list of options to set the size and number of bins used in the histogram.

▶ **3.** Click the **Bin width** option button, change the width of the bins from the default value of 9700 to **20000**, and then press the **Tab** key. See Figure 4-37.

Figure 4-37   Histogram with new bin widths

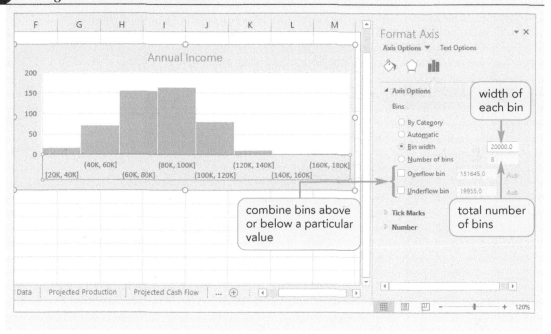

By changing the bin widths, you made the histogram easier to read and interpret. The distribution of the income values shows that there are a couple of outlying incomes in the 160,000 to 180,000 range, but almost all of the annual incomes are reported in the 60,000 to 100,000 range.

Creating a Pareto Chart

Another important statistical chart is the Pareto chart, which is used to indicate which factors are the largest contributors to an outcome value. Pareto charts are often used in quality control studies to isolate the most significant factors in the failure of a manufacturer process. They can also be used with market research to indicate which factor and combination of factors is the most crucial buying decision. Pareto charts appear as combination charts, combining a column chart and a line chart. The column chart lists the individual factors sorted from the most significant factor to the least significant. The line chart provides the cumulative percentage that each factor contributes to the whole.

Haywood's market survey asked respondents to list which one of the following factors was most important in choosing their pack: brand name, customer support, price, and quality. He wants you display this information in a Pareto chart that shows the factor that was listed most often in the survey results followed by the factor that was listed second-most often in the survey results, and so forth.

To create a Pareto chart showing buying factors:

▶ **1.** Go to the **Market Data** worksheet, and then select the range **H5:I8** containing the total responses in each of the four categories: brand name, support, price, and quality.

▶ **2.** On the ribbon, click the **Insert** tab.

▶ **3.** In the Charts group, click the **Insert Statistic Chart** button ▐▐▐▾, and then click the **Pareto** subtype (the second subtype in the Histogram section). The Pareto chart is inserted into the worksheet.

▶ **4.** Move the Pareto chart to the **Market Summary** worksheet, and then resize it to cover the range **F16:M26**.

▶ **5.** Change the chart title to **Factors in Buying**.

▶ **6.** Change the format of the chart title, chart area fill color, and plot area fill color to match the other charts on the sheet. See Figure 4-38.

Figure 4-38   **Pareto chart of buying factors**

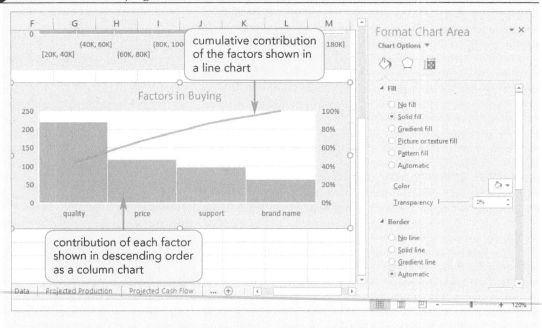

The Pareto chart quickly shows that quality is the most important factor in making a purchase for more than 200 of the respondents. The next most important factor is price, followed by support. Brand name is the least important factor. The line chart shows the cumulative effect of the four factors as a percentage of the whole. About 70 percent of the people in the survey listed quality or price as the most important factor in making a purchase, and about 90 percent listed quality, price, or customer support. Brand name, by comparison, had little impact on the respondent's buying decision, which is good for a new company entering the market.

Using a Waterfall Chart

A **waterfall chart** is used to track the effect of adding and subtracting values within a sum. Waterfall charts are often used to show the impact of revenue and expenses in profit and loss statements. The waterfall chart in Figure 4-39 is based on Backspace Gear's year 10 revenue and expenses projections.

Figure 4-39 Waterfall chart of Year 10 cash flow

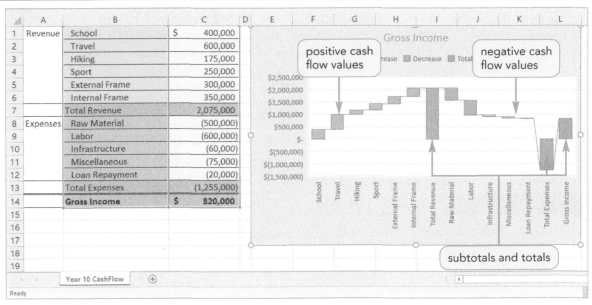

In waterfall charts, every positive value that adds to the total is represented by an increasing step, whereas negative values that subtract from the total are represented by decreasing steps. Subtotals such as the Total Revenue, Total Expenses, and Gross Income values are displayed in gray. The steps and colors in the chart show how each revenue and expense value contributes to the final gross income value.

Using a Hierarchical Chart

Hierarchy charts are like pie charts in that they show the relative contribution of groups to a whole. Unlike pie charts, a hierarchy chart also shows the organizational structure of the data with subcategories displayed within main categories. Excel supports two types of hierarchical charts: treemap charts and sunburst charts.

In a **treemap chart** each category is placed within a rectangle, and subcategories are nested as rectangles within those rectangles. The rectangles are sized to show the relative proportions of the two groups based on values from a data series. The treemap chart in Figure 4-40 measures the responses from the market survey broken down by gender and backpack type.

Figure 4-40 Treemap chart of preferences

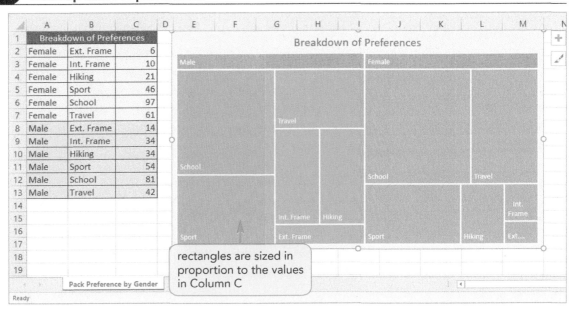

The size of the rectangles demonstrates how men and women in the survey differ in the types of packs they are likely to purchase. Men are more likely than women to purchase internal frame and hiking packs as indicated by the larger size of those rectangles in the treemap chart. Women, on the other hand, were more likely than men to purchase packs for school and travel. From this information, Haywood can tailor his product marketing to different segments of the population.

A **sunburst chart** conveys this same information through a series of concentric rings with the upper levels of the hierarchy displayed in the innermost rings. The size of the rings indicates the relative proportions of the different categories and subcategories. Figure 4-41 shows market survey results in a sunburst chart with three levels of rings showing the responses by gender, backpack category, and finally backpack type within category.

Figure 4-41   Sunburst chart of backpack preferences

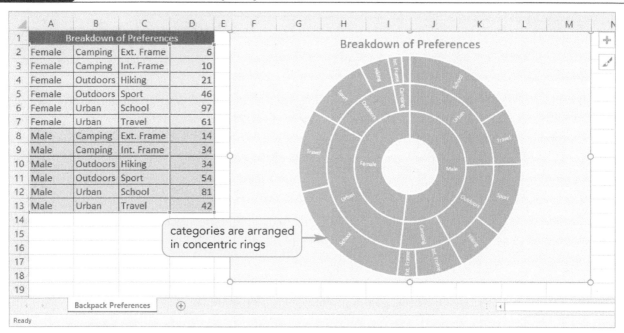

Sunburst charts are better than treemap charts at conveying information from multiple levels of nested categories and are better at displaying the relative sizes of the groups within each category level.

PROSKILLS

Decision Making: Choosing the Right Chart

Excel supports a wide variety of charts and chart styles. To decide which type of chart to use, you must evaluate your data and determine the ultimate purpose or goal of the chart. Consider how your data will appear in each type of chart before making a final decision.

- In general, pie charts should be used only when the number of categories is small and the relative sizes of the different slices can be easily distinguished. If you have several categories, use a column or bar chart.
- Line charts are best for categories that follow a sequential order. Be aware, however, that the time intervals must be a constant length if used in a line chart. Line charts will distort data that occurs at irregular time intervals, making it appear that the data values occurred at regular intervals when they did not.
- Pie, column, bar, and line charts assume that numbers are plotted against categories. In science and engineering applications, you will often want to plot two numeric values against one another. For that data, use **XY scatter charts**, which show the pattern or relationship between two or more sets of values. XY scatter charts are also useful for data recorded at irregular time intervals.

If you still can't find the right chart to meet your needs, you can create a custom chart based on the built-in chart types. Third-party vendors also sell software to allow Excel to create chart types that are not built into the software.

Creating Sparklines

Data can be displayed graphically without charts by using sparklines and data bars. A sparkline is a graphic that is displayed entirely within a worksheet cell. Because sparklines are compact in size, they don't include chart elements such as legends, titles, or gridlines. The goal of a sparkline is to convey the maximum amount of information within a very small space. As a result, sparklines are useful when you don't want charts to overwhelm the rest of your worksheet or take up valuable page space.

You can create the following types of sparklines in Excel:

- A line sparkline for highlighting trends
- A column sparkline for column charts
- A win/loss sparkline for highlighting positive and negative values

Figure 4-42 shows examples of each sparkline type. The line sparklines show the sales history from each department and across all four departments of a computer manufacturer. The sparklines provide enough information for you to examine the sales trend within and across departments. Notice that although total sales rose steadily during the year, some departments, such as Printers, showed a sales decline midway through the year.

Figure 4-42   Types of sparklines

line sparklines   column sparklines   win/loss sparklines

The column sparklines present a record of monthly temperature averages for four cities. Temperatures above 0 degrees Celsius are presented in blue columns; temperatures below 0 degrees Celsius are presented in red columns that extend downward. The height of each column is related to the magnitude of the value it represents.

Finally, the win/loss sparklines reveal a snapshot of the season results for four sports teams. Wins are displayed in blue; losses are in red. From the sparklines, you can quickly see that the Cutler Tigers finished their 10–2 season with six straight wins, and the Liddleton Lions finished their 3–9 season with four straight losses.

INSIGHT

Edward Tufte and Chart Design Theory

Any serious study of charts will include the works of Edward Tufte, who pioneered the field of information design. One of Tufte's most important works is *The Visual Display of Quantitative Information*, in which he laid out several principles for the design of charts and graphics.

Tufte was concerned with what he termed as "chart junk," in which a proliferation of chart elements—chosen because they look "nice"—confuse and distract the reader. One measure of chart junk is Tufte's data-ink ratio, which is the amount of "ink" used to display quantitative information compared to the total ink required by the chart. Tufte advocated limiting the use of nondata ink. Nondata ink is any part of the chart that does not convey information about the data. One way of measuring the data-ink ratio is to determine how much of the chart you can erase without affecting the user's ability to interpret the chart. Tufte would argue for high data-ink ratios with a minimum of extraneous elements and graphics.

To this end, Tufte helped develop sparklines, which convey information with a high data-ink ratio within a compact space. Tufte believed that charts that can be viewed and comprehended at a glance have a greater impact on the reader than large and cluttered graphs, no matter how attractive they might be.

To create a set of sparklines, you first select the data you want to graph, and then select the range where you want the sparklines to appear. Note that the cells in which you insert the sparklines do not need to be blank because the sparklines are part of the cell background and do not replace any content.

REFERENCE

Creating and Editing Sparklines

- On the Insert tab, in the Sparklines group, click the Line, Column, or Win/Loss button.
- In the Data Range box, enter the range for the data source of the sparkline.
- In the Location Range box, enter the range into which to place the sparkline.
- Click the OK button.
- On the Sparkline Tools Design tab, in the Show group, click the appropriate check boxes to specify which markers to display on the sparkline.
- In the Group group, click the Axis button, and then click Show Axis to add an axis to the sparkline.

Haywood's business plan for Backspace Gear involves rolling out the different types of packs gradually, starting with the school and travel packs, which have the most consumer interest, and then adding more pack types over the first five years. The company won't start producing all six types of packs until year 6. Haywood suggests that you add a column sparkline to the Financial Summary worksheet that indicates this production plan.

To create column sparklines that show projected production:

▶ 1. Go to the **Financial Summary** worksheet, and then select the range **C5:C10**. This is the location range into which you will insert the sparklines.

▶ 2. On the ribbon, click the **Insert** tab.

▶ 3. In the Sparklines group, click the **Column** button. The Create Sparklines dialog box opens. The location range is already entered because you selected it before opening the dialog box.

▶ 4. With the insertion point in the Data Range box, click the **Projected Production** sheet tab, and then select the data in the range **B5:K10**. This range contains the data you want to chart in the sparklines.

▶ 5. Click the **OK** button. The Create Sparklines dialog box closes, and the column sparklines are added to the location range in the Financial Summary worksheet. See Figure 4-43.

| Figure 4-43 | Column sparklines of projected production for pack type |

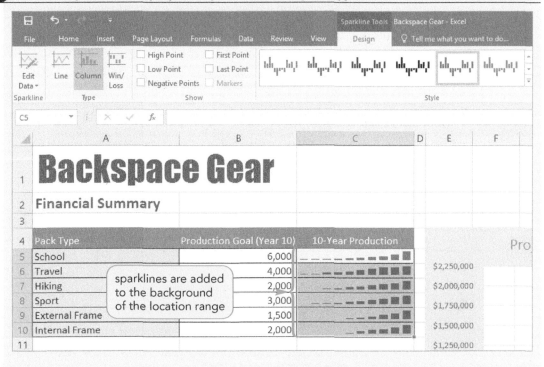

The column sparklines make it clear how the different product lines are placed into production at different times—school and travel packs first, and other models later in the production cycle. Each product, once it is introduced, is steadily produced in greater quantities as the decade progresses.

Formatting the Sparkline Axis

Because of their compact size, you have few formatting options with sparklines. One thing you can change is the scale of the vertical axis. The vertical axis will range from the minimum value to the maximum value. By default, this range is defined differently for each cell to maximize the available space. But this can be misleading. For example, the column sparklines in Figure 4-43 seem to show that Backspace Gear will be producing the same amount of each product line by the end of year 10 because the heights of the last columns are all the same. You can change the vertical axis scale to be the same for the related sparklines.

To set the scale of the column sparklines:

1. On the Financial Summary worksheet, make sure the range **C5:C10** is still selected. Because the sparklines are selected, the Sparkline Tools contextual tab appears on the ribbon.

2. On the Sparkline Tools Design tab, in the Group group, click the **Axis** button, and then click **Custom Value** in the Vertical Axis Maximum Value Options section. The Sparkline Vertical Axis Setting dialog box opens.

3. Select the value in the box, and then type **6000**. You do not have to set the vertical axis minimum value because Excel assumes this to be 0 for all of the column sparklines.

4. Click the **OK** button. The column sparklines are now based on the same vertical scale, with the height of each column indicating the number of packs produced per year.

Working with Sparkline Groups

The sparklines in the location range are part of a single group. Clicking any cell in the location range selects all of the sparklines in the group. Any formatting you apply to one sparkline affects all of the sparklines in the group, as you saw when you set the range of the vertical axis. This ensures that the sparklines for related data are formatted consistently. To format each sparkline differently, you must first ungroup them.

Haywood thinks the column sparklines would look better if they used different colors for each pack. You will first ungroup the sparklines so you can format them separately, and then you will apply a different fill color to each sparkline.

To ungroup and format the column sparklines:

1. Make sure the range **C5:C10** is still selected.

2. On the Sparkline Tools Design tab, in the Group group, click the **Ungroup** button. The sparklines are ungrouped, and selecting any one of the sparklines will no longer select the entire group.

3. Click cell **C6** to select it and its sparkline.

4. On the Sparkline Tools Design tab, in the Style group, click the **More** button, and then click **Sparkline Style Accent 2, Darker 25%** (the second style in the second row) in the Style gallery.

5. Click cell **C7**, and then change the sparkline style to **Sparkline Style Accent 4, (no dark or light)** (the fourth style in the third row) in the Style gallery.

6. Click cell **C8**, and then change the sparkline style to **Sparkline Style Accent 6, (no dark or light)** (the last style in the third row) in the Style gallery.

7. Click cell **C9**, and then change the sparkline style to **Sparkline Style Dark #1** (the first style in the fifth row) in the Style gallery.

8. Click cell **C10**, and then click **Sparkline Style Colorful #2** (the second style in the last row) in the Style gallery.

9. Click cell **A4** to deselect the sparklines. See Figure 4-44.

Figure 4-44   **Sparklines formatted with different styles**

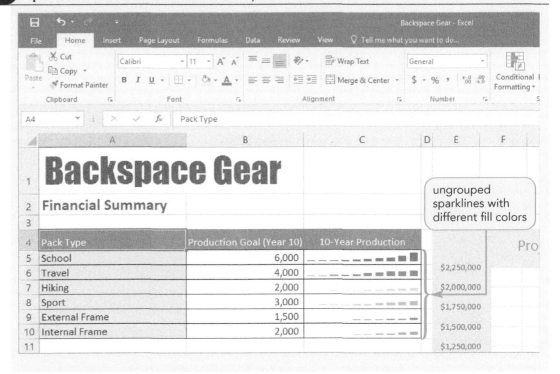

To regroup sparklines, you select all of the cells in the location range containing the sparklines and then click the Group button in the Group group on the Sparkline Tools Design tab. Be aware that regrouping sparklines causes them to share a common format, so you will lose any formatting applied to individual sparklines.

The Sparkline Color button applied a single color to the entire sparkline. You can also apply colors to individual markers within a sparkline by clicking the Marker Color button. Using this button, you can set a distinct color for negative values, maximum values, minimum values, first values, and last values. This is useful with line sparklines that track data across a time range in which you might want to identify the maximum value within that range or the minimum value.

Creating Data Bars

A data bar is a conditional format that adds a horizontal bar to the background of a cell containing a number. When applied to a range of cells, the data bars have the same appearance as a bar chart, with each cell containing one bar. The lengths of data bars are based on the value of each cell in the selected range. Cells with larger values have longer bars; cells with smaller values have shorter bars. Data bars are dynamic, changing as the cell's value changes.

Data bars differ from sparklines in that the bars are always placed in the cells containing the value they represent, and each cell represents only a single bar from the bar chart. By contrast, a column sparkline can be inserted anywhere within the workbook and can represent data from several rows or columns. However, like sparklines, data bars can be used to create compact graphs that can be easily integrated alongside the text and values stored in worksheet cells.

REFERENCE

Creating Data Bars

- Select the range containing the data you want to chart.
- On the Home tab, in the Styles group, click the Conditional Formatting button, point to Data Bars, and then click the data bar style you want to use.
- To modify the data bar rules, click the Conditional Formatting button, and then click Manage Rules.

The Market Summary worksheet contains a table of pack preferences from the market survey by gender. You've already charted the total values from this table as a pie chart in the previous session. Haywood suggests that you display the totals for men and women as data bars.

To add data bars to the worksheet:

1. Go to the **Market Summary** worksheet, and then select the range **C5:D10**.

2. On the Home tab, in the Styles group, click the **Conditional Formatting** button, and then click **Data Bars**. A gallery of data bar styles opens.

3. In the Gradient Fill section, click the **Green Data Bar** style (the second style in the first row.) Green data bars are added to each of the selected cells.

4. Click cell **A4** to deselect the range. See Figure 4-45.

Figure 4-45   Data bars added to the Market Summary worksheet

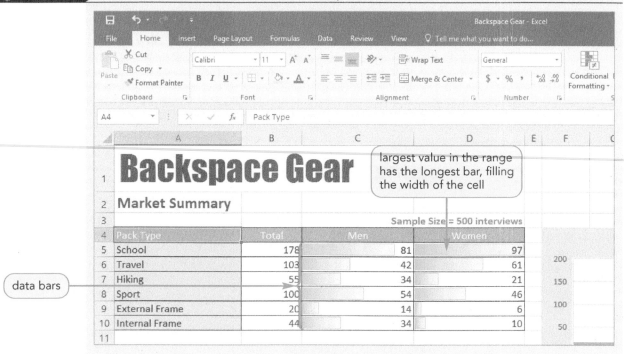

The data bars make it easy to compare the popularity of the different pack types among men and women. The bars clearly show that school packs are most popular followed by either the travel packs or the sport packs.

Modifying a Data Bar Rule

The lengths of the data bars are determined based on the values in the selected range. The cell with the largest value contains a data bar that extends across the entire width of the cell, and the lengths of the other bars in the selected range are determined relative to that bar. In some cases, this will result in the longest data bar overlapping its cell's data value, making it difficult to read. You can modify the length of the data bars by altering the rules of the conditional format.

The longest data bar is in cell D5, representing a count of 97 respondents. The length of every other data bar is proportional to this length. However, because it is the longest, it also overlaps the value of the cell. You will modify the data bar rule, setting the maximum length to 120 so that the bar no longer overlaps the cell value.

TIP

With negative values, the data bars originate from the center of the cell—negative bars extend to the left, and positive bars extend to the right.

To modify the data bar rule:

▶ **1.** Select the range **C5:D10** containing the data bars.

▶ **2.** On the Home tab, in the Styles group, click the **Conditional Formatting** button, and then click **Manage Rules**. The Conditional Formatting Rules Manager dialog box opens, displaying all the rules applied to any conditional format in the workbook.

▶ **3.** Make sure **Current Selection** appears in the Show formatting rules for box. You'll edit the rule applied to the current selection—the data bars in the Market Summary worksheet.

▶ **4.** Click the **Edit Rule** button to open the Edit Formatting Rule dialog box.

   You want to modify this rule so that the maximum value for the data bar is set to 120. All data bar lengths will then be defined relative to this value.

▶ **5.** In the Type row, click the **Maximum arrow**, and then click **Number**.

▶ **6.** Press the **Tab** key to move the insertion point to the Maximum box in the Value row, and then type **120**. See Figure 4-46.

Figure 4-46	Edit Formatting Rule dialog box

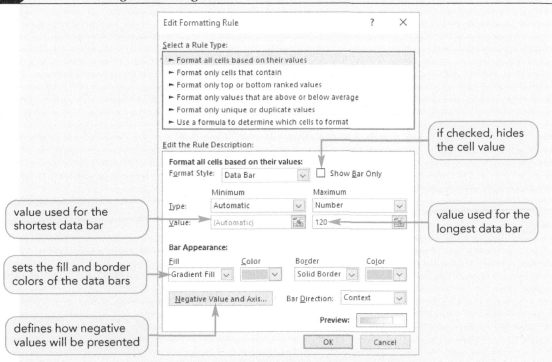

▶ **7.** Click the **OK** button in each dialog box, and then select cell **A4**. The lengths of the data bars are reduced so that no cell values are obscured. See Figure 4-47.

Figure 4-47   Revised data bars

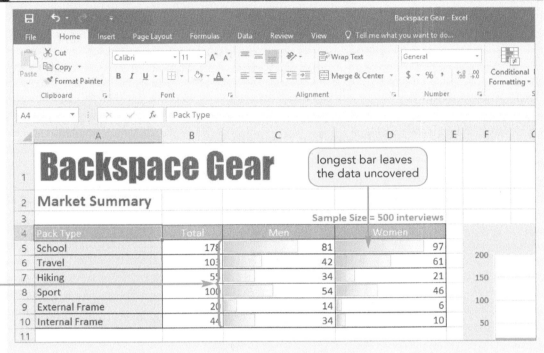

▶ **8.** Save the workbook.

You have finished your work on the Backspace Gear workbook. Haywood is pleased with the charts you created and feels that they provide useful visuals for anyone considering his business proposal.

REVIEW

Session 4.2 Quick Check

1. What is the difference between a line chart and a scatter chart?

2. A researcher wants to plot weight versus blood pressure. Should the researcher use a line chart or a scatter chart? Explain why.

3. What are major tick marks, minor tick marks, and chart gridlines?

4. How do you change the scale of a chart axis?

5. What is the difference between the chart area and the plot area?

6. What is a histogram?

7. When would you use a waterfall chart?

8. What are sparklines? Describe the three types of sparklines.

9. What are data bars? How do data bars differ from sparklines?

Review Assignments

Data File needed for the Review Assignments: Market.xlsx

Haywood is creating another workbook that will have market survey data on competing manufacturers as well as more demographic data on potential Backspace Gear customers. He wants you to add charts to his workbook that show this data graphically. Complete the following:

1. Open the **Market** workbook located in the Excel4 > Review folder included with your Data Files, and then save the workbook as **Market Analysis** in the location specified by your instructor.

2. In the Documentation worksheet, enter your name in cell B3 and the date in cell B4.

3. In the Business Loan worksheet, enter the data values and formulas required to calculate the monthly payment on a business loan of **$225,000** at **6.2%** annual interest to be repaid in **15 years**. Calculate both the monthly payment and the size of the annual payment.

4. In the Market Analysis worksheet, use the data in the range A4:B9 to create a pie chart in the range A11:C24 that shows information about competitors in the Northwest region.

5. Apply the Style 11 chart style to the pie chart, and then move the legend to the left side of the chart. Place the data labels on the inside end of each pie slice.

6. In the Market Tables worksheet, create a clustered column chart of the data in the range A5:F10 to show how many units each competitor sold in the Northwest region in the past five years.

7. Move the chart to the Market Analysis worksheet, and then resize it to cover the range E4:L13. Change the chart title to **Units Sold**. Apply the Style 9 chart style to the chart. Add both primary major horizontal and vertical gridlines. Change the fill color of the chart area to the Gold Accent 4, Lighter 80% theme color and the fill color of the plot area to white. Move the legend to the right side of the chart area.

8. In the Market Tables worksheet, use the data in the range A5:F10 to create a stacked column chart. Move the chart to the Market Analysis worksheet, and then resize it to cover the range E15:L24.

9. Change the chart title to **Total Units Sold**. Format the chart with the same fill colors and gridlines you used the clustered column chart. Move the legend to the right side of the chart.

10. In the Market Tables worksheet, select the nonadjacent range A5:F5,A11:F11,A29:F29, and then create a combination chart with Total Units as a clustered column chart and Total Revenue as a line chart displayed on the secondary axis.

11. Move the chart to the Market Analysis worksheet, and then resize it to cover the range E26:L40. Change the chart title to **Units Sold and Revenue**. Format the chart with the same fill colors and gridlines you used the clustered column chart. Remove the chart legend.

12. Add axis titles to the primary and secondary vertical axes with the title **Total Units** on the primary axis and **Total Revenue** on the secondary axis. Rotate the secondary axis text down. Change the color of the scales and axis titles for the primary and secondary axes to match the color of the clustered column chart and the line chart.

13. Change the scale of the Total Revenue axis to go from $3,500,000 to $5,000,000 in intervals of $250,000.

14. In the Market Tables worksheet, select the range A23:A28,F23:F28 containing the final year revenue for each brand, and then create a Pareto chart based on this data. Move the chart to the Market Analysis worksheet, and then resize it to cover the range A26:C40.

15. Change the chart title to **Market Revenue (2017)**. Format the chart with the same fill colors and gridlines you used the clustered column chart.

16. In the Survey Data worksheet, create a histogram of the distribution of customer ages in the range E7:E506. Change the chart title to **Age Distribution**. Resize the chart to cover the range G4:P22 in the Survey Data worksheet.

17. Change the width of the histogram bins to **5** units.

18. In the Market Analysis worksheet, add gradient fill orange data bars to the values in the range B5:B9. Set the maximum value of the data bars to **0.6**.

19. In the range C5:C9, insert line sparklines based on the data in the range B15:F19 of the Market Tables worksheet to show how the competitors' share of the market has changed over the past five years.

20. Save the workbook, and then close it.

Case Problem 1

Data File needed for this Case Problem: Stefanek.xlsx

Stefanek Budget   Edmund and Lydia Stefanek of Little Rock, Arkansas, are using Excel to track their family budget to determine whether they can afford the monthly loan payments that would come with the purchase of a new house. The couple is considering a $285,000 mortgage at a 4.30 percent interest rate to be paid back over 25 years. They want to know the impact that this mortgage will have on their budget. Complete the following:

1. Open the **Stefanek** workbook located in the Excel4 > Case1 folder included with your Data Files, and then save the workbook as **Stefanek Budget** in the location specified by your instructor.

2. In the Documentation worksheet, enter your name in cell B3 and the date in cell B4.

3. In the Budget worksheet, in the range B3:B8, enter the parameters for a **$285,000** mortgage at **4.3%** annual interest paid back over **25 years**. Calculate the interest rate per month and the total number of payments.

4. In cell B10, calculate the amount of the monthly payment needed to pay back the mortgage.

5. In the range C15:N15, calculate the total income from Edmund and Lydia's monthly salaries.

6. In the range C22:N22, use an absolute reference to insert the monthly mortgage payment you calculated in cell B10.

7. In the range C24:N24, calculate Edmund and Lydia's total expenses per month.

8. In the range C25:N25, calculate the couple's monthly net income by adding their income and their expenses. (Note that expenses are entered as negative values.)

9. In the range C28:C40, calculate the averages for the income and expenses from the 12-month budget.

10. In the range C28:C40, add data bars to the values. Note that negative data bars are displayed to the left of the center point in the cell, whereas positive data bars are displayed to the right.

11. In the range D28:D40, insert line sparklines using the values from the range C13:N25 to show how the different budget entries change throughout the year.

12. Create a pie chart of the income values in the range B28:C29 to show the breakdown of the family income between Edmund and Lydia. Resize the chart to cover the range E27:I40. Change the chart title to **Income** and apply the Style3 chart style to chart.

13. Create a pie chart of the expenses values in the range B31:C38. Resize the chart to cover the range J27:N40. Change the chart title to **Expenses** and apply the Style3 chart style to the chart. Change the position of the data labels to data callouts. If any data labels appear to overlap, select one of the overlapping data labels, and drag it to another position.

14. Save the workbook, and then close it.

Case Problem 2

Data File needed for this Case Problem: Circuit.xlsx

Circuit Realty   Alice Cho works at Circuit Realty in Tempe, Arizona. She wants to use Excel to summarize the home listings in the Tempe area. Alice has already inserted some of the new listings into an Excel workbook including descriptive statistics about the homes and their prices. She wants your help in summarizing this data using informative charts. Complete the following:

1. Open the **Circuit** workbook located in the Excel4 > Case2 folder included with your Data Files, and then save the workbook as **Circuit Realty** in the location specified by your instructor.

2. In the Documentation worksheet, enter your name in cell B3 and the date in cell B4.

3. In the Housing Tables worksheet, using the data in the range A4:B8, create a 2-D pie chart of the number of listings by region. Move the pie chart to the Summary worksheet in the range A4:E15. Change the chart title to **Listings by Region**. Add data labels showing the percentage of listings in each region, displaying the data labels outside the pie slices.

4. In the Housing Tables worksheet, using the range A10:B14, create a pie chart of the listings by the number of bedrooms. Move the pie chart to the Summary worksheet in the range A17:E28. Change the chart title to **Listings by Bedrooms**. Add data labels showing the percentage of listings in each category outside the pie slices.

5. In the Housing Tables worksheet, using the range A16:B22, create a pie chart of the listings by the number of bathrooms. Move the pie chart to the Summary worksheet in the range A30:E341. Change the chart title to **Listings by Bathrooms** and format the pie chart to match the two other pie charts.

6. In the Housing Tables worksheet, using the data in the range D4:E8, create a column chart showing the average home price in four Tempe regions. Move the chart to the Summary worksheet in the range G4:L15. Change the chart title to **Average Price by Region**.

7. In the Housing Tables worksheet, using the data in the range D10:E15, create a column chart of the average home price by age of the home. Move the chart to the Summary worksheet in the range G17:L28. Change the chart title to **Average Price by Home Age**.

8. In the Housing Tables worksheet, using the data in the range D17:E24, create a column chart of the average home price by house size. Move the chart to the Summary worksheet in the range G30:L41. Change the chart title to **Average Price by Home Size**.

9. In the Listings worksheet, create a histogram of all of the home prices in the range H4:H185. Move the histogram to the Summary worksheet in the range N4:U17. Change the chart title to **Home Prices**. Set the scale of the vertical axis to go from **0** to **50**. Set the number of bins to **6**. Set the overflow bin value to **350,000** and the underflow bin value to **150,000**.

10. Create a histogram of the distribution of home prices in each of the four regions, as follows:

    a. Use the data from the range H52:H107 in the Listings worksheet to create the North Region histogram. Place the chart in the range N18:U28 of the Summary worksheet. Change the chart title to **North Region**.

    b. Use the data from the range H5:H51 in the Listings worksheet to create the East Region histogram. Place the chart in the range N29:U39 of the Summary worksheet. Change the chart title to **East Region**.

    c. Use the data from the range H108:H143 in the Listings worksheet to create the South Region histogram. Place the chart in the range N40:U50 of the Summary worksheet. Change the chart title to **South Region**.

    d. Use the data from the range H144:H185 in the Listings worksheet to create the West Region histogram. Place the chart in the range N51:U61 of the Summary worksheet. Change the chart title to **West Region**.

11. The four regional histograms should use a common scale. For each histogram, set the scale of the vertical axis from **0** to **20**, set the number of bins to **6**, set the overflow bin value to **350,000**, and the underflow bin value to **150,000**.

12. In the Price History worksheet, use the data in the range A4:C152 to create a combination chart. Display the Average Price as a line chart on the primary axis and display the Foreclosure values as a column chart on the secondary axis. Move the chart to the Summary worksheet in the range A43:L61. Change the chart title to **Average Home Price and Foreclosure Rates**.

13. Add axis titles to the combination chart, naming the left axis **Average Home Price** and the right axis **Foreclosure (per 10,000)**. Change the horizontal axis title to **Date**. Change the minimum value on the left axis to **100,000**.

14. Change the color of the primary axis and axis title to match the color of the line in the line chart. Change the color of the secondary axis and axis title to match the color used in the column chart. Remove the chart legend.

15. Save the workbook, and then close it.

Case Problem 3

CHALLENGE

Data File needed for this Case Problem: Skyway.xlsx

Skyway Funds   Kristin Morandi is an accounts assistant at Skyway Funds, a financial consulting firm in Monroe, Louisiana. Kristin needs to summarize information on companies that are held in stock by the firm's clients. You will help her develop a workbook that will serve as a prototype for future reports. She wants the workbook to include charts of the company's financial condition, structure, and recent stock performance. Stock market charts should display the stock's daily opening; high, low, and closing values; and the number of shares traded for each day of the past few weeks. The volume of shares traded should be expressed in terms of millions of shares. Complete the following:

1. Open the **Skyway** workbook located in the Excel4 > Case3 folder included with your Data Files, and then save the workbook as **Skyway Funds** in the location specified by your instructor.

2. In the Documentation worksheet, enter your name in cell B3 and the date in cell B4.

3. In the Overview worksheet, add green data bars with a gradient fill to the employee numbers in the range B15:B19. Set the maximum value of the data bars to **20,000**.

4. Add a pie chart of the shareholder data in the range A22:B24. Resize and position the chart to cover the range A26:B37. Do not display a chart title. Add data labels to the pie chart, and then move the legend to the left edge of the chart area.

5. In the Income Statement worksheet, create a 3-D column chart of the income and expenses data from the last three years in the range A4:D4,A7:D7,A13:D13,A20:D20.

6. Move the chart to the range D6:I20 of the Overview worksheet. Change the chart title to **Income and Expenses (Thousands of Dollars)**. Remove the chart legend.

❖ **Explore** 7. Double-click the horizontal axis values to open the Format Axis pane. Expand the Axis Options list, and click the Categories in reverse order check box in the Axis position section to display the year value in reverse order so that 2015 is listed first.

❖ **Explore** 8. Add the data table chart element with legend keys showing the actual figures used in the column chart. (*Hint*: Use the Chart Elements button to add the data table to the chart, and use the data table submenu to show the legend keys.)

9. In the Balance Sheet worksheet, create a 3-D stacked column chart of the data in the range A4:D4,A7:D11 to show the company's assets over the past three years. Move the chart to the Overview worksheet covering the range D21:I37. Change the chart title to **Assets (Thousands of Dollars)**. Remove the chart legend.

❖ **Explore** 10. Use the Switch Row/Column button in the Data group on the Chart Tools Design tab to switch the categories used in the chart from the asset categories to the year values. Display the values on the horizontal axis in reverse order, and add a data table chart element with legend keys to the chart.

11. Repeat Steps 9 and 10 to create a stacked column chart of the company's liabilities in the range A4:D4,A15:D18 in the Balance Sheet worksheet. Place the chart in the range J21:P37 of the Overview worksheet. Change the chart title to **Liabilities (Thousands of Dollars).**

12. Create a line chart of the company's net cash flow using the data in the range A4:D4,A26:D26 of the Cash Flow worksheet. Place the chart in the range J6:P20 of the Overview worksheet. Display the values in the horizontal axis in reverse order. Change the chart title to **Net Cash Flow (Thousands of Dollars).**

⊕ **Explore** 13. In the Stock History worksheet, select the data in the range A4:F9, and then insert a Volume-Open-High-Low-Close chart that shows the stock's volume of shares traded, opening value, high value, low value, and closing value for the previous five days on the market. Move the chart to the Overview worksheet in the range A39:D54.

14. Change the chart title to **5-Day Stock Chart**. Remove the chart gridlines and the chart legend. Change the scale of the left vertical axis to go from **0** to **8**.

15. In the Stock History worksheet, create another Volume-Open-High-Low-Close chart for the 1-year stock values located in the range A4:F262. Move the chart to the Overview worksheet in the range E39:J54. Change the chart title to **1-Year Stock Chart**. Remove the chart legend and gridlines.

16. Create a stock chart for all of the stock market data in the range A4:F2242 of the Stock History worksheet. Move the chart to the range K39:P54 of the Overview worksheet. Change the chart title to **All Years Stock Chart** and remove the chart legend and gridlines.

17. Save the workbook, and then close it.

Case Problem 4

CREATE

Data File needed for this Case Problem: Datasports.xlsx

Datasports   Diane Wilkes runs the Datasports website for sports fans who are interested in the statistics and data that underlie sports. She is developing a series of workbooks in which she can enter statistics and charts for recent sporting events. She wants your help designing the charts and graphics that will appear in the workbook for college basketball games. She has already created a sample workbook containing the results of a hypothetical game between the University of Maryland and the University of Minnesota. She wants you to design and create the charts. For each chart, you need to:

- Include a descriptive chart title.
- Add horizontal and vertical gridlines.
- Add and remove chart elements to effectively illustrate the data.
- Change the colors and format of chart elements to create an attractive chart.
- Insert chart data labels as needed to explain the data.
- Resize and position charts to create an attractive and effective workbook.

Complete the following:

1. Open the **Datasports** workbook located in the Excel4 > Case4 folder included with your Data Files, and then save the workbook as **Datasports Report** in the location specified by your instructor.

2. In the Documentation worksheet, enter your name in cell B3 and the date in cell B4.

3. Create two column charts, as follows, and place them in the Game Report worksheet:

   a. Use the data in the range A6:A19,I6:I19 of the Box Score worksheet to chart the points scores by the University of Maryland players.

   b. Use the data in the range A23:A32,I23:I32 of the Box Score worksheet to chart the points score by the Minnesota players.

4. Add a line chart to the Game Report worksheet tracking the changing score of the game from its beginning to its end. Use the data in the range B5:D47 of the Game Log worksheet as the chart's data source.

5. Add eight pie charts to the Game Report worksheet in comparing the Maryland and Minnesota results for points, field goal percentage, free throw percentage, 3-point field goals, assists, rebounds, turnovers, and blocked shots. Use the data in the Box Score worksheet as the data source for these pie charts.

6. In the Game Log worksheet, in the range E6:E47, calculate the value of the Minnesota score minus the value of the Maryland score.

7. Add data bars to the values in the range E6:E47 showing the score difference as the game progresses. The format of the data bars is up to you.

8. In the Season Record worksheet, in the ranges C6:C19 and G6:G19, enter –1 for every game that the team lost and **1** for every game that the team won.

9. In the Game Report worksheet, create two sparklines, as follows:

   a. In cell D6, insert a Win/Loss sparkline using the values from the range C6:C19 of the Season Record worksheet to show a graphic of Maryland's conference wins and losses.

   b. In cell D7, insert a Win/Loss sparkline using the values from the range G6:G19 of the Season Record worksheet to show a graphic of Minnesota's wins and losses.

10. Save the workbook, and then close it.

Managing Multiple Worksheets and Workbooks

EXCEL

OBJECTIVES

Session 6.1
- Create a worksheet group
- Format and edit multiple worksheets at once
- Create cell references to other worksheets
- Consolidate information from multiple worksheets using 3-D references
- Create and print a worksheet group

Session 6.2
- Create a link to data in another workbook
- Create a workbook reference
- Learn how to edit links

Session 6.3
- Insert a hyperlink in a cell
- Create a workbook based on an existing template
- Create a custom workbook template

Summarizing Rental Income Data

Case | *Reveries Urban Centers*

Reveries Urban Centers is a rental agency with three locations in Michigan—Jackson, Fint, and Petosky. The agency specializes in innovative leasing of empty retail spaces to meet other community needs, including child care centers, medical clinics, religious centers, and music practice rooms, in addition to retail stores. Timothy Root is the COO (chief operating officer). Aubrette Caron manages the Jackson rental center, Gordon Warren manages the Petosky rental center, and Tammy Hernandez manages the Flint rental center.

As COO, Timothy is responsible for analyzing rental income at all locations. Each rental center tracks the rental amounts and types for each quarter in a workbook, which is sent to Timothy to consolidate and analyze. Timothy has received the workbooks with the quarterly rental income data for the past year from all three locations. You will create a worksheet in each workbook that summarizes the rental income totals.

STARTING DATA FILES

Excel6 →	**Module**	**Review**	**Case1**
	Flint.xlsx	FlintMI.xlsx	Tea.xlsx
	Michigan.xlsx	JacksonMI.xlsx	
	Petosky.xlsx	Midland.xlslx	
	UCMemo.docx	NewUC.xlsx	
	UCTotals.xlsx	NewUCMemo.docx	
		PetoskyMI.xlsx	

Case2	**Case3**	**Case4**
Barstow.xlsx	RoomGroom.xlsx	Delaware.xlsx
Carlsbad.xlsx		ELSSummary.xlsx
GoodieBag.xlsx		ELSTemplate.xltx
SanDiego.xlsx		Maryland.xlsx
		NewMD.xlsx
		Virginia.xlsx

Session 6.1 Visual Overview:

Anything you do in the active sheet—such as entering formulas, adding labels, and formatting—is automatically done to all sheets in the worksheet group, saving you time and ensuring consistency.

When worksheets are grouped, the workbook is in group-editing mode and "[Group]" appears in the title bar.

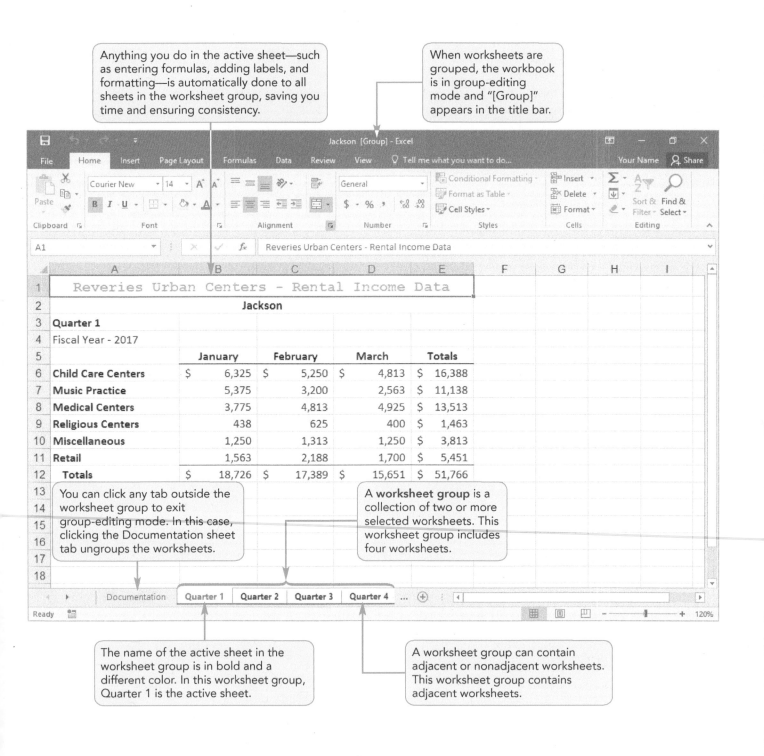

You can click any tab outside the worksheet group to exit group-editing mode. In this case, clicking the Documentation sheet tab ungroups the worksheets.

A worksheet group is a collection of two or more selected worksheets. This worksheet group includes four worksheets.

The name of the active sheet in the worksheet group is in bold and a different color. In this worksheet group, Quarter 1 is the active sheet.

A worksheet group can contain adjacent or nonadjacent worksheets. This worksheet group contains adjacent worksheets.

Worksheet Groups and 3-D References

A **3-D reference** is a reference to the same cell or range in multiple worksheets in the same workbook. This 3-D reference refers to cell E10 in Quarter1:Quarter 4 worksheets.

When two or more worksheets have identical row and column layouts, as the quarterly worksheets in this workbook do, you can enter formulas with 3-D references to summarize those worksheets in another worksheet.

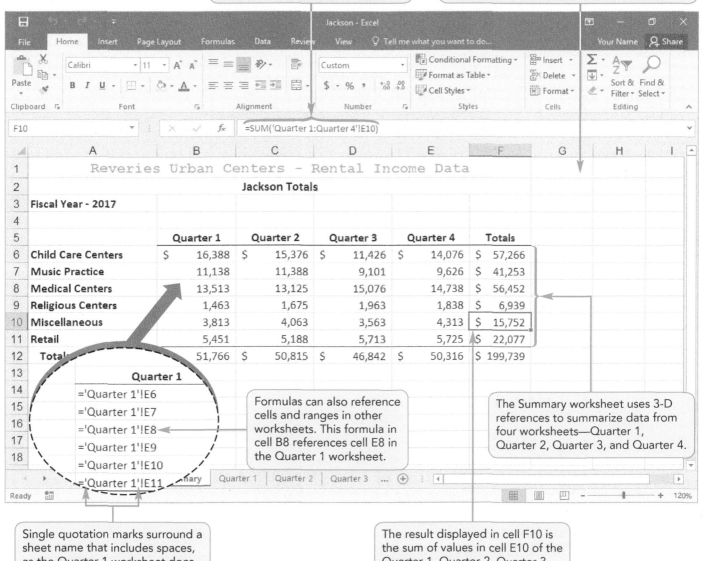

Formulas can also reference cells and ranges in other worksheets. This formula in cell B8 references cell E8 in the Quarter 1 worksheet.

The Summary worksheet uses 3-D references to summarize data from four worksheets—Quarter 1, Quarter 2, Quarter 3, and Quarter 4.

Single quotation marks surround a sheet name that includes spaces, as the Quarter 1 worksheet does in this formula.

The result displayed in cell F10 is the sum of values in cell E10 of the Quarter 1, Quarter 2, Quarter 3, and Quarter 4 worksheets.

Grouping Worksheets

Workbook data is often placed in several worksheets. Using multiple worksheets makes it easier to group and summarize data. For example, a company such as Reveries Urban Centers with locations in different cities within a geographic region can place income information for each site in a separate worksheet. Rather than scrolling through one large and complex worksheet that contains data for all locations, users can access collection information for a specific location simply by clicking a sheet tab in the workbook.

Using multiple worksheets enables you to place summarized data first. Managers interested only in an overall picture can view the first worksheet of summary data without looking at the details available in the other worksheets. Others, of course, might want to view the supporting data in the individual worksheets that follow the summary worksheet. In the case of Reveries Urban Centers, Timothy used separate worksheets to summarize the rental income for the Jackson location for each quarter of the 2017 fiscal year.

You will open Timothy's workbook and review the current information.

To open and review the Reveries Urban Centers workbook:

▶ **1.** Open the **Michigan** workbook located in the **Excel6 > Module** folder included with your Data Files, and then save the document as **Jackson** in the location specified by your instructor.

▶ **2.** In the Documentation worksheet, enter your name and the date.

▶ **3.** Go to the **Quarter 1** worksheet, and then view the rental income in Jackson for the first quarter of the year. See Figure 6-1.

Figure 6-1   **Quarter 1 worksheet for Jackson rental center**

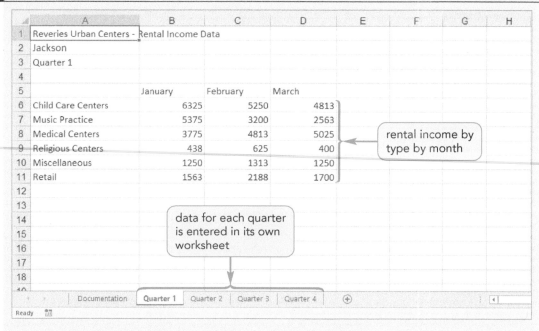

▶ **4.** Review the **Quarter 2**, **Quarter 3**, and **Quarter 4** worksheets. The layout for all four worksheets is identical.

Timothy didn't enter any formulas in the workbook. You need to enter formulas to calculate the total rental income for each column (columns B through D) and each row (rows 6 through 11) in all four worksheets. Rather than retyping the formulas in each worksheet, you can enter them all at once by creating a worksheet group.

A worksheet group, like a range, can contain adjacent or nonadjacent worksheets. In group-editing mode, most editing tasks that you complete in the active worksheet also affect the other worksheets in the group. By forming a worksheet group, you can:

- **Enter or edit data and formulas.** Changes made to content in the active worksheet are also made in the same cells in all the worksheets in the group. You can also use the Find and Replace commands with a worksheet group.
- **Apply formatting.** Changes made to formatting in the active worksheet are also made to all the worksheets in the group, including changing row heights or column widths and applying conditional formatting.
- **Insert or delete rows and columns.** Changes made to the worksheet structure in the active worksheet are also made to all the worksheets in the group.
- **Set the page layout options.** Changes made to the page layout settings in one worksheet also apply to all the worksheets in the group, such as changing the orientation, scaling to fit, and inserting headers and footers.
- **Apply view options.** Changes made to the worksheet view such as zooming, showing and hiding worksheets, and so forth are also made to all the worksheets in the group.
- **Print all the worksheets.** You can print all of the worksheets in the worksheet group at the same time.

Worksheet groups save you time and help improve consistency among the worksheets because you can perform an action once, yet affect multiple worksheets.

REFERENCE

Grouping and Ungrouping Worksheets

- To select an adjacent group, click the sheet tab of the first worksheet in the group, press and hold the Shift key, click the sheet tab of the last worksheet in the group, and then release the Shift key.
- To select a nonadjacent group, click the sheet tab of one worksheet in the group, press and hold the Ctrl key, click the sheet tabs of the remaining worksheets in the group, and then release the Ctrl key.
- To ungroup the worksheets, click the sheet tab of a worksheet that is not in the group (or right-click the sheet tab of one worksheet in the group, and then click Ungroup Sheets on the shortcut menu).

In the Jackson workbook, you'll group an adjacent range of worksheets—the Quarter 1 worksheet through the Quarter 4 worksheet.

To group the quarterly worksheets:

1. Click the **Quarter 1** sheet tab to make the worksheet active. This is the first worksheet you want to include in the group.

2. Press and hold the **Shift** key, and then click the **Quarter 4** sheet tab. This is the last worksheet you want to include in the group.

3. Release the **Shift** key. The four selected sheet tabs are white, the green border extends across the bottom of the four selected sheet tabs, and the sheet tab labels—Quarter 1 through Quarter 4—are in bold, indicating they are all selected. The text "[Group]" appears in the title bar to remind you that a worksheet group is selected in the workbook. See Figure 6-2.

TIP

If you cannot see the sheet tab of a worksheet you want to include in a group, use the sheet tab scroll buttons to display it.

Figure 6-2   Grouped worksheets

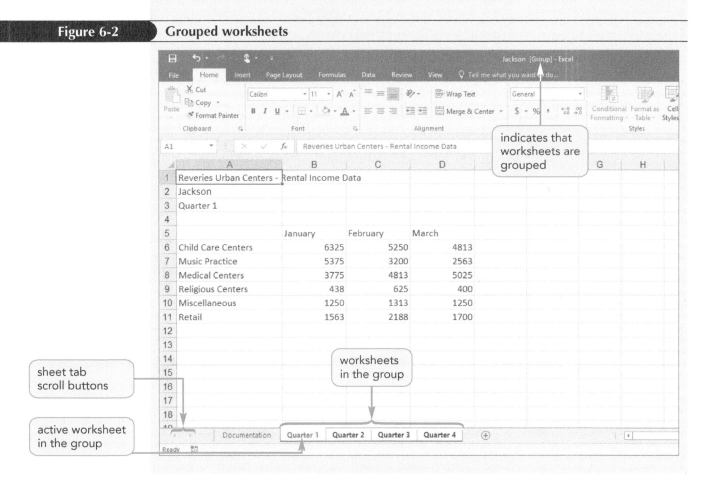

You can change which worksheet in a worksheet group is active. Just click the sheet tab of the worksheet you want to make active. If a worksheet group includes all the worksheets in a workbook, you cannot change which worksheet is the active sheet because clicking a sheet tab ungroups the worksheets.

To change the active sheet in the grouped quarterly worksheets:

1. Click the **Quarter 2** sheet tab to make the worksheet active. The Quarter 2 worksheet is now the active worksheet in the group.

2. Click the **Quarter 4** sheet tab. The Quarter 4 worksheet is now the active worksheet in the group.

Entering Headings and Formulas in a Worksheet Group

When you enter a formula in the active worksheet (in this case, the Quarter 4 worksheet), the formula is entered in the same cells in all the worksheets in the group. The grouped worksheets must have the exact same organization and layout (rows and columns) in order for this to work. Otherwise, any formulas you enter in the active worksheet will be incorrect in the other worksheets in the group and could overwrite existing data.

With the quarterly worksheets grouped, you will enter formulas to calculate the rental income totals for each month.

To enter formulas to calculate the rental income totals in the worksheet group:

▶ 1. Select cell **B12**. You want to enter the formula in cell B12 in each of the four worksheets in the group.

▶ 2. On the Home tab, in the Editing group, click the **AutoSum** button, and then press the **Enter** key. The formula =SUM(B6:B11) is entered in cell B12 in each worksheet, adding the total rental income at the Jackson rental center for the first month of each quarter. For Quarter 4, the October total of rental income shown in cell B12 is 15426.

▶ 3. Copy the formula in cell B12 to the range **C12:D12**. The formula calculates the rental income for the other months in each quarter. For Quarter 4, the rental incomes are 16427 in November and 18413 in December.

▶ 4. In cell **E6**, enter a formula with the SUM function to add the total rental income for Child Care Centers for each quarter at the Jackson rental center. The formula =SUM(B6:D6) adds the monthly rental income for Child Care Centers. In Quarter 4, the rental income was 14076.

▶ 5. Copy the formula in cell E6 to the range **E7:E12** to calculate the rental income for Music Practice, Medical Centers, Religious Centers, Miscellaneous, and Retail, as well as the grand total of rental income at the Jackson rental center for the quarter. For Quarter 4, the Jackson site had 9626 in rental income for Music Practice, 14738 for Medical Centers, 1838 for Religious Centers, 4313 for Miscellaneous, 5675 for Retail, and 50266 overall.

▶ 6. In cells **A12** and **E5**, enter **Totals** as the labels.

▶ 7. Click the **Quarter 3** sheet tab, and then click cell **B12** to make it the active cell. The formula =SUM(B6:B11), which adds the rental income for July, appears in the formula bar, and the formula result 15014 appears in the cell. See Figure 6-3.

| Figure 6-3 | Formulas entered in all worksheets in the group |

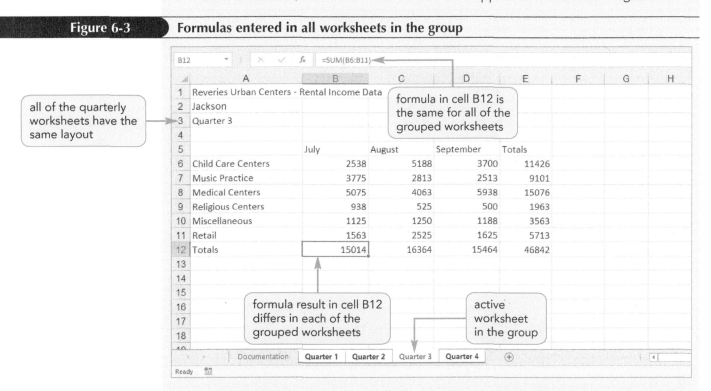

The formulas and labels you entered in the Quarter 4 worksheet were entered in the Quarter 1, 2, and 3 worksheets at the same time.

8. Click the **Quarter 2** sheet tab. Cell B12 is the active cell. The formula =SUM(B6:B11), which adds the rental income for April, appears in the formula bar, and the formula result 18938 appears in the cell.

9. Click the **Quarter 1** sheet tab. Cell B12 is the active cell. The formula =SUM(B6:B11), which adds the rental income for January, appears in the formula bar, and the formula result 18726 appears in the cell.

The grouped worksheets made it quick to enter the formulas needed to calculate the rental incomes for each quarter.

INSIGHT

Editing Grouped Worksheets

When you enter, edit, or format cells in a worksheet group, the changes you make to one worksheet are automatically applied to the other worksheets in the group. For example, if you delete a value from one cell, the content is also deleted from the same cell in all the worksheets in the group. Be cautious when editing a worksheet that is part of a group. If the layout and structure of the other grouped worksheets are not exactly the same, you might inadvertently overwrite data in some of the worksheets. Also, remember to ungroup the worksheet group after you finish entering data, formulas, and formatting. Otherwise, changes you intend to make in one worksheet will be made to all the worksheets in the group, potentially producing incorrect results.

Formatting a Worksheet Group

As when inserting formulas and text, any formatting changes you make to the active worksheet are applied to all worksheets in the group. Timothy wants you to format the quarterly worksheets, which are still grouped, so that they are easier to read and understand.

To apply formatting to the worksheet group:

1. In the Quarter 1 worksheet, click cell **A1**, and then format the cell with **bold**, 14-point, **Courier New**, and the **Dark Blue, Text 2, Lighter 40%** font color. The company name is formatted to match the company name on the Documentation worksheet.

2. Select cell **A12**, and then increase its indent once. The label shifts to the right.

3. Select the nonadjacent range **A2:A3,A6:A12,B5:E5**, and then bold the text in the headings.

4. Merge and center the range **A1:E1** and the range **A2:E2**.

5. Select the range **B5:E5**, and then center the text.

6. Select the nonadjacent range **B6:D6,B12:D12,E6:E12**, and then apply the **Accounting** format with no decimal places.

7. Select the range **B7:D11**, and then apply the **Comma style** with no decimal places. No change is visible in any number that is less than 1000.

8. Select the range **B5:E5,B11:E11**, and then add a bottom border.

9. Select cell **A1**. All the worksheets in the group are formatted.

> **10.** Go to each worksheet in the group and review the formatting changes, and then go to the **Quarter 1** worksheet. See Figure 6-4.

Figure 6-4 | **Formatting applied to the worksheet group**

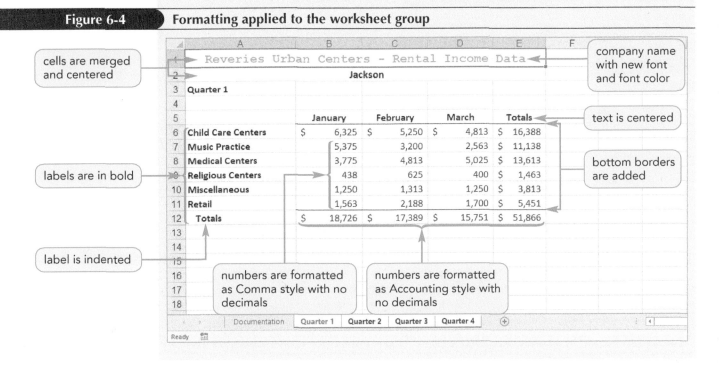

Ungrouping Worksheets

When you ungroup the worksheets, each worksheet functions independently again. If you forget to ungroup the worksheets, any changes you make in one worksheet will be applied to all the worksheets in the group. So be sure to ungroup worksheets when you are finished making changes that apply to multiple worksheets. To ungroup worksheets, click the sheet tab of a worksheet that is not part of the group. If a worksheet group includes all of the sheets in a workbook, click any of the sheet tabs to ungroup the worksheets.

You will ungroup the quarterly worksheets so you can work in each worksheet separately.

Be sure to ungroup the worksheets; otherwise, any changes you make will affect all worksheets in the group.

To ungroup the quarterly worksheets:

> **1.** Click the **Documentation** sheet tab. The worksheets are ungrouped because the Documentation worksheet was not part of the worksheet group. The text "[Group]" no longer appears in the Excel title bar.

> **2.** Verify that the worksheets are ungrouped and the word "[Group]" no longer appears in the title bar.

Timothy wants you to include a new Summary worksheet in the workbook. You'll start working on that next.

PROSKILLS

Written Communication: Using Multiple Worksheets with Identical Layouts

Using multiple worksheets to organize complex data can help make that data simpler to understand and analyze. It also makes it easier to navigate to specific data. For example, a workbook that contains data about a variety of products, stores, or regions could use a different worksheet for each rental type, store, or region. This arrangement provides a way to view discrete units of data that can be combined and summarized in another worksheet.

When you use multiple worksheets to organize similar types of data, the worksheets should have identical layouts. You can quickly group the worksheets with the identical layouts, and then enter the formulas, formatting, and labels in all of the grouped worksheets at once. This helps to ensure consistency and accuracy among the worksheets as well as make it faster to create the different worksheets needed.

Using multiple worksheets with identical layouts enables you to use 3-D references to quickly summarize the data in another worksheet. The summary worksheet provides an overall picture of the data that is detailed in the other worksheets. Often, managers are more interested in this big-picture view. However, the supporting data is still available in the individual worksheets when a deeper analysis is needed.

So, when you are working with a large and complex worksheet filled with data, consider the different ways to organize it in multiple worksheets. Not only will you save time when entering and finding data, but also the data becomes more understandable, and connections and results become clearer.

Working with Multiple Worksheets

As you develop a workbook, you might need to add a worksheet that has the same setup as an existing worksheet. Rather than starting from scratch, you can copy that worksheet as a starting point. For example, Timothy wants the workbook to include a Summary worksheet that adds the annual rental income from the quarterly worksheets. The formulas you create in the Summary worksheet will reference cells in each quarterly worksheet using 3-D references. You can then group the completed worksheets to develop a consistent page setup in all worksheets and then print them all at once.

Copying Worksheets

Often, after spending time developing a worksheet, you can use it as a starting point for creating another, saving you time and energy compared to developing a new worksheet from scratch. Copying a worksheet duplicates all the values, formulas, and formats into the new worksheet, leaving the original worksheet intact. You can then edit, reformat, and enter new content as needed to create the exact worksheet you need.

REFERENCE

Copying Worksheets

- Select the sheet tabs of the worksheets you want to copy.
- Right-click the sheet tabs, and then click Move or Copy on the shortcut menu.
- Click the To book arrow, and then click the name of an existing workbook or click (new book) to create a new workbook for the worksheets.
- In the Before sheet box, click the worksheet before which you want to insert the new worksheet.
- Click the Create a copy check box to insert a checkmark to copy the worksheets.
- Click the OK button.

or

- Select the sheet tabs of the worksheets you want to copy.
- Press and hold the Ctrl key as you drag the selected sheet tabs to a new location in the sheet tabs, and then release the Ctrl key.

Timothy wants you to create the Summary worksheet to provide an overall picture of the data in the detailed quarterly worksheets. The Summary worksheet needs the same formatting and structure as the quarterly worksheets. To ensure consistency among worksheets, you will copy the Quarter 1 worksheet to the beginning of the workbook and then modify its contents.

To copy the Quarter 1 worksheet and create the Summary worksheet:

TIP

You can move or copy a worksheet group within a workbook by dragging one of the group's sheet tabs and dropping it in the new location.

1. Click the **Quarter 1** sheet tab, and then press and hold the **Ctrl** key as you drag the worksheet to the left of the Documentation worksheet. The pointer changes to ⬚ and a triangle indicates the drop location.

2. Release the mouse button, and then release the **Ctrl** key. An identical copy of the Quarter 1 worksheet appears in the new location. The sheet tab shows "Quarter 1 (2)" to indicate that this is the copied sheet.

3. Rename the Quarter 1 (2) worksheet as **Summary**.

4. Drag the **Summary** worksheet between the Documentation worksheet and the Quarter 1 worksheet to make it the second worksheet in the workbook.

Timothy wants the Summary worksheet to show the rental income for each rental type by quarter and the total rental income for each rental type and quarter. You will modify the Summary worksheet to do this now.

To modify the Summary worksheet:

1. Make sure the **Summary** worksheet is the active sheet.

2. In cell **A2**, enter **Jackson Totals**. The new title reflects this worksheet's content.

3. In cell **A3**, enter **2017**. This is the year to which the summary refers.

4. Clear the contents of the cells in the range **B6:E11**. You removed the rental incomes and the formulas in column E, though the formatting remains intact.

5. Insert a new column **C** into the worksheet. The column appears between the January and February labels and has the same formatting as the January column.

▶ **6.** In the range **B5:E5**, enter **Quarter 1**, **Quarter 2**, **Quarter 3**, and **Quarter 4** as the new labels.

▶ **7.** Copy the formula in cell B12 to cell **C12**. See Figure 6-5.

| Figure 6-5 | Summary Worksheet created from the Quarter 1 worksheet |

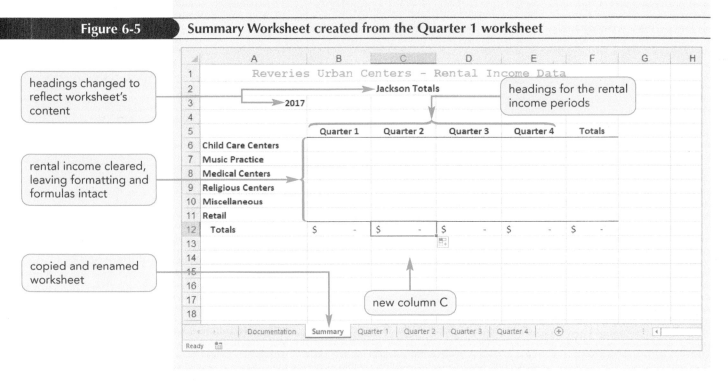

Referencing Cells and Ranges in Other Worksheets

When you use multiple worksheets to organize related data, you can reference a cell or a range in another worksheet in the same workbook. For example, the Summary worksheet references cells in the four quarterly worksheets to calculate the total rental income for the entire year. The syntax to reference a cell or a range in a different worksheet is

    =SheetName!CellRange

where *SheetName* is the worksheet's name as listed on the sheet tab and *CellRange* is the reference for the cell or range in that worksheet. An exclamation mark (!) separates the worksheet reference from the cell or range reference. For example, you could enter the following formula in the Summary worksheet to reference cell D10 in the Quarter1 worksheet:

    =Quarter1!D10

If the worksheet name contains spaces, you must enclose the name in single quotation marks. For example, the following formula references cell D10 in the Quarter 1 worksheet:

    ='Quarter 1'!D10

You can use these references to create formulas that reference cells in different locations in different worksheets. For example, to add rental income from two worksheets—cell C9 in the Quarter 1 worksheet and cell C9 in the Quarter 2 worksheet—you would enter the following formula:

    ='Quarter 1'! C9+'Quarter 2'!C9

You could type the formula directly in the cell, but it is faster and more accurate to use your mouse to select cells to enter their references to other worksheets.

REFERENCE

Entering a Formula with References to Another Worksheet

- Select the cell where you want to enter the formula.
- Type = and begin entering the formula.
- To insert a reference from another worksheet, click the sheet tab for the worksheet, and then click the cell or select the range you want to reference.
- When the formula is complete, press the Enter key.

Timothy wants you to enter a formula in cell A4 in each quarterly worksheet that displays the fiscal year entered in cell A3 in the Summary worksheet. All four quarterly worksheets will use the formula =Summary!A3 to reference the fiscal year in cell A3 of the Summary worksheet.

To enter the formula that references the Summary worksheet:

1. Click the **Quarter 1** sheet tab, press and hold the **Shift** key, and then click the **Quarter 4** sheet tab. The Quarter 1 through Quarter 4 worksheets are grouped.

2. Select cell **A4**. This is the cell in which you want to enter the formula to display the fiscal year.

3. Type = to begin the formula, click the **Summary** sheet tab, and then click cell **A3**. The reference to cell A3 in the Summary worksheet is added to the formula in cell A4 in the grouped worksheets.

4. On the formula bar, click the **Enter** button ✔. The formula =Summary!A3 is entered in cell A4 in each the worksheet in the group. The formula appears in the formula bar and 2017 appears in cell A4. See Figure 6-6.

| Figure 6-6 | Formula with a worksheet reference |

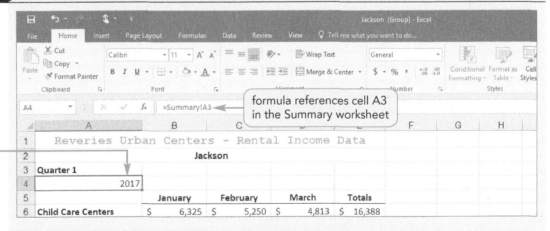

5. Go to each worksheet in the group and verify that the formula =Summary!A3 appears in the formula bar and 2017 appears in cell A4.

6. Go to the **Summary** worksheet. The quarterly worksheets are ungrouped.

7. In cell **A3**, enter **Fiscal Year - 2017**. The descriptive label in cell A3 is entered in the Summary worksheet and is also displayed in the quarterly worksheets because of the formula you entered.

8. Go to the **Quarter 1** through **Quarter 4** worksheets and verify that the label "Fiscal Year - 2017" appears in cell A4 in each worksheet. See Figure 6-7.

Figure 6-7   Edited content displayed in the cell with the worksheet reference

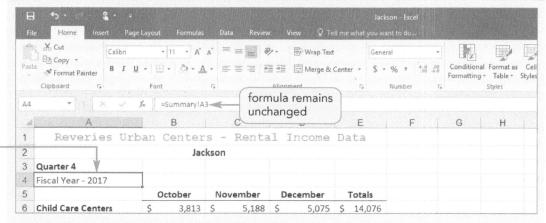

cell A4 in the Quarter 4 worksheet displays the contents of cell A3 in the Summary worksheet

The Summary worksheet needs to include the quarterly totals for each category. You will use formulas that reference the totals in the quarterly worksheets to calculate those totals.

To enter worksheet references for the quarterly totals:

1. Go to the **Summary** worksheet, and then select cell **B6**.

2. Type **=** to begin the formula.

3. Click the **Quarter 1** sheet tab, and then click cell **E6**. The cell is selected and added to the formula.

4. Click the **Enter** button ☑ on the formula bar to complete the formula and return to the Summary worksheet. Cell B6 remains selected, and the formula ='Quarter 1'!E6 appears in the formula bar. The formula result showing the rental income from Child Care Centers in the first quarter of 2017—$16,388—appears in cell B6.

5. Repeat Steps 2 through 4 to enter formulas with worksheet references in cells **C6**, **D6**, and **E6** that add the rental income from Child Care Centers in Quarter 2 (='Quarter 2'!E6), Quarter 3 (='Quarter 3'!E6), and Quarter 4 (='Quarter 4'!E6). The quarterly rental income totals from Child Care Centers are $15,376, $11,426, and $14,076, respectively.

6. Select the range **B6:E6**, and then drag the fill handle over the range **B7:E11**. The formulas with the worksheet references are copied to the rest of the item rows. The Auto Fill Options button appears below the copied range.

7. Click the **Auto Fill Options** button 🔲, and then click the **Fill Without Formatting** option button. You didn't copy the formatting in this case because you want to keep the Accounting format in the range B7:E11 and the bottom border formatting in the range B11:E11. The total values for the year appear in the range.

8. Click cell **B6** to deselect the range. The Summary worksheet now shows the 2017 totals for each rental type in Jackson by quarter and for all rental income in 2017. See Figure 6-8.

| Figure 6-8 | Rental income totals for Jackson in 2017 |

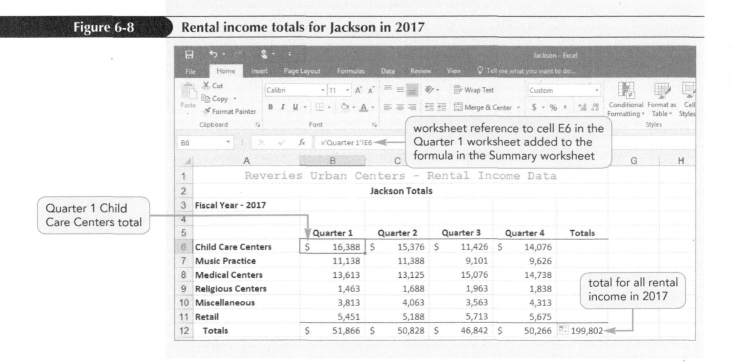

Quarter 1 Child
Care Centers total

worksheet reference to cell E6 in the
Quarter 1 worksheet added to the
formula in the Summary worksheet

B6   ='Quarter 1'!E6

total for all rental
income in 2017

Reveries Urban Centers — Rental Income Data

Jackson Totals

Fiscal Year - 2017

	Quarter 1	Quarter 2	Quarter 3	Quarter 4	Totals
Child Care Centers	$ 16,388	$ 15,376	$ 11,426	$ 14,076	
Music Practice	11,138	11,388	9,101	9,626	
Medical Centers	13,613	13,125	15,076	14,738	
Religious Centers	1,463	1,688	1,963	1,838	
Miscellaneous	3,813	4,063	3,563	4,313	
Retail	5,451	5,188	5,713	5,675	
Totals	$ 51,866	$ 50,828	$ 46,842	$ 50,266	199,802

Using 3-D References to Add Values Across Worksheets

Timothy wants you to calculate the rental income for each type of rental for the year and display the totals for the fiscal year in the Summary worksheet. To calculate the totals for the year, you can add the results from each quarterly worksheet and place the sum in the Summary worksheet. For example, in cell B6 of the Summary worksheet, you can enter the following formula:

```
='Quarter 1'!E6+'Quarter 2'!E6+'Quarter 3'!E6+'Quarter 4'!E6
```

This formula calculates the total rental income for Child Care Centers by adding the values in cell E6 in each of the quarterly worksheets. Continuing this approach for the entire worksheet would be time consuming and error prone.

Instead, when two or more worksheets have *identical* row and column layouts, as the quarterly worksheets in the Jackson workbook do, you can enter formulas with 3-D references to summarize those worksheets in another worksheet. The 3-D reference specifies not only the range of rows and columns but also the range of worksheet names in which the cells appear. The general syntax of a 3-D reference is

```
WorksheetRange!CellRange
```

where *WorksheetRange* is the range of worksheets you want to reference and is entered as *FirstSheetName:LastSheetName* with a colon separating the first and last worksheets in the worksheet range. If the sheet names include spaces, they are surrounded by ' ' (single quotation marks). *CellRange* is the same cell or range in each of those worksheets that you want to reference. An exclamation mark (!) separates the worksheet range from the cell or range. For example, the following formula adds the values in cell D11 in the worksheets between Monday and Friday, including Monday and Friday:

```
=SUM(Monday:Friday!D11)
```

If worksheets named Monday, Tuesday, Wednesday, Thursday, and Friday are included in the workbook, the worksheet range Monday:Friday references all five worksheets. Although the Tuesday, Wednesday, and Thursday worksheets aren't specifically mentioned in this 3-D reference, all worksheets positioned within the starting and ending names are included in the calculation.

INSIGHT

Managing 3-D References

The results of a formula using a 3-D reference reflect the current worksheets in the worksheet range. If you move a worksheet outside the referenced worksheet range or remove a worksheet from the workbook, the formula results will change. For example, consider a workbook with five worksheets named Monday, Tuesday, Wednesday, Thursday, and Friday. If you move the Wednesday worksheet after the Friday worksheet, the worksheet range 'Monday:Friday' includes only the Monday, Tuesday, Thursday, and Friday worksheets. Similarly, if you insert a new worksheet or move an existing worksheet within the worksheet range, the formula results reflect the change. To continue the example, if you insert a Summary worksheet before the Friday worksheet, the 3-D reference 'Monday:Friday' also includes the Summary worksheet.

When you create a formula, make sure that the 3-D reference reflects the appropriate worksheets. Also, if you later insert or delete a worksheet within the 3-D reference, be aware of how the change will affect the formula results.

3-D references are often used in formulas that contain Excel functions, including SUM, AVERAGE, COUNT, MAX, and MIN.

REFERENCE

Entering a Function That Contains a 3-D Reference

- Select the cell where you want to enter the formula.
- Type = to begin the formula, type the name of the function, and then type (to indicate the beginning of the argument.
- Click the sheet tab for the first worksheet in the worksheet range, press and hold the Shift key, and then click the tab for the last worksheet in the worksheet range.
- Select the cell or range to reference, and then press the Enter key.

In the Jackson workbook, Timothy wants to use 3-D references in the Summary worksheet to add the total rental income for each type of rental for the year. You will begin by entering a formula to add the total rental income for Child Care Centers in the first quarter. Then, you'll copy this formula to calculate the total rental income for Music Practice, Medical Centers, Religious Centers, Miscellaneous, and Retail in the first quarter.

To use a 3-D reference to enter the total rental income for Child Care Centers:

▶ 1. In the Summary worksheet, select cell **F6**, and then type **=SUM(** to begin the formula.

▶ 2. Click the **Quarter 1** sheet tab, press and hold the **Shift** key, click the **Quarter 4** sheet tab, and then release the **Shift** key. The quarterly worksheets are grouped to create the worksheet range.

▶ 3. In the Quarter 1 worksheet, click cell **E6**. Cell E6 is selected in each quarterly worksheet and added to the function. Notice that the worksheet names are enclosed in single quotation marks because the worksheet names include spaces. See Figure 6-9.

| Figure 6-9 | 3-D reference added to the SUM function |

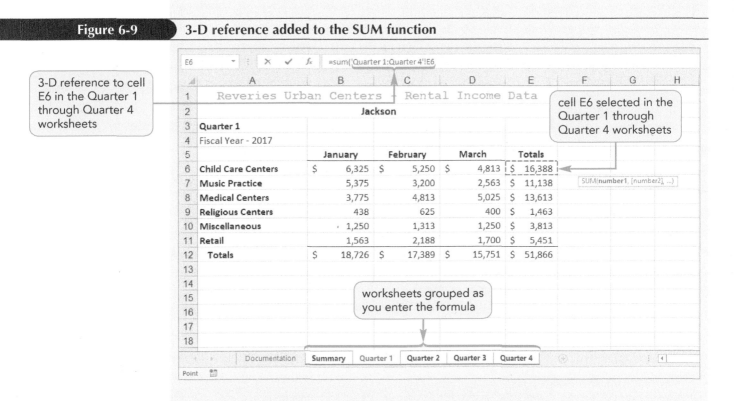

3-D reference to cell E6 in the Quarter 1 through Quarter 4 worksheets

cell E6 selected in the Quarter 1 through Quarter 4 worksheets

SUM(number1, [number2], ...)

worksheets grouped as you enter the formula

4. Press the **Enter** key. The completed formula in the Summary worksheet adds the total rental income for Child Care Centers in 2017.

5. In the Summary worksheet, select cell **F6**. The formula with the 3-D reference, =SUM('Quarter 1:Quarter 4'!E6), appears in the formula bar. The formula result—$57,266—appears in the cell. See Figure 6-10.

| Figure 6-10 | 3-D reference used in the SUM function |

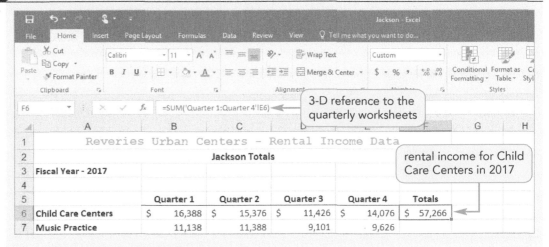

3-D reference to the quarterly worksheets

rental income for Child Care Centers in 2017

The next formula will add the total rental income for Music Practice in the first quarter.

To calculate the total rental income for Music Practice:

1. In the Summary worksheet, click cell **F7**, and then type **=SUM(** to begin the formula.

▶ 2. Click the **Quarter 1** sheet tab, press and hold the **Shift** key, click the **Quarter 4** sheet tab, and then release the **Shift** key. The quarterly worksheets are grouped to create the worksheet range.

▶ 3. In the Quarter 1 worksheet, click cell **E7**. Cell E7 is selected in each quarterly worksheet and added to the function.

▶ 4. Press the **Enter** key to complete the formula that adds the total rental income from Music Practice in 2017.

▶ 5. In the Summary worksheet, click cell **F7**. The formula with the 3-D reference, =SUM('Quarter 1:Quarter 4'!E7), appears in the formula bar, and the formula result $41,253 appears in cell F7.

Instead of entering formulas with 3-D references to create the totals for the remaining types of rental income, you can copy the formulas to the rest of the range. You copy formulas with 3-D references the same way you copy other formulas—using copy and paste or AutoFill.

Timothy wants you to calculate the remaining total rental incomes by rental type in 2017. You'll copy the formula with the 3-D references to do that.

To copy the formulas with 3-D references:

▶ 1. In the Summary worksheet, make sure cell **F7** is selected. This cell contains the formula with the 3-D reference you already entered.

▶ 2. Drag the fill handle over the range **F8:F11**. The formulas are copied for the rest of the rental income totals. The Auto Fill Options button appears below the copied range.

▶ 3. Click the **Auto Fill Options** button [icon], and then click the **Fill Without Formatting** option button. You don't want to copy the formatting in this case because you want to keep the bottom border formatting in cell F11. The total values for the year appear in the range.

▶ 4. Select cell **B6** to deselect the range. The Summary worksheet now shows the totals for 2017 in Jackson for each type of rental income. See Figure 6-11.

| Figure 6-11 | Summary worksheet with the Jackson rental income totals |

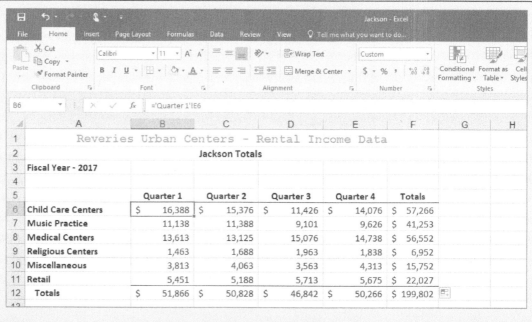

One benefit of summarizing data using formulas with 3-D references, like any other formula, is that if you change the value in one worksheet, the results of formulas that reference that cell reflect the change.

Timothy has discovered an error in the Jackson rental income data. In May, the rental income from Religious Centers was $425, not $438. You will correct the rental income.

To change the rental income in the Quarter 2 worksheet:

▶ **1.** In the Summary worksheet, note that the rental income for Religious Centers in Quarter 2 is 1,688.

▶ **2.** Go to the **Quarter 2** worksheet.

▶ **3.** In cell **C9**, enter **425**. The total rental income for Religious Centers for Quarter 2 is now $1,675.

   The results in the Summary worksheet are also updated because of the 3-D references in the formulas.

▶ **4.** Go to the **Summary** worksheet. The total rental income for Religious Centers in Quarter 2 is now 1,675. The Quarter 2 total is now $50,815, the 2017 total for Religious Centers is now $6,939, and the total rental income for 2017 is $199,789. See Figure 6-12.

| Figure 6-12 | Summary worksheet with updated Quarter 2 data |

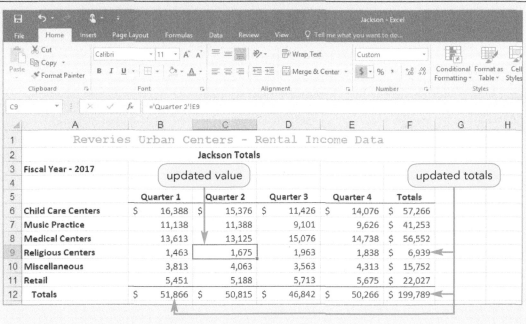

Printing a Worksheet Group

When you create a worksheet group, you apply the same page layout settings to all of the worksheets in the group at the same time. You can also print all of the worksheets in the group at once. The process for printing a worksheet group is the same as for printing a single worksheet, except that you must first group the worksheets you want to print.

Timothy wants a printed copy of the five rental income worksheets to include in his report. Each page should have the same setup. Because the layout will be the same for all the quarterly worksheets in the Jackson workbook, you can speed the page layout setup by creating a worksheet group before selecting settings.

To preview the Summary and quarterly worksheets with a custom header and footer:

Be sure to include all five worksheets in the group so you can apply page layout settings and print the worksheets at once.

1. Group the **Summary, Quarter 1**, **Quarter 2**, **Quarter 3**, and **Quarter 4** worksheets. The five worksheets are grouped.

2. On the ribbon, click the **Page Layout** tab.

3. In the Page Setup group, click the **Dialog Box Launcher**. The Page Setup dialog box opens with the Page tab active.

4. Click the **Margins** tab, and then click the **Horizontally** check box in the Center on page section to insert a checkmark. The printed content will be centered horizontally on the page.

5. Click the **Header/Footer** tab, click the **Custom Header** button to open the Header dialog box, click in the **Center section** box, click the **Insert Sheet Name** button to add the &[Tab] code in the section box, and then click the **OK** button. A preview of the header appears in the upper portion of the dialog box.

6. Click the **Custom Footer** button to open the Footer dialog box, type your name in the Left section box, click in the Right section box, click the **Insert Date** button to add the &[Date] code in the section box, and then click the **OK** button. A preview of the footer appears in the center of the dialog box.

7. Click the **Print Preview** button. The preview of the Summary worksheet, the first worksheet in the group, appears on the Print screen in Backstage view. See Figure 6-13.

| Figure 6-13 | Preview of the worksheet group |

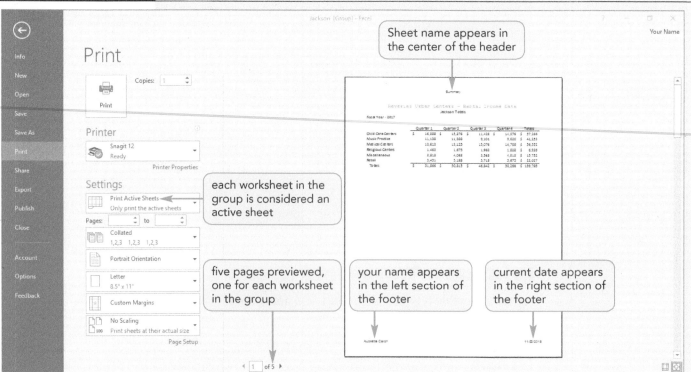

▶ **8.** Below the preview, click the **Next Page** button ▶ four times to view the other worksheets in the group. Each page has the same page layout, but the header shows the sheet tab names.

Trouble? If only one page appears in the preview, the worksheets are not grouped. Click the Back button to exit Backstage view, and then repeat Steps 1 through 8.

▶ **9.** Click the **Back** button ⬅ to exit Backstage view without printing the worksheet group.

▶ **10.** Go to the **Documentation** worksheet to ungroup the worksheets, and then go to the **Summary** worksheet.

In this session, you consolidated the data in Reveries Urban Centers Jackson workbook into a Summary worksheet so that Timothy can quickly see the collection totals for the rental income totals for each rental type. In the next session, you will help Timothy determine the annual totals for the other Reveries Urban Centers—Flint and Petosky.

Session 6.1 Quick Check

REVIEW

1. What is a worksheet group?

2. How do you select an adjacent worksheet group? How do you select a nonadjacent worksheet group? How do you deselect a worksheet group?

3. What formula would you enter in the Summary worksheet to reference cell C8 in the Quarter 2 worksheet?

4. What is the 3-D reference to cell E6 in the adjacent Summary 1, Summary 2, and Summary 3 worksheets?

5. Explain what the formula =AVERAGE(Sheet1:Sheet4!B1) calculates.

6. If you insert a new worksheet named Sheet5 after Sheet4, how would you change the formula =MIN(Sheet1:Sheet4!B1) to include Sheet5 in the calculation?

7. If you insert a new worksheet named Sheet5 before Sheet4, how would you change the formula =SUM(Sheet1:Sheet4!B1) to include Sheet5 in the calculation?

8. How do you apply the same page layout to all of the worksheets in a workbook at one time?

Session 6.2 Visual Overview:

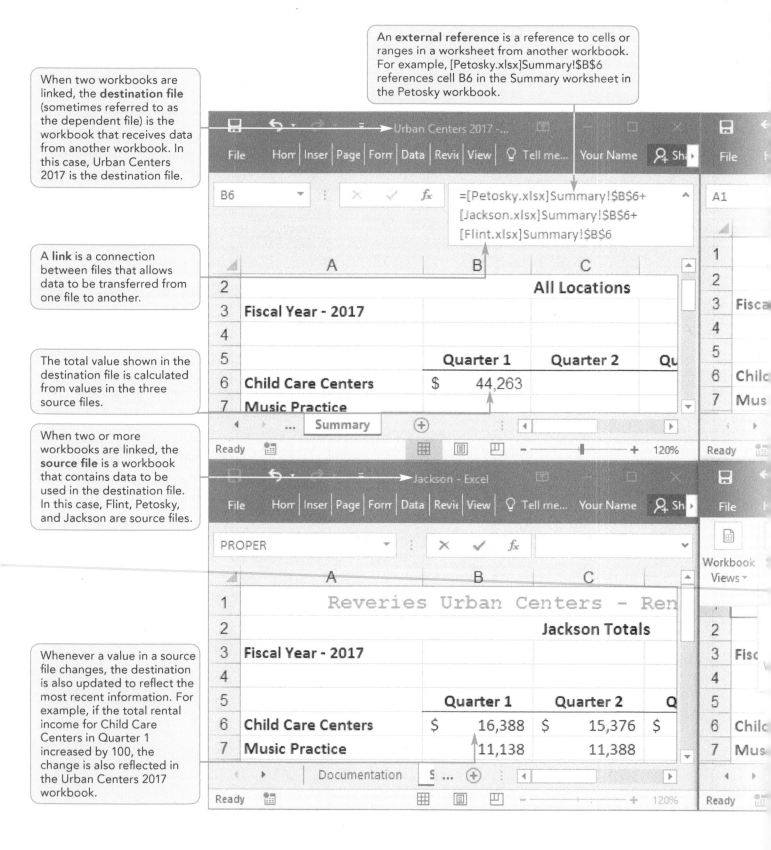

An **external reference** is a reference to cells or ranges in a worksheet from another workbook. For example, [Petosky.xlsx]Summary!$B6 references cell B6 in the Summary worksheet in the Petosky workbook.

When two workbooks are linked, the **destination file** (sometimes referred to as the dependent file) is the workbook that receives data from another workbook. In this case, Urban Centers 2017 is the destination file.

A **link** is a connection between files that allows data to be transferred from one file to another.

The total value shown in the destination file is calculated from values in the three source files.

When two or more workbooks are linked, the **source file** is a workbook that contains data to be used in the destination file. In this case, Flint, Petosky, and Jackson are source files.

Whenever a value in a source file changes, the destination is also updated to reflect the most recent information. For example, if the total rental income for Child Care Centers in Quarter 1 increased by 100, the change is also reflected in the Urban Centers 2017 workbook.

Urban Centers 2017 -...

B6   =[Petosky.xlsx]Summary!$B$6+[Jackson.xlsx]Summary!$B$6+[Flint.xlsx]Summary!$B$6

	A	B	C
2			All Locations
3	Fiscal Year - 2017		
4			
5		Quarter 1	Quarter 2	Qu
6	Child Care Centers	$ 44,263	
7	Music Practice		

Summary

Jackson - Excel

PROPER

	A	B	C
1	Reveries Urban Centers - Ren
2		Jackson Totals	
3	Fiscal Year - 2017		
4			
5		Quarter 1	Quarter 2	Q
6	Child Care Centers	$ 16,388	$ 15,376	$
7	Music Practice	11,138	11,388	

Documentation   S ...

Links and External References

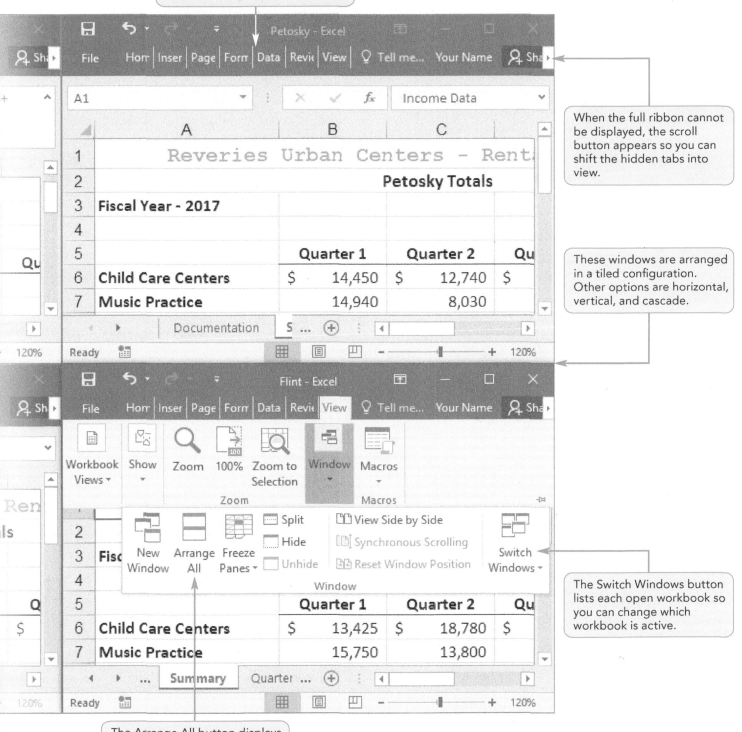

You can collapse the ribbon to make more space available for viewing the worksheet. This is helpful when you tile a workbook.

When the full ribbon cannot be displayed, the scroll button appears so you can shift the hidden tabs into view.

These windows are arranged in a tiled configuration. Other options are horizontal, vertical, and cascade.

The Switch Windows button lists each open workbook so you can change which workbook is active.

The Arrange All button displays all of the open workbooks in a tiled configuration within the program window.

Linking Workbooks

When creating formulas in a workbook, you can reference data in other workbooks. To do so, you must create a link between the workbooks. When two files are linked, the source file contains the data, and the destination file (sometimes called the dependent file) receives the data. For example, Timothy wants to create a company-wide workbook that summarizes the annual totals from each of the three Reveries Urban Centers. In this case, the Petosky, Flint, and Jackson workbooks are the source files because they contain the data from the three rental centers. The Urban Centers 2017 workbook is the destination file because it receives the data from the three rental center workbooks to calculate the company totals for 2017. The Urban Centers 2017 workbook will always have access to the most recent information in the rental center workbooks because it can be updated whenever any of the linked values change. See Figure 6-14.

Figure 6-14   Source and destination files

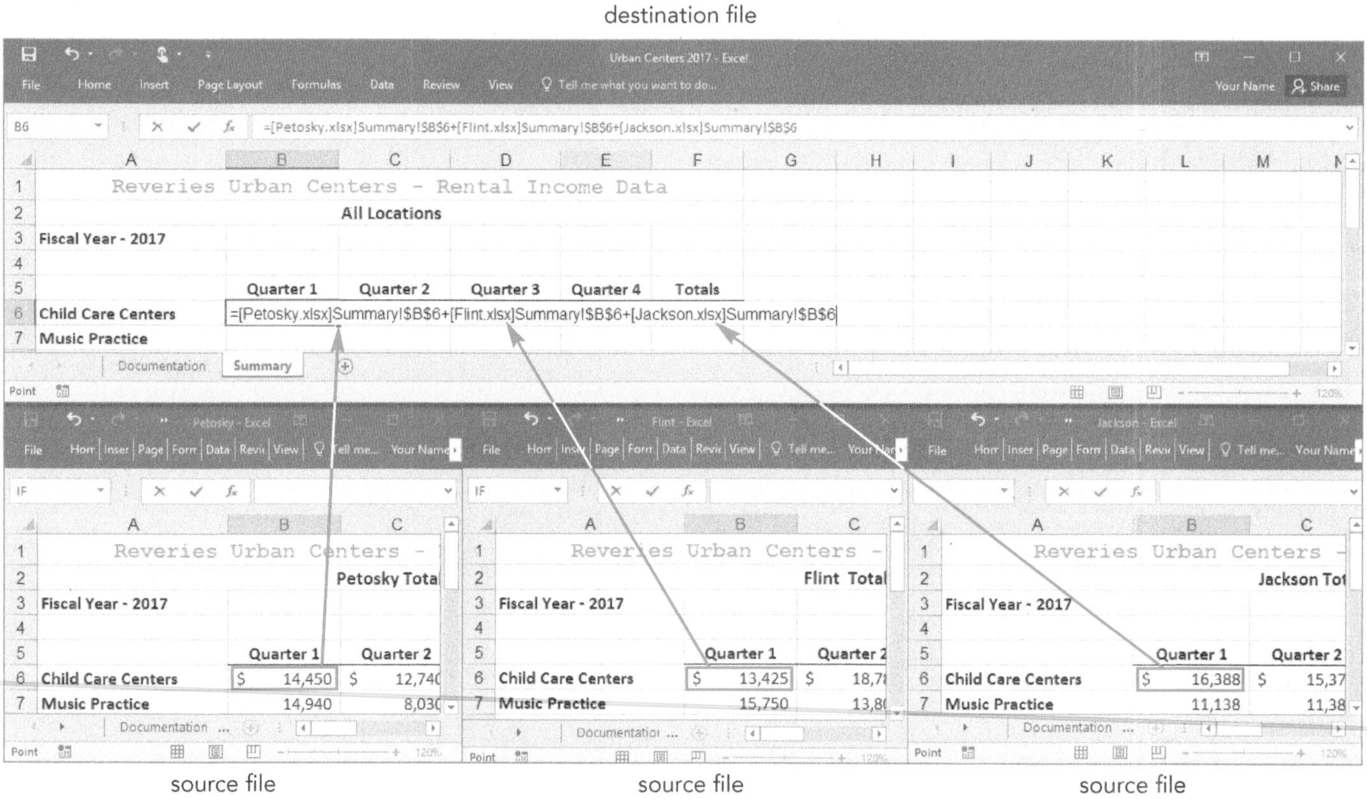

To create the link between destination and source files, you need to insert a formula in the UCTotals workbook that references a specific cell or range in the three rental center workbooks. That reference, called an external reference, has the syntax

[WorkbookName]WorksheetName!CellRange

where *WorkbookName* is the filename of the workbook (including the file extension) enclosed in square brackets; *WorksheetName* is the name of the worksheet that contains the data followed by an exclamation mark; and *CellRange* is the cell or range that contains the data. For example, the following formula references cell B6 in the Summary worksheet of the Jackson.xlsx workbook:

=[Jackson.xlsx]Summary!B6

TIP

When you click cells to include in formulas with external references, Excel enters all of the required punctuation, including quotation marks.

If the workbook name or the worksheet name contains one or more spaces, you must enclose the entire workbook name and worksheet name in single quotation marks. For example, the following formula references cell B6 in the Summary worksheet of the Flint 2017.xlsx workbook:

```
='[Flint 2017.xlsx]Summary'!B6
```

When the source and destination workbooks are stored in the same folder, you need to include only the workbook name in the external reference. However, when the source and destination workbooks are located in different folders, the workbook reference must include the file's complete location (also called the path). For example, if the destination file is stored in C:\Rental Income and the source file is stored in C:\Rental Income\Local Data, the complete reference in the destination file would be:

```
='C:\Rental Income\Local Data\[Flint.xlsx]Summary'!B6
```

The single quotation marks start at the beginning of the path and end immediately before the exclamation mark.

PROSKILLS

Decision Making: Understanding When to Link Workbooks

More than one person is usually involved in developing information that will be used in an organization's decision-making process. If each person has access to only part of the data, everyone's ability to see the whole picture and make good decisions is limited. Linking workbooks provides one way to pull together all of the data being compiled by different people or departments to support the decision-making process.
When deciding whether to link workbooks, consider the following questions:

- **Can separate workbooks have the same purpose and structure?** With linked workbooks, each workbook can focus on a different store, branch office, or department with the same products or expenditure types and reporting periods (such as weekly, monthly, and quarterly).
- **Is a large workbook too unwieldy to use?** A large workbook can be divided into smaller workbooks for each quarter, division, or product and then linked to provide the summary information.
- **Can information from different workbooks be summarized?** Linked workbooks provide a way to quickly and accurately consolidate information from multiple source workbooks, and the summary worksheet will always contain the most current information even when information is later updated.
- **Are source workbooks continually updated?** With linked workbooks, an outdated source workbook can be replaced and the destination workbook will then reflect the latest information.
- **Will the source workbooks be available to the destination workbook?** If the person who is working with the destination workbook cannot access the source workbooks, then the destination workbook cannot be updated.

If you can answer yes to these questions, then linked workbooks are the way to go. Creating linked workbooks can help you analyze data better, leading to better decision making. It also provides greater flexibility as data becomes more expansive and complex. However, keep in mind that workbooks with many links can take a long time to open and update.

Navigating Multiple Workbooks

When you create external reference formulas, you'll need to move between open workbooks. The Switch Windows button in the Window group on the View tab lists each open workbook so you can change which workbook is active. Another method is to click the Excel button on the taskbar and then click the thumbnail of the workbook you want to make active.

Timothy received workbooks from the Flint and Petosky managers that are similar to the one you helped prepare. These three rental income workbooks (named Petosky, Flint, and Jackson) contain the rental income for 2017. Timothy wants to create a company-wide workbook that summarizes the annual totals from each rental center workbook. You'll combine the three rental center workbooks into one rental center summary workbook. First you need to open the workbooks that you want to reference. Then you'll switch between them to make each Summary worksheet the active sheet in preparation for creating the external references.

To open the regional workbooks and switch between them:

1. If you took a break after the previous session, make sure the Jackson workbook is open and the Summary worksheet is active.

2. Open the **UCTotals** workbook located in the **Excel6 > Module** folder included with your Data Files, and then save the workbook as **Urban Centers 2017** in the location specified by your instructor.

3. In the Documentation worksheet of the Urban Centers 2017 workbook, enter your name and the date.

4. Open the **Petosky** workbook located in the **Excel6 > Module** folder included with your Data Files, and then go to the **Summary** worksheet.

5. Open the **Flint** workbook located in the **Excel6 > Module** folder included with your Data Files, and then go to the **Summary** worksheet. All three location workbooks have the same active sheet.

6. On the ribbon, click the **View** tab.

7. In the Window group, click the **Switch Windows** button. A menu lists the names of all the workbooks that are currently open.

8. Click **Urban Centers 2017** to make that the active workbook, and then go to the **Summary** worksheet. The Summary worksheet is the active sheet in each workbook.

Arranging Multiple Workbooks

Rather than continually switching between open workbooks, you can display all the open workbooks on your screen at the same time. This way, you can easily click among the open workbooks to create links as well as quickly compare the contents of worksheets in different workbooks. You can arrange workbooks in the following layouts:

- **Tiled**—divides the open workbooks evenly on the screen
- **Horizontal**—divides the open workbooks into horizontal bands
- **Vertical**—divides the open workbooks into vertical bands
- **Cascade**—layers the open workbooks on the screen

The layout you select will depend on the contents being displayed and your purpose.

REFERENCE

Arranging Workbooks

- On the View tab, in the Window group, click the Arrange All button.
- Select the layout in which you want to arrange the open workbooks.
- When arranging multiple workbooks, uncheck the Windows of active workbook option. When arranging multiple worksheets within one workbook, check this option.
- Click the OK button.

Currently, the four workbooks are open, but only one is visible. You'll make all the workbooks visible by displaying the workbooks in the tiled arrangement.

To tile the open workbooks:

1. On the ribbon, click the **View** tab.

2. In the Window group, click the **Arrange All** button. The Arrange Windows dialog box opens so you can select the layout arrangement you want.

> **TIP**
>
> You can click the Windows of active workbook check box to tile the sheets in the current workbook on the screen.

3. Click the **Tiled** option button, if necessary. The Tiled option will arrange the four Reveries Urban Centers workbooks evenly on the screen.

4. Click the **OK** button. The four open workbooks appear in a tiled layout.

5. Click in the **Urban Centers 2017** workbook to make it the active workbook, if necessary. In the tiled layout, the active workbook contains the active cell.

6. In the Summary worksheet, click cell **B6** to make it the active cell.

   The ribbon appears in each window, taking up a lot of the workbook space. To see more of the worksheets, you will collapse the ribbon in each window to show only the ribbon tabs.

7. In each window, click the **Collapse the Ribbon** button ⌃ in the lower-right corner of the ribbon (or press the **Ctrl+F1** keys). Only the ribbon tabs are visible in each window. If the ribbon includes more tabs than can be displayed, a ribbon scroll button ▶ appears to the right of the last visible tab, which you can click to display the other tabs. See Figure 6-15.

Figure 6-15   **Four workbooks arranged in a tiled layout**

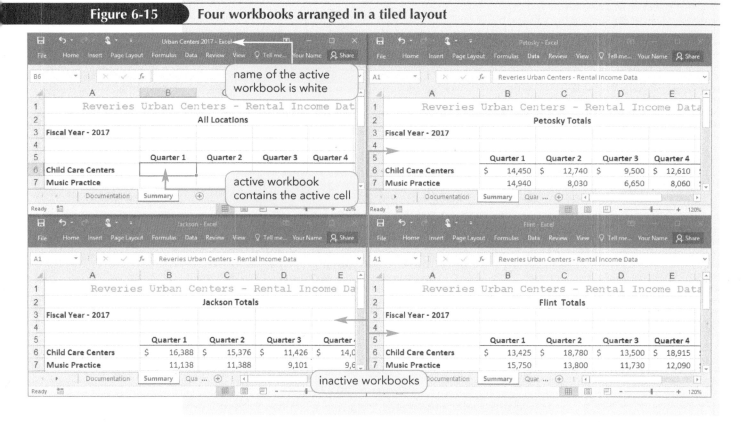

Creating Formulas with External References

A formula can include a reference to another workbook (called an external reference), which creates a set of linked workbooks. The process for entering a formula with an external reference is the same as for entering any other formula using references within the same worksheet or workbook. You can enter the formulas by typing them or using the point-and-click method. In most situations, you will use the point-and-click method to switch between the source files and the destination files so that Excel enters the references to the workbook, worksheet, and cell using the correct syntax.

You need to enter the external reference formulas in the Urban Centers 2017 workbook to summarize the rental center totals into one workbook for Timothy. You'll start by creating the formula that adds the total rental income for Child Care Centers in Petosky, Flint, and Jackson for Quarter 1 of 2017. You cannot use the SUM function with 3-D references here because you are referencing multiple workbooks, and 3-D references can be used only to reference multiple worksheets in the same workbook.

To create the formula with external references to add the total rental income for Child Care Centers:

1. In the Urban Centers 2017 workbook, in the Summary worksheet, make sure cell **B6** is the active cell, and then type **=** to begin the formula.

As you create the formula, be sure to verify each external reference before going to the next step.

2. Click anywhere in the **Petosky** workbook to make the Petosky workbook active and place the formula in its formula bar, and then click cell **B6** in the Summary worksheet. The external reference to cell B6 in the Summary worksheet of the Petosky workbook—[Petosky.xlsx]Summary!$B$6—is added to the formula in the Urban Centers 2017 workbook. See Figure 6-16.

Figure 6-16   Formula with an external cell reference

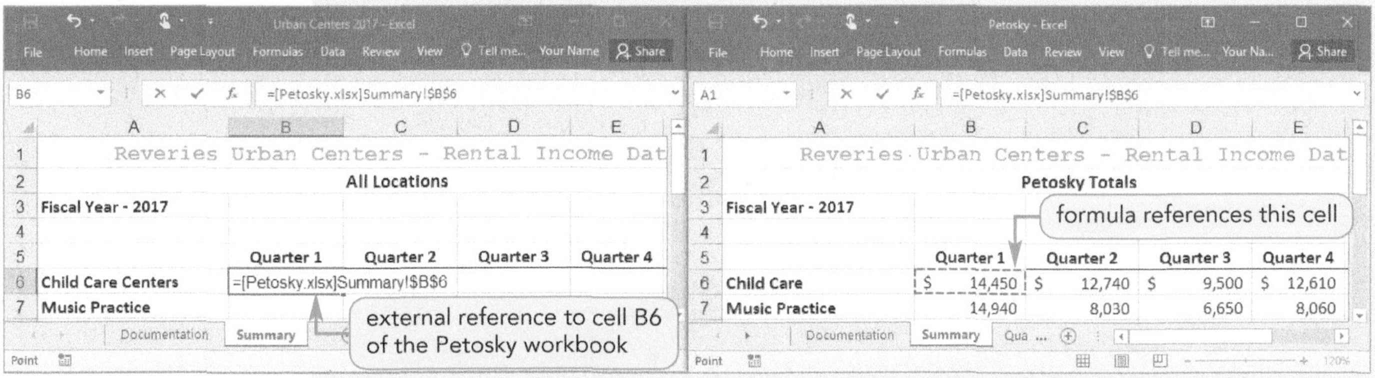

The reference created in a 3-D reference is an absolute cell reference, which does not change when the formula is copied. The formula remains in the formula bar of both the Urban Centers 2017 and Petosky workbooks until you make another workbook active. At that time, the formula will appear in the Urban Centers 2017 workbook and the active worksheet.

3. Type **+**. The Urban Centers 2017 workbook becomes active, and you can continue entering the formula. You need to create an external reference to the Flint workbook.

4. Click anywhere in the **Flint** workbook, click cell **B6** in the Summary worksheet, and then type **+**. The formula in the Urban Centers 2017 workbook includes the external reference to the cell that contains the total rental income for Child Care Centers in Flint during Quarter 1.

5. Click anywhere in the **Jackson** workbook, click cell **B6** in the Summary worksheet, and then press the **Enter** key. The formula with three external references is entered in the Summary worksheet in the Urban Centers 2017 workbook.

6. In the Urban Centers 2017 workbook, in the Summary worksheet, click cell **B6**. The complete formula is too long to appear in the formula bar of the tiled window. You will expand the formula bar so that it can display the full formula.

7. At the right edge of the formula bar, click the **Expand Formula Bar** button ⌄ (or press the **Ctrl+Shift+U** keys). The complete formula is now visible in the formula bar, and the Collapse Formula Bar button appears at the right edge of the formula bar, which you can click to return the formula bar to a single line. The formula results in cell B6 show that the Child Care Centers had rental income of 44263 during Quarter 1 in the three rental centers—$14,450 in Petosky, $13,425 in Flint, and $16,388 in Jackson. See Figure 6-17.

Figure 6-17   Total rental income for Child Care Centers from Petosky, Flint, and Jackson in Quarter 1

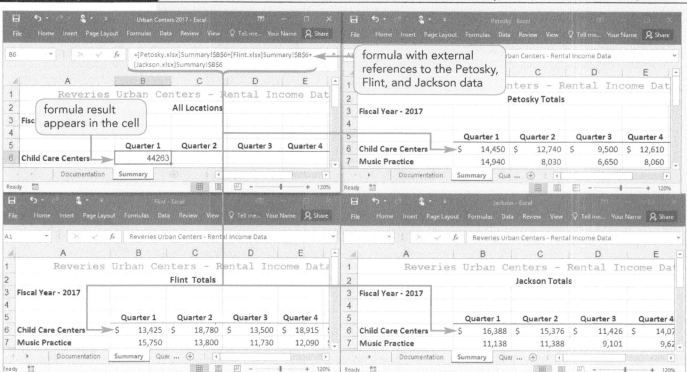

Trouble? If 44263 doesn't appear in cell B6 in the Summary worksheet in the Urban Centers 2017 workbook, you might have clicked an incorrect cell for an external reference in the formula. Repeat Steps 1 through 6 to correct the formula.

You'll use the same process to enter the external reference formula for cells C6, D6, and E6, which contain the total rental income for Child Care Centers in Quarter 2, Quarter 3, and Quarter 4, respectively. These formulas will calculate the total amounts from all three locations.

To create the remaining external reference formulas:

1. In the Urban Centers 2017 workbook, in the Summary worksheet, select cell **C6,** and then type **=** to begin the formula.

2. Click the **Petosky** workbook, click cell **C6** in the Summary worksheet, and then type **+**. The formula in the Urban Centers 2017 workbook includes the external reference to cell C6 in the Summary worksheet in the Petosky workbook.

3. Click the **Flint** workbook, click cell **C6** in the Summary worksheet, and then type **+**. The formula includes an external reference to cell C6 in the Summary worksheet in the Flint workbook.

4. Click the **Jackson** workbook, click cell **C6** in the Summary worksheet, and then press the **Enter** key. The external reference formula is complete.

5. In the Urban Centers 2017 workbook, in the Summary worksheet, click cell **C6**. Cell C6 displays 46896—the total rental income for Child Care Centers in Quarter 2 in Petosky, Flint, and Jackson, and the following formula appears in the formula bar: =[Petosky.xlsx]Summary!$C$6+[Flint.xlsx]Summary!$C$6 +[Jackson.xlsx]Summary!$C$6.

Next, you'll enter the external reference formulas in cells D6 and E6 to add the total rental income in Quarter 3 and Quarter 4.

▶ **6.** Repeat Steps 1 through 4 to enter the formula from cell **D6** in the Summary worksheet in the Urban Centers 2017 workbook. The formula result displayed in cell D6 is 34426—the total rental income for Child Care Centers during Quarter 3 in Petosky, Flint, and Jackson.

▶ **7.** Repeat Steps 1 through 4 to enter the formula from cell **E6** in the Summary worksheet in the Urban Centers 2017 workbook. The formula result displayed in cell E6 is 45601—the total rental income for Child Care Centers during Quarter 4 in Petosky, Flint, and Jackson.

You need to enter the remaining formulas for the other types of rental income. Rather than creating the rest of the external reference formulas manually, you can copy the formulas in row 6 and paste them in rows 7 through 11. The formulas created using the point-and-click method contain absolute references. Before you copy them to other cells, you need to change them to use mixed references because the rows in the formula need to change.

To edit the external reference formulas to use mixed references:

▶ **1.** Maximize the Urban Centers 2017 workbook, click the **Ribbon Display Options** button 🔳 in the title bar, and then click **Show Tabs and Commands** (or press the **Ctrl+F1** keys) to pin the ribbon to show both the tabs and the commands. The other workbooks are still open but are not visible.

▶ **2.** At the right edge of the formula bar, click the **Collapse Formula Bar** button 🔼 (or press the **Ctrl+Shift+U** keys) to reduce the formula bar to one line.

▶ **3.** In the Summary worksheet, double-click cell **B6** to enter Edit mode and display the formula in the cell.

TIP

You can also create the mixed reference by deleting the $ symbol from the row references in the formula.

▶ **4.** Click in the first absolute reference in the formula, and then press the **F4** key twice to change the absolute reference $B$6 to the mixed reference $B6.

▶ **5.** Edit the other two absolute references in the formula to be mixed references with absolute column references and relative row references.

▶ **6.** Press the **Enter** key, and then select cell **B6**. The formula is updated to include mixed references, but the formula results aren't affected. Cell B6 still displays 44263, which is correct. See Figure 6-18.

| Figure 6-18 | External reference formula with mixed references |

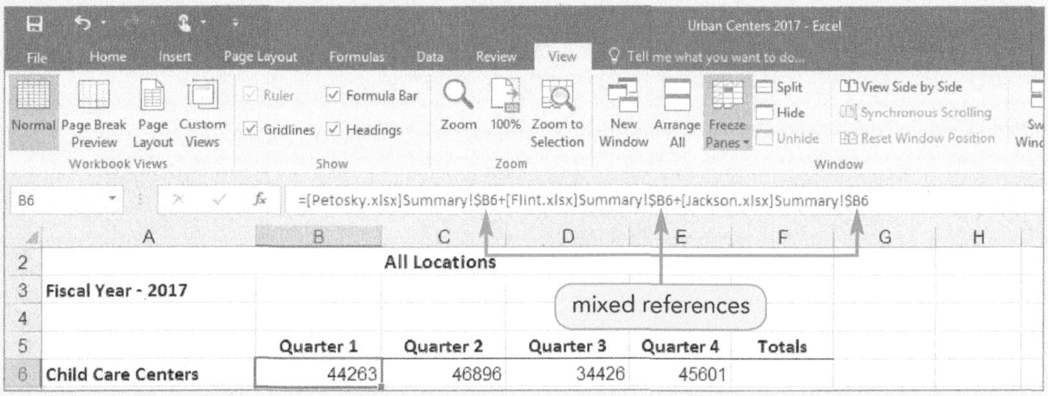

▶ 7. Edit the formulas in cells **C6**, **D6**, and **E6** to change the absolute references to the mixed references **$C6**, **$D6**, and **$E6**, respectively. The formulas are updated, but the cells in the range C6:E6 still correctly display 46896, 34426, and 45601, respectively.

With the formulas corrected to include mixed references, you can now copy the external reference formulas in the range B6:E6 to the other rows. Then you'll enter the SUM function to total the values in each row and column.

To copy and paste the external reference formulas:

▶ 1. Select the range **B6:E6**, and then drag the fill handle to select the range **B7:E11**. The formulas are copied to the range B7:E11, and the formula results appear in the cells. The Auto Fill Options button appears in the lower-right corner of the selected range, but you do not need to use it.

   Trouble? If all of the values in the range B7:E11 are the same as those in the range B6:E6, you didn't change the absolute cell references to mixed cell references in the formulas in the range B6:E6. Repeat Steps 3 through 7 in the previous set of steps, and then repeat Step 1 in this set of steps.

▶ 2. In cell **B12**, enter the SUM function to add the range **B6:B11**. The total rental income is 163016 in Quarter 1.

▶ 3. Copy the formula in cell **B12** to the range **C12:E12**. The total rental income is 152010 in Quarter 2, 144197 in Quarter 3, and 153921 in Quarter 4.

▶ 4. In cell **F6**, enter the SUM function to add the range B6:E6. The total rental income is 171186 for Child Care Centers at all rental centers in 2017.

▶ 5. Copy the formula in cell **F6** to the range **F7:F12**. The total for Music Practice is 132303, Medical Centers is 170087, Religious Centers is 20304, Miscellaneous is 44752, and Retail is 74512, with a grand total of 613144 for the year.

▶ 6. Format the nonadjacent range **B6:E6,F6:F11,** and **B12:F12** with the **Accounting** style and no decimal places.

▶ 7. Format the range **B7:E11** with the **Comma** style and no decimal places.

▶ 8. Format the range **B11:F11** with a bottom border, and then select cell **A1** to deselect the range. See Figure 6-19.

| Figure 6-19 | Completed summary of rental income data |

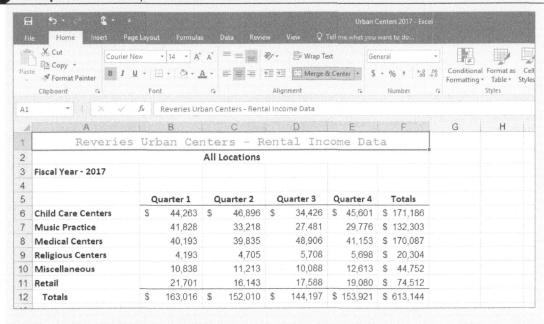

Timothy is pleased; the summary results match his expectations.

INSIGHT

Managing Linked Workbooks

As you work with a linked workbook, you might need to replace a source file or change where you stored the source and destination files. However, replacing or moving a file can affect the linked workbook. Keep in mind the following guidelines to manage your linked workbooks:

- If you rename a source file, the destination workbook won't be able to find it. A dialog box opens, indicating "This workbook contains one or more links that cannot be updated." Click the Continue button to open the workbook with the most recent values, or click the Change Source button in the Edit Links dialog box to specify the new name of that linked source file.
- If you move a source file to a different folder, the link breaks between the destination and source files. Click the Change Source button in the Edit Links dialog box to specify the new location of the linked workbook.
- If you receive a replacement source file, you can swap the original source file with the replacement file. No additional changes are needed.
- If you receive a destination workbook but the source files are not included, Excel will not be able to find the source files, and a dialog box opens with the message "This workbook contains one or more links that cannot be updated." Click the Continue button to open the workbook with the most recent values, or click the Break Link button in the Edit Links dialog box to replace the external references with the existing values.
- If you change the name of a destination file, you can open that renamed version destination file without affecting the source files or the original destination file.

Updating Linked Workbooks

When workbooks are linked, it is important that the data in the destination file accurately reflects the contents of the source file. When data in a source file changes, you want the destination file to reflect those changes. If both the source and destination files are open when you make a change, the destination file is updated automatically. If the destination file is closed when you make a change in a source file, you choose whether to update the link to display the current values or continue to display the older values from the destination file when you open the destination file.

Updating a Destination Workbook with Source Workbooks Open

When both the destination and source workbooks are open, any changes you make in a source workbook automatically appear in the destination workbook. Timothy tells you that the Jackson rental income for Medical Centers in March is actually $100 less than was recorded. After you correct the March value in the Quarter 1 worksheet, the amount in the Summary worksheet of the Jackson workbook and the total in the Urban Centers 2017 workbook will also change if both the source and destination files are open.

To update the source workbook with the destination file open:

▶ 1. Maximize the **Petosky**, **Flint**, and **Jackson** workbooks, and show the ribbon tabs and commands in each workbook.

▶ 2. Make the **Jackson** workbook active, and then go to the **Quarter 1** worksheet. You'll update the rental income for Medical Centers in March.

▶ 3. In cell **D8**, enter 4925. Jackson's rental income is updated, and the total rental income for March changes to $15,651.

▶ 4. Go to the **Summary** worksheet in the Jackson workbook, and then verify that the total rental income for Medical Centers in Quarter 1 (cell B8) is 13,513, the total rental income for Medical Centers in 2017 (cell F8) is $56,452, the total rental income in Quarter 1 (cell B12) is $51,766, and the total rental income in 2017 (cell F12) is $199,689. See Figure 6-20.

Figure 6-20   Summary worksheet in the Jackson workbook with revised Quarter 1 data

	A	B	C	D	E	F	G	H
1	Reveries Urban Centers - Rental Income Data							
2			Jackson Totals					
3	Fiscal Year - 2017							
4								
5		Quarter 1	Quarter 2	Quarter 3	Quarter 4	Totals		
6	Child Care Centers	$ 16,388	$ 15,376	$ 11,426	$ 14,076	$ 57,266		
7	Music Practice	11,138	11,388	9,101	9,626	$ 41,253		
8	Medical Centers	13,513	13,125	15,076	14,738	$ 56,452		
9	Religious Centers	1,463	1,675	1,963	1,838	$ 6,939		
10	Miscellaneous	3,813	4,063	3,563	4,313	$ 15,752		
11	Retail	5,451	5,188	5,713	5,675	$ 22,027		
12	Totals	$ 51,766	$ 50,815	$ 46,842	$ 50,266	$ 199,689		
13								
14								
15								

reflects the new value in the Quarter 1 worksheet

▶ **5.** Make the **Urban Centers 2017** workbook active, and then verify in the Summary worksheet that the rental income for Medical Centers in Quarter 1 (cell B8) is 40,093, the total rental income for Medical centers in 2017 (cell F8) is $169,987, the total rental income in Quarter 1 (cell B12) is $162,916, and the total rental income in 2017 (cell F12) is $613,044, reflecting the new value you entered in the Jackson workbook. Because both the destination and source files are open, Excel updated the destination file automatically. See Figure 6-21.

Figure 6-21   Summary worksheet in the Urban Centers 2017 workbook with the revised Quarter 1 data

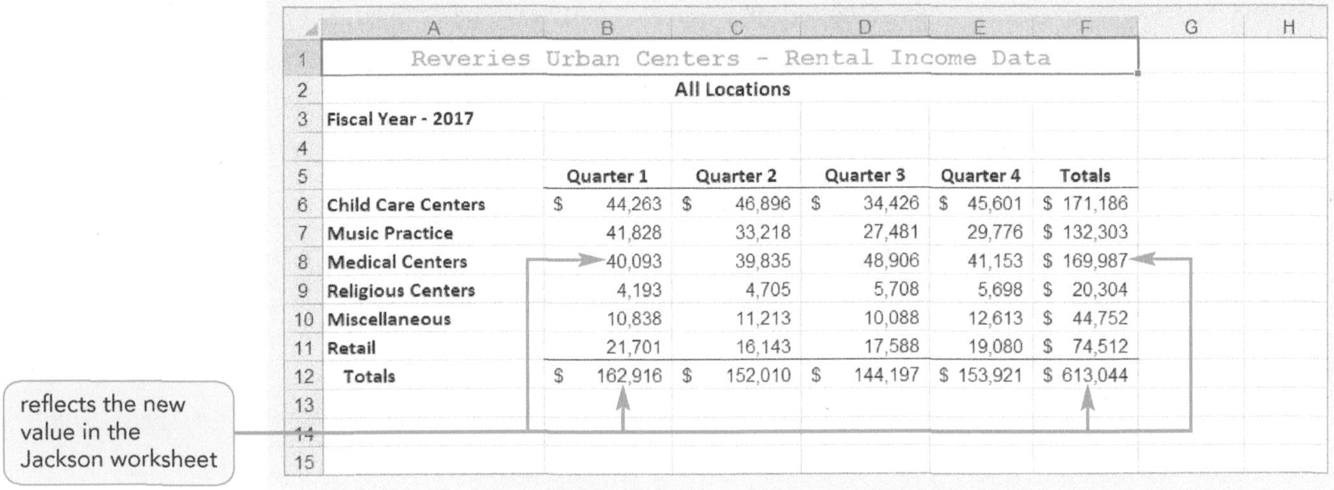

reflects the new value in the Jackson worksheet

▶ **6.** Save the Jackson and Urban Centers 2017 workbooks.

Updating a Destination Workbook with Source Workbooks Closed

When you save a workbook that contains external reference formulas, such as the Urban Centers 2017 workbook, Excel stores the most recent results of those formulas in the destination file. Source files, such as the Petosky, Flint, and Jackson workbooks, are often updated while the destination file is closed. In that case, the values in the destination file are not updated at the same time the source files are updated. The next time you open the destination file, the cells containing external reference formulas still display the old values. Therefore, some of the values in the edited source workbooks are different from the values in the destination workbook.

To update the destination workbook with the current data, you must specify that you want the update to occur. As part of the Excel security system that attempts to protect against malicious software, links to other workbooks are not updated without your permission. When you open a workbook with external reference formulas (the destination file), a dialog box appears, notifying you that the workbook contains links to an external source that could be unsafe. You then can choose to update the content, which allows the external reference formulas to function and updates the links in the destination workbook, or you can choose not to update the links, which lets you continue working with the data you have. The old values in the destination workbook are displayed and the links to the source files have an unknown status.

Timothy realizes that the Jackson workbook needs a second correction. In Quarter 4, the total rental income for Retail in December was $1,925 not $1,875 as currently entered in the Jackson workbook. He asks you to increase the rental income for Retail in December by $50. As a result, the totals in the Summary worksheet in the Jackson workbook and the rental income in the Urban Centers 2017 workbook will both increase by $50. You'll edit the source file, the Jackson workbook, while the destination file is closed.

To update the source workbook with the destination file closed:

▶ 1. Close the Petosky, Flint, and Urban Centers 2017 workbooks. The Jackson workbook remains open.

▶ 2. In the Jackson workbook, go to the **Quarter 4** worksheet.

▶ 3. In cell **D11**, enter 1,925. The rental income from Retail in Quarter 4 increases to $5,725.

▶ 4. Go to the **Summary** worksheet. The rental income from Retail for Quarter 4 (cell E11) is 5,725, the rental income from Retail for 2017 (cell F11) is $22,077, the total rental income for Quarter 4 (cell E12) is $50,316, and the total rental income in 2017 (cell F12) is $199,739. See Figure 6-22.

Figure 6-22   Revised Retail rental income for Quarter 4 in the Jackson workbook

	A	B	C	D	E	F	G	H
1	Reveries Urban Centers – Rental Income Data							
2			Jackson Totals					
3	Fiscal Year - 2017							
4								
5		Quarter 1	Quarter 2	Quarter 3	Quarter 4	Totals		
6	Child Care Centers	$ 16,388	$ 15,376	$ 11,426	$ 14,076	$ 57,266		
7	Music Practice	11,138	11,388	9,101	9,626	$ 41,253		
8	Medical Centers	13,513	13,125	15,076	14,738	$ 56,452		
9	Religious Centers	1,463	1,675	1,963	1,838	$ 6,939		
10	Miscellaneous	3,813	4,063	3,563	4,313	$ 15,752		
11	Retail	5,451	5,188	5,713	5,725	$ 22,077		
12	Totals	$ 51,766	$ 50,815	$ 46,842	$ 50,316	$ 199,739		
13								
14								
15								

reflects changes made to Retail rental income in Quarter 4

▶ 5. Save the Jackson workbook, and then close it.

Now you'll open the destination file (the Urban Centers 2017 workbook). The rental income from the source workbooks won't be updated until you specify that it should. When the destination file is open and the source files are closed, the complete file path is included as part of the external reference formula that appears in the formula bar.

To open and update the destination workbook:

▶ **1.** Open the **Urban Centers 2017** workbook, and then go to the **Summary** worksheet, if necessary. The value in cell E11 has *not* changed; it is still 19,080. A dialog box appears, indicating that the workbook contains links to one or more external sources that could be unsafe. See Figure 6-23.

Figure 6-23	Dialog box warning of possible unsafe links

Trouble? If the Message Bar appears below the ribbon with "SECURITY WARNING Automatic update of links has been disabled," click the Enable Content button. The values in the destination workbook are updated. Continue with Step 3.

You want the current values in the source files to appear in the destination workbook.

▶ **2.** In the dialog box, click the **Update** button. The values in the destination file are updated. The total rental income from Retail in Quarter 4, shown in cell E11 of the Urban Centers 2017 workbook, increased to 19,130, the rental income from Retail for 2017 (cell F11) is $74,562, the total Quarter 4 rental income (cell E12) is $153,971, and the grand total of all rental income in 2017 (cell F12) increased to $613,094.

▶ **3.** Click cell **E11**, and then look at the complete file path for each external reference in the formula. The full path appears because the source workbooks are closed. Note that the path you see will match the location where you save your workbooks.

▶ **4.** Save the workbook.

Managing Links

When workbooks are linked, the Edit Links dialog box provides ways to manage the links. You can review the status of the links and update the data in the files. You can repair **broken links**, which are references to files that have been moved since the link was created. Broken links appear in the dialog box as having an unknown status. You can also open the source file and break the links, which converts all external reference formulas to their most recent values.

After the fiscal year audit is completed and the source workbooks are final, Timothy will archive the summary workbook and move the files to an off-site storage location as part of his year-end backup process. You will save a copy of the Urban Centers 2017 workbook and then break the links to the source files in the copy.

To save a copy of the Urban Centers 2017 workbook and open the Edit Links dialog box:

1. Save the Urban Centers 2017 workbook as **Urban Centers Audited 2018** in the location specified by your instructor. The Urban Centers 2017 workbook closes, and the Urban Centers Audited 2018 workbook remains open.

2. On the ribbon, click the **Data** tab.

3. In the Connections group, click the **Edit Links** button. The Edit Links dialog box opens. Note that the path you see for source files will match the location where you save your workbooks. See Figure 6-24.

 Figure 6-24   Edit Links dialog box

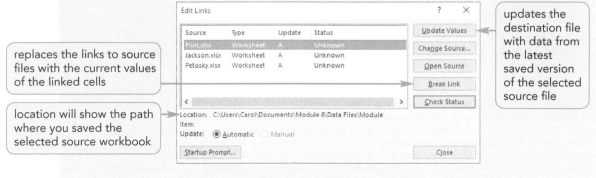

The Edit Links dialog box lists all of the files to which the destination workbook is linked so that you can update, change, open, or remove the links. You can see that the destination workbook—Urban Centers Audited 2018—has links to the Flint, Jackson, and Petosky workbooks. The dialog box shows the following information about each link:

- **Source**—indicates the file to which the link points. The Urban Centers Audited 2018 workbook contains three links pointing to the Flint.xlsx, Jackson.xlsx, and Petosky.xlsx workbooks.
- **Type**—identifies the type of each source file. In this case, the type is an Excel worksheet, but it could also be a Word document, a PowerPoint presentation, or some other type of file.
- **Update**—specifies the way values are updated from the source file. The letter *A* indicates the link is updated automatically when you open the workbook or when both the source and destination files are open simultaneously. The letter *M* indicates the link must be updated manually by the user, which is useful when you want to see the older data values before updating to the new data. To manually update the link and see the new data values, click the Update Values button.
- **Status**—shows whether Excel successfully accessed the link and updated the values from the source document (status is OK), or Excel has not attempted to update the links in this session (status is Unknown). The status of the three links in the Urban Centers Audited 2018 workbook is Unknown.

Timothy wants you to break the links so that the Urban Centers Audited 2018 workbook contains only the updated values (and is no longer affected by changes in the source files). Then he wants you to save the Urban Centers Audited 2018 workbook for him to archive. This allows Timothy to store a "snapshot" of the data at the end of the fiscal year.

TIP

You cannot undo the break link action. To restore the links, you must reenter the external reference formulas.

To convert all external reference formulas to their current values:

1. In the Edit Links dialog box, click the **Break Link** button. A dialog box opens, alerting you that breaking links in the workbook permanently converts formulas and external references to their existing values.

2. Click the **Break Links** button. No links appear in the Edit Links dialog box.

3. Click the **Close** button. The Urban Centers Audited 2018 workbook now contains values instead of formulas with external references.

4. Select cell **B6**. The value $44,263 appears in the cell and the formula bar; the link (the external reference formula) was replaced with the data value. All of the cells in the range B6:E11 contain values rather than external reference formulas.

5. Save the Urban Centers Audited 2018 workbook, and then close it. The Urban Centers 2017 workbook contains external reference formulas, and the Urban Centers Audited 2018 workbook contains current values.

In this session, you worked with multiple worksheets and workbooks, summarizing data and linking workbooks. This ensures that the data in the summary workbook is accurate and remains updated with the latest data in the source files. In the next session, you will create templates and hyperlinks.

Session 6.2 Quick Check

REVIEW

1. What is the external reference to the range B6:F6 in the Grades worksheet in the Grade Book workbook located in the Course folder on drive D?

2. What is a source file?

3. What is a destination file?

4. What are the layouts that you can use to arrange multiple workbooks?

5. How are linked workbooks updated when both the destination and source files are open?

6. How are linked workbooks updated when the source file is changed and the destination file is closed?

7. How would you determine what workbooks a destination file is linked to?

8. What happens to an external reference formula in a cell after you break the links in the worksheet?

Session 6.3 Visual Overview:

This Weekly Time Sheet workbook was created from one of the templates available from Office.com. Microsoft provides many templates that you can download.

Warrens Weekly Time Sheet –

| File | Home | Insert | Page Layout | Formulas | Data | Review | View | ♀ Tel |

PivotTable Recommended Table   Illustrations   Add-ins ▾   Recommended Charts   PivotChart

PivotTables

Tables

Charts

K4 | fx | Reveries Urban Centers Vacation Policy

A template is a workbook with labels, formats, and formulas already built into it with data removed. In other words, a template includes everything but the variable data.

A template can use any Excel feature, including formatting, formulas, and charts. The template used to create this workbook includes labels, formatting, and formulas.

Variable data is entered in the workbook created from the template. In this workbook, employee data was entered to fill out the weekly time record.

The formulas to calculate the total hours worked and total pay were included in the template.

Weekly time record

Reveries Urban Centers

Employee:	Gordon Warren
Manager:	Timothy Root

Employee phone:	
Employee email:	

Week ending: 8/26/2017

Day		Regular Hours	Overtime	Sick	Vacation	Total
Monday	8/20/2017	8.00				8.00
Tuesday	8/21/2017	8.00	1.50			9.50
Wednesday	8/22/2017					
Thursday	8/23/2017					
Friday	8/24/2017					
Saturday	8/25/2017					
Sunday	8/26/2017					
	Total hours	16.00	1.50			17.50
	Rate per hour	$15.00	$22.50			
	Total pay	$240.00	$33.75			$273.75

Weekly time record   ⊕

Ready

Templates and Hyperlinks

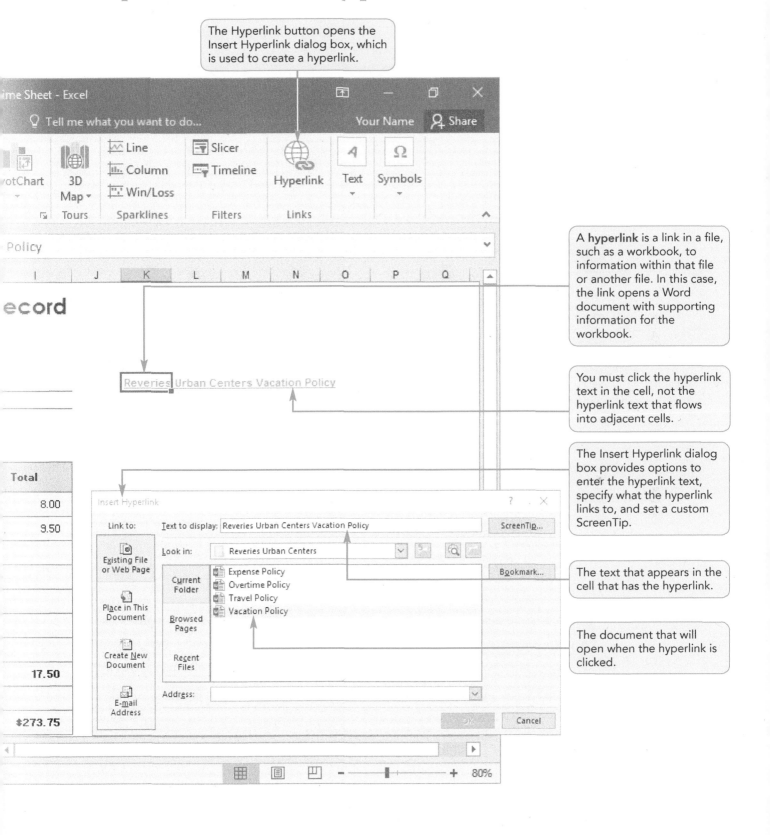

The Hyperlink button opens the Insert Hyperlink dialog box, which is used to create a hyperlink.

A **hyperlink** is a link in a file, such as a workbook, to information within that file or another file. In this case, the link opens a Word document with supporting information for the workbook.

You must click the hyperlink text in the cell, not the hyperlink text that flows into adjacent cells.

The Insert Hyperlink dialog box provides options to enter the hyperlink text, specify what the hyperlink links to, and set a custom ScreenTip.

The text that appears in the cell that has the hyperlink.

The document that will open when the hyperlink is clicked.

Creating a Hyperlink

A hyperlink is a link in a file, such as a workbook, to information within that file or another file. Although hyperlinks are most often found on webpages, they can also be placed in a worksheet and used to quickly jump to a specific cell or range within the active worksheet, another worksheet, or another workbook. Hyperlinks can also be used to jump to other files, such as a Word document or a PowerPoint presentation, or rental centers on the web.

Inserting a Hyperlink

You can insert a hyperlink directly in a workbook file to link to information in that workbook, another workbook, or a file associated with another application on your computer, a shared file on a network, or a website. Hyperlinks are usually represented by words with colored letters and underlines or images. When you click a hyperlink, the computer switches to the file or portion of the file referenced by the hyperlink.

REFERENCE

Inserting a Hyperlink

- Select the text, graphic, or cell in which you want to insert the hyperlink.
- On the Insert tab, in the Links group, click the Hyperlink button.
- To link to a file or webpage, click Existing File or Web Page in the Link to list, and then select the file or webpage from the Look in box.
- To link to a location in the current workbook, click Place in This Document in the Link to list, and then select the worksheet, cell, or range in the current workbook.
- To link to a new document, click Create New Document in the Link to list, and then specify the filename and path of the new document.
- To link to an email address, click E-mail Address in the Link to list, and then enter the email address of the recipient (such as name@example.com) and a subject line for the message.
- Click the OK button.

Timothy wrote a memo summarizing the collection results for Flint, Jackson, and Petosky in 2017. He wants the Urban Centers 2017 workbook to include a link that points to the UCMemo Word document. You'll insert the hyperlink to the memo now.

To insert a hyperlink in the Urban Centers 2017 workbook:

1. Open the **Urban Centers 2017** workbook, but don't update the links.

2. Go to the **Documentation** worksheet, and then select cell **A8**. You want to create the hyperlink in this cell.

3. On the ribbon, click the **Insert** tab.

4. In the Links group, click the **Hyperlink** button. The Insert Hyperlink dialog box opens. You use this dialog box to define the hyperlink.

5. If necessary, click the **Existing File or Web Page** button in the Link to bar, and then click the **Current Folder** button in the Look in area. All the existing files and folders in the current folder are displayed. See Figure 6-25, which shows the Excel6 > Module folder included with your Data Files.

| **Figure 6-25** | **Insert Hyperlink dialog box** |

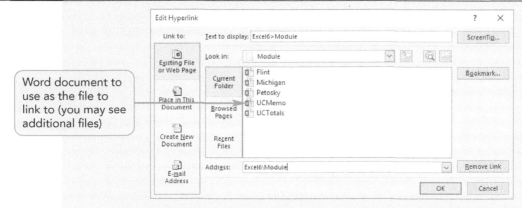

Word document to use as the file to link to (you may see additional files)

6. Click the **UCMemo** Word document in the list of files. This is the file you want to open when the hyperlink is clicked.

7. Click the **Text to display** box, select the filename in the box, and then type **Click here to read the Executive Memo** as the hyperlink text that will appear in cell A8 in the Documentation worksheet.

8. Click the **OK** button. The hyperlink text entered in cell A8 is underlined and in a blue font, indicating that the text within the cell is a hyperlink. See Figure 6-26.

| **Figure 6-26** | **Hyperlink to the Reveries Urban Centers memo** |

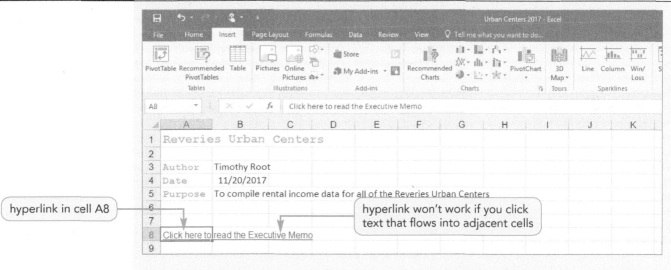

hyperlink in cell A8

hyperlink won't work if you click text that flows into adjacent cells

You will test the hyperlink that you just created to ensure it works correctly. To use a hyperlink in a worksheet, you must click the text inside the cell that contains the link. If you click white space in the cell or any text that flows into an adjacent cell, the hyperlink does not work.

To test the hyperlink to the UCMemo:

▶ **1.** Point to the text in cell **A8** so that the pointer changes to 🖑, and then click the **Click here to read the Executive Memo** hyperlink. The UCMemo document opens in Word.

Trouble? If the hyperlink doesn't work, you might have clicked the text that overflows cell A8. Point to the text within cell A8, and then click the hyperlink.

▶ **2.** Close the Word document and Word. The Documentation worksheet in the Urban Centers 2017 workbook is active. The hyperlink in cell A8 changed color to indicate that you used the link.

Editing a Hyperlink

TIP

You can right-click a hyperlink cell and then click Clear Contents to delete a hyperlink or click Remove Hyperlink to delete the hyperlink but keep the text.

You can modify an existing hyperlink by changing its target file or webpage, modifying the text that is displayed, or changing the ScreenTip for the hyperlink. ScreenTips, which appear whenever you place the pointer over a hyperlink, provide additional information about the target of the link. The default ScreenTip is the folder location and filename of the file you will link to, which isn't very helpful. You can insert a more descriptive ScreenTip when you create a hyperlink or edit an existing hyperlink.

Timothy wants you to edit the hyperlink to the memo so that it has a more descriptive ScreenTip.

To edit the hyperlink:

▶ **1.** In the Documentation worksheet, right-click cell **A8**, and then click **Edit Hyperlink** on the shortcut menu. The Edit Hyperlink dialog box opens; it has the same layout and information as the Insert Hyperlink dialog box.

▶ **2.** Click the **ScreenTip** button. The Set Hyperlink ScreenTip dialog box opens.

▶ **3.** In the ScreenTip text box, type **Click to view the Executive Summary for 2017**, and then click the **OK** button.

▶ **4.** Click the **OK** button to close the Edit Hyperlink dialog box.

▶ **5.** Point to the text in cell **A8** and confirm that the ScreenTip "Click to view the Executive Summary for 2017" appears just below the cell.

▶ **6.** Save the Urban Centers 2017 workbook, and then close it. Excel remains open.

Using Templates

If you want to create a new workbook that has the same format as an existing workbook, you could save the existing workbook with a new name and replace the values with new data or blank cells. The potential drawback to this method is that you might forget to rename the original file and overwrite data you intended to keep. A better method is to create a template workbook that includes all the text (row and column labels), formatting, and formulas but does not contain any data. The template workbook is a model from which you create new workbooks. When you create a new workbook from a template, an unnamed copy of the template opens. You can then enter data as well as modify the existing content or structure as needed. Any changes or additions you make to the new workbook do not affect the template file; the next time you create a workbook based on the template, the original text, formatting, and formulas will be present.

PROSKILLS

Teamwork: Using Excel Templates

A team working together will often need to create the same types of workbooks. Rather than each person or group designing a different workbook, each team member should create a workbook from the same template. The completed workbooks will then all have the same structure with identical formatting and formulas. Not only does this ensure consistency and accuracy, it also makes it easier to compile and summarize the results. Templates help teams work better together and avoid misunderstandings.

For example, a large organization may need to collect the same information from several regions. By creating and distributing a workbook template, each region knows what data to track and where to enter it. The template already includes the formulas, so the results are calculated consistently. If you want to review the formulas that are in the worksheet, you can display them using the Show Formula command in the Formula Auditing group on the Formulas tab or by pressing the Ctrl+` keys.

The following are just some of the advantages of using a template to create multiple workbooks with the same features:

- Templates save time and ensure consistency in the design and content of workbooks because all labels, formatting, and formulas are entered once.
- Templates ensure accuracy because formulas can be entered and verified once, and then used with confidence in all workbooks.
- Templates standardize the appearance and content of workbooks.
- Templates prevent data from being overwritten when an existing workbook is inadvertently saved with new data rather than saved as a new workbook.

If you are part of a team that needs to create the same type of workbook repeatedly, it's a good idea to use a template to both save time and ensure consistency in the design and content of the workbooks.

Creating a Workbook Based on an Existing Template

The Blank workbook template that you have used to create new, blank workbooks contains no text or formulas, but it includes formatting—General format applied to numbers, Calibri 11-point font, text left-aligned in cells, numbers and formula results right-aligned in cells, column widths set to 8.38 characters, one worksheet inserted in the workbook, and so forth.

Excel has many other templates available. Some are automatically installed on your hard drive when you install Excel. Other templates are available to download from the Office.com site or other sites that you can find by searching the web. These templates provide commonly used worksheet formats that can save you the time of creating the template yourself. Some of the task-specific templates available from the Office.com site include:

- **Family monthly budget planner**—builds projections and actual expenditures for items such as housing, transportation, and insurance
- **Inventory list**—tracks the cost and quantity reorder levels of inventory
- **Sports team roster**—organizes a list with each player's name, phone number, email address, and so forth
- **Employee time sheet**—creates an online time card to track employees' work hours
- **Expense report**—creates an expense report to track employee expenses for reimbursement

Using a template to create a new workbook lets you focus on the unique content for that workbook.

REFERENCE

Creating a Workbook Based on a Template

- On the ribbon, click the File tab, and then click New in the navigation bar.
- On the New screen, click a template category for the type of workbook you want to create (or type a keyword in the Search for online templates box, and then press the Enter key).
- Click the template you want to create, then click the Create button.
- Save the workbook based on the template with a new filename.

Gordon Warren, manager for the Petosky rental center, uses the Weekly time sheet template to submit his work hours to Timothy. You'll download this template and enter Gordon's most recent hours. *If you don't have an Internet connection, you should read but not complete the steps involving creating and using the online template.*

To create a workbook based on the Weekly time sheet template:

1. On the ribbon, click the **File** tab.

2. Click **New** in the navigation bar. The New screen in Backstage view shows the available templates on your computer and template categories on Office.com.

3. Click in the **Search for online templates** box, type **time sheets**, and then press the **Enter** key. All of the available time sheet templates are displayed. See Figure 6-27.

Figure 6-27	New screen with available time sheet templates

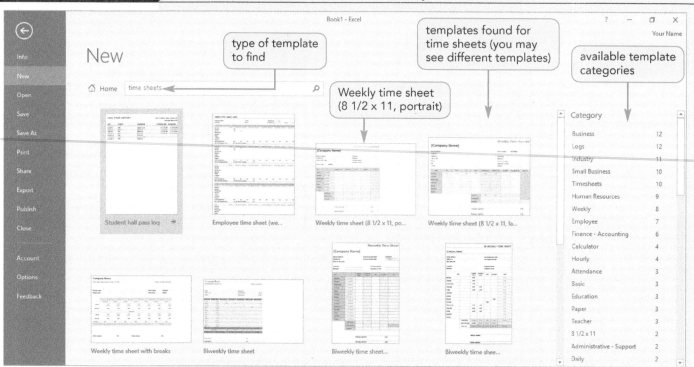

4. Click **Weekly time sheet (8 1/2 × 11, portrait)**. A preview of a worksheet based on the selected template appears in the center of the screen. If this is not the template you need, you can scroll through the time sheets by clicking the left or right arrow button. See Figure 6-28.

Figure 6-28   Weekly time sheet preview

Figure 6-28   Weekly time sheet preview

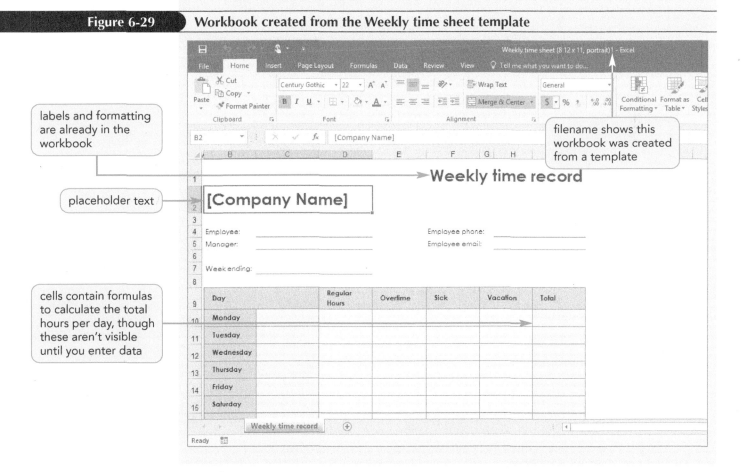

Back and Forward buttons appear so you can scroll through the available templates

preview of selected template

button to create a workbook based on this template

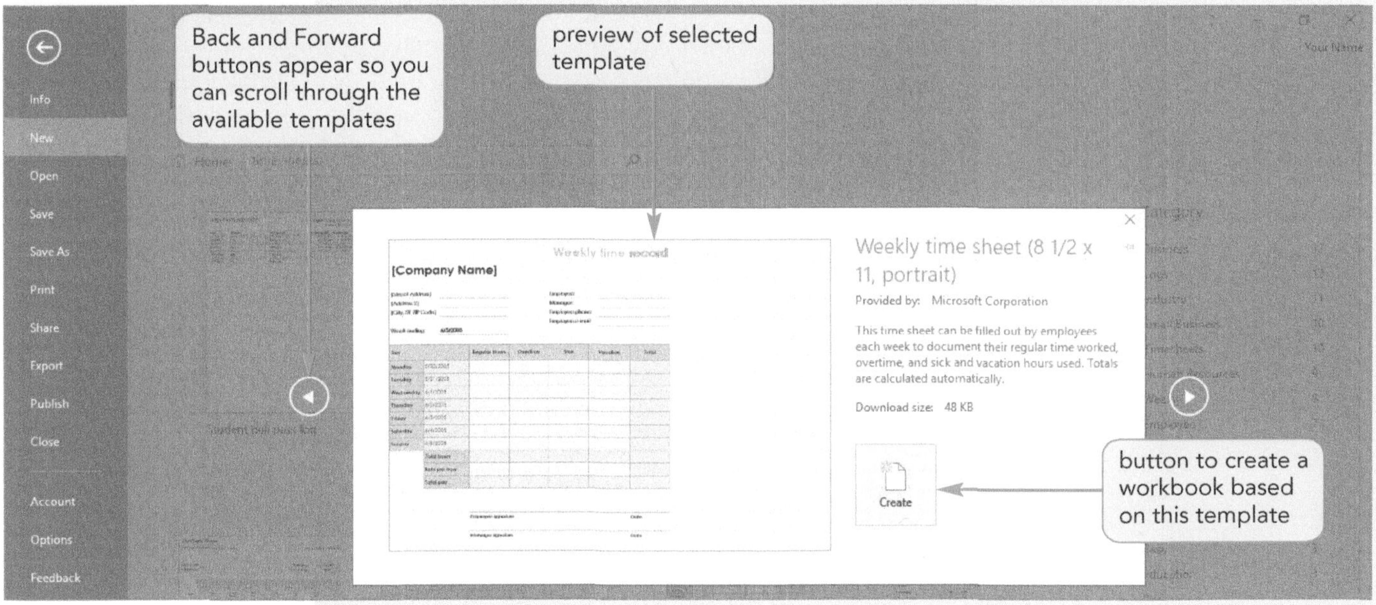

5. Click the **Create** button. A new workbook based on the selected template opens. See Figure 6-29.

Figure 6-29   Workbook created from the Weekly time sheet template

labels and formatting are already in the workbook

filename shows this workbook was created from a template

placeholder text

cells contain formulas to calculate the total hours per day, though these aren't visible until you enter data

A workbook based on a specific template always displays the name of the template followed by a sequential number. Just as a blank workbook that you open is named Book1, Book2, and so forth, the workbook based on the Weekly time sheet template is named "Weekly time sheet (8 ½ x 11, portrait)1" in the title bar, not "Weekly time sheet." Any changes or additions to data, formatting, or formulas that you make affect only this workbook and not the template (in this case, the Weekly time sheet template). When you save the workbook, the Save As screen opens so you can save the workbook with a new name and to the location you specify.

Look at the labels and formatting already included in the Weekly time sheet workbook. Some cells have descriptive labels, others are blank so you can enter data in them, and still other cells contain formulas where calculations for total hours worked each day and pay category will be automatically displayed as data is entered. The formulas aren't apparent unless you click in the cell and look at the cell contents in the formula bar, or you enter data and a calculation occurs.

Timothy asks you to enter Gordon's data for the previous week in the Weekly time record worksheet based on the Weekly time sheet template.

To enter Gordon's data in the Weekly time sheet (8 ½ x 11, portrait)1 workbook:

1. In cell **B2,** enter **Reveries Urban Centers** as the company name, and then format the text in **18** point font size.

2. In cell **C4,** enter **Gordon Warren** as the employee.

3. In cell **C5,** enter **Timothy Root** as the manager.

4. In cell **C7,** enter **8/26/2017** as the week ending date.

5. In cell **D10,** enter **8** for the regular hours Gordon worked on Monday. Totals appear in cells I10, D17, and I17 because formulas are already entered into these cells. Cell I10 shows the number of hours worked on Monday, cell D17 shows 8 regular hours worked that week, and cell I17 shows the total hours worked that week.

6. In cell **D11,** enter **8** for the regular hours Gordon worked on Tuesday.

7. In cell **E11,** enter **1.5** for the overtime hours Gordon worked on Tuesday. The totals are updated to 9.5 hours worked on Tuesday, 16 regular hours worked that week, 1.5 overtime hours worked that week, and 17.5 total hours worked that week.

8. In cell **D18** enter $15 for Warren's rate for Regular hours, and then, in cell **E18** enter $22.50 for his rate for Overtime hours. Gordon's total pay is calculated—$240.00 for Regular Hours pay (cell D19), $33.75 Overtime pay (cell E19), and $273.75 Total pay for the week (cell I19).

9. Save the workbook as **Warrens Weekly Time Sheet** in the location specified by your instructor, and then close the workbook. The Warrens Weekly Time Sheet workbook, like any other workbook, is saved with the .xlsx file extension. It does not overwrite the template file.

Each day Gordon works at Reveries Urban Centers, he or Timothy can open the Warrens Weekly Time Sheet workbook and enter the hours Gordon worked that day. The total hours are updated automatically. The template makes it fast and convenient to produce a weekly time sheet that contains all the necessary formulas and is fully formatted.

Creating a Custom Workbook Template

A **custom template** is a workbook template you create that is ready to run with the formulas for all calculations included as well as all formatting and labels. A template can use any Excel feature, including formulas and charts. To create a custom template, you build the workbook with all the necessary labels, formatting, and data, and then you save the workbook as a template. The template includes everything but the variable data. You can also create a template from a chart or chart sheet.

When you save a workbook as an Excel template file, the save location in the Save As dialog box defaults to the Templates folder. Although template files are usually stored in the Templates folder, you can store template files in any folder. However, custom template files stored in the Templates folder are available on the New screen in Backstage view.

All template files have the .xltx file extension. This extension differentiates template files from workbook files, which have the .xlsx file extension. After you have saved a workbook in a template format, you can make the template accessible to other users.

REFERENCE

Creating a Custom Template

- Prepare the workbook—enter values, text, and formulas as needed; apply formatting; and replace data values with zeros or blank cells.
- On the ribbon, click the File tab, and then click Save As in the navigation bar.
- Click the Browse button to open the Save As dialog box.
- In the File name box, enter the template name.
- Click the Save as type button, and then click Excel Template.
- If you don't want to save the template in the Custom Office Templates folder, select another folder in which to save the template file.
- Click the Save button.

or

- Create the chart you want to use for the template.
- Right-click the chart, and then click Save as Template.
- In the Save Chart Template dialog box, enter a filename, then select a folder in which to save the template file if you don't want to store it in the Charts subfolder of the Templates folder.
- Click the Save button.

The three rental income workbooks for 2017 have the same format. Timothy wants to use this workbook format for rental income data and analysis for next year. He asks you to create a template from one of the rental center workbooks. You'll save the Jackson workbook as a template file to use as the basis for the custom template.

To save the Jackson workbook as a template:

1. Open the **Jackson** workbook you created in this Module.

2. On the ribbon, click the **File** tab to open Backstage view, and then in the navigation bar, click **Save As**. The Save As screen appears.

3. Select the location where you are saving the files for this Module.

4. In the File name box, type **Urban Centers Template** as the template name.

5. Click the **Save as type** button, and then click **Excel Template**. The save location changes to the Custom Office Templates folder on your computer. You want to save the template in the same location as the other files you created in this Module.

6. Navigate to the location where you are storing the files you create in this Module.

Make sure you change the save location so you can easily find and use the template file later in the next set of steps.

7. Click the **Save** button. The Urban Centers Template is saved in the location you specified.

TIP

You can use a fill color or cell style to differentiate input cells from other cells in the worksheet.

When you create a template from an existing workbook, you should remove any values and text that will change in each workbook created from the custom template. Be careful not to delete the formulas. Also, you should make sure that all of the formulas work as intended, the numbers and text are entered correctly, and the worksheet is formatted appropriately.

Next, you will clear the data from the template file, so that the input cells are ready for new data. You will leave the formulas that you already entered. You will also add placeholder text to the template to remind users what labels they need to enter.

To prepare a custom template from the Urban Centers Template:

1. With the Urban Centers Template open, group the **Quarter 1** through **Quarter 4** worksheets. The worksheet group includes the four quarterly worksheets but not the Summary and Documentation worksheets.

2. Select the range **B6:D11.** This range includes the rental income data. You want to delete these values.

3. Right-click the selected range, and then click **Clear Contents** on the shortcut menu. The data values are cleared from the selected range in each of the quarterly worksheets, but the formulas and formatting remain intact. The cleared cells are blank. The ranges E6:E12 and B12:D12 display dashes, representing zeros, where there are formulas.

4. Change the fill color of the selected range to the **Dark Blue, Text 2, Lighter 80%** theme color. The blue fill color indicates where users should enter data for rental income in the quarterly worksheets.

5. In cell **A2,** enter **[Center Name]** as the placeholder text to remind users to enter the correct rental center name.

6. Go to the **Summary** worksheet. The quarterly worksheets are ungrouped, and dashes, representing zeros, appear in the cells in the ranges B6:F12, which contain formulas.

7. In cell **A2,** enter **[Center Name]** as the placeholder text to remind users to enter the correct rental center name.

8. In cell **A3,** enter **[Enter Fiscal Year - yyyy]**. This text will remind users to enter the year.

9. Group the **Summary** through **Quarter 4** worksheets, and then make sure column A is wide enough to see the entire contents of cell A3. See Figure 6-30.

Figure 6-30

Figure 6-30   **Worksheet modified to be used as a custom template**

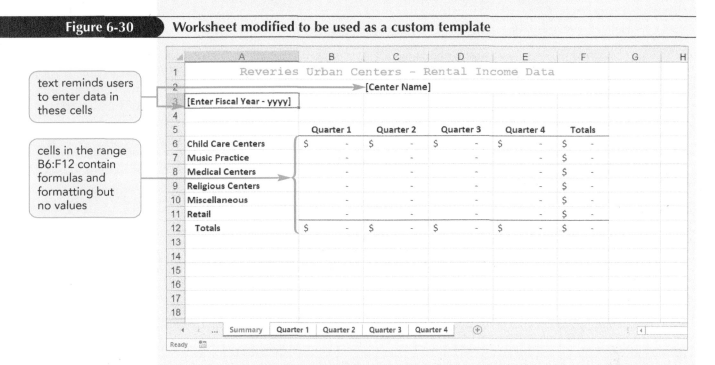

text reminds users to enter data in these cells

cells in the range B6:F12 contain formulas and formatting but no values

▶ **10.** Go to the **Documentation** worksheet, and then delete your name and the date from the range B3:B4.

▶ **11.** In cell **B5**, enter **To compile the rental income for [Center Name]**. The Documentation worksheet is updated to reflect the purpose of the workbook.

▶ **12.** Save the Urban Centers Template, and then close it.

Timothy will use the Urban Centers Template file to create the workbooks to track next year's rental income for each rental center and then distribute the workbooks to each rental center manager. By basing these new workbooks on the template file, Timothy has a standard workbook with identical formatting and formulas for each manager to use. He also avoids the risk of accidentally changing the workbook containing the 2017 data when preparing for 2018.

INSIGHT

Copying Styles from One Template to Another

Consistency is a hallmark of professional documents. If you have already created a template with a particular look, you can easily copy the styles from that template into a new template. This is much faster and more accurate than trying to recreate the same look by performing all of the steps you used originally. Copying styles from template to template guarantees uniformity. To copy styles from one template to another:

1. Open the template with the styles you want to copy.
2. Open the workbook or template in which you want to place the copied styles.
3. On the Home tab, in the Styles group, click the Cell Styles button, and then click Merge Styles. The Merge Styles dialog box opens, listing the currently open workbooks and templates.
4. Select the workbook or template with the styles you want to copy, and then click the OK button to copy those styles into the current workbook or template.
5. If a dialog box opens, asking if you want to "Merge Styles that have the same names?", click the YES button.
6. Save the workbook with the new styles as the Excel Template file type.

Creating a New Workbook from a Template

A template file has special properties that allow you to open it, make changes, and save it in a new location. Only the data must be entered because the formulas are already in the template file. The original template file is not changed by this process. After you have saved a template, you can access the template from the New screen in Backstage view or in the location you saved it.

Timothy wants all Reveries Urban Centers locations to collect rental income data in the same format and submit the workbooks to the central office for analysis. He wants you to create a workbook for fiscal year 2018 based on the Urban Centers Template file. You will enter Jackson as the rental center name where indicated on all of the worksheets and then enter test data for January.

To create a new workbook based on the Reveries Urban Centers Template file:

TIP

To create a copy of workbook based on a template stored in the Custom Office Templates folder, click the File tab, click New in the navigation bar, click Personal below the Search for online templates box, and then click the template.

1. On the taskbar, click the **File Explorer** button. The File Explorer window opens.

2. Navigate to the location where you stored the template file.

3. Double-click the **Urban Centers Template** file. A new workbook opens named "Urban Centers Template1" to indicate this is the first copy of the Urban Centers workbook created during the current Excel session.

4. Go to the **Summary** worksheet, in cell **A2** replace [Center Name] with **Jackson Total**, and then, in cell **A3**, enter **Fiscal Year – 2018**.

5. Group the **Quarter 1** through **Quarter 4** worksheets, and then in cell **A2**, replace [Center Name] with **Jackson**.

6. Go to the **Documentation** worksheet to ungroup the worksheets.

7. In cell **B5**, replace [Center Name] with **Jackson.**

8. Go to the **Quarter 1** worksheet. The text "Fiscal Year - 2018" appears in cell A4.

9. In each cell in the range **B6:B11**, which has the blue fill color, enter **100**.

10. Review the totals in the range E6:E11 (the cells that contain formulas to sum each column). See Figure 6-31.

Figure 6-31   New workbook based on the Reveries Urban Centers template file

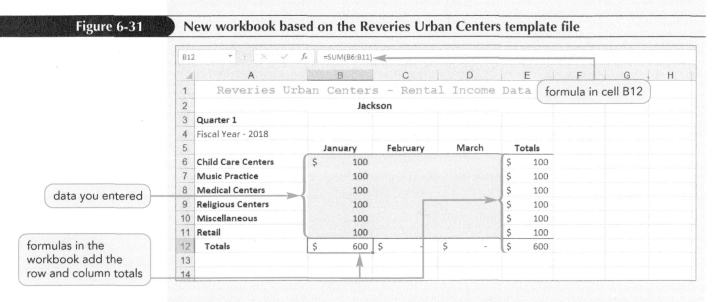

11. Go to the **Summary** worksheet. Totals appear in the ranges B6:B12 and F6:F12 as a result of the formulas in this worksheet. See Figure 6-32.

Figure 6-32   Summary worksheet with test data

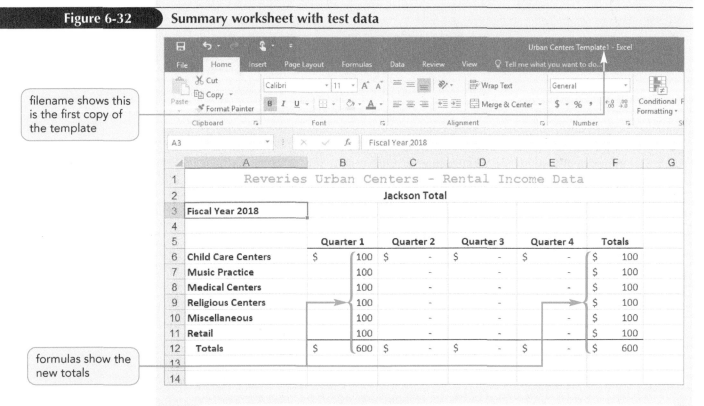

12. Save the workbook as **Jackson 2018** in the location specified by your instructor. The workbook is saved with the .xlsx file extension. The original template file is not changed.

Make sure the Save as type box shows Excel Workbook so that you create a new workbook file without overwriting the template.

You'll add data to the Quarter 2, Quarter 3, and Quarter 4 worksheets to verify that the Summary worksheet is correctly adding numbers from the four worksheets.

To test the Jackson 2018 workbook:

1. In the Jackson 2018 workbook, group the **Quarter 2, Quarter 3**, and **Quarter 4** worksheets. You did not include Quarter 1 in this group because you already entered test data in this worksheet.

2. In cell **C6**, enter **100**, and then in cell **D8**, enter **100**.

3. Go to the **Summary** worksheet. The total in cell F6 is $400, the total in cell F8 is $400, and the total for the year in cell F12 is $1,200.

   The formulas in the Summary worksheet correctly add values from all the quarterly worksheets. The template workbook is functioning as intended.

4. Save the workbook, and then close it.

The templates you created will ensure that all rental center managers enter data consistently, making it simpler for Timothy to add the rental income by rental type and time period for Reveries Urban Centers.

REVIEW

Session 6.3 Quick Check

1. How do you insert a hyperlink into a worksheet cell?
2. Why would you insert a hyperlink in a worksheet?
3. What is a template?
4. What is a custom template?
5. What is one advantage of using a custom template rather than simply using the original workbook file to create a new workbook?
6. What are some examples of task-specific templates available from the Office.com site?
7. How do you save a workbook as a template?
8. How do you create a workbook based on a template that is not saved in the Custom Office Templates folder?

Review Assignment

Data Files needed for the Review Assignments: Midland.xlsx, NewUCMemo.docx, NewUC.xlsx, JacksonMI.xlsx, PetoskyMI.xlsx, FlintMI.xlsx.

Reveries Urban Centers opened a new rental center in Midland, Michigan, on January 1, 2017. Michael Verhallen, the manager of the Midland rental center, collected the year's rental income in a workbook provided by Timothy Root at the central office. Before Michael can send the completed workbook to Timothy for the year-end reporting, he needs you to summarize the results and format the worksheets. Complete the following:

1. Open the **Midland** workbook located in the Excel6 > Review folder included with your Data Files, and then save the workbook as **Midland MI** in the location specified by your instructor.

2. In the Documentation worksheet, enter your name and the date, and then review the worksheets in the workbook.

3. Create a worksheet group that contains the Quarter 1 through Quarter 4 worksheets.

4. In the worksheet group, in the range B12:D12, enter formulas that sum the values in each column, and then in the range E6:E12, enter formulas that sum the values in each row.

5. Format the quarterly worksheets as specified below:

   a. In cell E5 and cell A12, enter the label **Totals**.

   b. Increase the indent of cell A12 by one.

   c. In the range A2:A3, A6:A12;B5:E5, bold the text.

   d. Merge and center the range A1:E1 and the range A2:E2.

   e. In the range B5:E5, center the text.

   f. Add a bottom border to the range B5:E5 and the range B11:E11.

   g. Format the range B6:D6,B12:D12,E6:E12 with the Accounting style and no decimal places.

   h. Format the range B7:E11 with the Comma style and no decimal places.

6. Ungroup the worksheets, make a copy of the Quarter 1 worksheet, rename it as **Summary**, and then place it after the Documentation worksheet.

7. In the Summary worksheet, make the following changes:

   a. In cell A2, change the heading to **Midland Total**.

   b. Change cell A3 to **Fiscal Year - 2017**.

   c. Insert a column between columns B and C.

   d. In the range B5:E5, change the headings to **Quarter 1**, **Quarter 2**, **Quarter 3**, and **Quarter 4**, respectively.

   e. Make sure that the text in the range B5:F5 is centered.

   f. Clear the contents of the range B6:F11.

8. Complete the formulas in the Summary worksheet, as follows, using the Fill Without Formatting paste option so that you can keep the bottom border on the range B11:F11.

   a. In the range B6:E11, create formulas that reference cells in other worksheets to display the quarterly totals for the rental income by type. For example, the formula in cell B6 will reference cell E6 in the Quarter 1 worksheet.

   b. In the range F6:F11, create formulas that use 3-D cell references to calculate the total for each type of rental income.

   c. Copy the formula from cell B12 to cell C12.

9. Change the March rental income for medical centers to **1976**, and then verify that the total rental income for Medical Centers in Quarter 1 in the Summary worksheet is $5,214, the total rental income in Quarter 1 is $19,538, the total rental income for medical centers in 2017 is $22,186, and the total rental income for 2017 is $82,286.

10. Group the Quarter 1 through Quarter 4 worksheets, and then enter a formula in cell A4 that references cell A3 in the Summary worksheet.

11. In cell A8 of the Documentation worksheet, insert a hyperlink that points to the **NewUCMemo** located in the Module6 > Review folder included with your Data Files. Make sure the text to display is **Click here to read Midland Executive Memo**.

12. Edit the hyperlink to use the ScreenTip **Midland Rental Center Summary for 2017**.

13. Save the Midland MI workbook, and leave it open.

14. Open the **NewUC** workbook located in the Excel6 > Review folder included with your Data Files, and then save the workbook as **New Urban Centers** in the location specified by your instructor. In the Documentation worksheet enter your name and the date. Open the **JacksonMI**, **PetoskyMI**, and **FlintMI** workbooks located in the Excel6 > Review folder included with your Data Files.

15. Make the New Urban Centers the active workbook, and then arrange the workbooks in a tiled layout. The New Urban Centers is the full height of the screen on the left with the remaining four taking the rest the screen. In each workbook, hide the ribbon so you can see as much data in the Summary worksheet as possible.

16. In the Summary worksheet of the New Urban Centers workbook, enter external reference formulas to create a set of linked workbooks to summarize the totals for JacksonMI, PetoskyMI, Midland MI, and FlintMI. Format the Summary worksheet in the New UC Totals workbook so that the numbers are readable and the range B11:F11 has a bottom border.

17. Maximize the New Urban Centers and Midland MI worksheets, making sure that the ribbon is displayed. Save the New Urban Centers workbook, and leave it open. Close the JacksonMI, PetoskyMI, and FlintMI workbooks.

18. In the New Urban Centers workbook, break the links. Select a cell, and notice that the formula has been replaced with a value. Save the workbook as **New UC Audited 2018**.

19. Create headers and footers for the Summary worksheet. Display the name of the workbook and the name of the worksheet on separate lines in the right section of the header. Display your name and the date on separate lines in the right section of the footer. Save the New UC Audited 2018 workbook, and then close it.

20. Use the Midland MI workbook to create an Excel template with the filename **Midland MI Template** in the location specified by your instructor.

21. Create a new workbook based on the Midland MI Template file, and then save the workbook as **Midland MI 2018** in the location specified by your instructor. In the Documentation worksheet, enter your name and the date.

22. In the Summary worksheet, enter **2018** as the fiscal year in cell A3. The Center Name should be Midland in all worksheets. In the Quarter 1 worksheet, enter **500** in each cell in the range B6:D11. In the Quarter 2 worksheet, enter **1000** in each cell in the range B6:D11. Confirm that the values entered in this step are correctly totaled in the Summary worksheet.

23. Save the Midland MI 2018 workbook, and then close it.

Case Problem 1

Data File needed for this Case Problem: Tea.xlsx

Paige's Tea Room   Paige's Tea Room has three locations: Atlanta, Georgia; Naples, Florida; and New Orleans, Louisiana. Paige Sapienza is the chief of operations and supervises the ongoing business operations of the three tea rooms. She uses Excel to summarize annual sales data from each location in separate workbooks. She wants you to total the sales by type of tea and location for each quarter and then format each worksheet. Paige also wants you to calculate sales for all of the locations and types of tea. Complete the following:

1. Open the **Tea** workbook located in the Excel6 > Case1 folder included with your Data Files, and then save the document as **Tea Room** in the location specified by your instructor.

2. In the Documentation worksheet, enter your name and the date.

3. Group the Atlanta, Naples, and New Orleans worksheets.

4. In the grouped worksheets, calculate the quarterly totals in the range B12:E12 and the types of tea totals in the range F4:F12.

5. In cells A12 and F3, enter **Totals** as the labels.

6. Improve the look of the quarterly worksheets using the formatting of your choice. Ungroup the worksheets.

7. Place a copy of one of the location worksheets between the Documentation and Atlanta worksheets, and then rename the new worksheet as **Summary Sales**.

8. In the Summary Sales worksheet, delete the values in the range B4:E11, and then change the label in cell A2 to **Summary Sales**.

9. In the range B4:E11, enter formulas that add the sales in the corresponding cells of the four quarterly worksheets. Use 3-D references to calculate the sum of each tea type per quarter.

10. Set up the Summary Sales and the three location worksheets for printing. Each worksheet should be centered horizontally, display the name of the worksheet centered in the header, and display your name and the current date on separate lines in the right section of the footer.

11. Make sure that any grouped worksheets have been ungrouped, and then save the Tea Room workbook.

12. Save the workbook as an Excel template with the name **Tea Room Template** in the location specified by your instructor.

13. In the Documentation worksheet, clear your name and date. In each of the location worksheets, clear the sales data but not the formulas. Save and close the Tea Room Template.

14. Create a new workbook based on the **Tea Room Template** file, and then save the workbook as **Tea Room 2017** in the location specified by your instructor.

15. In the Documentation worksheet, enter your name and the date.

16. In the three location worksheets, in the range B4:E11, enter **10**. Verify that the formulas in the three location worksheets and the Summary Sales worksheet summarize the data accurately.

17. Save the workbook, and then close it.

Case Problem 2

TROUBLESHOOT

Data Files needed for this Case Problem: Barstow.xlsx, SanDiego.xlsx, Carlsbad.xlsx, GoodieBag.xlsx

Clara's Goodie Bags   Clara Perry founded Clara's Goodie Bags to create unique party favor packages for private and corporate events. The first retail location opened on July 1, 2016, in Barstow, California. The San Diego location opened in 2017, and recently the Carlsbad location was added. Each location uses an Excel workbook to track the number of goodie bags sold in major categories—wedding, birthday, holiday, graduation, retirement, and custom. Clara wants you to use the workbooks to prepare a report showing the number of goodie bags sold by quarter and location for each category. Complete the following:

1. Open the **Barstow** workbook located in the Excel6 > Case2 folder included with your Data Files, and then save the workbook as **Barstow 2017** in the location specified by your instructor.

2. In the Documentation worksheet, enter your name and the date.

3. In the Barstow worksheet, calculate the total number of goodie bags sold in each category in the range B8:G8, and the total number sold each quarter in the range H4:H8.

4. Improve the look of the worksheet by using the formatting of your choice including a bottom border in the range A7:H7 and appropriate number formats for the total numbers of grab bags sold.

5. Save the Barstow 2017 workbook, and leave it open.

6. Repeat Steps 1 through 5 for the **SanDiego** and **Carlsbad** workbooks, naming them **San Diego 2017** and **Carlsbad 2017**, respectively.

7. Open the **GoodieBag** workbook located in the Excel6 > Case2 folder included with your Data Files, and then save the workbook as **Goodie Bags 2017** in the location specified by your instructor.

8. In the Documentation worksheet, enter your name and the date.

9. Rename Sheet1 as **Summary**. In cell A2, enter **Summary Sales** as the label.

⚙ **Troubleshoot** 10. The quarterly totals in the Goodie Bag 2017 Summary worksheet are not displaying the correct results. Make any necessary corrections to the formulas so that they add the correct cells from the Barstow 2017, San Diego 2017, and Carlsbad 2017 workbooks.

11. Insert formulas to calculate the totals for the range B8:G8 and the range H4:H8.

⚙ **Troubleshoot** 12. The Documentation worksheet in the Goodie Bag 2017 workbook includes hyperlinks in the range A9:A11 for each city's corresponding workbook (Barstow 2017, San Diego 2017, and Carlsbad 2017 located in the folder where you saved the workbooks). The text displayed for each hyperlink does not match its source file. Edit the hyperlinks so that each hyperlink points to its corresponding location workbook.

13. Add appropriate text for the ScreenTip to each hyperlink. Test each hyperlink.

14. Prepare each workbook for printing. For all worksheets except the Documentation worksheet, display the workbook name and the worksheet name on separate lines in the right section of the header and display your name and the current date on separate lines in the right section of the footer. Change the orientation so that each workbook will print on one page.

15. Save and close all of the workbooks.

Case Problem 3

APPLY

Data File needed for this Case Problem: RoomGroom.xlsx

Room and Groom   Room and Groom has been kenneling and grooming small, medium, and large cats and dogs in Topeka, Kansas, since June 2010. The standard kennel program includes access to the outside fenced play area, healthy meals, and private rooms. With the deluxe kennel program, the animal also has a daily playtime with a kennel employee, daily treats, and music or video playing in its room. Grooming services can occur during a kennel stay or as a standalone service. Samuel Wooten, the manager of Room and Groom, has been tracking the kennel and grooming services by month for the past year. Samuel wants you to analyze the data he has collected and create some preliminary charts. Complete the following:

1. Open the **RoomGroom** workbook located in the Excel6 > Case3 folder included with your Data Files, and then save the workbook as **RoomGroom 2017** in the location specified by your instructor.

2. In the Documentation worksheet, enter your name and the date.

3. Group the 12 monthly worksheets to ensure consistency in headings and for ease in entering formulas. Enter the heading **Total** in cells A11 and E4. For each month (January through December), enter formulas to calculate the total for each type of visit (the range B11:D11) and the total for each type of animal (the range E5:E11).

4. Improve the formatting of the monthly worksheets using the formatting of your choice. Be sure to include a bottom border in the ranges A4:E4 and A10:E10. Ungroup the worksheets.

5. In the Service by Month worksheet, in the range B5:B16, enter formulas with worksheet references to display the total grooming services for each month (the formulas will range from =January!B11 through =December!B11). Copy these formulas to the range C5:C16 (Room-Standard) and the range D5:D16 (Room-Deluxe).

6. In cells A17 and E4, enter the label **Total**. In the range B17:D17, enter formulas to add the total for each type of service, and then in the range E5:E17, enter formulas to add the total services each month by animal type.

7. Add a bottom border to the ranges A4:E4 and A16:E16. Improve the formatting of the Service by Month worksheet using the formatting of your choice.

8. Create a bar chart or a column chart that compares the types of services by month (the range A4:D16). Include an appropriate chart title and a legend. Format the chart so that it is attractive and effective. Position the chart below the data.

9. In the Service by Animal worksheet, in the range B5:D10, enter formulas using 3-D cell references to sum the services for the year for each animal. For example, in cell B5, the formulas for Small Dog Groom would be =SUM(January:December!B5).

10. In cells A11 and E4, enter the label **Total**. In the range B11:D11, enter formulas to add the total by type of service, and then in the range E5:E11, enter formulas to add the total services and total services by animal type.

11. Add a bottom border to the ranges A4:E4 and A10:E10. Improve the formatting of the Service by Animal worksheet using the formatting of your choice.

12. Create a pie chart based on the annual total for each animal type. Include an appropriate chart title and a legend. Format the chart so that it is attractive and effective. Position the pie chart below the data in the Service by Animal worksheet.

13. Group all of the worksheets except Documentation. Prepare the workbook for printing by displaying the workbook name and the worksheet name on separate lines in the right section of the header. Display your name and the current date on separate lines in the right section of the footer.

14. Save the workbook, and then close it.

Case Problem 4

Data Files needed for this Case Problem: Maryland.xlsx, Delaware.xlsx, Virginia.xlsx, ELSSummary.xlsx, NewMD.xlsx, ELSTemplate.xltx

Economic Landscape Supplies   Economic Landscape Supplies (ELS), a distributor of landscaping supplies, has offices in Delaware, Virginia, and Maryland. In December, each office submits a workbook that contains worksheets for all salespersons in that state. Each salesperson's worksheet contains the current year's sales by month and the projected increase that they will need to meet. Kyle Walker, the chief financial officer (CFO), wants you to calculate each salesperson's projected monthly sales based on the current sales and the projected increase. After you have added this information to each workbook, Kyle wants you to consolidate the information from the three workbooks into a single workbook. Complete the following:

1. Open the **Maryland** workbook located in the Excel6 > Case4 folder included with your Data Files, and then save the workbook as **ELS Maryland** in the location specified by your instructor.

2. In the Documentation worksheet, enter your name and the date.

3. Repeat Steps 1 and 2, opening the **Delaware** and **Virginia** workbooks and saving them as **ELS Delaware** and **ELS Virginia**, respectively.

4. Complete each salesperson worksheets in workbooks by doing the following:

   a. Group the Salesperson worksheets.

   b. Calculate the 2018 Projected Sales for each month by multiplying the 2017 Gross Sales by the Projected Increase. (*Hint*: Remember to use absolute cell references to the Project Increase cell.)

   c. Enter **Total** in cell A16, and then enter formulas to sum the totals of the 2017 Gross Sales and 2018 Projected Sales.

   d. Display all of the monthly sales numbers (the range B4:C15) with a comma and no decimal places. Display the total row values (the range B16:C16) with a dollar sign. Leave the Projected Increase value in cell B19 as formatted.

   e. Bold the ranges A4:A16 and B3:C3. Wrap the text and center the range B3:C3. Make sure all of the data and the headings are visible.

   f. Ungroup the worksheets.

5. In each of the state workbooks, do the following:

   a. Make a copy of the first salesperson's worksheet, rename it as **Summary**, and then place it after the Documentation worksheet.

   b. In cell A2, change the salesperson name to **Summary** and then clear the 2017 Gross Sales and 2018 Projected Sales data, leaving the formulas for the totals.

   c. Clear the label and data from the range A19:B19.

   d. In the range B4:C15, create 3-D reference formulas to calculate the total of each month's 2017 Gross Sales and 2018 Projected Sales. Widen columns as needed so you can see the totals.

   e. Group all worksheets except the Documentation worksheet. Prepare the workbook for printing by displaying the workbook name and the worksheet name on separate lines in the right section of the header. Display your name and the current date on separate lines in the right section of the footer.

   f. Ungroup the worksheets, and then save the workbook.

6. Open the **ELSSummary** workbook located in the Excel6 > Case4 folder included with your Data Files, and then save the workbook as **ELS Summary 2017** in the location specified by your instructor. Enter your name and date in the Documentation worksheet.

7. Make sure the three ELS state workbooks are open with the Summary worksheet active.

8. In the range B4:C15, enter external reference formulas to create a set of linked workbooks to summarize the 2017 Gross Sales and 2018 Projected Sales.

9. In cell A16, enter **Total**. In the range B16:C16, enter formulas to total the 2017 Gross Sales and 2018 Projected Sales.

10. Bold the range A4:A16. Bold, wrap text, and center the range B3:C3. Display all the monthly sales numbers with a comma and no decimal places. Display the total values (the range B16:C16) with a dollar sign and no decimal places.

11. Prepare the Summary worksheet for printing with the workbook name and the worksheet name on separate lines in the right section of the header. Display your name and the date on separate lines in the right section of the footer.

12. Save the Summary workbook.

⊕ **Explore** 13. The office manager for the Maryland ELS location found a newer workbook for that location's sales and commissions and has submitted it to you. Close the ELS Maryland workbook that you have been working with, open the **New MD** workbook located in the Excel6 > Case4 folder included with your Data Files, and then save the workbook as **New ELS Maryland** in the location specified by your instructor. Use Update Links to update the totals on the Summary worksheet in the ELS Summary 2017 workbook. The Totals before the update are 2017 Gross Sales $5,323,750 and 2018 Projected Sales $5,730,424. The totals after the update are 2017 Gross Sales $5,406,750 and 2018 Projected Sales $5,682,700.

14. Save and close all of the open workbooks.

⊕ **Explore** 15. Open the template named **ELSTemplate** located in the Excel6 > Case4 folder included with your Data Files, save the template as **ELS Template Revised** in the location specified by your instructor, and then change the company name in cell A1 of all the worksheets to **ELS**. Change the font for the company name to Bookman Old Style. Save the template.

16. Create a new workbook from the ELS Template Revised template. In the Documentation worksheet, enter your name and date.

17. In the Salesperson worksheet, enter **10,000** for each month's 2017 Gross Sales and Projected Increase of 1.20. Verify that the formulas are working correctly.

18. Save the workbook as **ELS Test** in a location specified by your instructor, and then close it.

INDEX

OBJECTIVES

Session 11.1
- Import data from a text file
- Work with connections and external data ranges
- Define a trusted location

Session 11.2
- Understand databases and queries
- Use the Query Wizard to import data from several tables
- Edit a query
- Import tables from Access for use with a PivotTable
- Manage relationships involving multiple tables

Session 11.3
- Create a web query
- Retrieve financial data using the WEBSERVICE function
- Access data from an XML document
- Work with XML data maps

Connecting to External Data

Building a Financial Report from Several Data Sources

Case | *Chesterton Financial*

Chesterton Financial is a brokerage firm in Burlington, Vermont. As part of its investment services business, the company advises clients on their investment portfolios. The investment counselors at the company need current financial data and reports, but they also must examine information on long-term trends in the market.

Some of this information comes from Excel workbooks, but other information is stored in specialized financial packages and statistical programs. In addition, the company maintains a database with detailed financial information about a variety of stocks, bonds, and funds. Company employees also use the Internet to receive up-to-the-minute market reports. Because much of the information that the counselors need comes from outside the company, they must retrieve information to analyze it and make decisions.

Rafael Garcia is an investment counselor at Chesterton Financial. He wants you to help him manage the different types of data available as he works on the Chalcedony Fund, one of the company's most important stock portfolios. You'll retrieve sample data from different sources and include them in a workbook.

STARTING DATA FILES

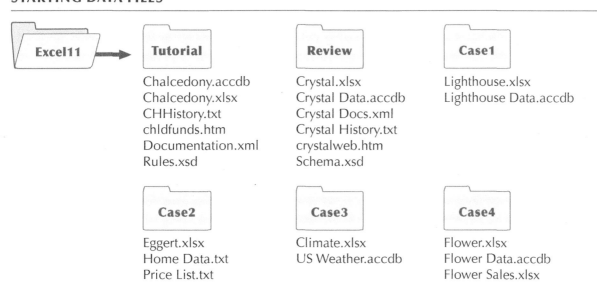

Excel11 →

Tutorial
Chalcedony.accdb
Chalcedony.xlsx
CHHistory.txt
chldfunds.htm
Documentation.xml
Rules.xsd

Review
Crystal.xlsx
Crystal Data.accdb
Crystal Docs.xml
Crystal History.txt
crystalweb.htm
Schema.xsd

Case1
Lighthouse.xlsx
Lighthouse Data.accdb

Case2
Eggert.xlsx
Home Data.txt
Price List.txt

Case3
Climate.xlsx
US Weather.accdb

Case4
Flower.xlsx
Flower Data.accdb
Flower Sales.xlsx

Microsoft product screenshots used with permission from Microsoft Corporation.

Session 11.1 Visual Overview:

The DATA tab contains commands for retrieving and refreshing data from external sources.

A **stock chart** displays the high, low, and closing values of a stock.

A **text file** contains only text and numbers without any formulas, graphics, special fonts, or formatted text.

Text files can be stored as **delimited text** in which a special character such as a space, comma, or tab marks the beginning of each column.

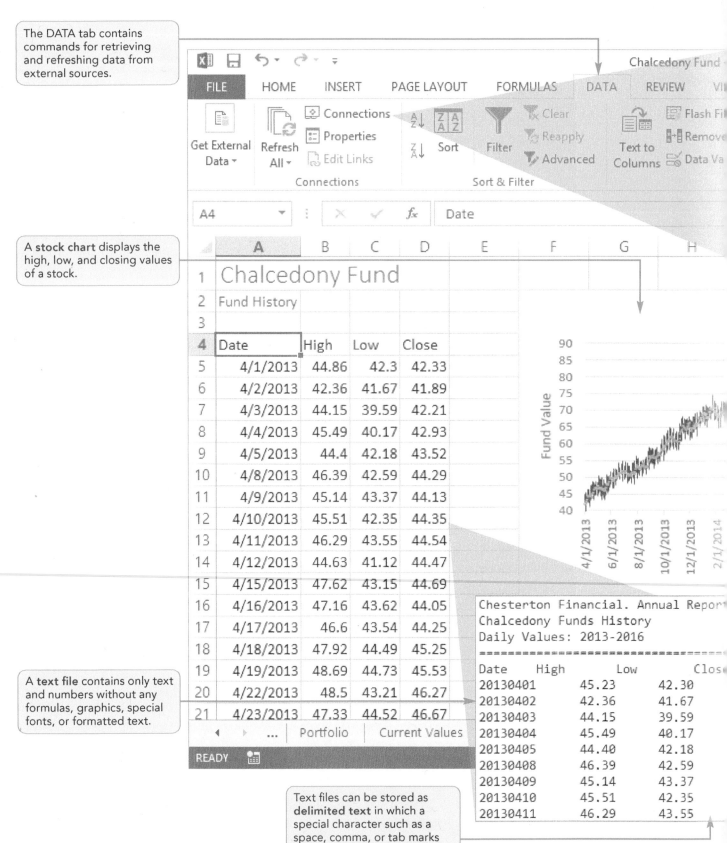

Chalcedony Fund

| FILE | HOME | INSERT | PAGE LAYOUT | FORMULAS | DATA | REVIEW | VI |

Get External Data ▾   Refresh All ▾   Connections   Properties   Edit Links
Connections

A↓ Z↓ Sort   Filter   Clear   Reapply   Advanced
Sort & Filter

Text to Columns   Flash Fi   Remove   Data Va

A4 | fx   Date

Chalcedony Fund

Fund History

	Date	High	Low	Close
5	4/1/2013	44.86	42.3	42.33
6	4/2/2013	42.36	41.67	41.89
7	4/3/2013	44.15	39.59	42.21
8	4/4/2013	45.49	40.17	42.93
9	4/5/2013	44.4	42.18	43.52
10	4/8/2013	46.39	42.59	44.29
11	4/9/2013	45.14	43.37	44.13
12	4/10/2013	45.51	42.35	44.35
13	4/11/2013	46.29	43.55	44.54
14	4/12/2013	44.63	41.12	44.47
15	4/15/2013	47.62	43.15	44.69
16	4/16/2013	47.16	43.62	44.05
17	4/17/2013	46.6	43.54	44.25
18	4/18/2013	47.92	44.49	45.25
19	4/19/2013	48.69	44.73	45.53
20	4/22/2013	48.5	43.21	46.27
21	4/23/2013	47.33	44.52	46.67

◄ ► ... | Portfolio | Current Values

READY

Chesterton Financial. Annual Report
Chalcedony Funds History
Daily Values: 2013-2016
=================================

Date	High	Low	Clos
20130401	45.23	42.30	
20130402	42.36	41.67	
20130403	44.15	39.59	
20130404	45.49	40.17	
20130405	44.40	42.18	
20130408	46.39	42.59	
20130409	45.14	43.37	
20130410	45.51	42.35	
20130411	46.29	43.55	

© 2014 Cengage Learning

Retrieving Text Data

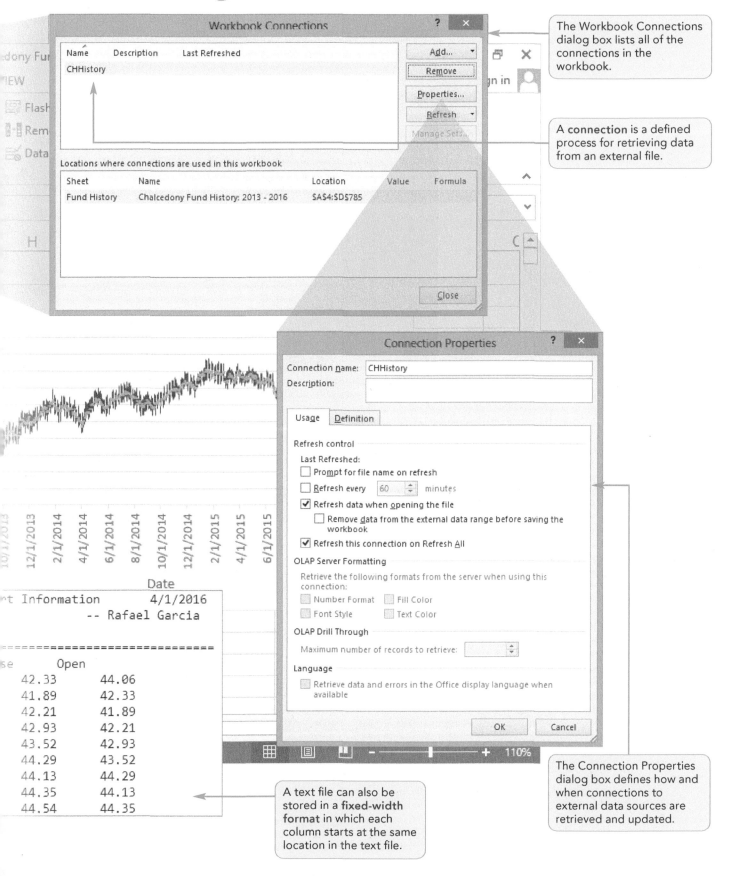

The Workbook Connections dialog box lists all of the connections in the workbook.

A **connection** is a defined process for retrieving data from an external file.

The Connection Properties dialog box defines how and when connections to external data sources are retrieved and updated.

A text file can also be stored in a **fixed-width format** in which each column starts at the same location in the text file.

Exploring External Data Sources

Many Excel projects involve working with data that is stored in locations other than the Excel workbook. These other locations are data files, known as **data sources**, that can be saved in a wide variety of formats. Learning how to retrieve and analyze data from different kinds of data sources is a key skill for any Excel user.

As an investment counselor, Rafael helps his clients plan their investment strategies. To do his job well, Rafael must look at the market from a variety of angles. He examines long-term trends so that his clients understand the benefits of creating long-term investment strategies. He tracks market performance in recent months to analyze current trends, and he also assesses the daily mood of the market by regularly viewing up-to-the-minute reports.

The information that Rafael needs comes from many data sources. As shown in Figure 11-1, long-term and historical stock information from the company's old record-keeping system has been retrieved from financial software packages and placed in text files that all counselors can use. Chesterton Financial stores its current market information in databases, which is where Rafael finds information on recent trends. Rafael can also access current market reports electronically from data sources located on the Internet.

Figure 11-1	Data sources for the Chalcedony Fund

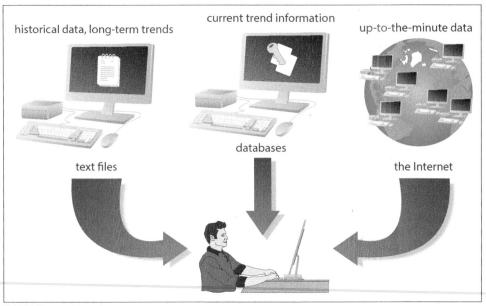

historical data, long-term trends   current trend information   up-to-the-minute data

text files   databases   the Internet

© 2014 Cengage Learning

Rafael's current project is to track the performance of the Chalcedony Fund, one of Chesterton Financial's oldest and most successful funds. The fund is composed of several stocks on the New York Stock Exchange (NYSE). He wants to develop a workbook that summarizes essential information from only a few stocks in the fund. Rafael wants the workbook to connect to sources containing (1) the fund's performance over the past few years; (2) more recent information on the fund's performance in the last year as well as the last few days; and (3) up-to-the-minute reports on the fund's current status. Figure 11-2 shows Rafael's strategy for the workbook he wants you to create.

Figure 11-2   Data plan for the Chalcedony Fund workbook

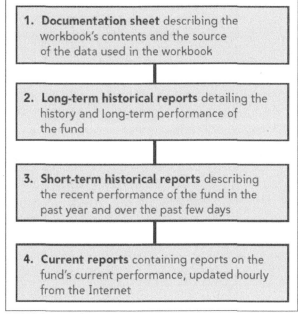

© 2014 Cengage Learning

To gather this data, you'll need to connect the workbook to several external data sources. First, you'll create a connection to the Chalcedony Fund's historical data. The daily values for the fund during the previous three years are stored in a text file, which you'll import directly into Excel.

Importing Data from Text Files

A text file contains only text and numbers without any formulas, graphics, special fonts, or formatted text. The text file is one of the simplest and most widely used formats for storing data because most software programs can save and retrieve data in this format. For example, Excel can open a text file in a worksheet, where you can format it as you would any data. Excel can also save a workbook as a text file, preserving only the data values without any of its formats. In addition, many types of computers can read text files. So, although text files contain only raw, unformatted data, they are very useful when you want to share data across a wide variety of software programs and computer systems.

REFERENCE

Connecting to a Text File

- On the DATA tab, in the Get External Data group, click the From Text button, and then select the text file containing the data.
- In the first step of the Text Import Wizard, choose how the data is organized, and then specify the row in which to start the import.
- In the second step, in the Data preview box, click to insert a column break, double-click a column break to delete it, and drag a column break to a new location.
- In the third step, click each column and select the appropriate data format option button or click the Do not import column (skip) option button.
- Click the Finish button.
- Specify where to insert the imported text, and then click the OK button.

Understanding Text File Formats

Because a text file doesn't contain formatting codes to give it structure, a program needs another way to understand the file contents. If a text file contains only numbers, the importing program needs to know where one group of values ends and another begins. One way to distinguish data that is organized within a text file is to use a **delimiter**, which is a symbol—usually a space, a comma, or a tab—that separates one column of data from another.

Figure 11-3 shows the same four columns of stock market data delimited by spaces, commas, and tabs. Columns in delimited text files are not always vertically aligned as they would be in a spreadsheet, but this is not a problem for a program that recognizes the delimiter. A tab delimiter is often the best way to separate text columns because tab-delimited text can include spaces or commas within each column.

Figure 11-3 **Delimited text files**

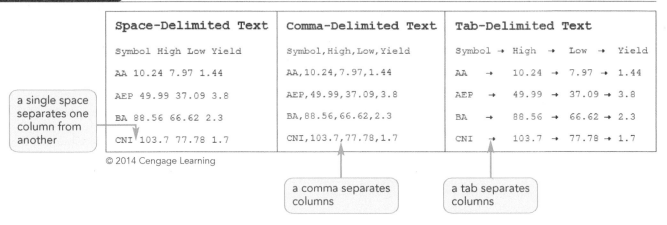

Space-Delimited Text	Comma-Delimited Text	Tab-Delimited Text
Symbol High Low Yield	Symbol,High,Low,Yield	Symbol → High → Low → Yield
AA 10.24 7.97 1.44	AA,10.24,7.97,1.44	AA → 10.24 → 7.97 → 1.44
AEP 49.99 37.09 3.8	AEP,49.99,37.09,3.8	AEP → 49.99 → 37.09 → 3.8
BA 88.56 66.62 2.3	BA,88.56,66.62,2.3	BA → 88.56 → 66.62 → 2.3
CNI 103.7 77.78 1.7	CNI,103.7,77.78,1.7	CNI → 103.7 → 77.78 → 1.7

a single space separates one column from another

a comma separates columns

a tab separates columns

© 2014 Cengage Learning

The other way to organize data is in a fixed-width text file in which each column starts at the same location in the file. For example, the first column starts at the first space in the file, the second column starts at the tenth space, and so forth. Figure 11-4 shows columns arranged in a fixed-width text file. In this example, all the columns line up visually because each one must start at the same location.

Figure 11-4 **Fixed-width text file**

each column begins at the same point in the text file

Fixed-Width Text			
Symbol	High	Low	Yield
AA	10.24	7.97	1.44
AEP	49.99	37.09	3.8
BA	88.56	66.62	2.3
CNI	103.7	77.78	1.7

© 2014 Cengage Learning

Starting the Text Import Wizard

When you use Excel to connect to a text file, the Text Import Wizard determines whether the data is stored in a delimited text file or a fixed-width text file—and if it's delimited, what delimiter is used. You can also tell Excel how to interpret the text file.

The text that Rafael wants you to import into Excel is stored in the file named CHHistory.txt. The file extension .txt identifies it as a text file. (Other common text file extensions are .dat, .prn, and .csv.) Although you know nothing about the file's structure, you can easily determine how the data is arranged by using the Text Import Wizard. You'll begin by creating a connection to the text file.

To create a connection to the CHHistory text file:

▶ **1.** Open the **Chalcedony** workbook located in the Excel11 ▶ Tutorial folder included with your Data Files, and then save the workbook as **Chalcedony Fund** in the location specified by your instructor.

▶ **2.** Go to the **Fund History** worksheet.

▶ **3.** On the ribbon, click the **DATA** tab. In the Get External Data group, click the **From Text** button. The Import Text File dialog box opens.

> **TIP**
>
> You can also open a text file by using the Open dialog box. When Excel detects the data in the text file, the Text Import Wizard opens.

▶ **4.** Click the **CHHistory** text file located in the Excel11 ▶ Tutorial folder included with your Data Files, and then click the **Import** button. The Text Import Wizard - Step 1 of 3 dialog box opens. In the Original data type section, the Fixed width option button is already selected, indicating that the Text Import Wizard has determined that the data is in a fixed-width text file. See Figure 11-5.

Figure 11-5	Text Import Wizard - Step 1 of 3

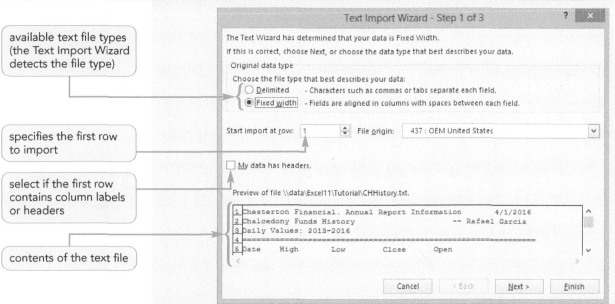

- available text file types (the Text Import Wizard detects the file type)
- specifies the first row to import
- select if the first row contains column labels or headers
- contents of the text file

▶ **5.** Scroll the preview box to view the data in the text file. The column labels for the data are in row 5, and the data list begins in row 6.

Specifying the Starting Row

By default, the Text Import Wizard starts importing text at the first row of the file. You can specify a different starting row if you want to skip those initial lines of text. In this case, Rafael wants the Text Import Wizard to skip the first four lines of the file, which contain titles and a description of the text file's contents. Because he is interested only in the data, he wants you to start importing at row 5, which contains the labels for each column of numbers—Date, High, Low, Close, and Open—that correspond to the date, the fund's high and low values on that date, and the fund's closing and opening values, respectively.

To specify row 5 as the starting row:

▶ 1. Click the **Start import at row up arrow** to change the value to **5**.

▶ 2. Click the **My data has headers**. check box to insert a checkmark. This specifies that the first row to be imported contains the column labels or headers.

▶ 3. Click the **Next** button to display the second step of the Text Import Wizard.

▶ 4. Scroll the Data preview box down four rows. The data to import from the text file starts with the column labels. See Figure 11-6.

Figure 11-6	Text Import Wizard - Step 2 of 3

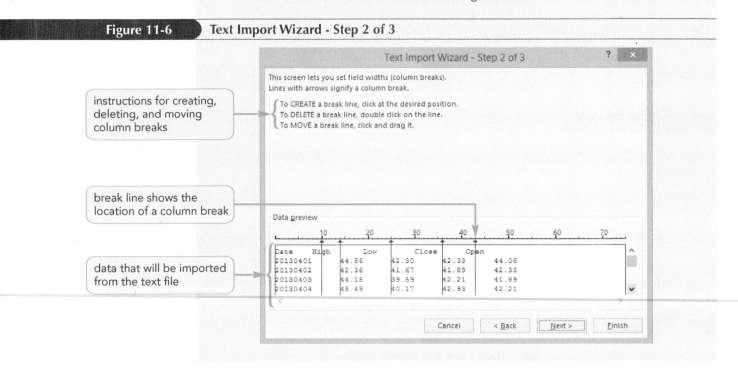

Editing Column Breaks

To correctly import a fixed-width text file, the Text Import Wizard needs to know where each column begins and ends. The point at which one column ends and another begins is called a **column break**. In a delimited file, the delimiter determines the column breaks. In a fixed-width file, the wizard guesses the locations of the column breaks. Sometimes, the wizard incorrectly defines the number and location of columns, so you should always check the Data preview box and edit the columns as needed.

You insert a new column break by clicking the position in the Data preview box where you want the break to appear. If a break is in the wrong location, you click and drag the break line to a new location in the Data preview box. You can delete an extra column break by double-clicking its break. Rafael wants you to make sure the column breaks in the CHHistory text file are accurate. You'll edit them to make sure the data is split into columns correctly.

To edit the column breaks in the CHHistory text file:

Make sure the column breaks do not intersect the data values in the column.

▶ **1.** Drag the first break line directly after the column of dates.

▶ **2.** Drag the second break line to the right directly after the values in the High column.

▶ **3.** Drag the third break line to the right directly after the values in the Low column.

▶ **4.** Drag the fourth break line to the right directly after the values in the Close column.

▶ **5.** Double-click the last break line to remove it from the Data preview window. See Figure 11-7.

Figure 11-7	Revised column breaks

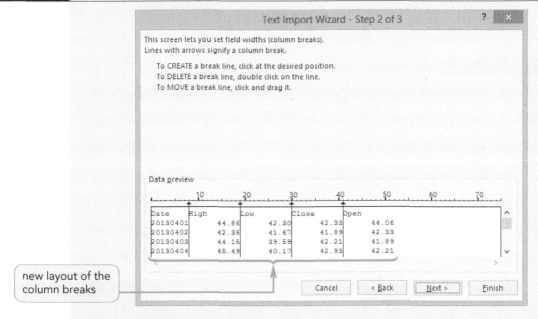

new layout of the column breaks

▶ **6.** Click the **Next** button to move to the third step of the Text Import Wizard.

Formatting and Trimming Incoming Data

In the third and final step of the Text Import Wizard, you format the data in each column. Unless you specify a format, the General format is applied to all of the columns. To specify a format, you select a column in the Data preview box, and then click the appropriate option button in the Column data format section. You can also indicate whether a column should not be imported. Eliminating columns is useful when you want to import only a few items from a large text file containing many columns.

The values from the Date column display each date with no separators between the four-digit year value and the month and day values. This is not a common date format. Rafael wants to make sure that the Text Import Wizard correctly interprets these values, so you'll change the General format style to a date format. He also wants to minimize the amount of data in the workbook, so you'll import only the date and the high, low, and closing values of the fund for each day, and not the fund's daily opening value, which is the same as its closing value from the previous day.

To specify a date format and remove the Open column:

1. If the first column is not selected in the Data preview box, click anywhere within the column to select it.

2. In the Column data format section, click the **Date** option button. The first column heading changes from General to MDY.

3. Click the **Date** box arrow to display a list of date formats, and then click **YMD**. The column heading for the first column changes to YMD, indicating the values in this column will be interpreted as dates formatted with the year followed by the month and the day.

TIP

For international data, click the Advanced button to apply a different number format.

4. In the Data preview box, click anywhere within the **Open** column to select it, and then click the **Do not import column (skip)** option button. The column heading for the Open column changes from General to Skip Column, indicating the data from this column will not be imported into the worksheet. See Figure 11-8.

Figure 11-8	Text Import Wizard - Step 3 of 3

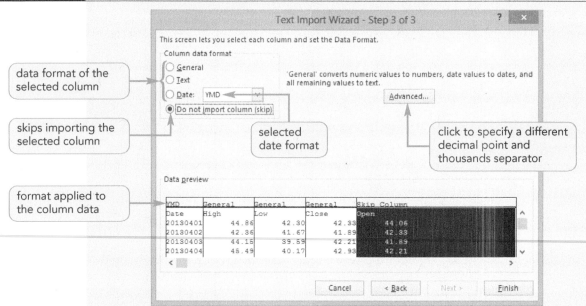

- data format of the selected column
- skips importing the selected column
- format applied to the column data
- selected date format
- click to specify a different decimal point and thousands separator

5. Click the **Finish** button. The Import Data dialog box opens so you can specify where to place the imported data in the worksheet. Note that if you used the Open dialog box to access the text file, its contents will be placed in the worksheet starting with cell A1.

6. Select cell **A4** in the Fund History worksheet, and then click the **OK** button. The data appears in the worksheet in the range A4:D785. Excel assigns the range a defined name that matches the name of the text file. See Figure 11-9.

Figure 11-9	Data imported into the Fund History worksheet

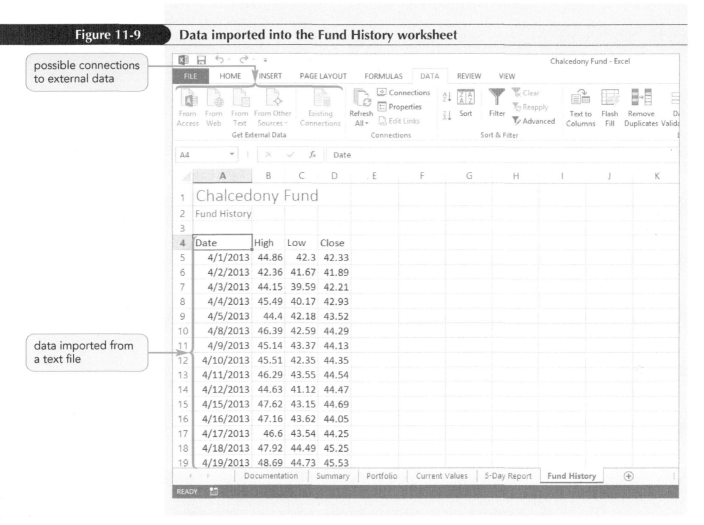

possible connections to external data

data imported from a text file

In addition to the fund values themselves, Rafael wants you to include a chart in the workbook displaying the fund's recent history. You will use a High-Low-Close chart designed to compare the high, low, and closing prices of a stock.

To create a High-Low-Close chart for the fund data:

1. Make sure cell **A4** is selected, and then press the **Ctrl+Shift+End** keys to select the range A4:D785. All of the fund data is selected.

2. Scroll to the top of the worksheet without deselecting the range.

3. On the ribbon, click the **INSERT** tab. In the Charts group, click the **Insert Stock, Surface or Radar Chart** button ☆▾, and then click **High-Low-Close** (the first chart in the gallery).

4. Resize the chart so that it covers the range **F2:M16**.

5. Change the chart title to **Historical Trends**, and then remove the legend.

6. Add Primary Major Vertical gridlines to the chart, and then change the minimum value of the vertical axis from its default value of 0 to **40**.

7. Add the Primary Vertical axis title **Fund Value**, and then add the horizontal axis title **Date**.

8. Close the Format pane, and then select cell **A3**. See Figure 11-10.

Figure 11-10   High-Low-Close chart

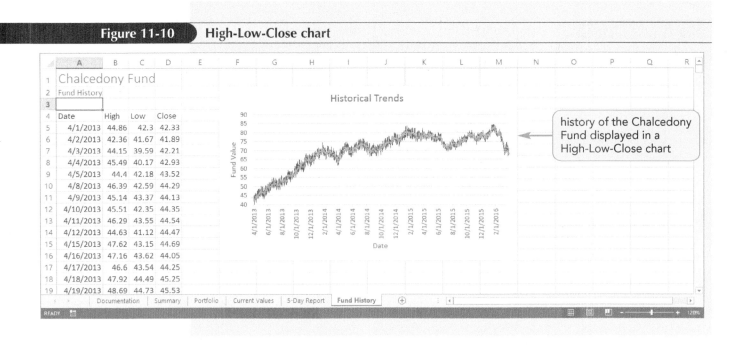

history of the Chalcedony Fund displayed in a High-Low-Close chart

Exploring External Data Ranges and Data Connections

When data is imported into a worksheet, it is stored within an **external data range**. Excel automatically assigns this data range a defined name based on the filename of the data source. You can change this to a more descriptive name that will help you and other users understand the purpose and content of the data stored in the external data range.

REFERENCE

Editing the Properties of an External Data Range

- Click any cell in the range containing the external data.
- On the DATA tab, in the Connections group, click the Properties button.
- To define a name for the data range, enter the name in the Name box.
- To specify how the external data is refreshed in the workbook, check the appropriate check boxes in the External Data Range Properties dialog box.
- Click the OK button.

The external data range in the range A4:D785 of the Fund History worksheet is named CHHistory, which was the filename of the original text file. Rafael wants you to change this name to something more descriptive. You'll edit the properties of the external data range.

To edit the properties of the CHHistory external data range:

1. Select cell **A4** to make the CHHistory external data range active.

2. On the DATA tab, in the Connections group, click the **Properties** button. The External Data Range Properties dialog box opens for the active external data range.

▶ **3.** In the Name box, select **CHHistory**, and then type **Chalcedony Fund History: 2013 - 2016**. See Figure 11-11.

Figure 11-11	External Data Range Properties dialog box

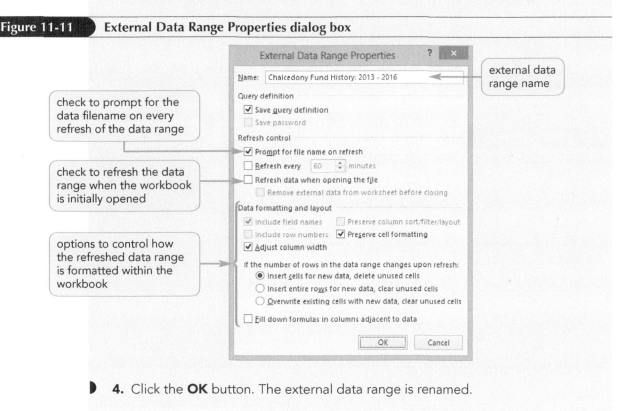

check to prompt for the data filename on every refresh of the data range

check to refresh the data range when the workbook is initially opened

options to control how the refreshed data range is formatted within the workbook

external data range name

▶ **4.** Click the **OK** button. The external data range is renamed.

Excel supports other properties for external data ranges, which include:

- Keep the contents of the external data range current by having Excel reimport or refresh the data from the external file when the workbook is opened or at specific intervals when the workbook is in use.
- Require the user to enter a password before data is refreshed, preventing other users from updating the data without permission.
- Define whether the refreshed external data range retains the formatting and layout you've already defined for those cells, or replaces the current format and layout based on the content of the new data.
- Define whether Excel inserts or overwrites cells when new rows are added to the data range.

Although you can change the properties of a data range, it is often more efficient to set the properties of the data connection from where the range gets its data.

Viewing a Data Connection

A data connection is like a pipeline from a data source to one or more locations in the workbook. The same data connection can link multiple data ranges, PivotTables, or PivotCharts. When you imported the contents of the CHHistory text file, Excel established a connection between a data range and that data source. To see where a data connection is being used, you can view that connection's properties.

Rafael wants you to review the data connections that are established in the Chalcedony Fund workbook. You'll do that from the Workbook Connections dialog box.

TIP

To delete a connection and separate the data from its source, select the connection in the Workbook Connections dialog box, and then click the Remove button.

To view the Chalcedony Fund workbook connections:

1. On the ribbon, click the **DATA** tab. In the Connections group, click the **Connections** button. The Workbook Connections dialog box opens, listing all of the connections in the workbook. Only one connection is listed—the one linked to the CHHistory text file.

2. Click the **Click here to see where the selected connections are used** link. The Workbook Connections dialog box shows that the connection to the CHHistory text file is used in only one location. See Figure 11-12.

Figure 11-12   Workbook Connections dialog box

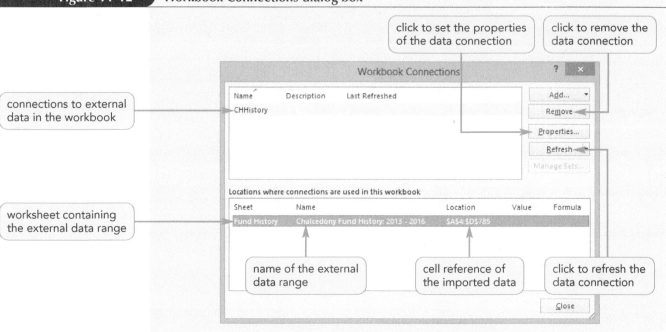

3. Click the **Close** button to close the dialog box.

Modifying Data Connection Properties

After a data connection has been established, you can modify its properties including how often the connection is refreshed or updated by the workbook. For example, you can set the connection to be refreshed whenever the workbook is reopened. In that case, every value in the workbook that relies on that data connection will also be refreshed.

REFERENCE

Refreshing External Data

- On the DATA tab, in the Connections group, click the Refresh All button.

or

- On the DATA tab, in the Connections group, click the Connections button.
- Select the connection, and then click the Refresh button.

or

- On the DATA tab, in the Connections group, click the Connections button.
- Select the connection, and then click the Properties button.
- Click the Refresh data when opening the file check box, click OK, and then click Close.

Rafael wants to automatically refresh the data connection to the CHHistory text file whenever the workbook is reopened. He also wants this data connection to have a more useful name and provide a description about the data source itself. You'll modify the properties of the CHHistory data connection to make these changes.

To modify the properties of a data connection:

▶ **1.** On the DATA tab, in the Connections group, click the **Connections** button. The Workbook Connections dialog box opens, again listing all of the data connections currently in the workbook.

▶ **2.** Click the **CHHistory** connection, if necessary, and then click the **Properties** button. The Connection Properties dialog box opens.

▶ **3.** In the Connection name box, type **Chalcedony Fund History** as a more descriptive name, and then press the **Tab** key.

▶ **4.** In the Description box, type **Daily values imported from the CHHistory.txt text file**.

TIP

To reduce the workbook's size when it is not in use, select the Remove data from the external data range before saving the workbook check box.

▶ **5.** Click the **Prompt for file name on refresh** check box to remove the checkmark. Excel will not always prompt you for the filename when refreshing the data.

▶ **6.** Click the **Refresh data when opening the file** check box to insert a checkmark. Now the connection to the CHHistory text file will be updated whenever the workbook is opened. See Figure 11-13.

Figure 11-13	Connection Properties dialog box

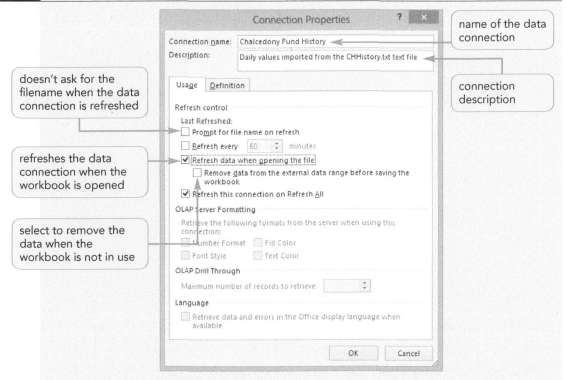

▶ **7.** Click the **OK** button to close the Connection Properties dialog box, and then click the **Close** button to close the Workbook Connections dialog box.

Rafael discovered an error in the CHHistory text file. The first value in the High column was entered incorrectly. You'll fix the error and verify that the workbook will be automatically updated to reflect the edit when it is reopened.

To edit the text file and refresh external data:

▶ **1.** Save and close the Chalcedony Fund workbook.

▶ **2.** In Notepad or another text editor, open the **CHHistory** text file located in the Excel11 ▶ Tutorial folder included with your Data Files.

▶ **3.** Change the High value in the first row from 44.86 to **45.23**. See Figure 11-14.

| Figure 11-14 | Revised CHHistory text file |

High value changed from 44.86 to 45.23

```
CHHistory - Notepad                                    –  □  ×
File  Edit  Format  View  Help
Chesterton Financial. Annual Report Information        4/1/2016
Chalcedony Funds History                         -- Rafael Garcia
Daily Values: 2013-2016
====================================================================
Date    High       Low        Close      Open
20130401    .45.23    42.30     42.33     44.06
20130402    42.36     41.67     41.89     42.33
20130403    44.15     39.59     42.21     41.89
20130404    45.49     40.17     42.93     42.21
20130405    44.40     42.18     43.52     42.93
20130408    46.39     42.59     44.29     43.52
20130409    45.14     43.37     44.13     44.29
20130410    45.51     42.35     44.35     44.13
20130411    46.29     43.55     44.54     44.35
20130412    44.63     41.12     44.47     44.54
20130415    47.62     43.15     44.69     44.47
20130416    47.16     43.62     44.05     44.69
20130417    46.60     43.54     44.25     44.05
20130418    47.92     44.49     45.25     44.25
20130419    48.69     44.73     45.53     45.25
```

▶ **4.** Save the CHHistory text file, and then close the file and the text editor.

▶ **5.** In Excel, open the **Chalcedony Fund** workbook. A security warning appears in the Message Bar below the ribbon, indicating that the external data connections have been disabled. Notice that the value in cell B5 has not yet been updated and still displays the original High value of 44.86. Disabling the connection is a security feature designed to prevent users from inadvertently opening workbooks infected with connections to invalid data sources.

▶ **6.** In the Message Bar, click the **Enable Content** button.

▶ **7.** If the Security Warning dialog box opens, prompting you to make this file a trusted document, click the **Yes** button. Excel refreshes the connection to the CHHistory text file, and the value in cell B5 changes from 44.86 to 45.23.

After opening the workbook, you can refresh external data manually by clicking the Refresh All button in the Connections group on the DATA tab. The Refresh All button provides two options—Refresh All refreshes all of the data connections in the workbook, and Refresh refreshes only the currently selected external data range.

PROSKILLS

Teamwork: Maintaining Data Security

Data security is essential for any business to maintain the integrity of its data and retain the trust of its colleagues and customers. It is critical to secure data to prevent lapses in security. If your Excel workbooks are connected to external data sources, keep in mind the following tips:

- **Apply data security controls.** Make sure your data files are set up with password controls to prohibit unauthorized access.
- **Keep software updated.** Be sure to diligently update the software that stores your data with the latest security patches.
- **Closely monitor data copying.** Have only one source of your data. When multiple copies of the data are allowed, data security, consistency, and integrity are compromised.
- **Encrypt data.** Use data encryption to prevent hackers from gaining unauthorized access to sensitive information.

Maintaining data security requires that everyone with access to your data files knows how to retrieve and process that data appropriately. In the end, your data will only be as secure as the work habits of the people who access it.

Defining a Trusted Location

Excel helps to maintain data security by using trusted locations. A **trusted location** is a data location that Excel will access without prompting you to confirm that the connection is secure. Any location that is not specifically identified as trusted requires users to accept it before proceeding to access the data. A trusted location is defined in the Trust Center from the Excel Options dialog box.

REFERENCE

Defining a Trusted Location

- On the ribbon, click the FILE tab, and then click Options in the navigation bar.
- Click Trust Center in the Excel Options list, and then click the Trust Center Settings button.
- Click Trusted Locations in the Trust Center list, and then click the Add new location button.
- Click the Browse button to locate the trusted location, and then specify whether to include subfolders.
- Click the OK button in each dialog box.

Rafael is concerned about Excel automatically disabling external data and forcing the user to enable it before the data can be refreshed. He asks you to override the default settings so that it always enables his data sources without prompting. You do this by defining all of the subfolders in the Excel11 folder as trusted locations.

To set up the Excel11 folder as a trusted location:

1. On the ribbon, click the **FILE** tab, and then click **Options** in the navigation bar. The Excel Options dialog box opens.

2. Click **Trust Center** in the left pane, and then click the **Trust Center Settings** button in the right pane. The Trust Center dialog box opens.

3. Click **Trusted Locations** in the left pane to display the list of locations that are trusted by Microsoft Office.

4. Only if your data files are located in a network folder, click the **Allow Trusted Locations on my network** check box.

5. Click the **Add new location** button. The Microsoft Office Trusted Location dialog box opens.

6. Click the **Browse** button, and then navigate to the **Excel11** folder included with your Data Files.

7. Double-click the **Excel11** folder icon to open it, and then click the **OK** button to return to the Microsoft Office Trusted Location dialog box.

8. Click the **Subfolders of this location are also trusted** check box to insert a checkmark. This option allows all of the subfolders in the Excel11 folder to be trusted.

9. In the Description box, type **Data sources for Tutorial 11**. See Figure 11-15.

Figure 11-15   **Microsoft Office Trusted Location dialog box**

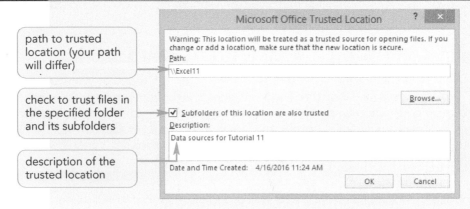

path to trusted location (your path will differ)

check to trust files in the specified folder and its subfolders

description of the trusted location

10. Click the **OK** button in each of the three dialog boxes to return to the workbook. Excel now trusts your data source from the Excel11 folder and will refresh the data from those sources without prompting.

11. Save and close the **Chalcedony Fund** workbook, and then reopen the workbook, verifying that you are not prompted to enable the data connections in the workbook when you reopen it.

By setting the Excel11 folder as a trusted location, Rafael will save time as he works with the Chalcedony Fund workbook.

INSIGHT

Moving a Data Source

When an Excel project is copied to another computer or when a data source is moved to a new folder, the path names to the external data sources might change and become unusable. To fix this problem, you must modify the properties of the connections established in the workbook. When you move or copy a workbook that is connected to external data, you must change the path to the external data. To update the connection, you modify the path on the Definition tab in the Connection Properties dialog box, which you open by clicking the Connections button in the Connections group on the DATA tab, selecting the connection, and then clicking the Properties button. With a revised definition established for the connection, other users can access and refresh the data from its new location.

You have set up the connection from the Chalcedony Fund workbook to the CHHistory text file. In the process, you've worked with connections, external data ranges, and trusted locations. In the next session, you'll learn about databases and how to connect an Excel workbook to a database.

REVIEW

Session 11.1 Quick Check

1. What is the difference between a fixed-width text file and a delimited text file?
2. Name three delimiters that can be used to separate data in a delimited text file.
3. How do you insert column breaks when importing a text file using the Text Import Wizard?
4. What is the relationship between a connection and an external data range?
5. Name two ways in which Excel automatically refreshes a connection.
6. What is a trusted location?
7. Describe how to reestablish a data connection when the data source is moved to a new location.

Session 11.2 Visual Overview:

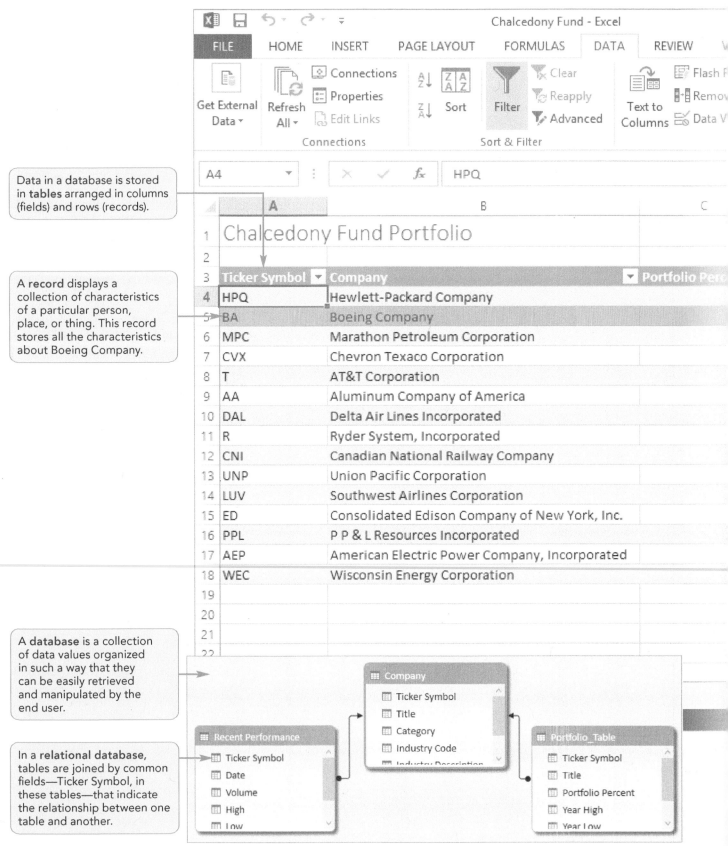

Data in a database is stored in **tables** arranged in columns (fields) and rows (records).

A **record** displays a collection of characteristics of a particular person, place, or thing. This record stores all the characteristics about Boeing Company.

A **database** is a collection of data values organized in such a way that they can be easily retrieved and manipulated by the end user.

In a **relational database**, tables are joined by common fields—Ticker Symbol, in these tables—that indicate the relationship between one table and another.

Chalcedony Fund - Excel

FILE   HOME   INSERT   PAGE LAYOUT   FORMULAS   DATA   REVIEW

Get External Data   Refresh All   Connections   Properties   Edit Links   Sort   Filter   Clear   Reapply   Advanced   Text to Columns   Flash   Remove   Data V

Connections   Sort & Filter

A4   fx   HPQ

	A	B	C
1	Chalcedony Fund Portfolio		
2			
3	Ticker Symbol	Company	Portfolio Per
4	HPQ	Hewlett-Packard Company	
5	BA	Boeing Company	
6	MPC	Marathon Petroleum Corporation	
7	CVX	Chevron Texaco Corporation	
8	T	AT&T Corporation	
9	AA	Aluminum Company of America	
10	DAL	Delta Air Lines Incorporated	
11	R	Ryder System, Incorporated	
12	CNI	Canadian National Railway Company	
13	UNP	Union Pacific Corporation	
14	LUV	Southwest Airlines Corporation	
15	ED	Consolidated Edison Company of New York, Inc.	
16	PPL	P P & L Resources Incorporated	
17	AEP	American Electric Power Company, Incorporated	
18	WEC	Wisconsin Energy Corporation	
19			
20			
21			
22			

Recent Performance
- Ticker Symbol
- Date
- Volume
- High
- Low

Company
- Ticker Symbol
- Title
- Category
- Industry Code
- Industry Description

Portfolio_Table
- Ticker Symbol
- Title
- Portfolio Percent
- Year High
- Year Low

© 2014 Cengage Learning

Excel Databases and Queries

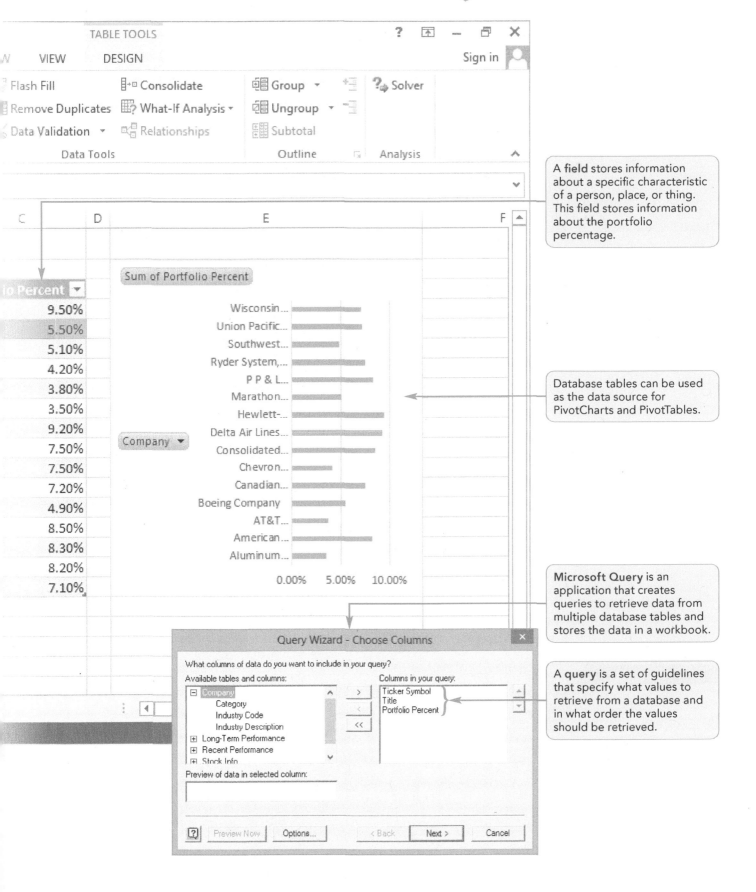

A **field** stores information about a specific characteristic of a person, place, or thing. This field stores information about the portfolio percentage.

Database tables can be used as the data source for PivotCharts and PivotTables.

Microsoft Query is an application that creates queries to retrieve data from multiple database tables and stores the data in a workbook.

A **query** is a set of guidelines that specify what values to retrieve from a database and in what order the values should be retrieved.

An Introduction to Databases

A database is a highly structured collection of data values organized to be easily retrieved and examined by the end user. Databases are commonly used as the data sources for Excel workbooks. A database is divided into separate tables. Each table is arranged in columns and rows, which are also referred to as fields and records. A field stores information about a specific characteristic of a person, place, or thing such as an individual's last name, a company address, or a stock value. A record is a collection of these fields. For example, a single record might contain a complete profile of an individual or a company, providing important information to the user. Excel can retrieve data directly from most database programs, including Microsoft Access, the database program that is part of Microsoft Office.

Analysts at Chesterton Financial store information about the Chalcedony Fund in an Access database named Chalcedony. Figure 11-16 shows the Company table, which contains fields—including the Ticker Symbol, Title, and Category fields shown in Figure 11-16—and records for 15 stocks that Rafael included in this sample database. Each stock is stored as a separate record in the table. For example, the first record in the Company table displays information for the Aluminum Company of America, which has the ticker symbol AA and is an industrial stock.

Figure 11-16	Company table in the Chalcedony database

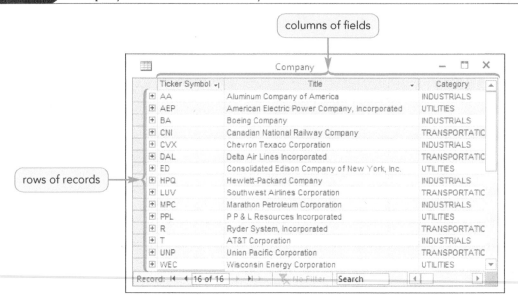

The Chalcedony database has four tables—Company, Long-Term Performance, Recent Performance, and Stock Info. Figure 11-17 describes the contents of each table.

Figure 11-17	Chalcedony database tables

Table Name	Description
Company	Includes data about each company in the fund and the percentage of the fund that is allocated to purchasing stocks for that company
Long-Term Performance	Summarizes the performance over the last 52 weeks for each stock, recording the high and low values over that period of time, and its standard deviation
Recent Performance	Daily high, low, closing, and volume values for each stock in the portfolio over the last five days
Stock Info	Description of each stock, including the yield, dividend amount and date, earnings per share, and average trading volume

© 2014 Cengage Learning

Different tables are connected through **database relationships** in which fields common to each table are used to match a record from one table to a record from another table. As shown in Figure 11-18, the Company table and the Stock Info table are related through the Ticker Symbol field. By matching the values of the Ticker Symbol field, information from both tables can be combined into a single data structure. This type of relationship is known as a **one-to-one relationship** because one record from the first table is matched to exactly one record from the second table. Another important relationship is the **one-to-many relationship** in which one record is matched to one or more records in the second table. A one-to-many relationship could be used in a customer orders database that matches a single customer record to a table describing the multiple orders made by that customer, for example.

| Figure 11-18 | Relating two tables based on a common field |

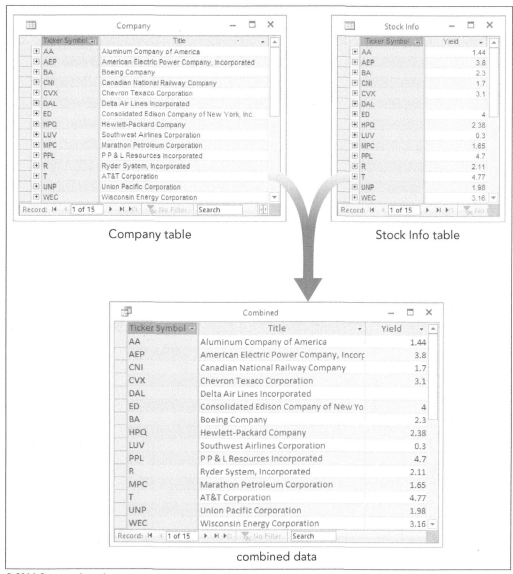

© 2014 Cengage Learning

Databases in which tables can be joined through the use of common fields are known as relational databases. Relational databases are extremely useful in that they allow similar pieces of information to be grouped in smaller, more manageable tables. Because the tables can be joined through a common field, it is unnecessary to duplicate the same piece of information across multiple tables. For example, a customer's name or address need only be entered in one table rather than several tables. By removing duplication, relational databases make it easier to manage large data sets and thus improve data quality and integrity.

Retrieving Data with Microsoft Query

Because a large database can contain dozens or hundreds of tables, and each table can have several fields and thousands of records, you need a way to retrieve only the information that you most want to see. To extract specific information from a database, you create a query. A query contains a set of criteria that specify what values to retrieve from a database and in what order the values should be retrieved. In the case of the Chalcedony database, Rafael might create a query to retrieve the ticker symbol, company title, and annual yield from the top-10 performing industrial stocks in the database. The query could further specify that any retrieved records be sorted alphabetically by company title.

Queries are written in a language called **SQL** or **Structured Query Language**. Writing a SQL query is beyond the scope of this tutorial, but you can create SQL-based queries using Microsoft Query, a program supplied with Microsoft Office and accessible from within Excel. Like the Text Import Wizard you used in the previous session, Microsoft Query uses a wizard containing a collection of dialog boxes that guide you through the entire query process.

Rafael wants the workbook to list the stocks in the Chalcedony Fund and describe their performance over the last year. According to the worksheet plan (refer back to Figure 11-2), you can extract this information from the Chalcedony database. You'll use the Microsoft Query Wizard to define your query.

To start the Microsoft Query Wizard:

◗ **1.** If you took a break at the end of the previous session, make sure the Chalcedony Fund workbook is open.

◗ **2.** Go to the **Portfolio** worksheet.

◗ **3.** On the ribbon, click the **DATA** tab. In the Get External Data group, click the **From Other Sources** button, and then click **From Microsoft Query**. The Choose Data Source dialog box opens. See Figure 11-19.

| **Figure 11-19** | **Choose Data Source dialog box** |

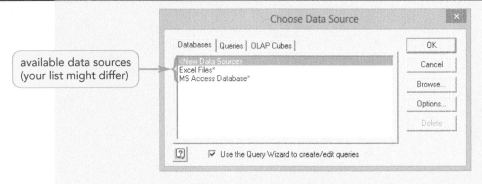

available data sources (your list might differ)

Connecting to a Data Source

In the first step of the wizard, you select the data source. The Choose Data Source dialog box lists several types of data sources from which you can retrieve data. You can also define your own data source by clicking <New Data Source> in the list of databases. In this case, Rafael wants you to connect to a Microsoft Access database, so you'll use the MS Access Database data source and connect to the Chalcedony database.

To connect to an Access data source:

▶ **1.** Click **MS Access Database*** in the list of data sources.

▶ **2.** Verify that the **Use the Query Wizard to create/edit queries** check box is checked, and then click the **OK** button. The Select Database dialog box opens.

▶ **3.** Navigate to the **Excel11 ▶ Tutorial** folder included with your Data Files, and then click the **Chalcedony** Access database file.

> **Trouble?** Microsoft Query does not reference network folders. If your data source is located on a network folder, you must map the folder to a drive letter. To do so, click the Network button in the Select Database dialog box to open the Map Network Drive dialog box.

▶ **4.** Click the **OK** button. Microsoft Query connects to the Chalcedony database file and opens the Query Wizard - Choose Columns dialog box. See Figure 11-20.

Figure 11-20	Query Wizard - Choose Columns dialog box

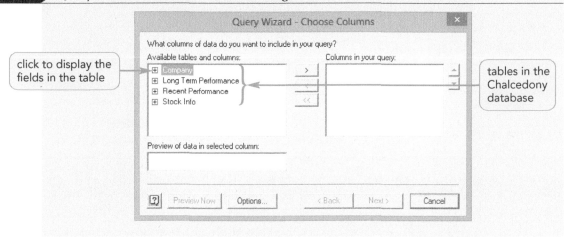

Choosing Tables and Fields

The next step in retrieving data from a database is to choose the table and fields to include in the query. You'll start by examining the fields in the Company table.

To view a list of fields in the Company table:

▶ **1.** In the Available tables and columns box, click the **Expand** button ⊞ next to Company.

▶ **2.** Verify that the columns (or fields) in the Company table are displayed in the Available tables and columns list box. See Figure 11-21.

| Figure 11-21 | Fields in the Company table |

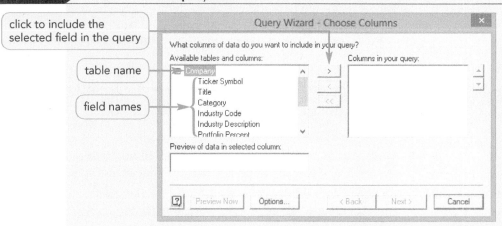

Because the Chalcedony database is relational, each of the tables listed by the Query Wizard is related by a common field, which in this case is the Ticker Symbol field. This means you can select fields from multiple tables and the Query Wizard will match records based on the Ticker Symbol value. Rafael's query will extract the ticker symbol, the company title, and the portfolio percent from the Company table. The portfolio percent is the percentage of the portfolio that is invested in each stock. The query will also include the Year High and Year Low fields from the Long-Term Performance table so that Rafael can identify the high and low market values from the previous year.

To select the fields to include in the query:

1. Click **Ticker Symbol** in the Available tables and columns box, and then click the **Select Field** button $>$ to move it to the Columns in your query box.

2. In the Available tables and columns box, double-click **Title**, and then double-click **Portfolio Percent**. These fields now appear in the Columns in your query box. Note that the order the fields are listed is the order they are retrieved and displayed within the workbook. You can reorder the fields if needed.

TIP

You can preview the selected field by clicking the Preview Now button.

3. Click the **Expand** button $+$ next to Long-Term Performance to display the list of columns in that table.

4. Double-click the **Year High** and **Year Low** column names. The five fields that Rafael wants to include in the query are selected. See Figure 11-22.

| Figure 11-22 | Fields selected for the query |

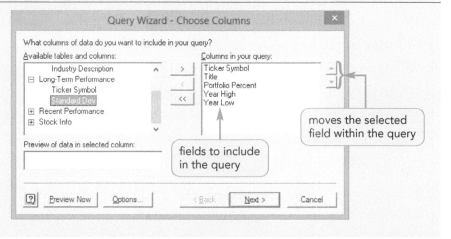

Filtering and Sorting Data

In the next step of the Query Wizard, you provide criteria to filter the records returned by the query. When you filter data, you specify which records you want to retrieve using specific criteria. For example, you can filter the data so that only a few specified stocks are retrieved, or limit the query to stocks that are bought and sold above a specified value.

You can include multiple filters in a query. To add another filter, you would fill in the next row of filter boxes in the dialog box. Select the And option button if all of the filter conditions must be matched to retrieve the record. Select the Or option button if a record will be retrieved if any of the filter conditions is met. Although the Query Wizard - Filter Data dialog box shows only three rows of criteria, the dialog box expands to provide additional rows as you specify requirements for your filter.

Rafael wants you to filter the query so that it retrieves information on stocks that constitute 7 percent or more of the Chalcedony Fund portfolio. To do this, you create a filter that returns records for stocks where the value of the Portfolio Percent field is 0.07 or greater.

To add a query to the filter:

1. Click the **Next** button to go to the Query Wizard - Filter Data dialog box.

2. In the Column to filter box, click **Portfolio Percent**, and then press the **Tab** key.

3. In the Only include rows where section, click the **arrow** button in the left column of the first row, and then click **is greater than or equal to** in order to select the type of comparison.

4. Enter **0.07** in the associated text box. See Figure 11-23.

Figure 11-23   **Query Wizard - Filter Data dialog box**

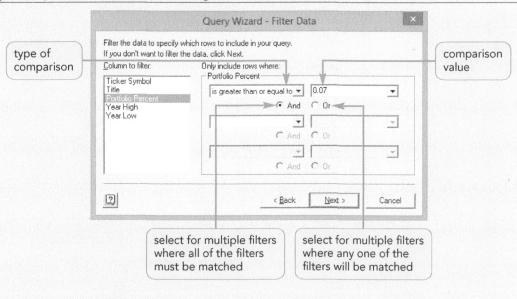

5. Click the **Next** button.

The last part of the Query Wizard lets you specify how to sort the data. You select the sort field and then specify either ascending or descending order. Microsoft Query allows you to specify up to three sort fields.

Rafael wants to display the portfolio information showing the stocks in which the Chalcedony Fund has the largest capital investment, and then showing the stocks with the smallest capital investment. Because the Portfolio Percent field tells you how much of the fund is invested in each stock, you'll sort the data by the values in that field in descending order (from highest percentage to lowest).

To sort the data in the query:

1. Click the **Sort by** arrow, and then click **Portfolio Percent** to select the sort field.

2. Click the **Descending** option button to sort the values from highest percentage to lowest percentage. See Figure 11-24.

Figure 11-24	Query Wizard - Sort Order dialog box

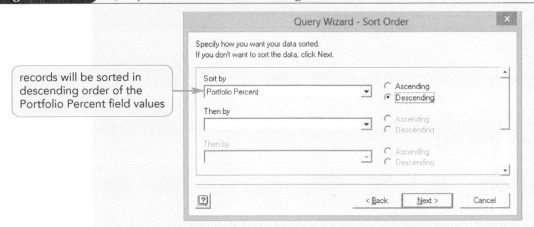

records will be sorted in descending order of the Portfolio Percent field values

3. Click the **Next** button to go to the final Query Wizard dialog box.

The Query Wizard - Finish dialog box provides three options. You can return (import) the data into the Excel workbook; you can display the results of the query in Microsoft Query, where you can further edit the data and the query definition; or you can save the query to a file. Saving the query to a file creates a text file containing the query's definition in SQL code. Because you don't need to refine the query at this point or save it to a file, you'll simply import the data into the Chalcedony Fund workbook. With Microsoft Query, you can import the query data in the form of an Excel table, a PivotTable, or a PivotTable and PivotChart, or you can simply create the connection to the query without actually importing the data. Rafael wants you to import the query data into an Excel table.

To import the query data into an Excel table:

1. Make sure the **Return Data to Microsoft Excel** option button is selected, and then click the **Finish** button. The Import Data dialog box opens so you can select where to insert the imported data.

2. Verify that the **Table** option button is selected so that the data is stored as an Excel table.

Be sure to select that the data should be imported into the workbook as an Excel table.

3. Click cell **A4** in the Portfolio worksheet to specify the location to create the Excel table. See Figure 11-25.

Figure 11-25   **Import Data dialog box**

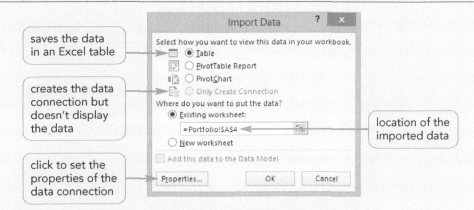

saves the data in an Excel table

creates the data connection but doesn't display the data

click to set the properties of the data connection

location of the imported data

4. Click the **OK** button. The data from the query is imported into the Portfolio worksheet at cell A4.

5. In the range **C5:C13**, format the data using the **Percentage** format with two decimal places, and then in the range **D5:E13**, format the data using the **Number** format.

6. Select cell **A4**. See Figure 11-26.

Figure 11-26   **Data imported into an Excel table**

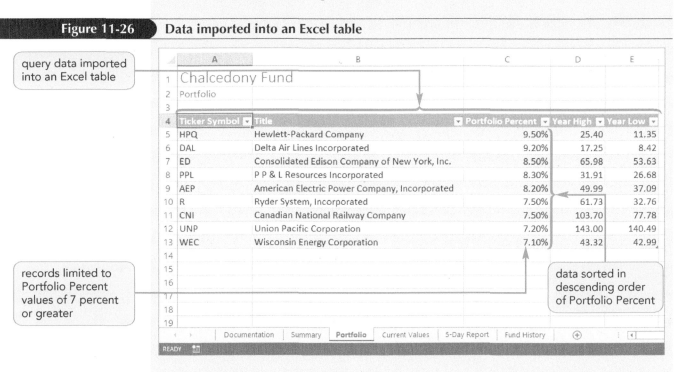

query data imported into an Excel table

records limited to Portfolio Percent values of 7 percent or greater

data sorted in descending order of Portfolio Percent

Ticker Symbol	Title	Portfolio Percent	Year High	Year Low
HPQ	Hewlett-Packard Company	9.50%	25.40	11.35
DAL	Delta Air Lines Incorporated	9.20%	17.25	8.42
ED	Consolidated Edison Company of New York, Inc.	8.50%	65.98	53.63
PPL	P P & L Resources Incorporated	8.30%	31.91	26.68
AEP	American Electric Power Company, Incorporated	8.20%	49.99	37.09
R	Ryder System, Incorporated	7.50%	61.73	32.76
CNI	Canadian National Railway Company	7.50%	103.70	77.78
UNP	Union Pacific Corporation	7.20%	143.00	140.49
WEC	Wisconsin Energy Corporation	7.10%	43.32	42.99

According to the retrieved data, 9.50 percent of the Chalcedony Fund is invested in Hewlett-Packard Company, and the value of that stock has ranged from a high of 25.40 points to a low of 11.35 points over the previous year. The table is sorted in descending order by the percentage of each stock in the portfolio, placing the most heavily invested stocks at the top of the list. The table shows only the nine stocks that constitute 7 percent or more of the total Chalcedony fund. After seeing these results, Rafael wants you to revise the query to show information about all of the stocks in the Chalcedony fund.

Editing a Query

By editing a query, you can add new columns to a worksheet, change the sort order options, or revise any filters. You edit a query by editing the definition of the connection. When you edit the connection, Excel recognizes that the Query Wizard was used to define the parameters of the connection and restarts the Query Wizard. You can then walk through the steps of the wizard, modifying the query definition as you go.

REFERENCE

Editing a Database Query

- On the DATA tab, in the Connections group, click the Connections button.
- Select the connection used by the database query, and then click the Properties button.
- Click the Definition tab, and then click the Edit Query button.
- Change the query definition using the dialog boxes provided by the Query Wizard.

Rafael wants you to remove the filter that limited the query to stocks with 7 percent or more of the portfolio, and he wants you to add the Category field to the query so that he can see each stock category (Industrials, Transportation, or Utilities). He also wants you to change the sort order so that the Excel table is sorted by Category field first, and then by descending order of the Portfolio Percent field within each category. You'll edit the query now.

TIP

You can view and edit the SQL code associated with the query by working with the contents of the Command text input box.

To edit the query:

1. On the DATA tab, in the Connections group, click the **Connections** button. The Workbook Connections dialog box opens.

2. Click the **Query from MS Access Database** connection, and then click the **Properties** button. The Connection Properties dialog box opens.

3. Click the **Definition** tab. From this tab, you can view the current definition of the Chalcedony Portfolio query. You can also edit the query.

4. Click the **Edit Query** button. The Query Wizard - Choose Columns dialog box reopens.

5. In the Available tables and column box, click the **Expand** button + next to the Company table entry, and then double-click the **Category** field. "Category" is added to the end of the list of columns in the query.

6. Click the **Next** button to go to the Query Wizard - Filter Data dialog box.

7. Select **Portfolio Percent** from the list of fields, click the first box arrow in the Only include rows where box, and then select the blank entry at the top of the list of comparison options. The Portfolio Percent filter is removed.

8. Click the **Next** button to go to the Query Wizard - Sort Order dialog box.

9. Click the **Sort by** arrow, click **Category**, and then click the **Ascending** option button. The sort order for the query is modified to first sort in ascending order by Category.

10. Click the **Then by** arrow, click **Portfolio Percent**, and then click the **Descending** option button. In each category, the records will be sorted in descending order by Portfolio Percent. See Figure 11-27.

| Figure 11-27 | Modified sort order for the query |

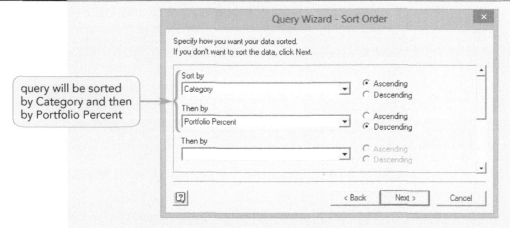

query will be sorted by Category and then by Portfolio Percent

11. Click the **Next** button, and then click the **Finish** button to close the Query Wizard.

12. Click the **OK** button in the Connection Properties dialog box, and then click the **Close** button in the Workbook Connections dialog box to return to the Portfolio worksheet. See Figure 11-28.

| Figure 11-28 | Revised Portfolio table |

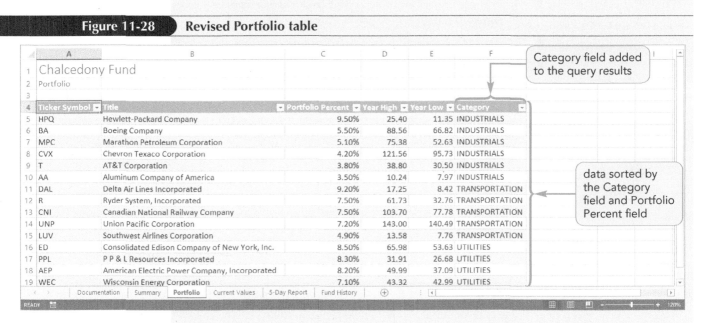

Category field added to the query results

data sorted by the Category field and Portfolio Percent field

The fund is composed of 15 stocks—with six industrial stocks, five transportation stocks, and four utility stocks. The most heavily invested stocks within each category are Hewlett-Packard Company, an industrial stock with 9.50 percent of the portfolio; Delta Air Lines Inc., a transportation stock with 9.20 percent of the portfolio; and Consolidated Edison Company of New York, Inc., a utility stock with 8.50 percent of the portfolio.

Excel has assigned the name Table_Query_from_MS_Access_Database to the Portfolio table containing the data imported from the Microsoft Query. The name reflects the fact that the data has been imported into a table using the Query from MS Access Database connection. Rafael wants you to change the table name to better describe the table's contents.

To rename the table:

▶ 1. On the ribbon, click the **TABLE TOOLS DESIGN** tab. In the Properties group, in the Table Name box, select the table name.

▶ 2. Type **Portfolio_Table** as the new table name, and then press the **Enter** key.

As you did with the data connection to the CHHistory text file, Rafael wants you to modify the properties of this data connection to give it a useful description and to have Excel automatically refresh the data whenever the workbook is reopened.

To edit the properties of the connection to the Chalcedony database:

▶ 1. On the ribbon, click the **DATA** tab. In the Connections group, click the **Connections** button. The Workbook Connections dialog box opens, listing the two data connections in the workbook.

▶ 2. Click **Query from MS Access Database** in the list, and then click the **Properties** button. The Connection Properties dialog box opens.

▶ 3. In the Connection name box, type **Chalcedony Portfolio Query**.

TIP

To disconnect an Excel table from its data source, click the Unlink button in the External Table Data group on the TABLE TOOLS DESIGN tab.

▶ 4. In the Description box, type **Stock data imported from the Chalcedony database using Microsoft Query**.

▶ 5. Click the **Refresh data when opening the file** check box to insert a checkmark.

▶ 6. Click the **OK** button to close the Connection Properties dialog box, and then click the **Close** button to close the Workbook Connections dialog box.

You are finished working with the query for the portfolio table. Next, Rafael wants you to directly connect Excel to an Access database.

INSIGHT

Saving a Data Connection

You can save the definition of a data connection as a permanent file in either the Office Data Connection (ODC) format or the Universal Data Connection (UDC) format. Connection files are used to share connections with other individuals, or to create a library of connection files for use with large database structures.

To manually save a connection to an ODC file, use the Export Connection File button on the Definition tab in the Connection Properties dialog box to specify the name and location of your Office Data Connection file. The default location for ODC files is the My Data Sources subfolder of your Documents folder. ODC files are added to the My Data Sources subfolder whenever you create a connection to an Access database table. UDC files are not created within Excel. To create a UDC file, you can use Microsoft InfoPath for creating and designing XML-based data entry forms for businesses.

To access a saved connection file, click the Existing Connections button in the Get External Data group on the Data tab to select the connection file from your workbook, your network, or your computer.

Importing Data from Multiple Tables into a PivotTable

You can import multiple tables from a database directly into Excel without using Microsoft Query. If the tables are related through a common field, Excel will automatically include the relationship between the tables as part of the data import. This method does not include defining a query, so the entire tables will be imported into the workbook.

Rafael wants to include an analysis of the most recent performance of each stock in the Chalcedony Fund. To do this, he wants to import the Company table and the Recent Performance table shown in Figure 11-29. The tables share a one-to-many relationship because one record from the Company table will be matched to many records (in this case, five records) in the Recent Performance table.

| Figure 11-29 | Relationship between the Company and Recent Performance tables |

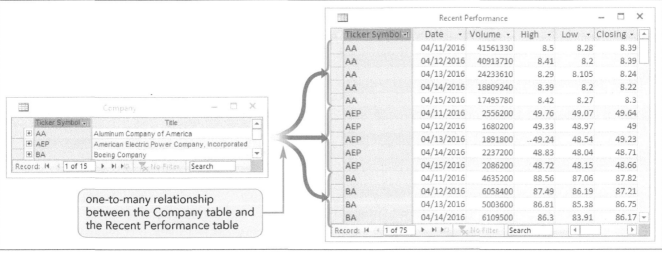

© 2014 Cengage Learning

You'll import these two tables now.

To import the Company and Recent Performance tables:

1. Go to the **5-Day Report** worksheet.

2. On the ribbon, click the **DATA** tab. In the Get External Data group, click the **From Access** button. The Select Data Source dialog box opens.

3. Select the **Chalcedony** database file located in the Excel11 ► Tutorial folder included with your Data Files, and then click the **Open** button.

   Depending on your system, the Data Link Properties dialog box might open with information about the link to this data source.

4. If the Data Link dialog box opens, click the **OK** button twice to open the Select Table dialog box.

5. Click the **Enable selection of multiple tables** check box so you can select more than one table from the database.

6. Click the **Company** and **Recent Performance** check boxes to select the two tables in the Chalcedony database. See Figure 11-30.

Figure 11-30   Select Table dialog box

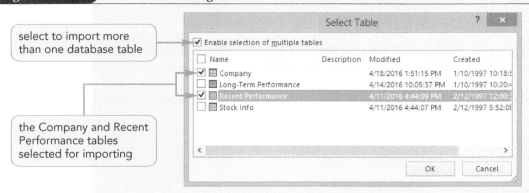

select to import more than one database table

the Company and Recent Performance tables selected for importing

> **7.** Click the **OK** button. The Import Data dialog box reappears.

Rafael wants the data to appear in an interactive report so that he can select the name of a company from the Chalcedony Fund and view the closing value and shares traded over the last five days. You'll import the data into a PivotTable report that summarizes each stock's activity. You will also change the properties of this data connection so that the data is automatically refreshed when the workbook is opened.

To import the Chalcedony database data into a PivotTable report:

TIP

The Table option creates multiple worksheets, and each sheet contains an Excel table with the complete contents of one of the selected database tables.

> **1.** In the Import Data dialog box, verify that the **PivotTable Report** option button is selected.
>
> **2.** Click in the **Existing worksheet** box, and then click cell **D4** in the 5-Day Report worksheet. This is the cell where you want to place the PivotTable.
>
> **3.** Click the **Properties** button. The Connection Properties dialog box opens.
>
> **4.** In the Connection name box, type **5-Day Performance Data**.
>
> **5.** In the Description box, type **Data from the Company and Recent Performance tables in the Chalcedony database**.
>
> **6.** Click the **Refresh data when opening the file** check box. Excel will refresh the data in this connection whenever the workbook is opened.
>
> **7.** Click the **OK** button. The Import Data dialog box reappears.
>
> **8.** Click the **OK** button. The data is imported, the PivotTable is inserted into cell D4, and the fields from the Company and Recent Performance tables are displayed in the PivotTable Fields pane organized by table.

Rafael wants the PivotTable to display the dates, closing value, and volume of shares traded for each of the stocks in the Chalcedony fund. He wants the company titles to appear in a slicer next to the PivotTable. You will create and format the PivotTable and slicer now.

To set up and format the PivotTable and slicer:

1. In the PivotTable Fields pane, scroll down to the list of fields in the Recent Performance table.

2. Drag the **Date** field to the Rows area. The list of five dates is displayed in the range D5:D9 in the worksheet.

3. From the list of fields in the Recent Performance table, drag the **Volume** field to the VALUES area, and then drag the **Closing** field to the VALUES area.

   The column labels include "Sum of" before the names of the Volume and Closing fields. This label is misleading because only one value will appear for these items for each stock on each day, so the PivotTable shows a "sum" of only one record. You'll revise the column labels to better reflect their contents.

4. In the range **D4:F4**, enter the following labels: **Date**, **Shares Traded**, and **Closing Value**.

5. In the range **E5:E9**, format the Volume values using the **Comma Style** with no decimal places.

6. In the range **F5:F9**, format the Closing values using the **Number** format with two decimal places.

7. On the PIVOTTABLE TOOLS DESIGN tab, in the Layout group, click the **Grand Totals** button, and then click **Off for Rows and Columns**. The Grand Totals are removed from the PivotTable because Rafael doesn't need to see grand totals for the five-day history.

   Next, you'll add a slicer containing the Title field from the Company table.

8. On the ribbon, click the **PIVOTTABLE TOOLS ANALYZE** tab. In the Filter group, click the **Insert Slicer** button. The Insert Slicers dialog box opens.

9. From the list of fields in the Company table, select the **Title** field, and then the **OK** button.

10. Move and resize the Title slicer so that it covers the range A4:C20.

11. In the Title slicer, click **Aluminum Company of America** from the list of company titles. The five most recent shares traded and closing values for that stock are displayed in the PivotTable. See Figure 11-31.

Figure 11-31   **Formatted PivotTable and slicer**

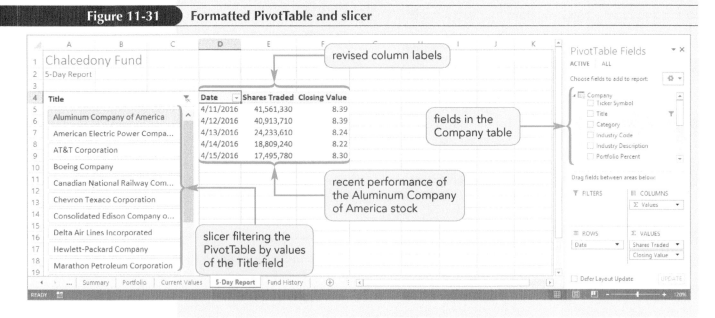

Rafael can use the PivotTable and slicer to quickly view the five-day history for each stock in the portfolio. As new data is added to the Chalcedony database, Rafael can refresh the data connection to view the results on the 5-Day Report worksheet.

Rafael wants to compare the recent values of the stocks in the Chalcedony Fund with their highest and lowest values from the previous year. He suggests that you add the Year High and Year Low values from the Portfolio worksheet (shown in Figure 11-28) to the PivotTable report. This requires joining the data in the Portfolio worksheet with the data from the Company and Recent Performance tables. You can do this with the data model.

INSIGHT

Opening Non-Native Files in Excel

Often, you can simplify the process of connecting to data sources by opening the data source files directly in Excel. You do this from the Open screen in Backstage view. If Excel supports the file format, it will open the appropriate dialog boxes to import the data into the Excel workbook. For example, opening a text file from the Open screen will launch the Text Import wizard. Opening an Access database will display a dialog box from which you can select one or more tables from the database. To choose other file formats in the Open dialog box, click the button directly above the Open button and choose the file format you want to display.

Exploring the Data Model and PowerPivot

TIP

The data model is supported in all versions of Excel 2013 except the tablet version found in Office RT.

The **data model** is a database built into Excel that provides many of the same tools found in database programs such as Access. Because the data model database is part of the Excel workbook, its contents are immediately available to PivotTables, PivotCharts, and other Excel features used for analyzing data.

The data model is constructed from different tables related by common fields. A table becomes part of the data model database when it is imported from an external database file like the Chalcedony database. When you imported the Company and Recent Performance tables, their data was added to the data model along with information about the relationship between the two tables. Excel tables can also be added to the data model, allowing database tools to be used to combine, analyze, and create queries among different Excel tables, or among Excel tables and tables imported from external database files.

Installing the PowerPivot Add-In

You interact with the data model using **PowerPivot**, which is an add-in supplied with the Professional Plus editions of Office or with the standalone edition of Excel. **The PowerPivot add-in is not supported in other versions of Excel.** With PowerPivot, you can:

- Apply filters to tables stored in the data model.
- Rename tables and fields within the data model.
- Define and manage the relationships among data tables joined by common fields.
- Create calculated fields based on data fields from multiple data sources.
- Create advanced data structures and models.

Rafael wants you to view the data model that is part of the Chalcedony Fund workbook. **Note:** If you are using a version of Excel that does not support PowerPivot, you need to complete the alternate steps posted online for the rest of this session. See your instructor for assistance.

To install the PowerPivot add-in:

▶ **1.** On the ribbon, look for the **POWERPIVOT** tab. If it appears on the ribbon, skip the rest of these steps because the PowerPivot add-in is already installed. If it doesn't appear on the ribbon, continue with Step 2.

▶ **2.** On the ribbon, click the **FILE** tab, and then click **Options** in the navigation bar. The Excel Options dialog box opens.

▶ **3.** In the Excel Options categories, click **Add-Ins**.

▶ **4.** Click the **Manage** box arrow, click **COM Add-ins**, and then click the **Go** button. The COM Add-Ins dialog box opens.

▶ **5.** In the list of available add-ins, click the **Microsoft Office PowerPivot for Excel 2013** check box.

▶ **6.** Click the **OK** button. The POWERPIVOT tab is added to the ribbon.

Adding a Table to the Data Model

The POWERPIVOT tab contains the commands for working with the data model. You use the Add to Data Model command to add Excel tables to the data model. PowerPivot displays the contents of the data model in a separate window from the Excel workbook window.

Rafael wants you to add the Excel table from the Portfolio worksheet to the data model so that it can be joined with the data imported from the Recent Performance and Company tables.

To add an Excel table to the data model:

▶ **1.** Go to the **Portfolio** worksheet, and then select cell **A4** to make the Excel table active in the worksheet.

▶ **2.** On the ribbon, click the **POWERPIVOT** tab. The PowerPivot commands are displayed on the ribbon.

3. In the Tables group, click the **Add to Data Model** button. The Portfolio table is added to the data model. See Figure 11-32.

Figure 11-32	Data view of the tables in the data model

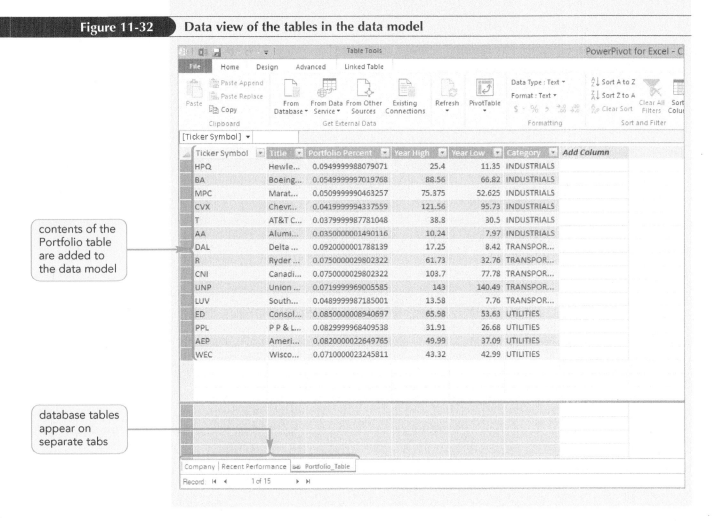

contents of the Portfolio table are added to the data model

database tables appear on separate tabs

Viewing the Data Model

You can view the contents of a data model in Data view and in Diagram view. Data view shows the contents of each database table in the data model on a separate tab. Diagram view shows each table as an icon, and relationships between tables are indicated by connecting arrows. To see which field joins the two tables, you click the arrow connecting the tables.

The data model currently includes three tables—the Company and the Recent Performance tables, whose data was imported from the Chalcedony database, and the Portfolio table you just added. You'll review the contents of each table in Data view, and then switch to Diagram view and review the relationship among the tables.

To view the data model in Data view and Diagram view:

1. In the PowerPivot for Excel window, click the **Company** tab. The contents of the Company table are displayed.

2. Click the **Recent Performance** tab to view contents of that table.

3. Click the **Portfolio_Table** tab to return to the Portfolio table.

4. On the Home tab, in the View group, click the **Diagram View** button. The tables and relationships within the data model are displayed graphically in the PowerPivot window. An arrow connects the Company and Recent Performance tables, indicating that those two tables are related by a common field.

5. Click the arrow connecting the Company table and the Recent Performance table. The Ticker Symbol field is highlighted, indicating that it is the common field joining the two tables. See Figure 11-33.

Figure 11-33 Diagram view of the tables in the data model

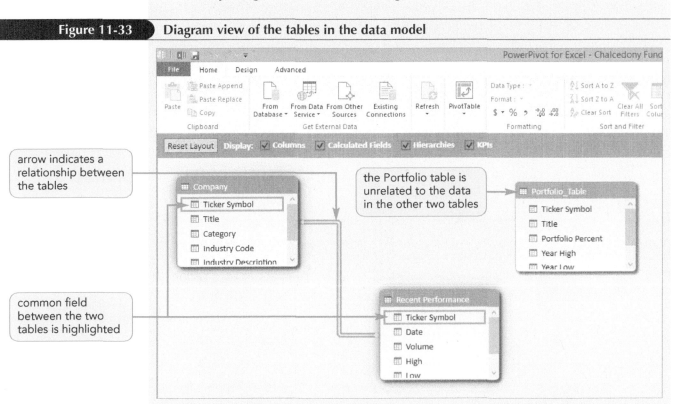

Managing Relationships in the Data Model

When no arrow connects a table to any of the other tables in the data model, there is no way to match the records of that table with the other tables. To fix this, you can create a relationship between tables. When creating a relationship, you need to identify a field in each table that will be used to match the table records.

Because no arrow is connecting the Portfolio table to another table in the data model, the records of the Portfolio table cannot be matched with the records of the two other tables. Rafael wants you to establish a relationship between the Portfolio table and the Company table using the Ticker Symbol field, which is the common field in all of the tables.

To create a relationship between two tables:

TIP

To define a relationship without PowerPivot, click the DATA tab in Excel, click the Relationships button in the Data Tools group, and then click the New button in the Manage Relationships dialog box.

1. On the ribbon, click the **Design** tab. In the Relationships group, click the **Create Relationship** button. The Create Relationship dialog box opens.

2. Click the **Table** arrow, and then click **Portfolio_Table**. This identifies one of the tables you want to use to create a relationship.

3. Click the **Column** arrow, and then click **Ticker Symbol**. This identifies the field you want to use to create the relationship.

4. Click the **Related Lookup Table** arrow, and then click **Company**. This identifies the other table you want to use to create a relationship. Ticker Symbol is selected in the Related Lookup Column box, identifying the corresponding field in the Company table. See Figure 11-34.

Figure 11-34	Create Relationship dialog box

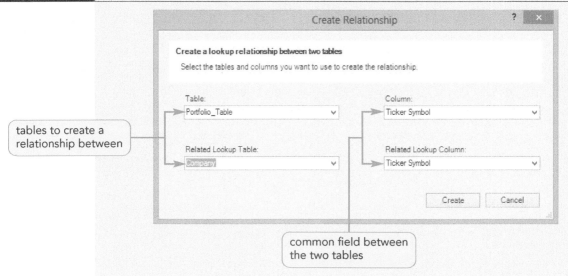

5. Click the **Create** button. An arrow appears linking the Portfolio table to the Company table.

   You don't need to create a relationship between the Portfolio and Recent Performance tables because they are related via the Company table.

6. On the ribbon, click the **File** tab, and then click **Close**. The PowerPivot window closes, and you return to the Excel workbook.

Rafael wants you to add the Year High and Year Low fields to the PivotTable to display the high and low values for each stock from the previous year. Because you established a relationship between the Portfolio table and the Company table, you can add the information in the Portfolio table to the PivotTable report.

To add the Year High and Year Low fields to the PivotTable:

1. Go to the **5-Day Report** worksheet, and then click cell **D4**, if necessary, to display the PivotTable Fields pane.

2. Click **ALL** from the PivotTable Fields menu to display all of the tables accessible to this PivotTable report. Verify that Portfolio_Table is listed between the Company and Recent Performance tables.

3. In the PivotTable Fields pane, click **Portfolio_Table** in the list of tables. The list of fields in that table is displayed.

4. Right-click the **Year High** field, and then click **Add to Values** on the shortcut menu. The Year High field is added to the PivotTable.

5. Right-click the **Year Low** field, and then click **Add to Values** on the shortcut menu. The Year Low field is added to the PivotTable. A Message Bar appears, indicating that relationships between tables may be needed. You can ignore this warning because you have already defined the table relationship.

6. In the range **G5:H9**, format the values with the **Number** format.

7. In cell **G4**, change the column label to **Previous High**, and in cell **H4**, change the column label to **Previous Low**. See Figure 11-35.

Figure 11-35   PivotTable with the Previous High and Previous Low values added

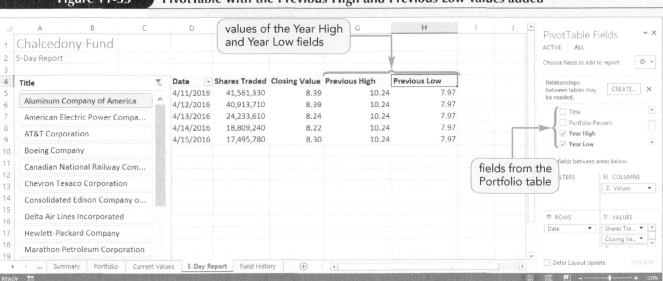

With the addition of the Year High and Year Low fields, Rafael can quickly compare the most recent values of the stock to the annual high and low values. For example, the most recent values of the Aluminum Company of America stock appear in the middle of the range of the low and high values from the previous year. To visualize this relationship, Rafael wants you to add a PivotChart to the worksheet displaying the values from the PivotTable. You'll create a combo chart with the Shares Traded values displayed as a column chart, and the Closing, Previous High, and Previous Low values displayed as a line chart on the secondary axis.

To add and format a PivotChart based on the PivotTable:

1. On the ribbon, click the **PIVOTTABLE TOOLS ANALYZE** tab. In the Tools group, click the **PivotChart** button.

2. Select **Combo** from the list of chart groups.

3. Select **Line** for the Closing Value, Previous High, and Previous Low data series, and then click the **Secondary Axis** button for each of those series.

4. Click the **OK** button.

5. Move and resize the PivotChart so that it covers the range **D10:H20**.

▶ **6.** On the ribbon, click the **PIVOTCHART TOOLS ANALYZE** tab. In the Show/Hide group, click the **Field Buttons** button. The field button is no longer displayed on the PivotChart.

▶ **7.** Position the chart legend at the top of the PivotChart.

▶ **8.** In the Title slicer, click each company name to display information about that company in the PivotTable and PivotChart, and then click **Union Pacific Corporation** to see the PivotTable and PivotChart for the recent performance of the Union Pacific Corporation stock. See Figure 11-36.

| Figure 11-36 | PivotChart of recent performance data |

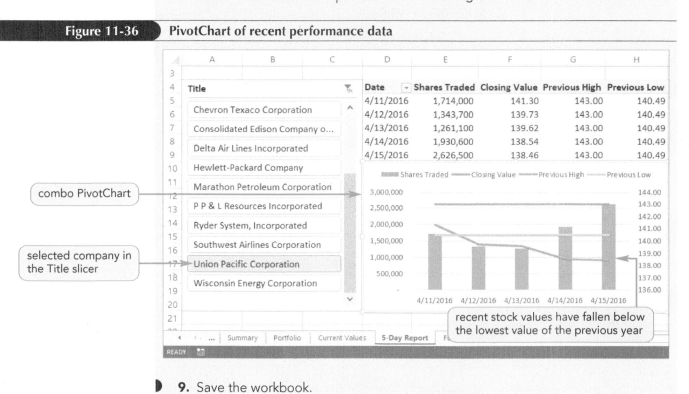

combo PivotChart

selected company in the Title slicer

recent stock values have fallen below the lowest value of the previous year

▶ **9.** Save the workbook.

The PivotChart makes it easy to identify stocks that have fallen below or risen above the annual benchmarks. For example, the PivotChart for the Union Pacific Corporation shown in Figure 11-36 makes it clear that the stock's value in the recent week has fallen below the previous year's low point. Rafael may want to investigate this issue further.

PROSKILLS

Written Communication: Designing a Database

When creating a database within either the Excel data model or Microsoft Access, keep in mind the following common, yet important, principles:

- **Split data into multiple tables.** Keep each table focused on a specific topical area. Link the tables through one or more common fields.
- **Avoid redundant data.** Key pieces of information, such as a customer's address or phone number, should be entered in only one place in your database.
- **Use understandable field names.** Avoid using acronyms or abbreviations that may confuse your users.
- **Maintain consistency in data entry.** For example, if you abbreviate titles (such as Mr. instead of Mister), include validation rules that ensure this rule is always followed.
- **Test the database on a small subset of data before committing all of the data.** The more errors you weed out early, the easier it will be to manage your database.

Databases are great tools to organize information, track statistics, and generate reports. When used in conjunction with Excel, a properly designed database can provide valuable information and help you make informed financial decisions. However, like any tool, databases must be used correctly. A badly designed or improperly used database will end up creating more problems rather than solving them.

This session only scratched the surface of what can be accomplished using database queries and the Excel data model. Databases are a powerful addition to any workbook, and Excel is an effective tool for analyzing and reporting on that data. Rafael is pleased with your progress and wants to examine other data sources that he can use in the workbook. In the next session, you'll explore how to integrate Rafael's workbook with data from the Internet.

REVIEW

Session 11.2 Quick Check

1. Define the following terms: (a) database, (b) table, (c) field, (d) record, (e) common field.
2. What is a relational database?
3. What is a query?
4. In database design, what is a one-to-one relationship? What is a one-to-many relationship?
5. What is SQL?
6. What is the Excel data model?
7. Name two sources for the data tables that can be added to the Excel data model.
8. What is PowerPivot?

Session 11.3 Visual Overview:

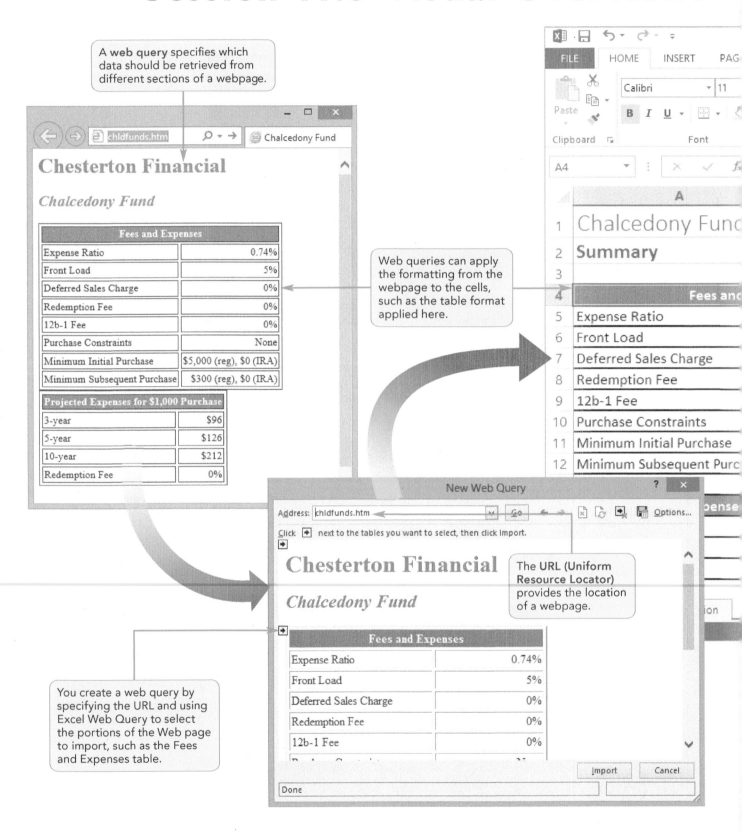

A **web query** specifies which data should be retrieved from different sections of a webpage.

Web queries can apply the formatting from the webpage to the cells, such as the table format applied here.

The URL (Uniform Resource Locator) provides the location of a webpage.

You create a web query by specifying the URL and using Excel Web Query to select the portions of the Web page to import, such as the Fees and Expenses table.

© 2014 Cengage Learning

Web and XML Connections

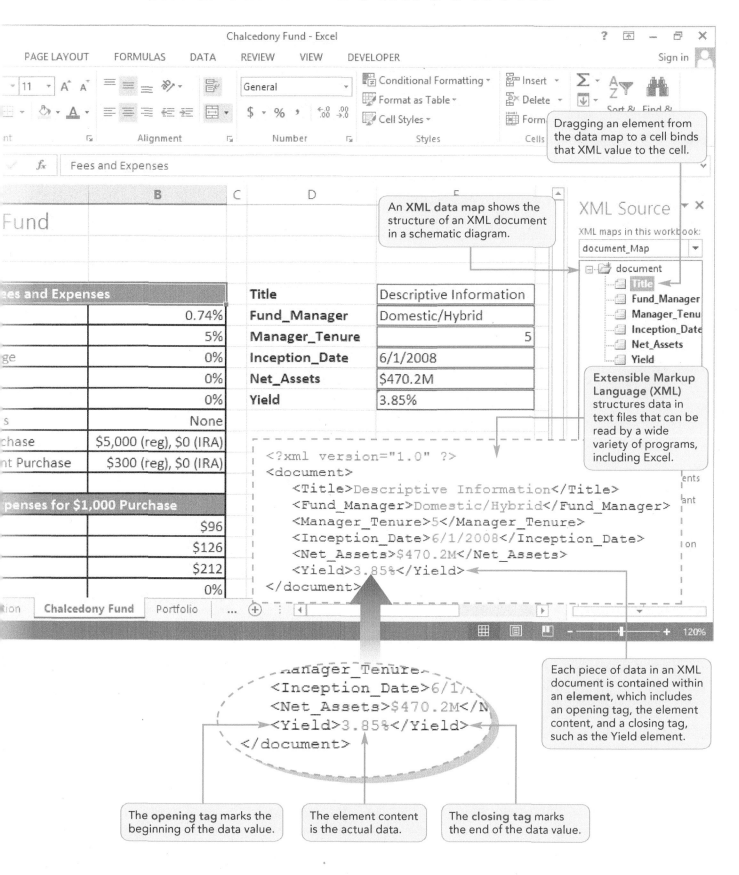

Chalcedony Fund - Excel

PAGE LAYOUT   FORMULAS   DATA   REVIEW   VIEW   DEVELOPER   Sign in

Dragging an element from the data map to a cell binds that XML value to the cell.

fx   Fees and Expenses

An **XML data map** shows the structure of an XML document in a schematic diagram.

XML Source

XML maps in this workbook:

document_Map

- document
  - Title
  - Fund_Manager
  - Manager_Tenu
  - Inception_Date
  - Net_Assets
  - Yield

Fund

	B		C	D	
es and Expenses			**Title**	Descriptive Information	
	0.74%		**Fund_Manager**	Domestic/Hybrid	
	5%		**Manager_Tenure**	5	
ge	0%		**Inception_Date**	6/1/2008	
	0%		**Net_Assets**	$470.2M	
	0%		**Yield**	3.85%	
s	None				
chase	$5,000 (reg), $0 (IRA)				
nt Purchase	$300 (reg), $0 (IRA)				

Extensible Markup Language (XML) structures data in text files that can be read by a wide variety of programs, including Excel.

penses for $1,000 Purchase

	$96	
	$126	
	$212	
	0%	

```xml
<?xml version="1.0" ?>
<document>
    <Title>Descriptive Information</Title>
    <Fund_Manager>Domestic/Hybrid</Fund_Manager>
    <Manager_Tenure>5</Manager_Tenure>
    <Inception_Date>6/1/2008</Inception_Date>
    <Net_Assets>$470.2M</Net_Assets>
    <Yield>3.85%</Yield>
</document>
```

ion   **Chalcedony Fund**   Portfolio   ...   ⊕

120%

```xml
    ...anager_Tenure...
    <Inception_Date>6/1/...
    <Net_Assets>$470.2M</N...
    <Yield>3.85%</Yield>
</document>
```

Each piece of data in an XML document is contained within an **element**, which includes an opening tag, the element content, and a closing tag, such as the Yield element.

The **opening tag** marks the beginning of the data value.

The **element content** is the actual data.

The **closing tag** marks the end of the data value.

Creating a Web Query

Chesterton Financial often stores corporate information on its web server to be displayed on the company webpage. To keep his Excel workbooks in sync with the data stored on the company's website, Rafael wants to create a query that retrieves data from the company webpage. The Chesterton Financial website includes pages that describe the various funds the company supports. The Chalcedony Fund webpage shown in Figure 11-37 provides descriptive information about the fund, such as the name of the fund manager and the fund's inception date.

Figure 11-37	Webpage about the Chalcedony Fund

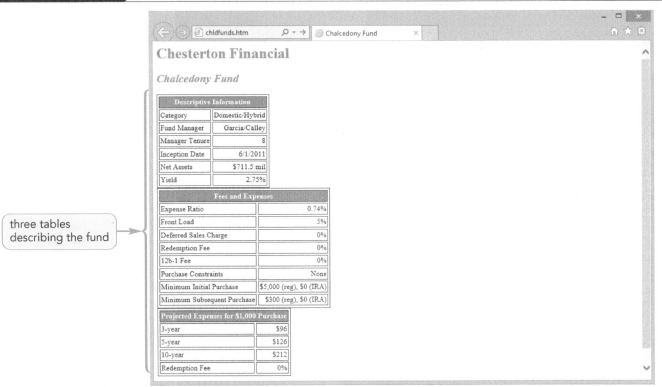

three tables describing the fund

You could copy and paste the data from the webpage into the workbook, but Rafael wants to create a query between the webpage and the workbook so that the workbook always matches the material on the company's website. To create this web query, you need to know the URL of the page you are accessing. A copy of the Chalcedony Fund's information webpage, chldfunds.htm, is included with your Data Files. If the file is stored on a web server, the URL would follow the format

        http://server/path/filename

where *server* is the name of the computer or web server storing the page, *path* is the path to the folder on the server in which the page is stored, and *filename* is the name of the webpage file. The following is an example of a URL in this format:

        http://www.example.net/docs/chldfunds.htm

When a file is stored locally and not on a web server, the URL follows the format

        file:///drive:/path/filename

where *drive* is the letter of the drive containing the file, *path* is the full path name of the folder containing the file, and *filename* is the filename of the webpage.

TIP

If you don't know the complete path to a webpage, open the page in your web browser and copy the path from the browser's Address box.

For example, if the Data Files are on drive Z and chldfunds.htm is located in the Excel11 ▸ Tutorial folder, the URL is as follows:

```
file:///Z:/Excel11/Tutorial/chldfunds.htm
```

If you don't include the `file:` prefix for the URL, your computer will attempt to locate the file on the web and not in a folder stored locally on your computer. If you don't want to enter this long string of text, you can also enter the path to the folder and webpage file in the following form, which is more standard:

```
Z:\Excel11\Tutorial\chldfunds.htm
```

The web query will replace this text with the URL form.

REFERENCE

Working with Web Queries

To create a web query:

- On the DATA tab, in the Get External Data group, click the From Web button.
- In the Address box, enter the URL of the website or the folder path to a local file.
- Click the selection arrows for the parts of the webpage you want to retrieve.
- Click the Import button.

To set the web query format options:

- Open the Connection Properties dialog box for the query.
- On the Definition tab, click the Edit Query button.
- Click the Options button, select format options, and then click the OK button.

To save a web query:

- Open the Connection Properties dialog box for the query.
- On the Definition tab, click the Edit Query button.
- Click the Save Query button, specify the filename and location, and then click the Save button.

You'll create a web connection to the Chalcedony Web page using the chldfunds. htm file included with your Data Files.

To create a web query to import the Chalcedony webpage:

1. If you took a break at the end of the previous session, make sure the Chalcedony Fund workbook is open. If a dialog box opens, prompting you to enter a password for the 5-Day Performance Data connection, click the Cancel button to proceed to the workbook.

2. Go to the **Summary** worksheet.

3. On the ribbon, click the **DATA** tab. In the Get External Data group, click the **From Web** button. The New Web Query dialog box opens.

   Trouble? If a Security Alert dialog box opens, click the No button in that and each subsequent dialog box to proceed to the New Web Query dialog box.

   Make sure you enter the complete path to the webpage file and not simply its filename.

4. In the Address box, enter the path to the **chldfunds.htm** file located in the Excel11 ▸ Tutorial folder included with your Data Files. For example, if the file is located in the Documents\Data\Excel11\Tutorial folder of drive E, you would enter E:\Documents\Data\Excel11\Tutorial\chldfunds.htm.

5. Press the **Enter** key. The contents of the chldfunds webpage appear in the dialog box. See Figure 11-38.

Figure 11-38 New Web Query dialog box

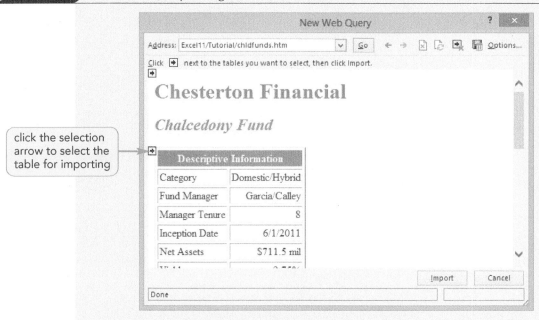

click the selection arrow to select the table for importing

6. Click the **selection** arrow ➡ next to the Descriptive Information table. The selection arrow changes to a green checkmark to indicate that this table is selected.

7. Scroll down, click the **selection** arrow ➡ next to the Fees and Expenses table, and then click the **selection** arrow ➡ next to the Projected Expenses for $1,000 Purchase table. The tables are selected.

8. Click the **Import** button. The Import Data dialog box opens.

9. Click cell **A4** in the Summary worksheet, and then click the **OK** button. The webpage content is imported into the Summary worksheet. See Figure 11-39.

Figure 11-39 Worksheet with imported webpage data

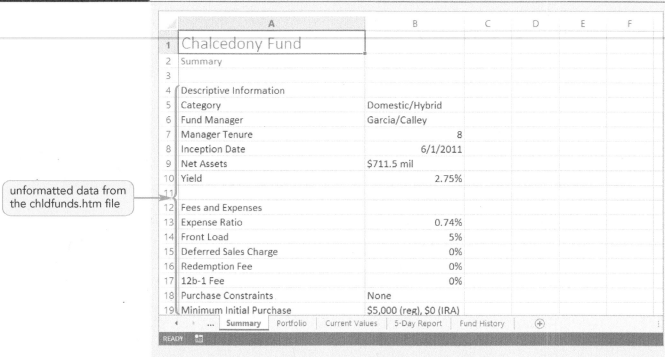

unformatted data from the chldfunds.htm file

	A	B	C	D	E	F
1	Chalcedony Fund					
2	Summary					
3						
4	Descriptive Information					
5	Category	Domestic/Hybrid				
6	Fund Manager	Garcia/Calley				
7	Manager Tenure	8				
8	Inception Date	6/1/2011				
9	Net Assets	$711.5 mil				
10	Yield	2.75%				
11						
12	Fees and Expenses					
13	Expense Ratio	0.74%				
14	Front Load	5%				
15	Deferred Sales Charge	0%				
16	Redemption Fee	0%				
17	12b-1 Fee	0%				
18	Purchase Constraints	None				
19	Minimum Initial Purchase	$5,000 (reg), $0 (IRA)				

Summary | Portfolio | Current Values | 5-Day Report | Fund History

READY

Formatting a Web Query

The text from the web query was placed in the worksheet as unformatted text. If you format this text, the formatting is preserved when Excel refreshes the data later. Another option is to retrieve both the webpage data and the styles used on the webpage.

You can retrieve the webpage format using None, Rich text formatting only, or Full HTML formatting. None, which is the default, imports the text but not the formatting. **Rich Text Format (RTF)** is a file format that allows for text formatting styles including boldface, italic, and color, but not advanced features such as hyperlinks or complicated table structures. The Full HTML formatting option retrieves all simple as well as advanced HTML formatting features, including hyperlinks. Full HTML formatting results in imported data that most closely resembles the appearance of the webpage.

Rafael wants the text on this page to resemble the webpage. You'll format the web query you just created to use full HTML formatting by modifying the connection properties.

To format the web query:

1. On the DATA tab, in the Connections group, click the **Connections** button. The Workbook Connections dialog box opens.

2. Click **Connection** in the Name column, and then click the **Properties** button. The Connection Properties dialog box opens.

3. Type **Chalcedony Fund webpage** in the Connection name box, type **Data from the Chalcedony Fund webpage** in the Description box, and then click the **Refresh data when opening the file** check box.

4. Click the **Definition** tab, and then click the **Edit Query** button. The Edit Web Query dialog box opens and displays the contents of the Chalcedony HTML file.

5. On the Edit Web Query toolbar, click the **Options** button. The Web Query Options dialog box opens.

6. Click the **Full HTML formatting** option button to specify that this web query should retrieve the HTML formatting along with the webpage text, and then click the **OK** button.

7. Click the **Import** button in the Edit Web Query dialog box, and then click the **OK** button in the Connection Properties dialog box. The Workbook Connections dialog box reappears.

8. Make sure the Chalcedony Fund webpage is still selected, click the **Refresh** button, and then click the **Close** button. The Workbook Connections dialog box closes. The worksheet is updated, reflecting the full HTML formatting of the original webpage. See Figure 11-40.

Figure 11-40   **Formatted web data**

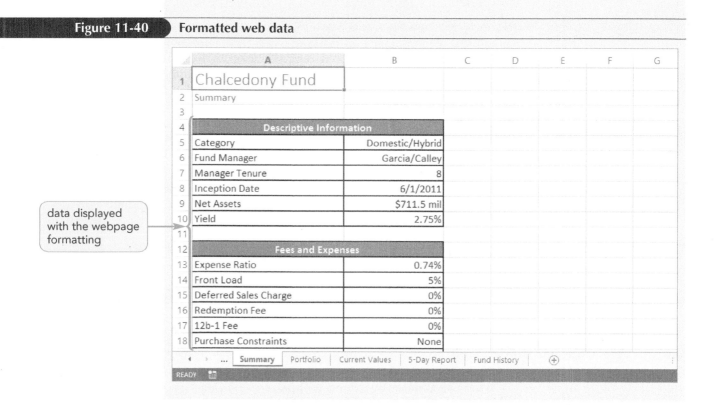

data displayed with the webpage formatting

Saving a Web Query

You can save the web query to a permanent file that you share among other Office documents. The saved connection file can then be loaded in any Office program. For example, after saving the Chalcedony Fund webpage web query, Rafael can retrieve the contents of the Chalcedony Fund webpage and display them in a Word document. Because Rafael wants to place the Chalcedony Fund information in other workbooks, you'll save the Chalcedony Fund webpage web query in a permanent file.

To save the Chalcedony Fund webpage web query:

TIP

You can view and edit web query files in Notepad. Using web query language, you can create sophisticated programs to retrieve and process web data.

1. On the DATA tab, in the Connections group, click the **Connections** button. The Workbook Connections dialog box opens.

2. Click **Chalcedony Fund webpage** in the Name column, and then click the **Properties** button. The Connection Properties dialog box opens.

3. Click the **Definition** tab, and then click the **Edit Query** button. The Edit Web Query dialog box opens.

4. On the Edit Web Query toolbar, click the **Save Query** button 🔲. The Save Workspace dialog box opens, displaying the contents of the Microsoft ▶ Queries folder. You'll save the query file in the location specified by your instructor.

5. Navigate to the location specified by your instructor, type **Chalcedony Web Query** in the File name box, and then click the **Save** button.

6. Click the **Import** button in the Edit Web Query dialog box, click the **OK** button in the Connection Properties dialog box, and then click the **Close** button in the Workbook Connections dialog box to return to the workbook.

Retrieving Live Stock Quotes from the Internet

Many financial applications need up-to-the-minute market data. Excel workbooks that display stock data need a way of downloading this information in a timely fashion. Many websites provide this service for a fee. There are also websites that provide stock market data for free, but slightly delayed from the fee-based services. One such website is *Yahoo Finance* located at the URL *http://finance.yahoo.com*. Excel can retrieve data from these kinds of web services uses the following function:

```
WEBSERVICE(url)
```

where *url* is the URL of the Web service from which you want to retrieve data. The URL needs to include tags that indicate what kind of data needs to be retrieved from the website. The actual tags are supplied by the website and will vary from one website to another. For example the following URL retrieves the most current value of the Hewlett-Packard stock (HPQ) from the Yahoo Finance website:

```
http://finance.yahoo.com/d/?s=HPQ&f=l1
```

To display this data in a worksheet cell, you place the URL within the following Excel function:

```
=WEBSERVICE("http://finance.yahoo.com/d/?s=HPQ&f=l1")
```

A more general approach would be to use a stock symbol entered into a worksheet cell rather than entered directly into the text of the URL. If the ticker symbol is entered into cell A5, you can reference that cell by making sure to enclose the beginning and end of the URL string in quotation marks and combining the text strings using the & symbol. The revised formula to return the last trading price of the stock symbol listed in cell A5 is, therefore:

```
=WEBSERVICE("http://finance.yahoo.com/d/?s="&A5&"&f=l1")
```

Stock values retrieved through the WEBSERVICE function do not act like web queries and are not treated as data connections. For example, they are not refreshed automatically when the workbook is reopened. The only way to refresh the values returned by the function is to recalculate the worksheet by selecting a worksheet cell and pressing the Enter key or by pressing the F9 key.

Rafael wants to use the WEBSERVICE function to retrieve current stock values for the stocks listed in the Chalcedony Fund portfolio. He would like to display the company name, the current stock price, the change in price, the percent change in price, and the volume of shares traded. You can retrieve this information from Yahoo Finance by using the URLs shown in Figure 11-41 (assuming that the ticker symbol is entered into cell A5).

Figure 11-41 **WEBSERVICE functions to retrieve stock quotes**

Company Name
```
=WEBSERVICE("http://finance.yahoo.com/d/?s="&A5&"&f=n")
```

Current Price
```
=WEBSERVICE("http://finance.yahoo.com/d/?s="&A5&"&f=l1")
```

Change in Price
```
=WEBSERVICE("http://finance.yahoo.com/d/?s="&A5&"&f=c1")
```

% Change in Price
```
=WEBSERVICE("http://finance.yahoo.com/d/?s="&A5&"&f=p2")
```

Volume
```
=WEBSERVICE("http://finance.yahoo.com/d/?s="&A5&"&f=v")
```

You'll use the WEBSERVICE function now to retrieve timely data on the stocks in the Chalcedony Fund. First you'll set up the worksheet.

To enter the ticker symbols and column titles:

1. Go to the **Portfolio** worksheet and copy the column heading and the ticker symbols in the range **A4:A19**.

2. Go to the **Current Values** worksheet, click cell **A4**, click the **Paste** arrow in the Clipboard group on the HOME tab, and then click **Paste Values** in the list of paste options. Excel pastes the column heading and the ticker symbols with no formatting.

3. Enter **Company Name** in cell B4, **Current Price** in cell C4, **Change in Price** in cell D4, **% Change in Price** in cell E4, and **Volume** in cell F4.

4. Resize the column widths to accommodate the text of the column headings, as shown in Figure 11-42.

Figure 11-42	Headings in the Current Values worksheet

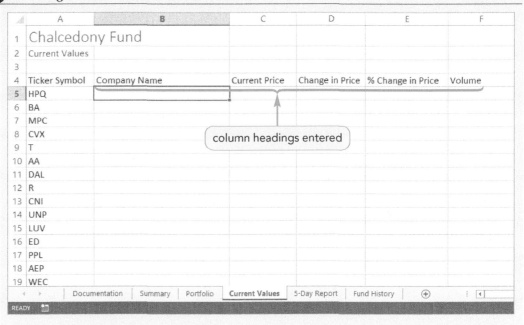

Next you'll insert the WEBSERVICE function in the first row of the table to retrieve stock data for the ticker symbol in cell A5. You can then copy the formulas from row 5 into the rest of the worksheet table.

To enter the WEBSERVICE function:

1. Click cell **B5** and enter the following formula to retrieve the company name from Yahoo Finance:

   =WEBSERVICE("http://finance.yahoo.com/d/?s="&A5&"&f=n")

2. In cell **C5** enter the following formula to retrieve the current stock price:

   =WEBSERVICE("http://finance.yahoo.com/d/?s="&A5&"&f=l1")

3. In cell **D5** enter the following formula to retrieve the change in the stock price:

   =WEBSERVICE("http://finance.yahoo.com/d/?s="&A5&"&f=c1")

4. In cell **E5** enter the following formula to retrieve the percent change in the stock price:

   =WEBSERVICE("http://finance.yahoo.com/d/?s="&A5&"&f=p2")

5. In cell **F5** enter the following formula to retrieve the volume of shares traded:

   =WEBSERVICE("http://finance.yahoo.com/d/?s="&A5&"&f=v")

   Figure 11-43 shows the stock values for the first stock listed in the table.

Figure 11-43   Current stock quotes for Hewlett-Packard stock (HPQ)

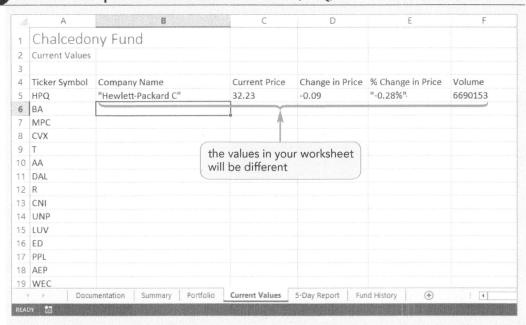

Trouble? If Excel returns an error message, check your formulas and make sure that you have not missed a quotation mark in the URL. Note that your values will not match the ones shown in Figure 11-43 because your quoted values will be retrieved at a different point in time.

6. Display the current values for the rest of the stocks by copying the formulas in the range **B5:F5** into the range **B6:F19**. Deselect the range by clicking cell **A4**. Figure 11-44 shows the current stock quotes for all of the stocks listed in the Chalcedony Fund.

Figure 11-44   Current stock quotes for stocks in the fund

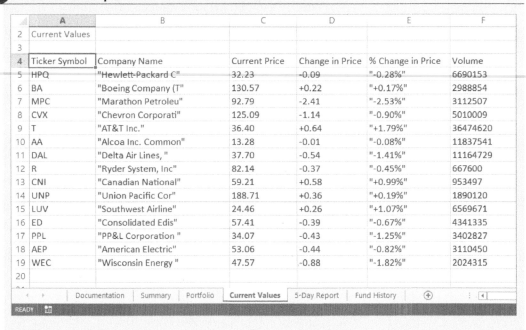

The WEBSERVICE function provides important information to Rafael about the stocks in the portfolio. For example, he can see that the value of the Hewlett-Packard stock has declined by 0.28% since the market closed the previous day. On the other hand, the value of the Boeing Company stock has increased by 0.17% from the previous day.

More than 90 different stock statistics can be retrieved from the Yahoo Finance website. To view the description of these different statistics and the URLs required to retrieve them, you can view documentation on the Yahoo Finance website.

Retrieving Data Using Office Apps

Another way to retrieve live data in your Excel workbook is through an **Office app**, which is a small specialized program that enhances the features of Excel, Word, PowerPoint, and other programs in the Office suite. There are apps to retrieve stock market data, weather information, and maps among other data sources.

Apps are downloaded from the Microsoft Office Store. Most apps are free. To download and use an Office app, you need an account with Microsoft Office. The account is free, requiring only a username and password to set it up. Once you have an account, you can add an app to your account and then download it to Excel. You can sign up and retrieve an app by clicking the Store button in the Apps group on the INSERT tab. You can view a list of your apps by clicking the My Apps button in the Apps group.

Be aware that apps are always being added and removed from the Microsoft Office Store, and Microsoft is not responsible for the quality and performance of third-party apps.

Importing Data from XML

Another important data source for Excel workbooks is XML documents. XML (the Extensible Markup Language) is a language used to create structured documents using only text. Because an XML document is a simple text file, a wide variety of programs and applications can read it. In fact, the internal code for Microsoft Office documents is saved in an XML format called the Office Open XML. XML documents are also easy to transfer over the Internet, which makes them ideal for web-based applications. Figure 11-45 shows an example of an XML document named Documentation created by a programmer at Chesterton Financial.

Figure 11-45   **Contents of the Documentation XML file**

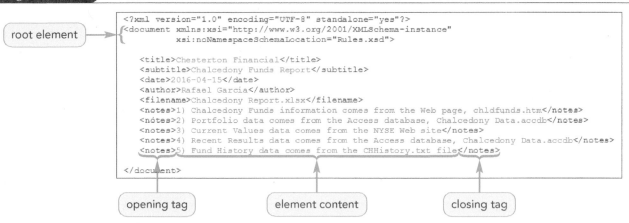

root element

```
<?xml version="1.0" encoding="UTF-8" standalone="yes"?>
<document xmlns:xsi="http://www.w3.org/2001/XMLSchema-instance"
          xsi:noNamespaceSchemaLocation="Rules.xsd">

  <title>Chesterton Financial</title>
  <subtitle>Chalcedony Funds Report</subtitle>
  <date>2016-04-15</date>
  <author>Rafael Garcia</author>
  <filename>Chalcedony Report.xlsx</filename>
  <notes>1) Chalcedony Funds information comes from the Web page, chldfunds.htm</notes>
  <notes>2) Portfolio data comes from the Access database, Chalcedony Data.accdb</notes>
  <notes>3) Current Values data comes from the NYSE Web site</notes>
  <notes>4) Recent Results data comes from the Access database, Chalcedony Data.accdb</notes>
  <notes>5) Fund History data comes from the CHHistory.txt file</notes>

</document>
```

opening tag   element content   closing tag

Each piece of data in an XML document is contained within an element. The data is marked by an opening and closing tag. For example, the following code shows the author element, Rafael Garcia, contained within an opening (<author>) and closing (</author>) tag:

```
<author>Rafael Garcia</author>
```

The opening and closing tags in Figure 11-45 are black and the data content is red to make it easier to differentiate the tags from the information they contain.

An XML document is structured like a tree in which elements are placed within one another, descending from a common **root element**. The structure of the document is displayed in a data map. The data map associated with the Documentation XML file is shown in Figure 11-46. Under this structure, the root element, document, contains six elements named title, subtitle, date, author, filename, and notes.

Figure 11-46   **Data map of the Documentation XML file**

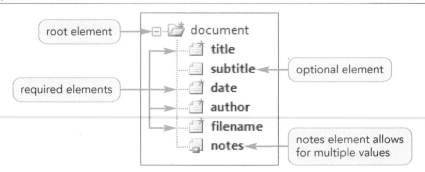

root element → document

required elements → title
subtitle ← optional element
date
author
filename
notes ← notes element allows for multiple values

One advantage of XML is that the document author can create rules specifying which elements are required and what types of values are allowed within each element. These rules are stored in a second document called the **schema**. Schemas are not required, but they are useful in ensuring the integrity and validity of XML data. Rules from the schema also appear in the data map. For example, required elements are marked with a red star. The required elements in the Documentation XML file are document, title, date, author, and filename. Elements that can contain multiple values are identified in the data map by a document icon with an arrow. In Figure 11-46, only the *notes* element allows multiple values.

Editing an XML File

Before you import the data from the Documentation XML file, you'll edit it by inserting your own name in the author element.

To edit the Documentation XML document:

▶ **1.** Start Notepad or another text editor, and then open the **Documentation** XML file located in the Excel11 ▶ Tutorial folder included with your Data Files.

▶ **2.** Select the author name **Rafael Garcia** located between the <author> and </author> tags, and then type your name. Do not delete the tags when you replace the name.

▶ **3.** Save the file, and then close it.

▶ **4.** Return to the **Chalcedony Fund** workbook in Excel.

The first step in connecting a workbook to an XML document is to generate the data map. After Excel has generated a data map, you can use it to place XML content anywhere within the workbook.

Loading an XML Data Map

The commands to access the data map of an XML document are part of the Excel Developer tools. To work with an XML data map, you must show the DEVELOPER tab on the ribbon. If the XML document has a schema file attached to it, you can load a data map without actually importing the data into the Excel workbook.

REFERENCE

Loading an XML Data Map

- On the DEVELOPER tab, in the XML group, click the Source button.
- In the XML Source task pane, click the XML Maps button.
- Locate and select the XML document file.
- In the XML Maps dialog box, click the Rename button to define a name for the map.

Rafael wants you to load the Documentation XML document and generate a data map for the workbook.

To generate an XML data map:

▶ **1.** If the DEVELOPER tab does not appear on the ribbon, right-click the ribbon, click **Customize the Ribbon** on the shortcut menu, click the **Developer** check box in the Customize the Ribbon box, and then click the **OK** button.

▶ **2.** Go to the **Documentation** worksheet.

▶ **3.** On the ribbon, click the **DEVELOPER** tab. In the XML group, click the **Source** button. The XML Source pane opens on the right side of the workbook window. From this pane, you can generate the data map for the Documentation.xml file.

▶ 4. Click the **XML Maps** button at the bottom of the XML Source pane. The XML Maps dialog box opens so you can add an XML data map to the workbook.

▶ 5. Click the **Add** button. The Select XML Source dialog box opens.

▶ 6. Click the **Documentation** XML file located in the Excel11 ▸ Tutorial folder included with your Data Files, and then click the **Open** button. The document map for the Documentation XML file is added to the list of XML maps in the current workbook and assigned the name document_Map.

▶ 7. Click the **Rename** button, type **Documentation information**, and then press the **Enter** key to give the data map a more descriptive name.

▶ 8. Click the **OK** button. The Documentation information data map is loaded into Excel and appears in the XML Source pane. See Figure 11-47.

| Figure 11-47 | XML Source pane |

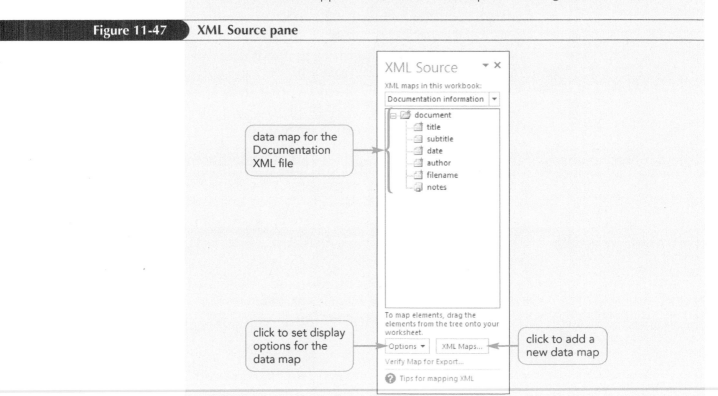

Binding XML Elements to a Worksheet

One advantage of using XML as a data source is that you can attach or **bind** elements to specific cells in the workbook, providing greater freedom in laying out the data. To bind an element to a cell, you drag the element name from the data map and drop it into the cell. After you drop the element, you can place the element name above or to the right of the cell (if those locations are available). If a Header Options button appears next to a cell, you can click the button to define where you want to place an element's name (if you want it displayed at all). The Header Options button does not appear for elements you place in the leftmost column of the worksheet because no room is available to place the element name to the left of or above the element data.

Rafael wants you to bind the elements of the Documentation XML file to cells in the Documentation worksheet.

To bind elements from the data map to the workbook:

TIP

To map an entire XML document into an Excel table, click the From Other Sources button in the Get External Data group on the DATA tab, and then click From XML Data Import.

1. In the XML Source pane, click **author** in the Documentation information data map and drag it to cell **B4** in the Documentation worksheet. No data appears in the cell because you have not actually imported the contents of the Documentation XML file. You've only defined where you want to bind the contents of the author element.

2. Click the **Header Options** button located to the right of cell B4 and click the **Place XML Heading to the Left** option button. The author element name appears in cell A4.

3. Repeat Steps 1 and 2 to bind the **date** and **filename** elements in cells **B5** and **B6**, respectively.

4. Drag the **notes** element from the data map to cell **B8**. Because this element can contain multiple values, Excel places it into the cell as an Excel table. The element name is placed above the table in cell B8. See Figure 11-48.

Figure 11-48   **XML elements bound to the worksheet**

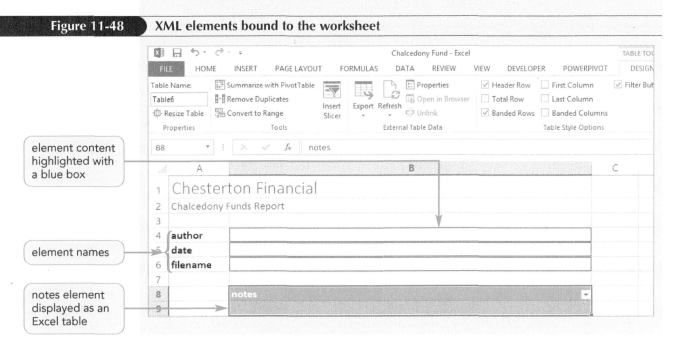

element content highlighted with a blue box

element names

notes element displayed as an Excel table

Importing XML Data

By using XML and the data map, you placed the elements in specific locations in the Documentation worksheet. Because these cells are now bound with elements from the XML file, you can import the XML data directly into the worksheet cells. To retrieve the XML data, you refresh the connection to the data source. Excel will automatically place the data in the correct worksheet cells.

Rafael wants you to import the data from the Documentation XML file into the Documentation worksheet.

To import data from the Documentation XML file:

1. In the Documentation worksheet, select cell **B4**. The active cell could be any of the cells in which an XML element is bound—in this case, cell B4, cell B5, cell B6, or cell B8.

2. On the ribbon, click the **DATA** tab. In the Connections group, click the **Refresh All button arrow**, and then click **Refresh**. Excel retrieves the XML data and places it in the workbook. See Figure 11-49.

Figure 11-49   XML data imported into the worksheet

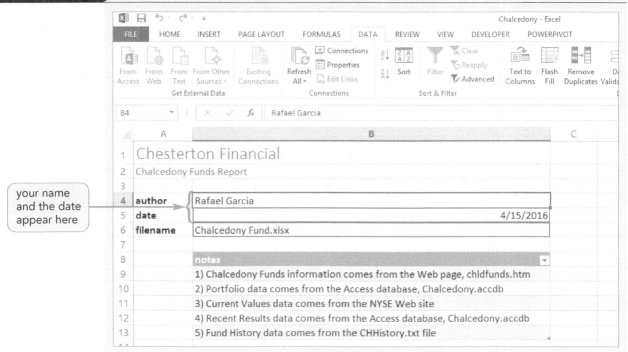

You will complete the XML data connection by defining the connection properties.

3. In the Connections group, click the **Connections** button. The Workbook Connections dialog box opens.

4. Click **Documentation** in the list of workbook connections, and then click the **Properties** button.

5. Type **Report Documentation** in the Connection name box, and then type **Retrieves information about the Chalcedony Fund Report from the Documentation.xml file** in the Description box to provide descriptive information about the connection established to the Documentation XML file.

6. Click the **OK** button to close the Connection Properties dialog box, and then click the **Close** button to close the Workbook Connections dialog box.

7. Remove the **DEVELOPER** tab from the ribbon.

As with database and webpage queries, you can automatically update the XML data in a workbook to reflect changes to the source XML document.

INSIGHT

Consolidating Data

When a workbook contains many data sources, you will often want to consolidate that information in one simple report. You can summarize or consolidate data from several data sources by doing any of the following:

- Create a PivotTable report. This method is extremely flexible in terms of choosing the data sources, calculating summary statistics, and laying out the appearance of the summary report and accompanying charts.
- Write formulas that include 3-D references to summarize data drawn from several worksheets or workbooks. This approach requires more work because you must lay out the report from scratch, but it can result in creative and visually appealing summary reports.
- Use the Consolidate button in the Data Tools group on the DATA tab to create a master worksheet that summarizes data from multiple worksheets within the same workbook. You can display the sum, count, average, or other summary statistics of data values from the worksheets.

The Consolidate command can be applied in two ways. One way is to consolidate by position, which requires data to be laid out exactly the same way and in the same ranges on all the worksheets. The second way is to consolidate by category, which uses labels in the top row or first column of the data ranges on the different worksheets to identify the categories to be summarized. This means that the data can be laid out differently on each worksheet as long as the worksheets use the same row and column labels. You can use Excel Help to learn more about the Consolidate command.

Using Real-Time Data Acquisition

For Rafael's workbook, you imported data from four sources—simple text files, databases, webpages, and XML documents. Scientists and researchers have a fifth possible data source—**real-time data acquisition** in which data values are retrieved from measuring devices and scientific equipment connected to a computer. For example, a climate researcher might connect a laptop to a temperature sensor and import temperature values at one-minute intervals directly into a workbook. To use real-time data acquisition, you usually need to purchase an add-in that manages the communication stream between Excel and the measuring device. To facilitate real-time data acquisition, Excel provides the RTD (real-time data) function. The syntax of the RTD function is

```
RTD(ProgID, server, topic1[, topic2][, topic3]...)
```

where *ProgID* is the program ID of the add-in that has been installed on the computer to manage the communication stream, *server* is the name of the server where the add-in is run (leave *server* blank if the add-in is being run on your computer), and *topic1*, *topic2*, and so forth are names assigned to the real-time data values. You can insert up to 28 different topics. After you insert the RTD function into a cell, the value of the cell displays the latest value retrieved from the measuring device. You can also write a VBA macro to run the RTD function in a range of cells, recording the last several values from the measuring device.

By using the RTD function along with an add-in program, the scientist or researcher can save hours of data entry time and concentrate on analysis.

PROSKILLS

Problem Solving: Best Practices for Data Storage

In the past, it was generally accepted that the solution to the ever-increasing need for data was to simply increase the amount of data storage. However, this is no longer the case as the cost of managing the stored data is outstripping the cost of purchasing and upgrading the physical data storage medium. In order to reduce costs and improve data quality, many information managers are looking at different ways to improve their data storage practices. Whether you are storing data in text files, databases, web servers, or XML documents, keep in mind the following practices:

- Maintain an inventory of your data, including where it is located and how it is stored. Know what you have and make that information available for others.
- Develop a system that searches for and removes duplicated data.
- Develop a policy for handling stale data. Many businesses will regularly purge records that are more than five years old or move them to offsite storage.

By developing a data storage policy, you can help ensure that the data you want to analyze can be easily retrieved and imported into your Excel workbooks. It also ensures that more of your time is spent understanding the data rather than trying to locate it.

The Chalcedony Fund workbook is complete. By tapping into a variety of data sources, you have created a file that Rafael can use to get current information on the fund as well as examine long-term and short-term data to look for important trends. He expects to find many ways to incorporate this new information into his daily work as an investment counselor at Chesterton Financial.

REVIEW

Session 11.3 Quick Check

1. Describe how to import data from a webpage into a workbook.
2. What are the three options for retaining the format styles found within an imported webpage?
3. Define the WEBSERVICE function.
4. What is an Office app?
5. What is XML?
6. What is an XML data map?
7. What Excel function would you use to retrieve real-time data from a measuring device connected to your computer?

ASSESS

SAM Projects

Put your skills into practice with SAM Projects! SAM Projects for this tutorial can be found online. If you have a SAM account, go to www.cengage.com/sam2013 to download the most recent Project Instructions and Start Files.

PRACTICE

Review Assignments

Data Files needed for the Review Assignments: Crystal.xlsx, Crystal History.txt, Crystal Data.accdb, Crystal Docs.xml, crystalweb.htm, Schema.xsd

Rafael has another fund he wants you to analyze. The Crystal Fund is based on dozens of stocks with information stored in text files, Access databases, webpages, and XML files. Current stock values can also be downloaded from the web using an Office app. Rafael wants you to create a workbook based on all of those data sources, displaying historic, short-term, and current information on the fund. Complete the following:

1. Open the **Crystal** workbook located in the Excel11 ▶ Review folder included with your Data Files, and then save the workbook as **Crystal Fund** in the location specified by your instructor.

2. In the Historic Record worksheet, retrieve 10 years of data on the fund by importing the contents of the **Crystal History** text file located in the Excel11 ▶ Review folder. Start the import from row 6 of the text file where the column labels are placed. The text uses a tab delimiter to separate one column from another. Format the Date column with the MDY date format, and format the Close column with the General format. Do not import the Open, High, and Low columns. Import the data into the Historic Record worksheet starting at cell A4.

3. Change the connection properties. Rename the data connection **Crystal Fund historical records**. Add the description **Data imported from the Crystal History.txt file**. Set the data to refresh whenever the workbook is opened, but do not have Excel prompt for the filename.

4. Create a line chart of the data you just imported. Move the chart to cover the range D4:K18. Add descriptive titles to the chart. Format the chart appropriately to best convey the data.

5. In the Stock Summary worksheet, use Microsoft Query to import data from the **Crystal Data** Access database located in the Excel11 ▶ Review folder. From the Profile table, include the Symbol, Name, and Sector fields. From the Summary table, include the Year High, Year Low, PE, EPS, Dividends, and Yield fields. From the Financial table, include the Profit Margin field.

6. Add a query to sort the data by ascending order of the Name field.

7. Import the selected data into cell A4 of the Stock Summary worksheet as an Excel table. Name the table **Stock_Summary**.

8. Rename the data connection **Crystal Fund Stocks**, and enter the description **Data retrieved from the Crystal Data Access database**. Refresh the data whenever the workbook is opened.

9. Import the Profile and Recent History tables from the Crystal Data Access database into Excel. Place the imported tables into a PivotTable report located in cell E4 of the Stock Performance worksheet.

10. Format the PivotTable report displaying the recent history of the stocks in the Crystal Fund with the following content:

    a. Place the Date field in the ROWS section of the PivotTable. Place the Volume and Close fields in the VALUES section of the table.

    b. Rename cells E4, F4, and G4 as **Date**, **Shares Traded**, and **Closing Value**, respectively.

    c. Format the shares traded values using the Comma style with no decimal places. Format the closing values with the Number format with two decimal places. Resize the columns to fit the column labels.

    d. Remove the grand totals from the PivotTable.

    e. In the range A4:D14, add a PivotTable slicer that contains the Name field.

11. Add the Stock_Summary Excel table displayed in the Stock Summary worksheet to the data model.

12. Create a relationship connecting the Recent History table to the Profile table using the Symbol field as the common field. Create another relationship that connects the Stock_Summary table to the Profile table using Symbol as the common field.

13. In the Stock Performance worksheet, add the Year High and Year Low fields to the VALUES section of the PivotTable. Change the column labels for the two fields to **Previous High** and **Previous Low**, respectively.

14. Add a Combo PivotChart to the A15:D26 range with the Shares Traded value displayed as a Column chart, and the Closing, Previous High, and Previous Low values displayed in the Line chart on the secondary axis. Format the chart as you wish to make the data easy to read and interpret.

15. Click different company names in the slicer and verify that you can view the recent history of each stock in the Crystal Fund.

16. In the Fund Summary worksheet, import data from the **crystalweb** HTML file located in the Excel11 ▶ Review folder. Select the contents of the Fund Overview, Performance Overview, and Sector Weightings tables. Import the webpage data into cell A4 using full HTML formatting.

17. Name the connection to the webpage **Crystal Fund webpage** with the description **Data retrieved from the webpage**. Set the connection to be refreshed when the workbook is opened.

18. In the Current Values worksheet, enter the titles **Ticker Symbol** in cell A4, **Company Name** in cell B4, **Current Price** in cell C4, and **Change in Price** in cell D4. Copy and paste the text of the ticker symbols from the Stock Summary worksheet into the range **A5:A19** in the Current Values worksheet.

19. In the Current Values worksheet, use the WEBSERVICE function to insert current stock values from Yahoo Finance into the range B5:D19.

20. Save the workbook, and then close it.

21. Open the **Crystal Docs** XML file located in the Excel11 ▶ Review folder using your text editor. Replace the name **Rafael Garcia** located in the author element with your name, and then save and close the file.

22. Reopen the **Crystal Fund** workbook. In the Documentation worksheet, load the XML data map for the **Crystal Docs** XML file located in the Excel11 ▶ Review folder.

23. Display the author element in cell B4 with the XML heading placed to the left, display the date element in cell B5 with the XML heading placed to the left, and then place the notes element in cell B6.

24. Refresh the XML data so that the documentation values appear in the worksheet.

25. Modify the connection properties for the Crystal Docs connection, changing the connection name to **Crystal Fund Documentation** and the description to **Documentation from the Crystal Docs.xml file**.

26. Save the workbook, and then close it.

Case Problem 1

APPLY

Data Files needed for this Case Problem: Lighthouse.xlsx, Lighthouse Data.accdb

The Lighthouse   Alicia Whitmore is the developmental director at The Lighthouse, a charitable organization in central Kentucky that works with poor and underprivileged youth. Data on donors and their contributions has been saved to an Access database. Alicia wants you to create a report that displays the total contributions from each donor.

Complete the following:

1. Open the **Lighthouse** workbook located in the Excel11 ▸ Case1 folder included with your Data Files, and then save the workbook as **Lighthouse Donor Report** in the location specified by your instructor.

2. In the Documentation worksheet, enter your name and the date.

3. Directly import the contents of the Contacts and Contributions tables from the **Lighthouse Data** Access database located in the Excel11 ▸ Case1 folder into new worksheets. Do not use Microsoft Query. Import the tables into Excel tables.

4. Name the worksheet containing the Excel table with the donor list **Donors**, and name the worksheet containing the list of contributions **Donations**.

5. Change the properties of the Lighthouse Data connection to **Lighthouse Donors and Donations** and enter the description **Data retrieved from the Contacts and Contributions tables in the Lighthouse Data.accdb file**. Refresh the connection whenever the workbook is reopened.

6. Create a relationship from the Contributions table to the Contacts table using ID as the common field.

7. In the Donor Report worksheet, in cell A3, insert a PivotTable report using the PivotTable button located in the Tables group on the INSERT tab. In the Create PivotTable dialog box, specify the Lighthouse Donors and Donations connections as the external data source.

8. From the Contacts table, add the Last Name, First Name, Address, City, State, and Postal Code to the ROWS section of the PivotTable in that order.

9. From the Contributions table, add the Date and Amount fields to the VALUES section of the PivotTable in that order.

10. On the PIVOTTABLE TOOLS DESIGN tab, in the Layout group, click the Report Layout button, and then click the Show in Tabular Form option. The PivotTable is displayed in a table format.

11. On the PIVOTTABLE TOOLS DESIGN tab, in the Layout group, click the Subtotals button, and then click the Do Not Show Subtotals option.

12. In cell G3, change the Count of Date label to **Donations**.

13. In cell H3, change the Sum of Amount label to **Total Contributions**. Display the contribution amounts in the range H4:H38 in the Currency format.

14. Save the workbook, and then close it.

Case Problem 2

Data Files needed for this Case Problem: Eggert.xlsx, Price List.txt, Home Data.txt

Eggert Realty   David Eggert is the owner of Eggert Realty, a large real-estate agency in New Braunfels, Texas. David wants to create an Excel workbook analyzing sales prices for homes in the area. He wants to import data from two text files. The Price List text file contains a list of home prices in the area and information about whether an offer is pending on a home. The Home Data text file contains information about each listed home including the size of the home, its age, its features, its location, whether it is located on a corner lot, and the annual property tax. The text files use a delimited format in which one column is separated from another using the forward slash (/) character. You'll import the data from these text files, and then use that data to create a PivotTable comparing homes of different ages and sizes. Complete the following:

1. Open the **Eggert** workbook located in the Excel11 ▸ Case2 folder included with your Data Files, and then save the workbook as **Eggert Realty** in the location specified by your instructor.

2. In the Documentation worksheet, enter your name and the date.

3. In the Home Listings worksheet, import the contents of the **Price List** text file located in the Excel11 ▸ Case2 folder starting at row 7. Use / as the delimiter character. Insert the contents starting at cell A4 in the Home Listings worksheet and add the data to the data model.

4. Add the description **Data retrieved from the Price List.txt file** to the Price List connection. Refresh the data when the workbook is reopened, but do not prompt for the filename when the data is refreshed.

5. In the Home Data worksheet, import the contents of the **Home Data** text file located in the Excel11 ▸ Case2 folder. Again, start at row 7 and use / as the delimiter character. Insert the contents starting at cell A4 in the Home Data worksheet and add the data to the data model.

6. Add the description **Data retrieved from the Home Data.txt file** to the Home Data connection. Again, refresh the data when the workbook is reopened, but do not prompt for the filename when the data is refreshed.

7. Create a one-to-one relationship between the Price List and Home Data tables using Listing ID as the common field.

8. In the Housing Summary worksheet, insert a PivotTable by selecting Choose Connection in the Create PivotTable dialog box and clicking Tables in the Workbook Data Model in the Tables tab of the Existing Connections dialog box.

9. Place the PivotTable report in cell A4 of the Housing Summary worksheet.

10. David wants to compare housing prices based on the size of the house in square feet, its age, and its location. Place the Square Feet field from the Home Data table in the ROWS section of the table. Place the Age field in the COLUMNS section and the Price field from the Price List table in the VALUES section.

11. Change the value field settings of the Price field to display the average price value in the PivotTable.

12. In cell A5, change the Row Labels text to **Square Feet**. In cell B4, change the Column Labels text to **Age Category**. In cell A4, change the label to **Average Price**. In cell E5 and cell A19, change the labels from Grand Total to **Overall Average**.

13. Format the PivotTable to make the content easy to read and understand.

14. Add a PivotTable slicer containing the NE Sector field to the range F4:J8.

15. Create a PivotChart of the PivotTable data using the Clustered Bar chart type with the Age field as the legend category. Place the chart to cover the range F9:J19. Format the chart so that it is easy to read and interpret.

16. Save the workbook, and then close it.

Case Problem 3

Data Files needed for this Case Problem: Climate.xlsx, US Weather.accdb

Climate Report   Monica Brecht is a professor of meteorology at Lake Academy in Lancaster, Pennsylvania. For an upcoming lecture, she wants to create a workbook that provides weather statistics for major U.S. cities. This data is stored in an Access database, which she wants you to import into Excel. She also wants you to create maps that graphically display the temperature, precipitation, and snowfall for regions across the United States. To do this, you'll use an Office app that maps data values. Complete the following:

1. Open the **Climate** workbook located in the Excel11 ▸ Case3 folder included with your Data Files, and then save the workbook as **Climate Report** in the location specified by your instructor.

2. In the Documentation worksheet, enter your name and the date.

3. In the Temperature worksheet, use Microsoft Query to import the City and Temperature fields from the US Cities table in the **US Weather** Access database file located in the Excel11 ▸ Case3 folder. Import the data as an Excel table into cell A4.

4. Name the data connection **Temperature data** and add the description **Data retrieved from the US Weather.accdb file using MS Query**. Refresh the data connection when the workbook is opened.

✦ **Explore**   5. Download and install the Bing Maps Office app from the Office Store.

⊕ **Explore** 6. Start the Bing Maps app to display a map app on the workbook. Select the range A4:B103, and then click the Show Locations icon at the top of the map. After several seconds, the app will map circles for each of the cities listed in the Excel table with the size of each circle proportional to the average annual temperature of each city in the selected range. (*Hint*: Because the Bing Maps app must download location data from the Internet, you will need an Internet connection to map the temperature values. If the app is temporarily unable to retrieve the location data for some of the cities, it might show an undefined warning message. You can reload the temperature data to try to show the location plots.)

7. Resize the map so that it covers the range D1:L30 in the worksheet. Zoom the map to display the continental United States, if necessary.

8. In the Precipitation worksheet, repeat Steps 3 through 7, importing the City and Annual Precipitation fields from the database. Plot the annual precipitation for each city on the map over the range D1:L30. Name the data connection **Precipitation Data**, add the description **Data retrieved from the US Weather.accdb file using MS Query**, and then refresh the data when the workbook is reopened.

9. In the Snowfall worksheet, repeat Steps 3 through 7 with the City and Annual Snowfall fields. Plot the annual snowfall in inches for each city in the map over the range D1:L30. Name the data connection **Snowfall Data** and use the same description you used for the first two data connections. Refresh the connection automatically when the workbook is reopened.

10. In the Rain Days worksheet, use Microsoft Query to retrieve the City, Precipitation Days, and Nonprecipitation Days fields from the US Cities database. Import the data into cell A4 of the worksheet.

11. Name the connection **Rainfall Days** and add the description **Data retrieved from the US Weather.accdb file using MS Query**. Refresh the connection automatically when the workbook is reopened.

⊕ **Explore** 12. Select the range A4:C103 and plot the selected data values on the map as pie charts.

13. Save the workbook, and then close it.

Case Problem 4

Data Files needed for this Case Problem: Flower.xlsx, Flower Data.accdb, Flower Sales.xlsx

Flower Pocket   Chris Barnes is the owner of Flower Pocket, an online company that sells and delivers flowers and gift baskets. Chris has been storing orders in an Access database and wants to import a subset of this data into an Excel worksheet. The database, named Flower Data, contains five tables. The Customers table lists the names and contact information for customers who have ordered during the past several weeks. The Orders table lists each order and the date it was submitted. The Products table lists products sold by Flower Pocket. The Customers_Orders table matches each order with the customer who ordered it. Finally, the Orders_Products table matches each order with the products in the order. You'll import the data from the Customers and Products tables into separate worksheets. You'll also create a PivotTable that displays details on each order. Complete the following:

1. Open the **Flower** workbook located in the Excel11 ▶ Case4 folder included with your Data Files, and then save the workbook as **Flower Pocket** in the location specified by your instructor.

2. In the Documentation worksheet, enter your name and the date.

3. In the Customers worksheet, import the Customers table from the **Flower Data** Access database located in the Excel11 ▶ Case4 folder. Import the data as an Excel table in cell A4 of the worksheet.

4. Edit the connection properties. Name the connection **Customers List** and add the description **Data retrieved from the Customers table in the Flower Data database**. Refresh the connection whenever the workbook is opened.

5. In the Products worksheet, import the Products table from the **Flower Data** Access database located in the Excel11 ▶ Case4 folder. Import the data as an Excel table starting in cell A4 of the worksheet. Format the Price values in column C with the Currency format.

6. Edit the connection properties. Name the connection **Product List** and enter the description **Data retrieved from the Products table in the Flower Data database**. Refresh the connection whenever the workbook is opened.

7. In the Order Report worksheet, use Microsoft Query to create a query based on the tables in the Flower Data database. The query should extract the fields in the following tables:
   * Customers—Name, Street, City, and State
   * Customers_Orders—CID and OID
   * Orders—Date
   * Orders_Products—PID
   * Products—Product and Price

8. Import the data from the query as a PivotTable Report into cell A5 of the Order Report worksheet.

9. Place the Name, Street, City, State, Date, and Product fields in the ROWS section of the PivotTable.

10. Place the Price field in the VALUES section of the table, showing the sum of the prices for the products ordered by customers.

11. Format the Sum of Price values using the Currency format.

12. On the PIVOTTABLE TOOLS DESIGN tab, in the Layout group, use the Report Layout button to change the layout of the PivotTable to a tabular form.

13. Do not display any subtotals in the PivotTable.

14. Change the column label for the Price field to **Order Price**, and then format the appearance of the table so that it is easy to read.

15. Name the connection for the PivotTable **Product Orders** with the description **Retrieves product orders from the Flower Data database**. Refresh the connection whenever the workbook opens.

Explore 16. Chris wants to save the connections you created as Office Data Connection (ODC) files for use in other projects. To save the connections as permanent files, open the Connection Properties dialog box for each of the three connections you have created, and then click the Export Connection File button on the Definition tab. Save the ODC files as **Customer List**, **Product List**, and **Product Orders** in the location specified by your instructor.

17. Save the Flower Pocket workbook, and then close it.

18. Chris wants an analysis of the most popular products sold by Flower Pocket. Open the **Flower Sales** workbook located in the Excel11 ▶ Case4 folder included with your Data Files, and then save the workbook as **Flower Sales Report** in the location specified by your instructor.

Explore 19. Test the connection files you created in Step 16. Click the Connections button in the Connections group on the DATA tab, and then click the Add button. Click the Browse for More button in the Existing Connections dialog box, and then locate and open the **Product Orders** ODC file you created in Step 16.

20. In the Sales Report worksheet, create a PivotTable report that lists each product retrieved from the Product Orders connection with the number of times the product was purchased by the customer and the amount of revenue generated by each product (in terms of the Price field). The layout of the PivotTable is up to you.

21. Save the workbook, and then close it.

Creating a Presentation

Presenting Information About an Event Venue

Case | *Lakeside Event Center*

Lakeside Event Center is a venue in Lake Havasu City, Arizona, that opened in 1981 and is available for functions of all types, including birthdays, bar mitzvahs, corporate events, and weddings. The event center, located on the shore of Lake Havasu, has rooms that can host from 50 to 900 people. The center underwent a recent renovation including planting new gardens and updating the décor inside. Caitlin Keough-Barton was recently hired as the events manager. One of Caitlin's responsibilities is to attract new bookings. Caitlin wants to advertise the hall at upcoming wedding and event-planning conventions.

Microsoft PowerPoint 2016 (or simply **PowerPoint**) is a computer program you use to create a collection of slides that can contain text, charts, pictures, sounds, movies, multimedia, and so on. In this module, you'll use PowerPoint to create a presentation that Caitlin can use to showcase everything Lakeside Event Center has to offer when she attends the Event Planners Association annual convention. After Caitlin reviews it, you'll add graphics and speaker notes to the presentation. Finally, you'll check the spelling, run the slide show to evaluate it, and print the presentation.

STARTING DATA FILES

Module	Review	Case1	Case2
Gazebo.jpg	DJ.jpg	After.jpg	Keyboard.jpg
Revised.pptx	Musicians.jpg	Before.jpg	Music.pptx
Tables.jpg	Photog.jpg	Clients.pptx	Richard.jpg
Wedding.jpg	Vendor2.pptx	Team.jpg	
		Windows.jpg	

Case3		Case4	
Beach.jpg	House4.jpg	Ballet.jpg	Jump.jpg
House1.jpg	House5.jpg	Dancing.mp4	Leap.jpg
House2.jpg	Realty.pptx	HipHop.jpg	Modern.jpg
House3.jpg		Jazz.jpg	Tap.jpg

Session 1.1 Visual Overview:

The **Quick Access Toolbar** contains buttons for frequently used commands. You can click the Customize Quick Access Toolbar button (the small arrow on the right) to add and remove commands.

The ribbon is organized into tabs. Each **tab** contains buttons related to particular activities or tasks.

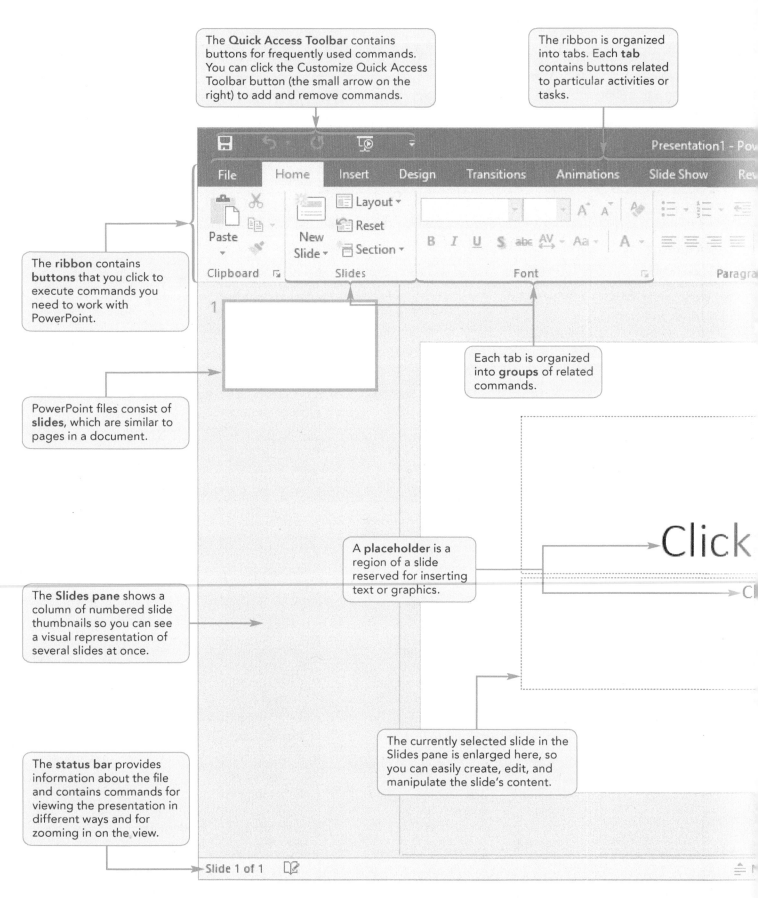

The **ribbon** contains **buttons** that you click to execute commands you need to work with PowerPoint.

Each tab is organized into **groups** of related commands.

PowerPoint files consist of **slides**, which are similar to pages in a document.

A **placeholder** is a region of a slide reserved for inserting text or graphics.

The **Slides pane** shows a column of numbered slide thumbnails so you can see a visual representation of several slides at once.

The currently selected slide in the Slides pane is enlarged here, so you can easily create, edit, and manipulate the slide's content.

The **status bar** provides information about the file and contains commands for viewing the presentation in different ways and for zooming in on the view.

The PowerPoint Window

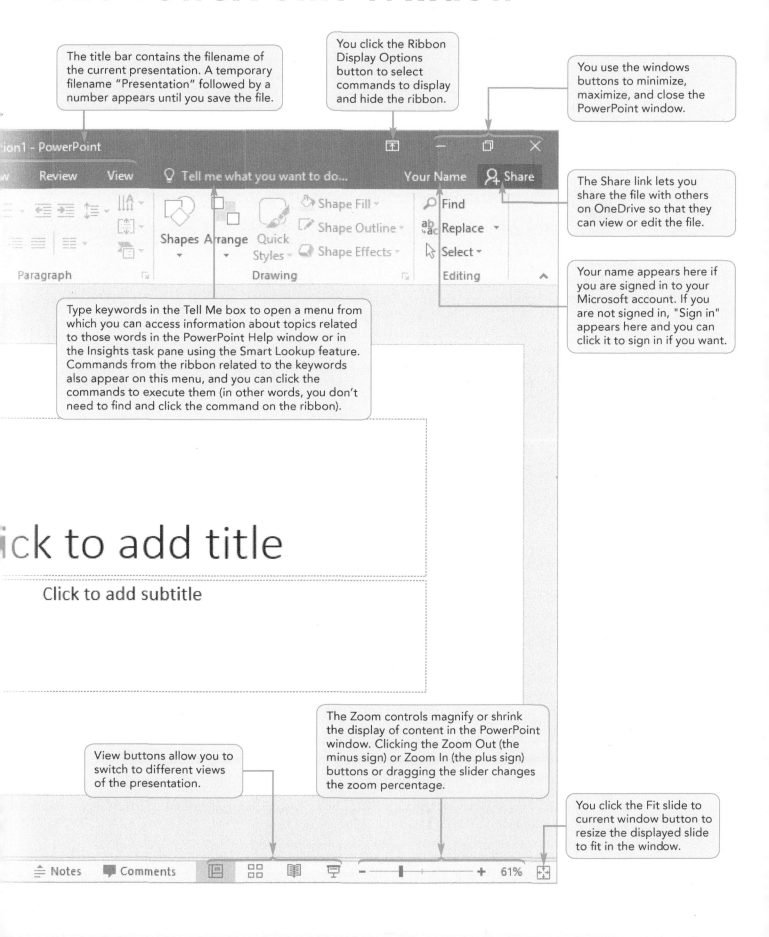

The title bar contains the filename of the current presentation. A temporary filename "Presentation" followed by a number appears until you save the file.

You click the Ribbon Display Options button to select commands to display and hide the ribbon.

You use the windows buttons to minimize, maximize, and close the PowerPoint window.

The Share link lets you share the file with others on OneDrive so that they can view or edit the file.

Type keywords in the Tell Me box to open a menu from which you can access information about topics related to those words in the PowerPoint Help window or in the Insights task pane using the Smart Lookup feature. Commands from the ribbon related to the keywords also appear on this menu, and you can click the commands to execute them (in other words, you don't need to find and click the command on the ribbon).

Your name appears here if you are signed in to your Microsoft account. If you are not signed in, "Sign in" appears here and you can click it to sign in if you want.

ick to add title

Click to add subtitle

The Zoom controls magnify or shrink the display of content in the PowerPoint window. Clicking the Zoom Out (the minus sign) or Zoom In (the plus sign) buttons or dragging the slider changes the zoom percentage.

View buttons allow you to switch to different views of the presentation.

You click the Fit slide to current window button to resize the displayed slide to fit in the window.

Planning a Presentation

A **presentation** is a talk (lecture) or prepared file in which the person speaking or the person who prepared the file—the presenter—wants to communicate with an audience to explain new concepts or ideas, sell a product or service, entertain, train the audience in a new skill or technique, or any of a wide variety of other topics.

Most people find it helpful to use **presentation media**—visual and audio aids to support key points and engage the audience's attention. Microsoft PowerPoint is one of the most commonly used tools for creating effective presentation media. The features of PowerPoint make it easy to incorporate photos, diagrams, music, and video with key points of a presentation. Before you create a presentation, you should spend some time planning its content.

PROSKILLS

Verbal Communication: Planning a Presentation

Answering a few key questions will help you create a presentation using appropriate presentation media that successfully delivers its message or motivates the audience to take an action.

- What is the purpose of your presentation? In other words, what action or response do you want your audience to have? For example, do you want them to buy something, follow instructions, or make a decision?
- Who is your audience? Think about the needs and interests of your audience as well as any decisions they'll make as a result of what you have to say. What you choose to say to your audience must be relevant to their needs, interests, and decisions or it will be forgotten.
- What are the main points of your presentation? Identify the information that is directly relevant to your audience.
- What presentation media will help your audience absorb the information and remember it later? Do you need lists, photos, charts, or tables?
- What is the format for your presentation? Will you deliver the presentation orally or will you create a presentation file that your audience members will view on their own, without you present?
- How much time do you have for the presentation? Keep that in mind as you prepare the presentation content so that you have enough time to present all of your key points.
- Consider whether handouts will help your audience follow along with your presentation or steal your audience's attention when you want them to be focused on you, the presenter.

The purpose of Caitlin's presentation is to convince people attending wedding conventions to book their weddings at Lakeside Event Center. Her audience will be members of the local community who are planning a wedding. She also plans to explain the service and price packages from which people can choose. Caitlin will use PowerPoint to display lists and graphics to help make her message clear. She plans to deliver her presentation orally to small groups of people as they visit her booth at the convention, and her presentation will be about 10 minutes long. For handouts, she plans to have flyers available to distribute to anyone who is interested, but she will not distribute anything before her presentation because she wants the audience's full attention to be on her, and the details are not complex enough that the audience will need a written document to refer to as she is speaking.

Once you know what you want to say or communicate, you can prepare the presentation media to help communicate your ideas.

Starting PowerPoint and Creating a New Presentation

Microsoft PowerPoint 2016 is a tool you can use to create and display visual and audio aids on slides to help clarify the points you want to make in your presentation or to create a presentation that people view on their own without you being present.

When PowerPoint starts, the Recent screen in Backstage view is displayed. **Backstage view** contains commands that allow you to manage your presentation files and PowerPoint options. When you first start PowerPoint, the only actions available to you in Backstage view are to open an existing PowerPoint file or create a new file. You'll start PowerPoint now.

To start PowerPoint:

1. On the Windows taskbar, click the **Start** button ⊞. The Start menu opens.

2. Click **All apps** on the Start menu, scroll the list, and then click **PowerPoint 2016**. PowerPoint starts and displays the Recent screen in Backstage view. See Figure 1-1. In the orange bar on the left is a list of recently opened presentations, and on the right are options for creating new presentations.

Figure 1-1	Recent screen in Backstage view

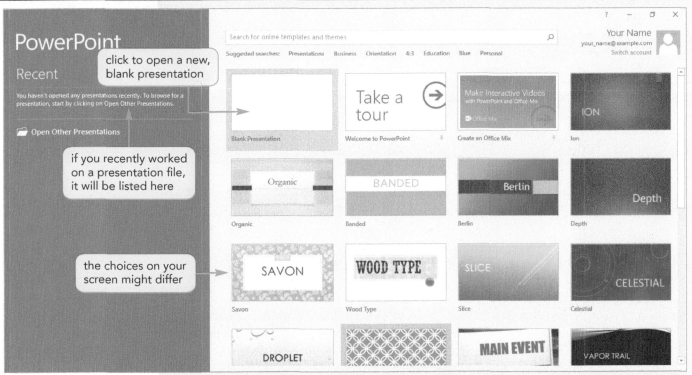

TIP

To create a new blank presentation when PowerPoint is already running, click the File tab on the ribbon, click New in the navigation bar, and then click Blank Presentation.

3. Click **Blank Presentation**. Backstage view closes and a new presentation window appears. The temporary filename "Presentation1" appears in the title bar. There is only one slide in the new presentation—Slide 1.

   Trouble? If you do not see the area on the ribbon that contains buttons and you see only the ribbon tab names, click the Home tab to expand the ribbon and display the commands, and then in the bottom-right corner of the ribbon, click the Pin the ribbon button 📌 that appears.

   Trouble? If the window is not maximized, click the Maximize button ◻ in the upper-right corner.

When you create a new presentation, it is displayed in Normal view. **Normal view** displays the selected slide enlarged so you can add and manipulate objects on the slide. The Slides pane on the left side of the program window displays **thumbnails**—miniature images—of all the slides in the presentation. The Home tab on the ribbon is selected when you first open or create a presentation. The Session 1.1 Visual Overview identifies elements of the PowerPoint window.

Working in Touch Mode

In Office 2016, you can work with a mouse or, if you have a touch screen, you can work in Touch Mode. In **Touch Mode** the ribbon increases in height so that there is more space around each button on the ribbon, making it easier to use your finger to tap the specific button you need. Also, in the main part of the PowerPoint window, the instructions telling you to "Click" are replaced with instructions to "Double tap." Note that the figures in this text show the screen with Mouse Mode on. You'll switch to Touch Mode and then back to Mouse Mode now.

   Note: The following steps assume that you are using a mouse. If you are instead using a touch device, please read these steps but don't complete them, so that you remain working in Touch Mode.

To switch between Touch Mode and Mouse Mode:

1. On the Quick Access Toolbar, click the **Customize Quick Access Toolbar** button ⬇. A menu opens. The Touch/Mouse Mode command near the bottom of the menu does not have a checkmark next to it.

   Trouble? If the Touch/Mouse Mode command has a checkmark next to it, press the Esc key to close the menu, and then skip Step 2.

2. On the menu, click **Touch/Mouse Mode**. The menu closes and the Touch/Mouse Mode button appears on the Quick Access Toolbar.

3. On the Quick Access Toolbar, click the **Touch/Mouse Mode** button 👆. A menu opens listing Mouse and Touch, and the icon next to Mouse is shaded orange to indicate it is selected.

   Trouble? If the icon next to Touch is shaded orange, press the Esc key to close the menu and skip Step 4.

4. On the menu, click **Touch**. The menu closes and the ribbon increases in height so that there is more space around each button on the ribbon. Notice that the instructions in the main part of the PowerPoint window changed by replacing the instruction to "Click" with the instruction to "Double tap." See Figure 1-2. Now you'll change back to Mouse Mode.

Figure 1-2   PowerPoint window with Touch mode active

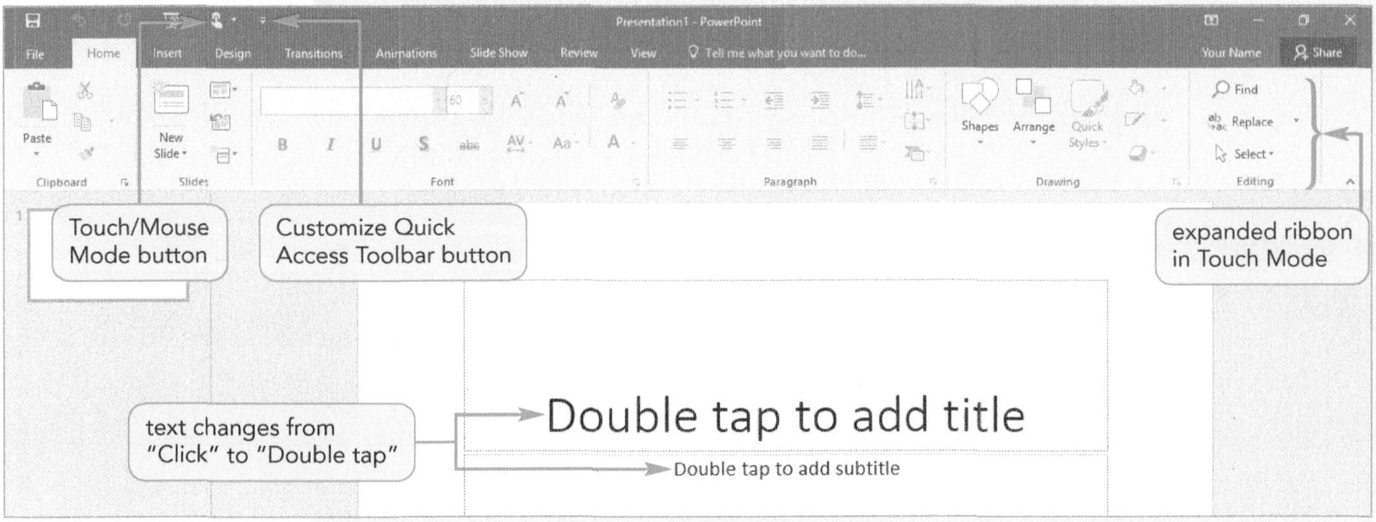

Touch/Mouse Mode button

Customize Quick Access Toolbar button

expanded ribbon in Touch Mode

text changes from "Click" to "Double tap"

Double tap to add title

Double tap to add subtitle

Trouble? If you are working with a touch screen and want to use Touch Mode, skip Steps 5 and 6.

5. Click the **Touch/Mouse Mode** button 🖑, and then click **Mouse**. The ribbon and the instructions change back to Mouse Mode defaults as shown in the Session 1.1 Visual Overview.

6. Click the **Customize Quick Access Toolbar** button 📥, and then click **Touch/Mouse Mode** to deselect this option and remove the checkmark. The Touch/Mouse Mode button is removed from the Quick Access Toolbar.

Creating a Title Slide

The **title slide** is the first slide in a presentation. It generally contains the title of the presentation plus any other identifying information you want to include, such as a company's slogan, the presenter's name, or a company name. The **font**—a set of characters with the same design—used in the title and subtitle may be the same or may be different fonts that complement each other.

The title slide contains two objects called text placeholders. A **text placeholder** is a placeholder designed to contain text. Text placeholders usually display text that describes the purpose of the placeholder and instructs you to click so that you can start typing in the placeholder. The larger text placeholder on the title slide is designed to hold the presentation title, and the smaller text placeholder is designed to contain a subtitle. Once you enter text into a text placeholder, it is no longer a placeholder and becomes an object called a **text box**.

When you click in the placeholder, the **insertion point**, which indicates where text will appear when you start typing, appears as a blinking line in the center of the placeholder. In addition, a contextual tab, the Drawing Tools Format tab, appears on the ribbon. A **contextual tab** appears only in context—that is, when a particular type of object is selected or active—and contains commands for modifying that object.

You'll add a title and subtitle for Caitlin's presentation now. Caitlin wants the title slide to contain the company name and slogan.

To add the company name and slogan to the title slide:

▶ **1.** On **Slide 1**, move the pointer to position it in the title text placeholder (where it says "Click to add title") so that the pointer changes to ⊥, and then click. The insertion point replaces the placeholder text, and the Drawing Tools Format contextual tab appears as the rightmost tab on the ribbon. Note that in the Font group on the Home tab, the Font box identifies the title font as Calibri Light. See Figure 1-3.

Figure 1-3	Title text placeholder after clicking in it

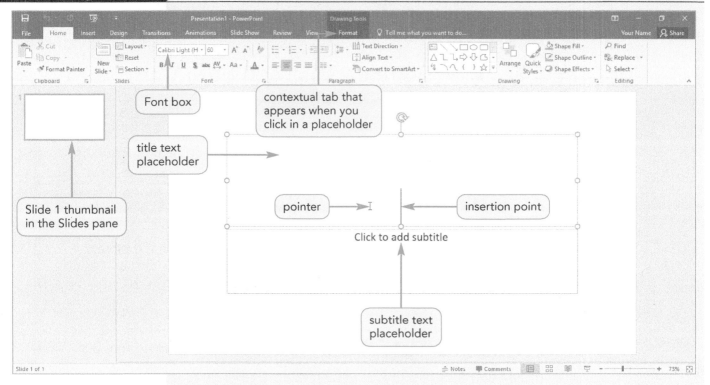

▶ **2.** Type **Lakeside Event Hall**. The placeholder is now a text box.

▶ **3.** Click a blank area of the slide. The border of the text box disappears, and the Drawing Tools Format tab no longer appears on the ribbon.

▶ **4.** Click in the **subtitle text placeholder** (where it says "Click to add subtitle"), and then type **Perfect venue for all occasions!**. Notice in the Font group that the subtitle font is Calibri, a font which works well with the Calibri Light font used in the title text.

▶ **5.** Click a blank area of the slide.

Saving and Editing a Presentation

Once you have created a presentation, you should name and save the presentation file. You can save the file on a hard drive or a network drive, on an external drive such as a USB drive, or to your account on OneDrive, Microsoft's free online storage area.

To save the presentation for the first time:

1. On the Quick Access Toolbar, point to the **Save** button 🖫. A box called a **ScreenTip** appears, identifying the button.

2. Click the **Save** button 🖫. The Save As screen in Backstage view appears. See Figure 1-4. The **navigation bar** on the left contains commands for working with the file and program options. Recently used folders on the selected drive appear in a list on the right.

Figure 1-4   Save As screen in Backstage view

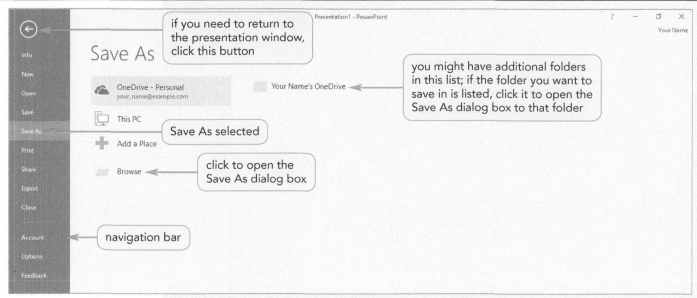

3. Click **Browse**. The Save As dialog box opens, similar to the one shown in Figure 1-5.

Figure 1-5   Save As dialog box

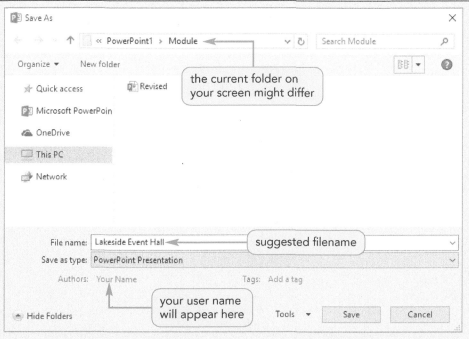

4. Navigate to the drive and folder where you are storing your Data Files, and then click in the **File name** box. The suggested filename, Lakeside Event Hall, is selected.

5. Type **Convention Presentation**. The text you type replaces the selected text in the File name box.

6. Click the **Save** button. The file is saved, the dialog box and Backstage view close, and the presentation window appears again with the new filename in the title bar.

Once you have created a presentation, you can make changes to it. For example, if you need to change text in a text box, you can easily edit it. The Backspace key deletes characters to the left of the insertion point, and the Delete key deletes characters to the right of the insertion point.

If you mistype or misspell a word, you might not need to correct it because the **AutoCorrect** feature automatically corrects many commonly mistyped and misspelled words after you press the spacebar or the Enter key. For instance, if you type "cna" and then press the spacebar, PowerPoint corrects the word to "can." If you want AutoCorrect to stop making a particular change, you can display the AutoCorrect Options menu, and then click Stop making the change. (The exact wording will differ depending on the change made.)

After you make changes to a presentation, you will need to save the file again so that the changes are stored. Because you have already saved the presentation with a permanent filename, using the Save command does not open the Save As dialog box; it simply saves the changes you made to the file.

To edit the text on Slide 1 and save your changes:

1. On Slide 1, click the **title**, and then use the ← and → keys as needed to position the insertion point to the right of the word "Hall."

2. Press the **Backspace** key four times. The four characters to the left of the insertion point, "Hall," are deleted.

3. Type **Center**. The title is now "Lakeside Event Center."

4. Click to the left of the word "Perfect" in the subtitle text box to position the insertion point in front of that word, type **Teh**, and then press the **spacebar**. PowerPoint corrects the word you typed to "The."

5. Move the pointer over the word **The**. A small, very faint rectangle appears below the first letter of the word. This indicates that an AutoCorrection has been made.

6. Move the pointer on top of the faint rectangle that appears under the "T" so that it changes to the AutoCorrect Options button ⚡▾, and then click the **AutoCorrect Options** button ⚡▾. A menu opens, as shown in Figure 1-6. You can change the word back to what you originally typed, instruct PowerPoint to stop making this type of correction in this file, or open the AutoCorrect dialog box.

   Trouble? If you can't see the AutoCorrection indicator box, point to the letter "T," and then slowly move the pointer down until it is over the box and changes it to the AutoCorrect Options button.

Figure 1-6 AutoCorrect Options button menu

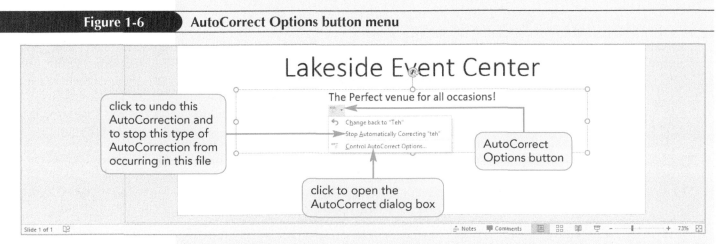

click to undo this AutoCorrection and to stop this type of AutoCorrection from occurring in this file

↺ Change back to "Teh"
→ Stop Automatically Correcting "teh"
⌐ Control AutoCorrect Options...

AutoCorrect Options button

click to open the AutoCorrect dialog box

Slide 1 of 1   ☰ Notes   💬 Comments   🔲 🔳 📊 🖵 − | + 73% 🔲

▶ **7.** Click **Control AutoCorrect Options**. The AutoCorrect dialog box opens with the AutoCorrect tab selected. See Figure 1-7.

Figure 1-7 AutoCorrect tab in the AutoCorrect dialog box

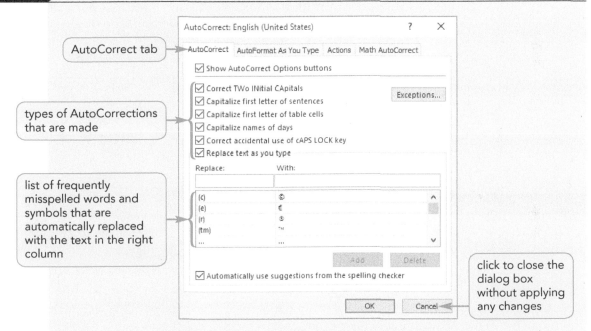

AutoCorrect tab

types of AutoCorrections that are made

list of frequently misspelled words and symbols that are automatically replaced with the text in the right column

click to close the dialog box without applying any changes

▶ **8.** Examine the types of changes the AutoCorrect feature makes, and then click the **Cancel** button.

▶ **9.** Click to the left of the "P" in "Perfect," if necessary, press the **Delete** key, and then type **p.**. The subtitle now is "The perfect venue for all occasions!" Now that you have modified the presentation, you need to save your changes.

▶ **10.** On the Quick Access Toolbar, click the **Save** button 🖫. The changes you made are saved to the Convention Presentation file.

Adding New Slides

Now that you've created the title slide, you need to add more slides. Every slide has a **layout**, which is the arrangement of placeholders on the slide. The title slide uses the Title Slide layout. A commonly used layout is the Title and Content layout, which contains a title text placeholder for the slide title and a content placeholder. A **content placeholder** is a placeholder designed to hold several types of slide content including text, a table, a chart, a picture, or a video.

To add a new slide, you use the New Slide button in the Slides group on the Home tab. When you click the top part of the New Slide button, a new slide is inserted with the same layout as the current slide, unless the current slide is the title slide; in that case the new slide has the Title and Content layout. If you want to create a new slide with a different layout, click the bottom part of the New Slide button to open a gallery of layouts, and then click the layout you want to use.

You can change the layout of a slide at any time. To do this, click the Layout button in the Slides group to display the same gallery of layouts that appears in the New Slide gallery, and then click the slide layout you want to apply to the selected slide.

As you add slides, you can switch from one slide to another by clicking the slide thumbnails in the Slides pane. You need to add several new slides to the file.

To add new slides and apply different layouts:

1. Make sure the Home tab is displayed on the ribbon.

2. In the Slides group, click the top part of the **New Slide** button. A new slide appears and its thumbnail appears in the Slides pane below Slide 1. The new slide has the Title and Content layout applied. This layout contains a title text placeholder and a content placeholder. In the Slides pane, an orange border appears around the new Slide 2, indicating that it is the current slide.

3. In the Slides group, click the **New Slide** button again. A new Slide 3 is added. Because Slide 2 had the Title and Content layout applied, Slide 3 also has that layout applied.

4. In the Slides group, click the **New Slide button arrow** (that is, click the bottom part of the New Slide button). A gallery of the available layouts appears. See Figure 1-8.

Figure 1-8 Gallery of layouts on the New Slide menu

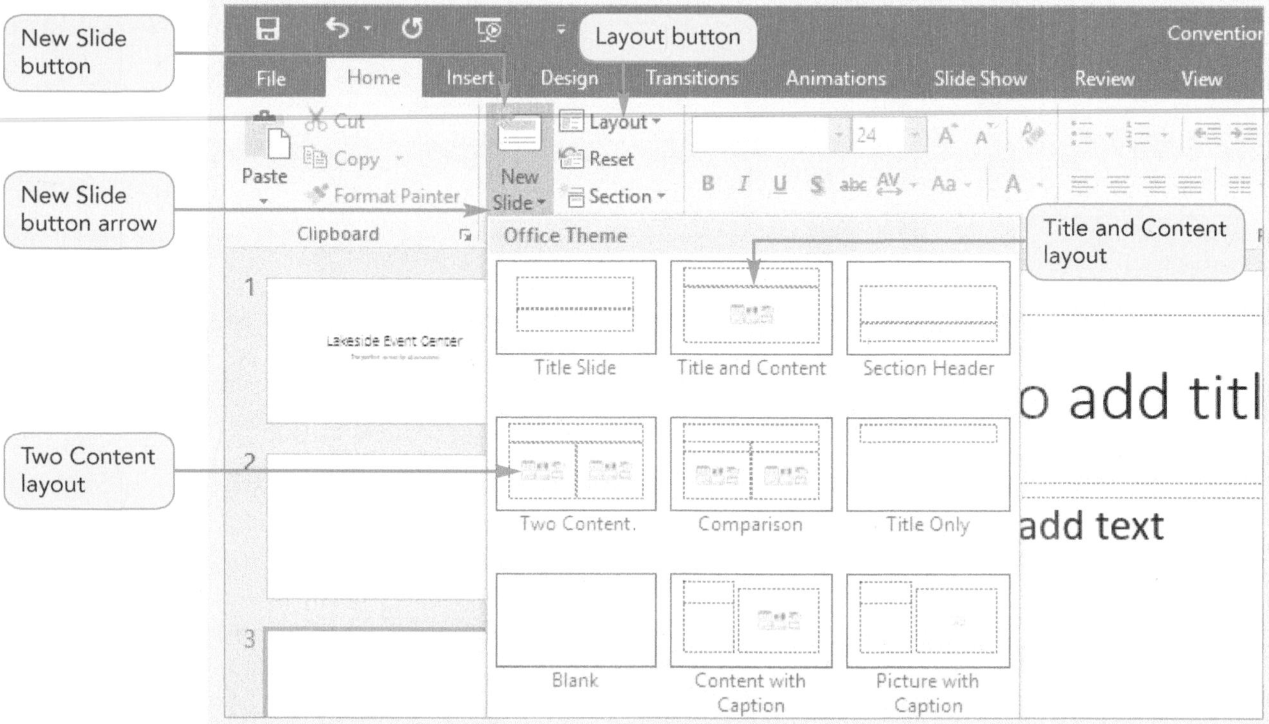

5. In the gallery, click the **Two Content** layout. The gallery closes and a new Slide 4 is inserted with the Two Content layout applied. This layout includes three objects: a title text placeholder and two content placeholders.

6. In the Slides group, click the **New Slide** button. A new Slide 5 is added to the presentation. Because Slide 4 had the Two Content layout applied, that layout is also applied to the new slide. You need to change the layout of Slide 5.

7. In the Slides group, click the **Layout** button. The same gallery of layouts that appeared when you clicked the New Slide button arrow appears. The Two Content layout is selected, as indicated by the shading behind it, showing you that this is the layout applied to the current slide, Slide 5.

8. Click the **Title and Content** layout. The layout of Slide 5 is changed to Title and Content.

9. In the Slides group, click the **New Slide** button twice to add two more slides with the Title and Content layout.

10. Add a new slide with the Two Content layout. There are now eight slides in the presentation. In the Slides pane, Slides 1 through 3 have scrolled up out of view, and vertical scroll bars are now visible in both the Slides pane and along the right side of the program window.

11. In the Slides pane, drag the **scroll box** to the top of the vertical scroll bar, and then click the **Slide 2** thumbnail. Slide 2 appears in the program window and is selected in the Slides pane. See Figure 1-9.

| Figure 1-9 | Slide 2 with the Title and Content layout |

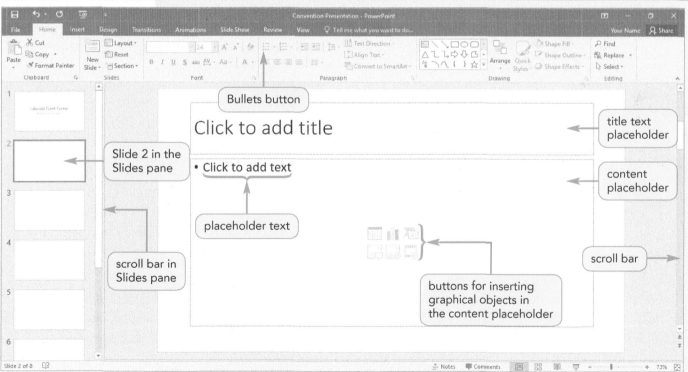

12. On the Quick Access Toolbar, click the **Save** button. The changes you made are saved in the file.

If you accidentally close a presentation without saving changes and need to recover it, you can do so by clicking the File tab, clicking Open in the navigation bar, and then clicking the Recover Unsaved Presentations button.

Creating Lists

One way to help explain the topic or concept you are describing in your presentation is to use lists. For oral presentations, the intent of lists is to enhance the oral presentation, not replace it. In self-running presentations, items in lists might need to be longer and more descriptive. However, keep in mind that PowerPoint is a presentation graphics program intended to help you present information in a visual, graphical manner, not create a written document in an alternate form.

Items in a list can appear at different levels. A **first-level item** is a main item in a list; a **second-level item**—sometimes called a **subitem**—is an item beneath and indented from a first-level item. Usually, the font size—the size of the text—in subitems is smaller than the size used for text in the level above. Text is measured in **points**, which is a unit of measurement. Text in a book is typically printed in 10- or 12-point type; text on a slide needs to be much larger so the audience can easily read it.

Creating a Bulleted List

A **bulleted list** is a list of items with some type of bullet symbol in front of each item or paragraph. When you create a subitem in the list, a different or smaller symbol is often used. You need to create a bulleted list that describes the amenities of the Lakeside Event Center and one that describes the catering packages available.

To create bulleted lists on Slides 2 and 3:

1. On **Slide 2**, click in the **title text placeholder** (with the placeholder text "Click to add title"), and then type **Amenities**.

2. In the content placeholder, click any area where the pointer is shaped as I— in other words, anywhere except on one of the buttons in the center of the placeholder. The placeholder text "Click to add text" disappears, the insertion point appears, and a light gray bullet symbol appears.

3. Type **Comfortable**. As soon as you type the first character, the icons in the center of the content placeholder disappear, the bullet symbol darkens, and the content placeholder changes to a text box. On the Home tab, in the Paragraph group, the Bullets button is shaded to indicate that it is selected.

4. Press the **spacebar**, type **indoor seating**, and then press the **Enter** key. The insertion point moves to a new line, and a light gray bullet appears on the new line.

5. Type **Dance floor**, press the **Enter** key, type **Surround sound for music**, and then press the **Enter** key. The bulleted list now consists of three first-level items, and the insertion point is next to a light gray bullet on the fourth line in the text box. Notice on the Home tab, in the Font group, that the point size in the Font Size box is 28 points.

6. Press the **Tab** key. The bullet symbol and the insertion point indent one-half inch to the right, the bullet symbol changes to a smaller size, and the number in the Font Size box changes to 24. See Figure 1-10.

Figure 1-10 **Subitem created on Slide 2**

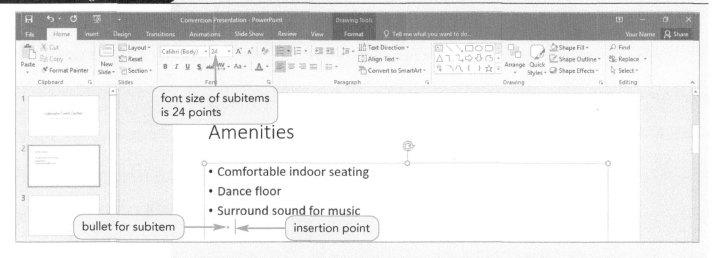

7. Type **DJs can easily plug in** and then press the **Enter** key.

8. Type **Live bands have plenty of room** and then press the **Enter** key. A third subitem is created. You will change it to a first-level item using a key combination. In this book, when you need to press two keys together, the keys will be listed separated by a plus sign.

TIP

You don't need to press the keys at exactly the same time—press and hold the first key, press and release the second key, and then release the first key.

9. Press the **Shift+Tab** keys. The bullet symbol and the insertion point shift back to the left margin of the text box, the bullet symbol changes back to the larger size, and 28 again appears in the Font Size box because this line is now a first-level bulleted item.

10. Type **Optional outdoor seating on patio**, press the **Enter** key, and then type **Additional appetizers and pasta stations available as add-ons**.

11. In the Slides pane, click the **Slide 3** thumbnail to display Slide 3, click in the **title text placeholder**, and then type **Packages**.

12. In the content placeholder, click the **placeholder text**, type **Basic--5 hours, standard catering package**, press the **Enter** key, and then type **Special-- 5 hours, deluxe catering package**. When you pressed the spacebar after typing 5, AutoCorrect changed the two dashes to an em-dash, a typographical character longer than a hyphen.

If you add more text than will fit in the text box with the default font sizes and line spacing, **AutoFit** adjusts these features to make the text fit. When AutoFit is activated, the AutoFit Options button appears below the text box. You can click this button and then select from among several options, including turning off AutoFit for this text box and splitting the text between two slides. Although AutoFit can be helpful, be aware that it also allows you to crowd text on a slide, making the slide less effective.

PROSKILLS

Written Communication: How Much Text Should I Include?

Text can help audiences retain the information you are presenting by allowing them to read the main points while hearing you discuss them. But be wary of adding so much text to your slides that your audience can ignore you and just read the slides. Try to follow the 7x7 rule—no more than seven items per slide, with no more than seven words per item. A variation of this rule is 6x6, and some presenters even prefer 4x4. If you create a self-running presentation (a presentation file others will view on their own), you will usually need to add more text than you would if you were presenting the material in person.

Creating a Numbered List

A **numbered list** is similar to a bulleted list except that numbers appear in front of each item instead of bullet symbols. Generally you should use a numbered list when the order of the items is important—for example, if you are presenting a list of step-by-step instructions that need to be followed in sequence in order to complete a task successfully. You need to create a numbered list on Slide 5 to explain how clients can reserve the event center for a function.

To create a numbered list on Slide 5:

1. In the Slides pane, click the **Slide 5** thumbnail to display Slide 5, and then type **Reserve Lakeside Event Center for Your Function!** in the title text placeholder.

2. In the content placeholder, click the **placeholder text**.

3. On the Home tab, in the Paragraph group, click the **Numbering** button. The Numbering button is selected, the Bullets button is deselected, and in the content placeholder, the bullet symbol is replaced with the number 1 followed by a period.

   Trouble? If a menu containing a gallery of numbering styles appears, you clicked the Numbering button arrow on the right side of the button. Click the Numbering button arrow again to close the menu, and then click the left part of the Numbering button.

4. Type **Specify date of function**, and then press the **Enter** key. As soon as you start typing, the number 1 darkens to black. After you press the Enter key, the insertion point moves to the next line, next to the light gray number 2.

5. Type **Choose package**, press the **Enter** key, type **Submit deposit**, and then press the **Enter** key. The number 4 appears on the next line.

6. In the Paragraph group, click the **Increase List Level** button. The fourth line is indented to be a subitem under the third item, and the number 4 changes to a number 1 in a smaller font size than the first-level items. Clicking the Increase List Level button is an alternative to pressing the Tab key to create a subitem.

7. Type **Credit card**, press the **Enter** key, type **Debit from checking account**, and then press the **Enter** key.

8. In the Paragraph group, click the **Decrease List Level** button. The sixth line is now a first-level item, and the number 4 appears next to it. Clicking the Decrease List Level button is an alternative to pressing the Shift+Tab keys to promote a subitem.

9. Type **Confirm**. The list now consists of four first-level numbered items and two subitems under number 3.

10. In the second item, click before the word "Choose," and then press the **Enter** key. A blank line is inserted above the second item.

11. Press the ↑ key. A light-gray number 2 appears in the blank line. The item on the third line in the list is still numbered 2.

12. Type **Specify number of guests**. As soon as you start typing, the new number 2 darkens in the second line, and the third item in the list is numbered 3. Compare your screen to Figure 1-11.

| Figure 1-11 | Numbered list on Slide 5 |

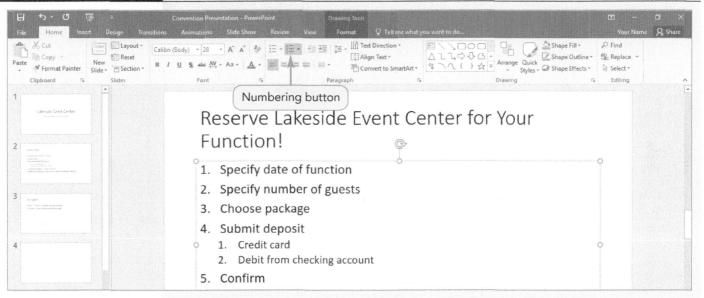

Creating an Unnumbered List

An **unnumbered list** is a list that does not have bullets or numbers preceding each item. Unnumbered lists are useful in slides when you want to present information on multiple lines without actually itemizing the information. For example, contact information for the presenter, including his or her email address, street address, city, and so on, would be clearer if it were in an unnumbered list.

As you have seen, items in a list have a little extra space between each item to visually separate bulleted items. Sometimes, you don't want the extra space between lines. If you press the Shift+Enter keys instead of just the Enter key, a new line is created, but it is still considered to be part of the item above it. Therefore, there is no extra space between the lines. Note that this also means that if you do this in a bulleted or numbered list, the new line will not have a bullet or number next to it because it is not a new item.

You need to create a slide that explains the event center's name. Also, Caitlin asks you to create a slide containing contact information.

To create unnumbered lists on Slides 4 and 7:

1. In the Slides pane, click the **Slide 4** thumbnail to display Slide 4. Slide 4 has the Two Content layout applied.

2. Type **About Us** in the title content placeholder, and then in the left content placeholder, click the **placeholder text**.

3. On the Home tab, in the Paragraph group, click the **Bullets** button. The button is no longer selected, and the bullet symbol disappears from the content placeholder.

4. Type **Lakeside**, press the **Enter** key, type **Event**, press the **Enter** key, and then type **Center**. Compare your screen to Figure 1-12.

Figure 1-12	Unnumbered list on Slide 4

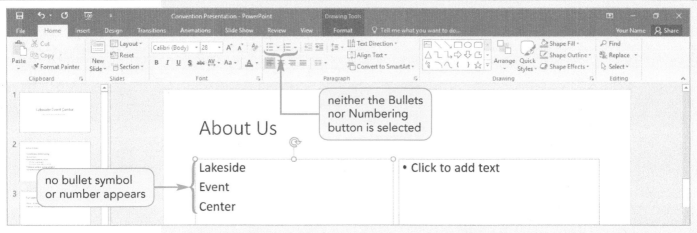

5. Display **Slide 7** in the Slide pane, type **For More Information** in the title text placeholder, and then in the content placeholder, click the **placeholder text**.

6. In the Paragraph group, click the **Bullets** button to remove the bullets, type **Lakeside Event Center**, and then press the **Enter** key. A new line is created, but there is extra space above the insertion point. This is not how addresses usually appear.

7. Press the **Backspace** key to delete the new line and move the insertion point back to the end of the first line, and then press the **Shift+Enter** keys. The insertion point moves to the next line, and, this time, there is no extra space above it.

8. Type **15680 Shore Drive**, press the **Shift+Enter** keys, and then type **Lake Havasu City, AZ 86403**. You need to insert the phone number on the next line, the general email address for the group on the line after that, and the website address on the last line. The extra space above these lines will set this information apart from the address and make it easier to read.

9. Press the **Enter** key to create a new line with extra space above it, type **(928) 555-HALL**, press the **Enter** key, type **info@lec.example.com**, and then press the **Enter** key. The insertion point moves to a new line with extra space above it, and the email address you typed changes color to blue and is underlined.

When you type text that PowerPoint recognizes as an email or website address and then press the spacebar or Enter key, the text is automatically formatted as a link that can be clicked during a slide show. To indicate this, the color of the text is changed and the text is underlined. Links are active only during a slide show.

10. Type **www.lec.example.com**, and then press the **spacebar**. The text is formatted as a link. Caitlin plans to click the link during her presentation to show the audience the website, so she wants it to stay formatted as a link. However, there is no need to have the email address formatted as a link because no one will click it during the presentation.

11. Right-click **info@lec.example.com**. A shortcut menu opens.

12. On the shortcut menu, click **Remove Hyperlink**. The email address is no longer formatted as a hyperlink. Compare your screen to Figure 1-13.

Figure 1-13   List on Slide 7

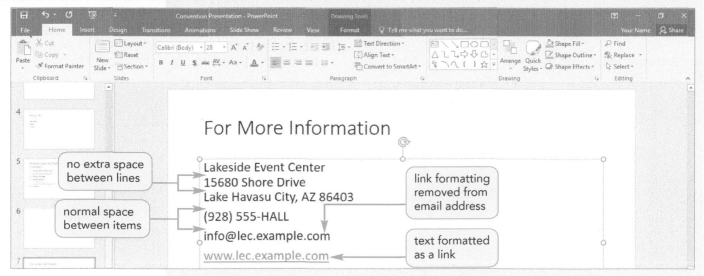

13. On the Quick Access Toolbar, click the **Save** button 💾 to save the changes.

Formatting Text

Slides in a presentation should have a cohesive look and feel. For example, the slide titles and the text in content placeholders should be in complementary fonts. However, there are times when you need to change the format of text. For instance, you might want to make specific words bold to make them stand out more.

To apply a format to text, either the text or the text box must be selected. If you want to apply the same formatting to all the text in a text box, you can click the border of the text box. When you do this, the dotted line border changes to a solid line to indicate that the contents of the entire text box are selected.

The commands in the Font group on the Home tab are used to apply formatting to text. Some of these commands are also available on the Mini toolbar, which appears when you select text with the mouse. The **Mini toolbar** contains commonly used buttons for formatting text. If the Mini toolbar appears, you can use the buttons on it instead of those in the Font group.

Some of the commands in the Font group use the Microsoft Office **Live Preview** feature, which previews the change on the slide so you can instantly see what the text will look like if you apply that format.

Caitlin wants the contact information on Slide 7 ("For More Information") to be larger. She also wants the first letter of each item in the unnumbered list on Slide 4 ("About Us") formatted so they are more prominent.

TIP

To remove all formatting from selected text, click the Clear All Formatting button in the Font group.

To format the text on Slides 4 and 7:

1. On **Slide 7** ("For More Information"), position the pointer on the border of the text box containing the contact information so that it changes to 🔲, and then click the border of the text box. The border changes to a solid line to indicate that the entire text box is selected.

2. On the Home tab, in the Font group, click the **Increase Font Size** button 🅰 twice. All the text in the text box increases in size with each click, and all the text in the text box is now 36 points.

3. Display **Slide 4** ("About Us").

4. In the unnumbered list, click to the left of "Lakeside," press and hold the **Shift** key, press the → key, and then release the **Shift** key. The letter "L" is selected. See Figure 1-14.

Figure 1-14 ▶ **Text selected to be formatted**

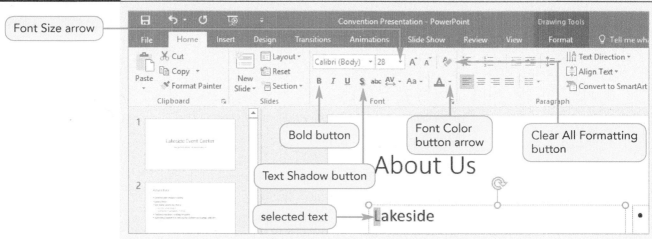

5. In the Font group, click the **Bold** button 🅱. The Bold button becomes selected, and the selected text is formatted as bold.

6. Make sure the letter "L" is still selected, and then in the Font group, click the **Text Shadow** button 🆂. The selected text is now bold with a slight drop shadow.

7. In the Font group, click the **Font Size arrow** to open the Font Size menu, and then click **48**. The selected text is now 48 points.

8. In the Font group, click the **Font Color button arrow** 🅰. A menu containing colors opens.

9. Under Theme Colors, move the pointer over each color, noting the ScreenTips that appear and watching as Live Preview changes the color of the selected text as you point to each color. Figure 1-15 shows the pointer pointing to the Orange, Accent 2, Darker 25% color.

Figure 1-15	Font Color menu

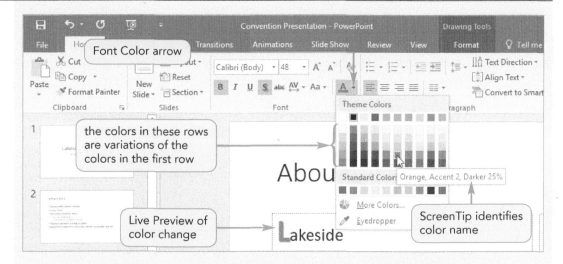

> **10.** Using the ScreenTips, locate the **Orange, Accent 2, Darker 25%** color, and then click it. The selected text changes to the orange color you clicked.

Now you need to format the first letters in the other words in the list to match the letter "L." You can repeat the steps you did when you formatted the letter "L," or you can use the Format Painter to copy all the formatting of the letter "L" to the other letters you need to format.

Also, Caitlin wants the text in the unnumbered list to be as large as possible. Because the first letters of each word are larger than the rest of the letters, the easiest way to do this is to select all of the text, and then use the Increase Font Size button. All of the letters will increase in size by four points with each click.

To use the Format Painter to copy and apply formatting on Slide 4:

> **1.** Make sure the letter "L" is still selected.

> **2.** On the Home tab, in the Clipboard group, click the **Format Painter** button, and then move the pointer on top of the slide. The button is selected, and the pointer changes to ▯.

> **3.** Position the pointer before the letter "E" in "Event," press and hold the mouse button, drag over the letter **E**, and then release the mouse button. The formatting you applied to the letter "L" is copied to the letter "E," and the Mini toolbar appears. See Figure 1-16. The Mini toolbar appears whenever you drag over text to select it.

Figure 1-16   The Mini toolbar

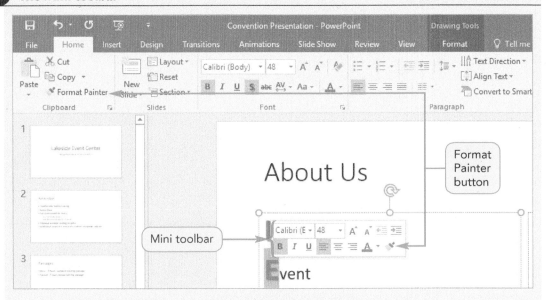

TIP

If you need to copy formatting to more than one location, double-click the Format Painter button to keep it selected until you deselect it.

4. On the Mini toolbar, click the **Format Painter** button , and then drag across the letter **C** in "Center."

5. Click the border of the text box to select the entire text box, and then in the Font group, click the **Increase Font Size** button five times. In the Font group, the Font Size button indicates that the text is 48+ points. This means that in the selected text box, the text that is the smallest is 48 points and there is some text that is a larger point size.

6. On the Quick Access Toolbar, click the **Save** button to save the changes.

Undoing and Redoing Actions

If you make a mistake or change your mind about an action as you are working, you can reverse the action by clicking the Undo button on the Quick Access Toolbar. You can undo up to the most recent 20 actions by continuing to click the Undo button or by clicking the Undo button arrow and then selecting as many actions in the list as you want. You can also Redo an action that you undid by clicking the Redo button on the Quick Access Toolbar.

When there are no actions that can be redone, the Redo button changes to the Repeat button. You can use the Repeat button to repeat an action, such as formatting text as bold. If the Repeat button is light gray, this means it is unavailable because there is no action to repeat (or to redo).

Moving and Copying Text

You can move or copy text and objects in a presentation using the Clipboard. The **Clipboard** is a temporary storage area available to all Windows programs on which text or objects are stored when you cut or copy them. To **cut** text or objects—that is, remove the selected text or objects from one location so that you can place it somewhere else—you select the text or object, and then use the Cut button in the Clipboard group on the Home tab to remove the selected text or object and place it on the Clipboard. To **copy** selected text or objects, you use the Copy button in the Clipboard group on the Home tab, which leaves the original text or object on the slide and places a copy of it on the Clipboard. You can then **paste** the text or object stored on the Clipboard anywhere in the presentation or, in fact, in any file in any Windows program.

You can paste an item on the Clipboard as many times and in as many locations as you like. However, the Clipboard can hold only the most recently cut or copied item. As soon as you cut or copy another item, it replaces the previously cut or copied item on the Clipboard.

Note that cutting text or an object is different from using the Delete or Backspace key to delete it. Deleted text and objects are not placed on the Clipboard; this means they cannot be pasted.

Caitlin wants a few changes made to Slides 5 and 3. You'll use the Clipboard as you make these edits.

To copy and paste text using the Clipboard:

▶ **1.** Display **Slide 5** ("Reserve Lakeside Event Center for Your Function!"), and then double-click the word **Reserve** in the title text. The word "Reserve" is selected.

▶ **2.** On the Home tab, in the Clipboard group, click the **Copy** button. The selected word is copied to the Clipboard.

▶ **3.** In the last item in the numbered list, click after the word "Confirm," and then press the **spacebar**.

▶ **4.** In the Clipboard group, click the **Paste** button. The text is pasted and picks up the formatting of its destination; that is, the pasted text is the 28-point Calibri font, the same font and size as the rest of the first-level items in the list, instead of 44-point Calibri Light as in the title. The Paste Options button 🗐 appears below the pasted text.

▶ **5.** Click the **Paste Options** button 🗐. A menu opens with four buttons on it. See Figure 1-17.

Figure 1-17   Buttons on the Paste Options menu when text is on the Clipboard

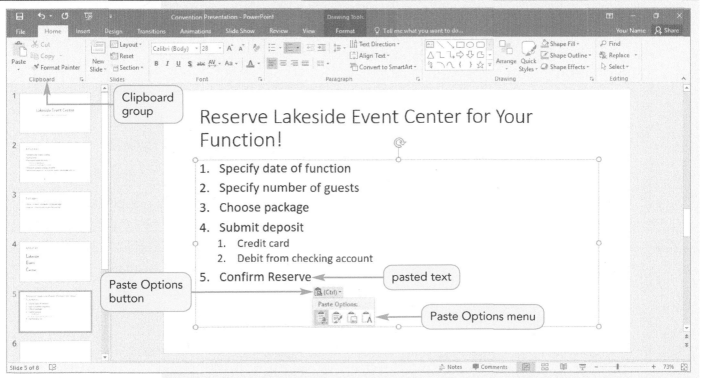

6. Point to each button on the menu, reading the ScreenTips and watching to see how the pasted text changes in appearance. The first button is the Use Destination Theme button 🔳, and this is the default choice when you paste text.

7. Click a blank area of the slide to close the menu without making a selection, press the **Backspace** key, type **ation**, click to the left of "Reservation," press the **Delete** key, and then type **r**. The word "reservation" in the numbered list is now all lowercase.

8. Display **Slide 2** ("Amenities"). The last bulleted item (starts with "Additional appetizers") belongs on Slide 3.

9. In the last bulleted item, position the pointer on top of the bullet symbol so that the pointer changes to ⁺⨥⁺, and then click. The entire bulleted item is selected.

10. In the Clipboard group, click the **Cut** button. The last bulleted item is removed from the slide and placed on the Clipboard.

11. Display **Slide 3** ("Packages"), click after the second bulleted item, and then press the **Enter** key to create a third bulleted item.

12. In the Clipboard group, click the **Paste** button. The bulleted item you cut is pasted as the third bulleted item on Slide 3 using the default paste option of Use Destination Theme. The insertion point appears next to a fourth bulleted item.

13. Press the **Backspace** key twice to delete the extra line, and then on the Quick Access Toolbar, click the **Save** button 🔲 to save the changes.

TIP

To cut text or an object, you can press the Ctrl+X keys; to copy text or an object, press the Ctrl+C keys; and to paste the item on the Clipboard, press the Ctrl+V keys.

INSIGHT

Using the Office Clipboard

The **Office Clipboard** is a special Clipboard available only to Microsoft Office applications. Once you activate the Office Clipboard, you can store up to 24 items on it and then select the item or items you want to paste. To activate the Office Clipboard, click the Home tab. In the Clipboard group, click the Dialog Box Launcher (the small square in the lower-right corner of the Clipboard group) to open the Clipboard task pane to the left of the displayed slide.

Converting a List to a SmartArt Diagram

A **diagram** visually depicts information or ideas and shows how they are connected. **SmartArt** is a feature that allows you to create diagrams easily and quickly. In addition to shapes, SmartArt diagrams usually include text to help describe or label the shapes. You can create the following types of diagrams using SmartArt:

- **List**—Shows a list of items in a graphical representation
- **Process**—Shows a sequence of steps in a process
- **Cycle**—Shows a process that is a continuous cycle
- **Hierarchy** (including organization charts)—Shows the relationship between individuals or units
- **Relationship** (including Venn diagrams, radial diagrams, and target diagrams)—Shows the relationship between two or more elements
- **Matrix**—Shows information in a grid
- **Pyramid**—Shows foundation-based relationships
- **Picture**—Provides a location for a picture or pictures that you insert

There is also an Office.com category of SmartArt, which, if you are connected to the Internet, displays additional SmartArt diagrams available in various categories on Office.com, a Microsoft website that contains tools for use with Office programs.

A quick way to create a SmartArt diagram is to convert an existing list. When you select an existing list and then click the Convert to SmartArt Graphic button in the Paragraph group on the Home tab, a gallery of SmartArt layouts appears. For SmartArt, a **layout** is the arrangement of the shapes in the diagram. Each first-level item in the list is converted to a shape in the SmartArt diagram. If the list contains subitems, you might need to experiment with different layouts to find one that best suits the information in your list.

REFERENCE

Converting a Bulleted List into a SmartArt Diagram

- Click anywhere in the bulleted list.
- In the Paragraph group on the Home tab, click the Convert to SmartArt Graphic button, and then click More SmartArt Graphics.
- In the Choose a SmartArt Graphic dialog box, select the desired SmartArt type in the list on the left.
- In the center pane, click the SmartArt diagram you want to use.
- Click the OK button.

Caitlin wants the numbered list on Slide 5 changed into a SmartArt diagram.

To convert the list on Slide 5 into a SmartArt diagram:

1. Display **Slide 5** ("Reserve Lakeside Event Center for Your Function!"), and then click anywhere in the numbered list to display the text box border.

2. On the Home tab, in the Paragraph group, click the **Convert to SmartArt** button. A gallery of SmartArt layouts appears.

3. Point to the first layout. The ScreenTip identifies this layout as the Vertical Bullet List layout, and Live Preview shows you what the numbered list will look like with that layout applied. See Figure 1-18. Notice that the subitems are not included in a shape in this diagram.

Figure 1-18   Live Preview of the Vertical Bullet List SmartArt layout

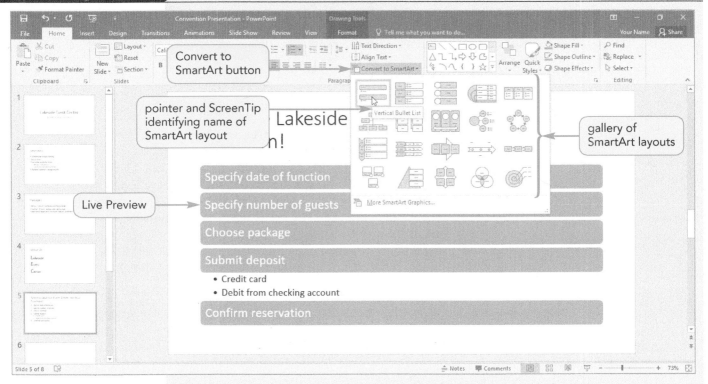

4. Point to several other layouts in the gallery, observing the Live Preview of each one. In some of the layouts, the subitems are included in a shape.

5. At the bottom of the gallery, click **More SmartArt Graphics**. The Choose a SmartArt Graphic dialog box opens. See Figure 1-19. You can click a type in the left pane to filter the middle pane to show only that type of layout.

Figure 1-19   Choose a SmartArt Graphic dialog box

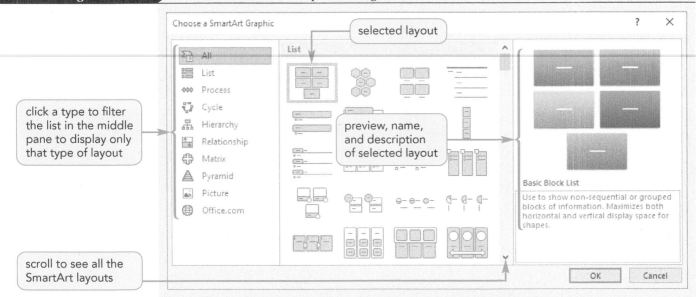

6. In the left pane, click **Process**, and then in the middle pane, click the **Step Up Process** layout, using the ScreenTips to identify it (it's the second layout in the first row). The right pane changes to show a description of that layout.

7. Click the **OK** button. The dialog box closes, and each of the first level items in the list appears in the square shapes in the diagram. The items also appear as a bulleted list in the Text pane, which is open to the left of the diagram. The SmartArt Tools contextual tabs appear on the ribbon. See Figure 1-20.

Figure 1-20	SmartArt diagram with the Step Up Process layout

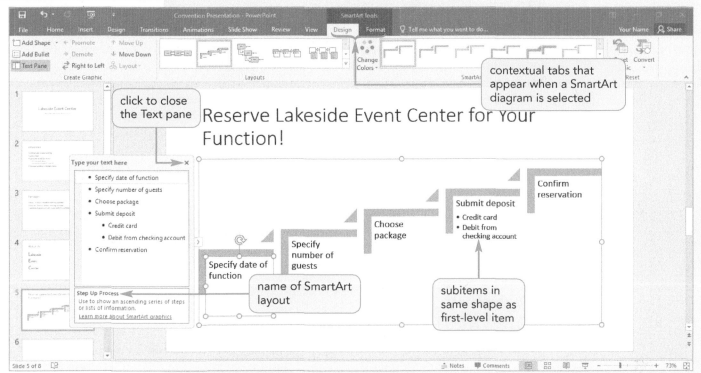

Trouble? If you do not see the Text pane, click the Text pane button ◁ on the left border of the selected SmartArt diagram.

In this layout, the subitems below "Submit deposit" are included in the fourth step shape; they are not placed in their own shapes in the diagram. Caitlin decides the information in the subitems does not need to be on the slide because people will see those options on the website when they submit their deposit.

8. In the "Submit deposit" shape, select **Debit from checking account**, and then press the **Delete** key. The text is deleted from the shape and from the Text pane.

9. In the Text pane, click to the right of the word "card," press the **Backspace** key as many times as necessary to delete all of the bullet text, and then press the **Backspace** key once more. The bullet changes to a first-level bullet and a new square shape is inserted in the diagram.

10. Press the **Backspace** key one more time. The empty bullet and the blank line are deleted in the Text pane, and the newly added shape is removed from the diagram. The "Submit deposit" shape now contains only the first-level item. Notice that AutoFit increased the size of the text in all the shapes so that the text still fills the shapes and is as large as possible. The "Submit deposit" shape is still selected. This shape should appear after the "Confirm reservation" shape.

> **11.** On the SmartArt Tools Design tab, in the Create Graphic group, click the **Move Down** button. The selected "Submit deposit" shape moves down one spot in the bulleted list in the text pane and one shape to the right in the SmartArt graphic on the slide.

> **12.** Click a blank area of the slide to deselect the diagram, and then on the Quick Access Toolbar, click the **Save** button 🖫 to save your changes.

Manipulating Slides

You can manipulate the slides in a presentation to suit your needs. For instance, if you need to create a slide that is similar to another slide, you can duplicate the existing slide and then modify the copy. If you decide that slides need to be rearranged, you can reorder them. And if you no longer want to include a slide in your presentation, you can delete it.

To duplicate, rearrange, or delete slides, you select the slides in the Slides pane in Normal view or switch to Slide Sorter view. In **Slide Sorter view** all the slides in the presentation are displayed as thumbnails in the window; the Slides pane does not appear. You already know that to select a single slide you click its thumbnail. You can also select more than one slide at a time. To select sequential slides, click the first slide, press and hold the Shift key, and then click the last slide you want to select. To select nonsequential slides, click the first slide, press and hold the Ctrl key, and then click any other slides you want to select.

Caitlin wants to display the slide that shows the name of the center at the end of the presentation. To create this slide, you will duplicate Slide 4 ("About Us").

To duplicate Slide 4:

> **1.** In the Slides pane, click the **Slide 4** ("About Us") thumbnail to display Slide 4.

> **2.** On the Home tab, in the Slides group, click the **New Slide button arrow**, and then click **Duplicate Selected Slides**. Slide 4 is duplicated, and the copy is inserted as a new Slide 5 in the Slides pane. Slide 5 is now the current slide. If more than one slide were selected, they would all be duplicated. The duplicate slide doesn't need the title; Caitlin just wants to reinforce the center's name.

> **3.** On Slide 5, click anywhere on the title **About Us**, click the **text box border** to select the text box, and then press the **Delete** key. The title and the title text box are deleted and the title text placeholder reappears.

You could delete the title text placeholder, but it is not necessary. When you display the presentation to an audience as a slide show, any unused placeholders will not appear.

Next you need to rearrange the slides. You need to move the duplicate of the "About Us" slide so it is the last slide in the presentation because Caitlin wants to leave it displayed after the presentation is over. She hopes this visual will reinforce the company's name for the audience. Caitlin also wants the "Packages" slide (Slide 3) moved so it appears before the "Amenities" slide (Slide 2), and she wants the original "About Us" slide (Slide 4) to be the second slide in the presentation.

To rearrange the slides in the presentation:

1. In the Slides pane, scroll up, if necessary, so that you can see Slides 2 and 3, and then drag the **Slide 3** ("Packages") thumbnail above the Slide 2 ("Amenities") thumbnail. As you drag, the Slide 3 thumbnail follows the pointer and Slide 2 moves down. The "Packages" slide is now Slide 2 and "Amenities" is now Slide 3. You'll move the other two slides in Slide Sorter view.

2. On the status bar, click the **Slide Sorter** button. The view switches to Slide Sorter view. Slide 2 appears with an orange border, indicating that it is selected.

3. On the status bar, click the **Zoom Out** button as many times as necessary until you can see all nine slides in the presentation. See Figure 1-21.

TIP

You can also use the buttons in the Presentation Views group on the View tab to switch views.

Figure 1-21 ▶ Slide Sorter view

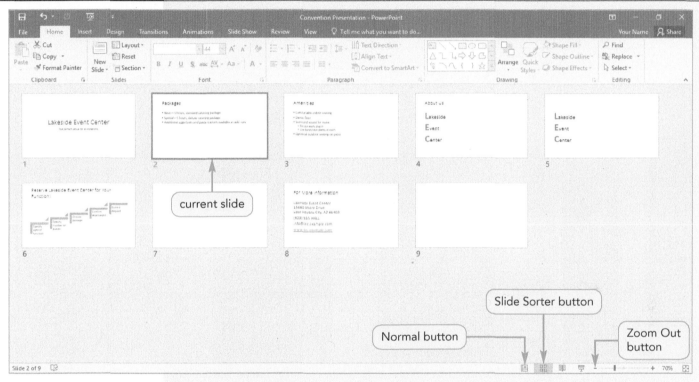

4. Drag the **Slide 4** ("About Us") thumbnail to between Slides 1 and 2. As you drag, the other slides move out of the way. The slide is repositioned, and the slides are renumbered so that the "About Us" slide is now Slide 2.

5. Drag the **Slide 5** thumbnail (the slide containing just the name of the company) so it becomes the last slide in the presentation (Slide 9).

Now you need to delete the two blank slides. To delete a slide, you can right-click its thumbnail to display a shortcut menu.

To delete the blank slides:

1. Click **Slide 6** (a blank slide), press and hold the **Shift** key, and then click **Slide 8** (the other blank slide), and then release the **Shift** key. The two slides you clicked are selected, as well as the slide between them. You want to delete only the two blank slides.

2. Click a blank area of the window to deselect the slides, click **Slide 6**, press and hold the **Ctrl** key, click **Slide 8**, and then release the **Ctrl** key. Only the two slides you clicked are selected.

3. Right-click either selected slide. A shortcut menu appears. See Figure 1-22.

Figure 1-22   **Shortcut menu for selected slides**

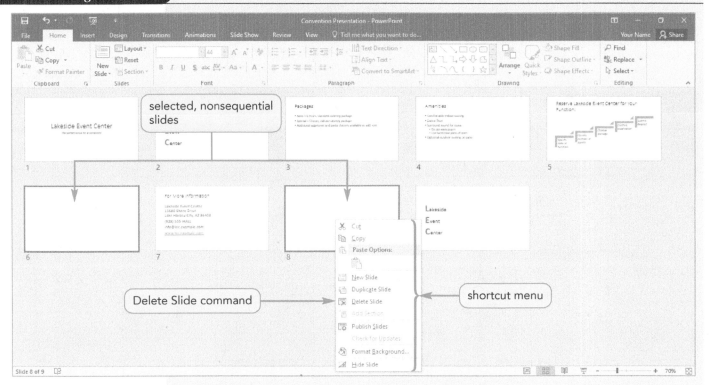

4. On the shortcut menu, click **Delete Slide**. The shortcut menu closes and the two selected slides are deleted. The presentation now contains seven slides.

TIP

You can also double-click a slide thumbnail in Slide Sorter view to display that slide in Normal view.

5. On the status bar, click the **Normal** button 🔲. The presentation appears in Normal view.

6. On the Quick Access Toolbar, click the **Save** button 🔲 to save the changes to the presentation.

Closing a Presentation

When you are finished working with a presentation, you can close it and leave PowerPoint open. To do this, you click the File tab to open Backstage view, and then click the Close command. If you click the Close button ☒ in the upper-right corner of the PowerPoint window and only one presentation is open, you will not only close the presentation, you will exit PowerPoint as well.

You're finished working with the presentation for now, so you will close it. First you will add your name to the title slide.

To add your name to Slide 1 and close the presentation:

1. Display **Slide 1** (the title slide), click the **subtitle**, position the insertion point after "occasions!," press the **Enter** key, and then type your full name.

2. Click the **File** tab. Backstage view appears with the Info screen displayed. See Figure 1-23.

Figure 1-23   Info screen in Backstage view

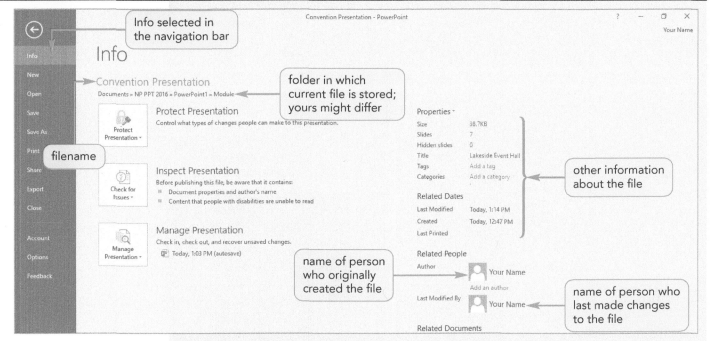

3. In the navigation bar, click **Close**. Backstage view closes, and a dialog box opens, asking if you want to save your changes.

4. In the dialog box, click the **Save** button. The dialog box and the presentation close, and the empty presentation window appears.

Trouble? If you want to take a break, you can exit PowerPoint by clicking the Close button ✕ in the upper-right corner of the PowerPoint window.

You've created a presentation that includes slides to which you added bulleted, numbered, and unnumbered lists. You also formatted text, converted a list to SmartArt, and manipulated slides. You are ready to give the presentation draft to Caitlin to review.

REVIEW

Session 1.1 Quick Check

1. Define "presentation."

2. How do you display Backstage view?

3. What is a layout?

4. In addition to a title text placeholder, what other type of placeholder do most layouts contain?

5. What is the term for an object that contains text?

6. What is the difference between the Clipboard and the Office Clipboard?

7. How do you convert a list to a SmartArt diagram?

Session 1.2 Visual Overview:

In **Slide Show view**, each slide fills the screen, one after another.

Benefits of Lakeside Event Center

▷ Beautiful venues for formal photos

　▷ Indoor private rooms

　▷ Outdoor gardens

　▷ Outdoor gazebo

▷ Friendly and accom

The pointer is not visible in Slide Show view until you move it or right-click it. When you move the pointer, this faint row of buttons appears in the lower-left corner of the screen. All of these buttons are also available in Presenter view.

Click the More slide show options button to display additional commands.

Click the Return to the previous slide and Advance to the next slide buttons to move from slide to slide in Slide Show view.

Click the Zoom into the slide button to zoom into a portion of the slide during the slide show.

Click the See all slides button to display all the slides, similar to Slide Sorter view.

©iStock.com/bloggityblog

Slide Show and Presenter Views

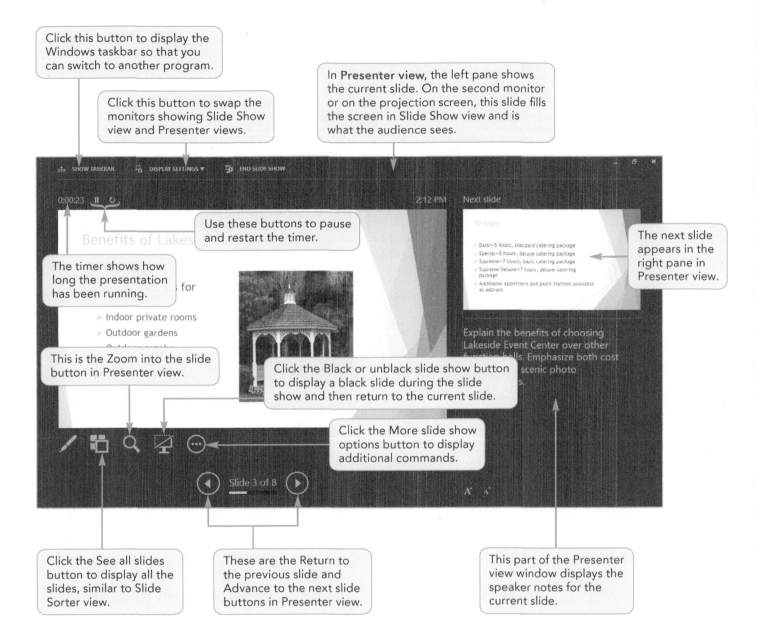

Click this button to display the Windows taskbar so that you can switch to another program.

Click this button to swap the monitors showing Slide Show view and Presenter views.

In **Presenter view**, the left pane shows the current slide. On the second monitor or on the projection screen, this slide fills the screen in Slide Show view and is what the audience sees.

Use these buttons to pause and restart the timer.

The next slide appears in the right pane in Presenter view.

The timer shows how long the presentation has been running.

This is the Zoom into the slide button in Presenter view.

Click the Black or unblack slide show button to display a black slide during the slide show and then return to the current slide.

Click the More slide show options button to display additional commands.

Click the See all slides button to display all the slides, similar to Slide Sorter view.

These are the Return to the previous slide and Advance to the next slide buttons in Presenter view.

This part of the Presenter view window displays the speaker notes for the current slide.

©iStock.com/bloggityblog

Opening a Presentation and Saving It with a New Name

If you have closed a presentation, you can always reopen it to modify it. To do this, you can double-click the file in a File Explorer window, or you can open Backstage view in PowerPoint and use the Open command.

Caitlin reviewed the presentation you created in Session 1.1. She added a slide listing the benefits of using Lakeside Event Center and made a few additional changes. You will continue modifying this presentation.

To open the revised presentation:

1. Click the **File** tab on the ribbon to display Backstage view. Because there is no open presentation, the Open screen is displayed. Recent is selected, and you might see a list of the 25 most recently opened presentations on the right.

   Trouble? If PowerPoint is not running, start PowerPoint, and then in the navigation bar on the Recent screen, click the Open Other Presentations link.

   Trouble? If another presentation is open, click Open in the navigation bar in Backstage view.

   Trouble? If you are storing your files on your OneDrive, click OneDrive, and then log in if necessary.

2. Click **Browse**. The Open dialog box appears. It is similar to the Save As dialog box.

3. Navigate to the drive that contains your Data Files, navigate to the **PowerPoint1 > Module** folder, click **Revised** to select it, and then click the **Open** button. The Open dialog box closes and the Revised presentation opens in the PowerPoint window, with Slide 1 displayed.

   Trouble? If you don't have the starting Data Files, you need to get them before you can proceed. Your instructor will either give you the Data Files or ask you to obtain them from a specified location (such as a network drive). If you have any questions about the Data Files, see your instructor or technical support person for assistance.

If you want to edit a presentation without changing the original, you need to create a copy of it. To do this, you use the Save As command to open the Save As dialog box, which is the same dialog box you saw when you saved your presentation for the first time. When you save a presentation with a new name, a copy of the original presentation is created, the original presentation is closed, and the newly named copy remains open in the PowerPoint window.

To save the Revised presentation with a new name:

1. Click the **File** tab, and then in the navigation bar, click **Save As**. The Save As screen in Backstage view appears.

2. Click **Browse** to open the Save As dialog box.

  3. If necessary, navigate to the drive and folder where you are storing your Data Files.

  4. In the File name box, change the filename to **Convention Final**, and then click the **Save** button. The Save As dialog box closes, a copy of the file is saved with the new name Convention Final, and the Convention Final presentation appears in the PowerPoint window.

Changing the Theme and the Theme Variant

A **theme** is a coordinated set of colors, fonts, backgrounds, and effects. All presentations have a theme. If you don't choose one, the default Office theme is applied; that is the theme currently applied to the Convention Final presentation.

You saw the Office theme set of colors when you changed the color of the text on the "About Us" slide. You have also seen the Office theme fonts in use on the slides. In the Office theme, the font of the slide titles is Calibri Light, and the font of the text in content text boxes is Calibri. In themes, the font used for slide titles is the Headings font, and the font used for the content text boxes is the Body font.

In PowerPoint, each theme has several variants with different coordinating colors and sometimes slightly different backgrounds. A theme and its variants are called a **theme family**. PowerPoint comes with several installed themes, and many more themes are available online at Office.com. In addition, you can use a custom theme stored on your computer or network.

You can select a different installed theme when you create a new presentation by clicking one of the themes on the New or Recent screen in Backstage view instead of clicking Blank Presentation, and then clicking one of the variants. If you want to change the theme of an open presentation, you can choose an installed theme on the Design tab, or you can apply a theme applied to another presentation or a theme stored on your computer or network. When you change the theme, the colors, fonts, and slide backgrounds change to those used in the new theme.

Caitlin wants the theme of the Convention Final presentation changed to one that has more color in the background. First you'll display Slide 2 so you can see the effect a different theme has on the text formatted with a theme color.

To examine the current theme and then change the theme and theme variant:

  1. Display **Slide 2** ("About Us"), and then, in the unnumbered list select the orange letter **L**.

  2. On the Home tab, in the Font group, click the **Font Color button arrow** [A▾]. Look at the colors under Theme Colors, and note the second to last color is selected in the sixth column, which contains shades of orange. Notice also the row of Standard Colors below the theme colors.

  3. In the Font group, click the **Font arrow**. A menu of fonts installed on the computer opens. At the top under Theme Fonts, Calibri (Body) is selected because the letter L that you selected is in a content text box. See Figure 1-24.

Figure 1-24 Theme fonts on the Font menu

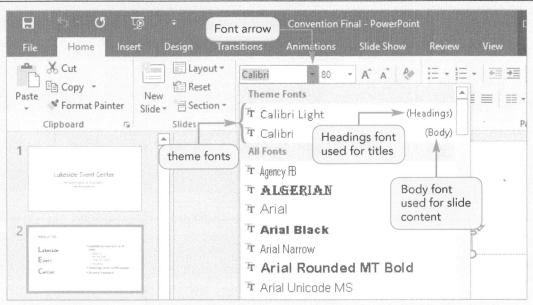

4. On the ribbon, click the **Design** tab. The Font menu closes and the installed themes appear in the Themes gallery on the Design tab. See Figure 1-25. The current theme is the first theme listed in the Themes group on the Design tab. The next theme is the Office theme, which, in this case, is also the current theme.

Figure 1-25 Themes and variants on the Design tab

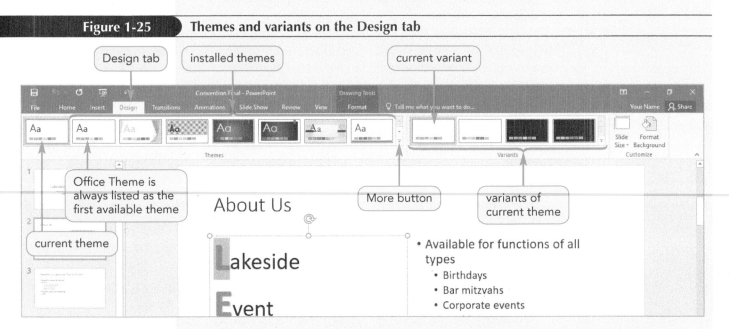

To see all of the installed themes, you need to scroll through the gallery by clicking the up and down scroll buttons on the right end of the gallery or clicking the More button to expand the gallery to see all of the themes at once. The **More button** appears on all galleries that contain additional items or commands that don't fit in the group on the ribbon.

5. In the Themes group, click the **More** button [▼]. The gallery of themes opens. See Figure 1-26. When the gallery is open, the theme applied to the current presentation appears in the first row. In the next row, the first theme is the Office theme, and then the rest of the installed themes appear. Some of these themes also appear on the Recent and New screens in Backstage view.

Figure 1-26   **Themes gallery expanded**

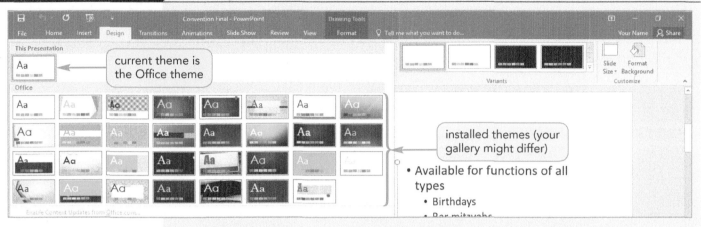

TIP

If the content of a slide is no longer positioned correctly or changes size when you apply a different theme, click the Reset button in the Slides group on the Home tab.

6. Point to several of the themes in the gallery to display their ScreenTips and to see a Live Preview of the theme applied to the current slide.

7. In the first row of the Office section of the gallery, click the **Facet** theme. The gallery closes, and the Facet theme is applied to all the slides with the default variant (the first variant in the Variants group). The title text on each slide changes from black to green, the letters that you had colored orange on Slide 2 are dark green, the bullet symbols change from black circles to green triangles, and in the Slides pane, you can see on the Slide 6 thumbnail that the SmartArt shapes are now green as well.

8. In the Variants group, point to the other three variants to see a Live Preview of each of them, and then click the **second variant** (the blue one).

   Trouble? If there are no variants, your installation of Office might have an extra version of the Facet theme installed. In the Themes group, click the More button, and then make sure you click the Facet theme in the first row.

9. Click the **Home** tab, and then in the Font group, click the **Font Color button arrow** $\boxed{A}$. The selected color—the color of the selected letter "L"—is now a shade of blue in the Theme Colors of the Facet theme. Notice also that the row of Standard Colors is the same as it was when the Office theme was applied.

10. In the Font group, click the **Font arrow**. You can see that the Theme Fonts are now Trebuchet MS for both Headings (slide titles) and the Body (content text boxes).

11. Press the **Esc** key. The Font menu closes.

After you apply a new theme, you should examine your slides to make sure that they look the way you expect them to. The font sizes used for the text in lists in the Facet theme are considerably smaller than those used in the Office theme. You know that Caitlin wants the slides to be legible and clearly visible, so you will increase the font sizes on some of the slides. The title slide is fine, but you need to examine the rest of the slides.

To examine the slides with the new theme and adjust font sizes:

1. On **Slide 2** ("About Us"), in the bulleted list, click the **first bulleted item**. In the Font group, the font size is 18 points, quite a bit smaller than the font size of first-level bulleted items in the Office theme, which is 28 points. You can see that the font size of the subitems is also fairly small.

2. In the bulleted list, click the **text box border** to select the entire text box. In the Font group, 16+ appears in the Font Size box. The smallest font size used in the selected text box—the font size of the subitems—is 16, and the plus sign indicates that there is text in the selected text box larger than 16 points.

3. In the Font group, click the **Increase Font Size** button [A] twice. The font size of the first-level bulleted items changes to 24 points, and the font size of the second-level bulleted items changes to 20 points.

   Trouble? If the Drawing Tools Format tab becomes selected on the ribbon, click the Home tab.

4. Display **Slide 3** ("Benefits of Lakeside Event Center"), click the **bulleted list**, click the **text box border**, and then in the Font group, click the **Increase Font Size** button [A] three times. The font size of the first-level bulleted items changes to 28 points, and the font size of the second-level bulleted items changes to 24 points.

5. On **Slide 4** ("Packages") and **Slide 5** ("Amenities"), increase the size of the text in the bulleted lists so that the font size of the first-level items is 28 points and of the subitems is 24 points.

6. Display **Slides 6, 7, 8,** and then **Slide 1** in the Slide pane. These remaining slides look fine.

7. On the Quick Access Toolbar, click the **Save** button [💾]. The changes to the presentation are saved.

INSIGHT

Understanding the Difference Between Themes and Templates

As explained earlier, a theme is a coordinated set of colors, fonts, backgrounds, and effects. A **template** has a theme applied, but it also contains text, graphics, and placeholders to help direct you in creating content for a presentation. You can create and save your own custom templates or find everything from calendars to marketing templates among the thousands of templates available on Office.com. To find a template on Office.com, display the Recent or New screen in Backstage view, type keywords in the "Search for online templates and themes" box, and then click the Search button in the box to display templates related to the search terms. To create a new presentation based on the template you find, click the template and then click Create.

If a template is stored on your computer, you can apply the theme used in the template to an existing presentation. If you want to apply the theme used in a template on Office.com to an existing presentation, you need to download the template to your computer first, and then you can apply it to an existing presentation.

Working with Photos

Most people are exposed to multimedia daily and expect to have information conveyed visually as well as verbally. In many cases, graphics are more effective than words for communicating an important point. For example, if a sales force has reached its sales goals for the year, including a photo in your presentation of a person reaching the top of a mountain can convey a sense of exhilaration to your audience.

Inserting Photos Stored on Your Computer or Network

Content placeholders contain buttons that you can use to insert things other than a list, including photos stored on your hard drive, a network drive, a USB drive, an SD card from a digital camera, or any other medium to which you have access. You can also use the Pictures button in the Images group on the Insert tab to add photos to slides.

Caitlin has photos that she wants inserted on three of the slides in the presentation. She asks you to add the photos to the presentation.

To insert photos on Slides 3, 5, and 8:

▶ 1. Display **Slide 3** ("Benefits of Lakeside Event Center"), and then in the content placeholder on the right, click the **Pictures** button 🖼. The Insert Picture dialog box opens. This dialog box is similar to the Open dialog box.

▶ 2. Navigate to the **PowerPoint1 > Module** folder included with your Data Files, click **Gazebo**, and then click the **Insert** button. The dialog box closes, and a picture of a gazebo appears in the placeholder and is selected. The contextual Picture Tools Format tab appears on the ribbon to the right of the View tab and is the active tab. See Figure 1-27.

| Figure 1-27 | Picture inserted on Slide 3 |

©iStock.com/bloggityblog

▶ 3. Display **Slide 5** ("Amenities"). This slide uses the Title and Content layout and does not have a second content placeholder. You can change the layout to include a second content placeholder, or you can use a command on the ribbon to insert a photo.

▶ 4. Click the **Insert** tab, and then in the Images group, click the **Pictures** button. The Insert Picture dialog box opens.

5. In the PowerPoint1 > Module folder, click **Tables**, and then click the **Insert** button. The dialog box closes and the picture is added to the slide, covering the bulleted list. You will fix this later.

6. Display **Slide 8** (the last slide). This slide has the Two Content layout applied, but you can still use the Pictures command on the Insert tab.

7. Click the **Insert** tab on the ribbon.

8. In the Images group, click the **Pictures** button, click **Wedding** in the PowerPoint1 > Module folder, and then click the **Insert** button. The picture replaces the content placeholder on the slide.

Cropping Photos

Sometimes you want to display only part of a photo. For example, if you insert a photo of a party scene that includes a bouquet of colorful balloons, you might want to show only the balloons. To do this, you can **crop** the photo—cut out the parts you don't want to include. In PowerPoint, you can crop it manually to any size you want, crop it to a preset ratio, or crop it to a shape.

Caitlin wants you to crop the photo on Slide 5 ("Amenities") to make the dimensions of the final photo smaller without making the images in the photo smaller. She also wants you to crop the photo on Slide 8 (the last slide) to an interesting shape.

To crop the photos on Slides 5 and 8:

1. Display **Slide 5** ("Amenities"), click the **photo** to select it, and then click the **Picture Tools Format** tab, if necessary.

2. In the Size group, click the **Crop** button. The Crop button is selected, and crop handles appear around the edges of the photo just inside the sizing handles. See Figure 1-28.

Figure 1-28 **Photo with crop handles**

©iStock.com/kai zhang; ©iStock.com/bloggityblog

---

3. Position the pointer directly on top of the right-middle crop handle so that it changes to ⊦, press and hold the mouse button, and then drag the crop handle to the left approximately two inches. See Figure 1-29.

Figure 1-29 Cropped photo

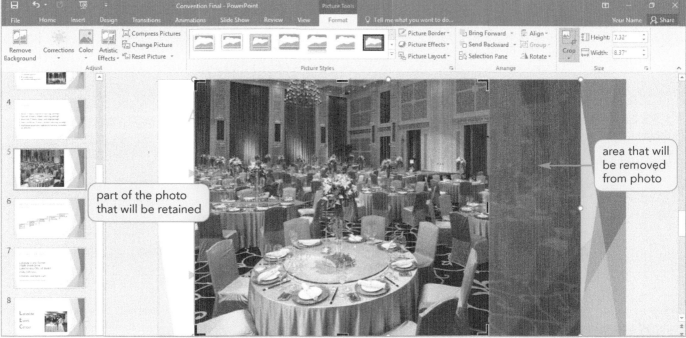

©iStock.com/kai zhang; ©iStock.com/bloggityblog; Courtesy of Dina White

4. Click the **Crop** button again. The Crop feature is turned off, but the photo is still selected and the Format tab is still the active tab.

5. Display **Slide 8** (the last slide), click the **photo** to select it, and then click the **Picture Tools Format** tab, if necessary.

6. In the Size group, click the **Crop button arrow**. The Crop button menu opens. See Figure 1-30.

Figure 1-30 Crop button menu

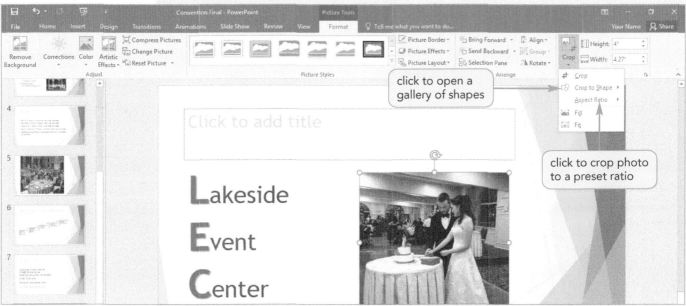

Courtesy of Dina White; ©iStock.com/kai zhang; ©iStock.com/bloggityblog

▶ **7.** Point to **Crop to Shape** to open a gallery of shapes, and then in the second row under Basic Shapes, click the **Plaque** shape. The photo is cropped to a plaque shape. Notice that the rectangular selection border of the original photo is still showing.

▶ **8.** In the Size group, click the **Crop** button. You can now see the cropped portions of the original, rectangle photo that are shaded gray.

▶ **9.** Click a blank area of the slide. The picture is no longer selected, and the Home tab is the active tab on the ribbon.

Modifying Photo Compression Options

When you save a presentation that contains photos, PowerPoint automatically compresses the photos to a resolution of 220 pixels per inch (ppi). (For comparison, photos printed in magazines are typically 300 ppi.) Compressing photos reduces the size of the presentation file, but it also reduces the quality of the photos. See Figure 1-31 for a description of the compression options available. If an option in the dialog box is gray, the photo is a lower resolution than that setting. Note that many monitors and projectors are capable of displaying resolutions only a little higher (98 ppi) than the resolution designated for email (96 ppi).

Figure 1-31   Photo compression settings

Compression Setting	Description
330 ppi	Photos are compressed to 330 pixels per inch; use when slides need to maintain the quality of the photograph when displayed on high-definition (HD) displays. Use when photograph quality is of the highest concern and file size is not an issue.
220 ppi	Photos are compressed to 220 pixels per inch; use when slides need to maintain the quality of the photograph when printed. This is the default setting for PowerPoint presentations. (Note that although this is minimal compression, it is still compressed, and if photograph quality is the most important concern, do not compress photos at all.)
150 ppi	Photos are compressed to 150 pixels per inch; use when the presentation will be viewed on a monitor or screen projector.
96 ppi	Photos are compressed to 96 pixels per inch; use for presentations that need to be emailed or uploaded to a webpage or when it is important to keep the overall file size small.
Document resolution	Photos are compressed to the resolution specified on the Advanced tab in the PowerPoint Options dialog box. The default setting is 220 ppi.
No compression	Photos are not compressed at all; used when it is critical that photos remain at their original resolution.

You can change the compression setting for each photo that you insert, or you can change the settings for all the photos in the presentation. If you cropped photos, you also can discard the cropped areas of the photo to make the presentation file size smaller. (Note that when you crop to a shape, the cropped portions are not discarded.) If you insert additional photos or crop a photo after you apply the new compression settings to all the slides, you will need to apply the new settings to the new photos.

REFERENCE

Modifying Photo Compression Settings and Removing Cropped Areas

- After all photos have been added to the presentation file, click any photo in the presentation to select it.
- Click the Picture Tools Format tab. In the Adjust group, click the Compress Pictures button.
- In the Compress Pictures dialog box, click the option button next to the resolution you want to use.
- To apply the new compression settings to all the photos in the presentation, click the Apply only to this picture check box to deselect it.
- To keep cropped areas of photos, click the Delete cropped areas of pictures check box to deselect it.
- Click the OK button.

You will adjust the compression settings to make the file size of the presentation as small as possible so that Caitlin can easily send it or post it for others without worrying about file size limitations on the receiving server.

To modify photo compression settings and remove cropped areas from photos:

1. On **Slide 8** (the last slide), click the **photo**, and then click the **Picture Tools Format** tab, if necessary.

2. In the Adjust group, click the **Compress Pictures** button. The Compress Pictures dialog box opens. See Figure 1-32. Under Target output, the Use document resolution option button is selected. Other than that option button, only the E-mail (96 ppi) option button is selected. This is because the currently selected photo's resolution is higher than 96 ppi but lower than the next largest photo size, Web (150 ppi).

Figure 1-32   **Compress Pictures dialog box**

3. Click the **E-mail (96 ppi)** option button. This setting compresses the photos to the smallest possible size. At the top of the dialog box under Compression options, the Delete cropped areas of pictures check box is already selected. This option is not applied to cropped photos until you open this dialog box and then click the OK button to apply it. Because you want the presentation file size to be as small as possible, you do want cropped portions of photos to be deleted, so you'll leave this selected. The Apply only to this picture check box is also selected; however, you want the settings applied to all the photos in the file.

Be sure you deselect the Apply only to this picture check box, and be sure you are satisfied with the way you cropped the photo on Slide 5 before you click OK to close the dialog box.

4. Click the **Apply only to this picture** check box to deselect it.

5. Click the **OK** button.

   The dialog box closes and the compression settings are applied to all the photos in the presentation. You can confirm that the cropped areas of photos were removed by examining the photo on Slide 5. (The photo on Slide 8 was cropped to a shape, so the cropped areas on it were not removed.)

6. Display **Slide 5** ("Amenities"), click the **photo**, and then click the **Picture Tools Format** tab, if necessary.

7. In the Size group, click the **Crop** button. The Crop handles appear around the photo, but the portions of the photo that you cropped out no longer appear.

8. Click the **Crop** button again to deselect it, and then save the changes to the presentation.

INSIGHT

Keeping Photos Uncompressed

Suppose you are a photographer and want to create a presentation to show your photos. In that case, you would want to display them at their original, uncompressed resolution. To do this, you need to change a setting in the PowerPoint Options dialog box before you add photos to slides. Click the File tab to open Backstage view, click Options in the navigation bar to open the PowerPoint Options dialog box, click Advanced in the navigation bar, and then locate the Image Size and Quality section. To keep images at their original resolution, click the Do not compress images in file check box to select it. Note that you can also change the default compression setting for photos in this dialog box—you can increase the compression or choose to automatically discard cropped portions of photos and other editing data. Note that these changes affect only the current presentation.

Resizing and Moving Objects

You can resize and move any object to best fit the space available on a slide. One way to resize an object is to drag a sizing handle. **Sizing handles** are the circles that appear in the corners and in the middle of the sides of the border of a selected object. When you use this method, you can adjust the size of the object so it best fits the space visually. If you need to size an object to exact dimensions, you can modify the measurements in the Size group on the Format tab that appears when you select the object.

You can also drag an object to reposition it anywhere on the slide. If more than one object is on a slide, **smart guides**, dashed red lines, appear as you drag to indicate the center and the top and bottom borders of the objects. Smart guides can help you position objects so they are aligned and spaced evenly.

In addition to using the smart guides, it can be helpful to display rulers and gridlines in the window. The rulers appear along the top and left sides of the displayed slide. Gridlines are one-inch squares made up of dots one-sixth of an inch apart. As you drag an object, it snaps to the grid, even if the grid is not visible.

Resizing and Moving Pictures

Pictures and other objects that cause the Picture Tools Format tab to appear when selected have their aspect ratios locked by default. The **aspect ratio** is the ratio of the object's height to its width. When the aspect ratio is locked, if you resize the photo by dragging a corner sizing handle or if you change one dimension in the Size group on the Picture Tools Format tab, the other dimension will change by the same percentage. However, if you drag one of the sizing handles in the middle of an object's border, you will override the locked aspect ratio setting and resize the object only in the direction you drag. Generally you do not want to do this with photos because the images will become distorted.

You need to resize and move the photos you inserted on Slides 3, 5, and 8 so the slides are more attractive. You'll display the rulers and gridlines to help you as you do this.

To move and resize the photos on Slides 3, 5, and 8:

1. Click the **View** tab, and then in the Show group, click the **Ruler** and the **Gridlines** check boxes. Rulers appear above and to the left of the displayed slide, and the gridlines appear on the slide.

2. On **Slide 5** ("Amenities"), click the **photo**, if necessary, and then position the pointer on the top-middle sizing handle so that the pointer changes to ↕.

3. Press and hold the mouse button so that the pointer changes to ╋, drag the top-middle sizing handle down approximately two inches, and then release the mouse button. The photo is two inches shorter, but the image is distorted.

4. On the Quick Access Toolbar, click the **Undo** button ↺. You need to resize the photo by dragging a corner sizing handle to maintain the aspect ratio.

5. Click the **Picture Tools Format** tab, and then note the measurements in the Size group. The photo is 7.32 inches high and about 8.4 inches wide. (The exact width on your screen might differ depending on how much you cropped.)

6. Position the pointer on the bottom-left corner sizing handle so that it changes to ⤢, press and hold the mouse button so that the pointer changes to ╋, and then drag the bottom-left sizing handle up. Even though you are dragging in only one direction, because you are dragging a corner sizing handle, both the width and height are changing proportionately to maintain the aspect ratio.

7. When the photo is approximately 4.5 inches high and approximately 5 inches wide, release the mouse button. Note that the measurements in the Height and Width boxes changed to reflect the picture's new size.

8. Drag the photo to the right so that the right edge of the photo aligns with the 6-inch mark on the horizontal ruler above the slide, and drag it down so that smart guides appear indicating that the bottom and top of the photo is aligned with the bottom and top of the text box that contains the unnumbered list as shown in Figure 1-33.

TIP

If you don't want objects you are moving to snap to the grid, press and hold the Alt key while you are dragging.

Figure 1-33   **Repositioning photo on Slide 5 using smart guides and gridlines**

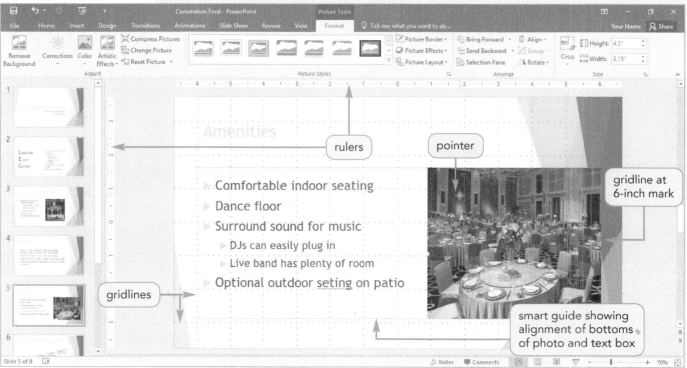

©iStock.com/kai zhang; ©iStock.com/bloggityblog

9. Release the mouse button. The photo is repositioned.

10. Display **Slide 3** ("Benefits of Lakeside Event Center"), click the **photo** to select it, and then click the **Picture Tools Format** tab if necessary.

11. In the Size group, click in the **Height** box to select the current measurement, type **4.5**, and then press the **Enter** key. The measurement in the Width box in the Size group changes proportionately to maintain the aspect ratio, and the new measurements are applied to the photo.

12. Drag the photo up and to the right until horizontal smart guides appear above and below the photo indicating that the top and bottom of the photo and the top and bottom of the text box containing the bulleted list are aligned, and so that the right edge of the photo aligns with the right edge of the title text box (at the 3.5-inch mark on the ruler), as shown in Figure 1-34.

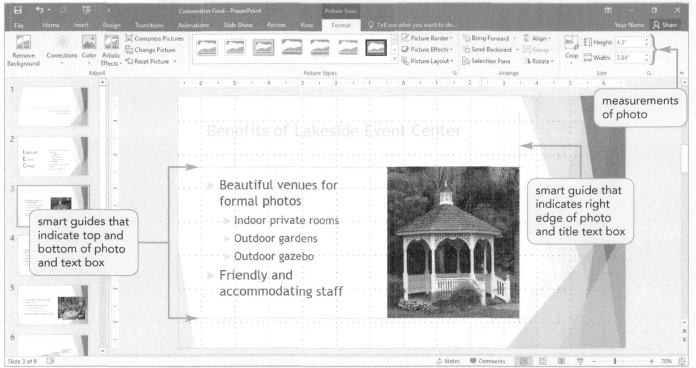

Figure 1-34   Moving resized photo on Slide 3

©iStock.com/bloggityblog; ©iStock.com/kai zhang

13. When the photo is aligned as shown in Figure 1-34, release the mouse button.

14. Display **Slide 8** (the last slide), resize the photo so it is 5.9 inches high and 6.3 inches wide, and then position it so that its bottom edge is aligned with the gridline at the 3-inch mark on the vertical ruler, and its right edge is aligned with the gridline at the 6-inch mark on the horizontal ruler.

15. Click the **View** tab, and then click the **Ruler** and **Gridlines** check boxes to deselect them.

Resizing and Moving Text Boxes

The themes and layouts installed with PowerPoint are designed by professionals, so much of the time it's a good idea to use the layouts as provided to be assured of a cohesive look among the slides. However, occasionally there will be a compelling reason to adjust the layout of objects on a slide, by either resizing or repositioning them.

Text boxes, like other objects that cause the Drawing Tools Format tab to appear when selected, do not have their aspect ratios locked by default. This means that when you resize a text box by dragging a corner sizing handle or changing one dimension in the Size group, the other dimension is not affected.

Like any other object on a slide, you can reposition text boxes. To do this, you must position the pointer on the text box border, anywhere except on a sizing handle, to drag it to its new location.

To improve the appearance of Slide 8, you will resize the text box containing the unnumbered list so it vertically fills the slide.

To resize the text box on Slide 8 and increase the font size:

1. On **Slide 8** (the last slide in the presentation), click the unnumbered list to display the text box border.

2. Position the pointer on the top-middle sizing handle so that it changes to ⇕, and then drag the sizing handle up until the top edge of the text box is aligned with the top edge of the title text placeholder.

3. Drag the right-middle sizing handle to the right until the right edge of the text box is aligned with the left edge of the photo.

4. Click the **Home** tab, and then in the Font group, click the **Increase Font Size** button Ａ three times. Even though the title text placeholder will not appear during a slide show, you will delete it to see how the final slide will look.

5. Click the **title text placeholder border**, and then press the **Delete** key. See Figure 1-35.

Figure 1-35	Slide 8 with resized text box

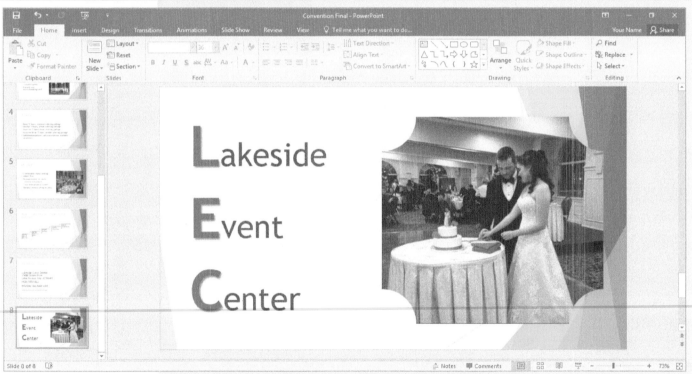

Courtesy of Dina White; ©iStock.com/bloggityblog; ©iStock.com/kai zhang

6. Save the changes to the presentation.

Adding Speaker Notes

Speaker notes, or simply **notes**, are information you add about slide content to help you remember to bring up specific points during the presentation. Speaker notes should not contain all the information you plan to say during your presentation, but they can be a useful tool for reminding you about facts and details related to the content on specific slides. You add notes in the **Notes pane**, which you can display below the displayed slide in Normal view, or you can switch to **Notes Page view**, in which an image of the slide appears in the top half of the presentation window and the notes for that slide appear in the bottom half.

To add notes to Slides 3 and 7:

1. Display **Slide 7** ("For More Information"), and then, on the status bar, click the **Notes** button. The Notes pane appears below Slide 7 with "Click to add notes" as placeholder text. See Figure 1-36.

Figure 1-36   Notes pane below Slide 7

Courtesy of Dina White

2. Click in the **Notes** pane. The placeholder text disappears, and the insertion point is in the Notes pane.

3. Type **Hand out contact information to audience. Use the link to demonstrate how to use the website**.

4. Display **Slide 3** ("Benefits of Lakeside Event Center"), click in the **Notes** pane, and then type **Explain the benefits of choosing Lakeside Event Center over other function halls**.

5. Click the **View** tab on the ribbon, and then in the Presentation Views group, click the **Notes Page** button. Slide 3 is displayed in Notes Page view. See Figure 1-37.

Figure 1-37   Slide 3 in Notes Page view

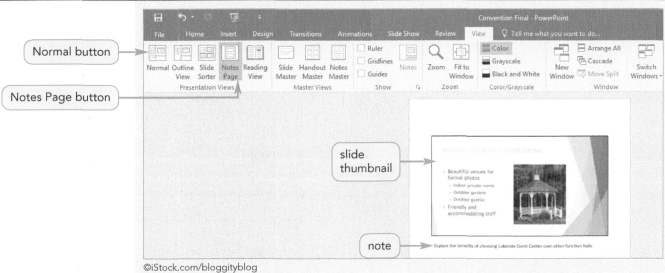

©iStock.com/bloggityblog

TIP

Use the Zoom in button on the status bar to magnify the text to make it easier to edit the note.

6. In the note, click after the period at the end of the sentence, press the **spacebar**, and then type **Emphasize both cost benefits and scenic photo opportunities**.

7. In the Presentation Views group, click the **Normal** button to return to Normal view. The Notes pane stays displayed until you close it again.

8. On the status bar, click the **Notes** button to close the Notes pane, and then save the changes to the presentation.

Checking Spelling

TIP

You can click the Thesaurus button in the Proofing group on the Review tab to look up synonyms of a selected word, or you can click the Smart Lookup button in the Insights group to open the Insights task pane listing search results from the web.

You should always check the spelling and grammar in your presentation before you finalize it. To make this task easier, you can use PowerPoint's spelling checker. You can quickly tell if there are words on slides that are not in the built-in dictionary by looking at the Spelling button at the left end of the status bar. If there are no words flagged as possibly misspelled, the button is 🗹; if there are flagged words, the button changes to 🗷. To indicate that a word might be misspelled, a wavy red line appears under it.

To correct misspelled words, you can right-click a flagged word to see a list of suggested spellings on the shortcut menu, or you can check the spelling of all the words in the presentation. To check the spelling of all the words in the presentation, you click the Spelling button in the Proofing group on the Review tab. This opens the Spelling task pane to the right of the displayed slide and starts the spell check from the current slide. A **task pane** is a pane that opens to the right or left of the displayed slide and contains commands and options related to the task you are doing. When a possible misspelled word is found, suggestions are displayed for the correct spelling. Synonyms for the selected correct spelling are also listed.

To check the spelling of words in the presentation:

1. Display **Slide 4** ("Packages"), and then right-click the misspelled word **Delux** in the fourth item in the list. A shortcut menu opens listing spelling options. See Figure 1-38.

Figure 1-38   **Shortcut menu for a misspelled word**

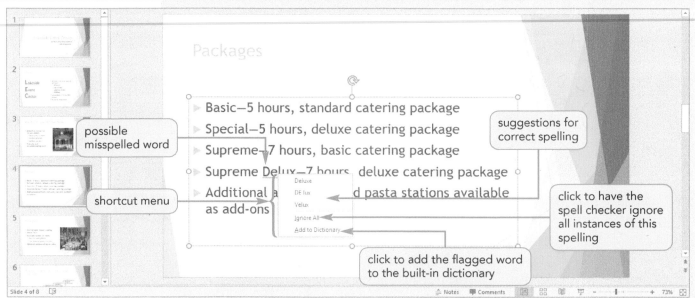

©iStock.com/bloggityblog; ©iStock.com/kai zhang

2. On the shortcut menu, click **Deluxe**. The menu closes and the spelling is corrected.

3. Click the **Review** tab, and then in the Proofing group, click the **Spelling** button. The Spelling task pane opens to the right of the displayed slide, and the next possible misspelled word on Slide 5 ("Amenities") appears with the flagged word, "seting," highlighted. See Figure 1-39. In the Spelling task pane, the first suggested correct spelling is selected. The selected correct spelling also appears at the bottom of the task pane with synonyms for the word listed below it and a speaker icon next to it.

Figure 1-39	Spelling task pane displaying a misspelled word

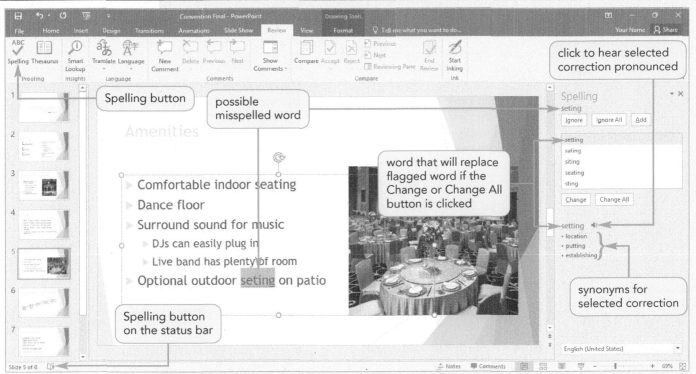

©iStock.com/kai zhang; ©iStock.com/bloggityblog

4. In the Spelling task pane, click the **speaker** icon 🔊. A male voice says the word "setting."

5. In the list of suggested corrections, click **sting**. The word at the bottom of the task pane changes to "sting," and the synonyms change also.

6. In the list of suggested corrections, click **setting**, and then click the **Change** button. The word is corrected, and the next slide containing a possible misspelled word, Slide 1, appears with the flagged word, "Keough," highlighted and listed in the Spelling task pane. This is part of Caitlin's last name so you want the spell checker to ignore this.

7. In the task pane, click the **Ignore All** button. Because that was the last flagged word in the presentation, the Spelling task pane closes, and a dialog box opens telling you that the spell check is complete.

   Trouble? If the spell checker finds any other misspelled words, correct them.

8. Click the **OK** button. The dialog box closes. The last flagged word, "Keough," is still selected on Slide 1.

9. Click a blank area of the slide to deselect the text, and then save the changes to the presentation.

Running a Slide Show

After you have created and proofed your presentation, you should view it as a slide show to see how it will appear to your audience. There are several ways to do this—Slide Show view, Presenter view, and Reading view.

Using Slide Show View and Presenter View

You can use Slide Show view if your computer has only one monitor and you don't have access to a screen projector. If your computer is connected to a second monitor or a screen projector, Slide Show view is the way an audience will see your slides. Refer to the Session 1.2 Visual Overview for more information about Slide Show view.

Caitlin asks you to review the slide show in Slide Show view to make sure the slides look professional.

To use Slide Show view to view the Convention Final presentation:

TIP

To start the slide show from the current slide, click the Slide Show button on the status bar.

1. On the Quick Access Toolbar, click the **Start From Beginning** button. Slide 1 appears on the screen in Slide Show view. Now you need to advance the slide show.

2. Press the **spacebar**. Slide 2 ("About Us") appears on the screen.

3. Click the mouse button. The next slide, Slide 3 ("Benefits of Lakeside Event Center"), appears on the screen.

4. Press the **Backspace** key. The previous slide, Slide 2, appears again.

5. Press the **7** key, and then press the **Enter** key. Slide 7 ("For More Information") appears on the screen.

6. Move the mouse to display the pointer, and then position the pointer on the website address **www.lec.example.com**. The pointer changes to 🖑 to indicate that this is a link, and the ScreenTip that appears shows the full website address including "http://". If this were a real website, you could click the link to open your web browser and display the website to your audience. Because you moved the pointer, a very faint row of buttons appears in the lower-left corner. The buttons provide access to commands you need in order to run the slide show. See Figure 1-40.

Figure 1-40	Link and row of buttons in Slide Show view

(928) 555-HALL

info@lec.example.com

www.lec.example.com

http://www.lec.example.com/

pointer on a link in Slide Show view

ScreenTip identifying the link

row of buttons that appears when you move the pointer

7. Move the pointer again, if necessary, to display the buttons that appear in the lower-left corner of the screen, and then click the **Return to the previous slide** button ⊙ four times to return to Slide 3 ("Benefits of Lakeside Event Center").

   Trouble? If you can't see the buttons at the bottom of the screen, move the pointer to the lower-left corner so it is on top of the first button to darken that button, and then move the pointer to the right to see the rest of the buttons.

8. Display the buttons at the bottom of the screen again, and then click the **Zoom into the slide** button ⊙. The pointer changes to ⊕, and three-quarters of the slide is darkened. See Figure 1-41.

Figure 1-41	Zoom feature activated in Slide Show view

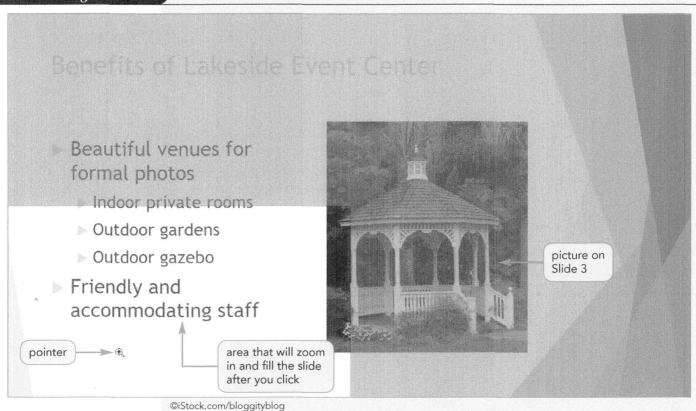

Benefits of Lakeside Event Center

▶ Beautiful venues for formal photos
   ▶ Indoor private rooms
   ▶ Outdoor gardens
   ▶ Outdoor gazebo
▶ Friendly and accommodating staff

picture on Slide 3

pointer ⟶ ⊕

area that will zoom in and fill the slide after you click

©iStock.com/bloggityblog

9. Move the pointer to the picture, and then click the **picture**. The view zooms so that the part of the slide inside the bright rectangle fills the screen, and the pointer changes to ⬦.

10. Press and hold the mouse button to change the pointer to ⬦, and then drag to the right to pull another part of the zoomed in slide into view.

11. Press the **Esc** key to zoom back out to see the whole slide.

Presenter view provides additional tools for running a slide show. In addition to seeing the current slide, you can also see the next slide, speaker notes, and a timer showing you how long the slide show has been running. Refer to the Session 1.2 Visual Overview for more information about Presenter view. Because of the additional tools available in Presenter view, you should consider using it if your computer is connected to a second monitor or projector.

If your computer is connected to a projector or second monitor, and you start a slide show in Slide Show view, Presenter view starts on the computer and Slide Show view appears on the second monitor or projection screen. If, for some reason, you don't want to use Presenter view in that circumstance, you can switch to Slide Show view. If you want to practice using Presenter view when your computer is not connected to a second monitor or projector, you can switch to Presenter view from Slide Show view.

Caitlin wants you to switch to Presenter view and familiarize yourself with the tools available there.

To use Presenter view to review the slide show:

1. Move the pointer to display the buttons in the lower-left corner of the screen, click the **More slide show options** button ⬦ to open a menu of commands, and then click **Show Presenter View**. The screen changes to show the presentation in Presenter view.

2. Below the current slide, click the **See all slides** button ⬦. The screen changes to show thumbnails of all the slides in the presentation, similar to Slide Sorter view.

3. Click the **Slide 4** thumbnail. Presenter view reappears, displaying Slide 4 ("Packages") as the current slide.

4. Click anywhere on Slide 4. The slide show advances to display Slide 5 ("Amenities").

5. At the bottom of the screen, click the **Advance to the next slide** button ⬦. Slide 6 ("Reserve Lakeside Event Center for Your Function!") appears.

6. Press the **spacebar** twice. The slide show advances again to display Slides 7 and then 8.

7. Press the **spacebar** again. A black slide appears displaying the text "End of slide show, click to exit."

8. Press the **spacebar** once more. Presentation view closes, and you return to Normal view.

PROSKILLS

Decision Making: Displaying a Blank Slide During a Presentation

Sometimes during a presentation, the audience has questions about the material and you want to pause the slide show to respond. Or you might want to refocus the audience's attention on you instead of on the visuals on the screen. In these cases, you can display a blank slide (either black or white). When you do this, the audience, with nothing else to look at, will shift all of their attention to you. Some presenters plan to use blank slides and insert them at specific points during their slide shows. Planning to use a blank slide can help you keep your presentation focused and remind you that the purpose of the PowerPoint slides is to provide visual aids to enhance your presentation; the slides themselves are not the presentation.

If you did not create blank slides in your presentation file, but during your presentation you feel you need to display a blank slide, you can easily do this in Slide Show or Presenter view by pressing the B key to display a blank black slide or the W key to display a blank white slide. You can also click the More button—⊙ in Slide Show view, ⬤ in Presenter view—or right-click the screen, point to Screen on the menu, and then click Black Screen or White Screen. To remove the black or white slide and redisplay the slide that had been on the screen before you displayed the blank slide, press any key on the keyboard or click anywhere on the screen. In Presenter view, you can also use the Black or unblack slide show button ◪ to toggle a blank slide on or off.

An alternative to redisplaying the slide that had been displayed prior to the blank slide is to click the Advance to the next slide button ⊙. This can be more effective than redisplaying the slide that was onscreen before the blank slide because, after you have grabbed the audience's attention and prepared them to move on, you won't lose their focus by displaying a slide they have already seen.

Using Reading View

Reading view displays the slides so that they almost fill the screen, similar to Slide Show view; however, in Reading view, a status bar appears, identifying the number of the current slide and providing buttons to advance the slide show. You can also resize the window in Reading view to allow you to work in another window on the desktop.

To use Reading view to review the presentation:

▶ 1. Display **Slide 2** ("About Us"), and then on the status bar, click the **Reading View** button ▦. The presentation changes to Reading view with Slide 2 displayed. See Figure 1-42.

Figure 1-42   **Slide 2 in Reading view**

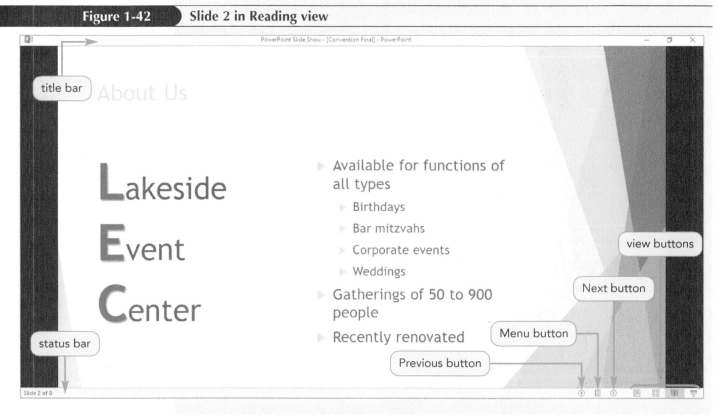

2. On the status bar, click the **Menu** button 🗒. A menu appears with commands for working in Reading view, some of which are also available in Slide Show and Presenter views.

3. Click **Full Screen**. The presentation switches to Slide Show view displaying the current slide, Slide 2.

4. Press the **Esc** key. Slide Show view closes, and you return to Reading view.

5. On the status bar, click the **Next** button ⊙. The next slide, Slide 3 ("Benefits of Lakeside Event Center"), appears on the screen.

6. On the status bar, click the **Normal** button 🗔 to return to Normal view with Slide 1 displayed in the Slide pane.

Printing a Presentation

Before you deliver your presentation, you might want to print it. PowerPoint provides several printing options. For example, you can print the slides in color, grayscale (white and shades of gray), or pure black and white, and you can print one, some, or all of the slides in several formats.

You use the Print screen in Backstage view to set print options such as specifying a printer and color options. First, you will add your name to the title slide.

To add your name to the title slide and choose a printer and color options:

1. Display **Slide 1**, click after Keough-Barton in the subtitle, press the **Enter** key, and then type your full name.

2. Click the **File** tab to display Backstage view, and then click **Print** in the navigation bar. Backstage view changes to display the Print screen. The Print screen contains options for printing your presentation, and a preview of the first slide as it will print with the current options. See Figure 1-43.

Figure 1-43	Print screen in Backstage view

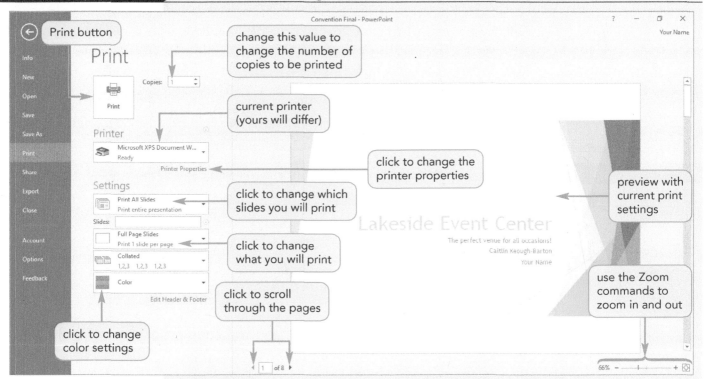

Trouble? If your screen does not match Figure 1-43, click the first button below Settings, and then click Print All Slides, and then click the second button below Settings and then click Full Page Slides.

3. If you are connected to a network or to more than one printer, make sure the printer listed in the Printer box is the one you want to use; if it is not, click the **Printer** button, and then click the correct printer in the list.

4. Click the **Printer Properties** link to open the Properties dialog box for your printer. Usually, the default options are correct, but you can change any printer settings, such as print quality or the paper source, in this dialog box.

5. Click the **Cancel** button to close the Properties dialog box. Now you can choose whether to print the presentation in color, black and white, or grayscale. If you plan to print in black and white or grayscale, you should change this setting so you can see what your slides will look like without color and to make sure they are legible.

6. Click the **Color** button, and then click **Grayscale**. The preview changes to grayscale.

7. At the bottom of the preview pane, click the **Next Page** button ▶ twice to display Slide 3 ("Benefits of Lakeside Event Center"). The slides are legible in grayscale.

8. If you will be printing in color, click the **Grayscale** button, and then click **Color**.

In the Settings section on the Print screen, you can click the Full Page Slides button to choose from among several choices for printing the presentation, as described below:

- **Full Page Slides**—Prints each slide full size on a separate piece of paper.
- **Notes Pages**—Prints each slide as a notes page.
- **Outline**—Prints the text of the presentation as an outline.
- **Handouts**—Prints the presentation with one or more slides on each piece of paper. When printing four, six, or nine slides, you can choose whether to order the slides from left to right in rows (horizontally) or from top to bottom in columns (vertically).

Caitlin wants you to print the slides as a one-page handout, with all eight slides on a single sheet of paper.

To print the slides as a handout:

1. In the Settings section, click the **Full Page Slides** button. A menu opens listing the various ways you can print the slides. See Figure 1-44.

Figure 1-44   **Print screen in Backstage view with print options menu open**

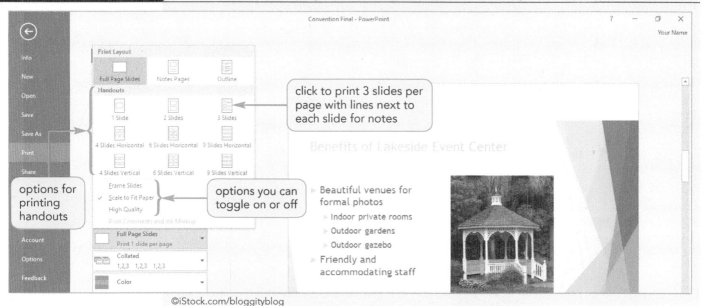

©iStock.com/bloggityblog

2. In the Handouts section, click **9 Slides Horizontal**. The preview changes to show all eight slides in the preview pane, arranged in order horizontally, that is, in three rows from left to right. The current date appears in the top-right corner, and a page number appears in the bottom-right corner.

3. At the top of the Print section, click the **Print** button. Backstage view closes and the handout prints.

Next, Caitlin wants you to print the title slide as a full-page slide so that she can use it as a cover page for her handouts.

To print the title slide as a full-page slide:

1. Click the **File** tab, and then click **Print** in the navigation bar. The Print screen appears in Backstage view. The preview still shows all eight slides on one page. "9 Slides Horizontal" appears on the second button in the Settings section because that was the last printing option you chose.

2. In the Settings section, click **9 Slides Horizontal**, and then click **Full Page Slides**. Slide 1 (the title slide) appears as the preview. Below the preview of Slide 1, it indicates that you are viewing Slide 1 of eight slides to print.

3. In the Settings section, click the **Print All Slides** button. Note on the menu that opens that you can print all the slides, selected slides, the current slide, or a custom range. You want to print just the title slide as a full-page slide.

4. Click **Print Current Slide**. Slide 1 appears in the preview pane, and at the bottom, it now indicates that you will print only one slide.

5. Click the **Print** button. Backstage view closes and Slide 1 prints.

Recall that you created speaker notes on Slides 3 and 7. Caitlin would like you to print these slides as notes pages.

To print the nonsequential slides containing speaker notes:

1. Open the Print screen in Backstage view again, and then click the **Full Page Slides** button. The menu opens.

2. In the Print Layout section of the menu, click **Notes Pages**. The menu closes, and the preview displays Slide 1 as a Notes Page.

3. In the Settings section, click in the **Slides** box, type **3,7** and then click a blank area of the Print screen.

4. Scroll through the preview to confirm that Slides 3 ("Benefits of Lakeside Event Center") and 7 ("For More Information") will print, and then click the **Print** button. Backstage view closes, and Slides 3 and 7 print as notes pages.

Finally, Caitlin would like you to print the outline of the presentation. Recall that Slide 8 is designed to be a visual Caitlin can leave displayed at the end of the presentation, so you don't need to include it in the outline.

To print Slides 1 through 7 as an outline:

1. Open the Print tab in Backstage view, click the **Notes Pages** button, and then in the Print Layout section, click **Outline**. The text on Slides 3 and 7 appears as an outline in the preview pane.

2. Click in the **Slides** box, type **1-7** and then click a blank area of the Print screen. See Figure 1-45.

Figure 1-45   **Print screen in Backstage view with Slides 1–7 previewed as an outline**

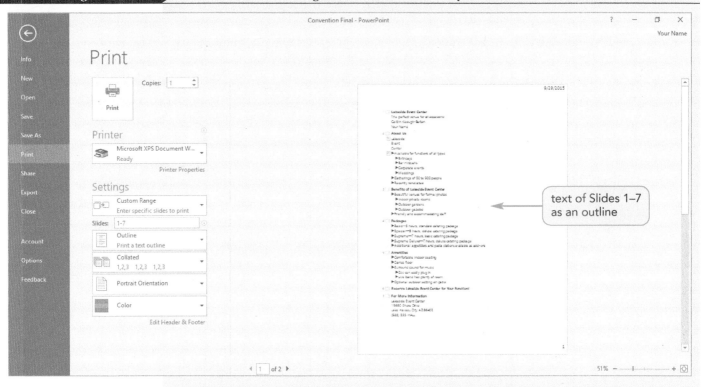

3. At the top of the Print section, click the **Print** button. Backstage view closes, and the text of Slides 1–7 prints on two sheets of paper.

Exiting PowerPoint

When you are finished working with your presentation, you can exit PowerPoint. If there is only one presentation open, you click the Close button ⊠ in the upper-right corner of the program window to exit the program. If more than one presentation is open, clicking this button will only close the current presentation; to exit PowerPoint, you need to click the Close button in each of the open presentation's windows.

To exit PowerPoint:

1. In the upper-right corner of the program window, click the **Close** button ⊠. A dialog box opens, asking if you want to save your changes. This is because you did not save the file after you added your name to the title slide.

2. In the dialog box, click the **Save** button. The dialog box closes, the changes are saved, and PowerPoint exits.

   Trouble? If any other PowerPoint presentations are still open, click the Close button ⊠ on each open presentation's program window until no more presentations are open to exit PowerPoint.

In this session, you opened an existing presentation and saved it with a new name, changed the theme, added and cropped photos and adjusted the photo compression, and resized and moved objects. You have also added speaker notes and checked the spelling. Finally, you printed the presentation in several forms and exited PowerPoint. Your work will help Caitlin give an effective presentation to potential clients of Lakeside Event Center.

REVIEW

Session 1.2 Quick Check

1. Explain what a theme is and what changes with each variant.
2. Describe what happens when you crop photos.
3. Describe sizing handles.
4. Describe smart guides.
5. Why is it important to maintain the aspect ratio of photos?
6. What is the difference between Slide Show view and Presenter view?
7. List the four formats for printing a presentation.

Review Assignments

Data Files needed for the Review Assignments: DJ.jpg, Musicians.jpg, Photog.jpg, Vendor2.pptx

In addition to booking new clients, Caitlin Keough-Barton, the event manager at Lakeside Event Center, maintains a preferred vendors list for providing additional services of entertainment, music, photography, and so on that clients might want. If clients who book the hall use a preferred vendor, they receive a discount on the price of the vendor's services. Caitlin wants to create a presentation that she can use when she meets with new vendors to describe their responsibilities to both the function hall and to the clients. She asks you to begin creating the presentation.

1. Start PowerPoint and create a new, blank presentation. On the title slide, type **Information for Vendors** as the title, and then type your name as the subtitle. Save the presentation as **Vendor Info** to the drive and folder where you are storing your files.

2. Edit the slide title by adding **Lakeside Event Center** before the word "Vendors."

3. Add a new Slide 2 with the Title and Content layout, type **Types of Vendors We Partner With** as the slide title, and then in the content placeholder type the following:
   - Photographers
   - Videographers
   - Florists
   - Music
     - DJs
     - Bands

4. Create a new Slide 3 with the Title and Content layout. Add **Requirements for Vendors** as the slide title, and then type the following as a numbered list on the slide:
   1) **Supply advertisement for brochure**
   2) **Pay annual fee by January 15**
   3) **Submit availability schedule for clients**
   4) **Contact Caitlin Keough-Barton**

5. Create a new Slide 4 using the Two Content layout. Add **Questions?** as the slide title.

6. Use the Cut and Paste commands to move the last bulleted item on Slide 3 ("Contact Caitlin Keough-Barton") to the left content placeholder on Slide 4.

7. On Slide 4, remove the bullet symbol from the text you pasted, and then add the following as the next two items in the unnumbered list:
   Email: c.keoughbarton@example.com
   Cell: 602-555-8723

8. Click after "Keough-Barton" in the first item in the list, and then create a new line below it without creating a new item in the list and so that there is no extra space above the new line. On the new line, type **Events Manager**.

9. Remove the hyperlink formatting from the email address.

10. Create a new Slide 5 using the Title and Content layout. Delete the title text placeholder. In the content placeholder, type **Thank You!** as a single item in an unnumbered list. Increase the size of the text "Thank You!" to 96 points, and then change the color of this text to Blue, Accent 1.

11. On Slide 3 ("Requirements for Vendors"), change the numbered list to a SmartArt graphic. Use the Vertical Circle List layout, which is a List type of diagram.

12. Save your changes, and then close the presentation.

13. Open the file **Vendor2**, located in the PowerPoint1 > Review folder included with your Data Files, add your name as the subtitle on the title slide, and then save it as **LEC Vendor Information** to the drive and folder where you are storing your files.

14. Change the theme to Basis and choose the third variant. On Slide 2, change the size of the text in the bulleted list so that the size of the text of the first-level items is 28 points and the size of the text of the second-level items is 24 points.

15. Change the layout of Slide 4 ("Photographers") to Title and Content, and then duplicate Slide 4. In the title of Slide 5 (the duplicate slide), replace the slide title with **Music Vendors**.

16. On Slide 4, insert the photo **Photog**, located in the PowerPoint1 > Review folder. Resize the photo so it is five inches high, maintaining the aspect ratio, and reposition it so its top and right edges are aligned with the top and right edges of the slide title text box.

17. On Slide 5, change the layout to Two Content, and then in the content placeholder on the left, insert the photo **DJ**. Crop the photo from the right about one-half inch and from the top about one-quarter inch. Resize the cropped photo so it is 2.4 inches high, maintaining the aspect ratio, and then reposition the photo so its left edge is aligned with the left edge of the slide title text box and its middle is aligned with the middle of the content placeholder on the right.

18. On Slide 5, in the content placeholder on the right, insert the photo **Musicians**. Resize it so that it is 2.5 inches tall. Position it so that its right edge is aligned with the right edge of the slide title text box and its middle is aligned with the middle of the photo on the left.

19. Move Slide 5 ("Music Vendors") so it becomes Slide 7.

20. On Slide 9 ("Questions?"), crop the photo to the Oval shape. Increase the size of the text in the unnumbered list to 20 points, and then resize the text box to make it wide enough so that the line containing the email address fits on one line. Remove the hyperlink formatting from the email address.

21. Compress all the photos in the slides to 96 ppi and delete cropped areas of pictures.

22. On Slide 4 ("Photographers"), add **Must be available for the entire event. Should be able to take both formal portraits and candids.** in the Notes pane. On Slide 7 ("Music Vendors"), add **Must be available for the entire time during the event. Should be versatile and be able to play music for all audiences.** as a note on this slide.

23. Delete Slide 3 ("Vendor Requirements") and the last slide (the blank slide).

24. Check the spelling in the presentation. Correct the two spelling errors on Slide 7, ignore all instances of Caitlin's last name, and ignore the flagged instance of "candids" in the Notes pane on Slide 3 ("Photographers"). If you made any additional spelling errors, correct them as well. Save the changes to the presentation.

25. Review the slide show in Slide Show, Presenter, and Reading views.

26. View the slides in grayscale, and then print the following in color or in grayscale depending on your printer: the title slide as a full-page-sized slide; Slides 1–9 as a handout on a single piece of paper with the slides in order horizontally; Slides 3 and 6 as notes pages; and Slides 1–8 as an outline. Save and close the presentation when you are finished.

Case Problem 1

Data Files needed for this Case Problem: After.jpg, Before.jpg, Clients.pptx, Team.jpg, Windows.jpg

Cleaning Essentials Suzanne Yang owns Cleaning Essentials, a home cleaning company in New Rochelle, New York. She markets her company at home shows in Westchester County and in New York City. She asks you to help her create PowerPoint slides that she will use at the home shows. Complete the following steps:

1. Open the presentation named **Clients**, located in the PowerPoint1 > Case1 folder included with your Data Files, and then save it as **New Clients** to the drive and folder where you are storing your files.

2. Insert a new Slide 1 that has the Title Slide layout. Add **Cleaning Essentials** as the presentation title on the title slide. In the subtitle text placeholder, type your name.

APPLY

3. Create a new Slide 2 with the Title and Content layout. Add **What Is Cleaning Essentials?** as the slide title, and **An affordable door-to-door cleaning service designed to make a homeowner's life easier.** as the only item in the content placeholder. Change this to an unnumbered list.

4. Apply the Savon theme, and then apply its second variant. (If the Savon theme is not listed in the Themes gallery, choose any other theme and variant that uses a white or solid color background, places the slide titles at the top of the slides, uses bullet symbols for first-level bulleted items, and positions the content in the bulleted lists so it aligns to the top of the content text box, not the middle.)

5. On Slide 2 ("What Is Cleaning Essentials?"), increase the size of the text in the text box below the slide titles to 28 points.

6. On Slide 3 ("What Services Do We Provide?"), Slide 7 ("Extra Services Offered"), and Slide 9 ("Book Us Now!"), increase the size of the text in the bulleted list so it is 28 points.

7. On Slide 4 ("Why Choose Cleaning Essentials?"), increase the size of the text in the bulleted list so that the first-level items are 24 points.

8. On Slide 2 ("What Is Cleaning Essentials?"), insert the photo **Team**, located in the PowerPoint1 > Case1 folder. Resize the photo, maintaining the aspect ratio, so that it is 3.6 inches wide, and then use the smart guides to position it so that its center is aligned with the center of the text box above it and its bottom is aligned with the bottom border of the text box.

9. On Slide 3 ("What Services Do We Provide?"), add the speaker note **All clients are welcome to request extra services needed to completely clean their homes.**

10. On Slide 6 ("Picture Proof"), change the layout to the Comparison layout, which includes two content placeholders and a small text placeholder above each content placeholder. In the small text placeholder on the left, add **Before**, and then in the small text placeholder on the right, add **After**. Change the font size in both text boxes to 24 points.

11. In the left content placeholder, insert the photo **Before**, and in the right content placeholder, insert the photo **After**.

12. On Slide 5 ("Polish wood floors"), cut the slide title, and then paste it in on Slide 3 ("What Services Do We Provide?") as the fifth bulleted item. If a blank line is added below the pasted text, delete it.

13. On Slide 7 ("Extra Services Offered"), add **Laundry** as a third bulleted item in the list, and then add **Use in-home machines** and **Send out and pick up dry cleaning** as subitems under the "Laundry" first-level item. Change the layout to Two Content.

14. On Slide 7, in the content placeholder, insert the photo **Windows**, located in the PowerPoint1 > Case1 folder. Resize the photo so it is 5 inches high, maintaining the aspect ratio, and then reposition it so that the top of the photo and the top of the title text box are aligned and the right edge of the photo is aligned with the right edge of the title text box.

15. Compress all the photos in the presentation to 96 ppi.

16. On Slide 8 ("Cleaning Visit Options"), add **Once a week** as the second item in the list, and then add **Most popular option** and **Visit is the same day each week** as subitems below "Once a week."

17. On Slide 8, convert the bulleted list to a SmartArt diagram using the Vertical Bullet List layout, which is a List type of diagram. In the Text pane, click before "Still produces a clean and uncluttered home," and then press the Tab key to make it the second subitem under "Once a month."

18. Delete Slide 5 (a blank slide). Move Slide 4 ("Why Choose Cleaning Essentials?") so it becomes Slide 6, and then move Slide 5 ("Extra Services Offered") so it becomes Slide 4.

19. Check the spelling in the presentation and correct all misspelled words.

20. Save the changes to the presentation, view the slide show in Presenter view, and then print the title slide as a full-page slide, print Slides 2–8 as a handout using the 9 Slides Horizontal arrangement, and print Slide 3 as a notes page.

TROUBLESHOOT

Case Problem 2

Data Files needed for this Case Problem: Keyboard.jpg, Music.pptx, Richard.jpg

Dillaire Music Richard Dillaire has owned Dillaire Music in Easton, Pennsylvania, since 1991. He sells, rents, and repairs musical instruments, and he teaches students how to play instruments. He wants to expand his business and attract new students, so he asks you to help him create a presentation. He created slides containing text and a few photos that he wants to include, and he wants you to finish the presentation by inserting additional photos and formatting the presentation. Complete the following steps:

1. Open the file named **Music**, located in the PowerPoint1 > Case2 folder included with your Data Files, and then save it as **Music School** to the drive and folder where you are storing your files. Add your name as the subtitle on Slide 1.

⚙ **Troubleshoot** 2. Review the presentation to identify the two slides that contain information that is repeated on another slide in the presentation, and delete those slides.

3. Display Slide 1 (the title slide), and then apply the Headlines theme to the presentation. Change the variant to the second variant.

⚙ **Troubleshoot** 4. Evaluate the problem that the theme change caused on Slide 1 and fix it.

⚙ **Troubleshoot** 5. Consider how changing the theme affected the readability of the lists on the slides and the size of the photos in the file. Make the appropriate changes to the slides. (*Hint:* On the slides that have pictures of a child playing an instrument on them, the first-level items should not be larger than 24 points.)

6. On Slide 8 ("Contact Info"), in the first item in the bulleted list, move "Easton, PA 18042" to a new line below the street address without creating a new bulleted item.

7. Move Slide 7 ("Lessons") so it becomes Slide 4.

8. On Slide 7 ("How to register online"), change the bulleted list to a numbered list. Add as a new item 2 **Click the green Apply button.**

9. Change the layout of Slide 8 ("Contact Info") to Two Content, and then insert the photo **Richard**, located in the PowerPoint1 > Case2 folder, in the content placeholder. Crop off about one-half inch from the top of the photo, and then increase the size of the picture, maintaining the aspect ratio, so that it is 3 inches wide. Reposition the photo so it is vertically centered below the slide title and bottom aligned with the bottom of the slide title text box.

10. On Slide 1 (the title slide), insert the photo **Keyboard** located in the PowerPoint1 > Case2 folder. Resize the photo so it is 5.25 inches square, and then position it so it is aligned with the right and bottom edges of the slide.

11. Compress all the photos in the presentation to 96 ppi and delete cropped portions of photos.

12. Check the spelling in the presentation, and then save the changes.

13. View the slide show in Presenter view, zooming in on the pictures in the presentation.

14. Print the title slide as a full-page slide in grayscale, and then print the entire presentation as an outline.

CREATE

Case Problem 3

Data Files needed for this Case Problem: Beach.jpg, House1.jpg, House2.jpg, House3.jpg, House4.jpg, House5.jpg, Realty.pptx

Shoreside Realty Karen Bridges owns Shoreside Realty, a real estate company in Scarborough, Maine, that specializes in selling and renting homes in local beach communities. As part of her marketing, she attends local events, such as the farmers' market, weekly summer concerts, and chamber of commerce events, and shows photos of houses near beaches for sale or rent. She created a presentation with slides containing the addresses and brief descriptions of newly listed properties. She asks you to finish the presentation. The completed presentation is shown in Figure 1-46. Refer to Figure 1-46 as you complete the following steps:

| Figure 1-46 | Shoreside Realty presentation |

Shoreside Realty

STUDENT NAME

1

General Information

Office hours:
Mon-Fri 9am-5pm

Appointments can be made outside of office hours

Main office phone:
(207) 555-4586

2

18 Oceanside Road

Only 5 houses away from Higgins Beach

Available for one week rentals June-August

Sleeps 10

3

27 Inner Cove Avenue

Views of Ferry Beach

For Sale: 4 bedroom, 2 bath

4

4 West Beach Road

Walking distance to Scarborough Beach

Available for week rentals June-August and 9 month winter lease September-May

Sleeps up to 14

5

17 Beachside Lane

Near Higgins Beach

For sale: 3 bedroom, 1½ bath

6

31 Island View Road

Charming original cottage near Ferry Beach

For sale: 3 bedroom, 1½ bath

7

To Schedule an Appointment

1. Call Main Office: (207) 555-4586.
2. Ask for Karen Bridges.
3. Specify house and location.
4. Specify date and time of tour.

8

Courtesy of Helen M. Pinard

1. Open the file named **Realty**, located in the PowerPoint1 > Case3 folder included with your Data Files, and then save it as **Shoreside Realty** to the drive and folder where you are storing your files.

2. Add a new slide with the Title Slide layout, and move it so it is Slide 1. Type **Shoreside Realty** as the title and your name as the subtitle.

3. Move Slide 8 ("General Information") so it becomes Slide 2, and then delete Slide 3 ("Newest Homes on the Market").

4. Change the theme to Retrospect, and the variant of the Retrospect theme to the seventh variant. (Note that in this theme, bulleted lists do not have any bullet symbols before each item.)

5. On Slide 2 ("General Information"), in the first item in the list, move the phone number so it appears on the next line, without any additional line space above the phone number. Then move the text "Mon–Fri 9am–5pm" so it appears on the next line, without any additional line space above it.

6. On Slide 2, move the "Main office phone" list item and the phone number so these appear as the last list items on the slide.

7. On Slide 2, insert the photo **Beach**, located in the PowerPoint1 > Case3 folder. Crop two inches from the top of the photo, and then resize the photo so that it is 3.4 inches high.

8. On Slide 2, position the photo so that its right edge is flush with the right edge of the slide and so that its bottom edge is slightly on top of the lighter blue line at the bottom of the slide.

9. Change the layout of Slides 3 through 7 to Content with Caption. On all five slides, move the unnumbered list from the content placeholder on the right to the text placeholders on the left, as shown in Figure 1-46, and then change the font size of the text in the unnumbered lists you moved to 16 points. Then insert the photos named **House1** through **House5** provided in the PowerPoint1 > Case3 folder on Slides 3 through 7, using Figure 1-46 as a guide.

10. Compress all the photos in the presentation to 96 ppi.

11. On Slide 8 ("To Schedule an Appointment"), change the list to a numbered list, and then add **Specify house and location.** as a new item 3.

12. Save the changes to the presentation, and then view the presentation in Reading view.

Case Problem 4

Data Files needed for this Case Problem: Ballet.jpg, Dancing.mp4, HipHop.jpg, Jazz.jpg, Jump.jpg, Leap.jpg, Modern.jpg, and Tap.jpg

Greater Dayton Dance Academy Paul LaCroix owns Greater Dayton Dance Academy, a dance studio that teaches students ages two through adult. He has an open house every September to attract new students. He asks you to help him create a presentation that includes photos and video that he can show at the open house. Complete the following steps:

🌐 **Explore** 1. Create a new presentation using the Striped black border presentation template from Office.com. (*Hint:* Use "striped black border" as the search term. If you get no results, type **white** as the search term, and then choose a template with a simple theme.)

2. Replace the title text on the title slide with **Greater Dayton Dance Academy**, and replace the subtitle text with your name. Save the presentation as **New Students** to the drive and folder where you are storing your files.

3. Delete all the slides except the title slide.

4. Add a new Slide 2 with the Two Content layout. Add **About Us** as the title, and then type the following as a bulleted list in the left content placeholder:

   - **Recreational classes meet once a week**
   - **Competitive classes meet 3 to 5 times a week**
   - **Private lessons available**
   - **Annual winter and spring productions**

CHALLENGE

5. On Slide 2, in the right content placeholder, insert the photo **Leap**, located in the PowerPoint1 > Case4 folder included with your Data Files. Resize it, maintaining the aspect ratio, so it is 3.8 inches high, and then reposition it so that the top edge of the photo is aligned with the top edge of the text box and the left edge of the photo is aligned with the right edge of the text box.

6. Add a new Slide 3 with the Title and Content layout. Add **Styles Offered** as the title, and then type the following as a bulleted list in the content placeholder:
   - **Ballet**
   - **Modern**
   - **Jazz**
   - **Tap**
   - **Hip Hop**

7. On Slide 3, convert the bulleted list to a SmartArt diagram with the Bending Picture Semi-Transparent Text layout, which is a Picture type of diagram.

⊕ **Explore** 8. Change the colors of the diagram to Colorful Range – Accent Colors 3 to 4 by using the Change Colors button in the SmartArt Styles group on the SmartArt Tools Design tab.

⊕ **Explore** 9. Insert the following pictures, located in the PowerPoint1 > Case4 folder, in the appropriate picture placeholders in the SmartArt diagram: **Ballet**, **Modern**, **Jazz**, **Tap**, and **HipHop**.

10. Add a new Slide 4 with the Two Content layout. Add **Call Today!** as the title. In the content placeholder on the left, type the following as an unnumbered list (no bullets) without extra space between the lines:

    Greater Dayton Dance Academy

    1158 North St.

    Dayton, OH 45417

11. On Slide 4, add the phone number **(937) 555-1254** and the website address **www.daytondance.example.com** as new items in the unnumbered list. Press the spacebar after typing the website address to format it as a link.

12. On Slide 4, change the size of the text in the unnumbered list to 22 point. (*Hint:* Click in the Font Size box, type **22**, and then press the **Enter** key.)

13. On Slide 4, add the photo **Jump**, located in the PowerPoint1 > Case4 folder, to the content placeholder on the right. Resize it so it is 3.6 inches high, maintaining the aspect ratio, and then position it so the top edge aligns with the top edge of the text box on the left and there is approximately one inch of space between the right side of the photo and the right edge of the slide.

14. Compress all the photos in the presentation to 96 ppi, and then save the changes.

15. Add a new Slide 5 with the Two Content layout. Add **Classic Ballet Technique Emphasized** as the title. In the content placeholder on the right, add **Because ballet is the foundation of all dance, all students are required to take ballet technique classes.** Remove the bullet from this item.

16. Move this slide so it becomes Slide 4.

⊕ **Explore** 17. On Slide 4 ("Classic Ballet Technique Emphasized"), insert the video **Dancing**, located in the PowerPoint1 > Case4 folder, in the content placeholder.

⊕ **Explore** 18. Open the Info tab in Backstage view. Use the Compress Media command to compress the videos to the lowest quality possible. Use the Back button at the top of the navigation bar in Backstage view to return to Normal view.

19. Save the changes to the presentation, and then run the slide show in Slide Show view. When Slide 4 ("Classic Ballet Technique Emphasized") appears, point to the video to make a Play button appear, and then click the Play button to play the 20-second video. (*Hint:* Point to the video as it plays to display the play bar again.)

POWERPOINT

Adding Media and Special Effects

Using Media in a Presentation for a Nonprofit River Cleaning Organization

Case | *RiverClean*

José Quiñones is a volunteer for RiverClean™, a nonprofit organization in New England that raises money and supports volunteer efforts to clean riverbanks in the area. José lives in Lowell, Massachusetts, where several intense storms have knocked down tree limbs, some of which block access to the Riverwalk trail next to the Merrimack River. In addition to the storm damage, portions of the trail are overgrown and in disrepair, and many areas along the trail have significant erosion problems. José wants to present this information to the city councilors so that he can get permission to organize a trail cleanup and obtain some funding for the project as well. José prepared the text of a PowerPoint presentation, and he wants you to add photos and other features to make the presentation more interesting and compelling.

In this module, you will modify a presentation that illustrates the poor conditions of the Riverwalk trail and estimates costs for addressing the problems. You will add formatting and special effects to photos and shapes, add transitions and animations to slides, and add and modify video.

STARTING DATA FILES

Module		**Review**	
Barrier.jpg	Sign.jpg	Cleared.jpg	NewView.mp4
Erosion1.jpg	Stairs.jpg	Landscape.jpg	Railings.jpg
Erosion2.mp4	Tree.jpg	NewSign.jpg	Renewed1.pptx
Mix.pptx	WalkTheme.pptx	NewStairs.jpg	Renewed2.pptx
Riverwalk.pptx		NewTheme.pptx	Wall.jpg

Case1	**Case2**	**Case3**	**Case4**
Equipment.jpg	Build.jpg	Paws.pptx	Candy.png
Exercise.mp4	Finish.jpg	PawsTheme.pptx	CarePak.pptx
FitTheme.pptx	Furniture.pptx		CPTheme.pptx
HomeFit.pptx	Sand.jpg		Games.png
	Sketch.jpg		Personal.png
	Trees.jpg		Salty.png

Session 2.1 Visual Overview:

Use the Shape Fill button to change the **fill**, the formatting of the area inside a shape.

To change the color, weight (thickness), or style (solid line, dashed line, and so on) of a shape's border, use the Shape Outline button.

The Drawing Tools Format tab appears when a drawing or a text box—including the slide's title and content placeholders—is selected.

The Shape Height box contains the height measurement of the selected shape, and the Shape Width box contains the width measurement.

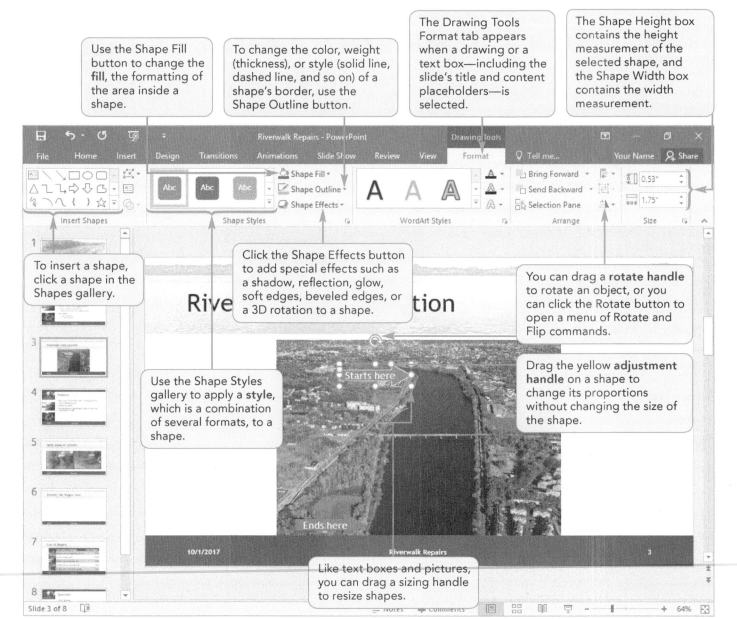

To insert a shape, click a shape in the Shapes gallery.

Click the Shape Effects button to add special effects such as a shadow, reflection, glow, soft edges, beveled edges, or a 3D rotation to a shape.

You can drag a **rotate handle** to rotate an object, or you can click the Rotate button to open a menu of Rotate and Flip commands.

Use the Shape Styles gallery to apply a **style**, which is a combination of several formats, to a shape.

Drag the yellow **adjustment handle** on a shape to change its proportions without changing the size of the shape.

Like text boxes and pictures, you can drag a sizing handle to resize shapes.

Courtesy of Helen M. Pinard; © Paul Mozell/Alamy

Formatting Graphics

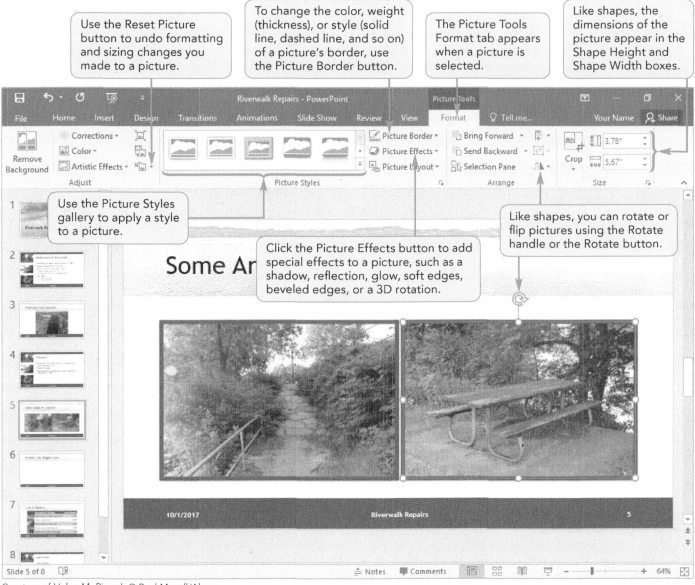

Use the Reset Picture button to undo formatting and sizing changes you made to a picture.

To change the color, weight (thickness), or style (solid line, dashed line, and so on) of a picture's border, use the Picture Border button.

The Picture Tools Format tab appears when a picture is selected.

Like shapes, the dimensions of the picture appear in the Shape Height and Shape Width boxes.

Use the Picture Styles gallery to apply a style to a picture.

Click the Picture Effects button to add special effects to a picture, such as a shadow, reflection, glow, soft edges, beveled edges, or a 3D rotation.

Like shapes, you can rotate or flip pictures using the Rotate handle or the Rotate button.

Courtesy of Helen M. Pinard; © Paul Mozell/Alamy

Applying a Theme Used in Another Presentation

As you learned earlier, an installed theme can be applied by clicking one in the Themes group on the Design tab. An installed theme is actually a special type of file that is stored with PowerPoint program files. You can also apply themes that are applied to any other presentation stored on your computer. For example, many companies want to promote their brand through their presentations, so they hire presentation design professionals to create custom themes that can be applied to all company presentations. The custom theme can be applied to a blank presentation, and this presentation can be stored on users' computers or on a network drive.

José created a presentation describing his concerns about the Riverwalk trail. He also created a custom theme by changing the theme fonts and colors, modifying layouts, and creating a new layout. He applied this theme to a blank presentation that he sent to you. He wants you to apply the custom theme to the presentation describing his concerns.

To apply a theme from another presentation:

1. Open the presentation **Riverwalk**, located in the **PowerPoint2 > Module** folder included with your Data Files, and then save it as **Riverwalk Repairs** in the location where you are saving your files. This is the presentation José created that describes his concerns. The Office theme is applied to it. You need to apply José's custom theme to it.

2. On the ribbon, click the **Design** tab.

3. In the Themes group, click the **More** button, and then click **Browse for Themes**. The Choose Theme or Themed Document dialog box opens.

4. Navigate to the **PowerPoint2 > Module** folder, click **WalkTheme**, and then click the **Apply** button. The custom theme is applied to the Riverwalk Repairs presentation.

5. In the Themes group, point to the first theme in the gallery, which is the current theme. Its ScreenTip identifies it as the WalkTheme. See Figure 2-1. Although variants appear in the Variants group, these are the Office theme variants, and if you click one of them, you will reapply the Office theme with the variant you selected.

Figure 2-1   **Custom WalkTheme applied**

Courtesy of Helen M. Pinard

6. Click the **Home** tab, and then on Slide 1 (the title slide), click **Riverwalk Repairs**, the title text.

7. In the Font group, click the **Font arrow**. Notice that Trebuchet MS is the theme font for both the headings and the body text. This is different from the Office theme, which uses Calibri for the body text and Calibri Light for the headings.

8. In the Slides group, click the **Layout** button. The Layout gallery appears. The custom layouts that José created are listed in the gallery, as shown in Figure 2-2.

| Figure 2-2 | Custom layouts in the WalkTheme custom theme |

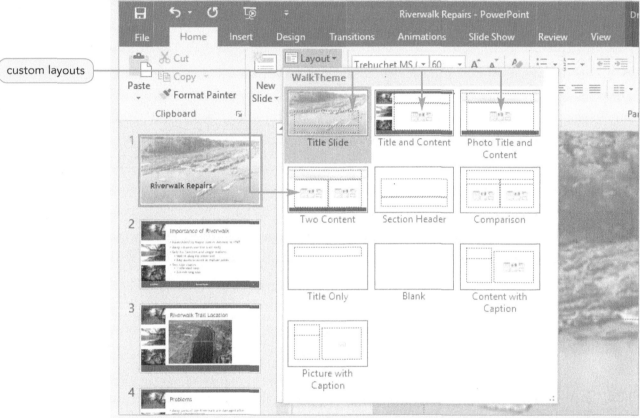

Courtesy of Helen M. Pinard; © Paul Mozell/Alamy

Notice the customized Title Slide layout has a photo as a slide background, the Title and Content customized layout has photos along the left edge of the slide, and the customized Photo Title and Content and the Two Content layouts include a photo under the slide title.

9. Press the **Esc** key to close the Layout gallery.

When you applied the custom theme from the WalkTheme presentation, the title slide and the slides with the Title and Content and Two Content layouts were changed to use the customized versions of these layouts. José wants you to change the layout of Slides 3, 6, and 7 to the custom layout he named Photo Title and Content.

To apply a custom layout to Slides 3, 6, and 7:

1. Display **Slide 3** ("Riverwalk Trail Location").

2. In the Slides group, click the **Layout** button. The Layout gallery appears.

▶ **3.** Click the **Photo Title and Content** layout. The custom layout is applied to Slide 3.

▶ **4.** Apply the **Photo Title and Content** layout to Slide 6 ("Erosion: The Biggest Issue") and Slide 7 ("Cost of Repairs").

▶ **5.** Save your changes.

INSIGHT

Saving a Presentation as a Theme

If you need to use a custom theme frequently, you can save a presentation file as an Office Theme file. A theme file is a different file type than a presentation file. You can then store this file so that it appears in the Themes gallery on the Design tab. To save a custom theme, click the File tab, click Save As in the navigation bar, and then click Browse to open the Save As dialog box. To change the file type to Office Theme, click the Save as type arrow, and then click Office Theme. This changes the current folder in the Save As dialog box to the Document Themes folder, which is a folder created on the hard drive when Office is installed and where the installed themes are stored. If you save a custom theme to the Document Themes folder, that theme will be listed in its own row above the installed themes in the Themes gallery. (You need to click the More button in the Themes gallery to see this row.) You can also change the folder location and save the custom theme to any location on your computer or network or to a folder on your OneDrive. If you do this, the theme will not appear in the Themes gallery, but you can still access it using the Browse for Themes command on the Themes gallery menu.

Inserting Shapes

You can add many shapes to a slide, including lines, rectangles, stars, and more. To draw a shape, click the Shapes button in the Illustrations group on the Insert tab, click a shape in the gallery, and then click and drag to draw the shape in the size you want. Like any object, a shape can be resized after you insert it.

You've already had a little experience with one shape—a text box, which is a shape specifically designed to contain text. You can add additional text boxes to slides using the Text Box shape. You can also add text to any shape you place on a slide.

José wants you to add labels identifying the trail in the aerial photo on Slide 3. You will do this with arrow shapes. First you will add an arrow that points to the start of the trail.

To insert and position an arrow shape with text on Slide 3:

▶ **1.** Display **Slide 3** ("Riverwalk Trail Location").

▶ **2.** Click the **Insert** tab, and then in the Illustrations group, click the **Shapes** button. The Shapes gallery opens. See Figure 2-3. In addition to the Recently Used Shapes group at the top, the gallery is organized into nine categories of shapes.

| Figure 2-3 | Shapes gallery |

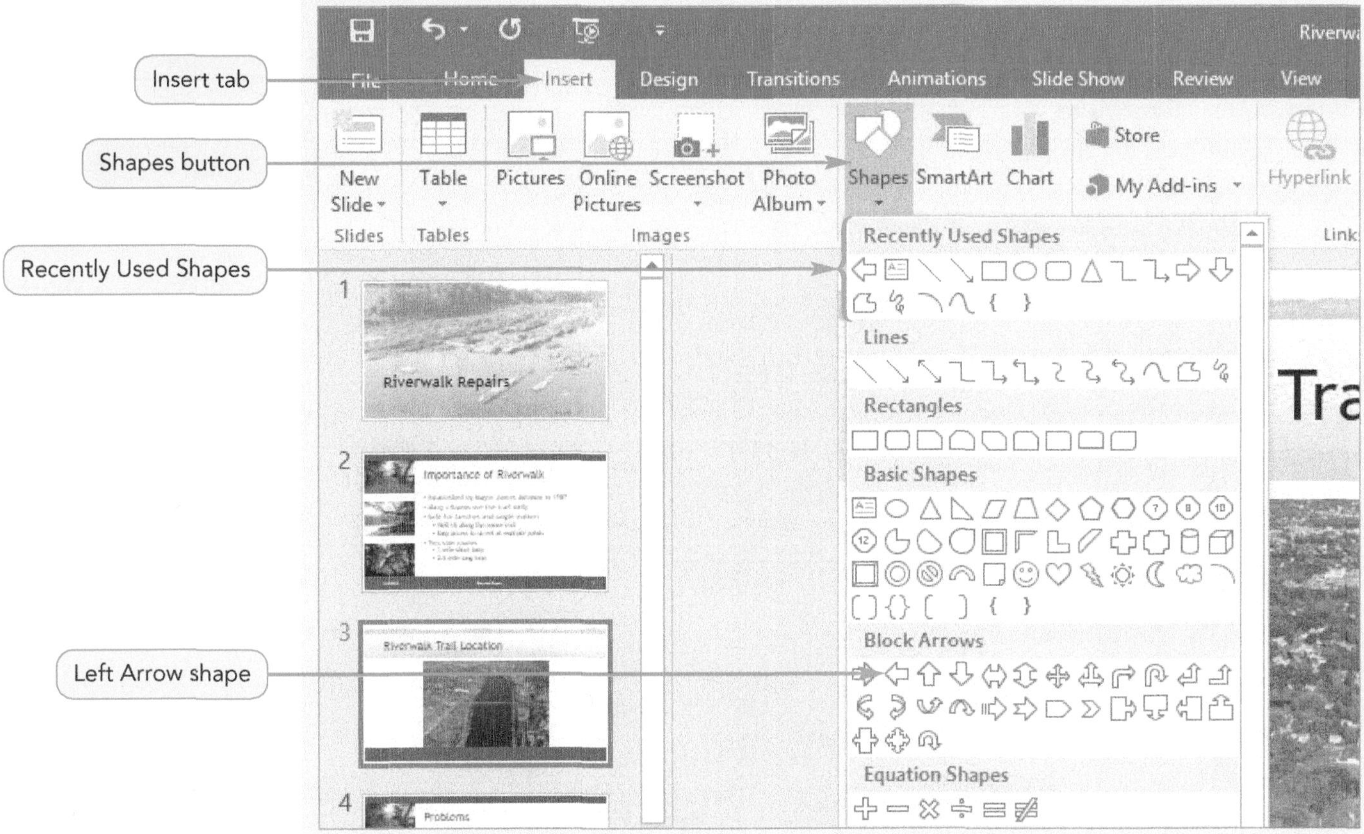

© Paul Mozell/Alamy; Courtesy of Helen M. Pinard

TIP

You can also insert a shape using the Shapes gallery in the Drawing group on the Home tab.

3. Under Block Arrows, click the **Left Arrow** shape ⬅. The gallery closes and the pointer changes to +.

4. On the slide, click to the right of the photo. A left-pointing arrow, approximately one inch long, appears. (Don't worry about the exact placement of the arrow; you will move it later.) Note that the Drawing Tools Format tab is the active tab on the ribbon.

5. With the shape selected, type **Starts here**. The text you type appears in the arrow, but it does not all fit.

6. Drag the middle sizing handle on the right end of the arrow to lengthen the arrow until both words fit on one line inside the arrow and the arrow is 1.75" long as indicated in the Shape Width box in the Size group on the Drawing Tools Format tab.

   Now you need to position the arrow shape on the photo. When you drag a shape with text, it is similar to dragging a text box, which means you need to drag a border of the shape or a part of the shape that does not contain text.

7. Position the pointer on the arrow shape so that the pointer changes to ⊹, and then drag the arrow shape on top of the photo so that it points to the left of the curve in the river near the top of the photo, as shown in Figure 2-4.

Figure 2-4	**Arrow shape with text on Slide 3**

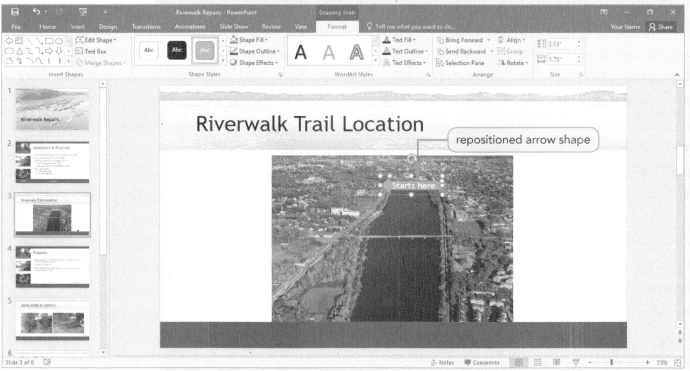

© Paul Mozell/Alamy; Courtesy of Helen M. Pinard

Next, you to need to add an arrow pointing to the end of the trail. You could draw another arrow, but instead, you'll duplicate the arrow you just drew. Duplicating is similar to copying and pasting, but nothing is placed on the Clipboard.

To duplicate the arrow on Slide 3 and edit the text in the shape:

1. On Slide 3 ("Riverwalk Trail Location"), click the **"Starts here"** arrow to select it, if necessary.

2. Click the **Home** tab, and then in the Clipboard group, click the **Copy button arrow**. A menu opens.

3. On the menu, click **Duplicate**. A duplicate of the "Starts here" arrow appears on the slide.

4. Double-click **Starts** in the duplicate arrow, and then type **Ends**.

5. Drag the duplicate of the arrow down so that it points to the left bank of the river at the bottom of the photo as shown in Figure 2-5.

| Figure 2-5 | Duplicate arrow positioned at the bottom of the photo on Slide 3 |

© Paul Mozell/Alamy; Courtesy of Helen M. Pinard

▶ **6.** Save your changes.

Rotating and Flipping Objects

You can rotate and flip any object on a slide. To flip an object, you click the Rotate button in the Arrange group on the Drawing Tools Format tab to access the Flip commands on the Rotate menu. To rotate an object, you can use the Rotate commands on the Rotate menu to rotate objects in 90-degree increments. You can also drag the rotate handle that appears above the top-middle sizing handle when the object is selected to rotate it to any position that you want, using the center of the object as a pivot point.

The arrows you drew on Slide 3 would look better if they were pointing from left to right. To make this change, you need to flip the arrows.

TIP

You can also click the Arrange button in the Drawing group on the Home tab to access the Rotate and Flip commands.

To flip the arrow shapes and reposition them on Slide 3:

▶ **1.** With Slide 3 ("Riverwalk Trail Location") displayed, click the **Starts here** arrow.

▶ **2.** Position the pointer on the Rotate handle so that the pointer changes to ↻, and then drag the Rotate handle clockwise until the Starts here arrow is pointing to the right. The arrow is pointing in the correct direction, but the text in the arrow is now upside down.

▶ **3.** On the Quick Access Toolbar, click the **Undo** button, and then click the **Drawing Tools Format** tab, if necessary.

4. In the Arrange group, click the **Rotate** button. The Rotate menu opens. See Figure 2-6.

Figure 2-6   **Rotate menu**

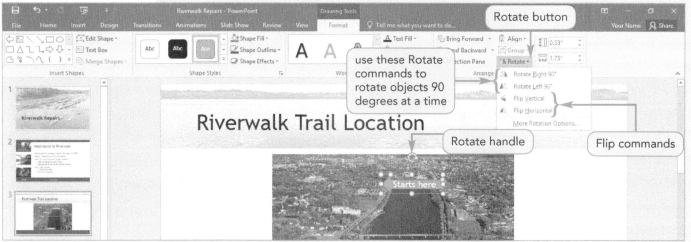

© Paul Mozell/Alamy; Courtesy of Helen M. Pinard

5. Click **Flip Horizontal**. The arrow flips horizontally and is now pointing right. Unlike when you rotated the arrow so that it pointed right, the text is still right-side up.

6. Drag the **Starts here** arrow to the left until it is pointing to the riverbank on the left side of the river at the curve at the top of the photo.

7. Click the **Ends here** arrow to select it, and then flip it horizontally. The Ends here arrow now points from the left to the right.

8. Drag the **Ends here** arrow to the left until it is pointing to the riverbank on the left side of the river at the bottom of the photo, and then click a blank area of the slide to deselect the arrow. Compare your screen to Figure 2-7, and then make any adjustments needed for your screen to match the figure.

Figure 2-7   **Arrows flipped and repositioned on Slide 3**

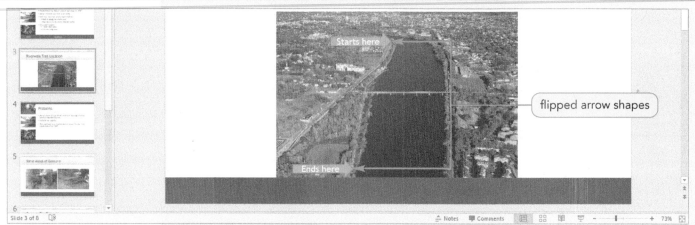

© Paul Mozell/Alamy; Courtesy of Helen M. Pinard

9. Save your changes.

Formatting Objects

Recall that both shapes and pictures, such as photos and clip art, are treated as objects in PowerPoint. The Picture Tools and Drawing Tools Format contextual tabs contain tools for formatting these objects. For both shapes and pictures, you can use these tools to apply borders or outlines, special effects such as drop shadows and reflections, and styles. You can also resize and rotate or flip these objects. Some formatting tools are available only to one or the other type of object. For example, the Remove Background tool is available only to pictures, and the Fill command is available only to shapes. Refer to the Session 2.1 Visual Overview for more information about the commands on the Format contextual tabs.

Formatting Shapes

You can modify the fill of a shape by filling it with a color, a gradient (shading in which one color blends into another or varies from one shade to another), a textured pattern, or a picture. When you add a shape to a slide, the default fill is the Accent 1 color from the set of theme colors, and the default outline is a darker shade of that color.

José wants you to change the default color of the "Starts here" arrow shape to green and the color of the "Ends here" arrow shape to red.

To change the fill and style of the arrow shapes:

▶ 1. On Slide 3 ("Riverwalk Trail Location"), click the **Ends here** arrow, and then click the **Drawing Tools Format** tab, if necessary.

▶ 2. In the Shape Styles group, click the **Shape Fill button arrow**. The Shape Fill menu opens. See Figure 2-8. You can fill a shape with a color, a picture, a gradient, or a texture, or you can remove the fill by clicking No Fill.

Figure 2-8   **Shape Fill menu**

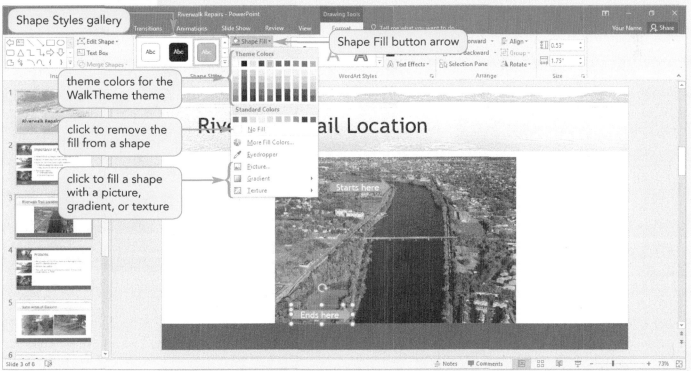

© Paul Mozell/Alamy; Courtesy of Helen M. Pinard

3. Under Standard Colors, click **Red**. The shape fill of the selected arrow changes to red. Next, you'll apply a style to the other arrow shape.

4. Click the **Starts here** arrow, and then in the Shape Styles group, click the **More** button. The Shape Styles gallery opens.

5. Click the **Light 1 Outline, Colored Fill – Dark Green, Accent 4** style. The style, which fills the shape with green and changes the shape outline to white, is applied to the shape.

On some shapes, you can drag the yellow adjustment handle to change the shape's proportions. For instance, if you dragged the adjustment handle on the arrow shape, you would change the size of the arrowhead relative to the size of the arrow.

You need to make the arrowhead larger relative to the size of the arrow shape.

To adjust the arrow shapes:

1. Click the **Starts here** shape, if necessary, to select it.

2. Drag the yellow adjustment handle at the top point on the arrowhead to the left so that the bottom point on the arrowhead aligns with the left side of the second "e" in "here."

3. Click the **Ends here** shape, and then drag the yellow adjustment handle at the top point on the arrowhead to the left so that the bottom point on the arrowhead aligns with the left side of the second "e" in "here." Compare your screen to Figure 2-9.

| Figure 2-9 | Formatted arrow shapes |

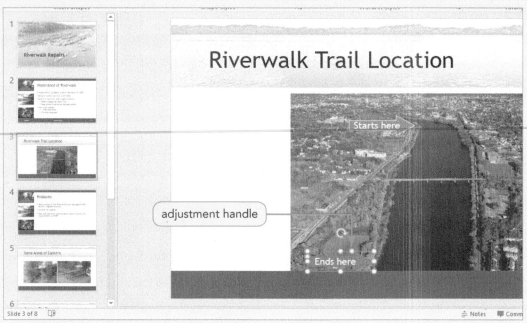

© Paul Mozell/Alamy; Courtesy of Helen M. Pinard

Formatting Pictures

You can format photos as well as shapes. To format photos, you use the tools on the Picture Tools Format tab.

José wants you to format the pictures on Slide 5 by adding a colored border. To create the border, you could apply a thick outline, or you can apply one of the styles that includes a border and then modify it.

To format the photos on Slide 5:

▶ **1.** Display **Slide 5** ("Some Areas of Concern"), click the photo on the left, and then click the **Picture Tools Format** tab.

▶ **2.** In the Picture Styles group, click the **Simple Frame, White** style. This style applies a seven-point white border to the photo.

▶ **3.** In the Picture Styles group, click the **Picture Border button arrow**, and then click the **Dark Blue, Accent 3** color. See Figure 2-10. You need to apply the same formatting to the photo on the right on Slide 5. You can repeat the same formatting steps, or you can copy the formatting.

Figure 2-10   **Picture with a style and border color applied**

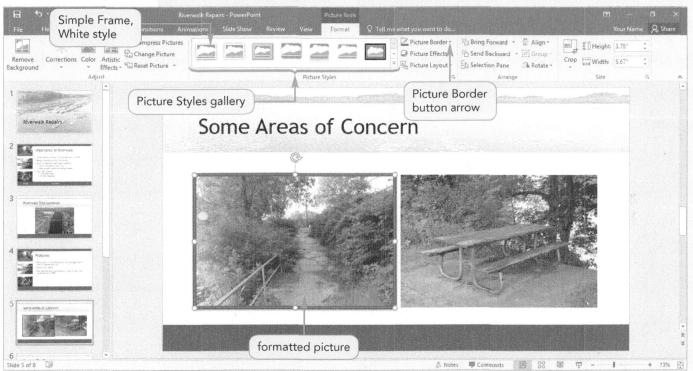

Courtesy of Helen M. Pinard; © Paul Mozell/Alamy

▶ **4.** With the left photo on Slide 5 still selected, click the **Home** tab.

▶ **5.** In the Clipboard group, click the **Format Painter** button, and then move the pointer to the slide. The pointer changes to ⬚ 🖌.

▶ **6.** Click the photo on the right. The style and border color of the photo on the left is copied and applied to the photo on the right.

▶ **7.** Save your changes.

Creating and Formatting Tables

A **table** is information arranged in horizontal rows and vertical columns. The area where a row and column intersect is called a **cell**. Each cell contains one piece of information. A table's structure is indicated by borders, which are lines that outline the rows and columns.

Creating a Table and Adding Data to It

José wants you to add a table to Slide 7 that itemizes the damages to the trail and associated repair costs. This table will have three columns—one to describe the damages, one to contain the expected costs for the repair, and one to list notes.

REFERENCE

Inserting a Table

- In a content placeholder, click the Insert Table button; or, click the Insert tab on the ribbon, click the Table button in the Tables group, and then click Insert Table.
- Specify the numbers of columns and rows, and then click the OK button.

or

- On the ribbon, click the Insert tab, and then in the Tables group, click the Table button.
- Click a box in the grid to create a table of that size.

José hasn't decided how many examples of trail damages to include in the table, so he asks you to start by creating a table with four rows.

To add a table to Slide 7:

1. Display **Slide 7** ("Cost of Repairs").

2. Click the **Insert** tab, and then in the Tables group, click the **Table** button. A menu opens with a grid of squares above three commands.

3. Point to the grid, and without clicking the mouse button, move the pointer over the grid. The label above the grid indicates how large the table will be, and a preview of the table appears on the slide. See Figure 2-11.

| **Figure 2-11** | **Inserting a 3x4 table on Slide 7** |

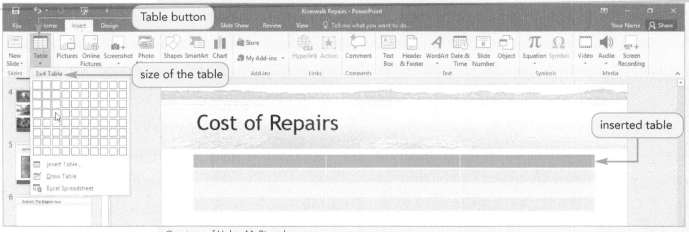

Courtesy of Helen M. Pinard

4. When the label above the grid indicates 3x4 Table, click to insert a table with three columns and four rows. A selection border appears around the table, and the insertion point is in the first cell in the first row.

Now you're ready to fill the blank cells with the information about the trail repairs. To enter data in a table, you click in the cells in which you want to enter data and then start typing. You can also use the Tab and arrow keys to move from one cell to another.

To add data to the table:

▶ 1. In the first cell in the first row, type **Description of Damages**. The text you typed appears in the first cell.

▶ 2. Press the **Tab** key. The insertion point moves to the second cell in the first row.

▶ 3. Type **Cost of Repair**, press the **Tab** key, type **Notes**, and then press the **Tab** key. The insertion point is in the first cell in the second row.

▶ 4. In the first cell in the second row, type **Broken stairs at beginning of trail**, press the **Tab** key, and then type **$700**.

▶ 5. Click in the first cell in the third row, type **Erosion along banks**, press the **Tab** key, and then type **$2500**.

▶ 6. Click in the first cell in the last row, type **Fallen trees blocking trail**, press the **Tab** key, and then type **$350**.

Inserting and Deleting Rows and Columns

You can modify the table by adding or deleting rows and columns. You need to add more rows to the table for additional descriptions of damage to the trail.

To insert rows and a column in the table:

▶ 1. Make sure the insertion point is in the last row in the table.

▶ 2. Click the **Table Tools Layout** tab, and then in the Rows & Columns group, click the **Insert Below** button. A new row is inserted below the current row. See Figure 2-12.

Figure 2-12   Table with row inserted

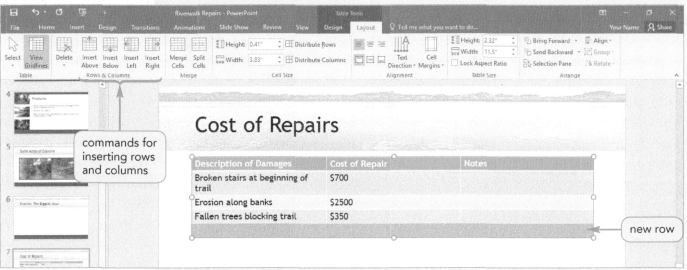

Courtesy of Helen M. Pinard

3. Click in the first cell in the new last row, type **Jersey barrier blocking trail**, and then press the **Tab** key.

4. Type **$300**, and then press the **Tab** key. The insertion point is in the last cell in the last row.

5. Press the **Tab** key. A new row is created, and the insertion point is in the first cell in the new row.

6. Type **Broken and vandalized signage**, press the **Tab** key, and then type **$250**. You need to insert a row above the last row.

7. In the Rows & Columns group, click the **Insert Above** button. A new row is inserted above the current row, and all the cells in the new row are selected.

8. Click any cell in the first column, and then in the Rows & Column group, click the **Insert Left** button.

   A new first column is inserted.

Make sure you click a cell in the first column before you insert the new column. Otherwise, you will insert three new columns.

José decided he doesn't want to add notes to the table, so you'll delete the last column. He also decided that the new row you added as the second to last row in the table isn't needed, so you'll delete that row.

To delete a column and a row in the table:

1. Click in any cell in the last column in the table. This is the column you will delete.

2. On the Table Tools Layout tab, in the Rows & Columns group, click the **Delete** button. The Delete button menu opens.

3. Click **Delete Columns**. The current column is deleted, and the entire table is selected.

4. Click in any cell in the second to last row (the empty row). This is the row you want to delete.

5. In the Rows & Columns group, click the **Delete** button, and then click **Delete Rows**. See Figure 2-13.

Figure 2-13   **Table after adding and deleting rows and columns**

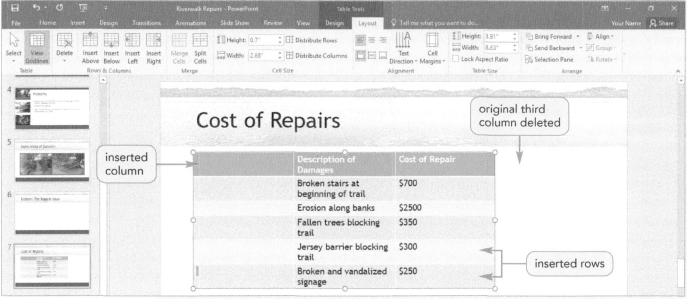

Courtesy of Helen M. Pinard

Formatting a Table

After you insert data into a table, you need to think about how the table looks and whether the table will be readable for the audience. As with any text, you can change the font, size, or color, and as with shapes and pictures, you can apply a style to a table. You can also change how the text fits in the table cells by changing the height of rows and the width of columns. You can also customize the formatting of the table by changing the border and fill of table cells.

You need to make the table text larger so that an audience will be able to read it.

To change the font size of text in the table:

▶ **1.** Click any cell in the table. You want to change the size of all the text in the table, so you will select the entire table. Notice that a selection border appears around the table. This border appears any time the table is active.

▶ **2.** Click the **Table Tools Layout** tab, if necessary, and then in the Table group, click the **Select** button. The Select menu opens with options to select the entire table, the current column, or the current row.

▶ **3.** Click **Select Table**. The entire table is selected. Because the selection border appears any time the table is active, the only visual cues you have that it is now selected are that the insertion point is no longer blinking in the cell that you clicked in Step 1 and the Select button is gray and unavailable. See Figure 2-14.

Figure 2-14 Table selected on Slide 7

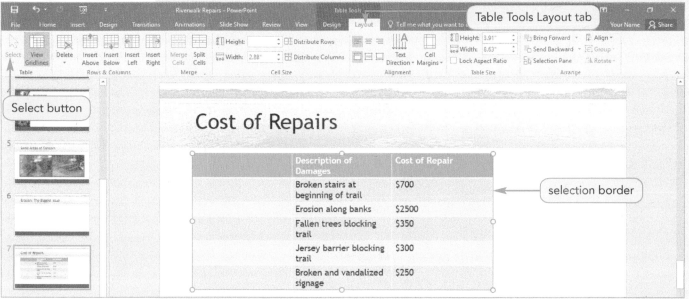

Courtesy of Helen M. Pinard

4. On the ribbon, click the **Home** tab.

5. In the Font group, click the **Font Size arrow**, and then click **28**. Because the entire table is selected, the size of all the text in the table changes to 28 points.

One of the rows is now off of the slide at the bottom. You will adjust the column widths so that all of the rows fit on the slide. To adjust column widths, you can drag a column border or type a number in the Width box in the Cell Size group on the Table Tools Layout tab. You can also automatically adjust a column to fit its widest entry by double-clicking its right border.

To adjust column sizes in the table:

1. Position the pointer on the border between the first and second columns so that the pointer changes to ◄‖►, and then drag the border to the left until it is below the "o" in the word "of" in the slide title.

2. Click the **Table Tools Layout** tab, click any cell in the first column, and then in the Cell Size group, examine the measurement in the Width box.

3. If the measurement in the Width box is not 1.6", click in the **Width** box, type **1.6**, and then press the **Enter** key. The width of the first column is changed to 1.6 inches.

4. Position the pointer on the border between the second and third columns so that it changes to ◄‖►, and then double-click. The second column widens to accommodate the widest entry in the column. See Figure 2-15.

| Figure 2-15 | Table column widths adjusted |

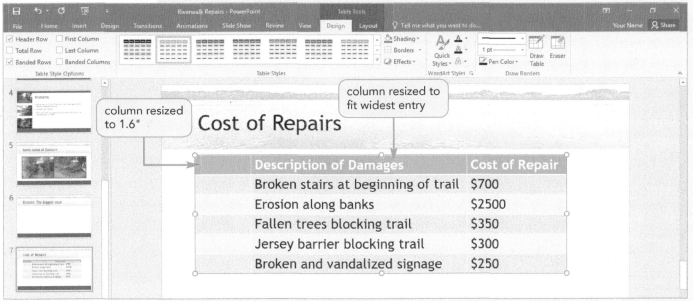

Courtesy of Helen M. Pinard

José wants you to change the format of the table so it looks more attractive and so that its colors complement the photo in the slide's layout. You will do this by applying a style to the table. When you apply a style to a table, you can specify whether the header and total rows and the first and last columns are formatted differently from the other rows and columns in the table. You can also specify whether to use banded rows or columns, that is, whether to fill alternating rows or columns with different shading.

To apply a style to the table:

1. Click the **Table Tools Design** tab on the ribbon, if necessary. In the Table Styles group, the second style, Medium Style 2 – Accent 1, is selected. In the Table Style Options group, the Header Row and Banded Rows check boxes are selected, which means that the header row will be formatted differently than the rest of the rows and that every other row will be filled with shading. See Figure 2-16.

Figure 2-16   Default formatting applied to the table

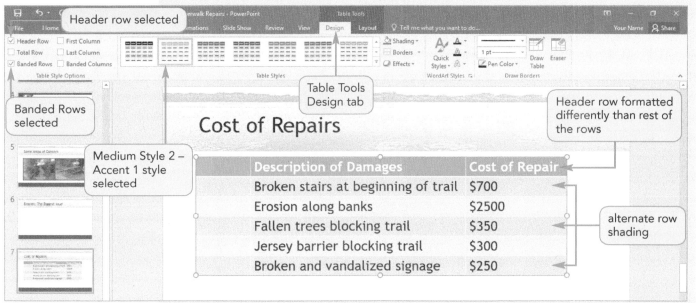

Courtesy of Helen M. Pinard

▶ **2.** In the Table Styles group, click the **More** button. The Table Styles gallery opens.

▶ **3.** Click the **Light Style 1** style, and then click a blank area of the slide to deselect the table. This style shades every other row with gray and adds a border above and below the top row and below the bottom row.

You can change the fill of table cells in the same manner that you change the fill of shapes. José wants the first row to be more prominent.

To change the fill of cells in the first row of the table:

▶ **1.** In the table, click any cell in the first row, and then click the **Table Tools Layout** tab.

▶ **2.** In the Table group, click the **Select** button, and then click **Select Row**. The first row in the table is selected.

▶ **3.** Click the **Table Tools Design** tab.

▶ **4.** In the Table Styles group, click the **Shading button arrow**. The Shading menu is similar to the Shape Fill menu you worked with earlier.

▶ **5.** Click **Dark Blue, Accent 3**. The menu closes and the cells in the first row are shaded with dark blue. The text is a little hard to read.

TIP

You can also change the font color of table text using the Font Color button in the Font group on the Home tab.

▶ **6.** In the WordArt Styles group, click the **Text Fill button arrow** [A ▾], and then click the **White, Background 1, Darker 5%** color. The text in the selected cells changes to the white color you selected.

In addition, the table might be easier to read if the horizontal borders between the rows were visible. You can add these by using the Borders button arrow and the buttons in the Draw Borders group on the Table Tools Design tab. When you use the Borders button arrow, you can apply borders to all the selected cells at once. The borders will be the style, weight, and color specified by the Pen Style, Pen Weight, and Pen Color buttons in the Draw Borders group. Note that borders are different than gridlines. Gridlines are the lines that form the structure of a table. Borders are drawn on top of the gridlines. Gridlines are always there, but they appear only if the View Gridlines button in the Table group on the Table Tools Layout tab is selected and if the table itself is selected.

You want to see how the table looks without gridlines, then you will remove the top border on the top row in the table and make the bottom border of that row thicker.

To view and hide gridlines and modify the borders of the table:

▶ **1.** Click the **Table Tools Layout** tab, and then in the Table group, click the **View Gridlines** button to deselect it. The faint vertical lines between the table columns disappear.

   Trouble? If the View Gridlines button was already deselected, click it again to deselect it.

▶ **2.** In the Table group, click the **View Gridlines** button again to select it. The faint vertical lines between the table columns are visible again.

▶ **3.** Make sure the first row of the table is still selected. You want to remove the top border on this row.

▶ **4.** Click the **Table Tools Design** tab, and then in the Table Styles group, click the **Borders button arrow**. A menu opens listing borders that you can apply to the selected cells. Notice that the Top Border and Bottom Border commands are selected on the menu. This is because the selected cells have a top and bottom border. As indicated in the Draw Borders group, the borders are solid-line borders, one point wide, and black. See Figure 2-17. You can change any of these attributes.

| Figure 2-17 | Current format of borders for top row of table |

Courtesy of Helen M. Pinard

▶ **5.** Click **Top Border**. The top border on the selected row is removed.

▶ **6.** In the Table Styles group, click the **Borders button arrow**. Only the Bottom Border command is selected on the menu now.

   Trouble? If the Top Border command is still selected, click Top Border again, and then repeat Step 6.

Next you will change the first row's bottom border to a three-point line.

7. In the Draw Borders group, click the **Pen Weight arrow**, and then click **3 pt**. The pointer changes to 🖉, and the Draw Table button in the Draw Borders group is selected. You could drag the pointer along the border you want to change, or you can use the Borders menu again.

8. In the Table Styles group, click the **Borders button arrow**. None of the options on the Borders menu is selected because even though the selected row has a bottom border, it is a one-point border, not a three-point border.

9. Click **Bottom Border**. The bottom border of the selected row changes to a three-point line. In the Draw Borders group, the Draw Table button is no longer selected.

Filling Cells with Pictures

Recall that one of the things you can fill a shape with is a picture. You can do the same with cells. Note that most of the table styles include shaded cells as part of the style definition, so if you want to fill table cells with pictures and apply a table style, you need to apply the table style first. Otherwise, the shading that is part of the table style definition will replace the pictures in the cells.

José wants you to add a picture to each row that shows an example of the described damage.

To fill the cells in the first column with pictures:

1. Click in the first cell in the second row in the table, and then click the **Table Tools Design** tab, if necessary.

2. In the Table Styles group, click the **Shading button arrow**, and then click **Picture**. The Insert Pictures window opens. See Figure 2-18.

| Figure 2-18 | Insert Pictures window |

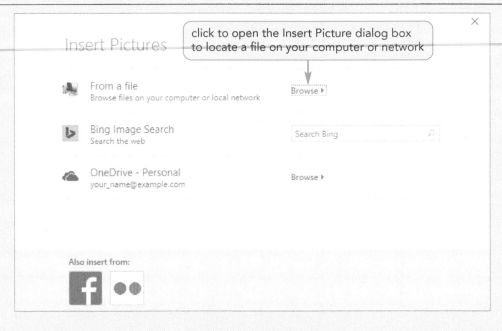

▶ **3.** Next to From a file, click **Browse**. The Insert Picture dialog box opens.

▶ **4.** Navigate to the **PowerPoint2** > **Module** folder, click **Stairs**, and then click the **Insert** button. The photo fills the cell.

▶ **5.** Insert the following photos, all located in the **PowerPoint2** > **Module** folder, in the first cells in the next four rows: **Erosion1**, **Tree**, **Barrier**, and **Sign**.

The text in the table is large enough, but the photos are too small, and some of them are distorted because they were stretched horizontally to fill the cells. To fix both of these problems, you'll increase the height of the rows containing the pictures.

To change row heights in the table:

▶ **1.** Position the pointer to the left of the second row in the table so that it changes to ➡.

▶ **2.** Press and hold the mouse button, drag down until the pointer is to the left of the bottom row in the table, and then release the mouse button. All the rows in the table except the first one are selected.

▶ **3.** Click the **Table Tools Layout** tab.

▶ **4.** In the Cell Size group, click in the **Height** box, type **.85** (make sure you type a decimal point before "85"), and then press the **Enter** key. The height of the selected rows increases to 0.85 inches.

The text in all cells in the table is horizontally left-aligned and vertically aligned at the top of the cells. The text in all the rows except the heading row would look better vertically aligned in the center of the cells. And because the data in the last column is dollar amounts, it would be better if these numbers were right-aligned. Finally, you also need to reposition the table on the slide to better fill the space. You move a table the same way you move any other object.

To adjust the alignment of text in cells and reposition the table:

▶ **1.** Make sure all the rows except the heading row are still selected.

▶ **2.** On the Table Tools Layout tab, in the Alignment group, click the **Center Vertically** button ▤. The text in the selected rows is now centered vertically in the cells.

▶ **3.** In the third column, click in the cell containing $700.

▶ **4.** Position the pointer in the last cell in the second row (the cell containing $700), press and hold the mouse button, drag down through the rest of the cells in the third column, and then release the mouse button. The cells you dragged over (all the cells in the third column except the heading cell) are selected.

▶ **5.** In the Alignment group, click the **Align Right** button ▤. The dollar amounts are now right-aligned in the cells. Now you will adjust the table's placement on the slide.

▶ **6.** In the Arrange group, click the **Align** button. A menu with commands for aligning the objects on the slide appears. Because only one object—the table—is selected, selecting a command will align the object to the borders of the slide.

7. Click **Align Center**. The table is horizontally aligned so that it is centered between the left and right borders of the slide. The bottom of the table slightly overlaps the blue bar at the bottom of the slide.

TIP

You could also drag the table by its border to reposition it on the slide.

8. On the Table Tools Layout tab, in the Table group, click the **Select** button, and then click **Select Table**. The entire table is selected.

9. Press the ↑ key as many times as needed to move the table up slightly so that the bottom of the table no longer overlaps the bar at the bottom of the slide. Compare your screen to Figure 2-19.

Figure 2-19   **Final formatted table**

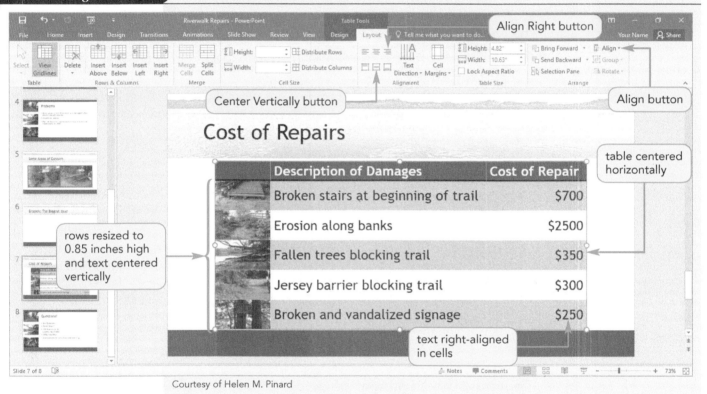

Courtesy of Helen M. Pinard

10. Click a blank area of the slide to deselect the table, and then save your changes.

Inserting Symbols

You can insert some symbols, such as the trademark symbol, the registered trademark symbol, and the copyright symbol, by typing letters between parentheses and letting AutoCorrect change the characters to a symbol. You can insert all symbols, including letters from another alphabet using a keyboard with only English letters, by using the Symbol button in the Symbols group on the Insert tab.

The nonprofit organization's name "RiverClean" is a trademarked name, so it usually appears with the trademark symbol ™ after it. You will add the trademark symbol after the organization's name on the last slide in the presentation.

To insert the trademark symbol by typing:

1. Display **Slide 8** ("Questions?"), and then in the bulleted list, click after "RiverClean" in the second bulleted item.

2. Type **(tm**.

3. Type **)** (close parenthesis). The text "(tm)" changes to the trademark symbol, which is ™.

TIP

To insert the copyright symbol ©, type (c). To insert the registered trademark symbol ®, type (r).

José's name contains two letters that are not in the English alphabet. You need to correct the spelling of José's first and last name. You'll do this using the Symbol dialog box.

To insert special characters:

1. In the first bulleted item, click after "Jose," and then press the **Backspace** key. The "e" is deleted.

2. Click the **Insert** tab, and then in the Symbols group, click the **Symbol** button. The Symbol dialog box opens.

3. Drag the scroll box to the top of the vertical scroll bar, click the **Subset** arrow, and then click **Latin-1 Supplement**.

4. Click the down scroll arrow three times, and then in the bottom row, click **é**. In the bottom-left corner of the Symbol dialog box, the name of the selected character is "Latin Small Letter E With Acute." See Figure 2-20.

Figure 2-20   Symbol dialog box

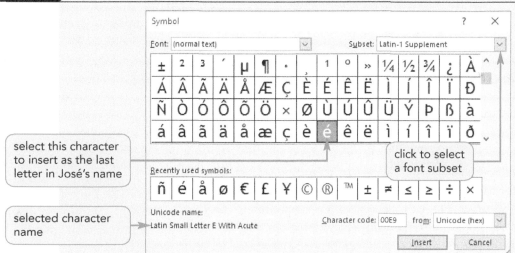

Trouble? If the letter does not appear in the row mentioned in Step 4, someone might have resized the Symbol dialog box. Refer to Figure 2-20 for help locating the symbol.

5. Click the **Insert** button. The letter "é" is inserted in the table, and the Cancel button in the dialog box changes to the Close button.

6. Click the **Close** button. The first word in the first bulleted item is now "José."

7. In the first bulleted item, click after the first "n" in "Quinones," and then press the **Backspace** key to delete the "n."

8. In the Symbols group, click the **Symbol** button to open the Symbols dialog box. The first row contains the é that you just inserted. You need to insert ñ, which appears in the row below the row containing the é.

9. In the second row in the dialog box, click **ñ**, which has the name "Latin Small Letter N With Tilde."

10. Click the **Insert** button, and then click the **Close** button. The first bulleted item is now "José Quiñones." See Figure 2-21.

Figure 2-21   **Symbols inserted on Slide 8**

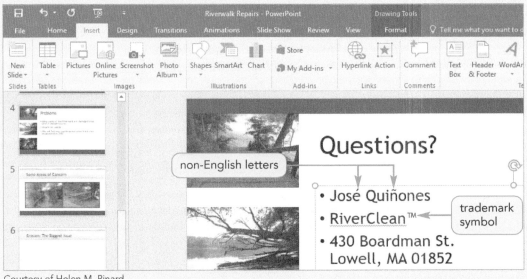

Courtesy of Helen M. Pinard

11. Click a blank area of the slide to deselect the text box, and then save your changes.

Adding Footers and Headers

Sometimes it can be helpful to have information on each slide such as the title of the presentation or the company name. This is called a **footer**. It can also be helpful to have the slide number displayed. For example, you might need to distribute handouts that reference slide numbers. And some presentations need the date to appear on each slide, especially if the presentation contains time-sensitive information. You can easily add this information to all the slides. Usually this information is not needed on the title slide, so you can also specify that it not appear there.

To add a footer, slide numbers, and the date to slides:

TIP

Clicking the Date & Time button and the Slide Number button also opens the Header and Footer dialog box.

1. Click the **Insert** tab on the ribbon if necessary, and then in the Text group, click the **Header & Footer** button. The Header and Footer dialog box opens with the Slide tab selected.

2. Click the **Footer** check box to select it, and then click in the **Footer** box. In the Preview box on the right, the middle placeholder on the bottom is filled with black to indicate where the footer will appear on slides. See Figure 2-22. Note that the position of the footer, slide number, and date changes in different themes.

Figure 2-22   Slide tab in the Header and Footer dialog box

Header and Footer   ?   ✕

Slide   Notes and Handouts

Include on slide   Preview

☐ Date and time

current date will appear here

○ Update automatically

10/1/2017

Language: Calendar type:

English (United States)   Gregorian

● Fixed

10/1/2017

type footer text here

☐ Slide number

☑ Footer

select this check box if you don't want the selected items to appear on the title slide

☐ Don't show on title slide

date position

footer position

slide number position

click to display selected items on all slides

Apply   Apply to All   Cancel

3. Type **Riverwalk Repairs**.

4. Click the **Slide number** check box to select it. In the Preview box, the box in the bottom-right is filled with black.

5. Click the **Date and time** check box to select it. The options under this check box darken to indicate that you can use them, and in the Preview box, the box in the bottom-left is filled with black.

   You don't want the date in the presentation to update automatically each time the presentation is opened. You want it to show today's date so people will know that the information is current as of that date.

6. Click the **Fixed** option button, if necessary. Now you want to prevent the footer, slide number, and date from appearing on the title slide.

7. Click the **Don't show on title slide** check box to select it, and then click the **Apply to All** button. On Slide 8, the footer, date, and slide number are displayed. See Figure 2-23.

Figure 2-23   Date, footer, and slide number on Slide 8

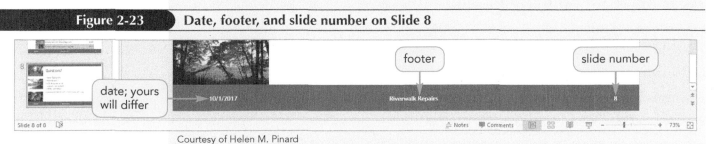

footer

slide number

date; yours will differ

10/1/2017

Riverwalk Repairs

8

Slide 8 of 8

≡ Notes   💬 Comments   – ──│── + 73%

Courtesy of Helen M. Pinard

8. Display **Slide 1** (the title slide). Notice the footer, date, and slide number do not appear on the title slide.

In common usage, a footer is any text that appears at the bottom of every page in a document or every slide in a presentation. However, as you saw when you added the footer in the Header and Footer dialog box, in PowerPoint a footer is specifically the text that appears in the Footer box on the Slide tab in that dialog box and in the footer text box on the slides. This text box can appear anywhere on the slide; in some themes the footer appears at the top of slides. This information does not appear on notes pages and handouts. You need to add footers to notes pages and handouts separately.

A **header** is information displayed at the top of every page. Slides do not have headers, but you can add a header to handouts and notes pages. Like a footer, in PowerPoint a header refers only to the text that appears in the Header text box on handouts and notes pages. In addition to headers and footers, you can also display a date and the page number on handouts and notes pages.

To modify the header and footer on handouts and notes pages:

1. On the Insert tab, in the Text group, click the **Header & Footer** button. The Header and Footer dialog box opens with the Slide tab selected.

2. Click the **Notes and Handouts** tab. This tab includes a Page number check box and a Header box. The Page number check box is selected by default, and in the Preview, the lower-right rectangle is bold to indicate that this is where the page number will appear.

3. Click the **Header** check box to select it, click in the **Header** box, and then type **Riverwalk Repairs**.

4. Click the **Footer** check box to select it, click in the **Footer** box, and then type your name.

5. Click the **Apply to All** button. To see the effect of modifying the handouts and notes pages, you need to look at the print preview.

6. Click the **File** tab to open Backstage view, and then in the navigation bar, click **Print**.

7. Under Settings, click the **Full Page Slides** button, and then click **Notes Pages**. The preview shows Slide 1 as a notes page. The header and footer you typed appear, along with the page number. See Figure 2-24.

| Figure 2-24 | Header and footer on the Slide 1 notes page |

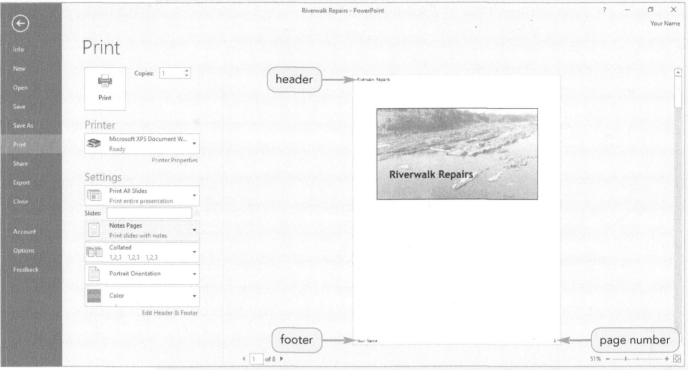

Courtesy of Helen M. Pinard

▶ **8.** At the top of the navigation bar, click the **Back** button ⊙ to return to Normal view.

▶ **9.** Save your changes.

You have modified a presentation by applying a theme used in another presentation, inserting and formatting pictures and shapes, and inserting a table and characters that are not on your keyboard. You also added footer and header information to slides and handouts. In the next session, you will continue modifying the presentation by applying and modifying transitions and animations, adding and modifying videos, and creating an Office mix.

Session 2.1 Quick Check

REVIEW

1. Which contextual tab appears on the ribbon when a shape is selected?
2. What is a style?
3. What is a shape's fill?
4. In a table, what is the intersection of a row and column called?
5. How do you know if an entire table is selected and not just active?
6. How do you insert characters that are not on your keyboard?
7. In PowerPoint, what is a footer?

Session 2.2 Visual Overview:

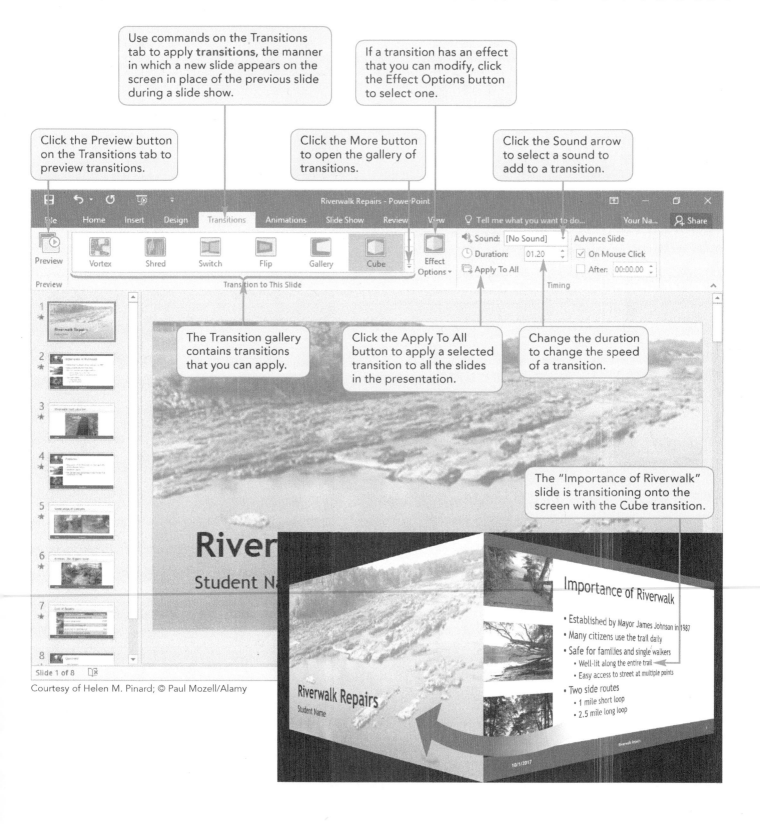

Use commands on the Transitions tab to apply **transitions**, the manner in which a new slide appears on the screen in place of the previous slide during a slide show.

If a transition has an effect that you can modify, click the Effect Options button to select one.

Click the Preview button on the Transitions tab to preview transitions.

Click the More button to open the gallery of transitions.

Click the Sound arrow to select a sound to add to a transition.

The Transition gallery contains transitions that you can apply.

Click the Apply To All button to apply a selected transition to all the slides in the presentation.

Change the duration to change the speed of a transition.

The "Importance of Riverwalk" slide is transitioning onto the screen with the Cube transition.

Courtesy of Helen M. Pinard; © Paul Mozell/Alamy

Importance of Riverwalk

- Established by Mayor James Johnson in 1987
- Many citizens use the trail daily
- Safe for families and single walkers
  - Well-lit along the entire trail
  - Easy access to street at multiple points
- Two side routes
  - 1 mile short loop
  - 2.5 mile long loop

Riverwalk Repairs
Student Name
10/1/2017

Using Animations and Transitions

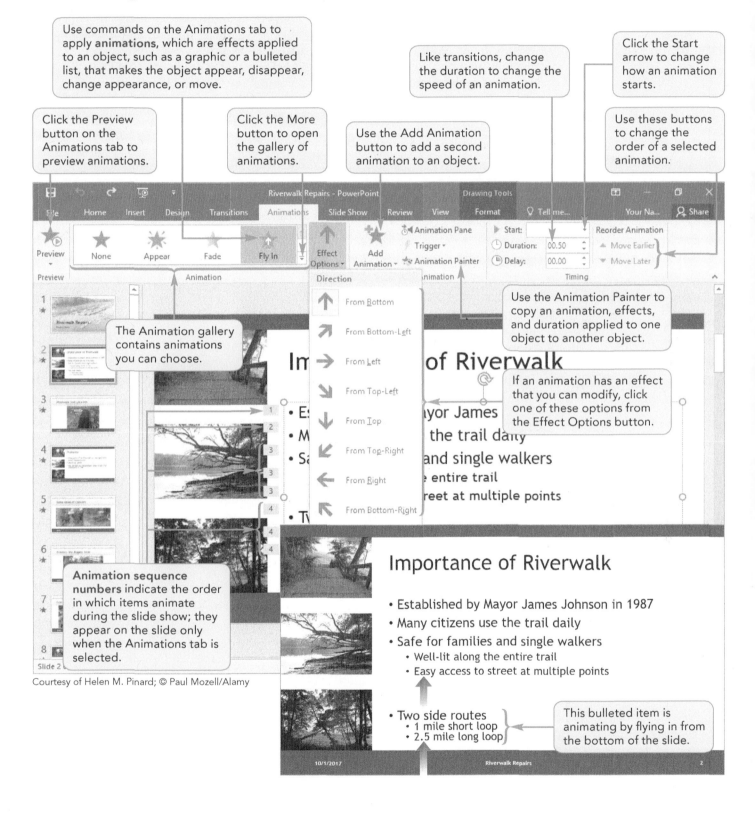

Use commands on the Animations tab to apply **animations**, which are effects applied to an object, such as a graphic or a bulleted list, that makes the object appear, disappear, change appearance, or move.

Like transitions, change the duration to change the speed of an animation.

Click the Start arrow to change how an animation starts.

Click the Preview button on the Animations tab to preview animations.

Click the More button to open the gallery of animations.

Use the Add Animation button to add a second animation to an object.

Use these buttons to change the order of a selected animation.

The Animation gallery contains animations you can choose.

Use the Animation Painter to copy an animation, effects, and duration applied to one object to another object.

If an animation has an effect that you can modify, click one of these options from the Effect Options button.

Animation sequence numbers indicate the order in which items animate during the slide show; they appear on the slide only when the Animations tab is selected.

This bulleted item is animating by flying in from the bottom of the slide.

Courtesy of Helen M. Pinard; © Paul Mozell/Alamy

Importance of Riverwalk

- Established by Mayor James Johnson in 1987
- Many citizens use the trail daily
- Safe for families and single walkers
  - Well-lit along the entire trail
  - Easy access to street at multiple points
- Two side routes
  - 1 mile short loop
  - 2.5 mile long loop

10/1/2017   Riverwalk Repairs   2

Applying Transitions

The Transitions tab contains commands for changing slide transitions. Refer to the Session 2.2 Visual Overview for more information about transitions. Unless you change it, the default is for one slide to disappear and the next slide to immediately appear on the screen. You can modify transitions in Normal or Slide Sorter view.

Transitions are organized into three categories: Subtle, Exciting, and Dynamic Content. Dynamic Content transitions are a combination of the Fade transition for the slide background and a different transition for the slide content. If slides have the same background, it looks like the slide background stays in place and only the slide content moves.

Inconsistent transitions can be distracting and detract from your message, so generally it's a good idea to apply the same transition to all of the slides in the presentation. Depending on the audience and topic, you might choose different effects of the same transition for different slides, such as changing the direction of a Wipe or Push transition. If there is one slide you want to highlight, for instance, the last slide, you can use a different transition for that slide.

REFERENCE

Adding Transitions

- In the Slides pane in Normal view or in Slide Sorter view, select the slide(s) to which you want to add a transition, or, if applying to all the slides, select any slide.
- On the ribbon, click the Transitions tab.
- In the Transition to This Slide group, click the More button to display the gallery of transitions, and then click a transition in the gallery.
- If desired, in the Transition to This Slide group, click the Effect Options button, and then click an effect.
- If desired, in the Timing group, click the Sound arrow to insert a sound effect to accompany each transition.
- If desired, in the Timing group, modify the time in the Duration box to modify the speed of the transition.
- To apply the transition to all the slides in the presentation, in the Timing group, click the Apply To All button.

José wants to add more interesting transitions between the slides.

To apply transitions to the slides:

1. If you took a break after the previous session, make sure the **Riverwalk Repairs** presentation is open, and then display **Slide 2** ("Importance of Riverwalk").

2. On the ribbon, click the **Transitions** tab.

3. In the Transition to This Slide group, click the **Reveal** transition. The transition previews as Slide 1 (the title slide) appears, fades away, and then Slide 2 fades in. The Reveal transition is now shaded in the gallery. In the Slides pane, a star appears next to the Slide 2 thumbnail. If you missed the preview, you can see it again.

4. In the Preview group, click the **Preview** button. The transition previews again.

5. In the Transition to This Slide group, click the **More** button. The gallery opens listing all the transitions. See Figure 2-25.

| Figure 2-25 | Transitions gallery |

Subtle transitions

Exciting transitions

Dynamic Content transitions

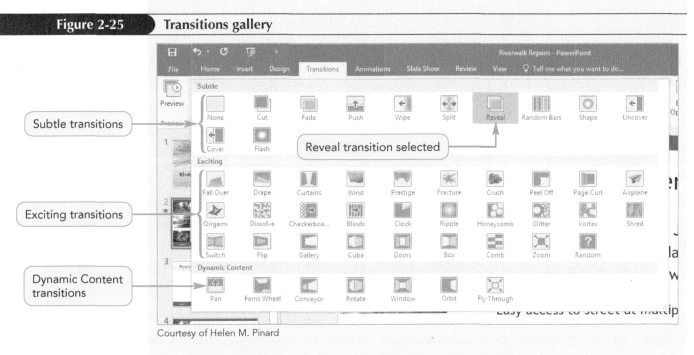

Reveal transition selected

Courtesy of Helen M. Pinard

▶ **6.** Click the **Push** transition. The preview shows Slide 2 slide up from the bottom and push Slide 1 up and out of view.

Most transitions have effects that you can modify. For example, the Peel Off transition can peel from the bottom-left or the bottom-right corner, and the Wipe transition can wipe from any direction. You'll modify the transition applied to Slide 2.

To modify the transition effect for Slide 2:

▶ **1.** In the Transition to This Slide group, click the **Effect Options** button. The effects that you can modify for the Push transition are listed on the menu.

▶ **2.** Click **From Right**. The Push transition previews again, but this time Slide 2 slides from the right to push Slide 1 left. The available effects change depending on the transition selected.

▶ **3.** In the Transition to This Slide group, click the **Shape** transition. The transition previews with a brief view of Slide 1, before Slide 2 appears in the center of Slide 1 and enlarges in a circular shape to fill the slide.

▶ **4.** Click the **Effect Options** button. The effects that you can modify for the Shape transition are listed.

▶ **5.** Click **Out**. The preview of the transition with this effect displays Slide 2 in the center of Slide 1 that grows in a rectangular shape to fill the slide.

Finally, you can also change the duration of a transition. The duration is how long it takes the transition to finish, in other words, the speed of the transition. To make the transition faster, decrease the duration; to slow the transition down, increase the duration. José likes the Shape transition, but he thinks it is a little fast, so you will increase the duration. Then you can apply the modified transition to all the slides.

To change the duration of the transition and apply it to all the slides:

▶ **1.** In the Timing group, click the **Duration** up arrow twice to change the duration to 1.50.

▶ **2.** In the Preview group, click the **Preview** button. The transition previews once more, a little more slowly than before. Right now, the transition is applied only to Slide 2. You want to apply it to all the slides.

▶ **3.** In the Timing group, click the **Apply To All** button.

In the Slides pane, the star indicating that a transition is applied to the slide appears next to all of the slides in the presentation. You should view the transitions in Slide Show view to make sure you like the final effect.

▶ **4.** On the Quick Access Toolbar, click the **Start From Beginning** button. Slide 1 (the title slide) appears in Slide Show view.

▶ **5.** Press the **spacebar** or the **Enter** key to advance through the slide show. The transitions look fine.

▶ **6.** End the presentation, and then save your changes.

Make sure you click the Apply To All button or the transition is applied only to the currently selected slide or slides.

Applying Animations

Animations add interest to a slide show and draw attention to the text or object being animated. For example, you can animate a slide title to fly in from the side or spin around like a pinwheel to draw the audience's attention to that title. Refer to the Session 2.2 Visual Overview for more information about animations.

Animation effects are grouped into four types:

• **Entrance**—Text and objects are not shown on the slide until the animation occurs; one of the most commonly used animation types.
• **Emphasis**—Text and objects on the slide change in appearance or move.
• **Exit**—Text and objects leave the screen before the slide show advances to the next slide.
• **Motion Paths**—Text and objects follow a path on a slide.

Animating Objects

You can animate any object on a slide, including pictures, shapes, and text boxes. To animate an object you click it, and then select an animation in the Animation group on the Animations tab.

REFERENCE

Applying Animations

• On the slide displayed in Normal view, select the object you want to animate.
• On the ribbon, click the Animations tab.
• In the Animation group, click the More button to display the gallery of animations, and then click an animation in the gallery.
• If desired, in the Animation group, click the Effect Options button, and then click a direction effect; if the object is a text box, click a sequence effect.
• If desired, in the Timing group, modify the time in the Duration box to modify the speed of the animation.
• If desired, in the Timing group, click the Start arrow, and then click a different start timing.

Slide 5 contains two pictures of damaged parts of the trail. José wants you to add an animation to the title text on this slide.

To animate the title on Slide 5:

▶ **1.** Display **Slide 5** ("Some Areas of Concern"), and then click the **Animations** tab on the ribbon. The animations in the Animation group are grayed out, indicating they are not available. This is because nothing is selected on the slide.

▶ **2.** Click the **Some Areas of Concern** title text. The animations in the Animation group are green to indicate that they are now available. All of the animations currently visible in the Animation group are entrance animations.

▶ **3.** In the Animation group, click the **Fly In** animation. This entrance animation previews on the slide—the title text disappears and then flies in from the bottom. In the Timing group, the Start box displays On Click, which indicates that this animation will occur when you advance the slide show by clicking the mouse or pressing the spacebar or the Enter key.

Notice the animation sequence number 1 in the box to the left of the title text box, which indicates that this is the first animation that will occur on the slide. You can preview the animation again if you missed it.

▶ **4.** In the Preview group, click the **Preview** button. The animation previews again.

▶ **5.** In the Animation group, click the **More** button. The Animation gallery opens. The animation commands are listed by category, and each category appears in a different color. At the bottom are four commands, each of which opens a dialog box listing all the effects in that category. See Figure 2-26. You will try an emphasis animation.

Figure 2-26	Animation gallery

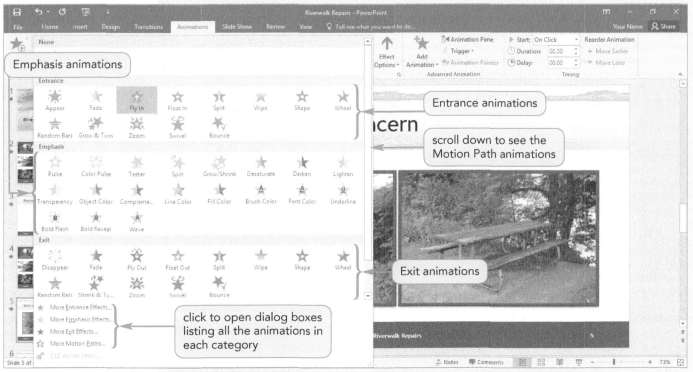

Courtesy of Helen M. Pinard

▶ **6.** Under Emphasis, click the **Underline** animation. The Underline animation replaces the Fly In animation, and the slide title is underlined in the preview.

The Underline animation you applied to the slide title is an example of an emphasis animation that is available only to text. You cannot apply that animation to objects such as pictures.

Slide 5 contains photos showing some areas of trail damage. To focus the audience's attention on one photo at time, you will apply an entrance animation to the photos so that they appear one at a time during the slide show.

To apply entrance animations to the photos on Slide 5:

▶ **1.** With Slide 5 ("Some Areas of Concern") displayed, click the picture on the right.

▶ **2.** In the Animation group, click the **More** button. Notice that in the Emphasis section, six of the animations, including the Underline animation you just applied to the slide title, are gray, which means they are not available for this object. These six animations are available only for text.

▶ **3.** In the Entrance section, click the **Split** animation. The picture appears starting from the left and right edges. In the Timing group, On Click appears in the Start box, indicating that this animation will occur when you advance the slide show. The animation sequence number to the left of the selected picture is 2, which indicates that this is the second animation that will occur on the slide when you advance the slide show.

You need to change the direction from which this animation appears, and you want to slow it down.

To change the effect and duration of the animation applied to the photo:

▶ **1.** In the Animation group, click the **Effect Options** button. This menu contains Direction options.

▶ **2.** Click **Vertical Out**. The preview shows the picture appearing, starting from the center and building out to the left and right edges.

▶ **3.** In the Timing group, click the **Duration** up arrow once. The duration changes from 0.50 seconds to 0.75 seconds.

After you have applied and customized the animation for one object, you can use the Animation Painter to copy that animation to other objects. You will copy the Split entrance animation to the other photo on Slide 5.

To use the Animation Painter to copy the animation on Slide 5:

▶ **1.** Click the photo on the right to select it.

▶ **2.** In the Advanced Animation group, click the **Animation Painter** button, and then move the pointer onto the slide. The pointer changes to ⬐ 🖌.

▶ **3.** Click the photo on the left. The Split animation with the Vertical Out effect and a duration of 0.75 seconds is copied to the photo on the left and previews.

After you apply animations, you should watch them in Slide Show, Presenter, or Reading view to see what they will look like during a slide show. Remember that On Click appeared in the Start box for each animation that you applied, which means that to see the animation during the slide show, you need to advance the slide show.

To view the animations on Slide 5 in Slide Show view:

▶ **1.** Make sure Slide 5 ("Some Areas of Concern") is displayed.

▶ **2.** On the status bar, click the **Slide Show** button 🖵. Slide 5 appears in Slide Show view. Only the photo that is part of the layout and the title appear on the slide.

▶ **3.** Press the **spacebar** to advance the slide show. The first animation, the emphasis animation that underlines the title, occurs.

▶ **4.** Press the **spacebar** again. The photo on the right appears starting at the center of the photo and building out to the left and right edges.

▶ **5.** Click anywhere on the screen. The photo on the left appears with the same animation as the photo on the right.

▶ **6.** Press the **Esc** key. Slide 5 appears in Normal view.

José doesn't like the emphasis animation on the slide title. It's distracting because the title is not the focus of this slide, the photos are. Also, it would be better if the photo on the left appeared before the photo on the right. To fix this, you can remove the animation applied to the title and change the order of the animations applied to the photos.

To remove the title animation and change the order of the photo animations:

▶ **1.** Click the **slide title**. In the Animation group, the yellow emphasis animation Underline is selected.

TIP

You can also click the animation sequence icon, and then press the Delete key to remove an animation.

▶ **2.** In the Animation group, click the **More** button, and then at the top of the gallery, click **None**. The animation that was applied to the title is removed, the animation sequence icon no longer appears next to the title text box, and the other two animation sequence icons on the slide are renumbered 1 and 2.

Now you need to select the animation applied to the photo on the left and change it so that it occurs first. You can select the object or the animation sequence icon to modify an animation.

▶ **3.** Next to the left photo, click the animation sequence icon **2**. In the Animation group, the green Split entrance animation is selected. See Figure 2-27.

| Figure 2-27 | Animation selected to change its order |

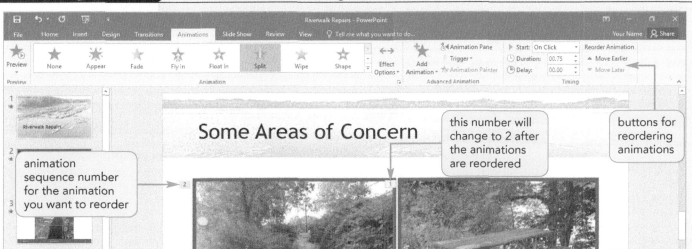

Courtesy of Helen M. Pinard; © Paul Mozell/Alamy

▶ **4.** In the Timing group, click the **Move Earlier** button. The animation sequence icon next to the photo on the left changes from 2 to 1, and the animation sequence icon next to the photo on the right changes from 1 to 2.

▶ **5.** In the Preview group, click the **Preview** button. The photo on the left appears, and then the photo on the right appears.

Changing How an Animation Starts

Remember that when you apply an animation, the default is for the object to animate On Click, which means when you advance through the slide show. You can change this so that an animation happens automatically, either at the same time as another animation or when the slide transitions, or after another animation.

José wants the photo on the right to appear automatically, without the presenter needing to advance the slide show.

To change how the animation for the photo on the right starts:

▶ **1.** With Slide 5 ("Some Areas of Concern") displayed, click the photo on the right. The entrance animation Split is selected in the Animation group, and in the Timing group, On Click appears in the Start box.

▶ **2.** In the Timing group, click the **Start** arrow. The three choices for starting an animation—On Click, With Previous, and After Previous—are listed on the menu.

▶ **3.** Click **After Previous**. Now this photo will appear automatically after the photo on the left appears. Notice that the animation sequence number next to this photo changed to 1, the same number as the animation sequence number next to the photo on the left. This is because you will not need to advance the slide show to start this animation.

When you preview an animation, it plays automatically on the slide in Normal view, even if the timing setting for the animation is On Click. To make sure the timing settings are correct, you need to watch the animation in a slide show.

To view and test the animations:

▶ **1.** On the status bar, click the **Slide Show** button 🖵. Slide 5 appears in Slide Show view.

▶ **2.** Press the **spacebar**. The photo on the left appears, and then the photo on the right appears.

▶ **3.** Press the **Esc** key to end the slide show.

When you set an animation to occur automatically during the slide show, it happens immediately after the previous action. If that is too soon, you can add a pause before the animation. To do this, you increase the time in the Delay box in the Timing group.

To give the audience time to look at the first photo before the second photo appears on Slide 5, you will add a delay to the animation that is applied to the photo on the right.

To add a delay to the After Previous animation:

▶ **1.** With Slide 5 ("Some Areas of Concern") displayed, click the photo on the right, if necessary, to select it. In the Timing group, 00.00 appears in the Delay box.

2. In the Timing group, click the **Delay** up arrow four times to change the time to one second. After the photo on the left appears (the previous animation), the photo on the right will appear after a delay of one second.

3. On the status bar, click the **Slide Show** button ⬚. Slide 5 appears in Slide Show view.

4. Press the **spacebar**. The photo on the left appears, and then after a one-second delay, the photo on the right appears.

5. Press the **Esc** key to end the slide show, and then save your changes.

Animating Lists

If you animate a list, the default is for each of the first-level items to animate On Click. This type of animation focuses your audience's attention on each item, without the distraction of items that you haven't discussed yet. José wants you to add an Entrance animation to the bulleted list on Slide 2. He wants each first-level bulleted item to appear on the slide one at a time so that the audience won't be able to read ahead while he is discussing each point.

To animate the bulleted lists:

1. Display **Slide 2** ("Importance of Riverwalk"), and then click anywhere in the bulleted list to make the text box active.

2. On the Animations tab, in the Animation group, click the **Fly In** animation. The animation previews on the slide as the bulleted items fly in from the bottom. When the "Safe for families" and "Two routes" items fly in, their subitems fly in with them. After the preview is finished, the numbers 1 through 4 appear next to the bulleted items. Notice that the subitems have the same animation sequence number as their first-level items. This means that the start timing for the subitems is set to With Previous or After Previous. See Figure 2-28.

| **Figure 2-28** | **Fly In entrance animation applied to a bulleted list with subitems** |

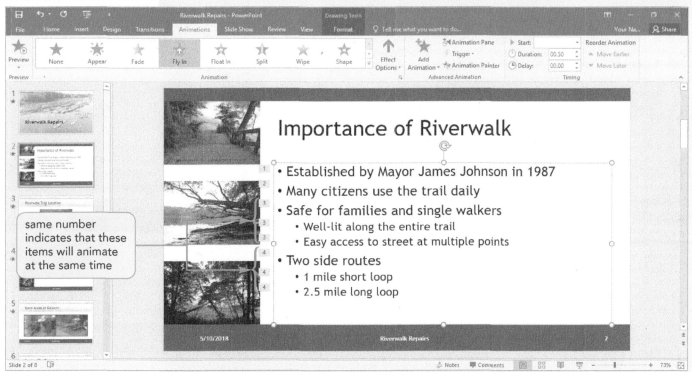

Courtesy of Helen M. Pinard; © Paul Mozell/Alamy

3. Next to the "Safe for families and single walkers" bulleted item, click the animation sequence icon **3** to select it. In the Timing group, On Click appears in the Start box.

4. Next to the subitem "Well-lit along the entire trail," click the animation sequence icon **3**. In the Timing group, With Previous appears in the Start box.

If you wanted to change how the items in the list animate during the slide show, you could change the start timing of each item, or you could change the sequence effect. Sequence effects appear on the Effect Options menu in addition to the Direction options when an animation is applied to a text box. The default is for the items to appear By Paragraph. This means each first-level item animates one at a time—with its subitems, if there are any—when you advance the slide show. You can change this setting so that the entire list animates at once as one object, or so that each first-level item animates at the same time but as separate objects.

To examine the Sequence options for the animated list:

1. Click in the bulleted list, and then in the Animation group, click the **Effect Options** button. The Sequence options appear at the bottom of the menu, below the Direction options, and By Paragraph is selected. See Figure 2-29.

Figure 2-29 Animation effect options for a bulleted list

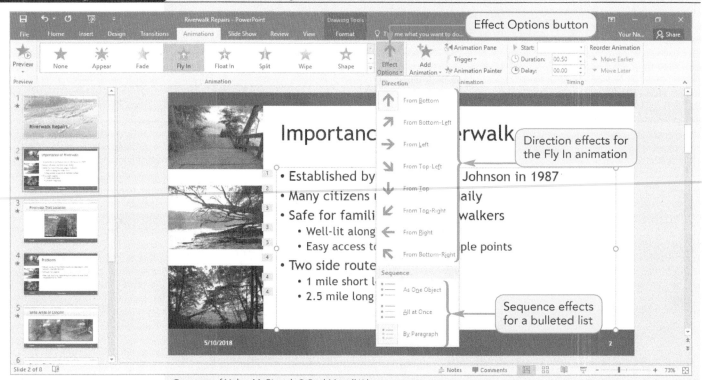

Courtesy of Helen M. Pinard; © Paul Mozell/Alamy

2. Click **As One Object**. The animation preview shows the entire text box fly in. After the preview, only one animation sequence icon appears next to the text box, indicating that the entire text box will animate as a single object. In the Timing group, On Click appears in the Start box.

3. In the Animation group, click the **Effect Options** button, and then under Sequence, click **All at Once**. The animation previews again, but this time each of the first-level items fly in as separate objects, although they all fly in at the same time. After the preview, animation sequence icons, all numbered 1, appear next to each bulleted item, indicating that each item will animate separately but you only need to advance the slide show once.

4. Next to the first bulleted item, click the animation sequence icon **1**. In the Timing group, On Click appears in the Start box.

5. Next to the second bulleted item ("Many citizens use the trail daily"), click the animation sequence icon **1**. In the Timing group, With Previous appears in the Start box.

6. In the Animation group, click the **Effect Options** button, and then click **By Paragraph**. The sequence effect is changed back to its original setting.

7. Save your changes.

PROSKILLS

Decision Making: Just Because You Can Doesn't Mean You Should

PowerPoint provides you with many tools that enable you to create interesting and creative slide shows. However, you need to give careful thought before deciding to use a tool to enhance the content of your presentation. Just because a tool is available doesn't mean you should use it. One example of a tool to use sparingly is sound effects with transitions. Most of the time you do not need to use sound to highlight the fact that one slide is leaving the screen while another appears.

You will also want to avoid using too many or frivolous animations. It is easy to go overboard with animations, and they can quickly become distracting and make your presentation seem less professional. Before you apply an animation, you should know what you want to emphasize and why you want to use an animation. Remember that animations should always enhance your message. When you are finished giving your presentation, you want your audience to remember your message, not your animations.

Adding and Modifying Video

You can add video to slides to play during your presentation. PowerPoint supports various file formats, but the most commonly used are the MPEG-4 format, the Windows Media Audio/Video format, and the Audio Visual Interleave format, which appears in Explorer windows as the Video Clip file type. After you insert a video, you can modify it by changing playback options, changing the length of time the video plays, and applying formats and styles to the video.

Adding Video to Slides

To insert a video stored on your computer or network, click the Insert Video button in a content placeholder, and then in the Insert Video window, in the From a file section, click Browse to open the Insert Video dialog box. You can also click the Video button in the Media group on the Insert tab, and then click Video on My PC to open the same Insert Video dialog box.

REFERENCE

Adding Videos Stored on Your Computer or Network

- In a content placeholder, click the Insert Video button to open the Insert Video window, and then in the From a file section, click Browse to open the Insert Video dialog box; or click the Insert tab on the ribbon, and then in the Media group, click the Video button, and then click Video on My PC to open the Insert Video dialog box.
- Click the video you want to use, and then click the Insert button.
- If desired, click the Video Tools Playback tab, and then in the Video Options group:
  - Click the Start arrow, and then click Automatically to change how the video starts from On Click.
  - Click the Play Full Screen check box to select it to have the video fill the screen.
  - Click the Rewind after Playing check box to select it to have the poster frame display after the video plays.
  - Click the Volume button, and then click a volume level or click Mute.

José gave you a video that he wants you to add to Slide 6. The video shows an eroded bank along the trail.

To add a video to Slide 6 and play it:

1. Display **Slide 6** ("Erosion: The Biggest Issue"), and then in the content placeholder, click the **Insert Video** button. The Insert Video window opens.

2. Next to From a file, click **Browse**. The Insert Video dialog box opens.

3. In the **PowerPoint2 > Module** folder, click **Erosion2**, and then click the **Insert** button. The video is inserted on the slide. The first frame of the video is displayed, and a play bar with controls for playing the video appears below it. See Figure 2-30.

Figure 2-30 ▶ **Video added to Slide 6**

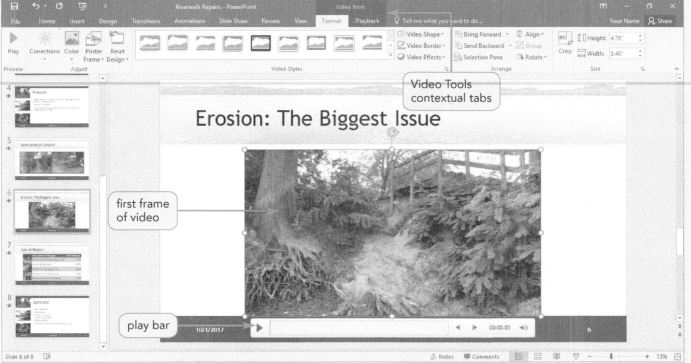

Courtesy of Helen M. Pinard

▶ 4. On the play bar, click the **Play** button ▶. The Play button changes to the Pause button ‖ and the video plays. Watch the 13-second video (note that this video does not have any sound). Next, you'll watch the video in Slide Show view.

▶ 5. On the status bar, click the **Slide Show** button 🖳. Slide 6 appears in Slide Show view.

▶ 6. Point to the **video**. The play bar appears, and the pointer changes to 🖑. You don't need to click the Play button to play the video in Slide Show view; you can click anywhere on the video to play it as long as the 🖑 pointer is visible. While the video is playing, you can click it again to pause it.

▶ 7. Click anywhere on the video. The video plays.

   Trouble? If Slide 7 appeared instead of the video playing, the pointer wasn't visible or you didn't click the video object, so clicking the slide advanced the slide show. Press the Backspace key to return to Slide 6, move the mouse over the video to make the pointer visible, and then click the video.

▶ 8. Before the video finishes playing, move the pointer to make it visible, and then click the **video** again. The video pauses.

▶ 9. Move the pointer to make it visible, if necessary, click the **video** to finish playing it, and then press the **Esc** key to end the slide show.

INSIGHT

Inserting Pictures and Videos You Find Online

In addition to adding pictures and video stored on your computer or network to slides, you can also add pictures and video stored on websites. To add pictures from a website, you click the Online Pictures button in a content placeholder. When you do this, the Insert Pictures window opens, in which you can use the Bing search engine to search for images stored on the Internet. Your results will be similar to those you would get if you typed keywords in the Search box on the Bing home page in your browser. However, in the Insert Pictures window, only images that are licensed under Creative Commons appear. (When you search using Bing in a browser, you see all results, not just the images licensed under Creative Commons.)

To add a video from a website, you click the Insert Video button in a content placeholder to open the Insert Video window. There, you can type search terms in the Search YouTube box to find a video on YouTube, or, if you have the embed code from a website, you can paste the embed code in the Paste embed code here box. When you search for a video on YouTube, videos that match your search terms appear in the window. You click the video you want to add, and then click Insert. To add a video whose embed code you copied, right-click in the Paste embed code here box, click Paste on the shortcut menu, and then click the Insert button in the box.

Trimming Videos

If a video is too long, or if there are parts at the beginning or end of the video that you don't want to show during the presentation, you can trim it. To do this, click the Trim Video button in the Editing group on the Video Tools Playback tab, and then, in the Trim Video dialog box, drag the green start slider or the red stop slider to a new position to mark where the video will start and stop.

José doesn't think the audience needs to watch all 13 seconds of this video, so he wants you to trim it to 10 seconds.

To trim the video on Slide 6:

1. With Slide 6 ("Erosion: The Biggest Issue") displayed, click the **video** to select it, if necessary, and then click the **Video Tools Playback** tab.

2. In the Editing group, click the **Trim Video** button. The Trim Video dialog box opens. See Figure 2-31.

Figure 2-31 ▶ **Trim Video dialog box**

Courtesy of Helen M. Pinard

3. Drag the red **Stop** tab to the left until the time in the End Time box is approximately 10 seconds, and then click the **OK** button.

4. On the play bar, click the **Play** button ▶. The video plays but stops after playing for 10 seconds.

5. Save your changes.

Setting a Poster Frame

The frame that appears on the slide when the video is not playing is called the **poster frame**. You can set the poster frame to be any frame in the video, or you can set the poster frame to any image stored in a file. The default poster frame for a video is the first frame of the video. You can change this so that any frame from the video or any image stored in a file is the poster frame. If the video is set to rewind, you can make the poster frame appear if you set the video to rewind after playing. José wants you to do this for the video on Slide 6.

To set a poster frame for the video on Slide 6:

1. With Slide 6 ("Erosion: The Biggest Issue") displayed, click the **video** to select it, if necessary, and then click the **Video Tools Format** tab.

2. Point to the **play bar** below the video. A ScreenTip appears identifying the time of the video at that point. See Figure 2-32.

Figure 2-32   Setting a poster frame

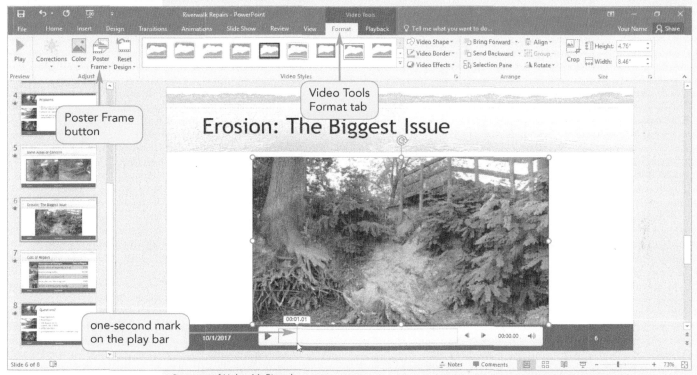

Courtesy of Helen M. Pinard

3. On the play bar, click at approximately the one-second mark. The video advances to the one-second mark, and the frame at the one-second mark appears in the video object.

4. In the Adjust group, click the **Poster Frame** button. The Poster Frame menu opens.

5. Click **Current Frame**. The message "Poster Frame Set" appears in the video's play bar, and the frame currently visible in the video object is set as the poster frame.

Modifying Video Playback Options

You can change several options for how a video plays. The video playback options are listed in Figure 2-33.

Figure 2-33   Video playback options

Video Option	Function
Volume	Change the volume of the video from high to medium or low or mute it.
Start	Change how the video starts, either when the presenter clicks it or the Play button on the play bar or automatically when the slide appears during the slide show.
Play Full Screen	The video fills the screen during the slide show.
Hide While Not Playing	The video does not appear on the slide when it is not playing; make sure the video is set to play automatically if this option is selected.
Loop until Stopped	The video plays until the next slide appears during the slide show.
Rewind after Playing	The video rewinds after it plays so that the first frame or the poster frame appears again.

One of the playback options you can modify is the start timing so that the video plays automatically when the slide appears during the slide show. When you insert a video, its start timing is set to On Click. This start timing means something different for videos than for animations. For animations, On Click means you can do anything to advance the slide show to cause the animation to start. For videos, On Click means you need to click the video object or the Play button on the play bar. If you click somewhere else on the screen or do anything else to advance the slide show, the video will not play. The start timing setting is on the Video Tools Playback tab.

In addition to changing the start timing, you can set a video to fill the screen when it plays during the slide show. If you set the option to play full screen, the video will fill the screen when it plays, covering the slide title and anything else on the slide. You can also set a video to rewind after it plays.

José wants you to change the start timing of the video on Slide 6 so that it starts automatically when Slide 6 appears during a slide show. He also wants the video to fill the screen when it plays during the slide show, and for the video to rewind after it plays. He asks you to set these options.

To modify the playback options of the video:

▶ **1.** With Slide 6 ("Erosion: The Biggest Issue") displayed, click the **video** to select it, if necessary.

▶ **2.** On the ribbon, click the **Video Tools Playback** tab. In the Video Options group, On Click appears in the Start box. See Figure 2-34.

Figure 2-34   Options on the Video Tools Playback tab

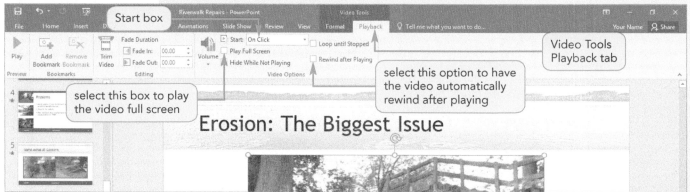

Courtesy of Helen M. Pinard

TIP

You can adjust the volume of a video while it plays, or you can set the default volume by clicking the Volume button in the Video Options group on the Playback tab and then clicking an option on the menu.

3. In the Video Options group, click the **Start** arrow, and then click **Automatically**. Now the video will start automatically when the slide appears during the slide show.

4. In the Video Options group, click the **Play Full Screen** check box to select it. The video will fill the screen when it plays.

5. In the Video Options group, click the **Rewind after Playing** check box to select it. The video will reset to the beginning after it plays and display the poster frame.

6. On the status bar, click the **Slide Show** button. Slide 6 appears briefly in Slide Show view, and then the video fills the screen and plays. After the video finishes playing, Slide 6 reappears displaying the poster frame of the video.

7. Press the **Esc** key to end the slide show, and then save the changes.

Understanding Animation Effects Applied to Videos

When you insert a video (or audio) object, an animation is automatically applied to the video so that you can click anywhere on the video to start and pause it when the slide show is run. This animation is the Pause animation in the Media animation category, and it is set to On Click. The Media animation category appears only when a media object—either video or audio—is selected on a slide. The Pause animation is what makes it possible to start or pause a video during a slide show by clicking anywhere on the video object. (When you click the video to play it, you are actually "unpausing" it.)

When you change the Start setting of a video on the Playback tab to Automatically, a second animation, the Play animation in the Media animation category, is applied to the video as well as the Pause animation, and the start timing of the Play animation is set to After Previous. If there are no other objects on the slide set to animate before the video, the Play animation has an animation sequence number of zero, which means that it will play immediately after the slide transition.

To see these animations, click the Animations tab on the ribbon, and then select a video object on a slide. The Pause and Play animations appear in the Animation gallery in the Media category.

You'll examine the video animations now.

To examine the Media animation effects for the video:

1. With Slide 6 ("Erosion: The Biggest Issue") displayed, click the **video** to select it, if necessary.

2. On the ribbon, click the **Animations** tab. Because you set this video to start automatically, two animation sequence icons appear next to it, one containing a zero and one containing a lightning bolt. In the Animation group, Multiple is selected because two animations are applied to this video. See Figure 2-35.

Figure 2-35   Two animations applied to a video

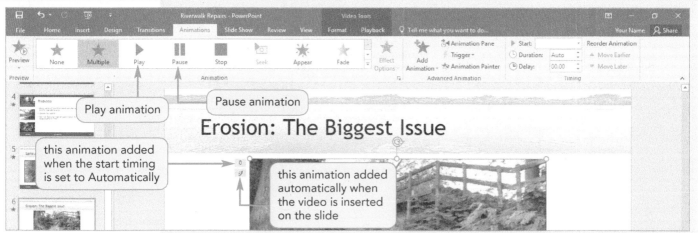

Courtesy of Helen M. Pinard

3. In the Animation group, click the **More** button. The Media category appears at the top of the Animation gallery because a media object is selected.

4. Press the **Esc** key. The gallery closes without you making a selection.

When more than one animation is applied to any object, you need to click each animation sequence icon to see which animation is associated with each icon.

5. Click the **lightning bolt** animation sequence icon. In the Animation group, the Pause animation is selected, and in the Timing group, On Click appears in the Start box. This animation is applied automatically to all videos when you add them to slides. It is because of this animation that you can click anywhere on the video object during a slide show to play or pause it.

6. Click the **0** animation sequence icon. In the Animation group, Play is selected, and in the Timing group, After Previous appears in the Start box. This Play animation was added to this video when you selected Automatically in the Start box on the Playback tab.

Compressing and Optimizing Media

TIP

If you might want to show the presentation using a projector capable of high-quality display, save a copy of the presentation before you compress the media.

As with pictures, you can compress media files. If you need to send a file via email or you need to upload it, you should compress media files to make the final PowerPoint file smaller. The more you compress files, the smaller the final presentation file will be but also the lower the quality. For videos, you can compress using the following settings:

• **Presentation Quality**—compresses the videos slightly and maintains the quality of the videos
• **Internet Quality**—compresses the videos to a quality suitable for streaming over the Internet
• **Low Quality**—compresses the videos as small as possible

With all of the settings, any parts of videos that you trimmed off will be deleted, similar to deleting the cropped portions of photos.

After you compress media, you should watch the slides containing the videos using the equipment you will be using when giving your presentation to make sure the reduced quality is acceptable. Usually, if the videos were high quality to start with, the compressed quality will be fine. However, if the original video quality was grainy, the compressed quality might be too low, even for evaluation purposes. If you decide that you don't like the compressed quality, you can undo the compression.

You will compress the media files you inserted. You need to send the presentation to José via email, so you will compress the media as much as possible.

To compress the videos in the presentation:

▶ 1. With Slide 6 ("Erosion: The Biggest Issue") displayed, click the **File** tab. Backstage view appears displaying the Info screen. See Figure 2-36.

Figure 2-36   **Compression options on the Info screen in Backstage view**

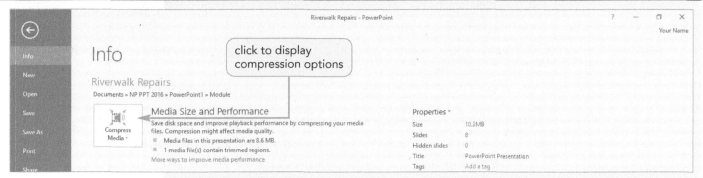

▶ 2. Click the **Compress Media** button. A menu opens listing compression choices.

▶ 3. Click **Low Quality**. The Compress Media dialog box opens listing the video file in the presentation with a progress bar to show you the progress of the compression. See Figure 2-37.

Figure 2-37   **Compress Media dialog box**

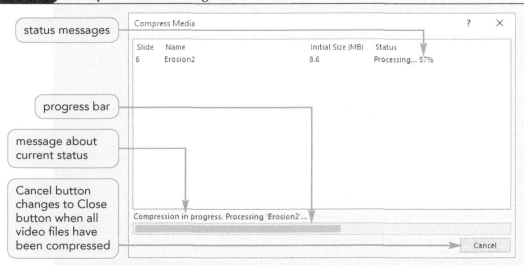

After the file is compressed, a message appears in the Status column indicating that compression for the file is complete and stating how much the video file size was reduced. A message also appears at the bottom of the dialog box stating that the compression is complete and indicating how much the file size of the presentation was reduced. Because there is only one video in this presentation, the amount the video was reduced and the amount the presentation was reduced is the same.

▶ **4.** Click the **Close** button. Next to the Compress Media button on the Info screen, the bulleted list states that the presentation's media was compressed to Low Quality and that you can undo the compression if the results are unsatisfactory. Now you need to view the compressed videos.

▶ **5.** At the top of the navigation bar, click the **Back** button ⊙ to display Slide 6.

▶ **6.** On the status bar, click the **Slide Show** button to display the slide in Slide Show view, and then watch the video. The quality is lower, but sufficient for José to get the general idea after you send the presentation to him via email.

▶ **7.** Press the **Esc** key to end the slide show.

▶ **8.** Display **Slide 1** (the title slide), add your name as the subtitle, and then save your changes.

Now that you have finished working on the presentation, you should view the completed presentation as a slide show.

To view the completed presentation in Slide Show view:

▶ **1.** On the Quick Access Toolbar, click the **Start From Beginning** button 🖳. Slide 1 appears in Slide Show view.

▶ **2.** Press the **spacebar**. Slide 2 ("Importance of Riverwalk") appears in Slide Show view displaying the photos on the slide layout, the slide title, and the footer, date, and slide number.

▶ **3.** Press the **spacebar** four times to display all the bulleted items, and then press the **spacebar** again to display Slide 3 ("Riverwalk Trail Location").

▶ **4.** Press the **spacebar** twice to display Slide 4 ("Problems") and then Slide 5 ("Some Areas of Concern").

▶ **5.** Press the **spacebar**. The photo on the left appears with the Split animation, and then after a one-second delay, the photo on the right appears.

▶ **6.** Press the **spacebar**. Slide 6 ("Erosion: The Biggest Issue") appears, the video fills the screen and plays automatically. When the video is finished, Slide 6 appears again with the poster frame you selected displayed in the video object.

▶ **7.** Press the **spacebar** to display Slide 7 ("Cost of Repairs"), and then press the **spacebar** to display Slide 8 ("Questions?"), the last slide.

▶ **8.** Press the **spacebar** to display the black slide that appears at the end of a slide show, and then press the **spacebar** once more to return to Normal view.

Using the Office Mix Add-In

The presentation with transitions, animations, and video is interesting and should enhance the presentation José will give to the city councilors. However, José wants to post the presentation to a website so that any city councilors—and any citizens—who do not attend the meeting can see the presentation.

To do this, he will use Office Mix, a PowerPoint add-in to create a mix. An **add-in** is software that you can install to add new commands and features to PowerPoint. A **mix** is an interactive video created from a PowerPoint presentation using Office Mix and posted to a website. When you use Office Mix, you can record your voice as you give your presentation and describe your slides. You can also record video of yourself as you speak; this video becomes part of the mix and appears on each slide as people view the mix. You can also record annotations (notes and drawings) that you add to slides while they are displayed. You can also add links to websites that viewers can click when they watch the mix. In addition, you can add quizzes to your mix that ask viewers questions that test their understanding of the content presented. After you create a mix, you can upload it to a Microsoft website using your Microsoft account, and anyone with the link can view it.

Installing Office Mix

In order to use Office Mix, you need to install the add-in. If the Mix tab does not appear on the ribbon to the right of the View tab, then Office Mix might not be installed.

If Office Mix is not installed as an add-in, you need to download it from Microsoft's website and then install it. You first need to close PowerPoint because you cannot install the Office Mix add-in while PowerPoint is running.

Note: The following steps were accurate at the time of publication. However, the Office Mix webpage is dynamic and might change over time, including the way it is organized and how commands are performed.

Also, if you are working in a lab or on a school-issued computer, get permission from your instructor before installing the Office Mix add-in.

To exit PowerPoint and then download and install the Office Mix add-in:

1. In the upper-right corner of the PowerPoint window, click the **Close** button ⊠ to close the presentation and exit PowerPoint.

   Trouble? If there is still a PowerPoint button on the taskbar, another presentation is open. Right-click the PowerPoint button on the taskbar, and then click Close window or Close all windows.

2. Start your browser, and then go to mix.office.com.

   Trouble? If the Internet address in Step 2 is not correct, use a search engine to search for Office Mix.

3. On the Office Mix webpage, click the **Get Office Mix button**. The Welcome to Office Mix page opens, asking you to sign in.

   Trouble? If you are already signed in with your Microsoft account, the Office Mix PowerPoint Add-in page appears instead. Skip Steps 4 and 5.

4. If you have a work or school account associated with Microsoft or Office, click the **Sign in with a work or school account button**; if you do not have a work or school account associated with the computer you are using, click the **Sign in with a Microsoft account button**. The sign in page appears.

   Trouble? If you don't have a Microsoft account, click the Sign in with a Microsoft account button, on the Sign in page that appears, click the Sign up now link, fill in the requested information to create a Microsoft account, and then sign in. Skip Step 5.

5. Enter your username and password in the appropriate boxes, and then click the **Sign in** button. The Office Mix PowerPoint Add-in page appears, and the Office Mix installation file starts downloading automatically.

   Trouble? If the software does not start downloading automatically, click the "click here" link next to "If your download doesn't start automatically."

6. After the file has finished downloading, click the **Run** button in the message box that appears at the bottom of the browser window to start installing the add-in. The Office Mix license dialog box appears.

Trouble? If you are using a browser other than Microsoft Edge, you might see the name of the file—OfficeMix.Setup.exe—in a button at the bottom of the browser window. Click that button to start installing the add-in. If the downloaded file does not appear at the bottom of the window, you need to locate the folder to which the file downloaded, and then double-click the OfficeMix.Setup file. If you can't find the file, ask your technical support person for assistance.

7. Click the **I agree to the license terms and conditions** check box to accept the software license, and then click the **Install** button. The license screen closes and the User Account Control dialog box appears, asking if you want to allow this app to make changes to your PC.

Trouble? If the dialog box displays "Modify Setup" instead of the license agreement, Office Mix is already installed on your computer. Click the Close button, close your browser, skip the rest of the steps in this section, and continue with the section "Creating a Mix."

8. Click the **Yes** button. The User Account Control dialog box closes and the Office Mix Preview Setup dialog box appears. After the add-in is installed, PowerPoint starts.

9. In the Office Mix Preview Setup dialog box, click the **Close** button.

Trouble? If you don't see the Office Mix Preview Setup dialog box, click the Office Mix Preview Setup button 🔲 on the taskbar, and then execute Step 9.

In the PowerPoint window, a Welcome to Office Mix slide is displayed, the Welcome task pane is open, and the Mix tab now appears on the ribbon to the right of the View tab and is the active tab. See Figure 2-38.

Figure 2-38   **Mix tab on the ribbon**

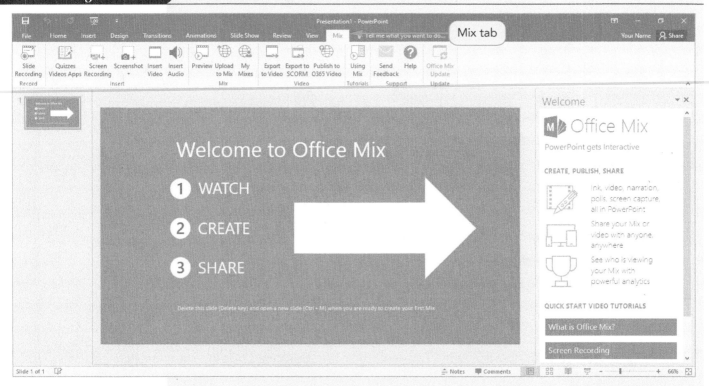

Trouble? If the Mix tab is not the active tab on the ribbon, click the Mix tab on the ribbon.

Trouble? If the Mix tab does not appear on the ribbon, click File, click Options, and then click Customize Ribbon. In the Customize the Ribbon list, click the Mix check box to select it, and then click the OK button.

TIP

If you want to watch video tutorials about Office Mix, on the Mix tab on the ribbon, click the Using Mix button in the Tutorials group to open the Welcome task pane, and then click a button to start a tutorial.

10. In the task pane title bar, click the **Close** button ⊠. The Welcome task pane closes.

Trouble? If the Welcome task pane does not appear on your screen, skip Step 10.

11. On the ribbon, click the **File** tab, and then in the navigation bar, click **Close**. The new presentation with one slide closes.

12. On the taskbar, click your browser's program button, and then close your browser.

Now you are ready to use Office Mix to create an interactive presentation.

Creating a Mix

To create a mix, you basically record the slide show and then post it to a website. In a mix, the recording of each slide is independent of the other slides in the presentation. This means that you can reorder the slides after you have recorded them for the mix, and the timing, annotations, audio, and video that you recorded for each slide will travel with that slide. It also means that you do not need to record all of the slides in one session. You can record each slide individually if you want.

José asked you to practice recording a mix. He wants you to record yourself explaining a few of the slides, but he does not want you to include video of yourself. Because this is just practice, you will use a version of the file that contains only three slides to reduce the file size and make the upload to the Microsoft Mix server faster.

To start recording a mix:

1. Start PowerPoint if necessary, open the file **Mix**, which is located in the **PowerPoint2 > Module** folder, and then save it as **Riverwalk Repairs Mix** to the location where you are storing your files. This file is similar to the file you created in this module, but it contains only three slides.

2. On Slide 1 (the title slide), add your name as the subtitle.

3. On the ribbon, click the **Mix** tab, if necessary. The Mix tab contains commands for recording and working with a mix.

Trouble? If the Mix tab is not on the ribbon, click File, click Options to open the PowerPoint Options dialog box, and then click Customize Ribbon in the navigation pane. In the Customize the Ribbon list, click the Mix check box to select it, and then click the OK button. If the Mix check box is not listed, click Add-ins in the navigation pane on the left, and then click the Go button at the bottom next to Manage COM Add-ins. In the COM Add-Ins dialog box, click the Office Mix check box to select it. (If it is already selected, do not click it.) Click the OK button. If the Mix tab still doesn't appear on the ribbon, open the Customize Ribbon screen in the PowerPoint Options dialog box again, click the Mix check box to select it, and then click the OK button.

4. In the Record group, click the **Slide Recording** button. The recording window appears with Slide 1 displayed. The ribbon in the recording window contains four groups of commands, and the Audio and Video task pane is open on the right side of the window. See Figure 2-39.

Figure 2-39 **Slide recording window in Office Mix**

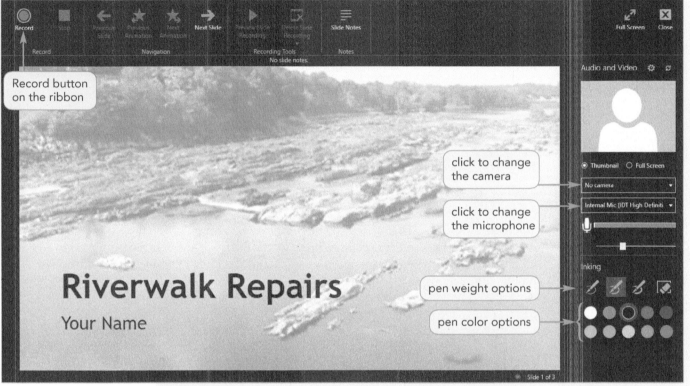

Courtesy of Helen M. Pinard

Before you start recording, you need to set the audio and video options. If you are going to record video of yourself, you need to select a camera. You also need to select a microphone if you are recording yourself speaking.

You can draw on slides while you are recording a mix. When you draw with the pointer, the lines you draw will be the color that is selected at the bottom of the Audio and Video task pane. The default color is black, and the Black color in the task pane has a faint gray border around it to indicate that it is selected. The default weight is medium, and the Medium Pen button is shaded to indicate that it is selected. You can change the pen color and weight during the recording, but it takes several seconds to do this. So in order to have a smooth recording session, you will change these options now.

To set video, audio, and pen options:

1. In the Audio and Video task pane, if the top button below the Thumbnail and Full Screen option buttons is not labeled "No camera," click it, and then click **No camera**.

2. Click the **microphone button** that appears below the No camera button. A menu of microphone options opens.

Trouble? If the only menu option is No microphone, you do not have a microphone built into or connected to your computer. You need to get a microphone and connect it to your computer in order to record yourself speaking. If you do not have a microphone, you can still create the mix, but skip the rest of the steps in this set of steps.

3. Click the microphone you want to use. The menu closes and the bar below the microphone box shows a moving white bar. The moving white bar indicates the volume level that is being detected by the microphone. You can test the microphone.

4. Say **Testing, testing** into the microphone. (If you are using the internal microphone on a laptop, you can speak sitting in front of the laptop and the microphone will pick it up.) When you speak, the white bar increases in size.

   Trouble? If the white bar does not move when you speak, you either selected the wrong option on the microphone menu or the microphone you selected is not enabled in Windows. Repeat Steps 2–4, making sure you select the correct microphone. If the white bar still doesn't move, in the upper-right corner of the window, click the Close button. At the right end of the Windows taskbar, right-click the speaker icon, and then click Recording devices. In the Sound dialog box that opens, on the Recording tab, right-click the microphone you want to use, and then click Enable. (If Enable is not listed on the shortcut menu, the microphone is already enabled.) Click the OK button. In the PowerPoint window, on the Mix tab, click the Slide Recording button to return to the Slide Recording window. Repeat Steps 2–4.

5. In the Audio and Video task pane, in the Inking section, click the **Thick Pen** button ✎.

6. In the Audio and Video task pane, click the **Red** color. When you draw on the slides, the lines you draw will be thick and red.

Now that the recording options are set up, you can record the mix. To do this, you click the Record button on the ribbon.

To record slides with audio for the mix:

1. On the ribbon, in the Record group, click the **Record** button. The Record button changes to the Pause your recording button ❙❙, and a moving, dashed line appears around the slide.

2. Move the pointer on top of the slide. The pointer changes to ✎. This indicates that you can use the pointer to draw on the slide. This also means that you cannot click to advance the slide show.

3. Say **The Riverwalk trail is badly in need of repairs.** and then press the **spacebar**. Slide 2 ("Importance of Riverwalk") appears. On the ribbon, the Move to your next slide button ➡ is no longer available. Instead, the Go to the next animation button ✦ is available. This is because the text on Slide 2 has animations applied, and you need to display the bulleted items before you can advance to the next slide.

   Trouble? If you do not have a microphone, skip the part of Step 3 in which you speak.

4. On the ribbon click the **Go to the next animation** button ⭐, pause for a moment, click the **Go to the next animation** button ⭐ again, pause, and then press the **spacebar**. Three first-level bulleted items and associated subitems appear on the slide.

5. In the second bullet, position the pointer below the word "Safe," press and hold the mouse button, drag below the word "Safe," and then release the mouse button. A red line appears along the path you dragged.

6. In the Navigation group, click the **Move to your next slide** button ➡. Slide 3 ("Some Areas of Concern") appears.

7. Press the **spacebar**. The photo on the left appears, and then after a brief delay, the photo on the right appears.

8. On the ribbon, click the **Stop your recording** button ⬛.

TIP

If you want to rerecord a slide, display that slide, click the Record button, keep the slide displayed for as long as you want, click the Stop your recording button, and then click Yes in the dialog box that asks if you want to overwrite the recording on the slide.

When you record a mix, a mix media object is placed on each slide that you record. The mix media object contains the slide timing, any drawings you added while recording, and any audio or video you recorded. You can see the mix media object on each slide when the slide is displayed in Normal view.

To close the recording window and view the mix media icons:

1. In the upper-right corner, click the **Close** button. The recording window closes, and Slide 3 ("Some Areas of Concern") appears in Normal view. In the upper-right corner of the slide, a mix media icon 🔊 appears. This is the mix media icon that appears when a microphone is selected while you record the mix.

   Trouble? If you do not have a microphone, the mix media icon looks like an analog clock showing three o'clock.

2. Display **Slide 1** (the title slide), and then point to the mix media icon 🔊. A play bar appears.

3. On the play bar, click the **Play** button ▶. The verbal recording you made plays.

Adding Interactive Content to a Mix

Mixes can include interactive content. If you include a link to a website in a mix, people watching the mix can click the link to open their browsers and display that webpage. You can also add slides containing quiz questions that users can answer as they watch the mix. The questions can be multiple choice, true/false, or free response.

To add a quiz to a mix:

1. Display **Slide 2** ("Importance of Riverwalk"), click the **Home** tab, and then click the **New Slide** button. A new Slide 3 with the Title and Content layout is added and is the current slide.

2. Click in the **title text placeholder**, and then type **Quick Quiz**.

3. Click the **Mix** tab, and then in the Insert group, click the **Quizzes Videos Apps** button. The Lab Office Add-ins window opens with the STORE tab selected. See Figure 2-40. Three types of quizzes and a poll are listed below Quizzes and Polls in the window.

Figure 2-40   **Lab Office Add-ins window**

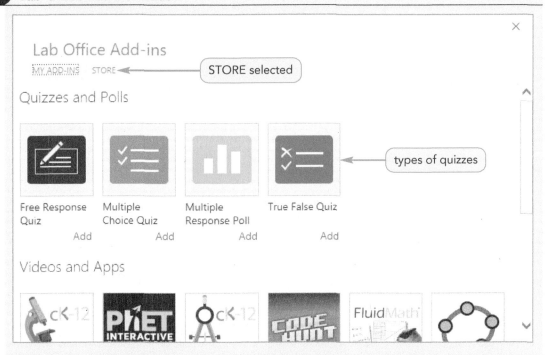

Trouble? If Quizzes and Polls does not appear in the window on your screen, at the top of the window, click STORE.

4. In the Quizzes and Polls section, click **True False Quiz**. The window changes to describe the True False Quiz.

5. Click the **Trust It** button. The window closes, and a True False Quiz object is inserted on Slide 3. See Figure 2-41.

Figure 2-41   **True False Quiz object on Slide 3**

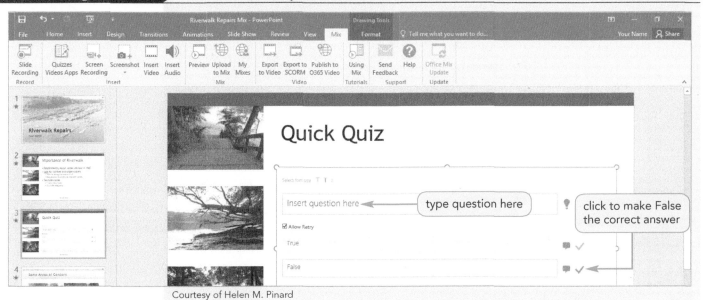

Courtesy of Helen M. Pinard

▶ 6. Click in the **Insert question here** box, and then delete all of the text in the box.

▶ 7. Type **The Riverwalk trail is poorly lit.** in the box. The answer to this is False, so you need to change the correct answer option.

▶ 8. To the right of the False box, click the **Select for correct answer** button ✓. The check mark changes to green to indicate that False is the correct answer.

▶ 9. At the bottom of the quiz object, click the **Preview** button. The borders around the question and answers disappear, and the Allow Retry check box changes to an instruction to select the correct answer. Also, the check marks that the user will click to choose True or False are both colored gray.

▶ 10. Save your changes.

INSIGHT

Recording a Mix of a Presentation That Includes Audio and Video

In a mix, only one media element—that is, audio or video—on a slide will play. This means that if a slide contains more than one media element, only the first element will play when the mix is viewed. Therefore, if you are going to create a mix of a presentation, do not create slides with more than one media element on them.

If a slide contains a media element, you cannot record audio or video of yourself on that slide when you make the mix. This is because you would be adding a second media element to that slide. If you are recording a mix of a presentation that contains media, the recording will stop when the slide containing media appears. To continue recording the mix, you need to move to the next slide, and then restart the recording. When you upload the mix to a website, the slide with the media on it will be included in the mix, and the media (either a video or recorded audio) will play automatically when that slide appears when someone watches the mix.

Previewing and Uploading a Mix

You can preview a mix on your computer. To do this, you click the Preview button in the Mix group on the Mix tab.

To preview the mix:

▶ 1. Display **Slide 1** (the title slide).

▶ 2. On the Mix tab, in the Mix group, click the **Preview** button. Slide 1 appears in Slide Show view, and the voice recording you made plays. Then Slide 2 ("Importance of Riverwalk") appears, the bulleted items animate onto the slide, and the word "Safe" is underlined in red. Next, Slide 3 ("Quick Quiz") appears. The mix will not move past this unless you do something.

▶ 3. Click **True**. "True" is highlighted in green, and its check mark changes to green.

▶ 4. Click the **Submit** button. This is incorrect, so a message appears indicating that, and the Submit button is replaced with the Retry and Continue buttons.

▶ 5. Click the **Retry** button, click **False**, and then click the **Submit** button. This is the correct answer, so a message appears indicating that.

▶ 6. Click the **Continue** button. Slide 4 ("Some Areas of Concern") appears and the two photos appear.

▶ 7. In the bottom-left corner, click the **Close and return to presentation view** button ✖. The mix preview closes and Slide 4 appears in Normal view.

Now that the mix is complete and you have previewed it, you can upload it so that others can view it. Before you upload a mix, you should review any quizzes you added and reset them if you answered them in a preview.

To upload the mix:

▶ **1.** Display **Slide 3** ("Quick Quiz"), and then at the bottom of the slide, click the **Preview** button. The quiz changes to Preview mode, and the Retry and Continue buttons appear at the bottom-right. The False option is selected. You need to reset this slide.

▶ **2.** Click the **Retry** button. The quiz resets and neither answer is selected.

▶ **3.** Save your changes.

▶ **4.** On the Mix tab, in the Mix group, click the **Upload to Mix** button. The Upload to Mix task pane appears on the right.

▶ **5.** At the bottom of the task pane, click the **Next** button. After a moment, the task pane changes to list buttons that you can click to sign in to your Microsoft account.

Trouble? If the task pane indicates that you are signed in, skip Steps 6 and 7 and continue with Step 8.

▶ **6.** If you have a work or school account associated with Microsoft or Office, click the **Sign in with a work or school account** button; if you do not have a work or school account or are using your own computer, click the **Sign in with a Microsoft account** button. The task pane changes to display boxes for your user name and password.

▶ **7.** Enter your username and password in the appropriate boxes, and then click the **Sign in** button. The task pane indicates that you are signed in, and the "This is a new Mix" option button is selected.

Trouble? If a message appears asking you if you want your browser to remember this password, click the Yes or No button depending on your preference. If the computer you are using is a school-issued or lab computer, it is safer to click the No button.

▶ **8.** In the Upload to Mix task pane, click the **Next** button. The task pane changes to show the progress of the upload and the publishing processes. When the mix is published, a message appears in the task pane indicating this, and the "Show me my Mix" button changes to orange.

▶ **9.** Click the **Show me my Mix** button. Your browser starts, and the webpage that contains the details for your mix appears. See Figure 2-42. You can edit the title, description, category, and tags (keywords that describe the mix content), and you can edit the permissions level (that is, change who can view the mix).

Figure 2-42   Riverwalk Repairs Mix Details webpage in the Edge browser

Courtesy of Helen M. Pinard

10. Click the **video**. The webpage containing the mix appears. See Figure 2-43.

Figure 2-43   Riverwalk Repairs Mix webpage

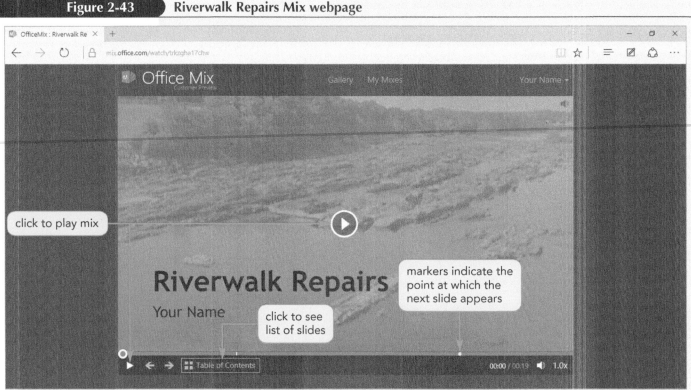

Courtesy of Helen M. Pinard

▶ **11.** Click the **Play** button ▶. The mix plays until Slide 3 ("Quick Quiz") appears. Notice that the transition between the slides is the Fade transition. The Fade transition is the only transition that is used in mixes. You can either answer the quiz or advance to the next slide without answering the quiz.

▶ **12.** In the play bar, click the **next** button ➡. Slide 4 ("Some Areas of Concern") appears, and then the photos appear.

▶ **13.** Click the browser's **Back** button to return to the page containing the details of your mix.

▶ **14.** If you want to sign out of your Microsoft account, click your username in the upper-right corner, click **Sign out**, and then close your browser.

▶ **15.** In the PowerPoint window, close the Upload to Mix task pane.

The final presentation file with transitions, animations, and video is interesting and should enhance the presentation that José will give to the city council. José also plans to record his presentation and create a new mix so that he can send the mix link to anyone who misses his presentation.

REVIEW

Session 2.2 Quick Check

1. What is a transition?

2. What are animations?

3. How do you change the speed of a transition or an animation?

4. When you apply an animation to a bulleted list with subitems, how do the first-level items animate? How do the second-level items animate?

5. What is a poster frame?

6. What does "On Click" mean for a video?

7. What animation is applied to every video that you add to a slide?

8. What is a mix created with the PowerPoint add-in Office Mix?

PRACTICE

Review Assignments

Data Files needed for the Review Assignments: Cleared.jpg, Landscape.jpg, NewSign.jpg, NewStairs.jpg, NewTheme.pptx, NewView.mp4, Railings.jpg, Renewed1.pptx, Renewed2.pptx, Wall.jpg

José Quiñones needs to explain the improvements RiverClean™ made to the Riverwalk trail in Lowell, Massachusetts. He decides to create a presentation that will include photos and video of the improved trail. This presentation will show the city council how the money allocated was spent. José also created a new custom theme to highlight the improvements. Complete the following:

1. Open the presentation **Renewed1**, located in the PowerPoint2 > Review folder included with your Data Files, add your name as the subtitle, and then save it as **Renewed Riverwalk** to the drive and folder where you are storing your files.

2. Apply the theme from the presentation **NewTheme**, located in the PowerPoint2 > Review folder.

3. Change the layout of Slide 4 ("Projects") and Slide 6 ("New Views of the River from the Trail") to the Photo Title and Content layout, and change the layout of Slide 5 ("Views of the Trail") to the Four Content layout.

4. On Slide 5 ("Views of the Trail"), in the top, empty content placeholder, insert the photo **Landscape**, located in the PowerPoint2 > Review folder. In the bottom, empty content placeholder, insert the photo **NewStairs**, also located in the PowerPoint2 > Review folder. Apply the Drop Shadow Rectangle style to the four pictures.

5. On Slide 5, add a Right Arrow shape anywhere on the slide. Type **Improved visibility** in the arrow, and then lengthen the arrow until the text you typed just fits on one line.

6. Change the shape style of the arrow to the Subtle Effect – Orange, Accent 1 style. Then change the outline of the arrow to the Red, Accent 2 color.

7. Make three copies of the arrow. Delete the text in one of the copies, and then type **Debris and brush cleared**. Resize this arrow so that the new text just fits on one line. Delete the text in another copy, and then type **Path set back to prevent more erosion**. Resize this copy so that the new text just fits on one line. Delete the text in the last copy, and then type **New stairs**.

8. Flip the "Path set back to prevent more erosion" and the "New stairs" arrows horizontally.

9. Position the "Improved visibility" arrow so it points to the top-left picture about one-half inch from the top of the photo and so its straight end is aligned with the left edge of the slide. Position the "Debris and brush cleared" arrow so it points to the bottom-left picture about one-half inch from the bottom of that photo and so its straight end is aligned with the left edge of the slide.

10. Position the "Path set back to prevent more erosion" arrow so it points to the top-right picture with its straight end aligned with the right edge of the slide and so that it aligns with the "Improved visibility" arrow. Position the "New stairs" arrow so it points to the bottom-right picture with its straight end aligned with the right edge of the slide and so that its middle aligns with the middle of the "Debris and brush cleared" arrow.

11. On Slide 4 ("Projects"), insert a 3x4 table. Refer to Figure 2-44 to add the rest of the data to the table. Add a row if needed.

Figure 2-44   Data for table on Slide 4 in the Renewed Riverwalk presentation

Improvement	Cost	Donated?
New sign	$0	Cushing Landscaping
New stairs	$1000	No
Cleared out debris and brush	$0	Martinez and Sons
Groundcover & retaining walls	$2000	No

12. On Slide 4, add a new row above the last row in the table. Type **New railings** in the new cell in the Improvement column, type **$0** in the new cell in the Cost column, and then type **Cushing Landscaping** in the Donated? column.

13. On Slide 4, apply the Light Style 2 – Accent 4 table style.

14. On Slide 4, insert a new column to the left of the Improvement column. Fill each cell in the new column (except the first cell) with the following pictures, all located in the PowerPoint2 > Review folder, in order from the second row to the bottom row: **NewSign**, **NewStairs**, **Cleared**, **Railings**, and **Wall**.

15. On Slide 4, format the table as follows:
    - Change the font size of all of the text in the table to 20 points.
    - Change the height of rows 2 through 5 to one inch.
    - Change the width of the first column to two inches.
    - Make the second and third columns just wide enough to hold the widest entry on one line.
    - Align the text in all of the rows except the first row so it is centered vertically.
    - Right-align the data in the Cost column (do not right-align the "Cost" column head).
    - Change the borders between rows 2 through 6 to a three-point black border.

16. Reposition the table so it is centered horizontally on the slide, and then move the table up so that the top half of the top row in the table overlaps the photo behind the slide title.

17. Apply the Uncover transition to any slide. Change the Effect Options to From Bottom, and then change the duration to 0.50 seconds. Apply this transition to all of the slides.

18. On Slide 2 ("Improvements Made"), animate the bulleted list using the Wipe animation. Change the Effect Options to From Left and the duration of the animation to 0.75 seconds.

19. On Slide 5 ("Views of the Trail"), apply the Fade entrance animation to each of the photos. Apply the Wipe animation with the From Left effect to each of the two arrows on the left, and then apply the Wipe animation with the From Right effect to each of the two arrows on the right.

20. On Slide 5, reorder the animations so that the arrow associated with each photo appears immediately after the photo with the top-left photo and arrow appearing first, then the top-right objects, then the bottom-right objects, and finally the bottom-left objects.

21. On Slide 5, add a 0.25-second delay to the animations applied to the arrows.

22. On Slide 6 ("New Views of the River from the Trail"), add the video **NewView**, located in the PowerPoint2 > Review folder. Trim three seconds from the beginning of the video. Set the poster frame to the four-second mark. Finally, set the playback options so that the video starts playing automatically, fills the screen, and rewinds after playing.

23. On Slide 7 ("Thank You!"), add the trademark sign after "RiverClean" and replace the "e" in "Jose" with "é" and the first "n" in "Quinones" with "ñ".

24. Add **Renewed Riverwalk** as the footer on all the slides except the title slide, and display the slide number on all the slides except the title slide. On the notes and handouts, add **Renewed Riverwalk** as the header and your name as the footer, and show page numbers.

25. Compress all the photos in the presentation to 96 ppi, and then compress the media to Low Quality.

26. Save your changes, and then close the Renewed Riverwalk presentation.

27. Open the file **Renewed2**, located in the PowerPoint2 > Review folder, and then save it as **Riverwalk Renewed Mix**.

28. Create a mix using this presentation. Make sure the Pen color is set to red. While Slide 1 is displayed, record yourself saying, "We've made many improvements to the Riverwalk trail," and then on Slide 3 draw an exclamation point after Jose's name.

29. After you record the slides, add a new Slide 3 with the Title and Content layout. Type **Do You Know?** as the slide title. Add a True False quiz to the new Slide 3 with the question **Views of the river from the trail have been greatly improved.** and with True as the correct answer.

30. Save the changes, and then upload the mix.

APPLY

Case Problem 1

Data Files needed for this Case Problem: Equipment.jpg, Exercise.mp4, FitTheme.pptx, HomeFit.pptx

HomeFit Sam Kim is the president of HomeFit, a company in Modesto, California, that sells exercise DVDs and subscriptions to online workout videos. To help advertise his videos, he created a PowerPoint presentation that he will use when he visits local colleges. He asks you to help him finish the presentation, which will include photos, a video, and a table to provide details his audience might be interested in knowing. Complete the following steps:

1. Open the file named **HomeFit**, located in the PowerPoint2 > Case1 folder included with your Data Files, add your name as the subtitle on Slide 1, and then save it as **HomeFit Videos** to the drive and folder where you are storing your files.

2. Apply the theme from the presentation **FitTheme**, located in the PowerPoint2 > Case1 folder.

3. On Slide 2 ("Videos Include"), apply the picture style Double Frame, Black to the picture on the slide, and then change the border color to the Dark Blue, Text 2, Darker 50% color. Apply this same style to the picture on Slide 3 ("Three Phases").

4. On Slide 2, animate the bulleted list using the Float In animation with the Float Down effect, and change the duration to 0.50 seconds. Animate the bulleted list on Slide 3 using the same animation.

5. On Slide 4 ("Sample Clip from a HomeFit Video"), insert the video **Exercise**, located in the PowerPoint2 > Case1 folder. Set the movie to play automatically, fill the screen when playing, and rewind after playing. Trim about eight seconds from the end of the video so the video ends at about the 16-second mark. Set the poster frame to the frame at approximately the seven-second mark.

6. On Slide 5 ("Packages"), add a new row below the row containing "HomeFit Original" in the first column with the following data: **HomeFit Plus, 15 hours of online video per week, More options for cardio and strength training, $45/month**.

7. Change the table style to Light Style 1 – Accent 1. In the header row, change the font to Century Gothic (Headings), change the font size to 20 points, and then align the text so it is centered horizontally. Select the text in the last column, and then center the contents of each cell horizontally.

8. On Slide 6 (the last slide), which has the Blank layout applied, insert the picture **Equipment**, located in the PowerPoint2 > Case1 folder. Crop about an inch off of the bottom of the picture, and then resize it to be the same height as the slide (it will be 7.5 inches high). Position the photo so its left edge aligns with the left edge of the slide.

9. On Slide 6, draw rectangle shape that is 3.5 inches high and 5 inches wide, and then position it so it is centered-aligned with the photo and approximately centered horizontally in the white space on the slide. Type **Subscribe or Order Your DVDs Today!**. Change the font to Century Gothic (Headings), change the font color to Black, make the text bold, and change the font size to 48 points.

10. On Slide 6, remove the fill from the rectangle containing the text, and remove the outline (that is, change the fill to No Fill and change the outline to No Outline).

11. On Slide 6, animate the rectangle containing the text using the entrance animation Grow & Turn. Set its duration to 1.25 seconds, set its start timing to After Previous, and set a delay of one-half second.

12. Compress the all the photos to 96 ppi, deleting cropped areas of pictures, and then compress the media to Low Quality.

13. Apply the Checkerboard transition to all the slides using the default From Left effect and with a duration of 1.25 seconds. Then remove the transition from Slide 1 (the title slide).

14. Save your changes, and then watch the slide show in Slide Show view. Remember, after the transition to Slide 6 (the last slide), wait for the text box to animate automatically.

15. Make sure you saved your changes, and then save a copy of the presentation to the location where you are saving your files as **HomeFit Mix**. Delete Slides 3–5, and then create a mix of the presentation. Change the Inking options to Thick Pen with the Red Color. On Slide 1, record your voice saying, "HomeFit Videos—quality instruction at a fair price." On Slide 2, circle the second subbullet under "Strength Training" after it appears.

16. Insert a new Slide 3 with the Title and Content layout. Type Quiz as the slide title, and then add a True False quiz. Type **HomeFit videos do not include warm-ups or cool-downs.** as the question, and then make False the correct answer.

17. Save your changes, and then upload the mix.

CREATE

Case Problem 2

Data Files needed for this Case Problem: Build.jpg, Finish.jpg, Furniture.pptx, Sand.jpg, Sketch.jpg, Trees.jpg

Cutting Edge Furniture Carl Bertoni is the manager for Cutting Edge Furniture, in Forest Lake, Minnesota. Carl's grandfather founded the business more than 50 years ago, and they now have the resources to expand the company. To advertise this, Carl created a PowerPoint presentation that describes his custom furniture and the painstaking process used to create the pieces. He will use the presentation at home shows around the country. He asks you to help him complete the presentation. Complete the following steps:

1. Open the presentation **Furniture**, located in the PowerPoint2 > Case2 folder included with your Data Files, add your name as the subtitle, and then save the presentation as **Cutting Edge Furniture** to the drive and folder where you are storing your files.

2. On Slide 1 (the title slide), add the trademark symbol after "Furniture."

3. Refer to Figure 2-45 and insert the pictures as shown on Slides 3 through 7, and format the tables on Slide 8. The picture files are located in the PowerPoint2 > Case2 folder.

Figure 2-45   **Slides 3 – 8 in the Cutting Edge Furniture presentation**

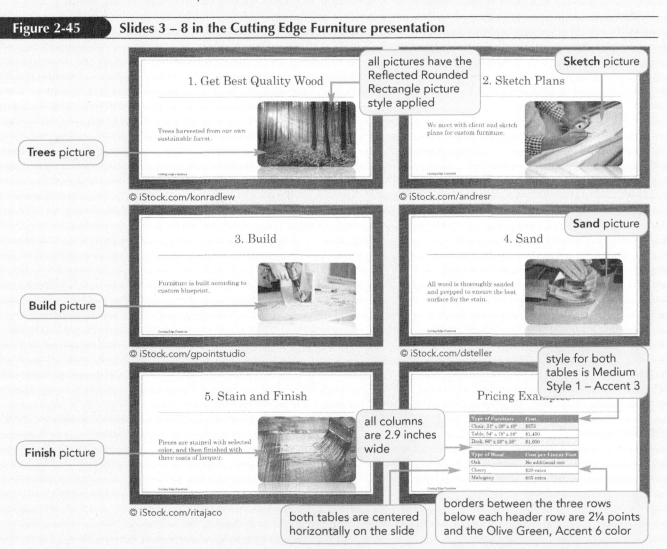

4. Compress all the photos to 96 ppi.

5. On Slide 2 ("What We Offer"), animate both bulleted lists so they appear with the Wipe animation with the From Top effect. Keep the start timing of the list on the left set to On Click, and change the start timing of the list on the right to After Previous with a delay of two seconds. Then, set the start timing of the animations applied to each of the three subitems in the list on the right to With Previous.

6. Apply the Fade transition to Slides 1, 2, 8, and 9. Apply the Conveyor transition to Slides 3 through 7.

7. Add **Cutting Edge Furniture** as a footer on all slides except the title slide. On the notes and handouts, display the current date to be updated automatically, and add your name as a header on the notes and handouts.

8. Save your changes, and then view the slide show. Remember to wait for the second bulleted list to appear on Slide 2 two seconds after the first list appears.

APPLY

Case Problem 3

Data Files needed for this Case Problem: PawsTheme.pptx, Paws.pptx

Primped Paws   Primped Paws is an animal-grooming service in Parkville, Maryland. Jasmine Feurman, the manager, needs to prepare a PowerPoint presentation that shows the care and attention that the groomers at Primped Paws give to animals. She will show the presentation to animal shelters and pet stores to convince them to recommend Primped Paws to new pet owners. Complete the following steps:

1. Open the presentation named **Paws**, located in the PowerPoint2 > Case3 folder included with your Data Files, add your name as the subtitle, and then save it as **Primped Paws** to the drive and folder where you are storing your files.

2. Apply the theme from the presentation **PawsTheme**, located in the PowerPoint2 > Case3 folder.

3. On Slide 3 ("Our Care"), change the font size of the text in the bulleted list to 24 points. On Slide 7 ("Make an Appointment Today"), change the size of the text to 28 points.

4. Change the layout of Slides 5 ("Canine Friends") and 6 ("Feline Friends") to Content Bottom Caption. On Slide 5, type **Daisy gets a bath** in the text placeholder below the picture. On Slide 6, type **Sam gets brushed** in the text placeholder below the picture.

5. On Slides 2 ("About Us") and 3 ("Our Care"), animate the bulleted lists on with the Appear entrance animation.

6. On Slide 3 ("Our Care"), add the Rounded Rectangle shape below the picture. Type **Two groomers keep animals calm** in the shape. Resize the shape so that all of the text appears on one line and the shape is one-half inch high and four inches wide. Center the shape below the picture and so that its middle is aligned with the top edge of the footer. Apply the Moderate Effect – Dark Teal, Accent 1 shape style, and then change the outline color to White. Animate the shape with the Appear animation.

7. On Slide 3, move the animation of the last bulleted item later so that it is the fifth item animated on the slide. Then move the animation of the third bulleted item later so that it is the fourth item animated on the slide. Then change the start timing of the animation applied to the rounded rectangle so that it animates at the same time as the second bulleted item. Watch the slide in Slide Show view to ensure that the rounded rectangle appears at the same time as the second bulleted item.

8. Apply the Metal Rounded Rectangle picture style to the photos on Slides 3 ("Our Care"), 5 ("Canine Friends"), and 6 ("Feline Friends").

9. On Slide 4 ("Pricing"), insert a 5x4 table. Enter the data shown in Figure 2-46.

Figure 2-46   Data for table on Slide 4 in Primped Paws presentation

Size	Wash and Brush	Trim Fur	Trim Nails	All Three
0-15 lbs.	$15	$10	$10	$35
16-40 lbs.	$20	$15	$10	$45
41-80 lbs.	$25	$20	$10	$55

10. On Slide 4, add a new bottom row to the table. Enter the following data in the new row: **81+ lbs.**, **$30, $25, $10, $65**.

11. On Slide 4, increase the size of all the text in the table to 28 points.

12. On Slide 4, horizontally and vertically center the text in the first row, and then right-align all of the dollar values.

13. On Slide 4, add a three-point border (using the default White color) between all the rows and columns.

14. Add **Primped Paws** as the footer, and display the footer and slide number on all of the slides except the title slide. Add your name as a header on the notes and handouts.

15. Apply the Honeycomb transition to any slide, change the duration of the transition to 1.75 seconds, and then apply that transition to all of the slides except the first one.

16. Save your changes, and then view the slide show.

Case Problem 4

CHALLENGE

Data Files needed for this Case Problem: Candy.png, CarePak.pptx, CPTheme.pptx, Games.png, Personal.png, Salty.png

CarePak CarePak markets care packages containing snacks and games to parents of college students. They are based in Carmel, Indiana, and ship to colleges nationwide. Tim King, a sales representative for CarePak, travels to colleges to convince the colleges to partner with CarePak. In return, CarePak will give a percentage of the sales to the college. He wants to use PowerPoint to give a presentation that describes the packages. He has asked you to help him prepare the presentation. Complete the following steps:

1. Open the presentation **CarePak**, located in the PowerPoint2 > Case4 folder included with your Data Files, add your name as the subtitle, and then save the presentation as **CarePak for Students** to the drive and folder where you are storing your files.

2. Apply the theme from the presentation **CPTheme**, located in the PowerPoint2 > Case4 folder.

3. On Slide 2 ("About Us"), animate the bulleted list using the Random Bars animation with the Vertical effect.

4. On Slide 3 ("Package Options"), insert a 2x4 table. Deselect the Header Row check box on the Table Tools Design tab. In the first column, enter **Sweet Snacks Package**, **Salty Snacks Package**, **Games Package**, and **Personalized Combo Package**. In the second column, fill the cells with the pictures **Candy**, **Salty**, **Games**, **Personal**, all located in the PowerPoint2 > Case4 folder.

5. On Slide 3, change the height of all of the rows in the table to 1.2 inches, and then change the width of the second column to 1.8 inches.

6. Make all of the text in the table bold, change the color of the text to the White, Text 1 color, and then change the font size to 24 points. Center the text in the first column vertically in the cells.

7. Remove the fill from all the cells in the first column, and then remove the table borders. (Hint: If the View Gridlines button in the Table group on the Layout tab is selected, you will still see the table gridlines after removing the borders.)

8. On Slide 3, insert a rectangle 1.25 inches high and 7.5 inches wide, and position it on top of the first row in the table so that the text and picture of candy is covered.

9. Apply the Wipe exit animation with the From Left effect to the rectangle. (*Hint*: Make sure you use the Wipe animation in the Exit category, not the Entrance category.)

10. Duplicate the rectangle three times, and then position the three copies on top of the other three rows in the table. (The shapes will slightly overlap.)

⊕ **Explore** 11. Change the fill of each rectangle to the same color as the slide background. (*Hint*: Use the Eyedropper tool on the Shape Fill menu.) Remove the outline from the rectangles.

⊕ **Explore** 12. On Slide 4 ("Customer Reviews"), apply the Appear animation to the bulleted list, and then modify the animation so that the letters appear one by one. (*Hint*: Use the Animation group Dialog Box Launcher, and then change the setting in the Animate text box on the Effect tab.) Speed up the effect by changing the delay between letters to 0.1 seconds.

⊕ **Explore** 13. Add the Typewriter sound to the animation. (*Hint*: Use the Animate text box again.)

14. Apply the Airplane transition to all the slides except Slide 1 (the title slide).

15. Save your changes, and then run the slide show.

16. Make sure you have saved your changes, and then save a copy of the presentation as **CarePak Mix** to the location where you are saving your files, Delete Slides 2 and 4, and then create a mix. Before you record it, change the microphone setting to No microphone and change the pen color to Red. When you record it, remember to advance the slide show to make the rectangles on top of the table disappear, and then after the fourth rectangle disappears, draw a red circle around the Personalized Combo Package on Slide 2.

⊕ **Explore** 17. Add a new Slide 4 titled **Survey** with the Title and Content layout, and insert a Multiple Response Poll. Enter **Which package appeals to you?** as the question, and **Sweet Snacks**, **Salty Snacks**, **Games**, **Combo** as the four options.

18. Save your changes, and upload the mix. Ask a few people to watch the mix and take the survey.

19. Add a new Slide 5 to the CarePak Mix presentation with the Blank layout.

⊕ **Explore** 20. View the responses to your survey by opening your browser, going to www.mix.office.com, and sign in to your Microsoft account if necessary. At the top of the window, click My Mixes. Below the CarePak for Students mix, click Analytics, and then click the slide containing the survey. (It can take up to 10 minutes for the statistics to be updated.)

⊕ **Explore** 21. Switch back to Slide 5 in the CarePak Mix presentation in the PowerPoint window, and then use the Screenshot button in the Insert group on the Mix tab or in the Images group on the Insert tab to take a screenshot of your Analytics screen and paste it on Slide 5. (Note: If you are using Edge as your browser and that window does not appear as an option on the Screenshot menu, switch back to Edge, and then press the Print Screen key (usually labeled PrtScr, PrntScr, or PrtScn on your keyboard). Switch back to Slide 5 in the CarePak Mix presentation, and then on the Home tab, in the Clipboard group, click the Paste button.) With the screenshot selected, on the Picture Tools Format tab, change the height to 7.5 inches and then position the picture on the slide if necessary (the picture will be the same size as the slide).

Applying Advanced Formatting to Objects

Formatting Objects in a Presentation for a Study Abroad Company

OBJECTIVES

Session 3.1
- Create a SmartArt diagram
- Modify a SmartArt diagram
- Add an audio clip to a slide
- Create a chart
- Modify a chart
- Insert and format text boxes
- Apply a WordArt style to text

Session 3.2
- Correct photos using photo editing tools
- Remove the background from a photo
- Apply an artistic effect to a photo
- Create a custom shape
- Fill a shape with a texture and a custom gradient
- Add alt text to graphics
- Use the Selection pane

Case | *International Study Crossroads*

International Study Crossroads (ISC), located in Baltimore, Maryland, arranges semesters abroad for college students. They have partnerships with more than 20 colleges and universities in five countries and will be expanding into three more countries soon. Robert Cloud is a registration councilor for ISC. One of his duties is to attend college fairs and advertise the services ISC offers. He has created a presentation to advertise ISC at these fairs. He asks for your help in enhancing the presentation with some more advanced formatting of the presentation's content.

In this module, you will add interest to the presentation by creating a SmartArt graphic and a chart and by inserting an audio clip. You will also create a text box and use WordArt styles. You will improve the photos in the presentation using PowerPoint's photo editing tools. In addition, you will create a custom shape and apply advanced formatting to the shape. Finally, you will add text to describe some of the graphics to make the presentation more accessible for people who use screen readers.

STARTING DATA FILES

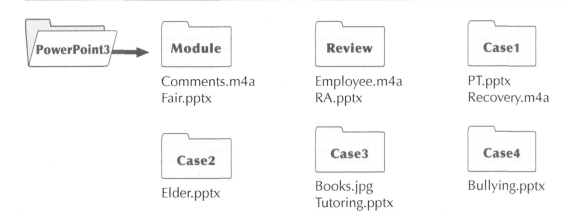

PowerPoint3 →

Module
Comments.m4a
Fair.pptx

Review
Employee.m4a
RA.pptx

Case1
PT.pptx
Recovery.m4a

Case2
Elder.pptx

Case3
Books.jpg
Tutoring.pptx

Case4
Bullying.pptx

Session 3.1 Visual Overview:

If you need additional tools and Excel is installed on your computer, click the Edit Data in Microsoft Excel button to open the spreadsheet in an Excel workbook.

When you insert a chart, a spreadsheet appears in which you enter the data to create the chart. A **spreadsheet** (called a worksheet in Microsoft Excel) is a grid of cells that contain numbers and text.

As in a table, the intersection of a row and a column is a **cell**, and you add data and labels in cells. Cells in a spreadsheet are referenced by their column letter and row number. This cell is cell B1.

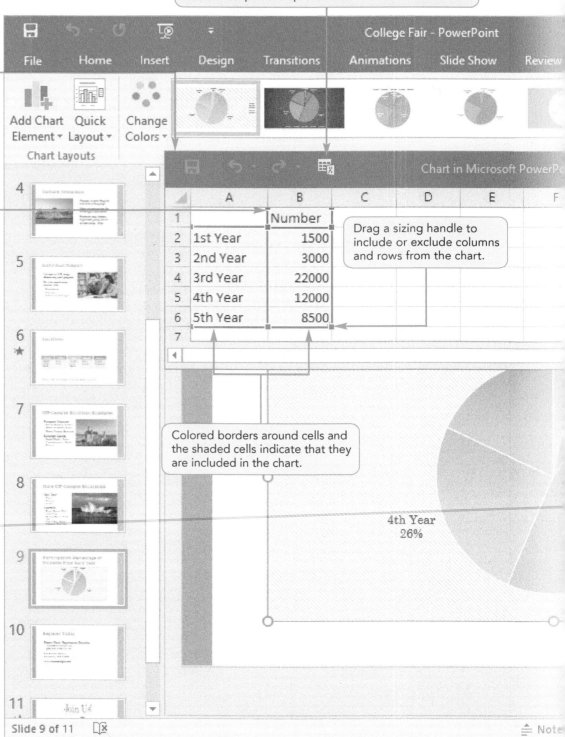

Drag a sizing handle to include or exclude columns and rows from the chart.

Colored borders around cells and the shaded cells indicate that they are included in the chart.

	A	B
1		Number
2	1st Year	1500
3	2nd Year	3000
4	3rd Year	22000
5	4th Year	12000
6	5th Year	8500
7		

4th Year
26%

Slide 9 of 11

© iStock.com/vichie81; © iStock.com/Susan Chiang; © iStock.com/Noppasin Wongchum; Courtesy of S. Scott Zimmerman

Creating a Chart on a Slide

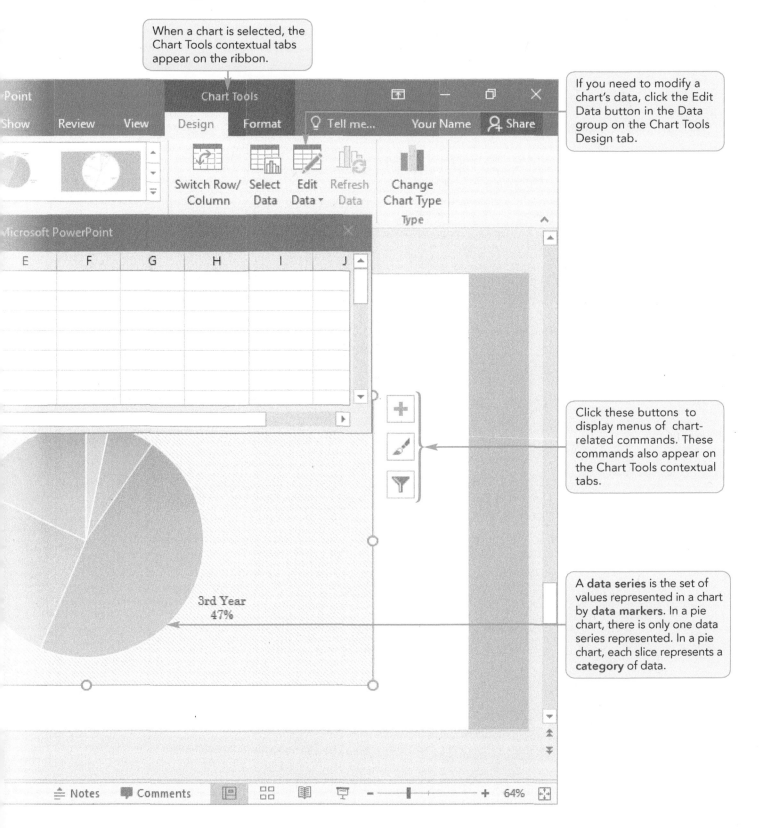

When a chart is selected, the Chart Tools contextual tabs appear on the ribbon.

If you need to modify a chart's data, click the Edit Data button in the Data group on the Chart Tools Design tab.

Click these buttons to display menus of chart-related commands. These commands also appear on the Chart Tools contextual tabs.

A **data series** is the set of values represented in a chart by **data markers**. In a pie chart, there is only one data series represented. In a pie chart, each slice represents a **category** of data.

Creating SmartArt Diagrams

In addition to creating a SmartArt diagram from a bulleted list, you can create one from scratch and then add text or pictures to it. Once you create a SmartArt diagram, you can change its layout; add or remove shapes from it; reorder, promote, or demote the shapes; and change the style, color, and shapes used to create the SmartArt. To create a SmartArt diagram, you can click the Insert a SmartArt Graphic button in a content placeholder, or in the Illustrations group on the Insert tab, click the SmartArt button to open the Choose a SmartArt Graphic dialog box.

REFERENCE

Creating a SmartArt Diagram

- Switch to a layout that includes a content placeholder, and then in the content placeholder, click the Insert a SmartArt Graphic button; or click the Insert tab on the ribbon, and then in the Illustrations group, click the SmartArt button.
- In the Choose a SmartArt Graphic dialog box, select the desired SmartArt category in the list on the left.
- In the center pane, click the SmartArt diagram you want to use.
- Click the OK button.

Robert wants you to create a SmartArt diagram on Slide 6 of his presentation. The diagram will list the countries and cities in which ISC has programs.

To create a SmartArt diagram:

▶ 1. Open the presentation **Fair**, located in the **PowerPoint3 > Module** folder included with your Data Files, and then save it as **College Fair** to the location where you are saving your files.

▶ 2. Display **Slide 6** ("Locations"), and then in the content placeholder, click the **Insert a SmartArt Graphic** button 🖻. The Choose a SmartArt Graphic dialog box opens.

▶ 3. In the list on the left, click **List**, click the **Vertical Bullet List** layout (in the second row), and then click the **OK** button. A SmartArt diagram containing placeholder text is inserted on the slide with the text pane open next to the diagram, and the SmartArt Tools Design tab is selected on the ribbon. See Figure 3-1. The insertion point is in the first bullet in the text pane.

   Trouble? If the text pane is not displayed, click the Text Pane button in the Create Graphic group on the SmartArt Tools Design tab.

Figure 3-1   **SmartArt inserted on Slide 6**

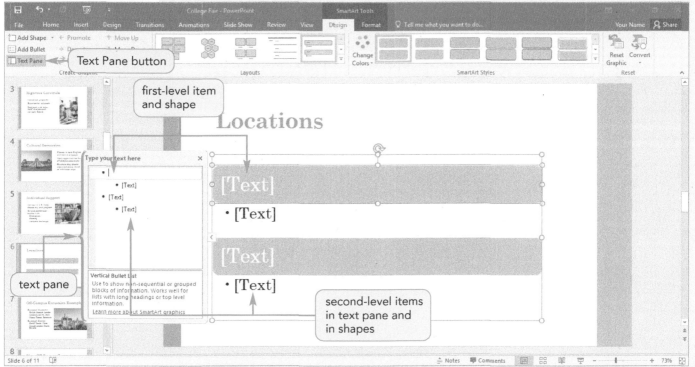

© iStock.com/sturti; © iStock.com/vichie81; © iStock.com/Susan Chiang; © iStock.com/Noppasin Wongchum

Now that you've added the diagram to the slide, you can add content to it. You will first add a first-level item and subitems to the diagram, and then reorder the shapes in the diagram.

To add text to the SmartArt diagram and move shapes:

1. With the insertion point in the first bulleted item in the text pane, type **England**. The text appears in the bulleted list in the text pane and in the top rectangle shape in the diagram.

2. In the text pane, in the first second-level bullet in the bulleted list, click **[Text]**. The placeholder text disappears and the insertion point appears.

3. Type **Oxford**. The text "Oxford" replaces the placeholder text in the second-level bullet.

4. Press the **Enter** key, type **London**, press the **Enter** key, and then type **Leeds**. The "London" bullet needs to be moved so it is the first second-level bullet.

5. In the text pane, click the **London** bullet, and then in the Create Graphic group, click the **Move Up** button. The London bullet moves up to become the first second-level bullet in the bulleted list.

With some SmartArt diagram layouts, you can click the Promote and Demote buttons in the Create Graphic group on the SmartArt Tools Design tab to move shapes up or down a level. But in other SmartArt diagrams, the insertion point must be in the text pane in order for this to work.

You need to add more first-level shapes to the SmartArt diagram. You do this using the Add Shape and Add Bullet buttons in the Create Graphic group on the SmartArt Tools Design tab.

To add additional first- and second-level shapes and bullets to the SmartArt diagram:

TIP

To change the shapes in the diagram, select all the shapes, and then click the Change Shape button in the Shapes group on the SmartArt Tools Format tab.

1. In the graphic, click the placeholder **[Text]** in the second first-level shape (below "Leeds,"), and then type **France**. The text you typed appears in the first-level shape in the diagram and in the text pane.

2. In the graphic, click the placeholder **[Text]** in the second-level item below "France," type **Paris**, press the **Enter** key, type **Nice**, press the **Enter** key, and then type **Spain**. The three items you typed appear as second-level bullets in the diagram and in the text pane. However, "Spain" should be in a first-level shape, at the same level as "England."

3. With the insertion point in the "Spain" bullet, click the **Promote** button in the Create Graphic group on the SmartArt Tools Design tab. "Spain" now appears in a first-level shape.

4. Press the **Enter** key. The insertion point moves to the next line in the "Spain" shape. The cities in Spain should be second-level items.

5. In the Create Graphic group, click the **Demote** button. Instead of creating a subbullet, the "Spain" bullet is demoted to a second-level item again. This is not what you wanted.

6. On the toolbar, click the **Undo** button 🔄 twice. "Spain" again appears in the first-level shape in the diagram.

7. In the Create Graphic group, click the **Add Bullet** button. A second-level bullet is added below the "Spain" shape.

8. Type **Barcelona**, press the **Enter** key, type **Madrid**, press the **Enter** key, and then type **Seville**.

9. Click in the **Spain** shape, and then in the Create Graphic group, click the **Add Shape** button. A new first-level shape is added to the bottom of the diagram.

10. Type **Germany**, and then add **Berlin** and **Munich** as second-level bullets below Germany.

11. Add **Australia** in a new first-level shape with **Sydney** and **Newcastle** as second-level bullets below it, and then add **Japan** in a new first-level shape. Compare your screen to Figure 3-2.

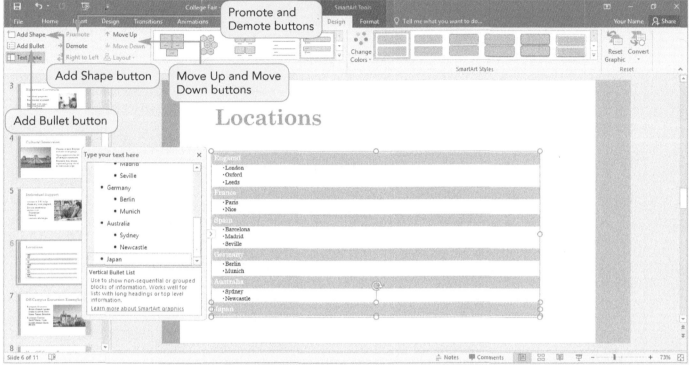

Figure 3-2   SmartArt with text added

© iStock.com/sturti; © iStock.com/vichie81; © iStock.com/Susan Chiang; © iStock.com/Noppasin Wongchum

Modifying a SmartArt Diagram

There are many ways to modify a SmartArt diagram. For example, you can change the layout of the diagram so the information is presented differently. You will do this next.

To change the layout of the SmartArt diagram:

1. On the SmartArt Tools Design tab, in the Layouts group, click the **More** button. The gallery of layouts in the List category opens.

2. Click the **Horizontal Bullet List** layout (the fourth layout in the second row). The layout of the diagram changes to the new layout.

3. Click the **Japan** shape, and then press the **Delete** key. The text and the shape are deleted.

   Trouble? If nothing happened when you pressed the Delete key, make sure you clicked the top part of the Japan shape—the part that contains the text "Japan," and then press the Delete key again.

   Trouble? If one of the letters in the word "Japan" was deleted when you pressed the Delete key, click the border of the top part of the Japan shape, and then press the Delete key again.

4. In the text pane, click the **Close** button ⊠. See Figure 3-3.

TIP

To switch the order of the shapes, click the Right to Left button in the Create Graphic group on the SmartArt Tools Design tab.

Figure 3-3   SmartArt after changing the layout

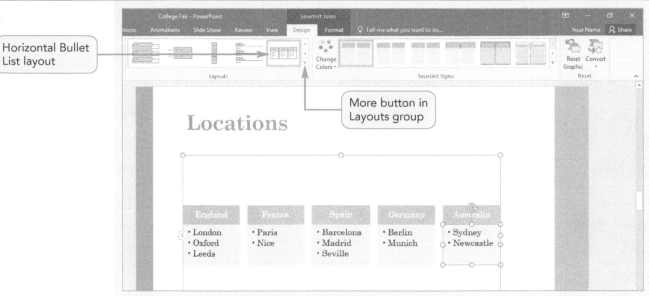

Horizontal Bullet List layout

More button in Layouts group

SmartArt diagrams contain multiple objects that are grouped as one object, which is then treated as a whole. So when you apply a style or other effect to the diagram, the effect is applied to the entire object. You can also apply formatting to individual shapes within the diagram if you want. You just need to select the specific shape first.

To apply a style to the SmartArt diagram and change its colors:

1. On the SmartArt Tools Design tab, in the SmartArt Styles group, click the **More** button to open the gallery of styles available for the graphic.

2. In the gallery, click the **Inset** style. The style of the graphic changes to the Inset style.

3. In the SmartArt Styles group, click the **Change Colors** button. A gallery of color styles opens.

4. Under Colorful, click the **Colorful – Accent Colors** style. See Figure 3-4.

| Figure 3-4 | SmartArt with color and style changed |

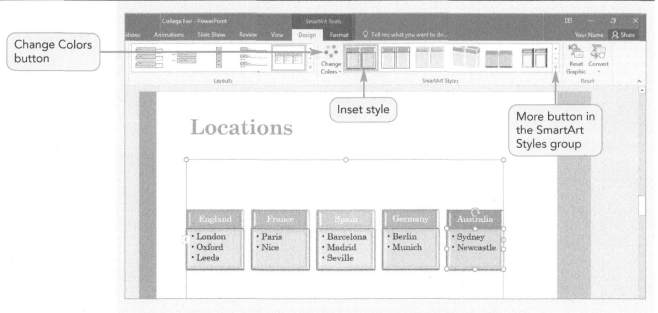

Animating a SmartArt Diagram

You animate a SmartArt diagram in the same way you animate any object. The default is for the entire object to animate as a single object. But similar to a bulleted list, after you apply an animation, you can use the Effect Options button and choose a different sequence effect. For example, you can choose to have each object animate one at a time.

Robert wants the shapes in the SmartArt diagram to appear on the slide one at a time during his presentation.

To animate the SmartArt diagram:

1. With Slide 6 displayed, on the ribbon, click the **Animations** tab.

2. In the Animation group, click the **Appear** animation. The animation previews, and the SmartArt diagram quickly appears on the slide. One animation sequence icon appears above and to the left of the diagram.

3. In the Animation group, click the **Effect Options** button. The selected effect is As One Object.

4. Click **One by One**. The animation previews, and each shape in the diagram appears one at a time. Ten animation sequence icons appear to the left of the diagram.

5. On the status bar, click the **Slide Show** button. Slide 6 appears in Slide Show view.

6. Advance the slide show twice. The first top-level shape, "England," appears, followed by the second-level shape containing the cities in England.

7. Advance the slide show eight more times. Each first-level shape appears, followed by its associated second-level shape.

8. Press the **Esc** key to end the slide show.

Robert wants the second-level shapes containing the cities to appear at the same time as the corresponding first-level shapes containing the countries. To make this happen, you need to change the start timing of each second-level shape to With Previous.

To change the start timing of the animations of the second-level shapes:

▶ 1. On Slide 6, click animation sequence icon **2**. The animation for the shape containing the cities in England is selected.

▶ 2. Press and hold the **Ctrl** key, click animation sequence icons **4**, **6**, **8**, and **10**, and then release the **Ctrl** key. The animations for the second-level shapes are selected.

▶ 3. On the Animations tab, in the Timing group, click the **Start** arrow, and then click **With Previous**.

▶ 4. On the status bar, click the **Slide Show** button 🖵. Slide 6 appears in Slide Show view.

▶ 5. Advance the slide show once. The first top-level shape, "England," and its associated second-level shape containing the cities in England appear.

▶ 6. Advance the slide show four more times. Each time the slide show is advanced, a first-level shape appears along with its associated second-level shape.

▶ 7. Press the **Esc** key to end the slide show.

▶ 8. Save the changes to the presentation.

INSIGHT

Converting a SmartArt Diagram to Text or Shapes

You can convert a SmartArt diagram to a bulleted list or to its individual shapes. To convert a diagram to a bulleted list, select the diagram, and then on the SmartArt Tools Design tab, in the Reset group, click the Convert button, and then click Convert to Text. To convert a group to its individual shapes, click Convert to Shapes on the Convert menu or use the Ungroup command on the Group menu on the Drawing Tools Format tab. In both cases, the shapes are converted from a SmartArt diagram into a set of grouped shapes. To completely ungroup them, you would need to use the Ungroup command a second time. Keep in mind that if you convert the diagram to shapes, you change it from a SmartArt object into ordinary drawn shapes, and you will no longer have access to the commands on the SmartArt Tools contextual tabs.

Adding Audio to Slides

Audio in a presentation can be used for a wide variety of purposes. For example, you might want to add a sound clip of music to a particular portion of the presentation to evoke emotion, or perhaps include a sound clip that is a recording of customers expressing their satisfaction with a product or service. To add a sound clip to a slide, you use the Audio button in the Media group on the Insert tab. When a sound clip is added to a slide, a sound icon and a play bar appear on the slide. Similar to videos, the options for changing how the sound plays during the slide show appear on the Audio Tools Playback tab. For the most part, they are the same options that appear on the Video Tools Playback tab. For example, you can trim an audio clip or set it to rewind after playing. You can also compress audio in the same way that you compress video.

REFERENCE

Inserting an Audio Clip into a Presentation

- Display the slide onto which you want to insert the sound.
- On the ribbon, click the Insert tab, click the Audio button in the Media group, and then click Audio on My PC.
- In the Insert Audio dialog box, navigate to the folder containing the sound clip, click the audio file, and then click the Insert button.
- If desired, click the Audio Tools Playback tab, and then in the Audio Options group:
    - Click the Start arrow, and then click Automatically.
    - Click the Hide During Show check box to select it to hide the icon during a slide show.
    - Click the Volume button, and then click a volume level or click Mute.

Robert wants you to add a sound clip to the presentation—a recording of a student praising the ISC. The recorded message is an MPEG-4 audio file, which is a common file format for short sound clips.

To add a sound clip to Slide 11:

1. Display **Slide 11** (the last slide), and then click the **Insert** tab on the ribbon.

TIP

To record an audio clip, click the Audio button, and then click Record Audio.

2. In the Media group, click the **Audio** button, and then click **Audio on My PC**. The Insert Audio dialog box opens.

3. Navigate to the **PowerPoint3 > Module** folder, click the **Comments** file, and then click the **Insert** button. A sound icon appears in the middle of the slide with a play bar below it, and the Audio Tools Playback tab is selected on the ribbon. See Figure 3-5. As with videos, the default start setting is On Click.

Figure 3-5   **Sound icon on Slide 11**

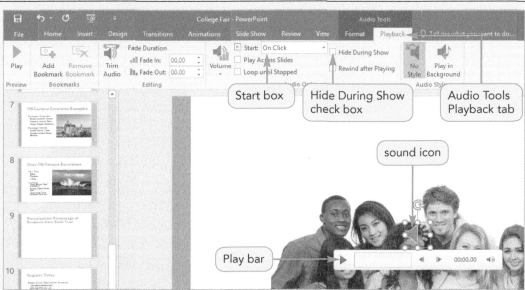

© iStock.com/Christopher Futcher; © iStock.com/Noppasin Wongchum; Courtesy of S. Scott Zimmerman

4. Drag the sound icon to the lower-right corner of the slide so it is positioned at the bottom of the blue bar.

> **5.** On the play bar, click the **Play** button ▶. The sound clip, which is a comment from a student complimenting the company on its programs, plays. Robert wants the clip to play automatically after the slide appears on the screen.
>
> **6.** On the Playback tab, in the Audio Options group, click the **Start** arrow, and then click **Automatically**. Because the clip will play automatically, there is no need to have the sound icon visible on the screen during a slide show.
>
> **7.** In the Audio Options group, click the **Hide During Show** check box to select it.
>
> **8.** Save the changes to the presentation.

INSIGHT

Playing Music Across Slides

You can add an audio clip to a slide and have it play throughout the slide show. On the Audio Tools Playback tab, in the Audio Styles group, click the Play in Background button. When you select this option, the Start timing in the Audio Options group is changed to Automatically, and the Play Across Slides, Loop until Stopped, and Hide During Show check boxes become selected. Also, the Play in Background command changes the trigger animation automatically applied to media to an After Previous animation set to zero so that the sound will automatically start playing after the slide transitions. These setting changes ensure the audio clip will start playing when the slide appears on the screen during a slide show and will continue playing, starting over if necessary, until the end of the slide show. To change the settings so that the audio no longer plays throughout the slide show, click the No Style button in the Audio Styles group.

Adding a Chart to a Slide

The terms "chart" and "graph" often are used interchangeably; however, they do, in fact, have distinct meanings. **Charts** are visuals that use lines, arrows, and boxes or other shapes to show parts, steps, or processes. **Graphs** show the relationship between variables along two axes or reference lines: the independent variable on the horizontal axis and the dependent variable on the vertical axis.

Despite these differences in the definitions, in PowerPoint a chart is any visual depiction of data in a spreadsheet, even if the result is more properly referred to as a graph (such as a line graph). Refer to the Session 3.1 Visual Overview for more information about creating charts and using spreadsheets in PowerPoint.

Creating a Chart

To create a chart, you click the Insert Chart button in a content placeholder or use the Chart button in the Illustrations group on the Insert tab. Doing so will open a window containing a spreadsheet with sample data, and a sample chart will appear on the slide. You can then edit the sample data in the window to reflect your own data to be represented in the chart on the slide.

REFERENCE

Creating a Chart

- Switch to a layout that includes a content placeholder, and then click the Insert Chart button in the content placeholder to open the Insert Chart dialog box; or click the Insert tab, and then, in the Illustrations group, click the Chart button to open the Insert Chart dialog box.
- In the list on the left, click the desired chart type.
- In the row of styles, click the desired chart style, and then click the OK button.
- In the spreadsheet that opens, enter the data that you want to plot.
- If you need to chart fewer rows or columns than are shaded in the spreadsheet, drag the handle in the lower-right corner of the shaded area up to remove rows or to the left to remove columns.
- In the spreadsheet window, click the Close button.

Robert wants you to create a chart on Slide 9 to illustrate the percentage of students from each grade level that typically make up the total of participating students in a given year. A pie chart is a good choice when you want to show the relative size of one value compared to the other values and compared to the total set of values.

To create a chart on Slide 9:

 1. Display **Slide 9** ("Participation Percentage of Students from Each Year"), and then, in the content placeholder, click the **Insert Chart** button. The Insert Chart dialog box opens. Column is selected in the list of chart types on the left, and the Clustered Column style is selected in the row of styles at the top and shown in the preview area. See Figure 3-6.

Figure 3-6   Insert Chart dialog box

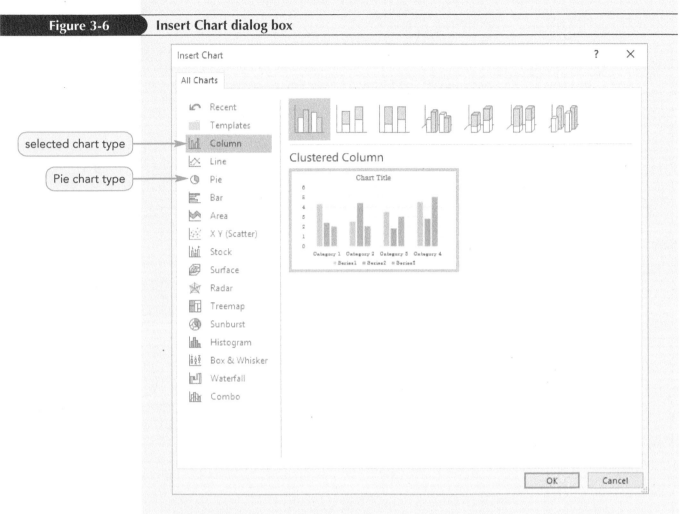

2. In the list of chart types, click **Pie**. The row of chart styles changes to pie chart styles. The Pie style is selected.

3. Click the **OK** button. A sample chart is inserted on Slide 9, and a small spreadsheet (sometimes called a datasheet) opens above the chart, with colored borders around the cells in the spreadsheet indicating which cells of data are included in the chart. See Figure 3-7.

Figure 3-7   Spreadsheet and chart with sample data

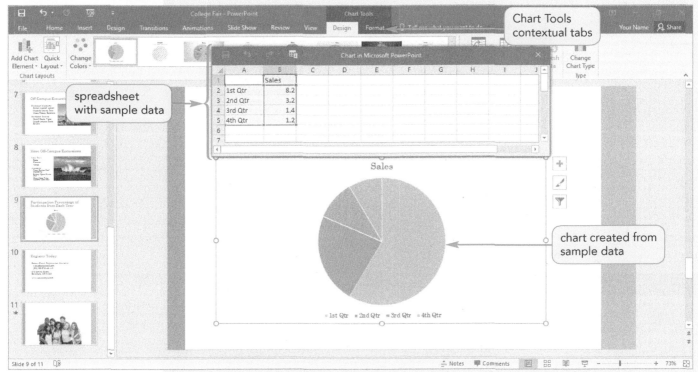

© iStock.com/Noppasin Wongchum; Courtesy of S. Scott Zimmerman; © iStock.com/Christopher Futcher

To create the chart for Robert's presentation, you need to edit the sample data in the spreadsheet. When you work with a spreadsheet, the cell in which you are entering data is the **active cell**. The active cell has a green border around it.

To enter the data for the chart:

▸ 1. In the spreadsheet, click cell **A2**. A green border surrounds cell A2, indicating it is selected.

▸ 2. Type **1st Year**, and then press the **Enter** key. Cell A3 becomes the active cell. In the chart, the category name in the legend for the blue pie slice changes to "1st Year."

▸ 3. Enter the following in cells **A3** through **A5**, pressing the **Enter** key after each entry:

   2nd Year

   3rd Year

   4th Year

TIP

To add or remove a row or column from the chart, drag the corner sizing handles on the colored borders.

▸ 4. In cell A6, type **5th Year**, and then press the **Enter** key. The active cell is cell A7, and the colored borders around the cells included in the chart expand to include cells A6 and B6. In the chart, a new category name is added to the legend. Because there is no data in cell B6, a corresponding slice was not added to the pie chart.

5. Click in cell **B1** to make it the active cell, type **Number**, and then press the **Enter** key. The active cell is now cell B2.

6. In cell **B2**, type **15000**, and then press the **Enter** key. The slice in the pie chart that represents the percentage showing the numbers of first-year students increases to essentially fill the chart. This is because the value 15000 is so much larger than the sample data values in the rest of the rows in column B. As you continue to enter the data, the slices in the pie chart will adjust as you add each value.

7. In cells **B3** through **B6**, enter the following values, and then compare your screen to Figure 3-8:

    3000

    22000

    12000

    8500

Figure 3-8 Spreadsheet and chart after entering data

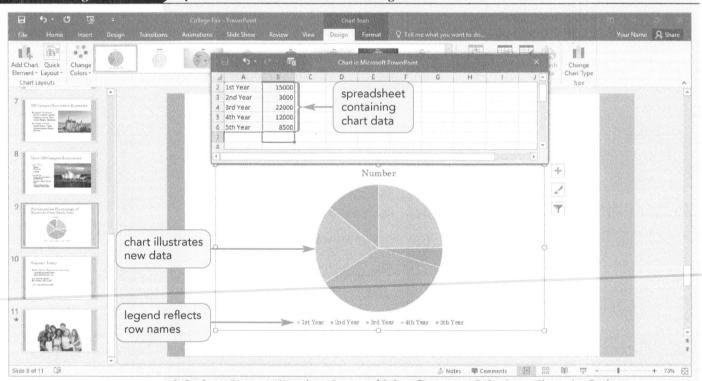

© iStock.com/Noppasin Wongchum; Courtesy of S. Scott Zimmerman; © iStock.com/Christopher Futcher

8. In the spreadsheet, click the **Close** button ✕. The spreadsheet closes.

9. Save the changes to the presentation.

PROSKILLS

Decision Making: Selecting the Correct Chart Type

To use charts effectively, you need to consider what you want to illustrate with your data. To represent values, column charts use vertical columns, and bar charts use horizontal bars. These types of charts are useful for comparing the values of items over a period of time or a range of dates or costs. Line charts and area charts use a line to connect points that represent values. They are effective for showing changes over time, and they are particularly useful for illustrating trends. Line and area charts are a better choice than column or bar charts when you need to display large amounts of information and exact quantities that don't require emphasis. Pie charts are used to show percentages or proportions of the parts that make up a whole. Treemap and sunburst charts also show the proportion of parts to a whole, but these chart types also show hierarchies.

Modifying a Chart

Once the chart is on the slide, you can modify it by changing or formatting its various elements. For example, you can edit the data; apply a style; add, remove, or reposition chart elements; add labels to the chart; and modify the formatting of text in the chart.

You need to make several changes to the chart you created on Slide 9. First, Robert informs you that some of the data he provided was incorrect, so you need to edit the data. Remember that a pie chart shows the size of each value relative to the whole. Therefore, if you change the value corresponding to one pie slice, the rest of the slices will change size as well.

To change the data used to create the chart:

TIP

To switch to another type of chart, click the Change Chart Type button in the Type group on the Chart Tools Design tab.

1. On the Chart Tools Design tab, in the Data group, click the **Edit Data** button. The spreadsheet opens again above the chart. You need to change the number of first-year students who participate in the program. The 1st Year slice is the blue slice.

2. Click cell **B2**, type **1500**, and then press the **Enter** key. The blue slice in the pie chart decreases significantly in size, and the other slices in the pie chart adjust to reflect the new relative values.

3. On the spreadsheet, click the **Close** button ☒. The spreadsheet closes.

Robert also wants you to make several formatting changes to the chart. There is no need for a title on the chart because the slide title describes the chart. Robert also wants you to remove the legend and, instead, label the pie slices with the category names and the percentage values. He also would like you to apply a different style to the chart.

To format and modify the chart:

1. On the Chart Tools Design tab, in the Chart Layouts group, click the **Quick Layout** button. A gallery of chart layouts specific to pie charts opens. Each layout includes different chart elements, such as the chart title and legend.

2. Point to several of the layouts to see which elements are added to the chart, and then click **Layout 1**. The category name and percentage of each slice is added as a label on the slices, and the legend is removed. With this layout, there is no need for the legend.

   3. To the right of the chart, click the **Chart Styles** button. A gallery opens with the Style tab selected at the top.

   4. Point to several of the styles to see the effect on the chart. In addition to changing the colors used, some of the styles include layouts and add or remove chart elements, similar to the Quick Layouts.

   5. Click **Style 6**. This style adds the legend and a background of thin, slanted lines. See Figure 3-9.

Figure 3-9 | Chart after changing the layout and applying a style

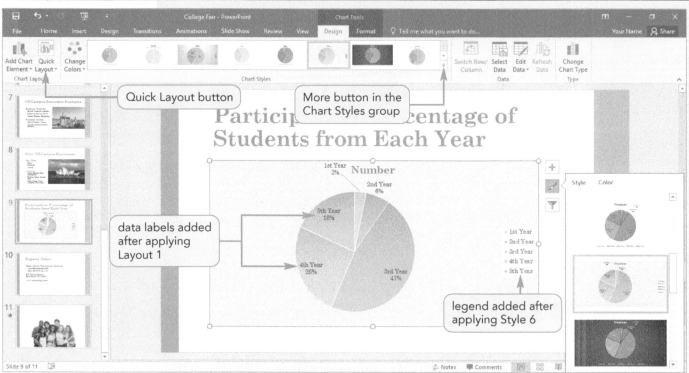

© iStock.com/Noppasin Wongchum; Courtesy of S. Scott Zimmerman; © iStock.com/Christopher Futcher

   6. To the right of the chart, click the **Chart Elements** button. The CHART ELEMENTS menu opens to the right of the chart. The Chart Title, Data Labels, and Legend check boxes are all selected, which means these elements are shown on the chart.

   7. On the CHART ELEMENTS menu, click the **Chart Title** check box, and then click the **Legend** check box to deselect them. The chart title and the legend are removed from the chart.

   8. On the CHART ELEMENTS menu, point to **Data Labels**. An arrow appears.

   9. Click the **arrow** to open the Data Labels submenu. See Figure 3-10.

TIP

Double-click a chart element to open a task pane containing additional commands for modifying that element.

Figure 3-10   Data Labels submenu on CHART ELEMENTS menu

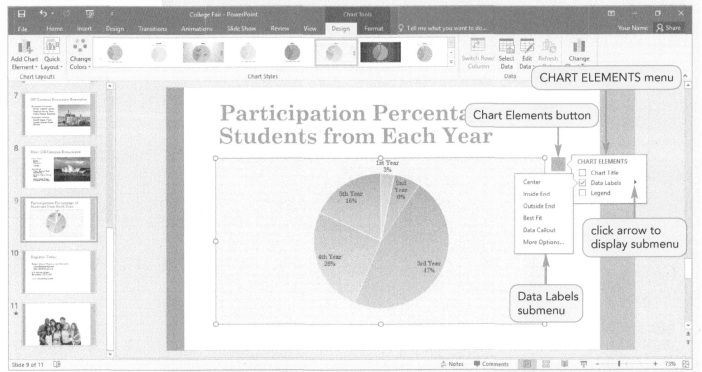

© iStock.com/Noppasin Wongchum; Courtesy of S. Scott Zimmerman; © iStock.com/Christopher Futcher

▶ **10.** On the submenu, click **Outside End**. The data labels are positioned next to each pie slice.

The data labels are a little bit small, so Robert asks you to increase their font size. When you change the font size of data labels on a pie chart, it is sometimes necessary to move a label so it is better positioned. You'll do this next.

To change the point size of the data labels and adjust their position:

▶ **1.** To the right of the chart, click the **Chart Elements** button 🔲 to close the menu, and then in the chart, click one of the data labels. All of the data labels are selected.

▶ **2.** On the ribbon, click the **Home** tab, and then change the font size of the selected data labels to **14** points. The 1st Year data label is now too close to the 2nd Year data label.

▶ **3.** Click the **1st Year** data label. Because all the data labels had been selected, now only the 1st Year data label is selected.

▶ **4.** Position the pointer on the edge of the selected **1st Year** data label so that it changes to ⁺🕂, and then drag it to the left a little so that it is not touching the 2nd Year data label and so that the "3" is above the blue pie slice. See Figure 3-11.

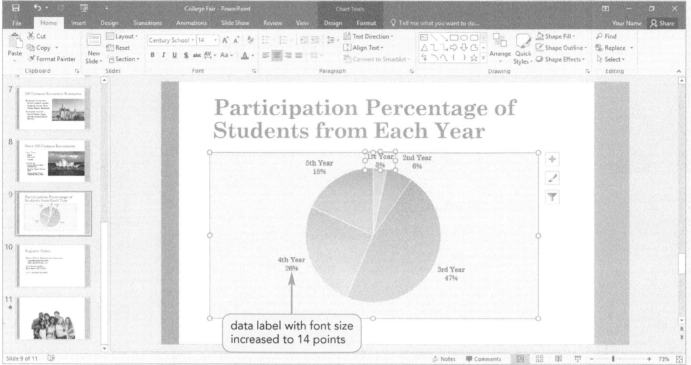

Figure 3-11 | Final chart on Slide 9

© iStock.com/Noppasin Wongchum; Courtesy of S. Scott Zimmerman; © iStock.com/Christopher Futcher

5. Save the changes to the presentation.

Inserting and Formatting Text Boxes

Sometimes you need to add text to a slide in a location other than in one of the text box placeholders included in the slide layout. You could draw any shape and add text to it, or you can add a text box shape. Unlike shapes that are filled with the Accent 1 color by default, text boxes by default do not have a fill. Another difference between the format of text boxes and shapes with text in them is that the text in a text box is left-aligned and text in shapes is center-aligned. Regardless of the differences, after you create a text box, you can format the text and the text box in a variety of ways, including adding a fill, adjusting the internal margins, and rotating and repositioning it.

Robert wants you to add text on Slide 6 that informs the audience of three new countries that will be available study abroad locations next spring. You will add a text box to accomplish this.

To add a text box to Slide 6:

1. Display **Slide 6** ("Locations"), and then click the **Insert** tab.

2. In the Text group, click the **Text Box** button, and then move the pointer to the slide. The pointer changes to $\downarrow$.

3. Position $\downarrow$ below the left edge of the first shape in the SmartArt, and then click and drag to draw a text box as wide as the England and France shapes and about one-half-inch high. See Figure 3-12.

Figure 3-12	Text box inserted on Slide 6

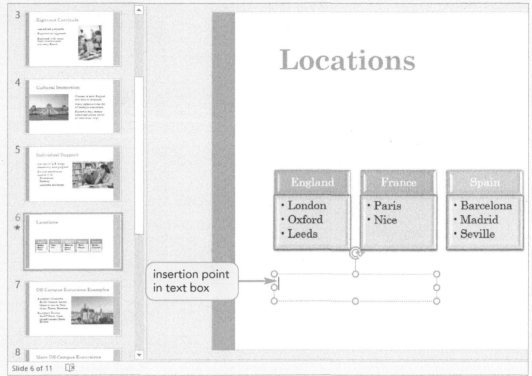

© iStock.com/sturti; © iStock.com/vichie81; © iStock.com/Susan Chiang; © iStock.com/Noppasin Wongchum

Trouble? If your text box is not the same size or is not positioned exactly as shown in Figure 3-12, don't worry. You'll adjust it later.

4. Type **Programs in South Africa, Japan, and Vietnam available next spring.** (including the period). As you type the text in the text box, the height of the text box changes, and the additional text wraps to the next line.

Trouble? If all the text fits on one line, drag the right-middle sizing handle to the left until some words appear on the next line so that you can complete the next sets of steps.

When you drag to create a text box, the default setting is for the text to wrap and for the height of the box to resize to accommodate the text you type. (If you simply click to place the text box, the text box will expand horizontally as wide as necessary to accommodate the text you type, even if it needs to flow off the slide.) This differs from text boxes created from title and content placeholders and shapes with text in them. Recall that text boxes created from placeholders have AutoFit behavior that reduces the font size of the text if you add more text than can fit. When you add text to a shape, if you add more text than can fit in that shape, the text extends outside of the shape.

Robert thinks the text below the SmartArt would look better if it were all on one line and italicized. You can widen the text box, or if you do not want the text to wrap to the next line regardless of how much text is in the text box, you can change the text wrapping option.

To modify and reposition the text box:

▶ **1.** Right-click the text box, and then on the shortcut menu, click **Format Shape**. The Format Shape task pane opens to the right of the displayed slide. At the top, the Shape Options tab is selected. This tab contains categories of commands for formatting the shape, such as changing the fill. See Figure 3-13.

Figure 3-13	Format Shape task pane and text box with wrapped text

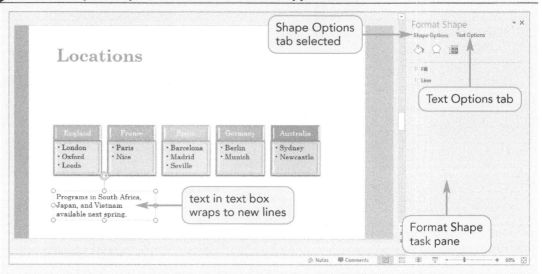

TIP

Clicking any of the Dialog Box Launchers on the Drawing Tools Format tab also opens the Format Shape task pane.

▶ **2.** In the task pane, click **Text Options** to display the Text Options tab. This tab contains commands for formatting the text and how it is positioned.

▶ **3.** Click the **Textbox** button [icon]. The task pane changes to show the Text Box section, containing options for formatting text in a text box. First you want to change the wrap option so the text does not wrap in the text box.

▶ **4.** Click the **Wrap text in shape** check box to deselect it. The text in the text box appears all on one line. Next, you want to decrease the space between the first word in the text box and the left border of the box. In other words, you want to change the left margin in the text box.

> **Trouble?** If the Wrap text in shape check box is not selected, you clicked instead of dragging to create the text box in Step 3 in the previous set of steps. In this case, do not click the check box; leave it unselected.

▶ **5.** Click the **Left margin down arrow**. The value in the box changes to 0", and the text shifts left in the text box.

▶ **6.** Click the text box border to select all of the text in the text box, and then, in the Font group on the Home tab, click the **Italic** button [I]. The text in the text box is italicized.

▶ **7.** Point to the border of the text box so that the pointer changes to [icon], press and hold the mouse button, and then drag the text box until its left edge is aligned with the left edge of the SmartArt and its top edge is aligned with the bottom edge of the SmartArt box, as shown in Figure 3-14.

Figure 3-14   **Formatted and repositioned text box**

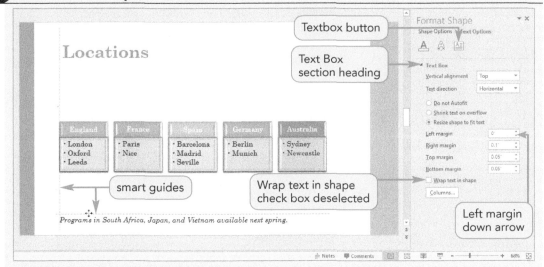

▶ **8.** Release the mouse button.

▶ **9.** In the Format Shape task pane, click the **Close** button ✕, and then save the changes to the presentation.

Applying WordArt Styles to Text

WordArt is a term used to describe formatted, decorative text in a text box. WordArt text has a fill color, which is the same as the font color, and an outline color. To create WordArt, you can insert a new text box or format an existing one. You can apply one of the built-in WordArt styles or you can use the Text Fill, Text Outline, and Text Effects buttons in the WordArt Styles group on the Drawing Tools Format tab.

Robert would like you to add a text box that contains WordArt to Slide 11 that reinforces the invitation to register with ISC.

To create a text box containing WordArt on Slide 11:

▶ **1.** Display **Slide 11** (the last slide), and then click the **Insert** tab.

▶ **2.** In the Text group, click the **WordArt** button to open the WordArt gallery. See Figure 3-15.

Figure 3-15   **WordArt gallery**

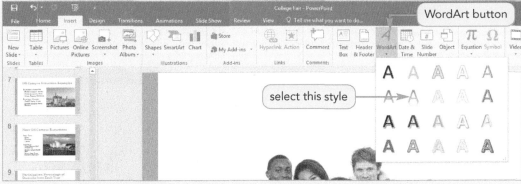

© iStock.com/Christopher Futcher; © iStock.com/Noppasin Wongchum; Courtesy of S. Scott Zimmerman

TIP

To format an existing text box on a slide with a WordArt style, select the text box, and then click a style in the WordArt Styles group on the Drawing Tools Format tab.

3. Click the **Gradient Fill – Green, Accent 1, Reflection** style. A text box containing the placeholder text "Your text here" appears on the slide, although it is a little hard to see because it is on top of the photo. On the ribbon, the Drawing Tools Format tab is selected. The placeholder text is formatted with the style you selected in the WordArt gallery. The placeholder text in the text box is selected.

4. Type **Join Us!**. The text you typed replaces the placeholder text.

5. Drag the text box to position it above the photo so that it is aligned with the middle of the slide and it is vertically centered between the top of the slide and the photo. You want to change the color used in the gradient fill from green to blue.

6. On the Drawing Tools Format tab, in the WordArt Styles group, click the **Text Fill button arrow**. The theme color palette appears.

7. Click the **Ice Blue, Accent 1, Darker 50%** color.

8. Change the font size of the text in the WordArt text box to **72** points.

The shape of text in a text box can be transformed into waves, circles, and other shapes. To do this, you use the options located on the Transform submenu, which is accessed from the Text Effects menu on the Drawing Tools Format tab.

Robert wants you to change the shape of the WordArt on Slide 11.

To change the shape of the WordArt by applying a transform effect:

1. With the WordArt on Slide 11 selected, click the **Drawing Tools Format** tab.

2. In the WordArt styles group, click the **Text Effects** button, and then point to **Transform**. The Transform submenu appears. See Figure 3-16.

| **Figure 3-16** | **Transform submenu on Text Effects menu** |

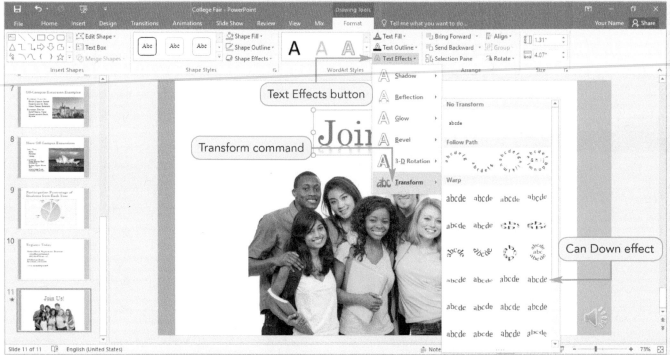

© iStock.com/Christopher Futcher; © iStock.com/Noppasin Wongchum; Courtesy of S. Scott Zimmerman

> **3.** In the fourth row under Warp, click the **Can Down** effect. See Figure 3-17.

Figure 3-17   WordArt after applying Can Down transform effect

© iStock.com/Christopher Futcher; © iStock.com/Noppasin Wongchum; Courtesy of S. Scott Zimmerman

> **4.** Save the changes to the presentation.

PROSKILLS

Decision Making: Selecting Appropriate Font Colors

When you select font colors, make sure your text is easy to read during your slide show. Font colors that work well are dark colors on a light background or light colors on a dark background. Avoid red text on a blue background or blue text on a green background (and vice versa) unless the shades of those colors are in strong contrast. These combinations might look fine on your computer monitor, but they are almost totally illegible to an audience viewing your presentation on a screen in a darkened room. Also avoid using red/green combinations, which color-blind people find illegible.

REVIEW

Session 3.1 Quick Check

1. How do you change the animation applied to a SmartArt diagram so that each shape animates one at a time?
2. What happens when you click the Play in Background button in the Audio Styles group on the Audio Tools Playback tab?
3. What is the difference between a chart and a graph?
4. What is a spreadsheet?
5. How do you identify a specific cell in a spreadsheet?
6. What is WordArt?

Session 3.2 Visual Overview:

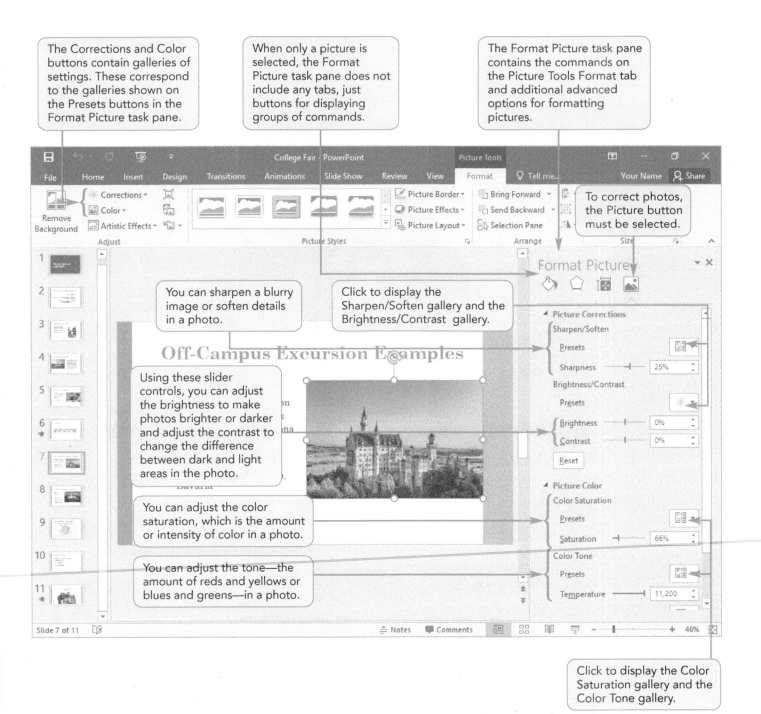

The Corrections and Color buttons contain galleries of settings. These correspond to the galleries shown on the Presets buttons in the Format Picture task pane.

When only a picture is selected, the Format Picture task pane does not include any tabs, just buttons for displaying groups of commands.

The Format Picture task pane contains the commands on the Picture Tools Format tab and additional advanced options for formatting pictures.

To correct photos, the Picture button must be selected.

You can sharpen a blurry image or soften details in a photo.

Click to display the Sharpen/Soften gallery and the Brightness/Contrast gallery.

Using these slider controls, you can adjust the brightness to make photos brighter or darker and adjust the contrast to change the difference between dark and light areas in the photo.

You can adjust the color saturation, which is the amount or intensity of color in a photo.

You can adjust the tone—the amount of reds and yellows or blues and greens—in a photo.

Click to display the Color Saturation gallery and the Color Tone gallery.

© iStock.com/sturti; © iStock.com/vichie81; © iStock.com/Susan Chiang; © iStock.com/Noppasin Wongchum; Courtesy of S. Scott Zimmerman; © iStock.com/Christopher Futcher

Formatting Shapes and Pictures

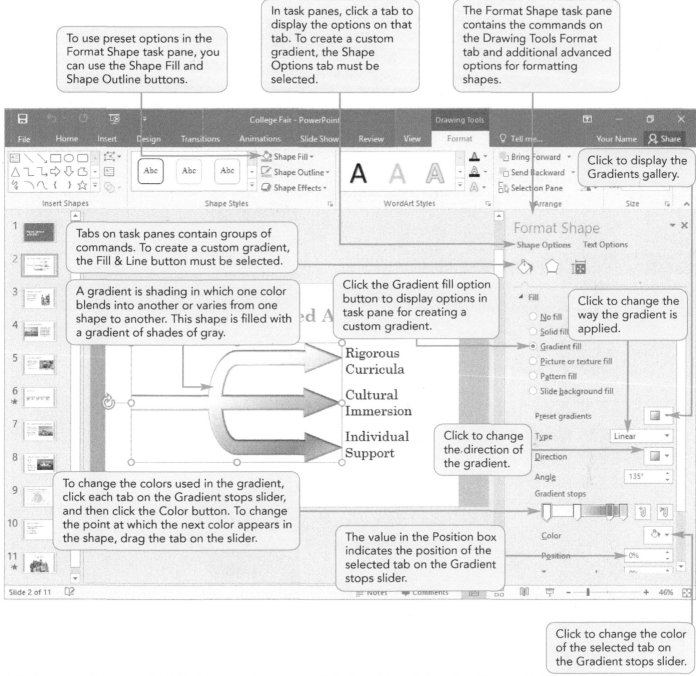

To use preset options in the Format Shape task pane, you can use the Shape Fill and Shape Outline buttons.

In task panes, click a tab to display the options on that tab. To create a custom gradient, the Shape Options tab must be selected.

The Format Shape task pane contains the commands on the Drawing Tools Format tab and additional advanced options for formatting shapes.

Click to display the Gradients gallery.

Tabs on task panes contain groups of commands. To create a custom gradient, the Fill & Line button must be selected.

A gradient is shading in which one color blends into another or varies from one shape to another. This shape is filled with a gradient of shades of gray.

Click the Gradient fill option button to display options in task pane for creating a custom gradient.

Click to change the way the gradient is applied.

Click to change the direction of the gradient.

To change the colors used in the gradient, click each tab on the Gradient stops slider, and then click the Color button. To change the point at which the next color appears in the shape, drag the tab on the slider.

The value in the Position box indicates the position of the selected tab on the Gradient stops slider.

Click to change the color of the selected tab on the Gradient stops slider.

© iStock.com/sturti; © iStock.com/vichie81; © iStock.com/Susan Chiang; © iStock.com/Noppasin Wongchum; Courtesy of S. Scott Zimmerman; © iStock.com/Christopher Futcher

Editing Photos

TIP

If you make changes to photos and then change your mind, you can click the Reset Picture button in the Adjust group on the Picture Tools Format tab.

If photos you want to use in a presentation are too dark or require other fine-tuning, you can use PowerPoint's photo-correction tools to correct the photos. These photo-correction tools appear on the ribbon and in the Format Picture task pane. Refer to the Session 3.2 Visual Overview for more information about correcting photos and the Format Picture task pane.

Robert thinks there is not enough contrast between the dark and light areas in the photo on Slide 11. You will correct this aspect of the photo.

To change the contrast in the photo on Slide 11:

1. If you took a break after the previous session, make sure the **College Fair** presentation is open and **Slide 11** (the last slide) is displayed.

2. Click the photo to select it.

3. On the ribbon, click the **Picture Tools Format** tab, and then in the Adjust group, click the **Corrections** button. A menu opens, showing options for sharpening and softening the photo and adjusting the brightness and the contrast. See Figure 3-18.

Figure 3-18	**Corrections menu**

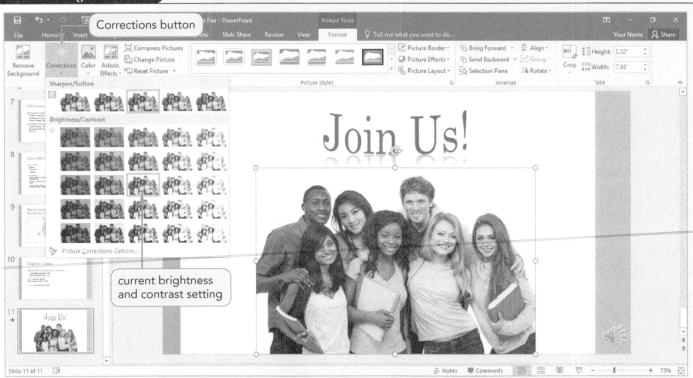

© iStock.com/Christopher Futcher

4. In the Brightness/Contrast section, click the **Brightness 0% (Normal) Contrast -20%** style (the third style in the second row). The contrast of the image changes. Because you chose a style with a Brightness percentage of 0%, the brightness of the photo is unchanged.

You want to decrease the contrast just a little more. However, the gallery provides options that change the contrast in increments of 20 percent, which will be more of an adjustment than you are looking for. For selecting a more precise contrast setting, you need to open the Format Picture task pane.

TIP

You can also right-click the photo, and then click Format Picture on the shortcut menu to open the Format Picture task pane.

5. Click the **Corrections** button again, and then click **Picture Corrections Options**. The Format Picture task pane opens with the Picture button selected and the Picture Corrections section expanded.

6. Drag the **Contrast** slider to the left until the box next to the slider indicates -30%. The contrast increases slightly.

    Trouble? If you can't position the slider exactly, click the up or down arrow in the box containing the percentage as needed, or select the current percentage and then type -30.

7. Close the task pane.

Next, Robert wants you to adjust the photo on Slide 7. He wants you to make the colors in the photo more realistic, by reducing the saturation and the tone.

To change the saturation and tone of the photo on Slide 7:

1. Display **Slide 7** ("Off-Campus Excursion Examples"), click the photo to select it, and then click the **Picture Tools Format** tab on the ribbon, if necessary.

2. In the Adjust group, click the **Color** button. A menu opens with options for adjusting the saturation and tone of the photo's color. See Figure 3-19.

| Figure 3-19 | Color menu |

© iStock.com/Noppasin Wongchum; Courtesy of S. Scott Zimmerman

TIP

To recolor a photo so it is all one color, click the Color button in the Adjust group on the Picture Tools Format tab, and then click a Recolor option.

3. Under Color Saturation, click the **Saturation: 66%** option. The colors in the photo are now less intense.

4. Click the **Color** button again.

5. Under Color Tone, click the **Temperature: 11200K** option. More reds and yellows are added to the photo, most noticeably in the skyline on the right side of the image.

Finally, Robert wants you to sharpen the photo on Slide 7 so that the objects in the photo are more in focus.

To sharpen the photo on Slide 7:

▶ 1. On Slide 7 ("Off-Campus Excursion Examples"), make sure the photo is still selected, and on the ribbon, the Picture Tools Format tab is the active tab.

▶ 2. In the Adjust group, click the **Corrections** button. The options for sharpening and softening photos appear at the top of the menu.

▶ 3. Under Sharpen/Soften, click the **Sharpen: 25%** option. The edges of the objects in the picture are sharper and clearer.

▶ 4. Save the changes to the presentation.

Removing the Background from Photos

Sometimes a photo is more striking if you remove its background. You can also layer a photo with the background removed on top of another photo to create an interesting effect. To remove the background of a photo, you can use the Remove Background tool. When you click the Remove Background button in the Adjust group on the Picture Tools Format tab, PowerPoint analyzes the photograph and marks parts of it to remove and parts of it to retain. If the analysis removes too little or too much of the photo, you can adjust it.

REFERENCE

Removing the Background of a Photograph

- Click the photo, and then click the Picture Tools Format tab on the ribbon.
- In the Adjust group, click the Remove Background button.
- Drag the sizing handles on the remove background border to make broad adjustments to the area marked for removal.
- In the Refine group on the Background Removal tab, click the Mark Areas to Keep or the Mark Areas to Remove button, and then click or drag through an area of the photo that you want marked to keep or remove.
- Click a blank area of the slide or click the Keep Changes button in the Close group to accept the changes.

Robert wants you to modify the photo of the Sydney Opera House on Slide 8 so that the background looks like a drawing, but the opera house stays sharp and in focus. To create this effect, you will need to work with two versions of the photo. You will use the Duplicate command to make a copy of the photo and then remove the background from the duplicate photo.

To duplicate the photo on Slide 8 and then remove the background from the copy:

▶ 1. Display **Slide 8** ("More Off-Campus Excursions" with the photo of the Sydney Opera House), click the photo to select it, and then, on the ribbon, click the **Home** tab, if necessary. The photo on Slide 8 is a photo of the Sydney Opera House in Sydney, Australia.

▶ 2. In the Clipboard group, click the **Copy button arrow**, and then click **Duplicate**. The photo is duplicated on the slide, and the duplicate is selected.

▶ 3. Point to the selected duplicate photo so that the pointer changes to ⬚, and then drag it left to position it to the left of the original photo. The duplicate photo is on top of the bulleted list and extends beyond the slide border.

4. With the duplicate photo selected, click the **Picture Tools Format** tab on the ribbon.

5. In the Adjust group, click the **Remove Background** button. The areas of the photograph marked for removal are colored purple. A sizing box appears around the general area of the photograph that will be retained, and a new tab, the Background Removal tab, appears on the ribbon and is the active tab. See Figure 3-20. You can adjust the area of the photograph that is retained by dragging the sizing handles on the sizing box.

Figure 3-20	Photograph after clicking the Remove Background button

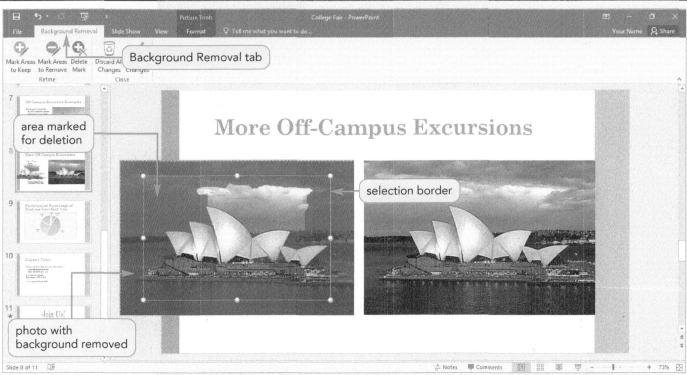

Courtesy of S. Scott Zimmerman; © iStock.com/Noppasin Wongchum; © iStock.com/Christopher Futcher

TIP

If the background of a photo is all one color, you can click the Color button in the Adjust group on the Picture Tools Format tab, click Set Transparent Color, and then click the color you want to make transparent.

6. Drag the top-middle sizing handle down to just above the tallest point of the opera house. Now only the opera house will be retained, and all of the sky and water will be removed.

Trouble? If any of the background of the photo is colored normally, click the Mark Areas to Remove button in the Refine group on the Background Removal tab, and then drag through the area that should be removed.

7. On the Background Removal tab, in the Close group, click the **Keep Changes** button. The changes you made are applied to the photograph, and the Background Removal tab is removed from the ribbon. See Figure 3-21.

| Figure 3-21 | Duplicate photo with background removed |

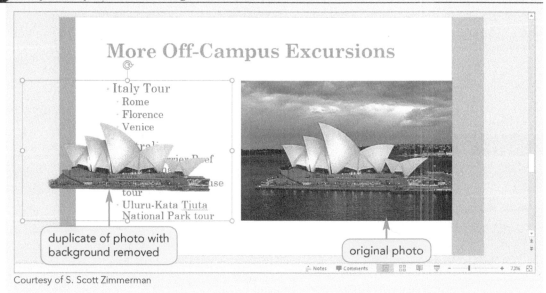

Courtesy of S. Scott Zimmerman

Applying Artistic Effects to Photos

You can apply artistic effects to photos to make them look like they are drawings, paintings, black-and-white line drawings, and so on. To make the opera house stand out in the photo, Robert wants you to apply an artistic effect to the original photo, and then place the photo with the background removed on top of it.

To apply an artistic effect to the original photo on Slide 8:

1. On Slide 8 ("More Off-Campus Excursions"), click the original photo with the visible background, and then click the **Picture Tools Format** tab, if necessary.

2. In the Adjust group, click the **Artistic Effects** button. See Figure 3-22.

| Figure 3-22 | Artistic Effects menu |

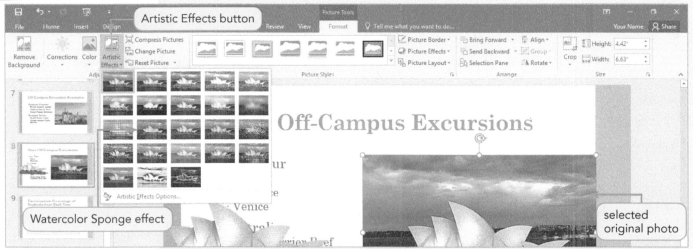

Courtesy of S. Scott Zimmerman; © iStock.com/Noppasin Wongchum

> **3.** Click the **Watercolor Sponge** effect in the third row. The watercolor sponge effect is applied to the photo. Now you will place the photo with the background removed on top of the photo with the artistic effect.

> **4.** Drag the photo with the background removed and position it directly on top of the opera house in the photo with the artistic effect applied. See Figure 3-23.

Figure 3-23   Final photo on Slide 8

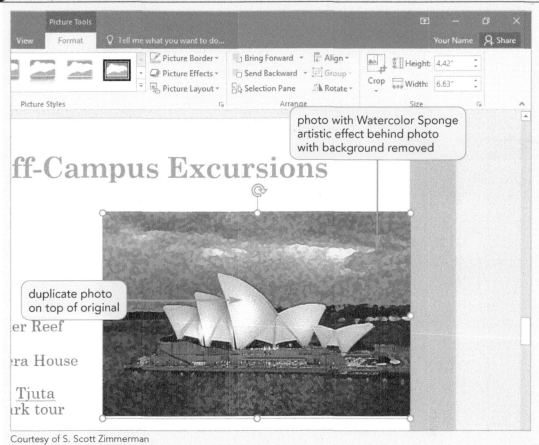

Courtesy of S. Scott Zimmerman

> **5.** Save the changes to the presentation.

Creating a Custom Shape

You have learned how to insert and format shapes on slides. In PowerPoint you can also create a custom shape by merging two or more shapes. Then you can position and format the custom shape as you would any other shape.

ISC advertises that it offers three main advantages: rigorous curricula, cultural immersion, and individual support. To illustrate this three-pronged approach, Robert wants to use a graphic, but none of the built-in shapes or SmartArt diagrams matches the idea he has in mind. He asks you to create a custom shape similar to the one shown in Figure 3-24 to illustrate this concept.

Figure 3-24 | **Robert's sketch of the shape for Slide 2**

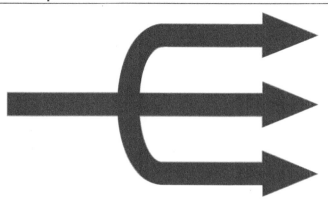

To create the custom shape for Robert, you will merge several shapes. Robert already placed three of these shapes on Slide 2. See Figure 3-25.

Figure 3-25 | **Slide 2 with three shapes**

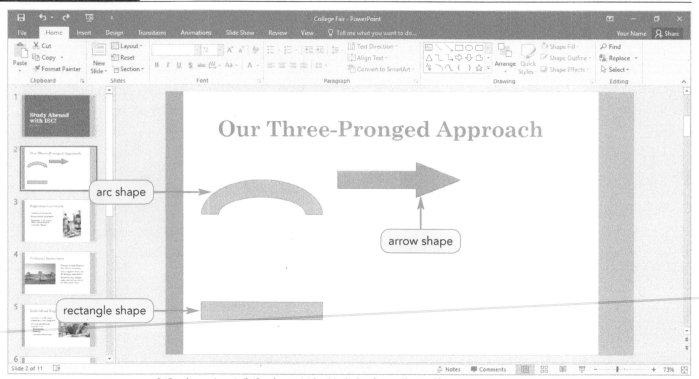

© iStock.com/sturti; © iStock.com/vichie81; © iStock.com/Susan Chiang

The first thing you need to do is duplicate the arrow shape twice to create the three prongs. Then you need to align the three arrow shapes.

To align the three arrow shapes on Slide 2:

TIP

You can also click the Align button in the Arrange group on the Format tab, and then click one of the alignment commands.

1. Display **Slide 2** ("Our Three-Pronged Approach"), and then duplicate the arrow shape twice.

2. Drag one of the duplicate arrows down until the smart guides indicate the bottom point of the arrow head is aligned with the top edge of the rectangle shape and so that its left and right ends are aligned with those of the original arrow.

▶ **3.** Drag the other duplicate arrow so it is halfway between the top and bottom arrow, until the smart guides indicate that its left and right ends are aligned with those of the top and bottom arrows and so that there is the same amount of space between the top and middle arrow and between the middle and bottom arrow, as shown in Figure 3-26.

Figure 3-26   **Smart guides showing alignment of arrow shapes**

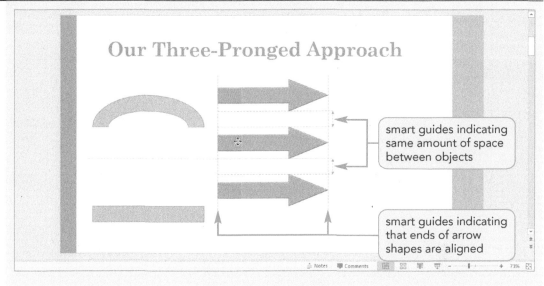

To create a custom shape, you need to use the commands on the Merge Shapes menu in the Insert Shapes group on the Drawing Tools Format tab. Each command has a different effect on selected shapes:

- **Union**—Combines selected shapes without removing any portions
- **Combine**—Combines selected shapes and removes the sections of the shapes that overlap
- **Fragment**—Separates overlapping portions of shapes into separate shapes
- **Intersect**—Combines selected shapes and removes everything except the sections that overlap
- **Subtract**—Removes the second shape selected, including any part of the first shape that is overlapped by the second shape

When you merge shapes, you place one shape on top of or touching another, and then you select the shapes. When you use the Union, Combine, Fragment, or Intersect command, the shape you select first determines the format of the merged shape. For example, if you select a red shape first and a blue shape second, and then you unite, combine, fragment, or intersect them, the merged shape will be red. When you use the Subtract command, the shape you select second is the shape that is removed.

You'll position the shapes and then merge them using the Union command.

To position the shapes and then merge them:

▶ **1.** Click the **arc** shape to select it.

▶ **2.** On the Home tab, in the Drawing group, click the **Arrange** button, point to **Rotate**, and then click **Rotate Left 90 degrees**.

Make sure the arc and arrow shape are touching or the shapes won't merge when you use the Union command.

▶ **3.** Drag the arc shape and position it so that its ends touch the left end of the top arrow and bottom arrow shapes, making sure the shapes touch.

▶ **4.** Drag the rectangle shape to position it so that its right end touches the end of the middle arrow. See Figure 3-27.

Figure 3-27 **Shapes arranged to form new shape**

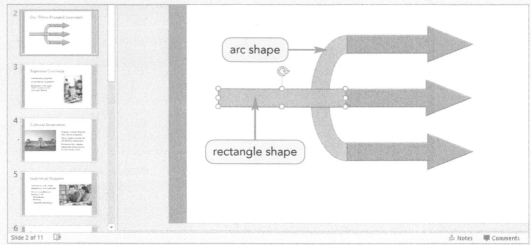

© iStock.com/sturti; © iStock.com/vichie81; © iStock.com/Susan Chiang

▶ **5.** On the ribbon, click the **Drawing Tools Format** tab. In the Insert Shapes group, the Merge Shapes button is gray and unavailable. At least two shapes need to be selected to use the commands on the Merge Shapes menu.

▶ **6.** Press and hold the **Shift** key, and then click the middle arrow. The rectangle and the middle arrow shape are now selected, and the Merge Shapes button is now available.

▶ **7.** In the Insert Shapes group, click the **Merge Shapes** button, and then click **Union**. The two shapes are merged into a new shape formatted the same tan color as the rectangle shape because you selected the rectangle shape first.

▶ **8.** Click the **arc** shape, press and hold the **Shift** key, click each of the arrow shapes including the merged shape, and then release the **Shift** key.

▶ **9.** In the Insert Shapes group, click the **Merge Shapes** button, and then click **Union**. The four shapes are merged into a blue shape.

Applying Advanced Formatting to Shapes

You know that you can fill a shape with a solid color or with a picture. You can also fill a shape with a texture—a pattern that gives a tactile quality to the shape, such as crumpled paper or marble—or with a gradient. You'll change the fill of the custom shape to a texture.

To change the shape fill to a texture:

▶ 1. Make sure the custom shape is selected, and then click the **Drawing Tools Format** tab, if necessary.

▶ 2. In the Shape Styles group, click the **Shape Fill button arrow**, and then point to **Texture**. The Texture submenu opens. See Figure 3-28.

Figure 3-28   Texture submenu on Shape Fill menu

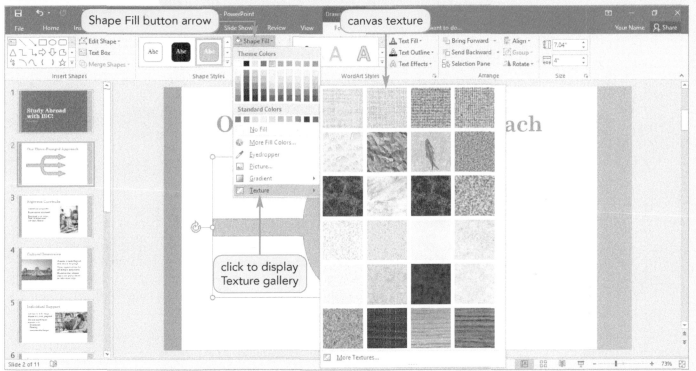

© iStock.com/sturti; © iStock.com/vichie81; © iStock.com/Susan Chiang

▶ 3. Click the **Canvas** texture, which is the second texture in the first row. The custom shape is filled with a texture resembling canvas. Robert doesn't like any of the textures as a fill for the shape. He asks you to remove the texture.

▶ 4. In the Shapes Styles group, click the **Shape Fill button arrow**, and then click **No Fill**. The texture is removed from the custom shape, and only the outline of the custom shape remains.

The texture did not achieve the effect Robert wanted for the shape. He now asks you to use a gradient to simulate the look of metal or silver. You can apply gradients on the Shape Fill menu that use shades of the Accent 1 color in the theme color palette. You can also create a custom gradient using the options in the Format Shape task pane. To create a custom gradient, you select the colors to use, specify the position in the shape where the color will change, and specify the direction of the gradient in the shape.

Refer to the Session 3.2 Visual Overview for more information about using the Format Shape task pane to create a custom gradient.

Creating a Custom Gradient in a Shape

REFERENCE

- Select the shape.
- Click the Drawing Tools Format tab.
- In the Shape Styles group, click the Shape Fill button arrow, point to Gradient, and then click More Gradients to open the Format Shape task pane.
- In the Format Shape task pane, on the Shape Options tab with the Fill & Line button selected, click the Gradient fill option button.
- On the Gradient stops slider, click a tab, drag it to the desired position on the slider, click the Color button, and then select a color.
- Repeat the above step for each tab.
- Click the Type arrow, and then click the type of gradient you want to use.
- Click the Direction button, and then click the direction of the gradient.

You will apply a custom gradient to the custom shape now.

To create a custom gradient fill for the custom shape:

1. In the Shape Styles group, click the **Shape Fill button arrow**, and then point to **Gradient**. The gradients on the submenu use shades of the Ice Blue, Accent 1 color. To create a custom gradient, you need to open the Format Shape task pane.

2. Click **More Gradients**. The Format Shape task pane opens with the Fill & Line button ◇ selected on the Shape Options tab.

3. In the Fill section, click the **Gradient fill** option button. The commands for modifying the gradient fill appear in the task pane, and the shape fills with shades of light blue. Under Gradient stops, the first tab on the slider is selected, and its value in the Position box is 0%. You will change the position and color of the second tab on the slider.

4. On the Gradient stops slider, drag the **Stop 2 of 4** tab (second tab from the left) to the left until the value in the Position box is **40%**.

   Trouble? If you can't position the slider exactly, click the Stop 2 of 4 tab, type 40 in the Position box, and then press the Enter key.

TIP

Click the Add gradient stop button to add another gradient stop to the slider; click the Remove gradient stop button to remove the selected gradient stop from the slider.

5. With the Stop 2 of 4 tab selected, click the **Color** button. The color palette opens.

6. Click the **White, Background 1, Darker 5%** color. Next you need to change the color of the third tab.

7. Click the **Stop 3 of 4** tab, click the **Color** button, and then click the **White, Background 1, Darker 50%** color.

8. Click the **Stop 4 of 4** tab, click the **Color** button, and then click the **Gray-50%, Accent 6, Lighter 60%** color.

   Next you will change the direction of the gradient. Above the Gradient stops slider, in the Type box, Linear is selected. This means that the shading will vary linearly—that is, top to bottom, side to side, or diagonally. You will change the direction to a diagonal.

9. Click the **Direction** button. A gallery of gradient options opens.

10. Click the **Linear Diagonal – Top Right to Bottom Left** direction. The shading in the shape changes so it varies diagonally. See Figure 3-29.

| Figure 3-29 | Custom shape with gradient fill |

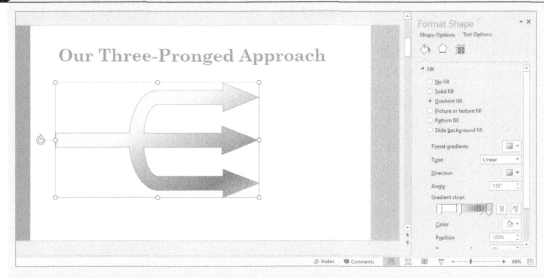

11. In the Format Shape task pane, click the **Close** button ⊠.

Although the gradient shading helped, the shape looks flat and doesn't really look metallic. To finish formatting the shape, you need to apply a bevel effect, which will give the edges a three-dimensional, rounded look.

To add a bevel effect to the custom shape:

1. On the ribbon, click the **Drawing Tools Format** tab, if necessary.

2. In the Shape Styles group, click the **Shape Effects** button. The menu that opens lets you choose from a variety of effects you can apply to shapes.

3. Point to **Bevel**, and then click the **Circle** bevel. The shape has a bevel effect.

TIP

To save a custom shape as a picture file so that you can use it in other files, right-click it, and then click Save as Picture on the shortcut menu.

Now you need to complete the slide by adding text boxes that list the three elements of the ISC approach. You will position the custom shape, and then place a text box next to each prong.

To add text boxes to Slide 2:

1. Drag the shape so its left edge aligns with the left edge of the title text box.

2. On the ribbon, click the **Insert** tab, and then in the Text group, click the **Text Box** button.

3. To the right of the shape's top arrow, drag to draw a text box approximately 2 inches wide, and then type **Rigorous Curricula**.

4. Change the font size of the text in the text box to **32** points. The text now appears on two lines in the text box.

   Trouble? If the text did not adjust to appear on two lines in the text box, drag the right-middle sizing handle to the left until it does.

5. Drag the text box to position it so that the top of the text box is aligned with the top of the shape and the left edge of the text box is aligned with the right edge of the shape.

6. Duplicate the text box, and then position the duplicate to the right of the shape's middle arrow, aligning the left and right edges with the left and right edges of the top text box and aligning the middle of the text box with the middle of the shape.

7. Duplicate the second text box. A third text box appears.

8. Point to the third text box so that the pointer changes to ↖, press and hold the mouse button, and then, if necessary, drag the third text box to the right of the shape's bottom arrow, aligning the left and right edges with the left and right edges of the other two text boxes and so that there is the same amount of space between each text box.

9. In the text box to the right of the middle arrow, replace the text with **Cultural Immersion**, and then in the text box to the right of the bottom arrow, replace the text with **Individual Support**. Compare your screen to Figure 3-30, and make any adjustments if necessary.

| Figure 3-30 | Text boxes next to custom shape with beveled edge |

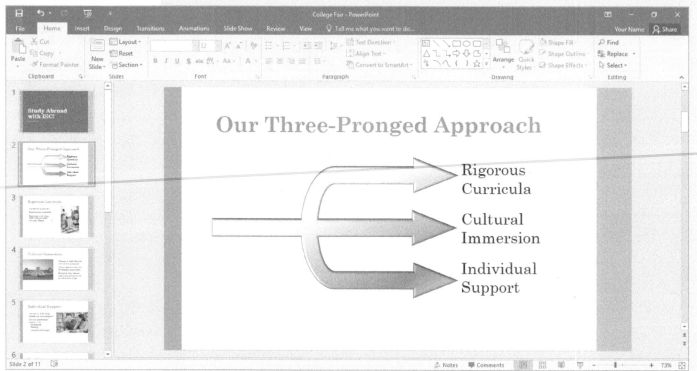

© iStock.com/sturti; © iStock.com/vichie81; © iStock.com/Susan Chiang

10. Save the changes to the presentation.

INSIGHT

Using the Format Shape and Format Picture Task Panes

Many options are available to you in the Format Shape and Format Picture task panes. Most of the commands are available on the Drawing Tools and Picture Tools Format tabs on the ribbon, but you can refine their effects in the task panes. For example, you can fill a shape with a color and then use a command in the Format Shape task pane to make the fill color partially transparent so you can see objects behind the shape. Because these task panes are so useful, you can access them in a variety of ways. Once a picture or shape is selected, you can do one of the following to open the corresponding task pane:

- Click any of the Dialog Box Launchers on the Drawing Tools or Picture Tools Format tab.
- Right-click a shape or picture, and then click Format Shape or Format Picture on the shortcut menu.
- Click a command at the bottom of a menu, such as the More Gradients command at the bottom of the Gradients submenu on the Fill Color menu or the Picture Corrections Options command at the bottom of the Corrections menu.

Making Presentations Accessible

People with physical impairments or disabilities can use computers because of technology that makes them accessible. For example, people who cannot use their arms or hands instead can use foot, head, or eye movements to control the pointer. One of the most common assistive technologies is the screen reader. The screen reader identifies objects on the screen and produces an audio of the text.

Graphics and tables cause problems for users of screen readers unless they have **alternative text**, often shortened to **alt text**, which is text added to an object that describes the object. For example, the alt text for a SmartArt graphic might describe the intent of the graphic. When a screen reader encounters an object that has alt text, it announces that an object is on the slide, and then it reads the alt text.

Adding Alt Text

You can add alt text for any object on a PowerPoint slide. Many screen readers can read the text in title text boxes and bulleted lists, so you usually do not need to add alt text for those objects. Most screen readers cannot read the text in SmartArt, in text boxes you draw, or in other shapes, so you will add alt text to the SmartArt diagram and the text box on Slide 6.

Make sure you select the entire SmartArt object and not just one shape. If you right-click a shape, the alt text will be applied only for that individual shape.

To add alt text for the SmartArt graphic:

▶ 1. Display **Slide 6** ("Locations").

▶ 2. Right-click the white area near any of the shapes in the SmartArt graphic to select the entire graphic.

▶ 3. On the shortcut menu, click **Format Object**. The Format Shape task pane opens with the Shape Options tab selected.

▶ 4. In the task pane, click the **Size & Properties** button 🖽, and then click **Text Box** to collapse that section, if necessary.

5. In the task pane, click **Alt Text** to expand the Alt Text section. A Title box and a Description box appear below the Alt Text section heading. See Figure 3-31.

| Figure 3-31 | Alt Text section in the Format Shape task pane |

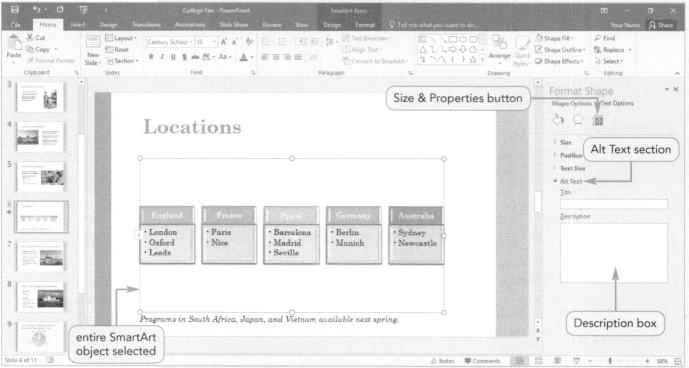

© iStock.com/sturti; © iStock.com/vichie81; © iStock.com/Susan Chiang; © iStock.com/Noppasin Wongchum; Courtesy of S. Scott Zimmerman

6. Click in the **Description** box, and then type **SmartArt graphic listing the ISC program countries and cities. The countries are England, France, Spain, Germany, and Australia.** (including the last period). This is the text a screen reader would read. (Note that in this case, if you were creating this slide for a real-life presentation, you should also add the city names to the Alt text.)

7. On Slide 6, click the text box at the bottom of the slide to select it. The Format Shape task pane changes to show an empty Description box. Now you will type alt text for the text box.

8. In the Format Shape task pane, click in the **Description** box, and then type **Note indicating that programs in South Africa, Japan, and Vietnam will be available next spring.** (including the period).

You also need to add alt text to the chart on Slide 9. To do this, you need to make sure that the chart area is selected and not just one element in the chart; otherwise the Alt Text commands will not be available in the task pane.

To select the chart area and add alt text to the chart on Slide 9:

1. Display **Slide 9** ("Participation Percentage of Students from Each Year"), and then click the chart.

2. On the ribbon, click the **Chart Tools Format** tab.

3. In the Current Selection group, click the **Chart Elements arrow** (the arrow on the top box in the group), and then click **Chart Area**, if necessary. Now the alt text will be added to the entire chart. In the task pane, the title is now Format Chart Area.

4. In the task pane, click the **Size & Properties** button ▨. In the Alt Text section, the Description box is empty.

5. In the task pane, click in the **Description** box, and then type **Pie chart illustrating that 47% of students in the program are in their 3rd year, 26% are in their 4th year, 18% are in their 5th year, and a small percentage are in their 1st or 2nd year.** (including the period).

6. Close the Format Chart Area task pane.

Robert will add alt text for the rest of the graphics in the presentation later. Next, you need to make sure that the objects on slides will be identified in the correct order for screen readers.

Checking the Order Objects Will Be Read by a Screen Reader

When a person uses a screen reader to access a presentation, the screen reader selects and describes the elements on the slides in the order they were added. In PowerPoint, most screen readers first explain that a slide is displayed. After the user signals to the screen reader that he is ready for the next piece of information (for example, by pressing the Tab key), the reader identifies the first object on the slide. For most slides, this means that the first object is the title text box. The second object is usually the content placeholder on the slide. To check the order in which a screen reader will describe objects on a slide, you can use the Tab key or open the Selection pane. You'll check the order of objects on Slide 8.

To identify the order of objects on Slide 8:

1. Display **Slide 8** ("More Off-Campus Excursions"), and then click a blank area on the slide. The slide is active, but nothing on the slide is selected.

2. Press the **Tab** key. The title text box is selected.

3. Press the **Tab** key again. The bulleted list text box is selected next.

4. Press the **Tab** key. The photo is selected. However, remember that there are two photos here, one placed on top of the other. To see which one is selected, you can use the Selection pane.

5. On the Home tab, in the Editing group, click the **Select** button, and then click **Selection Pane**. The Selection pane opens. See Figure 3-32.

Figure 3-32 Selection pane listing objects on Slide 8

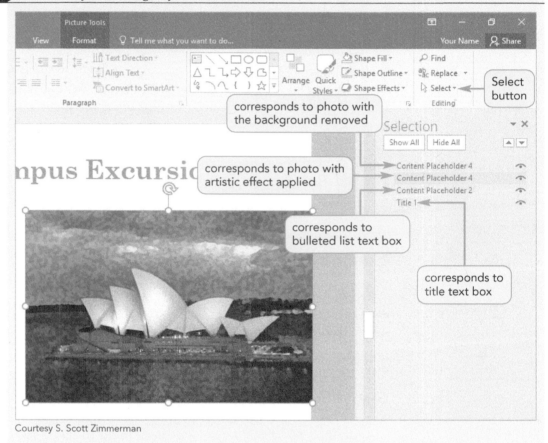

Courtesy S. Scott Zimmerman

In the Selection pane, the first object added to the slide appears at the bottom of the list, and the last object added appears at the top of the list. (The blue bar on the right side of the slide and the gray bar on the left side of the slide aren't listed in the Selection pane because they are part of the slide background.)

INSIGHT

Reordering Objects in the Selection Pane

If an object is listed in the wrong order in the Selection pane—for example, if the content placeholder was identified first and the title second—you could change this in the Selection pane. To do this, click the object you want to move, and then at the top of the pane, click the Bring Forward ▲ or Send Backward ▼ buttons to move the selected object up or down in the list.

Renaming Objects in the Selection Pane

In the Selection pane for Slide 8, there are two objects with the same name. This is because you duplicated the photo, so the name in the Selection pane was duplicated as well. To make it clearer which items on slides are listed in the Selection pane, you can rename each object in the list.

To rename objects in the Selection pane:

▶ **1.** On the slide, click the photo to select it, if necessary, and then drag left so that the version of the photo with the background removed is to the left of the version of the photo with the artistic effect applied. In the Selection pane, the top Content Placeholder 4 is selected.

▶ **2.** In the Selection pane, click the **selected Content Placeholder 4**. An orange border appears around the selected item. The insertion point appears in the selected text.

▶ **3.** Press the **Delete** and **Backspace** keys as needed to delete "Content Placeholder 4," type **Photo with background removed**, and then press the **Enter** key. The name is changed in the Selection pane.

▶ **4.** In the pane, click **Content Placeholder 4**, click it again, delete the text "Content Placeholder 4," type **Photo with artistic effect**, and then press the **Enter** key.

▶ **5.** Drag the photo with the background removed back on top of the photo with the artistic effect applied.

▶ **6.** Close the Selection pane.

▶ **7.** Display **Slide 1** (the title slide), replace Robert's name in the subtitle with your name, and then save and close the presentation.

PROSKILLS

Decision Making: Selecting the Right Tool for the Job

Many programs with advanced capabilities for editing and correcting photos and other programs for drawing complex shapes are available. Although the tools provided in PowerPoint for accomplishing these tasks are useful, if you need to do more than make simple photo corrections or create a simple shape, consider using a program with more advanced features, or choose to hire someone with skills in graphic design to help you.

You have created and saved a custom shape and used advanced formatting techniques for shapes and photos in the presentation. Robert is pleased with the presentation. With the alt text you've added, he is also confident that users of screen readers will be able to understand the slide containing the SmartArt and the text box and the slide containing the chart.

REVIEW

Session 3.2 Quick Check

1. What are the five types of corrections you can make to photos in PowerPoint?

2. What happens when you use the Remove Background command?

3. What are artistic effects?

4. What happens when you merge shapes?

5. How do you create a custom gradient?

6. What is alt text?

Review Assignments

Data Files needed for the Review Assignments: Employee.m4a, RA.pptx

Sara Allen is the human resources director at International Study Crossroads (ISC). Each year, she needs to hire resident advisors (RAs) for the program. The company requires one RA for every 50 students. Sara plans to attend career fairs at local colleges in Maryland, Washington, D.C., Virginia, Delaware, and southern Pennsylvania, and she asks you to help her create a presentation she can use to recruit new RAs. Complete the following:

1. Open the presentation **RA**, located in the PowerPoint3 > Review folder included with your Data Files, add your name as the Slide 1 subtitle, and then save it as **ISC RAs** to the location where you are storing your files.

2. On Slide 8 ("Interested in Applying?"), create a SmartArt diagram using the Circle Process layout, which is a Process type diagram. From left to right, replace the placeholder text in the shapes with **Fill out application**, **Submit information for CORI check**, and **Schedule drug test**.

3. Add a new first-level shape as the rightmost shape to the SmartArt diagram, and then replace the placeholder text in it with **Schedule interview**. Move the "Schedule interview" shape so it is the second shape in the diagram.

4. Change the style of the SmartArt diagram to the Powder style, and then change the color to Colorful – Accent Colors.

5. On Slide 9 (the last slide), add the audio clip **Employee**, located in the PowerPoint3 > Review folder. Set it to play automatically, and hide the icon during the slide show. Position the icon in the lower-right corner of the slide at the bottom of the orange bar.

6. On Slide 7 ("Number of Students by Country in 2016"), add a pie chart. In cells A2 through A6, type **England**, **France**, **Spain**, **Germany**, and **Australia**. In cell B1, type **2016**. In cells B2 through B6, type **14990**, **7233**, **9107**, **12997**, and **2673**.

7. Apply Layout 4 to the chart.

8. Click one of the data labels that was added, and then change the font color to Black, Text 1 and the font size to 16 points.

9. Change the position of the data labels to the Outside End option.

10. On Slide 5 ("Qualifications"), add a text box approximately 2 inches wide and one-half inch high. Type *****Criminal Offender Record Information**. Change the format of the text box so the text doesn't wrap and so that the left margin is zero.

11. Align the left edge of the text box with the left edge of the bulleted list text box, and align its top edge with the bottom edge of the picture and the bulleted list.

12. On Slide 9, insert a WordArt text box using the Fill - Orange, Accent 3, Sharp Bevel style. Replace the placeholder text with **Submit Your**, press the Enter key, type **Application**, press the Enter key, and then type **Today!**

13. Change the fill color of the WordArt text to Dark Red, Accent 1, and then change the font size of the text to 66 points. Add the Perspective Diagonal Upper Left shadow effect. (*Hint*: Use the Text Effects button in the WordArt Styles group on the Drawing Tools Format tab.)

14. Position the WordArt text box so it is entered horizontally and vertically on the slide. (*Hint*: Use the Align command in the Arrange group on the Drawing Tools Format tab.)

15. On Slide 5 ("Qualifications"), remove the background of the photo.

16. On Slide 6 ("Mandatory Training Dates"), change the color tone of the photo to Temperature: 7200K.

17. On Slide 3 ("What to Expect"), change the saturation of the photo to 66%.

18. On Slide 4 ("Locations"), sharpen the photo by 50%, and then change the contrast to 30%. Then apply the Pencil Sketch artistic effect to the photo.

19. On Slide 2, drag the gray doughnut shape on top of the large circle. Position the doughnut shape near the top right of the large circle so that smart guides appear indicating that the top and right of the two shapes are aligned. Subtract the doughnut shape from the larger circle by selecting the shape you want to keep—the large circle—first, and then selecting the shape you want to subtract—the gray doughnut shape—before using the Subtract command.

20. Drag the small yellow circle on top of the solid orange circle that was created in the merged shape. Position the yellow circle near the top right of the solid circle in the merged shape without overlapping the edges of the circles, and then subtract the yellow circle from the merged shape. The final shape should look like Figure 3-33.

Figure 3-33   **Merged shape**

21. On Slide 2, create a text box approximately 2 inches wide and 1 inch high. Type **ISC** in the text box. Deselect the Wrap text in shape option, if necessary. Change the font to Impact, and the font size to 48 points.

22. Drag the text box to the center of the white circle created when you subtracted the yellow circle in the merged shape. Select the merged shape first, and then select the text box. Use the Union command to combine the shapes.

23. Fill the merged shape with the From Bottom Left Corner gradient under Dark Variations on the Gradient submenu on the Shape Fill menu. Then customize the gradient by changing the position of the Stop 2 of 3 tab to 40% and changing the color of the Stop 3 of 3 tab to Dark Red, Accent 1, Lighter 80%.

24. Copy the merged shape. Display Slide 1 (the title slide), and then paste the copied shape to the slide. Resize the merged shape so that it is 1.4 inches square, and then position the shape to the left of "International Study Crossroads" so that its left edge is aligned with the left edge of the slide title text box and so that its top is aligned with the top of the "International Study Crossroads" text box. Delete Slide 2.

25. On Slide 6 ("Number of Students by Country in 2016"), add the following as alt text to the chart: **Pie chart showing the number of students in the program who went to each of the five countries.**

26. On Slide 7 ("Interested in Applying?"), add the following as alt text to the SmartArt shape: **SmartArt diagram listing four steps required to apply to be an RA.**

27. On Slide 7, edit the Content Placeholder 2 name in the Selection Pane to **SmartArt**.

28. Save and close the presentation.

Case Problem 1

Data Files needed for this Case Problem: PT.pptx, Recovery.m4a

PT PLUS   Ben and Helen Acosta, both physical therapists, opened their practice PT PLUS in Searcy, Arkansas, seven years ago. They have a state-of-the-art facility and equipment including a pool for aquatic therapy, and they have built a good reputation among local doctors and hospitals because patients referred to them have faster recovery times than average. They are preparing a bid for a local semi-pro football team to be the exclusive providers of physical therapy to the team members. As part of their bid, Helen prepared a PowerPoint presentation and asked you to finish it for her. Complete the following steps:

1. Open the presentation **PT**, located in the PowerPoint3 > Case1 folder included with your Data Files, add your name as the subtitle, and then save the presentation as **PT PLUS** to the location where you are storing your files.

2. On Slide 2 ("The PT PLUS Difference"), add a text box, and type ***American Board of Physical Therapy Specialties**. Turn off the Wrap text option, change the right margin to 0, and then right-align the text in the text box. Position the text box so that its right edge is aligned with the right edge of the title and bulleted list text boxes and its top edge is aligned with the bottom edge of the bulleted list text box.

3. On Slide 3 ("State of the Art Facility"), change the brightness of the photo on the left to -10% and the contrast to 30%.

4. On Slide 3, sharpen the photo on the right by 25%, change its saturation to 200%, and then change its tone to a temperature of 5900 K.

5. On Slide 4 ("Recovery Time Examples in Weeks"), add a clustered column chart in the content placeholder. Enter the date shown in Figure 3-34 in the spreadsheet to create the chart.

Figure 3-34   **Data for Slide 4**

	Industry Average	PT PLUS
Meniscus tear	8	5
Rotator cuff injuries	35	26
Achilles tendon rupture	24	18

6. Drag the small blue box in the lower-right corner of cell D5 up and to the left so that the blue border surrounds cells B2 through C4 and the data in column D and row 5 is removed from the chart.

7. Change the style of the chart to Style 2, and then change the colors of the chart to the Color 3 palette. (*Hint*: Use the Chart Styles button next to the chart.)

8. Move the legend so it appears below the chart, and then change the font size of the text in the legend to 16 points. Change the font size of the labels on the x-axis to 14 points, and then change the font size of the data labels to 16 points. (*Hint*: To modify all the data labels, select the data label above one color column and modify it, and then select the data label above a column of the other color and modify it.)

9. Remove the chart title.

10. On Slide 4, insert the audio clip **Recovery**, located in the PowerPoint3 > Case1 folder. Hide the icon during a slide show, and set it to play automatically. Position the sound icon centered below the chart.

11. Add the following alt text for the chart: **Chart showing that recovery times for certain injuries is faster at PT PLUS than the industry average.**

12. Save and close the presentation.

CHALLENGE

Case Problem 2

Data Files needed for this Case Problem: Elder.pptx

Keystone State Elder Services   Shaina Brown is the director of Keystone State Elder Services, a company that provides in-home services for elderly and disabled people in Youngstown, Ohio, and surrounding cities so that they can continue to live at home rather than in a nursing home. Shaina travels to senior centers, churches, and other locations to explain the services her company provides. She started creating a PowerPoint presentation and asked you to help complete it by creating a logo based on her design, correcting photos, and adding SmartArt. Complete the following steps:

1. Open the file named **Elder**, located in the PowerPoint3 > Case2 folder included with your Data Files, add your name as the subtitle on Slide 1, and then save it as **Elder Services** to the location where you are storing your files.

2. On Slide 2, duplicate the red filled square shape three times. These are the four squares behind the center square in Figure 3-35. Arrange them as shown in Figure 3-35 so that there is about one-quarter inch of space between each square. Merge the four squares using the Union command.

Figure 3-35   **Logo for Keystone State Elder Services**

3. Apply the From Center Gradient style in the Light Variations set of gradient styles to the square. Customize this gradient by changing the Stop 1 of 3 tab to the Red, Accent 1 color, changing the Stop 2 of 3 tab to the Red, Accent 1, Darker 50% color, and changing the Stop 3 of 3 tab to Red, Accent 1, Lighter 40% color and changing its position to 80%. Then change the gradient Type to Linear and the direction to Linear Down.

4. Create a text box, type **KS**, press the Enter key, and then type **ES**. Turn off the Wrap text option if necessary, change the font to Copperplate Gothic Bold, change the font size to 40 points, and then use the Center button in the Paragraph group on the Home tab to center the text in the box. Change the size of the text box to 1.5" square. Fill the text box shape with the White, Background 1 color. Apply the Preset 5 shape effect to this square (located on the Presets submenu on the Shape Effects menu).

5. Position the text box so it is centered over the custom shape, using the smart guides to assist you.

⊕ **Explore** 6. Group the custom shape and the text box. (*Hint*: Use the appropriate command on the Drawing Tools Format tab.)

⊕ **Explore** 7. Save the final grouped shape as a picture named **Logo** to the location where you are storing your files. (*Hint*: Right-click the shape.)

8. Delete Slide 2, and then insert the picture **Logo** on Slide 1 (the title slide). Resize it, maintaining the aspect ratio, so that it is approximately 2.6 inches by 2.6 inches (it may not be perfectly square). Position it to the left of the title so that it is bottom-aligned with the title text box and so that there is an equal amount of space between the logo and the slide title and the logo and the left side of the slide.

9. Add **Company logo** as alt text for the logo.

10. On Slide 2 ("Our Services"), change the saturation of the photo to 66%, and then change the tone to a temperature of 7200K.

11. On Slide 3 ("What We Do"), change the contrast of the photo to -20%, and sharpen it by 50%.

12. Add **Photo of a smiling woman at a keyboard** as alt text for the picture.

13. On Slide 4 ("How to Set Up Services"), insert a SmartArt diagram using the Sub-Step Process layout (in the Process category). Type the following as first-level items in the diagram:

    Schedule Services

    Set Up Assessment Appointment

    Answer Interview Questions

    Call Elder Line

14. Delete the second-level placeholders in the diagram. (*Hint*: Use the text pane.)

⚙ **Explore** 15. Reverse the order of the boxes in the diagram. (*Hint*: Use a command in the Create Graphic group on the SmartArt Tools Design tab.)

16. Change the style of the SmartArt diagram to the Cartoon style.

17. Add **SmartArt diagram listing the four steps to take to receive services.** as alt text for the SmartArt diagram.

18. On Slide 5 ("We Are Here for You"), insert the **Logo** file you created in the content placeholder on the left, and add **Company logo** as alt text for the logo on Slide 5.

19. Save and close the presentation.

Case Problem 3

Data Files needed for this Case Problem: Books.jpg, Tutoring.pptx

Total Learning Tutoring   Total Learning Tutoring (TLT), in Durham, North Carolina, offers tutoring services for students of all ages who need extra help to keep up with their classwork or who want to learn additional material not offered in their classes. They also offer SAT and ACT test prep courses. Over the past three years, the popularity of their test prep courses has exploded. In addition, the number of students who enroll in ACT test prep courses instead of SAT test prep has increased significantly. Tom Shaughnessy, the owner of TLT, wants to expand and asks you to help him create a PowerPoint presentation that he can use when he talks to potential investors. Complete the following steps:

1. Open the presentation **Tutoring**, located in the PowerPoint3 > Case3 folder included with your Data Files, add your name as the subtitle, and then save the presentation as **Total Learning Tutoring** to the location where you are storing your files.

2. On Slide 1 (the title slide), apply the Photocopy artistic effect to the photo.

3. On Slide 2 ("Our Services"), insert the photo **Books**, located in the PowerPoint 3 > Case3 folder, in the content placeholder to the left of the bulleted list. Resize it, maintaining the aspect ratio, so it is 3.5" high. Position it so that its left edge is aligned with the left edge of the slide and so it is aligned with the middle of the bulleted list text box.

⚙ **Explore** 4. On Slide 2, make the background of the photo transparent. (*Hint*: Use the appropriate command on the Color menu on the Picture Tools Format tab.)

5. On Slide 2, increase the saturation of the photo to 200%, and then sharpen it by 25%.

CHALLENGE

6. On Slide 2, insert a text box below the bulleted list. Type ***for original SAT score between 300 and 1150 or an original ACT score between 13 and 29** in the text box. Change the font size of the text in the text box to 14 points, and italicize it. Turn off the Wrap text option, change the left and right margins of the text box to 0 inches, and then resize the text box so it just fits the text inside it. Position the text box so its left edge is aligned with the left edge of the bulleted list text box and its top edge is aligned with the bottom of the bulleted list text box.

7. On Slide 3 ("Tremendous Growth in Just Three Years"), change the contrast of the photo by -30%.

8. On Slide 4 ("SAT and ACT Prep Course Enrollment"), insert a clustered column chart using the data shown in Figure 3-36.

Figure 3-36   Data for Slide 4

	SAT Prep	ACT Prep
2014	201	87
2015	587	334
2016	922	885

9. In the spreadsheet, drag the small blue selection handle in the lower-right corner of cell D5 up one row and left one column to exclude the Series 3 column of data and the Category 4 row of data.

10. Change the style of the chart to Style 4.

11. Remove the chart title and the legend.

Explore 12. Add the data table, and remove the data labels. (*Hint*: Use the CHART ELEMENTS menu.)

13. Change the font color of the text in the data table to Black, Text 2, and the font size to 14 points.

14. Add **Column chart showing that SAT and ACT Prep course enrollment has increased over the past three years.** as alt text for the chart.

15. Change the colors used in the chart to the Color 4 palette. (*Hint*: Use the Chart Styles button next to the chart.)

Explore 16. Animate the chart with the entrance animation Appear. Modify the animation so that the chart grid animates first, then the three data markers for the SAT Prep data series one at a time, then the three data markers for the ACT Prep data series one at a time. Finally, modify the start timing of the chart grid animation so it animates with the previous action.

17. On Slide 5 ("Proposed Test Prep Course Expansion"), change the color tone of the photo to a temperature of 7200 K.

18. On Slide 7, format the text "Thank You!" as WordArt using the Gradient Fill – Brown, Accent 4, Outline – Accent 4 style. Center the WordArt in the text box, and then change the font size to 60 points.

19. Save and close the presentation.

Case Problem 4

Data Files needed for this Case Problem: Bullying.pptx

Partners Counseling   Patricia Burrell is one of the owners of Partners Counseling in Middletown, Connecticut. Partners Counseling is a group of therapists who specialize in providing therapy to children. Patricia has been hired by several school districts to talk to teachers and school support staff about ways they can identify and stop bullying. She asks you to help her create her presentation by researching statistics about bullying and ways to identify and prevent bullying. Complete the following steps:

1. Research bullying online. For example, look for statistics about the number of children who are bullied, suggested ways others can help, and ways to identify bullying. While you are researching the topic, look for information that can be presented in a chart or in a SmartArt graphic. Make sure you note the webpage addresses of the pages that contain the information you are going to use because you will need to include that on your slides.

2. Open the presentation **Bullying**, located in the PowerPoint3 > Case4 folder included with your data files. Add your name as the subtitle, and then save the presentation as **Stop Bullying** to the location where you are saving your files.

3. Based on your research, on Slide 3, create a chart that shows statistics about bullying, and then add a slide title that describes the data in the chart. On Slide 4 ("How to Help"), insert SmartArt containing suggestions for how to stop bullying. On Slide 5, add any additional information you think is helpful, such as describing a list of things that adults should not do, suggestions on how to stop bullying when it happens, or descriptions of times when the police should be called.

4. On Slide 2 ("What Is Bullying?"), change the tone of the photo to a temperature of 5900 K. On Slide 5, sharpen the photo by 50%.

5. On each slide that contains information from a webpage, include a text box at the bottom of the slide that contains **Data from** followed by the name of the website and the name of the webpage followed by the webpage address in parentheses.

6. Add appropriate transitions and animations.

7. Check the spelling in your presentation and proof it carefully.

8. Save and close the presentation.

INDEX

A

accessible, making presentations, PPT 177–181

Action Settings dialog box, PPT 208–209

Add Animation button, PPT 99

add-ins described, PPT 118

adjustment handles, PPT 70

Advance to the next slide button, PPT 32

Advanced Animation group, Animation tab, PPT 190

advanced animations (visual overview), PPT 190–191

After check box, automatic slide timings, PPT 218

After Previous animation sequence, PPT 190, PPT 197

alignment of text in table cells, PPT 91

alt text, adding, PPT 177–179

anecdotes, sharing, PRES 16

animating

    lists, PPT 107–109

    objects, PPT 102–103

    SmartArt diagrams, PPT 145–146

    titles on slides, PPT 103

animation effects

    applied to videos, PPT 115–116

    options for bulleted list (fig.), PPT 108

animation emphasis effects, PA-8

Animation gallery, PPT 190

    described, PPT 99

    illustrated (fig.), PPT 103

Animation Painter

    copying and modifying animations, PPT 196–197

    using (visual overview), PPT 99

Animation Pane, working with, PPT 197–201

animation sequence icons (fig.), PPT 190

animation sequence numbers, PPT 99

animation triggers

    illustrated (fig.), PPT 191

    setting, PPT 201–202

animations

    adding more than one to objects, PPT 193–197

    advanced (visual overview), PPT 190–191

    Animation Pane, working with, PPT 197–201

    applying, PPT 102–109

    applying to videos, PPT 115–116

    changing start of, PPT 106–107

    copying and modifying, PPT 196–197

    testing, PPT 106

    triggers. See animation triggers

    using (visual overview), PPT 98–99

    viewing in Slide Show view, PPT 105

Animations tab, PPT 99

annotating webpages (Microsoft Edge), PA-15

Apply to All button, PPT 98

apps, productivity, PA-1–4

area charts, PPT 153

Arrange button, Drawing group, Home tab, PPT 77

arrow shapes, inserting, PPT 74–77

artistic effects, applying to photos, PPT 168–169

Artistic Effects menu (fig.), PPT 168

aspect ratio, PPT 44, PPT 47

audience

    analyzing needs and expectations of, PRES 9–11

    characteristics for presentations, PRES 3

    connecting to your, PRES 39–42

    gaining attention of, PRES 15

    needs of international, PRES 9

    way of gaining attention of (fig.), PRES 17

Audience Analysis worksheet (fig.), PRES 10

audio

    adding to slides, PPT 146–148

    inserting into presentations, PPT 147

    recording clips, PPT 147

    recording slides with, PPT 123–124

    setting options, PPT 122–123

Audio button, Media group, Insert tab, PPT 225

Audio Tools Playback tab, PPT 146

AutoCorrect, PPT 10

AutoCorrect Options button menu (fig.), PPT 11

AutoCorrect Options dialog box, PPT 10–11

AutoFit described, PPT 15

automatic slide timings (visual overview), PPT 218–219

B

backgrounds

    changing slide, PPT 202–206

    graphic, hiding, PPT 206

    removing photo's, PPT 166–168

Backspace key, deleting characters with, PPT 10

Backstage view, PPT 5

    Print screen in (fig.), PPT 57

    Save As dialog box in, PPT 9

bar charts, PPT 153

bevel effects, PPT 175

Black and White button, Color/Grayscale group, View tab, PPT 205

Black or unblack slide show button, PPT 33, PPT 55

body language, PRES 39–40

Bold button, PPT 20

borders

    colored, around spreadsheet cells, PPT 138

    picture, PPT 71

    table, PPT 82, PPT 89, PPT 89–90

Brightness/Contrast gallery, PPT 162

Bring Forward button, PPT 180

browsers. See Microsoft Edge

bulleted lists, PPT 14

    and alternatives (fig.), PRES 25

    creating, PPT 14–15

business jargon, avoiding, PRES 42

buttons. See specific button

C

Can Down transform effect, PPT 161

capturing video clips, PA-11

cards (Sway), PA-6–7

cases

    Division of Agricultural Development, PPT 189

    International Study Crossroads (ISC), PPT 137

    Lakeside Event Center, PPT 1

    RiverClean, PPT 69

    Ruff Streets dog rescue center, PRES 1

CDs, packaging presentations as, PPT 229–230

cells, spreadsheet

    charts in slides, PPT 138

    described, PPT 138

cells, table, PPT 82

    aligning text, PPT 91

    filling with pictures, PPT 90–91

characters

    deleting with Backspace or Delete keys, PPT 10

    inserting special, PPT 93–94

Productivity Apps for School and Work

Corinne Hoisington

OneNote
Sway
Office Mix
Edge

Lochlan keeps track of his class notes, football plays, and internship meetings with OneNote.

Zoe is using the annotation features of Microsoft Edge to take and save web notes for her research paper.

Nori is creating a Sway site to highlight this year's activities for the Student Government Association.

Hunter is adding interactive videos and screen recordings to his PowerPoint resume.

© Rawpixel/Shutterstock.com

Being computer literate no longer means mastery of only Word, Excel, PowerPoint, Outlook, and Access. To become technology power users, Hunter, Nori, Zoe, and Lochlan are exploring Microsoft OneNote, Sway, Mix, and Edge in Office 2016 and Windows 10.

Learn to use productivity apps!
Links to companion **Sways**, featuring **videos** with hands-on instructions, are located on www.cengagebrain.com.

Introduction to OneNote 2016

notebook | section tab | To Do tag | screen clipping | note | template | Microsoft OneNote Mobile app | sync | drawing canvas | inked handwriting | Ink to Text

Bottom Line

- OneNote is a note-taking app for your academic and professional life.
- Use OneNote to get organized by gathering your ideas, sketches, webpages, photos, videos, and notes in one place.

As you glance around any classroom, you invariably see paper notebooks and notepads on each desk. Because deciphering and sharing handwritten notes can be a challenge, Microsoft OneNote 2016 replaces physical notebooks, binders, and paper notes with a searchable, digital notebook. OneNote captures your ideas and schoolwork on any device so you can stay organized, share notes, and work with others on projects. Whether you are a student taking class notes as shown in **Figure 1** or an employee taking notes in company meetings, OneNote is the one place to keep notes for all of your projects.

Figure 1: OneNote 2016 notebook

Each **notebook** is divided into sections, also called **section tabs**, by subject or topic.

Use **To Do tags**, icons that help you keep track of your assignments and other tasks.

Type on a page to add a **note**, a small window that contains text or other types of information.

Personalize a page with a **template**, or stationery.

Write or draw directly on the page using drawing tools.

Pages can include pictures such as **screen clippings**, images from any part of a computer screen.

Attach files and enter equations so you have everything you need in one place.

Creating a OneNote Notebook

OneNote is divided into sections similar to those in a spiral-bound notebook. Each OneNote notebook contains sections, pages, and other notebooks. You can use One-Note for school, business, and personal projects. Store information for each type of project in different notebooks to keep your tasks separate, or use any other organization that suits you. OneNote is flexible enough to adapt to the way you want to work.

When you create a notebook, it contains a blank page with a plain white background by default, though you can use templates, or stationery, to apply designs in categories such as Academic, Business, Decorative, and Planners. Start typing or use the buttons on the Insert tab to insert notes, which are small resizable windows that can contain text, equations, tables, on-screen writing, images, audio and video recordings, to-do lists, file attachments, and file printouts. Add as many notes as you need to each page.

Learn to use OneNote!

Links to companion **Sways**, featuring **videos** with hands-on instructions, are located on www.cengagebrain.com.

Syncing a Notebook to the Cloud

OneNote saves your notes every time you make a change in a notebook. To make sure you can access your notebooks with a laptop, tablet, or smartphone wherever you are, OneNote uses cloud-based storage, such as OneDrive or SharePoint. **Microsoft OneNote Mobile app**, a lightweight version of OneNote 2016 shown in **Figure 2**, is available for free in the Windows Store, Google Play for Android devices, and the AppStore for iOS devices.

If you have a Microsoft account, OneNote saves your notes on OneDrive automatically for all your mobile devices and computers, which is called **syncing**. For example, you can use OneNote to take notes on your laptop during class, and then open OneNote on your phone to study later. To use a notebook stored on your computer with your OneNote Mobile app, move the notebook to OneDrive. You can quickly share notebook content with other people using OneDrive.

Figure 2: Microsoft OneNote Mobile app

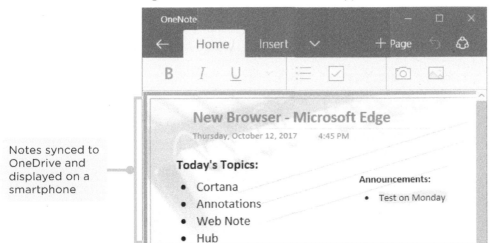

Notes synced to OneDrive and displayed on a smartphone

Taking Notes

Use OneNote pages to organize your notes by class and topic or lecture. Beyond simple typed notes, OneNote stores drawings, converts handwriting to searchable text and mathematical sketches to equations, and records audio and video.

OneNote includes drawing tools that let you sketch freehand drawings such as biological cell diagrams and financial supply-and-demand charts. As shown in **Figure 3**, the Draw tab on the ribbon provides these drawing tools along with shapes so you can insert diagrams and other illustrations to represent your ideas. When you draw on a page, OneNote creates a **drawing canvas**, which is a container for shapes and lines.

On the Job Now

OneNote is ideal for taking notes during meetings, whether you are recording minutes, documenting a discussion, sketching product diagrams, or listing follow-up items. Use a meeting template to add pages with content appropriate for meetings.

Figure 3: Tools on the Draw tab

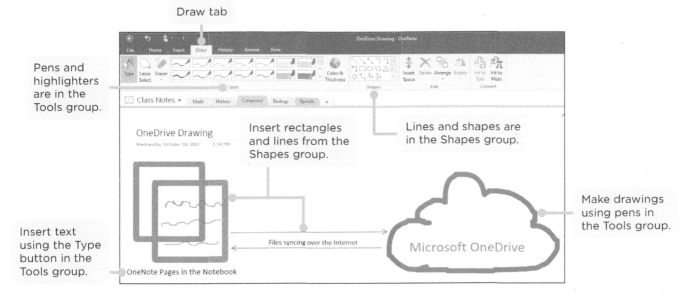

Pens and highlighters are in the Tools group.

Insert rectangles and lines from the Shapes group.

Lines and shapes are in the Shapes group.

Insert text using the Type button in the Tools group.

Make drawings using pens in the Tools group.

Converting Handwriting to Text

When you use a pen tool to write on a notebook page, the text you enter is called **inked handwriting**. OneNote can convert inked handwriting to typed text when you use the **Ink to Text** button in the Convert group on the Draw tab, as shown in **Figure 4**. After OneNote converts the handwriting to text, you can use the Search box to find terms in the converted text or any other note in your notebooks.

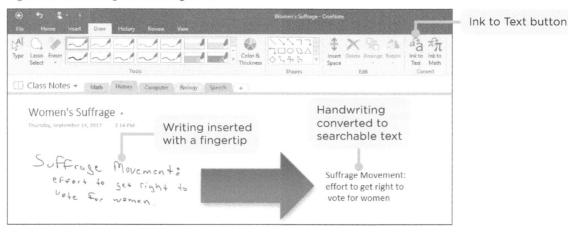

Ink to Text button

Writing inserted with a fingertip

Handwriting converted to searchable text

Women's Suffrage •
Thursday, September 14, 2017   2:14 PM

Suffrage Movement: effort to get right to vote for women

Suffrage Movement:
effort to get right to
vote for women

On the Job Now

Use OneNote as a place to brainstorm ongoing work projects. If a notebook contains sensitive material, you can password-protect some or all of the notebook so that only certain people can open it.

Recording a Lecture

If your computer or mobile device has a microphone or camera, OneNote can record the audio or video from a lecture or business meeting as shown in **Figure 5**. When you record a lecture (with your instructor's permission), you can follow along, take regular notes at your own pace, and review the video recording later. You can control the start, pause, and stop motions of the recording when you play back the recording of your notes.

Figure 5: Video inserted in a notebook

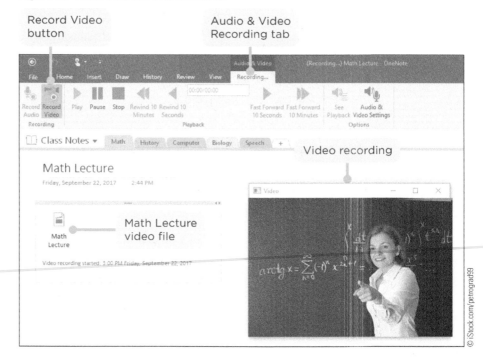

Record Video button

Audio & Video Recording tab

Video recording

Math Lecture
Friday, September 22, 2017   2:44 PM

Math Lecture video file

Video recording started: 3:00 PM Friday, September 22, 2017

© iStock.com/petrograd99

Try This Now

Learn to use OneNote!
Links to companion **Sways**, featuring **videos** with hands-on instructions, are located on www.cengagebrain.com.

1: Taking Notes for a Week

As a student, you can get organized by using OneNote to take detailed notes in your classes. Perform the following tasks:

a. Create a new OneNote notebook on your Microsoft OneDrive account (the default location for new notebooks). Name the notebook with your first name followed by "Notes," as in **Caleb Notes**.
b. Create four section tabs, each with a different class name.
c. Take detailed notes in those classes for one week. Be sure to include notes, drawings, and other types of content.
d. Sync your notes with your OneDrive. Submit your assignment in the format specified by your instructor.

2: Using OneNote to Organize a Research Paper

You have a research paper due on the topic of three habits of successful students. Use OneNote to organize your research. Perform the following tasks:

a. Create a new OneNote notebook on your Microsoft OneDrive account. Name the notebook **Success Research**.
b. Create three section tabs with the following names:

   - **Take Detailed Notes**
   - **Be Respectful in Class**
   - **Come to Class Prepared**

c. On the web, research the topics and find three sources for each section. Copy a sentence from each source and paste the sentence into the appropriate section. When you paste the sentence, OneNote inserts it in a note with a link to the source.
d. Sync your notes with your OneDrive. Submit your assignment in the format specified by your instructor.

3: Planning Your Career

Note: This activity requires a webcam or built-in video camera on any type of device.

Consider an occupation that interests you. Using OneNote, examine the responsibilities, education requirements, potential salary, and employment outlook of a specific career. Perform the following tasks:

a. Create a new OneNote notebook on your Microsoft OneDrive account. Name the notebook with your first name followed by a career title, such as **Kara - App Developer**.
b. Create four section tabs with the names **Responsibilities, Education Requirements, Median Salary**, and **Employment Outlook**.
c. Research the responsibilities of your career path. Using OneNote, record a short video (approximately 30 seconds) of yourself explaining the responsibilities of your career path. Place the video in the Responsibilities section.
d. On the web, research the educational requirements for your career path and find two appropriate sources. Copy a paragraph from each source and paste them into the appropriate section. When you paste a paragraph, OneNote inserts it in a note with a link to the source.
e. Research the median salary for a single year for this career. Create a mathematical equation in the Median Salary section that multiplies the amount of the median salary times 20 years to calculate how much you will possibly earn.
f. For the Employment Outlook section, research the outlook for your career path. Take at least four notes about what you find when researching the topic.
g. Sync your notes with your OneDrive. Submit your assignment in the format specified by your instructor.